Mexico

Are we meeting your travel needs?

Send written comments to:

AAA Member Comments
1000 AAA Drive, Box 61
Heathrow, FL 32746-5063

Published by:

AAA Publishing
1000 AAA Drive
Heathrow, FL 32746-5063
Copyright AAA 2004

**Advertising Rate and Circulation
Information**
Call: (407) 444-8280

Printed in the USA by Quebecor
World, Buffalo, NY

Photo Credit: (Cover & Title Page)
*Xel-Há National Park, Tulum,
Quintana Roo, Yucatán Peninsula
© Angelo Cavalli / SuperStock*

 Printed on recyclable paper.
Please recycle whenever possible.

Stock #5022

Mexico

TourBook Navigator

Follow our simple guide to make the most of this member benefit 9-25

Comprehensive City Index

Alphabetical list for the entire book 574

The Pacific Coast

Mexico City & Vicinity

Central Mexico

Southern Mexico

Featured Information

aaa.com
Travel Planning Made Easy!

Want to plan a fun and affordable trip quickly and easily? Visit **aaa.com** to get exclusive travel information, find ways to save money and access easy-to-use travel planning tools.

Searchable TourBook®guides. Find AAA's famous TourBook travel information including: Approved hotels (get Diamond ratings, member discounts on room rates, plus online reservations), Approved restaurants, recommended attractions, local events, and detailed destination descriptions.

AAA TripTiks®. Create your own customized TripTik: get door-to-door driving directions and maps, find AAA Approved hotels and reserve a room, locate AAA recommended restaurants, and discover things to do and see at your destination and along the way.

AAA Drive Trips*. Review AAA recommended drive trips.

Vacation Getaways. Take to the skies, hit the high seas or select a tour and receive exclusive benefits from AAA's Preferred Travel Partners.

Travel Guides. Get a 5% discount on AAA's famed travel guides at aaa.com/barnesandnoble.

Disney® Vacations. Get exclusive benefits and savings on AAA Vacations® Disney vacation packages.

Hertz Rental. Save up to 20% on car rental.

Show Your Card & Save. Search for savings on lodging, travel, entertainment, retail, and e-merchants.

AAA Travel Money. Get no-fee travelers cheques, foreign currency and prepaid cards.

AAA Map Gallery*. Know the best way to go wherever you travel.

Cash Back. Get up to a 5% rebate every time you use your AAA credit card to gas up.

AAA Approved Auto Repair. Find your nearest AAR shop to get your car ready for the road.

Travel to aaa.com to do all your vacation planning!

aaa.com

Travel With Someone You Trust®

*Products and Services available through participating AAA and CAA Clubs.

Mexico. From Coast to Coast.

With 13 outstanding properties throughout Mexico, catering to the leisure traveler, you can rest assured that whichever destination, hotel or resort you choose, you will find incomparable service.

Plus as a AAA member, you may take advantage of special AAA value rates. Just show your card and ask for the AAA preferred rate and start saving in style!

SHERATON CANCUN RESORT & TOWERS CANCUN
SHERATON HACIENDA DEL MAR RESORT & SPA LOS CABOS
SHERATON CENTRO HISTORICO HOTEL & CONVENTION CENTER MEXICO CITY
SHERATON MARIA ISABEL HOTEL & TOWERS MEXICO CITY
SHERATON SUITES SANTA FE MEXICO CITY
SHERATON AMBASSADOR HOTEL & TOWERS MONTERREY
SHERATON BUGANVILIAS RESORT & CONVENTION CENTER PUERTO VALLARTA
W HOTEL MEXICO CITY
THE WESTIN RESORT & SPA CANCUN
THE WESTIN SOBERANO CHIHUAHUA
THE WESTIN RESORT & SPA LOS CABOS
THE WESTIN RESORT & SPA PUERTO VALLARTA
THE WESTIN SAN LUIS POTOSI

Trust
the AAA TourBook® guide for objective travel information. Follow the pages of the TourBook Navigator to thoroughly understand this unique member benefit.

Making Your Way Through the AAA Listings

Attractions, lodgings and restaurants are listed on the basis of merit alone after careful evaluation, approval and rating by one of our full-time, professionally trained Tourism Editors. Annual evaluations are unannounced to ensure that our Tourism Editors see an establishment just as our members would see it.

Those lodgings and restaurants listed with an (fyi) icon have not gone through the same evaluation process as other rated properties. Individual listings will typically denote the reason why this icon appears. Bulleted recreational activity listings are not inspected but are included for member information.

An establishment's decision to advertise in the TourBook guide has no bearing on its evaluation or rating. Advertising for services or products does not imply AAA endorsement.

How the TourBook is
Organized

Geographic listing is used for accuracy and consistency. This means attractions, lodgings and restaurants are listed under the city in which they physically are located—or in some cases under the nearest recognized city. The Comprehensive City Index located in the back of the book contains an A-to-Z list of cities. Most listings are alphabetically organized by state, province, region or island; city; and establishment name. A color is assigned to each state or province so that you can match the color bars at the top of the page to switch from ❶ Points of Interest to ❷ Lodgings and Restaurants.

Destination Cities and Destination Areas

The TourBook guide also groups information by destination city and destination area. If a city is grouped in a destination vicinity section, the city name will appear at its alphabetical location in the book, and a handy cross reference will give the exact page on which listings for that city begin. Maps are placed at the beginning of these sections to orient you to the destinations.

❸ **Destination cities**, established based on government models and local expertise, are comprised of metropolitan areas plus nearby vicinity cities.

Destination areas are regions with broad tourist appeal. Several cities will comprise the area.

All information in this TourBook guide was reviewed for accuracy before publication. However, since changes inevitably occur between annual editions, we suggest you contact establishments directly to confirm prices and schedules.

Points of Interest Section

Orientation maps
near the start of each Attractions section show only those places we call points of interest. Coordinates included with the city listings depict the locations of those cities on the map. A GEM symbol (⬇) accents towns with "must see" points of interest which offer a *Great Experience for Members®*. And the black ovals with white numerals (**22** for example) locate items listed in the nearby Recreation Areas chart.

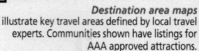

Destination area maps
illustrate key travel areas defined by local travel experts. Communities shown have listings for AAA approved attractions.

National park maps
represent the area in and around the park. Some campground sites and lodges spotted on the maps do not meet AAA/CAA criteria, but are shown for members who nevertheless wish to stay close to the park area.

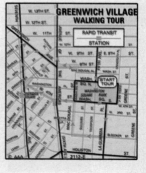

Walking or self-guiding tour maps
correspond to specific routes described in TourBook guide text.

City maps
show areas where numerous points of interest are concentrated and indicate their location in relation to major roads, parks, airports and other landmarks.

Lodgings & Restaurants Section

Destination area maps
illustrate key travel areas defined by
local travel experts. Communities
shown have listings for AAA-RATED®
lodgings and/or restaurants.

Spotting maps
show the location of lodgings and
restaurants. Lodgings are spotted with
a black background (**22** for example);
restaurants are spotted with a white
background (**23** for example). Spotting map indexes have
been placed immediately after each map to provide the user
with a convenient method to identify what an area has to
offer at a glance. The index references the map page number
where the property is spotted, indicates if a property is an
Official Appointment and contains an advertising reference
if applicable. It also lists the property's diamond rating, high
season rate range and listing page number.

Downtown/city spotting maps
are provided when spotted facilities are very concentrated.
GEM points of interest also appear on these maps.

Vicinity spotting maps
spot those properties that are outside the downtown or city area. Major
roads, landmarks, airports and GEM points of interest are shown on vicinity
spotting maps as well. The names of suburban communities that have
AAA-RATED® accommodations are
shown in magenta type.

Featured Information Section

Driving distance maps
are intended to be used only for trip-distance and
driving-time planning.

Sample Attraction Listing

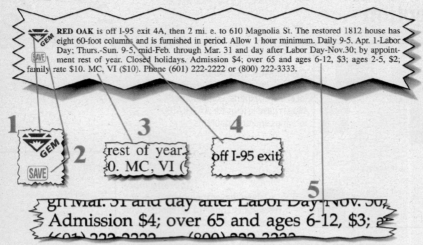

RED OAK is off I-95 exit 4A, then 2 mi. e. to 610 Magnolia St. The restored 1812 house has eight 60-foot columns and is furnished in period. Allow 1 hour minimum. Daily 9-5, Apr. 1-Labor Day; Thurs.-Sun. 9-5, mid-Feb. through Mar. 31 and day after Labor Day-Nov.30; by appointment rest of year. Closed holidays. Admission $4; over 65 and ages 6-12, $3; ages 2-5, $2; family rate $10. MC, VI ($10). Phone (601) 222-2222 or (800) 222-3333.

1

2

3 rest of year.
0. MC, VI (

4 off I-95 exit

5 git Mar. 31 and day after Labor Day-Nov. 30;
Admission $4; over 65 and ages 6-12, $3;

1   This attraction is of exceptional interest and quality and therefore has been designated a AAA GEM—offering a *Great Experience for Members*®.

2   Participating attractions offer AAA/CAA, AAA MasterCard or AAA Visa cardholders a discount off the attraction's standard admission; members should inquire in advance concerning the validity of the discount for special rates. The discount applies to the cardholder and up to six family members. Present your card at the admission desk. A list of participating points of interest appears in the Indexes section of the book. The SAVE discount may not be used in conjunction with other discounts. Attractions that already provide a reduced senior or child rate may not honor the SAVE discount for those age groups. All offers are subject to change and may not apply during special events, particular days or seasons or for the entire validity period of the TourBook. Shopping establishments preceded by a SAVE icon also provide discounts and/or gift with purchase to AAA/CAA members; present your card at the mall's customer service center to receive your benefit.

3
AX=American Express	DS=Discover	MC=MasterCard
CB=Carte Blanche	JC=Japan Credit Bureau	VI=VISA
DC=Diners Club		

4   Unless otherwise specified, directions are given from the center of town, using the following highway designations: I (interstate highway), US (federal highway), Hwy. (Canadian or Caribbean highway), SR (state route), CR (county road), FM (farm to market road), FR (forest road), MM (mile marker), Mex. (Mexican highway).

5   Admission prices are quoted without sales tax. Children under the lowest age specified are admitted free when accompanied by an adult. Days, months and age groups written with a hyphen are inclusive. Prices pertaining to points of interest in the United States are quoted in U.S. dollars; prices for Canadian province and territory points of interest are quoted in Canadian dollars; prices for points of interest in Mexico and the Caribbean are quoted as an approximate U.S. dollar equivalent.

Bulleted Listings: Casino gambling establishments are visited by AAA personnel to ensure safety; casinos within hotels are presented for member information regardless of whether the lodging is AAA approved. Recreational activities of a participatory nature (requiring physical exertion or special skills) are not inspected. Wineries are inspected by AAA Tourism Editors to ensure they meet listing requirements and offer tours. All are presented in a bulleted format for informational purposes.

These Show Your Card & Save® partners provide the listed member benefits. Admission tickets that offer greater discounts may be available for purchase at the local AAA/CAA club. The discount applies to the cardholder; the attraction, at its discretion, may also offer the discount to up to five family members.

Attraction Partners

SeaWorld/Busch Gardens    (aaa.com/seaworld)

SAVE Save $5 on general admission at the gate at SeaWorld and Busch Gardens

SAVE Save $3 on general admission at the gate at Sesame Place, Water Country USA and Adventure Island

SAVE Save 10% on select up-close dining. Reservations are required; visit Guest Relations for details

Six Flags Theme Parks

SAVE Save $4 on general admission at the gate

SAVE Save $12 on general admission at the gate each Wednesday

SAVE Save 10% on selected souvenirs and dining (check at main gate for details)

Universal Orlando   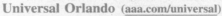 (aaa.com/universal)

SAVE Save $4 on a 2-day/2-park pass or $5 on a 3-day/2-park pass at Universal Orlando's theme parks (savings apply to tickets purchased at the gate)

SAVE Save 10% on select dining and souvenirs at both Universal Orlando theme parks and at select Universal CityWalk Orlando restaurants (except Emeril's)

Universal Studios Hollywood   (aaa.com/universal)

SAVE Save $3 on a 1-day Universal Studios pass (savings applies to tickets purchased at the gate)

SAVE Save 10% on select dining and souvenirs at Universal Studios Hollywood and Universal CityWalk

Gray Line   (aaa.com/grayline)

SAVE Save 10% on sightseeing tours of 1 day or less

Restaurant Partners

Landry's Seafood House, The Crab House, Chart House, Muer Seafood Restaurants, Joe's Crab Shack

SAVE Save 10% on food and non-alcoholic beverages at Landry's Seafood House, The Crab House, Chart House, Muer Seafood Restaurants and Joe's Crab Shack and 10% on merchandise at Joe's Crab Shack. Savings applicable to AAA/CAA member and up to five additional people

Hard Rock Cafe

SAVE Save 10% on food, non-alcoholic beverages and merchandise at all U.S. and select Canadian and international locations. Members also save 10% at The Hard Rock Vault. Savings applicable to AAA/CAA member and up to five additional people.

Visit aaa.com to discover all the great Show Your Card & Save® discounts in your area.

Sample Lodging Listing

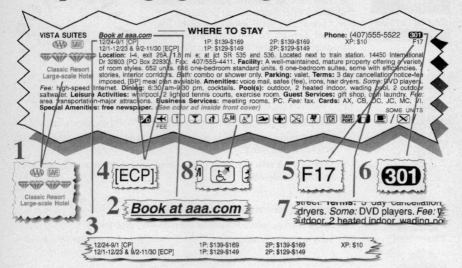

1. **AAA** or **CAA** indicates our Official Appointment (OA) lodgings. The OA program permits properties to display and advertise the **AAA** or **CAA** emblem. We highlight these properties with red diamonds and classification. Some OA listings include special amenities such as free continental breakfast; expanded continental breakfast or full breakfast; early check-in/late check-out; free room upgrade or preferred room, such as ocean view or poolside (subject to availability); free local phone calls; and free daily newspaper. This does not imply that only these properties offer these amenities. The **AAA** or **CAA** sign helps traveling members find accommodations that want member business.

   ◆◆◆ or ◆◆◆◆ The number of diamonds—not the color—informs you of the overall level of quality in a lodging's amenities and service. More diamond details appear on page 16.

   Classic Resort Large-scale Hotel or Classic Resort Large-scale Hotel: All diamond rated lodgings are classified using three key elements: style of operation, overall concept and service level. See pages 22-23 for details about our Lodging Classifications and Subclassifications.

Member Values

SAVE Official Appointment properties guarantee members a minimum 10% discount off the standard room rates published in TourBook guides or the lowest public rate available at the time of booking for the dates of stay, for standard rooms.

S$ Establishments offer a minimum senior discount of 10% off the listed rates. This discount is available to members 60 or older.

ASK Many properties offer discounts to members even though the lodgings do not participate in a formal discount program. The **ASK** is another reminder to inquire about available discounts when making your reservations or at check-in.

Discounts normally offered at some lodgings may not apply during special events or holiday periods. Special rates and discounts may not apply to all room types. Some Member Values may not apply in Mexico or the Caribbean.

To obtain published rates or discounts, you must identify yourself as a AAA or CAA member, request AAA rates when making reservations and have written confirmation sent to you. The SAVE or senior discount may not be used in conjunction with other discounts. At registration, show your membership card and verify the room rate.

Discounts normally offered at some lodgings may not apply during special events or holiday periods. Special rates and discounts may not apply to all room types. Some Member Values may not apply in Mexico or the Caribbean.

The rates listed for approved properties are provided to AAA by each lodging and represent the regular (rack) rate for a standard room. Printed rates, based on rack rates and last room availability, are rounded to the nearest dollar. Rates do not include taxes and discounts. U.S., Mexican and Caribbean rates are in U.S. dollars; rates for Canadian lodgings are in Canadian dollars.

2 Book at aaa.com - Internet Reservations
Indicates AAA/CAA members can conveniently check room availability and make reservations in a secure online environment at aaa.com.

3 Rate Lines
Shown from left to right: dates the rates are effective; meal plan provided with rates (see Meal Plan Indicators-if no plan noted, rate includes room only); rates for 1 person or 2 persons; extra person charge (XP); and any applicable family plan indicator.

Rates Guaranteed
AAA/CAA members are guaranteed that they will not be charged more than the maximum regular rate printed in each rate range for a standard room. Rates may vary within the range depending on season and room type. Listed rates are based on last standard room availability. Rates for properties operating as concessionaires for the U.S. National Park Service are not guaranteed due to governing regulations. Rates in the Mexico TourBook are not guaranteed and may fluctuate based on the exchange rate of the peso.

Exceptions
Lodgings may temporarily increase room rates, not recognize discounts or modify pricing policies during special events. Examples of special events range from Mardi Gras and Kentucky Derby (including pre-Derby events) to college football games, holidays, holiday periods and state fairs. Although some special events are listed in AAA/CAA TourBook guides, it is always wise to check, in advance, with AAA travel professionals for specific dates.

Discounts
Member discounts will apply to rates quoted, within the rate range, applicable at the time of booking. Special rates used in advertising, and special short-term, promotional rates lower than the lowest listed rate in the range, are not subject to additional member discounts.

4 Meal Plan Indicators
The following types of meal plans may be available in the listed room rate:
AP = American Plan of three meals daily
BP = Breakfast Plan of full hot breakfast
CP = Continental Plan of pastry, juice and another beverage
ECP = Expanded Continental Plan, which offers a wider variety of breakfast items
MAP = Modified American Plan of two meals daily
See individual listing "Terms" section for additional meal plans that are not included in the room rate.

> Check-in times are shown in the listing only if they are after 3 p.m.; check-out times are shown only if they are before 10 a.m.

5 Family Plan Indicators
F = Children stay free
D = Discounts for children
F17 = Children 17 and under stay free (age displayed will reflect property's policy)
D17 = Discount for children 17 and under

6 Lodging Locators
Black ovals with white numbers are used to locate, or "spot," lodgings on maps we provide for larger cities.

7 Unit Types
Unit types, amenities and room features preceded by the word "Some" indicate the item is available on a limited basis, potentially within only one unit.

8 Lodging Icons
A row of icons is included with each lodging listing. These icons represent the member values, member services, and facilities offered by that lodging. See page 19 for an explanation of each icon.

The Lodging Diamond Ratings

AAA Tourism Editors evaluate and rate each lodging based on the overall quality, the range of facilities and the level of services offered by a property. The size, age and overall appeal of an establishment are considered as well as regional architectural style and design.

While guest services are an important part of all diamond ratings, they are particularly critical at the four and five diamond levels. A property must provide a high level of service, on a consistent basis, to obtain and support the four and five diamond rating.

These establishments typically appeal to the budget-minded traveler. They provide essential, no-frills accommodations. They meet the basic requirements pertaining to comfort, cleanliness, and hospitality.

These establishments appeal to the traveler seeking more than the basic accommodations. There are modest enhancements to the overall physical attributes, design elements, and amenities of the facility typically at a modest price.

These establishments appeal to the traveler with comprehensive needs. Properties are multifaceted with a distinguished style, including marked upgrades in the quality of physical attributes, amenities and level of comfort provided.

These establishments are upscale in all areas. Accommodations are progressively more refined and stylish. The physical attributes reflect an obvious enhanced level of quality throughout. The fundamental hallmarks at this level include an extensive array of amenities combined with a high degree of hospitality, service, and attention to detail.

These establishments reflect the characteristics of the ultimate in luxury and sophistication. Accommodations are first-class. The physical attributes are extraordinary in every manner. The fundamental hallmarks at this level are to meticulously serve and exceed all guest expectations while maintaining an impeccable standard of excellence. Many personalized services and amenities enhance an unmatched level of comfort.

The lodging listings with **fyi** in place of diamonds are included as an "information only" service for members. The icon indicates that a property has not been rated for one or more of the following reasons: too new to rate; under construction; under major renovation; not evaluated; or may not meet all AAA requirements. Those properties not meeting all AAA requirements are included for either their member value or because it may be the only accommodation available in the area. Listing prose will give insight as to why the **fyi** designation was assigned.

Guest Safety

Room Security

In order to be approved for listing in AAA/CAA TourBook guides for the United States and Canada, all lodgings must comply with AAA's guest room security requirements.

In response to AAA/CAA members' concern about their safety at properties, AAA-RATED® accommodations must have dead-bolt locks on all guest room entry doors and connecting room doors.

If the area outside the guest room door is not visible from inside the room through a window or door panel, viewports must be installed on all guest room entry doors. Bed and breakfast properties and country inns are not required to have viewports. Ground floor and easily accessible sliding doors must be equipped with some other type of secondary security locks.

Tourism Editors view a percentage of rooms at each property since it is not feasible to evaluate every room in every lodging establishment. Therefore, AAA cannot guarantee that there are working locks on all doors and windows in all guest rooms.

Fire Safety

Because of the highly specialized skills needed to conduct professional fire safety inspections, AAA/CAA Tourism Editors cannot assess fire safety.

Properties must meet all federal, state and local fire codes. Each guest unit in all U.S. and Canadian lodging properties must be equipped with an operational, single-station smoke detector. A AAA/CAA Tourism Editor has evaluated a sampling of the rooms to verify this equipment is in place.

For additional fire safety information, read the page posted on the back of your guest room door, or write:

National Fire Protection Association
1 Batterymarch Park
P.O. Box 9101
Quincy, MA 02269-9101

Requirements for some features, such as door locks and smoke detectors/sprinkler systems, differ in Mexico and the Caribbean. If a property met AAA's security requirements at the time of the evaluation, the phrase "Meets AAA guest room security requirements" appears in the listing.

Access for Mature Travelers and Travelers with Disabilities

Qualified properties listed in this guide are shown with symbols indicating they meet the needs of the hearing-impaired or offer some accessible features for mature travelers or travelers with disabilities.

 ## *Hearing Impaired*

Indicates a property has the following equipment available for hearing-impaired travelers: TDD at front desk or switchboard; visual notification of fire alarm, incoming telephone calls, door knock or bell; closed caption decoder; text telephone or TDD for guest room use; telephone amplification device, with shelf or electric outlet next to guest room telephone.

 ## *Accessible Features*

Indicates a property has some accessible features meeting the needs of mature travelers and travelers with disabilities. Lodging establishments will provide at least one guest room meeting the designated criteria as well as accessible restrooms and parking facilities. Restaurants provide accessible parking, dining rooms and restrooms.

> AAA/CAA strongly urges members to call the property directly to fully understand the property's exact accessibility features. Some properties do not fully comply with AAA/CAA's exacting accessibility standards but may offer some design standards that meet the needs of some guests with disabilities.
>
> AAA/CAA does not evaluate recreational facilities, banquet rooms, or convention or meeting facilities for accessibility.

Service Animals

> No fees or deposits, even those normally charged for pets, may be charged for service animals. Service animals fulfill a critical need for their owners—they are *not* pets.

The Americans With Disabilities Act (ADA) prohibits U.S. businesses that serve the public from discriminating against persons with disabilities. Some businesses have mistakenly denied access to persons who use service animals. ADA, a federal mandate, has priority over all state and local laws, as well as a business owner's standard of business, which might bar animals from the premises. Businesses must permit entry to guests and their service animals, as well as allow service animals to accompany guests to all public areas of a property. A property is permitted to ask whether the animal is a service animal or a pet, and whether the guest has a disability. The property may not, however, ask questions about the nature of the disability, the service provided by the animal or require proof of a disability or certification that the animal is a service animal.

Note: These regulations may not apply in Canada, Mexico or the Caribbean.

What The Lodging Icons Mean

Member Values
(see p. 14)

AAA or **CAA** Official Appointment

SAVE Offers minimum 10% discount or lowest public rate *(see p. 14)*

ASK May offer discount

S Offers senior discount

fyi Informational listing only

Member Services

✈ Airport transportation

🐕 Pets allowed

🍴 Restaurant on premises

🍴→ Restaurant off premises (walking distance)

24 24-hour room service

🍸 Cocktail lounge

👶 Child care

Accessibility Feature
(see p. 18)

&M Accessible features

🦽 Roll-in showers

👂 Hearing impaired

Safety Features
(Mexico and Caribbean only)

S Sprinklers

D Smoke detectors

Leisure Activities

🎲 Full service casino

🏊 Pool

💪 Health club on premises

💪 Health club off premises

🎣 Recreational activities

In-Room Amenities

✕ Designated non-smoking rooms

AC No air conditioning

TV No TV

CTV No cable TV

VCR VCR

📽 Movies

DATA PORT Data port/modem line

☎ No telephones

🔲 Refrigerator

▣ Microwave

▢ Coffee maker

Availability and Additional Fees

If an in-room amenity is available only on a limited basis (in one or more rooms), the term "SOME UNITS" will appear above those icons. Fees may be charged for some of the services represented by the icons listed here. The word "FEE" will appear below each icon when an extra charge applies.

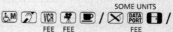

SOME UNITS

&M 👂 **VCR** 📽 ▢ / ✕ **DATA PORT** 🔲 /
        FEE FEE   FEE

Preferred Lodging Partners

AAA. Every Day.

SAVINGS. SELECTION. SATISFACTION. — When contacting one of the partners listed, you will be given AAA's best rates for your dates of stay. Your valid membership card must be presented at check-in.

SATISFACTION GUARANTEE — If you are not satisfied with any part of your stay, you must provide the property the opportunity to correct the situation during your stay. If the matter cannot be resolved, you will be entitled to recompense for a portion of, or your entire, stay. Satisfaction guarantee varies by chain.

Select the chain you want and have your membership card available when making a reservation and checking in.

| Visit | Over 1,100 AAA Offices | Click | aaa.com | Call | 866-AAA-SAVE |

Special rates and discounts may not apply to all room types. All discounts are off full rates and vary by location and time of year. Special rates and discounts are not available to groups and cannot be combined with other discounts. Restrictions apply to satisfaction guarantees. Valid AAA/CAA membership card must be presented at check-in. Offers good at time of publication; chains and offers may change without notice. Lodging partners offering discounts to AAA/CAA members may vary in Mexico and the Caribbean.

Making Reservations

When making reservations, you must identify yourself as a AAA or CAA member. Give all pertinent information about your planned stay. Ask about the lodging's pet policy, or the availability of any other special feature that is important to your stay. Request written confirmation to guarantee: type of room, rate, dates of stay, and cancellation and refund policies. At registration, show your membership card. Note: Age restrictions may apply.

Confirm Deposit, Refund and Cancellation Policies

Most establishments give full deposit refunds if they have been notified at least 48 hours before the normal check-in time. Listing prose will note if more than 48 hours notice is required for cancellation. However, when making reservations, confirm the property's deposit, cancellation and refund policies. Some properties may charge a cancellation or handling fee.

When this applies, "cancellation fee imposed" will appear in the listing. If you cancel too late, you have little recourse if a refund is denied.

When an establishment requires a full or partial payment in advance, and your trip is cut short, a refund may not be given.

When canceling reservations, phone the lodging immediately. Make a note of the date and time you called, the cancellation number if there is one, and the name of the person who handled the cancellation. If your AAA/CAA club made your reservation, allow them to make the cancellation for you as well so you will have proof of cancellation.

Review Charges for Appropriate Rates

When you are charged more than the maximum rate listed in the TourBook guide for a standard room, question the additional charge. If management refuses to adhere to the published rate, pay for the room and submit your receipt and membership number to AAA/CAA within 30 days. Include all pertinent information: dates of stay, rate paid, itemized paid receipts, number of persons in your party, the room number you occupied, and list any extra room equipment used. A refund of the amount paid in excess of the stated maximum will be made if our investigation indicates that unjustified charging has occurred.

Get the Room You Reserved

When you find your room is not as specified, and you have written confirmation of reservations for a certain type of accommodation, you should be given the option of choosing a different room or finding one elsewhere. Should you choose to go elsewhere and a refund is refused or resisted, submit the matter to AAA/CAA within 30 days along with complete documentation, including your reasons for refusing the room and copies of your written confirmation and any receipts or canceled checks associated with this problem.

How to Get the Best Room Rates

You'll find the best room rate if you book your reservation in advance with the help of a travel professional or agent at your local AAA/CAA office.

If you're not yet ready to make firm vacation plans or if you prefer a more spontaneous trip, take advantage of the partnerships that preferred hotel chains have arranged with AAA. Phone the toll-free number 866-AAA-SAVE that has been set up exclusively for members for the purpose of reserving with these Show Your Card & Save® chain partners.

Even if you were unable to make a reservation, be sure to show your membership card at the desk and ask if you're being offered the lowest rate available for that time. Many lodgings offer reduced rates to members.

Lodging Classifications

To ensure that your lodging needs/preferences are met, we recommend that you consider an establishment's classification when making your travel choices.

While the quality and comfort at properties with the same diamond rating should be consistent (regardless of the classification), there are differences in typical décor/theme elements, range of facilities and service levels. Please see the descriptions below.

Large-scale Hotel

A multistory establishment with interior room entrances. A variety of guest unit styles is offered. Public areas are spacious and include a variety of facilities such as a restaurant, shops, fitness center, spa, business center, or meeting rooms.

Hotel Royal Plaza, Lake Buena Vista, FL

Small-scale Hotel

A multistory establishment typically with interior room entrances. A variety of guest unit styles is offered. Public areas are limited in size and/or the variety of facilities available.

Baymont Inn, Dallas/Ft. Worth-Airport North, TX

Motel

A one- to three-story establishment typically with exterior room entrances facilitating convenient access to parking. The standard guest units have one bedroom with a bathroom and are typically similar in décor and design throughout. Public areas are limited in size and/or the variety of facilities available.

Best Western Deltona Inn, Deltona, FL

Country Inn

Similar in definition to a bed and breakfast, but usually larger in scale with spacious public areas and offers a dining facility that serves at least breakfast and dinner.

Greenville Inn, Greenville, ME

Bed & Breakfast

Small-scale properties emphasizing a high degree of personal touches that provide guests an "at home" feeling. Guest units tend to be individually decorated. Rooms may not include some modern amenities such as televisions and telephones, and may have a shared bathroom. Usually owner-operated with a common room or parlor separate from the innkeeper's living quarters, where guests and operators can interact during evening and breakfast hours.

1884 Paxton House Inn, Thomasville, GA

Evening office closures are normal. A continental or full, hot breakfast is served and is included in the room rate.

Condominium

Vacation-oriented or extended-stay, apartment-style accommodations that are routinely available for rent through a management company. Units vary in design and décor and often contain one or more bedrooms, living room, full kitchen, and an eating area. Studio-type models combine the sleeping and living areas into one room. Typically, basic cleaning supplies, kitchen utensils and complete bed and bath linens are supplied. The guest registration area may be located off-site.

Sands of Kahana, Kahana, Maui, HI

Cabin/Cottage

Vacation-oriented, small-scale, freestanding houses or cabins. Units vary in design and décor and often contain one or more bedrooms, living room, kitchen, dining area, and bathroom. Studio-type models combine the sleeping and living areas into one room. Typically, basic cleaning supplies, kitchen utensils, and complete bed and bath linens are supplied. The guest registration area may be located off-site.

Desert Rose Inn, Bluff, UT

Ranch

Typically a working ranch with an obvious rustic, Western theme. In general, equestrian-related activities are featured, but ranches may include other animals and activities as well. A variety of guest unit styles is offered in a family-oriented atmosphere.

Lost Valley Ranch, Deckers, CO

Vacation Home

Vacation-oriented or extended-stay, large-scale, freestanding houses that are routinely available for rent through a management company. Houses vary in design and décor and often contain two or more bedrooms, living room, full kitchen, dining room, and multiple bathrooms. Typically, basic cleaning supplies, kitchen utensils, and complete bed and bath linens are supplied. The guest registration area may be located off-site.

ResortQuest, Hilton Head Island, SC

Lodging Subclassifications

The following are subclassifications that may appear along with the classifications listed above to provide a more specific description of the lodging.

Casino

Extensive gambling facilities are available such as blackjack, craps, keno, and slot machines. **Note:** This subclassification will not appear beneath its diamond rating in the listing. It will be indicated by a dice icon and will be included in the row of icons immediately below the lodging listing.

Classic

Renowned and landmark properties, older than 50 years, well-known for their unique style and ambience.

Historic

These properties are typically over 75 years of age and exhibit many features of a historic nature with respect to architecture, design, furnishings, public record, or acclaim. Properties must meet one of the following criteria:
- Maintained the integrity of the historical nature
- Listed on the U.S. National Register of Historic Places
- Designated a U.S. National Historic Landmark
- Located in a U.S. National Register Historic District

Separate criteria designate historic properties in Canada, Mexico and the Caribbean.

Resort

Recreation-oriented, geared to vacation travelers seeking a specific destination experience. Travel packages, meal plans, theme entertainment, and social and recreational programs are typically available. Recreational facilities are extensive and may include spa treatments, golf, tennis, skiing, fishing, or water sports, etc. Larger resorts may offer a variety of guest accommodations.

Sample Restaurant Listing

1 **AAA** or **AA** indicates our Official Appointment (OA) restaurants. The OA program permits properties to display and advertise the **AAA** or **AA** emblem. We highlight these properties with red diamonds and cuisine type. The **AAA** or **AA** sign helps traveling members find restaurants that want member business.

   ▼▼▼ or ▼▼▼ The number of diamonds—not the color—informs you of the overall level of quality for food and presentation, service and ambience. Menus for red Diamond restaurants can be viewed on aaa.com.

   A cuisine type is assigned for each restaurant listing. AAA currently recognizes more than 90 different cuisine types.

2 Prices represent the minimum and maximum entree cost per person. Exceptions may include one-of-a-kind or special market priced items.

3 AX = American Express
   CB = Carte Blanche   DS = Discover   MC = MasterCard
   DC = Diners Club   JC = Japan Credit Bureau   VI = VISA

4 These three icons are used in restaurant listings. When present, they indicate: the presence of a cocktail lounge, the lack of air conditioning, and/or that the restaurant has a designated non-smoking section or is entirely smoke-free.

5 If applicable, restaurants may be further defined as:

   Classic—renowned and landmark restaurant operations in business longer than 25 years, known for unique style and ambience.

   Historic—properties must meet one of the following criteria:
   - Listed on the U.S. National Register of Historic Places
   - Designated a U.S. National Historic Landmark
   - Located in a U.S. National Register Historic District

   Separate criteria designate historic properties in Canada, Mexico and the Caribbean.

6 These white ovals with black numbers serve as restaurant locators and are used to locate, or "spot," restaurants on maps we provide for larger cities.

The Restaurant Diamond Ratings

AAA Tourism Editors are responsible for determining a restaurant's diamond rating based on established criteria.

These criteria were established with input from AAA trained professionals, members and restaurant industry experts. They are purposely broad to capture what is typically seen throughout the restaurant industry at each diamond rating level.

A one diamond restaurant must meet basic requirements pertaining to management, cleanliness and overall quality. The primary focus is on providing wholesome, straightforward and familiar food at an economical price. Generally, the menu selection is limited to a restaurant's specialty, such as hamburgers, fried chicken, pizza or tacos. Service is limited, in many instances self service, and the surroundings are often utilitarian.

A two diamond restaurant displays noticeable enhancements to food presentation such as the use of common garnishes in combination with the dishware. Typically, the menu offers a wide selection featuring familiar favorites or home-style foods often cooked to order and reasonably priced. The service, while often limited, is plain-speaking and relaxed. The surroundings, while limited in scope, typically reflect a clear theme. All elements combine to provide a familiar, often family-oriented experience.

A three diamond restaurant often employs a professional chef and a supporting staff of highly trained cooks. The menu is skillfully prepared and often reflects interpretations of the latest trends or a mastering of traditional cuisine. Typically, there are expanded offerings of beverages in compliment to the menu such as, international/regional wines, specialty beers, cocktails and soft drinks. The front of the house is headed by a professional dining room manager with a compliment of efficient service staff. The service reflects some degree of refinement such as reservations accepted, personal assistance or the ability to adapt to a guests's specific needs. The decor reflects the use of well-coordinated design mediums that provide a distinct theme and good comfort. Restaurants at this level convey an entry into fine dining and are often positioned as an adult-oriented experience.

A four diamond restaurant is geared to individuals in search of a distinctive fine-dining experience. Often orchestrated by an executive chef and an accomplished staff, menus reflect a high degree of creativity and complexity using imaginative presentations to enhance high quality, market fresh ingredients. The equally proficient service staff demonstrates a strong desire to meet or exceed guest expectations. A wine steward is typically available to provide menu-specific knowledge on wine selection. The ambiance is highly refined, comfortable and well coordinated incorporating quality materials and a variety of upscale design enhancements that give a first-class impression. The overall dining experience is typically expensive.

A five diamond restaurant is renowned and consistently provides a world-class experience. This is *haute cuisine* at its best. Menus are cutting edge, using only the finest ingredients available. Food is prepared in a manner that is highly imaginative and unique. The combination of technique and ingredients is extraordinary reflecting the impeccable artistry and awareness of highly acclaimed chefs. A maitre d' heads an expert service staff that exceeds guest expectations by attending to every detail in an effortless and unobtrusive manner.

The restaurants with **fyi** in place of diamonds are included as an "information only" service for members. These establishments provide additional dining choices but have not yet been evaluated.

Savings for all Seasons

Hertz rents Fords and other fine cars. ® REG. U.S. PAT. OFF. © HERTZ SYSTEM INC., 1999/2000-99.

No matter the season, Hertz offers AAA members exclusive discounts and benefits.

Operating in 150 countries at over 7,000 locations, Hertz makes traveling more convenient and efficient wherever and whenever you go. Hertz offers AAA members discounts up to 20% on car rentals worldwide.

To receive your exclusive AAA member discounts and benefits, mention your AAA membership card at time of reservation and present it at time of rental. **In addition**, to receive a free one car class upgrade, in the United States mention PC# 929714, in Canada mention PC# 929725 and in Puerto Rico mention PC# 929736 at the time of reservation. Offer available through 12/15/05.

For reservations and program details, call your AAA Travel office or the Hertz/AAA Desk at **1-800-654-3080**.

See how we got here.

Immerse yourself in a new museum experience and explore how transportation has changed America. **National Museum of American History, Washington, D.C.** americanhistory.si.edu/onthemove.

AMERICA
ON THE MOVE

Mexico

Popo's Splendor
Popocatépetl and its sister volcano Iztaccíhuatl are twin landmarks in this rugged nation

Beaches Galore
Mexico's beaches range from Cancún's powdery sand and aquamarine water to the Pacific's rolling breakers

Majestic Echoes of the Past
At Chichén Itzá, the remains of a great Maya city wait to be explored

Mountains & Sea
Puerto Vallarta blends old Mexico and modern amenities against a striking backdrop

Traipse Down to Tijuana
You can shop till you drop—and it's just a border hop away

Temple of the Inscriptions
Palenque, Chiapas
Southern Mexico
Guillermo Aldana
Mexico Tourism Board

long live mexico

Malecón, Puerto Vallarta, The Pacific Coast / Gibson Stock Photography

Mexico stands at a 21st-century crossroads of sorts. Perhaps nowhere else on earth is there such a difference between old and new, between the traditional past and the unpredictable future.

Timeless "Mexican" images still exist, of course. Donkeys amble down dusty paths, and ancient ruins stand silhouetted against the sky. But for every small village where a herd of goats comprises the local traffic, there is a vehicle-choked freeway. And for every local market displaying live chickens, handwoven baskets and piles of dried chilies, there is a glitzy mall offering the latest in upscale merchandise.

The extremes of wealth and poverty here can be shocking. Half an hour away

from Cancún's glittering resorts are windowless, thatch-roofed huts with dirt floors. In bursting-at-the-seams Mexico City, high fashion and haute cuisine coexist with sprawling shantytowns lacking running water.

But while a Third World way of life is still unfortunately the norm for many Mexicans, visitors benefit from a strong and growing first world of hotels, restaurants and related amenities, as well as a cultural heritage richly expressed through fiestas and national celebrations. This makes Mexico a fascinating country that can be explored rather easily. What are you waiting for?

Historical Overview

Mexican history has been particularly tumultuous, encompassing cultural peaks as well as the suffering borne out of conquest, war and subjugation. No one knows for sure where the native peoples of Mexico originally came from. Somewhere around 5000 B.C., in the valley of Tehuacán southeast of present-day Mexico City, a straggling community of seed gatherers discovered how to domesticate maize, becoming farmers in the process and beginning the establishment of permanent villages.

Eventually the stage was set for the building of cities. At a time when much of Europe was decidedly primitive, civilizations in the New World were carving out sophisticated architectural, scientific and artistic achievements. Scattered throughout central and southern Mexico, the ruins of pyramids, palaces and temples all bear witness to the highly developed skills of the Olmec, Maya, Toltec and Aztec cultures that flourished, in some instances, more than a thousand years before the arrival of Spain. Some waged war; all trafficked and explored, leaving behind a fascinating legacy.

Many historians consider the Maya to be the crown jewel of pre-Columbian cultures.

They developed the mathematical concept of zero and produced a calendar that enabled their priests to predict eclipses and plot the movements of the solar system. In contrast to these refined achievements, the Maya also participated enthusiastically in brutal games, human sacrifice and ritual bloodletting, which they believed helped them communicate with the gods. From about 200 B.C. through the eighth century, the vast Maya empire spread north from Guatemala to the Yucatán Peninsula.

In the early 1300s the fierce, nomadic Mexica, now known as the Aztecs, moved from place to place in search of a prophetic vision: an eagle perched on a cactus pad, clutching a serpent in its beak. According to legend, that vision was seen on an island in the middle of Lake Texcoco, within the Valley of Mexico—the site of present-day Mexico City. Aztec civilization was well advanced by the beginning of the 16th century, but ironically it was their ruthless dominance that led to their undoing at the hands of the Spanish *conquistadores*.

Destroying the Aztec empire gave Spain the infamous distinction of wiping out hundreds of years of Indian achievements in Mesoamerica. Spanish reign was insignificant

---

Mexico's first great urban civilizations are built, including Chichén Itzá, Palenque, Teotihuacán and Uxmal.

200 B.C.-A.D. 900

Father Miguel Hidalgo issues the *Grito de Dolores*, a call for freedom that sparks the War of Independence.

1810

Library of Congress

A new constitution is drafted proclaiming Mexico a federal republic.

1823

The Aztecs establish the city of Tenochtitlan, later to become Mexico City.

1325

eHistorical
Picture Archive
Corbis

1521

Tenochtitlan falls to conquistador Hernando Cortés, inaugurating three centuries of Spanish rule.

Mexico Historical Timeline

1848

The Treaty of Guadalupe Hidalgo forces Mexico to cede its territories north of the Rio Grande River to the United States.

politically but momentous socially. Mexico's colonial cities, its grand cathedrals and most of its historic buildings were constructed during three centuries of Spanish rule. Spain justified its continued presence in Mexico on the basis of converting the natives—considered barbarians—to Christianity. The church thus played a singular role in the colony of New Spain, which consisted of all Spanish possessions in North and Central America. Augustinian, Dominican and Franciscan friars (and later the Jesuits) all journeyed to New Spain to minister and teach, founding missions in the depths of the wilderness.

Mexico's push for independence came out of the divisiveness resulting from rigid societal classes that emerged over the course of colonial rule, and from continuing exploitation of the vast outpost off which the Spanish colonists profited. It was finally achieved in 1821, but political turmoil was the rule rather than the exception throughout the remainder of the 19th century and into the 20th.

Social change, rapid industrial growth and economic improvement came in the mid-20th century. The new Mexican prosperity was put on world view during the 1968 Summer Olympics, held in Mexico City. By the dawn of the 1990s the leap from developing nation to recognized world player seemed likely. Then a guerrilla uprising, a political assassination and a devastating currency devaluation (all in 1994) threatened hard-won stability. The United States bailed the country out of a monetary crisis with a $20 billion international financial aid package, but by 1997 Mexico had fully repaid its debt. The peso has yet to recover to pre-devaluation levels, however, so visitors with dollars to convert will find a country eager to accept them.

Natural Features

Mexico, while part of North America, also marks the transition from that vast continent's topographic and climatic extremes to the more uniformly tropical features of Central America and the Caribbean basin. Although its sun-scorched deserts and jagged mountain ranges look harsh, they also possesses an austere beauty. And not all is geographically forbidding—there are verdant valleys, cool highlands and mile after mile of sandy, palm-fringed beaches.

Roughly triangular in shape, Mexico narrows from an expanse of 1,300 miles across its northern frontier to a mere 140 miles at

French emperor Napoleon III is defeated at the Battle of Puebla.
1862

Growing opposition to the dictatorship of Porfirio Díaz sets off the bloody, protracted Revolution of 1910.
1910

Vicente Fox of the National Action Party defeats the PRI candidate in the presidential election, dethroning the country's ruling political dynasty.
2000

1929
Mexico's dominant political party, the Partido Revolucionario Institucional (PRI), is founded.

1994
Indian guerrillas calling themselves the Zapatista National Liberation Party lead a rebellion for land and self-rule in the state of Chiapas.

1968
Summer Olympics are held in Mexico City.

the Isthmus of Tehuantepec. Two peninsulas—Baja (Lower) California and the Yucatán Pebninsula—are appendages to the mainland.

Most of the country consists of hills or mountain ranges broken by level plateaus; the plateaus in turn are carved into many canyons and valleys. Central Mexico is a vast elevated landscape dominated by high mountains to the east and west, many of which are of volcanic origin. The east coast is low and flat, but in the state of Veracruz the lofty mountains advance almost to the coast. The northwestern coastal plain is another relatively flat area, broken in parts by low hills and mountains.

The Sierra Madre comprises three great mountain ranges. The Sierra Madre Oriental and the Sierra Madre Occidental form the eastern and western boundaries of the central plateau region. The Sierra Madre del Sur frames the Pacific coast through the states of Guerrero and Oaxaca.

The height of the mountains is accentuated by deep valleys and canyons, which can plunge more than 1,500 feet below the general level of the plateau. At the bottom of some of these canyons the climate and vegetation are subtropical and distinctly different from conditions at the canyon rim. This is particularly true of the Copper Canyon area in the state of Chihuahua. Shadowed by the lofty Sierra Madre Occidental, it derives its name from the rust coloring of many of the canyon walls.

There are hundreds of volcanic peaks in Mexico; in the state of Michoacán alone there are more than 80. Volcanoes active in the last half century or so include Volcán de Fuego de Colima, near the city of the same name; Paricutín, near Uruapan but now dormant; and El Chichonal. Born in the fall of 1943 when a cornfield suddenly erupted, Paricutín grew more than 1,700 feet in 10 months. In 1982 the long-dormant volcano El Chichonal spewed a billion tons of ash and rock across a wide area near the small town of Teapa in southeastern Mexico.

A recent increase in seismic activity has been noted within Popocatépetl, at 17,883 feet Mexico's second highest peak. Although snow perpetually covers its upper flanks, Popocatépetl has historically spewed ash over extensive areas. Tests conducted in 1994 measuring sulfur dioxide emissions showed the volcano to be among the world's five or six most active, although scientists cannot predict whether this is a significant indication of any future activity. Over time, dozens of villages have sprouted up on Popocatépetl's lower slopes, but as with earthquakes, most Mexicans treat the possibility of an erupting volcano as simply a fact of life.

The backbone of Baja California consists of several westward-sloping mountain ranges. The Yucatán Peninsula, on the other hand, is primarily flat or rolling; its highest point is barely 1,000 feet above sea level. Much of the subsurface rock is limestone, and subterranean erosion has produced many sinkholes (cenotes), some of which are used as natural swimming pools.

The Coasts

Mexico has four distinct coastal regions. The Baja California Peninsula, bathed by both the Pacific Ocean and the Sea of Cortés (Gulf of California), is marked by numerous bays and coves, as is the northwestern mainland coast. Farther south, Pacific breakers crash against the feet of the Sierra Madre Occidental and the Sierra Madre del Sur. The Pacific Coast cities of Manzanillo and Acapulco boast fine natural harbors.

The eastern coastal plain along the Gulf of Mexico is essentially featureless. The flat terrain is characterized by broad beaches, swamps and palm-lined lagoons. Sandbars and lagoons also are features of the western and northern coasts of the Yucatán Peninsula. The peninsula's eastern coast borders the Caribbean Sea and is marked by extensive coral reefs. The islands of Cozumel and Mujeres are off its northeast corner. Powdery sands and clear, aquamarine waters are the Yucatán's greatest natural resource.

For average monthly high and low temperatures and precipitation amounts for representative cities, see page 54.

People

The Mexican people are a vibrant and complex group, despite being the product of a historical legacy that is in many ways tragic and divisive. And just as the country is a land of extremes—from baked desert to dripping jungle, from craggy mountain to swampy coast—there are differences among the people as well. You'll likely encounter both ostentatious wealth and startling poverty, impeccable politeness and stony indifference, gracious manners and leering machismo.

The Indígenas

When Hernando Cortés arrived in 1519, the land now comprising Mexico was inhabited by some 15 to 20 million people, a number of whom were under the savage domination of the Aztecs. Many lived in the elevated plateau region of central Mexico, where the weather and soil were most favorable for agriculture. By 1521, a handful of Spanish *conquistadores* had toppled the vast Aztec empire and went on to subjugate an entire country.

Spaniards subsequently came to New Spain, amassed riches and returned to the mother country. The Indians, meanwhile, were put to work in the silver mines, toiled in fields or performed backbreaking manual labor constructing lavish cathedrals and public buildings, laboring side by side with Africans brought into the country for the same purpose. Although the Spanish contributed only minimally to growth—during 300 years of rule only about 300,000 settled in Mexico—a combination of introduced diseases, cultural upheaval and strict suppression decimated the natives.

The Indians, or *indígenas,* living in Mexico today—an estimated 15 percent of the total population—are direct descendants of the Aztec, Maya and other ancient civilizations. These natives speak a primary language other than Spanish, and many might express surprise if referred to as "Mexican." Some are small groups living in self-sufficient isolation; others occupy large territories. While it is convenient for the sake of categorization to lump all Indians together, Mexico's native peoples are characterized by linguistic and cultural differences that can be as distinct as those defining Norwegians and Italians.

Approximately 50 of the numerous ethnic groups populating Mexico at the time of the Spanish arrival remain in existence. They include the Tarahumara, who dwell in the Copper Canyon region of northwest Mexico; the Yaqui, in the state of Sonora; the Huichol and the Tarasco, near and along the central Pacific coast; the Nahua and the Otomí, in the central plateau region; the Zapotec and the Mixtec, in the state of Oaxaca; the Chamula, Tzeltal and Tzotzil, in the state of Chiapas; the Huastec, along the eastern Gulf of Mexico coast; and the Maya, throughout the Yucatán Peninsula.

The status of *indígenas* in today's Mexico, unfortunately, is not much better than it was during the colonial era. Poverty is a chronic, debilitating fact of life for more than three-quarters of the country's Indian communities, including many in the economically challenged states of Chiapas, Guerrero and Oaxaca. Indian rights—particularly the demand for self-rule—has been a thorny issue for the Mexican government since the January 1994 uprising led by the Zapatistas. Life is still hard for "Mexico's most forgotten people,"

as many *indígenas* refer to themselves, but their plight has garnered international attention and forced ongoing government negotiations.

Mestizos and the "Thousand Families"

The great majority of Mexicans—75 percent—are *mestizos,* of mixed European and Native American descent. They have perhaps the strongest sense of national identity, although occupying various levels of prosperity and social standing. The small percentage of citizens of purely European ancestry—some 10 percent of the population and often referred to as the "Thousand Families"—control the country's political power and economic wealth, just as the Spanish did more than three centuries earlier.

There are signs of change, however. The PRI's 1997 political defeats came largely at the hands of the youth vote. An estimated 65 percent of the population is under age 30, and this new generation of Mexicans may prove to be as influential on the nation's economics and culture as the baby boomers have been in the United States.

Mexico is the second most populous country in Latin America after Brazil. Within its 31 states and the Federal District live some 100 million citizens—up from just 30 million in 1950. But over the last several decades the fertility rate has fallen dramatically, and this generational shift has resulted in a trend toward smaller families that will have far-reaching social and economic effects.

The Mexican Character

Many Mexicans have a strong streak of fatalism. The country has weathered hurricanes, erupting volcanoes and severe earthquakes, particularly the one that leveled parts of Mexico City in 1985. More telling is the violence associated with history. Aztec ceremonies revolved around blood-spattered human sacrifice, with hearts literally torn from victims' chests. The Spanish conquest wiped out entire cities. Post-independence Mexico endured war, revolution, assassination and civil strife. Death is thus both honored and mocked in such celebrations as the Day of the Dead, when decorated sugar skulls are sold, costumed children bear mock coffins in street parades and families pay tribute to deceased members in front of lavish home altars.

This is a country that knows how to have fun, and priority is given to family and holidays. On weekends, city dwellers exit the concrete jungle en masse for beaches, parks and lakeside resorts. A minor saint's day is reason enough to hold a fiesta, and the birthday of a national hero or the date commemorating an important historical or religious event merits a major celebration.

Many Mexicans are rather formal in their dealings with strangers, and very polite as well; try to respond in kind. Older citizens can be very conservative, and provocative or skimpy dress—on men or women—is frowned upon if worn in churches or other inappropriate places. When sightseeing, dress with both comfort and common sense in mind. Mexican men also love to charm, and female travelers may receive openly admiring looks or remarks. If such behavior is bothersome, it's best to simply ignore it rather than to get angry, and to minimize or eliminate overtures by dressing conservatively.

Architecture

Mexico is particularly rich with reminders of its earliest architects' work. Innumerable archeological sites—some little more than a few earthen mounds or a crumbling platform, others the spectacular remains of cities—have left behind intriguing clues related to the puzzle of their abandoned cultures.

Early Builders

The first great architects were the Maya. They constructed numerous ceremonial centers connected by straight, wide roadways of crushed limestone called *sacbe.* (sack-BEH). These ancient roads were marvels of engineering, since the flat land denied builders an elevated vantage point while planning construction through the dense, scrubby jungle.

Maya buildings took three main forms: the pyramid, often with a temple capping the summit; the palace, consisting of a central court surrounded by chambers; and the ball court, a wide, flat area used for playing a mysterious but presumably sacred ball game.

Another early site is the ceremonial center of Teotihuacán, northeast of present-day Mexico City. Pyramids with sloping sides created an impression of great mass. They were adorned with stucco reliefs, murals and the carved heads of gods that frequently resembled animals. The Zapotecs, who dominated the Valley of Oaxaca in southern Mexico, created Monte Albán. Its ball court, raised platforms and temples bear the influence of Teotihuacán, Maya architects and the Pre-Classic Olmec people, who inhabited the coastal regions of the present-day states of Tabasco and Veracruz.

Mexican pyramids did not necessarily resemble the familiar form of the Egyptian variety—a square base with four sloping, triangular sides meeting at the top. Created essentially as religious monuments, they frequently had steps built into the sides. Exterior carvings not only served as decoration but also depicted historical and mythological events. The ceremonial centers from which these pyramids rose were dedicated to fanciful gods and paid tribute to the priest rulers who presided over rigidly hierarchical societies.

The medium of choice was stone, a common building material in Mexico and one suitable for long-lasting creations. Frequently employed was a porous, volcanic rock known as *tezontle,* also used by the Aztecs. Although the sheer scope of the structures is awe-inspiring, other archeological remnants—for example, the free-standing arch at Labná, on the Yucatán Peninsula—hint at the direction in which the Maya and other early architects might have headed.

Subsequent tribes such as the Toltecs, Mixtecs and Aztecs expanded on the architectural themes developed by the great Classic civilizations. Pyramids and palaces continued in importance, serving the needs of highly complex religious ceremonies. It was a period of military maneuvers and violent conquest, and the murals, carvings and bas-reliefs applied as decoration depicted scenes of war and human sacrifice.

European Influence

The arrival of Spain in the early 16th century brought an abrupt end to Indian achievements, as most of the existing civilizations were destroyed. The conquerors frequently chose such razed ground as the place to begin their own construction. The Spanish conquest ushered in a 300-year period during which ecclesiastical architecture predominated, often imitating prevailing European trends.

Augustinian, Dominican, Franciscan and Jesuit friars built churches throughout Mexico as part of a large-scale attempt to convert the natives to Christianity. These structures, distinguished by thick walls and simple interiors with vaulted ceilings, were impressively fortified to serve as protection against Indian attack. A monastery built around an enclosed patio was usually connected to the church. Decoration also served an educational purpose, as frescoes and stone carvings vividly depicted the symbolic themes of the new religion.

Several decorative motifs were developed to enhance the aesthetics of the buildings themselves. A combination dome and tower often was used; the dome, constructed of arched masonry, frequently was covered with colorful tiles arranged in geometric designs. Plateresque decoration foreshadowed the more extravagant flourishes of the 17th and 18th centuries. The word comes from the Spanish *platero,* or silversmith, and the delicate ornamentation that often was placed around doorways or entrances resembled silverwork designs. The Convent of San Agustín Acolman (Convento de San Agustín Acolman) in the town of Acolman, México, and the doorway of the Montejo House (Casa de Montejo) in Mérida, Yucatán, are two good examples of the Plateresque style.

The wealth amassed from Mexico's silver and gold mines and from the huge sugar-producing *haciendas* (plantations) led to a spate of ostentatious construction in the 17th and 18th centuries. The baroque style, characterized by lavish ornamentation, came into popularity, and baroque cathedrals began springing up in the central plazas of cities throughout the country. Notable examples are the Metropolitan Cathedral (Catedral Metropolitana) and the Church of Santo Domingo (Iglesia de Santo Domingo) in Mexico City and the Cathedral of the Immaculate Conception in Puebla.

The ultimate baroque expression was a Mexican development known as Churrigueresque, or ultra-baroque. It was named after Spanish artisan José de Churriguera, whose own work, curiously, was much more restrained. Buildings exploded with carved geometric forms, leafy vines, frolicking cherubs, scrolls and other imaginative accents, often to the point that formal structure seemed an afterthought.

The style extended inside as well, and Churrigueresque interiors were a cornucopia of extravagant embellishment, often executed in gold. The overall intent was literally to knock one's eyes out. Stunning examples of this ornate style are the Church of San Francisco Xavier (Iglesia de San Francisco Xavier) in Tepotzotlán, México; the Church of Santa Clara (Iglesia de Santa Clara) and the Church of Santa Rosa de Viterbo (Iglesia de Santa Rosa de Viterbo), both in the city of Querétaro; the Cathedral in the city of Zacatecas; and the interior of the Church of Santo Domingo (Iglesia de Santo Domingo) in the city of Oaxaca.

Another form used in Mexico during this period was *mudéjar,* derived from the Spanish Moors. The *mudéjar* style also favored lavish decoration; interiors and exteriors were plastered with colored tiles. Puebla is particularly noted for churches with intricate tiled designs; a secular example is the House of Tiles (Casa de Los Azulejos) in Mexico City, a former mansion occupied since 1919 by a Sanborn's restaurant.

After the excesses of the Churrigueresque, something had to give. The end of the colonial era saw a return to the more restrained neoclassic style. Buildings often incorporated several styles of architecture, however. Sometimes more than a century passed before work was finished; as a result, influences overlapped, particularly on the larger cathedrals. Mexico City's massive Metropolitan Cathedral took 240 years of off-and-on construction to complete; its facade is primarily baroque but also exhibits neoclassic elements, while the ornamentation of the altars is Churrigueresque.

During much of the 19th century Mexican life was disrupted by war and political turbulence, and architectural development was given short shrift. When relative prosperity returned under dictator Porfirio Díaz, a new round of public buildings appeared, mostly massive structures in a variety of styles that again imitated what was happening in Europe. Mexico City's Palacio de Bellas Artes (Palace of Fine Arts) was designed and executed by Italian architects following classic blueprints. Mérida's ornate mansions took on a Parisian influence, as wealthy hemp exporters strove to emulate the refined atmosphere of that French city.

The Modern Era

The early 20th century found Mexican architects struggling for a style to call their own. Attempts at monumentality produced such misguided curiosities as the gigantic statue of José María Morelos, a hero of the Mexican War of Independence. Built on an island in Lake Pátzcuaro, it depicts an ungainly-looking figure reaching toward the sky. Skyscrapers began to sprout in industrial centers like Mexico City and Monterrey, but their functional steel and concrete construction tended to resemble the tall buildings found in any big city.

In the last half of the century, innovative architecture resulted from the combination of old and new design elements, such as the buildings at the National University of Mexico (UNAM) in San Angel, the National Museum of Anthropology in Mexico City and large-scale resort properties in places like Cancún and Acapulco. One of the most recent examples is the National Center of the Arts, inaugurated in 1994. The complex, south of downtown Mexico City, incorporates futuristic forms—a vivid orange tower studded with exaggerated window frames—as well as a lecture hall resembling mission churches built during the colonial era.

Music and Dance

To a Mexican, a love of music is as fundamental a pleasure as the loving bonds of family. The country's musical traditions are exceedingly rich and abundantly varied. As with architecture and art, styles have tended to originate elsewhere before being assimilated and frequently adapted to suit the national preferences: passion, romance and insistent rhythms. Popular folk and dance music in particular vividly evokes the sights, sounds and moods of the country.

A broad distinction can be made between the music of Mexico's *indígena* and *mestizo* groups. Indian musical expression is ceremonial in nature, linked to religious rituals or village fiestas. Within the dominant, mixed *mestizo* population, on the other hand, music has a genuinely mass appeal that is strengthened by a healthy recording industry, ceaseless radio play and impromptu performances that enliven the central plazas of practically every town in the country.

From Marimba to Mariachi

Little is known about what sort of sounds were created by pre-Hispanic civilizations. Music, singing and dancing did, however, play a large role in daily ceremonial life. The mesmerizing beat of the drum was foremost among ancient instruments. Drums were fashioned out of clay, wood, bones and turtle shells. Rattles complemented the beat, and simple reed or clay flutes added a melodic counterpoint. It may well have sounded similar to what can be heard in some Indian villages today.

Spanish *conquistadores* and the missionaries who followed them imported European culture, which began to have an influence on native song and dance. Folk orchestras began to accommodate new instruments, chief among them various types of guitars. The *son* (also called *huapango*), a driving dance rhythm with plenty of instrumental flourishes, is the basic form of *mestizo* music. Regional styles have different names, such as *son huasteco* (northeastern Mexico), *son jarana* (the Yucatán Peninsula), *son jarocho* (around Veracruz) or *son mariachi* (the state of Jalisco). Whatever the region, the guitar is the lead instrument, replaced by violin in the *huasteco* style and harp in the *jarocho* style.

Another of Mexico's traditional sounds is that of the marimba, a percussion instrument similar to a xylophone. When struck with small rubber mallets, the marimba's hardwood bars produce clear, breezy-sounding tones. Marimba music is most commonly heard in southern Mexico and Guatemala, where on fiesta days town plazas resonate with lively rhythms, sputtering firecrackers and all manner of merriment.

Popular Mexican songs have long evoked the trials and tribulations of daily life. The *corrido*, a folk narrative descended from Spanish balladry, emerged during the turbulent period of the 1910 Revolution and served as a news service of sorts in the days before radio. In exchange for a meal, wandering minstrels would travel from one rural town to another, singing songs about historical events, heroes, villains and the travails of unrequited love.

The *canción* (literally, song or lyric) was usually a slow, unabashedly sentimental ballad appealing to the passionate aspect of Mexican character. No less dramatic were the *rancheras*, nostalgic paeans to home and country originally sung by Mexican cattlemen, thus giving them a sort of country-and-western flavor.

The music most emblematic of Mexico is the sound of the mariachis. The custom of hiring a group of professional musicians to play at weddings, birthdays and other special occasions began in the state of Jalisco; "mariachi" is said to be an adaptation of the French word *mariage*. Mariachi bands deck themselves out in the costumes of the *charro,* or Mexican cowboy: tight-fitting pants, wide-brimmed sombreros and lots of silver spangles. Today they can be found all over Mexico—regaling foreign tourists in flashy Cancún, playing to homesick laborers in border towns, or serenading the object of a young suitor's desire—all for a fee, of course.

Mariachi bands started out playing guitars, violins and harp, with the harp later replaced largely by the brassy sound of trumpets. The style reached its peak in the 1950s, when Mexican matinee idols in Hollywood films sang their love songs to the strains of mariachis. The two best places for visitors to see them in action today are Plaza Garibaldi in Mexico City and Plaza de Los Mariachis in Guadalajara. A mariachi band worth its salt will be able to reel off an astonishing variety of songs, from long-established classics to customer requests in styles from achingly sad to irresistibly upbeat—and all delivered with undeniable heart and soul.

With the shrinking of the global village over the last couple of decades, Mexico—like many countries throughout the world—has been exposed to a tidal wave of Americanized pop culture. In the cities, radios, bars and dance clubs *(discotecas)* blare the latest pop, rock and hip-hop. Beyonce, Justin Timberlake and other international acts are as popular here as anywhere. But despite the invasion, music with a Mexican feeling continues to thrive.

Norteña, appropriately, originated in the working-class *cantinas* and speak-easies of the northern border area. Springing from the *corrida* tradition of lyric-driven balladry, *norteña* songs often spin tales involving small-time thieves, drug runners, illegal immigrants and other antiheroes who buck a system they consider crooked. Musically, *norteña* is like a Mexican polka, with the accordion typically the lead instrument.

Cumbia, a seductive, danceable import from the Caribbean, was the most popular music in Mexico in the 1980s; the songs are distinguished by their flirtatious lyrics, often spiced with double entendres. Equally danceable salsa, which originated in Cuba and Puerto Rico and is influenced by jazz and rock, is popular as well. *Banda* musicians play various popular styles, all arranged with an emphasis on brass and percussion. And concerts given by brass bands fill parks and town halls throughout the country.

All of these influences—spliced together with bits of American rock 'n' roll, pop, country, jazz and rap—combine to produce *tejano,* a cross-cultural musical blend embraced by Americans of Mexican descent. The center of *tejano* music is Texas (specifically, the gulf coast city of Corpus Christi), although its popularity extends south of the border as well. *Tejano's* rising star, a young woman named Selena who was sometimes referred to as the "Mexican Madonna," actually hailed from Corpus Christi and was taught Spanish by her father to further her career. Selena was about to break into the English-language market when she was murdered in 1995 by her fan-club president.

Pole Flyers, Hats and Little Old Men

Rich in history and spectacle, native folk dances are one of Mexico's most enjoyable traditions for visitors. They include those that predate the Spanish arrival, as well as European dances adapted to suit the Mexican character. Although the *conquistadores* initially tried to eradicate what they viewed as simply pagan rites, Franciscan and Dominican missionaries encouraged the continuation of Indian dances and wove these age-old rituals into their ongoing efforts to convert the natives to the Catholic church. The symbolism may have been changed—substituting Moors and Christians in place of warring tribes, for instance—but the costumes and movements remained essentially the same.

Like musical styles, folk dances vary by region. Around Papantla in the state of Veracruz, Totonac Indians still perform the flying pole dance, originally a ceremony meant to appease the rain gods. In the states of Sonora and Chihuahua, Yaqui and Tarahumara Indians perform the deer dance, a ceremony once meant to impart good luck on the hunt. A dancer in this vivid re-enactment may even wear the stuffed head of a deer. *Los Viejitos,* the "Dance of the Little Old Men," originated in the state of Michoacán. It is danced by young boys wearing masks carved to resemble the visages of elderly men. The dancers begin by moving arthritically in a parody of old age; by the end, however, their pace has enlivened considerably.

Popular traditional dances are based, not surprisingly, on Spanish steps. Perhaps the one most widely known and closely associated with the country is the *jarabe tapatío,* or Mexican hat dance. The costumes for this passionate interlude are flamboyant: for men, the silver-embroidered shirt and trousers and wide-brimmed sombrero of the horseman (*charro*); for women, the national costume, a *china poblana* dress. The dance ends with the man's sombrero placed on the floor and the couple parading around it.

Food and Drink

Authentic Mexican dishes have many influences, among them Maya, Aztec, Spanish, French, Moorish and even Chinese. There is much more to the cuisine, however, than the commonly mistaken notion that it is always hot. Many items that are in use throughout the world originated in Mexico. Corn is the country's greatest contribution to global cookery, but the list also includes tomatoes, chocolate, avocados, squashes, beans, pumpkins, chilies and turkeys (the only bird bred in pre-Hispanic Mexico).

Corn, the centerpiece of the Indian diet, took on an almost magical significance in many cultures, being used in religious rituals and ceremonies. Called *teoxintle* until the Spaniards renamed it *maíz,* the different corn varieties enabled native cooks to put this versatile vegetable to assorted uses—grinding kernels to make tortillas, thickening soups, creating beverages.

Squash and beans were other basic foodstuffs, providing practical as well as nourishing applications. Gourds, for example, were fashioned into handy household items. The cacao bean, from which chocolate is made, was so valued that the Indians used it for money, and hot chocolate whipped to a fragrant froth was at one time a drink quaffed only by the upper classes. Another native plant highly prized in pre-Hispanic kitchens was the nopal (prickly pear) cactus. Its juicy fruit was cooked and added to soups and stews, or stuffed with meat.

Nopal cactus pads are a common sight in Mexican markets today.

It was with chilies, however, that early cooks could fully utilize their creative talents. Using the entire chile ensured maximum firepower, while removing the veins or seeds lessened the fiery impact. Although eaten alone as a garnish, chilies most often contributed to sauces—either salsa, made from a combination of ingredients, or mole (MOHleh), a blend of chilies.

All of this native bounty must have mesmerized the Spanish *conquistadores* who arrived in Mexico. Bernal Díaz, a historian who marched with Hernando Cortés, described the *tianguis* (the Aztec word for marketplace) at Tlatelolco, an important trading center located just north of present-day Mexico City. Wild game included pigeon, duck, rabbit, deer, boar and iguana. From fresh water came frog legs and the larvae of water gnats. Many of the exotic fruits, vegetables and herbs— among them chilies, avocado, cilantro, cumin, papaya, mango, guava and jicama—the Spaniards had never before seen.

The Spanish themselves influenced the native cuisine, introducing cattle, sheep, goats, pigs, chickens, sugar, olive oil, rice, citrus fruits, lettuce, pepper, cinnamon and other products. Many of Mexico's most enduring dishes were developed in the Spanish convents by nuns, who had the time and patience to painstakingly combine spices, herbs and chilies into complex sauces. Eggs, lard, sugar and milk formed the basis for pastries and candies, as well as new, improved versions of the traditional tortilla. The invading French also added to the culinary mix. Wine, butter and cream added a refined touch to sauces, and such herbs as dill and mustard lent flavor to French soufflés, omelettes and pâtes.

Mexican Staples

Corn anchors the Mexican diet. The tortilla, also common in Central America, is as ubiquitous in Mexico as a hamburger in the United States. This thin pancake made of coarse cornmeal appears in many guises. A basket of warm flour tortillas frequently replaces bread or rolls on a Mexican table. Tacos are rolled tortillas stuffed with beef, pork, chicken or cheese and customarily seasoned with avocado, onion, lettuce and chile sauce. When served with tomato sauce, soft rolled tacos are called enchiladas.

Crisp fried tortillas spread with minced chicken, meat or salad are called tostadas. Tortilla dough turnovers filled with cheese are quesadillas; when filled with potato, pork sausage (chorizo) or fried beans and then fried in fat, they are empanadas. Tamales are a mixture of corn and rice dough filled with bits of chicken, pork or sweets, wrapped in corn husks or banana leaves and then steamed. Tortas, the Mexican counterpart of sandwiches, are prepared with a small loaf of bread called *telera* or *bolillo* and then filled with different meats, lettuce, onion, tomato, cheese and avocado.

Other prevalent dishes are those made of either *frijoles* (beans) cooked in various ways or rice combined with vegetables, chicken livers, plantains or eggs. Guacamole is a salad or side dish that consists of mashed avocado seasoned with onion, hot peppers and tomato.

Festive and Regional Fare

The nation's favorite special preparation is *mole de guajolote,* turkey served with a rich, thick sauce made from various chilies, peanuts, spices, sesame seed and unsweetened chocolate. As many as 30 different ingredients, all of which must be ground or pureed, may go into the sauce's preparation.

Another distinctly Mexican concoction is *chiles rellenos,* or stuffed chilies. A dark green chili pepper—not the sweet bell variety popular in the United States—is stuffed with cheese or ground meat, fried in a coating of egg batter and then simmered in tomato sauce. A variation of this dish is called *chile en nogada.* Instead of tomato sauce, the chili (stuffed with beef, pork and fruits) is covered with ground fresh walnuts and a pureed white cheese similar to cream cheese. When sprinkled with red pomegranate seeds and garnished with parsley, the dish represents the red, white and green colors of the Mexican flag. It is frequently served in conjunction with independence celebrations during the month of September.

If you're fond of gastronomic adventure, Mexico has some exotic choices. At the time of the Spanish arrival, the staple diet of the Indians included such items as grasshoppers, ant eggs, rats, armadillos, monkeys, parrots and rattlesnakes. Fine restaurants in Mexico City and Oaxaca still offer insect dishes, including grasshoppers, ant eggs and the worm—crisply fried—found on the maguey plant, from which tequila is made. *Huitlacoche* is a black fungus that grows on ears of corn; it is often served with crepes. In the northern part of the country, broiled goat *(cabrito)* is popular.

Different areas of Mexico are known for their style of cooking or for specific dishes. In and around Veracruz the specialty is *huachinango a la Veracruzana,* red snapper broiled in tomato sauce and served with onions, olives and capers. Acapulco and other Mexican seaside towns are famous for their ceviche (say-VEE-cheh). Pieces of raw fish or shellfish are marinated in lime juice for at least eight hours, "cooking" the fish. Chopped tomatoes and onions, chilies and such herbs as cilantro are then added to this dish, which is served chilled and often as an appetizer. In Baja California and the northwestern coastal cities, lobster and shrimp are scrambled into eggs, or replace chicken and pork as tamale fillings.

Historical and geographical isolation have had perhaps their greatest impact on regional cuisine in the Yucatán Peninsula. Here the food has Cuban, Caribbean, European and Asian influences. The fiery habanero chile common in Yucatecan cookery grows nowhere else in Mexico. Achiote, the seed of the annatto tree, is the primary ingredient of a pungent spice with a distinctive orange-red color that seasons pork, chicken or fish cooked pibil style—sort of a distant relative of American barbecue.

Yucatecan menus offer such authentic dishes as cochinita pibil, suckling pig rubbed with achiote, wrapped in banana leaves and baked in an underground oven; puchero, a Sunday supper staple of chicken, pork, carrots, squash, cabbage, bananas and sweet potatoes simmered in broth flavored with cilantro and sour orange juice, the whole garnished with radishes; and huevos motuleños, a filling breakfast dish featuring a tortilla covered with refried beans, topped with a fried egg and smothered with tomato sauce, peas, diced ham and shredded cheese, usually served with slices of fried banana.

Soups and Desserts

Soups are tasty and varied. Mexican chicken soup is laden with chunks of chicken, rice, vegetables and often sliced avocado. Rich cream soups are made from such unlikely vegetable by-products as squash blossoms. Pozole, a hearty soup native to the state of Jalisco but popular in many parts of Mexico, incorporates hominy and pork or chicken in a flavorful broth. Shredded lettuce, chopped onions, strips of fried tortilla and splashes of lime juice are frequently tossed in. This stewlike concoction also takes on red or green hues from the addition of ancho chilies or green tomatoes mixed with various greens, respectively. **Note:** Most Mexican chilies are hot, and some are incendiary. If in doubt about their firepower, ask, "Es muy picante?" ("Is it very hot?").

Desserts are not the focal point of a good Mexican meal. Many are overwhelmingly sweet. Flan (browned custard), which is widely served, is a Spanish creation. Although there is a large variety of egg-based, pudding-like sweets, a better choice would be one of the country's tropical fruits, such as papaya, passion fruit, pineapple or mango. Remember to avoid those that are unpeeled. Mexican confections, or dulces, are most often fruit-flavored hard candies, sugar-glazed fruits in their natural form or little cakes made of honey, grated coconut, almonds and other ingredients. Some restaurants feature good ice cream (helado).

Beverages

A good way to begin the day in Mexico is to have a steaming cup of coffee. Cafe de olla is flavored with cinnamon and sugar, although you'll have to ask for cream (which usually turns out to be evaporated milk). Espresso and cappuccino are widely available—and undistinguished instant is frequently served in restaurants—but Mexicans favor cafe con leche, a combination of strong black coffee and hot milk that is often poured into a tall glass. Another favorite is Mexican hot chocolate, which is not as sweet as the American version.

Freshly squeezed fruit juices are inexpensive and refreshing. Ask for a licuado (fruit shake) made with bananas or papayas. Also inexpensive are soft drinks, the ubiquitous Coca-Cola as well as local brands (refrescos). They are not only safe to drink out of the can but one of the few luxuries that the country's poorer citizens can afford. Tehuacán, in the state of Puebla, is famous for bottled mineral waters made with and without natural fruit flavors. Local bottling plants draw from the mineral springs around the city.

Cerveza (beer) is as ubiquitous as Coke ("Coca"). Two Mexican varieties—Corona and Tecate—are sold everywhere (the latter is the country's No. 1 cheap alcoholic beverage). Quality brews like Dos Equis and Bohemia are appreciated throughout the world.

Mexico's viticultural history was relatively late in developing. Although pre-Hispanic peoples enjoyed fermented beverages, those derived from the grape were not among them. Spanish colonists introduced the first vine cuttings, and Mexican wines soon began competing with those of the homeland. A marauding insect almost destroyed the grape crop in the late 19th century, but plague-resistant cuttings from California were grafted onto the diseased ones, saving the wine industry. Today almost 80 percent of all domestic vintages are produced in the state of Baja California. Other major wine-producing areas are in the states of Aguascalientes, Querétaro and Zacatecas.

From the several varieties of the maguey (mah-GAY) plant, a cactuslike jack-of-all-trades, come highly intoxicating liquors that are uniquely Mexican. Tequila is the quintessential one, traditionally downed from a salt-rimmed glass and immediately followed by a bite into a lime wedge. Bottles of mezcal from the vicinity of Oaxaca sometimes include a worm that lives on the plant. Other alcoholic beverages produced from the maguey are *comiteco* (Chiapas), *charanda* (Michoacán), *sotol* (Chihuahua) and *bacanora* (Sonora).

Pulque, manufactured in central Mexico from the maguey's unfermented juice, has less of a kick and is considered to have both nutritious and medicinal properties. *Colonche* is prepared in the states of Aguascalientes, Guanajuato, Jalisco and San Luis Potosí with fermented fruit from the prickly pear cactus. *Rompope* originated in the state of Puebla as a family beverage for festive occasions. Similar to eggnog, its ingredients include milk, egg yolks, sugar, vanilla, cinnamon and a dash of rum.

Dining Tips

In large cities, restaurants serving top-quality French, Italian or Continental cuisine are easy to find. But it's worth the effort to seek out places that focus on traditional Mexican cooking, which is not necessarily the tacos and enchiladas so common north of the border. Native foods can be found in smaller restaurants called *cenadurías, taquerías* or *merenderos,* which cater more to Mexican customers than to foreign tourists. In such establishments diners can order *carne en su jugo* (meat in its juice), tamales and a great variety of *antojitos* (snacks). The sign "Antojitos Mexicanos" indicates that these and other specialties are on the menu. An added bonus at these country-style restaurants are the shows, accompanied by mariachi music, often put on for diners.

Another way to sample local fare is to buy it off the street. Even the smallest town square will have vendors selling roasted meat, cut-up fruit, soft drinks, sweets or other edibles. Levels of sanitation, however, vary greatly, and the advice of most veteran travelers who stay healthy is to avoid street vendor offerings.

For those accustomed to an early breakfast, Mexican restaurants are not particularly accommodating; many don't open until around 9 a.m. Markets, however, normally open early and are good places to pick up something for a morning meal. Another tip: Buy croissants or sweet rolls at a bakery the night before and have your own breakfast before starting the day.

Because many Mexicans make something of a ceremony out of meals, restaurant service tends to be slower than in the United States. If you follow the Mexican schedule for dining, you will have lunch no earlier than 2 p.m., cocktails at 7 p.m. and dinner at 9 or 10 p.m.

Lunch, or *la comida,* is the main meal of the day (*el almuerzo* also means lunch but tends to be a late morning snack eaten on the run). Many restaurants still offer a *comida corrida,* or lunch special, which usually includes soup, a main course, a dessert and coffee. For those on a budget, making lunch the big meal of the day is the most economical way to dine.

Gracious service is the rule rather than the exception. When you're ready for the check, simply say *"la cuenta, por favor"* ("the check, please"). Making scribbling motions on your hand to imply writing is commonly recognized international sign language.

Regardless of the establishment, always ask about policies and double check the total amount of the bill. You might assume, for example, that there are free refills for coffee when in actuality you'll be charged for each cup you drink (a free second cup is more common at breakfast). Some restaurants may compute the tab by adding up the number of glasses and plates on the table. The 15 percent I.V.A. service tax may be added (sometimes the charge is 17 percent, which includes local tax); again, double check the individual amounts. This does not take the place of a tip, so leave what you think is appropriate, usually 10 to 20 percent of the bill.

Celebrations

Perhaps the clearest view into the heart of a nation is through its celebrations. This is especially true in Mexico, with its distinctive yet endlessly varied blending of Indian and Hispanic cultures. Each town has its own traditions, stemming from centuries of ancestral practices and beliefs combined with the Christian influences introduced by the Spaniards.

Fiestas

The country's most dynamic—and ubiquitous—special event is the fiesta. A fiesta takes place somewhere in Mexico every day of the year, in the tiniest villages and the biggest cities. There's much to celebrate; in addition to observing national holidays and such countrywide fiestas as Carnaval and the Day of the Dead, every town salutes its patron saint's day.

Fiestas take on myriad forms, but almost every one includes a parade. The procession is usually in association with a revered religious image but also can be secular in nature, often capped off by fireworks. Music, dancing and an array of local edibles are essential elements. Costumed dancers may portray historical, mythological or imagined happenings to the accompaniment of indigenous instruments. Sometimes there are regional or folkloric dances representative of the area or state; mariachi or harp ensembles are the usual accompaniment. The Yucatán, for example, has its evocative *jaranas*, danced by couples in white costumes to the lilting sound of a band. Yucatecan fiestas, called *vaquerías,* brim with joy and merrymaking.

On a more official note is the observance of Independence Day on Sept. 16, commemorating the 1810 proclamation of the *Grito de Dolores,* a rallying cry for freedom from Spain, by Father Miguel Hidalgo y Costilla. The town of Dolores Hidalgo, where Father Hidalgo read the *grito* from his parish church, still figures prominently in Independence Day festivities. The biggest celebration by far, however, is in Mexico City, where the huge *Zócalo* swarms with crowds and fireworks fill the air.

Religious Observances

Some of Mexico's loveliest traditions center on Christmas, despite the American influence of Santa Claus and Christmas trees. Foremost are the *posadas,* which take place for nine days beginning Dec. 16 and represent the search for an inn *(posada)* in preparation for the holy birth. Bearing candles and figures of Mary and Joseph, guests circle a house begging for a place to stay, but are refused until the Pilgrims are identified. After that the party begins, with hot punch, sweets and the breaking open of *piñatas.* More and more, gift giving is on Dec. 25, although in smaller towns presents are still exchanged on the traditional Twelfth Night, or Epiphany (Jan. 6).

Another Christmas season tradition is the presentation of *pastorelas* in public plazas, schools and theaters. Based on the events immediately before Jesus' birth, they often have a comic touch. Over time *pastorelas* have come to include in their cast of characters such historical figures as Aztec emperor

Cuauhtémoc and revolutionary Emiliano Zapata, who take part as if they had lived during that first Nativity.

Mexico precedes the Lenten season with an uproarious celebration of Carnaval. Festivities usually begin on the Saturday before Ash Wednesday and end on Shrove Tuesday night, often with the burning of a papier-maché figure of Juan Carnaval to signal the beginning of Lent. Carnaval is particularly exuberant in Mazatlán and Veracruz.

The Lenten season culminates in Holy Week *(Semana Santa)* from Palm Sunday to Easter Sunday, which is marked by solemn *pastorelas* or a re-enactment of the Passion from Judgment to Resurrection. The young man chosen to portray Jesus undergoes rigorous preparation for his role, which in some places includes being whipped and then tied to a cross. Again, the observance often ends with the burning of a papier-maché figure, this time Judas. Many Holy Week celebrations also venerate the Virgin Mary, with processions bearing some form of her image.

Laughing at Death

Mexico's best-known celebration, one in which both Indian and Catholic traditions blend into a unique expression of love for the deceased, is *Los Dias de Muertos,* or Days of the Dead, which are celebrated on Nov. 1 and 2. A straightforward approach to the uncomfortable subject of mortality, the holiday—celebrated in Mexico for centuries—mixes mourning with macabre humor and pagan rites with the Catholic observances of All Souls' and All Saints' days.

Day of the Dead celebrations are similar to, although more serious than, the celebration of Halloween north of the border. But as with Christmas, the American influence has become pervasive, and some Mexican traditionalists worry that the proliferation of Halloween parties in Mexico City and elsewhere, as well as the sale of "spooky" items like vampire masks and plastic jack-o-lanterns, threatens to overshadow the meaning of their own holiday.

Families may honor departed loved ones by telling stories, eating candy skulls or even camping all night in the local cemetery, decorating gravesites, praying and sharing memories. The holiday tends to be downplayed by the wealthier and more educated segments of Mexican society as superstitious ritual or quaint religious holdover, although much of the country continues to explode each November with food, drink, flowers and skeletal figures (which are known as *calaveras;* literally, "skull"). The most traditional Day of the Dead celebration takes place on the island of Janitzio, in Lake Pátzcuaro, although local and regional variations abound.

The popular belief that the dead are permitted to visit their living kin provides the latter a chance to prepare sometimes ostentatious culinary offerings, which usually include sweet loaves of *pan de muerto* (bread of the dead). A lavish *ofrenda,* or altar, could include candles, mementos, pictures of the departed, a bottle of favorite liquor, dancing skeletons, a portrait of the Virgin of Guadalupe and a display of marigolds *(zempoalxóchitl),* known as the "flower of the dead." Everyone sings, dances and prays, simultaneously sending up and accepting the inevitability of death.

Note: Many Mexicans travel during Holy Week and the Christmas holidays, and visitors should make hotel reservations in advance if planning to be in the country during those times. Local transportation systems also tend to be jammed during Holy Week. For a listing of representative fiestas, fairs and celebrations in Mexico, *see "Fiestas and Holidays," pages 532-534.*

Recreation

Spectator Sports

The earliest known sport played in Mexico was a form of ball game; the ruins of courts on which it was played exist at various archeological sites. While the rules are unknown, it is believed that the final outcome for some of the players was death. Fortunately, today's organized recreational activities are decidedly safer. The national sport is **soccer. Baseball** and **football** also are popular.

Bullfighting was introduced by the Spaniards. More spectacle than sport, the bullfight, or *corrida de toros,* is an elaborate ceremony that begins with a parade and ends with the flamboyantly attired matador taking a tour of the ring to the accolades of spectators while a team of mules drags away the dead bull. In between is a series of encounters between man and beast, kept thrilling by the matador's dramatic skill and by the continual goading of the animal with viciously barbed lances. While bullfighting is very much a part of Mexican lore, those with an aversion to such brutality would be better off not attending. Bullfights can be seen throughout the country but are regularly scheduled in Mexico City, Guadalajara and Tijuana.

Equally spectacular but more humanitarian are the Mexican **rodeos** called *charreadas.* The *charro,* a gentleman cowboy, competes in various displays of skill. These events,

usually held on Sunday mornings, feature colorful costumes, music and a general air of showmanship; charro associations from all over Mexico compete. Guadalajara has some of the best exhibitions. **Jai alai,** an exciting game similar to squash that often is accompanied by spirited betting, is played countrywide but particularly in Mexico City and Tijuana. **Competitive cycling, horse racing** and **cockfights** (the last supposedly illegal) all take place in various locations; check at your hotel desk or consult the local tourist office for details.

Golf, Tennis and Riding

In Mexico you can play **golf** at a variety of world-class courses located in all of the major metropolitan areas and at the beach and vacation resorts. Los Cabos, at the southern tip of the Baja peninsula, is famed for its immaculately groomed and devilishly challenging courses, including three designed by old pro Jack Nicklaus. Many courses boast stunning backdrops, from Baja's deserts to Cancún's beaches to the colonial charm of San Miguel de Allende.

Among the outstanding courses are those located at the Moon Palace Golf Resort south of Cancún; the Cabo del Sol golf resort in Los Cabos; the Club de Golf México in Mexico City; the Tres Vida Golf Club in Acapulco; the Grand Bay Hotel at Isla Navidad, north of Manzanillo; and the Vista Vallarta Golf Club in Puerto Vallarta.

Almost all golf courses in Mexico are private and can be played by visitors only if they are accompanied by a member. Hotelowned courses give preference to guests, although the hotel might be able to arrange access to a nearby facility. Fees at the better course are comparable to those in the United States. Bring your own clubs if possible; purchasing equipment is even more expensive than playing.

The Mexican Ministry of Tourism (SECTUR) publishes an Official Golf Course Tourist Guide that provides general information about a number of courses throughout the country. The information also can be accessed through the Mexico Tourism Board's Web site *(see "Fast Facts").*

Tennis courts are plentiful in resort areas. Equipment can be rented but varies in quality; again, serious players should bring their own.

The horse was considered a strange, frightening beast to superstitious Aztecs who first laid eyes on the steeds brought over by Hernando Cortés. These fears were overcome, and today Mexicans are enthusiastic riders. **Horseback riding** is an invigorating way to explore the arid, beautifully scenic stretches of northern Mexico, and this part of the country has a number of stables and ranches that rent horses and arrange riding expeditions. Another popular activity is horseback riding along the beach, available at Acapulco, Mazatlán, Puerto Vallarta and along both coasts of Baja California.

The Lure of the Water

Mexico has some wonderful beaches along its Pacific and Caribbean coasts. The major resorts all offer the usual water sports, from **water skiing** and **windsurfing** to **sailing** and **parasailing,** and any necessary equipment is easily rented. Pay close attention to local warnings regarding surf conditions; many Pacific beaches have dangerous undertows and strong currents. In addition, some ocean waters can be polluted.

Snorkeling is best around Cancún and the islands of Cozumel and Isla Mujeres. The clear, shallow waters here brim with brilliantly hued fish and intricate coral formations. The Baja California and Pacific coasts are more suitable for **scuba diving,** although Baja's Pacific waters are quite cold and the diving spots tend to be hard to reach. La Paz, in southern Baja on the Gulf of California, and Guaymas, on the northwestern mainland coast, have inviting waters, equipment rentals and resort facilities. Other good bases for snorkeling and scuba explorations are Puerto Vallarta, situated amid the coves, rock formations and underwater ledges of the Bay of Banderas; Ixtapa/Zihuatanejo, where offshore rock formations create a variety of underwater sites; and Bahías de Huatulco, with nine lovely bays to explore.

Note: If you're taking scuba lessons or have a referral letter from your home training center, check to make sure that the instructor or dive center you choose in Mexico holds U.S.-recognized certification, such as NAUI, PADI, SSI or YMCA.

While **surfing** has little appeal to most Mexicans, American surfers claim that the country's Pacific breakers are some of the best. Accessible spots include the beaches in the vicinity of Cabo San Lucas at the southern end of Baja California; around Mazatlán and south toward San Blas; and at Puerto Escondido, west of Bahías de Huatulco. Those pursuing surfing opportunities in Mexico should keep in mind that very few boards are available for rent.

Getting Back to Nature

The most popular areas for **camping** are in Baja California and along the Pacific Coast beaches of the mainland. The desolate beauty of Baja is often accessible only via four-wheel-drive vehicle; campers straying off the beaten path should be experienced and properly equipped.

Some of Mexico's national parks permit camping as well. Many offer a backdrop of cool pine forests or sparkling lakes, as well as good **hiking** trails and scenic spots for **picnicking.** For listings of AAA-RATED campgrounds and trailer parks, *see "How to Read a Campground Listing," beginning on page 536.* **Note:** Avoid camping at deserted beaches or in other isolated areas, where banditry tends to occur.

For the prodigiously fit, Mexico has several challenging peaks for **mountain climbing.** Organized expeditions are available to the dormant volcano Iztaccíhuatl, near Mexico City, and to Citlaltépetl (Pico de Orizaba), in the state of Veracruz. Needless to say, experience is essential.

Major equipment is available in Mexico, but plan on bringing personal items (backpack, footwear, sleeping bag). Do not attempt to climb during the rainy season, June through September. For further information, contact the Exploration Club of Mexico (Club de Exploraciones de México, or CEMAC), Calle Juan A. Mateos #146, Col. Obrera, 06800 México, D.F.; phone (55) 5740-8032.

Fishing

Mexico offers some of the best deep-sea **fishing** in the world, particularly around the southern tip of Baja California, in the Gulf of California, along the Pacific coast and off the eastern coast of the Yucatán Peninsula; its excellence is attested to by the numerous tournaments held each year. As with hunting, Mexican authorities are taking greater steps to preserve the country's natural resources, and a catch-and-release policy is advocated for sports anglers.

Locations noted for their deep-sea fishing opportunities include Acapulco for pompano, barracuda and shark; Cabo San Lucas for blue and striped marlin, sailfish and swordfish; Cancún and Cozumel for sailfish, swordfish, marlin, dolphin and barracuda; Ensenada for yellowtail; Guaymas for marlin, sailfish, dolphin and yellowtail; La Paz and Loreto for marlin and sailfish; Los Mochis and Topolobampo for marlin, sailfish, pompano and roosterfish; Manzanillo for sailfish; Mazatlán for sailfish and marlin; Mulegé for snook; and Puerto Vallarta for sailfish, marlin, bonito, red snapper and shark.

Rivers and lakes contain many varieties of freshwater fish. A man-made lake near Valle de Bravo, in the state of México, is known for black bass and trout. Bass also is the lure at Vicente Guerrero, another man-made lake in the state of Tamaulipas. El Novillo Dam, east of Hermosillo in the state of Sonora, has good bass fishing. Whitefish, esteemed as a national delicacy, can be caught in Lake Catemaco, in the state of Veracruz; Lake Chapala, in the state of Jalisco; and Lake Pátzcuaro, in the state of Michoacán.

Fishing regulations, which apply to both freshwater and saltwater species, are not complicated—the only requirement is a license. A Mexican sport-fishing license covers all types of fishing and is valid anywhere in Mexico. If you intend to fish in Baja California or Pacific waters, contact the California office of the Secretaría de Pesca (Mexican Department of Fisheries) in San Diego for an application; phone (619) 233-6956, fax (619) 233-0344.

License fees vary depending on boat size and time spent fishing (one day to one year). They range from about $15 to $30 but are subject to change; contact the Department of Fisheries for updates. The cost is the same whether the angler is alone or part of a tour group. Everyone aboard private boats in Mexican waters must have a fishing license regardless of age and whether or not they are fishing. Licenses are not transferable. Skin divers and scuba divers who fish need a license as well.

Spear fishing is legal only with hand-held or spring-powered spears. The taking of mollusks, crustaceans, sea turtles, totoaba (totuava, or sea trout) and marine mammals is prohibited. It is illegal to sell, trade or exchange any fish caught.

The maximum catch per day varies by species. Generally authorized maximums are 10 fish caught per day, but not more than five of the same species. Catches of marlin, sailfish, swordfish and shark are limited to one per day per species; catches of tarpon, roosterfish, dorado and shad are limited to two per day per species. The limit on inland bodies of water is five fish per day, regardless of species. To preserve game species, many of Mexico's top sport fishing destinations emphasize a catch-and-release policy.

Major hotels and independent companies at the resorts and in port cities can arrange fishing expeditions or provide boats and gear for hire. All non-resident private boats entering Mexican waters must obtain certification and a temporary boat permit from the Mexican Department of Fisheries in San Diego, a Mexican consulate office or a customs broker.

The Mexican Ministry of Tourism (SECTUR) publishes an Official Sports and Recreation Fishing Guide that includes general information about the best salt and freshwater fishing opportunities in various parts of the country. The information also can be accessed through the Mexico Tourism Board's Web site (see "Fast Facts").

Spas

For some, the focus of recreation is on relaxation and restoration rather than physical activity. Visitors to a Mexican spa can benefit from the same therapeutic resources used for centuries by native peoples—the country's immense variety of native plants.

Mexico's botanical wonders are many. The nopal, a tropical prickly pear cactus, is a source of vitamin C and amino acids; helps the body pull fluids from tissues back into the bloodstream, thus diminishing cellulite and water retention; and is effective in regulating blood sugar for those who are diabetic. The so-called "magic bark" of the tepezcohuite tree, indigenous to the state of Chiapas, has skin-healing and regenerative properties used to treat sunburn, blisters and blemishes. Mexicans also have long extolled the use of mineral-rich volcanic mud to stimulate circulation and relieve muscular and arthritic pain.

The precursors to today's world-class spa facilities are the hot springs and mineral water bathing resorts that still can be found in places like Cuautla and Ixtapan de La Sal. But contemporary beauty and health services are increasingly adopting such pre-Hispanic spa techniques as the *temazcal*, a type of sweat house using hot stones and herbs to purify the body.

Mexico's spa offerings include resort facilities set against breathtaking natural backdrops, often incorporating golf, swimming or eco and adventure tourism activities to enhance the experience. The spa at the Las Ventanas al Paraíso resort in Los Cabos offers everything from an aromatic exfoliation and soak to non-traditional plant medicine therapies and sacred healing rituals. And Cabañas Copal, a secluded seaside resort an hour and a half south of Cancún, offers a spa where you can cleanse body and mind through holistic principles performed by local shamans.

Fast Facts

POPULATION: 100,124,800 (2002 estimate).

AREA: 1,972,554 sq km (761,603 sq. mi.).

CAPITAL: Mexico City, D.F.

HIGHEST POINT: 5,747 (meters 18,850 feet). Citlaltépetl (Pico de Orizaba), Ver.

LOWEST POINT: 13 meters (43 feet) below sea level. South of Mexicali, B.C.

LANGUAGE: Spanish; some 50 Indian languages and many more dialects are spoken outside of major cities and towns. English is widely spoken, particularly in larger cities and at resorts.

UNIT OF CURRENCY: The monetary unit is the peso. The exchange rate in September 2004 was about 11.3 pesos=$1 U.S., although the rate is subject to small daily fluctuations.

BANK HOURS: Most banks are open Mon.-Fri. 9-1:30; in some larger cities, they may reopen 4-6 and are open Sat. 10-1:30. Large hotels usually exchange money, although at varying rates. Banks are closed on all national holidays, and also may close to celebrate local holidays.

BUSINESS HOURS: In most cities, businesses operate Mon.-Sat. 9-7; many are closed from 2-4 for the traditional long lunch break. In resort areas stores and shops are often open into the evening and on Sunday. Shop hours may not always correspond to what is advertised. Shopping malls are generally open daily; they are closed Jan. 1, Good Friday, May 1 (Labor Day) and Dec. 25.

TAXES: Mexico levies a 15 percent value-added (Impuesto de Valor Agregado, or IVA) tax on all goods and services, even telephone and Internet services (10 percent in the states of Quintana Roo and Baja California). An additional tax on hotel and beverage services means that some items can carry a 17 percent IVA tax. The tax is supposed to be included in the posted price or rate but is not always itemized separately on your bill; inquire if you feel you are being doubly charged.

HOLIDAYS: New Year's Day; Constitution Day, Feb. 5; Birthday of Benito Juárez, Mar. 21; Holy Week (Semana Santa); Good Friday through Easter Sunday; Labor Day, May 1; Battle of Puebla (Cinco de Mayo), May 5; Independence Day, Sept. 16; Day of the Race (Columbus Day), Oct. 12; Christmas, Dec. 25. Banks, government offices and most stores are closed. Offices also may close the week between Christmas and New Year's Day.

MEDIA: Mexico has no national English-language newspapers. *USA Today* is usually available in big cities or resorts. The Sanborn's chain, with outlets in the larger cities, carries English-language magazines. Hotels usually provide free magazines that list what is happening around town; most hotels also offer U.S. TV channels. Some radio stations in larger cities broadcast in English.

ATTRACTION SCHEDULES: Before setting out for a day of sightseeing, check with the front desk at your hotel regarding schedules for local museums, archeological sites or historic buildings. Many museums in Mexico are open 9-5 and are closed on Monday. Admission fees are inexpensive, usually less than $5 (U.S.) The attraction listings in this TourBook provide hours and admissions where known.

PUBLIC RESTROOMS: Take advantage of those in hotels, restaurants, airports or bus stations wherever possible, as public restrooms otherwise are difficult to find. Those in out-of-the-way places, particularly at gas stations, often have primitive plumbing and are definitely not up to the standards of public restrooms in the United States. Always carry a roll of toilet paper and a small bar of soap; both of these necessities can be in short supply away from your hotel.

POLICE: Few tourists ever run into trouble with the law, but you may need to ask police for directions or seek assistance for other reasons. While officers normally are helpful, other encounters— mainly those involving alleged traffic violations— can be exasperating or even intimidating, especially if you don't speak fluent Spanish. Always cooperate if stopped, but try to resolve the situation right away.

RESOURCES: Bilingual telephone operators with the Mexico Ministry of Tourism (Secretaría de Turismo, or SECTUR) provide 24-hour information about tourist destinations and services. In Mexico City, phone (55) 5250-0123 or (55) 5250-0151; elsewhere in Mexico, phone (800) 903-9200 (toll-free long distance); in the United States, phone (800) 482-9832. The Mexico Tourism Board provides brochures and general information; phone (800) 446-3942 in the United States. The Web site address is www.visitmexico.com.

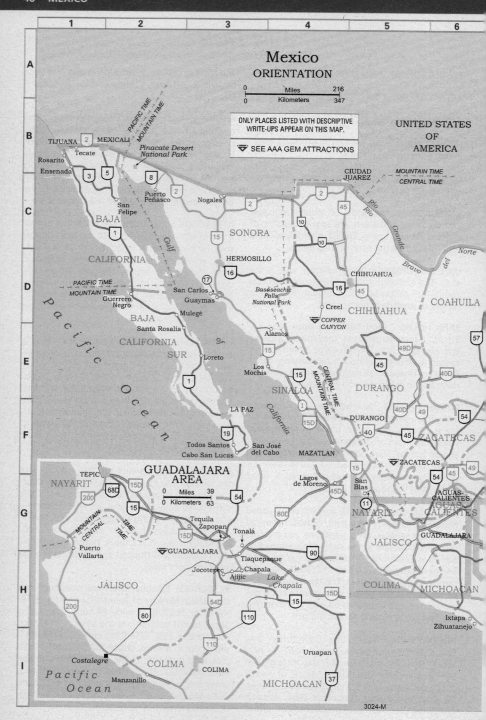

Mexico
ORIENTATION

Miles 216
Kilometers 347

ONLY PLACES LISTED WITH DESCRIPTIVE
WRITE-UPS APPEAR ON THIS MAP.

SEE AAA GEM ATTRACTIONS

UNITED STATES
OF
AMERICA

PACIFIC TIME
MOUNTAIN TIME

TIJUANA MEXICALI
Tecate
Rosarito
Ensenada

Pinacate Desert
National Park

CIUDAD
JUAREZ

MOUNTAIN TIME
CENTRAL TIME

Puerto
Peñasco

Nogales

BAJA

San
Felipe

CALIFORNIA

SONORA

HERMOSILLO

CHIHUAHUA

Rio

Rio

Grande

Bravo

del

Norte

COAHUILA

PACIFIC TIME
MOUNTAIN TIME
Guerrero
Negro

San Carlos
Guaymas

Mulegé

Basaseachic
Falls
National Park

Creel

CHIHUAHUA

BAJA

Santa Rosalía

CALIFORNIA
SUR

Loreto

COPPER
CANYON

Alamos

Pacific

Ocean

Los
Mochis

SINALOA

DURANGO

DURANGO

LA PAZ

California

Todos Santos
Cabo San Lucas

San José
del Cabo

MAZATLAN

ZACATECAS

ZACATECAS

AGUAS-
CALIENTES

NAYARIT

JALISCO

GUADALAJARA

COLIMA

MICHOACAN

Ixtapa
Zihuatanejo

GUADALAJARA AREA

Miles 39
Kilometers 63

TEPIC
NAYARIT

Lagos
de Moreno

San
Blas

MOUNTAIN

CENTRAL

TIME

TIME

Tequila
Zapopan

Tonalá

GUADALAJARA

Puerto
Vallarta

Tlaquepaque

Jocotepec
Ajijic

Chapala

Lake
Chapala

JALISCO

COLIMA

COLIMA

Costalegre

Pacific
Ocean

Manzanillo

Uruapan

MICHOACAN

3024-M

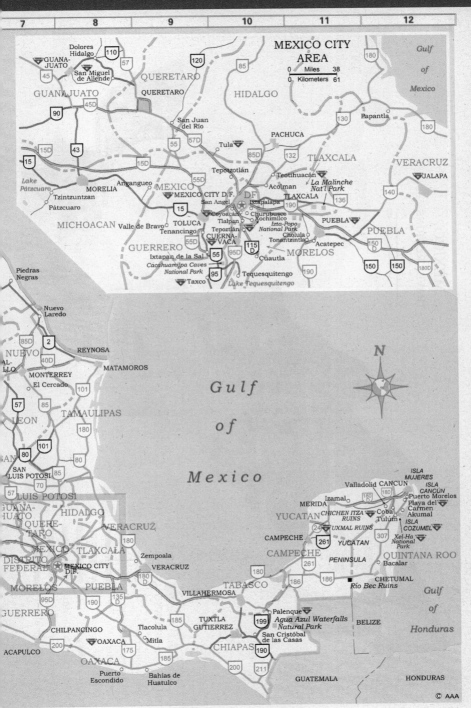

© AAA

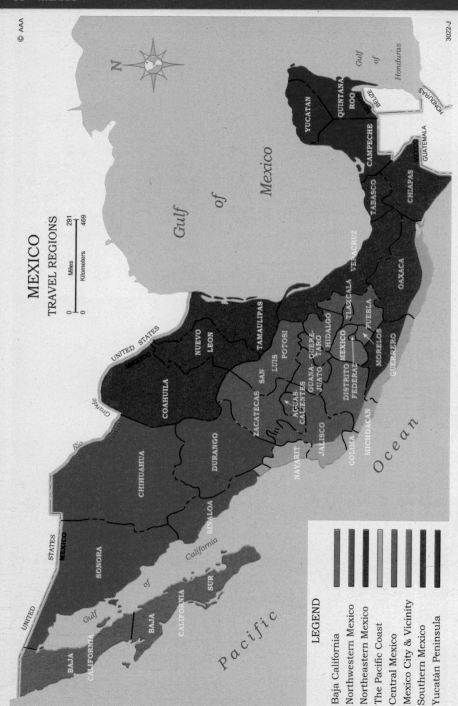

© AAA

3022-J

MEXICO
TRAVEL REGIONS

Miles   291
Kilometers   469

0
0

N

Gulf of Mexico

Gulf of Honduras

YUCATAN

QUINTANA ROO

MEXICO

BELIZE

CAMPECHE

TABASCO

CHIAPAS

GUATEMALA

UNITED STATES

MEXICO

VERACRUZ

OAXACA

NUEVO LEON

TAMAULIPAS

SAN LUIS POTOSI

QUERE-TARO

HIDALGO

TLAXCALA

PUEBLA

MEXICO

DISTRITO FEDERAL

MORELOS

GUERRERO

COAHUILA

ZACATECAS

AGUAS CALIENTES

GUANA-JUATO

CHIHUAHUA

DURANGO

NAYARIT

JALISCO

COLIMA

MICHOACAN

Río Grande

Río Bravo

SINALOA

SONORA

UNITED STATES

MEXICO

Gulf of California

BAJA CALIFORNIA

BAJA CALIFORNIA SUR

Pacific Ocean

LEGEND

Baja California
Northwestern Mexico
Northeastern Mexico
The Pacific Coast
Central Mexico
Mexico City & Vicinity
Southern Mexico
Yucatán Peninsula

Mexican State Chart

State	Abbreviation	Area (sq. miles)	Population	Capital
AGUASCALIENTES	Ags.	2,112	983,600	Aguascalientes
BAJA CALIFORNIA	B.C.	26,996	2,661,800	Mexicali
BAJA CALIFORNIA SUR	B.C.S.	28,369	450,000	La Paz
CAMPECHE	Camp.	19,619	705,900	Campeche
CHIAPAS	Chis.	28,653	4,121,700	Tuxtla Gutiérrez
CHIHUAHUA	Chih.	94,571	3,162,900	Chihuahua
COAHUILA	Coah.	57,908	2,346,900	Saltillo
COLIMA	Col.	2,004	561,700	Colima
DISTRITO FEDERAL	D.F.	571	8,665,800	Mexico City
DURANGO	Dgo.	47,560	1,449,400	Durango
GUANAJUATO	Gto.	11,946	4,790,900	Guanajuato
GUERRERO	Gro.	24,819	3,138,400	Chilpancingo
HIDALGO	Hgo.	8,038	2,283,500	Pachuca
JALISCO	Jal.	31,211	6,432,600	Guadalajara
MEXICO	Mex.	8,245	13,713,600	Toluca
MICHOACAN	Mich.	23,138	4,027,500	Morelia
MORELOS	Mor.	1,911	1,596,400	Cuernavaca
NAYARIT	Nay.	10,417	931,500	Tepic
NUEVO LEON	N.L.	25,067	3,937,700	Monterrey
OAXACA	Oax.	36,275	3,544,500	Oaxaca
PUEBLA	Pue.	13,090	5,276,400	Puebla
QUERETARO	Qro.	4,420	1,479,900	Querétaro
QUINTANA ROO	Q.R.	19,387	946,600	Chetumal
SAN LUIS POTOSI	S.L.P.	24,351	2,335,400	San Luis Potosí
SINALOA	Sin.	22,520	2,556,400	Culiacán
SONORA	Son.	70,290	2,240,500	Hermosillo
TABASCO	Tab.	9,756	1,943,300	Villahermosa
TAMAULIPAS	Tamps.	30,650	2,839,900	Ciudad Victoria
TLAXCALA	Tlax.	1,551	998,300	Tlaxcala
VERACRUZ	Ver.	27,683	6,947,200	Jalapa
YUCATAN	Yuc.	14,827	1,686,500	Mérida
ZACATECAS	Zac.	28,283	1,368,100	Zacatecas

Source: National Institute of Statistics and Geography (INEGI), 2000

Points of Interest Offering A *Great Experience for Members*®

Yucatán Peninsula

CHANKANAAB LAGOON PARK—Saltwater Chankanaab Lagoon is part of a national park that provides sanctuary for multicolored tropical fish and fun for swimmers and snorkelers. See Cozumel p. 106.

CHICHEN ITZA—The Yucatán Peninsula's best known and most visited ruin is one of the archeological wonders of the world. See p. 96.

TULUM RUINS—The remains of this Maya fortress-city overlooking the turquoise Caribbean are a popular day trip for visitors based in Cancún. See Tulum p. 118.

UXMAL—The majestic Pyramid of the Magician is a highlight of the Uxmal ruins, built by the Maya more than 1,000 years ago. See p. 120.

XCARET—Xcaret is a big seaside theme park of an attraction and a fun all-day destination. The ecological slant won't stop kids from loving it. See Playa del Carmen p. 116.

XEL-HA NATIONAL PARK—Xel-Há, a series of freshwater lagoons fed by underground springs, is a pretty place to swim and go snorkeling or scuba diving. See Tulum p. 119.

Northwestern Mexico

COPPER CANYON—A rail excursion through Copper Canyon country offers a chance to see some of Mexico's most spectacular mountain scenery. See p. 157.

Mexico City and Vicinity

BASILICA OF OUR LADY OF GUADALUPE—Two basilicas in the northern Mexico City suburb of Villa de Guadalupe honor the Guadalupe Virgin, the nation's patron saint and most revered iconic religious figure. See Mexico City p. 255.

DOLORES OLMEDO PATINO MUSEUM—Beautiful grounds and a notable collection of art make this tranquil retreat a worthwhile escape from Mexico City's hubbub. See Xochimilco p. 272.

FRIDA KAHLO MUSEUM—The house where Mexican surrealist Kahlo was born and where she died offers an intriguing look at the life of a groundbreaking artist. See Coyoacán p. 227.

METROPOLITAN CATHEDRAL—This towering church is a magnificent example of baroque architecture and also contains beautiful chapels and prized works of art. See Mexico City p. 244.

MUSEUM OF MODERN ART—The country's best modern art museum has works by Diego Rivera, Rufino Tamayo and other Mexican masters. See Mexico City p. 254.

NATIONAL MUSEUM OF ANTHROPOLOGY—One of the world's foremost museums, the National Museum of Anthropology exhibits its outstanding collection of treasures covering all of Mexico's early civilizations. See Mexico City p. 255.

NATIONAL PALACE—The chief attraction at the National Palace is a mesmerizing series of historical murals created by famed Mexican artist Diego Rivera. See Mexico City p. 245.

PALACE OF FINE ARTS—The Palacio de Bellas Artes is the capital's cultural center and a showcase for the music and dance performances  of the Ballet Folklórico. See Mexico City p. 251.

ROBERT BRADY MUSEUM—The wildly eclectic collection of art assembled by Robert Brady, an Iowan who settled in Cuernavaca in 1960, is displayed in his former home. See Cuernavaca p. 229.

TEOTIHUACAN—Teotihuacán is one of Mexico's most impressive and easily accessible archeological zones, and also one of its most mysterious. See p. 266.

Central Mexico

AMPARO MUSEUM—This collection of pre-Hispanic and colonial art is one of the best in the country, impressively displayed in a building that was formerly a college. See Puebla p. 305.

CABANAS CULTURAL INSTITUTE—Designated a World Heritage Site by UNESCO in 1997, Guadalajara's cultural and performing arts center is graced with powerful murals by Mexican artist José Clemente Orozco. See Guadalajara p. 287.

CHURCH OF LA VALENCIANA—Officially the Iglesia de San Cayetano (Church of San Cayetano), La Valenciana is a visual feast of wood carvings, gold leaf and lovely religious paintings. See Guanajuato p. 296.

DIEGO RIVERA MUSEUM—The birthplace of Mexico's celebrated muralist houses works tracing the development of his art, including sketches for his controversial mural commissioned by New York City's Rockefeller Center in the early 1930s. See Guanajuato p. 296.

DON QUIXOTE ICONOGRAPHIC MUSEUM—The hero of Miguel de Cervantes' novel is artistically celebrated in the form of paintings, sculpture and even clocks at this thoroughly enjoyable museum. See Guanajuato p. 297.

PARISH CHURCH—San Miguel's historic center is dominated by this beautiful church, which stands over the main plaza. See San Miguel de Allende p. 315.

RAFAEL CORONEL MUSEUM—The Rafael Coronel Museum features an incredible array of creative, colorful masks (máscaras) displayed in a gracious 18th-century building that was formerly a convent. See Zacatecas p. 322.

STATE HISTORICAL MUSEUM—The Alhóndiga de Granaditas, a former granary, played an important role in the fight for Mexican independence, and this excellent museum provides a historical perspective. See Guanajuato p. 298.

TULA RUINS—The Chac Mool figure, an international artistic symbol of Mesoamerican culture, was first discovered at this archeological site. See Tula p. 319.

Southern Mexico

CHURCH OF SANTA PRISCA—Built in the mid-18th century, Taxco's Santa Prisca Church is one of Mexico's finest examples of baroque architecture. See Taxco p. 341.

CHURCH OF SANTO DOMINGO—Mexico has no shortage of lovely churches, but Oaxaca's Iglesia de Santo Domingo boasts an especially  breathtaking interior of lavish gold leaf ornamentation. See Oaxaca p. 334.

MONTE ALBAN RUINS—The religious center of the Zapotec people, Monte Albán has a dramatic setting overlooking the Valley of Oaxaca. See Oaxaca p. 334.

MUSEUM OF ANTHROPOLOGY—Jalapa's Museo de Antropología houses a superb collection of artifacts focusing on the Indian groups that inhabited Mexico's gulf coast region. See Jalapa p. 329.

PALENQUE—What these Maya ruins lack in sheer scope is made up for by a primeval air that makes them worth visiting, despite the remote location. See p. 335.

SANTO DOMINGO CULTURAL CENTER—Priceless jewelry, precious stones and other treasures excavated from the Monte Albán site are the standout exhibits at the Santo Domingo Cultural Center. See Oaxaca p. 335.

Mexico Temperature Averages
Maximum / Minimum
Temperatures are in Fahrenheit, rainfall in Inches

	JAN	FEB	MAR	APR	MAY	JUNE	JULY	AUG	SEPT	OCT	NOV	DEC
Acapulco	88/72 .3	88/72 .1	88/72 .1	88/73 .1	90/76 1.1	90/77 10.4	91/77 8.9	91/77 10.4	90/76 15.0	90/76 6.3	90/75 1.9	88/73 .3
Chihuahua	64/36 .3	69/39 .1	75/44 .1	82/53 .1	89/59 .4	93/66 1.4	89/66 3.0	88/65 3.1	85/60 2.0	80/52 .7	72/42 .2	65/36 .3
Cancún	83/67 3.5	84/67 2.2	86/69 1.6	89/72 1.6	90/73 4.6	90/75 7.0	90/75 4.3	91/75 5.9	89/75 9.0	87/74 8.6	85/71 3.8	83/69 4.3
Cuernavaca	78/55 .5	81/56 .2	85/59 .2	86/62 1.1	85/63 2.7	81/62 10.3	79/60 10.0	79/60 9.0	77/60 9.8	78/58 3.7	79/57 .8	78/55 .1
Durango	66/40 .4	70/43 .2	75/46 .1	81/51 .1	84/56 .3	85/60 2.0	81/59 3.8	79/59 3.8	77/57 3.3	76/52 1.3	72/46 .3	66/42 .4
Guadalajara	74/44 .5	78/46 .2	82/49 .2	86/53 .3	88/57 1.0	84/61 6.4	79/60 9.8	79/59 7.6	78/59 5.8	78/54 2.3	77/48 .4	74/46 .5
Guanajuato	70/46 .5	73/48 .1	77/51 .2	81/54 .8	82/57 1.3	79/58 5.0	77/57 4.7	77/57 4.6	75/57 4.7	75/54 1.7	73/49 .6	70/47 .4
La Paz	73/55 .6	76/55 .1	79/56 .1	85/59 0	88/65 0	93/66 .1	96/74 .5	96/75 1.4	94/74 2.5	90/69 .5	83/62 .2	76/57 .8
Mazatlán	73/63 .6	73/62 .2	74/63 .1	77/66 .1	81/71 0	85/77 1.2	86/78 6.0	87/78 8.0	86/78 8.9	85/76 2.9	80/70 .5	75/65 .6
Mérida	82/64 1.2	84/64 1.1	89/68 .6	92/70 .6	92/72 2.9	91/73 5.1	91/73 5.0	91/73 6.0	89/73 7.7	86/71 4.4	83/67 1.4	82/65 1.4

Mexico Temperature Averages
Maximum / Minimum
Temperatures are in Fahrenheit, rainfall in Inches

	JAN	FEB	MAR	APR	MAY	JUNE	JULY	AUG	SEPT	OCT	NOV	DEC
Mexico City	70/42 .4	74/44 .1	78/48 .4	80/51 1.1	80/52 2.0	77/54 4.9	74/52 6.1	74/52 6.0	72/52 5.3	72/49 2.1	71/45 .6	69/43 .2
Monterrey	68/48 .5	73/52 .8	79/56 .6	86/64 1.1	89/68 1.4	92/71 2.5	94/72 1.8	93/72 3.8	87/69 5.9	81/63 3.3	74/55 .9	70/50 .4
Morelia	70/45 .6	73/47 .2	77/51 .2	80/54 .7	81/58 1.7	77/59 5.7	74/58 6.6	74/57 6.1	73/57 5.2	73/53 2.3	72/49 .6	70/46 .5
Puebla	71/44 .3	73/46 .2	77/51 .2	79/53 1.1	78/55 2.7	75/55 5.7	74/54 5.0	74/54 6.3	73/54 6.2	74/51 2.8	73/47 .9	71/44 .2
Querétaro	73/44 .6	77/46 .2	82/51 .3	86/54 .7	87/57 1.8	84/58 4.4	81/57 4.9	81/57 4.1	79/56 3.5	78/52 1.6	76/48 .4	74/45 .3
San Cristóbal de Las Casas	68/40 .3	70/40 .3	72/43 .7	73/45 2.2	72/48 4.5	71/51 9.4	71/50 6.5	70/50 6.8	70/50 9.5	69/48 4.8	69/44 1.4	68/40 .5
San Luis Potosí	71/43 .3	74/45 .2	82/50 .1	86/53 .5	86/56 1.3	82/58 2.4	80/56 1.3	81/56 2.0	77/56 2.7	75/51 .9	74/47 .4	71/44 .3
Taxco	78/55 .5	82/58 .5	87/62 .2	89/64 .7	87/65 4.1	80/64 10.9	79/62 9.9	78/62 11.5	77/62 10.2	78/61 4.2	78/59 .9	77/58 .2
Tijuana	68/43 1.6	68/45 1.3	69/47 1.1	72/50 .6	74/53 .2	76/57 0	82/61 0	83/64 0	82/60 .2	79/55 .2	74/49 1.2	70/45 1.3
Veracruz	76/65 .8	77/66 .6	79/69 .7	83/73 .6	86/76 2.5	87/77 10.6	88/75 15.1	88/76 11.7	87/75 13.8	85/73 6.8	82/70 2.4	78/67 1.1

Planning Your Trip

Planning for a Mexican vacation first depends on whether you'll be driving your own vehicle around the country, flying to one destination only, or flying to one destination and then driving a rental car to another. If you drive your own vehicle, specific regulations govern its temporary importation across the border. There's also your day-to-day, on-the-road itinerary to consider. Flying eliminates many of these additional details, particularly if a travel agency or tour operator is handling the logistics.

Trip cost will largely be determined by your agenda. If you want frills or as many of the comforts of home as possible, travel exclusively by air or take a guided package tour; stay at internationally recognized hotels or all-inclusive resorts; and eat and don't shop at establishments that cater primarily to tourists. Your vacation will be essentially hassle-free, but it also could be very expensive. But if you are willing to put up with the occasional lumpy bed or misguided detour and don't mind a few unexpected departures from an otherwise orderly schedule, you will not only reduce expenses but experience Mexico on a much more intimate level.

While not essential, a knowledge of Spanish is helpful. English is spoken widely, especially in large cities and at the popular beach resorts. Elsewhere, Mexicans who work in hotels, restaurants or other aspects of the tourism industry usually speak and understand basic English. Shop owners and market sellers likely will be familiar with numbers, which is helpful when bargaining.

Out-of-the-way places, particularly Indian villages and rural areas in the Yucatán Peninsula and southern Mexico, are another story. But if you know some words or phrases in the native tongue, Mexicans tend to overlook a visitor's halting pronunciation and mixed tenses. Speak slowly, distinctly and be patient if you have trouble making yourself understood. Where some

Palace of Fine Arts, Mexico City / Carlos Sanchez
Mexico Tourism Board

another. Practice is the only way to pick up such nuances.

Mexico Travel Regions

Tourism is big business in Mexico; the country welcomes more than 20 million visitors annually, and the 1994 currency devaluation means those with U.S. dollars can find some very good travel bargains. But no visitor takes on all of Mexico in one vacation. And with its sheer size and enormous variety, who would want to?

This book divides the country into eight regions, with geography the primary determining factor: Baja California, Northwestern Mexico, Northeastern Mexico, The Pacific Coast, Central Mexico, Mexico City and Vicinity, Southern Mexico and the Yucatán Peninsula. Each of these regions is color-coded on the Mexico Travel Regions map. Mexico provides varying levels of visitor amenities and many different things to see and do, so a knowledge of what each region offers can be an aid in trip planning.

Practical Advice and Tips

knowledge of the language is necessary, the "Speaking of Spanish" section in this TourBook provides words and phrases that identify common needs.

Keep in mind that the high-school Spanish many Americans learned—and promptly forgot—is based on the Castilian form of the language. Expressions that are innocuous in one Spanish-speaking country can take on an offensive tone in

Where To Go

Generally speaking, Mexico's priciest destinations are its big beach resorts. For the first-time visitor, they offer the exotic lure of a foreign country without too much cultural displacement. One will find American fast-food joints as well as thatch-roofed seafood shacks—and a large proportion of locals who speak English. Cancún, Los Cabos, Puerto Vallarta, Acapulco, Ixtapa,

Mazatlán, Manzanillo and Bahías de Huatulco all fall into this category.

Also pricey is Mexico City, which is not a place for those seeking laid-back relaxation. Museum lovers, however, will find some truly outstanding ones that exhibit the artistic and historical treasures associated with Mexico's long history.

Much of Mexico away from the resorts and the big cities provides a maximum of scenic splendor and local flavor and a minimum of pampering. Those with a taste for adventure and no need for luxury will relish the opportunity to camp along a deserted stretch of beach or explore little-visited archeological ruins.

Ecotourism is booming in Mexico among travelers and tour operators alike. Getting close to nature at relatively remote and unspoiled areas is a trend that goes hand in hand with the recognition that preserving the environment also benefits tourism. A bewildering number of tour companies offer specialized excursions based around biking, diving, hiking, kayaking and numerous other outdoor activities; consult a travel agency for details.

The Mexican government promotes ecological awareness in various ways. Biosphere reserves, such as Sian Ka'an in the state of Quintana Roo, protect the country's rich variety of indigenous flora and fauna. The El Rosario Monarch Butterfly Sanctuary, in the wooded mountains west of Mexico City, is a refuge for the insects, which annually migrate by the millions to the central Mexican highlands. In the Gulf of California commercial fishing is strictly regulated in order to protect the sport fishing industry, and a catch-and-release policy is advocated. California gray whales, which migrate to Baja's Pacific coast each winter, also are protected.

For travelers accustomed to a high level of comfort, an ecotour may not be a wise choice. But for those who prefer unspoiled environments and scientific authenticity over fine dining and

Travel Advisories

The U.S. Department of State issues Consular Information Sheets and Travel Warnings concerning serious health or security conditions that might affect U.S. citizens. They can be obtained at U.S. embassies and consulates abroad, regional passport agencies in the United States and from the Office of Overseas Citizens Services, 2201 C St. NW, Room 4811, Department of State, Washington, D.C. 20520; phone (202) 647-5225, fax (202) 647-3000. For the latest information about travel advisories or warnings, consult the Bureau of Consular Affairs home page; the Web site address is www.travel.state.gov.

Consular Information Sheets provide information about entry requirements, currency regulations, health conditions, security, political disturbances, areas of instability and drug penalties. A Travel Warning is issued when the situation in a country is dangerous enough for the Department of State to recommend that Americans not travel there.

five-diamond accommodations, Mexico offers a multitude of choices, from backpacking through the Baja desert to birdwatching along the northern Yucatán coast to mountain biking through the highlands of Oaxaca state.

Perhaps the best bet for combining affordable and acceptable comfort with the pleasure of experiencing new cultural perspectives is a visit to one of the interior cities. Such colonial cities as Guanajuato, Querétaro, San Miguel de Allende, Taxco and Zacatecas, built by the Spanish, have fascinating historical and architectural legacies.

Often overlooked on tourist itineraries is Morelia, the capital of Michoacán and perhaps the city in Mexico most reminiscent of Spain. Residents of Oaxaca, San Cristóbal de Las Casas and Mérida produce some of the best native handicrafts in Mexico. Guadalajara offers big-city amenities, Mexican atmosphere and Western familiarity, the last resulting in part from a large resident population of American retirees.

When To Go

When to go is as important a consideration as where to go. From a weather standpoint, the dry season—October through May—is the best time to visit most of the country. Rainfall patterns, however, vary greatly. In the highland region of central Mexico afternoon showers are likely at any time from June through September, but over a large portion of northern—and especially northwestern— Mexico, rain is infrequent throughout the year. In Chiapas and the normally wet coastal areas, heavy rains can wash out roads or cause mudslides. Much of northwestern Mexico and Baja California is uncomfortably hot in the summer; in the coastal regions summer heat is exacerbated by high humidity. Conversely, fall and winter evenings in high-altitude locations can get quite nippy.

December through February or March is the high season at Mexico's beach resorts, and accommodation rates at the major tourist destinations, such as Cancún and Puerto Vallarta, are at their peak. April through November is the off season, when rates come down and crowds let up. Each resort has its own timetable; Cancún, for example, is crowded with U.S. spring breakers during March and April.

Easter week is perhaps the most popular time of the year for

Mexican families to vacation. Many Mexicans also travel over the Christmas holiday period and during such major national celebrations as the Fiesta of the Virgin of Guadalupe on Dec. 12. For good weather, lower cost and crowd avoidance, a general rule of thumb is to go in the spring or fall. It's a good idea to obtain advance confirmed reservations for accommodations at beach resorts and in most other Mexican cities during the peak travel seasons—roughly speaking, December through June at the resorts and June through August at the inland cities. Reservations are imperative for the week preceding and following Easter.

You may want to time your arrival to coincide with a significant annual event, such as Oaxaca's Guelaguetza celebration in July or Guanajuato's International Cervantes Festival (Festival Cervantino) in October. The whole country celebrates occasions like Independence Day (Sept. 15 and 16) and the Days of the Dead (Nov. 1 and 2). And almost every day of the year some village or town honors its patron saint or commemorates a historical occasion.

All things considered, one of the nicest times to visit is in November: Temperatures are moderate, summer rains have turned much of the normally brown landscape a lusher green, and the peak holiday season is still a month away.

Calling Mexico

Trip planning may necessitate making phone calls to Mexico for the purpose of setting up hotel reservations, obtaining information about special events, etc. When calling Mexico from the United States and Canada, first dial 011 (the international access code), then 52 (the country code), then the area code and local phone number. For credit card and operator-assisted calls, dial 0152, then the area code and local phone number. While major hotels in tourist areas normally employ English-speaking staffs, a basic knowledge of Spanish will come in handy should you encounter an exception.

Packing Hints

Heed the old adage to "pack light." The weather in most areas ranges from mild to warm, and consequently you will not need a great deal of clothing. Bring items that are comfortable and easy to care for. In Mexico City and other high-altitude areas, a light coat is a good idea during the winter months, a sweater or jacket for other times. Sweaters also can ward off the chill of air conditioning, which can be icy in those establishments that have it. Lightweight summer clothing is necessary in tropical areas, which include practically all of the coastal lowlands.

Although Mexico is not a particularly formal country, neither is it lacking in modesty. Some of the native peoples are very conservative, and revealing clothing on either sex is frowned upon, regardless of the heat. Away from the main tourist areas women will attract much unwanted attention by going braless or wearing very short skirts or otherwise provocative attire.

Slacks or jeans are fine for sightseeing and shopping. Shorts and/or bathing suits are more appropriate at the beach and in cosmopolitan cities than they are in small towns or outlying areas, although personal comfort should be the deciding factor. If you plan to dine in an upscale restaurant, it's a good idea to keep casual evening clothes (a sports jacket and tie for men, a dress or suit for women) on hand. Bring a raincoat or umbrella for the rainy-season months of June through September.

A pair of sturdy, comfortable walking shoes is essential for exploring ruins, hiking through forests or climbing up hills, and even for walking the frequently cobblestoned streets of cities and towns. A luggage cart can be useful if you'll be traveling by bus, as stations in smaller towns rarely have porters, and it can save money at airports. For those who plan to be on the go much of the time, a shoulder bag may be more appropriate than a suitcase; make sure it fastens securely.

Take an extra pair of sunglasses, a good sunscreen, insect repellent (absolutely necessary in lowland and coastal areas and not always available in Mexico), a vacuum or plastic bottle for drinking water, eyedrops to ease discomfort from wind or glare, and a combination pocketknife with bottle opener and corkscrew attachments.

Mexico Tourism Board Offices

CHICAGO
225 N. Michigan Ave., Suite 1850, 60601; (312) 228-0517
MIAMI
5975 Sunset Dr., Suite 305, 33143; (786) 621-2909
NEW YORK
375 Park Ave., Suite 1905, 10152; (212) 308-2110
MONTREAL, QUEBEC
1 Place Ville Marie, Suite 1931, H3B 2C3; (514) 871-1103
TORONTO, ONTARIO
2 Bloor St. West, Suite 1502, M4W 3E2; (416) 925-0704
VANCOUVER, BRITISH COLUMBIA
999 W. Hastings St., Suite 1110, V6C 2W2; (604) 669-2845

Mexican pharmacies carry aspirin and other standard toiletry items, but you should bring your own prescription drugs. Toilet paper is often missing in out-of-the-way restrooms; bring several rolls, and always try to carry at least one. Purchase film and batteries before you leave, as they are more expensive in Mexico. Another useful item is a bathtub plug; in many hotel rooms they are missing or don't fit properly.

Electrical current in Mexico is 110-volt, 60-cycle AC—the same as in the United States and Canada—which permits the use of such small standard appliances as shavers, travel irons or hair curlers. In smaller towns, electricity may be weak or even unavailable, so bring a small flashlight and disposable razor.

For Assistance

Special needs frequently require a special kind of help, particularly when you are visiting a foreign country. The following sources of aid are suggested for travelers to Mexico.

Medical Assistance

Ask at your hotel desk or consular office for the name and address of the nearest hospital and English-speaking doctor. Several Mexican and U.S. companies offer medical evacuation service by air; the U.S. Embassy in Mexico City provides a list of these firms. Tourist publications often print names and addresses of local hospitals. Most Mexican cities and towns also have a *Cruz Roja* (Red Cross) facility.

The U.S. Department of State has a Web site link with general medical information for U.S. citizens traveling abroad: travel.state.gov/travel/abroad_ health.html. *Also see the "In Case of Emergency" sidebar under the listing for Mexico City, page 252, and "The Informed Traveler" page under the listings for Acapulco, page 180, Cancún, page 84, Guadalajara, page 282, and Puerto Vallarta, page 214.*

Legal Difficulties

Assistance often is provided by Tourist Assistance (*Protección*

Weather Notes

Mexico encompasses some 760,000 square miles and varies in elevation from sea level to more than 18,000 feet above. This wide range of terrain guarantees a correspondingly wide range of climatic conditions. The weather can be oppressively sultry or refreshingly cool, extremely dry or persistently rainy. Because much of the country lies within the tropics, altitude rather than latitude tends to determine the temperature. Two characteristics more or less stand out: a large number of hours of annual sunshine, and distinct wet and dry seasons.

Many of Mexico's major inland cities, including Mexico City, Guadalajara, Puebla, Guanajuato, Morelia and Querétaro, are at altitudes that give them spring-like weather year-round. Northwestern cities such as Chihuahua and Hermosillo experience greater seasonal extremes. Here summers are sizzling, while temperatures during winter can drop below freezing and occasional light snow falls. Cancún, Acapulco, Puerto Vallarta and other coastal resorts, on the other hand, show little temperature variation from month to month. The nicest weather in these cities is from November through March, when humidities are fairly low and little rain falls.

Severe weather and natural disasters in Mexico are sporadic in nature. Localized heavy rains—particularly in low-lying, tropical coastal areas—can cause flooding, bridge washouts and mud or rock slides that adversely affect transportation. Occasional hurricanes affect the eastern Yucatán Peninsula, the lower Gulf of Mexico coast, and the Pacific coast from the southern part of the normally arid Baja California Peninsula south to Acapulco. Earthquakes, however, cause the most catastrophic damage. While they are an ever-present possibility, the great majority of visitors will hopefully never experience these tremors.

---

al Turista). Offices are in Ensenada, Mexicali, Rosarito Beach, San Felipe, Tecate and Tijuana on the Baja California Peninsula and in the capital of each state on the mainland, normally in the same building that houses the State Tourism Office. The U.S. Embassy and Mexican consulate offices in the United States and Canada can provide lists of attorneys who speak English. Federal Consumer Protection Agency (*Procuraduría Federal del Consumidor*) offices are in all state capitals and other major cities.

If you run into problems with the police in Mexico, Tourist Assistance recommends that the following steps be taken:

Observe or ask for the officer's name (most police wear nameplates), badge number, department (federal, state or municipal), and vehicle number.

Go to the nearest police station to pay any traffic-related fine and ask for a receipt.

Write out the nature of the complaint and mail it to the Tourist Assistance Director.

Although the vast majority of tourists return home without encountering any legal difficulties, you could be arrested for breaking laws you didn't know about or for what would be considered a minor offense in Canada or the United States. For example, if you are involved in a traffic accident that causes injury you will

Selected Mexican Consulate Offices in the United States and Canada

ARIZONA

NOGALES—Consul de Mexico, 571 N. Grand Ave., 85621; (520) 287-2521

PHOENIX—Consul General de Mexico, 1990 West Camelback Rd., Suite 110, 85015; (602) 242-7398

TUCSON—Consul de Mexico, 553 S. Stone Ave., 85701; (520) 882-5595

CALIFORNIA

LOS ANGELES—Consul General de Mexico, 2401 W. Sixth St., 90057; (213) 351-6800

SACRAMENTO—Consul General de Mexico, 1010 8th St., 95814; (916) 441-3287

SAN DIEGO—Consul General de Mexico, 1549 India St., 92101; (619) 231-8414

SAN FRANCISCO—Consul General de Mexico, 532 Folsom St., 94105; (415) 354-1700

COLORADO

DENVER—Consul de Mexico, 48 Steele St., 80206; (303) 331-1110

DISTRICT OF COLUMBIA

WASHINGTON, D.C.—Consul de Mexico, 2827 16th Street N.W., 20009-4260; (202) 736-1000

FLORIDA

MIAMI—Consul General de Mexico, 5975 S.W. 72nd St., Suite 101, 33143; (786) 268-4900

ORLANDO—Consul de Mexico, 100 W. Washington St., 32801; (407) 422-0514

GEORGIA

ATLANTA—Consul General de Mexico, 2600 Apple Valley Rd., 30319; (404) 266-2233

ILLINOIS

CHICAGO—Consul General de Mexico, 204 S. Ashland Ave., 60607; (312) 855-1380

MASSACHUSETTS

BOSTON—Consul de Mexico, 20 Park Plaza, Suite 506, 02116; (617) 426-4181

MICHIGAN

DETROIT—Consul de Mexico, 645 Griswold Ave., Suite 1700, 48226; (313) 964-4515

MISSOURI

KANSAS CITY—Consul de Mexico, 1600 Baltimore Ave., Suite 100, 64108; (816) 556-0800

NEBRASKA

OMAHA—Consul de Mexico, 3552 Dodge St., 68131; (402) 595-1841

NEW MEXICO

ALBUQUERQUE—Consul de Mexico, 1610 4th St. N.W., 87102; (505) 247-4177

NEW YORK

NEW YORK—Consul General de Mexico, 27 E. 39th St., 10016; (212) 217-6400

NORTH CAROLINA

RALEIGH—Consul de Mexico, 336 E. Six Forks Rd., 27609; (919) 754-0046

OREGON

PORTLAND—Consul de Mexico, 1234 S.W. Morrison, 97205; (503) 274-1450

PENNSYLVANIA

PHILADELPHIA—Consul de Mexico, 111 S. Independence Mall East, Suite 310, 19106; (215) 922-3834

TEXAS

AUSTIN—Consul General de Mexico, 300 Brazos St., Suite 330, 78701; (512) 478-2866

BROWNSVILLE—Consul de Mexico, 724 E. Elizabeth St., 78520; (956) 542-4431

DALLAS—Consul General de Mexico, 8855 N. Stemmons Frwy., 75247-3855; (214) 252-9250

EL PASO—Consul General de Mexico, 910 E. San Antonio Ave., 79901; (915) 533-8555

HOUSTON—Consul General de Mexico, 4506 Caroline St., 77004; (713) 271-6800

LAREDO—Consul de Mexico, 1612 Farragut St., 78040; (956) 723-6369

SAN ANTONIO—Consul General de Mexico, 127 Navarro St., 78205; (210) 271-9728

UTAH

SALT LAKE CITY—Consul de Mexico, 155 E. 300 St. W, 3rd Floor, 84101; (801) 521-8502

WASHINGTON

SEATTLE—Consul de Mexico, 2132 Third Ave., 98121; (206) 448-3526

CANADA

MONTREAL—Consul General de Mexico, 2055 Peel St., Suite 1000, Quebec H3A 1V4; (514) 288-2502

TORONTO—Consul General de Mexico, 199 Bay St., Suite 4440, Commerce Court West Building, Ontario M5L 1E9; (416) 368-1847

VANCOUVER—Consul General de Mexico, 1177 W. Hastings St., Suite 710, British Columbia V6E 2K3; (604) 684-1859

automatically be taken into police custody, regardless of who is at fault. If detained or arrested, you should contact one of the following organizations:

Your embassy or consulate. By international law, you have the right to call a consular officer *(see "Embassies, Consulates and Consular Agencies," page 62).* **Note:** The long distance access code for the United States and Canada from within Mexico is 95 (station to station). For Mexico from within the country the code is 91. To make a direct international call to the United States or Canada from within Mexico, dial 001 before the area code and phone number; to call long distance from one Mexican destination to another, dial 01 before the area code and phone number.

Embassies and consulates advise and assist their nationals in case of accident, arrest, serious illness or death. Consular agents can help in such matters as lost passports. Important travel information, compiled by the U.S. Embassy in Mexico City, is contained in the brochure "Tips for Travelers to Mexico." Obtain a copy before your trip by enclosing $1 and writing the Superintendent of Documents, U.S. Government Printing Office, Washington, D.C. 20402, or the Consumer Information Center, Pueblo, CO 81009.

The International Legal Defense Counsel. This association allows access to a worldwide network of reputable attorneys. Their address is 1429 Walnut St., 8th Floor, Philadelphia, PA 19102; phone (215) 977-9982, fax (215) 564-2859.

The United States Embassy. The U.S. Embassy cannot represent U.S. citizens in court or provide legal counsel, but does maintain a list of local attorneys who speak English and who can provide advice on options and remedies within the Mexican legal system. For information phone (55) 5080-2000, ext. 4780.

Government Officials

Visitors who encounter trouble or require emergency services while in Mexico should contact the appropriate office of the State Tourism Department or, if there is no office nearby, notify local police. Outside major cities, Mexican government authority rests with the *delegado,* an elected official who presides over emergencies and civil or legal disputes. This individual can be found at the *delegación municipal* or *subdelegación.* Offices are often at the *palacio municipal* (city hall); ask at your hotel desk for directions. In isolated rural areas, authority is usually vested in an appointed citizen

Oaxaca / © Dallas and John Heaton / Stock Connection / PictureQuest

who reports to the nearest *delegado.* Tourist crime, however, occurs rarely in out-of-the-way places, so it shouldn't be necessary to resort to the last measure.

SECODAM, or the Comptroller and Administrative Development Secretariat, can help with complaints and also provides information about all government bureaus. Phone (55) 5604-1240 or (55) 5480-2000 in Mexico City; elsewhere within Mexico, phone (800) 001-4800 (toll-free long distance).

State Department Services

The U.S. State Department's Office of Overseas Citizens Services office deals with such situations as notifying home if you are caught in a natural disaster or political disturbance, locating someone in the event of an emergency, delivering emergency messages, making emergency money transfers and providing emergency loans. In these and other instances, have friends or family phone (202) 647-5225 (24 hours). Information also is provided for nonemergency questions. For emergency situations dealing with minors, contact the Office of Children's Issues; phone (202) 736-7000.

Note: Should you lose your money or other financial resources while in Mexico, the U.S. Embassy can help you contact your family, bank or employer to arrange for the transfer of funds. To transfer funds commercially to Mexico, contacts in the United States should go to the nearest Western Union office and have money sent to an "Elektra" store in Mexico. The funds should be sent in care of your name, either *Dinero en Minutos* (Money in Minutes) or *Va a Llamar* (Will Call).

The Elektra store closest to the embassy is the Insurgentes

Embassies, Consulates and Consular Agencies

Note: If calling or faxing from outside Mexico, dial 01152 before the area code and phone number. The U.S. Embassy's fax number is (55) 5525-5040; the Web site address is www.usembassy-mexico.gov. Office hours vary but are indicated where known. Offices are closed on U.S. and Mexican holidays.

U. S. EMBASSY:

Mexico City, Distrito Federal, Paseo de la Reforma #305, Colonia Cuauhtémoc, (55) 5080-2000; Mon.-Fri. 9-2 and 3-5

CANADIAN EMBASSY:

Mexico City, Distrito Federal, Calle Schiller #529, Colonia Polanco, (55) 5724-7900; Mon.-Fri. 8:45-5:15

U. S. CONSULATES:

Ciudad Juárez, Chihuahua, Avenida López Mateos #924-N, (656) 611-3000; Mon.-Fri. 8-4:45

Guadalajara, Jalisco, Progreso #175 at Avenida López Cotilla, (33) 3825-2700; Mon.-Fri. 8:30-noon and 2-3

Hermosillo, Sonora, Calle Monterrey #141 (between calles Rosales and Galeana), (662) 217-2375; Mon.-Fri. 8-4:30

Matamoros, Tamaulipas, Avenida Primera #2002, (868) 812-4402; Mon.-Fri. 8-noon and 1-5

Mérida, Yucatán, Paseo Montejo #453 at Avenida Colón, (999) 925-5011; Mon.-Fri. 7:30-4

Monterrey, Nuevo León, Avenida Constitución #411 Pte., (81) 8345-2120; Mon.-Fri. 8-5

Nogales, Sonora, Calle San José, about 3 miles south of the border and a block west of Avenida Obregón, (631) 313-4820

Nuevo Laredo, Tamaulipas, Calle Allende #3330, Col. Jardín, (867) 714-0512; Mon.-Fri. 8-12:30 and 1:30-5

Tijuana, Baja California, Avenida Tapachula #96, Col. Hipódromo, (664) 622-7400; Mon.-Fri. 8-5

U. S. CONSULAR AGENCIES:

Acapulco, Guerrero, Costera Miguel Alemán #121 (in the Hotel Acapulco Continental Plaza), (744) 469-0556; Mon.-Fri. 10-2

Cabo San Lucas, Baja California Sur, Boulevard Marina #C-4, Plaza Nautica, Colonia Centro, (624) 143-3566; Mon.-Fri. 8-3:30

Cancún, Quintana Roo, Plaza Caracol II, 3rd level (Boulevard Kukulcán, Km 8.5), (998) 883-0272; Mon.-Fri. 9-1 and 3-6

Cozumel, Quintana Roo, Villa Mar Mall, 2nd floor (avenidas Melgar and 5 Norte on the main plaza), (987) 872-4574

Ixtapa, Guerrero, Plaza Ambiente (Office 9), (755) 553-2100; Mon.-Fri. 10-2

Mazatlán, Sinaloa, Rodolfo T. Loaiza #202, Golden Zone (in the Hotel Playa Mazatlán), (669) 916-5889; Mon.-Thurs. 9-1

Oaxaca, Oaxaca, Calle M. Alcalá #407, Office 20, (951) 514-3054; Mon.-Fri. 9-2

San Luis Potosí, San Luis Potosí, Avenida Venustiano Carranza #2076-41 (Las Terrazas Building), (444) 811-7802; Mon.-Fri. 9-1

San Miguel de Allende, Guanajuato, Dr. Hernández Macías #72, (415) 152-2357; Mon. and Wed. 9:30-1 and 4-7, Tues. and Thurs. 4-7

CANADIAN CONSULATES:

Acapulco, Guerrero, Costera Miguel Alemán and Prolongación Farallón, Centro Comercial Marbella, (744) 484-1305; Mon.-Fri. 9-5

Cancún, Quintana Roo, Plaza Caracol II, 3rd floor (Boulevard Kukulcán, Km 8.5), (998) 883-3360; Mon.-Fri. 9-5

Guadalajara, Jalisco, Aurelio Aceves #225 on Minerva Circle (in the Hotel Fiesta Americana Guadalajara), (33) 3615-6215; Mon.-Fri. 8:30-2 and 3-5

Mazatlán, Sinaloa, Rodolfo Loaiza #202 (in the Hotel Playa Mazatlán), (669) 913-7320; Mon.-Fri. 9-1

Monterrey, Nuevo León, Constitución and Zaragoza #1300 Sur (Kalos Building), (81) 8344-2753; Mon.-Fri. 9-1:30 and 2:30-5:30

Oaxaca, Oaxaca, Pino Suárez #700, (951) 513-3777; Mon.-Fri. 11-2

Puerto Vallarta, Jalisco, Calle Zaragoza #160, (322) 222-5398; Mon.-Fri. 9-5

San José del Cabo, Baja California Sur, Boulevard Mijares at Plaza José Green, (624) 142-4333; Mon.-Fri. 9-1

Tijuana, Baja California, Avenida Germán Gedovius, Zona Río, (664) 684-0461; Mon.-Fri. 9-1

Elektra Store, Tonala #15, Colonia Juárez, 06600 Mexico, D.F.; phone (55) 5525-1608. The sender(s) must provide a 10-digit confirmation number along with their name and phone number, and the name, address and phone number of the Western Union office from which the money was sent. Photo identification is needed when the money is picked up.

Mexico's Highways

Mexico forever seems to be in the midst of a massive road-building program. Many old roads follow ancient Indian causeways or the cobblestoned *caminos carreteros* (carriageways) of colonial days. But new construction is ongoing, and bypasses and loop roads are standard features around cities and towns that have a central core with narrow streets and heavy traffic.

Roads in Mexico are generally not marked as clearly as those in the United States. Signs for turns and route directions will sometimes consist of city or town names only. Ideally, route numbers are posted every 5 kilometers (3 miles) on small roadside markers, but these also can be few and far between.

Each Mexican state is responsible for the maintenance of its roads, and some are better kept than others. Weather conditions, especially heavy rains, and such natural occurrences as mud or rockslides can keep roadways in disrepair. Lanes on nontoll roads tend to be narrow, and shoulders are either narrow or nonexistent.

If you plan to drive little-used or unpaved roads, inquire locally about conditions before heading out. Even a good map may not be accurate regarding the conditions of unpaved or ungraded routes; deep sand "roads" can stall even a four-wheel-drive vehicle, and seasonal downpours can render unpaved roads impassable. Put a protective covering over your luggage to keep out dust, and store camera equipment in plastic bags.

Toll Roads

A network of toll highways *(autopistas)* covers most parts of the country. Most of the newer tollways are four-lane, have road shoulders and are comparable in quality to U.S. highways. Emergency roadside phones often are spaced about every 2 kilometers (1.25 miles) along toll roads, and many are patrolled by the Green Angels as well. For the most part, toll roads are safe, speedy and scenic. Tolls are expensive, however—so much so that the highways are often all but deserted because Mexican motorists can't afford to use them.

Following are approximate charges (in pesos) for some major Mexican toll roads. Tolls may vary slightly due to the fluctuation in the exchange rate; in September 2004, the rate was about 11.3 pesos to the dollar.

Mex. 1-D (Tijuana to Ensenada): Runs about 114 kilometers (71 miles) south from the U.S. border to Ensenada in the state of Baja California. Tolls: 66 pesos for cars/motorcycles/vans/pickup campers, 135 pesos for trucks/motor homes.

Mex. 2-D (Tecate to Mexicali): Runs east-west along the U.S. border in the state of Baja California. Tolls: 42 pesos/85 pesos.

Mex. 15-D (Nogales to Mazatlán): Runs about 1,212 kilometers (727 miles) from the

U.S. border south to Mazatlán through the states of Sonora and Sinaloa. Tolls: 507 pesos/800 pesos.

Mex. 15-D (Tepic to Guadalajara): Runs about 228 kilometers (137 miles) southeast through the states of Nayarit and Jalisco. Tolls: 270 pesos/325 pesos.

Mex. 15-D (Guadalajara to Mexico City): Runs about 668 kilometers (401 miles) southeast through the states of Jalisco, Michoacán and México. Tolls: 282 pesos/442 pesos.

Mex. 57-D (Mexico City to Querétaro): Runs about 210 kilometers (126 miles) northwest from Mexico City through the states of México and Querétaro. Tolls: 100 pesos/204 pesos.

Mex. 85-D (Nuevo Laredo to Monterrey): Runs about 235 kilometers (141 miles) south from the U.S. border through the state of Nuevo León. Tolls 167 pesos/223 pesos.

Mex. 55-D/95-D (Mexico City to Acapulco): Runs about 415 kilometers (249 miles) south from Mexico City via Cuernavaca to Acapulco (states of Morelos and Guerrero). Tolls 75 pesos/130 pesos Mexico City to Cuernavaca, 396 pesos/661 pesos Cuernavaca to Acapulco (includes a tunnel toll).

Mex. 180-D (Mérida to Cancún): Runs about 242 kilometers (145 miles) from the junction

Floating Gardens, Xochimilco, Federal District / Guillermo Aldana
Mexico Tourism Board

with Mex. 180 east to the junction with Mex. 307 through the states of Yucatán and Quintana Roo. Tolls: 245 pesos/465 pesos.

Driving Precautions

Do not expect most free roads in Mexico to compare to the interstate highway system in the

Guillermo Aldana / Mexico Tourism Board

United States. Following the dictates of mountainous terrain, nontoll roadways are mostly rolling or winding, although there are many straight and/or level stretches in northern Mexico and the Yucatán Peninsula. Some of them have a sandpaper texture that affords better traction on curves but is wearing on tires.

Above all, motorists in Mexico should heed this advice: **Do not drive after dark if at all possible.** Few roads aside from the toll highways are equipped with street lights or shoulders, and night visibility is poor. Vehicles, which are sometimes driven with no headlights, might suddenly swerve to your side of the road to avoid potholes (which become invisible after dark). Bicycles without lights or reflectors are ridden, and pedestrians commonly use the roads at night. In addition, the Green Angels (see the "Emergency Road

Service" subheading) stop patrolling at 8 p.m. If you intend to cover a certain distance during any one day, get an early start and estimate your total driving time on the side of caution. *Never* pull off the road to sleep.

The possibility of robbery is another reason to curtail driving after dark. Bandits are likely to target foreign vehicles and have been known to pose as stranded motorists or police officers, so it's never a good idea to stop and offer assistance if you're unsure of the situation. You must stop, however, at designated police checkpoints (see the "Law Enforcement" subheading).

Livestock—principally cattle, goats and donkeys—may unexpectedly appear on rural roadways at night (and even during the day). A fence is no guarantee that an animal won't suddenly appear in the road. Slow down and give them a wide berth. Furthermore, animals will be almost invisible on unlighted roads at night—and can cause tremendous damage to your vehicle if they are struck.

Another requirement is to drive defensively. Always be alert to road conditions and other

motorists. Bus, truck and other drivers who are familiar with local routes will drive faster and negotiate maneuvers more boldly than tourists, who will likely find the highways more narrow, winding and weathered than those in the United States.

On some main corridors truck traffic is moderate to heavy, and truckers may drive aggressively or inconsiderately. If a truck begins to pass on a two-lane road, be prepared to pull off onto the gravel or graded dirt flanking the road surface if necessary to give the truck adequate room. Exercise caution; along the sides of roadways without shoulders there often is a full or partial covering of brush or undergrowth. Be particularly careful if you are attempting to pass a slow-moving truck—the driver isn't likely to pull over to give you more maneuvering room. Also be on the lookout for vehicles that are temporarily stopped in the roadway, particularly in rural areas.

Signaling one's intentions can have a different meaning than it does in the United States or Canada. For instance, a left turn signal in Mexico also means an invitation to pass on the left. Buses and trucks may flash their left blinker to guide you around them, but attempt to pass only when it can be done safely.

At intersections with a left-turn lane, there usually is a separate left-turn arrow; to turn left legally you must wait for the arrow. If making a left turn off a two-lane roadway where there is no separate left-turn lane, you are expected to pull over to the right as far as possible and wait for traffic to clear before making the turn. A right turn on red is generally not permitted unless there is a sign giving permission to do so; use your best judgement in situations when it is unclear whether you can legally turn right on red.

Heed the signals given by other drivers as well. When an oncoming truck flashes its headlights a couple of times, the driver is warning you to slow down or pull over. Since this signal is usually made when both you and the truck are approaching a one-lane bridge or narrow section of the road, you had better comply—the truck driver generally will not.

Speed bumps *(topes)* and potholes *(baches)* constitute perhaps the greatest danger to motorists on Mexican highways. Speed bumps are at the entrance to almost every town, no matter how small, and also can be encountered within towns. Warning signs will say *Topes, Vibradores* or *Reductor de Velocidad* (speed reducer) and give the distance in meters. Instead of words, some signs show a picture symbol and the distance in meters. In small towns these signs can appear suddenly, and not just at the entrance to town. Some speed bumps may not be preceded by a warning sign, however.

Topes are raised cobblestone bumps that can damage the underside of a vehicle unless negotiated at a very slow speed (in other words, you basically must come to a stop). *Vibradores* are corrugated, both lower and wider than *topes*. Speed bumps are prohibited on open sections of road and on toll roads, except at the entrance to toll stations.

Potholes are a particular problem along older free (nontoll) roadways and are exacerbated in areas that have a summer rainy season. Short-term maintenance may be nothing more than filling the pothole with sand or dirt. As some can be large enough to swallow a tire, caution is advised wherever potholes occur.

In the downtown sections of larger cities there are likely to be a number of one-way streets. Instead of signs, small arrows on the side of buildings or on lampposts often will indicate traffic direction. Follow the flow; if in doubt as to whether you are driving in the right direction, note

Michoacán / Bruce Herman / Mexico Tourism Board

which way parked vehicles are facing.

Recreational Vehicle Travel

Travel in recreational vehicles—campers, motor homes, trailers and similar vehicles—should be confined to the main highways. Do not park in isolated areas or camp along the highway or on beaches. Vehicles left unattended should be securely locked, with the shades or curtains drawn and all equipment (bicycles, chairs, etc.) removed from the outside. Never sleep in any vehicle parked along the roadside.

Propane gas is obtainable by vacationers traveling in recreational vehicles more than 50 kilometers (30 miles) below the U.S. border. This policy ensures that tourists who use propane for their engines, stoves and heaters will have an adequate supply.

Gasoline, Oil and Repairs

All gas stations in Mexico are concessions granted by the federally run oil company, Pemex. Fuel prices are fixed by the government. To avoid being overcharged by service station operators (a practice that targets

foreign motorists in particular), be certain you are charged the correct amount; make sure the pump is turned back to zero before your tank is filled; know exactly how many gallons/liters your tank holds; and keep smaller denominations of pesos in case attendants run out of change. Stations on major routes are spaced at adequate intervals but occasionally run out of supplies; it's a good idea to always keep your gas tank at least half full.

Most Pemex stations sell two grades of unleaded *(sin plomo)* gas: "Magna," dispensed from green pump handles, is the cheaper of the two; the "Premium" grade is dispensed from red pump handles. Pemex stations no longer offer Nova (leaded) gas, although diesel fuel is available.

The quality of the fuel tends to be somewhat lower than comparable U.S. unleaded grades, and prices are higher; at press time, Magna was equivalent to about $2.30 (U.S.) per gallon, Premium about $2.55 per gallon. Gas prices in border towns and cities tend to be a bit cheaper. Stations are full service; let the attendant fill the tank, but make sure he zeroes out the pump. Tipping is customary; a few pesos is fine.

Since unleaded pump nozzles in Mexico are sometimes larger than those in the United States, it's a good idea to keep a funnel in the car. Remember that pumps in Mexico register liters, not gallons; 10 liters is equal to about 2.5 gallons. For conversion information, *see the metric chart on page 544.* Stations with a "GasoPLUS" sign accept credit cards of the same name for gasoline purchases, but otherwise you'll have to pay cash, so keep peso amounts handy; payments must be made in pesos.

Service stations and private garages carry oils made in Mexico by foreign companies and by Pemex. Its brand, Brio, comes in several grades which are indicated by the color of the can; gold, black and blue are the best.

If your own vehicle or a rental car requires routine maintenance or major repairs while on the road, there are plenty of automotive repair shops (indicated by signs that say *taller mecánico*) in most parts of the country. Make sure you have a complete understanding about any work to be done as well as its cost. If a part must be ordered there could be additional expense and long delays, as permission from Mexican customs is needed to import parts. A knowledge of Spanish is usually necessary when negotiating with car repair shops, and it could be difficult finding a mechanic familiar with the make and model of your vehicle. Also keep in mind that businesses in Mexico may close from around 2-4 p.m. for *siesta*.

Jalisco / Nadine Markova / Mexico Tourism Board

The Green Angels

The idea of having a vehicle breakdown in Mexico can be unnerving, but motorists unfortunate enough to find themselves stranded do have a resource: the Green Angels. Since the early 1960s, these crews have patrolled roadways throughout the country. "Angeles Verdes" are identified by their distinctive green uniforms and green-and-white pickup trucks.

The Green Angels patrol more than 260 routes—both toll highways and "free" roads—that collectively cover every Mexico state capital and all major tourist destinations. Most Green Angel patrols are linked to 32 base stations, one in each of the 31 Mexican states plus the Federal District (Mexico City); routes are patrolled daily 8-8, year-round.

Green Angels personnel are carefully selected and should be familiar with the facilities along their routes. Services offered include vehicle mechanical aid, towing, adjustment or changing of tires, road condition information, medical first aid and protection. Motorists pay for the cost of automobile parts, gasoline and oil, but service is rendered free of charge. A tip is customary, although not required. Although all crew members are supposed to be bilingual, a knowledge of Spanish will still come in handy.

The program is in the midst of an expansion phase that will not only increase the capacity of Green Angels teams to respond to motorists in need of mechanical assistance, but also will provide advanced first aid and protection in conjunction with ambulance and emergency vehicle services. A prevention program focusing on the precautions visiting motorists need to take before and during their travels on Mexican roadways is being developed as well.

To enlist the assistance of a crew, pull completely off the highway and lift the hood of your vehicle. Contact the Mexico Ministry of Tourism (SECTUR) to obtain help or to have a crew dispatched; phone their national hotline, (800) 903-9200 (toll-free long distance).

If you break down in a remote area and don't have a cell phone, it may be necessary to hail a passing motorist, or preferably a bus or truck driver, and ask that he or she stop at the nearest available location to place the call. You also may be able to use one of the emergency telephones found along most of the newer toll highways and also along some older roads. Since Green Angel crews constantly cover their assigned sector, however, the chances are good that a patrol will soon locate you. Repairs, unfortunately, are another matter *(see the "Gasoline, Oil and Repairs" subheading)*.

Road Signs

Road signs are a mix of international picture symbols and signs in Spanish. A sign saying *Via Corta* indicates a short or alternate route. Toll roads are designated by the word *cuota* (and also by the letter "D" following the route number), nontoll roads by *libre*. Right turns on red are prohibited unless a sign is marked *Continua*. A sign with the word *Retorno* means a U-turn is permitted. Signs often posted just before entering small towns are *Poblado Proximo* (upcoming town), *Disminuya su Velocidad* (reduce your speed) or those that show the maximum speed limit allowed.

Common signs along highways include *Arbochate el Cinturon* (Buckle Your Seat Belt) and *No Deje Piedras Sobre el Pavimento* (Don't Leave Stones on the Pavement); the latter refers to the common practice of placing rocks in the road to denote a hazard or disabled vehicle. Some intersections without traffic signals have signs that say *Ceda el Paso a un Vehiculo* (Cede the Right of Way to One Vehicle); they are posted on each intersecting road and indicate that one vehicle at a time may proceed.

Be careful when approaching bridges. Those marked *Un Solo Carril* or *Puente Angosto* are narrow, one-way bridges. When two cars approach such a bridge from opposite directions, the first driver to flick his or her headlights has the right-of-way. The other should pull to the side of the road, allowing the first driver to cross. Although not a regulation, it is a general practice.

Many traffic signals are positioned horizontally rather than vertically. Also, on some signals the green light flashes three times before the yellow light appears. Motorists stopped at red lights in cities will often be approached by people attempting to earn money by washing windshields. If you're not interested, mouth the words *"no tengo dinero"* or shake your head "no" and rub your thumb and index finger together—the international symbol for "I have no money."

Parking

If possible, schedule daily activities so that your car does not have to remain unattended for

Church of Santa María Tonantzintla, Tonantzintla / Guillermo Aldana / Mexico Tourism Board

any length of time. Heed "no parking" signs, which depict a red circle with a diagonal line superimposed over a capital "E." Illegally parked cars will be towed, or their license plates will be removed. Recovering either item can result in a nightmare of time, expense and frustration. If in doubt, park in a guarded lot rather than on the street. Never leave valuables in plain sight in a parked vehicle.

On a one-way street, make certain your vehicle is parked on the left side, not the right. Parking on the street also likely means being approached by a youngster who will offer to watch your vehicle while you're gone. This often is a good idea, since the couple of pesos you hand over are a small price to pay for peace of mind. If a group of boys appears on your return, however, pay only one.

Law Enforcement

On main highways the speed limit is generally about 100 km/h

(60 mph) or as posted. In many cities the limit is about 40 km/h (25 mph); in some small towns it may be as low as 30 km/h (18-20 mph). Always obey the speed limit; while local police are generally lenient toward tourists who commit minor traffic violations, they make an exception in the case of speeding.

In Mexico City and those parts of the state of Mexico falling within the greater metropolitan area (particularly north and east of the Federal District), motorists with foreign license plates may be stopped by police for alleged driving infractions. If you commit an infraction and recognize it, accept the *boleta de infracción* (ticket) without arguing.

If you are stopped and did not do anything wrong, however, do not give in to a demand for graft. Take the officer's number and ask to speak with his *jefe* (HEH-feh), or boss, or to be taken to the nearest *delegación de policía* (police station) to explain your situation. In Mexico City, the Secretaría de Turismo (the Ministry of Tourism, or SECTUR) may be able to provide assistance if you feel you have been unfairly accused of a traffic violation; phone (55) 5250-0123 or (55) 5250-0151. Elsewhere within Mexico, phone (800) 903-9200 (toll-free long distance), or contact the nearest State Tourism Office.

Note: Motorists in northwestern Mexico—primarily those heading north toward the border—may occasionally be stopped by narcotics police, members of the military or inspection station personnel who are searching for arms or, more likely, drugs. These individuals may also speak only Spanish, which can make the situation stressful for those not fluent in the language.

While you should cooperate fully—even if it means explaining in English that you do not speak Spanish—by all means report any unfair treatment to the U.S. Embassy in Mexico City or to the nearest Mexican consulate office upon your return home. Such checkpoints are most likely to occur from Sinaloa north through Sonora, although they are a possibility practically anywhere in the country.

Bus Service

Mexico has a well-developed bus system, and this is an economical way to travel around the country. More than a dozen Mexican bus lines maintain frequent express service from U.S. border points to most cities, and also between major Mexican cities. Although service is less extensive in Baja California, buses travel practically everywhere. Among the major lines are Autobuses de Oriente (ADO), Enlases Terrestres Nacionales (ETN), Transportes del Norte (TN) and Elite.

Most of these companies offer first-class service that is comparable in quality to first-class U.S. bus service. Referred to as *ejecutivo, lujo, primera plus,* "deluxe," "super first class" and similar terms, these buses often include such amenities and extras as air conditioning, reclining seats, footrests, restrooms, movies, free snacks and beverages, as well as controlled 95 km/h (60 mph) speed. First-class buses also make few—sometimes no—stops and carry fewer passengers.

For long trips, bring your own food—in case you don't want to eat in the restaurant where the bus stops—drinking water and a roll of toilet paper. Seats on first-class buses are normally reserved in advance. Smoking is usually not permitted on these buses.

Note: Travel only during the day; avoid overnight trips. First-class and luxury buses use toll highways and are less likely to encounter incidents of robbery or assault.

Second- and third-class buses should by no means be compared to U.S. lines. You can hail one of these buses just about anytime and anywhere simply by standing at the side of the road and waving, and they're certainly a great way to experience local life. However, they make interminable stops, the vehicles themselves are frequently antiquated and can be unpleasantly hot, and you may have to share your seat with a pig or chicken. Furthermore, they cost only slightly less than first-class or luxury buses, and without the convenience of making advance reservations.

Many Mexican cities have one central bus station (*Central Camionera* or *Central de Autobuses*), which may or may not be near the main plaza or center of town. The various bus lines maintain offices at the central station. In some cities there may be several stations in different locations that serve specific companies or destinations. If you're unsure where to go, ask for the *estación del autobús* and give your destination. For trips between major cities, purchase a reserved-seat ticket from the station in advance; this is imperative for long weekends, and around school holidays, holiday seasons and important fiestas.

Note: Round-trip fares are not sold. Although buses frequently run behind schedule, be punctual—yours might depart the second it's supposed to. Routes, fares and departure times are always subject to change, and the only way to obtain this information is directly from the station. English is not likely to be spoken, so write your destination down and make certain you're getting on the right bus. Mexican bus schedules usually indicate whether the bus is *local* or *de paso* (which means it is en route from another location). *Directo* or *expresso* indicate a nonstop route. *Salida* means departure; *llegada,* arrival.

Do not use local buses for in-town transportation; a taxi, although more expensive, is safer. Exceptions are buses that travel specifically to tourist attractions; while these may be slow, they allow you to relax and enjoy the scenery.

The American bus line Greyhound Lines Inc. provides limited schedule and fare information for major Mexican bus lines and can ticket passengers to most U.S. border cities, in addition to Tijuana. Once across the border, passengers make arrangements with a Mexican bus line. Often there are buses that shuttle between the U.S. and Mexican stations. From Mexico City, bus trips to points of interest throughout the country are easily arranged; the major bus lines operate out of four huge terminals located in the northern, southern, eastern and western sections of the city.

One option to using buses as your main means of on-the-road transportation is to take a guided motor coach tour. Prior to 1991, U.S. and Canadian visitors were required by law to use Mexican buses and take Mexican tours once they crossed the border. Restrictions on bus travel have eased, and American buses now are able to make the entire journey. Such U.S. companies as Gray Line Tours offer transborder bus excursions from several hours to several days' duration that visit various parts of Mexico. Contact a travel agency for details.

Rail Service

Passenger rail service in Mexico is practically a thing of the past, eclipsed by first-class bus service that reaches just about all parts of the country. If you want to see Mexico while someone else does the driving, bus travel is recommended. One popular tourist train trip is the Chihuahua al Pacífico railway, which runs through the rugged Sierra Madre Mountains and the spectacularly scenic Copper Canyon region (*see Copper Canyon listing under Northwestern Mexico*).

Ferry Service

Passenger and vehicle ferry service is provided between the Mexican mainland and Baja California, connecting the ports of Santa Rosalía-Guaymas, La Paz-Topolobampo (Los Mochis) and La Paz-Mazatlán.

Normally, ferries run three times a week between Santa Rosalía and Guaymas (sailing time about 8 hours), and daily between La Paz and Topolobampo (sailing time about 5 hours).

Reservations, which are recommended, can be made by phone, as well as in person at one of the ferry offices, but a knowledge of fluent Spanish is necessary; it's easier to make reservations through a local travel agency at the port of departure.

The Web sites bajaferries.net and www.ferrysantarosalia.com provide fare, schedule and contact information.

Fares are one way and per person, sharing the accommodation. Cabin lodging with restroom facilities is available. Children ages 1-11 are charged half the adult fare. If you're prone to seasickness, bring the appropriate medications. Pregnant women are not allowed onboard. If transporting a vehicle, take everything you'll need out of it before the journey begins.

Note: If you plan on transporting a vehicle from Baja California to the Mexican mainland, it is necessary to obtain a temporary vehicle importation permit. To avoid frustration and disrupted travel plans, obtain the permit and have all related temporary vehicle importation documents filled out at the border before entering Mexico. When applying for a vehicle permit, acceptable proof of citizenship, a copy of the current registration and a notarized letter of permission from the lienholder (if a vehicle is not fully paid for) all must be presented for each vehicle being transported (including motorcycles). For additional details see "Temporary Importation of Vehicles," page 553.

Your vehicle must be weighed before you purchase your ticket. Arrive at the ticket office as soon as possible (check in advance; opening times vary from location to location), and inquire where to park your vehicle for weighing (la balanza). Passenger and vehicle tickets are usually sold in separate lines. Also keep in mind

that if you have entered Mexico via Baja California and then cross over to the mainland, you will have to go through customs before boarding the ferry and pay whatever duty fees are assessed.

In La Paz, the Grupo Sematur ticket office (for ferries to Mazatlán) is at Guillermo Prieto and Calle 5 de Mayo, two blocks inland from Jardín Velasco (Plaza Constitución). The Baja Ferries ticket office (for ferries to Topolobampo) is at the corner of Calle Isabel La Catolica and

ferry office is in the terminal building on Mex. 1, just south of the main entrance into town. In Topolobampo, Guaymas and Mazatlán, offices are at the ferry terminal. *Also see the separate listings for La Paz and Santa Rosalía under Baja California, the listings for Guaymas and Los Mochis under Northwestern Mexico and the listing for Mazatlán under The Pacific Coast.*

In the state of Quintana Roo, a daily ferry carries passengers and vehicles from Puerto Morelos to

Guadalajara / Pablo De Aguinaco / Mexico Tourism Board

Navarro. The ferry terminal is at Pichilingue, the deep-water port for La Paz, about 16 kilometers (10 miles) north of the city via Mex. 11. In Santa Rosalía, the

Cozumel; however, variable schedules can cause long waiting periods. Passenger boats also make several daily trips to Cozumel from Playa del Carmen. In addition, daily passenger trips run from Puerto Juárez, just north of Cancún, to Isla Mujeres; daily passenger/vehicle trips run from Punta Sam to Isla Mujeres. *See Cancún listing, page 88, and the separate listings for Playa del Carmen and Puerto Morelos under Yucatán Peninsula.*

Oaxaca / Guillermo Aldana / Mexico Tourism Board

Health and Safety

Sanitation and hygiene in Mexico have improved considerably in the last several decades. Several endemic infectious diseases have been eradicated, and today life expectancy at birth is 70 years for men, 78 years for women. Reasonable precautions will eliminate serious health risks for almost all foreign visitors.

Visiting High-Altitude Areas

If you live in or are used to a lower altitude, you may need a short adjustment period when visiting areas above 1,525 meters (5,000 feet). Don't push yourself too hard; a light diet and reduced intake of alcoholic beverages are recommended. Move about in a leisurely fashion for the first few days. If you're affected by the altitude (headache or nausea), rest quietly until you feel comfortable; it may take from 12 to 36 hours before you feel better. Another health consideration at high altitudes is overexposure to the sun; use a suntan lotion that has an effective sunscreen agent.

Persons with weak hearts or of very advanced age should consult their physician before undertaking prolonged visits to cities at high elevations. Travelers with specific health concerns should inquire about recommended immunizations or medications to carry with them.

Acute Mountain Sickness (AMS), which can strike at altitudes of 2,450 meters (8,000 feet) or more, is the body's way of coping with reduced oxygen and humidity. Also known as altitude sickness, its symptoms include headaches, double vision, shortness of breath, loss of appetite, insomnia and lethargy. Some people complain of temporary weight gain or swelling in the face, hands and feet. Even those used to high altitudes may feel the effects of AMS. If symptoms strike, stop ascending. A quick descent will alleviate the discomfort.

The negative reaction of your body to changes in altitude is lessened if you're in good physical shape and don't smoke. Ascend gradually, eat light but nutritious meals and drink plenty of bottled water. Alcohol consumption may aggravate AMS symptoms if they occur.

Note: The elevation for city and place descriptions is given when it is over 762 meters (2,500 feet).

Air Quality

As is common when traveling anywhere in the world, a change in weather or lifestyle can particularly affect the health of elderly visitors, young children or those who suffer from cardiac or respiratory conditions. Mexico City's dense traffic and air pollution, conditions present in any large metropolis, are factors that nevertheless should be taken into consideration. Air pollution also is a factor in Guadalajara and Monterrey.

Mexico City's location is partly responsible for its pollution problem: More than 7,000 feet above sea level, it is situated at the bottom of a valley ringed with mountains. Despite the unfavorable geography, a thin atmosphere and an estimated 3.5 million vehicles on the streets, federal and city authorities continue to take steps toward a cleaner environment.

Eating and Drinking

Follow the cardinal rule for fruits, vegetables and seafood: Do not eat anything that has not been peeled by you, or that cannot be cooked or boiled. Avoid unpasteurized dairy products as well. Otherwise, take every opportunity to enjoy the country's many distinctive regional dishes. Avoid food sold by street vendors, but at the better restaurants in Cancún, Mexico City, Puerto Vallarta and other cities where tourism is big business, virtually anything on the menu can be enjoyed without fear.

Mexican restaurants traditionally do not have a separate non-smoking area. One exception is Vips, a restaurant chain that is casual, clean, efficient and springing up everywhere.

Bottled water in liter or smaller sizes is sold throughout Mexico at gas station convenience stores, grocery stores and shops catering to tourists. Chemical disinfecting tablets also are available from pharmacies and supermarkets.

If the hotel has its own purification system, tap water can be used for brushing your teeth or rinsing contact lenses; ask to make sure, and also ask about the ice dispensed by ice machines. Most hotels routinely provide bottled water for drinking (some may charge for it when you check out). If in doubt about the water in smaller towns, ask for *agua purificada*. Remember that this includes ice cubes. If you find yourself in an area where bottled water is not available, boil water vigorously for one full minute to kill disease-causing organisms.

These precautions should serve to ward off the most common visitor ailment, diarrhea (which Mexicans call *turista*). Bed rest and a liquid diet (unsweetened tea is best) will cure most cases. If these preventive measures fail, see a doctor. There are physicians, surgeons, specialists, good hospitals and Mexican Red Cross clinics in all the major cities and larger towns. In many villages, the Instituto Mexicano del Seguro Social (IMSS), the Instituto de Seguridad y Servicios Sociales de los Trabajadores del Estado (ISSSTE) and the Secretaría de Salud run clinics or hospitals where visitors

can receive medical assistance.

Most of the better hotels have house doctors; if not, your hotel manager or the local police will help you find medical assistance. It's not a good idea to buy over-the-counter antibiotics.

Diseases

The risk of contracting typhoid or cholera is minimal, despite sporadic cholera outbreaks. Vaccinations will offer protection in areas off the tourist itinerary, where running water and drainage systems frequently are inadequate, but vaccinations should not be considered a substitute for caution in selecting food and drink. In the case of cholera or other intestinal ailments, this means avoiding raw or undercooked seafood and cold seafood dishes.

The presence of mosquitoes that transmit malaria is dependent on such local conditions as weather, altitude, mosquito control efforts and the prevalence of disease. Mosquitoes also can spread dengue fever. In coastal areas, the risks of being bitten are greater. Use mosquito repellent if you plan on spending time outdoors. Brands containing DEET are the most effective; be sure to read and follow the directions and precautions on the label. Try to avoid being outside

between dusk and dawn, when mosquitoes are most likely to bite.

According to the Centers for Disease Control and Prevention (CDC), the following states have a risk of malaria in rural areas: Campeche, Chiapas, Guerrero, Michoacán, Nayarit, Oaxaca, Quintana Roo, Sinaloa and Tabasco. If you plan to explore remote areas of any of these states, consult your physician or local health department before leaving for the advisability of taking a preventive drug.

Tourists arriving in Mexico from yellow fever-infected areas must have a yellow fever vaccination certificate; tourists arriving directly from the United States or Canada are not required to have the certificate.

The CDC operates a hotline with international health requirements and health recommendations for foreign travelers. Topics include general vaccinations, food and water guidelines and current disease-outbreak reports. Phone (877) 394-8747; for the immunization hotline, phone (800) 232-2522. The Web site address is www.cdc.gov.

Personal Safety

Crimes against tourists in Mexico are unlikely. But the possibility does exist, due in part to

Sarapes / Oaxaca Tourism

several factors: a criminal justice system that investigates few of these crimes and punishes even fewer perpetrators; law enforcement officers who may be in tacit partnership with organized criminal activity (and out-of-work former soldiers and police who turn to such activity); unemployment fueled by economic hardship; and the ever-growing gap between rich and poor that makes crime an increasingly lucrative career option.

The Mexico City metropolitan area, where an estimated 21 million people are crammed together, has been hit especially hard. Tijuana and Ciudad Juárez—both centers of the flourishing border drug trade—have seen violent crime escalate as well.

Political instability in the states of Guerrero and Chiapas has led to sporadic violence (although not directed at foreigners). Even the tourist haven of Cancún is not immune from hotel room thefts, purse snatchings and pickpocketing incidents. Other major visitor destinations, such as Cabo San Lucas, Puerto Vallarta and San Miguel de Allende, have seen fewer problems.

Regardless of your itinerary, employing the same common sense you would at home to maintain personal safety will reduce the chance of becoming a crime victim. For example, it is very important to look and act confident rather than bewildered when out in public. Don't, however, flaunt expensive watches, jewelry or clothing; you're more likely to be targeted for robbery or assault if you are easily identifiable as a well-off or wealthy tourist.

Avoid putting your wallet in a back pocket or wearing a purse with a shoulder strap that can be grabbed by a passerby. Petty thieves and pickpockets use a razor to slash pockets or bags, so keep your belongings close to you at all times. Put cameras in briefcases or bags with a chain-reinforced strap.

Stash traveler's checks and cash in different places; for example, in money belts and extra pockets sewn inside clothing. Keep photocopies of passports, credit cards and other documents in a separate place from the originals. Be very cautious around ATM machines. If possible, use one during the day inside a large commercial facility; avoid nighttime transactions at glass-enclosed street machines.

If you're driving, do not leave valuables in plain view in your car; stow possessions out of sight. Use parking lots or garages whenever possible. Parking areas are designated by a sign with the word *"Estaciona-miento"* and the international symbol of a red circle with a capital "E" inside.

Always lock your car, roll up the windows and park in a well-lighted area. If traveling by bus or train, be especially careful at the station; never leave your luggage unattended, and lock all items together with a chain or cable if possible.

As crime is an unfortunate byproduct of widespread poverty, highway robberies do occur, particularly outside of tourist areas and in the southern part of the country. To avoid becoming a target, stick to toll highways wherever possible, and above all do not pull off the road to sleep. **Never drive after dark.** Camp in designated national parks or at RV sites rather than along lonely beaches or other unsupervised wilderness areas.

In less-traveled areas of Mexico—particularly near the northern and southern international borders in Sonora and Quintana Roo, respectively, and in the states of Chiapas, Guerrero and Oaxaca—motorists may be stopped at military checkpoints and approached by official-looking men who request identification and ask where you are going.

If you are stopped at a roadblock, remain calm and polite, comply with instructions, speak as little Spanish as possible, and get badge numbers and names. If asked to hand over your wallet, give them *only* the proper identification; if necessary, remove all your money first. Report any irregularities to the appropriate embassy, consumer protection agency or consular office.

Poorly paid police may intimidate foreign motorists into paying "fines" for minor or alleged infractions. This is particularly true in and around Mexico City, where visitors with non-Mexican license plates may find themselves victims of harassment. You could also encounter a situation in which you are charged with an infraction that you are certain you did not commit.

Such an incident can be both frightening and infuriating, but if it happens, try to remain calm. Ask to be shown documentation of the rule you violated. Request to speak with someone of higher authority if necessary, and beware of "plainclothes policemen"; insist on seeing identification.

Very obviously writing down all the details of the incident—name, badge number, the nature of the alleged violation, the exact location where it occurred—may help defuse the situation. Avoid handing over an original driver's license, car rental contract, vehicle registration or any other document; always carry photocopies.

If resistance provokes further trouble, ask for the ticket, pay it at a bank and claim a receipt. To register a complaint, contact the Secretaría de Turismo (the Ministry of Tourism, or SECTUR) in Mexico City; phone (55) 5250-0123 or (55) 5250-0151, or (800) 903-9200 elsewhere within Mexico (toll-free long distance).

Women, either traveling alone or with others, normally do not need to take special precautions, but there are a few things that should be kept in mind. While ethnic or sexual stereotyping is unfortunate, it can occur. Female travelers who look obviously foreign, or those with fair skin and hair, may attract unsolicited attention. If this happens, the best response is no response. In *cantinas,* bars with a macho, often hard-drinking male clientele, female customers are unwelcome.

Sexual assault is not out of the question, particularly in Mexico City. In bars and nightspots (even those in areas frequented by tourists) avoid accepting a drink from a stranger; it may be drugged.

Currency

The monetary unit is the peso (its symbol is the dollar sign, or $). One peso equals 100 centavos. There are 10-centavo, 20-centavo and 50-centavo coins; peso coins are in denominations of $1, $2, $5, $10, $20, $50 and $100. Bills are in denominations of 20, 50, 100, 200 and 500 pesos.

The 10-centavo, 20-centavo and 50-centavo coins are not often used, but they come in handy as spare change to give to the needy, if you're so inclined, or to help facilitate souvenir purchases at markets. Hang on to smaller denomination bills and coins as you accumulate them, or exchange a dollar amount that will yield small-denomination coins or bills.

Cash payments for amounts that include centavos are rounded off to the nearest 10 centavos. An item costing 11.52 pesos, therefore, would be rounded off to a cash payment of 11.50 pesos; an item costing 11.56 pesos would be rounded off to a cash payment of 11.60 pesos. Check and credit card payments will show the exact amount and must be paid in that amount. Credit card charges are converted into dollars by the bank issuing the card, usually at a favorable bank rate.

In border cities and some tourist resorts, prices in Mexican currency may carry the abbreviation "m.n." (moneda nacional); prices in American currency, "dlls." (dollars). As a general rule, Mexican establishments rendering services to tourists quote and charge in pesos. In many of Mexico's resort areas, however, U.S. dollars are as readily accepted as pesos. Information sheets showing pictures of Mexican coins and bills are normally available at airports and border crossings, or appear in tourist publications.

Bruce Herman / Mexico Tourism Board

Note: As a convenient reference, any prices or rates appearing in this book are quoted in approximate U.S. dollars unless stated otherwise. In September 2004, the exchange rate was approximately 11.3 pesos to the dollar. However, the peso is a floating currency subject to small daily fluctuations.

Many banks in U.S. border cities handle currency exchanges, but rates are not likely to be as favorable as those offered by banks and airports south of the border. Although the services offered by Mexican banks are being upgraded, many exchange dollars for pesos only during morning business hours.

Credit cards should cover almost all hotel, restaurant and store charges, as well as airline tickets for flights within Mexico. (**Note:** Gasoline purchases cannot be charged unless you have a GasoPLUS credit card—issued only in Mexico—which can be used at Pemex gas stations.)

Automated teller (caja permanente) machines are available in major cities and resort areas; most accept the widely honored Cirrus and PLUS cards. Expect peso denominations in return, and to be charged a service fee by your bank for each transaction.

Using an ATM card avoids the commission charged by banks for exchanging traveler's checks into pesos (and the exchange rate is often better), but there is always the possibility that travelers will be forced to withdraw money. Make all ATM transactions during daylight hours, preferably at machines inside commercial establishments.

Unfortunately, the threat of purse or wallet snatching is ever present in crowded areas or a busy marketplace. Keep your money and important documents separate. Consider depositing surplus currency and jewelry in hotel vaults. When out in public, ignore remarks from strangers such as "What's that on your shoulder?"

or someone yelling "Thief!" in a crowded area—both may be set-ups used by pickpockets or scam artists to distract your attention or trick you into revealing where you carry your money.

Casas de cambio (private money exchangers) usually offer a better rate of exchange for dollars (cash or documents). These exchange offices often are located next to big hotels in cities, or in malls in resort areas. A driver's license is needed to cash U.S. traveler's checks.

Currency exchange also is a standard service at hotel front desks; call the hotel or hotels at which you'll be staying just prior to your trip to see what exchange rate is being offered. Trying to find the best rate usually boils down to a matter of convenience, since differences are normally minimal. If you're shopping around for the best rate or trying to save pennies a pocket calculator will come in handy.

If you're using traveler's checks, exchange only what you think you'll need for the next day or two. Keep in mind that all Mexican banks charge a service fee or commission to exchange dollars for pesos; beware of banks that charge a flat fee per traveler's check cashed.

Traveler's checks denominated in pesos can be purchased at banks and currency exchange offices in the United States and will be easier to cash in small towns and areas away from tourist centers, where banks may be less likely to cash a traveler's check.

Note: Banco de México is in the process of replacing the current 20-peso paper bills with plastic equivalents designed to have a longer life. The plastic bills look similar to their paper counterparts, with the addition of safety features such as a transparent window. If the transition is successful other denominations will follow.

Tipping

While tipping is virtually universal, the matter of whom, when and how much to tip varies. In Mexico, waiters, maids, porters and other workers whose wages are low must rely to a great extent on tips for their living. Let your conscience be your guide, and don't hesitate to reward outstanding service or penalize poor service.

Percentages for hotel and restaurant staff are similar to those in the United States and Canada. In restaurants, make sure that a service charge has not already been added onto the bill. Taxi

La Venta Museum, Villahermosa, Tabasco / Guillermo Aldana / Mexico Tourism Board

drivers are not usually tipped unless they've performed some special service, such as waiting while a bit of shopping is done. Gas station attendants, however, expect a tip.

Sightseeing tour guides should be tipped. There also are individuals whom you would not normally tip at home but should in Mexico; for example, theater ushers, washroom attendants and parking attendants.

Economic reality makes it necessary for some Mexicans to resort to begging as a means of survival. Women or children will ask for coins on the street or outside the town cathedral. Another frequently employed location, particularly in larger cities, is a busy intersection. Here an entire family may gather—washing windshields or even putting on an impromptu performance in costume—in return for small change from motorists stopped at the red light. Whether to give under such circumstances is up to the individual, of course, but considering the very real poverty with which many people must cope, any gift will be much appreciated.

Street vendors can be ubiquitous, particularly in the main plazas of towns, at archeological sites and other places where tourists are likely to be, and at beaches where vending is not prohibited. If you do decide to purchase something from a roving vendor, be very discreet; otherwise you will be inundated by insistent hawkers pushing everything from fruit to straw baskets. If you don't intend to buy, firmly communicate your lack of interest.

Young children frequently will offer special services to visitors. Even if it is performed in an unsolicited manner—for example, cleaning your windshield while you're stopped at a red light—compensation is expected. Again, if you are not interested in what a child is offering, whether it be carrying your bags at the airport or promising to guard your car while you shop or see the sights, be very firm about declining.

Youngsters also will charm coins or other gifts out of visitors, and it may be hard to resist these overtures. If you do succumb, hand something directly to a child. Children have been killed running across busy streets to pick up "gifts" tossed from car windows. Better yet, buy some pieces of fruit or other inexpensive foods at the local market. A few clothing items, pencils, pens or simple toys can be packed along with your own personal belongings if you enjoy contributing such gifts to the needy.

Mail Service

All letter mail to Mexico travels by air. First class mail service from Mexico to other countries is by air; parcel post and second class mail is by land. If you want to send mail from Mexico, use post mail only in those cities with airline service. **Note:** Mail service is notoriously slow, and mail can take up to a month to reach destinations in the United States, even that marked "via air mail." Do not expect postcards, letters or packages to arrive back home before you do.

Postal codes in Mexican addresses should be placed before the name of the destination town or city, as in the following example: Hotel Imperial, Avenida Guadalupe #210, 45040 Guadalajara, Jal., Mexico.

Addresses

If you've ever had difficulty hunting down an address in almost any large city in the United States, prepare for the same possibility in Mexico. Street names tend to change mysteriously on either side of a town's main square, or capriciously after traversing several blocks. Street signs may be outdated or even nonexistent. Addresses frequently do not include numbers. All of this can be frustrating if trying to locate an out-of-the-way shop or restaurant; however, there are some general guidelines that can be relied on to aid in the search.

Nadine Markova / Mexico Tourism Board

Although used where known in this book for purposes of clarification, designations such as *avenida* and *calle* usually are not posted, and streets are referred to by name only. That name may include a compass direction— *Nte.* or *Norte, Sur, Pte.* or *Poniente* and *Ote.* or *Oriente* for north, south, east and west, respectively.

When an address includes *s/n* it means there is no number. In numbered addresses, the number follows rather than precedes the name. Addresses on main routes outside of cities or towns will often be stated in terms of the number of kilometers from town; for example, *Km. 18 a Mérida.*

Sprawling urban areas (Guadalajara and Monterrey, for example) have their own inscrutable logic regarding street names and configurations, and trying to find something outside of well-known tourist areas can turn into an adventure. In a class of its own is Mexico City, where hundreds of new thoroughfares are added to the metropolitan area each year and existing streets are often renamed.

Streets in smaller cities are usually laid out in a simple grid pattern radiating from the central plaza (technically, only the square in Mexico City is referred to as the *zócalo*). Specific locations within the core downtown area can thus be pinpointed relatively easily in terms of the number of blocks north, south, east or west of the plaza.

If you become lost in an unfamiliar city or town, asking a local taxi driver for directions or having him lead you where you want to go can save a lot of headaches. A knowledge of Spanish is helpful in these situations, and agree on a price first if he transports you anywhere.

If you need to ask directions from someone on the street, you may be steered off course; Mexicans tend to improvise rather than admit they don't know. But again, there are certain strategies that can increase your chances of success. Keep questions brief and to the point, and ask them with a smile; most people will be happy to try and help. Women who were brought up not to talk to strangers may ignore you, and don't bother asking a child, particularly if your Spanish is rusty. Maps are not likely to be understood; pointing is more direct. If you ask how long it will take to reach a specific destination, or what the exact distance is, remember that the answer is likely to be subjective.

Phone Service

When making telephone calls within Mexico, keep two things in mind: Calling from your hotel, while convenient, is likely to be expensive; and using public phones, while less expensive, can be frustrating. If you do not speak fluent Spanish, local calls to businesses, police stations or public service agencies can easily grind to a halt. And busy signals are commonplace; if a call must be made and you experience difficulty getting through, keep trying.

If you want to connect directly to an international destination without speaking to an operator, use your calling card and dial 01 (for AT&T) or 001 (for MCI or Sprint) plus the 800 access number for your long-distance carrier. AT&T's USA DIRECT number is (800) 288-2872; MCI, (800) 674-7000; and Sprint, (800) 877-8000. To avoid having expensive hotel surcharges tacked on to your bill, don't call from your room. Some hotels may block one or more access code numbers if you try to call from the room; if that is the case, make the call from a public pay phone with a U.S. calling card. (**Note:** Some hotels add a charge for local calls made from the room in addition to the hefty surcharge placed on all international calls. Inquire when you check in whether local calls are extra.)

There are very few coin-operated public pay phones in Mexico, and they tend to be out of order. Most public phones are labeled Telmex, the name of the national telephone company, and are part of a system called Ladatel—literally, long distance (*lada*) telephone. Ladatel phones allow direct dialing without operator assistance and are less expensive than making phone calls from a hotel room. Local calls also can be made from Ladatel phones.

There are several types of Ladatel phones. Some have a coin slot that accepts pesos in the appropriate denomination and a slot in which to insert a disposable Ladatel phone card. Others have two slots—one for the Ladatel card and one for Mexican bank credit cards (Banamex, Bancomer or Carnet). Some phones also accept MasterCard or Visa, but not U.S. telephone calling cards. Ladatel phone cards can be purchased in

various peso denominations (typically 30, 50 or 100 pesos) at most pharmacies and gas station mini-markets, as well as from machines at airports and bus stations.

To make a call with a Ladatel card, insert the card into the appropriate slot and dial the access code (if necessary) plus the number you're trying to reach. The card is left in the slot while the call takes place. If the call does not go through, the card is returned. If the call is for less time than the value of the card, it is returned with a credit amount shown. If the call is still in progress when the card's value has been used up, the phone will beep and another card must be inserted to continue the call. Some phones have a digital display window that monitors the cost of the call.

When calling long distance from one Mexican location to another, dial 01 (the access code), then the three-digit area code (two-digit area code in metropolitan Guadalajara, Mexico City and Monterrey), then the seven-digit local phone number (eight-digit local number in metropolitan Guadalajara, Mexico City and Monterrey). Mexican phone numbers shown in this book include only the area code and the local number, not the access code that also must be dialed if making a long-distance call. Local calls in Mexico do not require dialing the access or area codes.

Note: All phone numbers in this book show the 10-digit format implemented in Mexico in November 2001. Free tourist publications usually include phone numbers for hotels, restaurants, attractions, travel agencies, airlines and so forth, as well as emergency and general information numbers. For additional assistance, consult a Telmex directory.

All Mexican toll-free numbers have an 800 area code. You must first dial the 01 access code, then the 800 prefix and the seven-digit number. Mexican toll-free numbers shown in this book do

not include the access code but are identified as being toll-free within Mexico. **Note:** Mexican numbers with an 800 prefix will work *only* in Mexico; the call will not go through if dialed from outside the country.

If you have a problem trying to make a specific local or long-distance call, enlist the aid of an operator; there are few recordings advising callers of phone number or area code changes. To reach a long-distance operator within Mexico, dial 020; for directory assistance, dial 040; for emergency assistance, dial 060 (similar to 911 in the United States); for an international operator, dial 090. Keep in mind that English may not be spoken.

To make an international call to the United States or Canada on a private phone line, dial 001, then the area code and phone number. If using a public phone, dial 95, then the area code and phone number. Calling collect is the least expensive option. If you call from your hotel room, however, you may be charged even if the call is not accepted.

Time Zones

Most of Mexico's states are on Central Standard Time. Exceptions are the states of Chihuahua, Nayarit, Sonora, Sinaloa and Baja California Sur, which are on Mountain Standard Time, and Baja California, which is on Pacific Standard Time.

Mexico began observing daylight-saving time (DST, referred to as "summer time" or "La Hora de Verano") in 1996 in accordance with the United States and Canada—from the first weekend in April through the last weekend in October. In 2001 the switchover was shortened by two months—from the first weekend in May to the last weekend in September. In the state of Baja California, however, daylight-saving time is still observed from the first weekend in April to the last weekend in October.

Cozumel, Quintana Roo / © Nik Wheeler / Corbis

Yucatán Peninsula

Consisting of three states—Campeche, Quintana Roo and Yucatán—the Yucatán (yoo-cah-TAHN) Peninsula is an intriguing juxtaposition of old and new, of the pristinely natural and the master-planned. Geographic, ethnographic and historical factors combine to separate the Yucatán somewhat from the rest of Mexico, a feeling shared by the people who live here—most think of themselves as *yucatecos* first, Mexicans second.

The first Spaniards who arrived at the Yucatán's eastern shore in the early 16th century believed it to be a huge island in between the Caribbean Sea and the Gulf of Mexico. Certainly the region's physical characteristics, which are more similar to the state of Florida than to the Mexican mainland, could qualify it as a separate country. The peninsula's most exploitable natural resource is its Caribbean coastline, bathed by aquamarine water and lined with gorgeous white-sand beaches, and the wealth of fishing, diving, snorkeling, swimming and boating opportunities draws multitudes of tourists to the Yucatán's shores.

It wasn't always so. As early as 400 B.C., the ancient Maya civilization was beginning to evolve in the Mexican state of Chiapas and the countries of Belize, Guatemala and Honduras. Its origins remain one of history's puzzles, although it is believed that the Maya were descended from the Olmec, whose own civilization flourished along Mexico's lower gulf coast in what is now the state of Tabasco. Over a period of time roughly parallel to the rise of the Roman Empire the Maya developed their own sophisticated civilization, as well as a reputation for bizarre, blood-spattered rites.

The Maya migrated northward from Central America to the present-day states of

Campeche and Yucatán. Between 1000 and 1500, such major cities as Chichén Itzá, Cobá, Dzibilchaltún, Edzná, Ek Balam, Mayapán, Tulum and Uxmal were built. Over time the focus of Maya civilization moved from the observance of elaborate religious rituals toward commercial, governmental and militaristic concerns. Some cities functioned as trade centers between the Caribbean and gulf coasts and Mexico's interior as the peninsula was infiltrated by various tribes. It was the squabbling among these different factions that set the stage for Spanish conquest of the Yucatán, which was absolute by the end of the 16th century.

The Yucatecan people—direct descendants of the Maya—are one of Mexico's largest *indígena* groups. They live throughout the peninsula, particularly in the state of Yucatán, and their short stature, dark-skinned complexions and sculpted cheekbones bear unmistakable witness to their forebears. Maya dialects are as readily spoken as Spanish, although residents employed in the tourist industry usually speak English as well. Yucatecans are friendly; don't be afraid to ask for the time or for directions, but return the kindness with a smile and a thank-you. You could also try thanking in Maya, which (spelled phonetically) is "dios boteek." Always ask first if you wish to photograph someone; this can be requested as simply as holding up your camera and saying *"por favor"?*

Adventurous travelers might want to head for Campeche, the least-explored state, where ancient ruins poke up out of thick jungle. Hardwoods traditionally furnished much of Campeche's wealth, although oil is the leading industry today. The capital of Campeche, walled in the 17th century as a defense against pirates, has the easygoing charm of a tropical port, and ongoing efforts are under way to renovate the city's numerous colonial-style buildings.

Rising from the flat scrubland of Yucatán state are the archeological sites of Chichén Itzá, Ek Balam and Uxmal. These former ceremonial centers contain monumentally scaled buildings created without benefit of such basics as the wheel, metal tools or proven beasts of burden. And among the small villages dotting the Yucatán's rolling hills, one bona fide city stands out: Mérida, one of the first cities to be built by the Spanish. Ornate mansions, fine old buildings and lively plazas combine to give this vibrant capital a distinctly European feel—despite the exotic flowers and sultry heat.

Quintana Roo, which occupies the eastern part of the peninsula, was almost wholly isolated from the rest of the country until the completion of two roads (Mex. 180 and Mex. 186). Today, however, the great majority of Quintana Roo's visitors fly in, and their destination of choice is Cancún, which as recently as the late 1960s was a sleepy, unknown fishing village. No more—hordes of spring breakers, winter-weary *gringos* and beach lovers have made this sun-splashed resort one of the world's top tourist destinations.

In stark contrast to Cancun's glittery newness is the primeval wilderness of the Sian Ka'an Biosphere Reserve, designated a World Heritage Site by UNESCO in 1987. This 1.3 million-acre ecological preserve, located on the Yucatán Peninsula's eastern coast, boasts a rich spectrum of habitats: tropical forests, lagoons, mangrove marshes and an offshore barrier reef, all protected from encroachment or commercial development.

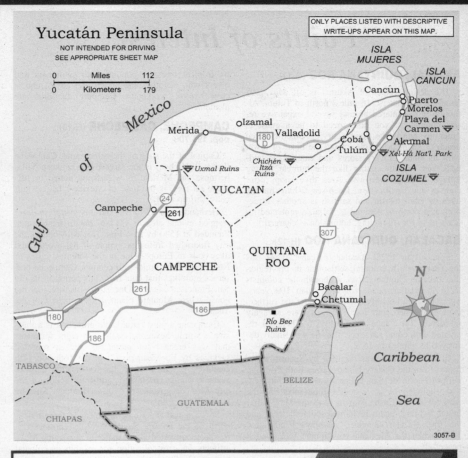

Yucatán Peninsula

NOT INTENDED FOR DRIVING
SEE APPROPRIATE SHEET MAP

ONLY PLACES LISTED WITH DESCRIPTIVE
WRITE-UPS APPEAR ON THIS MAP.

3057-B

Points of Interest

AKUMAL, QUINTANA ROO (G-12)

The diving center of Akumal is off Mex. 307 about 26 kilometers (16 miles) north of Tulum. Although it is centered around several expensive resort complexes, you don't need to be a guest in order to enjoy the long, curving, shell-covered beach or swim in the clear bay. The heart of town, with its small grocery stores and eateries, is laidback and friendly, rather like the humble fishing village Akumal once was. Area dive shops offer courses and certification. Deep-sea fishing for the likes of giant marlin and sailfish is another attraction. Just north of Akumal is Yalkú, a protected lagoon ideal for snorkeling; admission is charged.

BACALAR, QUINTANA ROO (H-12)

Founded in 1528, Bacalar (ba-cah-LAHR) was the first Spanish colonial settlement in the region that became Quintana Roo. Although the colonists lived in relative peace for more than 100 years, Spanish-Maya hostility simmered under the surface, exploding when four local farmers were savagely murdered. The Maya community in Chetumal retaliated with equal savagery; the site was finally destroyed by pirates in 1652.

In 1726, Bacalar was resettled by Spanish expatriates from the Canary Islands. They built Fort San Felipe (Fuerte de San Felipe), a massive fortification encircled by a crocodile-filled moat. At the outbreak of the Castes War in 1848 the Maya, after brutal fighting, again reclaimed the settlement and the fort. Bacalar remained in Maya hands until 1901, when the Mexican government reclaimed it peacefully.

Fort San Felipe, now surrounded by landscaped gardens rather than hungry reptiles, is a museum of history and archeology containing exhibits of weapons and regional artifacts. The fort's watchtower overlooks the fishing and boating activities on Bacalar Lagoon.

Bacalar Lagoon (Laguna de Bacalar) is east of town; follow the signs from Mex. 307. This 35-mile-long body of water is a spectacular natural wonder in the midst of the otherwise unremarkable jungle scrub of southern Quintana Roo. Salt and fresh water mix in the lagoon, accentuating beautiful hues from deep turquoise to almost black (it is also known as the "Lake of the Seven Colors"). The clear water is ideal for swimming, boating, snorkeling and scuba diving. Around the southern shore are some gracious, turn-of-the-20th-century lakefront homes.

About 5 kilometers (3 miles) south of town, almost at the edge of the lagoon, is Cenote Azul, a freshwater sinkhole said to be the world's largest. Some 600 feet across and more than 250 feet deep, its blue water is unusually clear. The cenote, shaded by tropical trees, is popular with swimmers and divers who negotiate the underwater caves, and is crowded on weekends. Camping facilities are available.

CAMPECHE, CAMPECHE (G-10)
pop. 195,700

Capital of the state of the same name, Campeche (kahm-PEH-cheh) is the largest city between Villahermosa and Mérida. Its waterfront, dotted by offshore oil rigs, is the base of Mexico's largest gulf coast shrimp fleet.

Hernández de Córdova and his *conquistadores* stopped in this area in 1517 to obtain fresh water. Founded in 1540 by Don Francisco de Montejo, the city flourished from the export of hardwoods and dyewoods to Europe. One of the foremost cities of New Spain in the mid-16th century, Campeche preserves buildings that date from this period in its old San Francisco section. One such structure was the house where Montejo planned his conquest of the Yucatán.

Campeche's most remarkable attraction is a massive 1.5-mile hexagonal wall with eight fortresses that was erected for protection against repeated sackings by European pirates in the 16th and 17th centuries. Begun in 1686, the fortification took 18 years to build. The historic fortified section of the city was designated a World Heritage Site by UNESCO in 1999.

Fort Soledad (Fuerte de la Soledad), three blocks north of the ancient Puerta del Mar entranceway, has been converted into a museum displaying Maya artifacts, an arms collection and exhibits on colonial history. On the outskirts of the city is one of the most impressive of all the fortresses, Fort San Miguel (Fuerte de San Miguel). Its moat supposedly contained crocodiles.

Fort San Carlos (Fuerte de San Carlos), a government-sponsored handicrafts market today, has intriguing secret underground passageways. Linked to many houses in the city, the tunnels provided a hiding place for women and children when pirate ships came to plunder. Most passageways are sealed off with bricks, but guides offer tours into the fort's basement for a small fee. The fort's roof, still equipped with ancient cannon, offers a spectacular view of the gulf.

Among the words coined in Campeche is *campechano*, used to describe a pleasant, easygoing person. Local tradition has it that the word "cocktail" originated here centuries ago because English pirates were served drinks adorned by palm fronds resembling cocks' tails. Happily, the root of Campeche's name, taken from the Maya words *kim* and *pech*, meaning "serpent" and "tick," has no modern application.

Although the city is studded with ancient walls and fortresses, it also contains such buildings as the Government Palace and the Legislative Palace, respectively referred to as "the jukebox" and "the flying saucer" for their modern architecture, which blends surprisingly well with the native buildings. Local markets sell such handicrafts as Panama hats and articles made of alligator skin. The regional cuisine includes such exotic dishes as shark stew.

Other points of interest include the 1540 Franciscan Cathedral, the oldest convent church in the Yucatán Peninsula; the 1546 Convent of San Francisco, the site of one of the first masses in Campeche; the Temple of San Francisquito, which now houses the Campeche Cultural Institute (Instituto Cultural Campechano); and the House of the King's Lieutenant (Casa del Teniente del Rey), which contains colonial furnishings. Alameda Park's Bridge of Dogs (El Puente de Los Perros), a colonial bridge guarded by carved stone dogs, honors the Dominican missionaries called the "Dogs of God" for their zealous hounding of converts.

Campeche State Tourism Office: downtown at Plaza Moch-Couoh, on Avenida Ruiz Cortines; phone (981) 816-6829.

EDZNA RUINS are about 53 km (33 mi.) southeast of Campeche; take Av. Central out of the city, following signs for the airport and Edzná. This Maya city was first inhabited about 600 B.C. and abandoned by the 15th century; as is true of other archeological sites in Mexico, the reasons for its decline remain a mystery.

The closest major ruins to Campeche may not be worth the trip if you've seen Chichén Itzá or Uxmal, but there is one standout building: the 98-foot-tall Temple of Five Stories (Templo de Cinco Cuerpos), a five-level structure with a central staircase and an impressive roofcomb. South of this temple is the Temple of Masks, with carvings of heads that have jaguar-like faces.

Site open daily 8-5. Admission around $4 (U.S.); the fee to use a video camera also is $4.

Cancún

Cancún's metamorphosis from drowsy fishing village to vacation paradise is a true Cinderella story. At the beginning of the 1970s, Mexico's most popular tourist destination didn't even show up on maps. Cancún was nothing but a handful of fishermen eking out a living in the northeastern corner of the Yucatán Peninsula, an area once home to the ancient Maya and later a refuge for pirates. Mexico's Caribbean coastline appealed to serious scuba divers and committed beach bums, but a lack of all but the most basic amenities—not to mention the marshy terrain and resident mosquitoes—discouraged widespread travel. Those in search of inviting beaches that actually had hotels at which to stay headed for Acapulco or Puerto Vallarta.

All that changed once the Mexican government, eager to develop the country's tourism potential, commissioned a study to determine a prime location for a new resort. A computer picked the little spit of land lying just off the Yucatán coast, and the fledgling playground was placed in the eager hands of developers.

A building boom began in the mid-1980s, and today Cancún has some 500,000 residents and receives some 3 million visitors annually. They come for year-round warm weather; for beaches of fine-grained sand and beautiful turquoise-hued water; for great snorkeling and scuba diving; for good restaurants, lively nightlife and a dose of Mexican atmosphere; and last but not least, to soak up sun on the beach. Cancún also is a spring break hotspot, a major convention city and a popular getaway for honeymooners.

There are actually two Cancúns. Ciudad Cancún (Cancún City), the commercial and business center located on the mainland, is very much like any other Mexican town. Resort facilities are concentrated on Isla Cancún (Cancún Island), known as the Zona Hotelera (Hotel Zone). This elbow-shaped sandbar is nearly 15 miles long but just a quarter-mile wide, separated from the mainland by narrow causeways at either end (blink and you'll miss them). In between are the calm waters of Laguna Nichupté (Nichupté Lagoon). The island's seaward side fronts Mujeres Bay from Ciudad Cancún east to Punta Cancún (Cancún Point). The point is the crook of the elbow; south of it the shoreline faces the open Caribbean.

All of the big hotels, upscale shopping areas and flashy nightspots are within the Hotel Zone. The hotels are Cancún's real "sights"—architecturally distinctive, lushly landscaped and opulently appointed, they are framed by the translucent Caribbean surf and etched under sunlight bright enough to make sunglasses a full-time accessory.

Often linked with Cancún in the minds of travelers, Cozumel *(see separate listing within this region)* is a separate destination with its own agenda. Mexico's largest populated island, it lies about 12 miles offshore opposite the mainland town of Playa del Carmen and has a deserved reputation among divers for water of unsurpassed clarity, inhabited by an amazing variety of marine life.

Isla Mujeres *(see separate listing within this region)*, a tiny island 4 miles off the Yucatán Peninsula's easternmost tip, is just north of Cancún opposite mainland Puerto Juárez. Recent growth is related directly to tourism, although Isla Mujeres is less developed and even more casual than Cozumel. It's a popular day trip from Cancún via passenger ferry.

Cancún also makes a convenient base for exploring other parts of the Yucatán. The ruins of Chichén Itzá *(see separate listing within this region)*, the remains of a once-great Maya city and the peninsula's best-known archeological site, are less than three hours away by car. About two hours south of Cancún are the ruins of Tulum *(see separate listing within this region)*, dramatically situated overlooking the Caribbean. The 100-mile stretch of coastline from Cancún south to Tulum, known as the "Riviera Maya," is a developing region of vacation resorts and such major tourist draws as Xcaret and Xel-Há, two theme park-style attractions with ecological overtones.

This is not colonial Mexico, steeped in time and tradition. Archeological ruins aside, it has a pervading sense of newness. Fast food and stateside franchises proliferate, and themed shopping complexes replace historical and cultural shadings. But there also is a comforting familiarity. English is commonplace—although Spanish might be spoken first. Dollars are routinely accepted. The widespread Americanization makes Cancún a good choice for travelers hesitant about vacationing in a foreign country, or for those who desire a higher level of amenities or fewer hassles than are routinely encountered in the country's less-developed areas.

The state of Quintana Roo faces a familiar dilemma: the specter of resort development taking over the coastline. Already on the drawing board is a plan to develop the now-isolated southern stretch between Punta Herrero and Xcalak (near the Belize border) for ecologically oriented tourism. As currently envisioned, the "Costa Maya" will feature small resorts of no more than 50 units spread out along the shore. Nature remains protected, however, in such places as the 1.5-million acre Sian Ka'an Biosphere Reserve.

Despite the environmental concern, Cancún does boast an unbeatable combination—sun, sea and sand. It offers plenty of options for visitors to enjoy these natural attributes, from economical tour packages to exclusive luxury hotels. Great care has been taken to craft this resort into a tourist's version of paradise, and planeloads of satisfied vacationers would say that the result is a job well done.

(continued on page 85)

© Bill Bachman / Alamy Images

© Demetrio Carrasco / Alamy Images

The Informed Traveler

City Population: 436,000 (estimated).

Location: Just off the northeastern tip of the Yucatán Peninsula in Quintana Roo.

Highlights: Beaches boasting powdery sand and clear, blue-green water; excellent snorkeling and scuba diving off Cozumel and Isla Mujeres and along the Caribbean coast; some of Mexico's most lavish hotels; abundant shopping and dining opportunities; easy accessibility to Chichén Itzá, Tulum and other Yucatán archeological sites.

WHOM TO CALL

Area Code: 998.

In Case of Emergency: To lodge a complaint with the Consumer Protection Agency (Procuraduría del Consumidor), phone (998) 884-2634. The office is at Av. Cobá #9 (2nd floor) in downtown Ciudad Cancún and is open Mon.-Fri. 9-3. If you lose your tourist card, contact the Immigration Office, avenidas J.C. Nader and Uxmal in Ciudad Cancún. Open Mon.-Fri. 9-noon; phone (998) 884-1404.

Standards of medical training, patient care and business practices vary widely in Cancún. Most of the major hotels have their own in-house or on-call doctor. If in doubt, obtain a list of physicians from the U.S. Consular Agency, located at Plaza Caracol Two (third level, #320-323), Boulevard Kukulcán Km 8.5; phone (998) 883-0272. Local clinics do not accept U.S. health insurance, often charge fees well above U.S. rates, and have been known to charge for services not rendered.

WHERE TO LOOK

Media

The *Miami Herald* and *USA Today* are available in the bigger hotels. Most hotels have a cable TV system that offers the ABC, CBS, NBC and Fox networks via a U.S. affiliate, such staples as CNN and ESPN, and HBO or another movie channel, in addition to Spanish-language channels.

Visitor Information

Quintana Roo State Tourism Office: in Ciudad Cancún at Av. Tulum #26 (between avenidas Cobá and Uxmal next to Banco Inverlat); phone (998) 884-8073.

Cancún Tips is a quarterly magazine with easy-to-read maps and information about restaurants, shopping, entertainment, sightseeing and local services. The *Mapa Pocket Guide*, published twice yearly, contains maps and useful phone numbers. Pick up these and other free tourist-oriented publications at the airport when you arrive.

Staff members of *Cancún Tips* magazine operate information booths at the airport and in the Plaza Caracol shopping center in the Hotel Zone.

WHAT TO KNOW

Weather

Cancún is warm year-round, and although constant sea breezes temper the summer heat, you will still feel it. Several of the big hotels have open-air public areas that can be uncomfortable (even with breezes) because of the high humidity.

The sun is intense, especially when it reflects off the water; use an appropriate sunblock for any long-term exposure. The beaches are warm enough for swimming all year. Rain can fall in any month, although May through October is the likeliest time. The greatest chance for hurricanes or other unsettled weather is in September and October.

Most visitors wear shorts and T-shirts; casual but stylish resort wear is appropriate at the nicer restaurants or for an evening out. Pack a sweater for the occasional cool winter day or air-conditioned summer interior.

Currency Exchange

Casas de cambio (currency exchange offices) and banks are along Avenida Tulum in downtown Ciudad Cancún. Exchange offices also are located in the Hotel Zone shopping areas around Cancún Point. Most banks are open Mon.-Fri. 9-1:30; currency exchange normally is confined to the morning hours.

Since the rates offered by exchange offices, banks and hotels don't differ that much and fluctuate daily, exchanging dollars boils down to a matter of convenience. Convert only what you'll need for bus and taxi fares, souvenir purchases and so forth.

Approaches

By Air

Cancún International Airport is on the mainland off Mex. 307, about 16 kilometers (10 miles) southwest of downtown Ciudad Cancún and about 10 kilometers (6 miles) from the southern end of Cancún Island. It receives regular flights from major cities in the United States and Mexico; many are daily. Aeroméxico, (998) 886-0003; American, (800) 904-6000 (toll-free long distance within Mexico); Continental, (800) 900-5000 (toll-free long distance within Mexico); and Mexicana, (800) 509-8960 (toll-free long distance within Mexico), offer direct flights from U.S. cities. **Note:** There are no direct flights from Canada to Cancún; most major U.S. airlines meet connecting flights from Canada in Dallas, Houston or New York. To confirm schedules, contact the appropriate airline or a travel agency. For additional information about airlines see "Arriving by Air," page 551.

Aerocaribe and Aerocozumel (both affiliated with Mexicana) are regional airlines with service to Cancún from various Mexican cities. They fly to nearby Yucatán destinations, including Chichén Itzá, Cozumel, Mérida and Playa del Carmen, as well as to Oaxaca. For information phone (800) 531-7921 (in the United States).

The airport is not very large but can be quite crowded, especially during the winter high season. Renting a luggage cart costs about $1 (U.S.). Airport staff hand out free maps and brochures, so you can pick these up if you need the information. Don't exchange dollars for pesos at the currency exchange office; you could get a better rate at your hotel. It's a good idea to exchange no more than what you'll need for a couple of days, as the rate fluctuates daily. The office is handy for changing Mexican currency back into dollars when you leave, although you'll be shortchanged by the rate.

All arriving passengers pass through Mexican customs; make sure your declaration form is properly filled out. After picking up your luggage, you must press the button on a machine that resembles a stoplight. If the light flashes green you may proceed; if it flashes red your luggage will be routinely searched.

Shuttle service via passenger van (colectivo) is available from the airport to the Hotel Zone for around $9.50 (U.S.). These vehicles usually take a maximum of 10 passengers at a fixed rate and are less costly than a private taxi. Expect to pay $35-$40 (U.S.) for a taxi to the Hotel Zone. You can purchase a ticket for a colectivo or a special airport taxi at the taxi counter in the terminal. Colectivos do not provide service back to the airport, making a cab ride necessary upon departure. Cabs affiliated with the bigger hotels often charge a fixed rate for service to the airport, which will be less than the trip from the airport.

Confirm your reservation and departure time with your airline at least 24 hours prior to departing Cancún. For international flights, arrive two hours before scheduled departure time to be on the safe side. The airport has a number of souvenir shops if you want to make last-minute purchases; prices are a bit steep, but U.S. dollars are accepted. Prices for merchandise sold at the duty-free store—mostly liquor, cigars and perfume—aren't that much of a bargain.

By Car

Mexico's easternmost city is located at the Yucatán Peninsula's northeastern tip. From the west, Mex. 180 via Veracruz, Villahermosa, Campeche and Mérida is the preferred route; it ends at Punta Sam, north of Cancún. From Villahermosa, an alternate route is Mex. 186 east to Escárcega, Camp., and then north on Mex. 281 to Champotón. It carries heavy truck traffic and has very few gas stations or mechanical services. This route should only be driven during daylight hours.

Mex. 180 is two lanes between Mérida and the small town of Hoctún. Four-lane toll highway Mex. 180-D begins at Hoctún and roughly parallels Mex. 180 for a distance of about 240 kilometers (144 miles). All of Mex. 180-D is in very good condition, lightly traveled and quicker than Mex. 180, which passes through towns—but also is isolated if you happen to break down.

Kilometer markers are along the right side of the road, and there are regular intervals, indicated by signs, to make a U-turn (retorno). Signage is good (both speed limit and mileage signs and the international blue highway signs). Toll plazas are located at the Chichén Itzá exit (Pisté) and at the Yucatán/Quintana Roo state line (Xcan), which also is a customs checkpoint. For cars, motorcycles, vans and pickup campers, tolls for the route are 245 pesos (around $26 U.S.). There are only a few gas stations along the length of the route, so make sure your tank is always at least half full.

Mex. 180-D ends about 16 kilometers (10 miles) west of the airport; follow the sign that says "Cancún/Puerto Juárez" to stay on the mainland, or the sign "Tulum/Aeropuerto" to get to the Hotel Zone.

An access route to Cancún from the south is Mex. 307, which begins about 19 kilometers (12 miles) west of Chetumal off Mex. 186 in southern Quintana Roo and proceeds north through Bacalar and Tulum. The section of Mex. 307 from Tulum north to Cancún closely parallels the Caribbean coast and offers access to a growing number of beach resorts.

A highway branching northwest at Tulum offers access to the Cobá archeological zone and joins Mex. 180 at the town of Xcan—a distance of about 85 kilometers (53 miles). It saves time and mileage if you want a more direct route from Tulum to Mérida.

By Bus

The bus terminal is in downtown Ciudad Cancún at the intersection of avenidas Tulum and Uxmal, in front of the Plaza Caribe Hotel. The ADO and

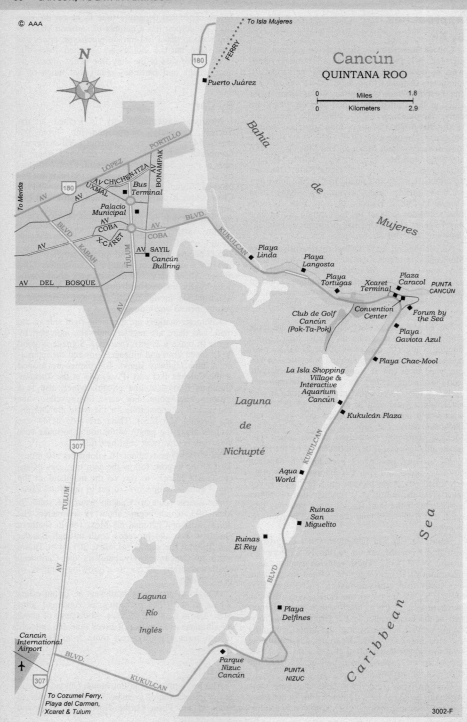

© AAA

To Isla Mujeres

FERRY

180

Puerto Juárez

Cancún
QUINTANA ROO

| 0 | Miles | 1.8 |
| 0 | Kilometers | 2.9 |

Bahía

de

Mujeres

LOPEZ

PORTILLO

AV BONAMPAK

AV CHICHEN-ITZA

To Merida

180

UXMAL

AV

AV

Bus
Terminal

Palacio
Municipal

AV
COBA

X-CARET

AV

BLVD

KABAH

TÚLUM

AV

BLVD

AV. COBA

AV. COBA

KUKULCAN

AV SAYIL

Cancún
Bullring

AV DEL BOSQUE

Playa
Linda

Playa
Langosta

Playa
Tortugas

Xcaret
Terminal

Plaza
Caracol

PUNTA
CANCÚN

Club de Golf
Cancún
(Pok-Ta-Pok)

Convention
Center

Forum by
the Sea

Playa
Gaviota Azul

Playa Chac-Mool

La Isla Shopping
Village &
Interactive
Aquarium
Cancún

Kukulcán Plaza

Laguna

de

Nichupté

KUKULCAN

Aqua
World

Ruinas
San
Miguelito

Ruinas
El Rey

BLVD

Laguna

Río

Inglés

Playa
Delfines

Cancún
International
Airport

307

AV

TULUM

307

BLVD.

KUKULCAN

Parque
Nizuc
Cancún

PUNTA
NIZUC

Caribbean

Sea

To Cozumel Ferry,
Playa del Carmen,
Xcaret & Tulum

3002-F

Linea UNO lines offer first-class service to and from various points on the Yucatán Peninsula, including Chetumal, Chichén Itzá, Mérida, Playa del Carmen, Tulum and Valladolid. Frequent first-class service is available from Mérida, with stops en route at Chichén Itzá and Valladolid. For additional information about buses *see "Bus Service," page 68*.

By Cruise Ship

Cancún has no docking facilities for cruise ships. Only an occasional ship stops offshore from Playa Tortugas, at Km 7 on Boulevard Kukulcán; passengers are ferried to land. If you're on a ship that docks at Cozumel and want to spend some time in Cancún, you'll be tendered from Cozumel to Playa del Carmen, about a 45-minute drive south of Cancún (or check with your ship's shore excursion desk to see if they offer a Cancún package). Depending on the length of shore leave, you could squeeze in a shopping trip or a visit to one of the beaches. **Note:** If you arrange a shore excursion through the ship it will wait for you; if you arrange it yourself the ship won't wait. Keep timing in mind.

Getting Around

City Layout

The main streets in downtown Ciudad Cancún (often called *El Centro*) are east-west Avenida López Portillo, the in-town section of Mex. 180, which extends from the western city limits northeast to Puerto Juárez and Punta Sam; and north-south Avenida Tulum, the in-town section of Mex. 307, which runs south toward the airport and on down the coast. Many souvenir shops and restaurants are along or near Avenida Tulum and Avenida Cobá which becomes Boulevard Kukulcán as it enters the Hotel Zone. Most souvenir shops, stores and restaurants are along or near Tulum and Cobá.

Ciudad Cancún is divided into districts called *super manzanas*, each containing several blocks unified by a central square or park. Driving can be daunting even if you know where you're going, however. There are numerous one-way streets and traffic circles *(glorietas)*, as well as speed bumps, potholed streets, crowds of pedestrians and inadequate traffic signals. If you're going into El Centro for dinner or shopping, take a bus or taxi.

Boulevard Kukulcán (also referred to as Paseo Kukulcán but usually just called "Kukulcán") runs the length of Cancún Island and is the only main traffic artery on this narrow island. It actually begins at Avenida Bonampak, on the eastern edge of Ciudad Cancún. Past Punta Nizuc (Nizuc Point), the island's southern tip, Kukulcán runs into southbound Mex. 307 at the overpass leading to the airport. **Note:** The speed limit along most of Kukulcán is 40 km/h (25 mph) and is strictly enforced; the limit increases to 60 km/h (37 mph) at the southern end of the island.

The approach to the Hotel Zone from the airport is not impressive—a two-lane road lined with tacky billboards. Once Cancún Island is reached, however, Kukulcán becomes a landscaped, four-lane divided highway with a couple of tantalizing glimpses of the Caribbean. Most of the Caribbean side is lined with big hotels set back from the road, and views of the water are few. Kukulcán's four lanes divide briefly to encompass Cancún Point, the elbow of the island's "seven" configuration. Where u-turns are permitted, signs in the median say *retorno*.

Numbered addresses are rarely given for places in the Hotel Zone; instead, median kilometer markers (from Km 1 on the mainland south to Km 25 beyond Nizuc Point) indicate locations. Directions also are given in reference to well-known landmarks or hotels. Because there is only one road, it's almost impossible to get lost.

Rental Cars

It's not really necessary to rent a car if you're limiting your vacation to Cancún and vicinity; bus and taxi service is frequent. But you'll need one if you plan a day or overnight trip down the coast toward Tulum or inland to the ruins of Chichén Itzá or Cobá and don't want to be part of an organized tour. The quality of most regional roads is good. Do not underestimate the amount of time it will take to arrive at your destination, however, and in general avoid driving after dark.

Rates are expensive if you rent on the spot; make reservations in advance through a U.S. 800 number to get the best deal. Arranging for pickup and drop-off at the airport will eliminate taxi fares. Make certain you fully understand the terms of any rental contract. If the car only has half a tank of gas when you pick it up, you can return it with half a tank; double check before you drive off.

Inspect the vehicle carefully inside and out, and check for the required in-car fire extinguisher. Inventory thoroughly for nicks and dents as well. Keep in mind that license plates on rental vehicles say "renta," marking you as a visitor. It is becoming more common for major rental car agencies to provide (for an added charge) a driver; consider this option if you don't feel entirely comfortable driving in unfamiliar surroundings. **Note:** In the event of damages caused by a hurricane, all insurance claims are void.

Hertz is one of several rental car agencies available, with offices at the airport, in downtown Ciudad Cancún and on Boulevard Kukulcán in the vicinity of Cancún Point. AAA/CAA members receive discounts through Hertz for vehicles booked in the United States or Canada; phone (800) 654-3080.

Buses

"Ruta 1" and *"Ruta 2"* buses (marked *"Hoteles"* or *"Zona Hotelera"* on the windshield) run regularly from the mainland to the southern end of the Hotel Zone and back daily 6 a.m.-10 p.m. The fare is inexpensive—6 pesos (about 60 cents U.S.).

For Your Information

Guides/Tours

The most popular day excursions from Cancún are to Xcaret, Xel-Há and Tulum, all south along the Caribbean coast. Guided tours to Chichén Itzá, Cobá and Uxmal also are available. There are numerous in-town tour operators, but many hotels have a travel agency on site or a concierge who can help with tour arrangements.

Gray Line Cancún, Km 3.5 on Boulevard Kukulcán (in Plaza Nautilus), offers motorcoach tours to various regional points of interest; including Chichén Itzá, Cozumel, Isla Mujeres, Tulum, Xcaret and Xel-Há; phone (998) 849-4545. Bus tours to Xcaret leave daily at 9, 10 and 11:30 a.m. from the Xcaret bus terminal in the Hotel Zone (across from Plaza Caracol), returning at either 4:30 or 9:30 p.m.; phone (998) 881-2400.

Staying Safe

Cancún is a destination of choice for college students on spring break, which begins in mid-February and lasts for about two months. Excessive alcohol consumption associated with partying has become a problem, and there has been an increase in crime—both petty and violent—as well as reported rapes. The legal drinking age in Mexico is 18, but it is not uniformly enforced. There also has been an increase in the number of reported incidents of police harassment and extortion.

Otherwise, crime directed at tourists is not prevalent, but do use common sense. Always put jewelry and other valuables in the hotel safe, or don't bring them at all. Be vigilant whenever using public transportation, as pickpocketing and purse snatching have become more common. Car break-ins can occur in the Hotel Zone's shopping areas; don't invite one by leaving valuables in plain view. Always take a taxi after dark, whether in Ciudad Cancún or the Hotel Zone.

The *"Ruta 8"* bus goes to Puerto Juárez and Punta Sam for the ferries to Isla Mujeres. You'll need Mexican currency; exact change isn't necessary. There are frequent designated stops throughout the Hotel Zone, and drivers also can be flagged from hotel driveway entrances along Boulevard Kukulcán. Using the bus is much cheaper than taking a cab, especially if you're staying at the southern end of the Hotel Zone. Buses are likely to be crowded mornings and evenings, when mainland locals use them to get to and from work.

The Linea Verde bus line offers round-trip excursions *(paquetes turísticos)* to such popular destinations as Chichén Itzá, Cozumel and Xcaret. Departures are from the main bus terminal in downtown Ciudad Cancún.

Taxis

Taxis within the Hotel Zone are very expensive; it can cost $5 (U.S.) just to ride from one hotel to the next. They also are not metered; fares are based on a zone system. Arranging for a cab directly at your hotel is convenient, but these cabs also tend to have the highest rates. Some hotels list fares to various destinations at the front entrance; if not, ask the doorman. Always confirm the rate with the driver before setting out. Better hotels will arrange "payouts," putting cab fares on the bill so they show up on your credit card receipt as a recorded expense.

Green city taxis can be hailed on the street in Ciudad Cancún. The driver should be able to provide a rate list if you ask, although it is likely to be in Spanish. If you're going from the Hotel Zone to Ciudad Cancún, Puerto Juárez or Punta Sam, take the Kukulcán bus to the mainland, then a taxi to your destination, since the city taxis have a cheaper rate structure than the Hotel Zone taxis.

Ferries

Enclosed, air-conditioned passenger ferries run between Puerto Juárez, about 3 kilometers (2 miles) north of Cancún, and Isla Mujeres. There are approximate hourly departures in each direction daily beginning around 6 a.m. until 6 p.m. The trip takes about 25 minutes; one-way fare is 40 pesos (about $4 U.S.). Schedules are posted at both docks but are subject to changes or delays; double-check the final departure time when you arrive at Isla Mujeres. Local *"Ruta 8"* buses make the short trip along Avenida Tulum in Ciudad Cancún to the Puerto Juárez public dock; you can also get there by taxi.

A passenger/car ferry operates daily, weather permitting, between Punta Sam, about 5 kilometers (3 miles) north of Puerto Juárez, and Isla Mujeres. The trip takes about an hour. The first of several departures is around 8 a.m.; the last, around 8:15 p.m. Double-check departure times at the public ferry dock. There are separate fees for vehicles and passengers. For additional information about ferry schedules, *see "Sightseeing."*

Parking

There are very few municipal parking lots in Ciudad Cancún or the Hotel Zone. Park on city streets at your own discretion. If you've rented a car or are driving your own vehicle, keep it in the hotel lot—most of them are guarded—and use buses or cabs for local excursions.

What To See

AQUA WORLD is at Km 15.2 on the lagoon side of Boulevard Kukulcán (opposite the Meliá Cancún Hotel). In addition to organizing deep-sea fishing and diving expeditions, Aqua World rents equipment for windsurfing, jet skiing and wave running. The Jungle Tour boat trip navigates Nichupté Lagoon's mangrove stands en route to a Caribbean reef for snorkeling. The *Sub See Explorer,* an air-conditioned, glass-bottomed boat, cruises from Nichupté Lagoon past Caribbean coral reefs to man-made Paradise Island for lunch and snorkeling. The Skyrider offers both ocean and lagoon-side parasail "flights" high above Cancún Island.

Scuba diving instruction is available. Arrange cruise excursions or fishing trips in advance. Aqua World sales kiosks are located at most major hotels. Daily 6:30 a.m.-9:30 p.m. Fees for activities, cruises and equipment rentals vary. AX, MC, VI. Phone (998) 848-8327.

CANCUN CONVENTION CENTER is at Km 8 on Boulevard Kukulcán near Cancún Point. It was rebuilt after being damaged in 1988 by Hurricane Gilbert. The complex offers a variety of performing arts events and provides extensive convention, exhibition and office space. The highlight of the four-story building is a huge ballroom overlooking the Caribbean. Phone (998) 991-0400.

Cancún Archeological Museum (Museo Arqueológico de Cancún) is next to the center. It exhibits a collection of pre-Hispanic artifacts gathered from around the state of Quintana Roo. Tues.-Sun. 9-7. Admission around $3.50 (U.S.); free to all Sun. and holidays. Phone (998) 883-0305.

EL REY RUINS (Ruinas El Rey) are on the lagoon side of Boulevard Kukulcán at Km 17; watch for signs. Although much smaller than other Yucatán archeological sites, El Rey is a nice change of pace from the pervasive newness. Temple platforms and a few larger buildings stand amid tropical trees. There is a separate entrance to the ruins, which are surrounded by the golf course at the Hilton Cancún.

Close by, on the Caribbean side of Kukulcán at Km 16.5, is San Miguelito, another Maya site that consists of a small building anchored by stone pillars. El Rey open daily 8-5. Admission around $4 (U.S.); free to all Sun.

INTERACTIVE AQUARIUM CANCUN is on the lagoon side of Blvd. Kukulcán at Km 12.5, in La Isla Shopping Village. Here you can swim with dolphins or feed sharks in a special underwater cage.

Touch exhibits allow visitors to observe sea urchins, starfish and other marine animals up close, and all guests can feed stingrays and young nurse sharks. Trained dolphins perform daily at 6 p.m. Food is available. Daily 9-7. Admission $13 (U.S.); ages 3-10, $9. Dolphin swim $115 per person, shark tank feeding $65 per person; advance reservations are recommended. Parking fee $2. AX, CB, DC, DS, MC, VI. Phone (998) 883-0411.

NICHUPTE LAGOON lies between the Hotel Zone and the mainland. It contains a combination of fresh and salt water. A few small islands are within the lagoon, and peninsulas punctuate the shoreline. Two smaller lagoons are connected to Nichupté by narrow waterways: Laguna Bojórquez, at the northeastern end, and Laguna Río Inglés, at the southwestern end. It is home to many different bird species.

PARQUE NIZUC CANCUN is at the southern end of Blvd. Kukulcán at Km 25, between the airport and the Hotel Zone. This Wet 'n Wild-type water park has three large waterslides, the Lazy River for inner-tube floating and a wave pool complete with sandy beach. You also can interact with dolphins as part of a program run by Atlantida or ride the Shotover jet boat, which spins 360 degrees.

Food is available. Changing facilities are available. Daily 10-5. Admission $29 (U.S.); ages 3-11, $23. Shotover jet boat $29. Call for Atlantida options and prices. Lockers, towels and inner tubes can be rented. AX, MC, VI. Phone (998) 881-3030.

SIAN KA'AN BIOSPHERE RESERVE— *see Tulum p. 119.*

 TULUM RUINS—*see Tulum. p. 118.*

 XCARET—*see Playa del Carmen p. 116.*

 XEL-HA NATIONAL PARK— *see Tulum. p. 119.*

What To Do

Dining

Many Hotel Zone restaurants offer standard Continental dishes of reliable quality and predictable expense. Most hotels go to great lengths to keep their guests on the premises, and some may charge for meals whether they are eaten or not. Dress is usually casual but not unkempt (no shorts or T-shirts). Don't expect much in the way of regional cookery; there are more U.S. fast-food franchises and Mexican chain restaurants than eateries offering local specialties.

Ciudad Cancún is a different story. Avenida Tulum is lined with restaurants, and most have outdoor tables. Look for places where locals congregate if you want authentically prepared Yucatecan dishes like *sopa de lima*—soup with a chicken broth base, vegetables and a tangy dose of fresh lime juice—or *pocchuc*, spicy marinated pork grilled with onions. One of the most popular with tourists is Los Almendros, at avenidas Bonampak and Sayil.

You can grab a reasonably priced Mexican breakfast at one of Cancún's coffee shops—perhaps *bistec de pollo encebollado* (chicken cutlets pounded thin and sauteed with onions) with a side of *chilaques* (tortilla strips, salsa and cheese with a dollop of sour cream) and refried beans. These, plus a basket of *pan dulce* (lightly sweetened breads), toast, a glass of fruit juice and good American-style coffee, can fill you up for most of the day.

Restaurants in the large hotels use purified water for cooking and for washing produce; inquire about this health procedure specifically at places on the mainland. In general, avoid ice cubes in drinks unless you know purified water has been used. For a list of AAA-RATED establishments in Cancún, *see the Lodgings & Restaurants section.*

Shopping

Shopping in Cancún's Hotel Zone usually focuses on two things: pricey specialty items, or T-shirts and beach supplies. As a duty-free zone, however, Cancún offers potential bargains on international merchandise. High-quality tequila and cigars are two of the most popular purchases. As far as garden-variety souvenirs, however, it pays to shop around, as merchants compete vigorously for tourist dollars and prices can be on the steep side. Inspect carefully before buying; quality can vary greatly.

In Ciudad Cancún, a variety of shops and open-air craft markets line Avenida Tulum. Ki-huic, near the intersection with Avenida Cobá, is a block-long flea market with more than 100 vendors offering handicrafts, knickknacks, marble chess sets, men's *guayabera* shirts, *huipil* (ee-PEEL) dresses and Panama hats. Another downtown crafts market is Mercado Plaza, at the corner of avenidas Tulum and Uxmal. Bargaining is expected at the markets; never offer to pay the initial asking price.

If you feel the need to shop for basics, branches of three familiar stateside retailers also are in Ciudad Cancún: Costco (Price Club), at the corner of avenidas Kabah and Yaxchilán; Sam's Club, at the corner of avenidas Xcaret and Yaxchilán; and Wal-Mart, at the corner of avenidas Kukulcán and Mayapán.

The Hotel Zone has both enclosed, air-conditioned malls and open-air complexes. Elegant Plaza Caracol, one of the largest malls, is at Km 8.5 across from the Cancún Convention Center. Cool marble walls and floors are the setting for some 200 shops and boutiques offering jewelry, designer clothing, resort wear, silver and decorative art. You'll also find pharmacies, art galleries, cafes and restaurants here. At Km 13 is Kukulcán Plaza, which caters to tourists with more than 250 stores and boutiques offering gifts, handicrafts, perfume, leather goods, jewelry and silver. It also contains a bank, currency exchange offices, drugstores, and fax and Internet service.

Forum-by-the-Sea, Km 9.5 next to the Hotel Krystal Cancún, is a bright, shiny shopping/entertainment complex with three levels of specialty boutiques like Tommy Hilfiger as well as a variety of restaurants and nightspots, including the Cancún branch of the Hard Rock Café. The shops, restaurants and watering holes at La Isla Shopping Village, Km 12.5 on Kukulcán (lagoon side), are linked by crisscrossing bridges and walkways running over small canals. Chili's, Johnny Rockets and McDonald's are some of the familiar stateside eateries here. There also are movie theaters, an aquarium and other family-friendly features. It's upscale, expensive and a fun place to spend a few hours.

Flamingo Plaza, Km 11.5 on Kukulcán (lagoon side), is a small, attractive shopping center with several duty-free stores and boutiques, as well as a currency exchange office and some fast-food outlets. Maya Fair Plaza, Km 8.5 on Kukulcán, is one of the Hotel Zone's oldest shopping centers. It has an open-air courtyard with restaurants, bars and shops that specialize in silver, leather and gifts.

If you enjoy haggling (in English) with persistent craft vendors, browse the stalls at the Mercado de Artesanías Coral Negro (Flea Market), a white stucco building on Kukulcán (lagoon side) just south of the convention center. The selection is large, and it's open daily.

Most of the mall stores are open daily 10-8 or 10 p.m. Outside the Hotel Zone many stores observe the traditional *siesta* and close for a few hours in the afternoon (usually 2-5); most are closed on Sunday. The sales tax is 10 percent, which may be waived at some shops if you pay in cash.

Beaches

Cancún's spectacular beaches are its main claim to fame, edged with golden-colored, tiny-grained sand. Composed of innumerable microscopic plankton fossils, it remains cool to the feet despite the strong sun. A gorgeous counterpoint is provided by the ever-shifting colors of the Caribbean, which range from opalescent green to vivid turquoise. The water is warm enough for swimming all year.

The beaches along the northern side of the island fronting Bahía Mujeres (Mujeres Bay) are narrow, with calm, shallow water. The Caribbean beaches are wider and more dramatic, with occasional crashing breakers and dangerous undertows.

The best beaches are in front of the big hotels. All beaches in Mexico, however, are federally owned property and therefore public, even stretches that may seem like they are on hotel property. Keep in mind that you cannot use hotel facilities unless you are a guest, and that beaches do not have shower facilities (although Playa Tortugas and Playa Chac-Mool have changing areas). Note the flags posted to indicate surf conditions. White, green or blue flags indicate safe conditions for swimming; yellow, caution; and red or black, dangerous.

The "inner" coast of Cancún Island borders saltwater Nichupté Lagoon. Nichupté, lined in some places with stands of mangrove, doesn't have the

Caribbean's beauty, but the calm water is ideal for scuba diving and water skiing.

The following designated public beaches are described in the order they appear along Cancún Island, beginning at the top of the island's "seven" configuration after leaving the mainland. *See map page 86.*

PLAYA LINDA is just before the bridge over Canal Nichupté, at Km 4. Boat tours to Isla Mujeres embark from the Playa Linda pier, and there are several snack and dive equipment shops in the vicinity.

PLAYA LANGOSTA is next to the Casa Maya Hotel at Km 5. The beach is close to several yacht clubs, water sports facilities and restaurants. Tour boats leave from the dock here.

PLAYA TORTUGAS is near the Intercontinental Presidente Cancún at Km 6. Frequented by locals, the beach faces the calm waters of Mujeres Bay.

PLAYA CARACOL is close to the Fiesta Americana Grand Coral Beach and the Xcaret bus terminal. Farther east is Cancún Point, the crook of the Cancún elbow. The very tip of the point, behind the Camino Real hotel, is where Mujeres Bay meets the open Caribbean. Isla Mujeres is visible in the distance. Waves crash against the rocks and send up plumes of spray on the Caribbean side, while just around the point the water is calm, shallow and translucent.

Reaching the point is an easy walk from the Camino Real's beachfront through shallow water and scattered rocks (wear nonslip shoes). Stand on the point and face west for a lovely view that takes in the peach exterior of the Fiesta Americana hotel, vividly colored water and coconut palms rustling in the breeze.

PLAYA CHAC-MOOL is at Km 9.5. Another popular stretch not associated with one of the big hotels, the beach is washed by the Caribbean surf and has sand that is incredibly powdery.

PLAYA DELFINES is at Km 18 at the southern end of the Hotel Zone. Delfines is far from the action, offering serenity and spectacular views.

Sightseeing

People come to Cancún not to sightsee but to sun, swim, eat, party and relax. There are options, however, particularly if you consider the surrounding area. One diversion is exploring the length of the Hotel Zone. Walk through the public and pool areas at a few of the big resorts. Buses marked "Hoteles" stop frequently along Boulevard Kukulcán, so use them to get from one place to another (keep in mind that you must pay bus fare each time you reboard).

Daytime cruises ply Nichupté Lagoon and the waters around Cancún Island, Cozumel and Isla Mujeres. Prices range from around $40-$60 (U.S.) per person. Boat operators and itineraries change, so check with your hotel or a local travel agency to see what's available. Aqua World's paddlewheeler the *Cancún Queen* cruises along the shores of Nichupté Lagoon at sunset. The excursion includes a gourmet dinner followed by dancing to live band music on the top deck. For reservation information phone (998) 848-8327.

The 340-person capacity *Dolphin Express* cruiser travels to Isla Mujeres; activities include shopping, snorkeling and dolphin observation. Cruises depart daily at 10 a.m. from the Playa Langosta Dock, next to the Casa Maya Hotel at Km 5 on Boulevard Kukulcán, and return at 4:30. For reservations and information phone (998) 849-4621.

If you would rather explore Isla Mujeres on your own, take one of the commercial passenger ferries that leave from the public dock at Puerto Juárez. There are approximate hourly departures in each direction daily beginning around 6 a.m. to around 6 p.m. The enclosed, air-conditioned boat holds about 30 passengers and docks at the northern end of the island; the trip takes 25 minutes. Double-check the final departure time when you arrive at Isla Mujeres. One-way fare is 40 pesos (about $4 U.S.) and is collected after you board. Crowds are a distinct possibility depending on the time of year.

A few miles north of Puerto Juárez is Punta Sam, from which a car/passenger ferry departs for Isla Mujeres several times daily (weather permitting). Because Isla Mujeres is so small, however, a car isn't necessary for routine day trips or an afternoon at the beach. Passengers not transporting a vehicle can use the Punta Sam ferry as well.

Extending south from Cancún is a 100-mile stretch of Caribbean coastline sprinkled with scenic beaches and protected by a series of offshore coral reefs. This region, sometimes referred to as the "Riviera Maya," is traversed by Mex. 307, which offers access to a growing number of resorts and ecologically oriented attractions. While organized tours frequent such tourist attractions as Xcaret, Xel-Há and Tulum, driving offers greater flexibility and the opportunity to see secluded spots the tour buses don't visit.

Note: Mex. 307 is a four-lane divided highway until a short distance south of Xcaret, with road expansion continuing to the south. Pavement markings and other improvements have yet to be completely installed throughout the stretch. Observe the speed limit—80 km/h (50 mph)—and drive defensively; many motorists, especially locals, tend to drive too fast for conditions. Avoid driving after dark. Almost all points of interest are a kilometer or so east of Mex. 307 via dirt or rutted roads; they are denoted by crude signs as well as prominent billboards. Mileage signs ("Chetumal 360") are posted in kilometers.

From Cancún, it takes a little less than two hours to reach Tulum. South from the Boulevard Kukulcán junction the highway is lined with tropical scrub and an occasional thatch-roofed hut. The turnoff for Puerto Morelos (*see separate listing within this region*) is about 36 kilometers (22 miles) south of Cancún; this laid-back fishing village has a safe (although seaweed-strewn) beach, and good snorkeling and diving due to a coral reef less than 2,000 feet offshore. The poverty of many locals is underscored by the scattered houses along the highway, which have thatched roofs, open doorways, dirt floors and no windows.

The turnoff for Punta Beté, a bumpy dirt road about 58 kilometers (36 miles) south of Cancún, leads to a jungle-lined beach sheltered by reefs and rocky lagoons; despite a growing number of resort-type accommodations, the atmosphere remains serene.

The turnoff to Playa del Carmen *(see separate listing within this region)* is about 68 kilometers (42 miles) south. This funky town is a laid-back alternative to Cancún's glitz. While there are condominiums, all-inclusive resorts and other signs of affluence, most visitors come for the simple thatched-roof restaurants, craft stalls and lovely beach. Also here is Playacar Club de Golf, a public, 18-hole course designed by Robert Von Hagge.

The turnoff for Xcaret *(see Playa del Carmen)* is about 72 kilometers (45 miles) south. Once a peaceful cove, it has been transformed into an all-day waterside theme park with an ecological slant. The highlight here is an underground river that flows through a series of caves to the beach; swimmers don life jackets and float along with the current.

The most popular day-trip excursion in the Mexican Caribbean is the organized bus tour to Xcaret

from Cancún; this also is the most convenient way to visit the park if you don't have a rental car. Colorfully painted buses depart for Xcaret from the Xcaret terminal, a large thatch-roofed building on Boulevard Kukulcán in the Hotel Zone (across from Plaza Caracol). Tour packages include round-trip transportation, park admission and a tour guide. Buses depart from the terminal daily at 9, 10 and 11:30 a.m.; the ride takes about an hour. Tickets can be purchased at the terminal. They return at either 4:30 or 9:30 p.m. The cost is $89 (U.S.); ages 5-12, $45. Phone (998) 881-2400.

Ten kilometers (6 miles) beyond Xcaret is the turnoff to Paamul, a crescent of sand fronting a calm lagoon. The clear water is good for snorkeling, and seashells wash up on the sandy sections of this rocky beach.

Puerto Aventuras, about 85 kilometers (53 miles) south, is a planned resort community with a challenging golf course (sinkholes and Maya ruins are among the hazards incorporated into its layout). Also at Puerto Aventuras is the CEDAM Museum *(see Playa del Carmen)*. Xpu-ha, about 90 kilometers (56 miles) south, is one of several "eco-parks" in development along the coast. It is similar to Xcaret but doesn't yet offer as many diversions. A separate beach is open to the public.

About 105 kilometers (65 miles) south are several marked turnoffs for Akumal *(see separate listing within this region),* a diving center located along a curving bay. Despite a spate of resorts, private homes and condominiums that have sprung up here, the atmosphere is friendly and low-key. Just north of Akumal off the access road to beachfront properties is Yalkú, a series of lagoons inhabited by tropical fish. A fee is charged to visit this spot, which—like many of the formerly deserted beaches along the Riviera Maya—is slated for further development.

About 108 kilometers (67 miles) south is Chemuyil *(see Tulum),* which used to promote itself as "The Prettiest Beach in the World." This claim has been compromised in recent years by an insect-spread blight known as lethal yellowing, which attacks palm trees and causes their fronds to drop off. Chemuyil does retain its horseshoe-shaped bay, and the protection of a coral reef ensures uniformly calm water. A few kilometers farther south is the signed turnoff to Xcacel, yet another crescent-shaped, white-sand beach. Both are examples of how commercial development is changing Mexico's Caribbean coast—and in the case of Xcacel, threatening the natural habitat of Atlantic green and loggerhead turtles, both on the endangered species list.

About 122 kilometers (76 miles) south is the well-marked turnoff to Xel-Há *(see Tulum),* a park in which interconnected freshwater lagoons form a natural aquarium. Xel-Há (shell-HAH) is a breeding ground for parrotfish and other tropical fish species. It's an ideal spot for kids and novice snorkelers. Tour buses regularly pack the parking lot, so try to get there early. On the west side of the highway

and close to the park entrance is a group of restored Maya ruins.

One look at the ruins of Tulum *(see separate listing within this region)*, about 131 kilometers (81 miles) south, and it's easy to see why the Maya chose this site: This is the only place on the low-lying Yucatán Peninsula where limestone deposits built up to form coastal cliffs. The most distinctive feature of these fortresslike ruins is their location overlooking the turquoise Caribbean. Visitors to the site can hike to the beach below and enjoy a swim in the sea. Tulum is a popular day trip from Cancún, often combined with a stop at Xel-Há.

South of Tulum Mex. 307 angles southwest into the scrubby flatlands of interior Quintana Roo. Hugging the coast directly to the south is the 1.3-million-acre Sian Ka'an Biosphere Reserve *(see attraction listing under Tulum)*, established as a protected area by the Mexican government in 1986 and designated a World Heritage Site in 1987 by the United Nations Educational, Scientific and Cultural Organization (UNESCO). This vast wilderness is a haven for numerous kinds of wildlife, some endangered.

From Mex. 307 at Tulum an unpaved road branches southeast to the Boca Paila Peninsula, within the far eastern edge of the Sian Ka'an Reserve. A bridge south of the Tulum ruins connects the peninsula to the mainland. This strip of land bordering the open Caribbean is dotted with lagoons, tidal pools and palm-lined beaches. Rustic lodges and campgrounds cater to anglers who come for the superb fishing. This stretch of coastline also is seeing the development of accommodations targeting the growing eco-tourism trend. Dedicated bird-watchers take boats to hidden cays to observe pelicans, frigate birds and other marine species that inhabit the mangrove flats. The journey ends at the tiny lobster-fishing village of Punta Allen.

The route, a circuitous trail of limestone covered with packed earth and sand that is riddled with potholes during the summer rainy season, passes through dense jungle. This trek is only for adventurous types with their own sturdy vehicle who don't mind the bugs, heat and lack of civilization. A few words of caution: Top off your gas tank in Tulum, and by all means do not attempt to negotiate any part of this route at night. Insect repellent is essential, as is a supply of drinking water.

Note: Tourists are restricted to the outer buffer (coastal) zone of Sian Ka'an; the core zone on the mainland is closed to visitors. Day trips organized by the nonprofit group Friends of Sian Ka'an (Amigos de Sian Ka'an) and led by licensed naturalist guides explore the coastal waterways and mangrove stands, and include bird-watching, a hike through the jungle and a float downstream in cold spring water. Tours of up to 18 people depart Mon.-Sat. at 9 a.m. (weather permitting) from the restaurant at the Cabañas Aña y José, south of Tulum on the road to the Boca Paila Peninsula. For reservations information contact the lodging; phone (998) 887-5470.

Recreation

Water sports, not surprisingly, top Cancún's list of leisure activities. **Fishing** is excellent; the open Caribbean, Mujeres Bay, the channel between Cozumel and the mainland, and the waters of Nichupté Lagoon together are home to some 500 species, including all types of game fish. Bonito, dorado and sailfish run from March into July; bluefin tuna from April through June. Barracuda, grouper, mackerel and red snapper can be hooked all year.

Hotel Zone marinas offer a range of crafts and top-of-the-line equipment. Larger boats are 35-40 feet long; single-engine diesel boats average 26-28 feet. Four- and eight-hour charter excursions normally include a captain, first mate, gear, bait and soft drinks. Cost varies and the marinas compete for business, so it pays to shop around; ask at your hotel for recommendations. Bluewater Adventures, Km 6.25 on Kukulcán, charters fishing trips; phone (998) 849-4444.

In addition to the islands, fishing opportunities are plentiful all along the Caribbean coastline and farther south at La Ascención and Espíritu Santo, two large bays along the shore of the Sian Ka'an Biosphere Reserve. Shark fishing is best in Laguna Yalahau, at the northern tip of Quintana Roo between Isla Holbox and Cape Catoche. Boats can be hired in the port town of Chiquilá, reached via a paved road branching north off Mex. 180 just east of Xcan.

Scuba diving and **snorkeling** also are rewarding, particularly at the southern end of Cancún Island around Nizuc Point, off Cozumel and Isla Mujeres, and in Nichupté Lagoon. Dive shops along Kukulcán rent equipment, give lessons and schedule trips; some hotels also can arrange dive excursions. Check credentials, boats and equipment, and if possible get the inside scoop from a diver familiar with the area. Conditions are best from May or June through August. Scuba Cancún, on the lagoon side of Kukulcán at Km 5 (across from Playa Langosta), offers a five-hour "resort course" that includes pool practice and a one-tank dive at a shallow reef with a certified PADI instructor. Phone (998) 849-7508.

Other activities include **water skiing, windsurfing, parasailing, swimming** and **boating.** The best place to water ski is Nichupté Lagoon; ski clubs along Kukulcán on the lagoon side rent boats and equipment. Windsurfing propels its participants across the water at exhilarating speeds; the sailboard used by windsurfers is comprised of a masted sail attached to a surfboard. The pools at the big resort hotels are masterfully designed, with the added bonus of the Caribbean as a backdrop.

For landlubbers there's **golf** at Club de Golf Cancún (Pok-Ta-Pok), a championship 18-hole course designed by Robert Trent Jones Jr. Located on an island between Laguna de Bojórquez and Laguna Nichupté (access is off Kukulcán at Km 7.5), it offers fine views of both lagoons and the Caribbean. Shoes, carts and clubs are available for rent, and there is a pro shop. Reservations are advised; phone (998) 883-1230 or (998) 883-1277. Another championship 18-hole course is at the Hilton Cancún Golf Club, off Kukulcán at Km 17; phone (998) 881-8016 or (998) 881-8000. Greens fees vary depending on the season and are less for hotel guests.

Horseback riding trips take in locations from jungle to seashore. Rancho Loma Bonita, off Mex. 307 just south of Puerto Morelos, provides transportation to and from the ranch, in addition to a guide and lunch. Phone (998) 887-5465, or make arrangements through your hotel or a local travel agency.

Bullfights are held during the winter season at Cancún's small Plaza de Toros bullring, at the intersection of avenidas Bonampak and Sayil in Ciudad Cancún. The action takes place on Wednesday afternoons at 3:30 and is preceded by a folkloric dance presentation and a performance by *charros* (elegantly costumed horseback riders). Tickets can be obtained at the bullring or from travel agencies and run about $45 (U.S.) for adults. **Note:** The bull is traditionally killed during these performances. Phone (998) 884-8372.

Tennis is offered at the big resort hotels; there are courts at the Camino Real Cancún, Cancún Sheraton Resort, Casa Maya, Fiesta Americana Condesa, Fiesta Americana Grand Coral Beach and Hotel Krystal Cancún, among others. A separate **jogging** and **bicycling** path—also used for roller blading—parallels the sidewalk along the northern (bay) side of Kukulcán, extending as far as Cancún Point; a path also parallels the sidewalk along most of the southern half of the Hotel Zone. Runners should make the circuit in the early morning before it gets too hot.

If you just want to relax—and are willing to pay the price—the spa at the J.W. Marriott Cancún, Km 14.5 on Kukulcán, offers hydrotherapy, massage and facial and body treatments, plus a state-of-the-art gym, an indoor pool, steam and sauna rooms and a natural juice bar. Phone (998) 848-9600, ext. 6837.

Nightlife

Cancún provides something for everyone after dark, from rowdy spring break hangouts to Mexican and Caribbean-themed dinner shows. The discos, needless to say, offer plenty of high-decibel action. Most of them open around 10 or 10:30 p.m., but they don't stay open all night. Most also collect a cover charge (as do many of the bars and nightclubs). Disco cover charges average around $12 (U.S.), more with an open bar, and may be waived on certain nights; at some places women are routinely admitted free of charge. Inquire about the dress code; some don't allow jeans or short shorts.

La Boom, at Km 3.5 on Kukulcán, has a video bar, light show and almost nightly special events. Coco Bongo, at Km 9.5 on Kukulcán in the Forum-by-the-Sea shopping complex, draws a young, raucous crowd with a mix of recorded techno, salsa

and '80s hits as well as live bands. With no actual dance floor, you gyrate wherever there's space. Ma'Ax'O, in the La Isla Village shopping complex, Km 12.5 on Kukulcán, has an ancient Maya motif, but up-to-the-minute music keeps the dance floor moving. Dady'O, at Km 9.5 on Kukulcán (near the convention center), has been around for a while but is still very popular; like other Cancún discos it's loud and wild, and the sound and lighting are first-rate.

A somewhat less frantic atmosphere prevails at Azucar, in the Camino Real Cancún, which features dancing to live salsa bands. Proper dress is required. Dady Rock, next door to Dady'O at Km 9.5 on Kukulcán, has live bands, karaoke, T-shirt giveaways, an open bar and food. La Madonna, an Italian restaurant in the La Isla Village shopping complex, has an upstairs martini bar offering more than 150 varieties. Pat O'Brien's, Km 11.5 on Kukulcán (in Flamingo Plaza), features "Hurricane" cocktails, an outdoor patio and live rock, jazz and country music If you prefer a quieter evening, most of the resort hotels have a nightclub or lobby bar with jazz or other live music.

For the partying crowd there are plenty of places that combine food, music and a frathouse sense of fun. Two Mexican chains—Carlos 'n Charlie's, at Km 5.5 on the lagoon side of Kukulcán (across from the Casa Maya Hotel), and Señor Frog's, at Km 9.5 on Kukulcán—are noisy and popular, with waiters who get as crazy as the patrons. Cancún's Hard Rock Cafe, in the Forum-by-the-Sea complex, has live rock bands every night except Wednesday, a menu of Mexican and American favorites and a view of the Caribbean.

Planet Hollywood, in Flamingo Plaza at Km 11.5 on Kukulcán (lagoon side), sticks to the movie memorabilia formula that has sustained the chain's worldwide popularity. Mango Tango, at Km 14.2 on the lagoon side of Kukulcán (opposite The Ritz-Carlton), accompanies dinner with a lively floor show staged outdoors nightly at 8, with live music (usually salsa or reggae) following at 9:30.

Those looking for Mexican-style entertainment amid the lasers and fog machines can still find it. The Ballet Folklórico de Cancún performs Tues.-Sat. at the Cancún Convention Center. The ticket booth is just inside the center; tickets can be purchased for a Mexican buffet dinner and the show, or for the show only. Dinner begins at 7 p.m.; the show begins at 8. Tickets are $50 (U.S.) for dinner and the show (ages 6-12, $25), $30 for the show only (ages 6-12, $15). For more information check with your hotel or a local travel agency.

The El Mexicano restaurant, in the Hotel Zone's Costa Blanca shopping complex (at Km 8.5 on Kukulcán), presents folkloric dinner shows, strolling mariachis and other entertainment.

Romantics will enjoy a moonlit cruise. The Columbus Lobster Dinner Cruise sets sail from the Captain's Cove Marina, at Km 16.5 on the lagoon side of Kukulcán (in front of the Omni Cancún), for a lagoon cruise and a lobster dinner aboard the

70-seat galleon *Columbus*. There are daily sunset and evening departures. Children are not permitted. Reservations are required; phone (998) 881-7206.

Special Events

Carnaval, a fiesta in the spirit of Mardi Gras, is held the week preceding Ash Wednesday. Locals dress up in elaborate costumes and parade down the streets of Ciudad Cancún. On Mar. 21 the vernal equinox is celebrated at Chichén Itzá. Jazz Festival Week takes place over the Memorial Day weekend and has in the past drawn such celebrated musicians as Carlos Santana and Ray Charles.

As in almost all of Mexico, Independence Day festivities take place Sept. 15-16 and include fireworks, a parade (on the 16th) and traditional food.

The ITU World Cup Triathlon, which attracts triathletes from around the world, is held in September at Playa Langosta. The Eve of All Souls' Day, Oct. 31, is observed throughout the Yucatán by placing flowers and candles at gravesites. Day of the Dead graveside and church ceremonies take place amid a party-like atmosphere Nov. 1 and 2.

Also in November is the Caribbean Cultural Festival, held in front of Municipal Hall in downtown Ciudad Cancún; it brings artists, dancers and singers from all over Mexico and the Caribbean. Christmas celebrations begin nine days prior to Dec. 25 and feature *posadas* (processions) of families and friends who take part in *pastorelas* (plays) portraying Jesus' birth. The colorful nativity scenes on display are a seasonal highlight.

**This ends listings for Cancún.
The following page resumes the alphabetical listings
of cities in Yucatán Peninsula.**

CHETUMAL, QUINTANA ROO (H-12)
pop. 126,700

One of the oldest cities on the Yucatán Peninsula, Chetumal (cheh-too-MAHL) was a former Maya stronghold. Three centuries of back-and-forth battles—some viciously barbaric—were waged as the Spanish attempted to wrest control of the region from the Maya. The city was renamed Payo Obispo in 1898 and recast as a border town dealing in jungle hardwoods, arms and smuggled goods. These profitable dealings came to an abrupt end in 1955, when a hurricane all but flattened the city.

The capital of Quintana Roo reflects the stages of its checkered history. It is at once a thriving port and a steamy backwater. The older part of town, with its rickety clapboard buildings huddled under trees ablaze with tropical blooms, has a marked Central American atmosphere (the nation of Belize, with which Chetumal shares tourist and commercial traffic, is just across the river). Boulevard Bahía, bordered by small plazas, follows the bay for several kilometers. The large, modern bus terminal is north of downtown near the intersection of avenidas Héroes and Insurgentes. First-class bus service to Cancún and Mérida is offered by ADO.

Day Trips

Chetumal itself is not resort-oriented, but it's a convenient base for fishing expeditions and trips to nearby points of interest. Decidedly off the beaten path is the fishing village of Xcalak (shka-LAK), at the tip of the peninsula extending across Chetumal Bay—just north of Belize's Ambergris Cay—about 55 kilometers (34 miles) southeast of Chetumal. To reach it, however, involves driving north on Mex. 307 to the Majahual turnoff (north of Bacalar). From there a paved but unmarked road leads to coastal Majahual, from which a dirt road proceeds south to Xcalak. Adventurers will appreciate the fishing, snorkeling and birdwatching at this idyllically remote seaside spot.

Xcalak is the jumping-off point for trips to Banco Chincorro, a Caribbean atoll that is a natural park. About two hours northeast of Xcalak by boat, Banco Chincorro is studded with the remains of sunken and grounded ships and is a favored dive site. Fishing, however, is not permitted. Boats and guides to explore the area can be arranged in Chetumal.

About a mile north of Xcalak at the Costa de Cocos resort is the Xcalak to Chincorro Dive Center, which offers complete dive services, equipment rentals and trips to Banco Chincorro atoll. Local dive excursions explore the spectacular coral and sponge formations of the offshore barrier reef, which extends south to the Honduras border. The center also organizes birdwatching, snorkeling and fishing trips. For additional information phone (983) 831-0461 in the United States.

Quintana Roo State Tourism Office (Secretaría de Turismo): Av. Del Centenario #622; phone (983) 835-0860, ext. 1809 or 1810.

Shopping areas: Many of Chetumal's stores line Avenida Héroes, which begins at the bay and runs west through the market area. An incongruous touch in this downtown shopping district are the numerous shops selling Dutch cheeses, Japanese stereo equipment, French perfume and other international products, all at duty-free prices. The chance to purchase such items draws crowds of Mexican and Belizean tourists. While it is possible to find good buys on Yucatecan hammocks, U.S. and Canadian visitors should save their pesos and purchase Mexican crafts elsewhere.

MUSEUM OF MAYA CULTURE (Museo de la Cultura Maya) is downtown on Av. de Los Héroes between Calle Cristóbal Colón and Av. Mahatma Gandhi, on the pedestrian mall. A visit to this museum is helpful if you plan on exploring the Río Bec archeological sites *(see separate listing within this region)*, as the exhibits provide insight into Maya society and beliefs. Scale models of major Maya ruins show how they might have looked when they were inhabited. Information is in Spanish and English. Tues.-Sun. 9-7 (also Fri.-Sat. 7-8 p.m.). Admission around $5.50 (U.S.).

▼GEM CHICHEN ITZA, YUCATAN
(G-11)

The pyramids, temples and shrines at Chichén Itzá (chee-CHEHN eet-SAH)—the magnificent remains of a once-great Maya city—were designated a World Heritage Site by UNESCO in 1988. It is believed that Chichén Itzá was founded sometime around A.D. 435; the first large-scale excavations of the site began around the turn of the 20th century. Of the several hundred buildings believed to have once stood, only about 30 are fully restored. A few more remain as they were found, and the rest are hidden under rough, underbrush-covered mounds in the thick jungle scrub of the north-central Yucatán Peninsula.

Northern Zone

Chichén Itzá is remarkable for both monumental scope and architectural variety. The ruins consist of two complexes connected by a dirt path. Generally speaking, the older southern section contains mostly Maya ruins and the structures in the northern section combine Maya and Toltec influences, although the blending of pre-Hispanic cultures is apparent throughout. The militaristic Toltec influence is evident in the images—jaguars, sharp-taloned eagles, phalanxes of marching warriors, feathered serpents—employed to decorate the exteriors of pyramids and temples.

El Castillo *(see attraction listing)* dominates the other Northern Zone ruins sprinkled over a level, grassy area. That this pyramid's builders were mathematically precise in their construction is borne out by a natural phenomenon that occurs at the spring and fall equinoxes (on or around Mar. 21 and Sept. 21). As the sun begins its descent, the shadows cast by the terraces on the north staircase form the body of a serpent, whose actual sculpted head rests at the base of the stairs. In the spring, the serpent appears to be slithering down the stairs; in the fall, the illusion is reversed. **Note:** Visitors from around the world attend this semiannual event, and although it is well worth seeing, expect large and boisterous crowds.

The staircases on three of the pyramid's sides can be climbed; most visitors use the one on the western side (the side you see as you first enter the site). The views from the summit are spectacular, with ruins poking above the surrounding green landscape. **Note:** The climb up is arduous but of fairly short duration (the pyramid is about 100 feet tall). It is, however, extremely steep, a fact much more apparent after you've reached the top. For those prone to vertigo or fearful of heights, the climb back down will be difficult. If you decide to brave it (and the views alone make the effort worthwhile), the easiest way to descend is backwards on hands and knees, facing the steps and proceeding slowly one step down at a time. For additional security, hold onto the link chain that extends up the middle of the staircase.

Temples are at both ends of the ball court *(see attraction listing)* near El Castillo. The temple at the northern end has a short stairway ascending to two columns supporting a roof. It retains only a few remnants of its former murals and sculptures. The Temple of the Jaguars, at the southeastern corner of the ball court, has columns carved in the shape of serpents and panels depicting jaguars and Maya warriors.

Just east of the ball court is the Temple of the Skulls (Tzompantli), decorated in macabre fashion with rows of human skulls. This artistic rendering reflects the gruesome act of human sacrifice that was integral to Maya religious rites, as the heads of victims were often stuck on the ends of poles. The adjacent Platform of the Eagles and Jaguars has carvings showing these creatures grasping human hearts. A short distance east of this structure and north of El Castillo is the Platform of Venus, which has depictions of a feathered serpent (a reference to the god Quetzalcóatl) holding a human head in its mouth. Serpent carvings ascend the stairways.

Just south of the Temple of the Warriors *(see attraction listing)* are the partially restored remains of what archeologists believe were steam baths and a market complex. Further to the southeast are unrestored mounds of rubble beneath the trees.

Central Zone

The southern complex of ruins (often mistakenly referred to as Old Chichén), accessible from the northern complex via a short dirt pathway, consists of mostly Maya ruins. The first structure you come to is the Ossuary (High Priest's Grave), thought to be a burial ground. This partially reconstructed pyramid is topped with the remains of a temple and has distinctive serpent head carvings at the base. Its

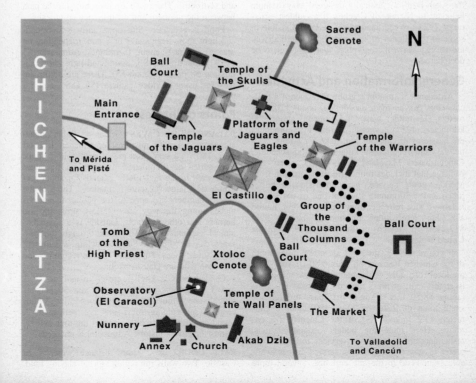

interior (not open to the public) leads to an underground cave in which human skeletons and offerings have been found.

Across the path and south of this pyramid is El Caracol (see attraction listing), an astronomical observatory dating from the 10th century that may have been one of the last Maya buildings erected at this site. The short stairway leading to the dome can be climbed, and there are fine views from the top of the wall, particularly of the nearby Nunnery.

East of El Caracol a winding path leads north through dense underbrush to the Cenote Xtoloc. Unlike the Sacred Cenote (see attraction listing), this well was not used for human sacrifice; it provided Chichén with its drinking water. South of El Caracol is the Nunnery (Casa de Las Monjas), so named by the Spaniards because it reminded them of a European convent. This large complex has exquisitely carved facades of animals, flowers and designs that are reminiscent of latticework. Next to the Nunnery is The Church (La Iglesia), also named by the Spanish. While it in no way resembles a church, this small building is lavishly decorated, primarily with beak-nosed carvings of Chac.

The exterior carvings on the Temple of the Carved Panels (Templo de Los Tableros Esculpidos), east of the Nunnery, are more difficult to discern, but may refer to Toltec warrior symbology. A rough path, also beginning east of the Nunnery, runs through the scrub for several hundred feet to the Akab-Dzib, a classically designed Maya temple believed to be one of Chichén Itzá's oldest structures. Traces of red handprints are faintly visible in some of the interior rooms, and above one doorway are carved Maya hieroglyphics that have yet to be deciphered.

General Information and Activities

Arrangements to join a group tour aboard a first-class bus can be made in Mérida, about 120 kilometers (75 miles) west, and Cancún, about 200 kilometers (125 miles) east. A group tour eliminates the hassle of driving but can make for a long, hectic day and requires sticking to a rigid schedule. Cancún-based Mayaland Tours offers a day trip package that includes round-trip transportation from Mérida, guide service, park admission, a buffet lunch and a 30-minute swim at one of the nearby hotels—a nice refresher after touring the hot, humid site. For reservations information phone (998) 887-2450 (in Mexico) or (800) 235-4079 (from the United States).

If you're driving, the ruins are a few miles south of the Chichén Itzá exit off Mex. 180-D; Yuc. 79 is the local road. One of the highway's two toll plazas is at this exit; at press time the toll was 85 pesos (about $8.50 U.S.). You'll first pass through the small town of Pisté, on Mex. 180 about 2 kilometers (1.2 miles) west of the Chichén Itzá entrance. Here there are budget accommodations, restaurants and basic travel services for those who prefer to stay overnight. Taxi service also is available from Pisté to the site entrance. Several more upscale hotels are grouped east of (and within walking distance) of the southern complex of ruins.

Chichén Itzá can be explored on your own or as part of a group led by a staff guide. A guide isn't necessary to appreciate the grandeur of the major landmarks, however, and information plaques in Spanish and English give a general architectural and historical background.

If you're visiting on your own, begin early in the morning if possible, before it gets too hot and the tour buses begin arriving. A hat or other headgear is advised for protection from the strong sun. Sturdy walking shoes with nonslip soles come in handy for clambering over rocks and especially for climbing El Castillo. Bring bottled water and/or snacks as well as insect repellent for any extended walking excursions. Three hours or so is enough to see everything, although archeology buffs could easily spend the entire day.

A sound-and-light show is presented nightly. The ruins are bathed in colored lights, and Spanish narration recounts the history of and legends associated with the site. Headsets in several languages can be rented. Confirm the start time at the visitor center ticket window.

The visitor center at the main entrance has an information desk (where admission tickets are purchased); a small museum; an air-conditioned auditorium, Chilam Balam, where an audiovisual presentation is shown; and a bookstore, restaurant and restrooms. There also are restrooms off the path between the northern and central zone complexes.

Food is available. Site open daily 8-5. Sound-and-light show begins at 7 or 8 p.m. (depending on season) and lasts about 45 minutes. Admission 87 pesos (around $9 U.S.). Sound-and-light show admission 50 pesos (around $5). There are additional fees for using a video camera ($6 U.S.) and for parking.

Points of Interest

BALANCANCHE CAVES (Grutas de Balancanché) are about 5 km (3 mi.) east of Chichén Itzá off Mex. 180 via a very short gravel road; follow signs. This series of illuminated underground passages, discovered in the mid-1960s, extends for about half a mile past large stalactite formations. Three of the seven chambers are open to the public. In various niches along the way are offertory urns, incense burners and other artifacts. Outside is a small botanical garden. **Note:** The walk through the passages can be slippery. Some crawling is required; wear sturdy shoes. The caves are not recommended for those who are claustrophobic.

Guided tours in English are given daily at 11, 1 and 3 for groups of between six and 30 persons (double-check tour times at the Chichén Itzá visitor center); self-guiding tours are not permitted. A sound-and-light show accompanies the tour and recounts the cave's history. Admission is charged.

BALL COURT is a short distance west of El Castillo. Two walls run parallel to the playing field.

The object of this ancient game was for two teams of players to maneuver a heavy rubber ball—without using their hands—through one of two stone rings placed high on each wall. Some participants (opinion is divided on whether they were winners or losers) apparently suffered death by decapitation. Stone carvings depict this act as well as players sporting protective padding and feathered headdresses. The acoustics are startling: Two people standing on opposite sides of the field and speaking in normal voices can easily hear each other.

THE CASTLE (El Castillo) is a short walk from the visitor center at the main entrance. Also called Kukulcán, the Maya name for the Toltec king Quetzalcóatl, this pyramid has a perfectly symmetrical design. Each of the four sides is scaled by 91 steps; the total of 364 steps plus the top platform equaled the number of days in the Maya year. An additional step underneath the pyramid, the 365th, signified a trip to the underworld. Each side also has 18 terraced sections—nine on either side of a central staircase, equaling the 18 months of the Maya year—and 52 panels, corresponding to the number of years in the Maya calendrical cycle.

Inside El Castillo is an older temple that can be entered twice a day (double-check times at the visitor center) via a stairway at the foot of the north staircase (on the western end). Narrow steps ascend to two humid inner chambers. One contains a reclining Chac Mool figure, the other a reddish throne in the shape of a jaguar with green jade eyes. Avoid entering this temple if you're claustrophobic.

OLD CHICHEN (Chichén Viejo) is about a 15-minute walk down a dirt path that begins southwest of the Nunnery. A sincere interest in archeology and a local guide are both recommended for a trek to this area of little-restored buildings, which is mosquito-infested (wear plenty of insect repellent) and overgrown with jungle scrub. Avoid exploring during the June-through-September rainy season, when the narrow pathways can become difficult to navigate.

The barely uncovered buildings feature masks of Chac and gargoyle-like creatures carved along cornices. The Date Group of ruins includes the House of the Phalli, so named for some sculptures carved into the walls of one room. The earliest date discovered in Chichén Itzá—the equivalent of A.D. 879—is carved into a lintel supported by columns; the rest of what was once a pyramid no longer remains.

SACRED CENOTE is about a five-minute walk due north of the Platform of Venus along a dirt path. This path was once a Maya *sacbe*, or paved causeway. Two cenotes, or limestone sinkholes, served Chichén Itzá. The Sacred Cenote is a 190-foot-wide pit that was used for human sacrifice to appease the rain god Chac. The skeletons of men, women and children have been excavated, which suggests that

in addition to young maidens—the preferred sacrificial victim—the diseased and mentally ill also may have been drowned in the well.

Excavations of the cenote have unearthed bones, idols, jewelry, jade objects and other artifacts from different parts of Mexico, leading archeologists to believe that pilgrimages to Chichén Itzá continued long after its abandonment.

THE SNAIL (El Caracol) is in the southern group of ruins. Also called "The Winding Stair," its name is a reference to the interior winding staircase (not open to the public) that leads to the dome (which can be entered). This ruin's round construction is quite possibly unique in Maya architecture. Stones could be removed from slits within the dome—nine in all—enabling Maya astronomers to study different parts of the heavens. Some interesting carvings decorate the dome's exterior.

TEMPLE OF THE WARRIORS is a short distance east of El Castillo. This Toltec-influenced temple has impressive rows of carved warriors and a roof boasting fine sculptural details of the rain god Chac, feathered serpents and mythical animals; it is guarded by a reclining Chac Mool figure. Next to the temple is the Group of the Thousand Columns, thought to have housed the residences of Chichén's ruling elite. The rows of Toltec-style pillars (in actuality, far fewer than 1,000) are covered with bas-relief.

COBA, QUINTANA ROO (G-11)

Cobá (coh-BAH) translates roughly as "waters stirred by wind." This small village is about 66 kilometers (40 miles) northwest of Mex. 307; the Tulum/Cobá road branches off Mex. 307 just north of the town of Tulum. From Cancún, take Mex. 180 west to Xcan, then the paved road south about 43 kilometers (26 miles). The village is about a mile west of the road via a turnoff.

COBA RUINS spread east from the shore of Lake Cobá just outside of town. This city/ceremonial center dates from between A.D. 600 to 900—older than both Chichén Itzá and Tulum—and at its height may have supported as many as 50,000 inhabitants. Archeologists theorize that Cobá was an important trade link between Maya outposts on the coast and cities in the interior.

The ruins were first discovered in the early 1890s, but excavations did not begin in earnest until 1973. It is believed that as many as 6,500 structures exist. Those temples, pyramids and elaborately carved stelae (vertical stone tablets) that have been excavated are surrounded by palm tree thickets, tropical hardwoods, roping vines and other vegetation.

Nohoch Mul, a 138-foot-high pyramid towering above the flat landscape (about a half-hour walk from the site entrance), is the tallest structure of its kind in the northern Yucatán—rising even higher than the Pyramid of the Magician at Uxmal. It can be climbed. The Cobá Group, a cluster of ruins on

The Maya Route

Enormous temples, intricately sculpted structures, lofty volcanoes, tropical rain forest—all are traversed by La Ruta Maya (The Maya Route), that region of Mesoamerica which includes all of Belize, most of Guatemala, portions of Honduras and El Salvador, and all or part of the Mexican states of Campeche, Chiapas, Quintana Roo, Tabasco and Yucatán.

Maya civilization began more than 2,000 years ago and reached its zenith between A.D. 300 and 900. At the same time Europe was suffering through the Dark Ages, the Maya people enjoyed a creative flowering more advanced than any of their contemporaries in the known world. They built temples and ceremonial centers that continue to evoke wonder; developed an astronomical calendar and predicted both solar and lunar eclipses; pioneered the mathematical concept of zero; and evolved a highly refined hieroglyphic writing system. The Maya also were accomplished artists, historians and road builders.

For reasons that are still unknown, major ceremonial centers such as Palenque and Tikal were abandoned by the early 10th century, as Maya civilization shifted northward to the Yucatán Peninsula and such cities as Chichén Itzá and Uxmal. Between about 1200 and the Spanish arrival in the early 16th century, El Mundo Maya (The Maya World) toppled. The exact causes remain a mystery, although invasion by other tribes, conflict between peasant farmers and the elite, overpopulation, drought and crop failure all likely had varying degrees of impact.

The first Spanish stronghold in the Yucatán Peninsula was established in 1542 at Mérida; the last Maya city to surrender was Tayasal, Guatemala, in 1697. The Maya retreated to the jungles of Quintana Roo, where fierce revolts continued through 300 years of Spanish domination. Even after Mexico won freedom from Spain, the Yucatán twice declared its independence.

the right after you enter the site, contains another large pyramid, the Temple of the Churches (this one cannot be climbed).

Guides can be hired at the entrance, and mountain bike rentals are available. Try to visit early in the morning; the heat, humidity and mosquitoes can be formidable. Sturdy walking shoes, insect repellent and drinking water are necessary for those planning to spend any time exploring the site. Daily 7-6. Admission around $4 (U.S.). Parking $1.25 (U.S.).

COZUMEL, QUINTANA ROO (G-12)
pop. 64,100

Cozumel (koh-soo-MEHL) offers a change of pace from Cancún's large-scale development. The relaxed rhythms of a tropical island prevail here, along with some real small-town atmosphere. But Cozumel's biggest claim to fame is the series of coral reefs that make this island 12 miles off the Quintana Roo coast one of the world's top diving destinations.

Cozumel was an important Maya ceremonial and trading center, and the people believed the island to be sacred. The present name descends from Cuzamil, or "the island of swallows." Cozumel's first foreign visitor was Spanish explorer Juan de Grijalva, who arrived in 1518 on a slave-hunting expedition; Hernando Cortés followed the next year, using the island as a base from which to launch attacks against mainland Indians. After the Spanish takeover Cozumel became an important port, but diseases introduced from Europe almost wiped out the local population by the late 1500s.

After a century of peaceful existence, Cozumel became a refuge for smugglers and pirates, who used the island's protected coves as hideouts. By the mid-19th century it had been all but abandoned, but Indian survivors of the racially triggered War of the Castes left mainland Yucatán and began to resettle the island. An economic boomlet then occurred when Cozumel became a port of call on the shipping route for chicle, a milky substance obtained from the trunk of the sapodilla tree that was used in making chewing gum. But as air freight became more widespread and synthetics replaced chicle in gum production, the island again lapsed into obscurity.

Growth began anew after U.S. servicemen stationed at Cozumel during World War II came back for vacations. The island's reputation as a choice dive spot was considerably enhanced in the early 1960s when undersea explorer Jacques Cousteau visited while making a television documentary. Resort development in the 1970s and '80s paralleled Cancún's, albeit at a slower pace. Although the tremendous growth of the cruise ship industry has resulted in a stream of daytripping visitors, serious divers still set the scene here, exploring the numerous offshore reefs, underwater caverns and sunken shipwrecks.

Island Layout

Cozumel is located off the coast opposite Playa del Carmen; a 3,000-foot-deep channel separates it from the mainland. Mexico's largest populated island, it has a total area of 189 square miles (about one-sixth the size of Rhode Island), is approximately 29 miles long and averages 9 miles wide.

Most of the interior comprises patches of insect-ridden jungle, expanses of thorny, uninviting scrub and scattered Maya ruins, none of them well preserved. The terrain is uniformly flat—the highest point is less than 50 feet above sea level—and inaccessible. It's a desolate landscape, which makes the beaches all the more inviting. Those on the western (leeward) side of the island are protected from the open Caribbean; they have calm waters and sandy shores. The eastern (windward) coast is rockier and faces the open sea. Pounding surf and powerful undertows create dangerous swimming conditions, but these beaches also have a wild beauty.

On the western coast is Cozumel's only town, San Miguel de Cozumel, usually referred to as San Miguel. The island's hub, it is a conglomeration of budget hotels, businesses, shops, restaurants and nightspots. Many of them line San Miguel's main street, Avenida Rafael Melgar, which runs north-south along the waterfront. A cement walkway, locally referred to as the *malecón,* divides the avenue from the beach. Avenidas run north-south, calles run east-west, forming an easy-to-negotiate grid pattern. (An exception is Avenida Benito Juárez, which begins at the passenger ferry pier and runs due east.)

A block inland from the *malecón* is Plaza del Sol, the central plaza, bounded on the north by Juárez and on the south by Calle 1 Sur. The plaza, graced with a statue of Mexican president and hero Benito Juárez, is especially pretty in spring when royal poinciana trees are covered with orange blooms. **Note:** Many downtown streets are closed to vehicular traffic, and parking is scarce.

Hotel zones comprising Cozumel's more exclusive accommodations are to the north and to the south of San Miguel. One paved road, the Carretera Transversal (the eastward extension of Avenida Benito Juárez), crosses the island east-west. There are no paved roads in the island's northern half, and very little development. The offshore reefs and the best beaches are toward the southern end of the island on the western (leeward) side and are accessible via the Costera Sur, the southern extension of Avenida Rafael Melgar.

Practicalities

Cozumel International Airport is about 3 kilometers (2 miles) north of San Miguel. Continental and Mexicana airlines offer direct flights from Houston and Miami, respectively. Make airline and hotel reservations well in advance if you'll be visiting during the peak tourist season, mid-December through mid-April. For side trips, the Mexicana subsidiary Aerocozumel has regular daily flights

The Maya Route *(continued)*

Maya descendants today number about 2 million in Mexico and Central America and speak more than 20 different dialects. In some small villages the *na*—an oval-shaped, thatched-roofed hut with *sascab* (lime dirt) floors—is still the principal dwelling, and timeless traditions manage to survive.

The Maya Route covers a 120,000-square-mile area from the Isthmus of Tehuantepec, Mexico's narrowest point, through the Yucatán Peninsula and south to Honduras and El Salvador. The "route" is actually a loosely tied-together network of existing roadways. The main highways are Mex. 186, which runs east-west across

Chichén Itzá
Nadine Markova
Mexico Tourism Board

the southern portions of Quintana Roo and Campeche; Mex. 307, which runs north-south along Quintana Roo's Caribbean coastline; and Mex. 180, which connects Cancún with Mérida before traveling southwest along the Gulf of Mexico coast. In addition, Mex. 180-D is a toll route roughly paralleling Mex. 180 between Cancún and Mérida. If you do decide to explore, make certain the vehicle you drive—whether rented or your own—is in top condition. Away from the cities, much of this part of Mexico remains primitive.

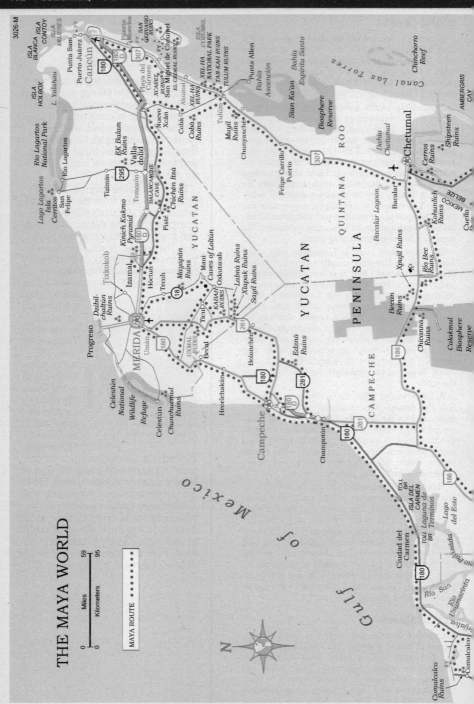

THE MAYA WORLD

MAYA ROUTE •••••••

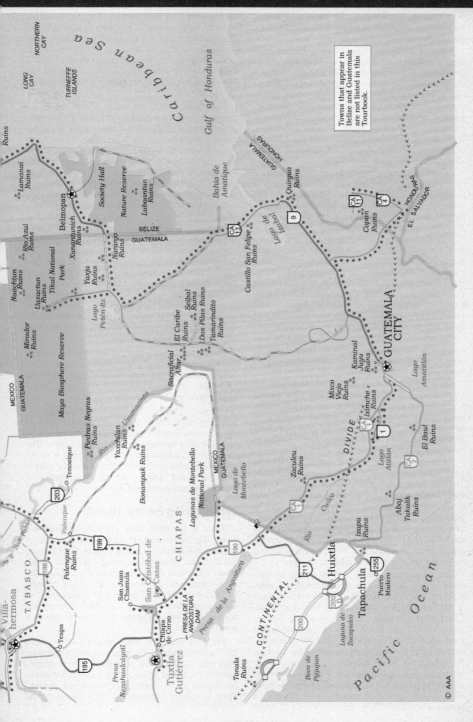

Towns that appear in Belize and Guatemala are not listed in this Tourbook.

© AAA

from Cancún, Isla Mujeres and Playa del Carmen; for schedule information phone (800) 531-7921 (in the United States).

Note: If flying to Cozumel from Cancún, you must purchase your ticket at the main terminal in the Cancún airport and then take a shuttle bus to a small terminal annex for the actual flight. Luggage can be checked at the main terminal. When returning to Cancún from Cozumel, request that your luggage be dropped off at the main terminal if you're continuing on another flight. If your connecting flight is with a Mexican airline, alert the Cozumel ticket agent and your luggage will automatically be forwarded to the connecting flight.

There is no taxi service from the airport; instead, *colectivos* (passenger vans) drop visitors off at their hotels. *Colectivo* tickets can be purchased at the airport exit. Take a taxi back to the airport upon departure. For additional information about airlines see *"Arriving by Air," page 551.*

Cozumel also is accessible by passenger ferry from Playa del Carmen *(see separate listing within this region).* The trip on the passenger-only ferry takes about 45 minutes. There are two types of ferries—older, open-air boats and the MV *Mexico,* an enclosed, jet-propelled, air-conditioned vessel (called a "water jet") offering refreshments and videos during the trip. Tickets can be purchased from the booth at the pier and cost around $10 (U.S.). Double check departure schedules, as they can change without notice. **Note:** Those prone to seasickness should take appropriate precautions on windy days.

There are approximate hourly crossings between Playa del Carmen and Cozumel daily from around 6 a.m. to 9 p.m., but schedules are subject to frequent change; verify arrivals and/or departures in advance at the ticket booth. The passenger ferry pier is at the west end of Avenida Benito Juárez, in the center of San Miguel.

Unless you need to bring a vehicle onto the island, avoid the Puerto Morelos passenger/car ferry. The trip itself takes from three to four hours, and there can be a tedious wait before departure. It also is necessary to arrive several hours in advance in order to purchase a ticket and secure a place in line. The ferry is docked during periods of bad weather; trucks carrying fuel and other cargo take precedence over automobiles. There is one crossing daily, and the schedule is subject to change.

The passenger/car ferry arrives at the international cruise ship pier, located a couple of miles south of San Miguel near the La Ceiba Beach hotel. A number of cruise lines, among them Caribbean, Commodore, Dolphin, Holland America, Norwegian, Princess and Royal, dock at Cozumel and/or Playa del Carmen. AAA/CAA members receive exclusive savings on cruising vacations by booking through a AAA Travel Agency.

Mopeds and motorcycles are popular ways to get around the island, but the potholed streets can make them a risky means of transportation. Wearing a helmet is required. There are several moped rental establishments in San Miguel. The rate averages $25-$30 (U.S.) per day; insurance is not included. Open-air jeeps also can be rented but entail a similar element of risk, as they can flip over easily. If you're staying on Cozumel more than a day, it might be worth your while to rent a car at the airport, since the beaches and other points of interest are spread out.

Taxis wait outside the major hotels and at the passenger ferry pier, and can be hailed on the street in San Miguel. Expect fixed rates within town, between downtown and the hotel zones to the north and south, and from downtown to such popular destinations as Chankanaab Lagoon Park or Playa San Francisco. If possible, share the cost with other passengers. You also can hire a taxi driver for a tour of the island; the standard fee should be around $60 (U.S.). Most hotels will call a taxi for their guests.

The Calling Station, Avenida Rafael Melgar at Calle 3 Sur, is open daily during the high season and has private booths for long-distance phone calls (minus high hotel surcharges), fax and currency exchange service, Internet access, and VCR and video rentals. The Cruz Roja (Red Cross) clinic is at Calle Rosada Salas and Avenida 20 Sur; phone (987) 872-1058. A 24-hour clinic and access to air ambulance service are available at the Cozumel Medical Center (Centro Médico de Cozumel), Calle 1 Sur #101; phone (987) 872-5664 or (305) 433-7490 (from the United States).

Money can be exchanged at banks in the vicinity of Plaza del Sol during the morning. Banks have better exchange rates than the hotels and the *casa de cambio* (exchange office) at the airport. Many island shops accept U.S. dollars.

Cozumel is balmy year-round. June through October, the rainy season, also is more humid. Most of the afternoon showers during these months are brief and pose little interruption to leisure activities. The possibility of a hurricane or tropical storm is likeliest in September or October. The rest of the year is dry, warm and sunny, with an occasional cool evening December through February.

What To Do on the Island

When in Cozumel, dive. From the international cruise ship pier south to Punta Celarain are miles of offshore coral reefs, including Paraíso, Chankanaab, Yucab, Santa Rosa, Palancar and Colombia. At the island's southern tip is Maracaibo Reef, where the coral formations are enormous and water currents make diving both exhilarating and challenging. For experienced divers only, Maracaibo is not on the regular dive boat itinerary and requires advance reservations.

The peak season is June through August, when the Caribbean waters are calm and warm and hotel rates tend to be lower. A wetsuit top is recommended for winter diving, when water temperatures are slightly lower. Night dives, underwater photography or making a customized video are among the available options. A scale map of all of Cozumel's reefs, complete with water depths and other information, can be obtained from most of the local dive shops.

A variety of packaged excursions, which usually include airfare, accommodations and diving costs, can be booked in the United States. In addition, the island's dive outfits compete vigorously for both seasoned divers and beginners, offering equipment rentals, instruction, guides and organized expeditions that range from an afternoon to several days.

Many hotels organize their own dive trips as well, and their facilities, while likely to be more expensive, also are more convenient. If you're not on a packaged trip or making your own arrangements, take the time to investigate credentials, boats and equipment; if possible, get the inside scoop from a diver familiar with the area.

Among the in-town outfits are Blue Bubble, Avenida 5 Sur at Calle 3 Sur, phone (866) 405-5749 from the United States; and Aqua Safari, Avenida Rafael Melgar at Avenida 5 Sur, phone (987) 872-0101. Note: Make certain the instructor you choose has PADI certification and is affiliated with the island's Buceo Médico Mexicano recompression chamber, located on Calle 5 Sur just off Avenida Rafael Melgar; phone (987) 872-2387.

Snorkeling is excellent in Chankanaab Bay, at Playa San Francisco and around the offshore reefs near Colombia Lagoon, at the island's southern tip. Morning feedings from the piers of the Stouffer Presidente and La Ceiba Beach hotels attract schools of hungry fish, some of which are bold enough to break the surface of the water and take food from outstretched hands (but beware of sharp teeth). An upside-down plane, deliberately sunk for a movie production, sits on the sandy bottom a short distance from the La Ceiba pier. Those who want to view the colorful marine life but don't want to get wet can take a glass-bottom boat trip.

Snorkeling gear can be cheaply rented at Playa San Francisco, Chankanaab Lagoon Park (see attraction listing) or from the larger hotels. In addition, the dive shops and travel agencies provide organized snorkeling excursions to the various reefs. A representative agency is Turismo Aviomar, which has a central office at Avenida 5 Norte between Calles 2 and 4 Norte; phone (987) 872-0588 or (987) 872-0477. Other Turismo Aviomar offices are in the lobbies of the major hotels, including the Presidente Intercontinental. The Fiesta Cozumel Holidays agency also has offices in the major hotels.

Sport fishing is superb, and from March through June world records are sometimes set for catches of swordfish, sailfish and marlin. At other times of the year barracuda, dorado, red snapper, tarpon and wahoo can be hooked.

The major hotels organize sport-fishing expeditions. You also can hire a boat and a guide yourself at the downtown ferry dock, or through Club Naútico de Cozumel, at the Puerto de Abrigo Marina on Avenida Rafael Melgar, just north of downtown; phone (987) 872-0118. To arrange a fishing trip in advance write Club Naútico at P.O. Box 341, Cozumel, Quintana Roo 77600. Boats can be chartered for a half or full day. Rates (including tackle, bait and guide) vary according to the size of the vessel, the number of people and the season. To get an idea of what's available and how much it costs, visit the marina in the late afternoon when the boats are returning and talk to a couple of the captains.

Sightseeing excursions to Cancún, Playa del Carmen, Xel-Há, Tulum and other nearby points of interest can be easily arranged; information is available at most hotels. Travel agencies also offer Cozumel tours that include such activities as sunbathing at the beach, snorkeling at Chankanaab Lagoon Park, a visit to the San Gervasio ruins or a day trip to the Xcaret ecological theme park on the mainland (see Playa del Carmen), which includes ferry transportation.

The Cozumel Country Club is on the north side of the island, near the airport. The island's first golf course has 18 holes, a pro shop, a driving range, and club and shoe rental. Carts are required. Guest privileges are available for those staying at the Playa Azul and Presidente Inter Continental hotels. For greens fees and additional information phone (987) 872-9570.

Rancho Buenavista offers a four-hour guided horseback riding trek into the interior jungle scrub, with stops at several Maya ruins. The tours depart from the Acuario Restaurant on Avenida Rafael Melgar and include round-trip transportation to the ranch; phone (987) 872-1537.

Carnaval, the island's version of Mardi Gras, is held in February on the three days preceding Ash Wednesday. Colorful float parades along the malecón, masquerade balls, street dances and the "burning" of Juan Carnaval (a Carnaval king) take place during this exuberant fiesta. The International Billfish Tournament is held in early May to take advantage of the narrow-jawed fishes' migrating season. Cozumel also celebrates the patron saint of San Miguel with a fiesta on Sept. 29.

Beaches and Ruins

As in the rest of Mexico, all of Cozumel's beaches are public, even those that appear to be the property of hotels. North of San Miguel are several of the more luxurious accommodations and some condominium developments. Playa San Juan extends to Punta Norte, where the highway ends. Beyond Punta Norte is miniscule Isla de la Pasión, in the middle of calm Abrigo Bay. Local boat owners can take you to this secluded spot, where there are deserted beaches and opportunities for fishing, but no facilities.

South of San Miguel, Avenida Rafael Melgar becomes the coastal highway (Costera Sur) and passes several beach and snorkeling spots. Playa San Francisco, south of Chankanaab Lagoon Park and off the Costera Sur (coastal highway, also known as the Carretera Sur), is one of Cozumel's most popular beaches. It has changing rooms and open-air restaurants, and beach chairs and snorkeling equipment can be rented. On weekends the beach is crowded with local families and cruise ship passengers.

The eastern (windward) coast is far less developed and thus more dramatic. The beaches, interspersed among rocky coves, are frequently empty. The open Caribbean is intensely turquoise, but the surf is often strong; swim at your own risk.

A paved road follows the coast from Punta Celarain north toward Punta Morena, halfway up the coast; there are a few restaurants and camping spots (no facilities) along the way. Playa Bonita, Playa Chen Río and Punta Chiqueros and (which is situated on a protected cove) are all good spots for beachcombing. At Punta Morena the road runs into the end of the Carretera Transversal (cross-island road), about 15 kilometers (9 miles) from San Miguel. The rocky beach here is scenic but not safe for swimming.

Several Maya ruins are scattered around the island. North of the Carretera Transversal the coastal route changes from paved to dirt and leads past waterfowl-filled lagoons and a smattering of ruins, among them Castillo Real, a former Maya fortification, where the few remains include a lookout tower. The snorkeling is outstanding in this little-visited area, but a four-wheel-drive vehicle is necessary to reach it. At the northern tip of Cozumel is the Punta Molas Lighthouse, where bird-watching is rewarding and it is possible to camp (again, no facilities).

The San Gervasio ruins *(see attraction listing)* are also north of and accessible from the cross-island road. At Km 17.5 on the Costera Sur, a turn-off leads about 3 kilometers (2 miles) east to the ruins of El Cedral. One small structure is all that remains at this site, believed to be the oldest on the island and the one first discovered by the Spanish. A tree grows from the roof, its roots snaking around the crumbled stones. Faint traces of paint and stucco are still visible. A tiny farming settlement has grown up here, dominated by a rural church painted bright green.

Shopping, Dining and Nightlife

For shoppers, Avenida Rafael Melgar is the place to go. Department stores, boutiques and craft shops offer duty-free imported goods, chic sportswear and high-quality folk art reproductions, as well as T-shirts and cheap souvenirs. Top-quality jewelry can be found at Van Cleef & Arpels, near the international cruise ship dock. Another concentration of shops line the side streets in the vicinity of Plaza del Sol. The two-story Plaza del Sol Mall is a small complex on the east side of the plaza. A crafts market is on Calle 1 Sur across from the plaza's south side.

Those for whom shopping is more of a sidelight can try Los Cinco Soles on Avenida Rafael Melgar, which sells a representative selection of clothing and Mexican craft items fashioned from papier maché, wood, glass, onyx and silver. More handicrafts are on display at Talavera, on Avenida 5 Sur near Plaza del Sol.

Most of Cozumel's restaurants are in San Miguel. Seafood, not surprisingly, stands out. For a morning pick-me-up, Zermatt, at the corner of Calle 4 Norte and Avenida 5 Norte, is a typical Mexican bakery where you can purchase fresh bread, rolls and pastries. Café Caribe on Avenida 10 Sur offers ice cream, carrot cake and other sweets along with fresh-roasted coffee. When mangos are in season (during spring and summer), street vendors sell them on a stick, peeled and carved into different shapes.

After a strenuous day of diving, swimming or exploring, most visitors are content to turn in early. For after-dinner relaxation, the outdoor cafés around Plaza del Sol are pleasant places to enjoy the evening breeze. On Sunday evenings the plaza comes alive when families gather to hear Latin bands or be serenaded by mariachis. This is a good opportunity to mingle with the locals, who take tourism in stride and are friendly toward visitors.

For those with energy to burn, the ever-reliable Carlos 'n Charlie's, in the Punta Langosta Plaza on Avenida Rafael Melgar, about four blocks south of Plaza del Sol, is a raucous spot with beer-drinking contests and high-decibel music. Patrons also know what to expect at the Cozumel branch of the Hard Rock Café, Av. Rafael Melgar #2A (second floor), just north of Plaza del Sol.

The Fiesta Americana Cozumel Reef, south of San Miguel at Km 7.5 on the Costera Sur (Avenida Rafael Melgar), sponsors a Mexican theme night on selected evenings during the high season. A buffet dinner is accompanied by folkloric dance performances, mariachis and other entertainment; phone (987) 872-9600.

Tourist information office: second floor of the Plaza del Sol building, on the east side of the main plaza. Open Mon.-Fri. 9-3; phone (987) 872-7563.

What To See

ATLANTIS XII **SUBMARINE** departs from a pier at Carretera Km 4 (across the street from the Casa del Mar Hotel); passengers are taken from the pier to the submarine in small boats. It accommodates 48 passengers for a 45-minute undersea tour of reefs in Chankanaab Lagoon Park at depths of up to 100 feet. Large portholes running the length of the sub offer views of coral formations and marine life in crystal-clear water. **Note:** Entering the sub involves climbing down steep stairs. Children under age 3 are not permitted, and the trip is not advised for those prone to motion sickness or claustrophobia.

Sub departs daily (weather permitting) at 9, 10, 11, noon and 1. Fee $76 (U.S.); ages 3-12, $38. AX, MC, VI. For reservation information phone (888) 732-5782 in the United States, or (987) 872-5671 or (800) 715-0804 (toll-free long distance) within Mexico.

CHANKANAAB LAGOON PARK (Parque Laguna de Chankanaab) is about 8 km (5 mi.) south of town off the Costera Sur (Coastal Highway), the southward extension of

Avenida Rafael Melgar. The saltwater lagoon, sheltered Chankanaab Bay and the offshore Yukab Reef all provide sanctuary for a fascinating diversity of marine life, including coral, sponges, crustaceans, turtles, moray eels and tropical fish. A sunken boat, a religious statue and encrusted anchors and cannons in the bay are popular with divers and snorkelers; swimming and snorkeling are prohibited in the protected lagoon itself. The beach fronting the bay, lined with thatched *palapas* (shelters), is wide and pretty.

Surrounding the lagoon is a shady botanical garden with hundreds of tropical and subtropical plant species, many native to Cozumel; for a tip, local youths will give impromptu tours and point out the different flora and fauna. A small museum has exhibits about local plant, animal and marine life. There are several dive shops on site, as well as restrooms, changing areas and showers. Snorkeling equipment can be rented. Food is available. Daily 8-5. Admission around $10 (U.S.).

MUSEUM OF THE ISLAND OF COZUMEL (Museo de la Isla de Cozumel) is on Avenida Rafael Melgar north of the main square, between calles 4 and 6 Norte. This museum's four exhibit halls chronicle the island's human history, from its reputation as a revered Maya religious destination through pre-Hispanic trade and navigation to its settlement by Maya refugees from the 19th-century War of the Castes. An overview of natural history (with information in Spanish and English) focuses on endangered species and local plant and animal life.

A restaurant on the second floor has expansive waterfront views. Guided tours in English are available. Daily 9-5 (may vary seasonally). Admission $3 (U.S.).

PUNTA SUR PARK (Parque Punta Sur) is at the southern end of the Costera Sur (coastal highway). This national ecological reserve focuses on the conservation of local wildlife, including crocodiles, iguanas, egrets and herons, and therefore has few facilities. The Celarain Lighthouse (Faro de Celarain) stands at Cozumel's southern tip. Sand dunes surround the lighthouse, now a museum of navigation displaying artifacts retrieved from historical sites.

The sandy portion of the beach in the vicinity of the lighthouse is a turtle hatching area that is blocked off to visitors. Round-trip taxi service from San Miguel can be arranged. Cars are not permitted within the park, but transportation is provided to the different eco-zones. Daily 8-6. Admission $10 (U.S.).

SAN GERVASIO RUINS are east on the Carretera Transversal (Avenida Benito Juárez) to the San Gervasio turnoff, then about 7 km (4 mi.) north on a dirt access road to the entrance gate. Not nearly as impressive as other archeological sites on the Yucatán Peninsula, San Gervasio was nevertheless inhabited for more than 1,000 years. The restored

buildings are little more than walls of block stone with door entrances; they were formerly small temples and shrines built atop platforms.

Tour guides are available, but it's just as easy to explore with the aid of a green site map, sold at most gift shops in San Miguel. Cold beverages and snacks are available at the entrance. Daily 8-5; closed holidays. Admission $5 (U.S.). The fee for use of a video camera is $5. There also is a $1 road access fee charged per vehicle (pay at the entry gate at the San Gervasio turnoff). For a fee (negotiable, but expect to pay up to $50), a taxi driver will take you to the site entrance and wait while you view the ruins.

ISLA MUJERES, QUINTANA ROO
(G-12) pop. 10,800

Isla Mujeres (EES-lah moo-HEH-rehs), about 5 miles long and only half a mile wide, lies in the Caribbean Sea about 5 miles off the easternmost tip of the Yucatán Peninsula. Single male travelers anticipating their dreams to be realized on the "Island of Women" might be disappointed to find its male-female ratio rather balanced.

Gold-seeking Spanish explorers led by Francisco Hernández de Córdoba accidentally discovered Isla Mujeres in 1517 after a storm blew their expedition off course. The origin of the name is attributed to two legends. One maintains that seafaring buccaneers used the island as a hideaway for their female captives; more likely, however, is that it refers to the terra-cotta female images, decorated with fruit and flower adornments, that were discovered by the Spaniards.

Pirates and smugglers took advantage of the island's isolation. After their era passed, Isla Mujeres became just another drowsy Caribbean fishing village. During the 1960s beach bums and hippies ambled over from the mainland, taken in by Isla's laid-back atmosphere and languid beaches. More recently it has experienced tourist spillover from neighboring Cancún, but Isla's small size prevents the intensive development that characterizes the bigger resort.

More typically Yucatecan than either Cancún or Cozumel, Isla Mujeres has a relaxed pace and also a greater natural beauty. Flat, sandy beaches mark the northern end; rocky bluffs and submerged coral reefs the southern.

Practicalities

Isla Mujeres is accessible by ferry or boat from mainland Puerto Juárez (passengers only) or Punta Sam (passengers and/or vehicles), and from the piers at Playa Linda and Playa Langosta on Cancún Island. There are approximate hourly departures in each direction between Puerto Juárez and Isla Mujeres. Schedules are posted at the passenger ferry dock but are subject to change or delay; double check when the last ferry leaves Isla Mujeres for Puerto Juárez (usually around 6 p.m.).

Enclosed, air-conditioned passenger vessels hold about 30 occupants and make the trip in about 20 minutes; one-way fare is 40 pesos (about $4 U.S.). The fare is paid after you board. Organized cruise excursions from Cancún usually sail once a day and cost considerably more. The car ferry from Punta Sam operates several times daily, barring bad weather; again, double check the schedule. For additional information about ferry service, *see "Sightseeing" under Cancún, page 91.*

There is no reason to bring a car onto the island for a day trip. If you're basing a vacation in Isla Mujeres and have several pieces of luggage, taxis line up by the two town docks for the short ride to the hotels concentrated in town and scattered along the beaches. The fare shouldn't be more than a dollar or two. Taxis also can be hired (at an hourly rate) for a tour of the island or to reach beaches at the southern end. A municipal bus travels from the Posada del Mar Hotel on Avenida Rueda Medina south to Playa Lancheros; the fare is inexpensive. The tourist information office *(see below)* can provide bus schedules.

Renting a "moto," the local term for mopeds, or an electric golf cart is an easy way to get around, and there are several places in town that rent both (many of the hotels also rent golf carts). Keep in mind, however, that the rental fee does not include insurance. Some hotels also rent bicycles, which cost considerably less.

The "downtown" section of Isla Mujeres occupies its northern end. The waterfront street, referred to locally as the *malecón,* is Avenida Rueda Medina. It also runs the length of the island. In town, the principal thoroughfares are north-south avenidas Guerrero and Hidalgo, and east-west avenidas Madero and Morelos. There is little traffic on these narrow, one-way, pedestrian-friendly streets. The ferry docks, most of Isla's hotels, restaurants and shops, City Hall, the police station, a supermarket, travel agencies, *casas de cambio* (currency exchange offices), a couple of *farmacias* (pharmacies), the post office and several Internet cafes are all within a compact area of about four by six blocks.

Islander, a monthly magazine available at hotels, provides tourist information. A Cruz Roja (Red Cross) clinic is about 5 kilometers (3 miles) south of town, just north of the Hacienda Mundaca; phone (998) 877-0280.

What To Do on the Island

The most popular beach is Playa Norte, located at the northern edge of town. This stretch used to be called Playa Cocos before Hurricane Gilbert destroyed most of its namesake coconut palms in 1988. The shallow, placid waters are good for swimming or wading; there are, however, no lifeguards on duty. The wide beach is lined with thatched-roof *palapas* selling cold drinks. Umbrellas, chairs, jet-skis, sailboards, three-wheeled water "trikes" and other equipment can be rented. **Note:** Topless sunbathers may be encountered at this beach.

Other options are Playa Lancheros and Playa Garrafón, both toward the opposite end of the island on the western (leeward) side (the surf is rougher along Isla's eastern coastline, which faces the open Caribbean). Playa Lancheros is the southernmost beach on the local bus route.

At the very southern tip of the island, on a bluff overlooking the sea, once stood the reconstructed remains of a Maya temple believed to have been built in honor of the fertility goddess Ixchel. Archeologists believe that the Maya, en route to Cozumel on pilgrimages to worship Ixchel, stopped over at Isla Mujeres. Gilbert reduced it to a pile of stones, but there are fine views of the sea. A 30-foot-tall lighthouse nearby was left standing. A taxi ride from downtown costs about $4 (U.S.).

Branching east off Rueda Medina, a paved road follows the eastern edge of the island back toward town. One justification for bringing a car to Isla Mujeres is to drive this route, stopping at one of the pull-offs for a view of the open sea.

Offshore coral reefs and the Cave of the Sleeping Sharks (Cueva de Los Tiburones Durmientes) attract scuba divers. The underwater cave, off the northern tip of Contoy Island National Park *(see attraction listing under "What To See"),* was discovered in the late 1960s. The reason for the sharks' seemingly narcotized state has been attributed to everything from varying salinity levels to lack of carbon dioxide in the underwater caverns to constant currents that supply the oxygen allowing the creatures to remain stationary. Whatever the cause, this is a challenging dive to depths of 150 feet or more, with no guarantee that the sharks will be around. Manchones Reef, just off the island's southern tip, also is good for diving and snorkeling.

The summer months of June, July and August, when the water is calm, are best for diving. The Bahía Dive Shop, on Avenida Rueda Medina across from the ferry dock, offers certification classes. Their knowledgeable instructors can arrange fishing excursions as well as a trip to the Cave of the Sleeping Sharks; phone (998) 877-0340. Coral Scuba Dive Center, Av. Matamoros #13-A at Avenida Rueda Medina (three blocks north of the passenger ferry dock), also offers certified instruction and organizes snorkeling and fishing trips; phone (998) 877-0763.

The Boatmen's Cooperative (Cooperativa Isla Mujeres), on Avenida Rueda Medina at the foot of Avenida Madero (near the ferry dock), handles snorkeling and sport fishing excursions as well as day trips to Isla Contoy *(see attraction listing).* Some outings require a minimum number of passengers. Billfish (swordfish and marlin) are a good possibility in April and May; during the rest of the year catches include bonito, grouper and red snapper.

Shopping, Dining and Nightlife

Although craft shop prices are lower than in Cancún, bargaining is still the best way to come out ahead. Wood carvings, ceramic and clay figurines, silver items, pottery, handmade clothing, T-shirts, and decorative objects made of sea and snail shells are among the possible purchases. Several small shops are along Rueda Medina near the passenger ferry dock. Van Cleef & Arpels, at avenidas Juárez and Morelos, has a great selection of jewelry.

One of the nicest restaurants on the island is Zazil-Ha, in the Hotel Na Balam on Calle Zazil (at Playa Norte). The seafood dishes are well-prepared, and diners have a choice of eating indoors or in an open-air garden setting. Pizza Rolandi, on Avenida Hidalgo between avenidas Madero and Abasolo, is a reliable chain that features pizza, calzones and pasta dishes along with fish. There are branches in Cancún and Cozumel as well. For something out of the ordinary, stop by the Mercado Municipal (Municipal Market), Avenida Guerrero next to the post office, and sample the fare at one of the cooking stalls.

Isla Mujeres is not known for frenetic nightlife, which suits most visitors just fine. The *palapas* along Playa Norte are a great place for sunset-watching. Most of the restaurant bars have a late afternoon happy hour, and a few offer live music and dancing.

Tourist information office: Av. Rueda Medina #130, between Madero and Morelos (just north of the ferry dock). Open Mon.-Fri. 8-8, Sat.-Sun. 8-2; phone (998) 877-0767.

What To See

CONTOY ISLAND NATIONAL PARK (Parque Nacional Isla Contoy) is about 32 km (20 mi.) north of Isla Mujeres. The uninhabited island is the site of a wildlife reserve and bird sanctuary. Four miles long and half a mile wide, Contoy has nature trails winding through tropical vegetation (bring insect repellent). Pelicans, egrets, cormorants and flamingos are among the species that nest here. In addition to park rangers, iguanas, turtles and hermit crabs live on the island, and marine life—which includes seasonal armies of migrating lobsters—is plentiful. There also is a fine outdoor nature museum.

Contoy is protected and can only be visited on a guided tour. Take one of the tours that leave from Isla Mujeres, which are run by people familiar with the island and dedicated to preserving its natural environment. Activities include birdwatching, snorkeling, trolling for fish and hiking on the island. The La Isleña travel agency, in town at avenidas Morelos and Juárez, organizes Contoy trips in boats that carry up to 15 passengers; life jackets, snorkeling equipment and lunch are provided. Tours around $40 (U.S.). Phone (998) 877-0578.

DOLPHIN DISCOVERY is on Treasure Island via a bridge across Makax Lagoon (Laguna Makax). At this facility visitors can enjoy an interactive swim with dolphins. The 1-hour program includes an educational video (watching it is required before you can enter the water) and 30 minutes in the water

along with a trainer. Ferry transportation from Cancún departs daily at 9 and 11 a.m. and 1 p.m. from the Playa Langosta dock, Km 5 on Boulevard Kukulcán, and leaves Isla Mujeres at noon, 4:15 and 6 p.m.; round-trip fare is $13 (U.S.).

Food is available. Allow 2 hours minimum. Encounters take place daily beginning at 10, noon, 2 and 3:30. The cost is $119 U.S. (adult or child over age 8). Advance reservations are necessary; for information phone (998) 877-0207, or (998) 849-4757 in Cancún.

GARRAFON is off Av. Rueda Medina at Punta Sur, the southern tip of the island. Formerly a national park but now managed by the owners of Xcaret (*see Playa del Carmen*), Garrafón has appropriated some of that attraction's theme park characteristics. Much of the offshore coral reef here was killed by Hurricane Gilbert in 1988, as well as by the dropped anchors of too many tour boats (a practice now outlawed), but snorkelers can still see tropical fish in calm, shallow water. Sea Trek allows you to observe marine life on an underwater stroll at depths of up to 13 feet via compressed air fed into a diving helmet.

In order to protect the environment, use of biodegradable sunscreen and insect repellent (available in the park's gift shop) is advised. Locker rooms and showers are available.

Daily 9-5:30. Admission includes use of all park facilities as well as life jackets, inner tubes and kayaks, plus transportation from Cancún (cruise boat) or downtown Isla Mujeres (taxi). All-inclusive packages from Cancún throw in a meal at one of the park's restaurants, snorkeling gear, and locker and towel use. Cancún trips depart from the El Embarcadero dock, Km 4 on the bay side of Boulevard Kukulcán. Admission $29 (U.S.); ages 4-8, $11.50. All-inclusive package $54 (U.S.); ages 4-8, $27. Snorkel gear rental $10 (U.S.), towels $2, lockers $2. Sea Trek and some other activities are extra. AX, MC, VI. Phone (998) 877-1100 or (998) 849-4950 (Garrafón cruise reservations).

HACIENDA MUNDACA is east off Av. Rueda Medina and across from the entrance to Playa Lancheros. A stone archway is practically all that's left of the former estate built by 19th-century pirate and slave runner Fermín Mundaca. Legend has it that Mundaca built the hacienda for La Trigueña (The Brunette), an 18-year-old girl with whom he had fallen in love. When she married a local man, Mundaca was inconsolable. His grave, in the municipal cemetery at the northern end of the island, is marked with the inscription "As you are I was, as I am you will be."

A dirt footpath leads to the ruins. Insect repellent is highly advised. Daily 10-6. Admission around $2 (U.S.).

IZAMAL, YUCATAN (G-11) pop. 14,300

A significant pre-Columbian political and religious center, Izamal (ee-sah-MAHL) developed around a Franciscan monastery. Diego de Landa, the Spanish bishop responsible for the annihilation of most of the Maya civilization's *codices* (picture books) and documents, deliberately chose Izamal as the seat of his diocese because it was a religious center of the Maya-speaking tribe known as the Itzae.

Izamal was a center of commerce and trade during the Spanish colonial period. When Mérida took over as the Yucatán's chief city, it slipped into obscurity. One recent momentous event in this slow-paced town was a 1993 visit by Pope John Paul II. The mustard-colored government buildings surrounding the central plaza give it the nickname "Ciudad Amarilla" (Yellow City). A relaxing way to view the colonial-era architecture is by horse-drawn carriage; rides can be arranged at the plaza, where the guides congregate.

Dilapidated houses and commercial buildings attest to the poverty that most Yucatecans endure. Downtown clusters around the small central plaza, shaded by trees and furnished with wrought-iron benches.

About 74 kilometers (46 miles) east of Mérida via two-lane Mex. 180, Izamal makes for an interesting day trip. From Mérida, watch for the signed turnoff that says "Yuc. 53"; if approaching from Cancún, the signed turnoff from toll highway Mex. 180-D says "Izamal" and also merges into Yuc. 53. The narrow, two-lane road, which has no shoulders and occasional potholes, passes through thick green scrubland interspersed with fields of spiky, blue-green agave plants.

Between the 180-D turnoff and Izamal—a distance of about 18 kilometers (11 miles)—are three small villages: Xanaba, Sudzal and Cuauhtémoc. Cobbled *topes* (speed bumps) force vehicles to slow to a crawl when entering each one, as do the wandering dogs, chickens, turkeys and children. Xanaba has a large yellow church with white trim opposite its small central plaza. In Sudzal and Cuauhtémoc you'll see typical Maya houses—thatch-roofed huts with open doorways, dirt floors and walls constructed of upright wooden stakes—surrounded by banana trees and other tropical vegetation. This is rural life at its most basic, a world away from Cancún's glitter and Mérida's big-city bustle.

From Izamal, there are two ways to return to Mex. 180: Backtrack on Yuc. 53, or take another local road to the small town of Hoctún (which is on Mex. 180). The latter route passes through Citilcum and Kimbila en route; all three villages are representative of the rural Yucatán countryside. Make certain you're back on Mex. 180 before dark.

Because of the slow-paced driving conditions and the fact that it's easy to lose your orientation in Izamal—small as it is—this trip is most conveniently taken with a hired taxi driver or guide from Mérida. Check with one of the city's tour operators or arrange for a driver through your hotel.

FRANCISCAN MONASTERY dominates the plaza. It was originally dedicated to St. Anthony of Padua and was later known as the Church of Our Lady of Izamal. It was completed in 1561 atop a Maya pyramid. In 1618, monks added the monastery and an arcade. The atrium of this enormous church is reputed to be second in size to that of St. Peter's Basilica in Rome. The church's simple, mustard-colored exterior contrasts with the rough-hewn, fortresslike monastery compound; the original access ramps and stairways built by the Maya remain.

KINICH KAKMO PYRAMID (Pirámide Kinich Kakmo) is a few blocks north of the central plaza. In the Maya language, its name means "Solar-Faced Macaw of Fire." Kinich Kakmo is one of Mexico's largest pyramids—some 115 feet high and almost 660 feet wide. It sits in the middle of town; there are houses just across the street. One of the four sides remains unexcavated and is covered with a thick green matting of tangled underbrush. Admission is charged.

MERIDA, YUCATAN (G-11)
pop. 680,300, metro area 875,200

Capital of the state of Yucatán and metropolis of the Yucatán Peninsula, Mérida (MEH-ree-dah) fits the description of a "colonial city" but somehow seems different from other places in Mexico. It is a peculiar mixture of the modern and the timeless, presenting the visitor with images both comfortingly familiar and exotically foreign.

Mérida was founded in 1542 by Francisco de Montejo (the son of Montejo the Elder) at the site of T'ho, an ancient Maya city. The crumbling temples and palaces at the site were razed to make way for cathedrals, ornate mansions and parks, many of which survive to this day. Over time Mérida became the commercial, governmental and religious center of the Yucatán, with the Spaniards living in luxury made possible by Indian toil.

Mérida became even wealthier in the last half of the 19th century because of a tough, thorny plant. Henequén, a member of the agave family, thrived in the rocky soil and seasonally dry conditions prevalent in the northern Yucatán. The fibrous leaves were made into a variety of products, including twine, burlap sacks, furniture stuffing and hammocks. Although sophisticated machinery now processes, weaves and dyes henequén fibers, in the heyday of the large haciendas (plantations) Indian field workers manipulated this intractable plant by hand.

By World War I the city claimed more millionaires per capita than any other in the world as a result of the monopoly on sisal fiber, the valuable henequén extract. The product was named after the port town of Sisal, 50 kilometers (31 miles) northwest of Mérida, from where it was once shipped.

Although plantation barons were swimming in the revenue generated by this profitable export, they were an island unto themselves. The Yucatán Peninsula was still considered Mexico's mosquito-ridden backwater, and a lack of road and rail access isolated it as well. As a result, privileged Meridanos looked to Europe as their model for cultural sophistication. Fueled by henequén's "green gold," they built imposing, Moorish- and rococo-style mansions with arched doorways and marbled tile interiors. These buildings line Paseo Montejo, Mérida's wide showcase boulevard, and give the city its air of graceful elegance.

The henequén haciendas are long abandoned now, although some have been turned into luxury hotels and spas. As in other large Mexican cities, tourism is becoming a leading industry. Mérida's tropical ambience and variety of cultural offerings make it an established destination among European travelers. It also is the most convenient base from which to explore nearby archeological ruins or the Yucatán's northern and western coasts.

Planning Your Stay

Many Yucatán travelers bypass Mérida in favor of Cancún and the Mexican Caribbean coast, but the city is a fascinating travel destination in its own right. There's plenty to do: visiting the museums and public buildings that cluster around the main square, Plaza de la Independencia (also called Plaza Grande); wandering through the bustling market district; taking a horse-drawn carriage ride down Paseo Montejo; or sampling authentic Yucatecan cuisine at local restaurants

Perhaps no other city in Mexico offers as many outdoor performances as Mérida, where there is something going on every day of the week. Better yet, most of the evening concerts or folkloric shows held at the downtown plazas are free.

For *Mérida en Domingo* (Mérida on Sunday), the streets surrounding Plaza de la Independencia are closed to traffic. Mexican families dressed in their Sunday best make for a great people-watching promenade as they stroll among the pushcart vendors selling *tortas* (sandwiches), corn on the cob and fruit drinks. Handicraft markets and food stalls set up shop around the plaza and also in Hidalgo Park and Santa Lucía Park.

Sunday also is one of the high points of Mérida's excellent public events program. In the late morning the city police orchestra performs typical Yucatecan music in Santa Lucía Park, on Calle 60 about three blocks north of Plaza de la Independencia. Groups of musicians in front of the Government Palace (Palacio del Gobierno), on Plaza de la Independencia, play everything from classical to jazz. A folkloric ballet interpretation of a Yucatecan wedding celebration is enacted at City Hall (Palacio Municipal), on the west side of Plaza de la Independencia, while marimba music percolates at Hidalgo Park (also called Cepeda Peraza Park), a block northeast of the main plaza at calles 59 and 60.

Saturday evenings also are active; the downtown area is closed to traffic, and restaurants move tables outside so diners can listen to the bands scattered around the plazas. The music starts at 8:30 and continues until around 2 a.m.

Guided tour operators abound in Mérida, and many of them offer the same destinations with differing forms of conveyance (from economical buses to luxurious private vehicles). City tours last a couple of hours and take in the public buildings around the main plaza, Paseo Montejo, and the Museum of Anthropology and History. Popular day trips travel to Chichén Itzá or Uxmal, with admission to the ruins, lunch, a guide and often a swim at a hotel pool included in the price.

Weatherwise, Mérida experiences sultry heat most of the year. April through September are quite hot and humid, and in May temperatures can soar above 100 degrees. If you're visiting during one of these months, sightsee in the morning, take it easy in the afternoon and venture out again in the evening, when it cools down somewhat. December through February have the most pleasant temperatures and lower humidity. The rainy season is June through September, but precipitation isn't usually heavy or persistent enough to affect travel plans. The greatest chance for hurricanes or other stormy weather is in September and October.

The city is very crowded in July and August, when many Mexican families go on vacation; if that's when you'll be there as well, make hotel reservations in advance.

Practicalities

Manuel Crecencio Rejon International Airport is off Avenida Benito Juárez, also called Avenida Itzáes (Mex. 180), about 7 kilometers (4 miles) southwest of the city center. Aeroméxico, phone (800) 021-4010 (toll-free long distance within Mexico) offers direct flights from Miami; Continental, phone (800) 900-5000 (toll-free long distance within Mexico), offers direct flights from Houston. Mexicana, phone (800) 509-8960 (toll-free long distance within Mexico), and the Mexicana subsidiary Aerocaribe, phone (999) 928-6790, offer connecting flights from various destinations in the Yucatán, including Cancún, Cozumel and Chetumal, as well as from Mexico City. For additional information about airlines see "Arriving by Air," page 551.

City bus #79 (designated "Aviación") takes airport passengers to the downtown area but is unreliable and slow; if you're carrying any amount of luggage it's more convenient to take a taxi. *Colectivo* (group) minivans transport passengers from the airport to downtown hotels for around $8 (U.S.) per person; taxi fare runs around $18 between the airport and downtown hotels.

The first-class bus station, Terminal CAME (CAH-me), is on Calle 70 between calles 69 and 71, about seven blocks southwest of Plaza de la Independencia. Buses travel frequently to and from Chichén Itzá, Uxmal, Cancún, Campeche, Playa del Carmen, Tulum and Palenque. "Deluxe" service to many of these destinations is offered by ADO's GL and UNO lines. For additional information about buses see "Bus Service," page 68.

Sitios (taxi stands) are located in the vicinity of Plaza de la Independencia, or use a cab affiliated with your hotel. Rates to in-town destinations are fixed and can be expensive; ask what the fare is before getting in the cab. *Colectivo* taxis (usually white Volkswagen minivans) also take passengers to various city destinations on a first-come, first-serve basis; look for these around Plaza de la Independencia.

Mérida has a tourist police force who patrol on foot and on motorcycle in the downtown core and also in the hotel zone, the area along Avenida Colón between Paseo Montejo and Calle 60. Officers wear white-and-brown or blue uniforms and a sleeve patch that says "Policia Turística." To contact police in case of an emergency, phone (999) 925-2555.

To register a complaint with the Consumer Protection Agency (Procuraduría del Consumidor), phone (999) 923-4927. If you lose your tourist permit, contact the Mexican Immigration Office; phone (999) 928-5823. In case of medical emergency, contact the Red Cross (Cruz Roja); phone (999) 924-9813.

Currency exchange is most conveniently expedited at your hotel front desk, as the rates offered by hotels, banks and *casas de cambio* (currency exchange offices) do not differ greatly. There's an exchange office next to the Hotel Fiesta Americana Mérida.

Approaches

By car, the main approach from the east is Mex. 180, which becomes east-west Calle 65 within the city limits. To get to the downtown hotel zone (where such major hotels as the Hyatt and the Fiesta Americana are located), take Calle 65 west to north-south Calle 60 and turn right.

Mex. 180 also approaches Mérida from the southwest via Campeche. Mex. 261 approaches from the south, joining Mex. 180 at the town of Umán, just south of the city limits. North of downtown, the northern extension of Calle 60 continues north as Mex. 261 to Progreso on the gulf coast.

A loop road, the Anillo Periférico, encircles Mérida, offering access to regional destinations without having to negotiate the downtown area. It can be confusing, however, unless you're familiar with the exits. If you're driving, the most direct way out of the city from the Paseo Montejo/hotel zone area is to take east-west Avenida Colón west to Avenida Itzaes, a major north-south thoroughfare on the west side of town. Turn left (south); you'll pass Centenario Park and the turnoff to the airport before reaching the Anillo Periférico—a distance of about 12 kilometers (7 miles).

Note: Avenida Itzaes changes names twice without warning—to Avenida Internacional and then to Avenida Benito Juárez—as it proceeds south. Don't get sidetracked by the name changes; stay on the avenue.

At the periférico junction there are signs for Cancún (Mex. 180 east), Progreso (Mex. 261 north) and Campeche (Mex. 180 southwest). To head south toward Uxmal and nearby archeological sites, continue south a mile or two on Avenida Itzaes/Internacional/Juárez to Umán. Watch for signs saying "To Campeche via Uxmal on Mex. 261," "Zona Arqueologica Uxmal" and "Ruta Puuc." Follow these signs to access Mex. 261 south.

To head east toward Cancún, turn left onto the periférico at the sign that says "Cancún/Motul." Take this four-lane divided highway about 15 kilometers (9 miles) to the Mex. 180/Cancún exit. From this point, two-lane Mex. 180 runs about 48 kilometers (30 miles) east to the town of Hoctún. At Km marker 66, Mex. 180 divides. The two-lane "libre" (free) road continues east toward the town of Kantunil, and the four-lane divided Mérida-Cancún "cuota" (toll) highway begins.

City Layout

Mérida has long been known as the "White City." Visual evidence does not automatically bear the name out (it could be the impression created by strong sunlight reflecting off the marble and stone surfaces of white buildings), but one thing is certain: The downtown core (often called *El Centro*) is compact, dense and an assault on the senses.

Downtown streets are laid out in a standard grid pattern radiating from the central plaza. They are numbered rather than named; even-numbered streets (calles) run north-south, odd-numbered streets run east-west. They are lined with many beautiful old buildings, and many more shabby ones. Most of these streets are narrow and one way. Vespa motor scooters and beat-up bikes abound, and traffic is heavy and slow. Elsewhere in the city thoroughfares are not well signed and change names without warning. They also can twist and turn confusingly, so know where you're going.

Note: In the *centro*, where buildings sit close together and sidewalks are very narrow, exhaust spewed by green city buses is a near-constant irritant. This central area is roughly bounded by Calle 49 on the north, Calle 67 on the south, Calle 52 on the east and Calle 66 on the west.

Fortunately Mérida also is a city of plazas, bursting with royal poinciana trees and other tropical greenery, that are oases of relative tranquility amid the street noise and traffic jams. Plaza de la Independencia is bounded east and west by calles 60 and 62 and north and south by calles 61 and 63. Here and at other city plazas you'll see *confidenciales*, S-shaped white stone benches that allow two people to face each other while talking. The cathedral and the aristocratic facades of government buildings border the plaza.

A good way to experience the local atmosphere is to stroll up and down Calle 60, a busy street filled with restaurants, handicraft shops selling clothing, jewelry and trinkets, and several fine examples of colonial architecture. From the northeast corner of Plaza de la Independencia, walk north. In the next block is cozy little Hidalgo Park, where there are several outdoor restaurants. At the corner of calles 60 and 57 is the imposing, Italianate Peón Contreras Theater (Teatro Peón Contreras); climb the marble steps and wander around inside.

Mérida's "show street" is four-lane Paseo Montejo, which begins at Calle 47, about seven blocks northeast of the main plaza. Broad and tree-lined, it also has much wider sidewalks than you'll encounter in other parts of the city, a relief from the cramped spaces of the *centro*. Montejo runs north for 10 blocks past hotels, shops, sidewalk cafés and several large, ornate 19th-century mansions. It culminates at the Monument to Patriotism (Monumento a la Patria), a grouping of sculptures within a traffic circle that depict various stages of Mexican history.

Mérida's streets were originally meant to accommodate *calesas* (horse-drawn carriages). Sunday is the best day to take a tour. Most of the carriages can be found in the vicinity of Plaza de la Independencia or along Calle 60, and they have designated routes. A 45-minute ride should cost from $15 to $20 (U.S.); determine the fare before you set out.

Shopping

Shopping is serious business in Mérida, where a multitude of goods are offered for sale. The city is particularly known for hammocks *(hamacas)*, clothing (especially the men's shirt called a *guayabera)*, Panama hats *(jipis)* and henequén handicrafts.

The market district spreads across several blocks and encompasses hundreds of shops and open-air stalls. Roughly, the area extends from calles 63 to 69 north-south and from calles 54 to 62 east-west (the area just southeast of Plaza de la Independencia). The Municipal Market (Mercado Municipal), centered at calles 65 and 56, is a dizzying hodgepodge of fruit, vegetables, live chickens, tortilla stands, spices and candy, all presided over by *huipil*-clad *señoras* who have brought their wares from the small Maya villages around Mérida. Among the items for sale are baskets, pottery, gold earrings, gold and silver filigree jewelry, and pieces of amber-colored incense.

Native handicrafts from all over Mexico, but particularly the Yucatán region, are in a separate building at calles 56 and 67. Look for table mats, purses, leather goods, hammocks, piñatas, clothing, ceramics and *huaraches* (sandals with leather straps and soles made from old tires). Fixed prices prevail at many shops, but you can bargain at some of the market stalls and with street vendors.

Note: Haggling in this crowded, noisy atmosphere is not for everyone. Although many vendors speak English, a knowledge of Spanish would be very handy for asking specific questions about merchandise. If you're uncomfortable around high-pressure sales tactics, stick to the fixed-price shops.

Hammocks—often used in the rural Yucatán in place of beds—are fashioned from various materials and come in several sizes. To judge the proper size, hold one end of the hammock even with the top of your head. Let the other end drop—if it reaches the floor and then some, it's probably big enough. Those made from cotton tend to be the most durable. Ask for a demonstration; loosely woven hammocks are an indication of poor quality.

Street vendors will assail prospective hammock purchasers, but their low prices may also indicate low quality. Shops specializing in hammocks offer a greater selection. Wherever you buy a hammock, check the workmanship carefully, since a poorly made one will wear out quickly.

The *guayabera,* a loosely worn, lightweight cotton shirt, is about as formal as men's clothing gets in sweltering Mérida. Upper-class Yucatecans in the late 19th century bought them during trips to Cuba. The garment is worn by businessmen and local politicians instead of a shirt and tie. Traditionally it is white, with a bit of colored embroidery around the front buttons, and has four pockets—two at the chest and two at the waist. Guayaberas Jack, on Calle 59, is one of the few city factories that still produces custom-made shirts.

Just as traditional as the *guayabera* is the *huipil,* a white cotton dress with a squared neck that often is edged with embroidered flowers. A similar but longer and more elaborate garment is the *terno.* Many women who live in rural areas still wear *huipils.* Handmade garments have largely been supplanted by machine-made ones, although the latter are usually of good quality.

A jauntily positioned *jipi* (HEE-pee) provides an effective screen against the hot Yucatán sun. The hats are made in several small towns in neighboring Campeche; residents store palm fronds in damp basements until they become soft and pliable, then weave them. Panama hats cost anywhere from about $6 to more than $60 (U.S.); the price is determined by the closeness of the weave and the quality of the fibers (coarse to fine). A good-quality, closely woven hat should bounce back into shape even after being folded into a suitcase or rolled up and stuck in a pocket.

Mexican markets are known for their exotica, and Mérida is no exception; here you can buy live "jeweled" beetle pins called *maquech* (maKETCH). The insects are displayed in glass bowls along with a few pieces of wood (their food). Bits of multicolored glass are glued to their backs, and the beetle is attached to a gold chain which hooks to a safety pin. If you do choose to indulge in a live lapel ornament, find another buyer before you leave the country; U.S. Customs and Border Protection officials won't allow it across the border.

Dining and Nightlife

Be sure to sample some of the culinary specialties associated with the Yucatán. *Papadzules* are tortillas stuffed with chopped hard-boiled eggs and topped with pumpkinseed or tomato sauce. *Pocchuc* is slices of pork marinated in the juice of sour oranges and served with pickled onions; *pollo pibil* is herb-infused chicken wrapped in banana leaves and baked.

Sopa de lima is a soup containing shredded chicken and strips of fried tortilla and flavored with lime juice. *Salbutes* are puffy fried tortillas topped with shredded turkey, lettuce and pickled onions. The incendiary habanero chile is provided on the side rather than in the dish at most establishments (ask to make doubly sure).

Beverages are intriguing as well. While *licuados*—liquified fruit drinks—are sold in many parts of Mexico, they are especially refreshing in Mérida, where the vendors can draw from a variety of melons, pineapple and other tropical flavors. *Licuado* stands are marked by rows of colorful fruit.

More unusual are drinks quaffed for centuries by the Maya and their descendants. One example is *horchata*, a blend of ground rice and almonds, water and ice, sweetened with raw sugar, cinnamon, vanilla or honey.

Café Montejo, in the lobby of the Hotel Fiesta Americana Mérida, is a pleasant spot for lunch or dinner. For a list of AAA-RATED establishments in Mérida, *see the Lodgings & Restaurants section.*

Mérida is a friendly city, and one that's fairly safe to walk around in after dark. At dusk, Plaza de la Independencia and adjoining Hidalgo Park are alive with crowds watching street performers, listening to musicians, grabbing a bite to eat or just relaxing on benches. Sidewalk vendors set up along nearby streets, and a head-spinning array of stores and walk-in eateries sell everything from *tortas* to heavy metal CDs. To fully experience this vibrancy, hit the streets on your own two feet.

There is free evening entertainment at downtown parks and plazas several nights a week, courtesy of an active cultural arts scene. On Monday beginning at 9 p.m. a folkloric dance troupe performs *vaquerías* (traditional Yucatecan dances) in front of City Hall (Palacio Municipal), on Calle 62 across from Plaza de la Independencia. For event schedule information, check with the information center in the Peón Contreras Theater or one of the city tourist offices.

Yucatán State Tourism Office: in the Peón Contreras Theater, on Calle 60 between calles 57 and 59. The office is open daily 8-8; phone (999) 924-9290 (English spoken). There also is a branch of the State Tourism Office inside the Government Palace (Palacio de Gobierno) on the main plaza. Another office is on the second level of the Century XXI Yucatán Convention Center, north of downtown on Calle 60 (the road to Progreso). It is open daily 9-7; phone (999) 930-3760.

The publication *Yucatán Today,* available at the airport and most hotels, has detailed information about city and state attractions and includes maps.

What To See
Downtown

CATHEDRAL (Catedral) is on the east side of Plaza de la Independencia, opposite the Government Palace. Much of the stone used in its construction came from the ruined buildings of T'hó, the ancient Maya city upon which Mérida was built. The interior is stark, in marked contrast to the lavish decoration of other Mexican colonial churches. One painting, hanging over a side door to the right of the main altar, depicts a meeting between the Spanish and the Xiu Indians.

To the left is a chapel containing a replica of the Christ of the Blisters (Cristo de las Ampollas), an image of Christ carved from a tree that was said to be struck by lightning but did not burn; it survived a fire in another church and was brought to the cathedral in 1645. Daily 6 a.m.-noon and 4-7. Free.

CITY HALL (Palacio Municipal) is on Calle 62 on the west side of Plaza de la Independencia. More commonly known as the Ayuntamiento, it was built atop a Maya pyramid. The exterior, yellow with white trim, shows a Moorish influence, and the clock tower is typical of Mexican government buildings. Adjoining it is the Olimpo, a cultural center with space for concerts and art exhibitions; schedules for upcoming performances are posted on the bulletin board in the pretty courtyard.

CITY MUSEUM (Museo de la Ciudad) is at calles 61 and 58 across the street from Plaza de la Independencia. It has paintings, photographs and drawings illustrating Mérida's history, with exhibit information in English. Tues.-Sun. 10-2 (also Tues.-Fri. 4-8). Free.

GOVERNMENT PALACE (Palacio de Gobierno) is on the north side of Plaza de la Independencia. It dates from 1892. Take the wide stairway to the second floor, where the walls of one room are adorned with murals by Meridano artist Fernando Castro Pacheco depicting traditional Maya symbology as well as the violent appropriation of their culture by the Spanish. A hall of history, also on the second floor, chronicles the destruction by Spanish bishop Diego de Landa of the Maya *codices*, pictorial history books. Daily 8-8. Free.

MACAY MUSEUM (Museo de Arte Contemporáneo Ateneo de Yucatán) is on Calle 60, facing the cathedral. It exhibits the work of regional artists in two floors of rooms built around an interior patio. Wed.-Mon. 10-6. Admission around $4 (U.S.); free to all Sun.

MONTEJO HOUSE (Casa de Montejo) is on Calle 63 (south side of Plaza de la Independencia). It was built in 1549 by the son of Francisco de Montejo, the Yucatán conqueror. Montejo the Younger employed Indian labor to create the richly ornamented facade and doors, fine examples of Plateresque decoration. A reminder of Spanish cruelty are the carvings of *conquistadores* with feet firmly planted on top of wailing Maya heads. This restored family home now houses a Banamex Bank branch with a huge, lushly landscaped patio. Business hours Mon.-Fri. 9-5, Sat. 9-2.

NATIONAL MUSEUM OF POPULAR ART (Museo Nacional de Arte Popular) is six blocks east of the plaza on Calle 59, between calles 48 and 50. It is housed in one of Mérida's venerable mansions. The collection of Yucatecan handicrafts here includes regional costumes, pottery, masks, woven baskets, musical instruments and beautifully carved conch shells. Tues.-Sat. 9-6. Admission around $2 (U.S.)..

PEON CONTRERAS THEATER (Teatro Peón Contreras) is on Calle 60 between calles 57 and 59, just north of Cepeda Peraza Park (Hidalgo Park). It was built in the early 20th century in the grand Italianate style of European opera houses. The main entrance features a staircase of Carrara marble, and the interior is typically and richly ornate. This venue for the performing arts also houses a tourist information center that is a good place to find out what's going on around town.

In and Around the City

ANTHROPOLOGY MUSEUM (Museo Regional de Antropología) is on Paseo Montejo at Calle 43. It is housed in the Palacio Cantón, the former home of Mérida's prominent Cantón family. The museum has an extensive collection of stone carvings, figurines and relics, including jade and gold objects retrieved from the Sacred Cenote at Chichén Itzá. Particularly interesting are the sections devoted to daily Maya life, showing how babies' heads were elongated and how teeth were filed to achieve their rather bizarre standards of beauty.

Exhibit information is mostly in Spanish. Tues.-Sat. 8-8, Sun. 8-2. Admission around $5 (U.S.); free to all Sun.

CENTENARIO PARK AND ZOO is about 12 blocks west of Plaza de la Independencia, running along Av. Itzáes between calles 59 and 65. Handsome, colonial-style yellow stone archways flank the park entrance. It is large, shady and particularly fun for children. The zoo displays a variety of animals and birds, from peacocks and flamingos to alligators, lions and jaguars, as well as species native to the Yucatán Peninsula. A miniature train offers rides through the park. Park open Tues.-Sun. 6-6, zoo Tues.-Sun. 8-5. Free.

DZIBILCHALTUN (zeeb-eel-chal-TOON) is about 15 km (9 mi.) north of Mérida; take Calle 60 north out of the city, following signs for Progreso and Mex. 261. The paved turnoff is marked by a sign that says "Dzibilchaltún/Universidad del Mavab." The site entrance is another 5 km (3 mi.) east. Although this is one of Mexico's largest archeological discoveries, not much remains of its former glory. More than 8,000 structures, mostly mounds of rubble or the remains of low platforms, have been uncovered so far.

The reconstructed Temple of the Seven Dolls (Templo de las Siete Muñecas) was named for the seven primitive figures discovered buried under the structure's floor. Exhibiting such deformities as a hunchback and a swollen belly, they may have served as spiritual "messengers" during ceremonies to cure illness. Museo del Pueblo Maya, a museum

on the grounds, exhibits Maya and Spanish artifacts from archeological sites throughout the Yucatán. Ruins daily 8-5; museum Tues.-Sun. 8-4. Admission (includes museum) around $7 (U.S.); free to all Sun. There is an additional fee for parking.

HERMITAGE OF SANTA ISABEL (La Hermita de Santa Isabel) is south of Plaza de la Independencia at calles 66 and 77. It was built in 1748. In colonial days it became known as the Convent of Safe Travel, since travelers on their way to the busy port of Campeche would stop to pray for a safe journey. The restored hermitage is surrounded by a serene, pretty garden accented with Maya and Toltec statues and a waterfall.

MAYAPAN is about 56 km (35 mi.) southeast of Mérida. To get there, take Mex. 18, a narrow, two-lane paved road that passes through the villages of Kanasin, Acanceh and Tecoh; about 10 km (6 mi.) south of Tecoh, watch for the signed turnoff to Mayapán. This walled city flourished after the heyday of Chichén Itzá and Uxmal; it was reduced to rubble in the 16th century by Spanish conqueror Francisco de Montejo's forces.

Numerous broken pyramids and buildings are overgrown with dense forest. One pyramid, Castillo de Kukulcán, can be climbed. A relative lack of restoration work means few visitors, and those fascinated by ruins will have the crumbling temple platforms and weathered sculptures of the feathered serpent-god Quetzalcóatl basically to themselves. Site daily 8-5. Admission around $4 (U.S.); free to all Sun. The fee to use a video camera is $5.

Nearby Destinations

A day trip possibility from Mérida is to the fishing village of Celestún, on the western Yucatán coast. To get there, take Mex. 281 (Calle 59A within the city) about 97 kilometers (60 miles) west. En route are the towns of Hunucma and Kinchil, as well as fields of henequén and old haciendas that drove this once-thriving industry.

The village sits at the tip of a strip of land separating the Celestún Estuary (ría in Spanish) from the Gulf of Mexico. The atmosphere is decidedly laid-back; there are no resort amenities here. A stretch of white-sand swimming beach is at the north edge of town, although constant winds make the water choppy and silt-laden. The harbor is picturesque in a scruffy sort of way, filled with small boats and fishing nets drying in the sun.

The main reason to visit Celestún is the surrounding wildlife refuge, home to a large colony of flamingos. While these spindly-legged, coral-plumaged birds are the area's most spectacular residents, numerous species of waterfowl also live here. In addition, Celestún is on the flyway of many species migrating from northern climates to South America.

Tours of the estuary can be arranged just past the bridge leading into town, where there is a parking lot, ticket window, restrooms and a snack bar. The fare for a 75-minute tour is about $45 (U.S.) per boat (cash only), in canopied boats that accommodate up to six passengers. Bring sunscreen and water. The tour includes birdwatching (in addition to flamingos, you're likely to see pelicans, herons, egrets, spoonbills and ducks) as well as an excursion through dense mangroves to a freshwater spring welling up within the saltwater estuary. The number of flamingos seen depends on the season, tide and time of day, but in any event refrain from encouraging your boat captain to get too close, which causes the birds undue stress.

Just outside the Mérida city limits via Mex. 180 (Avenida Itzáes), a short distance south of the Anillo Periférico loop road, is Umán, a typical Yucatecan small town. Around the main plaza, which is dominated by a large church, are small shops, sidewalk vendors and a lineup of *triciclos* that transport local passengers as well as sightseeing visitors.

Hacienda Yaxcopoil is about 34 kilometers (21 miles) south of Mérida via Mex. 180 to Umán, then south on Mex. 261 (follow the signs for Uxmal). The small village of Yaxcopoil (yawsh-koe-poe-EEL) is about 10 kilometers (6 miles) south of Umán; watch for the marked turnoff to the hacienda ("Antigua Hacienda y Museo Yaxcopoil") on your right.

Although now showing great age and some ruin, the Moorish-style architecture of the main buildings hints at the gracious lifestyle once enjoyed by wealthy 19th-century henequén plantation owners. The property is safe to visit and interesting to explore. Open Mon.-Sat. 8-6, Sun. 9-1. Admission around $4 (U.S.), under 12 free. Phone (999) 927-2606.

PLAYA DEL CARMEN, QUINTANA ROO (G-12) pop. 47,200

Playa del Carmen once was the mainland departure point for Maya pilgrims visiting the sanctuaries and temples on Cozumel. Its relation to the island continued as the canoes were supplanted by ferries bearing not worshippers but tourists. More than just a ferry stop, rapidly growing "Playa" has become a tourist destination in its own right.

The main road to town branches east off Mex. 307 about 68 kilometers (42 miles) south of Cancún. The rundown houses and small stores lining this scruffy street are typical of Mexican small towns. "Downtown" encompasses about 10 blocks and is easily walkable; north-south Avenida 5, just inland from the beach, is a pedestrian-only thoroughfare between calles 1 and 6 that is lined with cafes and shops.

Playa's beaches have the powdery sand and beautiful turquoise water characteristic of the entire Mexican coast, and an offshore reef guarantees good snorkeling and diving. The air of funky informality attracts both a young crowd and European vacationers, and topless sunbathing is nonchalantly accepted (although against the law in Mexico).

South of the ferry dock is the newer hotel zone, Playacar. Residential homes, condominiums, hotels and all-inclusive resorts frequented by Europeans are within this designated area; the cobblestoned main thoroughfare is called Paseo Xaman-Ha (sha-MAN hah). A genuine lodging bargain might be found here during the off season (after Easter through November). Cruise ship passengers and day visitors from Cancún take advantage of Playacar Club de Golf, a public, 18-hole golf course designed by Robert Von Hagge that includes an outstanding clubhouse and pro shop. Greens fees drop significantly if you're a guest at a hotel affiliated with the club.

Ferries carry passengers between Playa del Carmen and Cozumel *(see separate listing within this region)*. The centrally located ferry dock is off Avenida 5, about two blocks south of the main plaza. Cars are not transported; there is a guarded parking lot across the street from the dock. The trip to Cozumel takes about 45 minutes. There are two types of ferries—older, open-air boats and the MV *Mexico*, an enclosed, jet-propelled, air-conditioned vessel. Tickets are purchased at the dock's ticket booth and cost around $10 (U.S.).

There are approximate hourly crossings between Playa del Carmen and Cozumel daily from around 6 a.m. to 9 p.m. Double-check the regularly changing schedule at the dock, and in particular confirm the time of the last departure from Cozumel if you're planning a day trip to the island. **Note:** Ferry schedules also are subject to change due to weather conditions, as seas can sometimes be quite rough; make sure you carry appropriate medication if you're prone to seasickness.

Nearby Destinations

PUERTO AVENTURAS is 20 km (12 mi.) south of Playa del Carmen off Mex. 307. This planned resort community of hotels and condominiums has its own golf course, marina and dive center, plus shops and restaurants. The landscaped grounds are adorned with imported palms and orchids. Tennis, swimming, scuba diving, deep-sea fishing and a swim with dolphins are among the activities offered.

CEDAM Museum is at the resort. The Center for the Study of Aquatic Sports in Mexico salutes Mexico's divers. It displays the tools of their trade and the treasures—goblets, gold coins, medallions, weapons and other items—retrieved by CEDAM's members from 16th- and 17th-century ships that went down off Quintana Roo's coast. Mon.-Sat. 9-1 and 2:30-5:30. Donations.

XCARET is about 6 km (4 mi.) south of Playa del Carmen (follow the marked turnoff off Mex. 307). Xcaret (ISH-kah-ret) used to be a tranquil series of interlocking lagoons but has been turned into a full-scale, "eco-archeological" tourist attraction.

Swimmers, snorkelers and divers can paddle through interconnected cenotes (sinkholes) and natural pools. In addition to water-based recreation, Xcaret offers a butterfly pavilion, a breeding aviary with more than 30 species of birds, a botanical garden, an aquarium encompassing a natural coral reef habitat, a sea turtle nursery, an island habitat housing jaguars and cougars, horseback riding, a hot-air balloon ride over the park, a dolphinarium and educational programs that include an interactive dolphin swim. **Note:** Using suntan lotion is not permitted in the lagoons and other waterways because of its effect on the marine habitat.

The Xcaret Museum houses scale models of significant Maya archeological sites. Entertainment features performances of the ceremonial flying pole dance by the Papantla Flyers and the evening show "Xcaret at Night." Visitors are not permitted to bring food or beverages into the park.

Food is available. Daily 8:30 a.m.-10 p.m. Admission $49 (U.S.); ages 5-12, $25 (includes use of showers, changing rooms, beach chairs and hammocks, as well as all water rides, the aviary, botanical garden, butterfly pavilion and archeological sites). There are separate rental fees for snorkeling equipment, life jackets, lockers and towels. Depending upon crowds, however, the park may run out of supplies; bring your own towels and snorkeling gear if possible. There also are separate fees for scuba diving instruction, guided diving and snorkeling excursions, horseback riding, the hot-air balloon ride and the dolphin educational programs (the last activity can be reserved in advance but is not automatically confirmed; payment must be made at the dolphin cashier at the park museum at least one hour prior to the start of the program). AX, MC, VI. Phone (998) 881-2400, or (998) 887-6840 for dolphin program information.

PUERTO MORELOS, QUINTANA ROO (G-12)

The fishing village of Puerto Morelos (PWEHR-toh moh-REH-los) is about 36 kilometers (22 miles) south of Cancún off Mex. 307. The atmosphere is peaceful, with palm-shaded (although seaweed-strewn) beaches and restaurants serving fresh seafood. A large offshore coral reef offers excellent snorkeling and diving. There also is a large English-language bookstore, Alma Libre, on the main plaza, which is open November through April.

A passenger/car ferry leaves daily from the Puerto Morelos dock for Cozumel. The ferry takes about three hours to reach Cozumel, but the wait can be tedious and trucks carrying fuel and other cargo take precedence over automobiles. If you're not bringing a vehicle (which is advisable, as parking on the island is limited), a much quicker alternative is to board one of the passenger ferries departing from Playa del Carmen.

There is normally one departure daily from Puerto Morelos, which usually leaves in the early morning. Arrive several hours before the ferry is scheduled to depart in order to purchase a ticket and secure a place in line. In addition, double-check the return schedule to Puerto Morelos while you're on Cozumel. **Note:** This ferry has been

docked for as long as a week during prolonged periods of bad weather.

CROCO CUN is just north of the Puerto Morelos turnoff on Mex. 307, at Km marker 31. Advertised as a crocodile farm, it is actually a zoological park of sorts. Crocodile specimens of all ages and sizes are on view, along with rattlesnakes, boa constrictors, macaws, tapirs, spider monkeys, menacing-looking tarantulas and other regional species. Insect repellent is strongly advised. Guided tours are offered, and a restaurant is on the premises. Daily 8:30-5:30. Admission around $15 (U.S.); ages 6-12, $9.

DR. ALFREDO BARRERA BOTANICAL GARDEN (Jardín Botánico Dr. Alfredo Barrera) is just south of the Puerto Morelos turnoff; the entrance is right off Mex. 307. This protected area features a nature trail that winds through a variety of native and regional plants, including a grove of sapodilla trees (from which the sticky substance used to make chewing gum is extracted), a mangrove swamp, a section where epiphytes (air plants) grow and an area containing a small group of Maya ruins. Signs give plant names in Spanish and English. Wear plenty of insect repellent. Mon.-Sat. 9-5. Admission around $6 (U.S.).

RIO BEC, CAMPECHE (H-11)

Discovered at the turn of the 20th century, Río Bec (REE-oh bek) is the collective designation for an archeological zone comprising several Maya sites that once formed a large Maya city. All but one are in the state of Campeche. They generally flourished between about A.D. 400 and 1000 and are believed to have served as trade routes between Maya outposts established along the Caribbean and Gulf of Mexico coasts. The most interesting of these—Kohunlich, Xpujil, Becan and Chicanná—are all accessible from east-west Mex. 186.

Architecturally the sites exhibit what is referred to as the "Río Bec" style. Features include tower-like structures more impressive than functional and temple entrances carved to look like the open jaws of a snake, dragon or other monstrous creature. These ruins are largely unexplored, although more and more restoration efforts are being made. What remains intact is the mystery and sense of wonder surrounding these ancient cities.

One or more of the Río Bec sites can easily be visited in the course of a day, but the only tourist-class accommodations currently in this remote region are in Chetumal. Water and food are not available; bring your own. Insect repellent and sturdy shoes are essential for those who plan to do any amount of walking. The sites below are listed based on their distance from Chetumal.

Note: Mex. 186 is a long, hot route with few services of any kind. ADO operates first-class bus service from Chetumal west to Escárcega and Villahermosa; while the buses may stop at ruins along the way, it is much more convenient to drive your own vehicle. Make sure the car is in good condition and the tank is full (there is a gas station shortly before reaching Xpujil, near the Quintana Roo-Campeche state line). It is strongly recommended that Mex. 186 only be traveled during daylight hours.

KOHUNLICH ruins are about 68 km (42 mi.) west of Chetumal, just before the village of Francisco Villa, and about 8 km (5 mi.) south of the highway. Parklike and shady, Kohunlich (koh-hoon-LEECH) may once have been an oasis. The most notable structure among the rubble-strewn mounds is the pyramid-like Temple of the Masks (Templo de Los Mascarones), which has a central stairway flanked with carved faces, strongly Olmec-influenced, that resemble masks. Hints of red are still visible on these figures, which are protected by thatched coverings. Daily 8-5. Admission around $3 (U.S.); free to all Sun.

XPUJIL ruins are about 72 km (45 mi.) west of Kohunlich, on the north side of the highway just past the village of Xpujil. Xpujil (sh-pooh-HEEL), which means "place of the cattails" in the Maya language, flourished between A.D. 400 and 900. The largest building at the site consists of three towers that once had steep ornamental stairways extravagantly decorated with jaguar masks; traces of its former grandeur remain. Daily 8-5. Admission around $3 (U.S.); free to all Sun.

BECAN ruins are about 7 km (4 mi.) west of Xpujil on the north side of the highway and can be reached via a short, rutted dirt road (watch for the turnoff sign). Surrounded by a ditch that probably was used as a fortification (the name means "canyon"), the site once was accessed by seven causeway bridges. This is the most developed of the Río Bec sites and has the largest structures, including a twin-towered temple (Estructura VIII), plazas surrounded by low-rise buildings and a ball court. Daily 8-5. Admission around $3.50 (U.S.); free to all Sun.

CHICANNA ruins are about 5 km (3 mi.) west of Becán on the south side of the highway; a dirt road leads to the site. They stand within an enticing grove of tropical trees and other vegetation. The buildings are a mix of Río Bec and Chenes architectural styles. Most notable is the temple in Grupo A, which features a huge doorway fashioned after the jaws of a serpent's open mouth, complete with stone teeth; other structures are decorated with stone carvings of imaginative monster masks. Daily 8-5. Admission around $3 (U.S.); free to all Sun.

TULUM, QUINTANA ROO (G-12)

The town of Tulum (too-LOOM) straggles along the highway about a kilometer south of the junction with the access road to the Tulum Ruins. Past the south end of town Mex. 307 becomes a narrow, unpaved road as it heads toward the Boca Paila Peninsula. This area was once the site of four separate Maya cities—Solimán, Tankah, Xel-Há and Tulum.

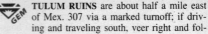 **TULUM RUINS** are about half a mile east of Mex. 307 via a marked turnoff; if driving and traveling south, veer right and follow the access road that crosses Mex. 307 and leads to the parking area. While not nearly as impressive architecturally as Chichén Itzá or Uxmal, Tulum is notable for its dramatic coastal setting. One of the later Maya outposts, it was constructed during the 10th century as a fortress overlooking the sea and abandoned some 75 years after the Spanish conquest of Mexico in 1521.

Some 60 structures are spread over a level, grassy area. The most imposing is The Castle (El Castillo), a clifftop pyramidal structure capped by a small temple. Also worth seeing is the Temple of the Frescoes, to the left of the site entrance. It features interior murals that display typical Maya motifs and exterior statues bearing still-discernible traces of paint. Just left of El Castillo, the Temple of the Descending God has a winged stucco figure over the doorway that suggests a plummeting diver.

Note: A few of the buildings can be climbed, but most have roped-off areas that visitors must stand behind. Wear nonslip walking shoes; the sandy, rocky terrain can be unexpectedly slippery. The porous limestone has created a few blowholes through which geysers of sea water can unexpectedly erupt. Weather permitting, bring a swimsuit—the lovely beach below is accessible from the ruins. Licensed, English-speaking guides are available, although the information you receive may or may not be historically accurate; a fee is charged. Tour group packages from Mérida include a buffet lunch and swim at a nearby hotel.

There are restrooms, a bookstore, a restaurant and a few souvenir stands in the visitor center next to the parking lot; the site is about a five-minute walk from the entrance. Daily 8-6 in summer; 8-5 rest of year. Admission Mon.-Sat. around $4 (U.S.), Sun. 37 pesos (around $3.50 U.S.). Parking $1 (U.S.). The fee for using a video camera is $4 (U.S.).

Nearby Destinations

CHEMUYIL is about 21 km (13 mi.) north of Tulum. Chemuyil (cheh-moo-YEEL), a sheltered cove, claims to be "La Playa Mas Bonita del Mundo" ("The Prettiest Beach in the World"). Unfortunately, its once-extravagant stand of coconut palms has been largely leveled by a disease called lethal yellowing, which causes the fronds to drop off and eventually kills the tree.

The blight has not, however, diminished Chemuyil's relaxed and friendly ambience. Facilities include camping areas, bungalows, restrooms, showers, thatched-roof pavilions and a restaurant/bar where such exotic animals as spider monkeys and baby ocelots mingle with the human patrons. A fee is charged for day use of the beach.

CHUNYAXCHE is about 26 km (16 mi.) south of Tulum on the east side of Mex. 307. Chunyaxche (choon-yahsh-CHEH) is the site of the Muyil ruins, a large, rarely visited Maya archeological site that contains a partially reconstructed ceremonial temple. Excavations are sporadic but ongoing; research continues to determine whether Muyil once functioned as a port, since canals join the site to the Caribbean, 15 kilometers (9 miles) east. Tours through the canals to jungle-lined lagoons along the coast can be arranged through the Cancún-based Friends of Sian Ka'an organization. Phone (998) 848-2136.

CUZAN BONEFISH FLATS is within the lobster-fishing village of Punta Allen, on the Boca Paila Peninsula about 60 km (37 mi.) south of Tulum. It can be reached via the access road that branches south off Mex. 307 at the town of Tulum. Boating excursions are offered to two nearby rookery islands to observe such tropical species as frigate birds and roseate spoonbills. Visitors can snorkel or fish against a backdrop of spectacular coral reefs. Guided fishing trips explore 20 square miles of uniformly shallow water at the northern entrance to Ascención Bay. The flats are home to bonefish, tarpon, barracuda and other game fish. Fly fishing is best from November through June.

Waterproof sunscreen, polarized sunglasses and insect repellent all are essential for a stay at Cuzan. **Note:** There is no public transportation to Punta Allen; the best way to reach Cuzan is to fly into Cancún and then rent a car. Allow up to two hours to reach Punta Allen from Tulum via an inferior road that passes through thick jungle.

Rates for trip packages ranging from 3 days to a week include accommodations, guided fishing and meals. Credit cards are not accepted. Reservations can be made by fax transmission to the mainland town of Felipe Carrillo Puerto. Phone (983) 834-0358; fax (983) 834-0292.

SIAN KA'AN BIOSPHERE RESERVE includes the Boca Paila Peninsula and the mainland south of Tulum and east of Mex. 307. Sian Ka'an ("place where the sky is born") encompasses tropical rain forest, drier areas of tree-speckled savanna, coastal mangrove flats and some 70 miles of offshore coral reefs. This vast wilderness is a haven for a variety of wildlife—including some endangered species—such as deer, jaguars, ocelots, tapirs, peccaries (a form of wild pig), howler monkeys, crocodiles, manatees and sea turtles.

Bird life is equally rich and diverse, and the 350 species inhabiting the reserve range from egrets and herons to toucans, parrots and the frigate bird. Areas of virgin jungle contain about 1,200 varieties of plants. Also within the reserve are some 30 archeological sites.

Note: Sian Ka'an's core zone is closed to visitors; tourism is restricted to the outer buffer zone. Biologist-escorted day tours of the peninsula are available on a seasonal basis. For further information about the biosphere reserve, contact the Friends of Sian Ka'an (Amigos de Sian Ka'an) in Ciudad Cancún. Office hours are Mon.-Fri. 9-5; phone (998) 848-2136.

TANKAH is about 3.5 km (2 mi.) north of the Tulum ruins and east of Mex. 307. It was one of the satellite cities of Tulum; the others were Solimán and Xel-Há. The few ruins that remain are hidden in the underbrush and have not been fully explored.

XCACEL is about 19 km (12 mi.) north of the town of Tulum off Mex. 307, about a quarter mile east of the highway. Although the crescent-shaped beach is one of Caribbean Mexico's prettiest, it is bypassed by most tourists. The calm water is ideal for swimming, snorkeling, diving and fishing. There are camping facilities, changing rooms, showers and a restaurant. A wrecked tour boat, which hit offshore rocks, sank and was pushed to the shore by the waves, is at the southern tip of the beach. A fee is charged for day use of the beach.

Note: At Xcacel, Paamul and other beaches along the Mexican Caribbean coast, volunteer groups sponsored by the state of Quintana Roo periodically organize programs designed to save sea turtles from extinction. The turtles' nesting sites are being destroyed by the development occurring along much of the coast. From May through August, rare loggerhead and green turtles laboriously leave the sea to build nests on the beach and lay their eggs. The volunteer groups help ensure that the turtles complete their task, and then tag and release the hatchlings. Visitors can ask to join a night patrol; flashlights are prohibited because they drive the turtles back toward the water. Donations are appreciated.

XEL-HA NATIONAL PARK is about 13 km (8 mi.) north of the Tulum ruins via a well-marked turnoff on the east side of Mex. 307 (Km marker 240). Fingers of limestone jutting into the labyrinth of inlets and lagoons form a natural aquarium and allow visitors to observe a variety of colorful tropical fish. Many of them gather around underwater rock formations. For landlubbers, platforms built over the lagoons offer easy viewing from above the water.

Snorkeling at Xel-Há (shell-HAH) can be enjoyed without the undertows or strong currents that can make the beaches dangerous, and the clarity of the water is excellent. Other activities include hiking, inner tubing and an interactive swim with dolphins. Cancún travel agencies often combine Xel-Há and Tulum as a single guided day-trip excursion. Dress casually and bring comfortable shoes to hike the park's Path of Conscience. Life jackets are provided, and there is a first-aid station on site. An ATM accepts international credit cards.

Food is available. Daily 9-6. To fully enjoy the park, get there early; when the tour buses arrive it can become very crowded. Admission Mon.-Fri. $26 (U.S.); ages 5-13, $13.50. Admission Sat.-Sun. $20; ages 5-11, $10. Snorkel gear rental $10 (U.S.), towel rental $3, locker rental $2 (you also may bring your own equipment). All-inclusive admission (includes towel, locker, snorkel gear and food/beverages) $52 (U.S.); ages 5-11, $26. There is a separate fee for the dolphin swim (make reservations in advance). AX, MC, VI. Phone (984) 875-6000 (park offices), (998) 884-9422 (Cancún offices); for dolphin swim reservations phone (998) 887-6840 or (800) 714-3672 (toll-free long distance within Mexico).

☗ UXMAL, YUCATAN (G-11)

If Chichén Itzá is considered the Yucatán Peninsula's most impressive archeological site, Uxmal (oosh-MAHL) is the most beautiful. Unlike the structures at Chichén Itzá, with their Toltec-influenced images of violent conquest, Uxmal's architecture is more purely Maya, with richly ornamented stone facades and a majestic pyramid. The ruins were designated a World Heritage Site by UNESCO in 1996; don't miss them.

Uxmal rose to prominence concurrently with the great civilizations at Palenque (see separate listing under Southern Mexico) and Tikal in Guatemala, flourishing between A.D. 600 and 1000. Little is known about its history. The name means "thrice built" in Maya, although it was actually reconstructed five times, suggesting that drought forced abandonment followed by resettlement. The subsequent importance of Chichén Itzá and the increased intermingling of Maya cultures with those from the central Mexican highlands were likely contributors to the city's decline, which appeared to be complete by the 14th century.

The first excavations were begun in 1929 by Danish archeologist and explorer Frans Blom, who also conducted research at other Maya archeological sites. The Mexican government has since worked with a number of archeologists to reconstruct the site, and the main buildings have all been restored.

Uxmal is the defining example of the Puuc architectural style (the name refers to the region's hilly terrain), which emphasized elegant, horizontal proportions and intricately detailed building exteriors of cut stones assembled in geometric patterns. Cornices and entryways often feature beak-nosed representations of the rain god Chac. The detail of the stonework is even more amazing when one considers that the Maya created their buildings without benefit of metal tools.

This part of the peninsula has a hot climate with seasonal precipitation and is subject to prolonged dry spells. Unlike other Maya cities, Uxmal did not have ready availability to a source of water. Instead, they depended upon the *chultun* (a man-made cistern) to collect precious rain.

Visitors enter the site via a short path that begins at the visitor center. The first building is immediately evident: The Pyramid of the Magician (see attraction listing). This structure probably functioned as a ceremonial building where Uxmal's rulers were crowned. **Note:** Climbing the pyramid is very risky if you're prone to vertigo. The stairways are sometimes roped off; inquire at the visitor center whether climbing is permitted.

The Nunnery (see attraction listing), named by the Spaniards, was probably used by Uxmal's elite ruling class. Just south of the Nunnery is a ball court, smaller and simpler than the one at Chichén Itzá. South of the ball court is the small, classically designed House of the Turtles (Casa de las Tortugas), named for the border of turtles carved along its upper molding. Stand on the south side of this temple and look through the central doorway (of three) for a nicely framed view of the Nunnery.

The Governor's Palace (see attraction listing) was most likely Uxmal's administrative center and may also have served an astrological purpose; it faces east while the other buildings face west, perhaps to better sight the planet Venus, which the Maya associated with war. From this elevated vantage point there is an expansive view of the Nunnery and the Pyramid of the Magician.

The Great Pyramid, partially restored, is just southwest of the Governor's Palace. Originally terraced with nine levels, it is topped by a palace decorated with Chac masks and bird carvings that probably represent parrots. The climb to the palace level is steep but doable (be particularly careful descending if you're prone to vertigo), with sweeping views of the surrounding jungle scrub.

Just west of the Great Pyramid are the remains of a building called the Dovecote because its lattice design somewhat resembles a bird nesting house. The view of this ruin is particularly fine from the summit of the Great Pyramid.

Other buildings at the site are only partially reconstructed, or unexcavated mounds hidden in the brush. The House of the Old Woman (Casa de la Vieja), an old, ruined pyramidal structure southeast of the Great Pyramid, is reached by an overgrown path. Further southeast is the Temple of the Phalli, another ruined structure with phallic-shaped sculptures along the cornices, presumably to divert and collect rainwater from the roof.

General Information and Activities

Mérida is the most convenient base from which to explore the Puuc region. Cancún-based Mayaland Tours offers two packages: a day tour of Uxmal and the nearby Kabah archeological site that departs at 9 a.m., and an afternoon tour of Uxmal that departs at 1:30 p.m. and includes the evening sound-and-light show. Both tours include round-trip transportation, guide service and lunch or dinner. For reservations information phone (998) 887-2450 (in Mexico) or (800) 235-4079 (from the United States). Tour groups usually have access to a swimming pool; bring a suit and towel, as they aren't provided.

Uxmal is about 79 kilometers (49 miles) south of Mérida via Mex. 261. If driving, take Avenida Itzaes (Mex. 180) south from downtown Mérida past the Anillo Periférico (loop road) to the town of Umán. Watch for signs saying "To Campeche via Uxmal on Mex. 261," "Zona Arqueologia Uxmal" and "Ruta Puuc"; follow these signs through Umán to access Mex. 261 south. The two-lane road (no shoulders) runs through largely undeveloped scrub country. Pass with care, as you will likely encounter an occasional slow-moving vehicle or stopped dump truck.

Note: En route to Uxmal a bypass branches off Mex. 261, rejoining it south of the town of Muna. Not having to drive through Muna cuts some time off the trip, which takes about an hour from Mérida. The old road passes through this typical Yucatecan small town of thatch-roofed stone dwellings and a large Franciscan church.

For those who want to spend the night near the ruins, there are comfortable hotels next to the site and along Mex. 261 near the entrance. More budget-minded travelers might consider an overnight stay in the nearby town of Ticul, about a 15-minute drive from Uxmal, which offers very basic services.

Guide fees are posted on a board next to the ticket window. Although you don't need a guide to appreciate the architecture, and the information may be embellished with fanciful details, a guide's general knowledge will be helpful to those unfamiliar with Maya history. If you'd rather explore on your own, the main buildings can all be viewed over the course of a few hours. Informational plaques at each one are in English, Spanish and Maya.

A 45-minute sound-and-light show is presented nightly from a vantage point overlooking the Nunnery quadrangle. Colored lights, recorded symphonic music under the stars and melodramatic narration provide an appropriate backdrop for Maya legends. Although the "history" can be taken with a grain of salt, the artificial lighting illuminates architectural details that are missed under sharp sunlight. The narration is in Spanish, but headsets offering the show in several languages (including English) can be rented.

Most of the site is unshaded; bring a hat or other headgear for protection from the strong sun. An early start will allow you to beat not only the heat but the tour bus crowds that begin arriving before noon. Comfortable, nonslip walking shoes are a must if you plan to do any climbing. It's also a good idea to bring bottled water and insect repellent (particularly if you're attending the sound-and-light show).

The visitor center at the entrance has restrooms, a bookstore, first-aid station, craft shop, ice cream parlor, casual restaurant and convenience store (where film and disposable cameras can be purchased). A few souvenir and T-shirt stands set up next to the visitor center parking lot. Uxmal is open daily 8-5. The sound-and-light show begins at 7 or 8 p.m., depending on the season. Admission (includes sound-and-light show) around $9 (U.S.). Parking fee 10 pesos (around $1 U.S.). Video camera fee 50 pesos (around $5 U.S.).

Points of Interest

GOVERNOR'S PALACE is south of the Nunnery and just southeast of the House of the Turtles. This building is widely considered to be among the finest Maya architectural achievements. The low, narrow structure, more than 300 feet long, is built on three levels. Its upper facade is covered with intricately carved stone figures and geometric designs. Serpents, masks and mosaic patterns all blend into a beautifully harmonious whole. Stand back from the palace's eastern side to discern the 103 stone carvings of Chac that together form the image of an undulating serpent (dramatically illuminated during Uxmal's sound-and-light show).

NUNNERY (Casa de las Monjas) faces the western stairway of the Pyramid of the Magician. More than 70 rooms are in the long, low buildings that surround a large quadrangle. Stand in the center of the courtyard to appreciate the overall harmony that prevails, even though the buildings are terraced and on different levels. The exteriors of each wing have beautiful decorative details, including stone masks of Chac (recognized by their elongated noses), entwined serpents, mosaic patterns and latticework designs. The southern wing has an arched entryway, once the complex's main entrance.

PYRAMID OF THE MAGICIAN is near the site entrance. Also called The Sorcerer (El Adivino), this impressive ruin is both taller (some 125 feet) and steeper than El Castillo, the pyramid at Chichén Itzá. It actually contains five superimposed layers that correspond to Uxmal's five separate periods of construction. The walls are rounded rather than sharply angular, an unusual feature. Stairways ascend the eastern and western sides. The western stairway is very steep (a 60-degree angle); the eastern stairway is not quite as steep.

Nearby Puuc Ruins

For true aficionados of Maya history and culture, a full day can be spent exploring the ruins along the "Puuc Trail" south and east of Uxmal, all within easy driving distance. Some tour buses visit these small archeological sites, but driving allows you to see them at your own pace. Roadside services are minimal, so make sure your gas tank is full and bring food, water, insect repellent and comfortable, nonslip walking shoes. The following sites are listed in order of location from Uxmal.

KABAH is about 19 km (12 mi.) south on Mex. 261; park in the small dirt lot on the east (left) side of the road. Although small—there are only two main buildings—it is well worth visiting to see the lavishly decorated Palace of the Masks, or Codz-Pop (in Maya, "rolled mat"). Its entire west exterior is emblazoned with elaborately carved stone masks of the rain god Chac. The busy architectural style reflects the ornate Chenes influence, which is not often seen in this region.

As amazing as the front is, make sure you walk around to the back (east) side. There are no Chac masks here, but jutting off the upper facade are the sculptures of two warriors who seem to be guarding the palace. Below them on one of the side panels (at ground level) are bas-reliefs depicting one warrior subjugating another in classic Maya fashion.

The other major building on this side of the road is the well-restored Palace (El Palacio), built on two levels, which features a Puuc-style colonnaded facade. Across Mex. 261 is the Great Temple, a large conical mound rising above the thick scrub. It is only partially restored. Beyond the Great Temple is a free-standing arch marking the spot where a Maya *sacbe* (limestone causeway) road once entered Kabah from Uxmal; compare it to the one at Labná *(see below)*.

Daily 8-5. Admission 37 pesos (around $4 U.S.). Video camera fee 50 pesos (around $5 U.S.).

SAYIL is about 5 km (3 mi.) from Kabah; take Mex. 261 to the junction with Mex. 184 (the road to Oxkutzcab), then east about 4 km (2.5 mi.) to the ruins. The aptly named site, which means "place of ants," contains several hundred known structures, almost all on the south side of the road. There is one standout: the Palace (El Palacio), a grand three-level building more than 200 feet long. The second level features rows of Grecian-style columns as well as a profusion of stone carvings. Most are of the rain god Chac, but there are additional depictions of an upside-down "diving god."

Most of the other buildings are in ruins or obscured by jungle. South of the Palace is El Mirador, a small temple, and beyond it a primitive stele (carved stone). Also at this site are a number of man-made cisterns that were built to catch seasonal rainfall. Daily 8-5. Admission 37 pesos (around $4 U.S.). Video camera fee 50 pesos (around $5 U.S.).

XLAPAK is about 6 km (3.5 mi.) east of Sayil. Xlapak (shla-PAHK) means "old walls" in Maya. The notable structure at this small site on the south side of the road is the partially restored Palace of Xlapak, which is decorated with Chac masks, some flaunting curled noses. The restored portions are lighter in tone than the weathered, unrestored sections. Daily 8-5. Admission 37 pesos (around $4 U.S.). Video camera fee 50 pesos (around $5 U.S.).

LABNA is about 3 km (2 mi.) east of Xlapak. Here the best-known ruin is a restored, free-standing stone arch larger and more ornately decorated than the one at Kabah. It features ornate decoration on the west side and a more geometric pattern on the east side. Pass through the arch to El Mirador, a pyramidal structure resting on a pile of rubble. Labná, like Sayil, contains the remains of many *chultunes* (cisterns) that collected rainwater.

Labná's impressive Palace building is similar to the one at Sayil, although not in as good condition. See it for the ornamentation, which is—as on so many Maya buildings—bizarrely imaginative. Daily 8-5. Admission 37 pesos (around $4 U.S.). Video camera fee 50 pesos (around $5 U.S.).

LOLTUN CAVES (Grutas de Loltún) are about 6 km (10 mi.) southwest of Oxkutzcab via the Sayil-Labná road. The entrance to the caves is reached from a gravel path that branches off the north side of the road; the turnoff is not signed. Hieroglyphic inscriptions and carvings of flowers on the cave walls are estimated to be some 1,000 years old; the name, loosely translated, means "one flower in the stone." Throughout the caves are *chultunes* (cisterns), stone troughs which were placed to collect water dripping from the roof. Natural formations include giant stalactites and stalagmites that emit an echoing hum when struck.

The caverns can be seen by guided tour only. Tours are given daily at 9:30, 11, 12:30, 2, 3 and 4; double-check this schedule at the Uxmal visitor center. Some passages are dark and the paths may be slippery or steep; wear comfortable, nonslip walking shoes. Most tours are given in Spanish; ask at the front ticket office regarding the availability of an English-speaking guide. Daily 8-5. Admission 50 pesos (about $5 U.S.).

Oxkutzcab, Ticul and Maní

Oxkutzcab (osh-koots-KAHB) is in a fertile farming region. In this and other small Yucatán towns, a popular means of conveyance is the *triciclo*, the reverse of a tricycle—two wheels in front supporting a cargo/carrier area and one in the back, below the driver's seat. Everything from human passengers to crates of produce and chickens ride through the streets by means of this cheap transportation.

Ticul is on the Mérida-Chetumal Highway (Mex. 184) about 19 kilometers (12 miles) northwest of Oxkutzcab. This busy regional center also specializes in the manufacture of pottery and women's shoes. It's larger than most of the other towns in this area; the streets are filled with *triciclos* (and dogs).

The domed 18th-century church stands next to Ticul's central plaza. An interesting exterior decoration is the facial features—two half-moon eyes and a nose—carved below the roof. Many of the shops lining the downtown streets sell nothing but shoes. Craft shops offer ceramic bowls, and street vendors hawk embroidered *huipiles* and Panama hats made from woven palm fronds.

East of Ticul is the village of Maní; believed to be the place where Diego de Landa, a Spanish bishop, ordered in 1562 the destruction by fire of the Maya *codices*, or hieroglyphic picture books, believing them profane. The historical loss resulting from this act was incalculable, leaving Landa's own treatise on Maya civilization, *"Relación de las Cosas de Yucatán"* ("Yucatán Before and After the Conquest"), the definitive account.

VALLADOLID, YUCATAN (G-11)
pop. 38,000

Valladolid (vah-yah-doh-LEED) was founded in 1543 by Francisco de Montejo, who established Spanish rule over much of the Yucatán Peninsula. The Spaniards constructed their churches over the site of a former Maya town, Zací. Many revolts occurred in this region during the mid-19th-century

War of the Castes, when rebellious and oppressed descendants of the Maya clashed with privileged landowners. Here too was one of the first uprisings against dictator Porfirio Díaz, which foreshadowed the Mexican Revolution of 1910.

The commercial center for an agricultural district, Valladolid is on Mex. 180 and is one of the three exits off toll highway Mex. 180-D. A colonial atmosphere, somewhat gone to seed, pervades this unpretentious market town, where old buildings still bear weathered Spanish coats of arms above their doorways. The main plaza is bounded by calles 39, 40, 41 and 42; here visitors can browse among shops selling leather goods or sit on one of the curved stone benches and observe the local scene.

CENOTE DZITNUP is about 4 km (2.5 mi.) southwest of town on the south side of Mex. 180 (there is a signed turnoff). This is a better alternative than Cenote Zací if you want to try swimming. The natural pool of clear, blue water is inside a cavern where artificial lighting illuminates the stalactites hanging from the roof. The short flight of stone steps leading down into the cavern can be slippery. Daily 7-6. Admission around $3 (U.S.).

CENOTE ZACI is on Calle 36 two blocks east of the main plaza, between calles 37 and 39. This huge underground sinkhole is reached by worn stone stairs that descend into a dark cavern, the upper reaches of which are populated by bats. The murky water is flecked with green scum that the locals call "lake lettuce." Zací (sah-KEE) is spookily atmospheric but unsuitable for swimming. It is located in a park that also contains traditional thatch-roofed Maya houses. Daily 8-5. Admission around $3 (U.S.).

CHURCH AND CONVENT OF SAN BERNARDINO DE SIENA is about six blocks southwest of the main plaza. The fortifications of this massive complex, founded in 1552 by the Franciscan Order, were built to ward off the warring Mayas, who sacked it repeatedly. Looting during the War of the Castes has robbed the church of much of its interior ornamentation; there is, however, a likeness of the Virgin of Guadalupe on the altar.

EK BALAM is about 32 km (20 mi.) northeast of Valladolid. To get there, take Calle 40 out of town to Mex. 295 and proceed north about 18 km (11 mi.) to the Ek Balam turnoff (watch for the sign marking the turnoff). Follow the narrow, winding road to the ruins, which are about 13 km (8 mi.) from the highway. Archeologists believe the site achieved its greatest prominence between A.D. 700 and 1000.

Ongoing restoration work has transformed piles of carved stones into beautifully reconstructed buildings at this site (the name means "black jaguar"). The fully restored structures are architecturally similar in style to the Puuc ruins found at sites near Uxmal. The largest pyramid, some 100 feet tall and 200 feet wide, is flanked by two smaller ones. The complex also contains a number of reconstructed altars and temples (one features a huge entryway in the shape of a toothed mouth), as well as an arch that once was connected to an ancient Maya road, or *sacbe*.

Wear comfortable walking shoes and bring drinking water. Daily 8-5. Admission around $7 (U.S.); free to all Sun. The fee to use a video camera is $5.

RIO LAGARTOS NATIONAL PARK is is about 100 km (62 mi.) almost due north of Valladolid at the end of Mex. 295. **Note:** The *topes* (speed bumps) along Mex. 295 can significantly damage the underside of a vehicle if negotiated at too fast a speed. Mexico's largest flamingo sanctuary comprises some 120,000 acres of protected mangrove swamps, sand dunes, mud flats and shallow estuaries along the Yucatán Peninsula's northern coast. In addition to flamingos, the park is home to herons, egrets, cormorants, ducks, pelicans and many other bird species.

Boat tours can be arranged with local guides at the dock area in the fishing village of Río Lagartos. Bring a hat or other protection from the sun, your own water and a snack. The winter months are a better—and cooler—time to observe young flamingos and other bird species. Don't allow the boatman to scare flamingos into flight for a photo opportunity, as this will eventually drive them from their habitat. Rates vary according to boat, destination and tour size, but an excursion for five people should be around $45 (U.S.).

Cabo San Lucas, Baja California Sur / © Artografika / Tom River / Alamy Images

Baja California

I n 1535, an officer under the command of Hernando Cortés became the first European to land in Baja (Lower) California. The reports he brought back, particularly with respect to the existence of pearls in the Gulf of California, were so tantalizing that a year later Cortés himself led settlers to the present site of La Paz, near the southern end of the Baja California Peninsula. The poverty of the land and the fierceness of the Indians led him to abandon the area a few years later, and Spanish *conquistadores*—busy plundering other parts of Mexico—all but forgot Baja.

It was not until 1697 that a permanent settlement was established, a Jesuit mission and presidio at Loreto *(see separate listing within this region)*. Throughout the 18th century, the Indians in this barren land were ministered to by the Jesuits, who founded the first missions and also taught the Indians how to farm. When the Jesuits were banished from Mexico in the 1760s, the Franciscans and the Dominicans followed. but along with churches, the missionaries brought disease. Smallpox had almost wiped out the indigenous population by the middle of the 19th century. Meanwhile, primitive settlements—

accessible only by boat or on foot—slowly developed.

Except for quintessential border town Tijuana and seaside Ensenada, Baja for the most part remained a lonely outpost for hardy fishermen through the first half of the 20th century. Much of it remains isolated, although the completion in 1973 of Mex. 1, the Transpeninsular Highway, opened the more far-flung parts to visitors and ushered in economic development.

The peninsula, nearly 800 miles in length and varying from about 30 to 110 miles in width, extends south from the U.S. border like a giant appendage paralleling the northwestern Mexican mainland. It broke off millions of years ago, in the process creating the Gulf of California (also known as the Sea of Cortés). Baja's backbone is made up of two westward-sloping mountain ranges. Sierra de San Pedro Mártir dominates the north; Sierra de la Giganta, the south. In the former, Picacho del Diablo attains an elevation of 10,073 feet, the highest point on the peninsula. Both the gulf and Pacific coastlines are indented by an endless string of bays and coves, with many islands scattered offshore. Both bodies of water are home to an amazing variety of fish, making the peninsula a sport-fishing paradise.

The state of Baja California, comprising all territory north of the 28th parallel, consists mostly of rugged mountains or harsh desert, although irrigation of the hot, arid valleys around the border city of Mexicali has turned them into a productive agricultural region. Easily accessible Tijuana—big, bustling, part trashy, part flashy—draws hordes of stay-for-a-day tourists, college-age partiers and dedicated shoppers. The port of Ensenada is a popular weekend destination offering beaches, dining and nightlife. Between the two is Rosarito Beach, a casual, rapidly growing resort area.

The state of Baja California Sur, occupying the southern portion of the peninsula, is even more barren. Occasional oases such as the village of San Ignacio, a mirage of date palms and pastel-colored buildings, pop up in the middle of the desert. At Baja's southern tip is its most popular vacation spot, the twin resorts of Cabo San Lucas and San José del Cabo, where sport fishing and surfing are augmented by an impressive string of championship golf courses.

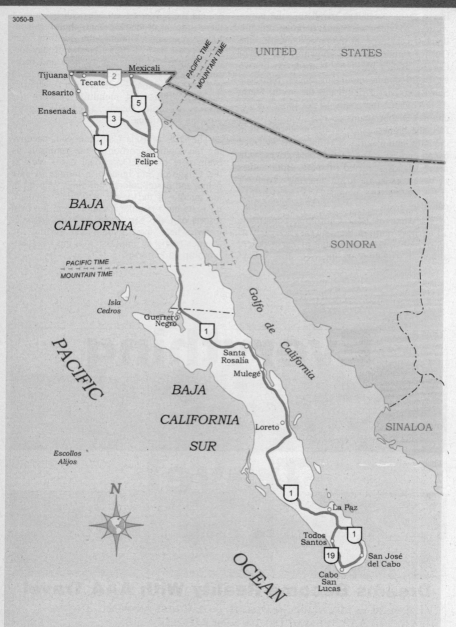

3050-B

UNITED   STATES

PACIFIC TIME
MOUNTAIN TIME

Tijuana
Tecate
Mexicali
2
Rosarito
5
Ensenada
3
1
San
Felipe

BAJA

CALIFORNIA

SONORA

PACIFIC TIME
MOUNTAIN TIME

Isla
Cedros

Guerrero
Negro
1

Golfo   de   California

PACIFIC

Santa
Rosalía
Mulegé

BAJA

CALIFORNIA

SUR

Loreto

SINALOA

Escollos
Alijos

N

1

La Paz
1

Todos
Santos
San José
del Cabo
19

OCEAN

Cabo
San
Lucas

Baja California

NOT INTENDED FOR DRIVING
SEE APPROPRIATE SHEET MAP

| 0 | Miles | 133 |
| 0 | Kilometers | 213 |

© AAA

ONLY PLACES LISTED WITH DESCRIPTIVE
WRITE-UPS APPEAR ON THIS MAP.

Points of Interest

CABO SAN LUCAS, BAJA CALIFORNIA SUR (F-3) pop. 40,300

See map page 128.

Cabo San Lucas (KAH-boh sahn LOO-kahs), at the southern tip of Baja California, marks the convergence of the Gulf of California and the Pacific Ocean. In the 16th and 17th centuries, gulfside Bahía San Lucas was a favored hiding place for pirates who plundered Spanish galleons. Cabo drowsed away the years until the 1950s, when the private yachts of well-to-do Americans began mooring in the bay. In the process, the town metamorphosed from unassuming cannery village to international resort. Together with neighboring San José del Cabo *(see separate listing within this region)*, the area known as Los Cabos (the Capes) is one of Mexico's fastest growing resort areas, rivaling Cancún/Cozumel in popularity.

Up until a few years ago Cabo San Lucas was primarily a destination for moneyed sportsmen and those escaping the crowds at Mexico's more established seaside getaways. But Baja's tip also has become a destination of choice for suntanned, fashionably unshaven Generation Xers who—unlike '80s yuppies and their sanitized Club Med tastes—relish southern Baja's nontouristy atmosphere, nearly deserted beaches and prime surfing spots.

Some 1,050 miles from the U.S. border, the two Cabos are accessible via Mex. 1 south from La Paz or Mex. 19 south from Todos Santos. Mex. 1 is a four-lane divided highway between San José del Cabo and Cabo San Lucas. The winding stretch provides views of rugged cliffs and glimpses of steely blue gulf water edged by white-sand beaches. Luxury resort developments with lushly groomed grounds are a dramatic counterpoint to the wild, rocky landscapes that surround them. **Note:** Avoid driving on Mex. 1 at night; as in many parts of Mexico, cattle are apt to cross the roadway unexpectedly.

Impressive proof of Cabo's popularity are the high-rise hotels, condominiums, boutiques and restaurants lining the hillsides and waterfront. They share space with trailer parks, markets, gift shops, shopping centers, auto repair shops and a marina. Glass-bottomed boats leave the marina daily for cruises to nearby rock formations, with views of a sea lion colony, pelican rookery and waters filled with brightly hued tropical fish along the way. A ferry terminal lies idle; service to Puerto Vallarta has been suspended indefinitely. The town is, however, a port of call for cruise ships.

Despite the growth, Cabo is easily negotiated. The main street, an extension of Mex. 1 (the Transpeninsular Highway) from San José del Cabo, is Lázaro Cárdenas. Branching off from it is Boulevard Marina, which follows the waterfront. Paseo Morelos (Mex. 19) enters town from the west. Other streets are clearly marked.

Buses also traverse the three main streets, providing inexpensive transportation to most points of interest. The main bus terminal is at avenidas Zaragoza and 156 de Septiembre, two blocks north of Lázaro Cárdenas. Taxis can take you from downtown to the outlying hotels or to secluded beaches along Bahía San Lucas. Local maps show beaches and other points of interest in relation to Mex. 1 km markers along the 33-kilometer (20-mile) distance between Cabo San Lucas and San José del Cabo.

Solitude seekers head for idyllic Playa del Amor (Lovers' Beach), which is overlooked by El Arco, a natural arch, and the rocky pinnacles of Los Frailes (The Friars). This idyllic spot is accessible only by boat. At the tip of the Baja California Peninsula is Cabo Falso, where an old lighthouse once guided ships between the U.S. west coast and Panama.

Local tour companies or travel agencies can arrange an all-terrain vehicle excursion over enormous sand dunes to visit the lighthouse and the remains of a shipwreck. Even more offbeat is another guided ATV tour to La Candelaria, an isolated Indian pueblo in the mountains north of Cabo San Lucas. An underground river provides water for uncharacteristically lush growths of mango, bamboo and palms. The locals here are said to still practice witchcraft.

To the east is Land's End (Finisterra), where the crashing of innumerable gulf and ocean waves have sculpted striking rock formations. Isolated beaches in the vicinity can be reached by boat or on foot from the Solmar Suites Resort. (Only those in good physical condition should attempt to clamber over the rocks here, and it is advisable to travel with a partner.) Both the approach to Cabo San Lucas via Mex. 1 and elevated spots in town offer panoramic views of this area, Baja's final frontier.

The weather in Cabo San Lucas is warm all year. Daytime highs are around 80 degrees in winter but can soar to over 100 during the summer months. In October the waters of the Pacific and the Sea of Cortez have been warmed by summer's heat to between 75 and 80 degrees, making conditions for swimming and snorkeling ideal. High season is October through April; bring a sweater for occasional cool evenings if visiting in January or February. **Note:** While it hardly ever rains in this part of Baja, the ravines (called arroyos) along Mex. 1 are subject to flash floods during infrequent storms. Flooding, although rare, can make vehicle travel impossible when it occurs.

Practicalities

The most useful number for emergencies is 060, which can be dialed to reach local police, the fire

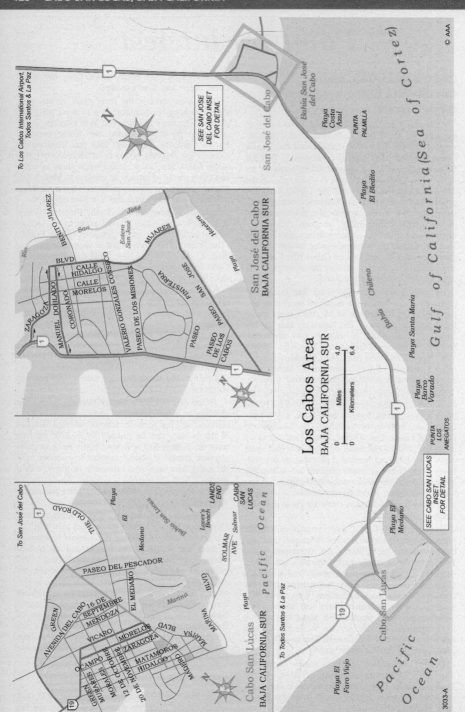

Los Cabos Area
BAJA CALIFORNIA SUR

SEE SAN JOSE DEL CABO INSET FOR DETAIL

San José del Cabo
BAJA CALIFORNIA SUR

Cabo San Lucas
BAJA CALIFORNIA SUR

SEE CABO SAN LUCAS INSET FOR DETAIL

To Los Cabos International Airport, Todos Santos & La Paz

To San José del Cabo

To Todos Santos & La Paz

Gulf of California (Sea of Cortez)

Pacific Ocean

Bahía San José del Cabo

Playa Costa Azul

PUNTA PALMILLA

Playa El Bledito

Bahía Chileno

Playa Santa Maria

Playa Barco Varado

PUNTA LOS ANEGATOS

Playa El Medano

Cabo San Lucas

Playa El Faro Viejo

San José del Cabo

Miles
0   4.0

Kilometers
0   6.4

© AAA

3033-A

department or the Red Cross. Other handy numbers are the IMSS Hospital, (624) 143-1548; post office, (624) 143-0048; Secretary of Fishing, (624) 143-0564; and the Highway Patrol (PFP), which provides updates on road conditions, (624) 146-1241 or (624) 146-0573.

Avoid the kiosks throughout town that claim to offer visitor information. Their real purpose is to lure the unsuspecting with free lunches and drinks and then attempt to sell time-shares in a new condominium development. These sales pitches can be long and arduous for those who are just in town to relax. The booth in front of the Hotel Plaza Las Glorias (on the marina in the center of town) is an exception; it has maps and information about the entire region.

Aero California, Alaska Airlines and Mexicana Airlines offer direct flights from Los Angeles to Los Cabos International Airport, which is about 13 kilometers (8 miles) northwest of San José del Cabo. Transportation to and from the airport is controlled by the local taxi service. *Colectivos* (shuttle vans) transport visitors from the airport to local hotels for around $9 (U.S.). A small airstrip just outside Cabo San Lucas accommodates single- and twin-engine aircraft and small private jets. Upon arrival, local cab drivers will race to the strip to inquire if a cab is needed into town. For additional information about airlines see *"Arriving by Air,"* page 551.

First-class bus service is provided by the Suburcabos line between Cabo San Lucas and San José del Cabo at about hourly intervals during daytime and early evening hours; the trip takes about 45 minutes. *Aguila* (local) buses traveling up and down Mex. 1 between the two towns can be flagged down along the highway and for a few pesos will drop you off at the downtown bus station. For the somewhat adventurous, this is one way to beat the high taxicab rates. *Aguila* buses also travel to La Paz; the trip takes between two and three hours and costs about $11 to $15 (U.S.). Tickets should be bought in advance in order to secure a seat.

Taxis in the area are expensive. Expect to pay from $20 to $30 (U.S.) for a ride into town if staying in an outlying resort or hotel between the two Cabos. Green taxis are for local fares only; yellow taxis are for fares heading out of town. Always negotiate the fare before getting in the cab. Most of the outlying hotels provide shuttles into Cabo San Lucas that may be free at certain times of the day; however, this service does not operate during evening hours.

If you're staying in town, one way to see the sights is by moped. Several agencies offer daily rentals for about $60 to $80 (U.S.). Keep in mind that the rental fee may not include insurance.

The English-language *Baja Sun* is a widely distributed monthly with information and advertisements pertaining to the Los Cabos region as well as the rest of Baja. *El Tiempo Los Cabos Times* is a bilingual newspaper. Radio station Cabo Mil (96 FM) broadcasts a variety of music.

Cash and traveler's checks can be exchanged at the Banca Serfin on Lázaro Cárdenas in the center of town. The commercial complex in which the bank is located also contains a travel agency and a Super Mercado grocery store. The Banamex Bank at Lázaro Cárdenas and Avenida Hidalgo has an ATM machine.

Outdoor Recreation

The waters of the Gulf of California and the Pacific Ocean are a breeding ground for hundreds of species of game fish, making the Los Cabos area a paradise for sport fishing. Striped marlin run year-round, and the season for the majestic blue marlin is June through mid-November. Others commonly hooked include amberjack, black marlin, bonito, black sea bass, corbina, dorado (mahi mahi), roosterfish, sailfish, snapper, wahoo, yellowfin tuna and yellowtail.

Fishing charters abound, and almost any of the bigger hotels can arrange an expedition. During the season it is advisable to book fishing trips well in advance; some anglers reserve boats as much as a year in advance for the Bisbee's Black and Blue Marlin Jackpot Tournament, held in October. The world's richest marlin fishing tournament, it has base fees of several thousand dollars.

A catch-and-release policy is emphasized; anglers experience the thrill of battle, and after their catch is reeled in it is tagged and set free, helping to preserve billfish species and ensure the continuation of the sport.

Pangas (small skiffs) can be rented by the hour and include fishing equipment, a license and a chest to ice the catch. Excursions can be easily arranged through one of the fleet operators at the marina sport-fishing dock; inquire at your hotel's front desk. More expensive sport-fishing cruisers normally rent for parties of four to six people so expenses can be shared; the cost usually includes tackle, bait, licenses, lunch, ice and a captain and mate, but not taxes or tips. Rates range from $200 to $700 per day, depending on the size of the boat. Trips depart around 7 a.m. and return by 2 or 3 in the afternoon. Most boats either travel east to the Gordo Banks or around Lover's Arch toward the Pacific.

Reputable in-town fleets include the Hotel Cabo San Lucas Fleet, phone (624) 143-3457; Hotel Finisterra Fleet, phone (624) 143-0366; Hotel Hacienda Fleet, phone (624) 143-0663; and Los Dorados Fleet, phone (624) 143-1630.

Medano Beach is the most popular local stretch of sand. Here you can rent snorkeling and water sports equipment or grab a bite at one of the outdoor restaurants. The Pisces Watersport Center, next to the Cascadas Resort, offers such activities as parasailing, snorkeling, water skiing, windsurfing and taking to San Lucas Bay in a catamaran sailboat. Phone (624) 143-1288. Cabo Aquadeportes, at the Hacienda Hotel on the bay and at Chileno

Beach next to the Hotel Cabo San Lucas, can arrange diving, kayaking, sailing and snorkeling expeditions; phone (624) 143-0117. Chileno Bay, near the hotel and about 14 kilometers (9 miles) north of Cabo San Lucas, is a prime location for snorkeling; octopus and lobster are among the many creatures on view.

The Gulf of California coast between San José del Cabo and Cabo San Lucas is sprinkled with surfing areas, hidden beaches and secluded little coves. Dirt paths branching off Mex. 1 lead to these spots. Playa Cemetario, about 4 kilometers (2.5 miles) north of Cabo San Lucas, is a white-sand beach ideal for swimming. Playa Barco Varado (Shipwreck Beach), about 10 kilometers (6 miles) north, curves around a rocky shelf and the remains of a Japanese freighter that sunk in the 1960s.

Santa María Bay, about 12 kilometers (7.5 miles) north, draws divers with its excellent visibility. Playa Palmilla, about 27 kilometers (17 miles) north, is near the Palmilla Hotel, itself a luxurious, hacienda-style accommodation. Thatched *palapas* at this exceptionally pristine beach are sandwiched between rock formations that look like king-size sand castles.

Note: Most of the beaches are safe for swimming; others are best appreciated for the scenery. Check locally for surf conditions; the currents and undertow at some beaches can carry swimmers far out to sea. Public transportation is generally not available to these sites, although buses that run between the two Cabos may let you disembark at beach turnoffs. It's easiest to use your own car. Fly-in visitors should keep in mind that rental cars in the Los Cabos area are expensive (at least $60 per day). All beaches in Mexico belong to the government and consequently are open to the public. Parking at or camping on deserted beaches is perfectly legal; it is not legal, however, to leave behind garbage of any kind.

Whale-watching excursions to San Ignacio Lagoon and the surrounding waters are offered from December through March. Gray whales can be seen along the mid-Baja coastline as they complete their long-distance migration from the Bering Sea to the Pacific's warm waters. Day tours depart by air twice a week from Cabo San Lucas at 7 a.m., returning around 4 p.m. The cost includes the round-trip flight, four hours of whale watching, lunch and a bilingual guide. Hotels in the downtown area can provide further information, or contact the regional airline Aereo Calafia; phone (624) 143-4255.

Rivaling the popularity of sport fishing is golf. Not so long ago, golf meant one nine-hole course, the Campo de Golf near San José del Cabo. A process that allows reclaimed water to be used for irrigation purposes made it possible to maintain manicured greens and fairways in the midst of arid conditions. Today world-class courses scattered between the two Cabos are laid out against a stunning backdrop of rugged seaside vistas and desert terrain. Course designers include Roy Dye, Robert

Trent Jones and Jack Nicklaus. Golfing in this resort area is by no means cheap, although greens fees normally include the use of a cart.

The signature hole at the Nicklaus-designed Palmilla, on the grounds of the Palmilla Hotel, is the par-4 fifth. The tee shot must carry over a cactus-filled arroyo; that same canyon wraps around in front of the green as well. The desert vegetation, which is in bloom year-round, makes this course not only challenging to play but breathtaking to view. The 27-hole course is open for play to resort guests only. Phone (800) 637-2226 in the United States.

The Golden Bear also designed Cabo del Sol, which features seven dramatic waterfront holes, including one where the tee shot is fired from a clifftop to a green surrounded by rock outcroppings rising from the cobalt-blue Sea of Cortés. Instead of negotiating long fairways, players tee off over deep arroyos to landing pads and then chip to the green. Phone (800) 386-2465.

Cabo Real Golf Club is a semi-private, 18-hole course with views ranging from mountaintop to sea, while the Eldorado Golf Club features six holes fronting the gulf. For both courses phone (800) 393-0400 in the United States.

Shopping, Dining and Nightlife

Downtown Cabo's small size lends itself to strolling. A pedestrian walkway wraps around the marina and can be traversed in about 30 minutes. Stop by in mid-afternoon, when local boats return from the day's fishing, for a first-hand look at the many varieties found in these waters. The Shrimp Bucket Restaurant provides a golf cart that transports visitors to points around the marina free of charge.

Most of the craft shops are on or near Lázaro Cárdenas and Boulevard Marina. They offer T-shirts and other touristy souvenirs in addition to blankets, folk art, woven goods and distinctive black coral jewelry. Galería El Dorado, at Boulevard Marina near Guerrero, is an arts and crafts store with a collection of paintings and ceramics executed by local artists. Open-air flea markets in the downtown area sell ceramics, pottery, silver jewelry, leather goods, blown glassware and hand-carved wooden animal figures. Bargaining is expected.

Faces of Mexico, in a bright blue building at Lázaro Cárdenas and Matamoros, is a combination art gallery-museum exhibiting a collection of religious masks dating back several hundred years. *Exvotos* have facial writings describing why the mask was made for a particular religious ceremony; *retablos* depict emotions without the use of words. The masks manage to convey great feeling despite their simplicity; their skilled creators come from all over Mexico. Most of the works are for sale. The gallery is open Mon.-Sat. 10-1:30 and 4-7.

If shopping works up an appetite, try the taco stands and food stalls scattered around the downtown area. Use the same common sense that applies whenever sampling street food in Mexico—if there's a crowd hovering around a cart and the food looks hot and fresh, it should be fine.

Tacos come in a variety of guises: *pescado* (fish), *camarones* (shrimp), *carnitas* (pork), *pollo* (chicken) and *carne asada* (beef). The open-air restaurants, many run by local families, also are good places for a hearty morning meal of *huevos rancheros* (eggs and black beans drenched in tomato salsa and sprinkled with cheese), tortillas and a cup of hot coffee.

With advance arrangements, hotel restaurants will prepare fish caught during the day for an evening meal. Seafood restaurants dot the marina area. The restaurant in the Hotel Cabo San Lucas serves fine cuisine on a patio overlooking the Sea of Cortez. Additional atmosphere is supplied by a nine-piece mariachi band playing music that is the essence of romantic Mexico. The musicians serenade diners nightly from 6 until 9 p.m.

Cabo San Lucas has a pretty active nightlife due to the preponderance of surfer types and other youthful revelers. Rather than the flashy discos common in other Mexican resorts, casual bars and rock 'n' roll are the preferred elements of a night on the town. The Cabo Wabo Cantina, downtown on Calle Vicente Guerrero (at Avenida Lázaro Cárdenas), is owned by rocker Sammy Hagar. Young crowds pack the place for occasional live shows by visiting bands; hard rock and dance pop blasts from the sound system on other nights. It's open daily until 4 a.m.

The Giggling Marlin, overlooking the marina west off Plaza Aramburo, has frequent live music and a well-attended happy hour. The attraction here is a pulley device that dangles patrons upside down—rather like a captured fish—to the great amusement of the masses. Also high on the see-and-be-seen circuit is El Squid Roe, on Boulevard Marina. The club resembles more than anything a two-story junkyard, with everything imaginable plastered on its walls. An outdoor patio accommodates those trying out the latest dance moves. Also on Boulevard Marina is the Río Bar and Grill, which offers free happy-hour munchies, '70s tunes, karaoke contests and live reggae bands on weekends.

The Whale Watcher's Bar in the Hotel Finisterra, off Boulevard Marina heading out toward Land's End, is a good place to sip a margarita and watch the sun slowly drop into the Pacific while mariachis play in the background.

Baja California Sur State Tourism Office (Secretaría de Turismo): Boulevard Mauricio Castro in the Plaza San José Mall, San José del Cabo. Open Mon.-Fri. 8-3; phone (624) 142-3310.

ENSENADA, BAJA CALIFORNIA (B-1)
pop. 237,700

One of Baja California's foremost summer resorts and its third largest city, Ensenada (ehn-seh-NAH-dah) spreads over scrub-covered hills that slope down to the shores of large, lovely Bahía de Todos Santos (Todos Santos Bay). The city (its name, not surprisingly, means "bay") boasts a scenic setting, attractive beaches, pleasant weather, duty-free shopping, fine sport fishing and close proximity to the United States; for many weekend visitors, Ensenada is the farthest they ever get into Mexico.

The area was relatively isolated before the completion of Mex. 1 from Tijuana and the development of port facilities in the mid-1930s. More than 300 years earlier, Spanish explorer Sebastián Vizcaíno sailed into the bay and, entranced by its beauty, named it Ensenada de Todos Santos—"All Saints' Bay." A lack of fresh water prevented any permanent settlement from taking hold, although the bay often sheltered whaling ships, treasure-laden galleons and the privateers who preyed upon them.

Ranchers securing a foothold in Mexico's northern frontier began to settle the area early in the 19th century. Ensenada temporarily boomed in 1870 with the discovery of gold at nearby Real del Castillo. The town became a supply depot for miners and was designated the capital of the Baja California Territory in 1882. By the early 20th century, however, the mines had given out, the capital was relocated to Mexicali and Ensenada lapsed back into obscurity.

After U.S. Prohibition went into effect in the late 1920s, Ensenada—along with Tijuana—became a favored drinking and gambling destination for Hollywood types. Real revitalization came with agricultural reform and development in the Mexicali Valley. A nearby port was needed to handle the export of farm produce to the United States and mainland Mexico, and Ensenada's harbor facilities made it an obvious choice for development. Tuna fishing provided further economic incentive. But it was the completion of paved highway Mex. 1 from Tijuana that opened up Ensenada to American vacationers and sport fishing enthusiasts.

Connected to Tijuana by the four-lane Mex. 1-D toll highway, Ensenada is the governmental seat of the *municipio* of Ensenada, which extends south to the Baja California Sur state line and includes shoreline on both the east and west coasts of the peninsula. The local economy has long relied on the cultivation of olives and grapes and the harvesting of halibut and yellowtail. A decline in commercial shipping activity and recent cutbacks in cruise ship schedules, however, have made tourism more important to the city than ever before.

While Ensenada is a little far for a day trip from the United States, it makes a great weekend getaway and a good choice for dining, strolling, perhaps a little shopping, and relaxing on the beach or on a boat. Summer is the high season; to avoid crowds, visit April-May or October-November.

Practicalities

Ensenada is about 109 kilometers (68 miles) south of Tijuana. The city's small airstrip currently accommodates only private planes, although regular service from Los Angeles via Air L.A. may eventually be initiated. A tourist permit is required, even for stays of less than 72 hours. For additional information about border crossing regulations *see* "Crossing the Border," page 550.

Four-lane toll highway Mex. 1-D is a quick, convenient route south from Tijuana. There are three toll booths between the two cities; restrooms are available near the booths. Although towing and Green Angels assistance are free, motorists who run out of gas on this stretch are required to pay for it. Emergency telephones also appear along Mex. 1-D approximately every 3 kilometers (2 miles). There are frequent panoramic views of the scenic Baja coastline, particularly around Punta Salsipuedes, just south of El Mirador and about 32 kilometers (20 miles) north of Ensenada. Some of the highway's curves can be daunting to drivers not used to them.

Free Mex. 1 (look for signs that say *Libre*) parallels Mex. 1-D most of the way, although it turns inland south of La Misión, out of sight of the ocean. The driving time is longer, and the road has some rough spots. Night driving along this and other two-lane secondary roads in northern Baja should be done with caution, as both cattle and pedestrians frequently cross them.

The bus station is in the northern section of town at Calle 11 and Avenida Riveroll. Bus service is inexpensive, and taking the bus is a good way for visitors who want to mix with the locals. Local bus routes are designated by street name, usually painted on the windshield. Intercity buses travel frequently between Ensenada along both Mex. 1 and Mex. 1-D; the ABC line offers "deluxe" service to Tijuana and Mexicali. For additional information about buses *see* "Bus Service," page 68.

Taxicabs congregate near the bus station and at the hotels along Avenida López Mateos. Although their ubiquitous solicitations can be annoying, drivers are normally courteous and knowledgeable. Make sure, however, that the fare is set before you get in the cab. Taxis can be hired for trips to such outlying destinations as La Bufadora.

One of Ensenada's best features is its mild climate, similar to coastal southern California but with fewer extremes of heat than almost any other Baja city. Winter evenings can be chilly, but the temperature seldom drops much below 40 F. Summers are warm and dry, with occasional hot spells caused by Santa Ana winds blowing in from the desert. Precipitation averages only 10 inches annually, with almost all of it falling between December and March. Fierce Pacific storms sometimes bring torrential winter rains.

Personal safety in Ensenada is a matter of common sense. Although it has experienced tremendous growth, the city still has a relaxed, laid-back atmosphere. Tourists are invariably welcomed, as it is their dollars that sustain many Mexican businesses. If traveling by car, the best advice is to drive safely; traffic accidents are often the biggest source of vacation headaches in Mexico. One way to minimize risk is to stop at every intersection, even those that don't have stop signs.

The English-language *Baja Sun* is a tourist-oriented newspaper containing travel information, articles about Baja cities and lots of local advertising. Radio Bahía Ensenada (1590 AM) has an English/Spanish program Saturdays from 4-6 p.m. ATM machines are located in the Serfin Bank, Avenida Ruíz #290, and the Banamex Bank, Avenida Reyerson and Calle 3. *Casas de cambio* (exchange booths), such as the one located at avenidas Juárez and Reforma on the east side of town, offer the best foreign exchange rates.

In the event of emergency, Clinica Hospital Cardiomed is located downtown at Av. Obregón #1018. Phone (646) 178-0351 (English spoken).

City Layout

Ensenada has two separate business districts that serve its commercial and resort interests. Local businesses, stores, banks, offices and *cantinas* line avenidas Ruíz and Juárez, which are extensions of Mex. 1 through the city. Closer to the waterfront, toll highway Mex. 1-D enters the city from the west. (**Note:** Negotiate the three metal speed bumps just west of downtown very carefully, as they can damage the underside of a vehicle.)

Along Avenida López Mateos and Boulevard Lázaro Cárdenas (also called Boulevard Costero) are hotels, restaurants, nightspots, sport-fishing outfits and shops that cater primarily to tourists. The Costero, which follows the bay, ends at Calle Agustín Sangines (also called Calle Delante), which proceeds east to Mex. 1; Mex. 1, the Transpeninsular Highway, then heads south down the length of the peninsula.

Away from the major arterials, Ensenada is easy to negotiate. The terrain is flat, and the layout is a basic grid. Avenues (avenidas) are named and run north-south; streets (calles) are numbered and run east-west. Streets and avenues are often unmarked, however. To orient yourself, count off city blocks inland from Avenida López Mateos, which is also known as Calle 1 (First Street); successive streets are Calle 2, Calle 3, etc. The prominent clock tower at the Historical and Cultural Center, Boulevard Lázaro Cárdenas and Avenida Club Rotario, can function as a downtown orientation landmark.

Driving tips to keep in mind: As in other Baja cities, traffic lights are small and often hard to spot from a distance. *Alto* (stop) signs placed at intersections can be obscure, so always proceed slowly and with caution. Some downtown streets are one way. On-street parking is usually available. The pay lot at the Plaza Marina shopping center, on Boulevard Costero just north of the sport-fishing piers, is convenient for nearby waterfront wandering.

The city's low skyline is distinguished by the twin spires of Our Lady of Guadalupe (Nuestra

Señora de Guadalupe), Calle 6 and Avenida Floresta. The church, built in typical Spanish colonial style, is one of Ensenada's most prominent structures. West of downtown, Avenida Alemán (accessible via Avenida Hidalgo Reyerson) encircles Chapultepec Hills, an attractive residential area. From this vantage point there is a bird's eye view of the entire city and Todos Santos Bay.

Special Events

Something always seems to be going on in Ensenada. Carnaval (Mardi Gras) is usually celebrated in mid-February on the six days prior to Ash Wednesday. A downtown street fair takes place each night, with rides, live music, food vendors, parades of flower-covered floats and other merriment. The festivities climax with a masquerade ball; prizes are awarded for the best costume.

The popular Newport to Ensenada Yacht Race from Newport Beach, Calif., to Ensenada is held each year in late April. Approximately 400 boats in different classes race to the finish line; most remain in the city for a day or two, and a huge party ensues. For information contact the Newport Ocean Sailing Association in California; phone (949) 644-1023.

The Estero Beach Volleyball Tournament takes place in late June on the sands in front of the Estero Beach Hotel. The tournament attracts some of the best volleyball players in North America.

Franciscan and Dominican missionaries first introduced wine culture to Baja California in the 16th century as a way to celebrate holy Mass, and today a thriving wine industry is centered in the Guadalupe Valley outside of Ensenada. With an ideal climate for grape production and rich volcanic soil, vineyards in northeastern Baja California state produce some 90 percent of Mexican wines.

For 10 days in early August the Harvest Festival (Fiesta de la Vendimia) celebrates the grape. Area wineries, many with vineyards in the nearby Guadalupe and El Escondido valleys, also offer tours (see Wineries below). For more information contact the Wine Workers Association of Baja California (Asociación de Vitivinicultores), downtown at Av. de la Marina #10, third floor; phone (646) 178-3038.

Local restaurants participate in the Seafood Fair, which takes place in late September. The Juan Hussong International Chili Cookoff, normally the second weekend in October, brings together chili cooks from around the region. Popular Mexican beers and a selection of local wines help their fiery concoctions go down more smoothly. Admission is charged.

Ensenada, like most of Mexico, honors the deceased during Day of the Dead celebrations Nov. 1-2. Beginning in mid-November is the SCORE Baja 1000 Off-Road Race (commonly known as the Baja Mil), one of the world's most prestigious off-road races. There are separate categories for cars, trucks, motorcycles and ATVs. The course alternates each year between a straight, 1,050-mile run

from Ensenada to La Paz and a shorter 620-mile loop that begins and ends in Ensenada. For information contact SCORE International in the United States; phone (818) 225-8402.

Another major festival is Our Lady of Guadalupe Day (Día de Nuestra Señora de Guadalupe), celebrated Dec. 12. It honors the nation's patron saint, the Guadalupe Virgin. All manner of amusement rides are set up in front of Our Lady of Guadalupe Church, and another attraction is the array of culinary specialties from all over Mexico.

Shopping

Some visitors prefer Ensenada's low-pressure shopping environment to Tijuana's more raucous atmosphere. Like that city, Ensenada is a duty-free zone, and savvy shoppers can purchase imported items at significant savings over U.S. prices.

The main tourist shopping area is along Avenida López Mateos. Gift shops carry such imported merchandise as silver and gold jewelry, onyx chess sets, leather boots and fine liquor. Some of the shops have fixed prices; English is usually spoken and credit cards are welcomed. Artesanías Castillo, Avenida López Mateos #656, and Los Castillo, Avenida López Mateos #815, carry Taxco silver jewelry guaranteed to be at least 92.5 percent pure (designated by the numerals ".925"). La Cucaracha, another gold and silver jewelry shop on Avenida Blancarte just off López Mateos, offers senior citizen discounts.

La Mina de Solomon, Avenida López Mateos #1000, sells jewelry by renowned designer Sergio Bustamante of Tlaquepaque, Jalisco. La Esquina de Bodegas, on Avenida Miramar and Calle 6 near the Santo Tomás winery, has a bookstore and gift shop and sells locally produced Baja wines.

Quality imported items also can be found in shops at the Estero Beach Resort south of Ensenada off Mex. 1. Importaciones carries Rolex watches, while Bazar Mexicano has sterling silver jewelry, onyx sculptures and decorative objects in copper, brass and glass. Also at the resort is a museum displaying a seashell collection and replicas of statues and ceramic figurines from various pre-Columbian cultures.

Curio shops up and down López Mateos stock traditional Mexican craft and clothing items like baskets, ceramics, guitars, jewelry, wrought-iron furniture, and leather jackets, purses and sandals. On Boulevard Lázaro Cárdenas (Costero) at Avenida Castillo is Centro Artesanal, a cluster of privately owned craft shops. One shop, Galería de Pérez Meillon, sells Casas Grandes pottery, Kumiai baskets and other handmade items fashioned by native artisans using age-old techniques.

Outdoor flea markets offer a chance to find the odd treasure amid piles of merchandise. Los Globos, at Los Globos and Calle 9 (three blocks east of Avenida Reforma), is especially busy on weekends. In one area there are foodstuffs—fruit, vegetables, nuts, grains, freshly made tacos and *churros,* a sweet fritter similar to a doughnut. Browse among the new and used tools, electrical appliances, clothing, toys and innumerable other items for sale.

For local shopping, try Dorian's, a branch of the Baja department store chain, at Av. Ruíz #328. Among the everyday goods are imported perfumes and clothing. Calimax, Calle 3 and Avenida Gastelum, carries grocery staples as well as Mexican liquors and wines.

Outdoor Recreation

Ensenada still proclaims itself "the yellowtail capital of the world," although catches have dwindled in recent years. The protected harbor and nearby waters yield barracuda, bonito and rockfish. The season for sport fishing is roughly June through mid-September, although such bottom-feeding species as sea bass, rock cod, halibut and whitefish can be caught all year.

Charter arrangements can be made at the piers off Boulevard Costero and at some shops along Avenida López Mateos. Rates for private groups range upward from about $550 per day, depending on the size of the craft and the number of passengers. These excursions usually leave at the crack of dawn and last until early afternoon. For those who would rather go it alone, surf fishing can be enjoyed along sandy stretches south of the city.

Gordo's Sport Fishing offers daily yellowtail excursions that leave around 7 a.m. The cost is about $35 (U.S.) per person; rod rental is extra. A fishing license costs $6.50. Night fishing for albacore also is available. For information phone (646) 178-3515.

Boat rides around the bay can be arranged; look for the small fishing boats *(pangas)* at the end of the fish market pier. This is also a good spot to watch local fishermen bringing in the daily catch.

From late December through March an estimated 15,000 whales pass by Todos Santos Island in Ensenada Bay, little more than a mile offshore, on a migration journey that begins in the Bering Sea and ends at Scammons Lagoon, midway down Baja's Pacific coast. Some of the whales come close enough to the shoreline to scratch their backs along the bay floor, removing barnacles and parasites. The Ensenada Clipper Fleet offers whale-watching excursions (December to March), fishing trips and party cruises aboard the *Clipper Deluxe.* For information phone (646) 178-2185.

There are no beaches within the city proper. Most visitors head for Estero Beach, about 12 kilometers (7 miles) south of downtown Ensenada via Mex. 1; the turnoff, about 7.5 kilometers (4.5 miles) south, is well marked. Here, along the shores of Estero Bay, there are gentle waves and a long stretch of sand. For surfing, the rocky beach near the village of San Miguel, north of Ensenada, is a favorite destination.

Punta Banda, the rocky peninsula forming the southern end of Todos Santos Bay, is popular for scuba and skin diving. This area also has an abundance of hot springs; at spots along the beaches here, it is possible to dig into the sand and create your own hole from which soothing hot waters bubble. There are a couple of RV parks along BCN 23, the paved road that traverses the peninsula. Several unmarked hiking trails also lead off this road.

Dining and Nightlife

Fishy delights await at Ensenada's open-air fish market, on Boulevard Costero at Avenida Miramar, just north of the sport-fishing piers. Known to locals as the Mercado de Mariscos, or Seafood Market, the covered sheds displaying freshly caught fish and shellfish have a suitably salty ambience. Handcart vendors hawk fresh clams, oysters shucked on the spot and ceviche, a mixture of salsa and marinated raw fish that is likely just hours out of the ocean.

Fish tacos are an Ensenada staple. Stands opposite the market offer strips of savory fried fish wrapped in a folded tortilla along with sour cream, guacamole, salsa (both *verde* and *roja,* green and red), cabbage, onions and cilantro; avoid the mayonnaise that is left out on the tables.

Other stands sell spicy shellfish cocktails *(cocteles)* made with clams or shrimp. Stumbling into a small, out-of-the-way seafood restaurant hidden on a side street is one of the joys of exploring the downtown area. Check the customers; if a place is full of locals, it's likely to be good. To be on the safe side, patronize only those places that use purified water in their preparations.

Although Ensenada is very quiet during the week—particularly in winter—it becomes a party town on weekends. Most of the nightspots catering to tourists are in the vicinity of avenidas Ruíz and López Mateos at the western end of downtown. Hussong's Cantina, on Ruíz just east of Mateos, revels in its reputation as one of Baja's rowdiest cantinas, although the designated driver in a group is treated to free soft drinks while his or her companions indulge in margaritas and Mexican beer. Discos roar with loud music as whistle-blowing waiters pour shots of tequila from their holstered pouches.

An offbeat alternative to all this raucousness can be found at Café Café, near the corner of avenidas Gastelum and López Mateos. This bohemian-style hangout offers local musicians, poetry readings, weekend jazz and arthouse film fare on Thursday evenings.

Behind Plaza Civica on Boulevard Costero is a Caliente sports betting facility, similar to those found in Tijuana, where wagers can be placed for just about every sporting event going on in Mexico and the United States. The complex, which has a bar and snack bar, is open daily.

Mexican dance, ballet and theatrical productions take place at the City Theater (Teatro de la Ciudad), on Calle Diamante between avenidas Pedro Loyola and Reforma. Chamber music concerts are given Thurs.-Sat. evenings at 8 p.m. (except mid-December through mid-January) by Pro Musica

Ensenada. Performances are given in the Sala de Barricas, an old winery warehouse at Avenida Miramar #666, across the street from the Bodegas de Santo Tomás winery.

Baja California State Tourism Office: across from the Corona Hotel in a one-story white building on Boulevard Lázaro Cárdenas (Boulevard Costero) and Calle Las Rocas. Open Mon.-Sat. 8-8, Sun. 9-1; phone (646) 172-3022 (English spoken). This office also can provide legal assistance to tourists.

The Convention and Visitors Bureau operates a booth on Boulevard Lázaro Cárdenas near the western entrance to the city. Open Mon.-Fri. 9-7, Sat. 10-4, Sun. 10-3; phone (646) 178-2411 (English spoken).

What To See in and Around Town

CIVIC PLAZA (Plaza Cívica) is at Blvd. Lázaro Cárdenas (Costero) and Av. Macheros. Also known as Three Heads Park, it has a small landscaped court with 12-foot-high busts of Mexican freedom fighter Father Miguel Hidalgo and former presidents Benito Juárez and Venustiano Carranza. Horse-drawn sightseeing carriages, or *calandrias,* depart from the plaza, and cruise ships dock offshore. There also are public restrooms. A block south at Avenida Alvarado is the Naval Base, where flag ceremonies with a drum and bugle corps take place at sunrise and sunset.

CONSTITUTION OF 1857 NATIONAL PARK (Parque Nacional Constitución de 1857) is northeast of the city. To get there, take Mex. 3 to Ojos Negros, a small farming community about 40 km (25 mi.) east of Ensenada. At Km 55, a dirt road branches northeast and steadily ascends for about 35 km (22 mi.) to the park entrance. Although ungraded, the road is normally negotiable in a passenger vehicle. In the high plateau country of the Sierra de Juárez range, the park offers a contrast to Ensenada's seaside air.

The rugged terrain, highlighted by unusual rock formations, is blanketed with thick forests of ponderosa pine. In the middle of the park is small Lake Hanson, surrounded by primitive campsites. Fishing is permitted (bass and catfish inhabit the lake when rainfall is adequate); hunting is prohibited. An entrance fee is charged. For information contact the Director of National Parks (Dirección de Parques Nacionales); phone (686) 554-4404 or (686) 554-5470.

LA BUFADORA (The Snort) is about 32 km (20 mi.) south of downtown Ensenada; take paved BCN 23, which splits west off Mex. 1 just north of Maneadero, passing olive orchards, cultivated fields, trailer parks and the private Baja Beach and Tennis Club before ending at a parking lot at the tip of the Punta Banda Peninsula. Climb the steps to observe this hollow rock formation that acts as a sea spout. During incoming tides, water rushes into an underground cavern, sending spray shooting into the air like a geyser.

Snack vendors congregate along the path to the blowhole, and there are curio shops where you can browse for souvenirs, but the main attraction is the dramatic mountain scenery en route. A parking fee is charged.

MUSEUM OF HISTORY AND ANTHROPOLOGY (Museo de Historia y Antropología) is at Av. Reyerson and Calle Virgilio Uribe. The oldest public building in the state of Baja California, it was built in 1887 by the International Co. of Mexico, an American firm established to promote the urban colonization of Baja. Since 1992 the two-story structure has been the regional headquarters for the National Institute of Anthropology and History (INAH).

Changing exhibits (with Spanish descriptions) chronicle the area's past. It is also said that a ghost inhabits the building. Tues.-Fri. 8-3, Sat.-Sun. 10-5. Donations. Phone (646) 178-2531.

SOCIAL, CIVIC AND CULTURAL CENTER OF ENSENADA (Centro Social, Cívico y Cultural de Ensenada) is on Blvd. Lázaro Cárdenas (Costero) at Av. Riviera. It occupies the Riviera del Pacífico, formerly a gambling casino and hotel. The mansion, with its elegant Moorish-style architecture, was a favored gathering place for wealthy Americans and Mexicans during the Prohibition era. The center now hosts conventions, civic and social events, and occasional art shows.

Visitors can view the murals in the entry hall, explore the restored ballroom and gambling rooms or relax in the patio gardens. The building also houses the Museum of Ensenada History (Museo de Historia de Ensenada), which has Baja-related exhibits. Tues.-Sun. 10-4 (but can close up to 2 hours for lunch). Donations. Phone (646) 176-4310, or (646) 177-0594 for the museum.

WINERIES

- **Bodegas de Santa Tomás** is downtown on Av. Miramar #666 (at Calle 7). Baja's oldest and largest winery began selling wine by the barrel in 1888, and today the firm's huge Ensenada complex produces a variety of wines and liquors. Forty-five-minute guided tours in English begin daily at 11, 1 and 3. Fee $2 (U.S.). Phone (646) 174-0836, ext. 22.
- **Casa Pedro Domecq** is on Mex. 3 (Carretera Tecate-El Sauzal), Km marker 73, a few miles north of the town of Guadalupe; from Ensenada, take Mex. 1-D north about 10 km (6 mi.) to the junction with Mex. 3, then proceed northeast toward Tecate. Tours and tastings Mon.-Fri. 10-4, Sat.-Sun. 10-1:30. Phone (646) 155-2249.
- **Château Camou** is off Mex. 3 in the Guadalupe Valley. One tour includes lunch. Tours and tastings Mon.-Sat. 8-3, Sun. 9-2. Fee $5-$40 (U.S.). Phone (646) 177-3303or (646) 177-2221.
- **L. A. Cetto Winery** is on Mex. 3 at Km 73.5. Tours and tastings daily 10-4. Phone (646) 177-2352.
- **Monte Xanic Winery** is off Mex. 3 near the village of Francisco Zarco. Tours and tastings Mon.-Fri. 9:30-4. Phone (646) 174-6155.

GUERRERO NEGRO, BAJA CALIFORNIA SUR (D-2) pop. 10,900

Guerrero Negro (geh-REH-roh NEH-groh) is located within the barren Vizcaíno Desert (Desierto Vizcaíno), just south of the Baja California Sur state border. The name, which means "black warrior" in Spanish, was the moniker of an American whaling ship wrecked at the entrance to nearby Scammon's Lagoon (Laguna Ojo de Liebre). Summer temperatures here are much cooler than in the interior of the peninsula due to the cold California Current, which extends north off the Pacific coast.

The area around Guerrero Negro is part of the El Vizcaíno Biosphere Reserve, designated a World Heritage Site by UNESCO in 1993. Encompassing bays, lagoons, vast expanses of the Sonoran Desert and the rugged Sierra mountains, El Vizcaíno is an important breeding and wintering site for the California gray whale and also is home to four species of endangered sea turtle.

Approximately 1,500 whales migrate south some 6,000 miles each year from the Bering Sea off Alaska to several lagoons along the central Baja coast: Scammon's Lagoon (Laguna Ojo de Liebre), Magdalena Bay (Bahía Magdalena) and San Ignacio Lagoon (Laguna de San Ignacio). The whales venture from their Arctic feeding grounds to mate and calve in these comparatively warm waters.

Most tours to view the whales depart from Magdalena Bay or San Ignacio Lagoon, about 100 miles to the south, although arranging for a boat to nearby Scammon's Lagoon is most conveniently arranged in Guerrero Negro.

To reach Scammon's Lagoon by car, take Mex. 1 south about 9 kilometers (5.5 miles) to the graded dirt turnoff (sandy but passable) that branches southwest; signs at this junction read "Laguna Ojo de Liebre" and "Parque Natural de la Ballena Gris/ Gray Whale Natural Park." There is a salt company checkpoint about 6 kilometers (4 miles) west of the turnoff. About 16 kilometers (10 miles) farther is a shack where admission to the natural park is charged. Just beyond the shack is a fork; the road to the left leads to the beach offering the best views. Since the whales are usually some distance offshore, bring a pair of binoculars.

From late December through March, group tours in small boats (*pangas*) are offered by local fishermen, who charge $30-$40 per person. Private boats are not permitted anywhere in the lagoon during the season; local operators receive special permits. Morning is the best time to spot whales, as afternoon fog frequently obscures visibility.

The easiest way to experience the whales up close is to take part in an organized trip from Guerrero Negro. Malarrimo Eco-Tours offers 4-hour excursions with English-speaking guides aboard a 23-foot outboard boat with a maximum of 10 passengers. In addition to the whales, marine birds, sea lions and dolphins can be seen. Van transportation to and from Scammon's Lagoon is included.

Warm clothing, a waterproof jacket or windbreaker, sunblock and rubber-soled shoes are recommended. Trips depart daily Dec. 15-Apr. 15 from the Malarrimo Restaurant and campground complex on Boulevard Zapata. The fee per person is $45 (U.S.); under 11, $35. For information phone (615) 157-0100.

Significantly more expensive, but worth it if you want convenience and a complete experience, is an all-inclusive package excursion under the guidance of an experienced naturalist. Most of these trips depart from San Diego and include transportation and accommodations. A representative package tour company is the environmentally oriented, San Diego-based Baja Expeditions, Inc.; phone (800) 843-6967.

LA PAZ, BAJA CALIFORNIA SUR (F-3) pop. 168,600

La Paz (lah PAHS) is the commercial as well as the governmental capital of the state of Baja California Sur. Its name means "peace," and the Dove of Peace Monument, a large contemporary sculpture that acts as a gateway to the city, bears the following (translated) inscription: "And if you want peace, I offer it to you in the sunny peace of my bay." Today's city spreads out from the curving shore of beautiful Bahía de la Paz, the largest bay along Baja's eastern coastline.

Ironically, La Paz's history is one of the most turbulent of any community on the entire Baja California Peninsula. Two years after the bay was discovered by a Spanish expedition in 1533, supply problems doomed a colonization attempt by Hernando Cortés. Nearly 300 years of isolation and hardship prevented a permanent settlement from taking hold. The most persistent inhabitants were the privateers who sought haven in the bay. The name of one—Cromwell—lives on (Hispanicized) in the *coromueles,* or offshore breezes, and in such local place names as Playa Coromuel.

Rich oyster beds below the surface of the Gulf of California attracted a handful of fortune seekers throughout the 17th century. The Jesuits founded a mission at La Paz in 1720 and kept it going despite a series of Indian uprisings. It was abandoned nearly 30 years later after disease had virtually wiped out the area's indigenous population; the city's cathedral stands on the site today.

A group of determined Spaniards finally established a settlement in 1811. Continued pearl diving and some mining provided impetus for growth, and when Loreto (see separate listing within this region) was destroyed by a hurricane in 1829, La Paz was named the territorial capital. Beautiful black and pink pearls from gulf waters filled the coffers of the Spanish royal treasury. But conflict broke out again, this time in the form of the Mexican-American War. Battles were fought in the city's streets, but American soldiers departed after the Treaty of Guadalupe Hidalgo was signed in 1848.

Southern Baja's remoteness continued to hinder any large-scale development. After the pearl and mining industries gave out toward the end of the 1930s, La Paz languished. But as was the case with Ensenada and Cabo San Lucas, sportsmen and tourists slowly rediscovered the area's balmy winter climate and fine fishing. After years of existence as a neglected territory, Baja California Sur—along with Quintana Roo, one of Mexico's two newest states—suddenly exploded with economic and population growth, and La Paz evolved from a sleepy port into a modern state capital.

This jolt into the Mexican mainstream has not come without a few rude awakenings—the traffic congestion on downtown's cramped, narrow streets being but one example. But the shady plazas and renovated, palm-fringed *malecón* (waterside Paseo Alvaro Obregón) still retain some of the colonial grace of old. And for every contemporary structure there is a quaintly arched doorway or an old cobblestone sidewalk.

The city sports a growing number of resorts and fleets of pleasure craft. La Paz also is a busy commercial port, and downtown streets are lined with small shops full of foreign goods. Some of these businesses still observe the traditional *siesta*, closing their doors in the early afternoon.

Despite its commercial bustle, La Paz is a laid-back city. Residents carry themselves with pride and respect; drivers actually stop for pedestrians crossing the street. While tourism is accommodated willingly, a thoroughly Mexican atmosphere prevails. This old-fashioned charm is most fully evident on Sunday evenings, when throngs of couples and families customarily promenade along the *malecón*, often against the backdrop of a spectacular sunset.

Practicalities

The airport is located 18 kilometers (11 miles) southwest of the city off Mex. 1 (north toward Ciudad Constitución). Aero California and Aeroméxico have daily flights from Los Angeles and Tijuana to La Paz. These two companies also fly to and from several Mexican mainland cities, including Guadalajara, Los Mochis and Mexico City. Alaska Airlines flies from Los Angeles, Portland, San Diego, San Francisco and Seattle Tuesday, Thursday and Saturday during the winter season.

Colectivos (shuttle vans) transport passengers from the airport into the city but not the other way around; you'll need to take a taxi when departing. *Also see "Arriving by Air," page 551.*

Buses to the beaches and the deep-water port of Pichilingue depart from the station at Paseo Alvaro Obregón #125 (the *malecón* terminal). Long-distance travel to other Baja cities is provided by Autotransportes Aguila; buses arrive and depart from the terminal at Jalisco and Héroes de Independencia, a couple of miles southwest of downtown. Regular passenger service is provided between La Paz and Tijuana—a 24-hour trip. Also arriving at this terminal are *Aguila* (local) buses from Cabo San Lucas, about 209 kilometers (130 miles) south

of La Paz. A taxi can take you from the terminal to the *malecón* area.

In-town routes cover the city. The fare is inexpensive, but a knowledge of Spanish is helpful and riders should be familiar with the city layout. The central depot is located at avenidas Revolución de 1910 and Degollado, next to the public market.

Taxis are plentiful, especially along the *malecón* and near the bigger hotels. Rates average about $4 (U.S.) for 2 miles, or about $11 from downtown to the airport. Make sure the fare is set before you get in the cab.

If you've arrived by air, a car will come in handy for exploring outlying beaches, but keep in mind that rental cars can be much more expensive in Mexico than in the United States. The city has several rental car agencies; unless otherwise specified, the vehicles tend to be Volkswagen Beetles.

Ferry service links La Paz with the mainland ports of Mazatlán and Topolobampo, near Los Mochis. Reservations to Mazatlán can be made in person at the Grupo Sematur ticket office, which is downtown on Guillermo Prieto at Calle 5 de Mayo, two blocks inland from Jardín Velasco (Plaza Constitución). The office is open Mon.-Fri. 8-3, Sat. 8-2; phone (612) 125-8899.

Reservations to Topolobampo can be made in person at the Baja Ferries ticket office, on the corner of Calle Isabel La Catolica and Navarro. The office is open Mon.-Sat. 8-5; phone (612) 125-7443 or (800) 122-1414 (toll-free long distance within Mexico). The terminal for both ferries is in Pichilingue, about 16 kilometers (10 miles) north of La Paz via Mex. 11.

Separate fares are charged for passengers and for vehicles; the rate for vehicles is determined by the length of the vehicle in meters. The maximum vehicle width is 2.6 meters (about 8.6 feet); vehicles that exceed this width are charged double the rate, as they will take up two spaces. Fares are subject to frequent change.

If you plan to transport a vehicle on the ferry, contact a Mexican consulate office prior to your trip for the latest updates regarding laws and regulations. Random but thorough searches may occur before vehicles are boarded. Owners are not permitted to retrieve articles from their vehicles after they have been boarded. For additional information, *see "Ferry Service," page 68.*

The English-language *Baja Sun* carries recreational articles and advertisements pertaining to La Paz and other Baja California cities. The Librería Contempo bookstore, on Agustín Arreola near Paseo Alvaro Obregón, sells several English publications. Radio station XERT, 810 AM, plays a variety of music; more traditional Mexican sounds can be heard on Radio Alegría, 90.1 FM. The satellite dish antennas at the large hotels bring in TV stations from Mexico City as well as the United States.

Currency can be exchanged at Banamex, on Esquerro at the corner of Agustín Arreola, in front of the La Perla de La Paz department store (just off the *malecón*). For medical emergencies, the Centro de Especialidades Médicas hospital is in the Fidepaz Building at the north end of town, on Mex. 1 at Km marker 5.5; phone (612) 124-0400.

Accommodations in La Paz range from budget hotels lining the *malecón* to more luxurious properties scattered along the road to Pichilingue. For adventurers or those traveling on shoestring budgets, there are several *pensións*, or boardinghouses, in the downtown area. These are no-frills places and frequently rundown-looking, although they tend to have a friendly, communal feeling. The Hostería del Convento, Av. Francisco Madero #85 Sur, has a lush tropical courtyard; the colonial building was once a Spanish mission.

November through April or May is the best time to visit La Paz, when days are warm and nights can be refreshingly cool. Summer's sticky heat and humidity is uncomfortable, to say the least, despite the presence of afternoon breezes coming off the bay. Rainfall in this desert region is scant and varies from year to year, although violent tropical storms called *chubascos* bring occasional downpours in late summer or fall.

City Layout

La Paz appears as somewhat of a mirage among the barren, cactus-covered foothills of southern Baja. Clearly marked signs indicate two routes. Following "Centro" will take you straight into downtown; the Mex. 1 fork proceeds south to San José del Cabo and Cabo San Lucas. Situated at Bahía de la Paz's southeastern end, the city faces northwest, an ideal location from which to appreciate the sunsets that turn the Gulf of California ablaze with color. A long, narrow sandbar, El Mogote, protects La Paz from the gulf's open waters.

The city is laid out in a simple grid pattern, with long, straight streets oriented northwest-southeast and southwest-northeast. The "tourist zone" runs along the *malecón* between avenidas Sinaloa and Colegio Militar. Adjoining the bayfront is old downtown, a congested section of irregular streets that is more easily navigated on foot than by car. Many streets in La Paz are one way, although clearly marked. The major thoroughfares are Paseo Alvaro Obregón, Avenida 16 de Septiembre and Avenida 5 de Mayo. Streets running inland from the waterfront are uphill, becoming primarily residential within 10 blocks.

What To Do

La Paz, like Cabo San Lucas and Ensenada, is famed for its sport fishing. Blue marlin weighing up to 1,000 pounds are found in offshore waters from mid-March through October; sailfish can be hooked from the end of May through October. Bonito, roosterfish and yellowtail are available all year. Other game species include black marlin, dorado, grouper, red snapper, triggerfish and yellowfin tuna.

Boats for a day of deep-sea fishing—either a *panga* (skiff) or a more expensive cruiser for four or more people—can be arranged through travel agencies along the *malecón* and at the fishing desk in the Los Arcos Hotel, on Paseo Alvaro Obregón between Allende and Rosales. Rental rates usually include tackle, bait and crew. Most boats depart from the Pichilingue docks. Reservations are advised from April to early July, when the big marlin are running.

One well-known outfit is the Dorado Velez Fleet, which operates out of the Los Arcos Hotel; for reservations information phone (612) 122-2744, ext. 608. If you're visiting on your own boat, Marina de la Paz, avenidas Topete and Legaspy near the western end of the *malecón*, has slips ranging from 30 to 70 feet and also provides a variety of shoreside services.

The nicest beaches are north of the city via Mex. 11 (known locally as the Pichilingue Highway) toward Pichilingue. The highway is not marked, although signs indicate that you are heading in the direction of Pichilingue and the ferry docks. Mex. 11 continues north all the way to Playa Tecolote.

A short distance north of the tourist wharf in town is Playa Coromuel, which has thatched-roofed bars and restaurants. About 10 kilometers (6 miles) north of downtown is Playa Comancito, located at La Concha (Km 5.5 on the Pichilingue Highway), the area's most exclusive resort. The beach, however—as are all beaches in Mexico—is open to the public. Here equipment for snorkeling, scuba diving and water skiing can be rented.

Pichilingue itself was once a haven for pirates plundering the bounty of black pearls harvested from oysters residing in the bay. By about 1940, however, the mollusks had mysteriously disappeared, presumably wiped out by disease. Today the town functions as the deep-water port for La Paz and a recreational getaway where sport-fishing boats bring in the day's catch.

The beaches become more secluded the farther you go. Playa Pichilingue is north of the ferry dock; stop here for a dip in the clear blue water followed by a cold beer and some freshly grilled fish at one of the beachside *palapas*. Next is Punta Balandra, a lovely series of quiet coves framed by dramatic rock formations. At the tip of the point is Playa Tecolote, where conditions for diving and snorkeling are just about ideal. There are few facilities other than outhouses and a few barbecue pits here, but camping and RV parking is currently free and the water is crystal clear.

Guided Tours

San Diego-based Baja Expeditions offers an array of exciting excursions, with a focus on environment, education and adventure. Sea kayaking, whale watching and scuba diving are among the trips offered. Serious naturalists or divers will relish scuba excursions of up to seven days' duration, exploring some of the peninsula's most beautiful spots. Most trips include accommodations, equipment, meals and a knowledgeable trip leader. Operations are based in La Paz; many trip organizers live in the city and are well acquainted with the area. For additional information, write Baja Expeditions at 2625 Garnet Ave., San Diego, Calif. 92109; phone (800) 843-6967.

Baja Diving Service, Paseo Alvaro Obregón #1665, Marina Pichilingue, offers scuba and snorkeling expeditions to various offshore locations, including Isla Espíritu Santo, site of the sunken vessel the *Salvatierra*. Isla la Partida, home to a large colony of friendly sea lions; the remote beaches on Isla Cerralvo, and underwater mountains, or seamounts. For further information phone (612) 122-1826 or (888) 279-6161 in the United States.

Trips to Magdalena Bay to view gray whales depart from the La Concha Beach Resort on Pichilingue Road (Mex. 11). After a three-and-a-half-hour drive to this bay on Baja's western coast, tour guests board a 16-foot *panga* for two hours of observation. The tour package is available from mid-January to mid-March. For information phone the resort at (800) 716-8603 (toll-free long distance within Mexico) or (800) 999-2252 (from the United States).

Shopping, Dining and Nightlife

As a free port, La Paz offers the savvy shopper good buys on imported merchandise as well as such handicrafts as coral jewelry, seashell knickknacks, leather goods and woven baskets. Tourist-oriented shops cluster along Paseo Alvaro Obregón. Curios La Carretera, on Morelos near the corner of Revolución de 1910, is a shopping complex featuring carved wood furniture, clothing and folk art from various parts of mainland Mexico.

A wide assortment of utilitarian goods fill the stalls of La Paz's Mercado (public market), in the center of town on Avenida Revolución de 1910 at Degollado. Produce, meats, fish and cheeses spill from the open-air stalls, and a juice bar offers orange, papaya, mango, grapefruit and strawberry liquid refreshment. Next to the market are several outdoor cafés that dish up freshly prepared tacos and locally caught fish prepared in a variety of ways.

La Perla de La Paz, in the thick of downtown on Mutualismo at Agustín Arreola, carries an impressive spectrum of upscale merchandise, while Dorian's, at avenidas 16 de Septiembre and 21 de Agosto, stocks typical department store items. Avenida 16 de Septiembre is chockablock with small storefronts selling name-brand stereos, car phones, word processors, TVs and Sony Walkmans. Clothing boutiques offer everything from high fashion to Levi 501's. You'll find clothing from Guatemala as well as Guadalajaran shoes, boots and hats.

Local artisans sell their wares at Cuauhtémoc Park (Parque Cuauhtémoc), on Paseo Alvaro Obregón between Bravo and Rosales, next to the State Tourism Office branch. At Artesanía Cuauhtémoc (The Weaver), southwest of downtown on Abasolo (Mex. 1) between calles Jalisco and Nayarit, Fortunato Silva makes and sells handwoven cotton and woolen articles—rugs, tablecloths, placemats and the like.

At Cerámica Acuario, Guillermo Prieto #625 near the Sematur ferry office, the Ibarra family fires pottery the old-fashioned way. Exquisite floral designs are carefully hand-painted on plates, pitchers, mugs and vases. Look for the various plates hanging on the shop's outside wall.

Steak and seafood head the bill of fare at local restaurants. There are a number of fast-food restaurants in the downtown area, but rather than burgers and fries these takeout cafés offer such Mexican basics as burritos, roasted *pollo* (chicken) and fish tacos.

Nightlife in La Paz doesn't compare to Cabo San Lucas, but there are still options. Las Varitas, on Calle Independencia at Domínguez, is a dance club where the music ranges from salsa to Mexican rock. There is a cover charge to get in. La Paz Lapa (Carlos 'n Charlie's) is typically rowdy, with live music on weekends. The Latin-themed nightclub La Cabaña, which also has a cover charge, is on the lobby floor of the Hotel Perla.

Local and visiting performing arts groups take to the stage at the City Theater (Teatro de la Ciudad), at Miguel Legaspy and Héroes de Independencia. The most enjoyable activity, though, might be to simply take a seat at an outdoor café along the *malecón* at sunset and watch as the waters of the bay turn to spectacular hues of red and gold.

Baja California Sur State Tourism Office (Coordinadora de Promoción al Turismo): on Mex. 1 at Km marker 5.5, at the north end of town in the Fidepaz Building (near the marina). Open Mon.-Fri. 8-8; phone (612) 124-0100 or (612) 124-0424. The staff is helpful and bilingual.

Another office is on the *malecón* at the intersection of Paseo Alvaro Obregón and Bravo (Cuauhtémoc Park); here visitors can obtain information about various city tour packages. It is open Mon.-Fri. 8-3 and 3:30-7; phone (612) 122-5939.

ANTHROPOLOGICAL AND HISTORICAL MUSEUM OF BAJA CALIFORNIA SUR (Museo de Antropología e Historia de Baja California Sur) is at Ignacio Altamirano and 5 de Mayo. It features exhibits on the geology, geography, flora and fauna of the state. Dioramas and photographs of cave paintings depict the region's Indian cultures, and an actual excavation site shows human bones being painstakingly extracted. Spanish mission settlement and Mexican ranch life are among the historical subjects covered. Most exhibit descriptions are in Spanish. Mon.-Fri. 9-6, Sat. 9-2. Donations. Phone (612) 125-6424.

OUR LADY OF LA PAZ (Nuestra Señora de la paz) is on the south side of Jardín Velasco (Plaza Constitución). The church was originally a Jesuit mission. Large bilingual plaques relate its history as well as La Paz's beginnings. The plaza has tiled, tree-shaded paths and is landscaped with colorful hibiscus shrubs. It's a peaceful place to relax and watch city life go by.

LORETO, BAJA CALIFORNIA SUR

(E-3) pop. 10,600

Loreto (loh-REH-toh) dates from 1697, when a mission was founded by Jesuit padre Juan María Salvatierra. It became the first capital of both Alta (the present state of California) and Baja California. Loreto also was the departure point from which Junípero Serra launched his northward quest in 1769 to establish a chain of missions in Alta California.

After Mexico won its independence from Spain in 1821, the missions began to decline. When a devastating hurricane struck in 1829, the capital was moved south to La Paz. Loreto fell into near oblivion until its impressive natural attributes began attracting U.S. sportsmen, who discovered that the fishing was outstanding.

Loreto is easily reached from points north via the transpeninsular highway (Mex. 1). The airport, about 7 kilometers (4 miles) southwest of town, receives regular flights from southern California. Direct flights are offered from Los Angeles by Aero California; for schedule and fare information phone (800) 237-6225.

The *malecón* (boardwalk) has benches for taking in the view, but beach lovers should skip the rocky public stretches in town and head for the indented shores of Bahía Concepción, about an hour's drive north up the Gulf of California coast toward Mulegé.

At Nopolo Bay, about 8 kilometers (5 miles) south of Loreto, there is a championship 18-hole golf course (located just south of the Camino Real Hotel). The challenging course features numerous sand traps and is laid out along the Gulf of California coastline, blending into the surrounding desert and the Sierra de la Giganta mountains. For information on tee times and facilities, phone (613) 133-0554.

There are several fishing outfits based in town. Alfredo's Fleet, on Boulevard Benito Juárez across from the marina, has knowledgeable guides; phone (613) 135-0165. Arturo's Sport Fishing, on Calle Hidalgo between the main plaza and the marina, is a family-owned business that offers diving, snorkeling, kayaking and whale-watching excursions in addition to fishing trips; phone (613) 135-0766.

A boat excursion can be taken to Coronado Island, about a mile and a half offshore, part of Bay of Loreto National Marine Park. The clear, tranquil water harbors a great variety of tropical fish. The best months for snorkeling and scuba diving are June through October, when the water is warmest. Whale sightings are possible in winter. Trip arrangements can be made through local hotels or Arturo's Sport Fishing.

Note: Few merchants in town take credit cards or traveler's checks for payment, although both pesos and U.S. dollars are readily accepted. Currency can be exchanged at the Bancomer bank, on the main plaza, Mon.-Fri. during the morning.

Adventurous travelers can make the trip to the San Javier Mission (Misión San Javier), which is west of town; from a signed junction about 2 kilometers (1.1 miles) south of the Loreto turnoff on Mex. 1, a rough access road (recommended only for high-clearance vehicles) proceeds southwest through stunning canyon and mountain scenery for about 37 kilometers (23 miles). The beautifully restored structure of dark volcanic rock in the *mudéjar* (Moorish) style sits at the bottom of a deep valley.

The second oldest of the Jesuit missions established on the peninsula, it was founded in 1699 but not completed until 1758. The towering walls feature exemplary stonework, and the gilded altar was brought from Mexico City. It's possible to climb the winding stairs to the roof and bell tower, which offers a panoramic view of the valley below. A guided tour can be arranged through Loreto hotels or Desert and Sea Expeditions; phone (613) 135-1979.

Tourist information office: in the Palacio de Gobierno building across from the main plaza. Hours vary; phone (613) 135-0411.

MISSION MUSEUM (Museo de Las Misiones) is next to the Mission of Our Lady of Loreto. Artifacts and manuscripts on display relate to Baja California's historic missions. Other exhibits include religious art and saddles used in colonial times. Tues.-Sun. 9-6. Admission around $3 (U.S.). Phone (613) 135-1831.

MISSION OF OUR LADY OF LORETO (Misión de Nuestra Señora de Loreto) is a block west of the main plaza. Severely damaged by earthquakes, the 1752 mission—including the tower with its modern clock—has been almost completely rebuilt and still functions as an active church. It features baroque stone ornamentation, a bell tower and a collection of gilded altar paintings.

MEXICALI, BAJA CALIFORNIA (B-2)

pop. 575,300, metro area 830,600

Mexicali (meh-hee-CAH-lih) developed as a market center for surrounding farms in the early 20th century. It became the capital of the territory of Baja California Norte in 1915. Visitors from across the border were attracted by legalized alcohol and gambling as well as by land speculation. *Maquiladoras,* foreign-owned businesses established in Mexican border areas because of low production costs, have further bolstered the economy.

Capital of the state of Baja California, Mexicali is a border city and duty-free port opposite Calexico, Calif. Mexican and U.S. Customs and Border Protection offices are open 24 hours daily.

A number of shops and restaurants are near the international border in an irregular rectangle bounded by avenidas Cristóbal Colón and Alvaro Obregón, the Río Nuevo and Calle C. Mexico's largest Chinatown (La Chinesca) also is near the border, concentrated south of Calzada López Mateos around avenidas Juárez and Altamirano. In the former state governor's residence at Avenida Alvaro Obregón #1209, between calles D and E, is The City Gallery (Galería de la Ciudad), an art gallery displaying works by Mexican artists.

Secture (Secretaría de Turismo del Estado): calzadas Montejano and Benito Juárez in the Hotel Zone (Zona Hotelera), south of Plaza Azteca. Open Mon.-Fri. 8-5, Sat. 10-3; phone (686) 566-1116 (English spoken). The office provides visitor information as well as tourist assistance.

REGIONAL MUSEUM, UNIVERSITY OF BAJA CALIFORNIA (Museo Regional, Universidad de Baja California) is at Av. Reforma and Calle L. It has exhibits focusing on paleontology, archeology, ethnography, landscape photography and the missions of Baja California. Mon.-Fri. 9-6, Sat.-Sun. 10-4. Admission around $1 (U.S.).

MULEGE,
BAJA CALIFORNIA SUR (E-2)

Mulegé (moo-leh-HEH) is an old, traditional Mexican town and an oasis in the middle of the inhospitable Baja California desert. Perched on a terrace above the Río Mulegé—one of the peninsula's few rivers—it has dirt streets and a laid-back air. Mulegé also offers easy accessibility to the stunning beaches and tucked-away coves of Bahía Concepción, which begins 19 kilometers (12 miles) south of town.

Mulegé's history dates back to 1705 with the founding of the Mission of Santa Rosalía Mulegé (*see attraction listing below*). Mulegé, which means "large creek," thrived as a producer of subtropical fruits and as a regional market center long before the completion of Mex. 1 brought tourists from the United States.

About 3 kilometers (2 miles) northeast of town is the public beach, at the end of a dirt road where the Río Mulegé empties into the Sea of Cortés. The beach has dark sand, a few waves and, in summer, jellyfish. Nearby El Sombrerito, at the mouth of the river, is a hat-shaped monolith with stone steps leading to a lighthouse at the summit.

Mulegé offers outstanding fishing and boating opportunities. Fishing arrangements can be made through most hotels or at one of the many RV parks along the river south of town. The area also attracts scuba divers and snorkelers; the underwater life in Bahía Concepción includes impressively large sea turtles. Cortez Explorers, Calle Moctezuma #75a (near the telegraph office), can arrange scuba and snorkeling expeditions and rents equipment; phone (615) 153-0500.

The shell-studded beaches of coarse white sand south off Mex. 1 along the shores of the bay are known for warm, clear and gloriously blue water. For a backdrop, there are mountains tinted shades of rose by the sun. All are accessible from Mex. 1, with signs posted at each turnoff; however, the access roads are likely to be sandy, rutted or both. If you wish to hike from the highway (wear sturdy shoes), bus drivers will make drop-offs at the access roads; double-check the time the last northbound bus heads back to town. Expect to share these beaches with an army of RVers and campers.

The first beach south of Mulegé is Playa Punta Arena, about 16 kilometers (9 miles) south. Palm-thatched *palapas* line the sand, and hillside caves south of the beach are littered with shells discarded by ancient inhabitants. Playa Santispac, crowded with campers, is the most active; craft from sailboats to yachts cruise on the bay.

Playa El Coyote fronts a cove and has several trees, rare on Baja's desert beaches. Playa El Requesón, a narrow point of land connected to an offshore island that can be reached by vehicle at low tide, is a prime windsurfing location. Don't expect much in the way of tourist facilities at any of these beaches, aside from some *palapa* shelters and a few toilets.

MISSION OF SANTA ROSALIA MULEGE (Misión Santa Rosalía de Mulegé) is just upstream from the Mex. 1 Bridge over the Mulegé River. It can be reached by a pathway shaded by broad-leafed banana plants. Sunday services are still held in the solid stone structure, which was abandoned as a mission in 1828. The hilltop view takes in date palm groves spreading toward the mountains.

ROSARITO, BAJA CALIFORNIA (B-1)
pop. 53,700

This rapidly growing resort town, easily reached from the United States, is about 29 kilometers (18 miles) south of Tijuana. Also known as Rosarito (roh-sah-REE-toh) Beach and Playas de Rosarito, it is located at the junction of free Mex. 1 and toll Mex. 1-D, both four lanes from Tijuana. The town commands a favored ocean site fronting several miles of gray-sand beach.

The opening of the Rosarito Beach Hotel in 1927 launched the town's vacation reputation, and it soon won favor as a secluded fly-in spot for movie stars. Still a village in 1960, it has since expanded in each succeeding decade—particularly the 1980s—mirroring the growth of tourism in general in Baja California. Numerous hotels now line the waterfront. Mex. 1 (the Old Ensenada Highway) through town is called Boulevard Benito Juárez and swarms with restaurants, bars and businesses.

Weekends bring bumper-to-bumper traffic as visitors converge on the beaches. Taxis make regular trips to Rosarito from Tijuana and also travel the stretch of Mex. 1 south of town. Rates are negotiable; decide on the fare in advance.

The beaches at the south end of town near the main hotels tend to offer more tourist facilities. Horses can be rented for rides up and down the beach or into the surrounding hills. Bicycle and motorcycle races are held in and around Rosarito as well, including the popular Rosarito-Ensenada 50-Mile Bicycle Ride, which usually takes place the last Saturday in April and September.

The bigger hotels have shopping arcades where visitors can poke around for Mexican handicrafts, although the selection is nowhere near as varied as in Tijuana. At the corner of Avenida Benito Juárez and Calle del Nogal, just north of the Rosarito Beach Hotel at the south end of town, is Festival Plaza, a phantasmagoria of watermelon sculptures, metallic streamers, tiled waterfalls and a giant concrete sombrero, all contained within an eight-story structure that resembles a wildly colorful roller coaster. This beachside complex has a village-style assortment of restaurants, shops and bars.

There's plenty for visitors to do. The Rosarito Beach Hotel, on Boulevard Benito Juárez at the south end of town, offers a Fiesta Mexicana dinner show Friday and Saturday nights in its main showroom, the Salón Mexicano. An all-you-can-eat Mexican buffet dinner is accompanied by costumed folkloric dancers, a live mariachi band and other family-oriented entertainment. For showtimes and prices contact the hotel; phone (661) 612-0144.

Papas and Beer, on the beach a block north of the hotel, claims to be the biggest bar in Baja and is a favorite local hangout for volleyball, dancing, music and knocking back an ice-cold beer.

Rosarito Beach Tourist Office: at the south end of town on Mex. 1 (the Rosarito-Ensenada free road) at Km marker 28; phone (661) 612-0200. The Rosarito Convention & Visitors Bureau is in the Centro Comercial Quinta Plaza; phone (800) 962-2252 in the United States.

FOXPLORATION is about 34 km (21 mi.) south of the San Ysidro, Calif., border crossing into Tijuana; take the last of four Rosarito exits off Mex. 1-D (signed "Popotla-Las Rosas"), then proceed south on Mex. 1 to Km 32.5. This movie theme park features outdoor sets, exhibits and memorabilia from films made entirely or in part at neighboring Fox Studios Baja, including the 2001 epic "Pearl Harbor." On Sundays, guides offer tours in English of "Titanic Expo," an exhibit that displays lifeboats, furniture and shipboard sets used in the motion picture.

Food is available. Wed.-Fri. 9-5:30, Sat.-Sun. 10-6:30. Admission $12 (U.S.); over 63 and ages 3-11, $9. MC, VI. Phone (866) 369-2252 (toll-free from the United States), or (661) 614-9444 in Mexico.

PUERTO NUEVO is about 21 km (13 mi.) south of Rosarito via the Old Ensenada Highway (Mex. 1). This tiny, unremarkable fishing village is known for one thing: some 30 restaurants specializing in Pacific lobster (*langosta*). Some have an ocean view and a touch of elegance; others are down-home places operated by local families. The menu at each is similar—a clawless lobster (ordered by size) sliced lengthwise and pan fried in lard, along with rice, beans and flour tortillas, plus melted butter and chili sauce on the side. Beverages are equally standardized, running to soft drinks, wine or beer.

Hucksters shout the merits of their particular establishment to potential customers, but the final decision boils down to ambience—or a line indicating popularity. Expect to pay about $15 per person for dinner. U.S. dollars are accepted, but few restaurants take credit cards. Summer weekends are the peak dining time.

SAN FELIPE, BAJA CALIFORNIA (C-2)
pop. 14,000

Although nomadic fishermen first gravitated to the area around San Felipe (sahn feh-LEE-peh) in the mid-19th century, the town was not permanently settled until the 1920s. The completion of Mex. 5 from Mexicali in 1951 brought a steady stream of American sportsmen who have helped transform San Felipe into a major winter vacation destination. Rapid expansion that began in the 1980s has produced a slew of waterfront trailer parks, condominiums and hotels. Even so, do not expect a luxury-style resort: San Felipe's style is distinctly no-frills.

About 193 kilometers (120 miles) south of Mexicali, the town's location combines the inviting—the Gulf of California's shimmering blue waters—with the forbidding—an extremely arid desert environment. Mex. 5 south from Mexicali is in excellent condition, including an initial stretch of four-lane divided highway. **Note:** There are only two gas stations between the village of La Puerta and San Felipe—a distance of some 100 miles—and only one selling unleaded fuel. Make sure your tank is full before starting out.

After traversing open desert, an archway heralds the arrival into town. The steep eastern flank of the Sierra San Pedro Mártir range—which includes Baja California's tallest mountain, Picacho del Diablo—is clearly visible to the west. The town spreads out under 940-foot-tall Punta San Felipe, a promontory that forms the northern end of Bahía San Felipe. Yellow-sand beaches line the coast southeastward from the crescent-shaped bayfront to Punta Estrella, about 19 kilometers (12 miles) distant. A splendid view of the town and coastline is available from the Virgin of Guadalupe Shrine, atop a hill just north of San Felipe.

The bay, along with the entire northern Gulf of California, has an extreme tidal range that often reaches more than 20 feet, requiring an experienced boater to successfully navigate the waters. At high tide waves break against the shore; at low tide it is possible to wade far out over sand and mud flats.

South of town, an unnumbered, very rough road passes the airport and continues 85 kilometers (53 miles) to Puertecitos. Along the way are turnoffs leading to vacation home communities and trailer camps, but very few motorist facilities.

About 21 kilometers (13 miles) south of San Felipe via the Gulf of California coast road is the Valley of the Giants (El Valle de Los Gigantes). Watch for the sign for Colonia Gutierrez Polanco, then take the sandy road going in the opposite direction—southwest—about 5 kilometers (3 miles). The cluster of very large, very old cardón cactuses and other desert vegetation makes for an intriguing sight. It is recommended that this excursion be made only in a sturdy, high-clearance vehicle.

San Felipe attracts campers, anglers, road racers and beachcombers. Dwellings are modest, vegetation scarce, and litter sometimes an eyesore. The town attracts a rowdy crowd of motorcyclists and dune buggy fanciers on holiday weekends and the two weeks around Easter. At these times noise and congestion reign. Also avoid the blistering summer months, when temperatures can soar to 120 degrees under cloudless skies. November through April is much more pleasant weatherwise, although still crowded on such holiday weekends as Washington's Birthday and Thanksgiving.

At this major fishing center shrimp are caught commercially, and surf fishing and package or chartered fishing trips are available. Cabrilla, white sea bass, yellowtail, dorado and other game species are found in the gulf waters. Boat rentals range from oar-propelled *pangas* to large craft that can accommodate a party for several days. Local boating outfits are concentrated along Mar de Cortés, as are San Felipe's restaurants, bars and nightspots.

Tourist information office: on the south side of town at Manzanillo and Mar de Cortés, the *malecón* (waterfront drive); phone (686) 577-1155.

SAN JOSE DEL CABO, BAJA CALIFORNIA SUR (F-4) pop. 33,000

San José del Cabo (sahn hoh-SEH dehl KAH-boh), situated where Mex. 1 meets the Gulf of California, was founded in 1730. The town is the local seat of government for the *municipio* of Los Cabos. Despite its emergence as a major resort area San José del Cabo has managed to retain a sleepy small-town charm, unlike Cabo San Lucas *(see separate listing within this region)*.

Boulevard Mijares runs through the center of town, divided by a landscaped mall ending at a fountain that is attractively lit at night. The central plaza, framed by stone arches, evokes some of the atmosphere of Old Mexico. Facing this tree-shaded space is a monument to Gen. José Antonio Mijares and the twin-steepled San José Church. On the church's exterior is an interesting tiled mural depicting a priest being dragged toward fire by Indians.

A block south of the plaza is the 1927 City Hall (Palacio Municipal), a traditionally designed structure with offices facing an interior patio. Commercial businesses and restaurants line Calle Zaragoza, where the town's two banks also are located, and Boulevard Mijares. Take time to explore the side streets, where shops and walk-in eateries are often nameless.

Palm groves and aquatic plants thrive around the freshwater estuary of the Río San José, a protected sanctuary just east of the Hotel Presidente where more than 200 bird species have been observed. Still primitive, the area is being developed for visitors; small boats can be rented to paddle through the serene habitat.

La Playita is a pretty swimming beach about 3 kilometers (2 miles) east of town and is accessible via two dirt roads. A taxi can take you there; negotiate the fare in advance. A fleet of *pangas* sit on shore; one of the small, outboard-equipped boats can be rented for a day of surf fishing. Negotiate the rate with the local fishermen.

Restaurants are concentrated along Boulevard Mijares, as are the tourist-oriented shops. You can bargain for souvenirs and handicrafts at a procession of open-air stalls. Chartered sport-fishing outings can be arranged through several local hotels. Some hotels also provide horse rentals by the hour for a breezy ride along the Gulf of California shore.

Vagabundos Del Mar Travel and Boat Club provides assistance to RV travelers in Baja. Services include roadside aid, RV park information, insurance needs, and medical air services and evacuation. Phone (800) 474-2252 in the United States.

Baja California Sur State Tourism Office (Secretaría de Turismo): Boulevard Mauricio Castro in the Plaza San José Mall. Open Mon.-Fri. 8-3; phone (624) 142-3310.

SANTA ROSALIA, BAJA CALIFORNIA SUR (D-3) pop. 11,300

A mining town that has been designated a national historic monument, Santa Rosalía (SAHN-tah roh-sah-LEE-ah) was established by the French-owned El Boleo Copper Co. during the 1880s. Prosperity reigned until the mines gave out in 1953. Mining operations were later reactivated with the discovery of new copper and manganese deposits, but these too failed. Commercial fishing and boat building contribute to today's economy.

The French left their mark on Santa Rosalía's narrow, bustling streets. Instead of Mexican-style stucco walls and tiled roofs, many houses are built of wood painted in pastel shades, and gardens are enclosed by picket fences. One of these residential neighborhoods sits on a plateau north of town and offers a panoramic view of the old copper smelter. Another European touch shows up on some of downtown's 19th-century buildings, which are topped with square clock towers.

Santa Rosalía also is known—somewhat incongruously—for bread. The El Boleo Bakery (Panadería El Boleo), Avenida Obregón and Calle 4, has earned a regional reputation for its fresh-baked specialties, particularly baguettes (arrive early if you want to stock up; they tend to sell out quickly).

Santa Rosalía's small harbor serves as the terminal for ferry service to Guaymas *(see separate listing under Northwestern Mexico)* on the Mexican mainland. Reservations are recommended; double-check rates and schedules prior to departure. The ferry office is in the terminal building just south of town on Mex. 1; phone (615) 152-1246 or (800) 672-9053 (toll-free long distance within Mexico). For reservations information phone (800) 505-5018 (toll-free long distance within Mexico). For additional information *see "Ferry Service," page 68*.

A pleasant side trip is the farming community of San José de Magdalena, reached via a well-marked turnoff that branches west off Mex. 1, about 27 kilometers (17 miles) south of Santa Rosalía. The road is graded dirt and can be negotiated by a high-clearance vehicle, but it becomes rough past the village. An oasis sheltered by palm groves, the village dates from Baja California's Spanish colonial period, when it served as a visiting station of the Mission Santa Rosalía Mulegé *(see Mulegé listing)*. In the vicinity are the ruins of a chapel built by the Dominicans in 1774.

SANTA BARBARA CHURCH (Iglesia Santa Barbara) is in the center of town at Av. Obregón and Calle 1. Santa Rosalía's most interesting architectural feature is this prefabricated, galvanized-iron church designed by Gustave Eiffel for the 1898 Paris World's Fair. It was shipped in pieces from France and reassembled here. Note the stained-glass windows.

TECATE, BAJA CALIFORNIA (B-1)
pop. 55,200

A port of entry about 51 kilometers (32 miles) southeast of San Diego, Calif., Tecate (teh-KAH-teh) has managed to maintain a Mexican small-town atmosphere. Daily life centers on the tranquil, tree-shaded main plaza. The town lies in a bowl-shaped valley below 5,884-foot Tecate Peak. Mexican customs offices are open daily 8-4; U.S. Customs and Border Protection offices are open daily 6 a.m.-midnight.

Tecate was first settled in the 19th century by farmers and ranchers attracted by its abundant water and fertile soil. Although it remains a commercial center for the surrounding grape-, olive- and grain-growing area, Tecate also attracts artists. As a result, shops and handicraft centers often sell locally made pottery, tile and glassworks instead of the typical border town curios and souvenirs.

Baja California State Tourism Office: Callejón Libertad #1305 on the south side of the main plaza. Open Mon.-Fri. 8-7, Sat.-Sun. 10-3; phone (665) 654-1095.

CUAUHTEMOC BREWERY is seven blocks from the border at avenidas Hidalgo and Obregón. This is where Baja's famed Tecate and Carta Blanca beers, among other brands, are brewed. The Tecate logo—is a red and gold symbol with a stylized eagle—is a familiar sight throughout Baja California. The beer garden offers one free beer per person. Beer garden open Mon.-Fri. noon-4, Sat. 10-4. Thirty- to 45-minute guided tours in English can be arranged by appointment. Phone (665) 654-9478.

TIJUANA, BAJA CALIFORNIA (B-1)
pop. 1,228,700

Tijuana (tee-HWAH-nah), some 29 kilometers (18 miles) south of San Diego, is the main U.S. point of entry to Baja California. A booming tourism industry has helped transform this former tawdry border town into a bustling metropolis of high-rise buildings, broad boulevards and an extraordinary assortment of shops, restaurants and bars aimed squarely at the thundering hordes of incoming visitors. "The World's Most Visited City" (as its boosters optimistically proclaim) extends for more than a dozen miles along the international border; its downtown core is less than a mile from the United States and about 6 miles inland from the Pacific Coast.

Tijuana is a window to Mexico, although it's not necessarily typical of how the rest of the country lives. It benefits from geographical location. To the north is San Diego, linked to the city via two border crossings. The bustling port city of Ensenada lies an hour south. To the east via Mex. 2 is the Baja California state capital, Mexicali.

Tijuana, often referred to as "TJ," is the farthest point in the country from Mexico City and does indeed seem apart. The area was settled relatively recently in comparison to other areas of Mexico—the 1860s—although the region has been inhabited by indigenous peoples for centuries. The city's name is derived from "Tia Juana," a former 10,000-hectare working ranch. When Mexico lost Upper California to the United States as a result of the Mexican-American War in 1848, the area around the ranch became the new border between the two countries.

The city's urban beginnings date from 1889, when the streets of the central downtown area were laid out. Californians first filtered across the border to watch horse races and boxing matches, shop around for souvenirs and enjoy hot springs bathing. Northwestern Baja has welcomed Golden State residents seeking an easily accessible weekend retreat ever since.

The 1920s brought important changes. Prohibition fueled tremendous growth as well as Tijuana's sinful reputation for drinking, gambling and worse. Upon Prohibition's repeal and the Great Depression's onset, the resort folded, the jetsetters moved on and Tijuana slumped. President Lázaro Cárdenas' administration closed down the casinos in the 1930s, furthering the city's decline. The government did, however, designate all of Baja California a duty-free port, and shoppers came calling in search of bargains.

U.S. servicemen kept alive the city's reputation as a bawdy center for illicit fun. Reform laws instituted in the 1930s began curbing some of the more undesirable aspects, but it was not until the 1960s that city leaders took steps to create a more family-friendly image for Tijuana.

This is one of Mexico's largest urban areas. Millions of people pour back and forth across the San Ysidro border crossing—said to be the world's busiest—each year, and the combination of tourism, manufacturing and commerce places Tijuana among the country's top destinations.

In the decades since 1970 the city really began reaping the rewards of a vast, money-spending *gringo* population just across the border. College students and weekend tourists flock to Tijuana to shop, play golf, have dinner, bet on sports and party the night away, although not all at once. But although the city receives 10 times as many annual visitors as Cancún, its challenge is to keep them for more than a day.

Tijuana is a hybrid—it's an Americanized place where English is widely spoken, yet has the curiosity appeal of a foreign country. It also is a city of contrasts. Viewed from the United States side, Tijuana looks decidedly ramshackle. But in the fashionable Zona Río district, Paseo de Los Héroes (roughly, "avenue of heroes") is lined with substantial hotels and office buildings. The avenue's name refers to the statues of historical figures, such as Aztec ruler Cuauhtémoc and U.S. President Abraham Lincoln, that stand in the center of several traffic circles.

The passage of the North American Free Trade Agreement (NAFTA) furthered the proliferation of foreign-owned businesses, the majority of them attracted by Tijuana's low production costs; an educated, relatively cheap labor force; and a prime location. *Maquiladoras*—the term for foreign-owned manufacturing operations—have sprung up here and at other Mexican border areas over the last several decades.

One example is the Otay Mesa Industrial District, a sprawling conglomeration of plants southeast of the same-named border crossing. Goods of all kinds are churned out of Tijuana factories, including several million TV sets each year; the big electronics manufacturers have all set up shop in the city.

Although industry has dramatically changed the city's face, tourism still bolsters the local economy, and Tijuana has shed some of the tackier aspects of its enduring appeal as a Mexican vacation spot. Avenida Revolución, the main street and traditional tourist zone, once was lined with cheap souvenir stands, rowdy bars and sleazy strip joints. But while many endearingly kitschy curio shops remain, much of the street has been extensively cleaned up.

Practicalities

Tijuana International Airport is on the eastern edge of the city near the Otay Mesa border crossing. Aeroméxico, (664) 685-4401, and Mexicana, (664) 685-7879, are among the airlines serving the airport. Aero California flies from Tijuana to La Paz, B.C.S. For additional information about airlines *see "Arriving by Air," page 551.*

Combis (shuttle vans) run between the airport, the border crossings and downtown. XPress Shuttle provides transportation between the airports in Tijuana and San Diego; for reservation information phone (800) 900-7433 in the United States.

Local bus lines cover all parts of the city and run along the major thoroughfares. Most fares are inexpensive, usually the equivalent of about 35 cents (U.S.), and payable in both dollars and pesos. Familiarity with the city layout and proficiency in basic Spanish both come in handy, as does a tolerance for frequently crowded conditions and old vehicles that don't offer the highest degree of comfort. Routes are usually designated by the city district *(colonia)* the bus is going to, announced by a sign in the windshield or whitewashed on it. The "Baja P" bus can be used to get to the Zona Río tourist district.

The Central Bus Terminal (Centro de Autobuses) is on Calzada Lázaro Cárdenas at Río Alamar in La Mesa, in the eastern part of the city near Tijuana International Airport. Regular passenger service is offered from Tijuana to the nearby cities of Ensenada, Mexicali and Tecate. The Autotransportes A.B.C. and Autotransportes del Pacífico lines both offer first-class service; phone (664) 683-5681 or (664) 621-2983.

Greyhound has terminals in San Diego, at the trolley stop in San Ysidro and at the Central Bus terminal. For fare and schedule information phone (800) 231-2222. For additional information about buses *see "Bus Service," page 68.*

Five Star Tours provides charter service from San Diego to locations in northern Baja. Buses depart from San Diego's Amtrak depot, Broadway at Kettner Boulevard, to Avenida Revolución in downtown Tijuana, Tijuana International Airport, Rosarito Beach, Foxploration, the Puerto Nuevo lobster village and the cruise terminal in Ensenada. For schedule and fare information phone (800) 553-8687 (in the United States) or (664) 622-2203 (in Mexico).

Mexicoach offers round-trip service from the Border Station parking lot (next to the San Diego Factory Outlet Center) or the trolley station in San Ysidro, Calif., to the downtown Tijuana Tourist Terminal. There also is round-trip shuttle service to Rosarito Beach and the Bullring-by-the-Sea. The bright-red buses depart every 15 minutes daily 9-9. A round-trip ticket is $3, shuttle service to Bullring-by-the-Sea $6, shuttle service to Rosarito Beach $8. Phone (619) 428-9517, or (664) 685-1470 in Tijuana.

The Tijuana Tourist Terminal (Terminal Turística Tijuana) is downtown at Av. Revolución #1025, betweeen Calles 6 and 7. A good base for a day visit, it has 40 clean, modern restrooms, an international ATM, a currency exchange office, public telephones, a coffee shop, consulate and tourist information, and a pharmacy. Medical assistance also is available. Terminal shops offer silver jewelry, leather goods and arts and crafts. Mexicoach and border shuttle buses stop here as well.

On-street city parking is available, and most shopping centers have free parking lots. A number of pay lots, some of them guarded, are located downtown. Many day visitors prefer to park on the California side and enter the city on foot via an elevated pedestrian promenade.

Taxis are convenient and easy to use, but always ask how much the fare is *("Cuanto?")* and state your destination before getting in, as drivers may try to get more money out of tourists or take you somewhere other than where you want to go. Cab drivers congregate around the stand just south of the border. Fares from the border to Avenida Revolución run about $5 (U.S.); within the downtown area $4 to $5; from downtown to the Grand Hotel Tijuana, racetrack and bullring about $8; and to the airport and the Central Bus Station about $10.

Route taxis *(taxis de ruta)* are generally large station wagons that hold up to 10 passengers; they have established routes but stop if they are flagged down. Destinations are painted on the vehicle. Fares are inexpensive and payable in both pesos and dollars.

The nearest RV park is the El Oasis Resort & Trailer Park, off Mex. 1-D about 5 kilometers (3 miles) north of Rosarito (southbound, Oasis exit; northbound, San Antonio exit). Another facility between Tijuana and Rosarito is KOA Rosarito, about 11 kilometers (7 miles) north of Rosarito via Mex. 1-D (San Antonio exit); phone (661) 613-3305. For listings of AAA-RATED campgrounds and trailer parks, *see "How to Read a Campground Listing," beginning on page 536.*

Note: Keep in mind that facilities, maintenance and services at trailer parks in Baja California may not be up to U.S. standards. Tap water is not fit for drinking, and bathroom facilities can be rustic. Campgrounds in the southern part of the peninsula may not have English-speaking employees; a knowledge of basic Spanish comes in handy.

Hospital General is located at Av. Centenario #10851 in the Zona Río neighborhood; phone (664) 684-0922. The U.S. consulate office is on Calle Tapachula near the Agua Caliente Racetrack. Assistance is offered to U.S. citizens who receive inappropriate treatment by Mexican police while traveling in northern Baja California. The office will furnish a questionnaire pertaining to incidents of mistreatment. In case of an after-hours emergency, phone (619) 585-2000, or write to P.O. Box 439039, San Ysidro, CA 92143.

The English-language *Baja Sun* newspaper is distributed free at tourist information centers, hotels and some stores. In addition to advertisements, it contains information about tourist attractions in Tijuana and other parts of Baja California. A number of California radio stations can be picked up in Tijuana and all over northern Baja. Tijuana stations feature Mexican music. The TV dial includes San Diego, Tijuana and Mexico City channels.

The weather in Tijuana is similar to that in southern California—mild, overcast and rather wet in winter, warm and dry in summer. Daily maximums are usually in the 60s during the winter months, rising to the low 80s in summer. While there are occasional hot spells, the moderating influence of the Pacific Ocean largely spares the city from the blazing temperatures common in many other parts of Baja. Precipitation averages only about 10 inches a year, with almost all of it falling during the winter; the months of May through September are essentially rainless.

Like many big cities, Tijuana has a rough side. Stick to the established tourist zone—roughly Avenida Revolución east to Paseo de los Héroes, the area just south of the San Ysidro border crossing, and along Boulevard Agua Caliente as it extends southeast off Avenida Revolución. At night, avoid side streets and unlighted areas.

Despite an emphasis on family entertainment, Tijuana still attracts a large contingent of partying revelers. Those who end an evening overindulging on margaritas or Tecate beer should take the appropriate measures to get back to their hotel room (or car) safely. Don't even consider purchasing drugs; penalties are swift and severe, with little possibility of intervention from U.S. sources.

Border Tips

There are two border crossings—at Tijuana-San Ysidro and at Otay Mesa, just east of Tijuana International Airport and south of SR 117 (Otay Mesa Road). U.S. Customs and Border Protection offices are open 24 hours daily. Mexican customs offices are open Mon.-Fri. 8 a.m.-9 p.m., Sat. 8-5. The San Ysidro border crossing is open daily 24 hours. The Otay Mesa border crossing is open daily 6 a.m.-10 p.m. and is particularly useful for travelers returning from weekend excursions to such Gulf of California spots as San Felipe. For additional information *see "Crossing the Border," page 550.*

Crossing the border into Tijuana can usually be accomplished without delay, but the same thing cannot always be said about returning to the United States. The best times to cross are before 10 a.m. and after 10 p.m. spring through fall, and before 2 p.m. and after 8 p.m. during the winter (except holidays). Occasional cloudy summer days—locally referred to as "June gloom"—often prompt weekend visitors to leave earlier on Sunday afternoons.

Crossing on or around major holidays—Memorial Day, July 4, Labor Day, Thanksgiving and Christmas—can entail waits of up to three hours. The two-week college spring break and the first two weeks of December, when citizens of both countries are traveling back and forth doing their Christmas shopping, are other times when significant delays can be expected, as are Mexican holidays.

For those who choose to leave their vehicle on the U.S. side and walk across the border, Border Station Parking, next to the San Diego Factory Outlet Center at the San Ysidro crossing, is open and attended 24 hours daily. It is fenced, lighted and equipped with surveillance equipment. Both short- and long-term parking is available. Mexicoach buses depart from the lot for Tijuana and Rosarito Beach. Phone (619) 428-1422.

San Diego Trolley provides transportation to its San Ysidro station (East Beyer Boulevard and East San Ysidro Boulevard) from various downtown San Diego stations, including America Plaza (West C Street and Kettner Boulevard), Civic Center (C Street and 3rd Avenue), 5th Avenue (5th Avenue and C Street) and Gaslamp (5th Avenue and Harbor Drive). There are public parking lots at each station; daily rates range from $5 to $7. One-way fare from downtown San Diego $2; over 59, $1. For information and schedules phone (619) 233-3004, 685-4900 (recording) or (619) 234-5005 (TTY/TDD); closed Thanksgiving and Dec. 25. Blue Border Shuttle buses take passengers from the San Diego Trolley's San Ysidro station to the Tijuana Tourist Terminal on Avenida Revolución.

City Layout

The intermittently flowing Tijuana River passes through the heart of Tijuana on its way northwest across the U.S. frontier, where it empties into the Pacific Ocean. The old downtown (referred to as El Centro) is just south of the river and less than a mile south of the San Ysidro border crossing. Busy Avenida Revolución, within the tourist zone, is lined with restaurants, nightclubs and souvenir shops. About a mile to the southeast rise Tijuana's newer, modern office buildings and shopping centers.

To reach the tourist zone after crossing the border, follow the signs that say "Downtown Centro"; they will lead you to Calle 3, which runs west to Avenida Revolución. Although a car is the most convenient means of transportation, city traffic is daunting. North-south avenidas Revolución and Constitución and east-west calles 2 and 3, which traverse the downtown core, are very congested. The old-fashioned traffic signals are not readily visible; watch carefully for them.

Traffic circles, or *glorietas,* along northwest-southeast Paseo de los Héroes and Paseo de Tijuana can be confusing; always bear right when entering a traffic circle, following the flow of traffic counterclockwise. There are many one-way street signs. Side streets away from the main business districts are often unpaved, rutted or potholed. Fortunately, several wide through streets facilitate traffic flow through central Tijuana.

Mex 1-D, a divided, fully access-controlled toll highway, provides a quick and safe route south to Ensenada and is preferable to old, free Mex. 1. From the international border, it proceeds west, paralleling the border fence and bypassing much of Tijuana's congestion (follow the "Ensenada Cuota" signs along Calle Internacional). You may, however, encounter detours that route traffic along downtown streets.

Mex. 1-D continues west to Playas de Tijuana, then turns south, with the ocean in view along most of the scenic route. There are three toll plazas between the two cities; the total charge is about $7 (U.S.). There also are emergency telephones along the highway at 3-kilometer (2-mile) intervals. Toll highway Mex. 2-D runs parallel to the border, linking Tijuana and Mexicali; expect to pay about $20 in tolls.

Shopping

Shopping is the No. 1 tourist activity in a city where the options range from French perfume to false teeth. Although the cheap souvenirs manufactured locally for the tourist trade are inescapable (yet somehow irresistible), there is much more to tempt the eyes and wallets of shoppers. Good buys can be found on many Mexican-made articles, including blankets, blown glass, ceramics, guitars, jewelry, leather goods, piñatas, pottery, silver and tin objects, stoneware, straw baskets, sweaters, wrought-iron furniture, hand-tooled saddles and decorative objects.

Because of its status as a duty-free port of entry, Tijuana also offers Rolex watches, Russian caviar, Italian shoes, French cosmetics, European designer fashions, Scottish cashmere sweaters, Oriental rugs, fine crystal, gold jewelry and other international goods, as well as fine-quality Mexican crafts. Merchants go out of their way to make the shopping experience as pleasant as possible. But although there are certainly bargains to be had, don't assume that prices will automatically be lower than back home; compare before you buy.

Some 10 blocks of Avenida Revolución downtown are lined with souvenir stalls and arcades filled with curio shops. Haggling is expected if you're buying from street vendors or open-air stalls; in more established shops, ask if bargaining is accepted. The only ground rule is to maintain a serious yet light-hearted approach, for a merchant's initial offering price will usually be about twice what the item is worth.

Avenida Constitución, a block to the west, caters more to local shoppers. Booths selling crafts and clothing crowd the Arts and Crafts Market (Mercado de Artesanías), on Calle 2 between avenidas Negrete and Ocampo. Mexico Curios, Av. Revolución #736, features watches, silver, gold rings, wool rugs, blankets and other items.

In this swirl of buying and selling, keep expectations in mind. For example, if you're looking for quality and authenticity in silver jewelry instead of a simple trinket, avoid the street vendors whose arms are garlanded with necklaces. Tijuana is considered the leather capital of Baja, and boots, shoes, sandals, luggage, purses, wallets, briefcases, belts and coats can all be bargained for—but again, check for quality before committing your dollars.

Tijuana has great bargains on such Mexican liquors as Kahlua, tequila, rum, brandy and local Baja wines. The best buys are found not in the smaller liquor stores but in the Mexican grocery stores called *super mercados*. Calimax is one of several chains in the city. Nondrinkers can stock up on gourmet coffees. The supermarkets also are a good place to pick up breads, pastries, sugar, aloe vera lotion and other items.

For those who would rather browse in a more concentrated area, Tijuana also has standard shopping malls. Plaza Río Tijuana, along Paseo de los Héroes next to the Tijuana Cultural Center, has more than a hundred stores and restaurants, including Sears, Comercial Mexicana and Dorian's, a Baja department store chain. For kids, there is a carousel in front of Sears. Next door is Plaza Zapato, or "shoe plaza," a two-story enclosed mall specializing in shoes, boots and upscale leather clothing.

Directly across the street is Plaza Fiesta, a collection of small shops and eateries in a traditional colonial-style complex. Pueblo Amigo, a five-minute walk from the border, has shops, restaurants, nightspots and a sports book betting facility. One of the newest and largest malls is Plaza Viva Tijuana, just south of the San Ysidro border crossing near the tourist information booth.

Across from the cultural center at Paseo de los Héroes and Avenida Independencia is the Hidalgo Market (Mercado M. Hidalgo), a typically lively public market filled with fresh produce stalls, art and craft shops, a mind-boggling array of spices, chilies and candy, and a great selection of piñatas.

In addition to merchandise, city businesses offer a wide variety of services at reasonable prices. In the area bounded by avenidas Ocampo and Pío Pico and calles 2 and 9 are a bevy of auto shops offering paint jobs, upholstering and body work for up to half the cost of similar repairs stateside. Most have English-speaking managers and will provide a written estimate of the cost and time involved to do the work.

Shoe and watch repair and clothing alterations are other services of which visitors may avail themselves. Optical and dental services can be a bargain, but seek out established businesses with professional, English-speaking staffs. Pharmaceuticals for personal use can be purchased at *farmacias* near the border, where the cost for some prescription drugs can be much less expensive than at pharmacies in the United States.

The Mexican peso and the American dollar are practically interchangeable in Tijuana. This is the one Mexican city where visitors rarely have to worry about currency exchange. Prices are fixed in department stores and the finer shops selling imported items; elsewhere, bargaining is expected. Some stores accept U.S. credit cards.

English is spoken in the main shopping centers and the shops along Avenida Revolución; for street haggling, some knowledge of Spanish is helpful. Most stores are open daily 10-9. U.S. Customs and Border Protection allows up to $800 in duty-free merchandise and one liter of spirits per adult to be brought back into the United States. For additional information *see* "What U.S. Citizens May Bring Back," page 557.

Sports and Recreation

Recreational diversions in Tijuana have changed little over the years. Some of the world's top matadors perform at two bullrings in town. Bullfights are held on selected Sunday afternoons from May through September; July and August are the busiest months. During the season sites alternate between Tijuana Bullring (El Toreo de Tijuana), about 3 kilometers (2 miles) east of downtown on Boulevard Agua Caliente, and the larger Bullring-by-the-Sea (Plaza de Toros Monumental), 10 kilometers (6 miles) west of downtown on Mex. 1-D. Reserved and general admission seating is available. Ticket prices start at around $7 (U.S.); seats on the shady side of each arena are more expensive. Tickets can be obtained at each bullring during events; phone (664) 686-1219 or (664) 686-1510.

The fast and furious action of jai alai once took place at the Jai Alai Palace (Frontón Palacio), at the corner of Calle 7 and Avenida Revolución. Matches (and the attendant betting) have been discontinued, although exhibition tournaments occasionally are held. The building itself is a Tijuana landmark, a Moorish-inspired structure with tile mosaics adorning its front.

Next to the Jai Alai Palace is a Caliente Race and Sports Book betting facility; other locations are scattered throughout Tijuana. Here wagers can be placed for just about any event; multiple giant-screen TVs broadcast the action. For information phone (800) 027-3354 (toll-free long distance in Mexico).

The Caliente Racetrack, about 5 kilometers (3 miles) east of downtown off Boulevard Agua Caliente, presents greyhound racing nightly at 7:45 and also at 2 on Tues. and Sat.-Sun.; closed Dec. 25. Another LF Caliente betting facility here is popular for wagering on U.S. horse races and professional sports teams. General admission is free. For additional information phone (619) 231-1910 in the United States or (664) 681-7811 in Tijuana.

The Tijuana Country Club (Club Social and Deportivo Campestre), also east of downtown via Boulevard Agua Caliente, boasts an 18-hole golf course designed by Alister MacKenzie, the man responsible for the Pebble Beach and Augusta National courses in the United States. The course is surrounded by resort hotels. Some tee times are reserved for members; nonmembers may play Wed. and Sat.-Sun. after noon, all day Mon.-Tues. and Thurs.-Fri. Reservations are accepted up to a month in advance; phone (664) 681-7855 and ask for the pro shop.

Dining and Nightlife

Gastronomic lore names Tijuana as the birthplace of the Caesar salad, originally intended to serve a crowd of late diners from a restaurant's depleted food supply. Victor's, on Boulevard Sanchez Taboada at Calle Juaquin Clausell in the Zona Río neighborhood, is said to have the best *carne asada* and Caesar salad in the city.

More meat, in the form of huge steaks and lamb chops, can be found at Restaurante Argentino de Tony, in the Pueblo Amigo Center in the Zona Río. For a gourmet Mexican dining experience, try Cien Años, Avenida José María Velazco in the Zona Río. The specialties here include such ingredients as poblano chilies, nopal cactus, tamarind and mango, and the food is stylishly presented.

Tijuana also abounds in local establishments that offer traditional Mexican fare. Meals of charbroiled chicken in a *mole* sauce with rice and beans, or *carnitas* (deep-fried pork) served with salsa, guacamole and onions, all wrapped in warm flour tortillas and washed down with a frosty *cerveza* (beer), are around $10-$15 (U.S.).

For those in search of quick, inexpensive street food, taco vendors line Calle 1 near Avenida Revolución downtown. These snacks are filling but can play bacterial havoc with stomachs not made of steel. If you indulge, look for food that is hot, freshly prepared and cooked using purified water. For the gastronomically unadventurous, Tijuana has a full complement of familiar franchises such as Dennys, Jack in the Box and McDonalds, along with local versions of such American staples as Southern fried chicken.

Do not include the 15 percent I.V.A. tax that is automatically added to the check in restaurants when deciding what to tip. A 20 percent tip is not expected in Mexico; 10 percent is acceptable, unless you feel the service has been truly outstanding. For a list of AAA-RATED establishments in Tijuana, *see the Lodgings & Restaurants section.*

Nightlife revolves around discos that are popular with locals and visitors alike. Music—both recorded and live—pouring out of the clubs along Avenida Revolución can be ear-splitting, and shills are stationed at every door luring potential customers with free drink cards.

If you do go in, don't look for bargains, as cover charges and drink prices are frequently equal to if not more than similar prices in the states. Most discos are open Thursday through Sunday evenings. The Tijuana branch of the Hard Rock Café, Av. Revolución #520 (between calles 1 and 2), is a popular hangout that draws a young, noisy crowd, as does Señor Frog's in the Pueblo Amigo shopping center, part of a Mexican chain.

Rodeo Santa Fe, in the Pueblo Amigo shopping center on Avenida Paseo Tijuana, sports glowing purple and gold icicles on its roof and three levels of music and dancing more or less modeled on the "wild, wild West." There's even a live rodeo at midnight. This club is open late and packed on weekends.

More sedate are the lobby bars and lounges in such hotels as the Lucerna, in the Zona Río neighborhood along Paseo de los Héroes. This area, which caters to the wealthy, also has a popular disco, Baby Rock, on Paseo de los Héroes and Avenida Río Tijuana at the Abraham Lincoln statue.

Expect a dress code; those in jeans and T-shirts won't get in.

Bacarat, in the Grand Hotel Tijuana on Boulevard Agua Caliente, offers a quiet and upscale evening of dinner and dancing. Local institution Tia Juana Tilly's, next to the Jai Alai Palace on Avenida Revolución at Calle 7, attracts the sports crowd.

Note: While Tijuana promotes fun, remember that you are in a foreign country where a different set of rules and laws are in effect. The police invariably arrest those who are inebriated and causing a disturbance in public, and nothing will ruin a vacation like a night in a Mexican jail and the ensuing bureaucratic hassle to get out.

Baja California State Tourism Secretariat (Secretaría de Turismo): Paseo de los Héroes #10289, on the fourth floor of the Nacional Financiera building; phone (664) 634-3961 or (664) 634-6330.

The Tijuana Tourism and Convention Bureau, at Paseo de los Héroes and Calle Mina, provides information as well; phone (800) 252-5363 in the United States, or (664) 684-0537 in Tijuana.

There is a tourist information center at the Border Station parking lot just north of the San Ysidro border crossing. It is open daily 9-5; phone (619) 428-6200. A tourist information booth inside the Plaza Viva Tijuana shopping center, a short distance from the Tijuana-San Ysidro border crossing, has free maps and brochures; staff members can help with basic questions about Tijuana and northern Baja. The booth is open Mon.-Sat. 9-7, Sun. 10-5; phone (664) 688-0555.

CANACO (Cámara Nacional de Comercio, Servicios y Turismo) operates an information booth on Avenida Revolución between Calles 2 and 3 that dispenses visitor information, sells stamps, and has restrooms and a public telephone; phone (664) 685-8472. **Note:** Good English is spoken at just about every tourism office in Tijuana.

What To See

TIJUANA CULTURAL CENTER (Centro Cultural Tijuana) is at Paseo de los Héroes and Calle Mina. The ultramodern complex includes a museum, exhibit halls, an Omnimax space theater (with daily showings in English), a 1,000-seat performing arts theater, art gallery, bookstore, restaurant and shopping arcade. The museum contains archeological displays and permanent exhibits chronicling pre-Hispanic, colonial and modern Mexico as well as the history of Tijuana.

During the summer months the Papantla Flyers perform the ancient "Flying Pole" dance in a park in front of the museum. "Baja P" buses drop passengers off here from the border. Museum open Tues.-Sun. 9-6. Museum admission $2 (U.S.). Omnimax films $4.50 (U.S.), children $2.50. Phone (664) 684-1111, ext. 303.

TIJUANA WAX MUSEUM is downtown at the corner of Calle 1 and Av. Madero. Figures depict both the famous and infamous from Mexico, the United States and around the world. While some of them bear little resemblance to the actual personage— John F. Kennedy, for example—Michael Jackson is suitably lifelike, and John Lennon, Marilyn Monroe and Mahatma Gandhi are here as well. Mon.-Fri. 10-7, Sat.-Sun. 10-8. Admission $2 (U.S.), under 6 free. Phone (664) 688-2478.

TODOS SANTOS, BAJA CALIFORNIA SUR (F-3)

An old farming and fishing community about 80 kilometers (50 miles) north of Cabo San Lucas, Todos Santos (TOH-dos SAHN-tos) was long isolated from visitors. That changed in 1986 with the completion of Mex. 19 from La Paz south to Cabo San Lucas. Even though large-scale resort development has begun to take shape south of town, Todos Santos ("All Saints") retains a relaxed air and the charms of a traditional Mexican town.

Located just south of the Tropic of Cancer, Todos Santos is tropical but not quite as torrid as the towns lying next to the warm Gulf of California waters. Underground water from the Sierra de la Laguna range, which rises to the east, provides irrigation for groves of mangoes, papayas and avocados. The town's 19th-century status as a sugar cane producer is evidenced by the ruins of a few sugar mills.

The peak tourist season is from October through February; many businesses are closed or open irregular hours from July through September, when the weather is hotter and more humid and the beaches are plagued by mosquitoes. From Oct. 10-14 Todos Santos puts on the Founder's Festival (Festival Fundador), which celebrates the town's founding in 1723.

The Hotel California, on Calle Juárez, is said to be the lodging with "plenty of room" referred to in the well-known song by the Eagles and shown on the cover of their same-named album. Dating to 1928, it is now being renovated. Caffé Todos Santos, on Calle Centenario at Calle Topete, is where visitors head for breakfast; the charming garden setting is perfect for lingering over a latte or espresso.

Todos Santos has become an established bohemian enclave. Local galleries include Galería de Todos Santos, Legaspi #33, where works by Mexican and American artists are on display, and Galería Santa Fe, Centenario #4 next to Café Santa Fe, where there is a delightful collection of Mexican folk art.

About 3 kilometers (2 miles) west of town on a dirt road is Playa Punta Lobos. Here local fishermen embark in their *pangas* for the day's catch; visitors can enjoy the dramatic Pacific surf. South of town via Mex. 19, dirt-road turnoffs offer access to unspoiled, unpopulated beaches—good for surfing—along the rocky coastline. Just 23 kilometers (14 miles) east the Sierra de la Laguna Mountains rise to 6,000 feet; pack trips to explore the area can be arranged in town.

Guaymas, Sonora / Nadine Markova / Mexico Tourism Board

Northwestern Mexico

Northwestern Mexico encompasses three of the country's four largest states—Chihuahua, Durango and Sonora—and vast expanses of insurmountable territory. Desolate plateaus stretch for miles, and the sun sets over panoramic mountain and desert vistas. This part of Mexico also is economically rich. Irrigated river valleys produce flourishing crops of cotton, peanuts, sugar cane, tobacco, fruits and vegetables. Extensive ranchlands in Sonora yield what is considered to be the country's best beef cattle. And mining remains important; looming over the city of Durango is one of the world's largest single iron deposits, Mercado Hill (Cerro de Mercado).

One of the most rewarding ways to view northwestern Mexico's rugged scenery is from the window of a passenger train traversing the Copper Canyon region, a complex of interconnected canyons almost four times larger and some 280 feet deeper than the Grand Canyon. Traveling across the rugged Sierra Madre Mountains between the cities of Los Mochis and Chihuahua, the Chihuahua al Pacífico railway traverses the spectacularly rugged scenery of this outstanding natural area.

The rail line was begun in the late 19th century, envisioned as the shortest trade route linking Kansas City with Mexico's Pacific coast. Finally finished in 1961, it made engineering history after intermittent work was delayed by lack of funds, the 1910 Revolution and what seemed like insurmountable terrain and engineering problems associated with crossing the Sierra Madre. Years of construction, 39 bridges and 87 tunnels were required to move a train from sea level to a maximum altitude of 8,056 feet.

Travel to this remote region, which has increased markedly in recent years, is seen as one way of stemming the uncontrolled logging that continues to take place. Copper Canyon travel packages—many emphasizing an ecotourism angle—feature coach tours, and some also include guided hiking or horseback riding expeditions or overnight camping trips to canyon-bottom locations.

The region's ruggedness also attracts devotees of extreme sports, and athletes from around the world make their way here to participate in mountain and desert biking competitions, triathlons and one ultra marathon covering 60 miles. For those who aren't prodigiously fit but still desire an active vacation experience, tour companies offer more moderate biking and hiking excursions to such natural wonders as Basaseáchic Falls.

The Copper Canyon is the domain of the Tarahumara Indians, Mexico's largest surviving tribe. Of all of this vast country's native peoples, they have perhaps been the most successful in preserving their centuries-old culture; many still dwell in the shadow of vast mountains and in the isolation of caves set in deep canyons.

The Tarahumara refer to themselves as *rarámuri*, or "foot runners," and it is said that they can run wild turkeys or deer to exhaustion. Both men and women compete in races called *rarajípari*, marathons of stamina that can last several days and cover hundreds of miles.

A harsh climate and landscape long impeded large-scale settlement of this part of Mexico, and there are few ancient ruins or cultural reminders of past greatness. One site that stands out is the Paquimé archeological zone, near the town of Nuevo Casas Grandes in the state of Chihuahua. Designated a World Heritage Site by UNESCO in 1999, these extensive ruins—which have only been partially excavated—were an important trade and cultural link between the Pueblo culture of the southwestern United States and the more advanced civilizations of Mesoamerica, before mysteriously vanishing around the time of the Spanish conquest.

The industrialized big cities are not as immediately appealing as, say, Mexico's beach resorts. Hermosillo was named after Jaliscan general José María González Hermosillo, a patriot in the Mexican War of Independence from Spain. A huge Ford assembly plant is representative of the region's industrial expansion. Appropriately, the city's most distinctive landmark is the rocky outcrop, right in the center of town, that is covered with a web of radio antennas.

Chihuahua, founded in 1709, is one of northwestern Mexico's major cities. *Perritos chihuahueños*, the very small dog breed that shares the city's name, is not originally from Mexico; it is thought that Jesuit priests brought the first chihuahuas to the country from the Philippines in the 18th century.

A day-trip destination and the gateway to north-central Mexico is the major border city of Ciudad Juárez, opposite El Paso. Home to nearly 1.5 million people, it is an interesting hybrid of both countries, much like Tijuana. The traditional tourist shopping area is within walking distance of the border, along Avenida Juárez. English is as widely spoken here as Spanish.

Durango, officially known as Victoria de Durango, is a major crossroads, sitting at the junction of Mex. 40, which connects Monterrey and Mazatlán, and Mex. 45, which leads to Mexico City. The city rises from the level Guadiana Valley, which is bordered by the foothills of the Sierra Madre Occidental. Visitors passing through on the main roadways linking Mex. 40 and 45 will see few of the city's attractions; much of Durango's charm lies in a 17th- and 18th-century architectural legacy, for which it has been designated a national historic monument. Fortunately, the mild climate (due to elevation) makes the city pleasant to explore on foot.

Two small but growing resorts are in the state of Sonora. San Carlos, just outside the port city of Guaymas, is in an area known for deep-sea fishing. Puerto Peñasco, on the northwestern Gulf of California coast, attracts weekenders from California and Arizona.

For a taste of authentic Mexico, head to Alamos, situated in the foothills of the Sierra Madre Occidental in Sonora's southeastern corner. This designated national historic monument is the site of an established expatriate community. Some 52 kilometers (32 miles) east of Navojoa via Mex. 10, it's about a five-hour drive from the U.S. border at Nogales. The presence of cottonwood trees, blooming flowers and elegantly restored colonial-era mansions make Alamos an oasis of sorts in the otherwise barren landscape of coastal Sonora.

Perhaps the spookiest place in all Mexico is the Zone of Silence (Zona del Silencio), a remote area at the point where the state borders of Chihuahua, Coahuila and Durango meet. For unexplained reasons it attracts meteor showers and also is said to prevent radio wave activity, hence the name. The mysteries associated with this remote area—about 130 kilometers (81 miles) north of the city of Torreón to the village of Ceballos, then about 40 kilometers (25 miles) east via a rough road—intrigue stargazers as well as proponents of UFOs.

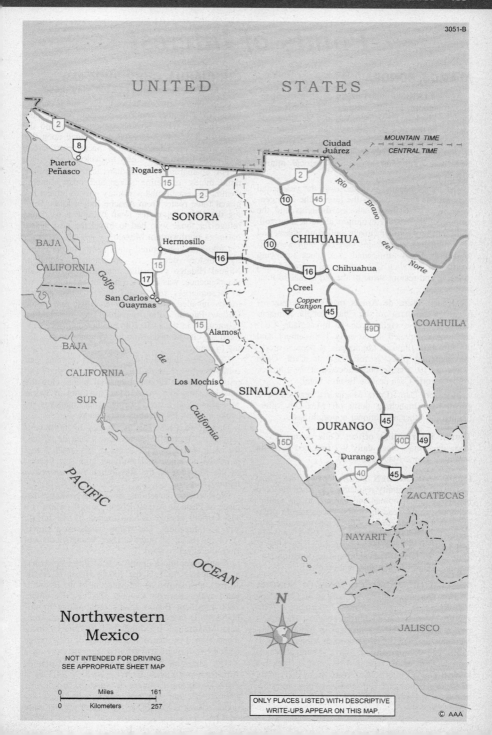

3051-B

UNITED STATES

MOUNTAIN TIME
CENTRAL TIME

Ciudad
Juárez

Puerto
Peñasco

Nogales

SONORA

Hermosillo

CHIHUAHUA

Chihuahua

Creel

Copper
Canyon

San Carlos
Guaymas

BAJA
CALIFORNIA

Golfo

Alamos

de

COAHUILA

BAJA

CALIFORNIA

SUR

Los Mochis

California

SINALOA

DURANGO

PACIFIC

Durango

ZACATECAS

NAYARIT

OCEAN

JALISCO

N

Northwestern
Mexico

NOT INTENDED FOR DRIVING
SEE APPROPRIATE SHEET MAP

| 0 | Miles | 161 |
| 0 | Kilometers | 257 |

ONLY PLACES LISTED WITH DESCRIPTIVE
WRITE-UPS APPEAR ON THIS MAP.

© AAA

Points of Interest

ALAMOS, SONORA (E-4)

Alamos (AH-lah-mohs) began as an early Spanish stronghold in the vastness of northwestern Mexico. Explorer Francisco Vásquez de Coronade camped in the area as early as 1540, unaware that the ground beneath him held rich deposits of silver. By the end of the 17th century, however, a settlement had sprung up to service regional mining operations.

The mines became depleted over the years, and were all but abandoned by the turn of the 20th century. Successive Indian attacks, droughts and the turmoil of the 1910 Revolution all took their toll. Many of the wealthier citizens pulled up stakes, and the colonial-style mansions they had built were left to deteriorate. A turnaround took place following World War II, when U.S. artists and retirees began to arrive and restore some of the old homes to their former glory.

Arcaded Plaza de Armas marks the center of town. On the plaza is the Church of the Immaculate Conception (Iglesia de la Inmaculada Concepción), completed in the early 19th century, and the City Hall (Palacio Municipal). A popular morning gathering place is the Casa de Café, Calle Obregón #10, a coffeehouse located at the entrance to the historic Casa de Los Tesoros hotel.

Mocuzari Dam (Presa Mocuzari), reached by a gravel road branching north off Mex. 10, offers fishing and other recreational opportunities.

Tourist information office: Calle Juárez #6 at Plaza de Armas. Open daily 9-7 (reduced hours in summer); phone (647) 428-0450.

HOME AND GARDEN TOUR departs from Plaza de Armas. Community residents open their restored Spanish colonial homes and gardens to the public; volunteer guides lead the tours. The nonprofit organization Los Amigos de Educación uses the proceeds to provide scholarships to local students. Tours depart Sat. at 10 a.m., mid-Oct. to May 1. Tour fee $8 (U.S.). For additional information contact the Alamos tourist information office.

MUSEUM OF SOCIAL CUSTOMS OF SONORA (Museo Costumbrista de Sonora) is at Guadalupe Victoria #1 on Plaza de Armas. It occupies a 19th-century colonial house with three patios. The state's past is preserved through displays of furniture, photographs, machinery and work tools, clothing, documents and ethnographic displays. There also is a reproduction of a typical 19th-century Mexican kitchen and a collection of coins from the former mints in Alamos and Hermosillo. Exhibit information is in Spanish. Wed.-Sat. 9-1 and 3-6, Sun. 9-6. Donations.

CHIHUAHUA, CHIHUAHUA (D-5)
pop. 678,000, metro area 822,100, elev. 4,690'

Chihuahua's (chee-WAH-wah) beginnings can be traced to a frontier mining settlement in the late 17th century. When Spanish governor Antonio de Deza y Ulloa arrived in 1709, he decided upon the spot where the Chuvíscar and Sacramento rivers met as the location for a new townsite.

The Spaniards drafted Indians to toil in labyrinthine mines, extracting silver and other mineral wealth, and established a military post to protect regional trade routes from Apache Indian raids. During the 19th century the town became a welcome refuge for those who had to travel the arid desert basins of northwestern Mexico.

Chihuahua has figured prominently in the country's history despite its geographical isolation. Miguel Hidalgo y Costilla, champion of Mexican independence, was executed here in 1811. It served as headquarters for Benito Juárez when French troops invaded Mexico between 1862 and 1867. Outlaw Pancho Villa frequented the surrounding countryside in the early 20th century and once captured the city by disguising his men as peasants going to market.

Chihuahua has evolved from its mining and cattle-breeding past to become a big, modern and prosperous state capital. Industrial plants clog the outskirts, but like many Mexican cities it has a well-preserved historic center that manages to evoke a bit of 19th-century atmosphere.

Downtown Chihuahua is divided by northwest/southeast Avenida Independencia; Plaza de Armas, the main square, is a block below this street. A taxi is needed to reach such outlying points of interest as the Museum of the Revolution (see attraction listing).

Most visitor attractions are within walking distance of Plaza de Armas. Rising from the plaza is a 115-foot-tall marble column topped by the bronze Angel of Freedom. The statue stands on a slowly revolving base; at night a laser beam shoots out from the angel's sword.

About three blocks northwest of Plaza de Armas at Av. Juárez #321 is the Juárez House (Casa de Juárez), also known as the Museum of the Republican Loyalty. Between October 1864 and December 1866 president Benito Juárez took refuge in this house while in exile during the brief reign of Archduke Maximilian. It exhibits historic objects, documents signed by Juárez and a replica of the carriage he rode in during a trip through the state.

The Museum of Contemporary Art (Museo de Arte Contemporaneo), which opened in 2003, is at calles Colón and Escudero. It is housed in a former railroad machine shop and also is called Casa Redonda (Round House), a reference to the early

20th-century structure's shape. In addition to modern paintings, sculpture and graphic arts, the museum exhibits tools and objects related to railroad operations.

The small Temple of Santa Rita, Calle 10 de Mayo #1601-A, Colonia Santa Rita, is very significant for Chihuahuans, who consider St. Rita the city's patron saint. The site was originally occupied by a hacienda and a smelting plant. The daughter of a general who acquired the property had a chapel built in honor of Santa Rita. In 1837 it became a hospice for the poor, initiating the popular devotion for Santa Rita. The chapel was restored in 1949 and retains its original beams.

The city's ancient aqueduct was begun in 1706, prior to its founding, in order for canoes to carry water from the Chuvíscar River to a smelting hacienda. The ditches dug for the canoes provided the foundation for a stone aqueduct completed in 1854; some of the semicircular arches can still be seen.

Lerdo Park, on Paseo Bolívar southeast of Plaza de Armas, is the scene of Sunday concerts. Seasonal Sunday afternoon bullfights take place at the 7,500-seat Plaza La Esperanza. For a good selection of Tarahumara and other regional crafts, visit the House of Crafts of the State of Chihuahua (Casa de las Artesanías del Estado de Chihuahua), at Av. Juárez #705 (across from the Federal Palace).

The El Tarahumara Trolley is a convenient way to sightsee in downtown Chihuahua. Service begins in front of the city's cathedral, facing the main plaza; the 19-passenger trolley completes the tour loop in 1 hour and runs daily 9-6. One ticket allows passengers to get on and off at different stops up to four times in the same day.

The 2-week Santa Rita Fair, which takes place in mid-May, is a major local event dating back to colonial-era celebrations of Chihuahua's patron saint. This family-oriented fair offers rides, arts and crafts, traditional food and cultural events.

About a 20-minute drive north of downtown Chihuahua via Calzada H. Colegio Militar, then down a well-signed dirt road, are the Nombre de Dios Caverns (Grutas de Nombre de Dios). An illuminated 1-mile path through the caverns passes stalactites, stalagmites and formations resembling Don Quixote, a dinosaur head and the Leaning Tower of Pisa. The tour takes about 90 minutes. Open Tues.-Sun. 9-4:30. Admission is charged.

Interesting day trips can be made to Aquiles Serdán (also known as Santa Eulalia), east of the city via Mex. 45, and to Aldama, north via Mex. 16. Reputedly the oldest mining town in northern Mexico, Santa Eulalia has been restored and has a cathedral, the Templo de Santa Eulalia de Mérida, that contains impressive religious artwork. Near Aldama, in the center of an important fruit-producing area, are the ruins of the Santa Ana de Chinarras Mission, founded by Jesuits in 1717.

Note: Many roads out of the city are four-lane and divided for a considerable distance, traversing open, desert-like areas; driving at night is not recommended.

Chihuahua State Tourism Office (Secretaría de Desarrollo Comercial y Turístico): Av. Tecnológico #1504, Colonia Santo Niño; phone (800) 508-0111 (toll-free long distance within Mexico) or (888) 654-0394 (from the United States).

CATHEDRAL faces Plaza de Armas. This ornate, twin-towered church of pink-hued stone is perhaps northern Mexico's finest example of baroque architecture. Although it was begun in 1725, Indian wars delayed completion until 1826. The Museum of Sacred Art (Museo de Arte Sacro) in the cathedral basement has a collection of 18th-century religious-themed paintings by Miguel Cabrera, José de Alcíbar and Antonio de Torres.

To the left of the main entrance is the beautiful Christ of Mapimí Chapel, where a cross-shaped niche holds a venerated image of Christ. Museum open Mon.-Fri. 10-2. Cathedral free, museum admission around $1.50 (U.S.).

CHURCH OF SAN FRANCISCO (Iglesia de San Francisco) is northeast of Plaza de Armas on Calle Libertad (at Calle 15). Begun by Franciscan missionaries and dedicated to St. Joseph, it was consecrated in 1721. Architecturally similar to Franciscan missions in northern Mexico, the church's exterior is relatively plain. The interior has a roomy cross-shaped nave, beamed roofing, 18th-century altarpieces and a majestic cupola. Bricklayer Nicolás Muñoz built the bell tower in 1740. Open daily. Free.

FEDERAL PALACE (Palacio Federal) is several blocks east of Plaza de Armas via pedestrian-only Calle Libertad, at Av. Juárez and Vicente Guerro. It dates from 1910 and houses the main post office. Within the building is Hidalgo's Dungeon, which preserves the cell in which Father Miguel Hidalgo was held prisoner by the Spanish while awaiting execution. It exhibits the freedom fighter's crucifix, pistol and other personal belongings, as well as a plaque inscribed with a message Hidalgo dedicated to his captors for their humane treatment.

Museum open Tues.-Sun. 9-6. Admission around 50 cents (U.S.).

GOVERNMENT PALACE (Palacio de Gobierno) is a block south of the Federal Palace, on the north side of Plaza Hidalgo at Calle Aldama. The Chihuahua state capitol dates from 1882; a third floor was added during reconstruction after a 1941 fire destroyed the building's woodwork. Beautiful stained-glass windows adorn the impressive main staircase landings.

It was here that Father Miguel Hidalgo was executed by firing squad in 1811 during the War of Independence. The Nation's Altar (Altar de la Patria) on the ground floor marks the exact spot where he died. The main patio walls are covered with noteworthy murals depicting Chihuahua history. Two museums devoted to Mexican independence—the Hidalgo Museum and the Gallery of

Arms—incorporate state-of-the-art interactive media displays. Daily 8-8. Free.

MUSEUM OF THE REVOLUTION (Museo de la Revolución) is south of the historic center at Calle 10 Norte #3014. It was the home of Pancho Villa, a bandit who nevertheless sympathized with the hardships endured by the Mexican peasant majority. It also is known as Quinta Luz in honor of Señora Luz Corral de Villa, Villa's only legal wife. The 50-room mansion, a museum dedicated to the Mexican Revolution of 1910, displays a collection of firearms, cartridge belts and uniforms, as well as Villa's archives. Exhibit information is in Spanish. The bullet-riddled Dodge in which he was ambushed and killed is parked in a courtyard.

An equestrian statue of the *generalísimo* by Chihuahuan sculptor Ignacio Asúnsulo stands at avenidas Universidad and División del Norte. Tues.-Sat. 9-1 and 3-7, Sun. 10-4. Admission around $1 (U.S.). Phone (614) 416-2958.

QUINTA GAMEROS is at Paseo Bolívar #401, about 8 blocks northwest of the main plaza. The cultural center for the University of Chihuahua occupies a restored turn-of-the-20th-century mansion—named for Manuel Gameros, the wealthy mining engineer who commissioned its construction—and furnished in Art Nouveau style. The main reason to visit is not the university's collection of art on the second floor but the building's stained-glass windows, intricately carved wooden staircases and lavish interior decoration and furniture.

Tues.-Sun. 11-2 and 4-7. Admission around $3 (U.S.). Phone (614) 416-6684.

CIUDAD JUAREZ, CHIHUAHUA (C-5)
pop. 1,257,200, elev. 5,000′

On the Rio Grande opposite El Paso, Tex., the sprawling border city of Ciudad Juárez (HWAH-res) is an overall economic success story: More than 400 manufacturing plants in 17 industrial parks employ some 250,000 people. Northern Mexico's principal highways and railroads converge here, making Ciudad Juárez a transportation center as well.

In 1581 Don Juan de Oñate crossed the Rio Grande River in the vicinity of present-day Juárez, the first Spanish explorer to do so. It wasn't until 1668, however, that Franciscan friar Father Garcia de San Francisco founded the Mission of Our Lady of Guadalupe (Misión de Nuestra Señora de Guadalupe), which still stands on the west side of Plaza de Armas in downtown Ciudad Juárez. While it has a very plain exterior, the interior beamed roofing is profusely decorated with geometric designs.

Next to the mission is the much newer Cathedral, built in 1935 but restored and enlarged in 1976. It boasts lovely stained-glass windows.

Much of the fighting during the 1910 Mexican Revolution took place around Ciudad Juárez and Chihuahua. The treaty ending the conflict and resulting in the resignation of president and dictator Porfirio Díaz was signed in the old Customs House, now the History Museum (Museo Histórico), on the east side of Plaza de Armas. This distinctive-looking building, which dates from 1889, features finely carved wood and beautiful ironwork. It re-opened in 2003 after being closed 2 years for renovations.

Just across the Bridge of the Americas off Avenida Lincoln is El Chamizal Park. Mexico claimed El Chamizal after the Mexican-American War established the Río Grande as the international border in 1848. However, the land fell into U.S. possession when the river changed its course 16 years later. It wasn't until 1967 that President Lyndon Johnson returned approximately 640 acres to Mexico, a goodwill gesture initiated by John F. Kennedy; the land was turned into a park.

Within the park is the Archaeology Museum. It contains mostly replicas of representative pre-Hispanic artifacts—such as a Chac Mool sculpture, an Olmec head and decorative motifs associated with the ruins of Uxmal and Teotihuacán—displayed in an outdoor garden.

Bullfights take place at the Plaza de Toros Monumental, on the east side of town just south of Avenida 16 de Septiembre (Mex. 45) and east of the junction with Avenida López Mateos. Famous bullfighters come here during the season, which runs from April to September.

Expo-Juárez is held each year in June and July. This major fair offers more than 200 booths displaying everything from locally made crafts and candy to furniture and jewelry, along with rides, theatrical performances, regional cuisine and performances by the Papantla Flyers. An arena, or *palenque*, is the setting for cockfights, bingo games and concerts by international singers.

Ciudad Juárez is accessed by several bridges. The Ysleta-Zaragoza Bridge (toll) on Zaragoza Avenue enters Mexico east of Ciudad Juárez. A newer border crossing at Santa Teresa in New Mexico, west of the El Paso/Ciudad Juárez area, can be used to bypass the cities. This port of entry also can process the paperwork necessary for travel into the interior. Do not use this crossing if you intend to visit Juárez, as it enters the city in an unfamiliar area off the beaten path for tourists.

From US 54 south of I-10, the Cordova Bridge (Bridge of the Americas, or the "free bridge") enters Juárez via Avenida Lincoln. **Note:** This is the only crossing that will process the paperwork necessary for vehicle travel beyond the border area.

The Santa Fe Street Bridge is the most convenient bridge to use if you are walking across the border for a day visit; there is plenty of parking on the U.S. side. Once across the border, Santa Fe Street becomes Avenida Juárez. The bridge is one way northbound for vehicles.

The Stanton Street Bridge (toll fee $2 per vehicle, 30 cents for pedestrians) is one way southbound, entering Juárez from Stanton Street in El Paso; once across the border the street becomes Avenida Lerdo.

Motorists returning to the United States from downtown Juárez must use the northbound-only Paseo del Norte Bridge (toll fee $2 per vehicle, 70 cents for pedestrians) via Avenida Juárez to Santa Fe Street, or the nontoll Bridge of the Americas via Avenida Lincoln. **Note:** Dollars or pesos are accepted when entering or departing Mexico or the United States. Baggage may be inspected at the customs offices.

Both Mexican and U.S. Customs and Border Protection offices are open 24 hours daily. AAA/CAA members can obtain Mexican auto insurance and make arrangements for bus tours of the city through the El Paso office of AAA Texas.

Note: In recent years Ciudad Juárez has become a center of rampant narcotics smuggling across the border, and violent crime has increased. While daytime sightseeing or shopping should not present any problems, avoid the area west of Avenida Juárez as it extends south toward Avenida 16 de Septiembre, especially after dark. If driving in the city, do not park in any area that appears to be restricted, as your license plates may be confiscated.

Tourist information center: in El Chamizal Park, just across the border via the Bridge of the Americas (Cordova Bridge). Open daily 9-9; phone (888) 654-0394 in the United States, or (800) 201-5589 within Mexico (toll-free long distance). The center offers travel guides and bilingual assistance to those visiting the state of Chihuahua, as well as general information about Mexico.

Shopping areas: Shoppers will want to visit the orange-and-blue Juárez Market (Mercado Juárez), on Avenida 16 de Septiembre a couple of blocks east of Plaza de Armas. It offers a variety of low-priced handicrafts from all over Mexico, including blankets, silver and turquoise jewelry, leather goods, pottery and curios. There also are a couple of open-air cafes in front of the market.

The Arts and Crafts Center (Centro Artesanal), at avenidas Lincoln and Ignacio Mejía across from the Museum of Art and History *(see attraction listing)*, also has a wide selection of high-quality crafts.

MUSEUM OF ART AND HISTORY is east of downtown and south of Chamizal Park at avs. Lincoln and Ignacio Mejía, in Plaza de las Americas (the PRONAF area). Built in 1964 and designed by architect Pedro Ramírez Vázquez, the museum contains exhibits pertaining to Mexico's ancient cultures and also displays works by local and national artists. Tues.-Sun. 11-7; closed Mexican holidays. Admission 75 cents.

GEM COPPER CANYON, CHIHUAHUA (D-4)

The Copper Canyon (Barranca del Cobre) area of northwestern Mexico was created by more than 60 million years of erosion, volcanic eruptions and faults. The name is something of a misnomer, as the "Copper Canyon" is actually six massive

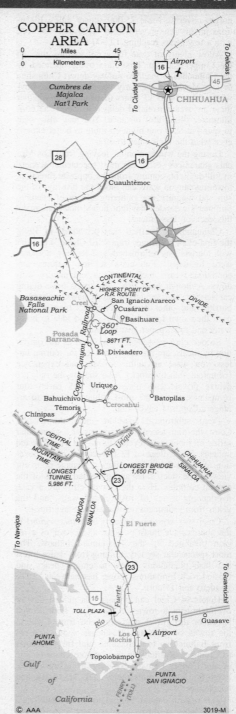

COPPER CANYON AREA

© AAA

3019-M

gorges covering some 25,000 square miles. Elevations in this region vary from 7,500 to 9,500 feet, with a few peaks reaching 12,000 feet.

Allow plenty of time for a rail journey through the Copper Canyon. First-class trains operated by the Chihuahua al Pacífico railway depart Chihuahua or Los Mochis in the early morning and take anywhere from 14 to 17 hours (depending on whether there are weather-related delays) to cover the 654-kilometer (406-mile) distance. You may also want to spend at least one night en route to better experience what the region has to offer.

During the winter months, leaving from Los Mochis guarantees seeing the most spectacular scenery in full daylight; coming from the opposite direction, towering canyon walls can block the last rays of the sun and magnify the gathering gloom of evening. Summer's extended daylight hours, however, make this decision less crucial.

Chihuahua al Pacífico was privatized in 1998; the first-class passenger train ("El Chepe") popular with tourists was refurbished, and security measures were tightened. First-class service features air-conditioned cars, reclining seats and picture windows. Although most first-class trains have dining car service, and vendors at stops hawk homemade burritos and other items, passengers may want to pack their own food. It's also a good idea to bring water and toilet paper, just in case.

Second-class passenger trains, used as transportation by locals, are not recommended for touring unless you want an authentic Mexican experience (complete with livestock). Also sharing the rails are deluxe private cars operated by U.S.-based tour companies; this is the most convenient way to arrange a Copper Canyon tour.

From subtropical lowlands near the Pacific Coast, the train ascends—by means of a spectacular series of loops and reverse turns—to pine-forested uplands. The village of El Divisadero, at an elevation of about 7,400 feet, offers a vantage point for viewing the steep sides and pine-clad ridges of the canyon complex. Here the canyon cliffs are a vast, overlapping series of rust-colored walls, and the vistas from prominent overhangs are magnificent.

Creel (see separate listing within this region) is the approximate midway point and center of a region inhabited by the Tarahumara Indians. The most spectacular scenery, ranging from dense forest and lush plantations below to craggy peaks and twisted rock formations above, lies between El Divisadero and Témoris.

Hotels in Creel can arrange for guided day or overnight trips to towns on the canyon floor. Rough paved or dirt-gravel roads descend from Creel to the towns of Cusárare, Basíhuare and Batopilas; from Bahuichivo to Cerocahui; and from Témoris to Chínipas. Rusticity is the keynote characteristic of any Copper Canyon exploring excursion. Many lodgings, while comfortable, lack electricity and telephones.

The ride to canyon-bottom towns—usually in a school bus—is dusty and can be bone-jarring.

Sturdy walking shoes are absolutely essential for exploring; even guided hikes may involve anything from fording a brook to clambering over fallen logs. Also make certain that a hired guide is thoroughly familiar with your destination, for much of this area still is authentic wilderness.

From the train station at Bahuichivo, a trip can be arranged to the mountain village of Cerocahui. The town has a Jesuit mission established in the late 17th century; Jesuit priests proselytized widely among the Tarahumara Indians. In addition, local hotels can arrange round-trip excursions from Bahuichivo to the canyon-bottom village of Urique. Cusárare, about 19 kilometers (12 miles) from Creel, also has a Jesuit mission built for the Tarahumara. In the vicinity is Lake Arareco (see Creel) and an area of volcanic rock formations that resemble mushrooms.

A trip to Batopilas, in the depths of a canyon about 129 kilometers (80 miles) southwest of Creel, is an eight-hour adventure if taken by local bus. The narrow, dusty dirt road to the bottom passes Cerro El Pastel ("Cake Mountain"), aptly named for its alternating layers of pink and white volcanic rock. The Urique and Basíhuare rivers trace tight, meandering paths before their headwaters lose themselves in unnamed chasms. As the route descends temperatures rise, and forests of cactus replace stands of pine.

Batopilas itself is a former silver-mining town. It began to boom in the 1740s, although mining operations had been in existence for more than 100 years before that. According to local legend, the town's cobblestone streets were once paved with silver.

Distinctly different from the canyon-top villages, Batopilas has whitewashed houses, swaying palm trees and gardens of subtropical flowers—temperatures here are some 30 degrees warmer than at the top of the canyon. Local ranchers ride into town on horseback, and even today it's not unusual to see the occasional goat or pig wandering the streets. Accommodations for overnight stays are modest.

U.S. travel agencies and tour companies offer various all-inclusive trip packages, and this is the easiest way to arrange a tour of the Copper Canyon. Campo David, owned by Dave Warner, offers a 7-day trip that begins with a visit to the nearby Gulf of California for a picnic lunch on the beach and includes overnight stays at Cerocahui and Posada Barranca, the latter a posada spectacularly perched on the side of a canyon wall.

The trip departs from Los Mochis. For additional information phone (866) 247-3464 in the United States or Canada; the Web site address is www.copper-canyon-tour.com.

Rail Travel Center offers an eight-day excursion aboard the "Sierra Madre Express," a private train with domed cars recalling the early days of leisurely train travel. Overnight stays in Divisadero and Cerocahui and a stop at Creel are included. The trip departs from Tucson, Ariz. For additional information, phone (800) 458-5394 in the United States or Canada; the Web site address is www.railtvl.com.

The best time of year to take the train trip is in October or November, when the weather is still warm, the June-September rainy season is over and the leaves are at their most colorful. Noteworthy fiestas focusing on Indian rituals are held during Holy Week (Palm Sunday to Easter Sunday) and during Christmas in Cusárare, Chínipas, San Ignacio Arareco and other Tarahumara towns.

URIQUE CANYON LOOKOUT TOUR departs from the village of Cerocahui. Even if you've traveled the Copper Canyon by train, this guided tour organized by the Hotel Misión is well worth it for breathtaking vistas of the region's deepest canyon. The tour includes a visit to a Tarahumara cave home/shop selling handmade baskets. The drive on dirt roads from Cerocahui to the lookout point takes about two hours.

Daily tours depart in the morning and afternoon. Fee $22 (U.S.). Phone (668) 818-7046.

CREEL, CHIHUAHUA (D-5) elev. 7,650′

The logging village of Creel (creh-EHL) was once the western terminus of the Chihuahua al Pacífico Railway; it is now the approximate midway point. Although the quantity of pine shipped from the vicinity has diminished over the years, active lumber camps still operate.

Creel retains much of its raw charm despite an ever-developing tourist industry. Almost every lodging, restaurant and service is on or within walking distance of the main street, López Mateos. Men ride by on horseback, and brightly dressed Tarahumara Indian women sell pottery and baskets from the curbsides. Several shops also sell Tarahumara arts and crafts, which include rugs, wood carvings, necklaces, dolls and violins. A concrete statue of Christ gazes down from the cliffs north of town, testimony to the Jesuit priests who have ministered to the Tarahumara since the early 17th century.

This is the largest settlement in the Copper Canyon area and makes a good base for exploration of the region. Dirt-gravel roads lead to Tarahumara villages at the edges of scenic canyons. **Note:** If you're planning to drive to the Copper Canyon area, fill the gas tank in Chihuahua or the town of La Junta, on Mex. 16. Driving time from Chihuahua to Creel is about 3.5 hours; a sturdy vehicle is recommended.

Basaseáchic Falls National Park is about 5 hours away via a paved road running from Creel north to the Mex. 16 junction, then west on Mex. 16 to the park. The falls plunge some 800 feet into an open cylinder formed by huge rock columns. The spray nourishes pine trees growing at the base of the falls, and a marked footpath allows hikers access to the bottom of the canyon. At the top there are basic camping facilities.

LAKE ARARECO is 7 km (4 mi.) south on a paved road. This horseshoe-shaped, man-made lake is surrounded by diversified forest and oddly-shaped rock formations. Lodging, horseback riding, boat rental and food service facilities are available. Fishing and camping are permitted.

DURANGO, DURANGO (F-5)
pop. 435,400, elev. 6,196′

Durango (doo-RAHN-goh) was founded in 1563 by Francisco de Ibarra and presumably named for Durango, Spain, the home of his parents. The settlement was an early Spanish outpost, and at one time the province known as Nueva Vizcaya covered a huge area equal to the present-day states of Chihuahua, Durango, Sinaloa and Sonora. After a railway was constructed between El Salto and Mexico City, Durango became an important shipping point for lumber and minerals taken from the surrounding mountains.

Local legend maintains that it was in a cave in one of the buttes punctuating the countryside north of Durango that Pancho Villa traded his soul to the Devil in return for mastery over other men. Villa was born Doroteo Arango in 1877 on a hacienda near the village of San Juan del Río, 110 kilometers (68 miles) north of Durango on Mex. 45.

Head straight for the historic downtown core, where there are two main plazas: Plaza de Armas, bounded by avenidas 20 de Noviembre and 5 de Febrero and calles Constitución and Juárez; and Plaza IV Centenario, two blocks west between 5 de Febrero and Pino Suárez. Plaza de Armas has pretty gardens and a circular bandstand, and is the scene of Sunday band concerts. The major attraction are all within a few blocks of these two plazas, making Durango a good city to explore on foot.

On the north side of Plaza IV Centernario is the Government Palace (Palacio de Gobierno), an 18th-century baroque building distinguished by its arcades. Inside are colorful murals depicting Durango state history. A block north, between Zaragoza and Martinez, is the Ricardo Castro Theater (Teatro Ricardo Castro), originally called the Teatro Principal but renamed for a Durangueño pianist and composer when it was renovated in 1990. Used for performances by visiting music, theater and dance troupes, it has beautiful marble and tile flooring.

The central bus station is northeast of downtown near the junction of avenidas Felipe Pescador and Colegio Militar (Mex. 40). Transportes del Norte offers first-class bus service from Chihuahua, Mazatlán, Mexico City, Zacatecas and other Mexican cities. The line running west from the station along Avenida 20 de Noviembre (the city's main east-west thoroughfare) to Plaza de Armas is closest to downtown points of interest.

The 320-kilometer (200-mile) journey west from Durango to Mazatlán via two-lane Mex. 40 passes some of Mexico's most spectacular scenery. The views of the Sierra Madre Occidental in this region are truly impressive, and the condition of the roadway is good. Make certain, however, that your vehicle is in tip-top shape; repair facilities between the two cities are nonexistent. About 100 kilometers (62 miles) west of Durango is the rustic timber town of El Salto; in the vicinity are interesting geological formations, waterfalls and thick forests at elevations of up to 8,500 feet.

Beginning about 46 kilometers (29 miles) west of El Salto is The Devil's Backbone (El Espinazo del Diablo), a narrow, 5-mile-long mountain ridge with steep cliffs slanting down from the edges of the highway. Mazatlán and the Pacific, more than 90 kilometers (55 miles) southwest, can be seen on clear days. Mex. 40 through this region is a triumph of man's ingenuity over a challenging environment. The town of La Ciudad offers basic services for those continuing the trek southwestward to the coast.

Durango State Tourism Office (Dirección General de Turismo y Cinematografía): downtown at Calle Florida #1106, on the second floor of the Barrio del Calvario; phone (618) 811-1107.

What to See

CATHEDRAL is on Av. 20 de Noviembre facing the north side of Plaza de Armas. Construction was begun in 1695 and completed in 1750. The massive structure is surmounted by two square towers. The exterior is a mixture of styles, with baroque predominating. The entrance is richly decorated. Inside are choir stalls adorned with finely carved wooden figures of saints and apostles. Bell ringers in the towers are visible from the plaza.

GANOT-PESCHARD MUSEUM OF ARCHEOLOGY (Museo de Arqueología de Ganot-Peschard) is 2 blocks west of Plaza de Armas at Calle Zaragoza #315 Sur, between avs. 20 de Noviembre and 5 de Febrero. It chronicles the indigenous cultures of this part of Mexico from prehistoric times through the Spanish conquest. Highlights are a photographic exhibition of cave paintings and an exhibit detailing the methodology of archeological research. Background information is in Spanish. Tues.-Fri. 10-6, Sat.-Sun. 11-7. Admission about 50 cents (U.S.)

HOUSE OF THE COUNT OF SUCHIL (Casa del Conde de Suchil) is 2 blocks east of the Plaza de Armas at Av. 5 de Febrero and Calle Madero. This is a fine example of mid-18th-century Spanish colonial architecture. Built for a wealthy landowner, the restored mansion's former grandeur is evident in such features as the tile accenting the floors and wooden wall paneling. The building is now occupied by a bank and several shops.

MERCADO HILL (El Cerro de Mercado) is just north of the city. A mound of high-content iron ore said to be one of the largest single iron deposits in existence, it rises some 700 feet above the surrounding plain and is still producing. The hill was named for the man who discovered it in 1552, Ginés Vázquez del Mercado.

MOVIE SETS (Escenarios) are permanent fixtures in this area. Durango's heyday as a moviemaking center began in the 1950s and continued through the '70s, as actors like John Wayne, Burt Lancaster and Robert Ryan came here to make Hollywood westerns. Among the classics shot in the vicinity was Sam Peckinpah's "The Wild Bunch."

Group tours of local movie sets can be taken on weekends. Make arrangements at the State Cinematography Office (Dirección Estatal de Cinematografía), located in the same building as the State Tourism Office.

Chupaderos is about 14 km (9 mi.) north of Durango on Mex. 45. An actual Mexican village, it has been used for filming more than any other area location. The town's original buildings have been augmented over the years by Old West-style structures. A few kilometers south on Mex. 45 is Villa del Oeste, a village that first came into being as a constructed "Western" town.

Los Alamos is about 29 km (18 mi.) south of Durango on the paved road to the village of La Flor; take Boulevard Domingo Arrieta (about 7 blocks east of the main plaza) south out of town. This set was built to re-create the town of Los Alamos, New Mexico, for the 1989 film "Fat Man and Little Boy," about the development of the atomic bomb. The canyon scenery en route is impressive.

GUAYMAS, SONORA (D-3) pop. 99,800

Backed by bare mountains that advance almost to the coast, Guaymas (GWAY-mahs) is one of Mexico's principal seaports. The surrounding area was originally occupied by Indians known as Guaymenas, thought to be an offshoot of the Seri tribe. Spanish explorers discovered the region in the 1530s, but it wasn't until 1701 that a nearby mission was established jointly by Fathers Eusebio Francisco Kino and Juan María Salvatierra. The settlement of Guaymas was founded in 1769.

The old city sits along the shore of a fine natural harbor crowded with freighters, tankers and shrimp boats. This part of Guaymas is divided by a mountainous peninsula from the newer resort area, which spreads out to the northwest along Bacochibampo and San Carlos bays. The mountain backdrop, brilliant blue sky and equally blue gulf waters are best appreciated by strolling along the waterfront section of Avenida Serdán, the main east-west thoroughfare.

Two blocks to the north is the 19th-century Church of San Fernando (Iglesia de San Fernando). In front of the church is a small park complete with white wrought-iron bandstand and benches set under trees that provide welcome shade. Nearby, at Avenida Serdán and Calle 23, is the Plaza of the Three Presidents (Plaza de Los Tres Presidentes). In front of City Hall (Palacio Municipal) on the plaza are statues honoring Plutarco Elías Calles, Adolfo de la Huerta and Abelardo Rodríguez, all former Mexican presidents born in Sonora.

Native heritage is evident in the celebrations and ritual dances of the Yaqui Indians, who still inhabit the villages in the Yaqui River valley southeast of Guaymas. One of Mexico's most fiercely independent ethnic peoples, the Yaqui staged frequent rebellions against ruling governments during the 18th and 19th centuries.

Politically assimilated into contemporary Mexico, the Yaqui have nevertheless maintained certain aspects of their culture, most notably the Deer Dance *(Danza del Venado)*, which is performed both locally and at folkloric festivals throughout the country. The main participant wears a deer's head to enact the dance's symbolic representation of the battle between good and evil.

The Guaymas area is well known to deep-sea fishing enthusiasts. Prized catches include marlin, sailfish, yellowtail, corbina, sea bass and red snapper. Even the local oysters are celebrated for their flavor. Fishing excursions and sunset cruises can be arranged in nearby San Carlos *(see separate listing within this region)*.

Practicalities

Aeroméxico offers direct flights to Guaymas from Tucson; for additional information about airlines *see "Arriving by Air," page 551*. Taxis provide service to and from the airport, which is located west of town. First-class bus service to border cities and other Mexican destinations is provided by several bus companies, including Elite, TAP, Transportes del Pacífico and Tufesa. Schedule and fare information can be obtained at one of the city's three downtown bus stations, all located in the vicinity of Calle 14 and Avenida 12. In addition, local buses to Playa Miramar and San Carlos make stops at various points along Avenida Serdán.

Despite breezes coming off the water, Guaymas is uncomfortably hot (and often humid) during the summer months. The winter season, roughly November through March, is much more pleasant— warm days, rather cool nights and mostly sunny skies.

Automobile-passenger ferry service links Guaymas and Santa Rosalía *(see separate listing under Baja California)* on the Baja California Peninsula. The ferry terminal is just east of downtown on Avenida Serdán. There are normally three departures a week; sailing time is 8-12 hours. Schedules and rates are subject to change and should be double-checked in advance. Phone (622) 222-0204 or (800) 672-9053 (toll-free long distance within Mexico) or check with the Guaymas tourist information office. For additional information about ferries *see "Ferry Service," page 68*.

Tourist information office: downtown at Calle 19 and Avenida 6. For information about the San Carlos area, contact the Sonora State Tourism branch office in San Carlos, located at Hacienda Plaza #264 Int. 6, Sector Crestón; phone (622) 226-0202.

HERMOSILLO, SONORA (D-3)
pop. 559,600, metro area 657,200

Capital of the state of Sonora, Hermosillo (ehr-moh-SEE-yo) rises abruptly from the sparsely settled terrain of northwestern Mexico. Big and spread out, the city is not conducive to sightseeing but is a popular stop for motorists proceeding south to Pacific coast resorts. Aeroméxico flies direct from Tucson and from Los Angeles via Tijuana, and has direct flights to Hermosillo from Mexico City, Guadalajara and other Mexican cities. Aero California flies direct from Los Angeles and Tucson. First-class bus service from Nogales is provided by several companies, including Elite, Norte de Sonora, TAP and Tufesa.

Aside from the colonial-era architecture of the 18th-century Cathedral of the Assumption (Catedral de la Asunción), the Government Palace (Palacio Gobierno) and the pink-hued City Hall (Palacio Municipal), most of Hermosillo looks blandly modern. Plaza Zaragoza, the central plaza, provides welcome shade trees and an oasis from the crowded and frequently dusty downtown streets. Also check out the colorful murals depicting Sonoran history in the Government Palace courtyard.

Mex. 15, also called the Pacific Coast Highway, extends from the U.S. border at Nogales south and east to Mexico City. It is mostly a divided four-lane highway except where it passes through some small towns and villages. Watch for occasional potholes and rocks, especially in the vicinity of hills or low mountains. Highway repair work is frequent, and traffic may be diverted to the two-lane stretch that is open. Periodic agricultural checkpoints and gun/drug checks may be encountered in each direction. These stops involve no monetary transactions and are normally routine; English is spoken, although a knowledge of Spanish is helpful.

There are presently 11 tollbooths along Mex. 15/15-D between Nogales and Mazatlán. Combined tolls for automobiles are a little over 500 pesos. **Note:** Toll charges can go up without warning, and rates for different types of vehicles aren't always posted. Avoid SIN-1 (Sinaloa Highway 1), a toll road between Guamúchil and Culiacán that has been known to be targeted by robbers.

Mex. 16 connects Hermosillo with Chihuahua and cuts through the Sierra Madre range. Before it opened, the only paved road running east-west through the Sierra Madres was Mex. 2, roughly paralleling the U.S. border between Agua Prieta and Janos in the state of Chihuahua. Mex. 16 is a narrow, two-lane blacktop without shoulders. There are many turns and steep grades, and horses, burros or grazing cattle may be encountered at almost any point. For the adventurous traveler with a reliable vehicle, the route offers breathtaking mountain scenery of canyons, cliffs, rivers and masses of vegetation.

Mex. 16 also can be used to access the Copper Canyon area *(see Copper Canyon listing)*. Those who do decide to travel on Mex. 16 should keep in mind that viewing scenic areas or dealing with a flat tire will require stopping on the roadway. There are no guardrails, and rock falls from the cliffs above may require sudden stops or veering into the opposite lane. Due to a lack of service stations, make sure your gas tank is full before starting out.

Saltwater fishing is the main attraction at the Gulf of California resort town of Kino Bay (Bahía Kino), some 105 kilometers (65 miles) southwest of Hermosillo via Mex. 16. Named for Jesuit missionary Francisco Eusebio Kino, this was long a hideaway known only to a few intrepid RV owners. Lately condominiums and secluded vacation homes have been springing up, although the mountain-backed beaches of golden sand for the most part remain unspoiled.

Tourist facilities are concentrated in Kino Nuevo (New Kino), which is separated by some 4 kilometers (2.5 miles) of open beach from Kino Viejo, the Mexican village. The beaches are practically deserted during the summer months, but they also are blazingly hot.

Across a narrow channel is Shark Island (Isla Tiburón), currently being developed into a game and wildlife refuge. A special permit is necessary to visit the island; check with one of the hotels or RV parks in town regarding guide service. About 24 kilometers (15 miles) north of Bahía Kino via a winding gravel road is the fishing village of Punta Chueca, where Seri Indians offer wood carvings and shell necklaces for sale.

Sonora State Tourism Office (Subsecretaría de Fomento al Turismo): on the third floor of the State Government Building, North Wing, located at Comonfort and Paseo Río Sonora Sur (about 7 blocks south of Plaza Zaragoza and 4 blocks east of Mex. 15); phone (662) 217-0076 or (662) 217-0060, ext. 125.

To receive visitor information from the Sonora Department of Tourism, phone (800) 476-6672 in the United States or (800) 716-2555 within Mexico (toll-free long distance).

What To See

REGIONAL MUSEUM OF SONORA (Museo Regional de Sonora) sits on the eastern slope of Cerra de la Campana (Hill of the Bells), which overlooks the city. It is housed in a former penitentiary dating from the beginning of the 20th century. Some of the underground dungeons and wards have been preserved. The museum's archeological, ethnological and historical exhibits emphasize northwestern Mexico. Open Wed.-Sun. Admission is charged.

REGIONAL MUSEUM OF THE UNIVERSITY OF SONORA (Museo Regional de la Universidad de Sonora) is at calles Luis Encinas and Rosales. It has exhibits relating to the Yaqui, Mayo, Pima, Pápago and Seri Indian groups. Also on view are photographs of Mexican Revolution activities in Sonora, exhibits pertaining to the local history of

the area and the university, and numismatic collections. Open Wed.-Sun. Admission is charged.

SONORA ECOLOGICAL CENTER (Centro Ecológico de Sonora) is about 3 km (2 mi.) south of the city on Mex. 15. A zoological park, it exhibits flora and fauna native to the region's varied ecosystems, from arid desert to the rich marine environment of the Gulf of California. Snakes, tortoises, sea lions and the Mexican gray wolf can all be seen. A highlight are the more than 300 species of cacti, many of them labeled. The zoo covers a large area and thus is more pleasant to walk during the cooler winter months. Bottled water is available. Open Wed.-Sun. Admission is charged.

LOS MOCHIS, SINALOA (E-4)
pop. 204,900

Los Mochis (los MO-chees) was founded in 1893 by Benjamin Johnston, who arrived from Pennsylvania to grow sugar cane. Johnston also founded the Ingenio Azucarero, an enormous sugar refinery around which the city developed; visitors can tour the building.

Los Mochis is the major coastal terminus of the Chihuahua al Pacífico Railway, which travels across the rugged Sierra Madre Occidental to Chihuahua via the spectacular Barranca del Cobre (Copper Canyon) region (see Copper Canyon listing).

Technically the end of the rail line is 24 kilometers (15 miles) south at Topolobampo. This deep sea port, known for its shrimp fleet and fishing, is connected by ferry to La Paz, B.C.S.

Topolobampo is the site of a colony developed in the late 19th century by a group of Americans headed by Alfred K. Owens, who originally conceived the Chihuahua-Pacífico Railway as part of a trade route linking Kansas City with Mexico's Pacific coast. Owens was an idealistic socialist intent on establishing a utopian community that would rival San Francisco in importance. Disillusioned followers and the ravages of typhoid eventually caused the colony to fail, and construction of the rail line faced a formidable obstacle burrowing through the Sierra Madre. Nevertheless, Owens' dream of success was realized in part; the completion of the line in 1961 brought new opportunities to the area.

Los Mochis is an agricultural boomtown and the export center of the state of Sinaloa. A dam on the Río Fuerte, part of a tri-river federal irrigation program in northern Sinaloa and southern Sonora, has increased the productivity of this semiarid region.

Direct U.S. flights to Los Mochis are offered by Aeroméxico. Aero California has daily flights to Los Mochis from Los Angeles. Baja Ferries service links Topolobampo with La Paz; the trip takes about 5 hours. Schedules and rates are subject to change and should be double-checked in advance with the Topolobampo ferry office; phone (668) 862-1003 or (800) 718-2796 (toll-free long distance within Mexico). For additional information *see* "Ferry Service," *page 68.*

The Hotel Santa Anita, downtown on Avenida Gabriel Leyva, is a good orientation landmark. Check with the Viajes Flamingo travel agency, on the hotel's first floor, for Copper Canyon train trip information. This travel agency also may be able to provide information about ferry service; phone (668) 812-1613. Elite offers first-class bus service; the bus station is nearby on Avenida Degollado.

Tourist information office: in the back of the State Government (Gobierno del Estado) building on Calle Allende.

NOGALES, SONORA (C-3)
pop. 164,700, elev. 3,674′

The border town of Nogales (noh-GAH-lehs) is separated by the international boundary fence from Nogales, Ariz. Following the ceding in 1848 of present-day New Mexico, Arizona and California to the United States as a result of the Mexican-American War, settlement on both sides of the new border was encouraged to help thwart across-the-border raids. With fewer defense resources at hand, Nogales became—and continues to be—larger than its U.S. counterpart, and also has maintained a stronger Mexican identity than other border towns.

Nogales also is the gateway into northwestern mainland Mexico and points south, although many visitors just come for the day. Things heat up on weekends, when the underage Arizona crowd makes the one-hour pilgrimage south from Tucson to patronize the local bars and nightspots.

Mexican and U.S. Customs and Border Protection offices are open 24 hours daily. A tourist card is not needed for in-town stays of less than 72 hours, but proof of citizenship is required. For motorists traveling into the interior, the official checkpoint—where your temporary vehicle importation permit must be presented, the $22 (plus tax) administrative fee paid and a windshield sticker obtained—is located 21 kilometers (13 miles) south of Nogales.

Note: Four-lane, divided Mex. 15 begins in Nogales. I-19 south from Tucson ends at Nogales, Ariz.; signs then point the way to the border crossing. This route, however, passes through the most congested part of town. Motorists intending to drive into the interior or to other points within Sonora can take the Mariposa exit west off I-19 and use the international truck crossing; the toll road bypasses downtown Nogales and connects with Mex. 15 to the south, at the 21-kilometer (13-mile) immigration checkpoint. At press time, the toll was about $2 (U.S.).

If you're driving through downtown Nogales back to the United States, watch for the sign that says "Linea International"; follow the directions for the road that leads to the border crossing.

Since almost all of the tourist-oriented shopping is within easy walking distance of the border, it is recommended that day visitors park on the Arizona side and head into Mexico on foot. From the Nogales-Santa Cruz, Ariz., Chamber of Commerce, 123 W. Kino Pkwy. (just off the intersection of Grand Avenue and US 82), it's about a 1.5-mile drive south to a series of guarded lots; parking fees are $3-$4. The turnstiles to Mexico are at the foot of the Port of Entry.

The shops and markets catering to tourists are concentrated near the border along Avenida Obregón. They offer pottery, baskets, leather goods, glassware, furniture, rugs, jewelry and more. Most business is conducted in English, bargaining is acceptable and even expected, and American currency is preferred. The more exclusive establishments carry crafts and gift items from all over Mexico. When buying at stalls or from street vendors, always check for quality.

The Cinco de Mayo Festival, held in early May, commemorates Mexico's defeat of Napoleon III's French army in 1862.

PUERTO PEÑASCO, SONORA (C-2)
pop. 31,600

Puerto Peñasco (PWEHR-toh peh-NYAHS-coh) is situated in the midst of some of Mexico's most inhospitable territory: blazingly hot, extremely arid and absolutely desolate. No matter. About 97 kilometers (60 miles) from the international border at Lukeville, Ariz., and just three hours from Tucson, Puerto Peñasco—like much of northern Baja California—attracts legions of weekenders.

The discovery of blue shrimp in the waters off Rocky Point (Cerro de Peñasco) in the 1920s established the village. Puerto Peñasco's shrimping industry took off in the 1950s, although overharvesting has depleted natural resources.

The town now benefits from its easy access for North American visitors. It remains a leisurely destination for California and Arizona RVers and campers, and is a popular beach getaway for college students on spring break. But a development program already under way—to include luxury hotels, a marina, a country club, two championship golf courses, an aquatic theme park, and upscale condominiums and beachfront homes—will likely change the character of this coast.

An extreme range between low and high tide, which can be more than 20 feet, characterizes the local waters. This phenomenon also occurs at San Felipe (see separate listing under Baja California), on the Baja side of the gulf. During low tide, marine life inhabiting the shallow tide pools can be explored. Tide calendars are available at the Desert and Ocean Studies Center (CEDO), on the eastern edge of town at Playa Las Conchas; the facility also can be toured.

Puerto Peñasco's beaches stretch for miles. They tend to be rocky, but the gulf waters are clear and warm. Summer temperatures in this region are among the hottest in all Mexico; the weather is much cooler November through March. **Note:** A temporary vehicle importation permit is not needed if visiting Puerto Peñasco from the United States. Motorists must, however, carry Mexican automobile insurance.

About 48 kilometers (30 miles) north of Puerto Peñasco Mex. 8 passes near the crater-strewn landscape of Pinacate Desert National Park, which was designated a biosphere reserve in the early 1990s to preserve the volcanic rock formations and protect endangered species. One of the world's most unique environments, it consists almost entirely of lava fields interspersed with sand dunes and moonlike craters. The park entrance is off Mex. 2, west of Sonoita. There are no facilities, although camping is permitted in designated areas (a permit is required). The tourist office in Puerto Peñasco can provide information about guided tours.

Tourist information office: phone (638) 383-6122.

SAN CARLOS, SONORA (D-3)

San Carlos, "just over the mountain" from the port city of Guaymas (see separate listing within this region), is actually about 8 kilometers (5 miles) north of Guaymas via Mex. 15, then 24 kilometers (15 miles) west on a four-lane highway. Guaymenas Indians occupied this area for a few thousand years before the Spanish arrival in the mid-16th century; Jesuit priests built a mission in 1710. San Carlos flourished as a major supply center during the Mexican-American and U.S. Civil wars, but following the Mexican Revolution of 1910 sport fishing took precedence over port activities.

Quiet San Carlos "went Hollywood" in the late 1960s when the movie "Catch 22" was filmed at nearby Playa Algodones. A Club Med followed, and today's resort was born. Natural beauty remains in the tranquil white-sand beaches and the clear, blue-green waters of the Sea of Cortés—which are inhabited by more than 650 species of game fish—and red-tiled roofs retain a Spanish flavor. Well-to-do Mexicans and foreign tourists will find upscale condominiums and the most luxurious accommodations in Sonora here, but there also are inexpensive motels and RV parks that cater to budget travelers.

Marina San Carlos, one of Mexico's largest yacht marinas, has extensive docking facilities as well as moorings on outer San Carlos Bay. The San Carlos country club, Avenida Cristobal #1390, has an 18-hole golf course; most hotels in the area can arrange a temporary membership. Gary's Dive Shop, on Avenida Bay, and the El Mar Diving Center, Avenida Creston #263, offer fishing and scuba excursions.

Sonora State Tourism Office: A branch office is located at Hacienda Plaza #264, Int. 6, Sector Crestón; phone (622) 226-0202.

Sierra Madre Oriental, Monterrey, Nuevo León / © Jonathan Blair / Corbis

Northeastern Mexico

Northeastern Mexico is not the Mexican vacation paradise touted in glossy travel brochures. Take the gulf beaches along the low-lying, marshy, lagoon-fringed coastal strip in the state of Tamaulipas, for example; they're muddy and rife with mosquitoes. The sprawling state of Coahuila is arid, largely undeveloped and sparsely populated, with tourist facilities few and far between. The clang of machinery is the pulsebeat of Nuevo León, where heavy industry—ironworks, steelworks, smelting plants—takes precedence over touristic charm.

Still, northeastern Mexico does have diversions for the visitor. Matamoros, Nuevo Laredo and Reynosa, all just across the southeastern Texas border, are easy day-trip destinations for shopping expeditions and a Mexican dinner. Matamoros, settled around 1700, was burned twice and pillaged several times, in the process earning the title "Thrice Heroic" city.

Nuevo Laredo is a center for *maquiladora* (foreign-owned) manufacturing plants utilizing inexpensive Mexican labor, and as a result the atmosphere is more industrial than picturesque. It does, however, offer an enormous variety of shops and souvenir stalls for those seeking bargains on Mexican crafts, and there are several good restaurants. While occasional Sunday bullfights are held, the city's racetrack, formerly a big attraction, is long gone.

A major gas-processing and oil-refining center, Reynosa is decidedly short on charm but does have a small tourist district, the Zona Rosa, where there are a few shops and restaurants. More shopping can be found in the vicinity of Plaza Principal, the main plaza (some 20 blocks in from the toll bridge), a typical Mexican square with a colonial-style cathedral upon which has been grafted an ultramodern addition.

Saltillo, in a broad valley surrounded by the imposing peaks of the Sierra Madre Oriental, was founded as a Spanish outpost in 1577 by Alberto del Canto. In 1591, Francisco de Urdiñola established a mining settlement populated by relocated Tlaxcaltec Indians. By the early 17th century, the town was a strategic center for Spanish expeditions embarking on explorations to the north. From 1835 to 1847 Saltillo was capital of a territory that included Texas and extended as far northward as present-day Colorado.

Capital of the state of Nuevo León, industrial powerhouse Monterrey is Mexico's third largest city. Numerous factories produce transportation equipment, electrical appliances, cement, steel, chemicals, clothing, beer, cut glass and many other products. Industrialization also has made the city a major Mexican rail center and an important point of commerce with the United States. Monterrey's business muscle is exemplified by the Centro Internacional de Negocios (CINTERMEX), said to be the largest trade and convention center in Latin America.

Passage of the North American Free Trade Agreement (NAFTA) in the early 1990s added further economic impetus to an already-healthy industrial environment. Multinational corporations drawn by the availability of cheap Mexican labor meant jobs for Mexican workers, and *maquiladoras*—assembly plants—sprang up here and in northeastern Mexico's border cities. Real prosperity, however, is a fact of life for only a small—although growing—percentage of the population.

Known locally as the "Sultana del Norte," or Sultan of the North, Monterrey is a favored weekend getaway for nearby Texans (just a 3-hour drive from the border). Sheer size can make it a daunting choice for the casual tourist. But Monterrey's old center—with its flower-filled plazas, narrow thoroughfares, centuries-old buildings and colorful patios—retains the flavor of Spanish colonial days, and a handful of pedestrian-only streets provide welcome relief from big-city congestion.

A world away from Monterrey's urban sprawl is the El Cielo Biosphere Reserve, south of the Tamaulipas state capital of Ciudad Victoria. This 357,000-acre refuge stretches from the eastern to western slopes of the Sierra Madre Oriental, encompassing a transition zone of tropical, semi-desert and temperate ecosystems.

Within the reserve is a cloud forest that is home to numerous species of orchids and birds. Several hiking trails begin in the little village of Gomez Farías, about 100 kilometers (62 miles) south of Ciudad Victoria and 40 kilometers (25 miles) north of Ciudad Mante on a side road branching west off Mex. 85. Guides are available in the village for this truly off-the-beaten-path ecotour adventure.

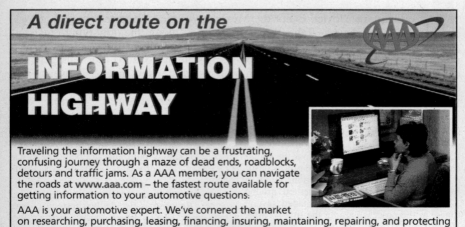

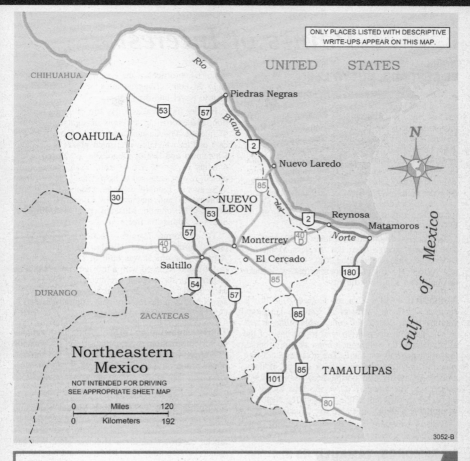

ONLY PLACES LISTED WITH DESCRIPTIVE
WRITE-UPS APPEAR ON THIS MAP.

UNITED STATES

CHIHUAHUA

Río

Bravo

Piedras Negras

53

57

2

Nuevo Laredo

COAHUILA

85

30

53

NUEVO
LEON

2

Reynosa

Matamoros

57

40

Monterrey

40

Norte

El Cercado

Saltillo

40

Gulf of Mexico

180

54

85

DURANGO

57

85

ZACATECAS

N

**Northeastern
Mexico**

NOT INTENDED FOR DRIVING
SEE APPROPRIATE SHEET MAP

| 0 | Miles | 120 |
| 0 | Kilometers | 192 |

101

85

TAMAULIPAS

80

3052-B

Points of Interest

EL CERCADO, NUEVO LEON (E-7)

About 36 kilometers (22 miles) south of Monterrey on Mex. 85, El Cercado (el sehr-KAH-doh) sits in the Río Escamillas Valley. This boat-launching site is on the lake impounded by Rodrigo Gómez Dam (Presa Rodrigo Gómez). The man-made lake, about 3.25 kilometers (2 miles) north of town, functions as a reservoir for the city of Monterrey. This is a popular spot for fishing, boating, swimming and water skiing. A rough road leads from the dam through Cañón Garrapatas (Tick Canyon) to the hamlet of Los Canelos, known locally for a warm spring and "El Bañito," a huge "bathtub" carved from solid rock.

The forests, mountains and lakes in this area are a refreshing change from hot, treeless Monterrey. Dozens of curio shops along Mex. 85 offer excellent variety and low prices, another reason to make this half-hour trip from the city.

HORSETAIL FALLS (Cascada Cola de Caballo) is about 5 km (3 mi.) west of El Cercado via steep, winding Mex. 20. A half-mile cobblestone access path leads from the parking area to the base of the falls; visitors can walk, rent a horse or hire a horse-drawn carriage to get there. The crystalline 75-foot waterfall is surrounded by a thick canopy of trees, unusual in mostly arid northeastern Mexico. Steps carved into the pathway allow the falls to be observed from different angles. Insect repellent and comfortable walking shoes are recommended.

Food is available. Picnicking is permitted. Daily 8-6. Admission around $4 (U.S.); ages 5-16, $3.

MATAMOROS, TAMAULIPAS (E-8)
pop. 395,400

Main port of entry to Mexico from the lower Rio Grande Valley, Matamoros (mah-tah-MOH-rohs) is connected with Brownsville, Tex. The city is a manufacturing center, the commercial hub of the surrounding cotton-producing and cattle-raising region, and is popular with border-hopping tourists.

Settled at the beginning of the 18th century, Matamoros also is the most historically significant of the Rio Grande border towns. U.S. Gen. Zachary Taylor and his troops entered the city in 1846 and waged the first major battle of the Mexican-American War. Matamoros profited during the U.S. Civil War, when Confederates smuggled contraband cotton across the border for shipment to European markets.

Two bridges span the Rio Grande. The B & M Bridge enters Matamoros via Mexico Street in Brownsville; the Gateway Bridge, also called the International Bridge, enters Matamoros via International Boulevard. U.S. Customs and Border Protection offices as well as Mexican customs and immigration offices at the Gateway Bridge are open daily 24 hours. Baggage must be inspected if you plan to travel into the interior.

Besides its appeal as a day trip shopping destination, Matamoros has a couple of sightseeing points of interest. The Casamata Museum, about 6 blocks east of Plaza Hidalgo (the main plaza) at avenidas Guatemala and Santos Degollado, is housed in the remains of a fort dating from 1845; never completed, it was supposed to help defend the city from U.S. attack. Exhibits include weapons, early city photographs and memorabilia associated with the Mexican Revolution. Museum open Mon.-Fri. 8-4, Sat. 8-2. Admission free.

The Reforma Theater (Teatro Reforma) is a block north of Plaza Hidalgo at Calle 6 and Avenida Abasolo. It was built in 1861, demolished in 1956 and replaced with a movie theater, and then restored to its original architectural style in the early 1990s. It now serves as the venue for events associated with the International Autumn Festival in October.

Tourist information office: The most reliable visitor information is available at the Brownsville Chamber of Commerce, a block from the international bridge at 1600 E. Elizabeth St. in Brownsville, Tex. The office is open daily 9-5; phone (956) 542-4341.

Shopping areas: The Juárez Market (Mercado Juárez) occupies the block between Calles 9 and 10 and avenidas Abasolo and Matamoros, about 4 blocks northwest of Plaza Hidalgo. Here you can wander among more than 100 stalls and bargain for a variety of crafts and souvenirs. Sections of Calle 9 and Avenida Abasolo in the vicinity of the market are pedestrian only. Avendia Alvaro Obregón, which runs south from the Gateway Bridge toward Plaza Hidalgo, is lined with shops selling good-quality handicrafts, gifts and silver jewelry.

MONTERREY, NUEVO LEON (E-7)
pop. 1,127,000, metro area 3,468,200

Founded in 1596 by Don Diego de Montemayor, Monterrey (mohn-teh-REY) was named for the Viceroy of New Spain, Don Gaspar de Zúñiga y Acevedo, Count of Monterrey. Real development began in the 18th century, when El Obispado, or the Bishop's Palace *(see attraction listing)*—initially built as a place of retirement for Catholic bishops—became the seat of the religious diocese.

The city lies in a valley ringed with craggy mountains, including 5,700-foot Hill of the Saddle (Cerro de la Silla) and 7,800-foot Hill of the Miter (Cerro de la Mitra). The former is saddle-shaped; the latter resembles a bishop's headdress. The

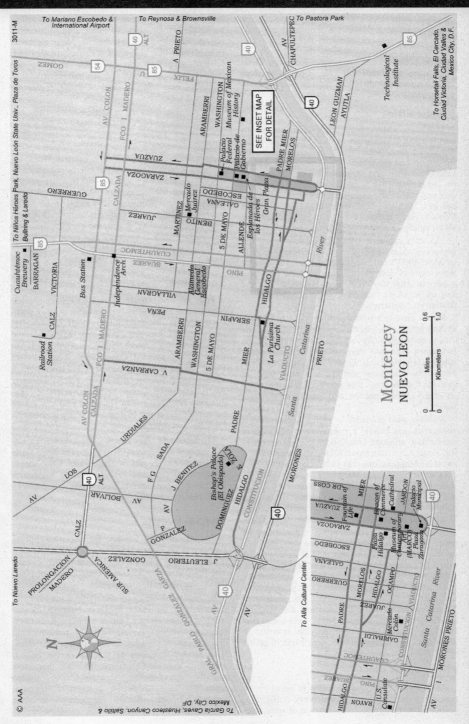

Monterrey
NUEVO LEON

To Mariano Escobedo & International Airport

To Reynosa & Brownsville

To Pastora Park

To Horsetail Falls, El Cercado, Ciudad Victoria, Ciudad Valles & Mexico City, D.F.

To Nuevo Laredo

To Garcia Caves, Huasteco Canyon, Saltillo & Mexico City, DF

To Cuauhtémoc Breivery To Niños Héroes Park, Nuevo León State Univ., Plaza de Toros

To Alfa Cultural Center

SEE INSET MAP FOR DETAIL

Miles
Kilometers
0   0.6
0   1.0

Museum of Mexican History

Palacio Federal
Palacio de Gobierno

Mercado Juárez

Esplanada de los Héroes
Gran Plaza

Independence Arch

Alameda General Escobedo

Bishop's Palace (El Obispado)

La Purisima Church

Bus Station

Railroad Station

Technological Institute

Inset map:

Fountain of Life
Beacon of Commerce
Cathedral
JARDIN
Palacio Municipal
Plaza Hidalgo
Museum of Contemporary Art (MARCO)
Plaza Zaragoza
Mercado Colón
U.S. Consulate

Santa Catarina River

© AAA

3011-M

mountains trap smog created by the dense concentration of industry, creating a significant pollution problem, and with an estimated metropolitan area population of nearly 3.5 million, the city faces formidable pollution and congestion problems. These urban pains are compensated for, however, by some impressive natural attractions outside the metropolitan area.

Practicalities

Monterrey's Mariano Escobedo International Airport is about 6 kilometers (4 miles) northeast of the downtown area. Taxis shuttle passengers between the airport and the central city. Aeroméxico, American, Continental and Mexicana airlines offer direct or connecting flights from U.S. cities. The Aeroméxico subsidiary Aeroliteral flies from San Antonio and McAllen, Tex.; reservations can be made through Aeroméxico. For additional information about airlines see "Arriving by Air," page 551.

Motorists can access the city via two major toll highways—Mex. 85-D from Laredo/Nuevo Laredo or Mex. 40-D from McAllen/Reynosa. These highways more or less parallel free Mex. 85 (the Pan-American Highway) and Mex. 40. Although the less scenic of the two, Mex. 40-D is convenient to downtown Monterrey.

Metro, the city's subway system (also referred to as Metrorrey), consists of two lines. Elevated Line 1 runs east-west along Avenida Colón, north of the downtown core, and then toward the northwestern suburbs. Underground Line 2 originates at Gran Plaza (the Zaragoza station) and runs west to Avenida Cuauhtémoc, then north-south to the vicinity of the Cuauhtémoc Brewery (the General Anaya station).

Metro is used primarily by office workers and is not particularly helpful for the visitor interested in sightseeing, although Line 2 does provide access to the Zona Rosa, downtown's upscale shopping/dining area. Magnetic one-way ticket cards can be purchased from vending machines at the entrance stations for 4.5 pesos (around 50 cents U.S.); multiple-trip cards also are available. Trains run daily from 5 a.m.-midnight. Check with the State Tourism Office (see below) for further information.

The downtown streets, wedged within a ring of expressways, tend to be narrow, one way and congested. Street parking in this area is difficult, and overnight parking is prohibited. The best way to see the sights is by taxi or bus tour. Taxis are plentiful and can be hailed on the street; always determine the fare in advance. First-class bus service to Monterrey from Dallas, Houston and San Antonio is offered by Transportes del Norte. Greyhound Bus Lines in Laredo, Tex., can provide information about bus lines serving northeastern Mexico; phone (956) 723-4324.

City Layout

At first glance, Monterrey seems to be all factories, grimy housing projects and noisy traffic congestion. But the city center is a haven of sorts from industrial sprawl, where modern hotels and office buildings stand next to venerable flat-roofed houses. One landmark symbolizes Mexico's break from Spain—the figure of "Patria" (Fatherland) holding a broken chain, which sits atop the Independence Arch (Arco de la Independencia) at Avenida Pino Suárez and Calzada Francisco Madero.

La Purísima Church, at Calle Serafín Peña and Avenida Hidalgo (west of Gran Plaza on the way to the Bishop's Palace), is considered an outstanding example of modern ecclesiastical architecture. The Nuevo León State University campus is in the northern section of the city. An interesting combination of contemporary and age-old building designs distinguishes the campus of Monterrey's Technological Institute. Considered by many to be Mexico's best engineering school, the institute is a short distance southeast of downtown on Mex. 85. Pastora Park (Parque la Pastora), east of downtown off Avenida Chapultepec, is a naturally landscaped recreation area featuring a lake and a zoo.

Shopping

Folk arts and handicrafts such as leather articles, blown glass and pottery are available at two downtown markets. Mercado Juárez is off Avenida Benito Juárez between avenidas Martinez and Aramberri; the more tourist-oriented Mercado Colón is on Avenida Constitución west of Gran Plaza. Other craft shops can be found around Plaza Hidalgo near the big downtown hotels; Carapan, Av. Hidalgo #305 Oriente, offers a variety of high-quality merchandise. The House of Crafts (Casa de las Artesanías) is just east of Gran Plaza at avenidas Dr. Coss and Allende.

Monterrey also has its own Zona Rosa, not unlike the one in Mexico City, which runs along Calle Morelos in the vicinity of Gran Plaza. Craft shops, fashionable boutiques, restaurants and nightclubs line an open mall several blocks long and 2 blocks wide, reserved for pedestrians only.

Special Events

Starting on Palm Sunday, the two-week Spring Fair (Feria de Primavera) festivities offer parades, art expositions, auto races and other sports events. The Festival of the Virgin of Guadalupe take place during the first half of December.

Bullfights are held periodically between May and December at the Plaza de Toros bullring, located south of Niños Heroes Park at avenidas Ruíz Cortines and Alfonso Reyes. Feats of horsemanship characterize charreadas, or Mexican-style rodeos, held Sunday mornings at ranches in the eastern suburb of Villa de Guadalupe. To reach them, follow the signs reading "Lienzo Charro" posted along free Mex. 40 in the direction of Reynosa. Contact Infotur Centro regarding schedule information.

Nuevo León State Tourism Office (Subsecretaría de Turismo): Av. 5 de Mayo #525 Ote. (West), on the third floor of the Elizondo Páez building; phone (81) 8345-1500, ext. 165 or 171.

Monterrey Infotur is at avenidas Zaragoza and Matamoros in Gran Plaza. The staff speaks English. The office is open Mon.-Fri. 9-1 and 3-7, Sat.-Sun. 10-5. In Monterrey, phone (81) 8345-0870; elsewhere within Mexico, phone (800) 832-2200 (toll-free long distance); in the United States, phone (800) 235-2438. Also check in Laredo, McAllen or other Texas border towns, particularly at places that sell Mexican automobile insurance.

What to See

ALFA CULTURAL CENTER (Centro Cultural Alfa) is southwest of downtown on Av. Manuel Gómez Morín (at Roberto Sada). Housed in a building that looks like a leaning cylinder, it has one of Mexico's best planetariums, an IMAX theater and numerous hands-on exhibits. Free buses run hourly to the center from the Alameda, a downtown park just west of Avenida Pino Suárez between avenidas Aramberri and Washington. Tues.-Sun. 3-9 (also Sat.-Sun. noon-3). Admission is charged.

BISHOP'S PALACE (El Obispado) is in the western part of the city at the west end of Av. Padre Mier. It was built by Fray José Rafael Verger in 1787, a year of famine, to employ Indian victims of a severe drought. During the Mexican-American War, it resisted an onslaught by the invading U.S. Army for two days after the city had fallen. The building also served as a stronghold against the French in 1864, as a hospital during a 1903 yellow fever epidemic, and as temporary quarters for Pancho Villa during the 1910 Revolution. On smog-free days, it offers a wonderful view of the city.

Regional Museum of Nuevo León (Museo Regional de Nuevo León) is inside the palace. It has displays tracing the industrial, cultural and artistic development of the Monterrey area. Of note are the guns that were used to execute emperor Archduke Maximilian. Tues.-Sun. 10-5. Admission is charged.

CUAUHTEMOC BREWERY (Cervecería Cuauhtémoc) is north of downtown at Av. Universidad #2002 Norte. Bohemia, Tecate and Carta Blanca beers are produced at the rate of more than a million bottles a day. A Sports Hall of Fame (Salón de la Fama) displays the memorabilia of Mexican professional baseball players. Tours of the brewery are offered during the week; beer is served in the garden. Open Tues.-Sun. Free. Phone (81) 8328-6060 for information about brewery tours.

Monterrey Museum (Museo de Monterrey) is in the old brewery warehouses. The museum displays original copper brewing vats and other artifacts, regional costumes, and works by Latin American artists.

GRAN PLAZA is bounded by Av. 5 de Mayo on the north and Av. Constitución on the south. Monterrey's immense central plaza is one of the world's largest city squares. Also known as the Macro Plaza, its construction during the 1980s helped revitalize the downtown area. Graced by fountains, statuary, gardens and boldly modern buildings, the 100-acre expanse stretches from City Hall (Palacio Municipal) north to the Government Palace (Palacio de Gobierno). Several streets pass beneath the raised plaza, helping to alleviate traffic congestion and giving it a surprisingly relaxed feel.

Beacon of Commerce (Faro del Comercio) stands in the center of Plaza Zaragoza. This 230-foot-tall, bright-orange laser beam tower dominates the plaza and bathes it with green light in the evenings.

Cathedral is on Calle Zuazua at the southern end of Gran Plaza. Built over a period of more than 2 centuries, it reflects several architectural styles. The pale yellow facade is baroque, while Plateresque decoration adorns the entrance door.

Esplanade of the Heroes (Explanada de Los Héroes) is just south of the Government Palace. This is the most formal looking part of Gran Plaza in terms of its resemblance to a traditional Mexican plaza. It contains monuments to Mexican historical figures Father Miguel Hidalgo, Benito Juárez and José María Morelos. Just south is the Hidden Garden (Bosque Hundido), a relaxing green space with trees, burbling fountains and sculptures.

Fountain of Life (Fuente de la Vida) is in the center of Gran Plaza between avenidas Matamoros and Padre Mier. This impressive fountain boasts a bronze statue of Neptune surrounded by cavorting steeds and nymphs.

Government Palace (Palacio Gobierno) anchors the north end of Gran Plaza, just south of Av. 5 de Mayo. The Nuevo León state capitol, this Spanish colonial-style building was built in 1908 of pink stone quarried from around San Luis Potosí; it has a typically Spanish patio.

Plaza Hidalgo is across Gran Plaza from the cathedral. Another traditional Mexican square, Hidalgo is framed with colonial-style buildings and dotted with shops and little outdoor cafes.

HEROIC CHILDREN'S PARK (Parque Niños Héroes) is on Av. Alfonso Reyes, just south of Nuevo León State University. It was named in honor of the young cadets who defended Mexico City's Chapultepec Castle from U.S. forces during the Mexican-American War. Within the park is the Museum of Fauna and Natural Sciences (Museo de la Fauna y Ciencias Naturales); the Nuevo León Art Gallery (Pinacoteca de Nuevo León), which surveys the state's artistic heritage; a baseball stadium; gardens; and a man-made lake. Tues.-Sun. 10-7. Admission is charged. Phone (81) 8331-3890.

MUSEUM OF CONTEMPORARY ART (Museo de Arte Contemporaneo) is at calles Zuazua and Ocampo at the southern end of Gran Plaza, next to the cathedral. MARCO, as this museum is popularly known, is a spacious, ultramodern building designed by noted Mexican architect Ricardo

Legorreta. Exhibits in the 14 galleries emphasize Mexican and Latin American artists. Works by 20th-century masters like Diego Rivera and David Alfaro Siqueiros share space with cutting-edge artists like Juan Soriano, who created the gigantic bronze sculpture of a dove, "La Paloma," that stands at the front entrance.

Food is available. Allow 2 hours minimum. Tues.-Sun. 10-6 (also Wed. 6-8 p.m.). Admission around $3.80 (U.S.); ages 1-6, around $2. Free to all Wed. Phone (81) 8342-4820.

MUSEUM OF MEXICAN HISTORY (Museo de Historia Mexicana) is on Plaza 400 Años, a few blocks east of the Government Palace It focuses on the Revolution of 1910. Multimedia exhibits, including a railroad car that transported rebels under leader Pancho Villa, chronicle the political turmoil of that era. Also on display is a collection of Huastec Indian artifacts. Guided tours in English are available. Daily 11-6:30 (also Fri.-Sun. 6:30-7:30 p.m.). Donations.

Nearby Destinations

GARCIA CAVES (Grutas de García) are northwest of downtown Monterrey via Mex. 40. A paved road runs to the caves, which are about 8 km (5 mi.) east of the village of Villa de García. Discovered about 1843 by parish priest Juan Antonio Sobrevilla, these caves are among the largest and most beautiful in Mexico. Their estimated age is 50 to 60 million years; it is presumed the caves were once submerged due to the shellfish fossils scattered over the walls and ceilings. Ten "rooms" contain stalagmite and stalactite formations.

A swimming pool, restaurants, and picnic and recreational areas cluster at the foot of the mountain where the caves are located. From the parking area, a cable car transports visitors past rugged scenery to the cavern entrance, tucked high on a cliffside. The cement passageways connecting the caves are well lighted. Open daily. Admission includes the cable car ride and a guided tour.

HUASTECA CANYON is about 32 km (20 mi.) west of Monterrey on Mex. 40 to the village of Santa Catarina, then 3 km (2 mi.) south. The magnificent rock gorge of Huasteca (wahs-TEH-kah) is located in Monterrey Heights National Park (Parque Nacional Cumbres de Monterrey). The sheer walls reach heights of 750 to 1,000 feet. In places the softer rock has been eroded into curious formations. Restrooms, a snack bar and picnic areas are available.

NUEVO LAREDO, TAMAULIPAS (D-7)
pop. 322,100, metro area 533,900

Nuevo Laredo (noo-EH-voh lah-REH-doh) is a major point of entry to the Mexican mainland from the United States. It is connected to Laredo, Tex., by four international toll bridges across the Río Grande. International Bridge 1 is open to vehicular and pedestrian traffic; International Bridge 2 (Juárez Lincoln) is open to vehicular traffic only. Both can be used by vehicles entering the interior. Bridge 3 (Columbia) primarily serves commercial vehicles, and Bridge 4 (World Trade Bridge) is reserved for commercial vehicles only.

For day trips to shop or dine, consider leaving your car in Laredo and walking across the border, which eliminates time-consuming crossing procedures. The Mexican customs and immigration office is open 24 hours daily. U.S. Customs and Border Protection offices at Bridge 1 and Bridge 2 are open 24 hours daily; the office at Columbia is open daily 8 a.m.-midnight.

The Falcon Dam, a joint Mexico/United States project on the Río Bravo (Rio Grande) River, can be reached on the Mexican side by taking Mex. 85 south to Mex. 2, then Mex. 2 about 101 kilometers (63 miles) southeast to the town of Nueva Ciudad Guerrero. Local outfits offer boat rentals for fishing, water skiing and cruising the dam's lake.

PIEDRAS NEGRAS, COAHUILA (D-7)
pop. 130,700

Piedras Negras (pee-EH-drahs NEH-grahs) faces Eagle Pass, Tex., across the Rio Grande. A toll bridge connects the two towns. The U.S. Customs and Border Protection office is open 24 hours daily; the Mexican customs office is open Mon.-Fri. 8-8, Sat. 10-2. This typical border city is notable chiefly as the beginning of Mex. 57—the Carretera de la Constitución (Constitution Highway), which runs south to Mexico City—and as the setting for the popular novel "Like Water for Chocolate."

REYNOSA, TAMAULIPAS (E-8)
pop. 431,900

On the Rio Grande just south of McAllen, Tex., Reynosa (reh-NOH-sah) is reached via the McAllen International Toll Bridge. The toll to enter Mexico is $1.50 per vehicle; to return the toll is $1.95 per vehicle (U.S. dollars are accepted). Both Mexican and U.S. Customs and Border Protection and immigration offices are open 24 hours daily. The city provides access to fishing camps around El Azucar (Sugar) Dam, some 81 kilometers (50 miles) to the west, which teems with bass and other freshwater game species.

SALTILLO, COAHUILA (E-7)
pop. 581,400, metro area 657,800, elev. 5,245'

About 85 kilometers (53 miles) southwest of Monterrey on Mex. 40, Saltillo (sahl-TEE-yoh) is the capital of and leading industrial city in the state of Coahuila. Its outskirts are a sprawl of manufacturing plants producing automobiles, engine parts and textiles. Saltillo's wool, silk and cotton mills are the source of brightly colored *sarapes*, the familiar woolen blanket worn as an outer garment. Although artificial fibers and chemical dyes are steadily replacing the old methods, *sarapes* and small throw rugs are still made by hand in shops clustered along Calle Victoria downtown; visitors are welcome to watch the weaving process. Unglazed terra-cotta tiles are another local product.

Because of its altitude and dry, mild climate, Saltillo is a popular summer resort. Golf, tennis, polo and swimming are popular recreational pursuits. The city's annual *feria* (fair) takes place the first half of August.

There are two downtown plazas. Dignified monuments and well-preserved colonial buildings line the streets around Plaza de Armas. The feeling of formality is reinforced by its paved surface, a central fountain overlooked by four female statues, and the lack of trees and benches. The plaza is flanked by the city's grand 18th-century cathedral and the Government Palace (Palacio de Gobierno), which contains murals illustrating regional history.

Much livelier is Plaza Acuña, 2 blocks northwest. Here there are an abundance of shops, and the square is ringed with little cafes and bars. Occupying one corner is Mercado Juárez, which is a good place to browse for handicrafts, *sarapes*, rugs, pottery, silverwork and bizarre-looking tin masks. Families and wandering musicians make this a fun spot to soak up the local atmosphere.

A monument to Emilio Carranza, who made the first nonstop flight from Mexico City to New York, stands along Calle Victoria. The street begins at the Alameda, a shady park just west of Plaza de Armas that is frequented by students and joggers. Here stands an equestrian statue of General Ignacio Zaragoza, hero of the 1862 Battle of Puebla. Zaragoza was born in 1829 in Bahía del Espíritu Santo, near what is now Goliad, Tex. The central bus station is southwest of downtown on Boulevard Luis Echeverría.

Coahuila State Tourism Office (Instituto Estatal de Turismo): Boulevard Venustiano Carranza #3206 in the Latinoamericana district of the city; phone (800) 718-4220 (toll-free long distance within Mexico).

What to See

FUENTE ATHENEUM (Fuente Ateneo) is on Boulevard Venustiano Carranza on the University of Coahuila campus. This Art Deco-style building contains an art gallery with works by well-known European and Mexican painters.

HERRERA MUSEUM is at Bravo Norte #342. It occupies the former home and studio of early 20th-century Mexican painter Rubén Herrera. The 18th-century residence contains more than 400 of his paintings, mostly Italian landscapes and pastoral scenes representing the artist's apprenticeship in Rome.

LA ANGOSTURA BATTLEGROUND is about a half-hour drive south of the city off Mex. 54. A monument on the east side of Mex. 54 marks the site of a bloody Mexican-American War battle on Feb. 22-23, 1847.

SANTIAGO CATHEDRAL is at calles Hidalgo and Juárez facing Plaza de Armas. Built 1746-1801, it exhibits a mix of architectural styles, most notably the Mexican Churrigueresque. Decorative baroque carvings representing plants and shells adorn its facade and doors. The interior features a gilded altarpiece and a pulpit covered in gold leaf. The 1762 chapel contains a Spanish image of Christ associated with numerous legends. A 200-foot tower dominates the church and offers a panoramic view of the city.

Acapulco / © Richard Cummins / SuperStock

The Pacific Coast

Also known as the Mexican Riviera, Mexico's Pacific Coast boasts hundreds of miles of surf-pounded shoreline and a string of destinations stretching from Mazatlán south to Bahías de Huatulco. They range from funky beach communities—traditional getaways for budget-conscious backpackers and Mexican families of modest means—to luxurious oceanside retreats catering to the well-heeled international set. The Mexican Riviera unofficially begins at Mazatlán, "the Pearl of the Pacific," a shrimping center, commercial port and beach resort that has long attracted sport-fishing enthusiasts. The name is derived from the Náhuatl Indian word *mazatl,* meaning "place of deer"—a reference to former inhabitants, as these fleet creatures are nowhere to be seen in the midst of today's oceanfront bustle.

Now a year-round resort, Mazatlán blends colonial charm with the modern allure of high-rise hotels. Strung along miles of scenic Pacific shoreline and with some 10,000 hotel rooms and condominium units covering all categories and rates, the city is northwest Mexico's major beach destination. The seaside boulevard, or *malecón,* stretches for more than 10 miles past golden sands and crashing waves. The combination of sun, sea and sand draws more than half a million visitors each year.

Balancing the tourist atmosphere are the activities of a busy commercial port. Minerals and agricultural products—tomatoes, cantaloupes, cotton—from throughout the fertile state of Sinaloa are brought to the city's harbor for export. Mazatlán maintains the largest fleet of shrimp boats in Mexico, and thousands of tons of the frozen crustaceans find their way to the United States and Japan, the two main foreign markets.

Those who opt for a more laid-back time head for Manzanillo, where sun, sea and sand mix with the matter-of-fact grime of a real working city. Manzanillo doesn't go out of its way to lay out the welcome mat for visitors, which gives it an unpretentious air. Again, sport fishing is one of the big draws. And Manzanillo all but shuts down on Sunday, when practically everyone heads for—where else—the beach.

Puerto Vallarta was a tiny fishing village blessed with a stunning natural backdrop until the early 1960s. The event that put it on the tourist map was the 1964 filming of "Night of the Iguana." John Huston's movie showcased the tropical beauty of Mismaloya Beach, and the torrid romance between star Richard Burton and tagalong Elizabeth Taylor—both of whom were married to others—titillated millions and generated an avalanche of publicity. Visitors came pouring in, hoping to glimpse a movie star, and an international destination was born.

Puerto Vallarta is basically a one-stop vacation destination, where an idyllic locale is complemented by a full spectrum of luxury amenities. It combines a leisurely, slow-paced ambience with such expected big-resort features as fine dining and flashy nightlife. Accommodations range from small and unpretentious to decidedly upscale. Most of the city's older section is postcard pretty and pleasant to stroll.

The surrounding region is rich in natural beauty as well, and ecotourism is in full swing here. Many day trips revolve around the inviting beaches lining Banderas Bay. Mismaloya, Quimixto and Yelapa, all south of Puerto Vallarta, are secluded spots (the latter two accessible only by boat) made to order for a relaxed outing away from the tourist hustle. More strenuous but equally rewarding options include taking in the jungle scenery by bike or on foot, or perhaps exploring coastal lagoons by kayak.

Ixtapa and Zihuatanejo are twin resorts, only 4 miles apart but decidedly different in atmosphere. Ixtapa, created in the early 1970s, has a glittery but planned look; Zihuatanejo, founded by Spanish conquistadores in the early 16th century, is much more down-home.

Perennially popular Acapulco now plays second fiddle to Cancún as Mexico's beach of choice, but its excess and boisterous nightlife remain in a class of their own. This Pacific playground instantly conjures images of idle days spent soaking up the sun and evenings of dining, dancing and revelry. Certainly Acapulco fulfills the scenic requirements for a tropical resort. Lofty mountains and green foothills extend to the sparkling blue of bay and ocean waters. Tall palm trees stand silhouetted against picturesque sunsets. And the view of Acapulco Bay at night, set off by thousands of city lights, is breathtaking.

Rounding out the Riviera is Bahías de Huatulco, built along a series of bays that scallop the Pacific coast like a necklace of aquamarine jewels. At some point in the future this fledgling resort might rival such hotspots as Acapulco, Cancún and Puerto Vallarta as one of Mexico's most desirable beach getaways. Located on the rugged Pacific Coast in Oaxaca, one of Mexico's poorest states, it has yet to graduate to major-league resort status, to date attracting mainly Mexican families, European tourists and diving enthusiasts.

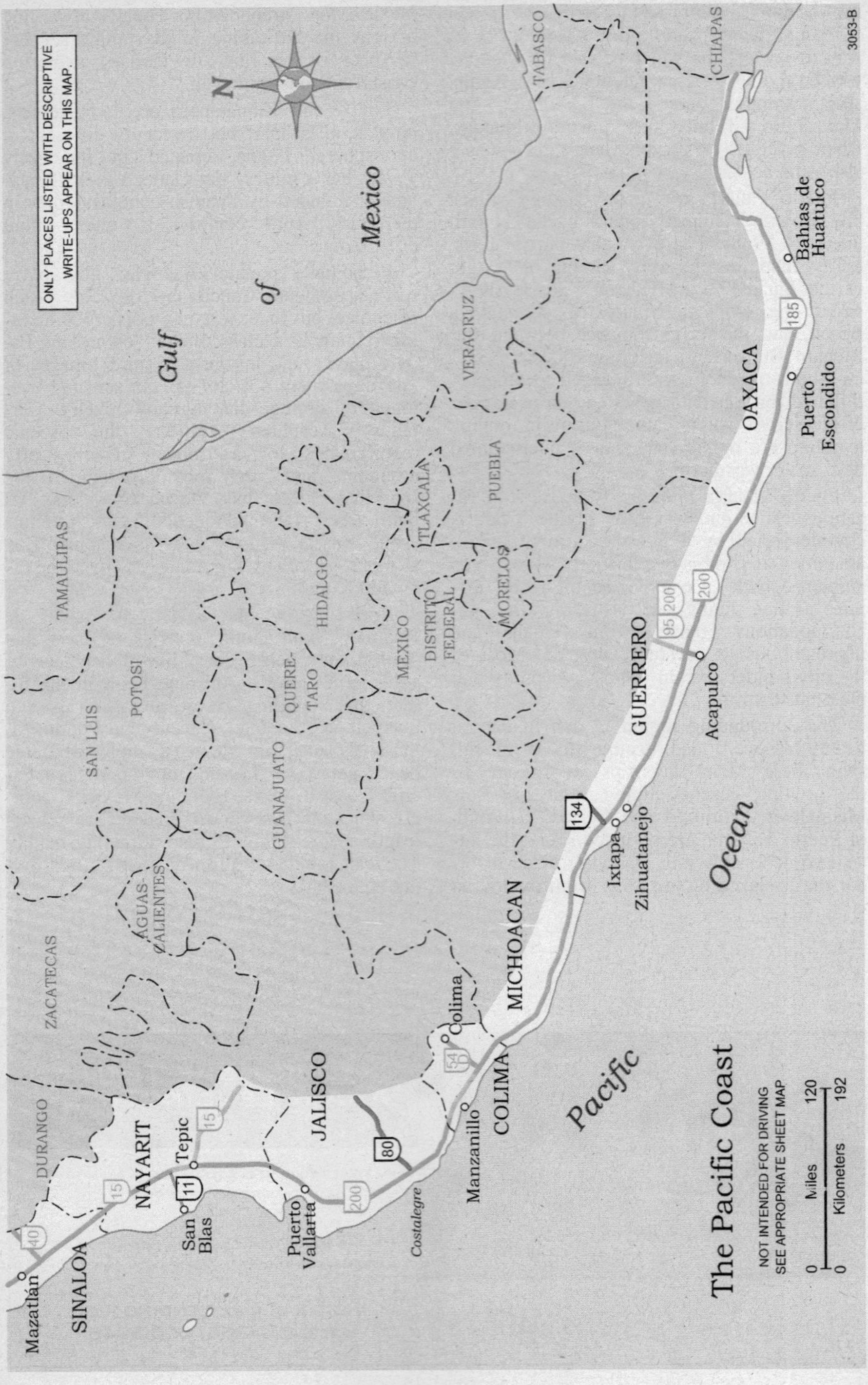

ONLY PLACES LISTED WITH DESCRIPTIVE
WRITE-UPS APPEAR ON THIS MAP.

N

3053-B

Gulf

of

Mexico

TABASCO

CHIAPAS

VERACRUZ

Bahías de
Huatulco

185

OAXACA

Puerto
Escondido

TAMAULIPAS

HIDALGO

TLAXCALA

PUEBLA

SAN LUIS

POTOSI

QUERE-
TARO

MEXICO

DISTRITO
FEDERAL

MORELOS

200

200

GUERRERO

95

GUANAJUATO

Acapulco

Ocean

AGUAS
CALIENTES

134

ZACATECAS

Ixtapa

Zihuatanejo

Colima

MICHOACAN

DURANGO

NAYARIT

Tepic

15

JALISCO

54

COLIMA

Pacific

SINALOA

15

80

Colima

Manzanillo

Mazatlán

40

San
Blas

11

Puerto
Vallarta

200

Costalegre

The Pacific Coast

NOT INTENDED FOR DRIVING
SEE APPROPRIATE SHEET MAP

0   Miles   120

0   Kilometers   192

Step into Paradise!

And step into a world of fun and relaxation with world-class beaches, dining, activities and so much more!

For more information or reservations, call or visit your local AAA Travel Office or log on to www.aaa.com.

Pleasant Holidays.

Travel With Someone You Trust.®

Acapulco

As early as the 1530s, ships for exploration purposes were built at a Spanish settlement occupying Acapulco's present site. Due to its excellent natural harbor, Acapulco (the name is an Indian word meaning "place where the reeds were destroyed") became the main west coast seaport for the Manila galleons and their treasures from the Orient. It was designated a city in 1599 and established as the only authorized trading port between the Americas and the Orient. From here silks, spices and other exotic goods were carried overland on mules to Mexico City and then Veracruz for shipment to Spain, while galleons moored in Acapulco Bay refilled their holds with silver and other Mexican products. That mercantile tradition continues, as the city remains a major export point for coffee, sugar and other products.

This rich trade with the Orient brought Mexico City merchants to annual unloading fairs. It also attracted Dutch and English pirates. Sir Francis Drake supposedly lay in wait for laden galleons near Puerto Marqués, just south of the present city, and pounced upon them as they left the sheltered harbor. To protect the ships from such raiders, the Spanish built the fort El Castillo de San Diego in 1616.

Commerce between Acapulco and Manila lasted some 250 years but came to a close in 1815 with the Mexican War of Independence. This conflict and the continued discovery and settlement of North and South America contributed to the rerouting of the China trade. As a result, Acapulco lapsed into the lethargy of an almost forgotten fishing village, punctuated by the excitement that accompanied a brief boom period during the California gold rush.

Not until 1927 was a road cut through the mountains to form an overland connection with the progressive cities to the north, particularly Mexico City. Acapulco's beaches are the country's closest to Mexico City by road, and although the trip took more than a week, the sleepy port was roused into a fever of development. When a new highway from Mexico City was completed in 1955, Acapulco was on its way to becoming Mexico's most notorious party spot.

Direct international air service began in 1964, ushering in the city's '60s and '70s heyday of glorious excess as it became a luxurious haven for the international and Hollywood jet sets, as well as one of the world's top resort destinations. The shore along Acapulco Bay was transformed into a 9-mile swath of glitter and indulgence patronized by *la gente bonita* (the beautiful people). Three decades of unmonitored growth, however, eventually tarnished Acapulco's image. Slums multiplied in the foothills behind the gleaming, high-rise bayfront buildings; traffic clogged the streets; some of the hotels became

Acapulco CVB

© SuperStock

worn around the edges. To maintain the city's standing as a world-class vacation destination, the Mexican government spent more than $500 million during the 1980s on redevelopment projects and planning for future improvements.

Although Cancún is Mexico's beach of choice for many foreign visitors, Acapulco retains its popularity, especially among Mexicans. A new condominium development or resort hotel project is always on the drawing board. Boat sweepers clean the bay daily (the beaches are swept daily as well), although pollution is evident in some locations, notably the area around La Quebrada, where Acapulco's famous cliff divers plunge into the surf.

Acapulco contains neither sober historical monuments nor venerable colonial architecture. Although it is a real city and important commercial center, the economy depends most heavily on the tourist trade. Visitors come not so much to sightsee but to relax. In addition to letting life's cares melt away at the beach, water recreation—from motorboat tours and fishing excursions to water skiing and parasailing—shopping and nightlife are favorite diversions.

For those with money to burn, the fun and flash are indeed heady. Big hotels—some of the finest in Mexico—pamper guests with private villas and every convenience. Dining here is an event, where al fresco tables at intimate restaurants overlook the bay. Night owls relish the city's flamboyant discos, which often don't wind down until the sun comes up. But Acapulco also has budget-friendly alternatives, simple fish shacks and a fun-filled atmosphere suitable for families. Those who keep coming back are drawn by those ever-reliable basics—sun, sand and water.

Approaches

By Air

Acapulco International Airport is about 23 kilometers (14 miles) southeast of the city and the hotel zone, near Puerto Marqués. Major carriers frequently fly into Mexico City, where connections can be made to Acapulco.

American, Continental, Delta and Mexicana airlines offer direct flights from U.S. cities. Within Mexico, Aeroméxico and Taesa airlines offer direct flights from Mexico City and other major cities; Aeroméxico also offers nonstop service from Los Angeles. For additional information about airlines *see "Arriving by Air," page 551.*

Transportes Terrestres is an airport taxi service that transports visitors to and from the airport and the city's hotel zone along Costera Miguel Alemán. The 30-minute ride costs about $6 (U.S.); phone (744) 762-1095 or (744) 762-1172.

(continued on page 181)

The Informed Traveler

City Population: 632,300, metro area 877,000 (estimated).

Location: On the southwestern Pacific coast.

Highlights: Dramatic Acapulco Bay, fringed with beaches and backed by jungle-covered mountain slopes; Mexico's liveliest nightlife, from torchlit cliff diving to pulsating discos to folkloric dance shows; a galaxy of options for dining out; accommodations from budget style to ultra luxurious.

WHOM TO CALL

Area Code: 744.

In Case of Emergency: If you need police assistance phone (744) 485-0650 or (744) 485-0862. English-speaking tourist police on the streets wear white uniforms and safari hats and are very helpful to tourists. The Highway Patrol (Policía Federal de Caminos) can be reached by phoning (744) 485-0647 or (744) 485-0439. LOCATEL, phone (744) 481-1111, can help locate missing persons or vehicles and gives assistance to those in need of public services.

In case of medical emergency contact the IMSS (Mexican Social Security Hospital), downtown at Av. Cuauhtémoc #95; phone (744) 483-5550. The Red Cross (Cruz Roja) is at Av. Ruíz Cortines #126; phone (744) 485-4100 or (744) 485-4101. Hospital Privado Magallanes, Wilfrido Massieu #2, provides medical services; phone (744) 485-6544. Most hotels have an in-house doctor or a doctor on 24-hour call.

Local phone calls in Acapulco cost 15 cents for three minutes. Many public phones take Ladatel credit cards only; these can be purchased in stores and other locations that display the Ladatel logo.

WHERE TO LOOK

Media

The bigger hotels offer *USA Today,* the *New York Times* and the *Los Angeles Times.* Sanborn's, a Mexican restaurant chain, has English-language books and periodicals. There are branches on Costera Miguel Alemán near Playa Condesa and in the old downtown area. *Adventure in Acapulco* is a monthly publication in English that offers information on what's happening around town.

Visitor Information

Guerrero State Tourism Office (Secretaría de Fomento Turístico): Costera Miguel Alemán #4455 in the Acapulco International Center (Centro Internacional de Acapulco); phone (744) 484-2423 (English spoken). The center also contains the local Green Angels office. It is open Mon.-Fri. 8-8, Sat.-Sun. 10-6.

For English answers to questions about hotels, restaurants, attractions, public facilities and sports, contact the Secretary of Tourism Promotion (Secretaría de Fomento Turístico). The office is open Mon.-Fri. 9-3 and 6-9 p.m.; phone (744) 484-7916 or (744) 484-2415.

CANACO (Acapulco Chamber of Commerce) also provides tourist information; it is at Quebrada #31 (second floor) at the corner of Hidalgo and is open Mon.-Sat. 9-2 and 4:30-8. Phone (744) 482-2095 (English spoken). City Hall Public Relations is open Mon.-Fri. 8-2; phone (744) 486-2676 or (744) 486-2666.

The post office building (Correo) is on Costera Miguel Alemán near Plaza Juan Alvarez. A branch office is on the Costera near Playa Caleta.

WHAT TO KNOW

Weather

Acapulco is always balmy: highs average in the upper 80s or low 90s, lows in the 70s. The ocean and bay are warm enough for swimming year-round. June through October is humid as well as hot, and these months also produce brief but torrential rains. Occasional hurricanes affect Mexico's Pacific coast. November is one of the nicest months, as high-season prices haven't yet kicked in.

Formality can be left at home with your coat; standard attire in Acapulco consists of shorts, T-shirts and scandalous bathing suits.

Currency Exchange

Most banks along the Costera, both in the downtown area and the hotel zone, are open Mon.-Fri. 9-1:30 (some stay open until 5 or 6) and may have better currency exchange rates than the hotels. *Casas de cambio* (currency exchange offices) line the Costera in the vicinity of the big hotels; these are open daily and often until 8 p.m.

By Car

From Mexico City, toll highway Mex. 95-D, the Autopista del Sol (Sun Highway), is by far the quickest and best option. Between Mexico City and Cuernavaca the funnel highway is toll Mex. 55-D. Mex. 95-D splits off from old Mex. 95 near Puente de Ixtla, proceeds south to Chilpancingo and Tierra Colorada, and then on to the international airport. Total driving time is about 3.5 hours.

The four-lane, largely traffic-free highway twists and turns through beautiful valleys and around mountainous curves. Signs denote scenic stops. About halfway to Acapulco a suspension bridge 600 feet above a river affords a spectacular view; acrophobes will probably want to keep their eyes shut.

The one drawback to traveling this well-maintained, 415-kilometer (249-mile) route is the cost: tolls are expensive. Tolls must be paid for and gas must be purchased in pesos. The highway is economically out of the question for the average Mexican driver; most of the traffic is luxury buses, long-distance trucks and tourists willing to pay for convenience.

Mex. 95, an older, free highway, begins at Mexico City and proceeds south through Cuernavaca, Taxco, Iguala and Chilpancingo to Acapulco, roughly paralleling toll Mex. 95-D. It's scenic, but also very winding. Coastal Mex. 200 links Acapulco with Bahías de Huatulco to the southeast and with Ixtapa/Zihuatanejo to the northwest.

Acapulco is a long way from the United States; from McAllen, Tex., one of the closest U.S. border points, the distance is nearly 900 miles. From points north or south along the Pacific coast, Mex. 200 is the only route. Portions of this roadway within the state of Guerrero, however, can be potholed or marked with detours that slow driving time. As a result, most visitors fly directly to the city or drive from Mexico City.

By Bus

First-class (ejecutivo) buses operated by Tres Estrellas de Oro make daily runs on the Autopista del Sol between Mexico City's southern bus terminal and Acapulco; the trip takes five to six hours and costs about $30 (U.S.) one way. This bus line also has service to Taxco, Ixtapa and Zihuatanejo. Buses coming from Mexico City on Friday and departing Acapulco on Monday are often very crowded. **Note:** This highway is very steep and winding in places. For additional information about buses see "Bus Service," page 68.

By Cruise Ship

Acapulco is a major port of call for cruise ships, most of which originate from Los Angeles. Ships dock at Puerto Acapulco, near the old downtown area. Lines that visit the city include Cunard, Holland America, Norwegian, Princess Cruises and Royal Caribbean. The ship's excursion manager plans tours of the city; on-shore visits include Fort San Diego (across the street from where the cruise ships are moored); La Quebrada, where the cliff divers perform; the city market; and the Mercado de Artesanías (flea market). The fine harbor and 4-mile-long bay also teem with smaller pleasure and commercial vessels.

Getting Around

City Layout

The oldest part of Acapulco fills a peninsula that forms the western side of the bay. This is where residents attend to such daily errands as grocery shopping and stopping at the post office. Plaza de Toros, where occasional bullfights are held, is south of the central downtown area. On the western side of the peninsula is La Quebrada.

Besides the Mercado Municipal (city market), Old Acapulco features a Moorish-looking cathedral—complete with onion-shaped blue bulb and yellow spires—that dominates Plaza Alvarez, the city's main square. The cathedral's appearance can be misleading: It was actually constructed from parts of an uncompleted movie theater. The main square, shaded by large trees, is a meeting place in which to stop and socialize, or peruse the newspaper over a cup of coffee. Band concerts are held here on Sunday evenings.

The waterfront contains the docks and fishermen's wharves, reminders of Acapulco's continuing importance as a commercial port. This is where both cruise ships and smaller fishing boats dock. Historic Fort San Diego is in this section.

Along the bay runs Costera Miguel Alemán, the scenic boulevard named for the former Mexican president who was responsible for much of Acapulco's resort development. Most of the luxury hotels, along with many restaurants and shops and the major beaches, are in the central bay area lining the "Costera," as the thoroughfare is commonly known. Beyond the junction with Mex. 95, the coastal drive follows Acapulco Bay toward Puerto Marqués and the airport, where another group of newer luxury hotels are clustered. Inland, the major route is Avenida Cuauhtémoc, which roughly parallels the Costera.

As in many other parts of Mexico, streets are bewilderingly named and frequently change names as well. Street signs are difficult to locate. Orient yourself by using the Costera as a reference point—the great majority of Acapulco's accommodations, restaurants, nightspots and attractions are on or a short distance off it.

Rental Cars

Hertz is one of several rental car agencies with offices in Acapulco. Be sure you fully understand the terms of any rental contract. Some luxury hotels provide jeeps for their guests.

Note: AAA/CAA members enjoy discounts through Hertz for vehicles booked in the United

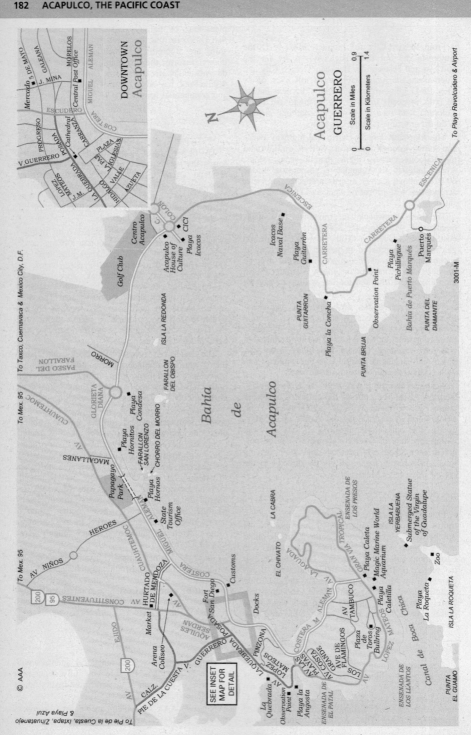

DOWNTOWN
Acapulco

Acapulco
GUERRERO

Scale in Miles
Scale in Kilometers

To Playa Revolcadero & Airport

States. Consult your local AAA/CAA club or phone Hertz, (800) 654-3080.

Buses

Local buses connect the city with the beaches and various points of interest; fares are inexpensive, and the newer tourist buses are air-conditioned. If you are taking a bus to one of the outlying areas, such as Pie de la Cuesta or Puerto Marqués, find out when and where to board the last bus going back into town. Buses run regularly all along the Costera, and maps at covered bus stops illustrate routes to major hotels and tourist attractions. Stay alert while on the bus and beware of pickpockets, who sometimes target foreign tourists.

Taxis

Hotel taxis are the most expensive, but they also are the most comfortable. A list showing the rates to which drivers must adhere is posted in most hotel lobbies. Rates usually go up at night. Taxis not affiliated with the hotels are usually white or blue-and-white Volkswagen Beetles. They usually charge by zone, destination or the distance traveled. Make certain that you come to an agreement on a rate before getting in the cab.

Parking

Old Acapulco has narrow streets and is better suited to walking than driving. It is illegal to park anywhere along Miguel Costera Alemán. An easier alternative is to use city buses or take a taxi where you want to go.

What To See

ACAPULCO HOUSE OF CULTURE (Casa de la Cultura de Acapulco) is 1 block east of CICI near the Acapulco International Center. This small complex of buildings displays pre-Columbian artifacts in addition to well-made reproductions of Mexican art and handicrafts, many of which are for sale.

CHILDREN'S INTERNATIONAL CENTER (CICI) is on Costera Miguel Alemán at Calle Cristóbal Colón. It contains a wave pool, waterslides, swimming pools with water pistols and boats, and an aquarium. There also are shows featuring performing dolphins and sea lions. Admission is charged.

FORT SAN DIEGO stands on a hill east of the main square in Old Acapulco, overlooking the harbor and the oldest section of the city's port. Originally built in 1616 as a series of ramparts to ward off Sir Francis Drake and other marauding pirates, the fort was extensively damaged by an earthquake and rebuilt in 1776 as a stout, star-shaped fortress. In 1813, during the War of Independence, Gen. José María Morelos attacked the fort; after a four-month siege, the Spanish capitulated, giving up their lucrative trading base.

Acapulco Historical Museum (Museo Histórico de Acapulco) is within the fort. It documents Acapulco's role in Mexican history from pre-Hispanic times through Mexican independence. Other exhibits include artifacts from the city's former lucrative trade with the Orient, including furniture and vases. Open Tues.-Sun. Admission is charged.

PAPAGAYO PARK is along the Costera between Hornos and Hornitos beaches. It features a children's amusement center offering a roller-skating rink, go-cart racing, a man-made lagoon with boats and a toboggan run down a hill (the summit is reached by cable car). Also in the park is an aviary where various exotic birds can be seen on a stroll along shaded paths. Admission is charged for rides.

PUERTO MARQUES is on a narrow neck of the bay east of Acapulco, accessible by car or bus. While this fishing village is in itself unremarkable, the water is calm and suitable for swimming or water skiing, and the beach is lined with seafood restaurants. The real attraction is the 18-kilometer (11-mile) drive east from Old Acapulco's Plaza Alvarez via the naval base at Icacos, which offers magnificent views of the city, Acapulco Bay and smaller Puerto Marqués Bay.

What To Do

Dining

Dining out is one of Acapulco's principal pleasures. Although the city has its share of local hangouts dishing out regional Mexican fare, get casually dressed up (no tie or jacket, but no shorts or jeans either) and splurge at one of the gourmet hotel restaurants. The view of the bay from a rooftop establishment at dusk is invariably glorious.

The bigger hotel restaurants offer a wide selection of international cuisine as well as local specialties. Prices tend toward the expensive side (dinner for two without drinks, wine or tip costs upwards of $40), but the quality of the food and luxury of the setting help compensate. Atmosphere and entertainment vary with the establishment. Dinner rarely begins before 9 p.m., although some hotel restaurants begin serving around 6 or 7.

Along Costera Miguel Alemán there are numerous *palapa* (thatch-roofed) places with a seafood menu and a funky air. Look for those where people are eating and not just having a drink. The Costera also has no shortage of rib and hamburger joints, where big portions, potent libations, wild decorations and a wilder crowd are the rule. Those homesick for fast food will find the usual American outlets lining the Costera, although prices are not cheap.

The area around the main square has many small, traditional restaurants where you can get a good Mexican meal. As elsewhere in the country, the *comida corrida* (lunch special) can be a good bargain, with soup, rice or noodles, an entree and dessert or coffee for a very reasonable price. Neighborhood street stands sell fresh seafood, but use caution when buying any food item from street vendors—if it's *not* fresh, your stomach could regret it.

For Your Information

Guides/Tours

With the focus on sunning, shopping and eating out, a guide is not really necessary in Acapulco. If you do hire one, make certain he or she is a reputable, bonded guide licensed by the State Department of Tourism. Guides can usually be found in the lobbies or at the entrances of the more expensive hotels.

Better yet, take one of the city's many organized tours. Excursions to the Old Acapulco market or to a nighttime Mexican fiesta are easily arranged. Tour operators often have offices at the large hotels. The Acapulco Convention and Visitors

Acapulco CVB

Bureau, Costera Miguel Alemán #3111, has information about various guided tours of the city and environs; phone (744) 484-8555 (English spoken).

Staying Safe

Areas frequented by tourists are generally safe, even after dark. However, tourists often are targeted for petty theft; stay alert in crowded public places like markets or on buses. Don't take large sums of money or other valuables to the beach, and always keep your hotel key with you.

In most restaurants it is customary to leave a tip (*propina*) of 10 to 15 percent. Establishments catering to tourists normally use purified water to cook vegetables and wash produce. At smaller places or if in doubt, ask for or order bottled water, juice, soda or beer. It's best to avoid ice cubes in drinks. For a list of AAA-RATED establishments in Acapulco, *see the Lodgings & Restaurants section.*

Shopping

Acapulco offers a wide variety of men's and women's clothing—both designer and casual—as well as Taxco silver items. The chief shopping districts are the air-conditioned complexes along the Costera and in the downtown area of Old Acapulco. Boutiques along the Costera are stocked with the usual resort wear, shoes and trendy fashions. The government-run FONART store on the Costera has crafts from all over the country.

The Plaza Bahía, on Costera Miguel Alemán next to the Acapulco Plaza Hotel, is an enclosed mall with stores and small restaurants on two levels. Most hotels have their own specialty shops as well; the plush shopping arcade at the Acapulco Princess is worth stopping by. Some establishments still shut down in the early afternoon for the traditional long lunch break from about 2-4 p.m.

For a more down-to-earth shopping experience, visit the Mercado de Artesanías (also called El Parazal), near Calle 5 de Mayo in the downtown area. About a 20-minute walk from the main plaza, this flea market is a melange of stalls with shopkeepers hawking replicas of archeological artifacts, rugs, papier-mâché souvenirs, ceramics and other assorted curios. Here the time-honored custom of bargaining prevails. The selling price is apt to be outrageous. If you don't have the time or patience to stand and haggle, pretending to walk away often brings the price down quickly. Go early in the morning, before it gets too hot or crowded.

The Municipal Market, a few blocks off the Costera at avenidas Cuesta Hurtado de Mendoza and Constituyentes, offers a distinct change from the upscale stores of the tourist strip. This is where the locals do their shopping, and stall after stall displays everything from fresh produce to good luck charms. Souvenirs abound, and fans of kitsch will appreciate the gaudy ashtrays and shell ornaments.

Beaches

Noisy band concerts and frivolous teeny-bikini contests notwithstanding, Acapulco's shoreline does have its business side. The bay is anchored by a commercial port at one end and a naval base at the other. Still, there is plenty of room in between for a swath of sand that is broken only by a few rock outcroppings, and more secluded beaches stretch northwest of the bay along the Pacific coastline. Keep in mind that all beaches in Mexico are federally owned property and therefore public, even stretches that may seem private because they are in front of one of the big hotels.

For safety's sake, avoid completely isolated beaches. Chairs, umbrellas, showers, hammocks and refreshments are available at most locations. Due to unpredictable or rough surf conditions, the beaches facing the open Pacific—northwest of more protected Acapulco Bay—are better suited for watching the sky turn a pretty pink at sunset or taking a romantic stroll along the shore than for swimming. The following beaches are listed alphabetically.

PIE DE LA CUESTA is about 16 km (10 mi.) northwest of Acapulco. "Foot of the Hill" is an uncrowded, golden-sand beach that makes a good day trip. Thatched *palapa* restaurants shaded by coconut palms are a perfect place to savor the local fish, caught fresh in the morning and broiled over charcoal fires. Crashing breakers and treacherous currents make swimming or bodysurfing at this beach very risky; there are no lifeguards.

Watching the sun go down over the water is a daily ritual. Families line up rows of chairs pointed toward the descending sun. Vendors mill around selling snacks and trinkets. All heads turn at sunset. If there are clouds in the sky, the patterns of color will be magnificent; even if the weather is perfect, the Pacific turns into pale gold as the sun drops.

PLAYA CALETA is along the peninsula where Old Acapulco is located. Caleta Beach and its twin, Playa Caletilla, used to be known as the "morning beaches." Once attracting the city's chic elite, the beaches today cater more to families. The ocean water is very calm here. Inner tubes and other water sports equipment can be rented.

Magic Marine World Aquarium (Mágico Mundo Marino) occupies a small island between Caleta and Caletilla beaches. The complex has indoor and outdoor marine life exhibits, as well as enclosures housing alligators, sea lions and turtles. Other facilities include a pool, waterslides and a scuba diving school. Rock platforms allow access into the ocean; snorkeling equipment and water skis can be rented.

Across from Caleta Beach is the secluded island of La Roqueta, reached by a 15-minute trip aboard a motorboat or glass-bottom boat. A lighthouse stands on the island. It's a peaceful place to sunbathe, snorkel or windsurf; boards, beach chairs, inner tubes and canoes all can be rented at Caletilla Beach.

Standing submerged in the harbor near the island is a bronze statue of the Virgin of Guadalupe. It is best seen on a glass-bottom boat ride, as the shrine is not easily visible from the surface.

PLAYA HORNOS is just off Costera Miguel Alemán. Twin beaches Hornos and Hornitos once were fashionable spots for afternoon bathers; both are now packed with Mexican tourists. Here the water of Acapulco Bay is calm, although not particularly clean. But palm trees shade the sand, and there are numerous casual, thatched-roof restaurants lining the beach.

PLAYA LA CONDESA faces the middle of Acapulco Bay. La Condesa Beach is crowded with singles—the place to see and be seen, view Acapulco's most daring swimwear (on both sexes) and watch the parasailers. Along Costera Miguel Alemán there are many lunch spots.

PLAYA REVOLCADERO is approximately three-quarters of a kilometer (half a mile) beyond Puerto Marqués. Revolcadero Beach is popular for swimming and surfing, although the waves can be rough and there is a powerful undertow; stay close to shore. The wide strip of sand is well suited for those who enjoy horseback riding along the beach. Puerto Marqués, which is lined with restaurants that are literally at the water's edge, is popular with Mexican tourists and is crowded on weekends.

Sightseeing

The sights here are scenic, not historic. Brightly decorated *calandrias* (horse-drawn carriages) regularly parade along Costera Miguel Alemán, a leisurely way to tour the city. They also can be hired as taxis. In Fraccionamiento Las Brisas, an upscale subdivision of homes, is La Capilla de la Paz, a simple, modern chapel. From this mountainside location a large white cross overlooks the east side of the bay. The attractive grounds offer a peaceful retreat from Acapulco's hectic pace.

Rental cars and jeeps are available for drives along the outlying coastal roads. An interesting side trip is through the Costa Chica (Little Coast), a 240-kilometer (150-mile) stretch of coastline that stretches southeast of Acapulco to the Guerrero-Oaxaca border. Mex. 200, in poor paved condition in some areas of this coastal route, runs past the town of San Marcos through a deserted terrain of lagoons and rocky cliffs in the shadow of the Sierra Madre mountains.

Costa Chica is inhabited by descendants of two boatloads of slaves who managed to evade their intended Acapulco destination. Many African customs have been preserved among the Costa Chicans, who are descendants of the Bantu tribe. This cultural enclave is most evident in and around the small mining village of Ometepec.

Driving northwest from Acapulco on Mex. 200 (the Costa Grande, or Big Coast) is another scenic excursion encompassing palm-lined lagoons and secluded beaches. Jungle-covered hills and high rock promontories finally yield to the high-rise hotels of Ixtapa.

Yachts that depart daily from the *malecón* offer morning, afternoon and moonlight cruises around Acapulco Bay. Tickets can be purchased at the boat or from any hotel travel agent. Lunch or dinner, music and dancing are frequently part of the package. The water also is a prime vantage point from which to view Acapulco's sunsets or the La Quebrada cliff divers. Glass-bottom boat tours of the bay are available at Caleta Beach and several other waterfront locations.

Outdoor Recreation

All forms of water recreation are natural choices for leisure activity. Big-game **fishing** for marlin, sailfish, dolphin, barracuda, yellowtail, shark, red snapper and pompano is excellent all year. An international sailfish tournament is held in late November or early December. Besides deep-sea fishing, there's fresh-water fishing in Tres Palos Lagoon and Coyuca Lagoon, near Pie de la Cuesta. Small boats can be rented, with catfish the frequent catch. Favored spots for inland river fishing are along the Río Papagayo, east of Acapulco just beyond Tres Palos Lagoon, and the Río Coyuca, just beyond Coyuca Lagoon and west of Pie de la Cuesta.

Guides are available for hire, and fishing trips also can be arranged through your hotel or the Pesca Deportiva, near the dock across from the main square. Rates at the dock are negotiable; select a reliable outfit whose equipment is in good, safe condition. Deep-sea boats with experienced crews can be rented by the day; these excursions usually leave in the early morning and return in the early afternoon. Make arrangements ahead of time. A fishing license is required, but local companies frequently will take care of this for you.

Almost every type of **boating** can be enjoyed. Sailboats, speedboats, catamarans and other pleasure craft prevail on the bay. Yachts and deep-sea fishing vessels are available as well; some host sunset and moonlight cruises complete with champagne. Arrange boat rentals through hotels or travel agents. For larger vessels with fully-equipped crews, make reservations in advance. An information booth at Caletilla Beach rents canoes, paddleboats and other small craft and can arrange water skiing and scuba diving excursions.

Swimming in certain areas of Acapulco Bay is not recommended, despite the enticing hue of its waters. Although cleanup efforts are ongoing, pollution is still evident. The beaches tend to have rough surf and strong undertows; pay particular heed to any warning flags posted. There also are periodic shark sightings. Fortunately, almost every hotel has a pool, if not several. Some of them are huge, set against a backdrop of rustling palms and tropical plantings, and have swim-up bars for the truly indolent. Luxury hotels feature private or semi-private pools.

All of the major hotels offer **scuba diving** lessons and equipment. The waters off Roqueta Island are especially suited to diving. Divers de México provides dive packages with English-speaking instructors, plus lessons beginning in a swimming pool; phone (744) 482-1398. Boats for **water skiing** can be booked at hotels as well. The gentler waters at Puerto Marqués and Caleta Beach are good for beginners. Exhibitions of barefoot skiing can be viewed at Coyuca Lagoon. **Surfing** is not permitted in Acapulco Bay; the best place to surf is Revolcadero Beach, near Puerto Marqués.

Another popular sport is **parasailing**, although it is not without risks. From a standing position, a speedboat hauls a "sailor" to an altitude of more than 325 feet. This thrill can be had at almost any beach, although many parachute operators set up at La Condesa. **Windsurfing** is good at Puerto Marqués and also can be arranged at Caleta Beach. **Horseback riding** is best at Playa Revolcadero and Pie de la Cuesta.

Bullfights are held on Sundays and some holidays from November through mid-April at the Plaza de Toros bullring, off Avenida López Mateos in Old Acapulco (up the hill from Caletilla Beach). Tickets are available through travel agencies or hotels; tickets purchased through agencies normally include transportation to and from the hotel. The

corrida begins promptly at 5:30, so arrive early, particularly if you plan to buy a ticket at the window. Prices average about $20 (U.S.) but vary with the location of the seat. *Sombra* (in the shade) seats are more expensive but more desirable than *sol* (in the sun). If it's your first bullfight, try to obtain seats near the top of the arena. They are less expensive than seats closer to the action but provide a sweeping view of the spectacle.

Fans of **jai alai** can watch this fast-paced sport at the Jai-Alai Stadium, also in Old Acapulco near the bullring. This state-of-the-art complex contains restaurants, specialty shops and an art gallery, in addition to a Racing & Sports Book betting facility where wagers can be placed.

Most accommodations provide **tennis** courts for their guests; non-guests can use the facilities but will pay more per hour for court fees. There are both indoor and outdoor courts; some are lighted for night play. Lessons with English-speaking instructors are available. A tennis center at the Vidafel Mayan Palace Hotel, in the Punta Diamante area at the eastern end of Acapulco Bay, has 12 clay and synthetic-floor courts surrounded by nylon netting that screens the sun but allows cooling breezes in.

Championship **golf** courses include the 18-hole course at the Acapulco Princess Hotel and the 18-hole course at the Pierre Marqués Hotel, both along Revolcadero Beach, and the Tres Vidas golf & Country Club at Punta Diamante, designed by renowned golf course architect Robert von Hagge. There also is a nine-hole public course off Costera Miguel Alemán, next to the Acapulco International Center. All four charge greens fees, although reduced fees are offered to Acapulco Princess and Pierre Marqués hotel guests. Advance reservations are suggested during the winter season. Try to schedule a weekday round, when courses are generally less crowded.

Opportunities for **jogging** are not plentiful. A morning run is possible along the sidewalk on the beach side of Costera Miguel Alemán; do it before traffic gets too heavy. The truly dedicated can run on the shifting sands of the beaches. For those unwilling to sacrifice regular workouts just because they're on vacation, the Villa Vera Hotel & Racquet Club has a **fitness center** with step aerobic machines and free weights. The center is open to nonguests.

Nightlife

Acapulco's reputation for wild nightlife is renowned: The fun usually begins after a long dinner and can last until dawn. Most activity centers on discos, nightclubs and hotel bars; for a full night on the town, try several establishments for dinner, dancing and drinks. Other options, such as flamenco dancers, drag shows, stand-up comedy or live salsa music, are plentiful.

The city's glitzy discos feature elaborate strobe lights, mirrored walls, video screens and dance beats pounding from state-of-the-art sound systems. Some have breathtaking views of Acapulco Bay. Discos start hopping after 10:30 p.m. and stay open until the wee hours. While always crowded, most are conveniently located along Costera Miguel Alemán and are grouped in clusters; if there's a line at one place, try another.

A dress code is standard (jeans and T-shirts are usually frowned on). Cover charges are steep, although they are sometimes waived to draw customers, and you can run up a hefty drink tab as well if you're not careful. Present hot spots include Andromedas, Baby'O, Enigma, Le Dome, News and Palladium. Another popular watering hole is the Acapulco branch of the Hard Rock Café, at Costera Miguel Alemán #37.

The city's most celebrated nighttime attraction, however, is the diving from La Quebrada cliff. From a torchlit spot atop a natural rock wall, men ranging in age from mid-teens to mid-40s plunge 135 feet into a narrow cove bordered by treacherous rocks. A diver hits the water at a speed of about 60 miles per hour.

The success of the spectacular dive depends not only on skill but also on split-second timing, since the tide fills the cove with swirling surf and then recedes quickly, leaving the water level as low as 12 feet during a brief period. Getting to the top of the cliff is risky as well—the divers scale the steep, vertical cliffside by grasping at rocky outcrops that occasionally snap off.

The cliff diving dates back to 1934, when La Quebrada first became a popular spot for local divers to display their talent. It is now presented with blazing torches each evening; dives can be viewed from a public platform where a small admission is charged or from the expensive nightclub of an adjacent hotel. There is a daily daytime dive as well, usually around 1 p.m.

In keeping with the local love for feats of daring, the celebrated Papantla Flyers (Voladores de Papantla) perform a flying pole act Wednesday and Friday evenings in Aztec Plaza at the Acapulco International Center, Costera Miguel Alemán #4455, as part of Fiesta Mexicana nights. With poles far higher than those traditionally used, the Indians' act is very hazardous and dramatic. The show begins at 8 p.m. Those who prefer less life-threatening drama can take in native dance performances of the Acapulco Ballet Folklórico. General admission or dinner show tickets can be purchased; phone (744) 484-7050 for reservations, or consult your hotel tour desk or a local travel agency.

The high-rise hotels frequently offer nightly entertainment, such as Mexican-style fiestas or theme parties. Live music accompanies the happy hour at these establishments, which also have the usual poolside cocktail bars and evening floor shows. The Acapulco International Center, in addition to hosting the flying pole dancers, has several entertainment facilities, including mariachi and piano bars and outdoor performance areas.

Special Events

The year's greatest influx of visitors is during Holy Week and the week after, marked by several religious observances. Many local businesses close, and the city becomes so crowded that some people sleep on the beach. Those wishing to visit during this time should make reservations far in advance.

For music lovers the Acapulco International Music Festival, which takes place in May, draws participants from many countries. The offerings encompass everything from top-of-the-charts pop to traditional boleros, and are performed by orchestras, bands, trios and individual artists. Concerts are given at the Acapulco International Center, the Plaza de Toros bullring and at beaches, hotels and other open-air spots around the city.

The Virgin of Guadalupe is the focus of a nationwide pilgrimage on Dec. 12 to the Basilica of Our Lady of Guadalupe, in a northern suburb of Mexico City *(see the Mexico City attraction listing, page 255)*. The event, celebrated with dancing and other forms of merriment, is observed with special exuberance in Acapulco. Also in December are the Cliff Diving Championships. Acapulco closes out the year with a huge party on New Year's Eve.

This ends listings for Acapulco.
The following page resumes the alphabetical listings
of cities in The Pacific Coast.

BAHIAS DE HUATULCO, OAXACA (I-9)

FONATUR, Mexico's government-funded tourist development agency, officially inaugurated Bahías de Huatulco (wah-TOOL-co) in 1988, selecting a 22-mile stretch of bays, coves and inlets as the site for a master-planned vacation getaway. But while its resort aspects are a recent development, the settlement of Huatulco has been around for quite awhile.

Zapotec, Mixtec and Aztec merchants established a trade route through this region during pre-Hispanic times, and the coastal settlement of Santa Cruz Huatulco became a thriving port and shipyard. By the late 16th century, however, Acapulco had absorbed the galleon trade, and pirate attacks brought about a further decline. Until recently, Huatulco and other small villages along this stretch of coast remained forgotten outposts.

Jagged boulders and small islands characterize this section of Mexico's Pacific coastline, much of which is backed by dense tropical forest. The resort area comprises nine bays in all. Thanks to their natural layout, large-scale development will be broken into a series of resort areas targeting budget, mid-range and upper-end travelers. Ecotourism is promoted heavily, and there are increasing opportunities for jungle hikes, river rafting, rappelling and other vigorous activities.

Planners also have vowed to set aside the majority of the resort's approximately 52,000 acres as ecological preserves in order to protect the area's natural environment. If projected development comes to pass, by the year 2018 the resort is expected to have some 30,000 hotel rooms (compared to about 2,300 now), bring in 2 million visitors annually, and generate nearly 25 percent of the state of Oaxaca's total revenue.

Practicalities

Huatulco International Airport is off Mex. 200, about 19 kilometers (12 miles) northwest of the Tangolunda resort area. To those travelers arriving by air, Huatulco from above resembles more than anything a vast green carpet of jungle descending from the foothills of the Sierra Madre del Sur to the ocean shore.

The tropical feeling is reinforced by the airport's appearance. The two terminals—one for international flights, one for domestic flights—are large, *palapa*-style hardwood structures with high ceilings and thatched roofs. Unfortunately, arriving visitors may encounter roaming time-share representatives; avoid their high-pressure sales tactics.

Mexicana Airlines flies from Chicago, Los Angeles, San Francisco, Toronto and other international cities to Huatulco via Mexico City. Mexicana and its subsidiary, Aerocaribe, also offer domestic flights to Huatulco from Mexico City, Oaxaca and other Mexican cities. For airport information phone (958) 581-9004. For additional information about airlines *see "Arriving by Air," page 551*.

Transportes Terrestres, phone (958) 581-9014 or (958) 581-9024, operates shared minivan *(colectivo)* service that shuttles passengers from the airport to the resort hotels; expect to pay around $9-$10 (U.S.) per person. A private taxi (often a Chevrolet Suburban) is much more expensive—around $40 and up, depending on the amount of luggage you have—and drivers can be aggressive about soliciting fares.

Taxi service also links the three separate areas of Tangolunda, Santa Cruz and La Crucecita. Cabs wait in front of the big hotels and also congregate around the plazas in Santa Cruz and La Crucecita. Fares average around $5 (U.S.) from La Crucecita to Tangolunda and $3 from Santa Cruz to Tangolunda or Santa Cruz to La Crucecita. Rates are posted at the travel booth on the main plaza in La Crucecita.

Since Huatulco is spread out and also has a good road network, a rental car can come in handy for exploring as well as for trips to nearby destinations. AAA/CAA members can reserve a rental car through their local club; it is recommended that you make all necessary arrangements prior to your departure. It also helps to know the peso equivalent of the dollar rate you are charged, since the charge in Mexico will be in pesos.

The climate is tropical, with an average annual temperature of 82 degrees. Temperatures in May, the hottest month, can reach 100. January through May is practically rainless; heavy rains fall July through September. As in Mexico's other Pacific coast resorts, the "winter" months, December through March, are the sunniest, driest and least oppressive. **Note:** Mosquitos can be fierce all along the coast. Pack an effective insect repellent or pick up Autan Classic, a widely available Mexican brand.

The Bays

From east to west, the nine bays of Huatulco are Conejos, Tangolunda, Chahué, Santa Cruz, El Organo, El Maguey, Cacaluta, Chachacual and San Agustín. Conejos, Tangolunda, Chahue, Santa Cruz, El Maguey and El Organo are accessible by car; others can be reached only by boat. Bahía Conejos has minimal tourist facilities but offers excellent snorkeling, diving and fishing at its four beaches.

Luxury hotel development in Huatulco is focused along Bahía Tangolunda, which means "place where the gods live" in the Zapotec dialect. High-rise buildings are absent—no structure here is more than six stories tall. As a result, the Mediterranean-, Moorish- and Mexican-style resorts that hug the bay offer unobstructed views from many different vantage points. Careful attention has been given to paving and landscaping, with sculptured rocks separating the roads running to and from the resort properties.

Several beaches line this bay, including Playa La Hierbabuena, Playa del Amor (Love Beach), Punta Paraiso and Playa La Entrega, where a coral reef lies just a few feet offshore. Most of the resorts are all-inclusive, with shuttle service to the beach and such diversions as themed evening shows and Mexican Fiesta nights.

Bahía Chahué (Chah-WAY) is the largest of the nine, with three separate stretches of sandy beach. A marina for private yachts is in operation. Many hotel employees live in La Crucecita, a planned town and residential area a mile or so inland off Mex. 200. Its main square, while not particularly authentic, is attractive, graced with a central bandstand, brick walkways, green lawns, shade trees and white stone benches.

Surrounding this plaza are modest hotels, restaurants, shops specializing in Oaxacan handicrafts and an Internet café, an establishment fast becoming ubiquitous in Mexico. Horse-drawn carriages depart from the plaza for leisurely tours. The central part of town is very lively in the evening, when locals and visitors mingle at the restaurants and in the square.

Bahía Santa Cruz is the site of the original fishing settlement of Huatulco. Day cruises to the other eight bays depart from the marina here; arrangements can be made at your hotel or through local travel agents. An international cruise ship dock was completed and opened in 2003 at the entrance to the Santa Cruz Marina.

The village of Santa Cruz, which developed in the wake of Huatulco's resort unveiling, has a shady main square surrounded by shops, restaurants, bars and a few Mexican-style, middle-class hotels. Playa Santa Cruz, the main beach, is a short distance from the marina. It has clear, calm water and refreshment facilities, making it a pleasant spot to snorkel or simply lay around after lunch. Nearby Playa Yerbabuena and Playa La Entrega are accessible by boat, either an outboard motor-propelled *panga* (skiff) or a deluxe cruise vessel.

Bahía El Organo has gentle surf, nearby parking facilities and a few open-air *palapa* restaurants. The four westernmost bays—El Maguey, Cacaluta, Chachacual and San Agustín—were designated a national park in 1998, protecting them from commercial development, although they can still be visited. Cacaluta and Chachacual have long, deserted stretches of beach; San Agustín is excellent for diving. All of the bays, in fact, boast lovely goldensand beaches and pristine waters, the result of a sewage system that permits nothing to be dumped into the ocean.

What To Do

Huatulco's cove-pocked coastline is its major attraction, and the best way to experience it is to take a cruise. Boat tours visit the more pristine of the nine bays, such as El Maguey or Chachacual, with time out for swimming or snorkeling in the crystal-clear water and lunch on the beach. Guided kayaking trips also are available up the Copalita River, which winds into the nearby mountains.

Isla La Blanquita, off Bahía Santa Cruz, looks white from a distance, crowded as it is with seagulls, ducks, pelicans and albatrosses. Bahía El Organo's U-shaped Playa Violín has very fine sand and gentle waves that form a sort of natural swimming pool. Here also are two natural phenomena: El Bufadero, a blowhole in a shoreline cliff from which spouts of water occasionally erupt, and the "Stone Face," a rock formation just above the water that resembles the visage of an old man.

The bays are ideal for swimming, sailing and snorkeling, but surf conditions can fluctuate greatly at Tangolunda Bay; heed the colored flags posted along the beach that advertise swimming conditions. Tangolunda and Santa Cruz bays have the most extensive equipment rental facilities. Among the prettiest beaches are Bahía Chahué's Playa Esperanza and Playa Tejón, and Bahía Chachacual's Playa la India. Swimming is best at Conejos, Tangolunda, Santa Cruz, El Organo and El Maguey bays.

In the mountains above Huatulco are coffee plantations begun by German immigrants. The tropical highlands in the vicinity offer ideal conditions for growing coffee, an evergreen shrub native to East Africa. Methods of harvesting and processing the plant's seeds, or beans, have changed little over time.

The trek up into this mountainous area is not for the faint of heart. Roads leading to the plantations must be traversed by four-wheel-drive vehicle. As the route ascends the vegetation changes, becoming more lush. Particularly beautiful are the intertwined limbs of saba trees, which are considered sacred. Scattered waterfalls and numerous streams in the vicinity feed into the Copalita River. Some of the plantations are only accessible via horseback.

For those who don't mind a rough journey, this is an opportunity to explore southern Mexico's rugged back country. Café Huatulco (*see "Dining and Nightlife" below*), a venture organized by the local coffee producers' association, can provide information about guided coffee plantation tours; phone (958) 587-0339.

Rancho Caballo del Mar, at Bahía Conejos, offers horseback rides along the beach, including hotel pickup. Reservations are required; phone (958) 587-0530.

The easiest way to arrange most activities is through a travel agency. Bahías Plus has offices in the major hotels and offers a variety of different tours, such as snorkeling and diving trips to the bays; sunset cruises; bird-watching excursions; ATV jungle trips; sport-fishing trips; ecotours to view turtles, crocodiles and native wildlife; and day trips to Puerto Angel and Zipolite Beach. The all-purpose "Huatulco Discovery" sightseeing tour includes a swim at El Maguey Bay, a stop in downtown La Crucecita and time out for shopping.

If necessary, bring comfortable shoes, sunblock, insect repellent and/or a bathing suit or change of clothes. Expect to get dusty on the ATV jungle trip. Some excursions (for example, the ATV trips) are advised only for those in good physical condition.

Bahía Plus agency's main office is at Av. Carrizal #704 in La Crucecita.

Dining and Nightlife

Dining choices in Huatulco are not necessarily limited to the expensive hotel restaurants. Restaurant Ve El Mar, on the water's edge at Playa Santa Cruz, is a casual, friendly place serving lobster, ceviche, shrimp and other seafood dishes.

El Sabor de Oaxaca, Avenida Guamúchil #206 in La Crucecita (just east of the plaza, in the Hotel Las Palmas), is airy and colorful and features such regional fare as chicken in *mole* sauce, *tlayudas* (big corn tortillas with cheese and other fillings), *chiles rellenos* (stuffed chilies) and tamales. For an inexpensive, tasty meal try Pollo Imperial, on Avenida Carrizal between Guamúchil and Boulevard Chahué. The healthy portions of rotisserie chicken come with charro beans and a macaroni and ham salad.

Café Huatulco has two branches, one on the plaza in Santa Cruz (near the marina) and one in the Plaza Esmeralda shopping center at Tangolunda. It serves a variety of caffeinated concoctions utilizing good locally grown coffee, and also sells whole beans.

Nightlife has a long way to go before catching up with Acapulco or Cancún. Most of the hotels have their own bars, and the bigger ones stage Mexican Fiesta nights. **Note:** Finding a cab late at night can be difficult. Make any necessary arrangements for transportation back to your hotel before stepping out for the evening.

Nightspots tend to open and close with regularity, but one local hangout that has been around awhile is the La Crema Bar, on the main plaza in La Crucecita (above the Tropicana Restaurant and across from the Hotel La Flamboyant). You can't miss the guitar-playing dude hanging from the outside of the building. Loud rock and a couple of PCs for Web surfing attract a young crowd. The wood-fired oven turns out a surprisingly good pizza.

Nearby Destinations

Northwest of the airport off Mex. 200, sitting at the foot of the jungle-carpeted Sierra Madre del Sur, is Santa María Huatulco, which functioned as a trade center for the coastal region during pre-Hispanic times. Today the town serves as the governmental center for the different districts that make up Huatulco. It is about 10 kilometers (6 miles) from the airport and west of the developed bays; watch for the marked turnoff on Mex. 200.

Unlike the resort area, Santa María Huatulco has the look of a typical Mexican small town. Activity centers on the main square, where there is a museum housing an interesting collection of masks. Also on the square is the 18th-century, red-and-white cathedral; inside is a fragment of wood that is said to be part of Jesus' cross.

A day trip can be made to the coastal town of Puerto Angel, about 49 kilometers (30 miles) west of Huatulco via Mex. 200 to the town of Pochutla, then about 12 kilometers (7 miles) south on the Puerto Angel-San Antonio highway. Buses travel from Huatulco to Pochutla, from which a taxi can be taken to Puerto Angel. This small fishing village was severely damaged by Hurricane Pauline in 1997 but has been rebuilt. The beaches are rocky but pretty, and the bay is dotted with *pangas*—small, motor-propelled skiffs.

Morning activity centers around Playa Principal and the town pier, where fishing boats arrive with the day's catch. The most popular in-town swimming and sunning beach is Playa Panteón, where there are sandy-floored *palapa* eateries and an oceanfront graveyard filled with colorful tombstones.

Playa Zipolite, about 5 kilometers (3 miles) west of Puerto Angel toward Mazunte, is one of the few beaches in Mexico where nudity is tolerated. In addition to *au naturel* sunbathers (who congregate at one end of the beach), Zipolite attracts a young crowd of surfers and backpackers. Strung along the sand are huts where one can eat, drink or just lounge in a hammock. Camping is permitted at the beach's trailer park. If you do venture here, don't bring anything valuable, as petty theft is common. **Note:** Zipolite faces the open ocean, and the undertow is treacherous; swimming is not advised. Also avoid walking on the beach after dark, as armed robberies have occurred.

Oaxaca State Tourism Office (Sedetur): on Boulevard Benito Juárez in Tangolunda; phone (958) 581-0176. Travel agents in the bigger hotels are probably the best sources for tourist information, however.

The Huatulco Hotel and Motel Association office (Asociación de Hoteles y Moteles de Huatulco) is at Blvd. Santa Cruz #303 in the town of Santa Cruz (near the main plaza). The staff can provide information about a variety of local excursions, including day trips to Puerto Escondido and Puerto Angel. The office is open Mon.-Fri. 9-6, Sat. 9-1; phone (958) 587-0848, or (866) 416-0555 from the United States.

NATIONAL MEXICAN TURTLE CENTER (Centro Mexicano de la Tortuga) is about 12 km (7 mi.) west of Puerto Angel on the Puerto Angel-San Antonio highway, in the small seaside village of Mazunte. It is dedicated to the ongoing preservation of endangered sea turtle species inhabiting Mexican coastal waters. Prior to 1990, when the government imposed a ban on turtle hunting, the local economy depended upon the slaughter of turtles for their meat and leathery hides; the center's opening refocused efforts toward conservation. Sea turtles are on view in large tanks.

Guided tours in English are available. Tues.-Sat. 10-4:30, Sun. 10-2:30. Tour fee around $5 (U.S.).

COLIMA, COLIMA (I-3) pop. 123,500

Although the city of Colima (koh-LEE-mah) is little visited, it makes it a very pleasant day trip from Manzanillo and a nice break from the beach. The 70-minute drive—via the Manzanillo-Colima toll highway to the town of Tecomán, then north on Mex. 110—passes beautiful tropical and mountain scenery. If you don't have a car, trips to Colima can be arranged through travel agencies at Manzanillo resorts *(see "What To Do" under the Manzanillo listing)*. **Note:** The toll charge is about $6.75 (U.S.) each way.

Colima itself lies in a fertile valley. Although tropical in appearance, it is cooler than the lowlands along the coast. The Río Colima divides the city in two, running through tropical fruit orchards and clusters of coconut palms (the region is an important producer of coconuts, bananas and lemons). Entering the city via Mex. 110 from Manzanillo, the first landmark visitors see is the King Colima Monument, a sculpture erected in 1955.

What makes Colima especially enticing—besides the remarkable cleanliness of its streets and parks—is the carefully preserved colonial atmosphere of the town center. Many of the downtown buildings were constructed in the neoclassic style during the later years of dictator Porfirio Díaz's regime. Earthquakes in 1932 and 1944 leveled some of the structures, which were later rebuilt.

Plaza Principal, the main square, is located between avenidas Madero, Hidalgo, Degollado and Reforma. The plaza is surrounded by the Liberty Garden (Jardín Líbertad), where there are white benches and huge, sculpted iron fountains shooting streams of water 20 feet into the air. Arcades on the north and south sides of the plaza shelter shops and commercial businesses.

On the plaza's east side are the Government Palace *(see attraction listing)* and the cathedral (Santa Iglesia), erected by the Spanish in 1527 but rebuilt several times since then. The Hidalgo Theater (Teatro Hidalgo), a block southwest of Plaza Principal at the corner of Degollado and Independencia, was originally completed in 1883 and reconstructed after earthquakes in 1932 and 1941. Its interior has a 19th-century elegance. Check with the State Tourism Office for information about scheduled performances.

Four blocks east of Plaza Principal is Jardín Nuñez, a park with lush greenery that makes it a good spot for relaxing. Just south of the House of Culture complex *(see attraction listing)* and east of Calzada Galván is Piedra Lisa Park (Parque Piedra Lisa). The name means "sliding stone," and those who do slide on the namesake rock will supposedly return to Colima one day.

For lunch, try Samadhi, about three blocks north of Jardín Nuñez on Avenida Filomena Medina (where it branches off Avenida Juárez). This vegetarian restaurant has a shady courtyard and serves a tasty, inexpensive *comida corrida*. Have a *licuado* (fruit shake) or juice rather than taking a chance on the water.

The Main Bus Terminal (Central Camionera Foránea), also called Terminal Nuevo, is a little

over a mile east of the city center via Avenida Guerrero to Avenida Niños Heroes.

About 7 kilometers (4 miles) north of Colima (via Avenida Herrera out of town) is the village of Comala ("the place of the griddles"). It's a quick trip by car or bus; "suburban" buses leave from the Central Camionera Suburbana station at Plaza Colimán, on the western outskirts of town via Carretera a Coquimatlán. Comala was once known as El Pueblo Blanco ("The White Town") for its all-white buildings with red-tiled roofs.

Passing time in the central plaza, with its shade trees and white benches, makes for a pleasant afternoon outing. A group of small restaurants on the plaza's south side (including local favorite Comala Bucaramanga) serve a variety of *botanas*, or appetizers, for the price of potent Mexican libations. As the afternoon wears on, the square fills with the sound of music as mariachi bands try to outdo each other for customers' business.

The Sociedad Artesanías Cooperativa Pueblo Blanco, a short walk south from the town center, is a factory and crafts school. Local artisans create colonial-style wood furniture and ironwork using traditional methods. Good buys are possible.

Twin volcanoes just 3 miles apart are the focus of Volcán Nevado de Colima National Park, about 40 kilometers (25 miles) north of the city via Highway 16 (the road to the villages of Comala, Suchitlán and San Francisco). Dormant Volcán Nevado de Colima, 14,365 feet tall, has flanks cloaked with forests of green conifers. Its neighbor, 12,989-foot Volcán de Fuego, has acted up numerous times since a disastrous eruption in 1941. The most recent outburst occurred in May 1999, spewing rocks and lava, necessitating the evacuation of nearby villages and creating spectacular night scenes for intrepid photographers.

From May through July, orchids line the paved, winding road to tiny San Antonio, just outside the national park. The clear, dry winter months, when the volcanoes are snowcapped, is the best time for viewing them. Experienced mountaineers often hike or climb to the summit of Nevado de Colima.

Colima State Tourism Office (Secretaría de Turismo): on the west side of Plaza Principal, across from the Government Palace at Calle Hidalgo #96. Open Mon.-Fri. 8:30-8, Sat. 10-2; phone (312) 312-4360 (English spoken).

What To See

COLIMA REGIONAL HISTORY MUSEUM (Museo Regional de Historia de Colima) is on Calle 16 de Septiembre at Av. Reforma, on the south side of Plaza Principal. It exhibits archeological and craft displays and a group of pre-Hispanic ceramics (primarily dogs and human figures), smaller than the collection at the Museum of the Western Cultures but just as fascinating. Tues.-Sat. 9-6. Admission around $3 (U.S.). Phone (312) 312-9228.

GOVERNMENT PALACE (Palacio de Gobierno) is on the east side of Plaza Principal. Built between 1884 and 1904, it has a cool inner courtyard. Covering four walls around an interior staircase is a mural by Jorge Chavez Carrillo illustrating scenes from Mexican history, beginning with the Spanish conquest and ending with the 1910 Revolution.

HOUSE OF CULTURE (Casa de la Cultura) is on Calzada Galván at Ejército Nacional, about half a mile east of Plaza Principal; it is most easily reached by bus. This is the University of Colima's arts center. The modern buildings of this extensive complex include a theater and an art gallery displaying a permanent collection of paintings by Colima artist Alfonso Michel, all set among landscaped grounds. Temporary art exhibits and traditional music and dance performances are regularly scheduled; contact the tourism office for information.

Museum of the Western Cultures (Museo de las Culturas de Occidente) is part of the Casa de la Cultura complex. It has a superb collection of pre-Columbian pottery and artifacts. Statues of both men and women depict many aspects of daily life in pre-Hispanic western Mexico. Noteworthy are the Izcuintli, or "Colima dog" figurines, playful representations of dancing canines that originated in this state. Deposited in the tombs of the departed, they were said to guide the dead in the journey toward *tlalocan* (paradise). Exhibit information is in Spanish. The museum's café has a smoky ambience accentuated by Salvador Dalí posters hanging on the walls. Tues.-Sun. 9-7. Admission around $2 (U.S.). Phone (312) 313-0608.

LA CAMPANA RUINS are on the city's northwest side in the village of Villa de Alvarez, next to the Plaza Diamante shopping center on Av. Tecnológico. The earliest remains of this important pre-Hispanic settlement are believed to date from around 1500 B.C. Seven pyramid-like buildings and a tomb have been excavated; structures No. 5 and 6 are the largest, and Structure No. 7 has a tunnel tomb beneath it. Buses run from the city center to the site. Tues.-Sun. 9-6. Admission around $2.50 (U.S.); free to all Sun.

UNIVERSITY MUSEUM OF POPULAR ARTS (Museo Universitario de Artes Populares) is about 8 blocks north of Plaza Principal at calles 27 de Septiembre and Manuel Gallardo. Here the emphasis is on traditional masks; there also are displays of musical instruments, textiles and furniture. Exhibit information is in Spanish. Tues.-Sat. 10-2 and 5-8, Sun. 10-1. Admission around $1 (U.S.); free to all Sun.

COSTALEGRE, JALISCO (I-1)

Travelers who want to experience a bit of seaside old Mexico should explore the Costalegre (Happy Coast)—also known as the Costa Careyes, or Turtle Coast—which extends from Chamela south to Barra de Navidad. A few expensive, exclusive, secluded resorts catering to celebrities and the wealthy are tucked among a string of modest beach towns that are popular weekend getaways for Guadalajarans.

To reach the area by car, simply take Mex. 200 south from Puerto Vallarta. (Buses traveling between Puerto Vallarta and Manzanillo also make stops along the coast.) At Boca de Tomatlán, south of Puerto Vallarta, the road swings inland, bypassing Cabo Corrientes (the southern tip of Banderas Bay) before nearing the Pacific again in the vicinity of Chamela. Although not strictly a coastal route, the highway does offer occasional views of the ocean.

The scenery is varied—hills spiked with cactus give way to palm groves as the route winds south, and views shift from craggy mountains to waterfowl-filled lagoons. Many of the villages, beaches and private resorts along the Costa Alegre are accessed from dirt roads branching off Mex. 200.

Just north of Chamela is the resort property of Las Alamandas, hidden off Mex. 200. A dirt road that passes through the village of Quémaro leads to the entrance of this small (six guest villas) but extravagantly appointed resort hideaway developed by the granddaughter of Bolivian tin baron Antenor Patiño.

The village of Chamela sits on bluffs overlooking Bahía Chamela. First settled in 1525, it served as a fortified anchoring ground for Spanish galleons returning from the Orient. Sea turtles and good-sized oysters inhabit the local beaches. During February and March, huge flocks of migrating sea birds settle on the small islands in the bay. A few rustic bungalows, restaurants and campsites accommodate travelers.

The next major development is Costa Careyes, where two luxury, all-inclusive resort developments—one of them a Club Med—are situated along a series of rocky, jungle-edged coves protected from the open ocean. Further south is the tranquil, mile-long beach at Tenacatita, which is reached by a 8-kilometer (5-mile) dirt road turnoff. There are a number of restaurants at the western end of the beach.

The most popular stretch of the Costalegre is anchored by the towns of Barra de Navidad and San Patricio Melaque (meh-LAH-keh), just north of the Colima state border. They lie about 2 miles apart along the shore of crescent-shaped Bahía de Navidad, which is edged by a long, curving beach. Small, inexpensive hotels and thatch-roofed restaurants line the beach, known for its blazing sunsets. This area is much less crowded during the week than it is on weekends (and particularly during the Easter and Christmas holidays).

Barra de Navidad, on a sandbar lying between the bay and a lagoon, is the more picturesque of the two towns and the one most dependent on tourism. While not luxurious, it has more upscale accommodations than San Patricio Melaque. Hotels line Avenida Lopez de Legazpi, the beachfront street (although it is actually a short walk to the beach from most of them). Simple, casual eateries serve standard Mexican dishes; Restaurante Pati, on Calle Jalisco, dishes up *carne asada* and barbecued chicken.

The redbrick-tiled *Zócalo*, on Calle Jalisco, is part of a pedestrian mall closed to traffic. This plaza is the place to relax, browse the many small shops *(tiendas)*, have a cup of coffee or a cold beer *(cerveza)*, or perhaps have your hair braided by one of the local women. On Thursdays, a street market sets up along Calle Guanajuato between avenidas Veracruz and Tampico.

There are views of the bay and beaches along the length of the *malecón* (sea wall), where *pangas* (small open-air ferries) and yachts can be seen entering and leaving the harbor. On the ocean side of the *malecón* stands the Nereida Triton, which commemorates the 400th anniversary of the discovery of the Philippine islands by a Spanish expedition that departed here in 1554.

An established group of American expatriates lives in Barra de Navidad; one of them runs Beer Bob's, a local gathering place and paperback book exchange located at Av. Tampico #8 (the first canalside street). It's usually open Mon.-Fri. 1-3.

The *panga* docks are at the south end of Avenida Veracruz, on the lagoon side of the sandbar. The local *cooperativa*—an association of individual boat operators—is further up the street. They can arrange fishing excursions, a tour of the lagoon or a quick trip across it to one of the half-dozen seafood restaurants in the little village of Colimilla. Lagoon tours are 150 pesos (around $15 U.S.).

Local buses connect Barra de Navidad with San Patricio Melaque, toward the northern end of Bahía de Navidad. Melaque is more like a typical Mexican town with its main plaza, church, municipal market and bus station. It has a greater number of hotels in the budget range. For RV owners, a designated camping area is located along the rather unattractive stretch of beach just west of town, as well as the Playa Trailer Park, closer to the main beach area.

IXTAPA/ZIHUATANEJO, GUERRERO
(H-6) pop. 75,900

Ixtapa (eeks-TAH-pa) and Zihuatanejo (see-wah-tah-NEH-ho) are geographically close resorts on Guerrero's Pacific coast, but they are altogether different in character. Ixtapa materialized in the 1970s, largely through the efforts of FONATUR, the Mexican government's tourism development agency. Zihuatanejo, in contrast, was a quaint little fishing town long before its northern neighbor's first lofty hotel rose from the sand. While Ixtapa indulges visitors with luxurious amenities at world-class hotels, Zihuatanejo beguiles them with centuries-old traditions and—despite its own increased growth—a relaxed village feel.

Artifacts, stone carvings and stelae found in the vicinity of Zihuatanejo offer evidence that the region has been inhabited as far back as 3,000 B.C. Spanish *conquistadores* first sailed from Bahía de Zihuatanejo in the 16th century, their galleons returned laden not only with silks and spices but with coconut palms brought from the Philippines (the graceful fronds of this palm are now a common sight at seaside resorts up and down the Mexican Pacific coast). However, Acapulco quickly took over the Orient trade.

During an early Spanish exploration of the area, an officer under Hernando Cortés is said to have asked his guide the name of the place. In the Náhuatl language, the guide replied "Cihuatlán," meaning "place of women"—a reference to the existing matriarchal society, in which weaving was the chief occupation. Along the way, Cihuatlán was mispronounced and the somewhat dismissive Spanish suffix "nejo" was tacked on at the end, resulting in the present name.

Ixtapa, on the other hand, blossomed almost overnight after FONATUR determined the stretch of sand a few miles northwest of Zihuatanejo Bay to be ripe for resort development. The construction of hotels, restaurants, shopping plazas and a marina created employment opportunities in a largely impoverished state. As Ixtapa grew, Zihuatanejo followed suit, albeit at a slower pace. For starters, many of the dirt streets were paved. Although restaurants and boutiques give the *malecón* (waterfront promenade) a touristy look, Zihuatanejo to a large degree has managed to hold on to its charm.

Those who decry Cancún level the same criticisms at Ixtapa—too big, too expensive, soulless, manufactured. But like Cancún, Ixtapa appeals to the traveler who craves a getaway from any and all daily concerns. Beauty and pampering come with a price, of course, but for those willing to pay it, the big-league resort trappings of Ixtapa definitely satisfy. Here, however, vacationers can have the best of both worlds—sampling Ixtapa's air-conditioned luxury as well as Zihuatanejo's down-to-earth informality.

Practicalities

Zihuatanejo International Airport is off Mex. 200 (referred to as the Carretera Costera, or Coastal Highway), about 10 kilometers (6 miles) east of Zihuatanejo and 17 kilometers (10.5 miles) southeast of Ixtapa. Continental flies direct from Houston, with connecting flights linking other U.S. cities. Alaska Airlines has direct flights from Los Angeles, San Francisco and Seattle. Mexicana offers flights from U.S. cities to Guadalajara and Mexico City, where connections can be made to Zihuatanejo. For schedule and reservation information, contact the individual airline. For information about Continental vacation packages to Ixtapa/Zihuatanejo, phone (800) 634-5555 in the United States.

Aeroméxico offers flights to Mexico City, where connections can be made to Zihuatanejo. Aerolitoral, an Aeroméxico subsidiary, has daily nonstop flights from Guadalajara. For Aeroméxico schedule information, phone the airport ticket office at (755) 554-2237 or 554-2634. For additional information about airlines *see "Arriving by Air,"* page 551.

Fixed-price *colectivos* (minivans) shuttle groups of passengers from the airport to hotels in either Ixtapa or Zihuatanejo. Tickets are purchased at the transportation desk in the arrival area. It will cost slightly more for a ride to Ixtapa. Private taxis from the airport are more than twice as expensive. Arrange transportation back to the airport through your hotel.

By car, the main—really the only—route is Mex. 200. Acapulco is about 256 kilometers (160 miles) to the southeast (a 3 1/2-hour drive); Manzanillo is 560 kilometers (356 miles) to the northwest. The condition of the roadway is generally good, although heavy summer rainstorms can create potholes or trigger mudslides. Numerous *topes* (speed bumps) are scattered along Mex. 200 between Zihuatanejo and Acapulco.

Mexico City is 576 kilometers (360 miles) to the northeast via Mex. 134, the most direct route. **Note:** Avoid Mex. 134 unless you have a four-wheel-drive vehicle. From Ciudad Altamirano to the junction with Mex. 200, Mex. 134 is filled with potholes, and portions of the roadway are likely to be washed out or blocked by rock slides. Regardless of the highway, **do not drive after dark.**

Taxis are a convenient way to shuttle between Zihuatanejo and Ixtapa's Hotel Zone (about a 10-minute ride), but they're expensive. It costs at least $5 (U.S.) to travel between the two, and a minimum of $2.25 within each town. Fares go up after midnight. Current rates are posted in hotel lobbies. Fortunately, both the Hotel Zone and downtown Zihuatanejo are easily negotiated on foot. Regardless of where you're going, agree to a fare before getting in the cab.

City buses run frequently between Ixtapa and Zihuatanejo. The fare is inexpensive, about 50 cents one way. Buses make numerous stops along Boulevard Ixtapa; in Zihuatanejo, they stop near the intersection of avenidas Morelos and Benito Juárez, some three blocks north of the city market. If you're driving from one town to the other, use caution; the road narrows and widens unexpectedly, and there are several speed bumps.

Moto Rent, located in the Los Patios shopping center on Boulevard Ixtapa, rents mopeds, mountain bikes and rollerblades; phone (755) 553-1630. **Note:** While a moped is a convenient way to get around, keep in mind that the rental fee may not include insurance.

Currency can be exchanged at hotels, banks and *casas de cambio* (exchange offices). Banks usually have the best rates and are open Mon.-Fri. 9-1. A Banamex branch is at the corner of Ejido and Vicente Guerrero in downtown Zihuatanejo. In Ixtapa, there are 24-hour Banamex automatic teller machines (designated *Caja Permanente*) on Boulevard Ixtapa next to the Hotel Fontan and at other locations. In Zihuatanejo, there are ATMs at Ejido and Vicente Guerrero and on Benito Juárez in the Comercial Mexicana, as well as several other locations. The machines accept MasterCard or Visa and dispense pesos.

For assistance or in case of an emergency, contact the Ixtapa tourist police; phone (755) 554-5360. The Red Cross (Cruz Roja), in Zihuatanejo, provides 24-hour ambulance service; phone (755) 554-2009. Major hotels should be able to provide the names and phone numbers of English-speaking doctors.

The average annual temperature at this tropical location is a balmy 79 degrees. Summers are hot, with temperatures ranging from the upper 70s to the low 90s. The winter months—high tourist season—are slightly cooler, with lows in the low 70s, highs in the upper 80s. The rainy season, from June through October, turns the normally brown countryside a brilliant green. Showers frequently fall at night, guaranteeing sunny days almost all year. Pacific hurricanes occasionally strike this section of the coast.

Layout

The coastal strips of both Guerrero and Michoacán states are essentially undeveloped and remote, giving Ixtapa/Zihuatanejo somewhat the feel of an oasis. This twin resort area encompasses some 16 miles of sandy beaches, tiny offshore islets, scalloped coves and placid lagoons, all backed by the Sierra Madre del Sur.

An impressive string of high-rise hotels, surrounded by clusters of palms, make up the 2-mile stretch of Ixtapa's Hotel Zone, which fronts broad Palmar Bay. Boulevard Ixtapa is the main street and runs behind the hotels. On the other side of this thoroughfare are a number of small shopping malls. At the Hotel Zone's eastern end is the Ixtapa Golf Club. Almost anything of interest to visitors will be on either side of Boulevard Ixtapa.

About a mile before the end of the Hotel Zone (if you're heading north), a road branching to the right off Boulevard Ixtapa leads to Mex. 200, and also is the way to get to Playa Quieta, Playa Linda and other beaches north of Ixtapa proper (watch for signs indicating the destination). Boulevard Ixtapa itself ends in a traffic circle at the 450-acre Marina Ixtapa complex, where luxury villas and condominiums share space with a 622-slip yacht marina, the Marina Golf Course and a dockside promenade lined with restaurants. Overlooking the marina is El Faro, an 85-foot-tall tower that offers a 360-degree view of the surrounding area.

Ixtapa is connected with Zihuatanejo, about 7 kilometers (4 miles) to the southeast, by Mex. 200 (which is referred to as the *carretera*) between the two towns. Zihuatanejo (affectionately referred to by locals as "Zihua") spreads along the shores of oyster-shaped Bahía de Zihuatanejo, a naturally protected harbor. Less than 2 miles wide, this is one of the more picturesque bays along Mexico's Pacific coast.

Zihuatanejo's small downtown lies north of the bay; to the east are unobstructed beaches and the foothills of the Sierra Madre del Sur. Locals and tourists alike congregate along the *malecón* (waterfront promenade), officially called Paseo del Pescador. In Zihuatanejo, the basketball court fronting the beach right in the center of town takes the place of the traditional Mexican main square.

East-west Avenida Juan Alvarez, a block north of and paralleling the *malecón*, is one of the main traffic arteries; it takes traffic out of the commercial area while Avenida Ejido, a block farther inland, takes traffic in. The main north-south thoroughfares are 5 de Mayo, Cuauhtémoc (which is pedestrian-only for a couple of blocks), Vicente Guerrero and Benito Juárez.

Hotels perch atop the cliffs surrounding the bay. A clifftop *mirador* (lookout point) along Camino a Playa la Ropa, the road that connects Zihuatanejo and La Ropa Beach *(see "The Beaches" below)*, offers a spectacular view of the town and the bay. A bronze plaque (in Spanish) commemorates the first commercial maritime expedition that left the port in 1527, bound for the Philippines.

The Beaches

The coastline between Ixtapa/Zihuatanejo and Acapulco is known as "La Costa Grande" because of its broad, open beaches. The swath fronting the Ixtapa Hotel Zone is called Playa del Palmar. The dramatic arc of white sand forms a wide curve, with clusters of rock formations rising out of the offshore waters. This beach faces the ocean, and the surf is rough at times. At the eastern end of the Hotel Zone, near the Ixtapa Golf Club, is Playa Vista Hermosa. Between Ixtapa and Zihuatanejo is Playa Majahua, a secluded, little-visited beach slated for resort development.

At the northwest end of Palmar Bay is Ixtapa Point (Punta Ixtapa). A residential and recreational complex is being constructed on this peninsula. Just off the tip of the point is Isla de a Pie ("island on foot"), so named because it can be reached at low tide by traversing the rocks. Marine birds, especially pelicans and seagulls, congregate on the islet. Along the west side of the peninsula is Playa Quieta (Quiet Beach), which is now largely devoted to the water sports facilities of Club Med and is closed to the public.

Playa Linda, about a mile up the coast from Playa Quieta, has a jungly backdrop of coconut plantations. Open-air restaurants along the beach serve fresh seafood. Outboard motor-powered skiffs *(pangas)* depart from the small jetty for the 10-minute boat ride to Isla Ixtapa, a short distance offshore. The wooded island is a pleasant place to spend a day sunning, snorkeling or diving. Playa Cuachalalate, the main beach, is lined with *palapa* restaurants. On the other side of the island, behind the El Marlin Restaurant, is tiny Playa Coral, with calm, crystal-clear water ideal for snorkeling. Basic gear is available for rent on the island.

Round-trip tickets for the boat ride to Isla Ixtapa can be purchased at the Playa Linda pier landing for about $2.25 (U.S.). The last boats leave for the mainland around 5 p.m.; keep your ticket stub for the return trip. **Note:** Only take a boat displaying the local *Cooperativa* emblem.

Zihuatanejo's main beach is Playa Principal, a sandy stretch in front of the *malecón* (Paseo del Pescador). At the *malecón's* western end is the town pier *(muelle)*. Local fishermen store their boats and gear on the sand after returning with the morning's catch. At the western end of the *malecón*, a concrete bridge crosses a narrow canal; to the south is the Puerto Mío resort and marina.

Just east of Playa Principal and the main part of town is Playa la Madera (Wood Beach). The name comes from colonial days, when pine, oak, cedar and mahogany cut from the mountain forests were shipped back to Spain. Small hotels, private bungalows and restaurants crowd Cerro la Madera (Madera Hill), which rises behind the narrow beach. A bayside footpath (known as "Continuación del Paseo del Pescador") cuts through the rocks that once separated the two beaches. It's a pleasant walk if not attempted at high tide, when you're bound to get wet. Also avoid the footpath after dark.

Particularly pretty is Playa la Ropa (Clothes Beach), on the protected eastern side of the bay and a five-minute taxi ride from downtown Zihuatanejo. The name refers to the cargo of silks that were strewn all over the beach when a Spanish galleon shipwrecked here. Palm trees fringe the mile of soft white sand, and several sand-floored, open-air *palapa* eateries offer both seafood and Mexican cooking. Playa la Ropa is good for swimming, water skiing, jet skiing, parasailing and windsurfing. A steep rock bluff separates this beach from Playa la Madera.

Divers and snorkelers head for the crystalline waters of Playa las Gatas, which is reached by boat. Harmless nurse sharks once populated the shallow, rocky bay bottom, hence the name. Legend has it that the long row of rocks that functions as a breakwater were deposited by a pre-Hispanic ruler as a shelter for his daughter's private beach, although it is possible they could also be ballast dumped from Spanish galleons. There are a number of *palapa* restaurants here.

Small, canopied *pangas* depart from the Zihuatanejo town pier for a scenic 10-minute ride across the bay to the small dock at Las Gatas. Round-trip tickets cost about $2.50 (U.S.) and can be purchased at the *Cooperativa* office at the head of the pier. The boats, often called "water taxis," run frequently; keep your ticket stub for the return trip.

Playa Blanca is about 10 kilometers (6 miles) east of Zihuatanejo; it is accessible via a dirt road that branches off Mex. 200. The scenic stretch of sand curves southeast to Barra de Potosí, off the tip of this hook-shaped peninsula is a group of rock islets, called *morros*, that are characteristic of this section of coastline. One of them, "The Iceberg,"

gets its name from the shower of white guano left behind by innumerable marine birds.

Outdoor Recreation

Although Mazatlán and Baja California are better-known Pacific coast sport-fishing destinations, anglers are discovering the offshore waters here. Sailfish is the pre-eminent big-game catch, along with blue and black marlin, dorado (mahimahi) and yellowfin tuna; smaller species like barracuda, grouper, roosterfish, Spanish mackerel and wahoo also put up a spirited fight. An environmentally friendly tag-and-release policy is promoted.

The Boat Cooperative (Cooperativa de Lanchas de Recreo) at the Zihuatanejo town pier can arrange an excursion; phone (755) 554-2056. Prices vary based on the size of the boat and the number of people and can be negotiated with the boat owners. Most of the boats depart the bay by 7 a.m. and return around 3. Your hotel may be able to arrange a fishing trip, although it will cost more.

Aeroméxico Vacations, an affiliate of the airline, offers Ixtapa/Zihuatanejo sport-fishing packages that include airfare, accommodations, licenses, a boat and all gear. Travel agencies can book a package; for general information and a brochure, phone (800) 700-3346 in the United States. Baja Fishing Adventures puts together similar package excursions departing from Los Angeles; for information phone (800) 458-3688 in the United States.

The Zihuatanejo Scuba Center arranges scuba and snorkeling trips and also organizes night dives and excursions for underwater still and video photography. Visibility is best from May through December, although diving is possible year-round. Juan Bernard, a marine biologist and the center's dive instructor, is very knowledgeable about the area's scuba sites, which range from shallow reefs to submerged shipwrecks to canyons 100 feet below the surface. One of the most recent discoveries was made by divers exploring the rock islets off Barra de Potosí; they found a series of caverns leading to a large dome rising above the water's surface. Snorkelers favor Playa Manzanillo, just south of Zihuatanejo Bay and accessible only by boat. Here, offshore in 15 to 20 feet of water, dwell an impressive variety of coral reef fish.

The scuba center operates two full-service dive shops. One is in downtown Zihuatanejo at Calle Cuauhtémoc #3 (across from the Banamex bank). The other is at the main dive facility within the private marina at the Puerto Mío resort, just inside the mouth of Zihuatanejo Bay. Full-day packages include separate morning and afternoon dives, all equipment, instructors and soft drinks on board. Morning, afternoon and night dives also are available. For information and reservations phone (755) 554-2147.

Yates del Sol's trimaran *Tristar* departs from the marina at the Puerto Mío resort for "sunshine" cruises to Ixtapa Island and a stop for lunch, snorkeling and swimming. A snorkeling cruise casts off for Playa Manzanillo, and a "magical sunset" cruise sails from the bay into the open Pacific for sunset watching and a view of Ixtapa's Hotel Zone. Reservations are required. Cruises can be arranged through a local travel agency, or phone Yates del Sol at (755) 554-2694 or (755) 554-8270.

The usual water sports—water and jet skiing, windsurfing, parasailing—can be enjoyed at both Ixtapa and Zihuatanejo. Facilities and equipment rentals are usually available at Playa del Palmar, Playa la Ropa and Playa las Gatas. Surfers favor Playa Troncones, which faces the open ocean northwest of Ixtapa. **Note:** Make certain that parasailing is arranged only through a reputable outfit. Not all boat operators have the required level of experience, and accidents have occurred.

There are two 18-hole golf courses in the area. The Ixtapa Golf Club, a Robert Trent Jones, Jr.-designed course at the eastern end of the Hotel Zone, extends to the ocean's edge. The grounds, considered a wildlife preserve, are lush with tropical vegetation and home to numerous exotic birds. Crocodiles inhabit some of the water hazards, discouraging any attempts to search for balls lost in the drink; zoologists from Mexico City visit once a year and retrieve the largest specimens for relocation to Mexican zoos. Clubhouse facilities include a pro shop, restaurant and pool with a lounge deck. For reservations information phone (755) 553-1062.

The Marina Golf Course, within the Marina Ixtapa complex just past the western end of the Hotel Zone, was designed by Robert von Hagge. Recreational boaters take advantage of the course's crisscrossing canals, and water hazards come into play on 14 holes. The challenging 600-yard, par-5 18th is known locally as "el hoyo del diablo" (the devil's hole). Golfers have the use of a clubhouse, restaurant, pro shop, pool and tennis courts, and the marina's dockside promenade is close by. For reservations information phone (755) 553-1410.

Tennis courts are located at the Ixtapa Golf Club, the clubhouse at Marina Ixtapa, at the major Ixtapa hotels, and at the Hotel Villa del Sol at Playa la Ropa in Zihuatanejo. Most courts are illuminated for night play; nonguests can usually play at the hotel courts for a fee.

At Playa Linda and Playa Larga, both northwest of Ixtapa's Hotel Zone, horses can be rented by the hour for rides along the beach or through one of the nearby coconut plantations. Sunset rides are especially nice (wear insect repellent). Local travel agencies can arrange a trip, or make reservations through Rancho Playa Linda; phone (755) 554-3085.

Shopping

There are no malls in the traditionally sprawling sense in either Ixtapa or Zihuatanejo. Instead, small complexes with (usually) air-conditioned shops line Boulevard Ixtapa, across the street from the big hotels. Fashionable resort wear, sportswear, jewelry, art and handicrafts fill the boutiques at Ixpamar, La Puerta, Las Fuentes and Los Patios, among other shopping plazas.

Laddi Guichi, in the Los Patios shopping center, specializes in woven goods made in the state of Oaxaca. La Fuente, also in the Los Patios center, has a fine selection of talavera pottery, hand-blown glass, ceramics and papier-maché figures. Mic-Mac, in the La Puerta center, offers native handicrafts, embroidered clothing and wall hangings. All of the shopping centers contain restaurants and snack shops for those in need of refueling. Most of the stores are open daily; many of them close from 2-4.

Downtown Zihuatanejo has its share of souvenir stands and T-shirt emporiums, but it's also a good place to search out Mexican crafts. Shops and stalls line Paseo del Pescador and the adjacent streets. Mario's Leather Shop, Calle Vicente Guerrero #12, features custom-made saddles, hats, vests, purses and belts. Galería Maya, Av. Nicolas Bravo #31, and Arte Mexicano Nopal, Av. Juan Alvarez #13B (at Calle Agustín Ramirez), display such items as pewter frames, straw baskets, wooden sculptures and handmade leather bags. Coco Cabaña, at Avenida Juan Alvarez and Calle Vicente Guerrero, also has a high-quality collection of handicrafts.

Casa Marina, Paseo del Pescador #9 (near Calle 5 de Mayo), consists of five family-owned folk art and handicraft shops under one roof. There are displays of pottery, rugs, pillows, regional costumes, silver jewelry, hammocks, hand-painted lacquer boxes and masks created by Guerrero artisans. Visitors can observe weaving demonstrations at La Zapoteca, one of the stores. Within the complex is Café la Marina, where you can have a pizza and a beer and then browse through the large collection of used books for sale and trade.

Vendors, formerly a persistent presence at the beaches, now hawk their wares at specially designated handicrafts markets. At the Mercado de Artesanía Turístico, on Boulevard Ixtapa across from the Ixtapa Sheraton, there are numerous souvenir and handicraft stands.

In Zihuatanejo, a similar tourist-oriented market is located along Calle 5 de Mayo across from the church. Families operate many of the stalls at these markets, producing hand-painted ceramics, seashell knickknacks and embroidered goods. Zihuatanejo's Central Market (Mercado Central) spreads along Avenida Benito Juárez several blocks inland from the waterfront. Here the emphasis is on foodstuffs—tropical fruits, vegetables, seafood and medicinal herbs. Good buys at the market include Guerrero coffee and leather *huaraches* (sandals).

Dining and Nightlife

For an expensive but reliably good dining experience, the Ixtapa Hotel Zone is an obvious choice. Zihuatanejo has a lower price range and a greater variety of eateries; imported fast-food chains are conspicuously absent. Fresh seafood—lobster, clams, squid, *huachinango* (red snapper) and a local specialty, *camarones al ajo* (shrimp encrusted with garlic)—are on many Zihuatanejo menus.

Sample the local bounty at Chez Arnoldo, the only tile-roofed structure among the thatched, open-air restaurants dotting Playa las Gatas. Here you can feast on expertly prepared seafood dishes in your bathing suit.

La Sirena Gorda (The Fat Mermaid), on the *malecón* next to the town pier, is known for its fresh seafood tacos—fish, shrimp, octopus and conch—and also is a pleasant spot for breakfast. Coconuts is a local gathering place on Calle Agustín Ramirez; Igorian Hacienda, the original building occupying the location, served as a weigh-in station for the coconut plantations that once surrounded Zihuatanejo.

Nueva Zelanda, Calle Cuauhtémoc #23 (at Avenida Ejido), is casual and family-oriented, specializing in *tortas* (Mexican sandwiches), enchiladas and *licuados* (fruit shakes). There is a branch in Ixtapa as well.

Pozole is a hearty, hominy-thickened soup with a chicken or pork stock base. Toppings include avocado slices, chopped onion, white cheese, lettuce and cabbage; herbs and spices vary depending on who is making the *pozole*. Less adventurous diners will appreciate the fact that pickled pig knuckles are normally served on the side. The addition of chilies gives *pozole* three different colors—red, green or white. Thursday is the traditional day to eat this thoroughly Mexican dish, and most lunch spots in Zihuatanejo include it on their Thursday *comida corrida* menu.

Mexican "Fiesta Nights" are popular evening entertainment in Ixtapa during peak tourist season (November to April). They start around 7 p.m. with a lavish buffet spread, after which live music and folkloric dance performances are presented. The cost, around $30-$40 (U.S.) per person, normally includes dinner, drinks and the show. The Westin Brisas Ixtapa offers its Fiesta Night on Sunday; the Hotel Krystal in Ixtapa on Monday; the Hotel Villa del Sol in Zihuatanejo on Friday. The Sheraton Ixtapa presents a Wednesday Fiesta Night all year. Reservations or advance tickets are necessary; call the hotel or make arrangements through a local travel agency.

Casual is the standard attire in both Ixtapa and Zihuatanejo, although shorts and sandals are frowned on for an evening out at an expensive restaurant or fashionable nightspot. For a list of AAA-RATED establishments in Ixtapa and Zihuatanejo, *see the Lodgings & Restaurants section*. Most restaurants use purified water to make the ice in drinks (check to see if the cubes have holes). If in doubt, order bottled mineral water (the brands Agua de Taxco or Tehuacán are good), beer or a soft drink; the *limón* flavor of Yoli, a soft-drink brand sold only in the state of Guerrero, is similar to 7-Up.

Nightlife is concentrated in Ixtapa. Christine, in the Hotel Krystal, is the splashiest of several discos. A laser light show set to music takes place at midnight; after that dancing takes over. Tiers of tables overlook the dance floor. The doors open nightly around 10:30 p.m. (the off-season schedule

varies); there is a cover charge. Shorts, jeans and tennis shoes are not allowed.

Other discos are Euforia, on Boulevard Ixtapa in front of the Best Western Posada Real, and Visage. Also on Boulevard Ixtapa (near the Best Western) is an outpost of Carlos 'n Charlie's, which offers food, drinks and dancing to rowdy rock on an elevated platform by the beach. Señor Frog's, in the La Puerta shopping center, also serves food to the accompaniment of loud rock 'n' roll. There is a cover charge here for dancing.

Special Events

Two major tournaments draw serious sportfishing enthusiasts to Ixtapa/Zihuatanejo: the Billfish Classic in January and the International Sailfish Tournament in May. Other sporting events include a Pro-Am tournament held at the Ixtapa Golf Club in June or July, a national triathlon in Ixtapa during September, and a high-powered boat race in Zihuatanejo in November. Amateur golf and tennis tournaments and a marathon are organized annually in Ixtapa as well; check with the tourism office for dates, which tend to be erratic.

Cultural Sunday takes place every Sunday at the basketball court in downtown Zihuatanejo. Young children are in the spotlight at this delightful event, performing regional dances from all over Mexico in full, colorful costume. The festivities begin around 6 p.m.

Guerrero State Tourism Office: in the La Puerta shopping center on Boulevard Ixtapa (across the street from the Presidente Forum Resort). Open Mon.-Fri. 9-2 and 4-7; phone (755) 553-1968.

The Ixtapa/Zihuatanejo Hotel Association also can provide general information about the area; phone (755) 553-1566. Avoid booths with "Tourist Information" signs (found mostly at the airport), which are essentially pushing time-sharing properties.

ARCHEOLOGICAL MUSEUM OF THE COSTA GRANDE (Museo Arqueológico de la Costa Grande) is on the Zihuatanejo waterfront at the eastern end of Paseo del Pescador (near Calle Vicente Guerrero). This small but nicely displayed museum contains artifacts, pottery and paintings relating to the Costa Grande, the section of coastline between Zihuatanejo and Acapulco. Exhibit information is in Spanish.

Allow 30 minutes minimum. Tues.-Sun. 10-6; closed Dec. 25. Admission 10 pesos (around $1 U.S.).

MANZANILLO, COLIMA (I-2) pop. 100,200

Manzanillo (mahn-sah-NEE-yoh) may have participated in trade with the Orient before the arrival of the Spanish. Settled by Europeans shortly after the Spanish conquest, it became an important departure point for Spanish expeditions, not only to other parts of Mexico but to such far-flung locations as the Philippines and Alta California (the present state of California). Hernando Cortés established what is believed to be Latin America's first shipyard at Manzanillo in 1531. This maritime legacy thrives today, and tourism—although well developed—takes a back seat to commerce.

Manzanillo began attracting foreigners in the 1970s, along with new seaside playgrounds like Cancún and Ixtapa. As with Puerto Vallarta, its neighbor some 259 kilometers (160 miles) to the north, Manzanillo was blessed with natural attributes. Twin bays, golden-sand beaches and a lush tropical backdrop of jungle and banana plantations drew U.S. and Canadian vacationers searching for something a little off the beaten track.

What put the city on the tourist map for good was the 1974 opening of Las Hadas, a luxurious beach retreat conceived by Bolivian tin magnate Antenor Patiño. The opulent hotel began attracting an international set of moneyed pleasure seekers. Manzanillo gained further exposure when the hotel was chosen as the setting for the 1979 film "10," although for many the movie's most striking image was a cornrowed Bo Derek jogging down the beach.

Practicalities

Playa de Oro International Airport is located about 47 kilometers (29 miles) northwest of Manzanillo, on the way to Barra de Navidad. Inside the small terminal building are rental car counters, several shops, a restaurant and a lovely mural. International flights are limited. Aeroméxico and Mexicana both offer flights from Los Angeles, with connections en route. America West flies from Phoenix; Aero California, from Los Angeles. Most flights to Manzanillo arrive via Mexico City.

The commuter airlines Aeromar and Aerolitoral both offer flights to Manzanillo from Mexico City, as well as from other Mexican destinations; phone (314) 333-0151 and (314) 333-2424, respectively. Charter packages to Manzanillo from various U.S. cities are available during the winter months; consult a travel agency for details. For additional information about airlines see "Arriving by Air," page 551.

Transportes Turísticos Benito Juárez provides shuttle service from the airport. The fare averages around $20-$25 (U.S.) per passenger. Make advance arrangements for a ride back to the airport upon your departure; a taxi ride between the airport and most hotels averages about $25 (U.S.).

First-class bus service from Manzanillo to Puerto Vallarta and Guadalajara is provided by ETN. The terminal is in the Santiago area, on Mex. 200 at Km marker 13.5. For additional information about buses see "Bus Service," page 68.

From Guadalajara, Manzanillo can be reached by car via two-lane Mex. 80, which runs into coastal Mex. 200 at Barra de Navidad, or by the toll highway Mex. 54-D, which passes through Colima. Driving Mex. 200 southeast from Puerto Vallarta or northwest from Ixtapa/Zihuatanejo can be an adventure, particularly during the July-through-September

rainy season, when downpours can create hazardous potholes and unexpected detours.

Layout

Manzanillo is first and foremost a commercial port. With a fine natural harbor and rail connections to the interior, it handles an enormous amount of Mexican industrial and agricultural output. The downtown district occupies a narrow isthmus at the southern end of Manzanillo Bay. It's a noisy, bustling jumble of shipyard activity and railroad tracks. Few tourist amenities will be found among the businesses, cheap hotels and no-frills restaurants, although an ongoing port beautification project—undertaken to help establish Manzanillo as a port of call for cruise ships—has resulted in a landscaped promenade.

Jardín de Obregón, the main plaza, is at the north end of downtown overlooking the harbor, which is studded with Mexican military vessels. This small square has an elaborate bandstand and a gazebo. Near the plaza are courts where pickup basketball and fútbol games attract lively crowds of spectators. Avenida México, the city's main commercial thoroughfare, runs south from the plaza.

The resort area spreads out north and then west of town along the shores of twin bays, Bahía de Manzanillo and Bahía de Santiago. Manzanillo Bay encompasses the harbor and some of the more reasonably priced hotels. The Santiago Peninsula, on which Las Hadas and the Hotel Sierra Plaza are located, separates the bays. This tourist-oriented area includes the Santiago and Salahua developments, where there are homes, restaurants and shopping centers. On the other side of the peninsula is Santiago Bay, where luxury homes and condominiums have begun springing up.

Note: In the Manzanillo area, Mex. 200 is referred to variously as the Santiago-Manzanillo Highway or the Costera Highway; the official name is Boulevard Miguel de la Madrid. Between the Santiago area and downtown, there are three major junctions along this highway: with the road to the Santiago Peninsula and Las Hadas; with the road to the Las Brisas Peninsula, the resort area closest to town (known as the crucero, or crossroads); and with the highway leading into downtown Manzanillo. At the last junction, Mex. 200 continues southeast down the coast toward Colima and Ixtapa/Zihuatanejo, while the Santiago-Manzanillo Highway bears south toward downtown, running into Calzada Niños Heroes.

Roads, many of them dirt, branch off Mex. 200, leading to resort and condominium developments. While Mex. 200 and other major roadways are in good condition, streets within the city can be potholed. City buses (the newer ones are blue and white) make a circuit from downtown north along Mex. 200 and the shores of the two bays. Destinations are marked on the left side of the windshield; for example, "Centro" (downtown), "Las Brisas,"

"Las Hadas" or "Santiago." The fare is inexpensive—just 25 cents (U.S.) from the main resort areas to downtown—and is an easy way to get a look at the coastline and some of the hotels without driving.

The Beaches

There are several beaches to choose from along the wide curve of Manzanillo's two bays. Playa las Brisas is the closest to town, although to reach it by road requires detouring around Laguna de San Pedrito to the narrow strip of land fronting Manzanillo Bay. Older hotels and restaurants line both sides of the bayfront drive, a popular destination for weekenders from Guadalajara.

Beyond Playa las Brisas is the long curve of golden-brown sand called Playa Azul. The water gets rougher heading north toward the Santiago Peninsula, and the bottom drops off sharply along much of this stretch, making it problematic for wading or swimming.

The water in Santiago Bay, which is not used for shipping, tends to be cleaner than at the beaches fronting Manzanillo Bay closer to town. One of the area's best swimming beaches is Playa la Audiencia, which occupies a pretty, sheltered cove below jungle-covered hills on the north side of the Santiago Peninsula. The rocky outcroppings here are one of Manzanillo's few good snorkeling spots.

Farther around Santiago Bay is Playa Miramar, another nice beach popular with windsurfers and boogie boarders. Beyond Playa Miramar, the shoreline curves to form the Juluapan Peninsula. Here the water becomes tranquil and the beach is dotted with thatch-roofed souvenir shops. Locals crowd this area on Sundays.

Swimmers should exercise care due to occasional rough surf; flags are posted at most beaches to indicate conditions. Red flags mean potentially dangerous conditions; white flags mean safe conditions.

About 49 kilometers (30 miles) southeast of Manzanillo and accessible by bus is Playa Cuyutlán, a beach known for the *Ola Verde,* or "Green Wave." This mountainous wave—with crests that are said to reach 30 feet or more from March through May—seems to be more talked about than actually seen. The greenish hue is due to the glow of phosphorescent marine organisms.

Despite their color, the waves pounding this beach are impressive at any time. The black sand is the result of crushed volcanic rock. The long, open beach, backed by coconut palms, is all but deserted during the summer; lifeguards are normally present during the high season (December to May). Swimmers should beware of rough seas and strong undertows.

The tiny village of Cuyutlán, which consists of a few budget hotels and small seafood restaurants, drowses away most days, although *Semana Santa* (Holy Week) brings an influx of Mexican families. Facilities are spartan, but it's an appealing day trip for those seeking solitude. To get there, take a local bus to the town of Armería, south of Manzanillo on Mex. 200; buses leave frequently from Armería for Cuyutlán. If you're driving, there is a signed turnoff for Cuyutlán on Mex. 200 about 5 kilometers (3 miles) before Armería, or take the Manzanillo-Colima toll highway that parallels the railroad line.

What To Do

Several of the major resort properties in Manzanillo are all-inclusive, providing guests with an array of entertainment and recreational options in addition to lodging and meals. It therefore tends to be easier to arrange such activities as tennis, horseback riding, scuba trips, sunset cruises, or fishing and golf packages if you are staying at a hotel that provides them. If you're not, try one of the local travel agencies, which have offices along Boulevard Miguel de la Madrid. These agencies can arrange tours of the city and trips to such nearby destinations as Colima, the state capital, and Barra de Navidad.

Like other resorts along Mexico's Pacific coast, Manzanillo claims to be the sport-fishing capital of the world, particularly with regard to sailfish. Marlin, dorado, tuna and wahoo are also hooked. The peak season is November through March. There are two annual fishing tournaments, one in early November and one in early February. Reservations for fishing excursions can be arranged through any of the resorts; booking as part of a group will lower costs.

Ocean Pacific Adventures offers deep-sea fishing excursions departing from La Perlita Plaza in downtown Manzanillo; phone (314) 335-0605. They'll also cook your catch for free at the Colima Bay Café. Again, going with a group will lower the cost. Less expensive are the *pangas* (outboard motor-powered launches) operated by individual owners; determined haggling can lower the fee.

Honeycombed with lagoons, the coastal region offers good birdwatching. Laguna de Cuyutlán, just south of Manzanillo, is populated by different species depending on the season. Herons, pelicans and flamingos can be seen at Laguna de las Garzas (Lagoon of the Herons), the waterway separating the Las Brisas Peninsula from the mainland. The views here are especially nice at sunset.

There are three area golf courses. The Club Santiago Resort has a nine-hole course. The 18-hole La Mantarraya, at the Las Hadas resort, offers plenty of water hazards, notably the water-encircled tee-off at the finishing hole. The course is open to the public, although hotel guests receive preferred tee times. To make reservations phone (314) 334-0000.

The 27-hole course at the Grand Bay Hotel on Isla Navidad, about 30 kilometers (19 miles) north of the airport and a 45-minute trip from Manzanillo, was designed by Robert von Hagge. Laid out along the ocean, with breathtaking views at the 13th and 14th holes, the course is lushly landscaped and immaculately maintained.

Tennis courts, all lighted for night play, are located at the following resorts: Club Maeva, on Boulevard Miguel de la Madrid at Playa Miramar; Las Hadas Resort, on the Santiago Peninsula off Boulevard Miguel de la Madrid; and the Hotel Sierra Manzanillo, on the Santiago Peninsula at Av. de la Audiencia #1.

Although Manzanillo is geared more toward relaxing at the beach than to sightseeing, its premier resort, Las Hadas, is an attraction in itself. Set against the eastern side of the Santiago Peninsula, this blindingly white hotel is a dazzling spectacle. With its minarets, cupolas and turrets, Las Hadas resembles a Moorish village. If you're not a guest, stop in and stroll the luxuriously landscaped grounds (although restaurant reservations are needed to enter the property through the guarded gate). The marina here accommodates up to 45 vessels; a fee is charged. Adjacent to the marina is a calm bay where boats can be moored without a fee.

Shopping, Dining and Nightlife

Manzanillo is not a shopper's paradise. A couple of shops on and around the main downtown plaza offer shell jewelry and a few handicrafts, but they're not worth a special trip. Pricey boutiques appear here and there along Boulevard Miguel de la Madrid and at the shopping arcade at the Las Hadas resort. Galería de Arte, in the Sierra Hotel, displays a selection of works by Sergio Bustamante. Plaza Manzanillo, on Boulevard Miguel de la Madrid in the Salahua neighborhood, is an air-conditioned mall with a Comercial Mexicana department store, specialty boutiques and a food court.

Fresh seafood is the specialty at Bigotes 1, Boulevard Miguel de la Madrid # 3157 (Mex. 200) at Playa Las Brisas. One of the house specialties is *pescado zarandeado*, a whole fish marinated in lime juice and soy sauce, grilled and served with a tomato sauce. American-owned Juanito's, on Boulevard Miguel de la Madrid at Km 14, Playa Olas Altas, is a relaxed hangout popular for breakfast as well as burgers, fries, crispy chicken tacos, ribs, milkshakes and fresh fruit smoothies. You also can check your e-mail and access the Internet here.

Casual dress is appropriate at all Manzanillo restaurants (resort wear at the more expensive places). Keep in mind that a service charge may automatically be added to the bill (in addition to the 15 percent I.V.A. tax). While purified water is used at the well-known restaurants, for gastrointestinal reasons it's best to steer clear of the *enramadas* (beach shack restaurants) and outdoor taco stands. For a list of AAA-RATED establishments in Manzanillo, *see the Lodgings & Restaurants section.*

Nightlife centers around the resorts. A Mexican "Fiesta Night" is offered at the Club Maeva resort during the high tourist season. Discos include Boom Boom, also at Club Maeva, and Disco Vog, in the vicinity of Playa Azul. There is a cover charge at both, and shorts and sandals are not permitted (this dress code is more likely to apply to men than to women). Hours at all discos may vary outside of the high season.

Colima State Tourism Office: Boulevard Miguel de la Madrid #1033 (Mex. 200), in the vicinity of Playa Azul. Open Mon.-Fri. 9-3 and 5-7, Sat. 10-2; phone (314) 333-2277 (English spoken).

The Manzanillo Foreign Community Association is a non-profit organization that assists foreign visitors with information about the Manzanillo/Santiago area in particular and Mexico in general, and also provides translation services, documentation assistance and help with emergency illness, legal or immigration matters. Phone (314) 334-0977 (English spoken).

UNIVERSITY MUSEUM OF ARCHEOLOGY (Museo Universitario de Arqueología) is on Av. Niños Héroes a few minutes north of downtown Manzanillo (on the San Pedrito campus of the University of Colima). Here are numerous metal and shell artifacts from western Mexico and a display of fabrics, looms and fabric-making implements. The university gallery mounts rotating exhibitions of contemporary Mexican art. Tues.-Sat. 10-2 and 5-8, Sun. 10-1. Admission around $1.25 (U.S.). Phone (314) 332-2256.

MAZATLAN, SINALOA (F-4) pop. 335,900

Mazatlán (mah-saht-LAHN) is a fairly young city by Mexican standards. Its earliest history predates the Spanish conquest, when itinerant sailors passing through the region dubbed it the "islands of Mazatlán" due to the many hills, lagoons and estuaries in the vicinity. It was officially founded on Easter Sunday in 1531 by a group of 25 Spaniards under the command of Nuño de Guzmán, but for many years thereafter remained a dormant settlement. Spanish galleons periodically departed the natural harbor laden with gold from inland mines, and legend has it that pirates buried their treasures in secret coves up and down the coast.

It wasn't until the early 1820s that a permanent colony took root. After years of virtual anarchy, municipal government was finally established by a group of enterprising German settlers who developed Mazatlán's port facilities in order to facilitate the import of agricultural equipment. Flourishing international trade followed.

The port was besieged several times over the years—first in 1847 by U.S. troops during the Mexican-American War, and again in 1864 during the French occupation of Mexico. At one point the city was even overrun by Southerners from the United States attempting to perpetuate Confederate ideals south of the border.

The Sierra Madre range retreats out of sight along this section of the coast, depriving Mazatlán of the scenic backdrop of mountains that frame other resorts along the "Mexican Riviera." The

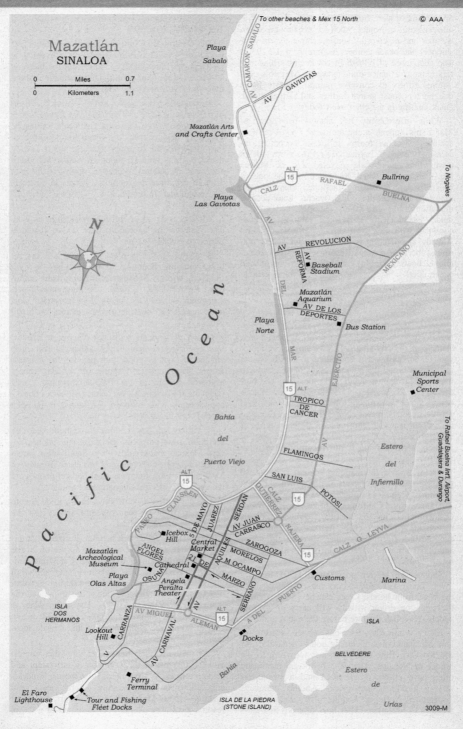

To other beaches & Mex 15 North

© AAA

Mazatlán
SINALOA

Miles	
0	0.7
0	1.1
Kilometers	

Playa
Sabalo

Mazatlán Arts
and Crafts Center

AV CAMARON SABALO

AV GAVIOTAS

AV

ALT
15

CALZ   RAFAEL
BUELNA

Bullring

To Nogales

Playa
Las Gaviotas

AV

AV   REVOLUCION

AV
REFORMA

AV
Baseball
Stadium

DEL

Mazatlán
Aquarium

AV DE LOS
DEPORTES

MEXICANO

Playa
Norte

Bus Station

MAR

EJERCITO

Municipal
Sports
Center

Pacific   Ocean

Bahía

del

Puerto Viejo

15   ALT

TROPICO
DE
CANCER

Estero

del

Infiernillo

AV

To Rafael Buelna Int'l, Airport,
Guadalajara & Durango

FLAMINGOS

SAN LUIS

ALT
15

CALZ
GUTIERREZ

15

POTOSI

NAJERA

15

Mazatlán
Archeological
Museum

Playa
Olas Altas

ISLA
DOS
HERMANOS

Lookout
Hill

CLAUSSEN

PASEO

ANGEL
FLORES

OSUNA

CARRANZA

5 DE MAYO

JUAREZ

Icebox
Hill

Central
Market

Cathedral

Angela
Peralta
Theater

AV MIGUEL

AV CARNAVAL

ALT
15

Ferry
Terminal

AV JUAN
CARRASCO

SERDAN

AQUILES

21 DE

ZAROGOZA

MORELOS

M OCAMPO

MARZO

AV

SERRANO

ALEMAN

ALT
15

Docks

A DEL   PUERTO

Customs

Marina

ISLA

BELVEDERE

Estero

de

El Faro
Lighthouse

Tour and Fishing
Fleet Docks

Bahía

ISLA DE LA PIEDRA
(STONE ISLAND)

Urias

CALZ G. LEYVA

3009-M

original lures were hunting and sport fishing. But other natural attributes, such as year-round warm weather and noteworthy sunsets, attracted sun worshippers and beachcombers beginning in the 1930s. The abundance of billfish in the Pacific's blue waters remains a major draw, although Mexico's continuing efforts to conserve natural wildlife mean that hunters must search farther and farther afield. Duck hunting is the chief sport today.

While affordability has always been part of Mazatlán's appeal, ambitious new construction to accommodate the tourist influx is becoming increasingly evident, particularly on the north side of town. One large-scale development is Marina Mazatlán, which when completed will be one of Mexico's largest boating facilities. Plans include moorings for more than 2,000 yachts, hotel accommodations, golf and tennis facilities, and a man-made island with a resort featuring cabanas equipped with their own slips for private docking. Already in operation is the deep-water access marina at the El Cid Mega Resort, with upscale recreational boating facilities tucked inside a protected ocean inlet.

Practicalities

One of Mazatlán's attractions is its relative closeness to the U.S. border. As a result, a greater percentage of the city's tourist traffic arrives by motor vehicle, at least when compared to beach resorts farther south and the colonial cities of the southern interior. Mazatlán is about 750 miles from the border at Nogales via Mex. 15/15-D. There are 11 toll-booths along this stretch; tolls for automobiles total a little over 500 pesos. **Note:** Toll charges can go up without warning, and rates for different types of vehicles aren't always posted. As in the rest of Mexico, **night driving is not recommended;** plan on a two-day journey from the United States.

Rafael Buelna International Airport is about 40 kilometers (25 miles) south of downtown via Mex. 15 and is a good 45-minute drive to the major resort areas. Aero California, Alaska, America West, Continental, Delta and Mexicana airlines offer direct flights from U.S. cities. Aeroméxico and Mexicana airlines fly in from other Mexican cities. For additional information about airlines *see "Arriving by Air," page 551.*

Shuttle van service costs about $7 (U.S.) into town. Taxis also take visitors into Mazatlán or to the beachfront hotels. Costs can be cut by sharing the ride; the driver usually will carry up to four people. Establish the fare before the cab sets off.

Elite provides first-class bus service to many inland Mexican cities, including hourly departures for Mexico City. Elite also offers service north to the border at Nogales, Ariz. The buses are clean and often have on-board television and a stewardess serving beverages and snacks. Another company, Transportes Norte de Sonora, offers service from Nogales to Mazatlán. Other lines offering first-class

service are Futura, Transportes del Pacífico and Tres Estrellas de Oro.

The Central Bus Station (Central de Autobuses) is just off Avenida Ejército Mexicano at Avenida de los Deportes, three blocks inland from the *malecón* at Playa Norte. For additional information about buses *see "Bus Service," page 68.*

Automobile-passenger ferry service links Mazatlán with La Paz *(see separate listing under Baja California)* on the Baja California Peninsula. The ferry departs from the Playa Sur terminal, at the southern end of town near the sport fishing docks; sailing time is about 18 hours. Schedules and rates are subject to change; double-check both prior to departure and purchase tickets in advance. For additional information *see "Ferry Service," page 68.*

The city is a port of call for cruise ships as well. The Carnival and Princess lines arrive regularly during the winter season.

Banks are generally open Mon.-Fri. 8-5 and set aside morning hours—8:30 to 11 a.m.—to cash traveler's checks. Banamex is the only bank authorized for ATM transactions; you must have a personal pin number to access your account. Most other banks will provide a cash advance on credit cards.

Casas de cambio (currency exchange offices) stay open longer than banks, although their rates are usually not as good; you pay for the convenience. The American Express office, on Avenida Camarón Sábalo in the Balboa shopping center (near the traffic circle), exchanges traveler's checks and accepts wire transfers of funds; it is open Mon.-Fri. 9-5, Sat. 9-1.

A variety of pay phones throughout the city serve different purposes. Beige plastic phones accept Mexican bank cards only. Small black street phones accept peso coins and buy three minutes of local calling time. Stainless steel Ladatel phones are the easiest to use for international calling.

The post office is downtown on Avenida Benito Juárez, in front of the cathedral and across the street from the main plaza.

Mazatlán's weather can be characterized as tropical, although not as hot as points farther down the coast. From November through May, daytime temperatures are in the 70s, nighttime temperatures in the 60s. It's hotter and more humid during the summer months, but afternoon highs are usually in the 80s rather than the sultry 90s. The ocean water is warmest in late summer and fall. Leave your heavy coat at home; the temperature at this seaside location has never dropped below 50 F.

July, August and September are the rainiest months; the rest of the year rain is infrequent and seldom a threat to vacation plans. Clothing is decidedly informal—bathing suits, shorts, jeans and T-shirts—unless you wish to "dress up" in casual resort wear for an evening out to dinner or a disco.

City Layout

Mazatlán occupies a peninsula that juts into the Pacific Ocean, forming Bahía del Puerto Viejo, a natural bay and protected harbor. The main approach into the city is via Mex. 15, which becomes the International Highway (Carretera Internacional).

Mex. 15 essentially loops around the city, changing names in the process. As Avenida Rafael Buelna, it veers west off Carretera Internacional, passing the bullring and ending at the Sábalo traffic circle at the waterfront. It then proceeds south as Avenida del Mar and Paseo Claussen. It skirts the southern edge of downtown as Avenida Miguel Alemán, running east to Port Avenue (Avenida del Puerto). At the customs office it becomes Avenida Gabriel Leyva and continues east toward the airport. Once out of town, Mex. 15 heads south to Tepic and Guadalajara.

The *malecón,* or waterfront boulevard, runs along the coast for some 17 kilometers (11 miles). In Mazatlán this thoroughfare also changes names—four times. At the southern end of the city (the old downtown area), it is called Paseo Claussen. North of downtown it becomes Avenida del Mar. At Punta Camarón (Shrimp Point, on which Valentino's Disco is perched), the name changes to Avenida Camarón Sábalo. At this point it runs inland and is paralleled by Avenida Rodolfo Loaiza, along which several of the city's luxury hotels sit. After a mile or so the two streets rejoin. Farther north the name changes again to Avenida Sábalo Cerritos, which runs north toward the marinas.

Stroll the *malecón* for a look at some of Mazatlán's sculptural monuments. The Fisherman's Monument (Monumento al Pescador), on Avenida del Mar north of Playa Olas Altas, is a local landmark. A woman and a fisherman dragging his net—both of them nude—present a curious sight. The Venado, La Mujer Mazatleca and La Continuidad de la Vida monuments honor a deer, a nymph and life, respectively.

The section of the *malecón* along Avenida Camarón Sábalo is known as the Golden Zone (Zona Dorada), which is the main tourist area. Here are hotels, restaurants, shops and nightspots, all within a compact area, and the nicest beaches.

Icebox Hill (Cerro de la Nevería), in the Olas Altas area, is a residential zone. A gradually ascending road reaches its summit, from which are views of a great part of the city, the immense blue bay and awe-inspiring sunsets that tint the sea and clouds a brilliant orange-red. Nearby El Mirador, off Paseo Claussen, is where daring locals plunge from a platform 45 feet above turbulent water surrounded by dangerous rocks. The feat requires expert timing; without the cushioning effect of a wave, a diver meets just 6 feet of water. In the evening these young daredevils carry torches for flamingly theatrical effect. Tips are expected.

Old Mazatlán, just inland from Playa Olas Altas, is the oldest part of the city. Here ongoing restoration efforts are preserving a number of historical structures. Blocks of buildings and private residences—including rows of town houses with wrought-iron and stone trim—line the narrow streets, especially along avenidas Heriberto Frias, Venus and Niños Héroes.

Although it remains unseen by many tourists staying at the substantial hotels to the north, Old Mazatlán is worth a look. This is where the city's daily business is conducted amid the rushing of people and vehicles. Plaza Principal, the main plaza (also called Plaza Revolución), has the usual vendors and shoeshine stands as well as an ornate, wrought-iron bandstand beneath which is a rather incongruous fast-food diner.

Outdoor art shows and music concerts take place on Sundays at Plazuela Machado, at avenidas Constitución and Carnaval a few blocks southwest of Plaza Revolución. This little plaza has a real tropical feel and is delightful in the evening, when music plays and the outdoor tables are full.

At the southern end of town are the ferry terminal, tour boat operators, sport fishing fleets and commercial port activities. Standing guard over the harbor's entrance is El Faro, said to be the tallest lighthouse in the Western Hemisphere and second only to Gibraltar in the world, with a range of some 35 nautical miles. Those undertaking the strenuous half-hour hike up the rocky pinnacle will be rewarded with an expansive view of the harbor and ocean.

Another great view of the city and its watery surroundings—particularly in the evening—can be seen from the top of Lookout Hill (Cerro de Vigía), a short distance north of El Faro. This climb, also steep, is better made via taxi.

Because of Mazatlán's waterfront sprawl, walking is an ill-advised choice for exploration. Fortunately, there are several public transportation options. A common sight are *pulmonías,* which are essentially open-air Volkswagen jeeps seating up to three people. They make the beach circuit and travel up and down the *malecón.* Unless money is no object, never hop in one of these vehicles and say, "Let's go." Always negotiate the fare in advance; it's expected. A word of caution: Those sensitive to exhaust fumes should avoid riding in a *pulmonía.*

The transit system is excellent and cheap: For about 20 cents (U.S.), one can get to just about any place in the city via local buses. The air-conditioned Sábalo Centro bus travels from the hotel zone to downtown; buses run every 10 to 15 minutes from 5:30 a.m. to 10 p.m. **Note:** During rush hour, about 5 to 7 p.m., buses that are full may pass waiting passengers. The Cerritos Juárez bus stops at the Gran Plaza shopping mall and the baseball stadium. The Sábalo Cocos bus stops at the Gigante supermarket.

Mazatlán is a favorite destination for RV travelers due to its access from the United States via Mex. 15. Most of the RV parks are at the north end of the city, along avenidas Camarón Sábalo/Sábalo Cerritos (the *malecón*). One of the largest is La

Posta, a few blocks east of the beach; phone (669) 983-5310.

Beaches

Mazatlán's beaches offer something for everyone and accordingly attract different groups of sunseekers. Some are patronized mainly by Mazatlecos; others draw tourists. The following beaches are described as they appear from south to north along the coast.

Stone Island (Isla de la Piedra), at the southern end of the city, is actually a peninsula offering miles of mostly undeveloped oceanside beaches that can be explored on horseback. Small motorboats carry passengers to and from the island (about a five-minute ride), departing from a launch along the harbor channel north of the ferry terminal. On weekends—and particularly Sunday—entire families spread out along the sand or under the coconut palm groves. Open-air restaurants offer smoked fish, shrimp and beer along with music and dancing.

Playa Olas Altas, off Old Mazatlán, was the city's first tourist beach and is where the *malecón* begins. The name means "high waves," and surfers congregate here during the summer. This is not the best beach for swimming; instead, enjoy the tremendous views of the surf from one of the many outdoor cafés that line the seaside walkway.

Playa Los Piños, located between the Marine House and the Fisherman's Monument, is where local fishermen sell their catch. If you're interested in purchasing fresh fish without angling for it, arrive early; the catch disappears quickly. Just north of Playa Los Piños is Playa Norte, which stretches between the Fisherman's Monument and Punta Camarón. This beach is popular with locals who play impromptu baseball and soccer games in the sand or take to the water on a three-wheeled floating trike.

Playa Martín fronts the seaside promenade along Avenida del Mar. A tunnel connects the beach with the Hotel Hacienda. Big Pacific rollers crash against the rocks at Punta Camarón. On the north side of this outcrop jutting into the water is Playa Las Gaviotas, popular with tourists who want to soak up some sun or play a game of beach volleyball.

Further up is Playa Sábalo, where the wide, white sands attract droves of tourists and what seems like equal numbers of Mexican vendors. Parasailers and windsurfers utilize these beaches fronting the Golden Zone. They are protected from the open surf by Bird, Deer and Goat islands, which rise out of the water a short distance offshore.

Beyond Playa Sábalo, at the north end of Mazatlán, are Playa Brujas and Playa Los Cerritos, which stretch north to Punta Cerritos (Cerritos Point). These beaches are the least crowded, although more and more condominiums are beginning to poke skyward. The more isolated Brujas is

frequented by local surfers. Open-air restaurants offer delicious seafood and a relaxed atmosphere.

Sports and Recreation

Fishing in Mazatlán ranks among the best anywhere. Striped marlin are hooked between November and April; sailfish and black marlin are caught between May and October. Other game species taken from the Pacific waters include blue marlin, bonito, dolphin and yellowfin tuna.

Because the migratory path of billfish includes the waters off Mazatlán, the city proclaims itself "the sailfish capital of the world." Well-equipped fleets are headquartered at the docks at the southern end of town, where the ferry and charter tour boats are moored. Charter fishing boat rates start at around $270 for the day and include lunch, bait, tackle and crew. Tipping the captain and first mate is customary, particularly if the day's catch has been bountiful. Many outfits promote a catch-and-release policy. Make fishing arrangements in advance of your arrival with either the fleet itself or through your hotel.

The marina and yacht club at the El Cid Mega Resort offers a variety of fishing packages utilizing its own fleet of boats. For information and reservations phone (800) 525-1925 or (888) 733-7308 in the United States, (800) 716-9800 in Mexico (toll-free long distance), or contact a travel agency. Local charter companies include Star Fleet, phone (888) 882-9614 (in the United States) or (669) 982-2665, and Flota Bibi Fleet, phone (669) 981-3640. Hotels will usually try to arrange group excursions, thereby sharing the cost of boats.

Baseball in Mazatlán is considered something of a tradition. Loyal fans fervently support the local Pacific Coast League team, which has produced players who have gone on to the American majors. Games are played at Teodoro Mariscal Stadium, off Avenida del Mar and convenient to the tourist zone. Check at the front desk of your hotel for game schedules.

Bullfights take place on Sundays at 4 p.m. from December to April at the bullring on Boulevard Rafael Buelna. Tickets can be purchased at the bullring, through most hotels or in front of Valentino's Disco. Prices depend on where you sit; seats in the shade are more expensive.

Kayaking is a popular activity in and around Mazatlán, offering a way to stay fit and the chance to observe secluded ecological sanctuaries at close range. Excursions travel to area rivers, streams and estuaries that abound with wildlife. The eco-friendly Mazatleco Sport Center offers four-hour guided trips that include state-of-the-art kayaks, instruction, snacks and transportation. Trips can be arranged through the tour desk at the Hotel Suites Las Flores; phone (669) 981-0302.

Another popular activity is parasailing, which provides 15 minutes of sheer thrills for those not prone to vertigo. Arrangements can be made in front of the Playa Mazatlán and Las Flores hotels in the Golden Zone. Other Golden Zone hotels rent jet skis, Hobie Cats and windsurfing equipment. Back on land, a 27-hole golf course designed by Robert Trent Jones is at the El Cid Mega Resort; play is reserved for those staying at the hotel and their guests.

Shopping

Shopping in Mazatlán is centered primarily around the Golden Zone running along avenidas Rodolfo Loaiza and Camarón Sábalo. The shops and galleries here feature the usual assortment of clothing, sportswear, resort wear, jewelry, handicrafts and leather goods. Most are open Monday through Saturday; some do not accept credit cards.

Be sure to stop by Sea Shell City, a combination museum and shop on Avenida Loaiza across from the Playa Mazatlán Hotel. A kaleidoscopic variety of shells from around the world are on display, and there are many shell craft items as well as Mexican handicrafts for sale. Upstairs is an amazing fountain covered in shells that holds living sea turtles.

Just north of Sea Shell City on Avenida Loaiza is Maya del Pacífico, an upscale shop selling high-quality arts and crafts, jewelry, pottery, leather boots, wallets and tableware. Prices are correspondingly high. For better bargains, visit the nearby Mazatlán Arts and Crafts Center, Avenida Loaiza and Calle Gaviotas, which stocks everything from tablecloths and rugs to pottery, *guayabera* shirts, embroidered dresses and footwear. Artisans can sometimes be seen creating both artwork and jewelry designs. Purchases here are cash only.

For a more authentic Mexican shopping experience, head downtown. In the Central Market (*mercado*), at avenidas Oampo and Juárez in Old Mazatlán, are piles of fresh shrimp, fish and produce, as well as open-air stalls packed with Mexican-made shoes, hats, belts, pottery and handicrafts. Good quality is harder to find, but for dedicated browsers the opportunity to haggle with local merchants is the real fun.

Nidart (Nido de Artesanos) occupies a bright purple and red-trimmed building next to the Angela Peralta Theater in Old Mazatlán. This gallery and studio complex (the name means "nest of artisans") features leather masks, sculptures, burlap dolls, decorated coconut shells, jewelry, clay figurines and other crafts expertly fashioned by local artisans. It is open Mon.-Sat. 10-5.

South of Avenida Rafael Buelna on Avenida de los Deportes, about 3 blocks inland from the *malecón* (Avenida del Mar), is La Gran Plaza, a mall offering American-style shopping. The supermarket and department stores make this a convenient place to stock up on basics. It is easily reached by taxi or the Sábalo Cocos bus.

Dining and Nightlife

Everything from American fast food to spicy Creole fare is available in Mazatlán. But for a city that touts itself as "the shrimp capital of Mexico,"

seafood understandably is the star on many local menus. Shrimp dishes are prepared in every way imaginable, and almost nowhere else is the crustacean fresher or more tempting.

In addition to the big hotel restaurants and fine dining spots, there are numerous establishments along the *malecón* serving fish filets, various shrimp concoctions or such Yucatecan specialties as *pollo pibil*, chicken slowly baked in a banana leaf wrapper.

The Hotel Playa Mazatlán on Avenida Rodolfo Loaiza in the Golden Zone presents "Fiesta Mexicana" on Tuesday, Thursday, Friday and Saturday evenings beginning at 6:45 p.m. An all-you-can-eat buffet of charbroiled steaks and chicken, tacos, burritos, guacamole, salsa and fresh fruit is followed by folkloric dance and music performances from various regions of Mexico. The entertainment includes an amazing display of rope twirling by a *charro,* or Mexican cowboy, and a flamboyantly costumed troupe who re-enact a bit of Carnaval.

Admittance to the shows is first-come-first served. Dress is casual, but shorts are not permitted. For information and tickets phone (800) 716-9567 (toll-free long distance within Mexico), or contact the tour desk inside the hotel lobby.

Most of the restaurants and hotels in Mazatlán offer purified water and ice. There should be no cause for concern about drinking the water in these establishments, but double check if in doubt. Purified water can be bought in any of the *mercados* (markets) around town. For a list of AAA-RATED establishments in Mazatlán, *see the Lodgings & Restaurants section.* **Note:** Some restaurants tack on a standard 10 to 15 percent gratuity to the bill. Be sure to differentiate between this charge and the I.V.A. tax that is added to every check, and tip accordingly.

Many of the big hotels in the Golden Zone have discos, bars or lounges, with plenty of evening happy hours featuring two-for-one drink prices. Valentino's an all-white structure perched atop Punta Camarón, the rocky outcrop near the Sábalo traffic circle, attracts a glamorous crowd into the wee hours. There are several discos within this complex, including one with a blown-up photograph of Rudolph Valentino above the dance floor; the Bora Bora Bar has a great view of the surf below. Another loud, rollicking nightspot is Joe's Oyster Bar, in the Los Sábalos Hotel along the Golden Zone beachfront.

Mellower options also exist. A romantic atmosphere prevails at the Mikinos Piano Bar, on Avenida Camarón Sábalo in the Golden Zone. Café Pacífico, in Old Mazatlán at the corner of calles Constitución and Heriberto Frias (on Plaza Machado), has a pool table, walls hung with old photographs and a relaxed air.

The Papantla Flyers, a folkloric group, perform their death-defying "Flying Pole" dance suspended from poles 50 feet tall. The dance originated in the state of Veracruz as part of pre-Hispanic agricultural ceremonies designed to ensure a bountiful harvest. The spectacle takes place in an open-air theater at the Mazatlán Arts and Crafts Center on Avenida Rodolfo Loiaza. Check at your hotel desk regarding schedule and admission information.

Events

The year's biggest party is the pre-Lenten Carnaval, or Mardi Gras, held in late February or early March. All Mazatlán—not to mention revelers from around the world—gathers for five days and nights of fireworks, parades with elaborate floats, the coronation of a festival queen and of course, plenty of music and dancing. If you'll be visiting around this time, make hotel reservations several months in advance and inquire regarding exactly when Carnaval begins. Expect prices to climb as well.

Historical records of the event date to 1827, when military men demanding salaries staged a protest by masquerading. Over the years the tradition grew, with mask wearing becoming part of the festivities at both public assemblies and private parties. By the end of the 19th century, French, German and Italian immigrants were adding facets of their own culture to Carnaval, and today the city claims that its celebration is the world's third largest after those in Rio de Janeiro and New Orleans.

Mazatlán celebrates Day of the Dead celebrations Nov. 1 and 2 with a combination of feasting and somber remembrances. Several sport fishing tournaments also occur in November.

Guided Tours

A guided tour is a good way to see both the city and several interesting towns in the surrounding area. Information about city and vicinity tours can be obtained through all of the major hotels or at any local travel agency.

A standard city tour hits Mazatlán's highlights, including Old Mazatlán, the central market and the waterfront. Vista Tours offers a selection of excursion packages both in and around the city; phone (669) 986-8610. Marlin Tours provides city excursions and tours to Concordia/Copala, Rosario and Teacapán; phone (669) 913-5301 or (669) 914-4616. **Note:** Beware the numerous sidewalk entrepreneurs who offer free tours; their real goal is to pitch the sale of time-share units.

A three-hour cruise aboard the double-deck *Fiesta* takes in the harbor and bay. Beverages are available for purchase, and there is dancing (to taped music) on board. The boat departs at 10:30 a.m. from the dock near the El Faro lighthouse. Reservations can be made through your hotel or a travel agency or by calling Yate Fiesta Mazatlán; phone (669) 985-2237.

Day excursions also can be arranged to several of the islands off the Golden Zone section of the coast, including Palmito de la Virgen, a haven for birdwatchers, and Deer Island (Isla del Venado), where little coves offer up a bounty of seashells

and schools of multicolored fish draw snorkeling enthusiasts. The El Cid Mega Resort offers a tour of the bay via trimaran, which includes drinks, lunch on Deer Island and the use of kayaks and snorkeling gear. The boat departs from the El Cid marina at 10 a.m. and returns at 3. For information contact the reservation desk; phone (800) 525-1925 in the United States.

A popular tour takes in the colonial town of Concordia, located east on Mex. 40 toward Durango. Founded in 1565, it is still a furniture and pottery making center. The main plaza contains a gazebo and an enormous wooden chair that provides an amusing photo opportunity. Across the street is the Church of San Sebastian, with an ornate stone facade.

A few kilometers east of Concordia is Copala. A walk down the town's cobblestone streets and past such landmarks as the Church of Saint Joseph is like a journey back in time. Tons of silver were once extracted from the surrounding mountains, and many homes here cling precariously to the hillsides. Charles Butter, an American entrepreneur, was responsible for much of the mining effort in this region, and a restaurant and small hotel in the center of town are named after him. The tour includes lunch at the restaurant, where one of the mouthwatering specialties is banana pie. Also on the premises is a small museum with exhibits depicting the process of melting down silver.

South of Mazatlán via Mex. 15 is Rosario, another old mining community. At the end of the 18th century it had a population of 7,000 and was one of the richest towns in northwest Mexico. Mining activities ceased in the 1940s. Of particular interest is Our Lady of the Rosary, the town's beautiful colonial church; its marvelous altarpiece is completely covered with intricate gold-leaf designs. Some 70 kilometers (43 miles) of underground tunnels, dug over a 300-year period to aid in extracting gold and silver, remain behind; locals attest that they outnumber the surface streets.

Sinaloa State Tourism Office (Coordinadora General de Turismo): Avenida Camarón Sábalo in the Banrural Building (Edificio Banrural), fourth floor. The staff is friendly and speaks English. Open Mon.-Fri. 9-7; phone (669) 916-5160.

What To See in Town

ANGELA PERALTA THEATER (Teatro Angela Peralta) is 3 blocks south of Plaza Principal at Av. Carnaval #47 (at Calle Libertad). It opened in 1874 as the Teatro Rubio. Renowned diva Angela Peralta, dubbed "the Mexican Nightingale," arrived for an engagement in 1883 but tragically died (in addition to most of her company) of cholera before uttering a single note.

After stints as a Mardi Gras ballroom, boxing arena and movie palace, the theater closed in 1964 and reopened in 1992. It houses a performing arts school, has an opulent interior and offers a wide range of cultural offerings, including regularly scheduled folkloric dance performances. Allow 30 minutes minimum. Daily 9-6. Admission 10 pesos (around $1 U.S.). Phone (669) 982-4447.

BASILICA OF THE IMMACULATE CONCEPTION (Basilica de la Inmaculada Concepción) is downtown on the north side of Plaza Principal, at avs. Juárez and 21 de Marzo. The city's cathedral is easily recognized by its gold-colored twin spires. The late 19th-century exterior is rather plain, but the beautifully preserved interior is very ornate, with numerous gold accents. Open daily. Free.

MAZATLAN AQUARIUM (Acuario Mazatlán) is half a block east of Av. del Mar at Av. de los Deportes #111. It displays 250 species of fresh and saltwater marine life, from colorful reef fish to moray eels to sea turtles, in some 50 tanks. A sea lion show is presented several times daily in an open-air amphitheater. There also is an exotic bird show utilizing birds confiscated from vendors who captured them illegally. Daily 9:30-5:30. Admission around $5.50 (U.S.), children $3. Phone (669) 981-7815.

MAZATLAN ARCHEOLOGICAL MUSEUM (Museo Arqueología de Mazatlán) is at Calle Sixto Osuna #76, just east of Paseo Claussen. The small but high-quality collection focuses on pre-Columbian pottery and artifacts. Exhibit information is in Spanish. Mon.-Sat. 10-6, Sun 10-3; closed Easter and Dec. 25. Admission 24 pesos (around $2.40 U.S.).

MAZATLAN JUNGLE TOUR is not really a jungle excursion but a tour of the bay. The tour boat passes shrimp fleets and a navy base, proceeds through inlets and waterways lined with mangroves, and ends up at Stone Island (Isla de la Piedra). A bus takes visitors to the island's beach. A charcoal-grilled fish lunch, prepared beachside, is included; horseback rides along the beach are extra. The boat departs at 9 a.m. and returns at 3; the schedule varies according to season. Reservations are required. All-inclusive fare around $42 (U.S.). Phone (669) 914-1444.

PUERTO ESCONDIDO, OAXACA (I-8) pop. 19,000

Puerto Escondido (PWEHR-to ehs-cohn-DEE-doh) means "hidden port," and until fairly recently the translation was quite appropriate. The town was named for Punta Escondida, the rocky outcrop that protects a half-moon bay. A port was established here in 1928 as a shipping point for coffee grown on the forested seaward slopes of the Sierra Madre del Sur. Coastal Mex. 200 came through in the 1960s, opening up the area to tourism.

Among the first visitors were surfers, who were drawn by the big waves and dirt-cheap lodgings. Today they're still here, but Puerto Escondido is no longer a hideaway and not quite as cheap. Instead, it's an established destination, frequented by an international group of travelers preferring a more laid-back alternative to the shiny expense of Bahías de Huatulco and other carefully planned seaside resorts.

Practicalities

Puerto Escondido is about 113 kilometers (70 miles) west of Huatulco via Mex. 200. This highway, often referred to as the Carretera Costera (Coastal Highway), divides the town roughly in half. The older, upper section, above the highway, is where most of Puerto Escondido's 40,000 or so residents live and conduct their daily business.

Below the highway is the newer, tourist-geared waterfront, where hotels, restaurants and shops spread for about a mile along the main thoroughfare, Avenida Peréz Gasga. At noon each day, chains are raised at the eastern and western ends of the beachfront strip, closing the street to vehicular traffic. At the western end of this pedestrian zone, Gasga begins winding uphill and crosses Mex. 200, where its name changes to Avenida Oaxaca (Mex. 131). The junction, marked by a traffic signal, is known as El Crucero.

The local bus stations are all within a block or so of the El Crucero intersection. Estrella Blanca provides first-class service along Mex. 200 between Acapulco and Bahías de Huatulco (be sure to specify the La Crucecita terminal as your destination if you're taking a bus to Huatulco from Puerto Escondido). The station is on Avenida Oaxaca, just north of the El Crucero junction.

By car, Puerto Escondido can be reached from Oaxaca by taking Mex. 175—a winding six- to eight-hour drive over mountainous terrain—to the junction with coastal Mex. 200 (just south of Pochutla), then west about 81 kilometers (50 miles). Avoid Mex. 131, a direct route between Oaxaca and Puerto Escondido but one that has long unpaved stretches.

Coastal Mex. 200 southeast from Acapulco or west from Bahías de Huatulco is generally negotiable, although the route winds between Acapulco and Puerto Escondido and is likely to be potholed in spots during the summer rainy season (roughly July through September). A word of caution: **Do not drive after dark.**

The international airport is about 3 kilometers (2 miles) west of town off Mex. 200, near the newer hotel and resort development around Playa Bacocho. It receives flights from Mexico City (via Mexicana/Aerocaribe) and Oaxaca (via Aerotucan). Taxis and less expensive *colectivos* (minibuses) operated by Transportes Terrestres shuttle airport passengers to and from hotels. For additional information about airlines see *"Arriving by Air,"* page 551.

There is a *casa de cambio* (currency exchange) office on each side of Peréz Gasga near the Rincón Pacífico Hotel. Graficom, Av. Peréz Gasga #302, has telephone, fax and Internet services.

The Beaches

A lighthouse atop Punta Escondida at the western end of the bayfront affords a panoramic view of town. Running east from the rocky cove beneath the lighthouse is Playa Principal, the in-town beach. Here the stretch of sand is narrow, the water calm and the beach backed by rustling palms. It can be crowded: Mexican families flock here on Sundays and holidays to wade and paddle in the shallows, and local fishermen cast their nets at the sheltered west side of the bay or launch small, colorfully painted boats. **Note:** Avoid walking along any of Puerto Escondido's beaches at night, as robberies and muggings have occurred.

To the east of Playa Principal is Playa Marineros, which begins at the jutting rocks below the Hotel Santa Fe. Here the shoreline begins curving toward the south and increasingly faces the open ocean. The surf gets rougher, and swimmers should exercise caution.

Farther to the southeast is Playa Zicatela, considered to be one of the world's best surfing beaches. The wide expanse of golden-colored sand stretches for miles, and the thundering Pacific breakers crashing onto it are impressive indeed. The biggest waves occur between August and November. Surfers from all over the world congregate at Zicatela, especially for the international tournament held annually in November. Spectators line the beach to watch these daredevils finesse the "pipeline," a long tubular swell of water. Needless to say, swim here at your own risk.

West of town are the coves of Puerto Angelito and Carrizalillo. With small beaches, submerged rock formations and close-in shelves of coral, these sheltered spots are ideal for snorkeling and scuba diving (bring your own gear, as facilities are limited at best). Both coves can be reached either by taxi, a boat launched from Playa Principal or a circuitous concrete footpath (wear a hat and bring water if you decide to walk). Farther west is Playa Bacocho, another open strip of sand; the waves and undertow make it better for sunning and hiking than swimming. Most of the more expensive hotels cluster around this beach.

What To Do

The main reason to visit Puerto Escondido is to relax at the beach; shopping and entertainment are not high on its list of diversions. The local *mercado* (municipal market) is in the upper section of town on Avenida 10 Norte, several blocks west of Avenida Oaxaca. It sells mostly produce, but one group of stalls offers a selection of regional handicrafts. Along the tourist strip, there are a few clothing shops and the usual hodgepodge of T-shirts, postcards and souvenirs.

Several restaurants line beachside Avenida Peréz Gasga, with fish and seafood—from sushi to octopus—the main menu items. Most places provide a view of the beach and the activity along it. The restaurant in the Hotel Santa Fe, on Avenida del Morro

at the eastern end of the bay (about half a mile southeast of the town center), has good food and a breezy atmosphere, with tables overlooking the Playa Zicatela surf.

Art and Harry's Surf Inn, as the name suggests, attracts the local surfer contingent. The fresh fish, salads and unobstructed sunset views are a good way to cap off a day at the beach. The restaurant is on Avenida del Morro, at the southern end of Zicatela.

The best places to watch the sun sink into the Pacific are along Playa Zicatela, where there is an unobscured view of the western horizon. The clifftop lawn on the grounds of the Posada Real Hotel, west of town overlooking Playa Bacocho, is an ideal perch for sunset watching. A taxi can get you there. There are a couple of noisy bars and discos in the tourist zone along Avenida Peréz Gasga and in the hotels around Playa Bacocho.

The surrounding coastal region is a natural paradise, and because most locations are inaccessible except by boat, ecotourism is actively promoted. Hidden Voyages Ecotours offers seasonal guided birdwatching and nature trips to some of the lagoons that indent the Oaxacan coast. Early morning trips visit Manialtepec Lagoon, about 15 kilometers (9 miles) west of Puerto Escondido, which is encircled by mangroves and home to a rich variety of wetland bird species and tropical vegetation.

An all-day excursion to Lagunas de Chacahua National Park, a larger series of lagoons west of Manialtepec, includes a midday swim and a visit to a crocodile hatchery. Sunset cruises also are available.

Round-trip transportation is provided from Puerto Escondido hotels. Food is not included; the Chacahua tour stops at a restaurant for lunch. The restaurant at the departure dock sells beverages to go. Bring a hat, sunblock and a dollar or two to tip the boatman. Binoculars are provided. There is a four-person minimum for tours. Fees range from $30 to $40 (U.S.) per person.

Reservations must be made through the Turismo Rodimar Travel Agency, Av. Peréz Gasga #905 on the beachfront. It is usually open daily 7:30 a.m.-10 p.m.; phone (954) 582-0734. This agency also can arrange three- or four-person fishing trips to the waters off Puerto Escondido for mackerel, sea bass, snook or tuna. Boats depart from Playa Principal.

Tourist information office: near the airport, at the intersection of Mex. 200 (Carretera Costera) and Avenida Benito Juárez. Open Mon.-Fri. 9-2 and 5-8, Sat. 9-1; phone (954) 582-0175 (English not likely to be spoken). An information booth operated by the Oaxaca Tourist Bureau, located near the western end of beachside Avenida Peréz Gasga, is normally open the same hours.

Puerto Vallarta

One of Mexico's top resorts, Puerto Vallarta is situated roughly at the midpoint of Bahía de Banderas (Banderas Bay). Spanish soldiers engaged in expeditions to Lower (Baja) California discovered the bay's shores in the early 16th century, stopping for supplies of water, firewood and food. Written chronicles of the time extolled the land's beauty and fertility, as well as the refuge the bay offered ships from marauding pirates.

A shipyard was built in 1644 to aid in the colonization efforts of Lower California. Entries in 17th-century ship logs made reference to whaling ships and fishing boats anchored in the bay, which at that time was also known as Bahía de los Jorobados (Humpback Bay) because of the number of humpback whale sightings. The first known settlement, called Las Peñas, was established in 1851. It consisted of families who farmed, raised cattle or brought in salt that was used in the refining process for silver-mining operations in the surrounding area.

Las Peñas was opened to national maritime traffic in 1885. There were both highs and lows over the next 50 years. A fire in 1888 destroyed more than half the town's homes (local legend maintains that the damage would have been far less severe if more of the male population had not been attending a cockfight at the time). In 1918, the town's name was changed to Puerto Vallarta, in honor of Jaliscan lawyer and state governor Don Ignacio L. Vallarta, who helped draft the Mexican Constitution. A yellow fever epidemic hit in 1922, but the town began to boom three years later with jobs created by the opening of banana plantations. And the first airplane landed in 1931.

Tourists began to arrive around 1930, and Mexican warships fired a 21-gun salute when the town celebrated its centennial in 1951. Improved road and air accessibility led to the construction of first-class hotels, and soon agriculture—previously the area's principal source of income—took a back seat to tourism (although tobacco and tequila production and cattle ranching still contribute to the regional economy).

Growth since then has been swift and steady, fueled by the annual invasion of sun-seeking visitors (some 2 million annually). Resort development, which has spread both north and south of the original village, is extensive but somehow does not overshadow the prevailing sense of charm that makes Puerto Vallarta (or "PV" as it is often called) so appealing. The city is simultaneously sophisticated, laid-back, very modern and timelessly Mexican.

Mismaloya Beach / © Gibson Stock Photography

Neptune and the Mermaid / © Gibson Stock Photography

The tourist influx peaks between mid-December and mid-April; if you plan on visiting during this period, reservations will need to be booked several months in advance. With all the activities at hand—sun, sand, strolling, shopping, swimming, fishing, boat trips or just kicking back and doing nothing—it's easy to spend a week or two.

Approaches

By Air

Gustavo Díaz Ordaz International Airport is on the main highway about 7 kilometers (4 miles) north of downtown. Aeroméxico, Alaska Airlines, American, America West, Continental, Delta and Mexicana all provide service to Puerto Vallarta from U.S. cities. Connections for flights from the United States are normally via Mexico City. Charter flights from Canada are available through Toronto and Vancouver. Aeroméxico and Mexicana also provide service from other cities within the country, including Guadalajara, León, Mexico City and Tijuana.

For flight information contact the individual airline; within Mexico, phone (800) 021-4010 for Aeroméxico, (800) 904-6000 for American, (800) 900-5000 for Continental, (800) 902-2100 for Delta and (322) 224-8900 for Mexicana. For additional information about airlines see *"Arriving by Air," page 551.*

The ticketing and arrival area is on the main level; customs is located in the baggage claim area. Beyond customs is the main lobby, where you can pick up tourist publications, make arrangements for ground transooprtation and exchange currency. The upper level is the departure area, which requires a boarding pass to enter. For airport information phone (322) 221-1298.

Colectivos (minivans) operated by Transportes Terrestres provide shared transportation from the airport to hotels. Tickets can be purchased at booths just outside the terminal. More expensive airport taxis *(taxi especial)* operated by Aeromovil also take passengers to hotels. In both cases, fares are based on a zone system. Zones are posted at the minivan and taxi ticket booths; ask if you don't know the zone in which your hotel is located. The *colectivos* depart as soon as they're full, so try to flag one as soon as possible after landing.

By Car

Reaching Puerto Vallarta by car involves a lengthy journey; the city lies some 1,200 miles south of the border at Nogales, Ariz., via Mex. 15/15-D and Mex. 200. Traffic slows considerably beyond Mazatlán. State and federal police conduct frequent inspections, particularly at state lines, which also can add time to the trip. Trucks can slow traffic down around Tepic,

(continued on page 215)

The Informed Traveler

City Population: 160,900 (estimated).

Location: On the Bay of Banderas along Jalisco's Pacific shoreline.

Highlights: A magnificent natural setting on Banderas Bay; El Centro, the heart of Vallarta, full of historic buildings along cobblestone streets; a bounty of restaurants offering fresh seafood and glorious views of the setting sun; better shopping than any other beach resort in Mexico; organized day trips to secluded coastal villages or into the surrounding jungle.

WHOM TO CALL

Area Code: 322.

In Case of Emergency: In the event of medical emergency, the CMQ Hospital, Basilio Badillo #365 at Insurgentes, is conveniently located and open 24 hours; phone (322) 223-0878 or (322) 222-3572.

Ameri+Med diagnostic medical center, in Plaza Neptuno at the entrance to Marina Vallarta (Boulevard Francisco Medina) also offers 24-hour emergency care; phone (322) 221-0023 or (800) 815-1921 (in the United States). The Red Cross is open 24 hours as well; phone (322) 222-1533.

For assistance with time share, taxi, store and similar issues, contact the Consumer Protection Agency (PROFECO). The office is at Calle Morelos #883 and is open Mon.-Fri. 9-3; phone (322) 222-2554. To contact the police in an emergency, dial 060; for non-emergencies, phone (322) 225-0000.

Use public phones marked "Ladatel" or "Lada 91" rather than calling from your hotel room, which almost always incurs a hefty charge. These phones require a Ladatel phone card, available in various denominations from most local stores. Avoid phones showing pictures of credit cards that advertise long distance calling to the United States and Canada.

WHERE TO LOOK

Media

Vallarta Today is an English-language daily newspaper geared toward tourists; it has information on everything from restaurants to currency exchange rates.

Visitor Information

Puerto Vallarta Tourist Office: in the City Hall (Presidencia Municipal) building on the main plaza downtown. The office is open Mon.-Fri. 9-8, Sat. 9-1; phone (322) 222-0242. It's a good source for city information.

The Web site www.virtualvallarta.com provides local news and comprehensive information about everything from airlines to restaurants to city services. In addition, Puerto Vallarta has Internet cafes where you can check your e-mail and surf the Web for about $3 per hour. Café San Angel, which also serves food and is a local gathering place, is at Olas Altas #449, south of the river.

WHAT TO KNOW

Weather

The weather in Puerto Vallarta is balmy year-round. Daily highs range from the 80s to the low 90s, nightly lows from the low 60s to low 70s. The temperature rarely drops below 60 degrees, making coats or jackets unnecessary. The nicest weather is during the high tourist season, from December through April. Bring along an effective insect repellent, as mosquitos can be a nuisance at any time of year; Autan Classic is a widely available Mexican brand.

Puerto Vallarta is very casual; most visitors wear shorts and T-shirts. Casual slacks for men and summer-type dresses for women are appropriate for more upscale restaurants and events. A sweater comes in handy for winter evenings; an effective sunblock is a must all year. Pack a hat, too.

Currency Exchange

Banks and currency exchange offices *(casas de cambio)* are concentrated in the downtown area. Banks are usually open Mon.-Fri. 9-1:30, although hours for exchanging foreign currency may be restricted. Currency exchange offices are open longer hours and may offer better rates. Stores, restaurants and even street vendors often will accept U.S. dollars, however, and credit cards are widely accepted. ATMs are plentiful; withdrawals are in pesos.

the Nayarit state capital. From Tepic, Mex. 200 is a slow, winding route south through mountains that reach to the coast.

A new shortcut connects San Blas, on the Nayarit coast, with Puerto Vallarta, bypassing the uphill route through Tepic. If heading south from San Blas (which is accessible from Mex. 15-D via local road Mex. 11), take the marked Puerto Vallarta turnoff (a short distance beyond the Santa Cruz de Miramar junction) south. A toll highway that will link Puerto Vallarta and Guadalajara is in the works.

From Guadalajara, it takes about 2 hours to reach Puerto Vallarta via toll highway Mex. 15. At Chapalilla, take the Compostela turnoff; at Compostela, proceed south on Mex. 200 for about 130 kilometers (80 miles) to Puerto Vallarta.

By Bus

Puerto Vallarta has a modern central bus station, Central Camionera de Puerto Vallarta, located just off the Tepic Highway about a kilometer north of the airport. Consolidating the small stations along Avenida Insurgentes that served different bus lines has considerably reduced the noise and pollution on downtown streets. The station has a ticket office, baggage storage, restaurants, long distance phone and fax services and guarded overnight parking.

The Elite line offers first-class bus service to and from Guadalajara (about 5 hours), as well as service north to Tepic, Mazatlán and Tijuana and south to Manzanillo, Zihuatanejo, Acapulco and Puerto Escondido. Some buses require transfers or stop along the way, while others do not; the ticketing agent will be able to clarify routes and answer questions. Phone (322) 223-1117.

Autotransportes del Pacífico and Primera Plus offer first-class service south along the coast. ETN (Enlaces Terrestres Nacionales) provides first-class service to Mexico City, while Flecha Amarilla has first-class service to Guadalajara and Manzanillo. Travel agencies around town can sometimes provide bus routes and schedules. For additional information about buses see "Bus Service," page 68.

By Cruise Ship

Puerto Vallarta is a major port of call for cruise ships, most arriving from Los Angeles during the peak tourist season. Cruise lines dock at the Terminal Marítima (Maritime Terminal), north of downtown at the Marina Vallarta complex, and include Carnival, Holland-America, Norwegian, Princess and Royal Caribbean.

Getting Around

Layout

From north to south, the different sections of the city north of the Río Cuale are connected by one primary thoroughfare. Officially called Boulevard Francisco Medina Ascencio, it changes names several times. As the Carretera Aeropuerto (Airport Highway), it brings traffic past the airport and the Hotel Zone before narrowing and becoming Avenida México and then Paseo Díaz Ordáz as it runs along the waterfront.

The downtown area is small and compact, hemmed in as it is between the mountains and the bay. The Río Cuale divides it into two sections. North of the river is the malecón, a mile-long oceanfront boardwalk that runs along Paseo Díaz Ordáz. White wrought-iron benches offer an opportunity to sit and contemplate the views, and the restaurants on the opposite side of the street are popular gathering places to watch the sun set over the bay.

Along the malecón are three nautically themed bronze sculptures. Fountain of the Dolphins (La Fuente de Los Delfines), next to the Los Arcos Amphitheater, sits atop a circular dome-shaped fountain. Each of the three dolphins faces in a different direction: the city, the sky and the sea. Nearby are Neptune and the Mermaid (Neptune y Serena) and Caballito de Mar, a boy riding a seahorse that is Puerto Vallarta's trademark. Across from the seawall are shops, nightspots, open-air cafés and fast-food outlets. The view is particularly nice from the second-story restaurant balconies.

Tree-shaded Plaza Principal is just off the malecón between avenidas Morelos and Juárez. This traditional-looking square has a bandstand in the middle and a statue of Don Ignacio L. Vallarta, for whom the city was named. Free concerts take place here on weekends.

On the east side of the plaza is the 20th-century Church of Our lady of Guadalupe (La Iglesia de Nuestra Señora de Guadalupe), which took 33 years to build. It's noted for the large crown atop the steeple, modeled after one worn by Carlota, wife of Archduke Maximilian, Mexico's ruler for 3 years in the 1860s. Made of fiberglass, it replaced the original crown, which collapsed during an earthquake in 1995. Angels clasping hands decorate the exterior. (**Note:** Do not wear shorts or T-shirts if you wish to enter the church.)

Whitewashed stucco walls and red-tiled roofs characterize El Centro, PV's heart. An irregular grid of narrow streets extends some 6 blocks up into the hills above the bay, forming the oldest section of Puerto Vallarta. Street names are denoted on Mexican tiles on the sides of buildings. El Centro exudes charm, although dusty cobblestones, street construction, sputtering taxicabs and the odd donkey are all reminders of a more prosaic Mexico.

Overlooking the river is the steep ravine dubbed Gringo Gulch, named for the well-connected Americans who settled in Puerto Vallarta during the 1950s and '60s.

Among the beautiful colonial-style villas—many tucked along narrow alleyways—is Elizabeth Taylor's former residence, Casa Kimberly, built in 1963 for $5,000 and sold years later for $450,000. It is now a bed-and-breakfast as well as a museum of sorts, as it contains everything Taylor left when she sold the house in the 1980s. Burton rented the

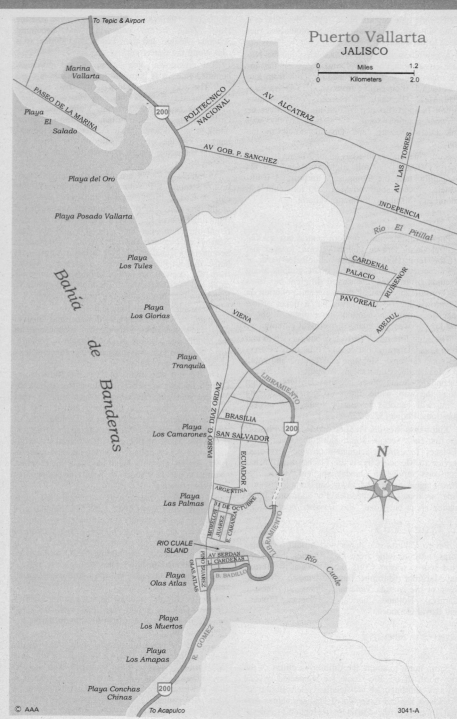

Puerto Vallarta
JALISCO

To Tepic & Airport

Marina
Vallarta

PASEO DE LA MARINA

Playa
El
Salado

200

POLITECNICO
NACIONAL

AV ALCATRAZ

AV GOB. P. SANCHEZ

AV LAS TORRES

Playa del Oro

INDEPENCIA

Playa Posado Vallarta

Río El Pitillal

CARDENAL

PALACIO

Playa
Los Tules

PAVOREAL

RUJEÑOR

Bahía

ABEDUL

Playa
Los Glorias

VIENA

de

Playa
Tranquila

LIBRAMIENTO

Banderas

PASEO G. DIAZ ORDAZ

BRASILIA

200

Playa
Los Camarones

SAN SALVADOR

ECUADOR

ARGENTINA

Playa
Las Palmas

31 DE OCTUBRE

MORELOS

JUAREZ

E. CARRANZA

ITURBIDE

RIO CUALE
ISLAND

AV SERDAN

L. CARDENAS

Río Cuale

PINO SUAREZ

OLAS ATLAS

Playa
Olas Atlas

B. BADILLO

LIBRAMIENTO

Playa
Los Muertos

Playa
Los Amapas

R. GOMEZ

Playa Conchas
Chinas

200

© AAA

To Acapulco

3041-A

N

Miles   1.2
Kilometers   2.0

house across the street and had a pink arched bridge built to connect the two. On Avenida Miramar, just north of the Río Cuale's north bank (near the Municipal Market) is a statue of the film couple.

Two stone bridges and a foot bridge connect the river with Río Cuale Island. The benches at this elongated sandbar's western end, overlooking the bay, are a prime spot for sunset watching. Between the bridges are souvenir stalls and casual little eateries in a parklike setting. Strolling the island is pleasant, although the river water in the canals is polluted. Just east of the Avenida Insurgentes bridge in a shady plaza is a life-size statue of actor/director John Huston.

The area south of the Río Cuale used to consist only of tucked-away coves and sandy beaches. Just below the river are more shops and restaurants, Plaza Lázaro Cárdenas Park, and motels catering to budget-minded travelers. Like El Centro, this area is easily traversed on foot.

Basilio Badillo, which runs east-west about five blocks south of the river, is appropriately known as Calle de Los Cafes, or "Restaurant Row." This part of town is the city's nightlife center, with everything from funky beach hangouts to martini bars. Farther south, heading toward Mismaloya Beach, is the upscale Conchas Chinas residential neighborhood, where expensive villas wedged into the rocky cliffs overlook the city and bay.

More luxury properties form a glittering Hotel Zone north of old Puerto Vallarta. Landscaped, four-lane Avenida de las Palmas (formerly called the Airport Highway) passes through this area. Approaching the city from the airport, this highway divides; downtown is to the right. **Note:** The 60 km/h (35 mph) speed limit is strictly enforced.

Many tourists stay at Marina Vallarta, at the northern edge of the Hotel Zone, which is a city unto itself. It encompasses major chain hotels, a flurry of upscale condominium developments, an enormous marina and yacht club and an 18-hole golf course. Along the marina boardwalk there are numerous shops, galleries, cafes and restaurants. There also is shuttle service to downtown Puerto Vallarta. Marina Vallarta is a good choice if you're a first-timer or part of a package tour, although it lacks the charm of Puerto Vallarta proper. This is the resort development closest to the airport, and as a result can be affected by noise from landing and departing aircraft.

Nuevo Vallarta, about 19 kilometers (12 miles) north of the airport, is just over the Nayarit state line at the mouth of the Río Ameca. This planned resort area, which seems removed from the rest of PV, has condominiums, time-share units, bayfront homes, a yacht marina and a sprinkling of all-inclusive accommodations. Water taxis make daily trips from the marina to downtown Puerto Vallarta.

A bit farther north is the village of Bucerías ("place of the divers"), an enclave of cobblestone streets, walled villas and tidy little hotels. Some travelers prefer this lower-cost alternative to Puerto Vallarta for its many shops, town square market and casual open-air restaurants. The 5-mile stretch of white sand is the longest along the Banderas Bay coastline. The shallow shoreline is perfect for wading, body surfing and shell collecting, and the beach draws throngs of local families on Sundays. Bucerías is most easily reached by bus; minivans also shuttle passengers from the airport to the village and back.

Rental Cars

If you've driven your own vehicle or rented one for exploring areas to the north or south, avoid driving after dark; cows wandering onto the roadway can be a very real hazard. For sightseeing in and around the city, take advantage of the green-and-white tourist buses that cover the area from Marina Vallarta south to Mismaloya Beach.

Note: AAA/CAA members enjoy discounts through Hertz for vehicles booked in the United States. Consult your local AAA/CAA club or phone Hertz, (800) 654-3080.

Buses

City buses are inexpensive and take passengers to almost all points along Banderas Bay, from the airport south through the Hotel Zone, into downtown via the Ignacio Vallarta Bridge, and to points as far south as Mismaloya Beach. The fixed fare is 4 pesos (about 40 cents U.S.). In addition to the newer minibuses (*combis* or *colectivos*) that are equipped with emission controls, there are still old public buses on the streets spewing clouds of exhaust.

Stops are designated by a white bus outlined on a dark blue sign. Destinations and routes (for example, *"Olas Altas," "Ixtapa," "Hoteles"* or *"Aeropuerto"*) are painted on the front of the bus or posted in the window. Local routes are normally covered from 6 a.m. to 11 p.m. Out-of-town service to Bucerías is 12 pesos (about $1.20); to Punta Mita, 14 pesos (about $1.40).

The local bus station is on Avenida Olas Altas at Plaza Lázaro Cárdenas, south of the Río Cuale and just inland from the beach. City buses also depart from Plaza de Armas, the main square.

Taxis

Taxis are plentiful and cover the same routes as buses, but are more expensive. Fares are based on set rates; the average fare is around 30 pesos ($3 U.S.). A ride across town from Marina Vallarta to Playa los Muertos will be about 60 pesos ($6 U.S.). Fares should be posted in each taxi and appear in the *Vallarta Today* newspaper. Even so, always ask how much the fare is (*"Cuanto?"*) and come to a decision before you get in the cab, which might save a few pesos. Many hotels post a list of rates to specific destinations, which can come in handy if you're unfamiliar with the city. It is customary not to tip drivers.

For Your Information

Guides/Tours

The standard city tour provides an all-purpose Puerto Vallarta orientation. A short version of the tour covers the local sights by air-conditioned minibus, including the main plaza and its crown-topped cathedral, the exclusive neighborhood of Conchas Chinas, Gringo Gulch, and the former homes of Elizabeth Taylor and Richard Burton.

The tropical tour is a longer version that throws in a trip to Mismaloya Beach and lunch in a jungle setting at Chico's Paradise. Hotel pickup and drop-off is included in the fee; lunch is not. City tours are given Mon.-Sat. 10-1, tropical tours Mon.-Sat. 10-3. Make arrangements through your hotel.

Caballito de Mar
Puerto Vallarta Tourism

Staying Safe

Tourist crime is uncommon, although visitors would do well not to carry large amounts of cash in public. If your hotel provides safety deposit boxes, they are a good place to keep money, airline tickets, tourist permits and so forth. Bilingual "tourist police" wearing white safari outfits and white (tourist) or blue (traffic) pith helmets patrol the downtown area and are generally friendly and helpful.

Parking

Parking in the compact downtown area is scarce, and driving around the city in general presents a challenge. During the winter tourist season from December through April the narrow streets are jammed; from July through October heavy rains can make them flooded and muddy. Many roads leading in to Puerto Vallarta are just two lanes and descend from the mountains; drive with caution.

What To Do

Dining

PV offers many options for dining well, if not particularly cheaply. A plus for foreign visitors is the purified water—including ice—that is universally used by licensed food and beverage establishments. (If in doubt, ask for bottled water, juice, beer or a soft drink.) While food quality is dependable, it is the striking water views that distinguish many restaurants. Most hotel establishments offer a standard steak and seafood menu. Seafood, Mexican and Argentinian are some of the choices at eateries along the 3 blocks of Calle Basilio Badillo between Pino Suárez and Insurgentes.

No Name Cafe, Calle Morelos #460 on the *malecón* (across from the sea horse statue), caters to families with an American-style menu of barbecued ribs, hot dogs and deep-dish pizza. This sports bar also has an extensive memorabilia collection.

Tourist-oriented "jungle" restaurants—easily reached by car or taxi—offer open-air dining amid beautiful tropical surroundings. One of the most popular is Chico's Paradise, Mex. 200 south to Km marker 20, past the village of Boca de Tomatlán. It features open-air *palapas* built atop boulders in a hilly riverside setting. If they wish, guests can swing Tarzan-style via rope and splash into a protected natural pool. Less active diners handpick their lunch from a fish-filled water tank in the middle of the restaurant.

A casual dress code is the rule, although wearing shorts to dinner may be frowned on at some of the nicer places. Some restaurants shut down for a month during the summer. For a list of AAA-RATED establishments in Puerto Vallarta, *see the Lodgings & Restaurants section.*

Shopping

Shopping is a major pastime in Puerto Vallarta. Merchandise from all over Mexico turns up, although prices tend to be higher than in the cities where the items originate. You'll find jewelry, especially silver; clothing ranging from beach T-shirts to designer fashions; colonial-style furniture; pottery and ceramics; hand-tooled leather goods, including *huaraches* (sandals); shoes (keep in mind that sizes are measured in centimeters); and sombreros and other hats. Fine handicrafts include beaded tapestries from Nayarit, lacquered boxes and ceremonial masks from Michoacán, and handwoven baskets, rugs and shawls from Central America.

A typical Mexican shopping experience can be had at the open-air Municipal Market, (Mercado Municipal), which spreads out under the trees below the steps leading down from the northern end of the Avenida Insurgentes Bridge. Clothes, crafts, leather goods, silver jewelry and trinkets fill the two-level maze of stalls—everything from piñatas to whips. Experienced hagglers may be able to persuade vendors to lower their prices *un poquito* (just a little bit).

Those interested in more than a souvenir should head for El Centro and its assortment of exclusive galleries, which display the wares of a resident community of painters, sculptors and artisans. Many of the merchants accept American dollars or credit cards, and store prices are usually fixed. Galería Uno, downtown at Calle Morelos #561 (at Calle Zaragoza), exhibits a range of Mexican fine art, including paintings, graphics and sculptures. It is open Mon.-Sat. 10-8; phone (322) 222-0908.

Galería Pacífico, Insurgentes #109, specializes in contemporary works by Mexican and Latin American artists. Olinalá Gallery, south of the river at Lázaro Cárdenas #274, has two floors of crafts and a particularly wide selection of masks. It is open Mon.-Sat. 10-2 and 5-9; phone (322) 222-4995. Galería de Ollas, Calle Morelos #101, carries the exquisite work of potters from the village of Mata Ortíz.; phone (322) 222-1045. Galería Manuel Lepe, Juárez #563, is run by the daughter of the late Puerto Vallartan painter, whose work is exhibited around the city.

Downtown shops carry an excellent selection of Mexican folk art. Prices tend to be high, but so does quality. La Rosa de Cristal, south of the river at Insurgentes #272 (between calles Lázaro Cárdenas and Madero) is the place to go for blown-glass items, which are made in the Guadalajara suburb of Tlaquepaque. On display at Alfarería Tlaquepaque, Av. México #1100, are baskets, woodcarvings, glassware and ceramics from various Mexican states. Mundo de Azulejos (World of Tiles), Venustiano Carranza #374 (south of the river), has a huge selection of handpainted Talavera tiles, as well as plates and murals.

Puerto Vallarta's shopping centers feature boutiques offering sportswear and casual yet fashionable evening wear. They are located primarily along the *malecón* and north into the Hotel Zone. Most stores are open until at least 8 p.m., and some may close from 2-4 for *siesta*. Many stores are closed on Sunday.

Among the arcades with browsing potential are Plaza Malecón, on the oceanfront at Paseo Díaz Ordaz and Calle Allende; Plaza Marina, within the Marina Vallarta complex; and Villa Vallarta, on Avenida de las Palmas in the Hotel Zone.

A flea market offering the usual T-shirts and souvenirs sets up at the Marina Vallarta docks where the cruise ships anchor. Gaggles of vendors also peddle their wares at the beaches, especially Playa de los Muertos. Their persistence can be annoying, so be very firm if you're not interested in purchasing anything.

Beaches

Puerto Vallarta's beaches are divided into three zones: north of town, in town and south of town. Perhaps the most popular is Playa los Muertos, or Beach of the Dead, which city officials have long tried to rename Playa del Sol. It stretches south from the river and can be accessed from Calle Olas Altas.

Better for sunning than for swimming (the water is somewhat polluted), Playa Los Muertos attracts locals, European tourists and budget travelers. Sunbathers crowd the sand (particularly on Sundays and holidays), parasailers soar above it and roaming vendors hawk barbecued fish on a stick—the PV equivalent of a Coney Island hot dog. At the southern end of the beach is El Púlpito, a rock formation shaped like a pulpit.

About 10 kilometers (6 miles) south of town off Mex. 200 (the southward extension of Avenida Insurgentes) is Playa Mismaloya, protected by a pretty cove. This is where "Night of the Iguana" was filmed, and it is still possible to hike to the ruins of the movie set, at the southern end of the cove.

Although the spot's tranquil beauty has been compromised by such sprawling developments as the La Jolla de Mismaloya hotel complex, the water is clear, the sand white and the beach backed by jungle-cloaked hills. A string of *palapa* restaurants sell beer and seafood, and also rent out tables and beach chairs. In the rugged country above Mismaloya another movie was made—Arnold Schwarzenegger's 1987 action opus "Predator."

On the north side of town is Playa de Oro, which is backed by the Hotel Zone. Although it may seem like the stretches of golden-brown sand in front of the big hotels are private, they are not; all beaches in Mexico are federal property and thus open to the public. The wide, flat expanse of sand, divided into sections by iron jetties and rocky in spots, faces the open bay; waves can be surprisingly rough.

At all of the beaches there are efforts to protect the eggs of endangered sea turtles, evidence of an increased ecological awareness throughout the country. Puerto Vallarta's program, known as "Vallarta-Tortuga 2000," involves regular patrols of turtle nesting grounds. Eggs are taken to protected nurseries, and hatchlings are released in the open water.

Sightseeing

Nearby beaches and islands make easy day trip destinations from Puerto Vallarta. More and more ecotourism activities allow participants to explore or learn about the local environment without disturbing it. Vallarta Adventures organizes a variety of sightseeing and eco tours; phone (322) 297-1212, ext. 3, or (866) 256-2739 from the United States.

Several companies organize guided trips into the surrounding region. Open Air Expeditions, downtown at Guerrero #339, specializes in adventure travel, taking small groups on hiking, kayaking, birdwatching and wildlife observation excursions; phone (322) 222-3310.

Terra Noble is an arts center and spa situated on a high plateau at the north end of town, surrounded by mountains and jungle. Visitors can attend hands-on clay or painting workshops utilizing pre-Hispanic techniques, or relax with a massage and an invigorating sea salt exfoliation. Reservations can be made through local travel agencies, or phone (322) 223-3530.

About 16 kilometers (10 miles) south of the city, just before Mex. 200 veers inland, is the village of Boca de Tomatlán, at the mouth of the Río Tomatlán. It is easily reached by taxi or bus (buses post their destination in the window or above the windshield). A relaxed tropical atmosphere prevails here amid lush hillsides, freshwater pools and water burbling past huge rocks. The small but enticing beach is sheltered by a narrow cove. For about $9 (U.S.) you can hire a *panga* (skiff) for a trip to the secluded beach at Las Animas, a bit farther southwest.

Separate daily cruises set sail for the coastal villages of Yelapa and Quimixto (key-MISH-toh). Cruises depart Marina Vallarta's Maritime Terminal at 9 a.m., returning around 4. The coastline here is punctuated by small coves set against a jungle backdrop.

At Yelapa, passengers can swim, snorkel or just stretch out in the sun; a short hike or horseback ride from Quimixto leads to a jungle waterfall. Lunch and snorkeling gear are normally provided. The trimaran *Bora Bora* sails to the beach at Las Animas, with snorkeling and lunch included on the all-day agenda. Many of these excursions provide music on board. Dinner and sunset cruises also are available. Make cruise reservations with one of the local travel agencies. For those who wish to tarry, rustic overnight accommodations are available in Yelapa.

About 36 kilometers (22 miles) north of Puerto Vallarta via Mex. 200 is the fishing village of Sayulita. The location boasts beautiful views of Banderas Bay and the rich tropical forest environment of the coastal Sierra Madre mountains. It's a popular getaway with a beautiful beach and a variety of homey thatch-roofed restaurants.

Within the village is Papa's Palapas, a collection of beachfront bungalows constructed in rustic Mexican *palapa* style but equipped with modern conveniences. A variety of eco-oriented activities can be arranged, including kayaking on the bay, nature hikes through an ecological reserve, bird and whale-watching expeditions, and organized mountain bike rides (more comfortably undertaken during the dry winter season) through the jungles surrounding Puerto Vallarta.

Transportation, guides and equipment are provided; wear a hat or cap and comfortable walking shoes, and bring insect repellent. For schedule and reservation information phone (800) 899-4167 in the United States, or (329) 291-3076 within Mexico.

Recreation

Water sports are a given in an environment where there is access to modern marine facilities within a protected bay. The Bay of Banderas extends north to Punta de Mita (Mita Point) and south to Cabo Corrientes (Corrientes Cape), where the foothills of the Sierra de Cuale range begin. It forms a natural barrier against most serious storms; the region's only hurricane was recorded in 1911.

Water depths of up to 1,500 feet give the bay characteristics normally associated with oceans, but it also is protected due to its shape and the surrounding geography. The result is generally calm water and clear visibility, which makes it ideal for **boating.** Favored by experienced divers are the Marietas Islands, off Punta de Mita at the bay's northern end. These islets were once used as a hiding place by pirates who plundered galleons loaded with silver from Sierra Madre mines.

For snorkelers, the bay teems with tropical fish. Dolphins, sea turtles, giant manta rays and migrating humpback whales also can be seen. A favorite **snorkeling** destination is the underwater park at Los Arcos (also called Las Peñas), a short distance offshore from Mismaloya Beach. The oddly eroded formations jutting out of the bay served as an early landmark for ships. Colorful marine life is particularly evident around these rocks.

A favored destination for divers, snorkelers and kayakers is the Marietas Islands (Islas Marietas), which comprise the tips of an undersea mountain range. Tropical fish thrive here, dolphins are frequently sighted, and the islands also are a protected bird sanctuary. Chico's Dive Shop, Paseo Díaz Ordaz #772 at the northern end of the *malecón*, rents equipment and organizes dive trips to the Marietas; phone (322) 222-1895.

Boats for **sport fishing** can be hired through the Fishing Cooperative (Cooperativo de Pescadores), at the northern end of the *malecón*. Rates for fishing vessels depend on the size of the boat, where you fish, and whether bait and tackle are supplied. Bring your own refreshments, since most trips don't include them.

Sailfish and blue marlin are hooked November through February; smaller game species such as dorado, roosterfish and tuna can be caught seasonally most of the year. A catch-and-release policy is stressed if the fish is not going to be eaten.

Marina Vallarta has more than 500 slips and offers boaters fresh water, as well as cable TV and telephone hookups. Hardware and boating supply outlets are located along the boardwalk of this sprawling complex, which also has an 18-hole golf course, luxury hotels and condominiums. Tour boats and fishing excursions depart from the marina's Maritime Terminal. Boaters can explore a variety of tiny coves and hidden beaches along the shore of Banderas Bay, or drop anchor for awhile at Bahía de Banderas in Nuevo Vallarta.

Swimming, water skiing, parasailing and other watery pursuits can be enjoyed at many spots along the bay. Surfers head for the open waters and bigger waves around Punta de Mita. For those who would rather view the bay than venture into it, saddle horses for shoreline rides can be rented through a travel agency or the beachfront hotels.

Rancho El Charro and Rancho Ojo de Agua organize guided two- to three-hour **horseback riding** excursions into the foothills of the Sierra Madre, past jungle plantations and rural villages. Transportation is included and reservations are necessary; phone (322) 224-0114 for Rancho El Charro, (322) 224-0607 for Rancho Ojo de Agua.

There are several 18-hole **golf** courses in the area. Water comes into play on 11 holes at the Marina Vallarta Golf Club course. A cart or caddy is mandatory, and member privileges are extended to guests staying at certain hotels. Greens fees range from $80-$115 (U.S.). Golfers wishing to play outside peak tourist season should check with the club; phone (322) 221-0073 or (322) 221-0545.

The Flamingos Golf Course and Country Club is about 13 kilometers (8 miles) north of the airport off Mex. 200, in the state of Nayarit. Greens fees at this older, par-71 course range from $55-$120 (U.S.); caddies and motorized carts are available. (**Note:** Nayarit observes Mountain Standard Time, which is an hour earlier than Puerto Vallarta and the rest of Jalisco.) Reservations and transportation can be arranged through your hotel, or phone (329) 298-0606.

The Vista Vallarta Golf Club, 653 Circuito Universidad, Colonia San Nicolas, is about 3 miles inland from Marina Vallarta. There are two courses, one designed by Jack Nicklaus and one by Tom Weiskopf. Greens fees range from $80-$170 (U.S.). For tee times and hotel package information phone (322) 290-0030.

Most of the resorts provide clay **tennis** courts for their guests. PV also has two tennis centers: the John Newcombe Tennis Center, at the Continental Plaza Puerto Vallarta in the Hotel Zone, and the Los Tules Tennis Center, near the Fiesta Americana Hotel. For **bullfighting** fans, the La Paloma Bullring is across Avenida de las Palmas from Marina Vallarta. Bullfights begin Wed. afternoons at 5, November through April; tickets can be obtained through travel agencies.

Nightlife

The cheapest after-dark option is strolling along the *malecón* (Paseo Díaz Ordaz). Sunday evenings in particular bring out local families, mariachi bands, street performers and the ubiquitous vendors.

Three popular watering holes along the *malecón* are The Zoo, Carlos O'Brien's and the PV branch of the Hard Rock Café, all of which tend to attract a younger crowd with loud rock, reggae and techno. The similarly boisterous Planet Hollywood is downtown on Calle Morelos (#518). Andale, Calle Olas Altas #425 at Avenida Rodriguez (near the Los Muertos Pier), caters to all ages with a video bar and upstairs restaurant.

Puerto Vallarta also has a number of American-style sports bars where you can grab a bite to eat, play a board game, watch sports on TV or just sit and chat. El Torito, on Ignacio L. Vallarta (#290), features satellite broadcasts of sports events and a casual menu with the likes of nachos, ribs and beer-battered shrimp. The Club, on Basilio Badillo across the street from Memo's Pancake House, is a

cozy, quiet Canadian pub frequented by locals and NASCAR enthusiasts.

Dance clubs are loud, flashy and stay open until the early hours of the morning. There is normally a cover charge, and drink prices can be steep; look for free passes that are available at tourist-frequented hotels and restaurants. Many hot spots are in the hotels. Christine's, next to the Krystal Vallarta Hotel, features a nightly laser light show set to music that begins around 11 p.m. Afterwards the dance music heats up. (**Note:** The dress code prohibits shorts for men.)

The Kit Kat Club, at Playa Los Muertos, is a hip, snazzy New York-style lounge with cool music, martinis and some outstanding desserts. For a more romantic evening, Café des Artistes has a nightly piano/jazz bar.

Mexican-style fiestas are another popular diversion and include dinner buffets, folk dancing, live music and even fireworks. One of the oldest is La Iguana, south of the river at Calle Lázaro Cárdenas #311 (at Constitución). A Mexican buffet dinner is accompanied by live music, mariachis, rope twirling, colorfully costumed folk dancers and breaking open a piñata. Shows begin Thurs. and Sun. at 7 p.m.; phone (322) 222-0105.

Other fiestas take place at big hotels like the Krystal Vallarta and the Sheraton Buganvillias. For schedule and reservation information, check with the hotels or a local travel agency.

Special Events

Luckily for visitors, Puerto Vallarta's biggest events occur during the peak tourist season. The Festival of the Sea (Fiesta del Mar) is celebrated during November. Tennis tournaments, art exhibits, an international boat show and a gourmet dining festival all take place, as well as a couple of fishing tournaments—the International Sailfish Tournament and the World Billfish Series Grand Championship—that attract anglers from all over Mexico and the United States. For dates and details on specific events, contact the Puerto Vallarta Tourist Office.

The yachting season kicks off in late fall with the San Diego to Puerto Vallarta Annual Regatta, which heralds the arrival of some impressive craft. The patron saint of mariachis is honored Nov. 23 during the Festival of Santa Cecilia, when a lineup of mariachi bands plays at the cathedral.

Perhaps the year's biggest celebration is the Fiesta de Guadalupe, honoring the Virgin of Guadalupe, Mexico's patron saint. Daily evening processions, called *peregrinaciones,* make their way to the Church of Our Lady of Guadalupe from various *colonias* (neighborhoods) and local businesses the week prior to Dec. 12. Young and old alike participate in the celebration, many carrying candles and offerings of food and flowers to be exchanged for a blessing by the priest. Mass is held in front of the cathedral, accompanied by dancing and singing. The festivities culminate on Dec. 12 with a grand fireworks display.

**This ends listings for Puerto Vallarta.
The following page resumes the alphabetical listings
of cities in The Pacific Coast.**

SAN BLAS, NAYARIT (G-5)

The fishing village of San Blas (sahn BLAHS) was a major port from the late 16th into the 19th centuries. Galleons involved in the Manila trade routinely stopped at San Blas here. During the mid-18th century it also became a shipbuilding center and was a garrison for the Spanish armada, which fought French, Dutch and British pirates; the ruins of a Spanish fortress occupy a hill looming above the town.

Adventurous travelers who want to avoid the hubbub of Mazatlán to the north or Puerto Vallarta to the south might consider San Blas, which is accessible via Mex. 11 branching off Mex. 15-D. (**Note:** Mex. 11 is isolated and jungle-lined; make sure the gas tank is full and your vehicle is in tip-top shape.)

The main draw for tourists are the tan-colored beaches, which encircle nearby Matanchen Bay. Playa Borrego is the most convenient to town. This typical Mexican beach has few amenities other than the open-air shacks serving cold beer and whole smoked fish. Playa Los Cocos, reachable by taxi, has a backdrop of palm trees. The rainy summer season is plagued by mosquitos; *jejenes* (hey-HAY-nays), or "no-see-ums," are bothersome biting gnats that materialize at dawn and dusk year-round. Needless to say, insect repellent is a necessity.

Tourist information office: in the Casa de Gobierno building on the east side of the main plaza (on Avenida Canalizo).

LA TOVARA is north of San Blas via the San Cristóbal Estuary (Estuario San Cristóbal). The jungle trip to this freshwater spring via motorized dugout *(lancha)* is a favorite of birdwatchers. The small boats (holding up to 12 passengers) pass through swampy lagoons and dense mangrove forests inhabited by herons, egrets, turtles, lizards and fish. The spring itself forms a cool, freshwater pool where swimming is possible. For the best wildlife views, go early in the morning. Most trips last about 3 hours.

Check with the tourist information office for trip information. An excursion also can be arranged with the boat owners themselves at the *embarcadero* (docking area), at the eastern end of Avenida Juárez leaving town. The fee is around $10 (U.S.) per person; lunch at the restaurant at the springs is not included.

TEPIC, NAYARIT (G-5) pop. 305,200

Tepic (teh-PEEK), the state capital, lies at the foot of the extinct Sangangüey (sahn-gahn-GWAY) volcano. The city dates from the 16th century, but grew slowly at first because of its isolated location. Today Tepic (a Náhuatl Indian word meaning "hard stone") functions mainly as a stopover for travelers en route to Guadalajara or Puerto Vallarta.

The cathedral bordering Plaza Principal has twin towers and a yellow exterior. At the summit of a hill south of the town center is the 18th-century Convent of the Holy Cross (Convento de la Santa Cruz). The restored former convent was built around a growth of grass in the shape of a cross, said to be a miraculous site.

The surrounding countryside is mountainous and isolated, although it has a wild beauty. Here live the Huichol and Cora Indians, among the least affected of Mexico's indigenous peoples by the intrusions of modern life. Appropriately, religion and ritual are an integral part of daily life. Huichol art, particularly the brightly colored wall hangings, incorporates symbols relating to fertility, nature and the heavens. Shops bordering Plaza Principal sometimes offer beads and other handicrafts made by local Huichol and Cora artisans.

The Regional Museum of Anthropology (Museo Regional de Antropología), south of Plaza Principal at Av. México #91 Norte (at Avenida Zapata), is housed in an 18th-century mansion, the former House of the Counts of Miravalle. On view are a collection of Huichol artifacts, including animal-shaped pottery, and an exhibit pertaining to the archeological site surrounding the town of Ixtlan del Río, which is distinguished by a circular pyramid. Open Tues.-Sun.

Nayarit State Tourism Office (Subsecretaría de Turismo): downtown at Avenida México and Calzada del Ejército, in the Ex-Convent of La Cruz (Ex-Convento de La Cruz); phone (311) 214-8071 or (800) 523-0160 (toll-free long distance within Mexico).

ZIHUATANEJO—*see Ixtapa/Zihuatanejo p. 194.*

Monument to the Child Heroes, Chapultepec Park, Mexico City / © Peter M. Wilson / Alamy Images

Mexico City and Vicinity

Floating on a lake bed a mile and a half high, Mexico City is, in a word, unique. This ancient land of the Aztecs is a thoroughly modern world capital, yet a city with roots deeply entrenched in its indigenous and colonial Spanish cultures. It is the oldest (more than 675 years) and second highest (7,350 feet) capital in North America, and one of the most populated cities in the world.

Distinguished colonial buildings fill Mexico City's historic center. More than 2,000 years of history unfurl at the city's wealth of museums and their collections of priceless artifacts. The world-famous Ballet Folklórico celebrates the history of Mexican folk music and dance. If you are a gourmand on a culinary quest, the capital offers memorable gastronomic experiences. And ardent shoppers will find a treasure trove of brightly colored bargains.

Mexico City's neighborhoods are as varied as the city itself. Polanco is a small residential area filled with art galleries, hotels, restaurants and foreign embassies. The shopping malls and exclusive international boutiques along Presidente Masaryk, the main street, are Mexico City at its chicest. La Condesa is another upscale neighborhood filled with parks and lovely turn-of-the-20th-century homes.

San Angel and Coyoacán are two distinctive neighborhoods in the city's southern sector. They offer a first-hand encounter with the colonial era in the form of venerable plazas, colorful markets and a vibrant sense of artistic expression. This is "old Mexico" at its most beguiling.

Sunday is the best time to visit Coyoacán, when it is the site of a lively street bazaar. City residents converge at Plaza Hidalgo against a heady backdrop of sights, colors

3055-B

QUERETARO

GUANA-
JUATO

HIDALGO

N

MICHOACAN

MEXICO

Tepotzotlán

Mexico City
San Angel

Toluca   Tlalpan

Valle de
Bravo   Tenancingo

Teotihuacán

Acolman

Ixtapalapa

Churubusco
Coyoacán
Xochimilco

DISTRITO
FEDERAL

Izta-Popo
National
Park

TLAXCALA

115

Tepoztlán
Cuernavaca

Cuautla

Ixtapan
de La Sal

MORELOS

PUEBLA

**Mexico City
and Vicinity**

NOT INTENDED FOR DRIVING
SEE APPROPRIATE SHEET MAP

Tequesquitengo

| 0 | Miles | 38 |
| 0 | Kilometers | 61 |

GUERRERO

ONLY PLACES LISTED WITH DESCRIPTIVE
WRITE-UPS APPEAR ON THIS MAP.

and aromas. Vendors display their wares—clothing, jewelry, balloons, trinkets, plants, paintings, puppies, paper flowers, incense, carved figurines, housewares and myriad other items—in stalls or spread on the ground on blankets.

Side trips are a relatively short hop away. Perhaps the most impressive is Teotihuacán, easily reached from Mexico City. While it lacks the lush jungle backdrop of Palenque, in southern Mexico, Teotihuacán is the most monumentally scaled of all the country's archeological zones. The temple remains and two majestic pyramids rise from a flat, open plain, with little surrounding vegetation to obscure the view. The wide open spaces and awe-inspiring ruins are the perfect antidote to the city's sometimes claustrophobic congestion.

Points of Interest

ACOLMAN, MEXICO (C-10) elev. 7,511'

Acolman is a small village off Mex. 132-D on the way to the ruins of Teotihuacán. From downtown Mexico City, take Avenida Insurgentes Norte (Mex. 85-D) northeast to the Mex. 132-D turnoff. The route is pleasantly scenic, although slow going because of heavy bus and truck traffic.

CONVENT OF SAN AGUSTIN ACOLMAN is in the town center. This fortresslike structure displays Mexico's first plateresque ecclesiastic facade. Completed in 1560, the convent was restored after falling into disuse. Two sets of columns, with the statue of a saint between each, flank the elaborate entrance.

The immense building, with its beautiful frescoes, sculptures and cloister, has some of Mexico's best examples of Renaissance art. It also contains a small museum housing more paintings as well as artifacts. At Christmas the convent's chapel provides the setting for nativity plays, or *pastorelas*. Daily 9-6. Admission around $3 (U.S.).

CHURUBUSCO, DISTRITO FEDERAL (C-10)

After having fought valiantly on the side of Gen. Antonio López de Santa Anna in several battles of the U.S.-Mexican War, members of St. Patrick's Battalion—a group of Mexican sympathizers—met disaster in Churubusco (choo-roo-BOOS-coh) in 1847. American forces captured and hanged most of the battalion of 260 Irish immigrants who had deserted the U.S. Army to fight for Mexico.

Thankfully, Churubusco is much more tranquil today. Mexico's major film studios also are concentrated in this suburb just east of Coyoacán.

EX-CONVENT OF CHURUBUSCO is between Calz. de Tlalpan and Av. División del Norte (M: General Anaya, line 2). It was built in 1678 over the ruins of an ancient Aztec temple. This former Franciscan convent, which includes the Church of St. Matthew, served as a fortress against invading U.S. forces in August 1847. There are lovely gardens on the grounds of the restored structure.

National Museum of Interventions (Museo Nacional de las Intervenciones) is within the convent complex. It chronicles the exploits of those adventurers, pirates and foreign armies—the United States and France chief among them—who have invaded Mexico over the past 4 centuries. Weapons, flags, medals and other war memorabilia make up the displays. Exhibit information is in Spanish.

Guide service in English is available. Tues.-Sun. 9-6. Admission around $3.25 (U.S.); free to all Sun. Phone (55) 5604-0699.

COYOACAN, DISTRITO FEDERAL (C-9)

About 10 kilometers (6 miles) south of downtown Mexico City and west of Avenida Insurgentes Sur, Coyoacán (coh-yoh-ah-KAHN) lies on the northern edge of the Pedregal. Established in 1521 by Hernando Cortés, Coyoacán was the third seat of Spanish government in New Spain. The name is loosely derived from the Náhuatl Indian term *coyohuacan,* or "place of the coyotes." Francisco Sosa, the main thoroughfare, connects it with neighboring San Angel.

This is an artsy neighborhood where the stucco buildings are painted bright purple, blue and yellow. Tall trees line the narrow streets. Bookstores, sweet shops, restaurants and sidewalk cafés all compete for the stroller's attention. The area is very congested; the easiest way to explore it is to hire a taxi driver who will drive you there, wait while you have a look around and then take you back to your hotel.

On Plaza Hidalgo stands the Palace of Cortés, now the Town Hall (Delegación de Coyoacán). The Spaniards allegedly tortured Aztec emperor Cuauhtémoc at the palace in an effort to obtain treasure.

Also of interest are the 1583 Church of San Juan Bautista, the 1530 Dominican Monastery and the Alvarado House, now a private home. The Alvarado House belonged to Pedro de Alvarado, Cortés' right-hand man in his conquest of Mexico and later governor of Guatemala.

Two blocks east of Plaza Hidalgo on Calle Higuera is the Malinche House (Casa de la Malinche), the former home of Cortés' Indian mistress, interpreter and chief aide on his march through Mexico. Malinche, a major and much-maligned figure in Mexican legend, was supposedly condemned to 300 years of martyrdom for her act of betrayal. The solemn-looking dwelling sits across from Plaza de la Conchita, a peaceful little park.

DIEGO RIVERA MUSEUM (Museo Anahuacalli) is on the south side of the city, off Av. División del Norte at Calle del Museo #150 (M: Coyoacán, line 3). It was designed by Rivera and constructed from black volcanic stone. This stark, pyramidal building contains the muralist's vast personal collection of pre-Hispanic art. The Aztec and Toltec civilizations and the ancient city of Teotihuacán are well represented, and there is an outstanding collection of objects from the states of Colima, Jalisco and Nayarit.

Rivera also set up a studio on the upper floor of the building; mementos and works in progress now occupy the restored space. There are spectacular views from the building's hilltop location, particularly of twin volcanoes Popocatépetl and Iztaccíhuatl. Tues.-Sun. 10-6 (closed 2-3 p.m.). Admission around $2.25 (U.S.). Phone (55) 5617-3797.

FRIDA KAHLO MUSEUM (Museo Frida Kahlo) is at Calle Londres #247 (at the corner of Allende), 5 blocks north of Plaza Hidalgo (M: Coyoacán, line 3). This adobe house was the celebrated Latin American painter's lifelong residence; from 1929 until her death in 1954 she shared it with her husband Diego Rivera, Mexico's equally celebrated muralist. Through their tempestuous relationship Rivera and Kahlo forged the nucleus of contemporary Mexican art.

"Casa Azul" is an explosion of color, not the least of which is the cobalt-blue, red-trimmed exterior. Personal possessions include the four-poster bed in which Kahlo was born and died. *Calaveras* (papier-mâché skeletons) and carved death masks are reminders of the physical suffering that plagued Kahlo's everyday life and provided the fuel for her creativity. Works on display by this self-taught artist include some surrealistic self-portraits.

A spacious studio contains the artist's wheelchair, paintbrushes and an easel on which rests an unfinished portrait of Joseph Stalin. Wooden spoons and ceramic jugs and bowls fill the kitchen. Be sure to stroll through the garden, full of luxuriant vegetation, sculptures, pre-Hispanic pottery and descendants of Kahlo's beloved cats. There is a cafe on the museum's first floor. The surrounding neighborhood, with its bookstores and coffee shops, has a bohemian air well suited to this iconoclastic figure. Tues.-Sun. 10-6. Admission around $3 (U.S.). Phone (55) 5554-5999.

LEON TROTSKY MUSEUM (Museo Casa de Leon Trotsky) is north of Plaza Hidalgo at Av. Río Churubusco #410 (M: Coyoacán, line 3). The Russian revolutionary took up residence here after being exiled from the Soviet Union in 1929. He was murdered at home on Aug. 20, 1940. An axe-wielding assassin (a Spanish communist) accomplished the deed, which had been attempted months earlier when Stalinist sympathizers showered the house with a hail of bullets.

The fortresslike dwelling is capped with turrets once occupied by armed guards. Inside are Trotsky's modest belongings, preserved largely as he left them, and newspaper clippings recounting the event. Tues.-Sun. 10-5. Admission around $2.25 (U.S.), students $1; free to all Sun. Phone (55) 5554-0687 or (55) 5658-8732.

CUAUTLA, MORELOS (D-10)
pop. 140,400, elev. 4,198′

Cuautla (coo-WOW-tlah), popular with the Aztecs for its mineral springs, became a fashionable Spanish spa early in the 17th century. The city witnessed one of the most dramatic battles of Mexico's War of Independence when patriot José María Morelos and 3,000 rebels managed to withstand a 58-day siege by Royalist troops.

Some 31 kilometers (19 miles) south of Cuautla is Chinameca, the hacienda where Emiliano Zapata was assassinated; the site has been designated a national historic monument. Another historical site is Ayala, about 6 kilometers (4 miles) south of Cuautla. In 1910, Zapata issued a declaration of land reform here; later the townsite was a battlefield during the Revolution of 1910.

AGUA HEDIONDAS are about 3 km (1.9 mi.) east of town. The "stinking waters" are a series of connected thermal pools. Aztec emperor Moctezuma is said to have spent time improving his health in the spa's sulphurous waters. Facilities include swimming pools, bathhouses, dressing rooms, a pavilion and gardens.

LAS ESTACAS is southwest off Mex. 115. This popular swimming resort is built over several deep and powerful springs. Blue Wells Spring is a skin diving and snorkeling spot. The resort also contains three swimming pools, a wading pool, a restaurant, sports facilities and camping and picnicking areas. **Note:** Pools are normally drained on Monday for weekly cleanings.

At the entrance road to Las Estacas is the town of Tlaltizapán, which was the site of Emiliano Zapata's headquarters during the Revolution of 1910. The town's Zapata Headquarters Museum (Museum Cuartel General de Zapata) displays photographs, weapons and clothing, including the clothes Zapata had on when he was assassinated.

CUERNAVACA, MORELOS (C-9)
pop. 334,400, metro area 737,000, elev. 5,058′
See map page 228.

Capital of the state of Morelos, Cuernavaca (kwehr-nah-VAH-cah) is one of the most attractive spots in Mexico. Pink, blue and yellow houses with red-tiled roofs, luxuriant vegetation and brilliant flowers add to its charm. Many affluent Mexico City residents have second homes here, with swimming pools and extravagant gardens hidden behind high walls. Some of the homes are opened to the public on Thursdays during the first 3 months of the year.

At Mex. 95 and Avenida Fundadores a grand equestrian statue pays tribute to Emiliano Zapata, the leader of the Revolution of 1910. Zapata's battle cry of "Land and liberty, and death to the haciendados" struck at the great hacienda owners throughout the state. His Plan de Ayala, the beginning of a program toward agrarian reform, was signed near Cuautla on Nov. 28, 1911. In 1914 Zapata briefly joined Pancho Villa in occupying Mexico City before returning to Cuernavaca to prevent its seizure by federal troops.

Those maintaining summer homes in Cuernavaca over the centuries have included Aztec emperors, Hernando Cortés, Archduke Maximilian and his wife Carlota, various Mexican rulers and José de la Borda, the "silver king" *(see Taxco listing under Southern Mexico).* On the outskirts of town in the suburb of Acapantzingo is the Olvido House, Maximilian and Carlota's summer home. The restored structure is now known as the Municipal Herb Museum (El Museo de Herbolaria).

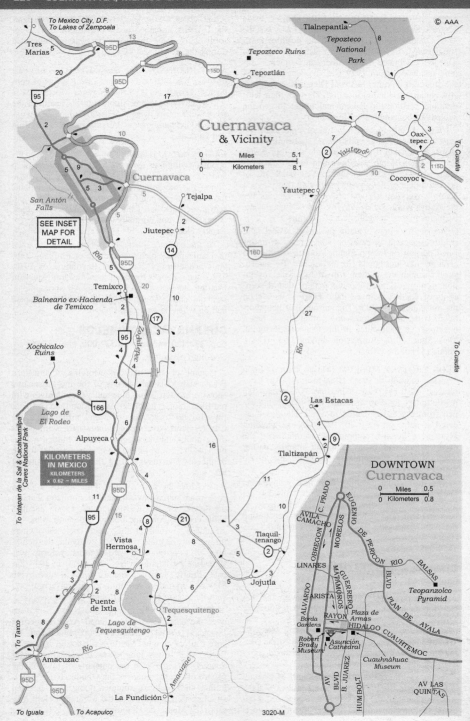

To Mexico City, D.F.
To Lakes of Zempoala

Tlalnepantla

Tepozteco
National
Park

© AAA

Tres
Marias

95D

13

8

Tepozteco Ruins

8

5

20

115D

Tepoztlán

13

95D

9

17

7

5

95

Cuernavaca
& Vicinity

7

3

Oax-
tepec

2

Yautepec

8

To Cuautla

115D

2

10

2

Miles   5.1
Kilometers   8.1

10

Cocoyoc

5

9

Cuernavaca

5

Tejalpa

Yautepec

5

3

2

San Antón
Falls

5

Jiutepec

2

SEE INSET
MAP FOR
DETAIL

14

17

160

Río

95D

5

To Cuautla

Temixco

20

10

Balneario ex-Hacienda
de Temixco

2

17

3

27

Xochicalco
Ruins

95

4

Río

N

4

3

4

4

To Ixtapan de la Sal & Cacahuamilpa Caves National Park

8

166

Lago de
El Rodeo

4

6

Las Estacas

2

Alpuyeca

6

4

KILOMETERS
IN MEXICO
KILOMETERS
x 0.62 = MILES

16

9

95D

11

Tlaltizapán

DOWNTOWN
Cuernavaca

95

15

4

8

21

10

Miles   0.5
Kilometers 0.8

Vista
Hermosa

1

8

3

Tlaquil-
tenango

EUGENIO

AVILA
CAMACHO

C. PRADO

SOTERO

DE PERICÓN

RÍO

4

1

6

5

2

OBREGÓN

MORELOS

BALSAS

3

3

6

5

Jojutla

LINARES

GUERRERO

BLVD

Teopanzolco
Pyramid

2

8

Puente
de Ixtla

ALVARADO

MATAMOROS

Plaza de
Armas

PLAN DE AYALA

8

9

Lago de
Tequesquitengo

2

ARISTATA

RAYON

Borda
Gardens

HIDALGO

CUAUHTEMOC

To Taxco

Río

7

Robert
Brady
Museum

Asunción
Cathedral

B. JUAREZ

Cuauhnáhuac
Museum

Amacuzac

AV
BLVD

HUMBOLT

AV LAS
QUINTAS

95D

Amacuzac

To Iguala

To Acapulco

La Fundición

3020-M

Quaint furniture, fine silver and leather articles, colorfully woven *huaraches* and straw hats can all be purchased in Cuernavaca; on market day wares are sold in the streets and plazas as well as at the market. The main plaza teems with vendors and also has restaurants and cozy cafés. Distinctive silver religious items are hand wrought by monks at the Emaus Monastery, Calle Laurel off Boulevard Zapata, and sold there on Sundays or in the atrium of the cathedral daily.

A colorful local fiesta is the Flower Fair, held the first week in April. It features exhibits and competitions in floriculture and gardening as well as a sound-and-light show and performances by popular entertainers.

Morelos State Tourism Office (Subsecretaría de Turismo): Av. Morelos Sur #187 in the Palmas neighborhood (south of the cathedral). Open Mon.-Fri. 8-5; phone (777) 314-3872 (English spoken). There also is a visitor kiosk on the cathedral grounds that is open daily.

What To See In and Around Town

ASUNCION CATHEDRAL (Catedral de la Asunción de María) is at avs. Hidalgo and Morelos, a block or so from the Borda Gardens. It was founded by Hernando Cortés in 1529 and is one of the oldest churches in Mexico. The cathedral was the focal point of activities by Franciscan missionaries in Far Eastern countries during the colonial era.

The interior was renovated in the 1960s in a spare, modern style, but remains of early frescoes can still be seen. At the back of the cathedral is the Chapel of the Third Order (Capilla de la Tercer Orden). Sculptures by Indian artists flank the atrium. Daily 8-2 and 4-10 p.m. Free.

BORDA GARDENS (Jardín Borda) are across Calle Morelos from the cathedral. They are part of the mansion, landscaped grounds and botanical gardens built by José de la Borda, a Frenchman who came to Mexico in 1716 and made a fortune in mining. Archduke Maximilian turned the palatial estate into his summer retreat in 1864. Borda is buried in the Church of Guadalupe (Parroquía de Guadalupe), next to the main house.

The gardens are formally laid out in a succession of terraces. The front buildings contain an art gallery; on the south side of the inner court is a cafe serving light snacks. Rowboats are available for rent. Tues.-Sun. 10-5:30. Admission around $1.25 (U.S.); free to all Sun.

CUAUHNAHUAC MUSEUM (Museo de Cuauhnáhuac) flanks the east side of the main plaza. This museum is housed in the Cortés Palace (Palacio Cortés), the former home of the Spanish conqueror. Begun in 1530, the medieval-style stone fortress has been considerably altered since that time.

The museum contains many interesting paintings and sculptures, as well as exhibits chronicling Mexico's evolution from the age of the dinosaur to contemporary Indians. Diego Rivera murals donated by former U.S. Ambassador Dwight Morrow depict the conquest of Mexico, the War of Independence and the Mexican Revolution of 1910. Tues.-Sun. 9-6. Admission around $2.50 (U.S.); free to all Sun.

LAKES OF ZEMPOALA NATIONAL PARK (Parque Nacional Lagunas de Zempoala) is 22 km (14 mi.) north on old Mex. 95 to the town of Tres Marías, then some 15 km (9 mi.) west on a narrow, winding road that passes the village of Huitzilac. The seven lakes comprising this national park—Zempoala, Compela, Tonatihagua, Quila, Hueyapan, La Seca and Ocoyotongo—lie about 9,500 feet above sea level. Some are stocked with trout, golden carp and bass. Several hiking paths radiate from the main open meadow. Camping is permitted. A toll is charged at a forest ranger station.

ROBERT BRADY MUSEUM (Museo Robert Brady) is next to the cathedral at Calle Netzahualcóyotl #4. The museum occupies Casa de la Torre, the former home of American artist Robert Brady (1928-86). Brady restored the 16th-century stone and adobe mansion, formerly a Franciscan convent. Within are more than 1,300 works of arts and crafts notable for their eclecticism.

Brady collected as well as created art, and the museum offers everything from Balinese masks to Mexican colonial carvings. Pieces from around the world are displayed on the shelves, walls and tables of 14 rooms, essentially as Brady left them. The bright yellow and deep red walls combine with the exuberantly colorful artwork for a surreal effect. Well-known artists represented are Diego Rivera, Rufino Tamayo, Frida Kahlo and several foreign painters influenced by Mexican art, among them Milton Avery and Marsden Hartley. Two patios are graced by sculptures and tropical plants; the main patio has a small cafe.

Guided tours in several languages are available by appointment. Allow 2 hours minimum. Tues.-Sun. 10-6. Admission 20 pesos (around $2 U.S.). Phone (777) 318-8554.

SAN ANTON FALLS (Salto de San Antón) are less than a mile west of the Borda Gardens. A walkway, where there are a few picnic tables, is cut into the rock behind the cascade. Clinging to a ledge above the falls is the tiny village of San Antón, where celebrated Cuernavaca pottery is produced. Tues.-Sun. 10-6. Free.

TEOPANZOLCO PYRAMID (Pirámide de Teopanzolco) is east of downtown near the railroad station, off Calle Río Balsas. Built by the Aztecs but never completed, it was discovered in 1910 during the Mexican Revolution, when a large hill on the outskirts of Cuernavaca was used as a platform for attacks on the city. Tremors resulting from gunfire shook away some of the earth and revealed the pyramid underneath, which surrounds an older pyramidal structure topped by the remains of two temples. Daily 9-5. Admission around $3 (U.S.); free to all Sun.

XOCHICALCO RUINS are about 37 km (23 mi.) southwest of Cuernavaca, reached by turning west onto Mex. 166 from Mex. 95 or Mex. 95-D at the town of Alpuyeca, then proceeding 8 km (5 mi.) beyond Alpuyeca on a paved road that winds north to the top of a mountain. The white-stone ruins, which cover about 6 square miles, are believed to have been a major pre-Hispanic ceremonial center.

The Pyramid of the Plumed Serpent (Pirámide de Quetzalcóatl) is the dominant structure, with well-preserved bas-reliefs and traces of hieroglyphs representing dates and eclipse signs. Close by is the entrance to a tunnel/maze that culminates in a stone-hewn, stepped chamber with a "telescope" orifice; through this aperture the astrologer-priests of Xochicalco were able to make corrections to their calendar.

Aside from its fortresslike position commanding views of the Valley of Cuernavaca, Xochicalco (so-chee-KAHL-coh, which means "place of flowers" in the Náhuatl Indian language) was possibly a communications center for drummed messages to and from the hinterlands. It was designated a World Heritage Site by UNESCO in 1999. Daily 9-5. Admission around $4 (U.S.); free to all Sun.

IXTAPALAPA, DISTRITO FEDERAL (C-10)

Long before it became a southeastern division of Mexico City, Ixtapalapa (ees-tah-pah-LAH-pah) was a flourishing Aztec town. Atop nearby Star Hill (Cerro de la Estrella), the Aztecs lighted fires to mark the beginning of their 52-year cycle. During the New Fire Ceremony, priests would ignite kindling on the chest of the unfortunate sacrificial victim. If the flame continued to burn, the continued existence of the world was assured. Flames would then be carried by runners to temples throughout the empire. Instead of human sacrifices, the hill today is the scene of a Passion Play performed on Good Friday.

The views of volcanoes Popocatépetl and Iztac-cíhuatl are exceptional from the hilltop; a road leads to the summit. Many visitors ascend the hill by foot, as there are caves and small ruins that can be explored along the way.

IXTAPAN DE LA SAL, MEXICO (D-9)
pop. 16,600, elev. 6,311'

Ixtapán de La Sal (ees-tah-PAHN deh lah SAHL) is a *balneario* (spa) town known for its warm mineral waters; bathing in them is certainly soothing, and reputed to aid arthritis and rheumatism as well. Public pools, flowing fountains, flowers and lush landscaping lend a cool, refreshing appearance to this popular resort. Golf, tennis, horseback riding and a variety of spa facilities are available at the Hotel Spa Ixtapan, which has been in business for more than 60 years.

The Balneario Ixtapan, off Mex. 55 (Boulevard Arturo San Román) next to the Hotel Spa Ixtapan, is a public spa along the lines of a Turkish bath. In addition to thermal pools of varying temperature

and such traditional spa treatments as massages and facials, it offers waterslides, a lazy river for inner tubing and other water park features.

Although Ixtapán de La Sal makes a nice day trip from either Taxco or Cuernavaca, weekends and holidays can be quite crowded. Tonatico, a town about 5 kilometers (3 miles) south via Mex. 55, also has swimming facilities.

STAR GROTTOES (Grutas de la Estrella) are about 12 km (7 mi.) south of Tonatico. They are most dramatic during the July-September rainy season, when waterfalls cascade among such spectacular rock formations as "The Holy Family" and "The Human Ear." Ancient Matlaltzinca Indians may have conducted religious ceremonies in the grottoes. Guided tours are possible along a lighted, protected footpath.

IZTACCIHUATL-POPOCATEPETL NATIONAL PARK, MEXICO (C-11)

Embracing the pass between Mexico's two most famous volcanoes, Iztaccíhuatl-Popocatépetl (shortened locally to Izta-Popo) National Park is about 83 kilometers (52 miles) east of Mexico City. Popocatépetl (po-po-kah-TEH-pet-el) and Iztac-cíhuatl (iss-tah-SEE-hwat-el) together form the Valley of Mexico's eastern rim. The volcanoes are Mexico's second and third highest mountains, and although located in a tropical latitude, both are high enough to be perpetually snowcapped.

Iztaccíhuatl (The White Lady), which rises 17,343 feet, is dormant. The mountain got its name from the legend of Popo, a warrior, and Izta, an Aztec princess, who fell in love and were turned into mountains by the gods, so the story goes, after Popo was betrayed by one of his enemies. Supporting the tale is the shape of Iztaccíhuatl, which bears a superficial resemblance to a reclining female form.

Immense quantities of sulphur have been taken from the crater of 17,887-foot Popocatépetl (The Smoking Mountain); Hernando Cortés' soldiers used it to make gunpowder. Aztec runners made daily trips up the mountain to fetch ice for Emperor Moctezuma's drinks and to preserve fish. The last significant eruption occurred in 1802, but sporadic spewings of ash resumed in December 1994 and have resulted in evacuations; Popo is off limits to the public.

The town of Amecameca, about 60 kilometers (37 miles) east of Mexico City via Mex. 190 and Mex. 115, lies at the foot of the national park at an elevation of about 7,500 feet. Although it doesn't offer much to do, there are views of Izta and Popo from the main plaza. From Amecameca, a paved road branches east to Cortez Pass (Paso de Cortés), a lookout point between the two volcanoes.

The Sanctuary of El Sacromonte (Santuario del Sacromonte) stands on a hill above Amecameca. From the arch on the southwest side of the plaza, walk about two blocks to the steps that ascend the hill to the sanctuary; the inspiring vistas en route are worth the effort.

Mexico City

Mexico City lies in the Valley of Mexico, or Anáhuac, a great basin about 60 miles long and 30 miles wide, bounded by mountains on all sides except the north. From the air, the vastness of the city sprawl is startling—a solid sea of buildings stretching across the valley floor to the distant horizon. The most conspicuous landmarks, however, are the snowcapped peaks of Popocatépetl and Iztaccíhuatl and to the southeast. The looming mountains hemming Mexico City in are chiefly responsible for creating the smog problem that threatens the environment. And at elevations ranging from about 7,200 to 8,000 feet, this is one of the world's loftiest cities.

Much of the valley, including the area occupied by Mexico City, is an old lake bed with no underlying bedrock. The combination of unstable subsoil and the volcanic nature of the region makes sinking and earthquakes the two greatest threats to the city's buildings. The metropolis, in fact, is settling under its own weight even as it continues to rise story upon steel, glass and stone story—although it only yields about an inch each year. But despite the preponderance of stone and concrete, Mexico City is surprisingly green (when it rains). Tamarind, cypress and rubber trees lines the streets, date palms adorn parks, clipped shrubs border sidewalks.

Earthquakes—the result of unfortunate geography—are in the back of every resident's mind. Mexico City's greatest natural catastrophe in modern times was the massive earthquake and aftershocks on Sept. 19 and 20, 1985. Some 10,000 people died, and scores of buildings were destroyed or later razed. There are still abandoned, decrepit structures here and there that were ruined but never torn down.

The entire city is designated a national historic monument, and the enormous *Zócalo*, or main square, is its centerpiece. (Although most Mexican cities and towns have a central plaza that may be locally referred to as the *zócalo*, it is only Mexico City's that receives the official designation.) It is the world's second largest public gathering place after Moscow's Red Square. Once a verdant green common strolled by privileged aristocrats, the *Zócalo* is now a vast expanse of concrete (the plaza was paved over during the Revolution of 1910) that, appropriately, is best known as a very public stage for political rallies.

Visitors will see sharp contrasts. As an important business center, Mexico City has a distinctly international air. In blatant contrast, however, are ragged children and the destitute elderly begging for a few coins, sad reminders of the rampant poverty suffered by millions trying to eke out a life. The green expanses of Chapultepec Park and the charm of colonial plazas are counterbalanced by the ceaseless noise and congestion of the city's traffic, some of the worst anywhere.

Zócalo / © Dallas and John Heaton / Stock Connection / PictureQuest

© Pictures & More / Alamy Images

But despite the big-city headaches, Mexico City is an enthralling experience. City residents are fond of saying—with an innate sense of pride—"*Como México no hay dos,*" or "There is no place like Mexico."

Historical Overview

Nomadic Indians from the north made their way to the Valley of Mexico in 1325 to fulfill a priestly prophecy: They were destined to settle where an eagle, carrying a serpent in its beak, was perched on a cactus (an image that appears on the Mexican flag). According to legend, that spot was an island in the middle of Lake Texcoco. Thus was the great capital of Tenochtitlan founded.

The Aztecs were named after their original homeland of Aztlán, thought by some archeologists to be the village of Mexcaltitlan in the present-day state of Nayarit. Built on a man-made island in a swampy lagoon area near the Pacific Coast, Mexcaltitán's layout resembles that of ancient Tenochtitlan. Soon they controlled the riches of the Valley of Mexico, an important trade center.

By the end of the 15th century Tenochtitlan was a beautiful and luxurious city of fountains, gardens and canals that encompassed the small islands dotting the lake. Eventual land reclamation resulted in the creation of one large island connected by causeways to the mainland and a political empire of Aztec nations. Tenochtitlan's population was about 300,000—possibly the world's largest city at its time. Then the Spanish arrived.

On Nov. 8, 1519, explorer Hernando Cortés became the first white man to enter Tenochtitlan's ceremonial center, today's *Zócalo*. One of world history's great mysteries is how an adventure seeker with a tiny band of followers could so successfully conquer the most aggressive warrior nation in the New World.

Although he led fewer than 400 men, Cortés was armed with formidable weapons; the sound of the Spanish cannons terrified the Aztecs. Furthermore, the Spaniards were aided by Indian allies only too eager to hasten the overthrow of their hated enemies. (The militant Aztecs exacted heavy payment from conquered tribes—gifts of tribute in large measure subsidized the lavish lifestyle of Tenochtitlan's inhabitants.) The presence of 16 horses, which the Aztecs took to be some sort of god-monsters, further awed and frightened them as well.

Moctezuma II, the Aztec emperor, met Cortés with rich gifts and offered no resistance to his entry into the city. He believed the Spaniard to be a divine envoy of Quetzalcóatl, the fair-skinned, golden-haired god of civilization who according to legend was to return in the year of One Reed (Ce Acatl). On the

(continued on page 235)

The Informed Traveler

City Population: 9,000,000, metropolitan area 20,965,400 (2002 estimate).

Elevation: 2,240 meters (7,347 feet).

Location: In south-central Mexico.

Highlights: Outstanding museums, notably the National Museum of Anthropology's collection of historical and cultural artifacts; magnificent colonial architecture, from ornate churches to stately mansions; the Polanco neighborhood's fashionable boutiques and fine dining; world-class performing arts, including music, theater, dance and folkloric productions.

WHOM TO CALL

Area Code: 55.

In Case of Emergency: *See In Case of Emergency p. 252.*

WHERE TO LOOK

Media

Tiempo Libre, published every Thursday, has information about restaurants, museums, galleries and cultural events. Major U.S. newspapers are available at many newsstands the day after they are printed.

The American Bookstore, Av. Francisco Madero #25 near Bolívar (M: Allende, line 2), has U.S. newspapers and magazines, books and an extensive selection of travel guides. The Sanborn's chain of drugstores also carries newspapers, magazines and books. Mexico City has numerous branches; one is in the House of Tiles, Av. Madero #4 (M: Bellas Artes, lines 2 and 8).

Visitor Information

Mexico Ministry of Tourism (Secretaría de Turismo, or SECTUR): Av. Presidente Masaryk #172 (ground floor), near the northeastern edge of Chapultepec Park in the Chapultepec Morales neighborhood (M: Polanco, line 7). Printed information can be obtained during office hours (Mon.-Fri. 8-6, Sat. 10-3), or phone (55) 5250-8555, ext. 111. A branch office is located at Av. Huevo León #56; phone (55) 5553-1901 or (800) 008-9090 (elsewhere within Mexico).

Contact SECTUR for answers in English to questions about tourist attractions, destinations and services. In Mexico City, phone (55) 5250-0123 or (55) 5250-0151; elsewhere within Mexico, phone (800) 903-9200 (toll-free long distance); from the United States phone (800) 482-9232. Phones are staffed 24 hours a day.

WHAT TO KNOW

Weather

Mexico City normally experiences no severe temperature extremes aside from a very occasional heat wave in May or early June. Days are generally sunny and pleasant and nights comfortably cool throughout the year. The arrival of spring somewhat diminishes the severe smog and pollution problem, which is exacerbated by the tremendous amount of automobile traffic. Afternoon showers are most likely from June through September.

Dress in the capital ranges from casual to elegantly formal, depending on your agenda. Expensive restaurants may require jackets and ties for men. A sweater, jacket or light topcoat is advisable for evenings or for trips to nearby mountain resorts.

Currency Exchange

While the rates charged by banks and *casas de cambio* (currency exchange offices) differ, they usually are better than the rates offered by hotels. Most banks exchange currency Mon.-Fri. 9-noon, but you may have to wait in line; exchange offices often are open weekdays until 5 and may be open Saturdays as well. Your hotel front desk is likely to be the most convenient option. Exchange offices are concentrated downtown near the major attractions, hotels and restaurants.

There are ATMs on Paseo de la Reforma in the vicinity of the Zona Rosa and in the Historic Center; almost all take Visa and MasterCard. Only use ATMs inside commercial establishments and be alert for suspicious behavior around the machine—criminals may target tourists withdrawing cash. Above all, do not make street transactions at night.

Aztec calendar, 1519 was that year. This case of mistaken identity brought about Moctezuma's downfall. Taking the ruler captive, Cortés and his troops remained in Tenochtitlan.

Sometime later, Moctezuma was wounded during a popular uprising by his people against the Spanish and died on June 30, 1520. On that evening, referred to as *La Noche Triste,* or "Night of Sadness," Cortés was driven from Tenochtitlan at the cost of about three-quarters of his force. The savagery of the hand-to-hand combat was horrific. It is said that Aztec warriors brandishing clubs embedded with shards of obsidian were able to decapitate the Spaniards' horses. The survivors, however, were allowed to escape, reaching Tlaxcala, an anti-Aztec stronghold.

After refortifying, open warfare ensued, marked by naval attacks on Lake Texcoco that cut off Aztec supplies and fresh water. After a long siege, the vaunted empire of the Aztecs collapsed with the fall of Tenochtitlan on Aug. 13, 1521.

The Spaniards built their own city atop the ruins of the capital, leaving the outer periphery to the vanquished. Aztecs gradually intermingled with the Spanish, resulting in *mestizos,* persons of mixed Spanish and Indian blood who comprise the great majority of Mexico's present-day population.

Although Spanish colonial rule was harsh, Mexico City benefited from the crown, becoming the most important city in New Spain and the capital of Spain's far-flung empire in the Americas. Lake Texcoco was gradually filled. Working together, Spanish and Indian architects developed a wildly ornamental baroque style that frequently utilized a light, porous volcanic rock known as *tezontle.* The 18th century—the golden age of Mexican architecture—produced some of the city's most impressive buildings.

Mexico City remained in the iron grip of Spanish rule for exactly three centuries, culminating in the decade-long fight for independence that followed *Grito de Dolores,* Father Miguel Hidalgo's impassioned speech advocating Mexican freedom, in 1810. It was finally taken by an army of patriots under Gen. Agustín de Iturbide, who entered the city on Sept. 27, 1821. Iturbide, a man hungry for power, appointed himself emperor of the new nation in 1822 and was crowned in Mexico City as Agustín I. His empire was short lived; in December 1822 the republic was proclaimed and Iturbide was forced to abdicate.

The Federal District was created in 1824 to centralize Mexico's new government. Mexico City continued as capital of the republic until the French installed Archduke Maximilian as emperor in 1864. His unhappy reign lasted three years, when, deserted by his original backer, Napoleon III, Maximilian was captured and executed. During these years, Benito Juárez was the president of Mexico's de facto liberal government, which instituted reform laws devoted to the separation of church and state. Besides raising living conditions in the country, he

took major steps to improve the physical layout of the capital.

It was during the 1860s that the first *colonias,* or residential districts, began to appear. Modernization began on a large scale during the reign of dictator Porfirio Díaz from 1876 to 1910. Mexico City benefited from the establishment of such amenities as electric lighting, streetcars and a drainage system. The Palace of Fine Arts (Palacio de Bellas Artes) and other monumental public buildings were constructed, their design modeled after prevailing European neoclassic styles.

As the governmental seat, the capital's history has obviously paralleled the history of the entire nation. Consequently, the political unrest that culminated in the Mexican Revolution of 1910 centered in the city. The protracted conflict turned the capital into a battlefield. But with only anarchy as a cause, the rebels, under their leaders Pancho Villa and Emiliano Zapata, occupied Mexico City in December 1914 for only a month; President Venustiano Carranza and his army soon returned to power.

Modernization continued after adoption of the Constitution of 1917, bringing a steady stream of impoverished *mestizos* and Indians from the countryside into Mexico City. They crowded into working-class *colonias,* while the creation of such luxurious residential districts as Lomas de Chapultepec (Chapultepec Hills) housed the wealthy few. Skyscrapers began to define the city's skyline in the 1930s.

One early renewal project was the relief of the centuries-old water shortage in the capital. The springs of Laguna del Río Lerma, beyond the mountains west of the city in the Valley of Toluca, now bring water by aqueduct to reservoirs in Chapultepec Park. The first sections of a modern subway system were completed in 1971; today the Metro's nine lines provide efficient and inexpensive city transportation. Construction of the system also brought to light some ancient archeological treasures, notably the Templo Mayor, or Great Temple of the Aztecs.

Since German traveler Baron Alexander von Humoldt described 18th-century Mexico City as a city of palaces centered on the *Zócalo,* the capital has expanded to become a metropolis. In addition to its business and commercial districts, Mexico City is honeycombed with hundreds of separate residential neighborhoods. In the last half of the 20th century the metropolitan area exploded in all directions, incorporating such former towns as Churubusco, Coyoacán, Ixtapalapa, San Angel, Tlalpan, Villa de Guadalupe and Xochimilco.

Approaches

By Air

Benito Juárez International Airport is in the northeastern part of the city, about 6 kilometers (4

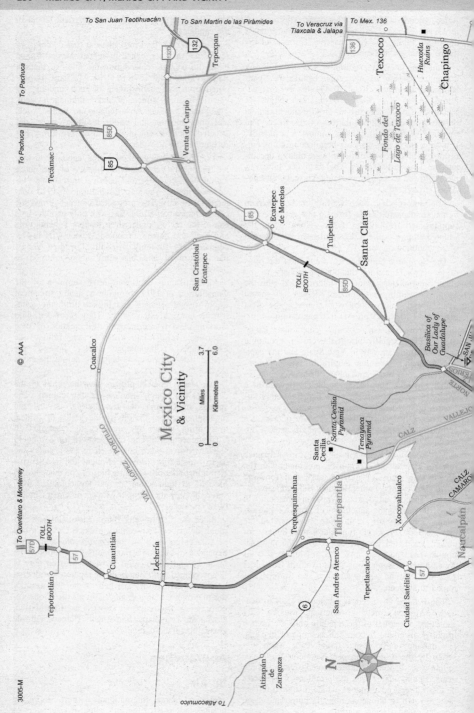

Mexico City & Vicinity

3005-M

© AAA

To Puebla, Oaxaca & Guatemala Border

To Puebla &

190

1900

150D

115

TOLL
BOOTH

ESTADO DE MEXICO

DISTRITO FEDERAL

136

San Vicente
Chicoloapan

Los Reyes

Chalco

Mixquic

190

San Juan
Ixtayopan

To Milpa Alta

Nezahualcóyotl

Acatitla

Acahualtepec

Santa Cruz
Meyehualco

Tlaltenco

Tlahuac

Tulyehualco

San Antonio
Tecómitl

Benito Juárez
International Airport

CALZ IGNACIO ZARAGOZA

Zapotitlán

San Luis
Tlaxialtemalco

San Gregorio
Atlapulco

San Juan
De Aragón

O DE
ADALUPE

Parque Nacional
Cerro de
la Estrella

Canal de
Cuemanco

Dolores Olmedo Patiño
Museum

Floating
Gardens

Santa Cruz
Alcapixca

San Andrés
Ahuayucan

ERMITA IZTAPALAPA

Ixtapalapa

Xochimilco

Nativitas

AV CONSULADO

A. MADERO

CHURUBUSCO

RIO

CALZ

TASQUEÑA

Southern
Bus Terminal

Tepepan

Santiago
Tepalcatlapan

TOLL
BOOTH

95D

95

FRANCISCO
MORAZAN

RAYON

FRAY SERVANDO
TERESA DE MIER

ANTONIO
ABAD

AV

Churubusco

CALZ

DE TLALPAN

CHURUBUSCO

DIVISION DE NORTE

To Cuernavaca,
Taxco & Acapulco

Xicalco

CARDENAS

LAZARO

SAN

UNIVERSIDAD

AV

CALZ

RIO

Coyoacán

Frida Kahlo
Museum

Diego Rivera
Museum

Netzahualcoyotl

Azteca
Stadium

Cuicuilco
Pyramid

Tlalpan

San Miguel Ajusco

DE LA REFORMA

AV INSURGENTES

CHAPULTEPEC

VIADUCTO

SAN ANTONIO

DIAGONAL

INSURGENTES
SUR

University
City

Convent of
El Carmen

Olympic
Stadium

EL PEDREGAL

PASEO

AV

CUBA

CALZ
M CAMACHO

MEXICO

Polyforum
Siqueiros

Plaza México
(Bullring)

San Ángel
(Villa Alvaro Obregón)

PERIFERICO

ANILLO

Contreras

AV AVILA
CAMACHO

Hippodrome
of the Americas

AV
CONSCRIPTO

Chapultepec
Park

AV CONSTITUYENTES

LOS LEONES

HIGHWAY CLOSED
FROM 6 PM TO
7 AM DAILY

DESIERTO DE

Cuajimalpa

San Bartolo
Ameyalco

Cuarto
Dinamo

130

134

San Rafael
Chimalpa

ESTADO DE MÉXICO
DISTRITO FEDERAL

15

La
Venta

CALZ

Desert
of the
Lions
National
Park

To Toluca

For Your Information

Guides/Tours

The services of a good guide can be expensive but invaluable, particularly for the first few days in this huge city. If you go with this option, obtain the services of a bonded guide licensed by the Secretaría de Turismo (the Mexican Ministry of Tourism, or SECTUR). Ask to see his or her official guide card marked with "Departamento de Turismo" and take special note of the expiration date to the right of the photograph. Additional fees are charged for guided trips outside Mexico City.

Taxi drivers also can function as a driver/bodyguard/guide, even if it means waiting by the car for an hour while you stroll one of the city's tourist-friendly neighborhoods. The rate begins at about $10 (U.S.) an hour; it goes up if the trip ventures outside Federal District borders. Most visitors will find the peace of mind that comes from not having to negotiate city traffic or use public transportation well worth the expense.

miles) east of the *Zócalo*. Some 35 airlines, both international and domestic, maintain regular flights to and from Benito Juárez.

Aeroméxico, (55) 5133-4010 or (800) 021-4010 (toll-free long distance within Mexico), and Mexicana, (55) 5448-0990 or (800) 509-8960 (toll-free long distance within Mexico), offer service from U.S. cities. Alaska Airlines, American, America West, Continental, Delta, Northwest, United and US Airways offer direct flights to Mexico City from Houston.

Numerous facilities cater to foreign travelers, including lockers for storing baggage; Ladatel (long-distance) phones (including some that accept international credit cards), rental car agencies, ATMs and *casas de cambio* (currency exchange offices), branches of the Mexican banks Banamex and Bancomer, car rental agencies (including Hertz), travel agents, restaurants and a variety of gift and duty-free shops.

The airport's hotel reservations service can book a room according to location and price specifications. There is no charge for making a reservation, but advance payment for one night is required. Authorized baggage handlers are identified by the "Union" ID placard attached to their hand carts. For airport information phone (55) 5571-3600.

Contact the airline directly when making reservations for flights to other cities within Mexico, or if you need price or schedule information. This can be frustrating if you reach someone who doesn't speak good English; airline numbers also change frequently. If possible, make all flight arrangements prior to your departure; then the only reason you may need to call is to confirm times.

When departing Mexico City, make sure to allow for sufficient travel time to the airport—a minimum of 45 minutes if you're based in the downtown area. Arrive at least an hour before departure for domestic flights, 90 minutes before departure for international flights. If you have an early morning flight, staying at the Marriott Aeropuerto is convenient; an elevated skywalk connects the hotel and Terminal B. For additional information about airlines *see "Arriving by Air," page 551.*

Authorized airport taxis are the safest way to reach the downtown area. The vehicles, sedans or minivans, have a black aircraft symbol on the door and are labeled "*Transportación Terrestre*" (Ground Transportation). Taxis require pre-payment at the official airport taxi counter; look for the "*Transportación Terrestre*" sign inside or just outside the terminal.

Rates are based on a zone system and vary according to distance. Beware of overcharging; confirm the rate by consulting the posted map, or ask to see a map if one isn't posted. Yellow-outfitted escorts show you to an available taxi; tickets are given to the driver. Do not negotiate with anyone who approaches you with the offer of a ride into town. There are no buses that travel directly to the city center.

If you're traveling light, you might consider using Metro, Mexico City's rapid transit system. Large pieces of luggage aren't likely to be allowed on board, however, and riding a crowded subway car weighed down with anything more than an overnight bag is not only cumbersome but unsafe. The airport station is Terminal Aérea (Air Terminal Building, line 5) on Boulevard Puerto Aéreo, a few minutes' walk from the main terminal; follow the signs. To reach the downtown area, take the subway to the Pantitlán station and switch to line 1.

By Car

Mex. 15-D, 57/57-D and 85-D are the major highways approaching Mexico City from the west and north. From the south and east come Mex. 95-D and Mex. 150-D. Other routes are likely to be slow, winding or of substandard quality, and one—Mex. 134, which travels northeast to Mexico City from Mex. 200 along the Pacific Coast—should be avoided entirely.

Leaving the city, the main thoroughfares are Avenida Insurgentes Sur, which becomes Mex. 95-D as it heads south to Cuernavaca, Taxco and Acapulco; running north, Avenida Insurgentes Norte becomes Mex. 85-D/85 heading toward Pachuca. The Periférico, which loops around the city's western and southern sides, is called Avenida Avila Camacho within the city and becomes Mex. 57-D heading northwest toward Querétaro. Avenida Constituyentes runs west past Chapultepec Park and becomes Mex. 15 as it heads toward Toluca; Calzada Ignacio Zaragoza leads east out of the city, becoming Mex. 190-D as it heads toward Puebla.

Try to time both arrival and departure times into and out of Mexico City as early in the morning as possible to avoid the near-constant traffic.

Note: Seat belt use by the driver and all passengers is required within the Federal District.

By Bus

With interconnections between Mexican and U.S. bus lines, it is possible to travel economically by bus from several U.S. border cities to Mexico City. Transportes del Norte, Tres Estrellas de Oro, Transportes Chihuahuenses and Omnibus de México are linked with Greyhound Lines Inc. From Tijuana it takes about 40 hours to reach Mexico City; from Ciudad Juárez, across the border from El Paso, Tex., about 24 hours; from Matamoros, across the border from Brownsville, Tex., about 14 hours.

Bus travel is available from Mexico City to nearly every town in the republic, but reservations must be made. Most major Mexican lines offer first-class (lujo) bus service; these companies include Autobuses Cristóbal Colón, Autobuses del Oriente (ADO), ETN, Omnibus de México, Primera Plus and Tres Estrellas de Oro. **Note:** Arrivals and departures at bus stations in Mexico are usually announced in Spanish only. For additional information about buses see "Bus Service," page 68.

For Your Information

Guides/Tours (continued)

Staying Safe

Street crime—from relatively benign offenses like pickpocketing and purse snatching to dangerous armed robbery—is an ever-present risk. No part of the city is immune, even the upscale Polanco neighborhood and other areas frequented by tourists. Do not wander around anywhere after dark, especially alone.

If you're going out for the evening, arrange designated hotel taxi transportation to and from your destination, particularly if you're unfamiliar with your surroundings. If you start feeling uneasy on the street, go to the nearest hotel or restaurant. But for safety's sake, it's advisable to arrange any excursion—even if only several blocks away—with a driver affiliated with your hotel.

Taxi robberies are among the most frequently reported crimes; never hail a circulating cab on the street. The Zona Rosa and the area behind

Digital Archives

the U.S. Embassy are particularly vulnerable to street crime against foreigners; also avoid taxis parked in front of the Palace of Fine Arts.

The capital's size and unfamiliarity can put you off your guard. Enjoy yourself, but stay alert at all times. Keep close watch over money, cameras or any other valuables in your possession, and avoid carrying large amounts of cash. Also see "Taxis" under "Getting Around" and "Health and Safety," page 71.

Mexico City has four main bus terminals that correspond to the four compass points. Each terminal has luggage storage facilities, a post office, ATMs, a cafeteria and long-distance (Ladatel) telephones.

By far the largest of the four is the Terminal Central de Autobuses del Norte, Av. Cien Metros #4907 (M: Autobuses del Norte, line 5). Most of the buses traveling from the northern border arrive at this terminal, also known as "Terminal Norte" or "Camiones Norte." From here, buses travel to almost every destination north of the capital, including the Pacific Coast resorts from Manzanillo northward; inland cities such as Aguascalientes, Guadalajara, Guanajuato, Monterrey, Morelia, Querétaro and San Miguel de Allende; and the nearby archeological sites of Teotihuacán and Tula.

The terminal offers currency exchange services (during normal banking hours) and has a hotel reservations booth. Taxis charge standard fares based on a zone system; tickets are purchased at booths inside the station. Count your change carefully, as overcharging is common.

Terminal de Autobuses de Pasajeros de Oriente (TAPO) is at Calzada Ignacio Zaragoza #200, near the airport (M: San Lázaro, line 1). The most modern of the four stations, it handles buses to and from such eastern destinations as Jalapa, Puebla, Veracruz, Villahermosa and cities on the Yucatán Peninsula, as well as Oaxaca, San Cristóbal de las Casas, Tuxtla Gutiérrez, Guatemala and other places to the south. Taxi ticket booths and currency exchange services are available.

Terminal Central de Autobuses del Sur is at Av. Taxqueña #1320 (M: Taxqueña, line 2). At the end of Metro's line 2, this also is a major terminus for local city buses from downtown and other points north. From here buses arrive and depart for Acapulco, Cuernavaca, Ixtapa/Zihuatanejo, Taxco and other points south of Mexico City. For day trips to Cuautla, Cuernavaca or Tepoztlán, take one of the Pullman de Morelos buses, which leave frequently for each of these tourist destinations. Estrella de Oro has first-class service to Acapulco and Zihuatanejo. The terminal also has a travel agency.

The smallest of the four is the western station, Terminal de Autobuses del Poniente, Av. Sur #122 at Tacubaya (M: Observatorio, line 1). This is the easiest way to take a day trip to Toluca by bus. Service also is available to Morelia and Guadalajara; the going is slow but the scenery is pleasant.

Getting Around

City Layout

Mexico City's *colonias*, or neighborhoods—more than 300 of them—are served by a maze of *calles*, *avenidas* and *calzadas*. Some narrow alleyways, or *callejones*, are cobblestoned relics from earlier days. Major thoroughfares, on the other hand, can have eight lanes.

Most of the signs tend to be more confusing than enlightening. There is no real logic to the city's streets, which are named after rivers, mountains, foreign cities and countries, musicians, writers, doctors, composers, the states of Mexico and just about everything else. They also change names frequently.

A system of connected highways combine to form the Circuito Interior, which roughly encircles the central city. Beginning at the airport, on the east side of town, Avenida Río Consulado runs north and then west, becoming Calzada Melchor Ocampo. Ocampo swings south, passing east of Chapultepec Park and intersecting Paseo de la Reforma, at which point it continues as Calzada Vasconcelos. Angling off Vasconcelos is Avenida de la Revolución, which runs south to Avenida Río Churubusco. Churubusco then proceeds east before turning north to connect with Río Consulado, southwest of the airport, and completing the circuit.

Theoretically, this loop provides a less congested alternative to the jam-packed streets within it. However, these roads themselves are usually crowded, particularly during the morning and evening rush hours.

Also within the Circuito Interior are axis roads *(ejes)*, a series of numbered boulevards running one way only, with special lanes reserved for trolleys and buses circulating in the opposite direction. East-west Eje 1 Norte and Eje 2 Norte are north of the Zócalo, Eje 2 Sur through Eje 8 Sur run progressively south of the Zócalo. North-south Eje 1 through 3 Oriente are east of Eje Central Lázaro Cárdenas, which divides the central city in half; Eje 1 through 3 Poniente are to the west.

The most magnificent of the broad principal arteries that intersect the central city is the Paseo de la Reforma. A legacy of French emperor Maximilian, it runs southwest to northeast for more than 7 miles. From the eastern end of Chapultepec Park to past Alameda Park, Reforma is exceptionally wide and beaded with monument-adorned *glorietas* (circles).

One good point of reference is the Independence Monument at the intersection of Reforma, Florencia and Tiber. The 150-foot-tall spire, topped by a gold angel, is easy to spot. Another is the major intersection at Paseo de la Reforma and Avenida Insurgentes, marked by the Cuauhtémoc Monument.

Insurgentes, the capital's longest thoroughfare, runs north/south, bisecting western and eastern sections of the city. East-west Viaducto Miguel Alemán runs south of downtown, connecting Calzada Ignacio Zaragoza at the eastern end of the city with the Anillo Periférico at the western end. The Periférico (Mex. 57) traverses the city's western and southern sections.

Driving just about anywhere within Mexico City is a daunting prospect and not recommended. The sheer number of vehicles makes for an extremely slow pace. Add to that aggressive tactics (the locals often disregard traffic signals), frequent construction, detours and a plethora of one-way streets, and visitors are far better off relying on taxi transportation provided by their hotel. Above all, never drive alone after dark due to the risk of car hijacking, robbery or assault.

If circumstances dictate that you must drive, carry a good city map and always park the vehicle in a guarded lot. Street parking is not only rare but chancy, as vandalism often occurs. Any vehicle parked illegally is likely to have its license plate removed by police; expect to pay a fee to get it back. Never leave valuables in your car, even if hidden.

Note: Motorists in Mexico City who are stopped for a red light at many downtown intersections are besieged by everyone from beggars to performing children (whose parents are often sitting on a nearby corner) to vendors selling newspapers, flowers, candy and trinkets. The best defense if you're part of this captive audience is to keep your door locked, your window rolled up and look straight ahead, avoiding eye contact.

Speed limits are shown in kilometers. If a road, avenue or street is unmarked, follow these general guidelines: school zones, 20 km/h (10-12 mph); residential streets, 30 km/h (20 mph); main streets, 50 km/h (30 mph); avenues, bypasses, loop roads and overpasses within the city, 60 km/h (35 mph); main roads, 100 km/h (60 mph); selected main roads and toll roads, 110-120 km/h (65-75 mph).

Taxis

Major hotels maintain fleets of *turismo* taxis associated specifically with the hotel. These can be used for short hops from your hotel to a nearby restaurant and back, or for longer excursions to shop or sightsee. For an hourly rate (and normally a 2-hour time minimum), you can arrange to have the driver wait at a specific location in addition to providing transportation. Rates for individual trips are negotiated with the driver; establish the fee for any excursion in advance. Although *turismo* taxis are expensive (a ride just a few blocks in length can cost several dollars), the peace of mind is well worth the cost.

J.R. Taxi is a reliable service; the driver speaks English, is familiar with all of the city's major tourist attractions and can pick passengers up at the airport or at designated bus stations. Phone (044) 5100-7542 (cellular number) within Mexico, or (55) 5100-7542 outside of Mexico.

If your hotel doesn't provide transportation or you otherwise need a cab, the U.S. Embassy strongly urges that you ride only in a taxi summoned by phone from a designated *sitio* (SEE-tee-oh) stand. They are considered safer than taxis that circulate because the driver can be easily traced back to the stand. Many of the stands list telephone numbers where the taxi can be called. Arrangements also can be made to have these cabs pick you up at a predetermined time and place.

Ask for the license plate number and the cab driver's name, and only use cabs with plates beginning with the letter "S," which are assigned to a particular site—such as a hotel—and registered. The number on the license plate should match the number painted on the side of the cab. Avoid the green and white Volkswagen Beetle taxis that constantly cruise the streets (often referred to as *ecologicos* or *magna sins*), or cabs with license plates containing the letter "L" (*libre* cabs). Never hail a cab on the street.

Authorized taxis at the airport and at bus stations charge fees based on a zone system; tickets to pay the fee are purchased at booths inside the terminal. *Also see "Approaches—By Air," page 235.*

Rental Cars

There are many car rental agencies in Mexico City. The larger companies also have branches in major cities where you can leave your car at trip's end. Be sure you fully understand the terms of any rental contract, especially in regard to insurance coverage. It's much less expensive to reserve before you leave home; make reservations at least 1 week in advance. AAA/CAA members enjoy discounts through Hertz for vehicles booked in the United States. Consult your local AAA/CAA club or phone Hertz, (800) 654-3080.

Note: Although having a vehicle at your disposal can be convenient for sightseeing trips outside the metropolitan area, keep in mind that a rental car driven by a foreigner may unfortunately become a target for police who will try to extract a bribe.

Vehicles in the Mexico City metropolitan area, including the Distrito Federal (Federal District) and parts of the state of Mexico, may *not* be driven on certain days based on the last digit of the license plate. Make certain your rental car can be driven when you wish to use it. A rental agency may inadvertently provide a vehicle with a license plate with a last digit that corresponds to the day on which it cannot be driven. For additional information, *see the "Day Without Car Program" box on page 246.*

Buses

City buses go just about everywhere and are inexpensive, but the system is not user-friendly for visitors. Routes and bus numbers change frequently, and route maps are practically nonexistent. Some signs at the downtown bus stops bear route descriptions. Buses run daily 5 a.m.-midnight, but show up much less frequently after 10 p.m.

Two major bus routes put visitors within walking distance of many of the city's attractions. The east-west route links the *Zócalo* with the National Auditorium in Chapultepec Park and continues to the Observatorio Metro station (line 1), traveling along avenidas Francisco I. Madero and Juárez and Paseo de la Reforma. These buses are usually marked *"Zócalo."*

Buses running north-south along Avenida Insurgentes connect the huge Terminal Norte station with the southern suburbs of San Angel and University City via the Zona Rosa. These buses are usually marked *"Indios Verdes-Tlalpan."* Routes are marked on the windshield.

Never carry valuables onto a city bus, and know exactly where you're going before you board. But unless you simply want to have the experience, it's safer and much more convenient to use a taxi associated with your hotel for getting around.

Peseros

These green-and-white vehicles resemble a minibus or van. *Peseros,* also called *colectivos,* travel along established routes and charged fixed rates (according to distance) that are a bit more than the bus but less than taxi fares. Route destinations (often a Metro station) are marked on the windshield or shown on a sign. Flag down a *pesero* as you would a bus, and tell the driver your destination when you board.

Major routes include the principal east-west and north-south tourist corridors (the *Zócalo* to Chapultepec Park and Avenida Insurgentes Sur, respectively). This is an alternative to the crowded and often chaotic city buses, although using a designated taxi is still the safest way to travel.

Metro

Metro—one of the world's busiest subway systems—is faced with the formidable task of moving some 6 million riders daily over both surface and subterranean track. The nine lines cover most of the city. In addition, a *tren ligero* (light rail) line provides service to the popular tourist attraction of Xochimilco.

Line 1 runs roughly west-east from the Observatory, near Chapultepec Park, to Pantitlán in the eastern suburbs, passing south of the Zona Rosa and the *Zócalo.* Subway riders bound for the airport switch to line 5 at the Pantitlán station. Line 2 begins in the northwest part of the city at the Cuatro Caminos station, proceeds east, burrows under the *Zócalo* and then runs above ground due south to the Taxqueña station.

Line 3 runs from the Indios Verdes station, north of the Basilica of Guadalupe, south past Alameda Park to University City (National University of Mexico campus). Line 4 runs north-south east of downtown, from the Martín Carrera to the Santa Anita stations. Line 5 runs from the Politécnico station south to the La Raza station, then east and south to Pantitlán, with a stop (Terminal Aérea) at the airport. **Note:** To switch from line 3 to line 5—or vice versa—at the La Raza station requires a 10- to 15-minute walk through a long tunnel.

Line 6 runs north of downtown, proceeding east from the El Rosario station to the Martín Carrera station via the Instituto del Petróleo and Deportivo 18 de Marzo stations. Line 7 runs north-south along the city's western edge from the El Rosario station to the Barranca del Muerto station. Line 8 runs from the Garibaldi station (one stop north of the Bellas Artes station on line 2) south and east to the Constitución de 1917 station, in the southeast section of the city. Line 9 parallels line 1 and runs south of it, from the Tacubaya station in the west to the Pantitlán station in the east.

Two additional lines provide light rail service. Line A runs from the Pantitlán station (the eastern terminus of lines 1, 5 and 9) south to the La Paz station; Line B serves the Buenavista Railroad Station and runs east to the Garibaldi station (the northern terminus of line 8), then north to the Ciudad Azteca station. The *tren ligero* line runs south from the Taxqueña station south to Xochimilco. The two lines most helpful to visitors are Lines 1 and 2, as they cover major sightseeing points of interest.

The flat fare, which includes transfers, is 2 pesos (about 20 cents U.S.). Tickets, which are valid indefinitely, are purchased at booths at the stations; the magnetically encoded stub allows passage through the turnstiles. If you plan on using the system, purchase several tickets at one time to avoid spending time standing in lines.

You also can purchase an *abono* ticket, which allows use of the entire system for a multiple-day period. (With this type of ticket, enter Metro stations only through the blue turnstiles; otherwise the ticket will be taken and not returned.)

At the stations, on signs and in guidebooks and brochures, Metro lines are designated by the following colors: lines 1 and A, bright pink; line 2, blue; line 3, olive green; line 4, light blue; line 5, yellow; line 6, red; line 7, orange; line 8, dark green; and line 9, brown. You can consult a color-coded subway guide at Metro information booths, or try obtaining a map of the system from the ticket booths at the larger stations.

The rubber-wheeled trains are fast and frequent, and the stations are modern. But keep in mind that Metro is used daily by millions for commuter travel, so sardine-can conditions usually prevail. During weekday rush hours (both morning and evening) the trains are crammed and guards are employed to control the crowds; avoid using the system during these times.

Single women, unfortunately, may have to fend off unwelcome advances or inappropriate male conduct. Foreign visitors are prime targets for pickpockets and purse snatchers, especially at stations near major tourist sights. There are separate cars for women and children during rush hours, but regulations are not strictly enforced.

Although it can be convenient to use the subway for sightseeing, especially to get to Xochimilco or the southern neighborhoods of Coyoacán and San Angel, for safety's sake it's best to hire a taxi affiliated with your hotel if you intend to visit these areas. If you do need to take Metro for any reason, make certain you know which direction the train is heading. Check the signs on the loading platforms *(andenes);* they denote the last station on the line in each direction. For example, *Dirección Pantitlán* and *Dirección Observatorio* indicate the last stations for line 1. Transfer gates, where more than one line shares a subway station, are marked *Correspondencia;* exits, *Salida.*

Metro is least crowded on weekends and holidays. In general trains begin running at 5 a.m.

METRO LINES

El Rosario
7 6
Tezozomoc
Aquiles
Serdán
Azcapotzalco
Ferrería
Norte 45
Vallejo
Camarones
Refinería
Politécnico
5
Instituto del Petróleo
Lindavista
Indios Verdes
3
Basílica
La Villa
6 4
Martín Carrera
Talisman
Bondojito

N

B
Ciudad Azteca
Plaza Aragón
Olímpica
Tecnológico
Muzquiz
Río de los Remedios
Impulsora
Continentes
Villa de Aragón
Bosque de Aragón
Deportivo Oceanía

Autobuses del Norte
Potrero

Cuatro
Caminos
2
Panteones
Tacuba
Cuitlahuac
Popotla
San Joaquín
Colegio Militar
Normal
Polanco
Auditorio
Constituyentes
San Cosme
Revolución
Juárez

La Raza
Misterios
Valle Gómez
Consulado
Eduardo Molina
Aragón
Oceanía

Garibaldi
8
Lagunilla
Tepito
Canal del Norte

Tlatelolco

Buenavista
Guerrero
B
Hidalgo
Bellas Artes
Allende
Morelos
Romero Rubio

Terminal Aérea
(Benito Juárez International Airport)

Hangares

San Juan de Letrán
Zócalo

Gran Canal

Balderas
Cuauhtémoc
Insurgentes
Sevilla
Chapultepec
Juanacatlán

Salto del Agua

Pino Suárez
Merced

Moctezuma
Balbuena
Aeropuerto
San Lázaro
Gómez Farías
Zaragoza

Pantitlán
1 5

Niños Héroes
Doctores
Obrera

Isabel la Católica
Candelaria
San Antonio Abad
Fray Servando

Tacubaya
1 9
Observatorio
San Pedro de los Piños
San Antonio
Mixcoac

Hospital General
Patriotismo
Chilpancingo
Centro Médico
Etiopía
Eugenia
División del Norte
Zapata

Chabacano
Lázaro Cárdenas
Viaducto
La Viga
Xola
Villa de Cortés
Nativitas
Portales
Ermita
General Anaya

Jamaica
Mixihuca
Velódromo
Ciudad Deportiva
Puebla
9 A

Santa Anita
Coyuya
Tezontle
Apatlaco
Aculco
Escuadrón 201
Atlalico
Iztapalapa
Cerro de la Estrella
La Purísima
Constitución de 1917
8

4

Barranca del Muerto
7
Coyoacán
Viveros
Miguel A. de Quevedo
Copilco

Universidad
3

Taxqueña
2

La Paz
A
Tren Ligero

Mon.-Fri., 6 a.m. Sat.-Sun. They run until at least midnight Sun.-Fri., later on Sat. Luggage and backpacks are technically not permitted on any of the subway cars, nor is the taking of photographs allowed.

Note: Points of interest and other locations described in the text for Churubusco, Coyoacán, Mexico City and San Angel include, where applicable, the name of the individual Metro station (M) and the subway line (1 through 9). Attraction listings without this designation are located away from Metro routes.

What To See

Note: To make it easier to plan a sightseeing itinerary in this sprawling city, the following attraction listings are grouped under nine separate, geographically based subheadings, and are spotted on three different maps. For a map of the greater Mexico City metropolitan area, see pages 236-237; for downtown Mexico City, see pages 248-249; for the Centro Histórico area, see page 256.

Around the Zócalo

CALLE MONEDA begins just east of the *Zócalo* at Av. Seminario (M: Zócalo, line 2). It takes its name from the country's first mint, which now houses the National Museum of the Cultures (*see attraction listing*).

Many of the colonial-era buildings lining this thoroughfare, one of the city's oldest, are constructed of *tezontle*, the reddish volcanic rock used by the Aztecs to build their pyramids and temples. Near the *Zócalo* they are carefully refurbished but become more dilapidated as the street heads east. Vendors add to the bustle of this downtown corridor, which is closed to traffic and therefore pleasant to stroll (during daylight hours only).

GRAN HOTEL is just west of the *Zócalo* at Av. 16 de Septiembre #82 (M: Zócalo, line 2). This five-story marble structure is an example of turn-of-the-20th-century architecture. The grand lobby is worth a peek; it features a spectacular Tiffany skylight and gilded, open-cage elevators.

GREAT TEMPLE (Templo Mayor) encompasses a city block just north of the *Zócalo;* the site entrance is on Av. Seminario (M: Zócalo, line 2). The only available parking is a commercial underground garage near the Palace of Fine Arts. The Great Temple, or Teocalli, of the Aztecs was a monumental pyramid that served as the religious, political and sacrificial center of the Aztec empire. The ruins, located in the heart of today's metropolis, are striking evidence of a separate civilization that flourished hundreds of years earlier.

Demolished and buried by the conquering Spaniards, the structure—originally thought to be beneath the nearby Metropolitan Cathedral—was rediscovered in 1978 by a subway construction worker. The excavated ruins reveal successive layers of older temples, each built atop the other as the

Aztecs consolidated their empire, and include other structures as well as a stone replica of a *tzompantli,* or wall of skulls. Plaques in Spanish explain the origin of the different temples. **Note:** Visitors must proceed through the complex in one direction and are not permitted to turn around and go back once inside the site.

Allow 1 hour, 30 minutes minimum. Site open Tues.-Sun. 9-4:30. Admission (includes site and museum) around $3.70 (U.S.), over 65 and under 6 free. The charge to use a video camera is $3.50. Phone (55) 5542-0606.

Great Temple Museum (Museo Templo Mayor) is at avs. Guatemala and Seminario within the site. The museum provides a valuable historical perspective, especially for those unfamiliar with Aztec lore. On display are more than 7,000 items recovered from the site and locations as far away as the present-day states of Veracruz and Guerrero. There are eight exhibit rooms (*salas*) on three levels, organized around a central open space dominated by the original discovery, the enormous stone depicting a beheaded and limbless Coyolxauhqui.

Among the more impressive artifacts are life-size, terra-cotta eagle warrior statues and stone masks that were offered as tributes by subjugated tribes. Open same hours as the site.

▼◢**GEM** **METROPOLITAN CATHEDRAL** (Catedral Metropolitana) is on the north side of the *Zócalo* (M: Zócalo, line 2). This enormous church seems even bigger rising up from the vast expanse of the *Zócalo*. A church built in 1525 was demolished in 1573 to make way for the present structure, which was not completed until 240 years later. The exterior presents a mingling of architectural styles, from baroque ornamentation to a neoclassic clock tower.

Along the interior side aisles are 14 chapels variously adorned with statuary, ornate altars, paintings, gilded surfaces, priceless tapestries and various representations of Christ, including a black Christ figure. The Chapel of the Kings, at the end of the nave behind the main altar, is graced by gilded wood carvings and an extravagantly Churrigueresque altarpiece. **Note:** Visitors to the cathedral (or any church in Mexico) should respect those who are there to worship.

All manner of crystals, herbs, gemstones and religious paraphernalia are sold in front of the cathedral. On the west side more vendors set up shop, selling everything from crafts to Mexican jumping beans, and laborers sit on the curb next to small signs advertising their trade. A sound-and-light presentation, "Voices of the Cathedral," features actors and musicians in period costume. Performances are Wed. at 8:30 p.m. Tickets are available through Ticketmaster; phone (55) 5325-9000. Daily 7-7. Free.

Sacristy (El Sagrario) adjoins the cathedral. This church, built in the mid-18th century to house vestments and sacred relics, has an elaborate baroque facade. Both the Sacristy and the cathedral were damaged in the 1985 earthquake, and each has tilted noticeably over decades as they ever so slowly sink into the underlying lake bed. Ongoing work to repair the effects of uneven settling has been successful, however, and some of the ever-present scaffolding that seemed to have become a permanent part of the cathedral has been removed.

MEXICO CITY HISTORIC CENTER (Centro Historico de México) is the area that radiates out from the *Zócalo*. It has been the city's hub since its founding by the Aztecs in 1325. Cortés and his followers decimated the Indian structures, building their own monuments atop the rubble. Today the district—designated a World Heritage Site by UNESCO in 1987—encompasses more than 1,500 historic structures, including the Templo Mayor, or Great Temple of the Aztecs, the National Palace and the Metropolitan Cathedral.

A multitude of businesses, including the National Pawn Shop, operate amid restaurants, museums, theaters, churches and the ubiquitous street vendors, who peddle everything from lottery tickets to holy water. Some of the streets around the *Zócalo*, where restoration efforts are ongoing, are closed to vehicular traffic. Visitors, at any rate, will definitely want to explore on foot.

MUNICIPAL PALACE (Palacio del Ayuntamiento) faces the *Zócalo's* south side (M: Zócalo, line 2). It serves as City Hall. The original building at the square's southwest corner dates from 1724. On the front arcade are coat-of-arms mosaics depicting Mexican cities, states and regions, including Coyoacán, site of the first city hall in the Valley of Mexico; the 1325 founding of Aztec capital Tenochtitlán; and the Villa Rica de la Vera Cruz, said to be the first city hall in the continental Americas. Inside are archives and portraits of Mexican rulers.

NATIONAL MUSEUM OF CULTURES (Museo Nacional de Las Culturas) is at Calle Moneda #13, near the cathedral and just east of the *Zócalo* (M: Zócalo, line 2). This museum once displayed the Mexican archeological treasures now housed at the National Museum of Anthropology in Chapultepec Park *(see attraction listing on page 255)*. Now it focuses on non-Mexican cultures, with exhibit halls grouped around a central patio. Especially notable are the African and South Seas groups. A striking Rufino Tamayo mural in the lobby depicts the 1910 Revolution.

Tues.-Sun. 9:30-5:30. Free. Phone (55) 5512-7452.

NATIONAL PALACE (Palacio Nacional) is along Av. Pino Suárez and faces the east side of the *Zócalo* (M: Zócalo, line 2). It has housed the offices of government officials since 1821. It took Diego Rivera some 25 years to execute the sweeping, lavishly detailed historical murals decorating the upper level of the central courtyard and the walls of the main staircase, which depict everything from romantically idealized views of Aztec life before the arrival of Hernando Cortés to the bloody 1910 Revolution.

Hanging over the central doorway is the Independence Bell, tolled by Father Miguel Hidalgo in 1810 to proclaim Mexican independence from Spain; on Sept. 15 Mexico's president rings the bell in an annual ceremonial re-enactment of Hidalgo's plea for freedom.

There also are two museums inside the palace. The Benito Juárez Museum consists of several large rooms displaying furnishings, manuscripts, artwork and other artifacts associated with the former Mexican president; the Parliamentary Museum has elegant fabric-covered walls, gold chandeliers, flags and the formal "well" used for parliamentary sessions. At the palace's far end is a relaxing garden with benches and stone fountains.

Allow 1 hour, 30 minutes minimum. Tues.-Sun. 9-4:30. Free (personal identification is required).

NATIONAL PAWN SHOP (Nacional Monte de Piedad) is near the northwest corner of the *Zócalo* at Monte de Piedad and Av. 5 de Mayo (M: Allende or Zócalo, line 2). This four-story, colonial-style structure stands on the site of Axayacatl, an Aztec palace occupied by the emperor Moctezuma and later entirely rebuilt by Hernando Cortés. The pawn shop was established in 1775 to provide poor citizens with loans on personal property at low interest rates, and houses a vast quantity of antiques and other merchandise. Mon.-Fri. 8:30-6, Sat. 8:30-3.

ZOCALO is bounded by avs. Corregidora, Seminario (Pino Suárez), Madero and Monte de Piedad (M: Zócalo, line 2). The *Zócalo* (SOH-cah-loh), or Plaza de la Constitución, is a vast, open expanse of concrete covering nearly 10 acres; only Moscow's Red Square is larger. Emperor Moctezuma's palace and the Templo Mayor stood on the site when the Spanish made their way into the city of Tenochtitlán and proceeded to tear it to the ground.

The *Zócalo* (the word means "base of a pedestal") follows the Spanish blueprint for colonial settlements staked out in the Americas: a central plaza surrounded by a cathedral and government buildings. A Mexican flag stands in the center of the square; residents come here to protest as well as to celebrate and stroll.

Special events are held regularly. An elaborate flag-lowering ceremony performed daily at 6 p.m. is filled with the flourishes of formal pomp and circumstance. Hundreds of thousands of people flock to the square for the Sept. 15 and 16 Independence Day celebrations. (For a panoramic view of either proceeding, sit outside on the seventh-floor dining terrace at the Majestic Hotel, Avenida Madero on the west side of the *Zócalo*.)

Note: This is a very crowded, congested part of the city. Do not even attempt to negotiate the traffic or find a place to park on your own. If you want to walk around and explore for an hour or so, hire a licensed guide, a private driver or a hotel taxi to drop you off, wait and then take you back to where

"Day Without Car" Program

In a continuing effort to reduce air pollution, city government officials in 1989 established driving restrictions on all vehicular traffic, including vehicles carrying non-Mexican registration and regardless of license plate origin. The restriction is based on the last digit of a vehicle's license plate and pertains to the days of the week. It is in effect throughout the Mexico City metropolitan area, which includes the Distrito Federal (Federal District) and parts of the state of México.

Vehicles may not be driven on certain days according to the following schedule: MONDAY—license plates that end with 5 or 6; TUESDAY—license plates that end with 7 or 8; WEDNESDAY—license plates that end with 3 or 4; THURSDAY—license plates that end with 1 or 2; FRIDAY—license plates that end with 9 or 0. All vehicles may be driven SATURDAY and SUNDAY. The restrictions **do not** apply from 11 p.m. to 5 a.m. Failure to comply with "Day Without Car" (Hoy No Circula) regulations will result in vehicle impoundment and a hefty fine.

These restrictions are ongoing and apply to both permanent and temporary plates. **There is no specific provision regarding plates with letters only.** If you are visiting Mexico City and plan to rent a car and drive anywhere in the greater metropolitan area, contact the rental car agency in advance and make certain the vehicle can be driven when you wish to use it. For information about designated no-driving days, contact the agency LOCATEL in Mexico City; phone (55) 5658-1111.

you're staying. Avoid the *Zócalo* and surrounding streets after dark.

Within the Historic Center

CHURCH AND HOSPITAL OF JESUS THE NAZARENE (Iglesia y Hospital de Jesús Nazareno) are 3 blocks south of the *Zócalo* on República del Salvador between 20 de Noviembre and Pino Suárez (M: Pino Suárez, lines 1 and 2). The first hospital in Mexico is said to stand on the site where Hernando Cortés and Aztec emperor Moctezuma had their first meeting in 1519; a stone monument on Pino Suárez next to the church commemorates the occasion. The chapel has an entrance on Salvador at Pino Suárez; inside are Cortés' remains. A plaque marking the tomb of the *conquistador* can be seen on the left wall of the main altar.

The dramatic José Clemente Orozco mural "Apocalypse" covers the ceiling and upper walls of the church's choir mezzanine. Mon.-Sat. 7 a.m.-8 p.m., Sun. 7-1 and 5-8. Free.

EX-CONVENT AND TEMPLE OF REGINA COELI (Ex-Convento y Templo de Regina Coeli) is about 5 blocks southwest of the *Zócalo* at calles Regina and Bolívar (M: Isabel la Católica, line 1). Construction began in 1655, although it was not consecrated until 1731. Once the Convent of the Nuns of the Conception in Mexico, it received its present name in 1756.

The sumptuous Medina-Picasso Chapel, built in 1733, encompasses an entire block and is considered a masterpiece of Churrigueresque architecture. It contains three altarpieces with works by Villalpando Rodríguez Juárez and other 18th-century painters. A striking niche in the main altar is adorned with tortoiseshell and mother-of-pearl.

FORMER COLLEGE OF SAN ILDEFONSO (Ex-Colegio de San Ildefonso) is north of the Great Temple at Justo Sierra #16 (M: Zócalo, line 2). This outstanding colonial edifice was built in 1749 as the Jesuit School of San Ildefonso. Converted to a museum, the renovated structure has three floors exhibiting colonial works of art, paintings by Fernando Leal and David Alfaro Siqueiros, and traveling exhibitions.

José Clemente Orozco murals depicting post-Revolutionary Mexico surround the main patio. The Patio of the Undergraduates (Patio de Los Pasantes), with just three corridors, has a small courtyard featuring Orozco and Diego Rivera murals painted in the 1920s. Tues.-Sun. 10-5:30. Admission around $3.25 (U.S.).

ITURBIDE PALACE (Palacio de Iturbide) is west of the *Zócalo* at Av. Madero #17 near Bolívar (M: Bellas Artes, lines 2 and 8). Commissioned by the Count of San Mateo de Valparaíso as a dowry for his daughter, this building exhibits the characteristic 18th-century baroque architectural style, with some Italian influence. It became a hotel in 1850 and was purchased by the National Bank of Mexico (Banco

Nacional de México) in 1966. It now houses the Banamex Cultural Promotion Institution.

The interior features an elegantly colonnaded courtyard. Daily 10-7. Free (a current ID is required to enter the palace).

JOSE LUIS CUEVAS MUSEUM (Museo José Luis Cuevas) is at Calle Academia #13, 2 blocks east of the *Zócalo*. The former Convent of Santa Inés was completed in 1612. The richly carved doors on the corner of Called Moneda depict the saint's life and death and portraits of the convent's founders. Cuevas, a highly regarded contemporary artist, created the monumental sculpture "The Giantess" that stands in the center of the courtyard. Of the museum's approximately 3,000 works, about a third are by Cuevas. Tues.-Sun. 10-6. Admission around $1 (U.S.).

MINISTRY OF PUBLIC EDUCATION (Secretaria de Educación Pública) is north of the Great Temple at República de Argentina #28 (M: Zócalo, line 2). The walls of this building were perhaps Diego Rivera's greatest canvas; almost every space on the three floors is covered with murals symbolizing Mexican life, history and culture.

The first floor contains images of daily rural life, depictions of industry and the celebration of such truly Mexican festivities as the Day of the Dead. Notably missing from these scenes is Rivera's customary political satire; instead, he emphasized national pride. Panels on the second and third floors focus on Mexican workers, the nation's heroic leaders, the 1910 Revolution and such familiar Rivera targets as capitalist greed. Mon.-Fri. 9-6. Free.

MUSEUM OF MEXICO CITY (Museo de la Ciudad de México) is 3 blocks south of the *Zócalo* at Pino Suárez #30, near República del Salvador (M: Pino Suárez, line 2). The building housing this museum was built shortly after the Spanish conquest as a private residence for the Count of Santiago de Calimaya. Constructed of reddish *tezontle* stone, it features timbered ceilings and friezes of cannons protruding from the outer walls. Supporting the building's northeastern corner, at Pino Suárez and Salvador, is a huge pre-Hispanic sculpture of a plumed serpent's head representing the god Quetzalcóatl.

In addition to some exhibits chronicling the city's history, the museum displays works by Mexican impressionist Joaquín Clausell. Tues.-Sun. 10-5. Free.

SANTO DOMINGO CHURCH (Iglesia de Santo Domingo) is on República de Venezuela (M: Allende, line 2), facing the north side of Santo Domingo Plaza. The original church, destroyed by a flood, was the first founded in Mexico by the Dominicans. The present building, dating from 1736, has a beautiful baroque exterior highlighted by ornately carved Corinthian columns. Inside is a chapel containing *milagros*, offerings given by the

"Day Without Car" Program (continued)

Physically disabled drivers are not exempted from the regulation. If you're driving your own vehicle, keep in mind that police officers in jurisdictions within the greater metropolitan area may stop drivers with foreign plates for "violating" driving restrictions in an attempt to extract a bribe. Signs explaining the program are posted along major highways entering the metropolitan area. Many of the signs, however, are in Spanish. There is a Web site that provides air quality reports and related information; the address is www.sima.org.mx.

Note: When pollution is extremely heavy (particularly during the winter months), emergency driving restrictions may be mandated. "Double Day Without Car" (Doble Hoy No Circula) means that driving is prohibited a second day during the week, based on whether the last digit of the license plate is odd (1, 3, 5, 7 or 9) or even (2, 4, 6, 8 or 0). Before any such decision is made, announcements are broadcast on radio and TV specifying the contingency days added to the normal restriction, and those vehicles affected.

Digital Archives

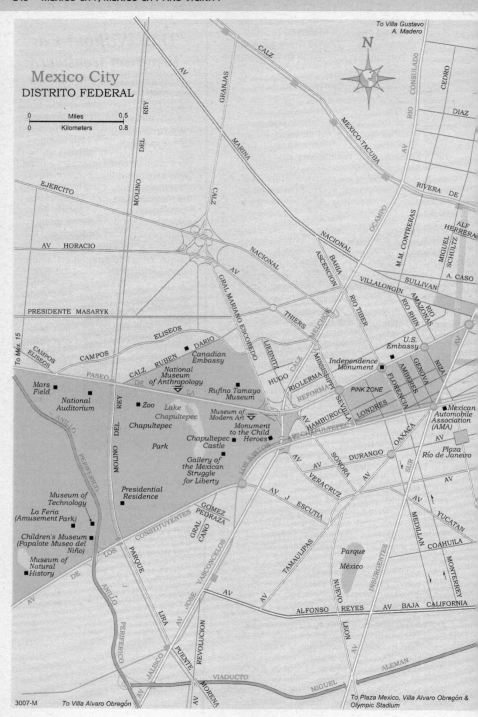

Mexico City
DISTRITO FEDERAL

| 0 | Miles | 0.5 |
| 0 | Kilometers | 0.8 |

To Villa Gustavo A. Madero

N

CONSULADO

CEDRO

RIO

DIAZ

CALZ

GRANJAS

AV

REY

DEL

MOLINO

MARINA

CALZ

MEXICO-TACUBA

RIVERA DE

EJERCITO

NACIONAL

OCAMPO

M.M. CONTRERAS

ALF HERRERA

MIGUEL SCHULTZ

AV HORACIO

NACIONAL

AV

GRAL MARIANO ESCOBEDO

ASCENCION

BAHIA

VILLALONGIN

SULLIVAN

A. CASO

PRESIDENTE MASARYK

THIERS

MELCHOR

RIO TIBER

RIO RHIN

RIO AMAZONAS

ELISEOS

DARIO

LIBERTAD

U.S. Embassy

NIZA

CAMPOS ELISEOS

CALZ RUBEN

Canadian Embassy

HUGO

MISSISSIPPI

RIOLERMA

Independence Monument

GENOVA

AMBERES

FLORENCIA

To Mex. 15

CAMPOS

National Museum of Anthropology

Rufino Tamayo Museum

REFORMA

SEVILLA

PINK ZONE

PASEO

DE

LA

Museum of Modern Art

HAMBURGO

LONDRES

Mexican Automobile Association (AMA)

Mars Field

National Auditorium

Zoo

Lake Chapultepec

Monument to the Child Heroes

AV CHAPULTEPEC

AV

Plaza Río de Janeiro

ANILLO

REY

DEL

MOLINO

Chapultepec Park

Chapultepec Castle

LOS SANTOS

OAXACA

SUR

AV

Gallery of the Mexican Struggle for Liberty

AV

DURANGO

SONORA

MEDELLIN

YUCATAN

PERIFERICO

Presidential Residence

VERACRUZ

AV

Museum of Technology

GOMEZ PEDRAZA

AV J ESCUTIA

COAHUILA

La Feria (Amusement Park)

CONSTITUYENTES

GRAL CANO

TAMAULIPAS

Parque México

INSURGENTES

MONTERREY

Children's Museum (Papalote Museo del Niño)

LOS

PARQUE

VASCONCELOS

NUEVO

Museum of Natural History

DE

JOSE

AV

AV

REYES

BAJA CALIFORNIA

ANILLO

PERIFERICO

LIRA

REVOLUCION

ALFONSO

LEON

AV

JALISCO

PUENTE

MORENA

VIADUCTO

MIGUEL

ALEMAN

3007-M   To Villa Alvaro Obregón

To Plaza Mexico, Villa Alvaro Obregón & Olympic Stadium

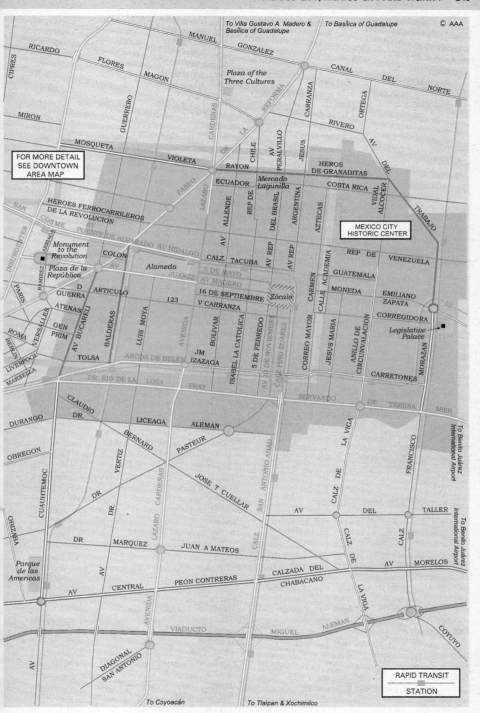

© AAA

To Villa Gustavo A. Madero &
Basílica of Guadalupe

To Basílica of Guadalupe

MANUEL GONZALEZ

RICARDO

CIPRES

FLORES

MAGON

GUERRERO

MIRON

CARRANZA

CANAL   DEL   NORTE

Plaza of the
Three Cultures

MOSQUETA

VIOLETA

RAYON

LA REFORMA

DE CARDENAS

CHILE

AV PERALVILLO

JESUS

RIVERO

AV DEL

ORTEGA

AV TRABAJO

FOR MORE DETAIL
SEE DOWNTOWN
AREA MAP

ECUADOR

Mercado
Lagunilla

COSTA RICA

HEROS
DE GRANADITAS

SAN COSME

HEROES FERROCARRILEROS
DE LA REVOLUCION

PUENTE DE ALVARADO AV HIDALGO

ARBEGA

ARRAGA

PASEO

LAZARO

AV ALLENDE

REP DE

DEL BRASIL

AV REP

ARGENTINA

AZTECAS

VIDAL ALCOCER

INSURGENTES

Monument
to the
Revolution

COLON

CALZ. TACUBA

AV REP

CALLE ACADEMIA

REP DE VENEZUELA

MEXICO CITY
HISTORIC CENTER

Plaza de la
República

RAMIREZ

AV

Alameda

5 DE MAYO

AV MADERO

GUATEMALA

PARIS

D
GUERRA

ARTICULO

JUAREZ

16 DE SEPTIEMBRE

Zócalo

CARMEN

MONEDA

EMILIANO
ZAPATA

ATENAS

123

V CARRANZA

CORREGIDORA

ROMA

GEN
PRIM

AV BUCARELI

BALDERAS

LUIS MOYA

AVENIDA

BOLIVAR

ISABEL LA CATOLICA

5 DE FEBRERO

AV 20 DE NOVIEMBRE

CALLE PINO SUAREZ

CORREO MAYOR

JESUS MARIA

ANILLO DE
CIRCUNVALACION

Legislative
Palace

MORAZAN

BERLIN

LIVERPOOL

VERSALLES

TOLSA

ARCOS DE BELEN

JM
IZAZAGA

CARRETONES

MARSELLA

DR. RIO DE LA   LOZA

FRAY

SERVANDO   DE   TERESA

MIER

DURANGO

CLAUDIO
DR.

LICEAGA

ALEMAN

AV LA VIGA

To Benito Juárez
International Airport

OBREGON

BERNARD

PASTEUR

LAZARO CARDENAS

SAN ANTONIO ABAD

CALZ DE LA VIGA

FRANCISCO

CUAUHTEMOC

VERTIZ

JOSE T CUELLAR

TALLER

To Benito Juárez
International Airport

DR.

DR

AV

DEL

CALZ

Parque
de las
Americas

DR

MARQUEZ

JUAN A MATEOS

CALZ DE

AV   MORELOS

VERACRUZ

AV

CENTRAL

PEON CONTRERAS

CALZADA DEL
CHABACANO

LA VIGA

AV

VIADUCTO

MIGUEL   ALEMAN

COYUYO

DIAGONAL
SAN ANTONIO

To Coyoacán

To Tlalpan & Xochimilco

RAPID TRANSIT
STATION

devout in thanks for a miraculous cure from infirmity or disease.

SANTO DOMINGO PLAZA is 3 blocks northwest of the Zócalo, bounded by República de Venezuela, República de Peru, República de Chile and República de Brasil (M: Zócalo, line 2). It is one of the best preserved colonial squares in the city. Dating from about 1550, the plaza is surrounded by charming old buildings. It also is the home of *los evangelistas*. These professional typists, writers and editors ply their trades from under arcades on the west side of the plaza, a service begun by public scribes in the 1850s for citizens unable to write.

Museum of Mexican Medicine (Museo de Medicina Mexicana) is at the opposite end of the plaza at Brasil and Venezuela. It is housed in the former headquarters of the Inquisition Palace (Palacio de la Inquisición). For more than two centuries, Mexican heretics and those who opposed Spanish rule were punished in the palace's dungeons. Exhibits chart Mexico's medical advances from pre-Hispanic herbal cures to modern vaccines. Daily 10-6. Free.

SUPREME COURT OF JUSTICE (Suprema Corte de Justicia) is just south of the National Palace at Pino Suárez and Corregidora. Built between 1935 and 1941 at the site of ancient Plaza del Volador, this building has a sober exterior, but the interior features an interesting set of staircases leading to the Hall of Lost Steps (Salón de los Pasos Perdidos), which contains two José Clemente Orozco murals depicting workers' rights, nationalism and concepts of justice.

Calle Corregidora runs between the court building and the National Palace. Prior to the Spanish conquest a canal traversed this area, part of a system that connected Tenochtitlán to other Aztec centers around Lake Texcoco. Today evidence of the ancient waterway can still be seen, although Corregidora is now a pedestrian-only thoroughfare filled with vendor stalls. Court open Mon.-Fri. 9-5:30. Free.

Alameda Park and Vicinity

ALAMEDA PARK lies just west of the Palace of Fine Arts between avs. Juárez and Hidalgo. Two Metro stations are close by: Hidalgo (lines 2 and 3) is at the intersection of Hidalgo and Paseo de la Reforma, a block off the park's northwest corner; Bellas Artes (lines 2 and 8) is at the park's northeast corner. A green retreat in the middle of Mexico City's concrete jungle, this rectangular, centrally located park—formerly an Aztec market—is surrounded by museums, theaters, hotels and restaurants.

Landscaped with poplars, ash and willow trees, the Alameda contains fountains, 19th-century French sculptures and a Moorish kiosk. Sundays bring out the crowds, with families, cotton candy and ice cream vendors, and lovers of all ages sharing the park. Organ grinders delight children, and there are free music concerts.

Juárez Monument (Juárez Hemiciclo) faces Av. Juárez along the park's southern boundary. "Hemiciclo" refers to the monument's semicircular design. It honors the liberal president of Mexico (1858-72); his marble statue sits on a pedestal surrounded by columns. Benito Juárez's March 21 birthday is celebrated at the park.

CHURCH OF THE CONVENT OF CORPUS CHRISTI is at Av. Juárez #44, opposite the south side of Alameda Park (M: Bellas Artes, lines 2 and 8). Part of the first convent to accept noble indigenous women and the daughters of Indian chieftains, this sober baroque building was later a training college for teachers and until 1985 housed the National Museum of Popular Art and Industries. The central portal has arched doors flanked by pilasters supporting a cornice and a small pediment.

DIEGO RIVERA MURAL MUSEUM (Museo Mural Diego Rivera) is at calles Balderas and Colón, just west of Alameda Park (M: Hidalgo, lines 2 and 3). It was built specifically to house the epic mural "Dream of a Sunday Afternoon in the Alameda Central," which had originally been painted on a wall of the Hotel del Prado across the street. Although the hotel was torn down following damage caused by the 1985 earthquake, the mural weathered the disaster and was carefully moved to this museum.

The central figures—among a gallery of Mexican historical characters—enjoying a Sunday promenade in the park are the artist (portrayed as a child); his wife, fellow painter Frida Kahlo; and a clothed skeleton representing satirist José Guadalupe Posada. Tues.-Sun. 10-6. Admission around $1.50 (U.S.); free to all Sun. Phone (55) 5510-2329.

FRANZ MAYER MUSEUM (Museo Franz Mayer) is at Av. Hidalgo #45 (Plaza de la Santa Veracruz), opposite the north side of Alameda Park (M: Bellas Artes, lines 2 and 8). A former convent dating from the second half of the 16th century, it was a hospital for much of its existence until closing in 1966; in 1989 it was restored to house an enormous and valuable collection of viceregal, European and Asiatic paintings and sculptures.

Among the objects on view are ceramics, silver, textiles, maps and navigation instruments. The museum also organizes temporary exhibits. Food is available. Tues.-Sun. 10-5. Admission around $1.50 (U.S.); free to all Tues. Phone (55) 5518-2265.

HOUSE OF TILES (Casa de Los Azulejos) is at Av. Francisco I. Madero #4, about 2 blocks east of the Alameda (M: Bellas Artes, lines 2 and 8). This is one of the city's finest colonial mansions. It was built in 1596 to be the residence of the Counts of Orizaba. The entire exterior is covered with decorative blue and white tiles from Puebla; the bronze balustrade was brought from China.

The flagship of the Sanborn's restaurant chain has occupied the building since 1919. Stop in for a look at the murals in the main dining room and the José Clemente Orozco mural that adorns the wall of the huge staircase. Daily 7 a.m.-1 a.m.

LATIN-AMERICAN TOWER (Torre Latino Americana) is at avs. Madero and Lázaro Cárdenas (M: Bellas Artes,-lines 2 and 8). At 595 feet, this slender, 44-story glass skyscraper was once the city's tallest but now ranks fourth. The tower rests on floating piers sunk deep into the underlying clay; as the city's first building to have an adequate foundation, it has survived every earth tremor that has occurred since its 1956 construction. The 40th floor has a bar that offers a panoramic vista.

Admission is charged to the observation deck at the top of the structure, where rare smog-free days offer magnificent views of the city and the surrounding mountains. Daily 9:30 a.m.-11 p.m. Observation deck admission around $3.50 (U.S.), children $3; tickets can be purchased at a booth near the elevators. Phone (55) 5130-2832.

MAIN POST OFFICE (Correo Mayor) is on the corner of avs. Tacuba and Eje Central Lázaro Cárdenas across from the Palace of Fine Arts (M: Bellas Artes, lines 2 and 8). Designed by Italian architect Adam Boari—who also was responsible for the Palace of Fine Arts—and in operation as a post office since 1907, this building incorporates Gothic, Moorish, Renaissance, Spanish and Venetian elements. The facade is covered with yellow-rose quarry stone from the state of Hidalgo. Most of the interior ironwork, banisters and furnishings were imported.

Within the building, the Philatelic Museum (Museo Filatélico) displays stamp collections and antique Mexican postal equipment. The post office also is the point of reference for the city's street numbering system. Museum open Mon.-Fri. 9-6, Sat. 10-2.

NATIONAL ART MUSEUM (Museo Nacional de Arte) is at Calzada Tacuba #8, directly east of the Palace of Fine Arts (M: Bellas Artes, lines 2 and 8). Formerly the Hospital of San Andrés and later the Palace of Communications, this building's gray stone facade is enhanced by wrought iron and wooden doors and window frames. The museum provides an overview of Mexican art, its 24 halls exhibiting works ranging from 17th- and 18th-century paintings of New Spain through 19th-century landscapes and portraits to 20th-century modernism.

Particularly noteworthy are the rooms devoted to José Guadalupe Posada and María Asúnsolo. Two elegant curved staircases at the back of the museum lead to the upper levels; at the bottom are two lions supporting a buttress with five lamps. The underside of one stairwell is decorated with the painting "Peace Defeating War." Tues.-Sun. 10-5:30. Admission around $3.25 (U.S.) but can vary by exhibition; free to all Sun. Phone (55) 5512-3224.

El Caballito stands in the center of the square fronting the museum. "The Little Horse" is the work of Manuel Tolsá. The 30-ton sculpture, showing King Charles IV of Spain astride his horse, is considered one of the world's finest equestrian statues. It was cast in 1803 from a single piece of bronze.

Palace of Mining (Palacio de Minería) is across from the museum at Tacuba #5. This impressive neoclassic building, also designed by Tolsá, has several patios and exhibits finely crafted stonework. Mon.-Fri. 9-8. Free.

NATIONAL MUSEUM OF ENGRAVING (Museo Nacional de la Estampa) is at Hidalgo #39 next to the Franz Mayer Museum (M: Bellas Artes, lines 2 and 8). Housed in a handsomely restored 16th-century building, it focuses on the graphic arts. The second floor has permanent exhibits, notably the pointed political cartoons and cavorting skeleton figures of 19th-century Mexican artist José Guadalupe Posada. Temporary exhibits of contemporary art are on the first floor. Tues.-Sun. 10-5:30. Admission around $1.50 (U.S.); free to all Sun.

PALACE OF FINE ARTS (Palacio de Bellas Artes) is on Calle Lopez Peralta at the east end of Alameda Park (M: Bellas Artes, lines 2 and 8). It was begun in 1904 by Italian architect Adamo Boari, interrupted by the Revolution of 1910 and finally dedicated in 1934, a legacy of Porfirio Díaz's economically progressive but politically oppressive regime. Because of enormous weight and a swampy subsoil, the building has settled considerably since its construction.

The decorative sculptures on the facade are the building's highlight. They include garlands, flowers, masks and a sculptural group called "Harmony." A sculpture of Pegasus stands in the outdoor esplanade. Inside the look is pure 1930s Art Deco, augmented by second- and third-floor murals by Diego Rivera, José Clemente Orozco and David Alfaro Siqueiros. Note in particular "Man in Control of His Universe," Rivera's caustic rendering of capitalism, originally commissioned for New York City's Rockefeller Center in 1933.

The city's premier cultural center is the home of the National Opera Company, the National Ballet of Mexico, the National Dance Company and the National Symphony Orchestra. The building also houses the National Museum of Architecture, which contains models, sketches, photographs and draft plans. Temporary exhibitions of art, sculpture and photography are regularly mounted.

Palace open Tues.-Sun. 10-6. Admission to museum and to view the murals 25 pesos (around $2.50 U.S.), students with ID and under 12 free; free to all Sun. Phone (55) 5512-2593, ext. 132.

Ballet Folklórico de México is presented in the palace theater. This theatrically colorful spectacle showcases many forms of Mexican folk music and dance. The theater is famed for its 22-ton crystal curtain; actually a double-walled steel curtain, the side facing the audience was crafted from 1 million pieces of opalescent glass that resemble a large

In Case of Emergency

Persons needing legal assistance should contact the Protección Legal al Turista (Tourist Protection) department at the Secretaría de Turismo (the Ministry of Tourism, or SECTUR). Headquarters is at Presidente Masaryk #172 (in the Polanco neighborhood); phone (55) 5761-4371 (English spoken). SECTUR's 24-hour hotline can also help tourists in difficulty or coordinate aid in an emergency; phone (55) 5250-0123 or (55) 5250-0151.

The U.S. Embassy, Paseo de la Reforma #305 (M: Sevilla or Insurgentes, line 1), has a protection officer on 24-hour duty to advise you in case of such serious trouble as robbery, assault, major loss, accident, illness or death. In any event, Mexican law takes precedence and must be observed. It also has lists of attorneys and translators on file. The embassy is open for general business Mon.-Fri. 9-2 and 3-5. Phone (55) 5080-2000; Web site address www.usembassy-mexico.gov. The Canadian Embassy is at Calle Schiller #529, just north of the National Museum of Anthropology (M: Auditorio, line 7). It is open Mon.-Fri. 8:45-5:15; phone (55) 5724-7900. Both embassies are closed on U.S./Canadian and Mexican holidays.

In general, the police in Mexico City should be contacted only as a last resort. If your car is stolen, however, you must report it to the police, for you will be liable for any subsequent crimes committed in or with the vehicle. To reach the highway police phone (55) 5684-2142; to report a robbery, assault or mugging, phone (55) 5625-8008 or (55) 5625-8646. An all-purpose emergency number (dial 060) can provide help to tourists who have been victims of a crime and need to file a police report; English is not likely to be spoken.

window and depict snowcapped peaks Popocatépetl and Iztaccíhuatl. The half-hour curtain show is given only before the Sunday morning performance.

Performances Sun. morning and evening and Wed. evening. Tickets $20-$35 (U.S.). For information phone Ticketmaster, (55) 5325-9000 *(also see "Concerts," page 263)*.

SAN FERNANDO CHURCH AND CEMETERY is northwest of Alameda Park at Vicente Guerrero #39 (M: Hidalgo, lines 2 and 3). At one end of the plaza is the church, a former monastery built in the mid-18th century. The Churrigueresque facade survived the monastery's dismantlement after the monks were expelled in 1860. The adjacent cemetery holds the remains of several prominent Mexican families; the last person buried here was former president Benito Juárez. Daily 8-3. Free.

SAN FRANCISCO CHURCH is on Av. Madero, 2 blocks east of Alameda Park and almost directly across from Sanborn's (M: Bellas Artes, lines 2 and 8). Begun in 1524 with money granted by Hernando Cortés, it was long the center of Catholicism in America and headquarters of the Franciscan Order. The original complex, fragments of which are still visible, also comprised a monastery and training school for Franciscan missionaries. The present church dates from the 18th century and has an elaborately Churrigueresque facade.

Chapultepec Park and Vicinity

CHAPULTEPEC CASTLE (Castillo de Chapultepec) is in Chapultepec Park (M: Chapultepec, line 1). It stands atop a 200-foot-high hill overlooking the central part of the city; the stony outcrop was once used by Aztec emperors as a summer retreat. Construction of the castle began in 1783. Completed in 1840, it was fortified and became a military college. When it was attacked and taken in 1847 by U.S. forces during the Mexican-American War, the castle was defended solely by its young cadets. After passing through a succession of leaders, the castle was finally bequeathed to the nation in 1939 by President Lázaro Cárdenas.

The climb to the castle along a paved walkway winding up Chapultepec Hill is fairly steep and takes about 20 minutes. En route there are frequent views of the downtown skyline. You also can board a train inside the park entrance that carries passengers up the hill. The rather dilapidated-looking castle houses the National Museum of History. Train fare around $2 (U.S.).

Gallery of the Mexican Struggle for Liberty (Galería de la Lucha del Pueblo Mexicano por su Libertad) is about halfway up the hill to Chapultepec Castle. It is popularly known as the Museo del Caracol for its spiral shape, which resembles a snail's shell.

The hallway leads past dramatic dioramas of decisive events in Mexican history. This walk through the past ends in a chamber of red *tezontle* (volcanic) stone dominated by three objects: the national flag, a carved-stone eagle and a facsimile of the 1917 Constitution. Explanations are in Spanish. Tues.-Sun. 9-5:30. Admission around $3.25 (U.S); free to all Sun.

National Museum of History (Museo Nacional de Historia) is in Chapultepec Castle. It has 11 *salas* (halls) tracing Mexican history from the Spanish conquest to the Revolution of 1910 and the adoption of the 1917 constitution. Weapons, paintings, clothing, furniture and maps are displayed, along with portraits of leading historical figures from Hernando Cortés to 20th-century presidents. Two striking Juan O'Gorman murals depict important events in the nation's history. Exhibit information is in Spanish. Tues.-Sun. 9-5. Admission around $4 (U.S.); free to all Sun. Flash photography is not permitted.

CHAPULTEPEC PARK (Bosque de Chapultepec) sprawls on either side of Paseo de la Reforma beginning about 4 blocks west of the Zona Rosa (M: Chapultepec, line 1; Auditorio and Constituyentes, line 7). It is the oldest natural park in North America and one of the largest and most varied in the world. After the establishment of Tenochtitlán, Aztec emperors used Chapultepec Hill, within today's park, for summer relaxation.

Despite the wear and tear it's fascinating to stroll along the cobbled walkways, as much for the people-watching as anything else. You won't see many foreign tourists here; the park is very much a gathering place for city residents. Sunday is the best day to visit, as families converge to enjoy their day off at this enormous green space.

Chapultepec is divided into three sections. Some of the city's most notable museums are grouped in the oldest (eastern) section ("1a Sección"), including the National Museum of Anthropology, the Museum of Modern Art and the National Museum of History in Chapultepec Castle. The section of the park west of Calzada Molino del Rey ("2a Sección") is newer and contains many of the kid-oriented attractions. The Pines (Los Piños), the Mexican president's residence, is just east of Molino del Rey; it is heavily guarded and cannot be visited.

If you plan to spend most of the day and would rather not sample the offerings of food vendors, bring a lunch. Eastern section open daily 5-5; some attractions are closed Mon. Free; separate admissions charged for attractions. Most are free on Sun.

Chapultepec Park Zoo (Parque Zoológico de Chapultepec) is in the eastern section, south of Paseo de la Reforma off Calz. Chivatito (near the National Museum of Anthropology). It displays giant pandas—this is one of the few zoos to have successfully bred them in captivity—a white tiger and other animals in natural habitats. There's also an aviary, a venomous snake exhibit and a miniature train ride. Tues.-Sun. 9-4:30. Free; admission to snake exhibit around $2.25 (U.S.).

In Case of Emergency (continued)

The city agency LOCATEL can help coordinate a search for missing persons and vehicles as well as provide assistance to those in need of public services; phone (55) 5658-1111 (English may not be spoken). For consumer protection issues, contact the Procuraduría del Consumidor (PROFECO); phone (55) 5568-8722.

Medical assistance is available from the American British Cowdray (ABC) Hospital, in the southern part of the city at Calle Sur #136 and Avenida Observatorio (M: Observatorio, line 1, west bus terminal); phone (55) 5230-8000. All major credit cards are accepted. The Mexican Red Cross (Cruz Roja), Ejército Nacional #1032 in the Polanco neighborhood, is open 24 hours; phone (55) 5395-1111.

© Jeff Greenberg / Index Stock

A list of doctors and hospitals in Mexico City is available from the U.S. Embassy, phone (55) 5080-2000, ext. 4780 (during working hours); the Canadian Embassy, phone (55) 5724-7900; the British Embassy, Av. Río Lerma #71 (2 blocks north of Paseo de la Reforma near the Sheraton María Isabel Hotel), phone (55) 5242-8500 Mon.-Fri. 8:30-3:30; or your hotel front desk.

The main Post Office (Correo Mayor) is at the corner of Tacuba and Avenida Lázaro Cárdenas in the first block north of the Palace of Fine Arts (M: Bellas Artes, lines 2 and 8).

Children's Museum (Papalote Museo del Niño) is at Av. Constituyentes #268 in the park's second (western) section (near the Anillo Periférico). Themed sections explore the human body, science, computers and artistic expression, among other subjects. Kids will love the contraption that makes giant soap bubbles. In addition to the many interactive, hands-on activities, the museum also has an IMAX theater alternating two different films several times daily.

Daily 10-2 and 3-7 (also Thurs. and Sat.-Sun. 7-11 p.m.). Admission 60 pesos (around $6 U.S.); over 59 and ages 2-11, 50 pesos (around $5). Combination museum and IMAX theater admission 110 pesos (around $11 U.S.); over 59 and ages 2-11, 100 pesos (around $10). Phone (55) 5224-1260.

Don Quixote Fountain (Fuente de Don Quijote) stands in Quixote Square, just off Gran Avenida, west of Lake Chapultepec and south of the Botanic Garden. The fountain is within a pavilion designed in the shape of a simple cube. A mural by Diego Rivera covering its bottom depicts the evolution of life by water. The hydraulic works in the vicinity receive water from the Río Lerma. Also on the square is a metallic structure housing two small sculptures of Quixote and sidekick Sancho Panza in the midst of an argument.

La Feria is in the park's second (western) section off the Circuito Bosque de Chapultepec, west of the Anillo Periférico. This amusement park is dominated by a giant roller coaster, the Russian Mountain (Montaña Rusa), and has a number of other rides, as well as bumper cars and go-carts. Tues.-Sun. 10-6 (also Sat.-Sun. 6-9 p.m.). Admission around $6.50 (U.S.), children $1.

Lake House (Case del Lago) is in the heart of the park's old section, on the western shore of Lake Chapultepec (Lago de Chapultepec). It functions as a cultural center and as a setting for public events. Rowboats can be rented. A short distance west of the lake is the park's Botanical Garden (Jardín Botánico).

Monument to the Child Heroes (Monumento de Los Niños Héroes) is near the park's main entrance. The group of columns memorializes six cadets who were among those defending Chapultepec Castle, then a military college, against American troops at the height of the Mexican-American War in 1847. They reputedly leaped to their deaths wrapped in the Mexican flag rather than be captured.

Museum of Natural History (Museo de Historia Natural) is in the park's second (western) section off the Circuito Bosque de Chapultepec. It consists of 10 interconnecting domes that house nature dioramas and biological, geological and astronomical exhibits. The museum's insect collection is a highlight. Tues.-Sun. 10-5. Admission around $1.75 (U.S.); free to all Tues.

Museum of Technology (Museo Tecnológico) is in the park's second (western) section off the Circuito Bosque de Chapultepec, south of the amusement park. Housed in a pyramidal structure, the museum has a planetarium and exhibits on aviation, energy, science and industry. The grounds feature installations of railroad cars and other industrial equipment. Tues.-Sun. 10-5. Free.

Rotunda of Illustrious Men (Rotonda de Los Hombres Ilustres) is in the western section of the park at avs. Constituyentes and Civil Dolores (M: Constituyentes, line 7). Dolores Cemetery, Mexico's national cemetery, is where many of the country's military leaders, political figures and important citizens have been laid to rest. The markers are arranged in circular fashion around an eternal flame. Artists Diego Rivera, David Alfaro Siqueiros and José Clemente Orozco are just a few of the notables interred. A map is available at the entrance building. Daily 6-6. Free.

COLONIA CONDESA is centered along Av. Michoacán off Calz. J. Vasconcelos, southeast of Chapultepec Park's eastern end (M: Juanacatlán, line 1). This trendy neighborhood was the early 20th-century home of Mexico City's well-to-do citizens, who abandoned the area 2 decades later and left behind dilapidated mansions. But Condesa has become fashionable again, renovated by an influx of young artists and expatriates. The neighborhood has a number of good restaurants and coffee bars, many of them concentrated near the intersection of avenidas Michoacán and Tamaulipas.

Avenida Michoacán also has a collection of clothing stores and shops selling CDs and other merchandise. Leafy Parque México, farther east on Michoacán near Avenida Insurgentes Sur, is delightfully well-kept and has plenty of benches.

INDEPENDENCE MONUMENT (Monumento a la Independencia) is in the circle at Paseo de la Reforma and Tiber (M: Insurgentes, line 1). A 150-foot-high column dating between 1901 and 1910, it is topped by a winged statue of Victory. The central figure at the base is Father Miguel Hidalgo; he is flanked by other leaders in the war for independence, including José María Morelos Nicolás Bravo. The female statues represent Law, Justice, War and Peace.

This is one of several commanding landmarks that stand in the middle of *glorietas* (traffic circles) at principal intersections along Reforma; locals and visitors alike use them as geographical reference points.

MUSEUM OF MODERN ART (Museo de Arte Moderno) occupies a circular building on the south side of Paseo de la Reforma (at Calle Gandhi), near the entrance to Chapultepec Park (M: Chapultepec, line 1). It celebrates the diversity of 20th-century Mexican modern art and also presents temporary exhibitions by important international artists.

The permanent collection is housed in Xavier Villaurrutia and Carlos Pellicer halls. Among its many highlights are works by Mexico's three leading muralists—Diego Rivera, David Alfaro

Siqueiros and José Clemente Orozco. Paintings by another major Mexican modern artist, Rufino Tamayo, include "The Sleeping Musicians" and "The Man Radiant in Happiness." This museum also contains Frida Kahlo's "The Two Fridas," one of the surrealist's most striking works.

José Guadalupe Posada, José Luis Cuevas and Juan Soriano are other well-known artists represented, along with contemporary figures like Oliverio Hinojosa and Irma Palacios. There is a sculpture garden surrounding the museum. Exhibit information is in Spanish. Food is available. Tues.-Sun. 10-5:30. Admission 15 pesos (around $1.50 U.S.); free to all Sun. and on official holidays. Phone (55) 5553-6233.

NATIONAL MUSEUM OF ANTHROPOLOGY (Museo Nacional de Antropología) is in Chapultepec Park off Calle Mahatma Gandhi, facing the north side of Paseo de la Reforma (M: Chapultepec, line 1 or Auditorio, line 7). A must-see stop for any Mexico City visitor, this is one of the world's finest museums. At the entrance looms a 217-ton, 25-foot-tall monolith of Tláloc, the Aztec god of rain.

Twelve exhibition halls are devoted to Mexico's early civilizations, with each focusing on a separate period or culture. The exhibits encompass every conceivable type of artifact and include temple reconstructions, stone carvings, sculptures, ceramics, antique furniture, jewelry, masks, decorative objects, and arts and crafts. There are pieces—such as a bowl with a hummingbird perched on the rim—of exquisite beauty. Dramatic lighting accentuates the remarkable artistry of the larger sculptures.

Guided tour tickets can be purchased in the main entrance hall, which also has a bookstore selling English-language museum guides and an orientation theater where a 20-minute orientation film is shown. Most exhibit labeling is in Spanish; newer exhibits also include an English translation.

Food is available. Wheelchairs are available. Restrooms are provided. Tues.-Sun. 9-7, Mon. 9-7 on official festival days. Guided tours in Spanish, English and French are given Tues.-Sat. 9:30-5:30. Admission 38 pesos (around $3.80 U.S.), over 59 and under 13 free; free to all on official festival days. Guided tour fee 60 pesos (around $6). The fee to use a personal video camera is 30 pesos (around $3). Phone (55) 5553-6381.

Aztec Hall (Sala Mexica) has as its focal point the 24-ton Aztec calendar stone, the Stone of the Sun (Piedra del Sol), with the face of the sun god carved in its center. The vivid statue of the goddess Coatlicue is rendered beheaded and wearing a skirt of snakes, and a scale model of the center of pre-Hispanic Tenochtitlán includes hundreds of detailed miniatures and an accompanying mural depicting the lake that once covered the area.

Maya Hall (Sala Maya) spotlights a culture that was arguably the most advanced in all Mesoamerica. While the artifacts displayed here may not equal the grandeur of their lavishly decorated temples—the singular Maya architectural achievement—they affirm the beauty of Maya art. Many of the ceramic figurines, pieces of jewelry and death masks were retrieved from burial sites.

Teotihuacán Hall (Sala Teotihuacána) is devoted to the first of Mexico's great pre-Hispanic cities. Here visitors can see a reproduction of the site's Temple of Quetzalcóatl, a huge statue of Chalchiuhtlicue, the Teotihuacán goddess of the "running waters," and displays from Cholula (see separate listing under Central Mexico).

RUFINO TAMAYO MUSEUM (Museo Rufino Tamayo) is in Chapultepec Park, on the north side of Paseo de la Reforma and west of Calzada Gandhi (M: Chapultepec, line 1). It displays the personal modern art collection of the Oaxacan painter and muralist, who died in 1991. Although Tamayo's work was initially criticized for its lack of political content, his reputation as a key figure of 20th-century Mexican art has grown over the years. In addition to Tamayo's own paintings, there are works by Pablo Picasso, Francis Bacon, Salvador Dali and Joan Miró. There also are changing international exhibitions. Tues.-Sun. 10-6. Admission around $2 (U.S.); free to all Sun. Phone (55) 5286-6519.

UNITED STATES EMBASSY is at Paseo de la Reforma and Río Danubio, just north of the Zona Rosa (M: Insurgentes, line 1). Like many city buildings, it was built to withstand the impact of a powerful earthquake. For Citizens Consular Services phone (55) 5080-2000.

ZONA ROSA (Pink Zone) is about halfway between Alameda Central and Chapultepec Park (M: Insurgentes or Sevilla, line 1), roughly bordered by Paseo de la Reforma on the north, Av. Chapultepec on the south, Insurgentes on the east and Sevilla on the west. This was long Mexico City's trendsetting neighborhood and favored tourist hotspot. However, its popularity has been eclipsed by the Polanco area, north of Chapultepec Park, which has many of the city's best hotels, restaurants and retailers.

Although still filled with shops, eateries and flashy nightspots, the Zona Rosa has become worn around the edges and also attracts groups of youth gangs who prey on anyone perceived to have money. Be careful if coming here for a night out, and arrange designated hotel taxi transportation both to and from your destination.

North of Downtown

BASILICA OF OUR LADY OF GUADALUPE (Basilica de Nuestra Señora de Guadalupe) is about 10 km (6 mi.) north of downtown's historic center (M: La Villa, line 6). The site is located on a rocky hill (Cerro del Tepeyac) in the suburb of Villa de Guadalupe; from the La Villa Metro station, walk north 2 blocks on Calzada de Guadalupe. The basilica, one of Roman Catholicism's holiest shrines, honors the Guadalupe Virgin, Mexico's patron saint.

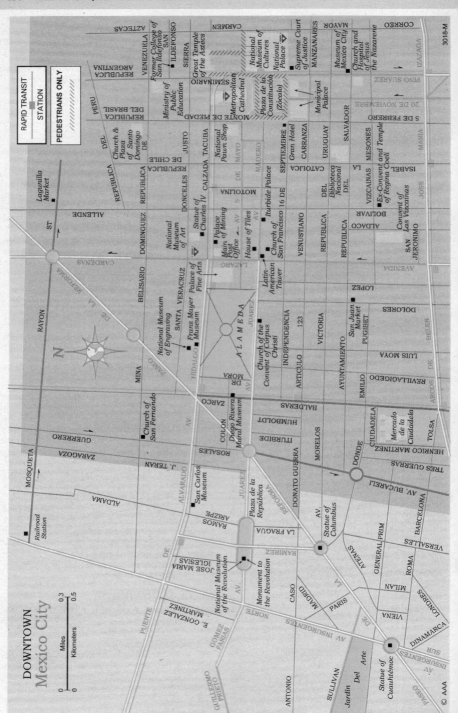

DOWNTOWN Mexico City

Mexican Catholics believe that at this site in December 1531 the Virgin appeared to Juan Diego, a peasant Indian, and asked him that a church be built. After hearing this story, the local bishop requested proof. Diego returned on Dec. 12, his cape filled with roses that the Virgin had directed him to pick (a rather miraculous occurrence itself, considering the time of year). When the cape was opened, the roses had disappeared and a vivid image of the dark-skinned Virgin appeared on the folds of cloth.

A plaza anchors the sprawling complex. A large underground parking lot is filled with a bazaar-like assemblage of religious-themed shops and street vendors selling handicrafts. Visitors enter the plaza through steel gates manned by armed guards. At the far end of the plaza is the ornate Basilica Antigua (Old Basilica), built about 1709 to house the sacred image.

Near the main entrance soars the Basilica Nueva, which can accommodate more than 10,000 people. Daringly modern in contrast, it was built in 1976. The cloth, in a gold frame and protected by bulletproof glass, hangs above the main altar; visitors pass beneath it via two moving walkways going in opposite directions. To the rear of the Old Basilica is a museum that displays religious artworks, including a collection of *retablos* (small devotional paintings). Other churches within the complex are the Church of the Indians (Parroquía de Indios) and the Chapel of the Well (El Pocito).

Allow 1 hour minimum. Tues.-Sun. 10-6. Churches free, museum admission around 55 cents (U.S.). Parking fee around $3, free with $10 worth of merchandise purchased from adjacent shops.

CONVENT OF SAN AGUSTIN ACOLMAN—
see Acolman listing p. 226.

PLAZA OF THE THREE CULTURES (Plaza de Las Tres Culturas) is north of the Historic Center and west of Paseo de la Reforma Norte, at Av. Lázaro Cárdenas and Ricardo Flores Magón (M: Tlatelolco, line 3). The name comes from three vastly different influences—pre-Hispanic Aztec, colonial Spanish and contemporary Mexican—that have left their individual imprints on this plaza.

The ceremonial and trading center of Tlatelolco (tlah-tay-LOHL-koh) considerably predated the Aztec capital of Tenochtitlán. Even after it was absorbed by the Aztec empire in 1473, Tlatelolco continued to function as an important market. It was from Tlatelolco that the Aztecs made their final stand against Spanish forces on Aug. 13, 1521.

Nearly 450 years later, the plaza was the scene of another massacre. On the eve of the 1968 Summer Olympic Games—with Mexico City in the world spotlight—a massive student protest over prevailing economic and social policies turned deadly when government troops were ordered to open fire.

The site ruins can be seen from raised walkways and give an indication of its former size. The Church of Santiago Tlatelolco, dating from 1609,

has a restored interior that contains several frescoes and a strikingly simple stone altar. Next to the church are the remains of a monastery and former college where Franciscan friars taught the sons of Aztec nobility.

SANTA CECELIA PYRAMID is about 3 km (2 mi.) north of the Tenayuca Pyramid *(see next attraction listing)* via the road to Santa Cecelia Acatitlán. Both pyramids are located east of Tlalnepantla (tlahl-neh-PAHN-tlah), an industrial city just north of the Federal District in the state of México. This small pyramid, of Aztec origin, is remarkably well reconstructed and has a shrine dedicated to Huitzilopochtli, the war god and a dominant deity of the Aztecs.

Also at the site is the Dávalos Hurtado Museum, which contains several representations of Aztec gods; original sculptures, engravings and paintings; and a reproduction of a Mexica (Mexican-Aztec) temple. Site and museum open Tues.-Sun.

TENAYUCA PYRAMID is just off Avenida de Los Cien Metros, about 12 km (7.5 mi.) north of downtown Mexico City via Eje Central Lázaro Cárdenas or Calzada Vallejo. Buses to the pyramid depart from Mexico City's Terminal Central de Autobuses del Norte. There is a Metro station at the terminal (Autobuses del Norte, line 5). Another way to reach the pyramid is by taxi.

This pre-Aztec site was once part of the 12th-century Chichimec empire. Passageways reveal the series of superimposed structures that excavations have uncovered within this pyramid, which is one of the most impressively reconstructed in Mexico. Its most striking features are the interlocking carved stone serpents that adorn three sides of the base. Tues.-Sun. 9-5. Admission is charged.

 **TEOTIHUACAN—**
see Teotihuacán listing p. 266.

West of Downtown

REVOLUTION MONUMENT (Monumento a la Revolución) stands in the Plaza de la República, north of Paseo de la Reforma and west of the Alameda (M: Revolución, line 2). Topped by an imposing copper dome that surmounts four arches, it rises 250 feet. Buried under the four columns are four former presidents—Venustiano Carranza, Plutarco Calles, Lázaro Cárdenas and Francisco I. Madero—as well as revolutionary Pancho Villa. Porfirio Díaz, the dictator deposed by the Revolution of 1910, intended the building to house the government's legislative offices, but the uprising halted construction; it was dedicated as a monument in the 1930s.

National Museum of the Revolution (Museo Nacional de la Revolución) is inside the lower part of the monument. It houses a collection of weapons, along with paintings and sculptures depicting the revolution's leading figures. Tues.-Sat. 9-5, Sun. 9-3. Admission around 65 cents (U.S.).

SAN CARLOS MUSEUM (Museo de San Carlos) is about 3 blocks north of Plaza de la República at Puente de Alvarado #50 (M: Revolución, line 2). It houses an impressive collection of paintings by European artists spanning the 15th through the 19th centuries, including works by Francisco José de Goya, Tintoretto, Titian, Anthony Van Dyck, Rembrandt and Peter Paul Rubens.

The lovely neoclassic building was the private home of such notable Mexican military figures as Gen. Agustín de Iturbide and Gen. Antonio López de Santa Anna. A small public park off Puente de Alvarado faces the rear facade. Wed.-Mon. 10-6. Admission around $2.75 (U.S.); free to all Sun. (55) 5566-8522.

STATUE OF COLUMBUS stands within the *glorieta* (traffic circle) on Paseo de la Reforma at Av. Morelos (M: Revolución, line 2). The work of Charles Cordier, it depicts the explorer (Cristóbal Colón in Spanish) and is one of several statues commissioned by Porfirio Díaz to grace major intersections along this stretch of the city's widest boulevard.

STATUE OF CUAUHTEMOC (Monumento a Cuauhtémoc) is on Paseo de la Reforma at Av. Insurgentes (M: Insurgentes, line 1). Cuauhtémoc, the last Aztec emperor, was tortured by Hernando Cortés in an unsuccessful attempt to force him to reveal the hiding place of the vast treasure of Moctezuma. The statue, created by Miguel Moreña, shows the proud ruler garbed in a plumed robe and standing imperiously with his spear, surrounded by warriors. Pedestal engravings depict Cuauhtémoc's torture and the burning of his feet. The circle at Insurgentes and Reforma is a major crossroads for city traffic.

South of Downtown

EL PEDREGAL covers 15 square miles at the southern end of Mexico City (M: Universidad, line 3, south terminal). The great basaltic lava bed is crossed by the Anillo Periférico, the loop highway traversing the western and southern sections of the city, and surrounded by such communities as Coyoacán, San Angel and Tlalpan. The lava flow is at its craggiest south of San Angel. In the 1950s ultramodern homes began cropping up in the middle of this barren rock landscape, incorporating the hardened formations to dramatic effect. Public transportation is scarce, although a taxi can be hired for a drive through the area.

El Pedregal is the result of the eruption of the volcano Xitle around A.D. 400. Excavations at the quarry of Copilco, just east of San Angel, have uncovered human remains and examples of primitive craftsmanship from a civilization that likely existed sometime during the Middle Preclassic period (1200-400 B.C.).

POLYFORUM SIQUEIROS is at Av. Insurgentes Sur and Filadelfia, on the grounds of the Hotel de México. An eight-sided, four-story exposition hall for the arts, it is the work of and a monument to muralist David Alfaro Siqueiros (1896-1974). Garish Siqueiros murals cover the building's exterior walls, and inside on the upper level a revolving floor permits an unimpeded view of his 26,150-square-foot ceiling mural "March of Humanity." Open daily. Admission is charged.

The Southern Suburbs

Churubusco, Coyoacán, Ixtapalapa, San Angel and Tlalpan, all within the Mexico City limits, were once individual *pueblos* (towns) that for the most part have maintained their distinct identities despite being swallowed up by the capital's rampant 20th-century growth. The Federal District, the 571-square-mile seat of national government, encompasses Mexico City and several separate municipalities, including Xochimilco, site of the popular floating gardens.

North-south Avenida Insurgentes Sur—a major thoroughfare lined with office buildings and commercial sprawl—is the easiest way to reach the southern suburbs, especially the tourist hotspots of San Angel and Coyoacán, both relatively quiet, well-to-do enclaves somehow removed from the rest of the city's clamor. Colonial charm, good restaurants, several museums, weekend arts and crafts shopping, and the cultural offerings of the National University of Mexico make this area a popular destination for visitors.

The safest and easiest way to reach the southern suburbs is to take a taxi; taxis also come in handy for making short trips from one point of interest to another. For an hourly fee you can hire a taxi driver to get you there and also wait while you shop or sightsee.

For more information about these destinations *see their individual alphabetical listings under this region.*

What To Do

Dining

For years, most of Mexico City's best known and most elegant establishments specialized in French and Continental, those two benchmarks of fine dining. More recently, however, traditional Mexican cooking has taken center stage. Many of the newest and trendiest restaurants are serving time-honored dishes that originated during pre-Hispanic days, but with a contemporary twist.

This is not necessarily the cheese-slathered, chile-spiked food that many people still think of as generically "Mexican," nor is it necessarily reminiscent of regional specialties that have ended up on menus across the country. Ingredients are frequently exotic—*nopales,* fleshy pads of cactus; *huitlacoche,* the earthy black fungus that is Mexico's version of the truffle; or *cajeta,* a sweet caramel flavoring made from goat's milk. Menu choices can be exotic, too: squash flowers, *chapulines* (fried grasshoppers) or *gusanos de maguey* (worms) fried and served with guacamole.

Diners still crave robustly traditional fare, of course—*sopa de tortilla* (tortilla soup); *chiles rellenos* (stuffed chilies); *huachinango a la Veracruzana* (a whole fish, usually sea bass or red snapper, awash in a sauce of tomatoes, onions, olives and capers); and *cochinita pibil* (pork wrapped in banana leaves and baked). La Fonda del Recuerdo is a boisterous, fun family restaurant featuring platters of delicious Mexican seafood accompanied by roving *jarocho* musicians. It's located at Bahía de las Palmas #37 in Colonia Veronica Anzures; take a taxi.

Café de Tacuba, Calzada Tacuba in the Historic Center, is a Mexico City institution that has been around since 1912. The colonial atmosphere is enhanced by brass lamps, colorful tiles and 18th-century paintings, including one of nuns working in a kitchen. The food is traditional Mexican; be sure to try the *mole poblano*. Students costumed in medieval garb serenade diners Thursday through Sunday evenings.

For those who demand world-class haute cuisine (with prices to match), Mexico City has some dependable choices. Such restaurants are usually located in the big, expensive hotels. Fouquet's de Paris, in the Camino Real Hotel at Mariano Escobedo #700—a branch of the Parisian outpost—offers as refined and elegant a setting as you'll find in the capital for food that is a combination of international and Mexican flavors.

Splurge at Maxim's de Paris, in the Hotel Intercontinental Presidente Mexico City at Campos Elíseos #218, which has a stylish art deco interior, an outstanding wine cellar and wonderfully attentive service. Also at the Presidente is Au Pied de Cochon, modeled closely after the Parisian original. The French cuisine here is top-notch, from roast leg of pork with béarnaise sauce to escargot, pigs' trotters and platters of perfectly prepared seafood. At these and other high-end restaurants, reservations are required or advised, and a jacket and tie are required for men.

Meson El Cid, Humboldt #61 in the Historic Center, dishes up Spanish classics like paella and roast Cornish hen during the week and offers a medieval banquet on Saturday evening, complete with costumed waiters and singers. Argentinian steakhouses are popular; Rincón Argentino, Presidente Masaryk #177 in Polanco, offers prime cuts of beef and stylish decor reminiscent of a hunting lodge.

If you're in a hurry or just want a casual meal, eat at Vips or Sanborn's, both Mexican chains with numerous Mexico City locations. The food is dependably prepared and reasonably priced; they're good choices for breakfast.

Another casual alternative is one of the sandwich stands that occupy almost every street corner. Try *tacos al pastor*—shreds of roast pork with grilled onions and cilantro heaped on a small tortilla, the whole thing rolled up burrito-style and popped in the mouth. At 5 pesos (about 50 cents) apiece, they're a popular late-night snack.

The El Globo bakery chain, with locations throughout the Federal District, offers good-quality breads and pastries at low prices. For the homesick and/or unadventurous, there are plenty of American fast-food outlets, including Burger King, McDonald's, Pizza Hut and Subway.

Many restaurants are concentrated in the Polanco and Zona Rosa areas; reservations are recommended or necessary. Another cluster of good restaurants and cozy sidewalk cafes are in the southern suburbs of San Angel and Coyoacán. Casual neighborhood eateries and family-style places are the rule in the downtown area and around the *Zócalo*. Many restaurants close on Sunday. Pay with a major credit card if possible, as the rate of exchange is better than that offered by banks or currency exchange offices.

Approach cocktails and liquors with caution if you are unaccustomed to the altitude. Also be aware that imported wines and spirits are heavily taxed; Mexican beers and wines are much less expensive. Although the better restaurants customarily use purified water, avoid green salads, unpeeled raw vegetables and unpeeled fruit if you have a sensitive stomach. To be completely safe, order drinks without ice cubes, or drink bottled water.

In general, restaurants cater to the local custom of eating the main meal of the day in the early afternoon, then a lighter supper around 9 p.m. or later. Most begin to serve breakfast around 7:30 a.m., *comida* (lunch) about 1 p.m. and dinner after 7:30 p.m. From 2 to 4, restaurants can be crowded with lingering diners; if you eat dinner before 9, on the other hand, you might have the place to yourself.

Even in the finer establishments, don't expect every server to have a fluent command of English. A knowledge of basic Spanish or a handy phrase book not only helps in communication but also in deciphering menus. For a list of AAA-RATED establishments in Mexico City, *see the Lodgings & Restaurants section.*

Shopping

Whether it's a cheap souvenir or an expensive, finely crafted work of art, chances are you'll find it here. In particular, look for intricate silverwork, hand-carved masks, jewelry, tinted onyx and obsidian, carved wooden chests, boxes of inlaid wood, furniture, paintings, picture frames, fine glassware and pottery, lacquerware, hand-tooled leather and textiles—especially *sarapes, rebozos* (shawl-like garments), embroidery and fine table linens. Merchandise is sold either in fixed-price shops where you pay the posted sale price or in markets where bargaining determines the cost.

One of Mexico City's major shopping areas is the Zona Rosa, off Paseo de la Reforma and encompassing calles Amberes, Génova, Hamburgo, Niza and Londres (M: Sevilla or Insurgentes, line 1). Galleries and boutiques abound, and outdoor cafes provide a relaxing break. For music purchases, there is a Tower Records at Niza #19-A.

Another exclusive shopping area is the Polanco neighborhood (M: Polanco, line 7). Armani, Cartier, Perry Ellis, Hermes and other chic fashion boutiques line a section of Avenida Presidente Masaryk that is Mexico City's version of L.A.'s Rodeo Drive.

More modest shopping—and lower prices—prevail at hundreds of shops and vendor stalls along avenidas Juárez and Francisco I. Madero in the vicinity of the Zócalo. This old downtown section of Mexico City is packed with stores and shops. From the Zócalo west to Avenida Lázaro Cárdenas, every other side street is closed to traffic and paved with brick tiles.

The government-run FONART stores offer a variety of arts and crafts—rugs, glassware, folk art, pottery—from all parts of the country at reasonable prices. A centrally located outlet, also known as Exposición Nacional de Arte Popular, is at Av. Juárez #89, just west of Alameda Park (M: Hidalgo, line 2).

The major department stores are Liverpool, Palacio de Hierro and Sanborn's. The first two have several city branches, while Sanborn's has numerous locations throughout Mexico City, including the original store in the House of Tiles (see attraction listing) and several along Paseo de la Reforma and in the Zona Rosa. In addition to carrying quality craft items and ceramics, Sanborn's outlets are convenient places to pick up toiletries and English-language publications, and most have a restaurant or coffee shop, a pharmacy and an ATM machine.

Among the suburban shopping malls, the largest is Centro Santa Fe, in the western part of the city. Although inconvenient for tourists because there is no Metro station nearby, it does have nearly 300 stores, as well as movie theaters, restaurants and play areas for kids. To get there, take the Anillo Periférico expressway (Avenida Avila Camacho) south to the exit marked Centro Santa Fe. Another big, pricey mall is Perisur, located on the southern outskirts close to where the Periférico expressway connects with Avenida Insurgentes Sur.

Mexico City's mercados were once areas of stalls open to the weather, roving dogs, and plagues of insects and bacteria. Long on merchandise, they were short on sanitation. City officials stepped in, and the markets are now housed in clean, properly ventilated buildings. Here you can haggle to your heart's content—and should, for a vendor normally asks at least 25 percent more than he or she expects to receive.

A suitable arena in which to practice the art of bargaining is the San Juan Market (Mercado de Curiosidades San Juan). The principal section is in a modern three-story building at Ayuntamiento and Dolores, 4 blocks south of Alameda Park (M: Salto del Agua, line 1). It offers an assortment of such wares as baskets, leather goods, jewelry, linens and shawls and is open Mon.-Sat. 9-7, Sun. 9-4.

The huge Buenavista Artisan Center (Centro Artesanal Buenavista), Aldama #187 near the Buenavista train station northwest of the Historic Center, markets handicrafts from throughout Mexico. Specialties include leather goods, pottery, stained-glass lamps and clothing. Prices are fixed. Open daily 9-6.

The city's biggest food market is La Merced, several blocks east of the Zócalo along Circunvalación (M: Merced, line 1). The huge buildings are crammed with a multitude of vendors selling produce, housewares and other everyday items. The selection of fruits, vegetables and spices in particular is staggering. While you're not likely to find many souvenirs, the sheer scope of the commerce makes it a fascinating place to wander through.

The Mercado Insurgentes, also called the Mercado Zona Rosa, fills an entire block along Calle Londres between Florencia and Amberes in the Zona Rosa (M: Insurgentes, line 1). A typical neighborhood crafts market, it has a maze of stalls selling everything from baskets to ponchos. Bargaining is expected, and good buys are possible. Open Mon.-Sat. 9:30-7:30, Sun. 10-4.

The Lagunilla Market is east of the intersection of Lázaro Cárdenas and Paseo de la Reforma, between República de Chile and Calle Allende (M: Allende, line 2). A modern triple-roofed building of enormous proportions, Lagunilla is especially busy on Sunday, when vendors from all over the city set up tables or booths to sell used clothing, silver of varying quality and other goods. Antiques, coins, blankets and rare books are good buys here. Watch out for pickpockets. Within walking distance, north of Paseo de la Reforma, is the Plaza of the Three Cultures (see attraction listing).

Serious silver fanciers should head for Tane, Amberes #70 in the Zona Rosa and several other city locations, where the jewelry, candelabra and museum-quality reproductions are expensive but exquisitely crafted. The striking work of contemporary Mexican artist and sculptor Sergio Bustamente is available at his gallery on Amberes #13 in the Zona Rosa; another outlet is in the Hotel Nikko México, at Campo Elíseos #204 in the Polanco neighborhood.

Handcrafted items from all over the country are sold at the Mercado de la Ciudadela, about 6 blocks southwest of Alameda Park on Plaza de la Ciudadela at Avenida Balderas (M: Balderas, line 1). More than 300 covered booths display everything from leather moccasins to custom guitars. Some of the most interesting items at La Ciudadela are the handcarved wooden masks, with colorful and creatively rendered visages ranging from whimsical to demonic. Expect to bargain here.

Scores of Mexican artists exhibit and sell paintings and sculpture in the city's many art galleries. Of special interest is the Saturday Bazaar (Bazar Sábado), at Plaza San Jacinto #11 (M: Miguel A. de Quevedo, line 3) in San Angel. Set up in a beautifully renovated 18th-century mansion—but usually spilling out of it as well—the bazaar is held only on Saturdays from 10-7.

The emphasis here is on art and features works by a tightly knit group of contemporary artisans, some of them U.S. expatriates. Paintings, sculpture, ceramics, textiles and garments, rugs and high-quality jewelry are sold; prices are high, but so is quality. Search out the *animalitos*, bizarrely carved and painted wooden creatures for which Oaxaca is famous, and the "Tree of Life" candelabras exploding with flowers, animals and other figures.

Gilded statues of the Virgin Mary, Our Lady of Guadalupe and other Mexican patron saints are exquisite examples of handiwork and command high prices. More affordable merchandise—and a greater chance to bargain—can be found outside the bazaar, where merchants offer wooden toys, decorative gourds and beaded bracelets. Local artists exhibit their work, and the lively scene frequently includes dancers and other entertainment.

Sightseeing

Mexico City's enormous size makes it difficult to plan a sightseeing itinerary. Although many museums and other points of interest are concentrated in certain areas—the Historic Center, Chapultepec Park, the southern suburbs of San Angel and Coyoacán—getting to them can take effort, given the formidable traffic congestion. If the prospect of hitting the streets on your own seems too stressful, consider taking a guided tour.

The easiest way to obtain guided tour information is to check with the staff at your hotel; the hotel may either have its own travel agency or be able to recommend a reliable one. An alternative is to visit one of the city's tourist information modules (Módulo de Información y Orientación Turística) operated by the Tourism Secretariat of Mexico City. A number of these modules are located in the Historic Center, in the vicinity of Alameda and Chapultepec parks, in the Pink Zone (Zona Rosa) and along Paseo de Reforma.

Guided tours of the Historic Center and Coyoacán are conducted aboard buses built to resemble the trams that used to ply Mexico City streets. For schedules and other information, check at any tourist information module.

Turibuses travel a route encompassing some 130 different attractions, including museums, monuments, art galleries, recreational parks and areas with a concentration of restaurants. Each bus can hold up to 70 passengers, and the tour includes a simultaneous translation in five languages. One ticket allows you to use the service all day, disembarking and reboarding at 25 stops. The buses run daily 9-9. For more information check with your hotel or at a tourist information module.

Another easy way to see the sights is to have your hotel arrange for a private car and a guide, either by the hour or by the day. Although you'll pay for the convenience, this option allows greater flexibility and more personal service. The larger hotels should be able to arrange such an excursion; check with the concierge. Guests at the Four Seasons Hotel, for example, can take advantage of guided weekend cultural tours.

The best day to sightsee in Mexico City is Sunday, when many attractions are free. For additional information about guided tours *see the "For Your Information" sidebar.*

Sports and Recreation

For the spectator, opportunities in Mexico City are legion. Besides the major sports mentioned below, there are basketball games, boxing and wrestling matches and a growing collegiate schedule of American-style football. Refer to the sports pages of the newspapers for current activities and schedules. Your hotel can help you get tickets.

The best **bullfighting** in the republic can be found at the Monumental Plaza México, also known as the Plaza Monumental (M: San Antonio, line 7). Accommodating about 50,000 spectators—the world's largest bullring—it is located on Calle Agusto Rodín a few blocks west of Avenida Insurgentes, about 6 kilometers (4 miles) south of the traffic circle at Paseo de la Reforma (the Cuauhtémoc Monument).

The season for top matadors runs from mid-October to April. During other months novice bull-fighters *(novilleros)* take the ring. Bullfights start promptly at 4 p.m. on Sunday; buses marked "Plaza México" travel along Insurgentes Sur throughout the afternoon. Plan on arriving early to get a good seat, and hang on to your ticket stub so you can reclaim your seat if you need to leave it.

The scene at these *corridas* is as rollicking as that at any American football or baseball game. Vendors hawk programs, gum and peanuts; hundreds of stalls outside the ring sell cold beer and snacks.

To avoid long lines at the bullring's ticket windows *(taquillas),* buy tickets in advance or book a tour that includes a bullfight through your hotel or a travel agency. Ticket prices range from around $5 to $50 (U.S.); they vary according to proximity to the ring and the side on which you sit. Sun *(sol)* is cheap, shade *(sombra)* is expensive. Seats in the sun tend to attract the more unruly fans. For more information phone (55) 5563-3961. **Note:** The bull is traditionally killed during these performances; plan not to attend if you find the spectacle's inherent cruelty upsetting.

The country's most popular game is **soccer** *(fútbol).* It is played almost every weekend by the big leagues at Azteca Stadium, in the southern part of the city on Calzada de Tlalpan, north of the Periférico Sur. Shuttles are available from the Taxqueña Metro station (line 2). There are winter (August to December) and summer (January to May) seasons. The city's most popular team, América—nicknamed Las Aguilas (the Eagles)—draws huge crowds, especially when they play archrival Guadalajara in a match called El Clásico.

The university-sponsored Pumas play soccer at Olympic Stadium (Estadio Olímpica) on the National University of Mexico campus. Reconstructed and enlarged for the 1968 Summer Olympics, it can accommodate some 72,500 people. The oval design somewhat resembles the crater of a volcano. A Diego Rivera mosaic of colored rocks, illustrating human endeavor in sports, covers the stadium's sloping walls. Tickets for all games are normally available right up to game time and range from around $2 to $11 (U.S.).

NBA **basketball** exhibition games are played at the Sports Palace (Palacio de Deportes), Avenida Río Churubusco and Calle Añil (M: Velódromo or Ciudad Deportiva, line 9). Designed by Félix Candela for the 1968 Olympic Games, it seats 25,000.

Professional **baseball** is popular in Mexico City, where teams in the Mexican League play from the beginning of April through mid-September. Games are announced in Spanish, but little is lost in the translation as the rules are the same. Some key terms: *el lanzador* is the pitcher, *la entrada* is the inning, *pegar* means hit, *un sencillo* is a single.

Many games are played at the Parque Foro Sol, a very modern facility on Avenida Río Churubusco in front of the Sports Palace. It is shared by two teams, the Diablos Rojos and the Tigres; the season is from March through August. General admission seats are inexpensive, less than $5 (U.S.). Tickets can be purchased through Ticketmaster; phone (55) 5325-9000.

Horse races are held at the lovely Hippodrome of the Americas (Hipódromo de las Américas). The track is in the northwestern part of the city between avenidas del Conscripto and Industria Militar, west of the Anillo Periférico. Buses and *peseros* (minivans) marked "Hipódromo" travel west along Paseo de la Reforma to the track. Races are held Friday through Sunday throughout the year beginning at 3 p.m.

General section admission 15 pesos (around $1.50 U.S.); box seats are more expensive. Tickets are available through Ticketmaster. There are fast-food outlets, the fashionable restaurant La Terraza and a sports book facility on the premises. For further information phone (55) 5387-0600.

Tennis and **golf** clubs are private; if you want to play tennis, make arrangements to stay at a hotel that offers courts. The Bella Vista Golf Club, an 18-hole course northwest of the city off Mex. 57-D (the Querétaro Highway), offers playing privileges to guests staying at the Camino Real and Sheraton María Isabel hotels. Greens fees are expensive, especially on weekends. Phone (55) 5360-3501.

Nightlife

More often than not, nightlife in Mexico City means nightclubs—both independent establishments and the lobby bars in the big hotels. Nightclub tours are an easy way to visit some of the city's hot spots, since transportation and reservations are arranged for you. These tours usually last several hours and include dinner at a nice restaurant and perhaps a floor show or a stop at Plaza Garibaldi (*see below*). For more information check with your hotel desk or a travel agency. The weekly publication *Tiempo Libre*, published on Thursday and available at newsstands, provides entertainment and performing arts listings in Spanish.

Just as they do in Acapulco and Cancún, people in Mexico City tend to keep the evening going practically all night. Dinner might begin at 9 or 10 p.m., and most of the discos don't kick into high gear until midnight. Many nightspots are closed on Sunday. Keep in mind that altitude can greatly magnify the effects of alcohol.

Note: Always be careful when venturing out after dark anywhere in Mexico City, even in tourist-frequented areas like the Zona Rosa and Polanco. Metro is not recommended as a way of getting around at night, and never hail a taxi on the street. The safest way to travel is to make drop-off and pickup arrangements with your hotel taxi service. Thieves also frequent the popular nightlife districts, so carry a minimum of cash and guard your personal belongings carefully.

Hotel lobby bars offer an elegant atmosphere, a sophisticated clientele and music for dancing. Good bets include the bars in the Intercontinental Presidente Mexico City, Campos Elíseos #218, Colonia Polanco; the Camino Real Mexico, Mariano Escobedo #700 (near the main entrance to Chapultepec Park); the Sheraton María Isabel Hotel and Towers, Paseo de la Reforma #325 (opposite the Independence Monument); and the Westin Galería Plaza, Hamburgo #195 in the Zona Rosa.

Avoid *cantinas*, small, dimly lit places that tend to attract hard-drinking patrons. An exception is the La Opera Bar, Av. 5 de Mayo #10 at Filomeno Mata, 3 blocks east of Alameda Park (M: Bellas Artes, lines 2 and 8). By day this is a crowded lunch spot, with jacketed waiters and formal service. In the evening dinner is served, but the gilded ceiling, mirrored walls, dark paneled booths and clubby feel also make La Opera an intimate place for an early evening cocktail. Your waiter is likely to show you the bullet hole Pancho Villa supposedly fired into the ceiling.

Dance to live salsa and merengue at Bar León, República de Brasil #5 in the Historic Center (behind the Metropolitan Cathedral). The cover charge begins at around $5.50 (U.S.). The club is open Thurs.-Sat. evenings; phone (55) 5510-3093.

The Art Deco Bar Mata, Filomena Mata #11 at Avenida 5 de Mayo in the Historic Center (near the La Opera Bar), occupies two floors in a colonial building near the Palace of Fine Arts. Dancing is to jazz, blues and rock. The rooftop bar offers fresh air and great views of the illuminated city. El Hijo del Cuervo, Jardín Centenario #17 in Coyoacán, attracts hip students and a mix of locals and foreigners. The music is hip as well; there is a cover charge for occasional live shows.

Floor shows are another option. International headliners appear at El Patio, an old-fashioned nightclub at Atenas #9 (east of the Zona Rosa and a block south of Paseo de la Reforma). Bar Jorongo, in the Sheraton María Isabel Hotel and Towers at Paseo de la Reforma #325, is a popular nightspot where well-known mariachi trios play in upscale surroundings. There is a cover charge. The rooftop bar at the Hotel Majestic, Av. Francisco I. Madero #73 (M: Zócalo, line 2), often has live entertainment in a setting overlooking the *Zócalo.*

For those seeking an indubitably Mexican nightlife experience, Plaza Garibaldi offers it. Bounded by calles República de Peru and República de Honduras, about five blocks north of the Palace of Fine Arts (M: Garibaldi, line 8), this square is ruled by the city's mariachi bands, who serenade paying customers every night of the week. The typical outfit includes violin, trumpet, guitar and a heart-tugging vocalist, and the songs almost always address the travails of love (usually at the hands of an unfaithful woman—a nod to Mexican *machismo*).

Decked out in tight, silver-spangled costumes and wide-brimmed sombreros, the musicians unabashedly solicit business from the throngs of people crowding the plaza (about $5 U.S. for a song). Sunday night is the best time to hear music in the square itself. Mariachis also perform in the surrounding *cantinas* and clubs, which stay open into the wee hours.

Plaza Santa Cecilia nightclub, across Calle Amargura from the plaza, puts on first-rate mariachi shows. At the establishments El Tenampa and Tlaquepaque you can sit and listen to the mariachis while nibbling *botanas* (snacks).

Note: Plaza Garibaldi is at its most exuberant late at night and is a traditional last stop for an evening on the town, but the surrounding neighborhood is unsavory, filled with cheap hotels and gaudy burlesque theaters. Unfortunately, street crime has become all too common here, even during daylight hours. If you do go, exercise caution. Guard closely against pickpockets, and arrange in advance for safe transportation to the plaza and back to your hotel. Some places have been known to gouge money from tourists by raising quoted prices for food and/or drinks, so stick to the larger, well-known establishments.

Concerts

Your hotel or a travel agency may be able to obtain tickets for popular performances, such as those by the Ballet Folklórico de México, which should be obtained in advance. Tickets for many events also can be purchased through Ticketmaster. Phone (55) 5325-9000; www.ticketmaster.com.mx. There is a Ticketmaster outlet in the National Auditorium, Paseo de la Reforma #50 in Chapultepec Park (M: Auditorio, line 7).

The Palace of Fine Arts (M: Bellas Artes, lines 2 and 8) is the home of the National Symphony Orchestra. The National Opera Company also stages productions here, usually January through March and August through October. The Mexico City Philharmonic Orchestra (Filarmonica de la Ciudad de México) gives concerts at Silvestre Revueltas Hall (Sala Silvestre Revueltas). It is located at Anillo Periférico Sur #5141, just east of Avenida Insurgentes at the southern end of the city (near San Angel). International symphony, ballet and opera companies also perform at the National Auditorium, phone (55) 5280-9250.

The acclaimed National University Symphony mounts its concert program at Justo Sierra Auditorium (M: Universidad, line 3, south terminal), on the National University of Mexico campus. The hall is famed for its acoustics. Nezahualcoyotl Hall regularly presents performing artists and groups, including the University of Mexico Philharmonic Orchestra. It is located within the University Cultural Center, which is off Avenida Insurgentes south of the main campus buildings.

Music al fresco is particularly popular and can be heard on the street or at parks throughout the capital. Better yet, many of these performances—which range from mariachi music to heavy metal—are free. Sunday concerts often take place in Alameda Park, usually around noon, and near the Lake House (Casa del Lago) in Chapultepec Park.

The central plazas in the southern suburbs of Coyoacán and San Angel often are the scene of weekend musical offerings. Big-name pop, rock and hip-hop concerts by international acts take place at the National Auditorium; the Sports Palace (Palacio de Los Deportes), Avenida Río Churubusco and Calle Añil; and Parque Foro Sol stadium, in front of the Sports Palace.

The Ballet Folklórico de México *(see Palace of Fine Arts attraction listing)* is one of the city's standout offerings. Although tickets are sold in advance at the Palace of Fine Arts box office (on the ground floor at the main entrance), they may be difficult to obtain unless you purchase them at least a day ahead or book a tour that includes the ballet. **Note:** The troupe is occasionally moved to another venue, usually the National Auditorium, to accommodate visiting performing arts groups. Check with Ticketmaster regarding specific schedule information.

Theater and Cinema

Theaters are not centralized in an entertainment district but are located throughout the city. Plays are almost always presented in Spanish, but other theaters present shows in a cabaret or variety format that can be enjoyed by non-Spanish speakers.

The Insurgentes Theater (Teatro de Los Insurgentes), Av. Insurgentes Sur #1587, presents plays and musicals in a building that boasts a striking Diego Rivera mosaic on its facade. The Blanquita Theater (Teatro Blanquita), four blocks north of the Latin-American Tower on Avenida Lázaro Cárdenas (M: Bellas Artes, lines 2 and 8), offers variety shows performed by Mexico's top singers, dancers, comedians and magicians.

Other theaters include the Hidalgo, Av. Hidalgo #23 (M: Hidalgo, line 2); and the Virginia Fábregas Theater, Calle Velasquez de León #29, a few blocks from the Zona Rosa (M: Allende, line 2). For listings, check *Tiempo Libre.*

American and foreign films are shown in their original language with Spanish subtitles. Hollywood blockbusters and first-run films open in Mexico soon after they do in the United States, and admission is inexpensive (around $3.75 U.S.; half-price on Wednesdays). For listings, check *Tiempo Libre*.

Cineteca Nacional, Av. México-Coyoacán #389, the southern extension of Avenida Cuauhtémoc (M: Coyoacán, line 3), is a multiplex with a wide range of movie choices; phone (55) 5422-1100. Closer to the city center is Cinepolis Diana, Paseo de la Reforma #423, Colonia Cuauhtémoc; phone (55) 2122-6060. Cinemex Casa de Arte, Av. Anatole France #120 at Avenida Presidente Masaryk in the Polanco neighborhood, has four small theaters that show arthouse films from around the world; phone (55) 5257-6969.

Special Events

Mexico City residents observe many of the celebrations listed in the "Fiestas and Holidays" section on page 532. The capital also gives an extra flourish to historical commemorations that helped secure independence and pave the way for modern Mexico. Several religious holidays are of special importance as well.

Flower-garlanded cows, beribboned dogs and cats and irreverent roosters are paraded on Jan. 17 for the Feast of San Antonio Abad, or the "blessing of the animals." This whimsical ceremony takes place at the Metropolitan Cathedral on the *Zócalo*. Holy Week *(Semana Santa)* celebrations take place in mid-April.

On May 1, Labor Day *(Día del Trabajo)*, the president reviews a huge parade of workers from the central balcony of the National Palace. For the Feast of Corpus Christi, families dress children in native costumes or their Sunday best and gather at the Metropolitan Cathedral for a priest's blessing. The date is variable, occurring between late May and mid-June.

The fall of Tenochtitlán to Hernando Cortés and his followers is commemorated on Cuauhtémoc Day, Aug. 21, with wreath-laying ceremonies at the Plaza of the Three Cultures and the Cuauhtémoc Statue at the intersection of Paseo de la Reforma and Avenida Insurgentes.

Father Miguel Hidalgo's *"El Grito de Dolores,"* the rallying cry of Mexican independence, is repeated by the president of Mexico and echoed by hundreds of thousands on the evening of Sept. 15 in Plaza Constitución (the *Zócalo*). One of the year's biggest events, it is nationally televised. A morning military parade on Independence Day, Sept. 16, proceeds from the *Zócalo* to the Independence Monument, past buildings draped with streamers in the national colors of red, green and white.

Columbus Day *(Día de la Raza)* on Oct. 12 commemorates Christopher Columbus' discovery of the Americas. Families build altars in their homes and decorate the graves of loved ones with extravagant flower garlands to celebrate the Day of the Dead Nov. 1. Revolution Day, Nov. 20, features a spirited parade down avenidas Madero, Juárez and Reforma in commemoration of the start of the Revolution of 1910.

The venerated Virgin of Guadalupe, patron saint of the country, is the focal point of a nationwide celebration of dancing, fireworks and religious processions on Dec. 12, the Feast Day of the Virgin of Guadalupe. Devout believers from throughout the country and abroad make the journey to the Basilica of Guadalupe, in the northern suburb of Villa de Guadalupe. Mexico City is decorated in high style for Christmas and the nine days leading up to it, during which there are traditional re-enactments of the Holy Family's search for an inn *(posada)*.

This ends listings for Mexico City.
The following page resumes the alphabetical listings
of cities in Mexico City and Vicinity.

SAN ANGEL, DISTRITO FEDERAL (C-9)

San Angel (sahn AHN-hehl) was once a small town far removed from colonial Mexico City. Like other southern suburbs, however, it has been overtaken by the capital's inexorable growth. Even so, a leisurely stroll past San Angel's elegant colonial mansions and bougainvillea-draped walls is a trip back through history and a welcome respite from downtown Mexico City's noise and congestion.

In the beautifully leafy Bombilla Park (Parque de la Bombilla), at the junction of avenidas La Paz and Insurgentes Sur, stands a granite monument honoring Gen. Alvaro Obregón. Obregón helped draft the Constitution of 1917 and was the first president of post-revolutionary Mexico. He was assassinated in San Angel by a religious fanatic in 1928.

A few blocks southwest of the park off Avenida La Paz is Plaza San Jacinto, a pleasant square bordered by cobblestone streets, tucked-away restaurants and outdoor cafés. A plaque in the square honors members of St. Patrick's Battalion, a group of Irish immigrants who deserted the U.S. Army and sided with Mexico during the Mexican-American War. Today the plaza is known for its Saturday Bazaar (Bazar del Sábado) *(see description under the Mexico City "Shopping" section, page 260).*

West of San Angel on the Mexico-Toluca Highway (Mex. 15) is Miguel Hidalgo National Park (Parque Nacional Miguel Hidalgo), known locally as La Marquesa for the name of the small town nearby. Surrounded by mountains, the park contains picnic sites, a government trout hatchery and a man-made lake stocked with trout. Horseback rides can be arranged at several park locations.

CARRILLO GIL ART MUSEUM (Museo de Arte Carrillo Gil) is about 3 blocks north of Plaza San Jacinto at Av. Revolución #1608 (Metro: Miguel A. de Quevedo, line 3). It displays the collection amassed by Dr. Carrillo Gil, focusing on paintings and graphics by noted 20th-century Mexican artists but including European works as well. José Clemente Orozco, Diego Rivera, David Alfaro Siqueiros and Pablo Picasso are among those represented. Tues.-Sun. 10-6. Admission around $1.75 (U.S.); free to all Sun.

CASA DEL RISCO is at Plaza San Jacinto #15 (Metro: Miguel A. de Quevedo, line 3). The building contains an extensive library and one of Mexico City's finest collections of European paintings from the 14th through the 17th centuries. Don't miss the colorful, wildly abstract fountain in the patio that appears to be made primarily of broken crockery. Tues.-Sun. 10-5. Free.

DIEGO RIVERA STUDIO MUSEUM (Museo Casa Estudio Diego Rivera) is on Calle Diego Rivera, across the street from the San Angel Inn (Metro: Miguel A. de Quevedo, line 3). Designed by architect Juan O'Gorman in 1931, it was Rivera's last home, where he died in 1957. Surrounded by different kinds of cacti, it has interior and exterior staircases leading up to the artist's large studio, which contrasts sharply with the small bedrooms. A roof bridge links the house to one occupied by fellow artist and partner Frida Kahlo. Temporary exhibitions are mounted.

Tues.-Sun. 10-6. Admission around $1 (U.S.); free to all Sun. Phone (55) 5550-1189.

EL CARMEN MUSEUM (Museo del Carmen) is just south of Av. La Paz at Av. Revolución #4 and Monasterio (Metro: Miguel A. de Quevedo, line 3). It occupies a former Carmelite convent dating from 1615. The building is distinguished by carved doors, baroque altarpieces, a fine collection of religious paintings and three domes, each tiled in a different color. The cloister's garden has a tropical look, unusual for Mexico City. Tues.-Sun. 10-5. Admission around $3.50 (U.S.); free to all Sun.

NATIONAL UNIVERSITY OF MEXICO (Universidad Nacional Autonoma de México) is south of San Angel (M: Copilco or Universidad, line 3), roughly between avs. Insurgentes Sur and Universidad. The National University of Mexico, or UNAM, spreads over some 800 acres. Its mosaic-covered modern buildings and academic reputation have made University City (Ciudad Universitaria), as the complex is commonly referred to, world famous.

The best reason to visit is to see the murals that decorate the exterior of the main campus buildings, most of them concentrated just east of Insurgentes Sur. One of the most visually arresting is the Main Library (Biblioteca). This rectangular tower is covered with stone mosaic work, augmented in places by colored tiles.

Near the library is the Administration Building (Rectoría), dominated by a huge David Alfaro Siqueiros mural that incorporates pieces of colored glass. A mosaic that includes a three-headed mask symbolizing Indian, Spanish and *mestizo*—the three peoples of Mexico—adorns one wall of the School of Medicine.

The easiest way to get to the university is to take a taxi or line 3 of the Metro, getting off at one of the last two stops. City buses marked "Ciudad Universitaria" travel regularly down Avenida Insurgentes Sur and stop in front of the main complex of buildings. Weekends, when students are noticeably absent, are the best time to view the buildings.

TENANCINGO, MEXICO (C-9)
pop. 31,600, elev. 6,632'

Tenancingo (teh-nahn-SEEN-goh)—its name an Indian term meaning "place of little walls"—was founded in 1425. Overlooking the town from atop a hill is a large Christ statue; this vantage point provides a sweeping view. Tenancingo produces wood and palm furniture, *rebozos* (shawl-like woven garments) and fruit liqueurs, all of which are for sale at the huge open-air market held on Sundays.

MALINALCO is about 25 km (16 mi.) east of Tenancingo via a graded road to the village of Malinalco, then approximately 2 km (1.2 mi.) west on a good dirt road. Buses from Toluca travel to Malinalco. Partially restored, the site is hewn into a cliffside.

The Temple of the Eagles and Jaguars, one of the world's few archeological remains carved from solid stone, has a reconstructed thatch and wood roof entrance, in front of which sits a headless stone figure. The doorway resembles an open-mouthed serpent. A beautifully carved wooden drum retrieved from the Temple of the Sun (Building IV) resides in the Museum of Anthropology at the Mexiquense Cultural Center in Toluca *(see attraction listing under Toluca)*.

The staircase that leads to the site is carved into the mountainside. It's an arduous climb of more than 400 steps that takes 30 minutes, but the view of the surrounding valley is magnificent. Tues.-Sun. 9-5:30. Admission around $3.50 (U.S.); free to all Sun.

SANTO DESIERTO DEL CARMEN MONASTERY NATIONAL PARK is about 12 km (7 mi.) southeast of Tenancingo on a graded road, a short distance from Malinalco. The park's main feature is a late 18th-century Carmelite monastery that sits in a lovely wooded setting.

TEOTIHUACAN, MEXICO (C-10)

San Juan Teotihuacán (teh-oh-tee-wah-KAHN) is one of the most widely known and easily accessible of Mexico's major archeological zones. Very little is known about this religious center, the people who built it, or even what the city was originally called. It was designated a World Heritage Site by UNESCO in 1987.

Teotihuacán is thought to have been founded as early as 700 B.C., although it was not until around 100 B.C. that construction of its two great pyramids began. Archeologists estimate that at its height around A.D. 500, up to 200,000 people lived there, making it bigger than Rome at the time and one of the largest cities in the world. The city was burned and abandoned for unknown reasons around A.D. 750; it is believed the decline was gradual and perhaps facilitated by overpopulation and a resulting depletion of natural resources.

The area was later inhabited by the Toltecs; by the time the Aztecs discovered the site, it was in such an advanced state of ruin that they named it Teotihuacán, which means "place of the gods," or more broadly, "where men become gods." The gray stone structures seen today are to a large degree reconstructed, and the barren landscape barely hints at what the city must have looked like during its heyday some 1,500 years ago.

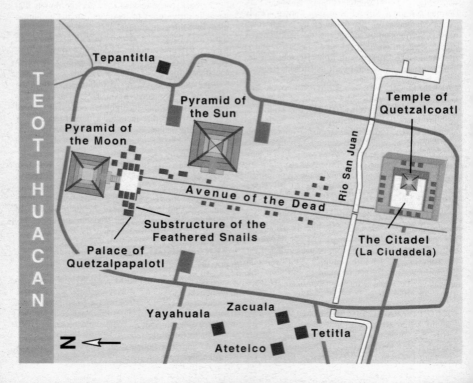

Exploring the Site

Teotihuacán was once paved with volcanic stone and mica slabs, and buildings were plastered with lime and mortar and then decorated with bas-relief sculptures and murals, often painted red; traces of the color are still discernible. The typical structural arrangement was often a courtyard surrounded by several levels of temples and rooms.

The ruins are aligned along a north-south axis traversed by the Avenue of the Dead (Avenida de Los Muertos). The name was given by the Aztecs, who believed that the low structures lining both sides of the avenue were burial sites. All similar in size and style, they accentuate the grandness of the pyramids. Touches of paint can still be detected on some of the building fragments. This wide thoroughfare (paved for today's visitors) is more than a mile long; it seems even longer when you're trekking from one building to another.

The Pyramid of the Sun, on the east side of the Avenue of the Dead, dominates the ruins and is the oldest of Teotihuacán's structures. It is the world's third-largest pyramid; only those at Cholula and Cheops, Egypt, are bigger. The structure rises in five sloping levels to a height of more than 250 feet; each side of its base measures about 735 feet.

Built of adobe brick faced with volcanic stone, the pyramid is visible for some distance from the highway approaching the site. When first discovered it was a gigantic mound covered with vegetation, but even the subsequent reconstruction fails to detract from the achievement of those who originally built this enormous monument without benefit of the wheel or metal tools.

A stairway on the west flank begins at the pyramid's base and leads to the summit, where a temple probably once stood. The 248 steps make for an arduous climb, but the five levels each provide a chance to stop, take a breather and take in the view. In clear weather, the panorama from the top is simply breathtaking. Because of the gentle slope, descending is significantly easier than clambering down the steep sides of some of Mexico's other pyramids, such as El Castillo at Chichén Itzá. If you still feel vulnerable, hold onto the link chain that runs the length of the stairway.

The Plaza of the Moon constitutes a remarkable cluster of buildings. The plaza is surrounded by staired platforms and has a square altar in the middle. The Pyramid of the Moon, at the north end of the Avenue of the Dead, is 140 feet high; stairs scale its south face. It appears as tall as the Pyramid of the Sun because it was built on higher ground. The pyramid is connected to a temple with sloping walls. The climb to the summit of this pyramid is shorter (although no less taxing). It's worth the effort, though, for the panoramic vista of the Avenue of the Dead. **Note:** The apex is rocky and uneven; watch your footing.

At the southwest corner of the Plaza of the Moon is the restored Palace of Quetzalpapalotl, Teotihuacán's most elaborate building. Presumed to have been the home of a prominent citizen or supreme priest, it has some well-preserved murals. In the inner courtyard are pillars decorated with bas-reliefs depicting the *quetzal-papalotl*, a feathered butterfly, and various symbols related to water. Beneath this palace is the Palace of the Jaguars, so called because of the jaguar images in the rooms ringing the courtyard, and the Substructure of the Feathered Snails, part of a beautifully decorated temple beneath the Quetzalpapalotl Palace that features carvings of large snails garlanded with feathers.

In 1998 excavations uncovered a tomb and offerings inside the Pyramid of the Moon that archeologists hope will provide additional clues to help solve the riddle of the site's origination. Objects at what has initially been described as a burial site—most likely someone of high social standing—include obsidian and jade sculptures and skeleton fragments.

At the southern end of the zone is The Citadel (La Ciudadela). Teotihuacán was ruled from this vast sunken square, which encompassed nearly 17 acres and was surrounded by a low wall. The inner esplanade once held thousands of standing people.

Within the courtyard are several temples; the most elaborate is the restored Temple of Quetzalcóatl (the Feathered Serpent). The god Quetzalcóatl was worshipped by the Maya, Toltec and Aztec civilizations, although it is unknown whether the inhabitants of Teotihuacán paid tribute to the same being. Carved stone slabs face part of the structure; writhing serpents, their heads sticking out from ruffles of feathers, adorn some of the walls.

Other structures are located off the Avenue of the Dead. Tepantitla, east of the Pyramid of the Moon, may have been the residence of a high priest. Several walls have traces of paintings showing Tláloc, the rain god, amid swimming male figures and water imagery. Tetitla, west of the loop road that surrounds the archeological zone, has a labyrinthine maze of rooms with patchy murals depicting jaguars, snakes, quetzals and aquatic life. Also west of the loop road is Atetelco, another large-sized group of structures with murals that depict priests. Nearby are Zacuala and Yayahuala, fortresslike one-story structures with many rooms, halls and passageways.

The museum (Museo Teotihuacán) near the Pyramid of the Sun has archeological, historical and diagrammatic exhibits, some of them interactive, that pertain to the peoples who once inhabited the area. Scale models of the zone (which you walk above and view through a glass floor) will help orient the first-time visitor.

General Information and Activities

The archeological site is about 49 kilometers (30 miles) northeast of downtown Mexico City. Buses for Teotihuacán depart regularly from the Terminal Central de Autobuses del Norte in Mexico City, on Avenida de los 100 Metros; Metro has a subway station at the terminal (Autobuses del Norte, line

5). The trip takes about an hour. Ascertain from the bus driver when the last bus returns to Mexico City and where it picks up passengers. Numerous Mexico City travel agencies offer Teotihuacán sightseeing tours.

If driving, take Avenida Insurgentes Norte out of the city, which becomes Mex. 85-D, and take the exit for Mex. 132-D. From the toll plaza, the site entrance is about 22 kilometers (14 miles) east (about a 30-minute drive); signs along the way are marked "Pirámides."

Wear sturdy, nonslip walking shoes if you plan to climb the pyramids, because the rocks can be slippery. On warm, sunny days wear lightweight clothing, sunscreen and a hat. During the summer months (June through September) afternoon showers are frequent. Fall and winter days can be cloudy, chilly and breezy. The altitude is more than 7,000 feet, so walk and climb at a relaxed pace.

Note: Numerous souvenir vendors roam the site, and you will be approached on many occasions to purchase items ranging from jewelry to carved figurines to lace shawls. The vendors are persistent but usually not aggressive. If you have no intention of buying anything, keep walking; a negative shake of the head and a polite *"gracias"* will convey a "thanks, but no thanks" response. If you stop, chances are you'll never get away. But if you want to buy something, by all means bargain; a vendor will initially offer three to four times what he or she is willing to settle for.

Avoid going on weekends, which can be very crowded. Try to visit during the week and early in the day before the tour buses begin arriving.

Snacks are available at the entrance and there are a few restaurants just outside the site, but most hotels will pack a box lunch to take along on a bus tour. Bring bottled water, particularly if it's a hot day. There are very basic restrooms at the entrance. The site is open daily 8-5; the museum is open Tues.-Sun. Admission 25 pesos (about $2.50 U.S.); free to all Sun. There is an additional 30-peso (about $3) fee for the use of a video camera.

TEPOTZOTLAN, MEXICO (C-10)
pop. 40,500, elev. 7,577'

Tepotzotlán (teh-poht-soh-TLAHN), about 35 kilometers (22 miles) north of Mexico City, is an easy day trip destination from the capital. From the downtown area, take Avenida Avila Camacho (Mex. 57) northwest out of the city and watch for the Tepotzotlán turnoff; the town lies about a mile west. Buses depart regularly for Tepotzotlán from the Cuatro Caminos Metro station (the western terminus of line 2); ask for the bus going to Tepotzotlán. To return, take a bus going to the Cuatro Caminos station.

The town is the perfect antidote for visitors tired of Mexico City's grinding congestion and noise: It has clear air, wonderful mountain views, colonial charm and a commercial yet laid-back atmosphere. After visiting the Church of San Francisco Xavier,

Tepotzotlán's main attraction, have a relaxed lunch at one of the eateries surrounding the central plaza.

CHURCH OF SAN FRANCISCO XAVIER faces the plaza. It was founded by the Jesuits in the late 16th century, serving as a seminary for the religious training of the children of Otomí Indians. The richly detailed stone carvings of angels and saints on the building's facade—a masterful example of Mexican baroque architecture—reflect the Jesuit order's wealth and influence.

A tree-lined atrium leads to the Aljibes Cloister (Claustro de Los Aljibes), which contains paintings by Miguel Cabrera. The interior is filled with gold gilt, carvings of cherubs and saints, and five extravagant altarpieces. A highlight is the Camarín de la Virgen, or altar room, behind the Chapel of the Virgin of Loreto (Capilla de la Virgen de Loreto). This small, octagonal-shaped chamber is a jewel box of intricate interior design.

Outside the Orange Cloister (Claustro de Los Naranjos), planted with orange trees, are carefully tended gardens. Church and National Museum of the Viceroyalty open Wed.-Sun. 9-6, Tues. 10-5. Museum admission around $3.80 (U.S.), under 14 free.

National Museum of the Viceroyalty (Museo Nacional del Virreinato) is adjacent to the church, within the restored monastery. It houses 3 centuries' worth of colonial and religious art. Rare 16th-century vestments and altar hangings, gold and repoussé silver monstrances from the 17th century and a painting of the Virgin attributed to Bartolomé Esteban Murillo are among its many treasures.

Pastorelas, traditional re-enactments of Christ's birth, are performed during the Christmas season. Travel agencies in Mexico City can arrange for reservations, which should be booked well in advance. Admission is charged for the *pastorela* performances.

TEPOZTLAN, MORELOS (C-9)
pop. 15,200, elev. 5,579'

Tepoztlán (teh-pohs-TLAHN), a name that means "place of copper," is secluded on the lush green slopes of the Sierra del Ajusco and protected by the Sierra de Tepoztlán. The latter's scarred cliffs constitute Tepozteco National Park, which surrounds the village of Tlalnepantla, northeast of Tepoztlán. Tepoztlán's sequestered location was perfect for Emiliano Zapata, regarded locally as a folk hero, who used the village as his revolutionary stronghold in 1910.

Despite proximity to urban Cuernavaca and Mexico City, traditional customs of the town's Aztec predecessors remain. Older residents still speak Náhuatl, the ancient Aztec tongue, and mingle Christian and pre-Christian religious practices. Tepoztlán's mystical aura attracts proponents of new-age philosophies in addition to weekend visitors from Mexico City.

Celebrations include Mardi Gras, held on the 5 days preceding Ash Wednesday, in which villagers perform Aztec dances and dress as Spanish *conquistadores*. On Sept. 7, a celebration honors both the Nativity of the Virgin and the town's patron god Tepoztécatl, the Mexican Bacchus credited with the perfection of pulque, the fermented drink extracted from the maguey plant. Tepoztlán also has a vibrant Saturday and Sunday market overflowing with regionally produced handicrafts as well as '60s-style hippie jewelry.

EX-CONVENT OF DOMINICO (Ex-Convento Dominico de la Navidad) is just off the main plaza. It was built by Dominicans in the 16th century. The massive structure has some walls that are more than 6 feet thick. The upper floor offers a fine view of the surrounding mountains and also houses a museum with exhibits on the region's natural history, people and religion. Tues.-Sun. 10-6. Free.

TEPOZTECO PYRAMID stands high on a hill overlooking the town and is accessible by a trail beginning at the end of Av. Tepozteco. Now a ruin, this pre-Hispanic monument, built by the Tlahuica Indians, honored the god Tepoztécatl. The vista from the hillside and the top of the pyramid is superb but the ascent is steep (although shaded and beautiful); make sure you wear comfortable hiking shoes. Site daily 9-5:30. Admission around $3 (U.S.); free to all Sun.

TEQUESQUITENGO, MORELOS (D-10)
elev. 3,083'

South of Cuernavaca lies the resort area of Tequesquitengo (teh-kehs-kee-TEHN-goh), on Lake Tequesquitengo. The village was moved to its present location in 1820 when rising lake waters forced the abandonment of an earlier site. Between 1957 and 1958 the lake rose nearly 13 feet, inundating lakeside homes and the first floor of a hotel. To restore the water level, a 1.7-mile tunnel was bored through a nearby mountain rim.

The lake, about 3,000 feet above sea level, has calm, spring-fed waters ideal for water skiing; it is the site of championship exhibitions. Swimming, boating and fishing also are possible.

TLALPAN, DISTRITO FEDERAL (C-9)

Tlalpan (TLAHL-pan), south of University City, can be reached by bus from the Taxqueña Metro station (line 2). The name means "place of solid ground"; in this area south of the Valley of Mexico, regional civilizations flourished as early as 1200 B.C. The Olympic Village (Villa Olímpica), built to house athletes during the 1968 summer games, is now a residential area.

Near Plaza de la Constitución, Tlalpan's main square, is the 1532 church of San Agustín de las Cuevas, which contains paintings by Miguel Cabrera. To the southwest is the extinct 13,097-foot Volcán Ajusco. Buses that leave from Azteca Stadium on Calzada de Tlalpan travel to the volcano, which offers excellent views of the surrounding area if the weather is clear.

CUICUILCO PYRAMID is near the intersection of Av. Insurgentes Sur (Mex. 95) and the Anillo Periférico, close to Olympic Village. The city of Cuicuilco was a major urban center, believed to have developed as early as 700 B.C. It eventually had a population estimated to be 20,000, but was abandoned around the end of the fourth century after several eruptions by the volcano Xitle.

Today the site consists of a round platform, discovered in the early 1920s, and a ramp that once led to an altar at the temple's summit. The original structure was some 370 feet in diameter and 59 feet high; it was enlarged several times over the centuries. A small museum at the site has geologic exhibits and displays objects found during the excavations. Daily 9-5. Admission is charged to the museum. Phone (55) 5606-9758.

TOLUCA, MEXICO (C-9)
pop. 461,400, elev. 8,790'

Capital of the state of México, Toluca (toh-LOO-cah)—about 65 kilometers (40 miles) west of Mexico City—is a commercial center in the middle of the flat Toluca Valley. One of the highest Mexican cities in elevation, it thus enjoys cool weather despite the tropical latitude. Although it is heavily industrial, low buildings characterize Toluca's skyline, and there are many little plazas and manicured parks.

Toluca was an Indian settlement as early as 1200; the name is derived from the Náhuatl Indian expression *tollocan*, or "those who bow their heads." Spaniards under Hernando Cortés began settling the region in the early 16th century after the conqueror was granted 22 towns in central and southern Mexico by King Carlos V.

Plaza of the Martyrs (Plaza de Los Mártires), the main plaza, is between avenidas Sebastian Lerdo de Tejada and de la Independencia. It was named for a group of revolutionaries who were executed in 1811 for their part in Mexico's struggle to win freedom from Spain, an uprising started by Father Miguel Hidalgo. On the plaza's south side is the cathedral, where traditional dances are presented on various Mexican holidays. Check with the State Tourism Office (*see below*) for more information about these colorful spectacles.

Among several downtown museums is the Museum of Fine Arts (Museo de Bellas Artes), on Avenida Santos Degollado a block north of the plaza. The collection of paintings and sculptures spans the 16th through the 19th centuries.

A block or so south of the plaza along Avenida Miguel Hidalgo is Los Portales, a pedestrian-only walkway fronting an arcade of shops and restaurants protected by arches and buzzing with sidewalk vendors. It's an interesting place to stroll. Here rows of candy stands offer Toluca's local fruit confections, and liquor stores sell an orange-flavored liqueur called *moscos*.

From Mexico City, the easiest way to reach Toluca by car is to take toll highway Mex. 15-D.

This direct route is expensive but fast. Buses to Toluca depart regularly from Mexico City's Terminal de Autobuses del Poniente, the western bus terminal; to get there, take Metro to the Observatorio station (at the western end of Line 1). Buses marked "Toluca—Directo" make the trip in the least amount of time.

Several towns and villages to the east and south of Toluca offer a first-hand look at the way Mexico's rural population has engaged in manufacturing and marketing since pre-Hispanic days. Visiting these places during the morning is a good way to acquire locally made items at the various *tianguis* (open-air markets), even without benefit of bargaining expertise.

East of Toluca on Mex. 15 to the paved turnoff for the village of San Pedro Cholula, then south, is appropriately named Tianguistenco. The Tuesday *tianguis* (open-air market) fills roughly half the streets in town with baskets, *sarapes* and other crafts from throughout the Toluca Valley. Visiting during the morning is a good way to acquire locally made items, even without benefit of bargaining expertise.

México State Tourism Office (Dirección General de Turismo): Avenida 1 de Mayo #731 at the corner of Roberto Bosch, second floor, Industrial Zone; phone (722) 275-8108 or (722) 275-8109.

What To See in and Around Town

BOTANIC GARDEN (Cosmovitral Jardín Botánico) is just east of the main plaza at calles Lerdo de Tejada, Degollado and Ignacio Rayón. Hundreds of plant species native to Mexico are exhibited within the walls of this Art Nouveau-style building. Most impressive, however, are the magnificent stained-glass panels, which replaced the original windows. They were designed and built in 1980 by local artist Leopoldo Flores, who utilized some 45 tons of glass, 65 tons of metal and 25 tons of lead in their creation. Tues.-Sun. 10-6. Admission around $1.25 (U.S.).

CALIXTLAHUACA ARCHEOLOGICAL ZONE is 8 km (5 mi.) north on Mex. 55 to the site turnoff, then about 3 km (2 mi.) west. The site is located on a hilltop above the village of the same name. Not much is known about its origins, although it was taken over by the Aztecs around 1476. Several buildings have been uncovered: the conical Temple of Quetzalcóatl-Ehecatl; the Pyramid of Tláloc; and the Altar of Skulls (Tzompantli), which was probably used for human sacrifice. Buses make frequent trips from Toluca to Calixtlahuaca; there is a short uphill walk to get to the site entrance. Daily 9-5. Admission around $3 (U.S.); free to all Sun.

CASA DE ARTESANIAS is at Paseo Tollocan Oriente #700, at the corner of Uracua. This government-run crafts store offers contemporary crafts produced in the state of México, including textiles, carved wood figures, ceramics and blown glass. It also is possible to watch the artisans as they work. The store is staffed with multilingual personnel. Daily 10-7.

FELIPE S. GUTIERREZ MUSEUM is downtown at Calle Nicolas Bravo #303, at the corner of Av. Lerdo de Tejada. It features works by the 19th-century portrait painter who taught figure drawing to José María Velasco. Gutiérrez was one of the first Mexican artists who rendered his subjects' Indian lineage, making no attempt to give them European features. Guided tours are available. Tues.-Sun. 10-6. Free. Phone (722) 213-2647.

JOSE MARIA VELASCO MUSEUM is at Av. Lerdo de Tejada #400, adjoining the Felipe S. Gutiérrez Museum. It exhibits paintings and sculptures by one of Mexico's most influential 19th-century painters. One of Velasco's more notable works, "Vista desde Molino del Rey," was donated to the museum by former president Ernesto Zedillo. One room contains a re-creation of the artist's workshop. Guided tours are available. Tues.-Sun. 10-6. Free. Phone (722) 213-2647.

METEPEC is about 8 km (5 mi.) southeast of Toluca and an hour west of Mexico City. It is best known for the Trees of Life (*Arboles de la Vida*) meticulously created by local artisans. Against a backdrop of clay trunks and branches, these delightful trees depict stories populated by a diverse cast of religious and secular characters and inanimate objects. Many families in town are engaged in the craft.

Buses depart frequently for Metepec from Toluca's central bus station. The town is an easy day trip from Mexico City as well. By car, leave the capital via Paseo de la Reforma or Avenida Constituyentes, picking up either toll Mex. 15-D or free Mex. 15 west toward Toluca. Take the Mex. 15-D exit for Taxco/Ixtapan de La Sal and follow signs for Metepec. Pottery shops line the main street; ask for directions to the artisans' workshops (alfarerías), where bargaining for purchases is expected. (Note: Many are closed from 2-4 for afternoon siesta).

MUSEUM OF WATERCOLOR (Museo de la Acuarela) is at Melchor Ocampo #105. It occupies one of Toluca's oldest buildings, a two-story house with a central courtyard. It is known as "El Gallito," a reference to the brand of thread that was once distributed from the building. The permanent collection of 176 paintings is displayed in six halls, each named after a popular artist from the state of México. Guided tours are available. Tues.-Sun. 10-6. Free. Phone (722) 214-7304.

NEVADO DE TOLUCA NATIONAL PARK (Parque Nacional Nevado de Toluca) is about 25 km (16 mi.) southwest of Toluca on Mex. 134 to the junction with Mex. 10, then south on Mex. 10 about 8 km (5 mi.) to the park entrance. From the entrance, a paved road winds about 3.5 km (2 mi.) to the main gate, then a rough, unsurfaced road ascends the 17 km (11 mi.) to the crater. This 15,032-foot-high extinct volcano is Mexico's fourth highest summit.

Nevado de Toluca's summit is snowcapped from November to March and frequently obscured by clouds. Within the crater are two deep-blue lakes, El Sol (Lake of the Sun) and La Luna (Lake of the Moon). With care and a good guide, you can drive to the top of the mountain and then hike down into the crater; on a clear day, the views are splendid. Check with the State Tourism Office in Toluca for information about guided excursions. Park admission around $1 (U.S.).

STATE OF MEXICO CULTURAL CENTER (Centro Cultural Mexiquense) is off the Paseo Tollocan loop road; from its southwest section (between the monument to Christopher Columbus, at the junction with Mex. 134, and the University of the State of México), follow the signs about 1.6 km (1 mi.) southwest to the cultural center. This large, spread-out complex comprises a mix of architectural styles from colonial to contemporary.

Several museums here are dedicated to the conservation and exhibition of Mexican cultural traditions. The center can be reached from downtown Toluca via bus or taxi. Guide service in English is available. Museums open daily 10-6. Admission around $2 (U.S.). Phone (722) 274-1200.

Museum of Anthropology (Museo de Antropología) exhibits artifacts from the state's archeological zones, including Malinalco and Calixtlahuaca. It was designed by Pedro Ramírez Vasquez, the architect who supervised construction of Mexico City's National Museum of Anthropology.

Museum of Modern Art (Museo de Arte Moderno) has works by Mexican muralists José Clemente Orozco, Diego Rivera and David Alfaro Siqueiros, among others.

Museum of Popular Arts (Museo de Artes Popular) is housed in a hacienda dating from the 17th century. Colorful murals decorate its walls, and a variety of regional handicrafts are on display. A huge "tree of life" sits in the front hall. The museum's exhibits of saddles, clothing and other items used by charros (cowboys) are considered among the best of their type in the country.

TEOTENANGO ARCHEOLOGICAL ZONE is about 25 km (16 mi.) south of Toluca via Mex. 55, overlooking the village of Tenango de Arista. Teotenango was probably a ceremonial center for nearby Malinalco (see Tenancingo listing). This walled, hilltop site covers more than 2 square miles, spread across a flat bluff. The impressive reconstructions include a good-sized ball court, large pyramids and squat temples faced with broad staircases. An uphill walk to the ruins passes a small museum displaying artifacts recovered during restoration efforts. Bus transportation is available from Toluca. Tues.-Sun. 9-5. Admission (site and museum) around $1.25 (U.S.).

ZACANGO ZOO is about 7 km (4 mi.) southeast of the city via Mex. 55 to the Metepec exit, then approximately 6 km (3.5 mi.) west, following signs. The zoo displays more than 200 species of animals on the grounds of the former Hacienda de Zacango, home of the Order of Franciscan Priests in the 16th century. Features include an African compound with free-roaming animals, a walk-through aviary and a petting zoo. Food is available. Daily 9-5. Admission is charged.

VALLE DE BRAVO, MEXICO (C-8)
pop. 26,600, elev. 5,937'

Situated on a forested mountain slope about 140 kilometers (87 miles) west of Mexico City, Valle de Bravo (VAH-yeh deh BRAH-voh) overlooks large, man-made Lake Avándaro, part of a vast hydroelectric project serving the Valley of Mexico. The town is a popular weekend resort for well-to-do residents of Mexico City and Toluca.

Hang gliding, hiking, horseback riding, kayaking mountain biking, sailing and windsurfing are among the recreational activities available. Nearby Avándaro Reort and Spa has an 18-hole golf course. Valle de Bravo also hosts an international hang-gliding competition. Due to the elevation, the region is blessed with some of Mexico's nicest weather—mild, dry and sunny.

Buildings with whitewashed stucco walls and red-tiled roofs give the town an attractive colonial look. Further color is supplied by masses of bougainvillea cascading over walls and terraces, and—from November through May—fluttering clouds of monarch butterflies en route to and from their nearby wintering grounds *(see Angangueo listing under Central Mexico)*. In the vicinity of Plaza Independencia, the main square, are boutiques, restaurants, a two-story artisans' market and a bookstore.

XOCHIMILCO, DISTRITO FEDERAL (C-10)

Xochimilco (soh-chee-MEEL-coh) is about 24 kilometers (15 miles) southeast of downtown Mexico City, within the Federal District but outside the city limits. Designated a World Heritage Site by UNESCO in 1987, the "place where the flowers grow" was once a Chichimec Indian stronghold.

The best way to reach Xochimilco is to take Mexico City's Metro (line 2) to the Taxqueña station, then board a light rail train *(tren ligero)* and get off at the Xochimilco stop. *Peseros* (minibuses) also make the trip from the Taxqueña Metro station to Xochimilco, as do buses that travel down Avenida Insurgentes Sur and Calzada de Tlalpan to the Anillo Periférico.

By car, Xochimilco can be reached via the Periférico, exiting at Jardines del Sur. The tourist-oriented "floating gardens" area is busiest on Sunday, when Mexican families come on their traditional day off. It's much less crowded in the middle of the week.

Xochimilco is threaded by numerous waterways, the last remains of a once-extensive lake. Today's floating gardens were originally *chinampas,* or rafts woven of twigs, covered with earth and planted with flowers or vegetables. The rafts often carried a small hut and were propelled about the lake with oars. Gradually the roots of vegetation on the rafts attached to the lake bottom, and the gardens became islands threaded by canals. Other *chinampas* were anchored by planting willows or *ahuehuetes* (cypresses) around their perimeters.

Over the years the government has waged battle against tenacious water hyacinths, stagnation, pollution and falling water levels. Ongoing canal cleanup efforts seem to be proving successful, and Xochimilco continues to be a prime tourist attraction as well as a local weekend outing of choice.

For a real taste of Mexican merrymaking visit on Sunday, when Xochimilco is thronged by families and a freewheeling carnival atmosphere prevails. Signs marked "Embarcadero" point the way to the boat launches. The rental rate is per boat rather than per person, so it's cheaper—and more fun—to join a group.

Restaurants and souvenir stands line the canals. Everywhere there are hawkers, ashore and afloat in canoes, peddling tacos, beer, drinks, trinkets, balloons, flowers and fruit. Music is an integral part of the fun, and some boats are occupied by mariachi bands or guitar trios, in full costume and of varying degrees of polish, who paddle up to prospective customers and serenade them for a fee.

The government sets authorized rates for the different sizes of boats. If an operator tries to charge more, complain to the police, who usually patrol the principal pier. If a police officer is not available, you must resort to bargaining, at which the boat operators are uncannily skillful; many have learned some English for just this purpose. Be sure to agree on the price and the length of your ride before embarking. Bargaining is easier during the week when there are fewer visitors.

North of the town center is a more recently developed area of canals and *chinampas* where produce is raised, most of it bound for Mexico City markets. Boats can be hired to cruise these canals as well, although the area is kept separate from the tourist-targeted floating gardens. Picnicking is permitted along the banks of a man-made lake, where there also is a visitor center.

Although the floating gardens are the reason most people come here, Xochimilco has other attractions. Facing the main square is the early 16th-century Franciscan Convent and Church of San Bernardino, one of the first in New Spain. Stone carvings of angels and flowers adorn the church's exterior. Inside are several chapels and a main altar resplendent with gold gilt, sculptures and paintings. Also in the central part of town are garden centers and the market, liveliest on Saturdays when Indians come from miles around to sell their wares.

DOLORES OLMEDO PATIÑO MUSEUM is at Av. México #5843; take Metro line 2 to the Taxqueña station, then the *tren ligero* (light rail) to the La Noria station. The museum is about 2 km (1 mi.) west of Xochimilco. Street parking is limited; it's easier to hire a taxi from Mexico City. Philanthropist, art collector and benefactor of Diego Rivera, Olmedo bequeathed her hacienda, La Noria, and her outstanding art collection to the Mexican people upon Rivera's death in 1957.

Featured are Rivera paintings, drawings and engravings; paintings by Frida Kahlo (including some of her best-known works); watercolors and engravings by Russian artist Angelina Beloff; sculptures; and Mexican folk and religious art. The lovely grounds of this immense complex—with their lush gardens, orange and fig trees, Aztec and Maya artifacts, wandering peacocks and a friendly pack of *xoloitzcuintle,* a rare, mid-size hairless dog with black skin dating from pre-Hispanic times—are alone worth a visit. Children's programs, concerts and other special events take place Sat.-Sun.

Food is available. Restrooms are provided. Allow 2 hours minimum. Tues.-Sun. 10-6. Guided tours are given Wed.-Sun. at 10, noon and 4. Admission around $3 (U.S.), over 64 and under 6 free; free to all Tues. Headphone and cassette player rental fee $1. Phone (55) 5555-1016.

Querétaro / Guillermo Aldana / Mexico Tourism Board

Central Mexico

The "heartland of Mexico" evokes more reminders of Spain's legacy than any other part of the country. It is in this region that Spanish explorers capitalized upon abundant mineral resources, particularly silver, and built Mexico's first colonial cities. Many of the country's grand cathedrals and historic buildings were constructed during three centuries of Spanish rule. But Spanish colonists put most of their effort into exploiting the natural resources of their far-flung colony rather than developing an infrastructure to improve it, and the emergence of a rigid class society that put Indians on the bottom rung had bred widespread divisiveness by the turn of the 19th century.

As a result, history figures strongly in this region. The push for independence began with secret meetings in Morelia, Querétaro and San Miguel de Allende. These revolutionaraues plotted Spain's downfall to coincide with the rising of Nueva España ("New Spain"), an independent nation. It was in the town of Dolores Hidalgo that Father Miguel Hidalgo first declared Mexico's freedom from Spain in his 1810 proclamation *Grito de Dolores*.

Father Hidalgo, an intriguing mix of flawed cleric (he sired several children) and committed champion for Indian rights, became the leader of a group of like-minded intellectuals intent on securing Mexican independence. He and two of his chief officers, Ignacio Allende and Ignacio Aldama, were captured outside the city of Chihuahua and executed in 1811, and it would be 10 more long years before independence was finally achieved. Although Hidalgo died in disgrace as a failed rebel and defrocked priest, he is revered in Mexico today.

The Treaty of Guadalupe Hidalgo was signed in the city of Querétaro in 1848. It ended the Mexican War and forced Mexico to give up its territory north of the Rio Grande to the United States, an enormous area comprising Arizona, New Mexico, California, Nevada, Utah and part of Colorado.

In May 1862, invading French forces under emperor Napoleon III were soundly defeated in battle at Puebla, a triumphant event celebrated in today's *Cinco de Mayo* festivities both north and south of the border. And in 1867, Archduke Maximilian, de facto "ruler" of Mexico while then-president Benito Juárez's government was in disarray due to political turmoil, was executed by firing squad at Querétaro. Querétaro also is where the present Mexican constitution was drafted in 1917, and where Mexico's dominant 20th-century political party, the Partido Revolucionario Institucional (PRI), was organized in 1929.

Central Mexico's so-called "colonial" cities—including Guanajuato, Morelia, Puebla, Querétaro, San Miguel de Allende and Zacatecas—are noted for their historic centers. Here you'll find pretty plazas, carefully preserved old buildings, and beautiful cathedrals and churches. Puebla also is known for buildings covered with geometrically patterned Talavera tiles—a Spanish import.

Guadalajara, Mexico's second city and the capital of Jalisco, offers much to see. But it also is a magnet for Mexico's poor, who pour into the city hoping for a better life, putting a strain on already overburdened public services. While visitors are likely to be enchanted by the colonial plazas and stately architecture, they must also contend with traffic jams, air pollution and other urban ills. Still, to many people Guadalajara embodies the essence of Mexico, and its residents are known for their hospitality.

Guadalajara preserves the Spanish colonial past but also celebrates such homegrown pleasures as the *jarabe,* or Mexican hat dance, the heartfelt strains of mariachi music and the flashy horsemanship that characterizes a *charreada,* or Mexican rodeo. And be sure to investigate Chapala, Ajijic and the other resort towns along the shore of nearby Lake Chapala; pleasant year-round weather plus cultural and recreational opportunities have helped make this area a major destination for U.S. and Canadian retirees.

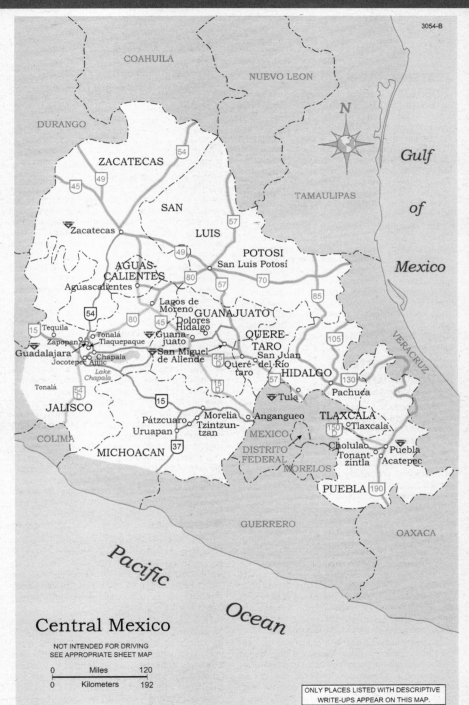

3054-B

COAHUILA

NUEVO LEON

DURANGO

N

Gulf

ZACATECAS

54

TAMAULIPAS

of

45   49

SAN

57

Mexico

Zacatecas

LUIS

POTOSI

49

San Luis Potosí

AGUAS-
CALIENTES

80

57   70

Aguascalientes

Lagos de
Moreno

85

Dolores
Hidalgo

GUANAJUATO

54

15   Tequila

80   45

QUERÉ-
TARO

105

Zapopan   Tonalá
Tlaquepaque

Guana-
juato

San Juan
del Río

Guadalajara   Chapala
Jocotepec   Ajijic

San Miguel
de Allende

45
b

Queré-
taro

HIDALGO

130

*Lake
Chapala*

57

Tonalá

15
b

Pachuca

Tula

54
b

15

JALISCO

Pátzcuaro

Morelia
Tzintzun-
tzan

Angangueo

TLAXCALA

150
b   Tlaxcala

COLIMA

Uruapan

MEXICO

Cholula
Tonant-
zintla

Puebla

MICHOACAN

37

DISTRITO
FEDERAL

Acatepec

MORELOS

PUEBLA   190

GUERRERO

OAXACA

Pacific

VERACRUZ

Ocean

Central Mexico

NOT INTENDED FOR DRIVING
SEE APPROPRIATE SHEET MAP

0	Miles	120
0	Kilometers	192

ONLY PLACES LISTED WITH DESCRIPTIVE
WRITE-UPS APPEAR ON THIS MAP.

Points of Interest

ACATEPEC, PUEBLA (D-11)

The small villages of San Francisco Acatepec (ah-kah-teh-PEHK) and Tonantzintla *(see separate listing within this region)* are just off Mex. 190 a few miles south of Cholula. Both are distinguished by baroque churches that are magnificent examples of Indian craftsmanship—local artisans employing pre-Hispanic imagery to depict Christian beliefs—and are well worth seeing for their visual splendor. The two towns are close to each other, and both churches can be visited by taking a local bus designated "Chipilo." Buses make the trip to Acatepec and Tonantzintla from either Cholula or Puebla.

The beautifully preserved and refurbished Church of San Francisco Acatepec, in the center of this little town, dates from the 18th century and is considered one of the most ornate in the Americas. The facade is an extravagantly colorful feast of blue, yellow and orange tiles fastidiously arranged in dazzling geometric patterns. The interior is somewhat more restrained but still lovely, with paneled doors, wall paintings and folk art decoration. Both this church and the one in Tonantzintla strongly reflect the culture of the Indians who labored to build them.

AGUASCALIENTES, AGUASCALIENTES (G-6)

pop. 618,400, metro area 734,400, elev. 6,193'

The name Aguascalientes (ah-guahs-ka-lee-EHN-tehs) is derived from nearby thermal springs, which were already known at the time of the city's founding. An extensive system of underground tunnels has earned Aguascalientes the nickname "La Ciudad Perforada" (the perforated city). This maze of catacombs, presumably excavated by an ancient people, has never been completely explored. Visitors, however, are not allowed in them.

The first inhabitants of this region were an indigenous people known as the Chichimecas (brave dogs), many of whom belonged to nomadic tribes with distinctive names. Soon after the Spaniards arrived, orchards began to be cultivated; the settlements around them led to the development of the city's oldest neighborhoods. Aguascalientes was founded in 1575 as "Villa de Nuestra Señora de la Asunción de Las Aguas Calientes," a reference to the abundant thermal waters in the vicinity, and provided shelter for those traveling the "Silver Route" between Zacatecas and Mexico City.

Modern Aguascalientes is a manufacturing center, and companies from Japan and the United States have set up operations here. Impressive reminders of a colonial past, however, can still be seen in the area around Plaza de la Patria, the main plaza. The city's warm, dry climate also makes it pleasant to explore on foot.

The cathedral and various government buildings flank Plaza de la Patria. The Government Palace (Palacio de Gobierno), on the plaza's south side, is built of red sandstone; it features hand-carved pillars and a fine interior patio. A highlight is the mural by Chilean painter Oswaldo Barra, which depicts all manner of mercantile scenes as well as miners grimly ascending from underground. The building is open Mon.-Sat. 9-4; closed holidays.

Next door, City Hall (Palacio Municipal), another imposing building, has an attractive fountain inside the entrance. The baroque Cathedral, on the west side of Plaza de la Patria, is the oldest church in Aguascalientes and contains valuable religious paintings. The plaza itself, with its beautiful fountain and a park-like garden furnished with benches, is a pleasant spot to relax.

The House of Culture (Casa de la Cultura), 2 blocks west of Plaza de la Patria on Calle V. Carranza, is housed in an old colonial convent and is worth a stop for the beauty of the building, which has courtyards festooned with vividly colored bougainvillea. The Church of San Antonio, about 6 blocks northeast of Plaza de la Patria, has a cupola adorned with stained-glass windows.

Aguascalientes' annual San Marcos Fair (Feria de San Marcos), honoring the city's patron saint, has been held since 1604. Mexico's oldest and largest state fair takes place from late April to early May at the Expo Plaza, southwest of Plaza de la Patria near the bullring. The celebrations include fireworks, amusement rides, craft exhibits, agricultural and industrial expositions, cultural events (including an international film festival), the crowning of a festival queen and a huge parade on Apr. 25, the saint's day. Bullfights and cockfights generate a great deal of wagering. Those planning a visit during this time should make reservations for accommodations well in advance.

Practicalities

Jesús Terán International Airport is about 34 kilometers (21 miles) south of the city via Mex. 45 (the Aguascalientes-León Highway). There is air service to Aguascalientes via Aero California *(see "Arriving by Air," page 551).* Taxi service is available between the airport and downtown; one-way fare is about $8 (U.S.).

Highway signs in and around Aguascalientes can be outdated, and it is easy to get lost; visitors should plan their itinerary and obtain specific directions before negotiating the city on their own. Roadways within the state are narrow, with little or no shoulders and much truck traffic, but are well maintained. Toll highway Mex. 45-D proceeds southeast, linking Aguascalientes with Lagos de Moreno.

Day Trips

Although Aguascalientes is a fairly large city, the attractions of interest to tourists are concentrated around or near the main plaza. It should take no more than a day or two to see the sights. Another option is to stroll the plaza area in the morning and then arrange an afternoon excursion to a nearby winery or spa. Peñuelas Hacienda is a breeding ranch said to produce some of Mexico's most spirited bulls; make arrangements to visit beforehand, either through your hotel or the State Tourism Office.

Ojocaliente Sports Center (Centro Deportivo Ojocaliente) is about a kilometer east of downtown on Mex. 70. This spa has thermal pools, steam baths, saunas and tennis courts. Plaza Vestir, about 10 kilometers (6 miles) south on Mex. 45, is a collection of shops selling locally made clothing, embroidered items and shoes. A city bus or taxi will take you to the center.

In the nearby town of Pabellón de Hidalgo, 33 kilometers (20 miles) north of Aguascalientes on Mex. 45, then 5 kilometers (3 miles) west, is the Hacienda San Blas de Pabellón, which houses the Museum of the Insurgency. Here, after losing two important battles against the Spanish in 1811, insurgent leader Father Miguel Hidalgo y Costilla was relieved of his command and replaced by Ignacio Allende. The hacienda produces woolen goods on hand-powered looms.

The mining town of Asientos, easily reached by bus, is about 45 kilometers (28 miles) northeast. Many 16th- and 17th-century paintings are on display in the local churches, and a colonial atmosphere prevails. Encarnación de Díaz, about 42 kilometers (26 miles) south on Mex. 45, has old baroque churches and a central plaza with living trees sculpted into various shapes, including Christopher Columbus' ships the *Niña,* the *Pinta* and the *Santa María.*

Aguascalientes State Tourism Office (Coordinadora de Turismo): Calle Manuel M. Ponce #134 in the historic city center; phone (800) 949-4949 (toll-free long distance within Mexico) or (449) 915-1155.

CITY MUSEUM (Museo de Aguascalientes) is about 6 blocks northeast of Plaza de la Patria at Calle Zaragoza #507, opposite the Church of San Antonio. It exhibits 20th-century art, including a collection of paintings by Saturnino Herrán, who was born in the city. His work depicts the common people with uncommon sensitivity and fostered a sense of nationalist pride. Tues.-Sun. 11-6. Admission around $1.25 (U.S.); free to all Sun.

JOSE GUADALUPE POSADA MUSEUM is about 6 blocks south of Plaza de la Patria on Plaza Encino, next to Encino Church (Templo del Encino). It houses a fascinating collection of works by Posada, a 19th-century Mexican engraver and cartoonist who was another native son. He was best known for his *calaveras,* skeletal-like figures that satirized events leading up to the Mexican Revolution of 1910. These humorous political scenarios influenced public opinion in their day. Tues.-Sun. 11-6. Admission around 50 cents (U.S.); free to all Sun.

AJIJIC, JALISCO (H-3) pop. 13,300

Ajijic (ah-hee-HEEK) is about 8 kilometers (5 miles) west of Chapala on the northern shore of Lake Chapala. This artists' and writers' colony, one of several resort/retirement communities along the lake, is populated by many former U.S. residents.

Along Calle Morelos between the main square and the waterfront are shops and boutiques selling everything from local handicrafts to designer fashions. Easily reached from Guadalajara, Ajijic has a picturesque waterfront area and cobblestone streets and is a pleasant destination for shopping, strolling and perhaps lunch. The town's Fiesta of St. Andrew, held in late November, is celebrated with parades, dancing and fireworks.

ANGANGUEO, MICHOACAN (C-8) elev. 7,997'

Anganueo (ahn-gahn-GEH-oh), which sits in a canyon carved by the Río Puerco, was a pueblo inhabited by Tarascan Indians long before the arrival of the Spanish. The name means "mouth of the cave." Towering above are the 10,000-foot peaks of Cerro de Guadalupe, El Campanario and Cerro de la Gotera.

Anganueo's heyday was in the early 20th century, when it was a mining center. Today this hamlet, dominated by two imposing Catholic churches facing each other across the main plaza, survives as a tourist departure point for the surrounding butterfly sanctuaries.

Every winter an estimated 100 million monarchs—the last generation of butterflies that have spent the spring and summer in Canada and the United States east of the Rockies—arrive in this part of the country as part of their remarkable migratory cycle. Scientists do not know for sure what inner navigational system guides the insects into making this 2,500-mile journey, although one possible explanation is that more than half of North America's species of milkweed—the caterpillars' food source—are native to Mexico, indicating that the urge to migrate is passed along genetically.

After reaching their wintering grounds the monarchs hibernate, forming enormous colonies in tall pines and firs. In a semi-dormant state they burn almost no energy, but begin to grow more active as the weather warms, preparing for the northward migration in the spring. Several generations hatch along the way, thus continuing the monarch's life cycle for another year.

Note: In the winter of 2002 an unusual combination of heavy rainstorms followed by freezing weather decimated the migratory monarch population; it remains to be seen whether this will have a lasting impact on succeeding migrations.

EL ROSARIO MONARCH BUTTERFLY SANCTUARY (Santuario de Las Mariposas Monarca, El Rosario) is about 6 km (4 mi.) northeast of Angangueo, near the small village of El Rosario. The steep and rough dirt road to the sanctuary should be negotiated only in a truck or four-wheel-drive vehicle. An alternate entry can be made via a dirt road from the village of Ocampo, a few miles southwest of Angangueo; this route is longer but can be made adequately in a small car. This is one

of several butterfly refuges in the highlands of Michoacán and México, some 100 miles west of Mexico City.

Organized daylong bus or van tours to the sanctuary from Mexico City or Morelia can be arranged through travel agencies in those cities. But while a tour saves time and effort, it also necessitates getting up before dawn. If you're driving, leave your car in Angangueo and ride in a four-wheel-drive vehicle to the sanctuary. This is easier than it sounds; numerous freelance guides are available, and tourists are approached the moment they set foot in town. The slow, steep route to the sanctuary takes about an hour.

Another alternative is to spend the night in the region for a more relaxed trip. In Angangueo, the hotel Albergue Don Bruno has comfortable rooms; phone (715) 156-0026.

Wear sturdy, comfortable walking shoes and bring a jacket or sweater in case the weather is chilly. Weekends are crowded with Mexico City residents; go during the week if possible. Sanctuary open daily 9-6, Dec.-Mar. Admission around $2.25 (U.S.).

CHAPALA, JALISCO (H-4) pop. 19,600

Along with Ajijic and Jocotepec, Chapala (chah-PAH-lah) is the largest of several resort communities lining the northern shore of Lake Chapala. During the early 20th century it was the summer residence of dictator Porfirio Díaz. At that time the town attracted a rich international clientele who spent weekends at lavish estates, enjoying the area's tranquil beauty; D.H. Lawrence wrote "The Plumed Serpent" here in the mid-1920s. Today it caters to Mexican families and a resident population of American and Canadian retirees.

Commercial activity is centered along Avenida Madero, which leads to the lake and town pier. The street is lined with shops and small cafes. Near the pier is the main square, a pleasant spot to relax; band serenades are held here on Sunday evenings. Along the lakeshore is Cristiania Park, where vendors gather on the weekend.

The lake itself, some 53 miles long and 18 miles wide, is the largest natural lake in Mexico, surrounded by lushly forested mountains. The weather is delightfully springlike all year, a bit cooler in summer and warmer in winter than Guadalajara. The lake, however, is the chief source of water for the city, and because of tremendous population growth in the surrounding area, the water level has dropped by half since the turn of the 20th century. Cutting down trees has caused millions of cubic feet of mud to seep into the lake over the years, and the stench of pollution is strongly evident in some areas. Engineers and Mexican environmental groups have worked to promote reforestation programs to reverse this trend.

Mezcala Island can be reached by boat from the Chapala pier. The ruins of a fort and bastion here date from the Mexican War of Independence, when rebels successfully defended the island against the Spanish army and navy from 1812-16. Hunger and sickness finally forced these 1,500 courageous souls to surrender, but their valor prompted the Spaniards to present them with an honor guard and a military pardon.

CHOLULA, PUEBLA (C-10)
pop. 125,000, elev. 7,039'

The Cholula (choh-LOO-lah) of today is practically a suburb of ever-expanding Puebla, but at the time of its destruction in 1519 by Hernando Cortés it was a religious city built on the foundations of a ceremonial center that had flowered by the second century A.D. At its peak Cholula was inhabited by 100,000 Cholultecs—a mixture of Olmec, Toltec, Aztec, Mixtec and Mazatec Indians.

When Cortés arrived in Cholula en route to Tenochtitlán, the Aztecs mistook the conqueror for the god Quetzalcóatl, which their mythology described as being fair skinned and with light hair. Consequently, the 100,000 inhabitants showed deference to Cortés and his band of 500 men. The conqueror promptly shattered this illusion by having his second in command, Pedro de Alvarado, carry out the slaughter of 6,000 Indians and the destruction of their temples and shrines.

Following custom, the Spanish conquerors erected a church atop the rubble of each temple they razed. An example sits atop Tepanapa Pyramid, one of the New World's largest structures. Burrowing into the earth near the base of this brush-covered hill, archeologists discovered that the Cholultecs, in fact, appeared to be better builders than the Aztecs who last occupied the city. An earthquake in 1999 caused extensive damage to this church, which has since been restored by the state.

ROYAL CHAPEL (Capilla Real) faces the main square. The chapel is within the walls of the Church of San Gabriel. Originally built for defensive as well as religious purposes, it contains seven naves and has 49 domes.

TEPANAPA PYRAMID (Pirámide Tepanapa) rises near the main square. Its base length is about 1,315 feet—each side some 500 feet longer than the Pyramid of the Sun at Teotihuacán. An arduous stone trail leads to the Santuario de Los Remedios, the church that crowns the hill 230 feet above ground level. Climbers reaching the top are rewarded with excellent views. Some of the nearly 5 miles of tunnels are lighted; guides identify structures and decorative highlights.

A museum near the entrance exhibits pottery and artifacts dating from pre-Hispanic times, Indian knives and arrowheads used in sacrifices, and a scale model of the pyramid as it is believed to have appeared prior to Hernando Cortés' arrival. Site open Tues.-Sun. 9-5. Admission around $2 (U.S.).

DOLORES HIDALGO, GUANAJUATO
(A-8) pop. 52,100, elev. 6,517'

Known in Mexico as Cuna de la Independencia Nacional (The Cradle of National Independence) and designated a national historic monument, Dolores Hidalgo (doh-LOH-rehs ee-DAHL-goh) lies in the valley of the Río Laja. Just before midnight on Sept. 15, 1810, Father Miguel Hidalgo y Costilla called together his parishioners by ringing the village church bell. He then gave the venerated *Grito de Dolores,* a speech announcing Mexican independence that ignited the 11-year war to achieve it.

A statue of Hidalgo stands in Plaza Principal, the main plaza, where various vendors ply their wares among comfortable old benches and square-trimmed trees. The former homes of other Mexican heroes are here as well; guides are available for town tours.

The annual Independence Day celebrations held Sept. 15-16 re-create Father Hidalgo's historic rallying cry, and the president of Mexico often officiates.

HIDALGO HOUSE MUSEUM (Museo Casa de Hidalgo) is on Morelos #1 at Hidalgo, a block south of the main plaza. Miguel Hidalgo lived here when he was the town's parish priest. It contains many items relating to the life of the patriot, including paintings, portraits, books, period furniture and a room filled with wreaths and other memorials. Tues.-Sat. 10-5:30, Sun. 10-4:30. Admission around $2.50 (U.S.); free to all Sun.

Guadalajara

Guadalajara's (gwah-dah-lah-HAH-rah) history dates to 1530, just 38 years after Christopher Columbus first reached North America and nine years after the conquest of Mexico by Hernando Cortés. Another Spanish explorer, Nuño de Guzmán, founded the settlement. Guzmán was a cruel conqueror; he and his soldiers slaughtered entire Indian communities in the course of exploring the lands west and north of Mexico City. He established Guadalajara—named for his hometown in Spain—at the site of present-day Nochistlán in the state of Zacatecas, about 60 miles to the northeast. Early settlers moved several times after Indian attacks before finally settling in the Valley of Atemajac in 1542. It was a wise choice, for the mile-high plateau ensured unimpeded expansion.

When the Spanish Crown learned of Guzmán's atrocities, he was deported back to Spain and the name of his self-appointed "country" was changed from La Gran España to Nuevo Galicia. Early on Guadalajara figured prominently in the history of this area. The town grew rapidly and by 1769 had become a provincial capital. Spanish expeditions left from Guadalajara to gain control of such far-flung lands as the Philippine and Molucca Islands and the island of Guam, and to establish missions in northern Mexico and present-day California. Wealth from the surrounding farms and silver mines was channeled into the construction of lavish churches, mansions and monuments.

After abolishing slavery and launching the War of Independence in September 1810, Father Miguel Hidalgo briefly occupied the city. In the late 1850s and early 1860s Guadalajara withstood army attacks led alternately by Archduke Maximilian and Benito Juárez, who made the city the capital of his reform government for a few months during his forced exile from Mexico City.

Guadalajara today is a sprawling metropolis, Mexico's second largest. Nearly 4 million residents jam the city and its suburbs. The surrounding high plains of the Valley of Atemajac, part of Mexico's great central plateau, are noted for fine horse, cattle and grain ranches. The city's factories convert metals, hides and foodstuffs into many different products.

Guadalajara also has become an electronics center. Plants operated by Hewlett-Packard, IBM and Motorola produce cellular phones and desktop and laptop computers, leading some local business boosters to refer to the city as "Silicon Valley South."

The city even has its own word—*tapatío*. Reputedly derived from *tlapatiotl*, a term used to denote cacao or other small units of exchange frequently used in the Indian marketplace, it now refers to any person, thing or quality that is indisputably Guadalajaran. *Tapatío* indeed

Pablo De Aguinaco / Mexico Tourism Board

Cathedral / © Danny Lehman / Corbis

are such characteristically Mexican pleasures as the *jarabe,* or Mexican hat dance, and the music of the mariachis.

Approaches

By Air

Miguel Hidalgo International Airport is about 17 kilometers (11 miles) southeast of the city off Mex. 23. Aeroméxico, Continental, Delta, Mexicana and United airlines offer direct flights from U.S. cities; Aero California serves Guadalajara from Tijuana. International connections are usually via Mexico City. Numerous half-hour flights connect Guadalajara with Puerto Vallarta. Always check with a travel agency or the airline prior to booking a flight, as routes and direct-flight availability differs depending on the time of year. For additional information about airlines *see "Arriving by Air," page 551.*

Airport Transportation (Autotransportaciónes Aeropuerto) offers shared-ride shuttle van service to and from any place in the metropolitan area. Tickets are sold at a booth outside the terminal exit; fares are based on a zone system and can cost anywhere from around $10-$15 per person (U.S.). For details phone (33) 3612-4278. Taxis also take passengers to and from the airport; the fare to the downtown area is around $15 (U.S.).

By Car

Guadalajara's location between the Pacific coast and central Mexico makes it an ideal base from which to explore Jalisco and the surrounding states of Nayarit, Zacatecas, Aguascalientes, Guanajuato, Michoacán and Colima. Mex. 15/15-D is the major highway from the northwest; Mex. 54 from the north and northeast. Mex. 80 proceeds southwest to coastal Mex. 200, which heads south to Manzanillo or north to Puerto Vallarta. With the exception of Mex. 15-D, all of the above routes are old (free) highways.

The Guadalajara-Manzanillo toll highway, Mex. 54-D, begins at El Cuarenta, on Mex. 15 south of the city. Although the distance to Colima is not much shorter than that traveled on free Mex. 54, the toll road avoids the latter's narrow, winding stretches.

The Mex. 15-D toll highway is a multilane route linking Guadalajara with Mexico City. It takes between five and six hours to drive the 506-kilometer (316-mile) route, which runs south of Mex. 90, Mex. 45-D and Mex. 57-D via Irapuato and Querétaro—previously the most direct route between the two cities.

South of and roughly parallel to Mex. 15-D is old Mex. 15, a winding road that hugs the southern shore of Lake Chapala and passes through the cities of Morelia, Zitácuaro and Toluca on its way to Mexico City—a scenic but much more time-consuming alternative. The road is in poor condition in places, and

(continued on page 283)

The Informed Traveler

City Population: 1,659,400, metropolitan area 3,847,000 (2002 estimate).

Elevation: 1,552 meters (5,091 feet).

Location: In west-central Mexico, due east of Puerto Vallarta.

Highlights: A pedestrian-friendly historic center sprinkled with colonial plazas, museums and architectural landmarks; Mercado Libertad, an enormous covered city market selling everything from pottery to dried iguanas; Plaza Tapatía, a seven-block-long promenade that is Guadalajara's best place for people watching; the suburbs of Tlaquepaque and Tonalá, where high-quality pottery and other handicrafts are produced and sold.

WHOM TO CALL

Area Code: 33.

In Case of Emergency: Dial 080 and ask for an English-speaking operator if you need emergency assistance. To contact the municipal police department, phone (33) 3617-6060 (no English spoken). Hospital México-Americano, Colomos #2110, provides full medical services and 24-hour emergency service; phone (33) 3642-7152. Major hotels and the U.S. Consulate can provide lists of doctors who are on 24-hour call.

WHERE TO LOOK

Media

English-language newspapers, including the weekly *Guadalajara Reporter,* are available at newsstands and the Best Western Hotel Fenix, downtown at avenidas Corona and López Cotilla. The free *Huésped* (Guest Magazine) has information about Guadalajara and the Lake Chapala area.

Sandi Bookstore, Av. Tepeyac #718 in the Chapalita neighborhood west of downtown, has English-language newspapers and books. The Sanborn's chain has several area locations and also offers books, newspapers and magazines in English; the downtown branch is at avenidas Juárez and 16 de Septiembre, a block south of Plaza de Armas.

Visitor Information

Jalisco State Tourism Office (Secretaría de Turismo): Calle Morelos #102 at Plaza Tapatía (behind the Degollado Theater). The office is open Mon.-Fri. 9-8, Sat.-Sun. and holidays 9-1; phone (800) 363-2200 (toll-free long distance within Mexico). It has lots of information about Guadalajara and other destinations within the state, and also provides listings for hotels, restaurants and cultural events, as well as walking tour maps of the historic center. The staff speaks English.

A tourist information booth is inside the southern doorway of the Government Palace (Palacio de Gobierno), facing Plaza de Armas; it is open Mon.-Fri. 9-3 and 6-8, Sat. 9-1.

The Citizens Consular Services office of the U.S. Consulate, Progreso #175 at Avenida López Cotilla, provides a reference list of English-speaking lawyers, doctors and translators for those in difficulty; a duty officer is available for after-hours emergencies. Phone (33) 3825-2700.

WHAT TO KNOW

Weather

Guadalajara enjoys springlike temperatures much of the year, along with abundant sunshine. High temperatures are normally in the 70s and 80s; uncomfortably humid days are rare. In April and May, the warmest months, it can creep into the low 90s, but always cools off in the evening. The rainy season is June through September. Air pollution is a problem, although not as severe as in Mexico City.

Bring appropriate attire for an evening at the theater or dinner in a good restaurant. A sweater or light jacket will come in handy on cool nights.

Currency Exchange

A number of *casas de cambio* (currency exchange offices) are located downtown along Avenida López Cotilla between calles Corona and Degollado, about 3 blocks south of the cathedral. Almost all offices post their rates, and they normally don't have the lines that banks often have. Cash and traveler's checks can be changed at branches of Banamex banks Mon.-Sat. 9-1. A Banamex branch is at Calle Corona and Avenida Juárez.

driving the stretch from Morelia to Mexico City is not recommended because of the possibility of encounters with *banditos*.

Mex. 15-D begins east of Guadalajara near the suburb of Tonalá, bypassing cities and towns for the most part as it traverses rolling farmland and upland valleys and skirts the southern shore of Lake Cuitzeo. The route reaches its highest elevation—and also ends—near Atlacomulco in the state of México; from there Mex. 55 and Mex. 15 proceed south and east, respectively, to Mexico City. Toll charges are typically expensive, but toll highways in general are in much better condition than free roads throughout Mexico.

By Bus

Bus lines out of Guadalajara's big, modern New Bus Station (Nueva Central Camionera), about 10 kilometers (6 miles) southeast of downtown outside the suburb of Tlaquepaque (on the way to Tonalá), service all cities and most towns in the country. Several of the biggest lines are connected with Greyhound Lines Inc. Cross-country buses make frequent trips between Guadalajara and border points. First-class travel compares favorably with major U.S. lines; these buses are the standard size but carry half as many passengers. ETN is one of the lines offering first-class service.

Seven terminal buildings (*módulos*) accommodate different lines. Amenities include shuttle bus service, luggage storage (referred to as *guarda equipaje*), restaurants, Ladatel long-distance telephones and hotel information. City buses and *colectivos* designated "Centro" or "Central" travel between the bus station and downtown. You also can take a taxi from the station to the downtown area. Taxi tickets are sold inside each terminal building; fares are based on a zone system.

For shorter bus trips to Tequila, the Lake Chapala suburban communities or other towns within a 60-mile radius of the city, use the Old Bus Station (Antigua Central Camionera), located off Avenida Dr. R. Michel at calles Los Angeles and 28 de Enero (just northeast of Parque Agua Azul). A convenient way to obtain route, schedule and fare information for the main Mexican lines is to stop at the Servicios Coordinados office, Calz. Independencia #254 in Plaza Tapatía. Reservations can also be made here. For additional information about buses *see "Bus Service," page 68.*

Getting Around

City Layout

Sprawling Guadalajara is divided into four sectors; street names change when a new sector is entered. The major north-south routes are Calzada Independencia/Calzada Gobernador Curiel, which divides Guadalajara into east and west sectors; Avenida Alcalde/Avenida 16 de Septiembre, which passes through the Historic Center (Centro Histórico); Avenida Federalismo/Avenida Colón, which runs a few blocks west of Alcalde; and

Avenida López Mateos, the main thoroughfare passing through a concentration of malls, upscale shops and restaurants west of downtown that cater to the city's wealthy business class.

The major east-west routes are Avenida Circunvalación, which runs north of downtown; Avenida Avila Camacho, which provides access to the northwestern suburb of Zapopan; Avenida Independencia/Calzada Independencia (not to be confused with Avenida Industria), which runs through the historic center a block north of the cathedral; Avenida Vallarta/Avenida Juárez/Avenida Javier Mina, which also runs through the historic center and divides the city into north and south sectors; and Avenida Guadalupe/Avenida Niños Héroes/Calzada González Gallo, which links points of interest in the southern part of the city.

For visitors, Guadalajara's chief attraction is the careful preservation of its downtown historic district. Forming a shape somewhat like a giant cross are four different plazas, each offering a distinct personality: Plaza Tapatía, Plaza de la Liberación, Plaza de Armas and Plaza de los Laureles. They all surround the cathedral (*see attraction listing*), which is the heart of the old city. Centuries of history unfold along the narrow cobblestone lanes and in the weathered two- and three-story buildings that constitute the center of old Guadalajara, where street vendors and shoeshine boys are an immutable part of the landscape.

Plaza Tapatía (*see attraction listing*) is Guadalajara's gathering place, conveniently located close to museums, monuments and grand examples of colonial architecture. Here are tree-lined parks, stone walkways, burbling fountains and numerous restaurants. On Sundays, throngs of dressed-up families parade up and down Plaza de la Liberación, just east of the cathedral at the western end of Plaza Tapatía. A narrow waterway runs along this plaza, bordered on both sides by shops and more restaurants. A statue of Father Miguel Hidalgo shows the priest holding a broken chain, a symbol of his call to end slavery in Mexico.

Plaza de Armas, a block south of the cathedral, is the city's traditional main square, bordered on the east side by the Government Palace (*see attraction listing*). Plaza de los Laureles (just west of the cathedral) is, as the name suggests, planted with Indian laurel trees. The church on the plaza's north side, built in the mid-20th century, is one of the newer buildings in the historic center.

West and south of the historic center the boulevards are wider, the buildings newer and taller. Along north-south Avenida Chapultepec between Avenida Niños Héroes and Avenida México—about 20 blocks west of the cathedral—are modern offices, fine shopping and some good restaurants. Farther west, along Avenida López Mateos between Avenida Vallarta and Avenida Mariano Otero, are many of Guadalajara's major hotels and nightlife venues as well as the big Plaza del Sol mall.

Lending a unifying appearance to this structural and human diversity are the vibrant purple of

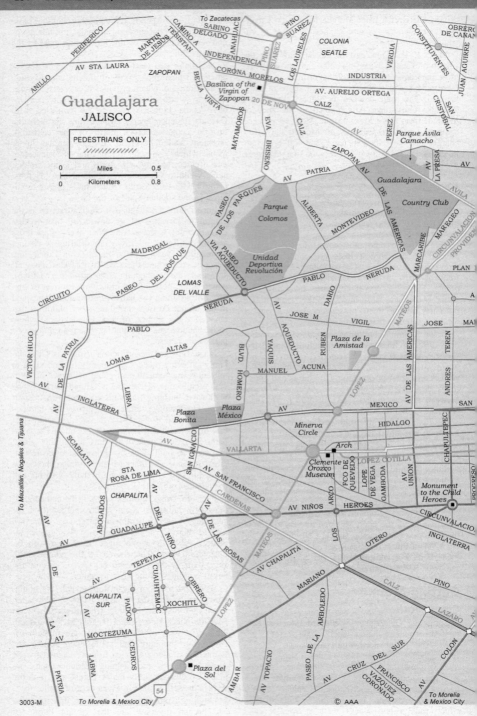

Guadalajara
JALISCO

PEDESTRIANS ONLY

Miles	
0	0.5
Kilometers	
0	0.8

Parque Colomos

Guadalajara Country Club

Basílica of the Virgin of Zapopan

Parque Ávila Camacho

Unidad Deportiva Revolución

Lomas del Valle

Plaza de la Amistad

Plaza Bonita

Plaza México

Minerva Circle

Arch

Clemente Orozco Museum

Monument to the Child Heroes

Plaza del Sol

To Zacatecas

To Mazatlán, Nogales & Tijuana

To Morelia & Mexico City

To Morelia & Mexico City

3003-M

© AAA

DOWNTOWN
Guadalajara

To Zacatecas

To Mex. 44

To Miguel Hidalgo International Airport & Morelia

For Your Information

Guides/Tours

Tour guides with name tags who congregate at the bus terminal are likely to be agents on commission with hotels. The major hotels usually have a list of licensed bilingual guides. Bus tours of the downtown area and nearby points of interest are offered by Panoramex, at Av. Federalismo Sur #944; phone (33) 3810-5109 (English spoken). For visitors without a car, this is the easiest way to explore the city and outlying suburbs.

Rides in horse-drawn *calandrias* (carriages) can be taken throughout the central downtown area and are a relaxing way to see the sights. Excursions

depart from the Regional Museum of Guadalajara, Liberty Market and San Francisco Park. Few drivers speak English, so you may want to familiarize yourself with the layout of the city before embarking.

© Nik Wheeler / Corbis

Staying Safe

The rules in Guadalajara are the same as those in any big city. At night, avoid urban neighborhoods that are away from the downtown core or other tourist areas; dark side streets in particular can be dangerous. If going out for the evening or taking a side trip during the day, it's a good idea to hire a taxi driver affiliated with your hotel. Keep an eye on personal items at all times, especially in the crowded shopping districts, and avoid wearing jewelry or carrying large sums of money. Women are not welcome in *cantina* bars and other bastions of heavy drinking and *machismo* attitudes.

blooming jacaranda trees and cascading bougainvillea, which seems to grow just about everywhere. Fountains, most of them delightfully ornate, also are scattered throughout the city.

Two thoroughfares loop around Guadalajara. The inner Avenida de la Patria travels around the western half of the city between Avenida de las Américas and Avenida López Mateos. The outer Anillo Periférico encircles the entire metropolitan area; navigating this two-lane route can be slow going, however, due to potholes and heavy truck traffic. **Note:** During and after the summer rainy season, roads both within the city and the state of Jalisco may develop dangerous breaks in the pavement and potholes that can cause accidents.

City traffic is heavy and moves slowly, and many streets are equipped with *topes* (speed bumps). Significant truck traffic adds to the overall congestion. *Glorietas* (traffic circles) are common at busy intersections. **Note:** Air pollution levels have risen to the point where state officials have instituted a tune-up test that all vehicles with Jalisco license plates must pass. Vehicles with out-of-state plates, however, are exempted.

Rental Cars

Hertz is one of many rental car agencies with offices at the airport and downtown. Be sure you fully understand the terms of any rental contract, especially with regard to insurance coverage. It's significantly less expensive to reserve before you leave home; make reservations at least one week in advance.

Note: AAA/CAA members enjoy discounts through Hertz for vehicles booked in the United States. Consult your local AAA/CAA club or phone Hertz, (800) 654-3080.

Buses

Buses are the preferred—and most economical—means of local transportation, for they cover every part of town. City buses run daily every 5 to 10 minutes from 6 a.m.-10 p.m. School bus-style vehicles are the cheapest (around 40 cents U.S.), but conditions tend to be substandard to what visitors are used to. They also are quite likely to be very crowded.

Tur buses (operated by Linea Turquesa), turquoise in color and with the letters "TUR" designated on the side, cost more (around 70 cents U.S.) but are air conditioned, do not carry standing passengers and travel to such outlying tourist destinations as Tlaquepaque, Tonalá and Zapopan. *Par Vial* buses travel a central east-west route along avenidas Independencia/Hidalgo as far west as Minerva Circle (at Avenida López Mateos); from there, they double back along Avenida Vallarta/Juárez, a few blocks south.

Privately operated *colectivos* (minivans) cost about the same as city buses; some have their destination marked on the windshield, although routes and pick-up points change frequently.

Taxis

Compared to the bus, a taxi ride in Guadalajara is expensive. Even short 10-minute rides are likely to cost at least $5 (U.S.). Rates go up at night. All cabs are equipped with a meter, but drivers can be reluctant to use them, quoting a flat fee instead; make certain you agree on a destination and a fare with the driver before entering the cab. Check at your hotel's front desk for current fares; bellboys can often assist those who don't speak Spanish. Most cabs are found at or called from a cab stand (*sitio*). *Sitios* are located near all the major hotels and attractions. The safest option is to stick with cab drivers who are affiliated with your hotel.

Parking

On-street parking in the city center is scarce. Public parking garages generally charge a fixed rate per hour; few are insured for customers. Parking lots charge less than garages. An underground lot is below Plaza de la Liberación, just east of the cathedral. Always avoid areas marked *"No E," "Estacionamiento Prohibido"* (No parking) or *"Exclusivo"* (Reserved). License plates are removed from illegally parked vehicles, and a fine must be paid to retrieve them.

Public Transportation

Guadalajara's *tren ligero* (light rail) rapid-transit system has two lines. Line 1 runs north-south along Avenida Federalismo-Colón for a distance of about 10 miles, between the northern and southern stretches of the Periférico. More helpful to visitors is Line 2, which runs east-west along avenidas Vallarta/Juárez and Javier Mina (the street name changes at Calzada Independencia). Trains run about every 15 minutes or so daily 6 a.m.-11 p.m.; the fare is inexpensive. Stops are marked by a "T" symbol.

What To See

AGUA AZUL PARK (Parque Agua Azul) is at the intersection of calzadas Independencia Sur and González Gallo, about 20 blocks south of the city center. This is the oldest of the city's parks. Trees, flowers, fountains and a man-made lake make it a popular spot for city residents and a pleasant place to while away an afternoon. On the grounds are an orchid house, an aviary and an outdoor theater. On the other side of Calzada González Gallo is Plaza Juárez, which has a monument encircled by the flags of other Latin American countries. Daily 8-6. Admission around 40 cents (U.S.), children 20 cents.

Jalisco House of Handicrafts (Casa de las Artesanías de Jalisco) is just past the park entrance, with a separate entrance on Calzada Gallo. This state-run store sells fixed-price regional handicrafts, including leather saddles, furniture, blown glass, ceramics, pottery, textiles, tinwork and woodcarvings. Mon.-Fri. 10-6, Sat. 11-3, Sun. 11-2.

ARCHEOLOGICAL MUSEUM OF WESTERN MEXICO (Museo de Arqueología del Occidente de Mexico) is on Plaza Juárez (at calzadas Independencia Sur and del Campesino), across from the entrance to Agua Azul Park. It exhibits a small but select group of figurines, pottery and other artifacts from sites in Colima, Jalisco and Nayarit. Daily 10-2 and 5-7. Admission around 40 cents (U.S.).

CABAÑAS CULTURAL INSTITUTE (Instituto Cultural Cabañas) is at the eastern end of Plaza Tapatía at Cabañas #8; take a taxi, as this is a congested area. It was built in the early 19th century and financed by Bishop Juan Cruz Ruíz de Cabañas. Originally offering shelter for crippled, destitute and orphaned men, women and children, the building provided education and medical care for children through the 1970s before being renovated for use as a cultural center.

This architecturally fascinating complex encompasses 23 patios linked by pink-tiled corridors. Known locally as El Hospicio Cabañas, it is the showplace for some of José Clemente Orozco's most powerful murals, particularly *"El Hombre de Fuego"* ("Man of Fire"), which graces the lofty ceiling. The art is memorable, although it depicts scenes of horrific violence from Mexico's history.

In addition to contemporary art and changing exhibitions, the institute has a movie theater, performing arts theater and an outdoor patio where ballet, music and dance performances take place. Tues.-Sat. 10-6, Sun. 10-3. Admission 10 pesos (around $1 U.S.). Phone (33) 3818-2800.

CATHEDRAL faces Av. Alcalde. Begun in 1561, it was consecrated in 1618. Its twin 200-foot towers were erected in 1848 after an earthquake destroyed the original, much shorter structures. Emblazoned with yellow and blue tiles, they are a city landmark. Inside are three cavernous naves and 11 elegantly appointed altars, a gift from King Ferdinand VII of Spain. A lovely sculpture, "Our Lady of the Roses," was given to the city by the 16th-century Spanish king Carlos V. The priceless painting "The Assumption of the Virgin" in the sacristy is thought to be by Bartolomé Murillo. Open daily. Free.

CHURCH OF OUR LADY OF ARANZAZU (Iglesia de Nuestra Señora de Aranzazu) is at avs. 16 de Septiembre and Prisciliano Sánchez, bordering the south side of San Francisco Park (Parque San Francisco). It has a plain exterior, but inside is an extravagantly ornate *retablo* (altarpiece) that is a dazzling example of Spanish baroque design; its niches contain life-size statues of the saints. Also impressive are the colorful walls and ceilings.

Next to this church stands the less-ornate San Francisco Church (Iglesia de San Francisco). San Francisco Park is a starting point for horse-drawn carriage rides.

CITY MUSEUM (Museo de la Ciudad) is west of the historic center at Av. Independencia #684 (at Av. Mariano Bárcenas). It opened in 1992 to commemorate Guadalajara's 450th anniversary. The old stone convent housing the museum is a fine example of late 17th-century colonial architecture. Eight *salas* (halls) present a chronological timeline of the city's history and development. Among the more interesting displays are equestrian trappings, reminders of Guadalajara's *charreada* tradition. Exhibit information is in Spanish. Tues.-Sat. 10-5, Sun. 10-3. Admission around 50 cents (U.S.). Phone (33) 3658-2531.

CLEMENTE OROZCO MUSEUM is at Av. Aurelio Aceves #29, just east of Minerva Circle off Av. Vallarta. This is the former workshop and residence of José Clemente Orozco, Jalisco's leading muralist (1883-1949). Distinguished by a three-story window, it displays photographs, tools, clothing and his personal easel. The wall facing the window is covered by a huge mural entitled *"Alegoría del Vino"* ("Wine Allegory"). The museum also has a collection of documents, handwritten letters, posters, diplomas and other tributes to Orozco. Mon.-Fri. 9-5. Free. Phone (33) 3616-8329.

DEGOLLADO THEATER (Teatro Degollado) is on Calle Belén between Calle Morelos and Av. Hidalgo, just east of the cathedral. This impressive neoclassic structure, completed in 1866, has been compared to Milan's La Scala Opera House, although it has the grimy look of stone buildings exposed to years of vehicle exhaust. The relief above the columned entrance depicts Apollo and the Nine Muses. The plaque on the outside back wall commemorates Guadalajara's 1542 founding ceremony.

Inside are opulent red and gold balconies and a dome with murals painted by Gerardo Suárez that depict Dante's "Divine Comedy." The remodeled theater is the home of the Jalisco Philharmonic Orchestra and presents concerts, live theater performances and film festivals year-round. Performances are given by the University of Guadalajara Folkloric Ballet every Sunday at 10 a.m. If you can't attend an event, the theater is open Mon.-Sat. 10-1 for tours. Phone (33) 3658-3812 for performance and ticket information.

EXPIATORY TEMPLE (Templo Expiatorio) is west of the historic center, bounded by avs. López Cotilla, Juárez and Enrique Díaz de León. This massive structure covers a city block. One balcony of the Gothic-style church, built at the turn of the 20th century, features mechanical representations of the 12 Apostles who make an appearance, accompanied by a carillon playing classical music, three times daily (9 a.m., noon and 6 p.m.). The clockwork figures can be viewed from the square in front of the church.

GOVERNMENT PALACE (Palacio de Gobierno) faces the east side of Plaza de Armas. The Spanish baroque building dates from 1643 and was completed in 1774. Note the stone gargoyles, used to divert water from the roof, and the pillared front entrance. Enormous murals by José Clemente Orozco depict Mexico's history.

This building was the site of Father Miguel Hidalgo's decree abolishing slavery in 1810, as well as Guillermo Prieto's plea saving president Benito Juárez from assassination in 1858. The cannon and armor carved on the building's facade are a symbol of colonial authority. Daily 9-9.

GUADALAJARA REGIONAL MUSEUM (Museo Regional de Guadalajara) is at Av. Liceo #60, a block north of the Government Palace. Housed in a former theological seminary dating from around 1700, it has been a museum since 1918. Exhibits focus on the history of Jalisco and western Mexico, and include pre-Hispanic artifacts, ethnological displays and a 1,715-pound meteorite discovered in the state of Zacatecas in 1792.

A collection of Spanish and Mexican art on the second floor features paintings from the school of Bartolomé Murillo. Tues.-Sat. 9-5, Sun. 9-3. Admission around $3.50 (U.S.), under 13 free; free to all Tues. Phone (33) 3614-9957.

GUADALAJARA ZOO (Zoológico de Guadalajara) is about 6 km (4 mi.) north of Plaza Tapatía at the junction of Calzada Independencia Norte and Paseo del Zoológico. Overlooking Río Santiago Canyon, it contains a variety of large mammals, birds, reptiles and monkeys. A train and well-marked footpaths traverse the major viewing areas. There also is a children's petting zoo.

Next to the zoo is a planetarium and the Selva Mágica amusement park, which has a pool with performing dolphins. Parking is provided. Wed.-Sun. 10-6; daily during Holy Week. Admission around $3 (U.S.), children $1.50.

JALISCAN CULTURAL CENTER (Casa de la Cultura Jalisciense) is at avs. 16 de Septiembre and Constituyentes, near Agua Azul Park. This state-supported center houses a movie theater, two art exhibition halls, artists' studios and the offices of various culture-oriented organizations. The 300,000-volume Guadalajara Public Library also is in this building.

OBLATOS CANYON (Barranca de Oblatos) is 10 km (6 mi.) northeast of downtown Guadalajara via Calzada Independencia Norte, near the Guadalajara Zoo. This 2,000-foot-deep gorge was cut by the Santiago and Verde rivers. Thermal rivulets plunge down the red walls (except during the dry season). The greater the depth, the more tropical the climate: Papayas, oranges, guavas, bananas, mangoes and other fruits grown at the canyon bottom are marketed in Guadalajara.

A cable car leaves the rim daily at 8 a.m. to take workers to the power plant on the canyon floor. The best views are from the Parque Huentitán el Alto Mirador lookout area at the top of the gorge.

PLAZA TAPATIA is along Av. Hidalgo. A seven-block-long pedestrian pathway connects the Degollado Theater at the west end to the Cabañas

Cultural Institute at the east end. The walkway enables visitors to see several of Guadalajara's downtown attractions without having to cross major streets. Underground parking lots also are along the route.

Plaza Tapatía is a prime spot for strolling and people watching. Vendors sell everything from candy to canaries. The festive atmosphere unfolds against a backdrop of flower beds, statues, fountains and reflecting pools, and there are myriad storefronts in which to browse or window shop.

An unusual but practical service is offered by the *escritorios* who set up shop in the arcade close to the State Tourism Office. For centuries these typists, writers and editors have helped illiterate people fill out documents or write messages and correspondence, particularly love letters.

ROTUNDA OF ILLUSTRIOUS MEN (Rotonda de Los Hombres Ilustres) is on the north side of the cathedral in a park bounded by Calle Hidalgo and avs. Alcalde, Independencia/Industria and Liceo. The mausoleum is where six of Jalisco's foremost native sons—representing artistic, philanthropic and musical fields as well as the military—are buried. Sculptures of the men, plus other Jaliscan notables, are surrounded by a circular grouping of columns.

SANTA MONICA CHURCH (Iglesia de Santa Monica) is at calles Santa Mónica and Reforma, about 4 blocks northwest of the cathedral. It dates from around 1720. The baroque facade features exquisite stone carvings in 18th-century Spanish style. The interior is elaborate as well.

UNIVERSITY OF GUADALAJARA is on Av. Juárez at Av. Enrique Díaz de León, behind the Expiatory Temple and 4 blocks west of Revolución Park. The main building, French Renaissance in style, contains an Orozco mural. On the north side of Avenida Vallarta is the university tower, where cultural events are held regularly.

University of Guadalajara Museum of Arts (Museo de las Artes de la Universidad de Guadalajara) is opposite the main building. It occupies a beautiful early 20th-century edifice that was once a primary school. The permanent collection consists primarily of contemporary Jaliscan and Mexican artists; traveling exhibitions are mounted regularly. Also here are early Orozco murals. Tues.-Sat. 10-8, Sun. noon-8.

What To Do

Dining

Guadalajaran restaurants offer diners a number of meaty options. Typically *tapatío* fare includes grilled steaks; *carne asada a la tampiqueña,* spicy broiled or roasted meat served with bacon and beans; *pozole,* a thick, satisfying hominy-based soup with hunks of *carnitas* (pork), tomatoes, cilantro and frequently chickpeas; and *birria* (stewed goat or pork in a thick, spicy tomato broth). But the city also has elegant Continental

dining rooms, vegetarian eateries, Italian-style trattorias and *loncherías,* stand-up lunch counters offering sandwich fixings piled on a fresh *bolillo* roll. Such options should satisfy anyone's taste and pocket.

Perhaps the most authentic of the city's eateries are the *restaurantes campestres,* country-style establishments serving big steaks with such hearty Mexican side dishes as beans, quesadillas and tortillas. The food is accompanied by mariachi music and entertainment. Some establishments also present a modified form of *charreada,* or rodeo, which gives willing customers the opportunity to fight a young bull; cheers or laughs ensue depending on the outcome. *Restaurantes campestres* are located within the city and also along main highways outside the urban area.

Gastronomic adventurers will be sorely tempted by the astounding variety of street food. Numerous inexpensive *taquerías* (taco stands) operate up and down the length of Plaza Tapatía; the freshly made corn tortillas are wrapped around a wide variety of meat or vegetable fillings. The Mercado Libertad (*see "Shopping" below*) has hundreds of tiny stands offering full-course *comida corrida* meals, tamales, enchiladas, quesadillas and other treats. You can also find cheese, fruit and pastries. Cleanliness levels vary, however, and anyone planning to nibble their way from stall to stall should keep in mind the possibility of bacterial contamination, especially if the food has been sitting for a long time.

Travelers longing for a taste of home need not despair. Whether it's due to the many U.S. and Canadian expatriates residing in Guadalajara or the changing tastes of local residents, U.S. fast-food franchises are everywhere. And for a meal on the run, Guadalajara has a number of pizza carryouts.

Except at first-class hotels and restaurants where purified water is customarily used, be careful of drinking water; this includes the ice cubes in drinks. Avoid unpeeled raw vegetables and fruit as well as untreated milk and dairy products. For a list of AAA-RATED dining establishments in Guadalajara, *see the Lodgings & Restaurants section.*

Shopping

Fashionable shops and boutiques line Avenida Chapultepec between avenidas México and Niños Héroes, west of the historic center. This is Guadalajara's Zona Rosa (Pink Zone), an upper-class area frequented by tourists.

Malls dot the metropolitan landscape as well. La Gran Plaza is a sleek three-story collection of stores and a movie theater multiplex on Avenida Vallarta near the Camino Real Hotel. The largest is Plaza del Sol, at avenidas López Mateos Sur and Mariano Otero southwest of downtown. Restaurants and outdoor garden areas offer a break from shopping. City buses designated "Plaza del Sol" travel to the mall from Calzada Independencia in the vicinity of the Liberty Market.

Guadalajara also has an amazing number of shoe stores. Calle Esteban Alatorre, northeast of the historic center, is known locally as "shoe street." Galería del Calzado, at the corner of avenidas México and Yaquis (on the west side of town near Plaza México), is a shoe shopping center covering a square block. Shoe and boot prices at its stores are reputed to be among the best in Mexico.

Just off Calzada Independencia at Avenida Javier Mina is the Liberty Market (Mercado Libertad), a huge, timeless Mexican market under a 20th-century roof. Shoppers bargain for an encyclopedic array of tropical fruits and vegetables, like chewy *zapotes* (fruit from the sapodilla tree). Also available for haggling over are such handicrafts as baskets, woodcarvings and pottery; watches; chess sets; jewelry; leather goods; electronic gadgets; computer software programs; and such time-tested exotica as speckled quail eggs and herbal potions to cure impotence.

The market also sells a tremendous variety of food, from tacos to the delicately carved mango slices sold by fruit vendors. Those with squeamish stomachs will want to avoid some of the more unappetizing stalls, which offer the likes of *menudo* (tripe stew) and calves' heads.

El Baratillo, Guadalajara's Sunday morning flea market, offers shopping that is more for fun than for serious purchasing, unless you're an expert haggler. It stretches for blocks along Avenida Javier Mina in an area east of the Liberty Market; take a local bus along Avenida Gigantes, 2 blocks south of the market, to get there. The enormous melange makes up just about everything, most of it used.

Sightseeing

Guadalajara is a convenient base for day excursions to the Lake Chapala communities of Ajijic, Jocotepec and Chapala; to the suburban handicraft centers of Tlaquepaque and Tonalá; to the town of Tequila, known for the production of one of Mexico's more potent brews; and to the suburb of Zapopan, home of the revered Virgin of Zapopan.

Casual attire is suitable for almost any sightseeing excursion in the Guadalajara area; shorts are frowned upon in churches, however. For more information about these destinations *see their individual alphabetical listings under this region.*

Sports and Recreation

Bullfighting fans head for the 25,000-seat Plaza de Toros Nuevo Progreso, northeast of downtown on Calzada Independencia Norte (across from Jalisco Stadium). From October through March, bullfights *(corridas)* take place on Sunday afternoons starting at 4:30. Tickets are sold at the bullring. Spectators can opt for seats in the sun *(sol)* or shade *(sombra);* those in the shade are more expensive. For further information phone (33) 3637-9982, or ask at your hotel about dates and ticket prices.

Although they resemble the Western rodeos of the United States, **charreadas** are unmistakably Mexican. When Spanish explorers and conquerors reintroduced the horse (which had roamed the North American plains some 45,000,000 years earlier), only noblemen were permitted to ride. But the Indians soon acquired their own horseback skills, with the *charro* (male rider) evolving from the requirements of livestock raising in open country.

Charros were resourceful, self-reliant men, familiar with the land and able to live off it. *Charro* contingents fought in the war to achieve Mexican independence, and *charreadas,* where native horseback riders gathered to show off their skills, became part of Mexican folklore. The National Association of Charros was founded in 1921, and in

Guadalajara these events have remained particularly popular.

Both *charros* and *charras* (female riders) are expert at fancy horsemanship and roping. The focus is on style and finesse rather than competition, although some of the feats performed are of the daredevil variety. One of the chief pleasures of a *charreada* is viewing the elegantly ceremonial costumes on display. Men are decked out in white pleated shirts, black pants encrusted with silver buttons and a sombrero embroidered with gold or silver thread. *Charras*—often the daughters or wives of *charros*—wear lacy petticoats, brightly colored skirts decorated with lace and ribbons, and braided, beribboned hair.

Charreadas take place throughout the year. Lienzo Charros de Jalisco, Av. Dr. R. Michel #577 near Agua Azul Park, presents a rodeo Sundays at noon with different events as well as folkloric music and dance. Admission begins at around $3 (U.S.); phone (33) 3619-0315.

Soccer (*fútbol*) is the city's most popular spectator sport. Professional teams play at Jalisco Stadium (Estadio Jalisco), on Calzada Independencia Norte across from the bullring. Schedules vary; for ticket and other information, check with your hotel or the Jalisco State Tourism Office.

Guadalajara's year-round mild, sunny weather is ideal for **golf.** Some private courses allow visitors to play for a greens fee and proof of membership in a U.S. club; others are closed to nonmembers on weekends and holidays. Admittance to the immaculately maintained, 18-hole course at the Guadalajara Country Club is through a member, although the better hotels may be able to get their guests in. The country club is off Avenida Avila Camacho, about 8 kilometers (5 miles) northwest of the downtown historic center.

The Atlas Golf Club (18 holes) is southeast of the city, on Mex. 23 just south of Tlaquepaque (on the way to Lake Chapala); phone (33) 3689-2620. The Santa Anita Golf Club is on Mex. 15, about 7 kilometers (4 miles) south of the Periférico loop road; phone (33) 3686-0962.

Some of the larger hotels, such as the Crowne Plaza Guadalajara and the Camino Real Guadalajara, permit nonguests to use their **tennis** courts for a fee. Colomos Park (Parque Colomos), south of Avenida Patria and west of the country club in the city's western sector, has a track and tree-lined paths for **jogging.**

Nightlife

Unlike Mexico City or the big beach resorts, Guadalajara's nightlife is not particularly frenetic. Nightclubs, bars and discos tend to be concentrated in two places: downtown and in the Plaza del Sol area. Inquire at the front desk of your hotel or ask a bellboy what is happening in town during your stay.

The lobby bar in the Fiesta Americana Hotel, Av. Aurelio Aceves #225 on Minerva Circle, is a classy club/lounge with live music. La Diligencia in the Camino Real Hotel, Avenida Vallarta #5005, has a romantic atmosphere and music for dancing. Maxim's Disco in the Hotel Frances, downtown at Calle Maestranza #35 (near Plaza de la Liberación), has live music and a dance floor. The Frances also has an intimate lobby bar with piano music.

Several theaters show foreign and repertory films, including the Cine Cinematógrafo, Av. Vallarta #1102 (2 blocks west of the University of Guadalajara Museum of Arts), and Cine-Teatro Cabañas, in the Cabañas Cultural Institute at the eastern end of Plaza Tapatía. Malls such as Plaza del Sol have multiplexes showing the latest American releases.

Soak up the local ambience at Plaza de los Mariachis, on Calzada Independencia Sur between avenidas Javier Mina and Alvaro Obregón (on the south side of the Mercado Libertad). This pretty plaza is staked out by the roving bands of musicians. For a fee (usually around $5 U.S.) they will perform with guitar, violin, trumpet and an enthusiasm second to none. It costs nothing to listen to these serenades from another table, but if you're the one requesting a song, negotiate the price first.

The numerous sidewalk cafés clustered around the plaza are pleasant places to relax during the day; it's advisable not to linger in this area after it gets dark. Use the pedestrian overpass from the market to avoid the heavy traffic congestion. **Note:** Pickpockets frequent the plaza; keep an eye on your valuables.

On Thursday and Sunday evenings the Jalisco State Band gives free performances at Plaza de Armas, across from the Government Palace. The music starts at 6:30 p.m., but if you want a seat at one of the benches arrive at least half an hour early.

Theater and Concerts

Probably the grandest spectacle in town is the presentation of the University of Guadalajara's Ballet Folklórico in the Degollado Theater. Regional dances are complemented by *estudiantinas* or *rondallas* string ensembles, the Mexican counterpart of American high school marching bands or drum-and-bugle corps. Performances take place Sunday mornings at 10 a.m. Tickets for each performance go on sale Thursday afternoon; phone (33) 3614-4773.

The Jalisco Philharmonic Orchestra (Orquesta Filarmónica de Jalisco) performs following the Ballet Folklórico on Sundays and seasonally at other times at the Degollado Theater. National and international artists appear at the theater as well. The Cabañas Cultural Institute presents various theater, dance and musical performances throughout the year. Chamber music recitals take place in the institute's Tolsá Chapel. The English-language *Guadalajara Reporter* publishes schedules of current events.

For something a little out of the ordinary, take in a performance at the Experimental Theater of Jalisco (Teatro Experimental de Jalisco), on Calzada Independencia Sur next to the entrance to

Agua Azul Park. The University of Guadalajara's theater company is headquartered here. Performances are in Spanish.

Special Events

Guadalajara's chief annual event is the October Fair, or Fiestas de Octubre. This monthlong artistic and cultural festival offers concerts, ballet, opera, theater, movies, folk art expositions and live music. Events take place at various locations, many in the vicinity of Plaza Tapatía, where outdoor stages and pavilions sprout. Hotel and ticket reservations are highly advised for the entire month of October and should be made in advance.

Guadalajarans celebrate many of the occasions listed in the "Fiestas and Holidays" section on page 532. Some are of particular interest, such as Independence Day celebrations in mid-September, or the return of the Virgin of Zapopan to the Basilica of Zapopan on Oct. 12 *(see Zapopan)*. A series of cultural events take place the last 2 weeks of February before the beginning of Lent.

Other festivities with a special *tapatío* flavor are the Day of the Three Wise Men on Jan. 6; the Tlaquepaque Ceramics Fair, beginning June 15; the Day of St. James the Apostle in Tonalá on July 25, which features a mock battle between Indians and Spaniards; and Day of the Dead celebrations Nov. 1-2. Most of these are characterized by *tianguis* (open-air markets), *charreadas* (rodeos), fireworks, dancing, mariachi bands and tempting spreads of regional food.

The Christmas holidays in Guadalajara are celebrated with *pastorelas*, folk representations of the birth of Christ, and *posadas*, re-enactments of Mary and Joseph's search for an inn. The city's museums often participate, offering traditional dance programs and providing special refreshments. Families also get together to take part in candlelight processions to each other's homes, and nativity scenes are set up in churches and plazas. If you'll be visiting during December, check with your hotel, the Jalisco State Tourism Office or the bulletin boards at museums for further information.

This ends listings for Guadalajara.
The following page resumes the alphabetical listings
of cities in Central Mexico.

GUANAJUATO, GUANAJUATO (A-7)

pop. 76,900, elev. 6,649'

See map page 296.

Guanajuato (gwah-nah-HWAH-toh) is one of Mexico's most beautifully preserved colonial cities. Steeped in history, rich with culture and perched at the bottom of a delightfully scenic canyon, it offers numerous pleasures for the traveler. Leafy plazas, ornate mansions and flowerpot-bedecked alleyways add to Guanajuato's charm. So much of the city's colonial aspect endures, in fact, that it was designated a World Heritage Site by UNESCO in 1988. Guanajuato also—in an age of global information sharing and pop culture predominance—remains thoroughly Mexican in character.

Capital of the state of the same name, Guanajuato (the name means "place of frogs") was founded in 1548. Silver is its reason for being. For a while the fabulous strike at La Valenciana Mine alone supplied more than half of all the silver received by the Spanish monarchs.

This mineral wealth made Guanajuato the commercial and financial center of a region known as the Bajío, or heartland, for its green, rolling hills and fertile farmland. The establishment of a university by the Jesuits in 1732 began Guanajuato's reputation as an intellectual center and seat of learning.

Ironically, the city which had become wealthy under Spanish rule took an integral role in the struggle for Mexican independence. In 1810, Guanajuato was invaded by a motley army of peasant farmers, miners and other disenfranchised citizens under the leadership of Father Miguel Hidalgo de Costilla, venerated as the "Father of Mexican Independence."

Spanish Royalists—mining barons and the landowning elite—holed up in the massive town granary, Alhóndiga de Granaditas, which is now a museum (see attraction listing). Under orders from Hidalgo, a young miner nicknamed El Pípila heroically made his way to the wooden door of the fortresslike structure, setting it on fire and allowing the insurgents to storm the interior, giving them the first major military victory of the War of Independence.

Although Guanajuato was sacked and many of the town's Spanish aristocracy massacred, the revolutionaries did not remain in control for long. In 1811, Hidalgo and three of his leaders were executed near Chihuahua and their heads sent to Guanajuato to be hung on hooks protruding from the four outside corners of the granary, grisly reminders that this particular conflict was far from over. The heads remained impaled until 1821, when Mexico finally won its independence.

Happily, those Spanish legacies that remain add immeasurably to the city's picturesque air. It crowds the slopes of a dry, narrow, rugged canyon. Houses hug the canyon's different levels, with the foundation of one house sitting at the rooftop level of the one below. The Spanish architectural influence is unmistakably evident, but because Andalusians were among the early arrivals, there is a Moorish touch to some early buildings.

Guanajuato's downtown core maintains architectural integrity by restricting gas stations and other concessions to contemporary living to the suburbs and outlying areas. The city's twisting streets are interspersed with little plazas, perfect for relaxing on a shaded bench or perhaps chatting over coffee with one of the students who attend the prestigious University of Guanajuato.

Planning Your Stay

If you're basing a vacation in Guanajuato, plan on at least 2 days to fully appreciate the city's fine museums, colonial churches and outstanding university. A third day could be spent simply enjoying the compact city center—wandering from plaza to plaza, browsing through the Hidalgo Market and having a leisurely dinner at one of the outdoor cafes near the centrally located Jardín Unión, a park with an old-fashioned, romantic atmosphere.

Add another day for exploring attractions in the environs, such as the Church of La Valenciana, the La Valenciana Mine, Cubilete Mountain or the Mummy Museum (see attraction listings). Drive the Panoramic Highway (Carretera Panoramica), the loop road that roughly encircles the city and offers several memorably scenic vantage points, or have a picnic at Olla Dam (Presa de la Olla), site of a man-made lake and the pretty gardens at Acacia Park.

Allow even more time to attend performances if your visit coincides with the International Cervantes Festival (see "Special Events"), held from mid- to late October. Hotel reservations, however, will need to be booked up to 6 months in advance.

It's an easy trip from Guanajuato to the nearby colonial cities of San Miguel de Allende, Querétaro and Dolores Hidalgo (see separate listings within this region). Northwest of Guanajuato is León. It's a sprawling industrial center, but diehard shoppers should note that it also is the country's leading producer of shoes. Spend an afternoon bargaining for footwear and leather goods at several of the many downtown shops.

For those who cannot or would rather not negotiate Guanajuato's hilly streets, Transportes Turísticos de Guanajuato offers guided tours of such attractions as the Church of Valenciana, the Statue of El Pípila and the Mummy Museum. The office is underneath the Basilica of Our Lady of Guanajuato (Basilica Nuestra Señora de Guanajuato) on Plaza de la Paz; phone (473) 732-2134.

Practicalities

The nearest airport is in León, about 56 kilometers (35 miles) northwest. Aeroméxico offers flights from Mexico City; the taxi ride to Guanajuato takes about an hour. For additional information about airlines see "Arriving by Air," page 551.

Central Camionera, the main bus station, is about 6 kilometers (3.5 miles) southwest of downtown. First-class bus service is offered by ETN and Omnibus de México. There is frequent service between Mexico City's Terminal del Norte (North Bus Terminal) and Guanajuato. The Flecha Amarilla line has service from Guanajuato to San Miguel de Allende several times daily. For additional information about buses see "Bus Service," page 68.

Local buses navigate several routes. One runs from downtown east along Mex. 110, passing several hotels along the way, and heads toward the La Valenciana Church and Mine and the town of Dolores Hidalgo. Buses designated "Presa-Estación" basically travel from one end of town to the other; they use the subterranean avenue if going toward the La Olla Reservoir and above-ground streets if going toward the train station. Another line takes tourists to the popular Mummy Museum. All schedules are subject to frequent change; the State Tourism Office (see below) can provide helpful bus information.

The city's high altitude guarantees mild weather year-round. Daytime highs are usually in the low or mid 70s except in April and May, when they climb into the low 80s. Nighttime lows are usually in the 40s and 50s, although winter nights can be chillier. Showers or thunderstorms occur from June through September, but the weather is usually dry and sunny. Bring a couple of sweaters and a jacket or light coat if you're visiting in the fall or winter. Comfortable walking shoes are a must, not only for the cobblestoned street surfaces but for climbing the numerous hills.

Guanajuato has a large student population and an active social and cultural life. The city is small, and most establishments are casual and friendly. Tourist crime occurs infrequently, and personal safety is essentially a matter of taking the usual common sense precautions.

City Layout

Attempting to negotiate Guanajuato's narrow, congested and utterly illogical streets by car is a classic exercise in frustration. Furthermore, there are practically no local car rentals available. Most maps, including those available from the State Tourism Office, fail to show the winding, often unmarked streets in perspective. If you're staying at a hotel outside of the city, use local transportation for forays into and around downtown. Taxi stands (sitios) are located around Plaza de la Paz and the Jardín Unión, and taxis also can be hailed on the street. Always establish the fare before setting out.

Unlike many Mexican cities, where the streets are laid out in an orderly grid pattern radiating from a central plaza, downtown Guanajuato's twisting thoroughfares simply follow the dictates of the terrain. The two main streets, Avenida Juárez and Calle Pocitos, run one way roughly east to west. Juárez is closed to vehicular traffic east of the basilica, and past Jardín Unión its name changes to Avenida Sopeña. Pocitos runs north of Juárez and changes names from Lascuraín de Retana to Pocitos to 28 de Septiembre as it travels from east to west.

Traffic going west to east uses Avenida Subterránea Miguel Hidalgo, an antiquated tunnel which in the mid-1960s was transformed into a vehicular route for inbound traffic. It follows the original course of the Río Guanajuato under the city—roughly parallel with Avenida Juárez/Sopeña—for about 1.5 miles. Mexican engineers rerouted the river following a flood in 1905. Street-level exits are just beyond the Hidalgo Market, at Plazuela de los Angeles, at Jardín Unión and at the subway terminus at Plaza Allende. Little more than illumination and paving stones were required to turn the tunnel into a traffic artery.

A confusing network of subsidiary tunnels have since been added in a not-too-successful effort to alleviate the heavy traffic; the city's layout was never intended to accommodate automobiles. Even horse-drawn carriages cannot fully negotiate the steep streets. It's best to travel on foot whenever possible.

The best starting point for the Panoramic Highway (Carretera Panoramica), the delightfully scenic loop road that travels around Guanajuato's periphery, is from Mex. 110 just south of the Real de Minas Hotel (north of downtown). This route offers easy access to such attractions as the El Pípila Statue, Acacia Park, La Olla Dam, the Mummy Museum at the city cemetery (El Panteón) and the Church of La Valenciana.

Events

Guanajuato's biggest cultural event is the annual International Cervantes Festival (Festival Cervantino). University of Guanajuato students first began presenting entremeses—skits—of Spanish author Miguel de Cervantes' work in the early 1950s at the Plaza de San Roque.

The festival has grown ever since, and for 2 to 3 weeks in October, Mexican as well as international actors, dance companies and symphony orchestras perform at plazas and in theaters across the city. Theater performances are reserved, paying events, while the open-air performances in the plazas are often free. The farcical entremeses, presented mostly in pantomime, are easily grasped even if you don't understand Spanish.

Ballet, films, and classical, jazz and rock concerts round out the offerings. Reservations need to be made months in advance for the top events; if Guanajuato hotels are full, an alternative is to stay in San Miguel de Allende. For information about the festival, contact Festival Cervantino, Plaza San Francisquito #1, 36000 Guanajuato, Gto.; phone (473) 731-1221. Tickets can be ordered through Ticketmaster in Mexico City; phone (55) 5325-9000.

Note: The festival draws huge crowds to the city and the already-narrow streets can become extremely congested, something to keep in mind if you're staying in Guanajuato.

Day of the Dead, or Día de Los Muertos, is celebrated Nov. 1 and 2. *Posadas,* re-enactments of Mary and Joseph's search for an inn, take place during the Christmas season. The arrival of the Virgin of Guanajuato is commemorated in late May and again on Aug. 9. These festivals usually include fireworks, regional dance groups and sometimes a parade.

Shopping

The Hidalgo Market (Mercado Hidalgo), on Avenida Juárez west of the city center, occupies a hangarlike 1910 building that resembles, with its glass windows and elaborate iron grillwork, a Victorian train station.

The market has two levels. A peripheral walkway above is roamed by souvenir vendors and contains shops selling crafts, clothing and sombreros. Below are the produce, meat and sweet stands, where local families do their marketing, and little eateries offering quick bites of typical Mexican fare. Everything from fruit to honey-laced candy is offered along row after row of these tidy stalls. In contrast to the market's timeless look are the miniature-screen TVs hidden beneath some of the counters. Flower vendors congregate on the sidewalks outside. The market is open daily.

Bargainers may want to focus their skills on pottery purchases. Numerous types are sold, including the highly glazed, pale green and blue ceramic designs known as majolica or Talavera, a style introduced by the Spaniards. Ceramic mugs and other items fashioned by Gorky González, a local artisan renowned for his Talavera-influenced work, are available at lower prices here than at his studio, which is located on Calle Pastita near Embajadoras Park (Parque de las Embajadoras).

Touring Guanajuato's Parks and Plazas

Guanajuato's meandering, often steep streets and tiny alleyways were made to be explored on foot. Several streets are closed to traffic, and those that aren't frequently are congested and filled with the fumes of idling vehicles. Strolling, therefore, is not only a more practical but a more pleasurable alternative. All you really need for a jaunt through the city's plazas is a good pair of shoes.

The Jardín Unión, in the center of town, is the city's lively focal point. This elegant park has old-fashioned lampposts, tiled, tree-shaded walkways, outdoor cafes and a band shell that is the scene of frequent musical performances. Most of Guanajuato's downtown attractions are within easy walking distance. It's just off Avenida Juárez/Sopeña, which can be used as a point of orientation when exploring the downtown area.

Facing one side of the triangle-shaped plaza are the opulent Teatro Juárez and the Church of San Diego, another of Guanajuato's picturesque colonial churches. Commissioned by Franciscan missionaries, it was almost destroyed by floodwaters and rebuilt in the late 18th century. The doorway in

particular is representative of the flamboyant Churrigueresque architectural style.

Just off Jardín Unión is Plazuela del Baratillo, a peaceful spot for relaxing in the *sol* (sun) or *sombra* (shade) to the sounds of a gurgling fountain, a gift to the city from Emperor Maximilian.

West from the Jardín Unión is Plaza de la Paz, anchored by the Basilica of Our Lady of Guanajuato, or Parish Church (La Parroquia). Behind the plaza is the University of Guanajuato. Palatial private residences dating from the 18th and 19th centuries surround the plaza, recalling the days when silver poured out of the region's mines.

Continue down Avenida Juárez to Plazuela de Los Angeles, where the walls of the shops and houses are painted in bright colors. Close by is the Alley of the Kiss (Callejón del Beso), an intimate passageway narrow enough to permit a smooch from balconies on either side of the street; according to local legend, two lovers who were kept apart did just that.

Near Jardín de la Reforma, a shady park along Avenida Juárez a block or so from the Hidalgo Market, is Plaza de San Roque, a small square that is the site of many of the *entremeses* presented by university students as part of the Cervantes festival in October.

Equally engaging are the *callejoneadas* (kah-yeh-hoh-neh-AH-dahs), or serenades, that take place at Guanajuato's plazas or in the city streets on various weekend evenings. During these frolics, strolling student ensembles called *estudiantinas* dress in medieval costumes and sing songs with guitar and mandolin accompaniment. The public is welcome to join in the merriment.

The reservoir impounded by La Olla Dam (Presa de la Olla), built in the mid-18th century, provides Guanajuato's supply of drinking water as well as a recreational setting favored by local weekenders. This residential area at the east end of town can be reached via Paseo de la Presa or by taking a city bus designated "Presa."

Antillón Park is just below the dam. Flower gardens and a large statue of Father Miguel Hidalgo distinguish Acacia Park; picnicking is permitted, and rowboats can be rented for paddling around on the man-made lake.

Guanajuato State Tourism Office (Coordinadora Estatal de Turismo): Plaza de la Paz #14, across from the Basilica of Our Lady of Guanajuato. Open Mon.-Fri. 9-7, Sat. 10-4, Sun. 10-2; phone (800) 714-1086 (toll-free long distance within Mexico).

What To See in and Around Town

CHURCH OF LA COMPAÑIA (Iglesia de la Compañía) is at Calle Pocitos and Navarro near the University of Guanajuato. It was built by the Jesuits 1747-65 and then abandoned when the order was expelled from New Spain. Restored in the 19th century, the church has a lovely, typically ornate Churrigueresque exterior of rose-colored stone,

To The Mummy Museum

© AAA

Avenida Subterránea Miguel Hidalgo is for inbound traffic only with street level exits just beyond the Hidalgo Market, at Plazuela de los Ángeles, at Jardín Unión and terminus at Plaza de Allende. It is 3 km. long.

To Mexico City, D.F. or León & Pípila Statue

Hospital

C. PARDO

Cantador Park

ESCALERA SALGADO

To Valenciana Church & Mine, Dolores Hidalgo & Cubilete Mountain

AV. SUBTERRÁNEA MIGUEL HIDALGO

S. DEMANO

JUAREZ

MENDIZABAL

State Historical Museum (Alhóndiga de Granaditas)

Hidalgo Market

JUAN VALLE

POCITOS

Plazuela de los Ángeles

ALONZO

Plaza de la Paz Parish Church (La Parroquia)

Diego Rivera Museum

State Historical Museum

University of Guanajuato

Church of La Compañía

House of Crafts

TENAZA

San Diego Church

Jardín Unión

Juárez Theater

EL SOL

Don Quixote Iconographic Museum

MANUEL DOBLADO

HIDALGO

Post Office

CALLE BELAUNZARAN

Plaza de Allende

CALLE SANGRE DE CRISTO

Las Embajadoras Park

C. SEBASTIAN

San Jerónimo Park

N

PASEO DE LA PRESA

CALLE PASTITA

Government Palace

Antillón Park

Presa de la Olla

Guanajuato

GUANAJUATO

Acacia Park

Miles		0.2
0		
Kilometers		0.3
0		

3017-L

intricately carved wooden doors and a large dome. The interior contains paintings by 18th-century artist Miguel Cabrera.

CHURCH OF LA VALENCIANA (Iglesia de la Valenciana) is about 4 km (2.5 mi.) northwest of downtown on Mex. 110, toward Dolores Hidalgo; some parking is available along the road by the church. The Church of San Cayetano (Iglesia de San Cayetano) is commonly referred to as La Valenciana. It dates from 1788 and was constructed by the Don Antonio de Obregón Alconcer family, wealthy owners of the La Valenciana Mine.

The pink-stone facade, with its profusion of delicate carvings, is a fine example of the florid Churrigueresque architectural style. But it is the interior that is truly breathtaking, adorned with a soaring gilt and gold-leaf, ornately carved retablo (wall behind the main altar), which includes many life-size statues of saints and biblical figures. Two additional retablos, each as tall and as magnificent as the central decoration, grace the transepts on either side. Three huge oil paintings by Luis Monray Pinto depicting biblical stories hang along the side walls of the narthex.

On Dec. 8 a fiesta honors The Immaculate Conception (La Purísima). Designated "Valenciana" buses take visitors to the church, which has operated continuously since its inception. Allow 30 minutes minimum. Mass daily at 10 a.m.; church open all day. Free; donations accepted.

CUBILETE MOUNTAIN (Cerro del Cubilete) is about 16 km (10 mi.) west of Guanajuato off Mex. 110, on the way to Silao. It is said to be the geographical center of Mexico and draws many pilgrims. A gravel road climbs to the 9,440-foot summit, which is surmounted by a 65-foot-tall bronze statue of Christ the King (Cristo Rey). From here are superb views of the Bajío region, a fertile green plain dotted with lakes and isolated mountain peaks. City buses travel to the summit; the trip takes about 90 minutes.

DIEGO RIVERA MUSEUM (Museo Casa Diego Rivera) is at Calle Pocitos #47, 3 blocks north of the Guanajuato State Museum; street parking is very limited. The city's most celebrated native son and one of Mexico's most esteemed muralists lived here the first 9 years of his life. The first floor of the home has been restored and is furnished with turn-of-the-20th-century antiques. The second and third floors contain more than 90 paintings, sketches and watercolors that trace the development of his style, influenced by both 20th-century Cubism and ancient Maya techniques.

Political beliefs strongly informed Rivera's work, as evidenced by a sketch for the 1933 mural commissioned by Rockefeller Center in New York City that was destroyed because it included a portrait of Vladimir Lenin. Exhibit information is in Spanish. Restrooms are provided. Allow 1 hour minimum.

Tues.-Sat. 10-6:30, Sun. 10-2:30. Admission 15 pesos (around $1.50 U.S.). Phone (473) 732-1197.

DON QUIXOTE ICONOGRAPHIC MUSEUM (Museo Iconográfico del Quijote) is at Manuel Doblado #1, about 2 blocks southeast of Jardín Unión in an area of very limited street parking. Housing more than 700 pieces of art, this fascinating museum provides a look at the enduring literary character created by Spanish author Miguel de Cervantes as seen through the eyes of Pedro Coronel, Salvador Dalí, Pablo Picasso and other artists.

The pieces are displayed in rooms surrounding a three-story courtyard. Quixote and trusty companion Sancho Panza are executed in a variety of media, including paintings, sculpture, stained-glass windows, clocks, painted eggs, woodcarvings and one large leaf, complete with veins, that shows Cervantes' hero in profile on horseback. There also are huge wall murals and quartz, bronze, silver and porcelain statuary.

Exhibit information is in Spanish. Restrooms are provided. Allow 1 hour minimum. Tues.-Sat. 10-6:30, Sun. 10-2:30; closed national holidays. Admission 20 pesos (around $2 U.S.). Phone (473) 732-6721.

GOVERNMENT PALACE (Palacio de Gobierno) is on Paseo de la Presa near the La Olla Dam. It stands on the site of the old house of the Marqués of San Clemente. The original building was destroyed by a flood; the present structure was completed in 1903. It evokes a European elegance, enhanced by the use of Guanajuato green sandstone.

GUANAJUATO STATE MUSEUM (Museo del Pueblo de Guanajuato) is at Calle Pocitos #7 near the University of Guanajuato. An art museum housed in a 17th-century mansion, it has an extensive collection of colonial-era religious paintings amassed by muralist José Chávez Morado, as well as Morado murals. Also displayed are works by contemporary Mexican artists. Tues.-Sat. 10-2 and 4-7, Sun. 10-2. Admission around $2 (U.S.). Phone (473) 732-2990.

HOTEL POSADA SANTA FE is at Plaza Principal #12 at Jardín Unión. The hotel houses a collection of paintings by Don Manuel Leal, a Guanajuatan who dramatically documented his perceptions of the city's history. The paintings hang in the hotel's lavishly appointed, colonial-style public areas. Phone (473) 732-0084.

JUAREZ THEATER (Teatro Juárez) faces Jardín Unión; street parking is very limited. It is a deliciously opulent reminder of Guanajuato's late 19th-century prosperity. The exterior is impressive, with tall columns, ascending steps, branching lampposts, bronze lions and statues of the Greek muses at the roof line.

Inside there are four levels of seating, private boxes and a smoking room with circular velvet settees, heavy drapes and a marble floor. The Moorish-style ornamentation includes dazzlingly intricate red-and-gold patterns on the walls and ceiling. Theater, symphony performances and productions associated with the *Festival Internacional Cervantino* all take the stage.

Note: The upper portion is closed for renovations and was expected to reopen in late 2004 or early 2005. Allow 30 minutes minimum. Tours given daily 11-2. Tour fee 15 pesos (around $1.50 U.S.). Phone (473) 732-1542.

LA VALENCIANA MINE is across the highway from the church. Discovered in 1760, it ranks as one of the greatest silver mines in history, at one point said to produce more than a fifth of the world's silver. The outer walls of the mine area are peaked to symbolize the crown of Spain. The shaft is exceptionally wide and more than 1,500 feet deep; visitors can look down it but are not permitted to descend. The mine was reactivated in the late 1960s after decades of lying in ruin, and still brings up silver, lead and nickel. Daily 8-7. Admission around 50 cents (U.S.).

MARFIL is about 3 km (2 mi.) southwest of Guanajuato off Mex. 110; the old road to Marfil (Camino Antiguo a Marfil) winds into a valley. At the height of this former mining town's prosperity in the late 19th century, numerous silver mines operated and luxurious mansions lined the streets. Marfil was devastated in 1905 when La Olla Dam burst, killing many of the residents. In recent years Marfil has experienced a rebirth, with ongoing renovations sprucing up some of the long-neglected haciendas of the mine owners.

Ex-Hacienda of San Gabriel de Barrera (Museo Ex-Hacienda San Gabriel de Barrera) is at Camino Antiguo a Marfil Km 2.5, opposite the Hotel Misión Guanajuato. This former hacienda, which contains paintings and elegant Victorian-era furniture as well as a small chapel with an ornately carved retablo (decorative wall) behind the altar, offers a peek at the lifestyle enjoyed by privileged late 19th and early 20th-century Mexicans. The gardens are a delight—more than a dozen, all beautifully maintained, whimsically named and distinctive with regard to plants and statuary.

Food is available. Allow 1 hour minimum. Daily 9-6. Admission 22 pesos (around $2.25 U.S.). The fee to use a camera is 20 pesos ($2), a video camera 25 pesos (around $2.50).

MUMMY MUSEUM (Museo de Las Momias) is west of downtown on Calzada del Panteón, next to the city cemetery (El Panteón). This is the city's ghastliest attraction. Dryness, minerals and natural salts in the soil all helped preserve some 120 corpses, which escaped decomposition to a remarkable degree.

The mummies—men, women and children, some still with shoes and hair—are displayed behind glass with various frozen expressions, giving visitors the morbid thrill of viewing them face to face. This museum is not recommended for the squeamish or the claustrophobic (it's small and often crowded). City buses and taxis that can be boarded or hailed along Avenida Juárez will stop within walking distance of the museum. Daily 9-6. Admission around $3 (U.S.), children around $2. The charge for using a camera is around $1, a video camera around $2. Phone (473) 732-0639.

PARISH CHURCH (La Parroquía) is on Plaza de la Paz. It also is known as the Basilica of Our Lady of Guanajuato. The church, which has a baroque facade that is an interesting yellow-orange in color, dates from 1671. The celebrated image of the Virgin of Guanajuato, brought from Granada, Spain, in 1557, was a gift from King Philip II. Mounted on a pedestal of solid silver, the jewel-bedecked wooden statue is said to date from the seventh century and is considered to be the oldest piece of Christian art in Mexico. The church also contains ornamental frescoes and Miguel Cabrera paintings.

STATE HISTORICAL MUSEUM (Alhóndiga de Granaditas) is at Mendizábal and 28 de Septiembre (Calle Pocitos), northwest of the city center; street parking in the immediate area is very limited. This massive 1809 structure was originally a seed and grain warehouse.

Among the varied exhibits are Indian weavings, saddles, leather clothing, hats, tools, pottery, *Carnaval* masks and a full-sized kitchen with period displays of pots and foods. Upstairs are historical exhibits and a number of pre-Columbian stone artifacts. Murals by José Chávez Morado depicting revolutionary themes embellish the Alhóndiga's stairwells. Bronze busts of War of Independence heroes Hidalgo, Jiménez, Aldama and Allende preside in a hall illuminated by an eternal flame.

Permanent and temporary exhibitions feature the work of Mexican and international artists, and a fine exhibit depicts Guanajuato's historical, social and mining importance through photographs and various artifacts. Exhibit information is in Spanish. Restrooms are provided. Allow 1 hour minimum. Tues.-Sat. 10-2 and 4-5:30, Sun. 10-2:30; closed state holidays. Admission 30 pesos (around $3 U.S.). Phone (473) 732-1112.

STATUE OF EL PIPILA (Estatua de El Pípila) overlooks Guanajuato from a steep hill to the east of the Jardín Unión. It immortalizes Juan José Martínez, a miner who set fire to the front door of the Alhóndiga de Granaditas, the massive granary where Spanish Royalists took refuge in 1810 during an attack on the city by Mexican revolutionaries. The dramatic, 30-foot-high figure, bearing a torch, keeps watch over the city below. This vantage point affords an outstanding view of Guanajuato's architectural landmarks.

Buses designated "Pípila" take visitors to the monument; parking for other vehicles is free. El Pípila also is accessible by a steep climb on foot (wear sturdy walking shoes). To get there, take Calle Sopeña east to Callejón del Calvario and watch for the sign that says "Al Pípila." An incline railway (funicular) takes passengers up the hill to a terminal just below the monument. Funicular runs Mon.-Sat. 9 a.m.-10 p.m., Sun. 10-9. Monument free; funicular around $1.25 (U.S.) one way, $2.25 round trip.

UNIVERSITY OF GUANAJUATO is on Calle Pocitos/Lascurain de Retana. The school has been in almost continuous operation since it was opened by Jesuits in 1732 at the request of Spain's King Philip V. It became a state university in 1945. Ten years later a modern new addition with interconnecting patios and open-air hallways was built, complete with Moorish-style facade. The city's cultural arts showcase, it offers theater, symphonies and student performances of Cervantes' *entremeses* (short comic presentations).

JOCOTEPEC, JALISCO (H-3) pop. 15,900

Founded in 1528, Jocotepec (hoh-koh-teh-PEHK) sits at the western end of Lake Chapala. This popular retreat still manages to exude a relatively unspoiled Mexican atmosphere. It is known for handwoven items, which are still produced on old-fashioned looms. Local artisans turn out bedspreads, table coverings, wall hangings and *sarapes*. Several small shops line Calle Hidalgo, and it's possible to watch the weavers at work.

LAGOS DE MORENO, JALISCO (G-4)
pop. 81,300, elev. 5,917′

Lagos de Moreno (LAH-gos deh moh-REH-noh) is an attractive town in the Jaliscan highlands, strategically situated at the intersection of two major highways, Mex. 45 and Mex. 80. Although it is an important commercial hub, Lagos de Moreno retains a sense of timelessness. Designated a national historic monument, it has a downtown riverside park, colonial mansions with central patios, streets brightened by flowers and tiny plazas in unexpected places.

Worth visiting are the Montecristo House of Antiques, downtown, and its remodeled Hacienda de Montecristo, just southwest of town on Mex. 80. Although the monastery that overlooks Lagos de Moreno from a hillside perch is not open to visitors, those who make the climb will be rewarded with beautiful views, especially around sunset.

MORELIA, MICHOACAN (B-7)
pop. 562,400, elev. 6,399′
See map page 300.

Capital of the state of Michoacán. Morelia (Moh-REH-lee-ah) was founded in 1541. It was first known as Valladolid, after the Spanish birthplace of New Spain's first viceroy, Antonio de Mendoza. In 1828, the name was changed to honor native son José María Morelos, who became a general for and hero of the Mexican War of Independence.

Morelia retains a strong Spanish flavor that has earned it the title "Aristocrat of Colonial Cities"; the historic center was designated a World Heritage Site by UNESCO in 1991. In an effort to retain this atmosphere of Old World charm, building ordinances require that all new construction conform to the architectural blueprint of the city's richly decorated 17th- and 18th-century buildings. Morelia's early planners also had the foresight to lay out wide, straight boulevards, which for the most part accommodate today's vehicle traffic.

The city's famed Boy's Choir, which has sung in Rome and at Carnegie Hall, has its base in the Church and College of las Rosas (Templo y Colegio de las Rosas), established in the late 16th century as a Dominican convent and the home of the oldest school for liturgical music in the Western Hemisphere. Visitors are welcome to attend the rehearsals at Las Rosas, which occupies a magnificent colonial building on Avenida Santiago Tapia, 2 blocks north of the northwest corner of Plaza de Armas. A statue of Vasco de Quiroga stands opposite the statue of Cervantes in the nearby Garden of the Roses (Jardín de las Rosas).

An aqueduct (El Acueducto) dating from 1789 was once the primary means of bringing water to the city. It extends for more than a mile and is made up of 253 arches, the tallest 25 feet in height. They're impressively lit at night. Concealing small shops and private homes, some of the arches line two sides of Parque Villalongín.

Extending east from this small park is Calzada Fray Antonio de San Miguel, a tree-shaded, three-block-long pedestrian street lined on both sides with stone benches. It runs to the Guadalupe Sanctuary (Santuario de Guadalupe) on Calzada Ventura Puente. This typically lavish baroque church was built in the early 18th century, although the highly ornate interior dates from the early 20th century.

Cultural events assume special importance in this university city. Folkloric dance performances and music recitals take place regularly at several locations around town. For schedule information, check with the State Tourism Office (see below) or at the Casa de Cultura. Band concerts take place at Plaza de Armas on Sundays. The Morelia Fair (Feria de Morelia), held in mid-May, is an old-fashioned state fair showcasing livestock and produce displays; it also features regional dance performances and a celebration of the city's founding in 1541.

Musicians perform at various locations during the International Music Festival (Festival Internacional de Música), which occurs in late July and early August. Michoacános also celebrate Independence Day Sept. 15-16, the Birthday of José María Morelos on Sept. 30, Day of the Dead (Día de Los Muertos) Nov. 1-2 and the Feast of the Virgin of Guadalupe, honoring Mexico's patron saint, on Dec. 12.

Practicalities

Aeroméxico offers daily flights between Mexico City and Morelia's Francisco Mújica Airport, about 30 kilometers (19 miles) north of the city. Schedules change frequently, and flight times should be confirmed in advance. Airport taxi services charge about $17 (U.S.) between the airport and the city center.

First-class bus service is offered by ETN between Morelia and Mexico City's Terminal de Autobuses del Poniente (Western Terminal), as well as to Guadalajara and Guanajuato. The central bus station is near the intersection of avenidas Eduardo Ruíz and Gomez Farias, a couple of blocks northwest of the main plaza; a newer bus station is on Periférico República, opposite the football stadium on the northwestern city outskirts.

Buses, taxicabs and combis (usually white VW vans) all provide public transportation. Buses can be helpful for getting to and from Cuauhtémoc Woods Park and the Aqueduct via Avenida Madero, but they move slowly along the crowded streets during rush hours. Combi vehicles have different-colored stripes depending on their destination. Taxis are not metered. The average in-town fare is normally around $2.50 (U.S.); agree on the amount before getting in the cab.

City Layout

Large, tree-lined Plaza de Armas, the main square, is bounded on the north by Avenida Francisco I. Madero and on the south by Calle Allende. It also is known as the Plaza of the Martyrs (Plaza de los Mártires) in honor of the rebel priests who were executed during Mexico's War of Independence. The square is surrounded by colonial-era buildings, and this part of the city is pedestrian-friendly (although congested with vehicles and vendors). Almost all of Morelia's visitor attractions are within walking distance of the plaza.

Downtown street names change north and south of Avenida Madero (Mex. 15), which is the city's principal east-west artery. Two blocks west of Plaza de Armas, Avenida López Rayón becomes Gómez Farias north of Avenida Madero. A block west, Calzada Galeana becomes Nigromante north of Madero. Avenida Abasolo, which runs along the west side of Plaza de Armas, becomes Guillermo Prieto north of Madero; a block east of Plaza de Armas, Avenida García Obeso becomes Juárez north of Madero.

East-west thoroughfares change names at the cathedral. West of the cathedral Avenida Madero is Poniente (Pte.); to the east it is Oriente (Ote.). Calle Allende, which runs along the south side of Plaza de Armas, becomes Valladolid once east of the cathedral.

Nearby Destinations

About 32 kilometers (20 miles) north of Morelia on Mex. 43 is an unusual 19th-century causeway across Lake Cuitzeo. The town of Cuitzeo, on the lake's north shore, contains one of the region's two fortresslike 17th-century Augustinian monasteries; the other is in the city of Yuríria, north of Cuitzeo and a short distance east off Mex. 43.

Two national parks with scenic views are east of Morelia on Mex. 15. José María Morelos National Park (Parque Nacional Insurgente José María Morelos) is about 26 kilometers (16 miles) east of the city. Cerro de Garnica National Park (Parque Nacional Cerro de Garnica), which has two *miradores* (observation points) overlooking the rugged Mil Cumbres (Thousand Peaks) landscape, is another 24 kilometers (15 miles) farther east. From here, Mex. 15 continues winding through steep mountains and dense forests to the town of Ciudad Hidalgo.

Michoacán State Tourism Office (Secretaría de Turismo): adjoining Clavijero Palace, downtown at Calle Nigromante #79. In addition to maps and

visitor information, the office can provide details about free guided walking tours of the city center. Open Mon.-Fri. 9-8, Sat.-Sun. 9-4; phone (800) 450-2300 (toll-free long distance within Mexico).

What To See in and Around Town

BALNEARIO SPA (Balneario Cointzio) is 9 km (6 mi.) west of Morelia on Mex. 15, then about 6 km (4 mi.) south. The spa, at the base of a cliff where mineral waters of 100 F (37 C) emerge, includes two swimming pools, a wading pool, bathhouse, refreshment facilities and bungalows. Open Wed.-Mon. Admission is charged; there are additional fees for parking, pool and bungalows.

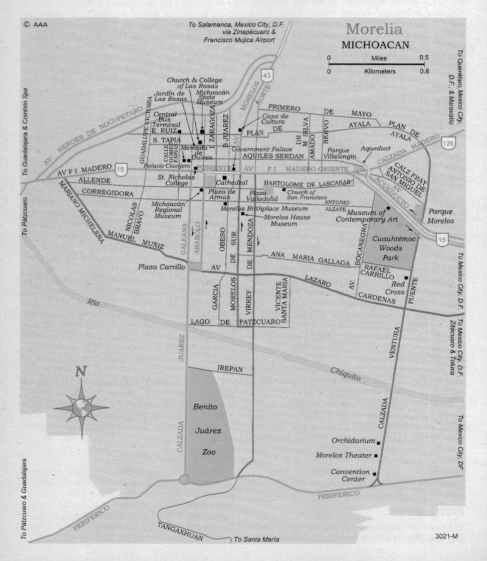

BENITO JUAREZ ZOO (Parque Zoológico Benito Juárez) is about 3 km (1.9 mi.) south of the city center via Av. Juárez. It houses an extensive collection of animals and birds amid landscaped grounds. The zoo also contains a small lake (rowboats are available for rent) and a children's playground. Picnicking is permitted. Daily 10-5. Admission around $1.50 (U.S.).

CATHEDRAL is on the east side of Plaza de Armas, facing Av. Madero. One of Mexico's most beautiful churches, it took more than a century (1640-1744) to build. Exterior highlights are the rose-colored stone facade, two elaborately decorated towers, and a colonial fence and gates. Inside are religious relics and paintings as well as a magnificent three-story organ with 4,600 pipes, reputed to be one of the world's largest. The cathedral is the site of the International Organ Festival, held annually in early May.

CLAVIJERO PALACE (Palacio Clavijero) is at Calle Nigromante #79. A former Jesuit college, it now functions as the state library. The main patio features lofty colonnades and beautiful pink stonework. Cultural events take place in the large open-air gallery.

Under the arcade on the western side of the complex is the Candy Market (Mercado de Dulces). Candy-making traditions begun by European nuns are still carried out at this shrine to Mexican confections. Worth trying are the many flavors of *ate*, a pastelike concoction made with fresh fruit to which sugar and water are added. Perhaps the biggest holiday for sweets shops is the *Day of the Dead* Nov. 1-2, when they turn out an array of sugar skulls, skeletons and other ghostly creations. Market open daily 9 a.m.-10 p.m.

CONVENTION CENTER (Centro de Convenciones) is southeast of downtown, at the intersection of Calzada Ventura Puente and the Periférico (loop road) that encircles the city. This complex of buildings is situated in a reasonably well-groomed park. Convention meetings and cultural events take place at the Morelos Theater (Teatro Morelos). The Orchid House (Orquidario) is a greenhouse containing more than 3,000 varieties that bloom at various times. The Planetarium (Planetario de Morelia) presents star shows on a domed screen.

Orchid greenhouse open Mon.-Fri. 9-6, Sat.-Sun. 3-6; planetarium shows Tues.-Sun. at 7 p.m. Greenhouse admission around 50 cents (U.S.), planetarium shows around $2.25.

CUAUHTEMOC WOODS PARK (Bosque Cuauhtémoc) is about 12 blocks east of Plaza de Armas, off Av. Acueducto (Mex. 15). This is the city's largest green space and a popular Sunday picnic spot. On the park's northeast side, in the small Plaza Morelos, is a statue of the patriot on horseback.

Museum of Contemporary Art (Museo de Arte Contemporaneo) is on the park's northern border at Av. Acueducto #18. Housed in an early 19th-century mansion, it exhibits works by both local and international artists. Tues.-Sat. 10-2 and 4-8, Sun. 10-5. Free.

EX-CONVENT OF SAN FRANCISCO (Ex-Convento de San Francisco) is on Calle Bartolomé de las Casas at Plaza Valladolid, 2 blocks east of the cathedral. It dates from 1531. The founding of Morelia took place in the square in front of the church. Closely set columns give its interior courtyard a medieval look, unlike the open archways that characterize others in the city.

House of Crafts (Casa de las Artesanías) is in the church cloister. This combination museum and workshop displays lacquerware, woodcarvings, pottery, copper items, ceramics and other crafts from throughout the state. Artisans also can be observed at work. The quality of the handicrafts is excellent, and prices are accordingly high. Daily 10-3 and 5-8; individual shop hours may vary.

GOVERNMENT PALACE (Palacio de Gobierno) faces the cathedral across Calle Allende. This baroque building, a former semniary, serves as the state capitol and is the colonial prototype for all new city edifices. Murals painted by Alfredo Zalce, Morelia's famed artist, depict scenes from Mexico's often violent history. Open daily.

HOUSE OF CULTURE (Casa de Cultura) is 4 blocks north of Plaza de Armas on Av. Morelos Norte. This peach-colored, architecturally striking building was salvaged from the ruins of a 350-year-old Carmelite monastery. The central courtyard serves as an open-air theater for drama, dance and music groups, and also provides studio space for artists. Ask about the free monthly brochure that lists upcoming city events.

Within the complex is the Museum of Masks, which displays a collection of ceremonial masks from around the country. Building open Mon.-Fri. 10-3 and 4-8, Sat.-Sun. 10-6. Free.

MICHOACAN REGIONAL MUSEUM (Museo Regional Michoacano) is at Calle Allende #305 near Plaza de Armas. A palace dating from the 18th century, it contains an art gallery, archeological and natural history exhibits, displays of colonial-era furniture and weaponry, and other historical items. Note the stairway mural by Alfredo Zalce depicting figures who have made a positive contribution to Mexico's national identity, as well as those who have not.

Tues.-Sat. 9-7, Sun. 9-2. Admission around $2.50 (U.S.); free to all Sun. Phone (443) 312-0407.

MICHOACAN STATE MUSEUM (Museo del Estado) is at Av. Guillermo Prieto #176. It offers an overview of Michoacáno history, from pre-Columbian figurines to a collection of 18th-century apothecary jars to exhibits of contemporary crafts. The mansion in which the museum is housed was once the residence of self-designated Mexican emperor Agustín Iturbide. Daily 9-2 and 4-7 (also Mon.-Fri. 7-8 p.m.). Free. Phone (443) 313-0629.

MORELOS BIRTHPLACE MUSEUM (Museo Casa Natal de Morelos) is at Corregidora #113 at García Obeso, a block south of Plaza de Armas. The Mexican revolutionary was born here in 1765. The house, erected more than a century earlier, is a national monument and contains a public library. An eternal flame burns in a courtyard garden behind the building. Eight rooms are devoted to Morelos memorabilia, portraits and documents. Mon.-Fri. 9-7. Free.

MORELOS HOUSE MUSEUM (Museo Casa de Morelos) is 3 blocks southeast of Plaza de Armas at Av. Morelos Sur and Calle Aldama. A typical example of domestic colonial architecture, this was José María Morelos' residence beginning in 1801. His descendants lived in the house until 1910, when it was converted into a museum. Inside are personal belongings, manuscripts and exhibits relating to the War of Independence. Daily 9-7. Admission around $2.50 (U.S.); free to all Sun.

ST. NICHOLAS COLLEGE (Colegio de San Nicolas) is at the corner of Calle Nigromante and Av. Madero Poniente, a block northwest of Plaza de Armas. This is the oldest Mexican university still in operation, and was the second educational institution to be established in the Americas. Among its distinguished alumni were War of Independence leaders José María Morelos and Father Miguel Hidalgo. Interesting frescoes decorate the inner walls of the main building's colonial patio. Open Mon.-Fri. Free.

PACHUCA, HIDALGO (B-10)
pop. 278,100, elev. 7,957'

Capital of the state of Hidalgo, Pachuca (pah-CHOO-kah) is the center of a rich mining district that produces much of the world's silver. It is believed that silver was mined before the arrival of the Spanish, who founded the city in 1534. The surrounding hills are honeycombed with tunnels and heaped with slag piles, although industrialization has increased to counteract declining mineral production. The Pachuca area also is known for the production of pulque, a mildly alcoholic drink made from the fermented juice of the maguey (mah-GAY) cactus.

Government offices are in the Red Houses (Casas Coloradas), a complex built as a school toward the end of the 18th century by the Count of Regla, who made his fortune from Pachuca's silver mines. Also of interest is the 1596 Convent of San Francisco. Housed within the convent is the Casasola Archives (Archivo Casasola), which contains an extensive collection of photographs chronicling Mexican history from the late 19th to early 20th centuries. The Mexican Revolution of 1910-20 is particularly well documented.

Nearby Destinations

Northwest of Pachuca along Mex. 85 is the town of Actópan (ahk-TOH-pahn). The name, meaning "in thick and fertile soil," is appropriate, as the town lies in a rich agricultural region. It was founded July 8, 1546, 10 years after Augustinian friars had first journeyed to the area to Christianize the indigenous people. The Toltecs, meanwhile, had arrived even earlier—perhaps as far back as the seventh century.

In the nearby mountains are rock formations known locally as "The Friars," or Los Frailes. According to legend, these rocks were formed when God, angry with two friars who fell in love with a beautiful woman, turned all three people into stone.

Actópan's St. Nicholas Church and Monastery (Templo y Convento de San Nicolas), built in 1546, is distinguished by its massive and harmonious proportions. Among the building's impressive features are its patio, Renaissance-style doorway, frescoes and Gothic cloisters.

The 125-foot-tall bell tower, between the church entrance and the door to the monastery, resembles a giant vertical prism and suggests a Moorish influence. In the chapel ruins outside the church, parts of a mural fresco painted on the walls and ceiling can still be seen. Painted to impress newly converted Indians, it depicts the various punishments their souls would receive in hell if they were not good Christians.

Farther west along Mex. 85, between Actópan and Ixmiquilpan, is El Mezquital, an Otomí Indian region known for its embroidered clothing. Ixmiquilpan (ees-mee-KEEL-pahn) was once the Otomí capital. The town's Church and Monastery of St. Michael the Archangel is a huge, medieval-style fortress/complex and former monastery dating from 1550 and founded by the Order of St. Augustine. Inside the main church are Indian frescoes depicting imaginary beasts and warriors engaged in classic combat. The Church of El Carmen, graced by gilded altars, also is noteworthy.

Monday is market day in Ixmiquilpan; beautifully worked bags, mother-of-pearl-encrusted miniatures, guitars, wine bottle racks and Otomí belts are all for sale. Maguey is an important local crop. From this versatile plant paper, vinegar, molasses, medicines, rope and thread all are made. More potent derivatives include such alcoholic drinks as aguamiel, pulque and mezcal.

About 11 kilometers (7 miles) northeast of Pachuca via Mex. 105 is Mineral Real del Monte, an old mining town that overlooks Pachuca. Its narrow, extremely steep cobblestone streets and old buildings are reminiscent of a Cornish village. Most of the houses were built more than 200 years ago, after the Count of Regla abandoned area mining operations and an English firm took over. Mex. 105 continues on to the picturesque town of Omitlán.

About 3 kilometers (1.9 miles) past Omitlán a road branches eastward off Mex. 105 to Huasca, another village, and the nearby 18th-century smelting haciendas of Santa María Regla and San Miguel Regla. The two complexes have been converted into historical lodgings, with rooms, restaurants and other facilities occupying many of the original buildings.

From Mineral Real del Monte a paved road travels northwest to another old mining town, Mineral El Chico. En route is El Chico National Park, an area of enormous rock formations and cool pine woods.

Hidalgo State Tourism Office (Secretaría de Turismo): Av. Revolución #1300. Open Mon.-Fri. 8:30-4:30; phone (800) 718-2600 (toll-free long distance within Mexico).

PATZCUARO, MICHOACAN (C-7)
pop. 48,400, elev. 7,131′

Pátzcuaro (PAHTZ-kwah-roh), built on the hills sloping back from Lake Pátzcuaro, has red and cream-colored churches, mansions and other buildings erected during three centuries of Spanish rule. It also boasts one of Mexico's loveliest colonial plazas: Plaza Vasco de Quiroga, named for the first Spanish bishop of Michoacán, who introduced Christianity and various craft industries to the region's Tarascan Indians. A statue of "Tata Vasco" gazes down from a stone fountain in the center of the plaza.

A block north of Plaza Vasco de Quiroga is Plaza Gertrudis Bocanegra, named in honor of a woman who was executed by firing squad in 1818 for staunchly supporting the War of Independence. This is the commercial center of town; the market on the plaza's west side bustles with food, clothing and craft stalls.

Many of the colorful native dances performed throughout Mexico originated in this area. One of the most widely known is "Los Viejitos" (the little old men), a witty commentary on the manners and foibles of age.

First-class bus service is provided by the Herradura de Plata line between Mexico City's Terminal de Autobuses del Poniente (Western Terminal) and Pátzcuaro's Central Bus Station (Central Camionera), on the southwest outskirts on Avenida Circunvalación, a loop road encircling town.

Michoacán State Tourism Office: A branch office (Delegación Regional de Turismo) is at Calle Buena Vista #7, on the northwest side of Plaza de la Basilica (about 2 blocks northeast of Plaza Vasco de Quiroga, near the basilica). Open daily 9-3 and 4-7; phone (434) 342-1214 (English may not be spoken).

BASILICA (Basilica de Nuestra Señora de la Salud) is on a hill 2 blocks northeast of Plaza Vasco de Quiroga. The church dates from 1554. The venerated Virgin of Health, on the main altar, is made from a paste of crushed cornstalks mixed with a substance extracted from orchids. On Dec. 8 a fiesta honors the Virgin.

Every morning local women set up shop in Plaza de la Basilica to serve a breakfast of *corundas,* triangular tamales with a filling of pork, beans and cream, and *atole,* a warm drink made of ground cornmeal or rice that has a thick consistency and often is flavored with vanilla.

HOUSE OF THE ELEVEN COURTYARDS (Casa de Los Once Patios) is about a block southeast of Plaza Vasco de Quiroga. Once a Dominican convent, it now houses the studios and galleries of painters and artisans, whom visitors can watch at work. The building also contains small shops *(artesanías)* selling regional handicrafts. Most shops open daily 10-7.

JANITZIO ISLAND (Isla Janitzio) is in the middle of Lake Pátzcuaro. The town of the same name is built in terraced fashion. Day of the Dead ceremonies held Nov. 1-2 include an all-night candlelight vigil in the village cemetery. The island is accessible by launch and is crowded with day visitors on weekends and holidays.

Statue of Morelos is on Janitzio Island. It has been called "quite an accomplishment in ugliness." José María Morelos' raised arm tops the 130-foot-tall figure. A balcony offering a panoramic view of the lake is in the cuff of his sleeve. A spiral staircase leads to the top. The climb is arduous, but the stairway walls are adorned with more than 50 somewhat deteriorated murals depicting the life of the priest turned freedom fighter. Admission around 60 cents (U.S.).

LAKE PATZCUARO, its placid waters dotted with islands, is one of the highest lakes in the country. Around its shoreline are a score or more of tiny Tarascan villages, many accessible only by boat. The distinctive "butterfly" nets that once were the main tool of local fishermen now appear mostly for photographers. The lake still yields the *pescado blanco,* a small, almost transparent whitefish that is a local favorite.

MUSEUM OF POPULAR ARTS (Museo de Artes Populares) is a block south of the Basilica in the former Colegio de San Nicolás. The exhibits of Michoacán arts and crafts here include white lace *rebozos* (shawls), hand-painted ceramics and copperware. Behind the museum are the remains of some pre-Columbian stone structures. Tues.-Sat. 9-7, Sun. 9-3. Admission around $3.50 (U.S.); free to all Sun. Phone (434) 342-1029.

STIRRUP PEAK (El Estribo) is about 4 km (2.5 mi.) west of the main plaza via Calle Ponce de León (beginning at the southwest corner of Plaza Vasco de Quiroga), following signs. Reached by a steep cobblestone road, it overlooks the lake and surrounding villages. The road can be walked or driven; if you choose to hike to the summit, which takes about an hour, it's safer to go on a weekend when there are other people around. Picnicking is permitted.

PUEBLA, PUEBLA (C-11)

pop. 1,320,600, metro area 2,500,000, elev. 7,091'

See map page 306.

Puebla (PWEH-blah), capital and commercial center of the state of Puebla, lies in a large valley flanked by four volcanoes: Popocatépetl, Iztaccíhuatl, Malinche and Citlaltépetl (Pico de Orizaba). A product of the Spanish conquest, Puebla was established in 1531 by colonists to whom Spain had granted lands and Indian slaves.

Strategically located between the Gulf of Mexico coast and Mexico City, the city protected the capital from military attack, became a stopover for the rich and famous, and developed into a major religious center. History was made at forts Loreto and Guadalupe on May 5, 1862, when about 4,500 poorly armed Mexicans defeated some 6,500 French troops who were attempting to establish the reign of Archduke Maximilian.

Vivid Talavera tile, used in combination with a dark red tile, is evident throughout Puebla. Tilemakers who settled from Talavera de la Reina, near Toledo, Spain, introduced this colorful form of decorative art. Puebla was the first city in Mexico to produce these handmade Spanish wares, and they are still made today.

The city also is known for its distinctive cuisine. *Mole* (mo-LEH), the Náhuatl Indian word for sauce, comes in a variety of guises; many of these complex concoctions were painstakingly developed by convent nuns. Popular versions are *poblano*, a blend of chilies and bitter chocolate; *pipian*, which mixes chilies and pumpkin seeds; and *adobo*, a pairing of cumin and a variety of regional chilies.

Another signature dish is *chiles en nogada*, a spicy mix of large green chilies stuffed with ground beef and fresh fruit, topped with creamy white walnut sauce and red pomegranate seeds. Sweets include *camotes*, a confection of sweet potato paste molded into a stick shape and flavored with fruit. *Camote* street vendors also sell sweet potatoes and plantains baked in wood-burning stoves.

Celebrations include Holy Week, observed Palm Sunday to Easter Sunday, and the Huey Atlixcóyotl Fiesta, held during the last Sunday in September. This native dance festival takes place at the hill of San Miguel in the town of Atlixco, southwest of Puebla via Mex. 190-D.

City Layout

Just as Puebla was long second in importance to Mexico City in New Spain, it is bypassed by many travelers today. There is much to see here, however; the city was designated a World Heritage Site by UNESCO in 1987. A mix of old and new, Puebla has both imposing glass towers and colonial-era buildings featuring ornamental wrought iron and walls adorned with Talavera tiles.

The main plaza, or *Zócalo*, flanked by arcades, has iron benches and a large fountain. Most of Puebla's museums and other tourist attractions are within a four-block walk of the *Zócalo*. The surrounding narrow, cobblestoned streets, which become poorer and more dilapidated the farther you go from the plaza, form a grid pattern that adheres to the classic blueprint for cities built by the Spanish in Mexico.

Noted for its French Renaissance design is City Hall (Palacio Municipal), on the north side of the *Zócalo* at Portal Hidalgo #14. The antique Theater (Teatro Principal), about 4 blocks northeast of the *Zócalo* at Avenida 8 Oriente and Calle 6 Norte, dates from 1760, making it among the oldest in the Americas (although it was rebuilt in the 1930s). The interior can be toured when the theater is not in use; phone (222) 232-6085.

About 6 blocks northwest of the *Zócalo* at Calle 11 Norte #1005 (at Avenida 10 Poniente) is the National Museum of Mexican Railways (Museo Nacional de Los Ferrocarriles Mexicanos), located on station property of the former Mexican and Mexican Southern railways. The collection of vintage rolling stock includes steam, electric and diesel locomotives as well as passenger, baggage and freight cars and cabooses.

The downtown street system is based on numbers rather than names. The northwest corner of the *Zócalo* is the city center; from here, the main thoroughfares are north-south Avenida 5 de Mayo/16 de Septiembre and east-west Avenida Palafox y Mendoza/Reforma. East-west streets are even-numbered north of the *Zócalo* and odd-numbered south of it. Likewise, north-south streets are odd-numbered west of the *Zócalo* and even-numbered east of it.

Street names also include a direction—north/*norte*, south/*sur*, east/*oriente* or west/*poniente*—based on the Avenida Reforma/Avenida 5 de Mayo axis.

Note: An earthquake in June 1999 damaged a number of Puebla's churches and other historic structures, some significantly. Extensive, ongoing repairs (scheduled to be completed by the end of 2004) have resulted in the restoration of almost every damaged building, but check reopening times in advance before planning your sightseeing itinerary, just in case.

Puebla State Tourism Office (Secretaría de Turismo): Calle 5 Oriente #3, in the downtown historic center; phone (222) 246-2044. There also is a visitor information office at Boulevard Hermanos Serdán and Avenida 6 Poniente, and another at Calle 24 Sur and Avenida 11 Oriente (third floor); the latter office is open Mon.-Fri. 8-3.

Shopping areas: Among the city's long-established Talavera workshops is Uriarte Talavera (Taller de Cerámica Uriarte), 5 blocks west of the *Zócalo* at Av. 4 Poniente #911. Factory tours to observe the ceramics being molded, hand painted, fired and cooled are given Mon.-Sat. at 11, noon and 1. They also will ship purchases; phone (222) 232-1598.

El Parián Market, 3 blocks east of the *Zócalo* between calles 6 and 8 Norte, offers typical crafts from this part of Mexico, including Talavera pottery, trees of life and onyx jewelry. The open-air shops are in a pedestrian-only area. Bargaining is expected.

Plazúela de Los Sapos (Plaza of the Toads), bounded by avenidas 3 and 5 Oriente and calles 4 and 8 Sur, is lined with shops offering antique furniture and collectibles as well as new furniture made to look old. The Artists' Neighborhood, in a pedestrian passageway at Avenida 6 Oriente and Calle 6 Norte (behind the Theater), is a concentration of studios where local artists create and sell their work.

What To See in and Around Town

AFRICAM is about 16 km (10 mi.) south of Puebla on the road to Valsequillo, at Km marker 16.5 (follow signs). This ecological park is a bit of Africa on the Mexican high plains, where such animals as lions, tigers, giraffes, buffaloes, deer and peacocks roam freely. Visitors can get out of their cars at certain locations for picture-taking opportunities. Guided tours are available. Buses to Africam depart Tues.-Sun. from the *Zócalo*. Daily 10-5. Admission 125 pesos (around $12.50 U.S.), children 120 pesos. Phone (222) 281-7000.

AMPARO MUSEUM is 3 blocks s. of the *Zócalo* at Calle 2 Sur #708 (at Calle 9 Oriente). It contains one of the finest collections of pre-Hispanic art in Mexico, as well as colonial, modern and contemporary works. The exhibits are housed in a yellow stucco mansion that has a tranquil central courtyard. Near the museum entrance a 20-foot-tall stone sculpture pays tribute to corn's pre-eminent role in Mexico's early cultures.

Two floors are filled with Olmec art, Nayarit clay figurines and other objects. One of the museum's most delightful works is a mural, completed in 1990 by Pedro Diego de Alvarado, that depicts four angels creating the colonial town of Puebla. Colonial art (arte virreinal) is on the second floor. Exhibit information is presented in both Spanish and English; English-speaking guides also can be hired. Large-screen TVs broadcast explanations in English and several other languages.

Note: The museum is expected to reopen in early 2005 after being closed for remodeling and repairs. Food is available. Wed.-Mon. 10-6. Admission 25 pesos (about $2.50 U.S.); senior citizens, students with ID and ages 3-12, 15 pesos (about $1.50). Free to all Mon. Audio headphones with English commentary can be rented for the pre-Hispanic exhibit areas. Phone (222) 246-4646.

BELLO GONZALEZ MUSEUM is at Av. 3 Poniente #302. The museum's collection of art and artifacts was donated to the city by the son of José Luis Bello, a textile magnate and collector. Beautifully handcarved furniture, glassware, porcelain, gold and silver articles, paintings and ironwork from the 17th to 19th centuries are all on display. The museum's collection of Talavera pottery is among the largest in the country. Guided tours are available. The museum is currently closed but is expected to reopen in December 2004. Tues.-Sun. 10-5. Admission around $1.25 (U.S.).

BELLO ZETINA MUSEUM is at 5 de Mayo #409 next to the Church of Santo Domingo. It displays turn-of-the-20th-century antiques and religious art. Open Tues.-Sun. Free. Phone(222) 232-4720.

CATHEDRAL OF THE IMMACULATE CONCEPTION stands on the south side of the *Zócalo*. The plans for the cathedral, one of the largest in Mexico, were approved in 1562 by Philip II of Spain, but construction was not completed until 1641; it was consecrated in 1649. The immense building is noted for its elaborately carved facade, great doors, 14 chapels and two bell towers that were erected in 1678. The interior features a gray onyx altar designed in 1799 by Manuel Tolsá, onyx sculptures carved by Tolsá, wood inlay in the choir, lovely tapestries and a collection of rare paintings.

CHURCH OF LA COMPAÑIA (Iglesia de la Compañia) is a block east of the *Zócalo* on Calle 4 Sur. The sacristy of this blue and white tiled, Churrigueresque-style church, also known as the Iglesia del Espiritu Santo (Church of the Holy Ghost), is the final resting place of a local legend, La China Poblana. Her standard dress, a white embroidered peasant blouse and a green and white skirt, is known as a *china poblana* dress and is the national costume for women. The skirt now includes a colorful, sequin-studded design of the Mexican eagle and is worn by young women dancing the *jarabe tapatío* (Mexican hat dance).

CHURCH OF SAN FRANCISCO (Templo de San Francisco) is about 6 blocks northeast of the *Zócalo*, just off Av. 14 Oriente at the corner of Blvd. Héroes del 5 de Mayo. The oldest church in Puebla was founded in 1535; the present edifice was completed in 1667 and is noted for its facade of colorful rectangular tiles. The church has a small chapel off the main altar with a funerary glass box containing the remains of Franciscan friar Sebastián de Aparicio. Before taking his vows, Fray Sebastián was famed as the first roadbuilder in the Americas. He was beatified for his good deeds and purported miracles.

CHURCH OF SANTO DOMINGO (Iglesia de Santo Domingo) is 3 blocks north of the *Zócalo* on Av. 5 de Mayo, between avs. 4 Poniente and 6 Poniente. It was completed in the early 17th century and features colorful tile decoration.

Don't miss the spectacularly ornate Chapel of the Rosary (Capilla del Rosario), which has walls and a ceiling completely covered with gold leaf and gilded stucco figures of angels, saints, children and animals. The extravagant altar features a statue of the Virgen del Rosario, crowned and adorned with jewels.

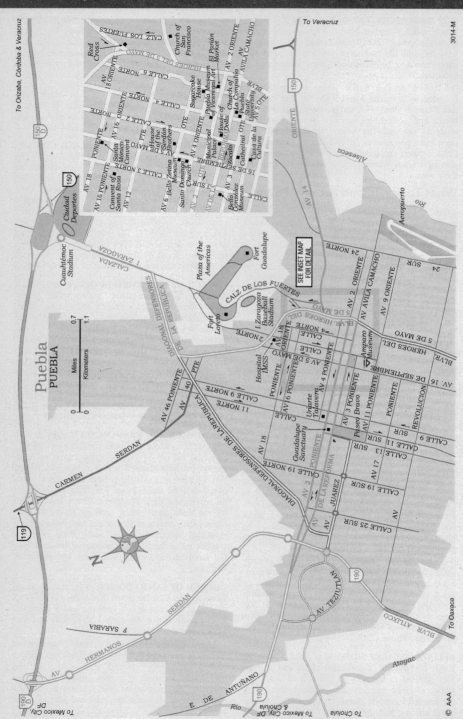

PUEBLA

Puebla

To Onzaba, Córdoba & Veracruz

To Veracruz

To Oaxaca

To Cholula

To Mexico City, DF

To Cholula & Cholula

To Mexico City, DF

SEE INSET MAP FOR DETAIL

Miles
Kilometers

Ciudad Deportes

Cuauhtémoc Stadium

CALZADA I. ZARAGOZA

DIAGONAL DEFENSORES DE LA REPÚBLICA

Plaza of the Americas

Fort Guadalupe

CALZ DE LOS FUERTES

Fort Loreto

I. Zaragoza Baseball Stadium

BLVR HEROES DEL 5 DE MAYO

Hospital IMSS

AV 46 PONIENTE

AV 40

PTE

CALLE 9 NORTE

CALLE 2 NORTE

AV 18 PONIENTE

AV 6 PONIENTE

AV 5 DE MAYO

AV 4 PONIENTE

AV 3 PONIENTE

Uriarte Talavera

Guadalupe Sanctuary

AV 18 PONIENTE

CALLE 19 NORTE

AV 2

DE LA REFORMA

JUAREZ

Paseo Bravo

Amparo Museum

AV 11 PONIENTE

REVOLUCION

AV 16

HEROES DEL 5 DE MAYO

BLVR DE SEPTIEMBRE

AV 17

AV 9 ORIENTE

AV 2 ORIENTE

AV AVILA CAMACHO

24 NORTE

24 SUR

Aeropuerto

Río Alseseca

AV 14

ORIENTE

Atoyac

BLVR ATLIXCO

AV TEZIUTLA

CALLE 25 SUR

CALLE 19 SUR

CALLE 13 SUR

CALLE 11 SUR

CALLE 9 SUR

SERDAN

CARMEN

HERMANOS

F SARABIA

E DE ANTUÑANO

Río

© AAA

3014-M

Inset map

Red Cross

Church of San Francisco

CALZ LOS FUERTES

El Parián Market

AV AVILA CAMACHO

HEROES DEL 5 DE MAYO

AV 18 ORIENTE

CALLE 6 NORTE

CALLE 4 NORTE

CALLE 2 NORTE

AV 16 ORIENTE

Sugarcake House

Puebla Museum of Viceregal Art

AV 2 ORIENTE

Church of La Compania

Puebla University

BLVR 5 DE MAYO

CALLE 5 OTE

AV 18 PONIENTE

AV 16 PONIENTE

Santa Monica Convent

Convent of Santa Rosa

CALLE 3 NORTE

AV 6

Bello Zetina Museum

Santo Domingo Church

AV 12

PONIENTE

AV 4 ORIENTE

OTE

House of the Serdán Brothers

House of Dolls

Municipal Palace

Zócalo

16 DE SEPTIEMBRE

Cathedral

Casa de la Cultura

Bello & González Museum

AV 3 SUR

AV DEL

ORIENTE

EX-CONVENT OF SANTA MONICA (Ex-Convento de Santa Mónica) is 9 blocks north of the *Zócalo* at Av. 18 Poniente #103, just off Av. 5 de Mayo. It was ordered closed when the 1857 Reform Laws abolished monasteries and convents in Mexico; the convent's nuns continued their work in semi-secrecy until 1934.

The museum preserves the dark corridors and austere rooms and includes a collection of religious art; the paintings on velvet by Rafael Morante have retained their brilliant colors after centuries. Guides are available. Entry to the museum is through a house and passageway. Tues.-Sun. 9-5. Admission 24 pesos (around $2.50 U.S.).

EX-CONVENT OF SANTA ROSA (Ex-Convento de Santa Rosa) is 7 blocks northwest of the *Zócalo* at Av. 14 Poniente #305, between calles 3 and 5 Norte. This partially restored convent has a museum with handicraft exhibits and a splendid 18th-century tiled kitchen. According to legend, the traditional chocolate and chile sauce called *mole poblano* was invented here by nuns who wanted to prepare a special dish for the saint's day of their bishop.

A government-sponsored craft shop on the premises sells embroidery, lace and *poblano* craft items. Tues.-Sun. 10-5. Admission 10 pesos (around $1.25 U.S.), children 5 pesos.

FORTS LORETO AND GUADALUPE (Fuertes de Loreto y Guadalupe) stand on a hill (Cerro de Guadalupe) in a park about 2 km (1.2 mi.) northeast of the *Zócalo*. They commemorate the defeat of 6,500 French troops by a force of 4,500 Mexicans led by General Ignacio Zaragoza on May 5, 1862.

Fort Loreto contains original cannons, a chapel that dates from 1780, and a museum dedicated to the battle as well as other aspects of Mexican history. Fort Guadalupe, also a site of the May 5 battle, stands just 1,500 feet away across the Plaza of the Americas. Mon.-Fri. 9-5. Admission to each 33 pesos (around $3.35 U.S.), children free.

GUADALUPE SANCTUARY (Santuario de Guadalupe) is on Av. Reforma, 6 blocks west of the *Zócalo*. This is one of the finest examples of the region's traditional architecture.

HOUSE OF CULTURE (Casa de la Cultura) is 1 block south of the *Zócalo* on Av. 5 Oriente #5, facing the south side of the Cathedral. It is housed in the former Archbishop's Palace (Palacio del Obispado), a building in the classic *poblano* style—patterned red brick interspersed with glazed blue-and-white tiles, windows framed in white stucco, and a flat roof embellished with a row of white spikes. It contains a concert and lecture hall as well as the Palafox Library. Free maps of the city can be obtained here. Daily 10-8. Phone (222) 242-1966 or (222) 246-6922.

Palafox Library (Biblioteca Palafoxiana) is on the second floor. The immense room, just 20 feet wide but more than 200 feet long, contains thousands of volumes, mostly priceless bound manuscripts in Latin. Other valuable books include a 1584 atlas printed in Antwerp, Belgium, and a 16th-century Bible in four languages. Exquisitely carved cedar bookshelves protected by wire stand in three tiers above the worn red-tile floors. The reading tables are onyx with inlaid wood. Marble busts of Aristotle, Plato and other philosophers line one wall. Open Tues.-Sun. Admission 10 pesos (around $1 U.S.), children 5 pesos.

HOUSE OF DOLLS (Casa de Los Muñecos) is across from the northeast corner of the *Zócalo* on Calle 2 Norte. This 17th-century building is a particularly colorful example of talavera craftsmanship, with tiles in combinations of blue and yellow and yellow and green. The house is known for its mosaic caricatures of the builder's supposed enemies. Within the building is the University Museum (Museo Universitario). The museum is currently closed but is expected to reopen in December 2004. Admission around 60 cents (U.S.).

HOUSE OF THE SERDAN BROTHERS (Casa de Aquiles Serdán) is at Av. 6 Oriente #206, between calles 2 and 4 Norte. It contains the Museum of the Revolution (Museo de la Revolución). In their poblano-style home, which they had turned into an arsenal, the Serdán family played an important role in launching the revolution against dictator Porfirio Díaz. On Nov. 18, 1910, the house was surrounded by 500 federal army soldiers and policemen, who were alerted to the family's plot. During a 14-hour gunfight, several members of the family were killed; the rest were imprisoned.

Bullet holes still scar the walls, floor and ceiling of the living room. Tues.-Sun. 10-4:30. Admission 11 pesos (around $1.15 U.S.), children 5 pesos.

PLAZA OF THE AMERICAS is about 2 km (1.2 mi.) northeast of the *Zócalo* in the exposition park complex that includes Forts Loreto and Guadalupe. Within this complex, which commemorates the centennial of the Battle of Puebla, are the Planetarium (Planetario de Puebla), phone (222) 235-2099; the Puebla Regional Museum (Museo Regional de Puebla), phone (222) 235-9720; and Imagina, an interactive children's museum. A bubble-domed auditorium seats 2,000.

Museums open Tues.-Sun. 10-5. Natural History Museum admission around $2.50 (U.S.), Puebla Regional Museum around $3.50, planetarium light shows around $3.

PUEBLA MUSEUM OF VICEREGAL ART (Museo Poblano de Arte Virreinal) is 2 blocks northeast of the *Zócalo* at Calle 4 Norte #203. Puebla's newest museum is housed in the restored Hospital of San Pedro. The permanent collection of colonial-era paintings is augmented by rotating temporary exhibitions devoted to contemporary Mexican artists. Daily 10-5. Admission around $2 (U.S.).

SUGARCAKE HOUSE (Casa de Alfeñique) is 3 blocks northeast of the *Zócalo* at Av. 4 Oriente and Calle 6 Norte. This 17th-century colonial mansion, named for its ornate exterior, was once a residence for visiting dignitaries. Now a museum, it has an archeological and historical collection on the first two floors; the third floor is furnished in period. Tues.-Sun. 10-5. Admission around $2 (U.S.).

QUERETARO, QUERETARO (A-9)
pop. 565,400, metro area 825,500, elev. 6,078'

Querétaro (keh-REH-tah-roh) lies in a valley at the base of a hill called the Sangremal. The city, founded by the Otomí Indians long before Europeans discovered the New World, became part of the Aztec Empire in the 15th century. It was captured by the Spanish in 1531 and developed as the headquarters for the Franciscan monks who established missions throughout Central America, Mexico and California.

Querétaro has played a pivotal role in Mexican history. The early 19th century saw the city as the center of rebellion against Spain. Doña Josefa (La Corregidora) and her husband, the local magistrate, formed the Society for the Study of Fine Arts to discuss poetry and politics; two of Mexico's greatest revolutionary heroes, Father Miguel Hidalgo and Capt. Ignacio Allende, often attended. In 1810, when budding plots for national independence were uncovered, Doña Josefa alerted the principal insurgents of their impending arrest.

The city also was Mexico's capital 37 years later when U.S. troops took over Mexico City; the Treaty of Guadalupe-Hidalgo, which ceded California, Arizona and New Mexico to the United States, was formulated in 1848 at Querétaro's Academy of Fine Arts. During the War of Reform (1857-59), President Benito Juárez made Querétaro his headquarters. Emperor Maximilian's headquarters were here as well; he ended his 3-year reign before a firing squad on the nearby Hill of the Bells (Cerro de las Campañas), thus ending Europe's dream of controlling Mexico.

Elegant colonial architecture is concentrated in the historic downtown area, which was designated a World Heritage Site by UNESCO in 1996. The cobblestoned streets are narrow but well maintained, with pedestrian-only thoroughfares (*andadores*) linking several plazas.

The central plaza is called Jardín Zenea; north-south Avenida Corregidora, downtown's main street, runs along its east side. Band concerts take place at the plaza on Sunday evenings at 6 p.m. Six blocks south is the large, tree-shaded Alameda.

Two blocks east of Jardín Zenea is Plaza de Armas (also called Plaza de la Independencia). On the plaza's west side, at the Portal de Dolores (Avenida Pasteur #6), is Ecala's House (Casa de Ecala). This building has what might be the most beautiful 18th-century baroque facade in the city; note the brick and stone staircases and the small window with an elaborate ornamentation of drapes sculpted in stone.

Visitors can walk around the inner courtyard during normal business hours.

Among other notable downtown buildings is the Casa de la Marquesa, at Av. Madero #41. In the 18th century this elegant mansion was the residence of a wealthy family of royal blood; it now houses a hotel. The interior courtyard is graced with Moorish-style arches. Another hotel, the Mesón de Santa Rosa (on Plaza de Armas at Av. Pasteur #17) has three spectacular courtyards; in the middle one stands an old trough that once served to water guests' horses.

A block north of the Jardín Zenea at the corner of avenidas Corregidora and Hidalgo is the Theater of the Republic (Teatro de la República), built in neoclassic style between 1850 and 1852 and embellished with accents of olive leaves, crowns and shields. The Mexican Constitution was signed there in 1917.

A block west of the Jardín Zenea at Avenida Madero and Calle Allende is the Neptune Fountain (Fuente de Neptuno). It was designed by Eduardo Tresguerras, who was responsible for a number of the city's neoclassic buildings.

Another landmark is the 6-mile-long, 50-foot-high aqueduct (*acueducto*), constructed by the Spanish more than 200 years ago and still supplying the city with water. Its 74 arches run along the center of east-west Avenida Zaragoza.

The state of Querétaro is known for its gemstones, especially opals. These should be purchased only at reputable shops; avoid sidewalk vendors. Lapidaria de Querétaro, a few blocks north of the Jardín Zenea at Av. Corregidora Norte #149-A, sells locally mined opals and other semiprecious stones.

The Plaza de Toros Santa María, south of downtown on Avenida Constituyentes, is one of Mexico's best bullrings, drawing top matadors from Mexico and Spain. The main season runs from November through January.

Querétaro State Tourism Office (Secretaría de Turismo): Av. Luis Pasteur #4 Norte off Plaza de Armas. Open daily 9-8; phone (800) 715-1742 (toll-free long distance within Mexico) or (888) 811-6130 (from the United States).

What To See

CHURCH OF SAN FRANCISCO (Iglesia de San Francisco) is opposite the Jardín Zenea on Calle 5 de Mayo. It dates from 1545 and dominates the plaza. The dome's colored tiles were brought from Spain in 1540. The church houses a collection of 17th-, 18th- and 19th-century religious paintings, and a figure of Santiago adorns the doorway.

CHURCH OF SANTA CLARA (Iglesia de Santa Clara) is on Calle Allende, just north of the Neptune Fountain. Founded in 1633 and reconstructed during the 18th century by architect Eduardo Tresguerras, Santa Clara had one of Mexico's richest nunneries. It is noted for its ornately carved interior, gilded altarpieces and delicate exterior ironwork.

CHURCH OF SANTA ROSA DE VITERBO (Iglesia de Santa Rosa de Viterbo) is about 5 blocks southwest of the Jardín Zenea at Av. General Arteaga and Calle Ezequiel Montes. Oriental influences are visible in this 1752 church's bell tower, fashioned after a pagoda, and in its flying buttresses, flanked by dragon faces. The interior exhibits a profusion of gilt, carved wood with inlaid marble and filigree work.

CONVENT OF SANTA CRUZ (Convento de la Santa Cruz) is east of the city center at Av. Venustiano Carranza/Independencia and Calle Acuña. As many as 200 monks once lived in the mission compound, a well-preserved series of cloisters and cells complete with an orchard, a kitchen with a cold storage chamber, several schools and an enclosed reservoir. The monastery's gardens have trees with cross-shaped thorns.

Standing watch over the church plaza are statues of Querétaro's founders and other figures important to the city's early history. The monastery also served as Maximilian's army barracks and later, after his defeat in 1867, as his prison. The ashes of the heroine La Corregidora are encased in a monument behind the church. Guided tours are available. Open Tues.-Sat. Donations.

GOVERNMENT PALACE (Palacio Gobierno) is at the north end of Plaza de Armas. Now housing the state of Querétaro offices, it was once the home of Doña Josefa Ortiz, or "La Corregidora" (the mayor's wife), the heroine of the 1810 War of Independence. Under house arrest, she whispered instructions through a keyhole to a messenger to warn insurgents Father Miguel Hidalgo and Capt. Ignacio Allende in the nearby town of Dolores. As a result, Hidalgo immediately issued his famous cry *(grito)* for independence. More than 50 years later, Archduke Maximilian presided over many meetings here. Open during normal business hours.

HILL OF THE BELLS (Cerro de las Campañas) is on the western outskirts of the city. It was the site of Archduke Maximilian's last battle, and it was at this location that he was executed by a firing squad on June 19, 1867.

A monument erected by the government in honor of Benito Juárez, who defeated the ill-fated "Emperor of Mexico," is at the top of a hill behind the Capilla de la Piedad. This neoclassic chapel, erected by the Austrian government in 1901, is dedicated to Maximilian. Stelae mark the spots where Maximilian and his two Mexican generals, Miramón and Mejía, fell. In the small Museum of the Siege of Querétaro (Museo del Sitio de Querétaro) near the chapel are several photographs documenting the event. Museum open Tues.-Sun. 10-5. Admission around $1 (U.S.).

MUSEUM OF ART (Museo de Arte) is at Calle Allende Sur #14. It is housed in a former monastery, the Convent of San Agustín (Convento de San Agustín), an outstanding example of baroque architecture built in 1731 by Mexican architect Ignacio Mariano de las Casas. The building's exterior ornamentation is as impressive as the collection of Mexican colonial and European art inside. Tues.-Sun. 11-5. Admission around $2 (U.S.).

REGIONAL MUSEUM (Museo Regional) is on Av. Corregidora next to the Church of San Francisco. Housed in the former monastery, it displays colonial relics; uniforms and weaponry; 17th-, 18th- and 19th-century paintings by Juan Correa, Villalpando, Miguel Cabrera and Luis Rodríguez; and a library of more than 8,000 books, mostly parchment tomes from the 17th and 18th centuries. Tues.-Sun. 11-5. Admission around $3.25 (U.S.).

SAN JUAN DEL RIO, QUERETARO
(B-9) pop. 105,600, elev. 6,498′

San Juan del Río (sahn hwan dehl REE-oh), noted for semiprecious stones, woodcarvings, baskets and palm furniture, is located in a prosperous agricultural region that yields corn, dairy products and wine. This picturesque city was once an important stop on the stagecoach route to Mexico City. San Juan del Río features many buildings painted white and enhanced by decorative elements of dark brown carved stone.

Also near San Juan del Río are the Trinidad opal mines. Opals and amethysts are polished in town; gems should be purchased only at established shops.

A short distance northeast of San Juan del Río via Mex. 120 is the resort town of Tequisquiapan (teh-kees-kee-AP-an). This weekend retreat was once popular for its hot-water thermal springs, but competition from local industries for the available water has hurt the spa business. It remains a pretty place to stroll, however, with narrow streets planted with flowering fruit trees and cloaked in brightly colored bougainvillea, and a quaint main plaza surrounded by arcades *(portales)*.

On the plaza's north side is the neoclassic Church of Santa Maria of the Assumption (Templo de Santa María de la Asunción). A crafts market (Mercado de Artesanías) near the plaza sells rattan furniture and other locally made items.

From Tequisquiapan, continue north on Mex. 120 to Ezequiel Montes; from here, take the paved turnoff west about 10 kilometers (6 miles) to Bernal. Another popular weekend destination, this picturesque little town has craft shops offering wool and cotton clothing. The main attraction, however, is La Peña de Bernal, a huge, pyramid-shaped monolith.

About 38 kilometers (24 miles) north of Tequisquiapan on Mex. 120 is the town of Cadereyta; ask in town for directions to La Quinta Schmoll, a botanical garden devoted to cacti (more than 4,000 varieties). The garden is open daily; admission is free.

This stretch of Mex. 120 through northeastern Querétaro state traverses the Sierra Gorda, part of the eastern Sierra Madre mountain range and a green oasis at the edge of central Mexico's vast semi-desert region. The scenery is impressively rugged; forested peaks rise more than 10,000 feet, while the valleys between them are hot and humid.

Mex. 120 passes through the town of Pinal de Amoles, then makes a series of dramatic ascents and descents to Jalpan. Beginning in the 1750s, Franciscan priest Father Junípero Serra established five missions in this region to evangelize the Chichimeca Indians; he later went on to found another chain of missions in Alta (upper) California. These five missions—Jalpan, Concá, Landa, Tancoyol and Tilaco—were designated World Heritage Sites by UNESCO in 2003.

Jalpan's old mission church, the Misión de Jalpan, is beautifully restored. Also in town is the Museum of the Sierra Gorda (Museo de la Sierra Gorda), a former military fort with exhibits offering insight into the region's Indian cultures and Father Serra's evangelical work.

SAN LUIS POTOSI, SAN LUIS POTOSI (F-7)

pop. 670,500, metro area 936,000, elev. 6,157′

San Luis Potosí (sahn loo-EES poh-toh-SEE), capital of the state of the same name, dates from the late 1500s when it was established as a mining settlement. The city was seat of the national government under President Benito Juárez in 1863 and again in 1867. While here in 1854, González Bocanegra wrote the Mexican national anthem, first sung in Mexico City's Santa Ana Theater on Sept. 15 of that year. The San Luis Plan, drafted by Francisco I. Madero while he was imprisoned in the city by dictator Porfirio Díaz, set the stage for the Revolution of 1910.

A distribution point for foreign and domestic merchandise, San Luis Potosí's atmosphere is largely industrial. Tanneries, flour mills, smelters, textile mills, breweries and furniture factories are among the manufacturing concerns, and highways around the city and within the state are busy with truck traffic.

San Luis Potosí is not all soot and smoke. It has a well-preserved colonial center, anchored by Plaza de Armas, the main square. The plaza is flanked by the city's 18th-century cathedral on the east and the Government Palace (Palacio de Gobierno) on the west.

Two blocks northwest of Plaza de Armas is Founders' Plaza (Plaza de Los Fundadores); 2 blocks east and a block south of Plaza de Armas is Plaza del Carmen. Two blocks west and 2 blocks south of Plaza de Armas is Plaza San Francisco. Each of these plazas is a pleasant spot to take in city life.

The Plaza España bullring is on Avenida Universidad, at the eastern end of downtown near the southeastern corner of Alameda Park. On the north side of this large park is the city's modern train station, where a series of Fernando Leal frescoes depict the history of transportation in Mexico.

The city's newest museum, the Federico Silva Museum of Contemporary Sculpture (Museo Federico Silva Escultura Contemporánea), opened in 2003. This is the only museum in Mexico devoted to sculpture, and the first in Latin America to focus on contemporary sculpture. It is located in the historic center at Av. Alvaro Obregón #80, at Plaza San Juan de Dios (about three blocks east of Plaza de Armas). Open Mon. and Wed.-Sat. 10-6, Sun. 10-2; phone (444) 812-3848.

Holy Week (Semana Santa) celebrations are among the city's most traditional as well as most solemn. Various cultural, artistic and gastronomic events lead up to Good Friday, when there is a silent procession through the historic city center. More down to earth is the San Luis Potosí National Fair (Feria Nacional Potosina), normally held the latter half of August, which features bullfights, cockfights, rodeos, and agricultural and livestock exhibitions.

About 56 kilometers (35 miles) south of the city via Mex. 57 are two spas known for their medicinal waters. Lourdes Spa, just outside Santa María del Río, has strongly alkaline, radioactive waters that purportedly benefit intestinal ailments. El Gogorrón National Park is accessible from a paved road that branches southwest off Mex. 57 to the village of Villa de Reyes; its thermal pools and many springs are reputed to alleviate circulatory problems and rheumatism.

San Luis Potosí State Tourism Office (Secretaría de Turismo): downtown at Av. Alvaro Obregón #520, less than a block west of Plaza de Los Fundadores. Open Mon.-Fri. 8-8, Sat. 9-2; phone (444) 812-9939.

Shopping areas: Among the wares on display at the huge Hidalgo Market (Mercado Hidalgo), 4 blocks north of Plaza de Armas, are prized Santa María *rebozos* (shawl-like garments), so gauzy in texture they can be pulled through a woman's wedding ring; pottery; and a candy called *queso de tuna* made from the fruit of the prickly pear cactus. Calle Hidalgo between the market and Plaza de Armas is a pedestrian-only street flanked by numerous shops and stores.

The best place in the city to shop for handicrafts is the government-run FONART store on Plaza San Francisco, which stocks items from all over Mexico. Another good place to browse is La Casa del Artesano, Av. Carranza #540 about 5 blocks west of Plaza de Armas; it sells crafts from the state of San Luis Potosí.

What To See

BULLFIGHTING CENTER MUSEUM (Museo del Centro Taurino Potosino) is east of Alameda Park at

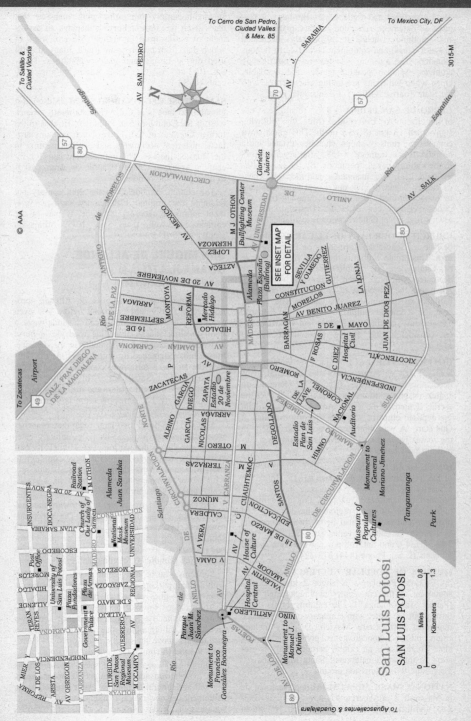

San Luis Potosí
SAN LUIS POTOSI

Av. Universidad and Calle López Hermosa. It features an extensive collection of photographs, posters, clothing (including elaborately decorated matador capes) and equipment belonging to famous matadors. The museum also features a bullfighting archives. Spanish-speaking guides are available. Open when bullfights are taking place; check with the State Tourism Office for a schedule. Free.

CERRO DE SAN PEDRO is 8 km (5 mi.) east out of the city on Av. Universidad (Mex. 70) following signs, then 13 km (8 mi.) north. This ghost town contains the ruins of shops, churches, estates and a hospital. It was founded in 1583 after several mines in the vicinity began operations. By the late 1940s, the gold, lead, iron, manganese and mercury deposits finally began to give out. Local firms continue to extract limited quantities of minerals from the mines. Visitors can enter La Descubridora, the town's first mine. Guide service is available.

CHURCH OF OUR LADY OF EL CARMEN (Iglesia de Nuestra Señora del Carmen) is on Plaza del Carmen. This ornate church is the city's finest example of Churrigueresque architecture. Its domes are decorated with blue, green, yellow and white tiles. Also note the profusion of carved stone angels, a hallmark of indigenous craftsmanship. The interior contains a carved pulpit, a reredos by Eduardo Tresguerras, paintings by Vallejo and a baroque altar considered one of the most impressive in Mexico.

GOVERNMENT PALACE (Palacio de Gobierno) is across Plaza de Armas from the cathedral. This neoclassic structure dates from 1770. Here Benito Juárez, despite petitions for mercy from all over the world, denied clemency to Archduke Maximilian; the deposed emperor was subsequently executed at Querétaro. A wax tableau and a portrait gallery in the Juárez Room recall the event. Open during normal business hours. Free.

HOUSE OF CULTURE (Casa de la Cultura) is west of the city center at Av. Carranza #1815. Housed in a turn-of-the-20th-century neoclassic building surrounded by landscaped gardens, this museum exhibits works of art, regional handicrafts, and historical and archeological items. It also functions as a venue for cultural events. Tues.-Sat. 10-2 (also Tues.-Fri. 4-6 and Sat. 6-8 p.m.). Admission around 50 cents (U.S.). Phone (444) 813-2247.

MUSEUM OF POPULAR CULTURES (Museo de las Culturas Populares) is about 2 km (1.2 mi.) southwest of the city center in Tangamanga Park (Parque Tangamanga 1). It exhibits crafts from throughout the state, with emphasis on the Huastec region of northeastern Mexico. Displays include chairs, baskets, wooden items, pottery and a wax altar. There also is an exhibit pertaining to the creation of the area's celebrated Santa María shawls. Tues.-Sun. 9-4. Admission around 30 cents (U.S.).

NATIONAL MASK MUSEUM (Museo Nacional de la Máscara) is at Villerías #2, north of Calle Guerrero and just south of Plaza del Carmen. Housed in

an architecturally interesting pink mansion that dates from the 18th century, it displays an assortment of masks from throughout Mexico, some of which date from pre-Hispanic times. Many are still used during fiestas and other celebrations. Tues.-Sat. 10-2 and 5-7, Sun. 10-2. Admission around 50 cents (U.S.).

SAN POTOSI REGIONAL MUSEUM (Museo Regional Potosino) is at Calle Galeana #450, a block west of the Church of San Francisco. Housed in the former Convent of San Francisco, it contains artifacts, historical documents and exhibits relating to the Huastec Indians. The impressively lavish 17th-century Aranzazú Chapel (Capilla de Aranzazú) is in the rear of the building.

The church, remodeled in the 20th century but retaining the original 17th-century sacristy (vestment room) of carved pink stone, is part of the complex as well. Tues.-Sun. 10-5. Admission around $2.50 (U.S.).

SAN MIGUEL DE ALLENDE, GUANAJUATO (A-8)
pop. 62,200, elev. 6,134′

You sense that San Miguel de Allende (pronounced a-YEHN-deh) is special before you even get there. The feeling is reinforced in subtle ways: a family selling snacks along the roadside, a horse and rider clip-clopping contentedly in the distance, brown hills brightened by wildflowers. At this altitude the air has a refreshing coolness, even though the sun is bright. Small clusters of dwellings—tiny cement cubes with tin roofs—and dirt yards exhibit obvious poverty, but somehow seem less grim than the vast shantytowns ringing Mexico City.

Mex. 111, a local two-lane road that branches west off highway Mex. 57-D, is an unlikely gateway to the charm that defines San Miguel. Its outskirts have that everyday scruffiness common to most Mexican towns—dilapidated gas stations mix with newer commercial development in a small-scale version of "suburban sprawl."

But as Mex. 111 twists and turns toward the center of town, things start to change. The street narrows and becomes cobbled. Aged buildings rub shoulders along a sidewalk barely wide enough for one pedestrian, let alone two. Open shop doorways offer quick glimpses of clothing and crafts.

Suddenly you're at a scenic overlook, a pulloff with a small parking area. A few vendors sit beside their wares—piles of woven baskets, perhaps, or neatly arranged rows of painted ceramic figurines. Below a protective wrought-iron fence the town spreads out, filling a bowl-shaped valley. One structure towers above the others: multispired La Parroquia, the parish church *(see attraction listing)*.

San Miguel began as a mission where Indians were evangelized and also taught European weaving and agricultural techniques. As it prospered, the settlement became a local market center for the surrounding haciendas trading in cattle and textiles.

Historical significance made its mark as well: Here native son Ignacio Allende, along with Father Miguel Hidalgo y Costilla, a priest from the neighboring town of Dolores Hidalgo, planned the original uprising that led to Mexico's bitter and protracted War of Independence.

In 1926, the Mexican government designated the city a national historic monument, and preservation measures began in earnest. Modern construction was prohibited in the city center; crumbling old buildings were carefully restored. Foreigners began moving in during the 1930s, and today there is an established North American expatriate community of artisans, teachers, writers and part-time residents.

Practicalities

The León-Guanajuato Airport is in León, about a 90-minute drive away. Several airlines, including Aeroméxico, American, Continental and Mexicana, offer flights from selected U.S. cities. Travel agencies such as American Express and Viajes San Miguel offer passenger shuttle van service between the airport and San Miguel. More expensive taxi service also is available. For additional information about airlines *see "Arriving by Air," page 551.*

"Deluxe" bus service from Mexico City's Terminal Central de Autobuses del Norte is provided daily by ETN; Primera Plus and Pegaso Plus provide first-class service. The trip is nonstop and takes about 3 hours. Second-class service by Flecha Amarilla and Herradura de Plata takes 4 hours and includes a stop in Querétaro and local stops en route. Flecha Amarilla buses also provide frequent service between San Miguel and Guanajuato. The central bus station is on the westward extension of Calle Canal, about 1.5 kilometers (1 mile) west of the center of town. For additional information about buses *see "Bus Service," page 68.*

Taxis provide flat-rate service between the bus station and downtown, as well as to other locations around the city. There is a *sitio* (cab stand) at the main plaza.

By car, the 180-mile journey from Mexico City takes 3 to 4 hours via Mex. 57-D to the Querétaro toll bypass (watch for the San Miguel exit). The bypass highway crosses Mex. 57-D north of Querétaro and connects with Mex. 111, which proceeds northwest to San Miguel. The trip along two-lane Mex. 111 is slow but scenic, offering views of typical Mexican rural life. From Guanajuato, take Mex. 45 and 45-D south and east toward Celaya, then Mex. 51 north.

Note: Street parking is scarce in the congested historic center, and local police do not hesitate to issue violators a ticket. If driving from Mexico City or elsewhere, you may have to park several blocks from the center. If you're staying in town and have a car, leave it at your hotel and use public transportation. The altitude may initially tire visitors not used to walking at higher elevations.

Banks along Calle San Francisco exchange currency Mon.-Fri. 9-1:30, but the *casas de cambio* (currency exchange offices) located in the vicinity of the main plaza are a quicker alternative.

For Internet access try Internet 2000, on Avenida Juárez opposite the plaza Jardín de San Francisco. It's open daily 9-9. Unisono, in the heart of town at Hernández Macías #72-B (on the second floor of Plaza Golondrinas), offers full cyber cafe services, and the staff speaks English. Hours are Mon.-Fri. 9-2 and 4-6; phone (415) 152-6331.

San Miguel's weather is similar to Guanajuato's: warm and dry most of the year. April and May are the warmest months, but the city rarely experiences the extremes of heat common to much of Mexico. Winter nights can be chilly, and many hotels aren't heated (although some have fireplaces). The rainy season is June through September.

Exploring Around Town

Some travelers complain that San Miguel's "gentrification," so to speak, has replaced authentic Mexican atmosphere with a touristy vibe—trendy restaurants, pricey boutiques and a lack of local grit. But a stroll through the historic center proves that these complaints are primarily quibbles. Here there is atmosphere to spare, whether it's intricate stone carvings adorning the doors and windows of handsome old buildings or the extravagant beauty of their sheltered inner patios, cool retreats filled with trees, burbling fountains, clipped hedges and flowerpot urns.

There's a sense of discovery along the narrow streets that sparks curiosity as to what's around the next corner. You'll see other tourists but also have plenty of opportunities to mingle with locals—perhaps children who shyly ask if you want to buy some gum *("Chicle"?),* or an elderly gentleman whiling away the afternoon at El Jardín, the main plaza.

Make the plaza, located between calles San Francisco and Correo, your first stop. Shaded by Indian laurel trees, it's a great place to relax on a wrought-iron bench, listen to the tolling bells of La Parroquía and observe the local scene. Buy a cold drink from a vendor and plan the day's itinerary. Most of the city's attractions are within easy walking distance of the plaza, and the historic center is compact. **Note:** Wear comfortable shoes; the streets tend to be steep and cobblestoned.

San Miguel's reputation as an arts center was established by the opening of the Allende Institute, southwest of downtown at Calle Ancha de San Antonio #20. One of its American founders, Stirling Dickinson, came to Mexico as a tourist in the 1930s and fell in love with the city. Fountains, arcades and courtyard gardens grace the grounds of the campus, which has extensive classroom space, two art galleries, a theater and a library.

The Bellas Artes Cultural Center (Centro Cultural Bellas Artes), about 2 blocks west of the main plaza at Calle Hernández Macías #75, also is called the Centro Cultural el Nigromante (its official name) and the Centro Cultural Ignacio Ramírez. It is a branch of the well-known National Institute of Fine Arts (Instituto Nacional de Bellas Artes) in Mexico City. The impressive building dates from the mid-18th century and has an immense, tree-shaded courtyard. Several murals are exhibited, including one by David Alfaro Siqueiros.

Saturday morning "adventure" tours to local handicraft workshops and out-of-town points of interest such as haciendas, ranches, vineyards or a monastery benefit the Centro de Crecimiento, a school for children with disabilities that is supported through donations. The 3-hour tours depart from the main plaza at 10:30 a.m.; tickets can be purchased from the Casa Maxwell shop at Calle Canal #14, about half a block west of the plaza. The suggested donation is 150 pesos (around $15 U.S.).

The Promotion of Mexican Culture, Calle Cuna de Allende #11 in the Hotel Vista Hermosa Taboada, sponsors city walking tours, adventure and nature tours, and field trips to colonial and archeological sites. Their offices are open Mon.-Sat. 9-7; phone (415) 152-1630. For information about local happenings, consult the weekly English-language newspaper *Atención San Miguel,* which is available at the public library *(see attraction listing)* and the El Colibri bookstore, about two blocks east of the main plaza at Calle Sollano #30.

Siesta Tours, Inc. specializes in tours of San Miguel as well as nearby Guanajuato, Pátzcuaro and Morelia *(see separate listings within this region).* For information phone (800) 679-2746 in the United States.

Shopping

San Miguel is known for the variety and quality of its regionally produced handicrafts. Metalwork—masks, trays, lanterns, picture frames and decorative objects made of tin, copper, brass, bronze and wrought iron—and the designs of local silversmiths are particularly worth seeking out. Also available are pottery, weavings, sculpture, straw items, hand-loomed *cambaya* cloth (a material frequently used to make skirts), and folk and traditional art. The colonial furniture is some of the finest produced in Mexico.

Most craft and gift shops are open Mon.-Sat. 9-7 and close from 2-4 for the traditional *siesta;* a few may open briefly on Sunday. Many accept U.S. dollars and/or MasterCard and Visa, and some will pack and ship purchases.

The open-air City Market fills the plaza near the Church of San Felipe Neri, several blocks northeast of the main plaza, and usually spreads onto the surrounding streets. Livestock and fresh produce share space with inexpensive everyday items and souvenirs at the cheaper end of the price scale. The Crafts Market (Mercado de Artesanías) consists of vendor stalls in an alley off Calle Loreto, near the Quinta Loreto Hotel and the City Market.

Pricier boutiques are scattered throughout the downtown area. Casa Canal, Calle Canal #36, specializes in hand-carved wooden furniture. Casa Maxwell, Calle Canal #14, has an array of Mexican and Latin American folk art, plus ceramics, jewelry, glassware and furniture. Veryka, Calle Zacateros #6A, sells indigenous art—masks, ceramics, Huichol crafts.

Casa Anguiano, at the corner of calles Canal and Hernández Macías, features embroidered fabrics and copperware. For a large selection of antiques, colonial art and home furnishings, browse through La Antigua Casa Canela, Calle Umaran #20.

Art galleries are concentrated around the main plaza, and exhibit openings are big social events. Two that showcase both regional and national talent are Galería San Miguel, Plaza Principal #14, and Galería Atenea, Calle Jesús #2.

Dining, Nightlife and Events

Despite its small size, San Miguel has a number of restaurants offering a wide range of cuisines—from reliable French and Italian to regional Mexican to such unexpected choices as Tex-Mex and vegetarian. Much of this variety has to do with the American expatriate community. Restaurants also open and close with regularity. The most expensive establishments are in upscale hotels, where a jacket and tie for men may be advised.

If you want a change of pace from these restaurants' standard Continental offerings, there are plenty of options. Bella Italia, Calle Hernández Macías #59, offers spinach ravioli, risotto and other Italian standbys, plus a good tiramisu. The nouvelle cuisine at La Capilla, Calle Cuna de Allende #10 next to La Parroquía, is complemented by lovely city views as well as a garden patio and upstairs terrace for outdoor dining.

Tío Lucas, Calle Mesones #103 (at Hernández Macías), is known for its steaks and also has an open patio featuring live jazz and blues nightly. La Fragua, Calle Cuna de Allende #3, is a popular San Miguel gathering place housed in an old colonial building. Traditional Mexican music is performed evenings in the courtyard. Rock, reggae, country and blues bands play at Pancho and Lefty's, a local institution at Calle Mesones #99 near the main plaza.

San Miguel's biggest event is San Miguel Arcángel the third Saturday in September, which honors the town's patron saint. The festivities, which extend for several days, take place around the main plaza and along the adjoining streets and include parades, fireworks and regional dance performances.

Holy Week celebrations, which begin about 2 weeks before Easter Sunday, include a lavish procession on Good Friday and the burning of Judas effigies on Easter. The Chamber Music Festival takes place the first 2 weeks of August at the Bellas Artes Cultural Center. The city's Christmas *posadas* also are well known. For information about event happenings and schedules, stop by the State Tourism Office.

Guanajuato State Tourism Office: A tourism office branch is on the southeast side of the main plaza, to the left of La Parroquía. Open Mon.-Fri. 10-2:45 and 5-7, Sat.-Sun. 10-noon; phone (415) 152-6565 (English spoken).

What To See

ALLENDE HOUSE MUSEUM (Museo Casa de Allende) is on Calle Cuna de Allende #1, opposite the southwest corner of the main plaza; street parking is limited. It was the birthplace of Ignacio Allende, one of the few early leaders of the War of Independence with actual military training. Together, he and Father Miguel Hidalgo organized a ragtag army and plotted strategies for overthrowing Spanish rule. Exhibits include a collection of pre-Columbian pottery and ceremonial stone pipes; information is in Spanish.

Allow 30 minutes minimum. Tues.-Sun. 10-4. Admission 32 pesos (around $3.25 U.S.); free to all Sun.

CHURCH OF THE CONCEPTION (Iglesia de la Concepción) is a few blocks west of the main plaza at calles Canal and Hernández Macías. It was begun in the mid-17th century, although the domed roof—one of the largest in Mexico—was not completed until 1891. While the exterior is worn, inside is a breathtaking retablo more than 30 feet tall, decorated with gilded wood and numerous statues. Also notable are the huge oil paintings in both transepts portraying events in the lives of Jesus and Mary. Allow 30 minutes minimum. Open daily; Sun. Mass at 10 a.m. Free; donations accepted.

CHURCH OF SAN FELIPE NERI (Oratorio de San Felipe Neri) is at calles Insurgentes and Loreto, two blocks northeast of the main plaza. It was built by San Miguel's Indian population in the early 18th century. The original structure's facade of pink stone can be seen at the church's eastern end, along with a figure of Our Lady of Solitude (Nuestra Señora de Soledad). The southern exterior is newer and incorporates a baroque style. The church is notable for its differently shaped domes. The adjoining chapel, Santa Casa de Loreto, is behind the church.

CHURCH OF SAN FRANCISCO is on Calle Juárez between calles San Francisco and Mesones. Built in the late 18th century, it is thought to be the work of Eduardo Tresguerras, who contributed to the design of many churches in central Mexico. Construction was financed through donations from wealthy families and the proceeds from bullfights. The intricate stone carvings gracing the exterior are a fine example of the ornate Churrigueresque style. The high-ceilinged interior contains statues, paintings and more carved stone.

PARISH CHURCH (La Parroquía) is on Calle Correo, facing the south side of the main plaza; street parking is limited. Soaring over the plaza, La Parroquía dominates the city.

Originally built in the late 17th century in a plain Franciscan style, it was given an imposing facelift 2 centuries later by a local Indian artisan, Zeferino Gutiérrez. With no formal training, he added the present facade of pink-hued sandstone, allegedly using postcard pictures of French Gothic cathedrals as his inspiration.

Inside are murals, vaulted ceilings, side chapels and statues of saints, including St. Michael the Archangel (the church's official name is Parroquía de San Miguel Arcángel). The tomb of Anastasio Bustamante, president of Mexico from 1832-33 and again from 1839-41, is open to the public on Nov. 2. The original bell, cast in 1732, begins ringing early in the morning to summon parishioners. Allow 45 minutes minimum. Church staff do not speak English. Open daily; Sun. mass 6 a.m.-1 p.m. and at 6 and 8 p.m. Free; donations accepted.

PUBLIC LIBRARY (Biblioteca Pública) is 2 blocks north of the main plaza at Calle Insurgentes #25. A repository for some 22,000 English volumes and an equal number of books in Spanish, it is the second largest bilingual library in Latin America. Scanning the variety of notices posted at the entrance (many in English) is a good way to find out what's going on around town.

A 2-hour house and garden tour of selected homes departs from the library on Sundays at 11:30 (doors open at 11), except three specified Sundays celebrating Mexican and religious holidays; phone

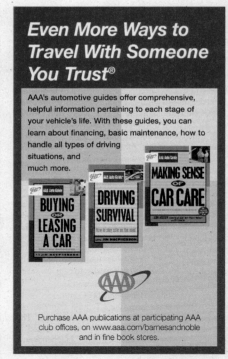

(415) 152-0293. A fixed donation of about $15 U.S. ($20 for the annual Christmas tour) is charged, which benefits a scholarship fund for the education of San Miguel youth. Library open Mon.-Fri. 10-2 and 4-7, Sat. 10-2.

SANCTUARY OF ATOTONILCO (Santuario de Atotonilco) is about 15 km (9 mi.) north on Mex. 51, then about 3 km (1.9 mi.) southwest off the highway in the village of Atotonilco. "El Santuario" minibuses make this trip, departing from the bus stop on Calle Puente Umarán (opposite the city market). The village itself is uninteresting, and the church's exterior is plain and worn. Inside, however, is true beauty—walls and arched ceilings covered with writings, poems, paintings and frescoes, most in full color. The Chapel of the Rosario, dedicated to Our Lady of Guadalupe, has an entire wall adorned with gold-framed stations of the cross surrounding a life-size statue of the saint.

Hiring a guide in San Miguel to show you around the church and explain its historical significance makes for a more rewarding experience. Allow 30 minutes minimum. Open daily. Free; donations accepted.

TABOADA SPRINGS are about 8 km (5 mi.) north of San Miguel on Mex. 51. The mineral springs feed a thermal spa, which provides a hot soaking and reputed skin benefits. There also are two swimming pools and a large lawn area. Snacks and drinks are available. The buses that go to Atotonilco also stop within walking distance of the spa, but a more reliable means of transportation is to hire a taxi. Wed.-Mon. 9-6. Admission around $5 (U.S.).

TEQUILA, JALISCO (F-3) pop. 24,400

This typical Mexican town is about 56 kilometers (35 miles) northwest of Guadalajara, just off Mex. 15. It sits amid extensive plantations devoted to the cultivation of the agave plant, from which the same-named beverage is extracted. Local distilleries (the major one is Sauza) have obtained a patent that prohibits other producers, even those within Mexico, from calling their drink tequila.

Cultivated agave plants resemble a field of spiny blue bayonets. Although the region's indigenous peoples had long drunk the fermented sap, the Spaniards introduced the distilling process. The tough, swordlike fronds are stripped from the plant, exposing its "heart," which can weigh more than 100 pounds. The hearts are "cooked" in large copper kettles, and the resulting liquid is transferred to huge tanks. Clear tequila is bottled at once; the golden variety ages in oak casks for up to seven years.

The Guadalajara Chamber of Commerce organizes a Tequila day trip, the "Tequila Express," in conjunction with Mexican National Railways. The train leaves the Guadalajara rail station, located at Avenida Washington and Calzada Independencia Sur (near Agua Azul Park), Saturdays around 11 a.m. en route to the Herradura distilllery in the town of Amatitán.

The trip includes mariachi music and tequila tastings on board, a tour of the distillery and a buffet-style lunch. Tickets cost 650 pesos (around $65 U.S.); under 12, 400 pesos (around $40). They can be purchased at the chamber, Av. Vallarta #4095, phone (33) 3880-9099, or through Ticketmaster in Guadalajara, phone (33) 3818-3800.

Tequila lies at the northern base of extinct, 9,797-foot Volcán de Tequila, which has a stopper of hardened lava in its crater. Shards of obsidian, a volcanic glass, are visible in cuts flanking the highway near town. La Toma, a picnic spot with a waterfall and swimming pool, is about 4 kilometers (2.5 miles) northwest of Tequila off Mex. 15; the Santiago River Canyon, through which the river winds, is particularly scenic.

TLAQUEPAQUE, JALISCO (H-4)
pop. 467,900

A southeastern suburb of Guadalajara, Tlaquepaque (tla-keh-PAH-keh) is an important crafts center. Distinctive, hand-painted Tlaquepaque pottery is prized throughout Mexico. The fragile earthenware is decorated by hand. Many artisans still use the potter's wheel, and visitors can view the work in progress at some pottery shops. Tlaquepaque also is known for blown glass, textiles, jewelry, furniture, copperware and carved wood. The town is a tourist magnet and can get very crowded, but dedicated shoppers won't want to miss out on the huge selection of high-quality handicrafts.

The word "mariachi" seems to have originated in Tlaquepaque. French soldiers garrisoned in the city in the mid-19th century noted that the strolling troubadours performed primarily at weddings, or *mariages*, hence the possible derivation of the term. Mariachi bands perform in the gazebo within Jardín Hidalgo, the main plaza (bounded by the streets Independencia, Guillermo Prieto, Morelos and Francisco I. Madero).

Browsing is easiest along pedestrian-only Calle Independencia. Many of the shops and galleries are housed in refurbished old mansions with thick stone walls and iron gates. Most of the larger shops accept U.S. dollars or payment by credit card, and will arrange to have purchases packed and shipped as well. Many are closed or open limited hours on Sunday. Under the circular roof of El Parián, a building in the middle of town, are many sidewalk cafes, pleasant spots to relax over a leisurely lunch while the shops close for afternoon *siesta* (usually between 2 and 4).

La Casa Canela, Independencia #258, has showrooms arranged around a lush garden patio. This tasteful shop offers Mexican furniture, papier-mâché artworks and antiques. Tierra Tlaquepaque, Independencia #156, offers wood sculpture, pottery and decorative objects. Sergio Bustamente's fanciful sculptures, known around the world, are featured at the Galería Sergio Bustamante, Calle Independencia #236.

Linea Turquesa (TUR) buses depart regularly for Tlaquepaque and Tonalá (see separate listing within this region) from downtown Guadalajara; the trip takes about half an hour. They carry only seated passengers; cheaper city buses carry both standing and seated passengers and are likely to be crowded. Tell the driver you want to get off at the stop nearest El Parián.

If driving, take Avenida Revolución off Calzada Independencia Sur, heading southeast away from downtown Guadalajara. This road becomes Boulevard Tlaquepaque as it heads into town. At the traffic circle, bear right onto Avenida Niños Héroes, which runs into Calle Independencia after a block.

Tourist information office: Calle Guillermo Prieto #80, across from the main plaza. Open Mon.-Fri. 9-3, Sat. 9-1; phone (33) 3635-5756.

REGIONAL MUSEUM OF CERAMICS (Museo Regional de la Cerámica) is at Calle Independencia #237, at Calle Alfareros. Housed in an 18th-century building that was formerly a private home, it contains several rooms displaying mostly modern regional pottery pieces as well as some pre-Columbian artifacts. Exhibit information is in Spanish. Mon.-Sat. 10-6, Sun. 10-3; closed Easter and Dec. 25. Free.

TLAXCALA, TLAXCALA (C-11)
pop. 77,000, elev. 7,387'

A highland city in the middle of a wooded region, Tlaxcala (tlas-KAH-lah), the state capital, is about 75 miles east of Mexico City. The Tlaxcala Indians, a Chichimec group, settled in this region after defeating the Aztecs at Lake Texcoco. Alliance with the Otomí Indians provided the military protection that gave the Tlaxcaltecs the freedom to advance their civilization. Leaders of this small, powerful nation were the second, after the Totonacs, to align their forces with Hernando Cortés.

Apparently, joining the wrong side has been forgiven. This amiable colonial town, off the usual tourist track, is one of Mexico's most picturesque and makes for a pleasant side trip from Mexico City or Puebla. The downtown area is a delightful assemblage of structures in shades of sepia, deep red and orange. Plaza Constitución, the main square, is distinguished by neatly trimmed trees, a bandstand and a burbling fountain presented to the city by King Philip III.

Most points of interest in town surround the plaza. On its north side is the Government Palace (Palacio de Gobierno), with a brick exterior punctuated by ornately decorated windows and doorways. Inside are extravagantly colorful murals depicting agricultural life and the history of the Tlaxcaltec people, painted in the early 1960s by local artist Desiderio Hernández Xochitiotzin.

Also on the plaza is the baroque Palace of Justice (Palacio de Justicia), with neoclassic touches added in the 18th century. Inside the Parish Church

of St. Joseph (Parroquía de San José), a peach-colored building, is the Chapel of St. Joseph (Capilla de San José), which has an arched ceiling with plaster ornamentation and impressive altarpieces.

Perhaps the finest examples of pre-Columbian artwork in all of Mexico are the mural paintings on view at the ruins of Cacaxtla (see attraction listing). Discovered only in 1975, they remain vividly colorful more than a thousand years after their execution. Archeological evidence suggests the city that once stood here reached a peak of development between A.D. 650 and 900, and was abandoned by the beginning of the 11th century.

Cacaxtla (ca-CASHT-la) is thought to have been the capital of the Olmecan-Xicalancas, one of several groups who moved into this region of Mexico during a period of widespread unrest. Their domain encompassed the Valley of Puebla and the southwestern corner of present-day Tlaxcala state. The city was built atop a rise that facilitated contact with other Mesoamerican tribes but was also vulnerable to raids. As a result, the perimeter was walled and moated to ward off attack.

Cacaxtla's earliest structures were a group of adobe edifices that over time were demolished and filled in to form a large platform. This process was repeated several times until the foundation reached its present height. Most of the structures that visitors see today are vestiges dating from the latest period of construction. Ceremonial courtyards, tombs and enclosures were repeatedly reconfigured during the site's centuries of occupation.

About 45 kilometers (28 miles) southeast of Tlaxcala is La Malinche National Park, which has as its centerpiece La Malinche, an extinct volcano 14,632 feet high. At the entrance to the park is Malintzin, a vacation resort run by the Mexican Social Security Institute (IMSS) that offers lodgings, sports facilities and medical services in a wooded setting. Malintzin lies at a 9,840-foot elevation on the northern slopes of the mountain; from a marked exit on Mex. 136 between the towns of Apizaco and Huamantla (the sign reads "Centro Vacacional Malintzi"), a road ascends 14 kilometers (9 miles) to the retreat.

Tlaxcala State Tourism Office (Secretaría de Turismo): at the intersection of avenidas Benito Juárez and Lardizábal (behind the Government Palace). The staff speaks English. Open Mon.-Fri. 9-7, Sat.-Sun. 10-6; phone (800) 509-6557 (toll-free long distance within Mexico).

CACAXTLA RUINS are about 17 km (12 mi.) southwest of Tlaxcala. To reach them by car from the center of town, take the road to Nativitas (follow signs) and then watch for the sign about 1.5 km (1 mi.) west of that town indicating the direction to Cacaxtla and the nearby village of San Miguel del Milagro. The hillside entrance to the site is about a 1-mi. walk from the parking lot.

Climb the stairs to reach the Gran Plaza, a broad platform protected by a huge metal roof. The largest and most dramatic of the murals flanking the plaza is the mythological Mural of the Battle, painted between A.D. 650 and 700. It depicts two groups of warriors—one outfitted in birdlike plumage and feather headdresses, the other cloaked in the skins of jaguars. The colors—rich blues, reds, yellows and browns—and the depth of detail are startling. Daily 10-5. Admission (ticket also good for Xochitécatl site) around $4 (U.S.); free to all Sun. The fee for the use of a video camera is around $4.

Xochitécatl is about 2 km (1.2 mi.) from Cacaxtla and can be reached on foot. A much older site, it was not uncovered until 1994. It consists of three pyramids and the base of a fourth. The Pirámide de la Espiral, named for its circular shape, is thought to have been used for astronomical explorations or built in dedication to Ehecatl, the god of wind. The Pyramid of the Flowers (Pirámide de las Flores), also constructed of rounded stones, has an exceptionally wide base. Tues.-Sun. 10-5:30.

EX-CONVENT OF THE ASSUMPTION (Ex-Convento Francisco de la Asunción) is southeast of the main plaza and off a smaller plaza, Plaza Xicoténcatl; a cobblestone path leads up a hill to the cathedral. It dates from the early 16th century. The original chapel with its stone baptismal font can be seen. In the Franciscan church are gilded altars, 17th-century religious paintings and an intricately carved and decorated wooden ceiling in *mudéjar* (Moorish) fashion. A lovely open-air chapel features Moorish-style pointed arches.

Tlaxcala Regional Museum (Museo Regional de Tlaxcala) occupies the church's cloister. Exhibits in the whitewashed rooms depict the state's history from prehistoric times to the present. Tues.-Sun. 10-5. Admission around $3.50 (U.S.).

MUSEUM OF POPULAR ARTS AND TRADITIONS (Museo de Artes Populares y Tradiciones) is at Blvd. Sanchez and Av. 1 de Mayo, 3 blocks west of the main plaza. This small museum exhibits such items as clay water jugs and animal skins. Tues.-Sun. 10-6. Admission around 80 cents (U.S.), under 6 free.

SANCTUARY OF THE VIRGIN OF OCOTLAN (Santuario de la Virgen de Ocotlán) sits atop a hill about a mile east of town. It commemorates the supposed appearance of the Virgin of Guadalupe to the Indian Juan Diego Bernardino at this site in 1541. A masterpiece of baroque architecture in the indigenous Puebla-Tlaxcalan style, the shrine has a dazzlingly white, elaborately carved stucco facade and towers supported by twin tiled bases of red clay. The interior is a riot of gilded wood ornamentation. The octagonal Dressing Room (Camarín), a chamber where the Virgin's robes were said to be changed, explodes with carvings of angels and saints.

Visitors can hike to the shrine from the center of town, or take an inexpensive *colectivo* (minivan) designated "Ocotlán"; the driver stops at the front steps and will wait while you tour the sanctuary.

SANTA ANA CHIAUTEMPAN is less than 3 km (2 mi.) from Tlaxcala; it can be reached via the paved road that branches east from town. At this weaving center, artists fashion hand-loomed *sarapes* and beautiful bolts of cloth. The village's main street is lined with shops selling rugs and *sarapes*. Native craftwork is supplemented by the tweeds and woolen bedspreads produced in the region's modern textile plants.

TIZATLAN RUINS are about 4 km (2.5 mi.) northeast of town via Mex. 117 to the Tizatlán turnoff. A wool-weaving settlement established by the Tlaxcaltecs in the mid-14th century, Tizatlán developed into a major trade center. The ruins include a palace built on a small platform and small sanctuaries with murals painted on the altars. These paintings depict wars with the Aztecs, who failed in their attempt to incorporate the Tlaxcaltec nation into their empire.

TONALA, JALISCO (G-4) pop. 335,900

Tonalá (toh-nah-LAH), about 7 kilometers (4 miles) east of Tlaquepaque, was the original site of Guadalajara until 1531, when the Spaniards, repeatedly harassed by hostile Indians, abandoned the area. Many homes in this noted pottery-producing center double as family-run pottery workshops, or *talleres*, and factories here produce many of the wares displayed in Tlaquepaque.

The best days to visit are Thursdays and Sundays, when there is a large open-air *tianguis* (market). Savvy shoppers can obtain excellent buys on glassware, ceramics and papier-mâché crafts, all spread out on the sidewalks in a colorful, enticing hodgepodge.

Tonalá's factories and workshops are concentrated along north-south Avenida de Los Tonaltecas, the main thoroughfare, and in the vicinity of the main plaza, at calles Juárez and Hidalgo. An excellent selection of ceramics can be found at Casa de Artesanos, Av. Tonaltecas Sur #140. The workshop of Jorge Wilmot, who combined modern technology with traditional methods to produce distinctive ceramic designs, is at Calle Morelos #88. The shop/studio of Ken Edwards, Calle Morelos #184, features lovely stoneware items.

The public buses that travel to Tlaquepaque *(see separate listing within this region)* go to Tonalá. You also can get there by taxi; one-way fare should average about $4 (U.S.) from Tlaquepaque, $7 from Guadalajara. If driving, take the Zapotlanejo Highway (Carretera Zapotlanejo) east out of Tlaquepaque.

Tourist information office: in the Casa de Artesanos, Av. Tonaltecas Sur #140. Open Mon.-Fri. 9-3, Sat. 9-1; phone (33) 3683-1740. Inquire about the free walking tours on non-market days (Mon.-Wed. and Fri.-Sat.) that include visits to local workshops; English-speaking guides can be requested.

NATIONAL MUSEUM OF CERAMICS (Museo Nacional de la Cerámica) is at Av. Constitución #104,

2 blocks north of City Hall. Housed in a two-story mansion, it displays a quality collection of pieces from different regions of Mexico dating from pre-Columbian to modern times, as well as displays showing the various methods of creating and firing pottery. Exhibit information is in Spanish. Tues.-Fri. 9-5, Mon. and Sat. 9-3. Free.

TONANTZINTLA, PUEBLA (D-11)

Tonantzintla (toh-nahn-TSEEN-tlah) *(see Acatepec listing)* is worth a visit just for its amazing church, which dominates the tiny village.

CHURCH OF SANTA MARIA TONANTZINTLA is a couple of miles south of Cholula via Boulevard Miguel Alemán, across from the main plaza. While the yellow and white exterior looks fairly disciplined, the riotously ornate interior of this church is a definitive example of the Churrigueresque architectural style. The walls and ceiling are completely covered with gilded decorations, painted cherubs and saints garlanded in plumed headdresses. The colorful motifs include fruits, flowers, birds and Christmas themes, and the faces and dress of the human figures are strongly Indian in character.

Although it was under construction for nearly 300 years—from 1607 to 1897—the church exhibits such harmonious ornamental continuity that it all appears to date from the early 17th century. Both this church and the one in neighboring Acatepec are an easy side trip from Cholula, Puebla or Mexico City. Free.

TULA, HIDALGO (B-10)
pop. 27,300, elev. 6,776'

Tula (TOO-lah) was founded by Franciscans in the early 16th century; their fortresslike church, which also dates from that time, still stands. Typical of smaller Mexican towns, it has a busy market and a quiet central plaza bordered with taco stands. Evening band concerts occasionally take place in the square. Archeologists long believed that the remains of the Toltec capital of Tollan, which means "metropolis" or "large city," were somewhere in this region; however, the exact whereabouts remained a mystery until the Tula ruins were determined to be the site in 1938.

Tula's dominance as a major city in pre-Hispanic Mexico was relatively brief—from about A.D. 950 to 1174, when the Chichimecs, forerunners of the Aztecs, attacked, sacked and burned it. The sculptural figure known as Chac Mool, first found at this site, has become an international artistic symbol of Mesoamerican culture. But the reclining figure—holding a vessel that presumably received still-beating hearts torn from victims' chests during sacrificial ceremonies—underscores the violent nature of Toltec culture.

 TULA RUINS are about 32 km (20 mi.) off Mex. 57-D (the toll highway to Querétaro) north through the center of Tula, then 4 km (2.5 mi.) northwest to the site, following signs.

The Legend of Quetzalcóatl

One of Mexican history's most intriguing mysteries surrounds Quetzalcóatl, a man known for his advocacy of peace and who was believed to have opposed the practice of human sacrifice. Over time, fact and myth have become almost impenetrably tangled, although certain events are reasonably established. The son of Toltec chieftain Mixcóatl, Quetzalcóatl took the full name Ce Acatl Quetzalcóatl (literally, "One Reed Feathered Serpent"). It is believed that he founded the Toltec city of Tollan (Tula); the plumed serpent motif is noticeably evident at this archeological site. A power struggle ensued, and according to legend Quetzalcóatl's rivals conspired to get him drunk and thereby shame him into exile. (A

© Richard Nebesky
Lonely Planet Images

more likely scenario is that the continued invasion of warlike tribes caused a decline in Toltec power.) The king led his followers, it is said, out of Tula and east toward the Gulf coast, where he either sailed off, promising to return in a future era, or burned himself alive and was reincarnated as the morning star. Meanwhile, Quetzalcóatl the myth continued to be invoked, a personage described as light-skinned, blue-eyed and bearded—features different from those of any person the Indians had ever before seen. When Hernando Cortés arrived in the Aztec capital of Tenochtitlán, the emperor Moctezuma believed him to be the returning god—a case of mistaken identity the *conquistador* craftily used to his advantage.

Taxis departing from Tula's main plaza drop visitors off at the ruins. They constitute what is left of the capital and chief ceremonial center of the Toltecs. The focal point of the ruins is the five-tiered pyramid with a tongue-twisting name, the Temple of Tlahuizcalpantecuitli (Lord of the House of the Morning Star Venus). It dominates the north side of a plaza flanked by colonnaded buildings.

On top of the pyramid stand four colossal figures known as the Atlantes (one is a replica). They once supported the roof of a temple that stood atop the pyramid. Each Atlantean is swaddled in a loincloth, its chest protected by stylized butterfly breastplates and its back by shields in the shape of the sun. The figures wear headdresses decorated with feathers and carry a spear-thrower in the right hand, a supply of spears in the left. This pyramid as well as several others can be climbed, but their steepness makes descending more difficult than ascending.

The museum near the entrance houses professional displays of artifacts found at the site, including huge sandal-clad feet carved from solid rock. Vendors hawking artifact replicas line the path from the museum to the ruins. Allow 1 hour minimum. Site daily 10-5, museum Tues.-Sun. 10-5. Admission around $3 (U.S.). Guided tour fees are negotiable.

TZINTZUNTZAN, MICHOACAN (C-8)
elev. 6,724′

Once the capital of a powerful Tarascan kingdom, Tzintzuntzan (tseen-TSOON-tsahn) is now a small village on the shores of Lake Pátzcuaro. The curious name means "the place of the hummingbirds" in the Tarascan Indian language.

This area is one of the largest sources of inexpensive hand-painted pottery in Mexico. Local artisans decorate their pottery with simple, childlike drawings of swans, fish and native net fishermen. They also weave figurines and table and floor mats out of reeds. Another cottage industry is woodcarving; items range from small wall decorations, dishes and flowerpots to doors, windows and columns.

The restored 16th-century Franciscan Convent of Santa Ana can be visited. The church courtyard is noted for its olive trees, which were planted by Don Vasco de Quiroga despite a Spanish injunction against planting the trees in the New World. Restored *yácatas,* ruins of Tarascan pyramids, are visible from Mex. 120; a paved side road leads to the edge of the site.

Holy Week ceremonies culminate with a series of concerts and performances of classical Spanish plays, staged by residents in the atrium of the Santa Ana Convent. The village's *pastorelas,* medieval dramas based on the Nativity, begin Dec. 16.

Tzintzuntzan also participates in Day of the Dead ceremonies Nov. 1-2. During this all-night vigil, families visit the local cemetery to bring food, drink and other *ofrendas* (offerings) to their deceased relatives. This ritual, as well as those observed during Holy Week, attract many visitors to towns on the islands of and around Lake Pátzcuaro. If you'll be visiting during either of these times, book hotel reservations in Pátzcuaro or nearby Quiroga well in advance.

URUAPAN, MICHOACAN (I-4)
pop. 229,400, elev. 5,491′

Uruapan (oo-roo-AH-pahn) means "place where the flowers bloom," and the lush vegetation seen throughout the city is a testament to the warm climate (it is nearly 2,000 feet lower in elevation than nearby Pátzcuaro). Orange groves and plantations growing coffee, bananas and especially avocados flourish in the fertile farmland that surrounds the

city. Uruapan also is known for hand-painted lacquerware carved from cedar and other native woods.

Michoacán State Tourism Office (Delegación de Turismo): Av. Ayala #16, 2 blocks northwest of the main plaza. Open Mon.-Sat. 9-2 and 4-7; phone (452) 524-7199.

EDUARDO RUIZ PARK (Parque Eduardo Ruiz) has an entrance at the end of east-west Av. Independencia (off Calzada La Quinta), about 8 blocks west of the main plaza. This shady subtropical park has lush vegetation along the banks of the Río Cupatitzio and fountains with dancing waters propelled by gravity alone; no pumps are used. Numerous footpaths wind along the riverbank.

The river rises at Devil's Knee (Rodilla del Diablo) spring, named—according to legend—for the spot where Lucifer left a kneeling imprint. Daily 8-6. Admission around $1 (U.S.), children 50 cents.

PARICUTIN is north on Mex. 37 for about 16 km (10 mi.) to the junction with a paved road branching west 21 km (13 mi.) to the town of Angahuan. Paracutin (pah-ree-koo-TEEN), a now-dormant volcano, sprang from a cornfield in 1943. The blunt-topped cone rises some 1,700 feet above the surrounding valley.

During its brief period of activity, Paricutín destroyed two villages (part of a church protruding from the jumble of boulders is the only remaining evidence of their existence) and forced more than 4,000 people to abandon their homes. The volcanic cone and the weirdly blackened surrounding lava fields can be reached on horseback or by hiking on foot. Guided trips can be arranged in Angahuan, or check with the State Tourism Office in Uruapan.

REGIONAL MUSEUM OF POPULAR ART (Museo de Arte Popular) faces the northeast side of the main plaza. It is housed within La Huatapera, a colonnaded building that is a fine example of 16th-century architecture. It was built under the direction of Spanish bishop Vasco de Quiroga and was originally a hospital. The museum exhibits skillful examples of Tarascan Indian workmanship, including primitive dolls, statues, lacquerware and copper handicrafts. Currently closed for major restoration work.

TZARARACUA WATERFALL (Cascada de Tzaráracua) is just off Mex. 37 about 10 km (6 mi.) south of town. Here the Río Cupatitzio rushes through a natural stone amphitheater, then drops about 90 feet into a pool within a cool, leafy setting. There is a fairly steep half-mile descent from the parking area down to the falls, but the trail is well marked, and handrails are provided. Buses to Tzaráracua (tsah-RAH-rah-kwah) depart from Uruapan's main plaza on weekends and drop passengers off at the parking lot; a cab ride to the falls is about $4 (U.S.).

ZACATECAS, ZACATECAS (F-6)

pop. 115,700, elev. 8,115'

Zacatecas (sah-kah-TEH-kahs), capital of the state of the same name, is built in a ravine on the slopes of Cerro de la Bufa, a rock-crowned hill 8,748 feet high. Long a mining center, the settlement was taken by the Spaniards in 1548. In 1588, it was named "The Very Noble and Loyal City of Our Lady of the Zacatecas" because of the vast quantities of silver shipped from the region to Spain. Although now surrounded by agricultural and cattle-raising lands, Zacatecas continues to be a center for silver mining. The largest mine in the region is 200-year-old El Bote, which is still in operation.

Elaborate old mansions, an aqueduct and stone steps connecting steeply inclined flagstone streets lend Zacatecas a charmingly medieval atmosphere; the historic city center was designated a World Heritage Site by UNESCO in 1993. The beautiful baroque buildings also attest to the great wealth that was generated by the mines. A magnificent cathedral *(see attraction listing)* and several excellent museums also are reasons to visit.

A wide, divided avenue 5 kilometers (3 miles) long leads east from downtown Zacatecas to the suburb of Guadalupe, the site of an early 18th-century convent. It once served as a base for Franciscan missions established to the north of Mexico in what is now the southwestern United States. The town is noted for colonial architecture as well as for marquetry (inlaid woodwork) and wool *sarapes* with portraits woven into their designs.

Trancoso, 22 kilometers (14 miles) east off Mex. 45/49, has one of the most elegant and best preserved old haciendas in Mexico. In Bracho, on the north side of the loop road encircling the city, La Morisma is celebrated the last week in August. During this fiesta, hundreds of local boys and men dressed in Moorish-style costumes act out a battle against a European army for several consecutive days.

Zacatecas State Tourism Office (Consejo Estatal de Turismo): downtown at Av. Hidalgo #403 (second floor); phone (492) 924-4047 or (800) 712-4078 (toll-free long distance within Mexico). From the United States, phone (877) 297-8319.

What To See in and Around Town

CATHEDRAL is on the south side of Plaza de Armas. Begun in 1612 and completed in 1752, it is one of the ultimate expressions of the Mexican baroque style. The extravagant exterior carvings of pink sandstone (called *cantera* in Spanish) are notable. This is still an active church, and Mass is held daily. Open for services (closes after dark); there is no tour schedule, but visitors can enter the building and look around. Free.

CERRO DE LA BUFA overlooks the city from the northeast. There are panoramic views from the summit, which can be reached by the Zacatecas Cable Car*(see attraction listing).*

Battle of Zacatecas Museum (Museo Toma de Zacatecas) is next to the chapel. It chronicles the 1914 battle led by Pancho Villa to gain control of the city, one of the decisive conflicts of the Revolution of 1910. Information is presented in Spanish. Daily 10-5. Admission around $2 (U.S.).

Patrocinio Chapel (La Capilla de la Virgen del Patrocinio) is at the summit. Erected in 1728, it is named for the patron saint of miners.

EDEN MINE (Mina el Edén) can be reached by car from Mex. 54; when entering the city, turn northeast at the Hotel Parador en Zacatecas and then proceed down the hill about half a kilometer, following signs. From downtown, go past Alameda Park and the Social Security building. First operated in the 16th century, this mine produced great quantities of silver, copper and zinc during its most active period.

A small powered train takes visitors through the mine's 1,950-foot-long tunnel entrance; a guided tour then travels through several other tunnels. Talks in Spanish tell of the gruesome living conditions of the original Indian miners. Tours daily 10-6. Admission around $2.50 (U.S.).

FRANCISCO GOITIA MUSEUM (Museo Francisco Goitia) is south of the city center at Av. Estrada #102, across from Enrique Estrada Park. Housed in the former Governor's Mansion, it exhibits works by Goitia (1882-1960) that include a dramatic self-portrait, as well as sculpture and paintings by other 20th-century Zacatecano artists. Tues.-Sun. 10-5. Admission around $2.50 (U.S.).

GUADALUPE CONVENT (Convento de Guadalupe) is about 7 km (4 mi.) southeast of the city via Mex. 45/49, in the town of Guadalupe. Local *Ruta* 13 buses depart regularly for Guadalupe from the corner of Calle Salazar and Blvd. López Mateos, near the old bus terminal in downtown Zacatecas.

The convent dates from 1707. This enormous baroque church and former monastery once housed Franciscan monks. Seemingly endless corridors, all lined with paintings and portraits, pass rows of cells where the monks spent their time when not ministering to the Indians.

Museum of Viceregal Art (Museo de Arte Virreinal) is within the convent. It contains 18th-century Miguel Cabrera paintings of the Virgin of Guadalupe and other colonial religious art, as well as a library with a collection of hand-printed books. Especially noteworthy is the Chapel of Napoles (Capilla de Napoles), which has a domed roof covered with beautifully ornate gold-leaf decoration. The chapel is not always open, so a tip for the guide who grants entrance is appreciated. Guided tours of the museum also are available. Daily 10-4:30. Admission around $3 (U.S.); free to all Sun.

LA QUEMADA RUINS lie on the hillside of a valley, about 56 km (35 mi.) southwest of Zacatecas off Mex. 54. Also known as Chicomostoc Ruins, this archeological site bears traces of narrow streets and the foundations of homes and temples of the Náhuatlac Indians, who settled the valley around 1170. Thought to be destroyed by fire, the city was already a ruin when the Spaniards discovered it in 1535.

Among the remaining structures are a restored pyramid, a palace with 11 standing columns, and the substantial surrounding walls. Since local transportation is unreliable, the ruins are much easier to reach if you have your own vehicle. From the highway it's an uphill, 30-minute walk to the site entrance. Visitors should wear comfortable hiking shoes and bring water. Daily 10-5. Admission around $3 (U.S.).

PEDRO CORONEL MUSEUM is on Plaza Santo Domingo, about 2 blocks west of Plaza de Armas. It houses the outstanding private collection of noted Zacatecan artist and sculptor Pedro Coronel, which includes works by Pablo Picasso, Salvador Dalí, Joan Miró and Marc Chagall.

Other displays include Coronel's tomb and exhibit of his own sculpture and paintings; pre-Columbian pieces and colonial-era works by Zacatecano artists; Chinese, Indian, Greek and Egyptian art; and a fine collection of Mesoamerican and African masks. Fri.-Wed. 10-5. Admission around $2.50 (U.S.). Phone (492) 922-8021.

RAFAEL CORONEL MUSEUM (Museo Rafael Coronel) is on Calle Chevano, a short distance north of the cathedral; from the cathedral front, walk up Av. Hidalgo 2 blocks to Calle Abasolo, proceed left at the fork for 2 short blocks to Calle Chevano, then take the right fork to the museum. It is housed in the Convento de San Francisco, a gracious 18th-century edifice abandoned as a convent in 1857, which has an exterior colored in tones of mellowed pink. Lush flowering plants fill the gardens in the interior courtyard.

On display in large, high-ceilinged galleries is an amazing collection of several thousand masks from all over Mexico, donated by Rafael Coronel, younger brother of Pedro. They depict saints as well as grotesque-looking, devilish figures, *conquistadores* and bizarrely imaginative animals. Entirely handmade and decorated with everything from human hair and glitter to steel wool and bones, the masks are a remarkable testament to Mexican artistic ingenuity. There also are impressive dioramas of puppets engaged in such activities as warfare, a bullfight and a wedding, all created by a family of puppet makers from Huamantla, Tlaxcala.

Food is available. Tues.-Sun. 10-5. Admission 20 pesos (around $2 U.S.). Phone (492) 922-8116.

ZACATECAS CABLE CAR (Teleférico), next to the Del Bosque Motel, can be reached from Mex. 54, following signs. Built by Swiss engineers, it connects the hills Cerro de la Bufa and Cerro Grillo, spanning the northern section of the city. The journey takes 8 minutes, covers a distance of 2,100 feet and overlooks Zacatecas from varying heights. The two enclosed cars are capable of holding 15 passengers at a time. Parking is available at either end of the run. Trips every 15 minutes, weather permitting, daily 10-6. One-way fare around $2.50 (U.S.), round trip $4.50.

ZAPOPAN, JALISCO (G-3) pop. 932,700

About 7 kilometers (4 miles) northwest of downtown Guadalajara via Avenida Avila Camacho, the sprawling "suburb" of Zapopan (sah-POH-pahn) is the home of the Virgin of Zapopan—often referred to as La Zapopanita ("Little Zapopaner") since her image. made of corn paste. stands a mere 10 inches tall.

Legend alleges that Chimalhuacano Indians, awed by a Franciscan friar's display of La Zapopanita during the heat of battle against the Spanish, surrendered and were converted to Christianity. In 1734, at the height of an epidemic, she was taken to the towns and villages around Guadalajara. Wherever the virgin appeared, sickness reputedly ceased, and many miracles were subsequently attributed to her.

Each summer the statue of the virgin is encased in a protective glass shell and embarks on a 4-month pilgrimage to the more than 100 parish churches throughout the state. Transported by

special car, the virgin begins a final journey at dawn on Oct. 12 from Guadalajara's cathedral back to her home church, the massive 17th-century Basilica of the Virgin of Zapopan (Basilica de la Virgen de Zapopan), on the west side of Zapopan's central plaza.

Piety and merrymaking are both in evidence on this occasion. In addition to solemn marchers holding banners, there are marching bands, cowboys on horseback, police cars with screaming sirens, dancers in native costume and assorted revelers dressed up as if for a giant Halloween party.

Many pilgrims show their devotion by crawling the last kilometer or two on their knees, underscoring the importance of this annual event for the nation's devout Catholics. The homecoming procession from the cathedral to the basilica—a 5-mile route—often involves more than 1 million participants and spectators and is a highlight of Guadalajara's *Fiestas de Octubre* celebration *(see page 532).*

The basilica features an ornate Plateresque exterior and a tiled *mudéjar* dome. In the church courtyard a statue commemorates Pope John Paul II, who gave a mass at the plaza during his 1979 visit. Within the Franciscan monastery next door is the small Huichol Museum (Museo Huichol), which has displays of beadwork and other handicrafts (all for sale) made by the Huichol Indians of northern Jalisco, Nayarit and Zacatecas.

Guadalajara city buses traveling northbound on Avenida 16 de Septiembre/Alcalde go to the basilica; the trip takes about half an hour.

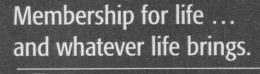

Church of Santa Prisca / © Witold Skrypczak / SuperStock

Southern Mexico

This is Mexico's poorest region economically but among its richest in cultural traditions. The states of Oaxaca and Chiapas are home to the country's largest concentration of Indian communities. Most of the people are descended from the Zapotec, Mixtec and Maya civilizations that flourished hundreds of years before the Spanish conquest of Mexico. The Zapotecs settled in the Valley of Oaxaca and created the ceremonial center of Monte Albán, which eluded discovery by Spanish *conquistadores*. Much more recently Chiapas, Mexico's southernmost state, made international headlines with the 1994 emergence of the Zapatista National Liberation Army, a guerrilla movement that demanded greater economic opportunities for the region's Indians, or *indígenas*.

The Maya left behind the ruins of Palenque, Bonampak, Yaxchilan and Tonina, also in Chiapas. Palenque's crumbling but intricately decorated structures seem to be inhabited by ghosts of the distant past. The primordial feeling is heightened by the occasional chattering of monkeys or the shriek of an exotic bird. Similarities between the architecture at Palenque and that of palaces in southeast Asia hint at a possible link between Mexico and the Orient, although the mysteries of Maya civilization related to this particular puzzle will probably lay forever buried beneath the rubble.

Oaxaca, meanwhile, just might be the quintessential Mexican destination. It offers excellent museums, beautiful churches, a delightfully vibrant central plaza, Indian markets overflowing with native handicrafts, and a distinctive regional cuisine incorporating everything from subtly spiced *mole* sauces to *panuchos,* pizzas made of cornmeal and topped with pork and onions.

Oaxaca state's Sierra Norte, characterized by a cool, damp climate, forested mountains and a wealth of native plant and animal species, is distinctly different from the dry central valleys and the flat, steamy Isthmus of Tehuantepec to the south. A network of Zapotec hamlets northeast of Oaxaca city called the Commonwealth of Villages (Pueblos Mancomunados) have worked together to develop this impoverished but beautiful region as an ecotourism center. Villagers have created more than 100 miles of signposted trails, some designated for hikers and others for mountain biking. You can explore on your own or take a trip led by a trained local guide.

For a different experience, head to Veracruz. It has the langorous ambience of a tropical port (Mexico's oldest and largest) as well as the energy provided by lively music, folk dances and a jolt of *café con leche*—strong black coffee laced with hot milk—that can be enjoyed at one of the city's sidewalk cafes.

The city also has played an important role in Mexican history, from the arrival of Hernando Cortés through the Mexican Revolution of 1910. In addition to coffee, Veracruz is noted for cigars, distinctive cuisine and the *quexquémetl,* a capelike garment decorated with multicolored embroidery. Totonac Indians produce some of the finest traditional designs.

Jalapa isn't on most Mexican tourist itineraries, but this little-visited city is an altogether charming blend of old and new. Built on the slopes of Macuiltépetl, a large, tiered hill, Jalapa was a Spanish stronghold and an important stagecoach stop between Veracruz and Mexico City. The colonists who followed in the wake of Hernando Cortés almost certainly found the higher altitude and cooler climate a welcome respite from steamy Veracruz, as well as a more suitable environment for the cultivation of coffee and fruit trees.

Much of Veracruz state is green, and the natural lushness makes it an ideal choice for ecotourism. More than 40 rivers flow from the Sierra mountains through the jungle to the Caribbean Sea, etching the hillsides with cascading waterfalls. Tour companies offer white-water rafting trips down such rivers as the Antigua and the Filobobos, with fearsomely named rapids like La Brujita (The Little Witch) and Las Puertas del Infierno (The Doors to Hell) providing the thrills.

True adventurers will be enchanted by the Los Tuxtlas Biosphere Reserve. Created in 1998 in the southern part of the state, Los Tuxtlas preserves a remnant of tropical rain forest from the devastating effects of deforestation due to human activity. The reserve has a biodiversity rivaled by few other areas in Mexico: nearly 2,700 species of plants, more than 100 species of fish and some 570 species of migratory and native birds. In addition to bird watching, available tours include kayking into the mangroves of Lake Sontecomapan and visits to Hidden Lagoon (Laguna Escondida) and Monkey Island (La Isla de los Monos).

Taxco, a delightfully picturesque old silver-mining town in the state of Guerrero, is a designated national historic monument and a popular tourist stop between Mexico City and Acapulco. Sprawled over a rugged hillside in the heart of the Sierra Madre, Taxco has changed little in appearance since the 18th century. The Mexican government prohibits the building of modern structures; older ones proliferate, in various stages of preservation, along with whitewashed houses, red-tiled roofs and cobblestoned streets.

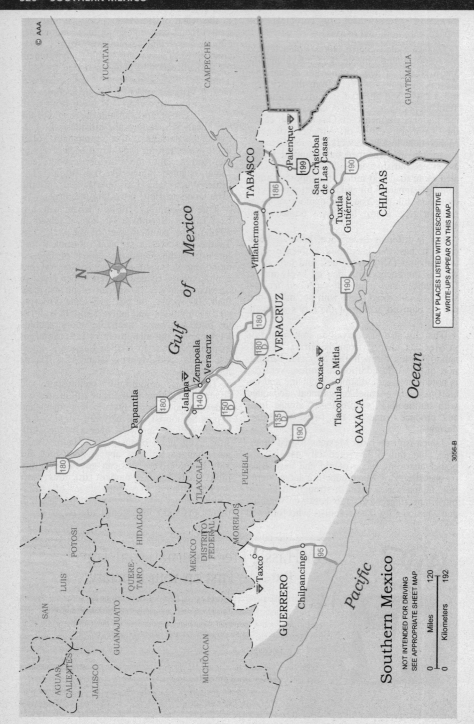

© AAA

N

Southern Mexico

NOT INTENDED FOR DRIVING
SEE APPROPRIATE SHEET MAP

Miles   0   120
Kilometers 0   192

ONLY PLACES LISTED WITH DESCRIPTIVE
WRITE-UPS APPEAR ON THIS MAP.

3056-B

Gulf of Mexico

Pacific Ocean

YUCATAN
CAMPECHE
GUATEMALA
TABASCO
CHIAPAS
VERACRUZ
OAXACA
PUEBLA
TLAXCALA
MEXICO
DISTRITO FEDERAL
MORELOS
HIDALGO
QUERETARO
GUANAJUATO
GUERRERO
MICHOACAN
JALISCO
AGUAS CALIENTES
SAN LUIS POTOSI

Palenque
San Cristóbal de Las Casas
Tuxtla Gutiérrez
Villahermosa
Papantla
Jalapa
Zempoala
Veracruz
Oaxaca
Mitla
Tlacolula
Taxco
Chilpancingo

180   140   150   180   135   190   95   186   199   190

Points of Interest

CHILPANCINGO, GUERRERO (I-7)
pop. 149,200, elev. 4,460'

Capital of the state of Guerrero and home to the University of Guerrero, Chilpancingo (cheel-pahn-SEEN-goh) is a bustling college town. It also has historical credentials—the first Congress of Mexico met here in 1813.

Points of interest include the House of the First Revolutionary Congress (Casa del Primer Congreso Revolucionario), La Asunción Church, the city's ancient cemetery and the State Capitol (Palacio de Gobierno), which has some fine murals. The Indian village of Acatlán, 55 kilometers (34 miles) northeast of Chilpancingo via a partially paved road, is noted for hand-loomed and embroidered shawls.

In Chilapa, 54 kilometers (33 miles) east of Chilpancingo, the Day of St. Gertrude on Nov. 16 features whimsically named native dances, including The Seven Vices, The Eight Lunatics, The Old Woman and The Mule. In Chichihualco, 33 kilometers (20 miles) northwest of Chilpancingo, the Fiesta of St. James Sept. 28-29 includes a parade, regional foods and such native dances as Fishermen and Devils.

JUXTLAHUACA CAVES are reached via a paved road that leaves Mex. 95 at Petaquillas, about 11 km (7 mi.) south of Chilpancingo. Rivaling the caves in Cacahuamilpa Caves National Park *(see Taxco listing)* in size and beauty, these caves are little known outside the region. They contain walls decorated with 3,000-year-old Olmec paintings and unusual geological formations, including translucent salt "veils" and flowerlike crystal formations.

Subterranean ponds and streams support a variety of sightless creatures. A lantern-lit guided tour takes about 5 hours. Explorers should wear comfortable, sturdy walking shoes and bring a light snack; rainwear is advised against spray from subterranean waterfalls. Admission is charged.

JALAPA, VERACRUZ (C-12)
pop. 387,900, elev. 4,681'

Capital of the state of Veracruz and home to nearly 400,000 people, Jalapa (hah-LAH-pah, but spelled Xalapa in Mexico) doesn't seem like a big city. The natural setting is breathtaking—the black volcanic peaks of the Sierra Madre Oriental rise in the distance, towered over by Pico de Orizaba, Mexico's tallest mountain. Practically every corner offers a vista of the mountainous terrain that surrounds the city.

Jalapa's colonial legacy is evident in the structures flanking its older, cobblestone avenues; their red-tiled roofs, wrought-iron balconies, carved wooden doors and window grilles are unmistakably Spanish. Shops and homes are painted in vibrant shades of white, green and deep red. The streets are steep and curving, and also change names and directions frequently; a good city map is an effective navigational aid. Taxis and local buses provide inexpensive transportation to points within the city center.

Begin a morning stroll of downtown Jalapa at the Café la Parroquía, on Calle Zaragoza near the south side of the Government Palace (Palacio de Gobierno). A local meetingplace, it has an old-fashioned '50s look and attracts everyone from university professors to families. As in Veracruz, a favorite morning beverage is a *lechero*, a tall glass of strong espresso to which hot milk is added. Tapping your glass with a spoon signals the waiter, who pours the milk from a steaming kettle.

At the corner of calles Enríquez and Revolución, just north of the Government Palace, stands the city's 18th-century Cathedral. Its plain white facade is accented by Moorish-style arches and a bell tower clock transported from London. The religious paintings inside are worth a look, as is the sloping floor.

The *chipichipi,* a light but persistent winter rain, and evening mists in summer contribute to Jalapa's reputation as the "flower garden of Mexico." The warmth and moisture create a natural greenhouse effect, and the city is filled with roses, bougainvillea and pine trees. Tree-shaded Juárez Park (Parque Juárez), across Calle Enríquez from the City Hall (Palacio Municipal), is representative of the prevailing lushness. White wrought-iron benches are scattered among pruned hedges and well-tended flower beds at this park, which also is the city's central plaza.

Mexico's equivalent of Cambridge is a hip cultural center as well, being home to the University of Veracruz. The Agora Arts Center, just off Juárez Park, is a hangout for students and artists and has extensive events listings. The State Theater (Teatro del Estado) on Ignacio de la Llave hosts performances by the ballet and the symphony. All Jalapa celebrates on Sept. 30, the Day of St. Jerome, when streets are bedecked with flowers and candlelight processions are held.

A few blocks south of Juárez Park on the grounds of an attractively landscaped lakeside park is the state-run Casa de Artesanías, where there are handicrafts for sale by Veracruzan artists, as well as packaged coffee beans. The indoor market on Calle Altamirano, about 2 blocks north of Juárez Park, is a typically colorful hodgepodge displaying assorted trinkets, heaps of dried chilies and beans, and containers of bubbling *mole* sauces.

Street vendors frequent Callejón Diamante, a steep little alley off Calle Enríquez (a block or so east of Juárez Park), along which are several casual

Travel Advisory

It is recommended that visitors check on current conditions before traveling to the states of Chiapas, Guerrero (outside the established tourist destinations of Acapulco, Ixtapa/Zihuatanejo and Taxco) and Oaxaca. Although not directed specifically at tourists, blatant crime continues in the isthmus area of southern Mexico (Chiapas and Oaxaca), and there is the possibility of sporadic violence in the more remote parts of these states. The most potentially dangerous areas in Guerrero are the mountainous, remote interior and undeveloped sections of the Pacific coast. For additional information, consult a Mexico Tourism Board Office *(see page 58),* a Mexican consulate *(see page 60)* or the U.S. State Department's Bureau of Consular Affairs Web site *(see page 57).*

Digital Archives

restaurants specializing in regional fare. Locals and visitors alike head to La Sopa, which serves a filling *comida corrida* (fixed-price lunch).

Macuiltépetl Park (Parque Macuiltépetl), north of downtown, is an ecological preserve that showcases indigenous flora and fauna. The winding paths are a bracing climb up one of Jalapa's hillsides, but the views are outstanding.

Practicalities

The nearest international airport is in Veracruz. From Veracruz, Jalapa is about a 2-hour drive north on Mex. 180 to the town of Cardel, then east on Mex. 140 past numerous coffee plantations.

The central bus station (CAXA) is on Avenida 20 de Noviembre, about a mile east of the downtown area. From this clean, modern building you can make first-class bus connections and long-distance phone calls, arrange for a taxi into town (an otherwise hilly walk) and even grab a bite to eat. It also has a tourist information booth that is open daily. First-class bus service is offered by Autobuses del Oriente (ADO).

Nearby Destinations

Formal plantings, an arboretum and a palm collection make up Clavijero Botanical Gardens, about 3 kilometers (1.5 miles) south of downtown via the road to Coatepec. En route are views of coffee and banana plantations. Coatepec, a colonial town about 8 kilometers (5 miles) south of Jalapa, is known for the raising of ornamental plants, chiefly orchids. The main plaza is surrounded by small shops selling coffee beans and *heladerías* (ice cream parlors) dishing up exotic flavors.

About 11 kilometers (7 miles) past Coatepec is Xico (HEE-coh), a village where sacks of coffee beans are one of the most common sights. Nearby Texolo Waterfall (Cascada de Texolo) has been put to good scenic use in such films as "Romancing the Stone" and parts of the Harrison Ford espionage adventure "A Clear and Present Danger." The falls cascade into a gorge surrounded by lush greenery. A restaurant is at the site, and pathways allow visitors to observe the falls from different vantage points. Local buses to Coatepec and Xico depart from Jalapa's central bus station.

Veracruz State Tourism Office (Subsecretaría de Turismo): Blvd. Cristóbal Colón #5 in the Torre Animas building, about 3 kilometers (1.9 miles) east of downtown; phone (800) 712-6666 (toll-free long distance within Mexico).

What To See

GOVERNMENT PALACE (Palacio de Gobierno) is on the east side of Plaza Juárez. Ornate fountains face this long, pink, colonial-style building, which serves as the state capitol. Inside are murals by José Chávez Morado, including "Liberation," which depicts humanity's struggle for freedom.

HACIENDA EL LENCERO is about 10 km (6 mi.) east of Jalapa off Mex. 140 (toward Veracruz);

watch for the signed turnoff on the right. A tour of this country estate, a former inn for stagecoaches traveling between Veracruz and Mexico City, offers insight into 19th-century hacienda life, a relatively luxurious existence reserved for wealthy plantation owners. Particularly impressive are the finely crafted Mexican rugs and expensive imported furniture that fill the house, and the carefully landscaped gardens that surround it. Tues.-Sun. 10-6. Admission around $3 (U.S.).

GEM **MUSEUM OF ANTHROPOLOGY** (Museo de Antropología de Xalapa) is northwest of downtown on Av. Xalapa, between avs. Acueducto and 10 de Mayo. It houses a superb collection of artifacts encompassing most of Mexico's gulf coast Indian groups, with an emphasis on the Olmec, Totonac and Huastec cultures. Contrasting vividly with the antiquity of the exhibits is the ultramodern museum building, which incorporates a series of tropically landscaped outdoor patios.

A massive Olmec head is stationed at the museum entrance; several other heads, the largest almost 9 feet tall, are on display in outdoor gardens and indoor galleries. Additional highlights include dramatically lifelike ceramic statues of women wearing belts in the form of writhing serpents; a carved figure in green stone holding an infant with jaguar-like facial features that are characteristically Olmec; and beautifully crafted jade and bone jewelry. The carefully organized displays are augmented by maps that note excavation sites and show where the civilizations flourished.

Information about the exhibits is presented in Spanish only, but bilingual guides are available for tours. Allow 2 hours minimum. Daily 9:30-5. Admission around $3.50 (U.S.); there is an extra fee for the use of a video camera. Phone (228) 815-0920.

MITLA, OAXACA (I-9)

The town of Mitla (MEE-tlah) is about 42 kilometers (26 miles) southeast of Oaxaca and about 1.9 kilometers (3 miles) off Mex. 190. The original city, a religious and ceremonial center, was inhabited by the Zapotecs as early as 800 B.C.; by the 11th or 12th century, the Mixtecs had expelled the Zapotecs from both Mitla and Monte Albán and began to establish their own culture. Mitla prospered up until the time of the Spanish conquest. The name means "place of rest" and refers to the catacombs beneath the Mitla ruins.

Weaving is the principal commercial activity today; woven goods can be purchased almost everywhere. Around Mitla and south along Mex. 190 are outlet stores selling mezcal, a locally produced liquor that packs a wallop. Derived from a variety of the maguey plant, mezcal is a specialty of the state of Oaxaca. The bottle often includes a pickled *gusano* (worm). If imbibed at all, mezcal is best diluted with fruit juice.

MITLA RUINS are about 1 km (.6 mi.) north of the main plaza via Av. Morelos. This site was begun by the Zapotecs but taken over by the Mixtecs, and the architectural style of elaborate cut stonework reflects the latter group. Unlike many Maya ruins, Mitla was never buried under encroaching jungle, and the structures are well preserved.

Rectangular patios are surrounded by buildings or long, narrow rooms. Underground chambers and cruciform tombs honeycomb the soil beneath these structures. The Hall of Columns, the most important group, is supported by six enormous pillars, each a single stone, and more than 100,000 pieces of cut stones form the intricate mosaic decorating its walls. The most common design is a zigzag pattern. What sets Mitla apart from other North American archeological sites is the lack of human, animal or mythological figures—abstract representations predominate.

Note: Vendors congregate outside the ruins, vociferously hawking fake archeological pieces and a variety of crafts. There also is a craft market near the ruins entrance. Keep in mind, however, that many of the same items can be purchased in town as well, sometimes at lower prices. Daily 8-5. Admission around $3 (U.S.). The fee to use a video camera is around $5.

MUSEUM OF ZAPOTEC ART (El Museo Frisell) is in town, just off the main plaza. Maintained by the University of the Americas, this museum contains an impressive collection of Mixtec and Zapotec artifacts, housed in a lovely restored hacienda. Exhibit information is in English. **Note:** The museum, which had been closed for remodeling, is scheduled to reopen in August 2005. Admission around $3 (U.S.).

OAXACA, OAXACA (I-8)
pop. 257,000, elev. 5,084'
See map page 330.

Oaxaca (wa-HAH-ka), the state capital, is situated in a high valley surrounded by the towering summits of the Sierra Madre del Sur. It also lies in the shadow of the Mixtec and Zapotec civilizations. Highly religious, these tribes erected elaborate ceremonial centers, were knowledgeable in astronomy and developed systems of writing that are reputed to be the oldest on the North American continent.

The coastal areas of Oaxaca state are steamy and the low-lying Isthmus of Tehuantepec region hot and dry, but the capital is sheltered by the encircling mountains. This fertile valley is one of Mexico's oldest continuously inhabited regions; evidence of human settlement dates back to 8,000 B.C.

Zapotec culture was at its zenith from about the third through the seventh centuries; it was challenged by the Mixtecs, who built their own center at Mitla. The two tribes fought for control of the valley until the Aztecs came and conquered in the late 15th century. The Spanish followed, and the city of Oaxaca was founded by Hernando Cortés in 1529. Today's city retains a strongly Indian character, and both the downtown historic center and the ruins of Monte Albán *(see attraction listing)* were designated World Heritage Sites by UNESCO in 1987.

Oaxaca produced two of Mexico's best known presidents. Benito Juárez was born in the nearby village of Guelatao. A Zapotec with no formal childhood education, he nevertheless entered politics, serving as governor of the state, chief justice of the Mexican Supreme Court and later as president of Mexico (1858-72). Streets, statues and a university bear this national hero's name.

Porfirio Díaz, on the other hand, is not nearly so highly regarded. Of Mixtec rather than Zapotec heritage, Díaz embarked on a military career and assumed the presidency in 1876. The Díaz government soon took on the trappings of a dictatorship, however. Important Mexican advances in railroads, manufacturing, oil production and investment abroad were made during his regime, but at the expense of the country's poor and indigenous citizens.

Indian traditions and heritage have remained largely intact in both Oaxaca and neighboring Chiapas, encouraging richness and diversity in handicrafts, ethnic celebrations and regional cookery. Descendants of the Zapotec and Mixtec peoples live in small villages throughout the valley and in the mountains. Regional dialects abound, and for many residents—known as Oaxaqueños—Spanish is a second language.

This strong cultural identity has made Oaxaca one of Mexico's leading art centers. In the last few decades a group of artists, all native to the state, have converged here to produce artwork that is stylistically diverse but rooted in themes relating to the lives of the Indians who populate the many rural villages surrounding the city.

The setting would certainly inspire many an artist. The older buildings are constructed of an unusual greenish volcanic stone that takes on a golden

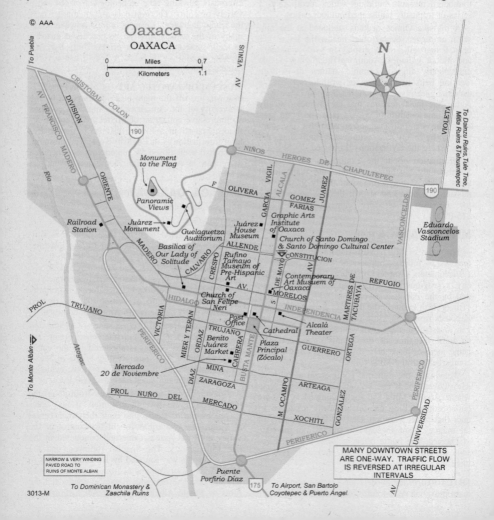

3013-M

tone when the sun is low on the horizon. Others are painted bright turquoise or pink. Bougainvillea and roses tumble over walls, geraniums spill out of huge clay pots, and when the jacaranda trees are in bloom they form masses of purple. Completing this colorful palette is the sky, which is most often an azure blue.

Be sure to sample the local cuisine. The state is known in particular for *mole* sauces, which incorporate a number of spices. There are distinct varieties, only *mole negro* employing the chocolate that also turns up in the *mole poblano* sauce of Puebla.

Other specialties are chicken and mole-filled *tamales oaxaqueños; tlayudas,* king-size tortillas that are topped with almost anything; *picadillo,* spicy shredded pork; and *quesillo,* a stringy Oaxacan cheese. The adventurous can try *chapulines* (fried grasshoppers) with a squeeze of lime and a dash of chili powder or garlic, sold in the food markets and by vendors at Plaza Principal.

The *comida corrida,* a fixed-item midday meal available at many local restaurants, is a good way to enjoy Oaxacan cooking at reasonable prices.

Planning Your Stay

The peak tourist seasons in Oaxaca are Holy Week *(Semana Santa)* and the Christmas season. But there are so many things to see and do that visitors could easily spend four or five days at any time of year. Allow at least a day to visit the principal downtown attractions; if you have a particular interest in colonial architecture, spend a day touring the cathedral and churches and another visiting the museums.

The bustling city markets are certainly worth a visit, especially on Saturdays; spend the morning shopping and take in a few downtown attractions in the afternoon. For nighttime entertainment—music, atmosphere, people watching—there's no better place than the main plaza.

Bus tours to nearby craft villages or town markets will fill up a full day. Of the nearby archeological sites, Monte Albán and Mitla *(see place listing)* are the most significant; plan on a full day at Monte Albán and half a day at Mitla. Excursions to these two sites could also be combined with a shopping expedition *(see "Village Day Trips").*

Many potholed detours lead in and out of Oaxaca; if you'd rather not drive, take a guided tour. Hotels and travel agencies offer various sightseeing packages. Itineraries include nearby market villages, craft centers and archeological sites, a general tour of the city or tours of churches and museums. A more expensive option is to hire a licensed guide, available through the State Tourism Office *(see "Practicalities").*

Practicalities

There are no direct U.S. flights to Oaxaca, but both Aeroméxico and Mexicana offer nonstop connecting flights from Mexico City. The domestic airlines Aero Caribe and Aviacsa have flights from nearby cities, including Cancún, Mérida, Tuxtla Gutiérrez and Villahermosa.

Oaxaca's Benito Juárez Airport is about 8 kilometers (5 miles) south of the city off Mex. 175. Transportes Terrestres minibus *(combi)* and taxi service between the airport and downtown hotels is easily arranged. Taxi fare averages around $8 (U.S.); *combis* are cheaper. For additional information about airlines *see "Arriving by Air,"* page 551.

A toll road running north to the city of Tehuacán reduces the amount of time it takes to travel by car between Oaxaca and Mexico City. The two-lane roadway features wider lanes, fewer curves and better-engineered grades than most other routes that travel through the mountains. It parallels Mex. 190 from Oaxaca northwest to the town of Nochixtlán, then travels north-northwest to Tehuacán, paralleling Mex. 131 for part of the way. Northwest of Tehuacán the road ties into Mex. 150-D, which proceeds west to Mexico City.

Bus service is available to and from Mexico City, but there are many stops along the 565-kilometer (350-mile) route. "Deluxe" service is provided by UNO and Cristóbal Colón, first-class service by ADO. The first-class bus station is about 1.5 kilometers northeast of downtown at Calzada Niños Héroes de Chapultepec #1036.

Local buses depart from the second-class bus station (about one kilometer west of Plaza Principal via Avenida Trujano). They're an economical way to travel to the archeological ruins and Indian villages, although trips can be excruciatingly slow along the narrow, winding mountain roads. For additional information about buses *see "Bus Service," page 68.*

Taxis are another way to get around town, and the fare to nearby destinations can be shared among several riders; negotiate the rate before you set out. Fares within the city center average around $2.25 (U.S.). Taxis line up around Plaza Principal.

Personal safety while staying in Oaxaca means such common-sense precautions as keeping your car in a lot overnight rather than parking it on the street, storing all valuables out of sight, and staying alert in such public places as markets and bus stations—professional pickpockets can be very smooth. Stick to established tourist areas, and avoid driving after dark.

Temperatures are mild to warm throughout the year, averaging in the 70s or 80s during the day and the 50s or 60s at night. May is the hottest month and the height of the dry season; the rainy season is from June through September. At this tropical latitude the sun can be quite strong; take the necessary precautions if you'll be outside all day. Sturdy, comfortable walking shoes also come in handy for exploring the ruins and trekking around the village markets. Avoid wearing skimpy or revealing clothing inside churches.

Special Events

Oaxaca's festivals, like the city itself, are dynamic, colorful and expansive. They draw big crowds, so hotel space should be booked well in advance for the Easter holiday and in July, November and December.

The Guelaguetza, meaning "offering," is a centuries-old festival celebrated throughout the state. Community troupes present their regional costumes, dances, songs and music in a specially designed, open-air theater (Auditorio Guelaguetza) built into the side of Cerro del Fortín, the hill in the northern part of the city. To reach the site, take Calzada Madero north to the Mex. 190 junction, then go east on Mex. 190 about 1.6 kilometers (1 mile).

A dizzying whirl of Oaxacan folk dance and musical performances comprise the Guelaguetza, as participating singers, dancers and musicians throw *guelaguetzas* (gifts) to spectators. An evening show presents the legend of Princess Donají, which includes staged re-enactments of battles between Zapotec and Mixtec warriors. Even if you have tickets, arrive early—at least by 8 a.m.—for the best seats. **Note:** Bring water, and wear a hat or appropriate headgear for protection from the strong sun.

Performances are given on the two successive Mondays following July 16. (In years when July 18—the anniversary of Benito Juárez's death—falls on a Monday, the dates are July 25 and Aug. 1.) Check in advance with a travel agency, the Oaxaca State Tourism Office or your hotel for the exact dates. Tickets, necessary for the main performances, should be reserved no later than May, preferably through a travel agent; confirm the exact festival dates when you make your reservations.

Holy Week, beginning the Friday before Easter Sunday, brings parades and communion services, and local churches sponsor fairs, concerts and other activities. Oaxaca celebrates the Day of the Dead (Día de Los Muertos) Oct. 31 and Nov. 1 and 2. The markets are ablaze with marigolds and sell all manner of offerings with which to decorate altars built to honor the deceased.

The Fiesta of the Virgen de la Soledad in mid-December is a Christmas season highlight and honors the city's patron saint with processions, fireworks, floats and dances. Dec. 23 brings the Night of the Radishes. For this competition the main plaza is filled with booths displaying local radishes carved into every conceivable shape. Sweets are served in clay dishes; after finishing the treat, fling your dish to the ground so it smashes.

Shopping

Oaxaca's markets are among Mexico's most exciting, with head-turning displays of crafts, foodstuffs, household products and curios. If you don't mind the crowds and noise, Saturdays provide the biggest spectacle, drawing Indians who come for miles around to buy and sell. Arrive unburdened so you can maintain your bearings amid the jostling, and be prepared to bargain—begin by offering to pay half the selling price for any item.

Look for leather goods, hand-loomed cottons, jewelry, carved idols and black pottery from the village of San Bartolo Coyotepec. Teotitlán and Ocotlán are weaving and pottery centers, respectively. Local artisans also create carved, brightly painted wooden animals that have whimsical or surreal expressions. Gold, silver and jade jewelry is often a reproduction of actual pieces found at Monte Albán or designed in a similar style.

The enormous Abastos Market (Mercado de Abastos), southwest of downtown on the periférico loop road, is one of Oaxaca's busiest. It is open daily but is most active on Saturday, when villagers dressed in native garb convene to display their merchandise in a huge warehouse and across blocks of open-air lots and canopied stalls.

This market is crammed with such items as shawls, embroidered blouses, pottery, woven baskets, rugs, toys, religious ornaments, woodcarvings and jewelry. The air is filled with the smells of incense, chocolate and tortillas. Abastos also is a produce and livestock market, and there are piles of dried chilies in a rainbow of colors, mounds of garlic bulbs, herbs, unfamiliar vegetables and tropical fruits.

One block south of Plaza Principal along Calle 20 de Noviembre is the indoor Benito Juárez Market, also busiest on Saturday. There are numerous food stalls here. Use appropriate caution when deciding whether or not to sample snacks; if you can see something being cooked it's usually safe to eat. Among the clothing items for sale are coarse-weave woolen sweaters, shawls and capes. In the next block south is the Mercado 20 de Noviembre, which offers *mole* sauces, Oaxacan chocolate and other foodstuffs, as well as a few craft stalls.

The Handicrafts Market (Mercado de Artesanías), a block southwest of the Mercado 20 de Noviembre at the corner of calles J.P. García and Zaragoza, specializes in textiles. The artisans can be observed as they weave rugs, wall hangings and *sarapes* on simple looms. Expect to bargain for any purchase.

If you don't relish the give-and-take of haggling, try one of Oaxaca's many fixed-price stores. The government-run FONART store, at Cempoaltépetl #409, Colonia Volcanes, sells a variety of representative crafts from all over the country. The state-run ARIPO (Artesanías y Industrias Populares del Estado de Oaxaca), Calle García Vigil #809, has rooms filled with Oaxacan black pottery, rugs and textiles. The store has an English-speaking staff and will ship purchases.

The Galería Arte de Oaxaca, 3 blocks north and 1 block east of Plaza Principal at Calle Murguía #105, is a gallery featuring the work of noted Oaxacan painters and sculptors. Víctor Artes Regionales, Porfirio Díaz #111 between Independencia and Morelos, is housed in a 17th-century monastery and specializes in locally handcrafted textiles, basketry, toys, masks and ceramics.

Calle M. Alcalá between the main square and the Church of Santo Domingo is a pedestrian boulevard lined with high-quality shops. La Mano Mágica,

Calle M. Alcalá #203, is a combination art gallery and crafts shop. It's known for finely woven rugs, particularly those by Teotitlán weaver Arnulfo Mendoza, and lovely pieces of regional folk art. Corazón del Pueblo, Calle M. Alcalá #307-329, stocks a distinctive collection of ceramic figurines, Huichol bead work, masks, painted wooden animals, jewelry and likenesses of Frida Kahlo by artisans from Oaxaca and elsewhere in Mexico.

If you'd like to support local artisans, visit MARO (Mujeres Artesanas de las Regiones de Oaxaca), Av. 5 de Mayo #204 between Morelos and Murguía. This cooperative benefiting women in the villages of the Oaxaca Valley offers a variety of handicrafts, including Atzompa and Coyotepec pottery, stamped tinware, leather bags, sandals, belts and toys.

Note: While it's easy to accumulate a trove of treasures, they may need to be shipped home. The better shops and stores can usually arrange for shipping, but this is not the case with items purchased at the markets or from craftspeople in the villages. The most important thing to remember in such cases is to procure a written receipt.

Village Day Trips

Excursions to area villages can be as rewarding as shopping in the city. The second-class bus station *(see "Practicalities")* has bus service to most of the villages; another option is to take an inexpensive taxi from a lot near the Abastos Market. Taxis serve the local population as well and fill up quickly in the morning; a per-person rate is charged.

Tianguis (open-air markets) take place on different days. Green-glazed pottery, including bowls from which breasts or lilies unexpectedly sprout, is the specialty at Atzompa, about 6 kilometers (4 miles) northwest of Oaxaca on Mex. 190. Also look for clay dolls. Market day is Tuesday. A variety of cheeses and mole sauces can be purchased at the Wednesday market at San Pablo Etla, 14 kilometers (9 miles) northwest on Mex. 190. Thursday's market at Ejutla, 61 kilometers (38 miles) south on Mex. 175, is agriculturally oriented as well.

Zaachila, about 18 kilometers (11 miles) southwest on the road to Cuilapan, also has a Thursday market that does not target tourists but is interesting for its produce and livestock displays and slice of Mexican village life. The raucous Friday market at Ocotlán, about 40 kilometers (25 miles) south on Mex. 175, is the busiest outside of Oaxaca. *Rebozos* (scarves or shawl-like garments), produce, leather goods, cutlery and whimsical ceramic figurines of women are among the many items for sale.

Other towns are known for a particular craft in which the entire populace seems to be involved. Arrazola, a tiny village southwest of Oaxaca near the ruins of Monte Albán, is noted for carvers who fashion fanciful wooden creatures painted in vivid colors. Second-class buses travel to Arrazola, and local youngsters will take you to the artisans' homes for a small tip.

San Bartolo Coyotepec, about 16 kilometers (10 miles) south of Oaxaca on Mex. 175, is the source of the distinctive black pottery sold in many Oaxaca shops. Buses and tours travel frequently to this village. Items can be purchased at the local factory, in shops around the plaza or from the potters' homes. Friday is market day.

The village of Guelatao, 63 kilometers (39 miles) north on Mex. 175, is the birthplace of Mexican president Benito Juárez. Guelatao's monument-studded plaza honors this native son, and lively celebrations are held on his birthday, Mar. 21. Although the journey to Guelatao offers impressive views at around 7,000 feet, motorists should exercise caution when negotiating the roadway's serpentine bends and potholes. Frequent drizzle also can make the road surface slippery. To fully enjoy the scenery, take a bus.

Oaxaca State Tourism Office (Secretaría de Desarrollo Turístico): downtown at Murguía #206. Open daily 8-8; phone (951) 514-0570 or (951) 516-0123.

What To See in and Around Town

ALCALA THEATER (Teatro Macedonio de Alcalá) is on Av. Independencia at Calle Armienta y Lopez, 2 blocks northeast of Plaza Principal. Built around the turn of the 20th century, the Alcalá reflects the grandiose style public buildings took under the rule of native son and dictator Porfirio Díaz. The interior in particular is plushly opulent. Open only for events; check with the State Tourism Office for schedule information.

BASILICA OF OUR LADY OF SOLITUDE (Basilica de la Soledad) is at Av. Independencia #107 (at Av. Galeana), about 5 blocks west of Plaza Principal. This massive 17th-century structure, actually a complex of several buildings and a garden, has a richly carved exterior. The basilica is dedicated to the Virgin of Solitude (Virgen de la Soledad). A statue of the Virgin, Oaxaca's patron saint, is displayed above the altar, draped in jewel-encrusted black velvet.

The interior is an extravagant showcase of baroque ornamentation. A museum to the rear of the church displays a replica of the Virgin statue. It also contains glass panels depicting the legend of her arrival in the city and an enormous assemblage of gifts (primarily miniature glass figurines) sent in tribute. Basilica open daily 7-2 and 4-9; museum Mon.-Sat. 10-2 and 4-6. Museum admission around 25 cents (U.S.).

CATHEDRAL faces the north side of Plaza Principal. Begun in 1563, the church was completed about 2 centuries later. Although severely damaged by earthquakes, the rebuilt cathedral, which is constructed of the native greenish stone, still reflects much of its original grandeur. The clock, its works made of wood, was presented by a Spanish king. The facade and central panel above the door are fine examples of baroque craftsmanship. Daily 7 a.m.-9 p.m. Free.

CHURCH OF SAN FELIPE NERI (Iglesia de San Felipe Neri) is on Av. Independencia at Calle Tinoco y Palacios, about 3 blocks northwest of Plaza Principal. The interior of this 17th-century baroque church features a lavish altar of carved, gilded wood and impressive wall frescoes. Daily 8 a.m.-10 p.m. Free.

 CHURCH OF SANTO DOMINGO (Iglesia de Santo Domingo) is at Gurrión, M. Alcalá, Berriozábal and Reforma, about 4 blocks north of Plaza Principal. Founded by the Dominicans in the mid-16th century, it took about a century to build. Even in a city (and country) of impressive churches, Santo Domingo has a well-deserved reputation as one of the most ornate. Every square inch of the interior walls and ceilings is covered with gold leaf, polychrome reliefs and plaster statues. Try to visit in the afternoon, when sunlight pouring through the stained-glass window casts everything in a golden glow.

One particularly noteworthy decoration, on the ceiling under the raised choir loft near the entrance, depicts crowned heads appearing on the branches of the family tree of Santo Domingo de Guzmán, founder of the Dominican order. The adjoining monastery now houses the Santo Domingo Cultural Center *(see attraction listing)*. Allow 2 hours minimum. Daily 7-1 and 5-8 p.m. Free.

CONTEMPORARY ART MUSEUM OF OAXACA (Museo de Arte Contemporáneo de Oaxaca, or MACO) is at Calle M. Alcalá #202, 2 blocks north of Plaza Principal. It occupies a turn-of-the-18th-century building also known as the House of Cortés (Casa de Cortés), so named for supposedly being a former residence of the conqueror (historians and chronology insist otherwise). Changing exhibits in this beautifully restored colonial building feature the work of contemporary artists, both regional and international. Wed.-Mon. 10:30-8. Admission around $1.25 (U.S.); free to all Sun. Phone (951) 514-2818.

DAINZU RUINS are about 24 km (15 mi.) southeast of Oaxaca on a dirt road off Mex. 190, on the way to Mitla; watch for the turnoff. They date from 600 to 200 B.C. and are believed to be one of the final evidences of Olmec civilization in the Oaxaca region. A pyramidal structure (Edificio A) shows artwork portraying ball players, and there also is a partially restored ball court. A caretaker is available to guide visitors around the site. Daily 8-5. Admission around $2.50 (U.S.); free to all Sun.

DOMINICAN MONASTERY is in the town of Cuilapan, about 16 km (10 mi.) southwest of Oaxaca via a paved road. Never completed, it dates from 1555. A roofless cloister stands beyond the monastery; another church has been restored and is in use. It has a Renaissance-style facade and contains a

number of frescoes. Vicente Guerrero, one of Mexico's first presidents, was executed at this site on Feb. 14, 1831; a monument marks the spot. His remains lie in the base of the Independence Monument in Mexico City. Daily 9-5. Admission around $4 (U.S.).

GRAPHIC ARTS INSTITUTE OF OAXACA (Instituto de Artes Gráficas de Oaxaca) is at M. Alcalá #507, across from the Church of Santo Domingo. It was created primarily through the efforts of celebrated Oaxacan artist Francisco Toledo. The institute has a collection of more than 5,000 engravings that includes his work, that of fellow Mexicans Rufino Tamayo and José Guadalupe Posada, and international artists. There also is an extensive library of art-related volumes. Daily 10:30-8. Donations requested. Phone (951) 516-2045.

JUAREZ HOUSE MUSEUM (Museo Casa de Juárez) is about 6 blocks north of Plaza Principal at García Vigil #609. This 19th-century colonial home was once owned by Padre Antonio Salanueva. The Salanuevas brought a young Oaxaqueño, Benito Juárez, from the village of Guelatao to live with them; Juárez's resulting education was the springboard for his careers in law and politics. The house is furnished to reflect a typical Oaxacan middle class lifestyle in the 19th century. Tues.-Sun. 10-7. Admission around $3 (U.S.); free to all Sun. Phone (951) 516-1860.

MONTE ALBAN RUINS are about 10 km (6 mi.) southwest of Oaxaca; if driving, take Calle Trujano west out of town across the Río Atoyac; it becomes the narrow, winding road to the ruins. One of Mexico's greatest pre-Columbian sites, Monte Albán presides over the valley of Oaxaca from a mountaintop location. This major religious center was built by the Zapotecs around 600 B.C. atop a summit that was deliberately flattened. At its height around A.D. 300, Monte Albán supported 40,000 inhabitants. The city was taken over in the 10th century by the Mixtecs, who were in turn conquered by the Aztecs, and fell into ruin around the time of the Spanish conquest.

The site's focal point is the Great Plaza, a grassy area about 970 feet long and 650 feet wide, bounded by four large ceremonial platforms. It was leveled by hewing away rock outcroppings. All of the buildings are aligned on a precise north-south axis except for one, an observatory believed to be placed in relation to the stars rather than to compass directions. Many of the structures are roped off from visitors.

An I-shaped ball court dominates one corner of the plaza. One of the most fascinating buildings is the Temple of the Dancers *(danzantes)*, on the west side of the plaza. The oldest building at the site, it is named for the elaborate figures carved into its stone slabs. They were first thought to be dancers but may be representations of the diseased or cadavers used for study in a school of medicine.

Some 170 subterranean tombs are scattered throughout the ruins. These contain numerous slab paintings, glyphs, frescoes and stone carvings. Tombs 104 and 105 can be entered by climbing down a ladder, but aren't always open. In 1932, Tomb 7 (near the site entrance) yielded a priceless collection of items, which are on display at the Santo Domingo Cultural Center.

Autobuses Turísticos tour buses depart for Monte Albán several times a day from the Rivera del Angel Hotel at Calle Mina #518 (round-trip fare around $4 U.S.). The journey to the site is very slow but very scenic. There is a museum (with exhibit information in Spanish only), a bookstore and a casual restaurant at the site entrance. Licensed guide service is available for a fee.

Note: Sporadic outbursts of politically motivated violence occur from time to time in the states of Chiapas, Guerrero and Oaxaca. The U.S. Department of State's Bureau of Consular Affairs recommends that visitors to this part of Mexico—and Chiapas in particular—contact the U.S. Embassy for additional security information before traveling. Food is available. Allow 3 hours minimum. Daily 8-6. Admission around $4 (U.S.); free to all Sun. The fee for using a video camera is around $5.

PLAZA PRINCIPAL is bordered by avs. Hidalgo, Miguel Cabrera, Guerrero and Valdivieso. Old World charm makes this one of Mexico's most enjoyable plazas. Indian laurel trees shade the square; fountains decorate some of the walkways, and a wrought-iron gazebo and bandstand stands at its center. Early evening, when a formal flag-lowering ceremony is performed and people start to gather, is a good time to visit.

Plaza Principal really comes alive as darkness falls. Street musicians materialize and offer impromptu performances. Vendors hawk ice cream, roast corn, pineapple chunks, *chorizo* (sausage), musical instruments, balloons, children's toys and tin skeletons dancing on the end of sticks. Band concerts—from brass to marimba to Oaxacan rock—take place regularly.

RUFINO TAMAYO MUSEUM OF PRE-HISPANIC ART (Museo Rufino Tamayo de Arte Prehispanico) is at Av. Morelos #503, 4 blocks northwest of Plaza Principal. It spotlights the private collection of artist Rufino Tamayo, which he donated to his native city. Housed in a restored, 16th-century colonial mansion, it includes artifacts from Teotihuacán, Nayarit state, and the Olmec, Maya, Totonac and Aztec civilizations. Figurines, sculpture and other works are handsomely displayed in the series of brightly colored rooms. Exhibit information is in Spanish.

Wed.-Sat. and Mon. 10-2 and 4-7, Sun. 10-3. Admission around S2.75 (U.S.). Phone (951) 516-4750.

SANTO DOMINGO CULTURAL CENTER is next to the Church of Santo Domingo. Housed in a beautifully restored former Dominican convent, it charts the course of human development in the Valley of Oaxaca.

The showcase exhibits focus on some 500 pieces of priceless jewelry and art objects—goblets, urns, masks, breastplates—made of gold, turquoise, jade, amber and obsidian that were found in Tomb 7 of the Monte Albán ruins. The museum also contains fascinating, carefully organized collections of regional handicrafts, costumes worn by the different Indian groups within the state, and archeological artifacts. Information is presented in Spanish.

Tours with English-speaking guides are available; inquire at the information desk. Allow 2 hours minimum. Tues.-Sun. 10-7:45. Admission around $4.50 (U.S.); free to all Sun. Phone (951) 516-2991.

TULE TREE (Arbol del Tule) is in the village of Santa María del Tule, about 10 km (6 mi.) southeast of Oaxaca on Mex. 190. This colossal specimen of a Mexican cypress, or *ahuehuete,* is believed to be at least 2,000 years old. The tree stands in the local churchyard and measures more than 150 feet both in height and around its base. Churchyard open daily 9-5. Admission around 50 cents (U.S.).

ZAACHILA RUINS are in Zaachila, about 18 km (11 mi.) southwest of Oaxaca past the village of Cuilapan; the site, behind the town church on the main plaza, is marked "Zona Arqueológica." Archeologists exploring this final stronghold of the Mixtec empire uncovered two tombs built between 700 A.D. and 1050. The treasures within Tomb 2 were excavated in 1962 and transferred to the National Museum of Anthropology in Mexico City. There also are several pre-Hispanic remains in the vicinity of the plaza. Archeological site open daily 9-4. Admission around $2 (U.S.).

PALENQUE, CHIAPAS (H-10)

The Maya ruins of Palenque (pah-LEHN-keh), designated a World Heritage Site by UNESCO in 1987, are among the most impressive and perhaps the most haunting in Mexico. They occupy the lower foothills of the Sierra Madre in one of the country's wettest, most lushly forested regions.

Palenque most likely began as a farming settlement around 150 B.C. and flourished between A.D. 600 and 800, when the city ruled an area covering much of the present-day states of Chiapas and Tabasco. It was abandoned around A.D. 900 for reasons unknown but still debated by historians.

The ruins, near the town of Palenque, are some 145 kilometers (90 miles) southeast of Villahermosa. Large-scale excavations in the 1920s under the supervision of Danish explorer Frans Blom (*see San Cristóbal de las Casas*) began clearing away centuries of earth and encroaching jungle. Subsequent excavations have brought to light significant knowledge about Palenque, its inhabitants, its culture and its central role within the Maya empire.

The excavated section—small in relation to the city's size during its heyday more than 1,000 years ago—spreads a mile or so from east to west. The structures here are among the best preserved in Mesoamerica. Stone plaques at the individual temples offer descriptions in English, Spanish and Maya.

One of the most impressive is the 90-foot-tall Temple of the Inscriptions (Templo de las Inscripciones), to the right as you enter the site. The climb to the top of this stairstepped, pyramidal structure is slow going but manageable, and well worth the effort for the panoramic view of the surrounding buildings.

This temple was the final resting place of Pacal, the king who ruled Palenque for almost 70 years beginning at the ripe old age of 12. It is believed to be one of the only temples in Mexico constructed expressly to be a tomb. The royal crypt has relief carvings on the walls and contains the massive carved stone sarcophagus lid. It is reached by descending a steep flight of stone block stairs. The steps can be slippery, and those subject to claustrophobia will want to avoid the dank, stuffy atmosphere and stay above ground. **Note:** The crypt was closed for restoration work in 2001, and both it and the temple may have restricted visitor access.

Next to the Temple of the Inscriptions is Temple XIII, where another tomb was discovered in 1994. Just east is the Palace, a complex of stepped buildings and four courtyards connected by corridors and an extensive system of underground passageways. The exterior walls are adorned with the beautifully carved, unusually well-preserved panels and stucco reliefs for which Palenque is famous.

Other groups of structures are in various stages of restoration. Cross the Río Otolum (little more than a stream) to reach the Temple of the Cross, at the southeastern edge of the ruins. It is one of several structures ringing a spacious plaza. Projecting upward from the temple are vertical roof combs, a decorative architectural feature favored by Maya builders. Inside the building is a small shrine.

Nearby are Temple 14, which contains more stone tablets with carved inscriptions, and the Temple of the Sun, believed to contain the tomb of Pacal's son, Chan-Bahlum, his successor to the throne.

At the site's northern end is the Northern Group of buildings, including a ball court 'and the Temple of the Count, named for Frederick Waldeck, an early explorer. This structure, the best preserved of the group, is made up of five stepped tiers; its main facade faces east.

General Information and Activities

Travel agencies in Villahermosa, Tuxtla Gutiérrez and San Cristóbal de Las Casas can provide information on reaching Palenque by first-class bus; the trip takes 2 to 3 hours from Villahermosa and about 6 hours from Tuxtla Gutiérrez. Although the ruins can be adequately toured in half a day, staying overnight makes for a less hurried agenda.

From Villahermosa, motorists should take Mex. 186 to Catazajá, then Mex. 199 south to the ruins. Passing through lush countryside, the roadway is generally straight, although slick during the June-through-October rainy season and potholed at any time of year. Mex. 199 intersects Avenida Juárez about half a mile west of the town of Palenque's main plaza; the junction is designated by a large statue of a Maya chieftain's head. The road to the ruins branches west off Mex. 199 less than half a mile south of this junction; the site entrance is about 8 kilometers (5 miles) from the turnoff.

Palenque town has little to offer tourists, although there are hotels and restaurants around the main plaza. If you arrive by first-class bus, *colectivo* shuttle buses and taxis run between the center of town and the ruins.

The winter months—November through February—are a better time to visit than in the summer, which is oppressively hot and humid. Arrive early to avoid both the heat and the crowds, and wear a hat and sunblock for protection from the sun. An all-weather jacket or other rain gear will come in handy at any time. Insect repellent is necessary if you plan on doing any exploring or clambering around the ruins, particularly in the late afternoon.

A combined museum and visitor center, located on the ruins access road about a mile before the site entrance, contains a refreshment stand and shops selling Chiapan handicrafts. The museum displays reproductions of hieroglyphic panels and other artifacts uncovered at the ruins, with explanations in both Spanish and English. Local vendors peddle souvenirs in the large parking lot at the site entrance, where the ticket booth is located.

Note: Sporadic outbursts of politically motivated violence occur from time to time in the states of Chiapas, Guerrero and Oaxaca. The U.S. Department of State's Bureau of Consular Affairs recommends that visitors to this part of Mexico—and Chiapas in particular—contact the U.S. Embassy for additional security information before traveling. Food is available. Allow 3 hours minimum.

Site open daily 8-5; museum daily 9-4. Admission (includes museum) 48 pesos (around $5 U.S.); the fee to use a video camera is $4 (U.S.).

Chiapas State Tourism Office: intersection of Avenida Juárez and Abasolo, a block from the main plaza; open Mon.-Sat. 9-9, Sun. 9-1. Information on transportation to the ruins can be obtained here.

Points of Interest

AGUA AZUL WATERFALLS NATURAL PARK (Parque Nacional Cascadas de Agua Azul) is about 62 km (39 mi.) south of Palenque off Mex. 199, toward the town of Ocosingo; the park entrance is about 5 km (3 mi.) off the highway via a turnoff. A series of cascades plunge into turquoise pools that have a tropical jungle setting. Swimming is permitted, but the current can be strong and submerged rocks are hazardous. Outdoor restaurants serving fish dishes line the walking path (an uphill trek) along the falls. Intentional burning in April and May to clear the jungle can result in a thick haze of smoke. The water also is murky and silt-laden after heavy rains.

A closer waterfall, Misol-Ha, is about 19 kilometers (12 miles) south of Palenque off Mex. 199; watch for the signed turnoff. Equally beautiful, it drops 90 feet into a wide pool. Weekends and holidays at both locations are crowded. Travel agencies in Palenque offer day trip packages; inquire along Avenida Juárez near the main plaza. Open daily. Admission to Agua Azul 10 pesos (around $1 U.S.) per vehicle, 10 pesos per person; to Misol-Ha, 10 pesos per person.

PAPANTLA, VERACRUZ (B-11)
pop. 48,600

Papantla (pah-PAHN-tlah) spreads out over the green foothills of the Sierra Madre Oriental, about 243 kilometers (150 miles) northwest of Veracruz. This was the capital of the Totonac kingdom in the mid-15th century, before it fell to the conquering Aztecs. The vanquished Totonacs extracted a revenge of sorts by aiding Hernando Cortés in defeating the Aztec empire. The city remains a center of Totonac culture today, and visitors are likely to see locals wearing native garb: billowing white pants and sailor shirts for men, lacy skirts and embroidered white blouses for women.

This is Mexico's vanilla-producing center, and the distinctively sweet scent frequently hovers in the air. Vanilla bean pods are fashioned into small figures that are sold around town, along with textiles, embroidered clothing and baskets. Souvenir hunters also can try the Hidalgo Market (Mercado Hidalgo), on Avenida 20 de Noviembre just off the northwest corner of the main plaza, for handmade men's and women's clothing.

Papantla is celebrated for its Papantla Flyers (Voladores de Papantla), Totonac Indians who give an exciting rendition of the "Flying Pole" dance. Ropes that have been wound around a 70-foot-tall pole are tied around their waists. Four dancers jump backward off a tiny revolving platform atop the pole, whirling downwards as the ropes unwind. A fifth man, who dances while playing a flute and beating a drum, remains on top of the platform. Each performer revolves around the pole 13 times; the total number of revolutions, 52, equals the number of years in the Aztec religious life cycle.

Before it evolved into a crowd-pleasing spectacle of its own, the dance was part of a pre-Hispanic agricultural ceremony designed to secure the favor of the rain gods and to celebrate the vanilla harvest. The dancers perform up to three times a day during the Festival of Corpus Christi in late May and early June. Papantla's signature annual event, the festival is celebrated with art exhibitions, traditional dances, cockfights and fireworks displays.

Overlooking the city from a hilltop is a giant likeness of a flute-playing *volador*, a monument erected in 1988. There are good views of the surrounding countryside from the base of the statue, which can be reached by walking up Avenida Reforma from the cathedral.

The first-class Autobuses del Oriente (ADO) bus station is at the intersection of avenidas Venustiano Carranza and Benito Juárez, north of Plaza Tellez (*see attraction listing*). From the station there is service to Jalapa and Veracruz.

Tourist information office: on Avenida 16 de Septiembre in a building opposite the cathedral.

EL TAJIN is about 13 kilometers (8 miles) west of Papantla via a paved road. The main reason to come to Papantla is to visit El Tajín (tah-HEEN). Some of the site has been restored, although archeologists estimate that hundreds of ruined buildings remain hidden beneath the jungle growth. The ruins were discovered in the late 18th century; a major restoration project began in 1992, the same year that El Tajín was designated a World Heritage Site by UNESCO. More than 30 buildings have since been restored, although many more hidden under grassy mounds await excavation.

The excavated structures are divided into two main groups. In the main group is the most impressive structure, the Pyramid of the Niches. Its seven terraces are punctuated with a total of 365 corniced, deeply recessed square niches. A steep staircase with bordering ramps ascends the east side. A smaller pyramid, Building 5, is just south, as is the South Ball Court, the largest and best-preserved of the site's several ball courts.

North of the Pyramid of the Niches, an uphill pathway leads to a newer group of buildings called El Tajín Chico (Little Tajín). Overlooking this complex is the Building of the Columns; the six richly carved column shafts—three on each side—once supported a ceiling. A Maya arch forms the entrance to Building A. Building C, a pyramid, features stone fretwork similar to that adorning the Pyramid of the Niches.

A museum at the entrance displays artifacts retrieved from the excavations as well as a scale model of the entire site. The flying pole dance performed in town also takes place here (the pole is near the museum) whenever there are enough tourists—usually touring groups—to form an appreciative crowd. A $2 (U.S.) donation is requested to watch the spectacle, which is not without risk to its daredevil performers.

Note: Visitors should stay on the cleared pathways between the buildings; the thick underbrush in this part of Mexico is likely to be inhabited by poisonous snakes. Climbing the pyramids is not permitted. Bring a water bottle and wear a hat and sunblock for protection, as the site has little shade.

White minibuses marked "Chote/Tajín" depart for the site from Avenida 16 de Septiembre (running along the uphill side of the cathedral) on the main plaza. The tourist information office can provide information about bus or minibus service to the ruins, although English is not likely to be spoken. It's easier to reach the site in your own vehicle or visit it as part of an organized bus tour. Daily 8-5. Admission (includes site and museum) around $5 (U.S.); free to all Sun. The fee to use a video camera is $3.50.

PLAZA TELLEZ is terraced into a hillside in the center of town. White-tiled and palm-shaded, it has benches inlaid with tile mosaics. On the plaza's south side is the Cathedral of Our Lady of the Assumption (Catedral de Nuestra Señora de la Asunción). Carved into the church's north wall is the Tribute to the Totonac Culture (Homenaje a la Cultura Totonaca), a 165-foot-long stone mural. It depicts Totonac folkloric figures and is dominated by a rendering of the plumed serpent Quetzalcóatl that runs its entire length.

SAN CRISTOBAL DE LAS CASAS, CHIAPAS (I-10) pop. 118,200, elev. 6,888´

San Cristóbal (sahn krees-TOH-bahl) de Las Casas was settled in 1528 by troops of Hernando Cortés under the command of Diego de Mazariegos, who later became the governor of Cuba. In a fertile basin ringed by the Chiapas Mountains, it was once capital of the state. San Cristóbal, a beautiful colonial city that has been designated a national historic monument, is located in an especially scenic, though remote, part of Mexico where rain-laden clouds brush the tops of forested ridges.

Although well into the tropics, the altitude and frequent heavy cloud cover lend San Cristóbal a decidedly nontropical feeling. The air is redolent with the smoky fragrance of burning *ocote* (a Náhuatl Indian word meaning "kindlewood"), a pitch-pine kindling sold in the markets. This also is where Central America begins, culturally if not politically; the border with Guatemala lies little more than 160 kilometers (100 miles) southeast.

The city center's narrow streets were designed for carriages rather than cars. Old houses with grilled windows give it a look that is stylistically Spanish, although the atmosphere is definitely Indian. The local population supplies the markets with handwoven fabrics, handcrafted leather articles, ornamental candles, wooden toys, and earthenware jugs and vases. While most men in San Cristóbal wear contemporary-style clothing, you'll see older women dressed in traditional Maya garb.

Plaza 31 de Marzo, the main plaza, is a good starting point for exploring. Some of the carvings adorning San Cristóbal's 16th-century Cathedral, flanking the plaza's north side, are missing their heads. The bright yellow exterior is particularly lovely in the late afternoon sun.

Three blocks south of the plaza, just off Avenida Miguel Hidalgo, is the 1587 Church of El Carmen (Templo del Carmen), which has a street passing through the middle of its four-story arch. In the hills east of the center of town is the Church of the Virgin of Guadalupe.

The Spring Fair (Feria de Primavera) takes place the week after Easter. The merriment includes parades, bullfights, band concerts, handicraft exhibits, amusement rides and stalls serving an array of regional foods. The Fiesta of San Cristóbal, held July 17-25, honors San Cristóbal's patron saint. Pilgrims carrying torches climb the steep hill to the Church

of San Cristóbal *(see attraction listing)* to attend special services.

Mex. 190 runs through the southern part of town; the official name is Boulevard Juan Sabines, but it's known locally as "El Bulevar." From San Cristóbal west to Tuxtla Gutiérrez, Mex. 190 winds for some 83 kilometers (51 miles) in a series of S-curves around high mountain peaks, frequently above cloud level. The altitude drops some 5,000 feet between the two cities. A drive through this region passes beautiful, unspoiled scenery, but slippery pavement can make the roadway dangerous. Motorists should maintain a speed appropriate to conditions and exercise caution, particularly around curves.

"Deluxe" and first-class bus service to and from Mérida, Oaxaca, Tuxtla Gutiérrez and Villahermosa is offered by Autotransportes Cristóbal Colón, ADO and UNO. These three lines share a bus terminal at the intersection of Mex. 190 and Avenida Insurgentes, about 9 blocks south of the main plaza.

Nearby Destinations

The ethnic peoples populating the nearby communities north of San Cristóbal are among the most interesting in the country. They have managed—over hundreds of years and despite the drastic modernization much of Mexico has undergone—to maintain their cultural identity. Although almost all are members of the Tzeltal and Tzotzil tribes, the inhabitants of these mountain villages maintain a striking variety of differences in manner of dress, dialect, and religious customs and ceremonies.

Among the handicrafts produced by village artisans are wooden musical instruments, leather goods, ceramics, furniture and woven baskets. The best time to visit is during a fiesta or on Sunday, when most of the villages have their own market and tourists are most welcomed.

San Juan Chamula, about 10 kilometers (6 miles) northwest of San Cristóbal via a paved road, is the best known. The municipality of Chamula is divided into three areas—San Juan, Sebastian and San Pedro—that are home to some 70,000 people. Spanish is not spoken, and English is rarely heard.

Daily dress varies according to the village. In San Juan Chamula, men wear short or long white trousers secured by a leather belt and a black, grey or white wool *jorongo* (a sort of sleeveless jacket). Standard garb for women, regardless of the village, is the *huipil* (a white blouse with colorful embroidery), a black wool skirt and a blue or red shawl. Many women run colorful ribbons through their hair, which is traditionally worn in long braids.

The town church (Templo de San Juan Bautista) stands next to the main plaza and has a beautifully carved wooden door. Inside the floor is strewn with pine needles, and the smell of incense wafts throughout. Statues of saints line the walls, although they play a part in church rituals in name only; Catholicism is not observed by the Chamulans. You must obtain a 10-peso ticket (around $1

U.S.) to enter the church; tickets are available at the local tourist office on the main plaza. **Note:** Visitors may stand and observe quietly in the background while rituals are being performed, but photography is strictly forbidden. Do not wear a hat inside.

The town is noted for its religious observances, particularly those celebrated during Holy Week (between Palm Sunday and Easter Sunday). A blend of Christian and pagan rites, the ceremonies take place both inside the church and in the plaza in front of it. On June 24, a Catholic priest visits the village to baptize newborn children.

Carnaval celebrations, featuring a parade of vivid costumes, take place just before Lent. The Feast of St. John the Baptist (San Juan Bautista), the patron saint of San Juan Chamula, is observed June 22-25 with much merriment. Chamulans also celebrate— along with the rest of Mexico—the Day of the Dead Nov. 2, the Feast Day of the Virgin of Guadalupe Dec. 12 and celebrations of Jesus' birth during the Christmas season.

Zinacantán is about 11 kilometers (7 miles) northwest of San Cristóbal; the road to this village forks west off the road to San Juan Chamula and descends into a valley. It's a bit more prosperous than Chamula; villagers' clothing often incorporates the colors pink and purple and is adorned with tassels. Zinacantán's side-by-side churches also have floors covered in pine needles, but the rituals here incorporate Catholicism to a greater degree. Photography, both inside and out, is strictly prohibited, and you may be escorted rather than being allowed to enter on your own.

A visit to any local village involves sensitivity, as you are an outsider and may well be made to feel like one. Picture taking is forbidden at most events, particularly so inside churches, and residents may not take kindly to being stared at. Photography of any sort is generally objected to, so keep cameras packed. Youthful vendors in San Juan Chamula, many of whom live in desperate poverty, will hawk tourists aggressively.

Chiapas State Tourism Office (Secretaría de Turismo): Av. Hidalgo #1B, just south of the main plaza. Open Mon.-Sat. 8-8, Sun. 9-2; phone (967) 678-6570. The municipal tourist office is located in the City Hall (Palacio Municipal) building on the main plaza, opposite the cathedral. Open Mon.-Sat. 9-8; phone (967) 678-0665.

Check the bulletin board there for notices pertaining to cultural events and guided tours, and at each office about arranging excursions to points of interest in and around San Cristóbal.

Shopping areas: The Central Market, 8 blocks north of the main plaza between Avenida General M. Utrilla and Belisario Domínguez, stands out due to the colorful outfits worn by merchants and customers. It's open every morning but Sunday, when the local village markets take over. Produce and household items dominate the open-air portion; butcher stalls are within the covered section. **Note:**

Avoid taking pictures of vendors or shoppers at the market.

If you're searching for handicrafts, try the shops along Calle Real de Guadalupe in the blocks just east of the main plaza.

What To See

AMBER MUSEUM (Museo del Ambar) is 4 blocks west of the main plaza on Av. Mazariegos. Housed in a former convent, this is perhaps the only museum in Mexico devoted to amber, a brownish-yellow, translucent fossil resin that is mined in the nearby Simojovel Valley. On view are sculpted amber pieces carved by local artisans, as well as ancient chunks with fossilized insects inside. Tues.-Sun. 10-2 and 4-7. Admission 10 pesos (around $1 U.S.).

CHURCH OF SAN CRISTOBAL (Templo de San Cristóbal) perches atop a hill at the end of Calle Hermanos Domínguez; walk 3 blocks south of the main plaza along Av. Miguel Hidalgo, then turn right. Although you'll have to climb what seems like an endless series of steps up the hill to reach the church, the view of the city from the lookout point (*mirador*) at the top is worth it.

NA-BOLOM MUSEUM is about 10 blocks northeast of the main plaza at Av. Vicente Guerrero #33. It celebrates the work of Danish explorer and ethnologist Frans Blom. The colonial-style building, dating from 1891 and now a museum, was purchased by Blom in 1950.

Blom conducted extensive research at the Maya ruins around Palenque, and oversaw some of the first excavations at Uxmal (*see separate listing under Yucatán Peninsula*). His wife Gertrude, a journalist and photographer, devoted herself to preserving the rain forest homeland of the reclusive Lacandón Indians. Na-Bolom continues to operate as a private, nonprofit institute dedicated to the preservation of the environment and native cultures.

Guided group tours of the home take in a collection of pre-Hispanic artifacts put together by Blom; the library, with thousands of volumes about the Maya and Chiapas; a walk through the extensive gardens; and a showing of the film "La Reina de la Selva," about the Lacandón forest and its inhabitants. Tours are offered Tues.-Sun. at 11:30 and 4:30. Tour fee 45 pesos (around $4.50 U.S.). Phone (967) 678-1418.

TEMPLE AND EX-CONVENT OF SANTO DOMINGO is about 5 blocks north of the main plaza, entered from Av. 20 de Noviembre. Construction of the church was begun in 1547; the extravagantly detailed carvings on its baroque exterior have weathered to a dusty pink. Inside are numerous representations of saints. An adjacent convent houses a handicraft showroom selling wool capes, clothing, woven goods and other Indian-made items. Showroom open Tues.-Sat. 9-2 and 4-6. Church admission free.

Altos Cultural Center (Centro Cultural de Los Altos) is within the convent complex. This museum has exhibits pertaining to San Cristóbal and Maya history, set around a courtyard overlooked by wide balconies. Information is in Spanish. Tues.-Sun. 10-5. Admission 30 pesos (around $3 U.S.).

TAXCO, GUERRERO (D-9)
pop. 51,500, elev. 5,897′

Probably the oldest mining town in North America, Taxco (TAHS-coh) originated as the Indian village of Tlachco (meaning "place of ball game") when Hernando Cortés' captains discovered rich gold deposits. The restored Hacienda del Chorrillo, where they handled smelted silver shipments, is now the governor's guest house and can be visited. Bermeja Hill still bears the scar of a cavernous mining shaft called the King's Shaft, reputed to be the oldest on the continent. The town's real development dates from the time of José de la Borda, a French miner who arrived in 1716 and amassed an immense fortune.

Borda's initial impact on the mining industry was carried on by a young American named William Spratling, who came to Taxco in 1929 to write a book. Stranded in Mexico after his publisher went broke, Spratling turned to the silver business. He opened a retail outlet and found apprentices among the local youth, many of whom went on to become proprietors of Taxco's silver shops.

Plaza Borda, Taxco's main square, is typical of those in other old Mexican towns, shaded by trees, offering benches for relaxation and providing a bandstand for musical performances. The shops in and around the plaza specialize in silver, and shopping for it is undoubtedly the most popular tourist activity in town. The range of items in Taxco's more than 300 silver shops covers everything from inexpensive trinkets to artistic pieces selling for hundreds of dollars.

The price of most pieces is determined primarily by weight, and many shops sell both retail (*menudeo*) and wholesale (*mayoreo*). Always check for the stamp bearing the numerals ".925," which certifies that it is at least 92.5 percent sterling silver, and for the two-letter initials signifying the manufacturer. If you're looking for items at the less expensive end of the scale, try the Silver Market (Mercado de Artesanías Plata), a block or so southeast of Plaza Borda; the stalls here carry a huge selection of rings, chains and other jewelry.

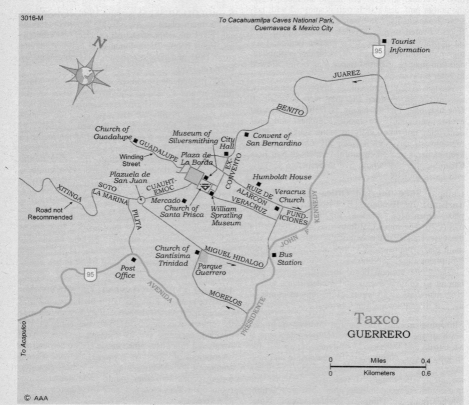

3016-M

To Cacahuamilpa Caves National Park, Cuernavaca & Mexico City

Tourist Information

95

JUAREZ

BENITO

Church of Guadalupe

GUADALUPE

Museum of Silversmithing

City Hall

Convent of San Bernardino

Winding Street

Plaza de La Borda

EX-CONVENTO

Plazuela de San Juan

CUAUHTEMOC

Humboldt House

SOTO

LA MARINA

RUIZ DE ALARCON

Veracruz Church

XITINGA

Mercado

VERACRUZ

Road not Recommended

PILITA

Church of Santa Prisca

William Spratling Museum

FUNDICIONES

KENNEDY

JOHN F.

Church of Santisima Trinidad

MIGUEL HIDALGO

Bus Station

Post Office

95

Parque Guerrero

AVENIDA

MORELOS

PRESIDENTE

Taxco
GUERRERO

To Acapulco

Miles   0   0.4
Kilometers   0   0.6

© AAA

Much pageantry is associated with Holy Week (Semana Santa). On Palm Sunday an image of Christ on a donkey departs the nearby village of Tehuilotepec, east of town, for a processional to Taxco. Candlelit processions by *penitentes* take place nightly, culminating on Holy Thursday, when the Last Supper is staged in front of the Church of Santa Prisca (*see attraction listing*). The Resurrection re-enactment takes place on Saturday evening, and another processional occurs on Easter Sunday. If you plan on being in town during Holy Week, make hotel reservations in advance.

The weeklong National Silver Fair (Feria Nacional de la Plata), held the last week in November or the first week in December, is Mexico's most important silversmithing contest. Each year judges confer international recognition to artisans whose designs and workmanship are deemed superior.

Another annual event of interest to visitors is Alarcón Days (Jornadas Alarconianas). This cultural and artistic festival offers painting expositions, band serenades in Plaza Borda and musical performances during the last three weekends in May; check with the State Tourism Office (*see below*) for exact dates. Presentations of plays by Juan Ruiz de Alarcón, a Taxco native born of noble Spanish parentage who wrote his works during the same period as Miguel de Cervantes, are given in plazas and city streets.

Steep, narrow roads, infrequent street name designations and many one-way streets make driving in Taxco difficult. Walking is the best way to explore. *Combis* are a convenient and inexpensive means of local transportation; rides in these white Volkswagen minibuses are around 30 cents (U.S.) in town. Taxi fares in town average around $1.50; taxis also are available for visiting points of interest in the surrounding area.

"Tour guides" will eagerly approach visitors around Plaza Borda. Ask to see their credentials, and beware of freelance guides who are not federally licensed or government sponsored. The State Tourism Office can recommend a reliable licensed guide. The Hotel Loma Linda, at the southern end of town at Av. de Los Plateros #52, organizes city walking tours; for information phone (762) 622-0206 or 622-0753.

Malasia Tours, a local travel agency, offers guided tours to Cacahuamilpa Caves National Park (*see attraction listing*) and the Xochicalco Ruins (*see Cuernavaca listing under Mexico City and Vicinity*). The agency is located at Plazuela de San Juan #5; phone (762) 622-3808 (English spoken).

Guerrero State Tourism Office (Secretaría de Fomento Turístico): Av. J.F. Kennedy #1 (Mex. 95), at the north end of town where the aqueduct arches cross the highway. Open daily 9-8; phone (762) 622-6616.

CACAHUAMILPA CAVES NATIONAL PARK (Parque Nacional Grutas de Cacahuamilpa) is at the intersection of Mex. 166 and Mex. 55, about 32 km (20 mi.) northeast of Taxco. Spelunkers have burrowed more than 8 miles through the passageways of Grutas de Cacahuamilpa (kah-kah-wah-MEEL-pah) and still haven't reached the end. About half a mile of the vast labyrinth can be viewed from wide, paved pathways.

Huge chambers—100 feet high, 200 feet long and nearly as wide—hold an array of fantastic formations, some of which are enhanced by lighting. Comfortable walking shoes are recommended. Spanish-speaking guides lead regularly scheduled, 90-minute tours of the caverns. Daily 10-6. Admission around $3.50 (U.S.), children around $2.25.

CHURCH OF SANTA PRISCA (Iglesia de Santa Prisca) faces the main square. It was funded by José de la Borda in gratitude for his good fortune in mining. Begun in 1751 and completed 7 years later, the church has a beautifully carved facade with twin 130-foot spires flanking a tiled dome. The interior is even more elaborate, a breathtaking profusion of gold-leaf saints and cherubs, 12 highly decorated altars and lovely paintings by Miguel Cabrera, one of Mexico's most celebrated colonial-era artists; Borda spared no expense in making this a beautifully appointed church.

Guides approach visitors outside offering tours. For a few pesos you'll receive some enlightening background information, but determine whether the fee applies to an individual or group tour and make sure the guide speaks understandable English. Allow 1 hour minimum. Daily 6:30 a.m.-8 p.m. Free. Phone (762) 622-0184.

CONVENT OF SAN BERNARDINO is off the Plaza del Convento. It was founded in 1592. The Plan of Iguala was drafted here in 1821 by Agustín de Iturbide, a pivotal character in the battle for Mexican independence from Spain. The plan drew the various Mexican social classes into the freedom movement, consolidating previously ineffective efforts. Mexico finally achieved independence several months later.

HUMBOLDT HOUSE (Casa Humboldt) is at Calle Juan Ruíz de Alarcón #12. It dates from the 16th century. German naturalist Baron Alexander von Humboldt spent the night in April 1803 while on a scientific journey that included South America and Cuba, hence the name. The restored house, boasting a rich Moorish facade, has also served as a convent, hospital and Taxco's first movie theater. It now houses the Museum of Viceregal Art (Museo de Arte Virreinal), which displays a small but interesting collection of religious paintings.

Tues.-Sat. 10-6. Admission around $1.75 (U.S.). Phone (762) 622-5501.

SILVERSMITHING MUSEUM (Museo de la Platería) is in the Patio de las Artesanías building on Plaza Borda, next to the Church of Santa Prisca; after entering turn left, go down the hallway and then down the stairs. It houses a collection of exquisite silver items that have won prizes in national contests, and seeing them may whet your appetite to do some shopping. Exhibit information is in Spanish. Tues.-Sun. 10-5:30. Admission around $1.50 (U.S.).

WILLIAM SPRATLING MUSEUM (Museo Guillermo Spratling) is directly behind the Church of Santa Prisca at Av. Porfirio A. Delgado #1. On display are pre-Columbian art and artifacts, many from Spratling's private collection. Tues.-Sat. 9-6, Sun. 9-3. Admission around $3.50 (U.S.), under 13 free.

TLACOLULA, OAXACA (I-8) pop. 11,400

Tlacolula (tlah-coh-LOO-lah), dating from around 1250, is an important market center for the surrounding Indian communities and the area's mezcal and castor oil producers. Its 16th-century *mudéjar* (Moorish-style) chapel is one of the most ornate in the state of Oaxaca. Known as the Chapel of Silver, it is built of cut stone and decorated with intricate carvings. Tlacolula's Sunday market is notable for its size and selection, and all kinds of intriguing items turn up among the mundane housewares and utilitarian clothing. In mid-October a regional festival is held, highlighted by the celebrants' dancing from Tlacolula to nearby villages.

The Yagul Ruins are 2.75 kilometers (1.7 miles) east of town, then 2 kilometers (1.2 miles) north of Mex. 190 by paved road. This Zapotec-Mixtec city, with well-preserved tombs, mosaics and buildings,

flourished about 500 B.C. Resembling a huge palace with six patios, the site may have served a civic rather than a religious function. The ball court here is in excellent condition.

TUXTLA GUTIERREZ, CHIAPAS (H-9) pop. 445,100

Tuxtla Gutiérrez (TOOX-tlah goo-TYEH-rehs) replaced San Cristóbal de Las Casas as the capital of the state of Chiapas in 1892. The discovery of vast oil reserves brought an influx of people and wealth to this prosperous commercial hub, which is lower in elevation and therefore steamier than many of the surrounding mountain communities. Tuxtla Gutiérrez also is a distribution point for the region's coffee and tobacco plantations.

Mex. 190 passes through the city; its approach from the west is cluttered with hotels. The hectic downtown area is divided by Avenida Central, the principal thoroughfare, which runs east-west. The main square constitutes two plazas separated by Avenida Central. It is fronted by imposing government buildings, shaded by manicured trees and filled with benches. In the marketplace and in shops near the plaza, such articles as appliqued scarves, gold filigree jewelry, boxes of inlaid wood and brightly painted gourds are sold.

At Blvd. Belisario Domínguez #2035 is the government-run Casa de las Artesanías, which has Chiapan handicrafts on display and for sale. First-class bus service is provided by Autotransportes Cristóbal Colón. The first-class bus station is 2 blocks west of the main plaza at Avenida 2 Norte and 2 Poniente.

This is Chiapas' economic and transportation center, and there is little for tourists to see. If you're touring this part of Mexico, however, you may need to spend the night here. The surrounding countryside is noted for lush scenery, including mountains, canyons, forests and such waterfalls as El Chorreadero.

Chiapas State Tourism Office (Secretaría de Turismo): in the western part of the city at Boulevard Belisario Domínguez #950 (in the Plaza de las Instituciones building); phone (961) 602-5299 or (800) 280-3500 (toll-free long distance within Mexico).

SUMIDERO CANYON (Cañon del Sumidero), about 23 km (14 mi.) north of the city, is reached by a paved mountain road. It features five different lookout points that provide spectacular views of the canyon's sheer walls as they plunge to the Río Grijalva below. Boat tours can be arranged in the town of Chiapa de Corzo, east of Tuxtla Gutiérrez, to observe not only the canyon's gaping cliffs but the river's murky green waters and the surrounding forest's alligators, exotic birds and colorful butterflies.

ZOOMAT (Zoológico Miguel Alvarez del Toro) is about 8 km (5 mi.) southeast of downtown; a taxi ride is about $3 (U.S.). This is one of Mexico's most noteworthy zoos. On exhibit is an impressive

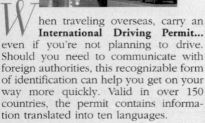

collection of more than 150 animal species native to Chiapas, including monkeys, tapirs, toucans, anteaters, eagles, boa constrictors, iguanas, scorpions and jaguars. The animals are housed in simulated habitats so roomy they appear to roam free through the lush vegetation. Tues.-Sun. 8:30-5. Admission 20 pesos (around $2 U.S.).

VERACRUZ, VERACRUZ (H-9)
pop. 544,800, metro area 607,000

Veracruz (veh-rah-CROOS) has long served as a doorway leading into the heart of Mexico. Spanish rule began in 1519 with the arrival of Hernando Cortés, who named the new settlement La Villa Rica de la Vera Cruz (Rich Town of the True Cross). Cortés then went inland to discover the Aztec capital and to launch the campaign that resulted in the colonization of the continental Americas.

Veracruz was the point of arrival for African slaves and served as a support base for Spanish colonial activities in Florida. Ironically, Spanish rule ended in the city as well. Three centuries after Cortés' landfall, the Spanish flag was lowered at the Fortress of San Juan de Ulúa across the bay.

This is the only place where the celebrated privateer John Hawkins, accompanied by his nephew Francis Drake, met defeat. His powerful fleet was thwarted at the hands of Spanish and Mexican men in 1568.

U.S. forces also landed in Veracruz on their way to Mexico City during the Mexican-American War of 1846-48. In 1862, French troops marched inland from Veracruz to subdue the country for Archduke Maximilian's arrival. U.S. forces again landed in 1914 to protest the actions of the Mexican military under Victoriano Huerta, who had seized the presidency after assassinating President Francisco I. Madero. These three invasions, along with the city's role in the struggle for Mexican independence, earned it the title *"Cuatro veces heroica Veracruz"* (four times heroic).

Plaza de Armas, the city's main square and one of the oldest Spanish plazas in North America, serves as a focal point for today's decidedly more peaceful but still spirited activity. The sidewalk tables of the Gran Café del Portal (long known as the Gran Café de la Parroquía until a change in ownership), on the plaza, are ideal for lounging and enjoying an order of *cafe con leche,* concentrated coffee mixed with boiled milk served in tall glasses, or perhaps a thick ice cream soda in a glass with inky black coffee at the bottom. For coffee refills, clink your knife against your glass.

The plaza is the site of strolling mariachi players, string trios—jarana, guitar and harp—and frequent band concerts. Music is a major contributor to the city scene; the popular song "La Bamba" originated in Veracruz. Crowds also gather to watch *jarocho* folk dances, part of a rich cultural tradition.

Extending a couple of miles from downtown along the Gulf of Mexico, the *malecón* seawall is a popular walkway from which to view such colonial buildings as the Customs House (Aduana Marítima) and La Parroquía Cathedral, specialty shops and the bustling harbor. A few blocks from the Customs House are remnants of a protective wall that surrounded Veracruz in the 18th century.

A drive southward along the shore via Boulevard M. Avila Camacho leads to Playa Villa del Mar, about 3.5 kilometers (2.2 miles) from the Plaza de Armas, and Playa Mocambo, 10 kilometers (6 miles) south. Both beaches are somewhat muddy, and sharks sometimes lurk offshore. The beaches are, however, a pleasant place to stroll and watch fishermen mending their nets or making repairs on their boats. On weekends they are filled with bathers, dancers and vendors proffering beer and seafood, all against a backdrop of nonstop band music.

Beyond Playa Mocambo, at the mouth of the Río Jamapa, is Boca del Río, noted for its fine open-air seafood restaurants. Diners are frequently treated to performances of the *son jarocho* dance by local children, accompanied by harp players.

The city's pre-Lenten Carnaval rivals New Orleans' in spectacle and enthusiasm, if not in size. The Veracruz version begins with the "burning of ill humor" and concludes with the funeral of Juan Carnaval. Parades wend their way down waterfront Boulevard Avila Camacho during the 9 days prior to Ash Wednesday, replete with lavishly decorated floats and outrageously attired revelers. Other events, including fireworks, folkloric dance shows and plenty of salsa and other music, take place around Plaza de Armas. Local hotels are booked solid for Carnaval, so if you plan on attending the party make reservations well in advance.

Veracruz State Tourism Office: on the ground floor of City Hall (Palacio Municipal), on the east side of Plaza de Armas. Open Mon.-Sat. 9-8, Sun. 10-6; (229) 989-8817 (English may not be spoken).

CASTLE OF SAN JUAN DE ULUA (Castillo de San Juan de Ulúa) is in the harbor on Gallega Island, reached by car or foot over a free causeway from extensions of avs. Morelos and República. This massive fort was built by the Spanish to protect their New World interests; construction took place 1582-1707. The dungeons, ramparts and barracks are open. From the fortress there are fine views of the port. "San Juan de Ulúa" buses depart for the fort from the east side of Plaza de República, in front of the Customs House. Tues.-Sun. 9-5. Admission around $3.25 (U.S.); free to all Sun.

LA ANTIGUA is about 32 km (20 mi.) north of the city via Mex. 180. This small village, shaded by big trees, was the original site of Veracruz. It contains a ruined 16th-century customs house (known as the "Casa de Cortés") as well as the Hermitage (La Ermita del Rosario), reputed to be the oldest church on the American mainland. This is a popular day trip, and there are a couple of small seafood eateries in the vicinity.

NAVAL HISTORY MUSEUM (Museo Histórico Naval) is about 4 blocks southeast of Plaza de Armas on Calle Arista. This impressively restored late 19th-century building once housed Mexico's naval academy. Displays include model ships, weapons and nautical apparatus, and there are exhibits on the American occupation of Veracruz in 1914 and the history of the naval academy. Information is in Spanish. Guided tours are available. Tue.-Sun. 9-5. Free.

VERACRUZ CITY MUSEUM (Museo de la Ciudad de Veracruz) is at Calle Zaragoza #397. Exhibits focus on historical and social themes, including slavery, the colonial era and the Revolution of 1910. Wed.-Sun. 10-6. Admission around $2.50 (U.S.).

VILLAHERMOSA, TABASCO (H-10)
pop. 342,200, metro area 625,500

Villahermosa (vee-yah-ehr-MOH-sah) was founded in 1519 under the name Santa María de la Victoria. Hernando Cortés established the settlement to commemorate his defeat of an army of Indian warriors who had attacked him during his march toward the Aztec capital of Tenochtitlán. In tribute to their conquerer, the Indians gave Cortés an Indian princess. Baptized Doña Marina, she became Cortés' mistress and trusted translator, an invaluable asset in his conquest of Mexico.

Villahermosa's strategic location on the banks of the navigable Río Grijalva, which flows northward out of rubber, cacao and coffee country, makes it an important distribution center. This river and the Río Usumacinta carry the largest volumes of water in a country not known for extensive river systems.

For years the area suffered from a stagnant economy. However, the 1970s discovery of some of the world's richest oil fields, as well as the development of extensive hydroelectric projects and successful agricultural programs, energized this hot, humid port. Oil drilling has created blight as well as wealth, however, and the quest for timber and rangeland has depleted Tabasco's natural forests.

Villahermosa has two main commercial centers. The central downtown area of stores, hotels and restaurants is known as the Zona Luz. It extends from Juárez Park (Parque Juárez) south to Plaza de Armas, the main plaza, and is roughly bounded by Avenida Zaragoza on the north, Avenida 5 de Mayo on the west, Avenida Allende on the south and waterfront Calle Madrazo (the *malecón*) on the east. A few of the streets here are pedestrian malls, closed to traffic.

The newer hotel and shopping district, Tabasco 2000, is about 6 kilometers (4 miles) northwest of the Zona Luz; it can be reached via Avenida Ruiz Cortines (Mex. 180), the main east-west thoroughfare. The wealth generated by oil is evident in this complex's contemporary government buildings, upscale hotels and sleek Galerías Tabasco 2000 mall. If you plan on spending the night in Villahermosa, Tabasco 2000 has the nicest accommodations.

First-class bus service to Campeche, Mérida, Mexico City, Palenque, San Cristóbal de Las Casas, Veracruz and other cities is offered by ADO. The ADO bus terminal is at Calle Javier Mina #297, about 10 blocks northwest of downtown and 3 blocks south of Avenida Ruiz Cortines. Taxi fares within the area encompassing the city center north to Avenida Ruiz Cortines average around $1.50 (U.S.). Villahermosa's streets, unlike those in other Mexican cities, are well marked, with arrows indicating the direction of traffic flow—a boon for navigating the hectic, congested central city.

West of the city are prosperous cacao plantations and the important archeological site of Comalcalco *(see attraction listing)*. A driving tour of this region reveals lush countryside that contrasts sharply with Mexico's more common arid expanses. Along Mex. 180 toward Cárdenas are masses of banana plants laden with clusters of fruit, which is sold at roadside stands.

Cárdenas itself is a cacao processing center, and some chocolate plantations and factories offer guided tours (check with travel agencies in Villahermosa). The cacao tree grows everywhere; its large, elliptical pods bear the seeds from which cocoa and chocolate are made. The harvesting season is November through April. Small family-run operations throughout this region grow and process cacao beans that end up as boxes of chocolate.

Tabasco State Tourism Office (Subsecretaría de Turismo): Avenida de Los Ríos at the corner of Calle 13 in the Tabasco 2000 complex, past the La Venta Museum and heading west out of downtown. Open Mon.-Fri. 9-3 and 6-8 p.m.; phone (993) 316-5134.

What To See

COMALCALCO RUINS are west on Mex. 180 to the town of Cárdenas, then north about 35 km (22 mi.) on Mex. 187 to the town of Comalcalco; the site is about 3 km (2 mi.) farther on the right. There are no highway signs from Villahermosa en route to Comalcalco; watch for signs in town that direct you to the ruins.

This large site consists of several tall pyramids spread out over grassy meadows and small hills. The structures here were constructed of thin, flat bricks called *tabiques*, covered with a plaster made from ground seashells, rather than the stone used elsewhere in pre-Hispanic Mexico. Heed the signs warning *No Subir* (Do Not Climb). A small one-room museum contains carved stone figures.

Descendants of the Chontal Maya, who originally inhabited Comalcalco around A.D. 600-900, still live in the area and earn a livelihood as their ancestors did by processing cacao and raising bananas and other fruits. **Note:** This is one of Mexico's hottest regions; visit early in the day and bring a hat or umbrella as a sunscreen. Daily 9-5. Admission around $3.50 (U.S.), under 8 free.

LA VENTA MUSEUM (Parque Museo La Venta) is west of downtown off Av. Ruiz Cortines (Mex. 180), just east of the Tabasco 2000 complex. This open-air park-museum spreads along the shores of man-made Lake of the Illusions (Laguna de las Ilusiones). Its 30 monuments, some weighing as much as 30 tons, were discovered in the late 1930s at the ruins of La Venta, an Olmec ceremonial center in the river country near the Veracruz state line. When oil exploration threatened to destroy the archeological zone, most of the artifacts were transported to this site.

Three colossal stone heads wear war helmets and display the characteristic facial features of Olmec art: wide noses, infantile expressions and full, downward-turning lips resembling the mouth of a jaguar. Other artifacts include sculptures, stone altars, stelae (stone tablets) and a tomb. All are scattered along a trail through junglelike grounds inhabited by free-roaming monkeys and deer, twittering birds, crocodiles (confined to a moat) and some caged animals.

This lush sanctuary should be toured in the morning before it gets too hot. Insect repellent is strongly advised. Daily 8-4. Admission around $3.75 (U.S.). Phone (993) 314-1652.

MUSEUM OF ANTHROPOLOGY (Museo Regional de Antropología) is south of downtown at Periférico Carlos Pellicer #511, along the west bank of the Río Grijalva within the Investigation Center for the Olmec and Maya Cultures, or CICOM (Investigaciones de Culturas Olmeca y Maya).

Exhibit halls contain representative pieces from Teotihuacán and the Aztec, Totonac, Mixtec and Zapotec cultures, as well as artifacts from the states of Nayarit and Colima. Featured are jade, ceramic and clay figurines, stelae, burial urns and gold objects. Special attention is given to the Olmec and Maya civilizations. The displays are complemented by photographs and maps of the archeological sites from which they were taken; descriptions are in Spanish. Tues.-Sun. 9-7:30. Admission around $3 (U.S.). Phone (993) 312-6344.

ZEMPOALA, VERACRUZ (H-8)

About 40 kilometers (25 miles) north of Veracruz off Mex. 180, Zempoala (sehm-poh-AH-lah), also known as Cempoala, is the site of remains that once comprised the ceremonial center and fortress of the Totonac Indians. Zempoala was a Classic Period contemporary of El Tajín (*see Papantla*), although it continued to thrive after the latter's abandonment sometime during the 13th century.

It was here that Hernando Cortés gained the first Indian allies in his 1519 campaign to conquer the Aztecs. The *conquistadores* took note of the city because the white stucco buildings, gleaming in the tropical sun, most likely reminded them of silver. He gained the trust of the Totonac chief (reputedly celebrated for his enormous girth) and his followers, who had been under Aztec rule for the previous 50 years.

ZEMPOALA RUINS are on the northern edge of town. The site is about a 45-minute drive from Veracruz; watch for the sign indicating the Zempoala turnoff about 7 km (4 mi.) north of the town of Cardel.

Six major structures remain. The Main Temple (Templo Mayor), constructed of riverbed stones, rises on 13 platforms to about 35 feet and probably resembled similar temples in the Aztec capital of Tenochtitlan. The Temple of the Chimneys (Templo de las Chimeneas) derives its name from a series of semicircular pillars. The Little Faces (Las Caritas), a three-story edifice of boulders and cement, is adorned with niches that once contained small carved faces. At the west end of the site is the Great Pyramid (La Gran Pirámide), which has two staircases that climb to a three-level platform.

First-class buses travel regularly from Veracruz north to Cardel; from Cardel, *colectivos* (minivans) or a taxi can take you to the ruins. Daily 9-5. Admission around $5 (U.S.); free to all Sun.

Smithsonian
National Museum of American History
Behring Center

America on the Move is made possible by generous support from
General Motors Corporation, AAA, State Farm Companies Foundation, The History Channel,
United States Congress, U.S. Department of Transportation, ExxonMobil, American Public
Transportation Association, American Road & Transportation Builders Association,
Association of American Railroads, National Asphalt Pavement Association, The UPS Foundation.

See how we got here.

Immerse yourself in a new museum experience and explore how transportation has changed America. **National Museum of American History, Washington, D.C.** americanhistory.si.edu/onthemove.

AMERICA
ON THE MOVE

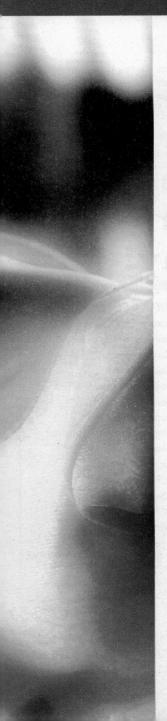

_____

_____

_____

_____

3 hotel lines.
Over 60 locations.
1 unforgettable experience!

No matter where you find yourself in Mexico, Fiesta Americana Hotels & Resorts -honored as "The Best Hotel Chain in Mexico" by the World Travel Awards- is there to welcome you with 19 architecturally renowned properties, traditional hospitality and a warm smile.
For an even more Grand experience, luxuriate in Fiesta Americana Grand's highest-caliber resorts in Los Cabos, Cancun and Mexico City.

BOOK NOW!
1-800-FIESTA1
or www.fiestamericana.com

 -

_____

_____

_____

_____

3 hotel lines.
Over 60 locations.
1 unforgettable experience!

Experience Mexico at its most accommodating at your choice of charming Fiesta Inns. Located in its most exciting city destinations, these 33 properties cater to business and leisure travelers with friendly staff, warm hospitality and top-value services.

BOOK NOW!
1-800-FIESTA1
or www.fiestamericana.com

Mexico

Temple of the Inscriptions
Palenque, Chiapas
Southern Mexico
Guillermo Aldana
Mexico Tourism Board

YUCATAN PENINSULA

AKUMAL, QUINTANA ROO

———— **WHERE TO STAY** ————

———— *The following lodging was either not evaluated or did not* ————
meet AAA rating requirements but is listed for your information only.

BAHIA PRINCIPE AKUMAL   **Phone:** 984/875-5000
(fyi)   Not evaluated. **Location:** KM 250 Carr Chetumal, Benito Juarez Local B. KM 250 Carr Chetumal, Benito Juarez.
Facilities, services, and decor characterize a mid-range property.

CAMPECHE, CAMPECHE pop. 195,700

———— **WHERE TO STAY** ————

———— *The following lodgings were either not evaluated or did not* ————
meet AAA rating requirements but are listed for your information only.

HACIENDA UAYAMON   **Phone:** 981/829-7525
(fyi)   Not evaluated. **Location:** In northern Campeche. KM 20 Carr Uayamon-China-Edzna 24000. Facilities, services, and
decor characterize an upscale property.

HOTEL DEL MAR   **Phone:** 981/816-2233
(fyi)   Not evaluated. **Location:** Center; facing the gulf. Ave Ruiz Cortines #51 24000. Facilities, services, and decor
characterize a mid-range property.

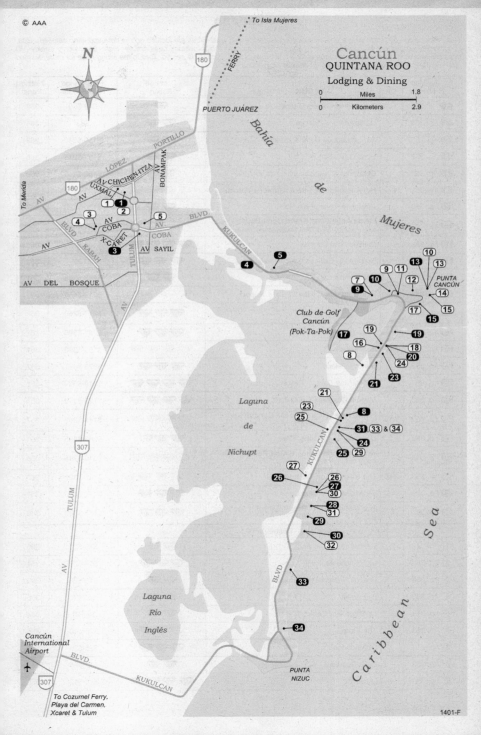

Cancun

This index helps you "spot" where approved accommodations and restaurants are located on the corresponding detailed maps. Lodging rate ranges are for comparison only and show the property's high season; rates are per night, unless only weekly (W) rates are available. Restaurant rate range is for dinner, unless only lunch (L) is served. Turn to the listing page for more detailed rate information and consult display ads for special promotions.

Spotter/Map Page Number	OA	CANCUN - Lodgings	Diamond Rating	Rate Range High Season	Listing Page
1 / p. 353		Best Western Plaza Caribe	◆	$79-$90	357
3 / p. 353		Oasis America Cancun	◆◆	$63	361
4 / p. 353		Sunset Lagoon Hotel & Marina	◆◆	$150-$340	362
5 / p. 353		Hotel Oasis Beach	◆◆	$162-$215	358
8 / p. 353		Occidental Caribbean Villages Cancun	◆◆	$150-$246	362
9 / p. 353	AAA	**Hotel Presidente InterContinental Cancun**	◆◆◆◆	$190-$250	358
10 / p. 353		Ambiance Villas at Kin-Ha	◆◆	$120-$220	357
13 / p. 353	AAA	**Fiesta Americana Grand Coral Beach** - see color ad p 359, back cover, card inserts	◆◆◆◆◆	$290-$590	358
15 / p. 353		Camino Real Cancun	◆◆◆◆	$149-$199	357
17 / p. 353		Holiday Inn Express Cancun Hotel Zone	◆◆◆	$120	358
19 / p. 353		Hotel Sierra Cancun	◆◆	$268-$368	361
20 / p. 353	AAA	**Hyatt Cancun Caribe Villas & Resort**	◆◆◆◆	$219-$450	361
21 / p. 353		Sheraton Cancun Resort & Towers - see color ad p 8	◆◆◆	$217-$260	362
23 / p. 353		Porto Real	◆◆◆	$237-$396	362
24 / p. 353	AAA	**Le Meridien**	◆◆◆◆	$150-$300	361
25 / p. 353		Cancun Palace	◆◆◆	$378-$491	357
26 / p. 353		JW Marriott Cancun Resort & Spa	◆◆◆◆	$219-$569	361
27 / p. 353		Marriott CasaMagna Cancun	◆◆◆◆	$129-$349	361
28 / p. 353	AAA	**Fiesta Americana Condesa Cancun** - see color ad card inserts	◆◆◆◆	$148-$280	357
29 / p. 353		Omni Cancun Hotel & Villas	◆◆◆	$260-$895	362
30 / p. 353	AAA	**Hilton Cancun Beach & Golf Resort** - see color ad p 360	◆◆◆◆	$310-$465	358
31 / p. 353	AAA	**The Ritz-Carlton Cancun**	◆◆◆◆◆	$185-$390	362
33 / p. 353		Crown Paradise Club Cancun	◆◆◆	$210-$360	357
34 / p. 353		The Westin Regina Resort Cancun - see color ad p 8	◆◆◆	$143-$308	363
		CANCUN - Restaurants			
1 / p. 353		Restaurant El Calamar	◆◆	$10-$20	366
2 / p. 353		La Habichuela	◆◆◆	$15-$25	364
3 / p. 353		Pericos Restaurante-Cantina	◆◆	$10-$26	365
4 / p. 353		La Parrilla	◆◆	$6-$20	365
5 / p. 353		La Dolce Vita Centro	◆◆	$8-$21	364
7 / p. 353	AAA	**The Palm**	◆◆◆	$25-$40	365
8 / p. 353		La Madonna	◆◆◆	$25-$35	365
9 / p. 353		Casa Rolandi's	◆◆	$11-$25	363
10 / p. 353		Le Basilic	◆◆◆◆	$23-$47	365

Spotter/Map Page Number	OA	**CANCUN** - Restaurants (continued)	Diamond Rating	Rate Range High Season	Listing Page
⑪ / p. 353		La Fisheria	♦♦	$12-$28	364
⑫ / p. 353		Savio's	♦♦	$16-$25	366
⑬ / p. 353		La Joya Restaurant	♦♦♦♦	$30-$50	365
⑭ / p. 353		Maria Bonita	♦♦♦	$12-$22	365
⑮ / p. 353		La Brisa	♦♦♦	$10-$30	364
⑯ / p. 353	AAA	**The Plantation House**	♦♦♦	$25-$40	366
⑰ / p. 353		Hacienda El Mortero Restaurante	♦♦♦	$14-$32	364
⑱ / p. 353		Cafe Cocay	♦♦♦	$12-$22	363
⑲ / p. 353		Lorenzillo's	♦♦	$40-$50	365
㉑ / p. 353		Ruth's Chris Steak House	♦♦♦	$50-$60	366
㉓ / p. 353		Cenacola Il Ristorante Italiano	♦♦♦	$14-$22	363
㉔ / p. 353		Blue Bayou	♦♦♦♦	$18-$30	363
㉕ / p. 353		La Destileria	♦♦	$14	364
㉖ / p. 353		La Capilla Argentina	♦♦♦	$15-$30	364
㉗ / p. 353		La Dolce Vita	♦♦♦	$12-$28	364
㉙ / p. 353	AAA	**Aioli**	♦♦♦♦	$30-$65	363
㉚ / p. 353		Mikado	♦♦♦	$18-$30	365
㉛ / p. 353		Rosato Ristorante	♦♦♦♦	$15-$35	366
㉜ / p. 353		Mitachi	♦♦♦	$18-$35	365
㉝ / p. 353	AAA	**The Club Grill**	♦♦♦♦♦	$32-$45	364
㉞ / p. 353	AAA	**Fantino**	♦♦♦♦	$35-$40	364

CANCUN, QUINTANA ROO pop. 167,700 (See map and index starting on p. 353)

WHERE TO STAY

AMBIANCE VILLAS AT KIN-HA — Phone: (998)883-1100 — 10

Small-scale Hotel

All Year — 2P: $120-$220

Location: On the north beach. Blvd Kukulcan KM 8.5 77500. Fax: 998/883-1101. **Facility:** 150 units. 87 one-bedroom standard units. 63 one-bedroom suites with kitchens. 3-4 stories, interior corridors. *Bath:* shower only. **Parking:** on-site. **Terms:** [AP] & [MAP] meal plans available, package plans. **Amenities:** safes, hair dryers. *Some:* video games (fee). **Pool(s):** outdoor. **Leisure Activities:** exercise room. *Fee:* sailboats, windsurfing, scuba diving, snorkeling, fishing. **Guest Services:** gift shop, valet and coin laundry. **Business Services:** meeting rooms, fax (fee). **Cards:** AX, MC, VI.

SOME UNITS

DATA PORT / /

BEST WESTERN PLAZA CARIBE — Phone: (998)884-1377 — 1

Small-scale Hotel

12/1-4/20	2P: $79-$90
7/18-8/17	2P: $90
4/21-7/17 & 8/18-11/30	2P: $79

Location: Across street from main bus terminal. Located in the heart of Old Town Cancun. Tulum y Uxmal Lote 19 77500 (Apdo Postal 487). Fax: 998/884-6352. **Facility:** 140 one-bedroom standard units. 2 stories (no elevator), exterior corridors. *Bath:* shower only. **Parking:** on-site. **Terms:** [AP] & [MAP] meal plans available. **Amenities:** safes, irons, hair dryers. **Pool(s):** outdoor. **Guest Services:** gift shop, valet laundry. **Business Services:** meeting rooms, fax (fee). **Cards:** AX, DC, JC, MC, VI.

SOME UNITS

/ /

CAMINO REAL CANCUN — Book at aaa.com — Phone: (998)848-7000 — 15

Resort Large-scale Hotel

All Year — 2P: $149-$199

Location: On the beach at Punta Cancun. Punta Cancun Zona Hotelera KM 8.5 77500 (Apdo Postal 14). Fax: 998/848-7001. **Facility:** Set in a scenic area featuring Mayan ruins and palm-tree-shaded beaches, this hotel offers rooms with balconies and ocean or lagoon view. 381 units. 355 one-bedroom standard units, some with whirlpools. 26 one-bedroom suites ($305-$1650), some with efficiencies (no utensils) and/or whirlpools. 5-16 stories, interior/exterior corridors. *Bath:* combo or shower only. **Parking:** on-site. **Terms:** 7 day cancellation notice-fee imposed. **Amenities:** voice mail, safes, honor bars, hair dryers. *Some:* CD players, dual phone lines, irons. **Dining:** Maria Bonita, La Brisa, see separate listings. **Pool(s):** heated outdoor. **Leisure Activities:** steamroom, rental boats, boat dock, spa. *Fee:* paddleboats, sailboats, windsurfing, waterskiing, scuba diving, snorkeling, fishing, charter fishing, 3 lighted tennis courts. **Guest Services:** gift shop, valet laundry. **Business Services:** conference facilities, business center. **Cards:** AX, CB, DC, MC, VI.

SOME UNITS

FEE 24 DATA PORT / VCR /

CANCUN PALACE — Book at aaa.com — Phone: (998)881-3600 — 25

Resort Large-scale Hotel

All Year [AP] — 1P: $378-$393 — 2P: $463-$491

Location: Blvd Kukulcan; windward side of Cancun Island. Blvd Kukulcan KM 14.5 77500. Fax: 998/881-3601. **Facility:** This all-inclusive resort features lagoon- or ocean-view rooms with balconies and an extensive selection of resort activities. 565 one-bedroom standard units, some with whirlpools. 8-12 stories, interior corridors. **Parking:** on-site. **Terms:** 21 day cancellation notice, in season. **Amenities:** safes, irons, hair dryers. **Pool(s):** 3 outdoor, wading. **Leisure Activities:** boating, canoeing, paddleboats, marina, miniature golf, 2 lighted tennis courts, recreation programs, exercise room. *Fee:* windsurfing, waterskiing, scuba diving, fishing. **Guest Services:** gift shop, complimentary evening beverages, valet laundry. **Business Services:** conference facilities, fax (fee). **Cards:** AX, DC, MC, VI.

SOME UNITS

24 D / /

CROWN PARADISE CLUB CANCUN — Phone: (998)848-9000 — 33

Large-scale Hotel

All Year [AP] — 1P: $210-$225 — 2P: $320-$360 — XP: $75

Location: On the beach; windward side of Cancun Island. Blvd Kukulcan KM 18.5 77500. Fax: 998/885-1707. **Facility:** 508 units. 500 one-bedroom standard units, some with whirlpools. 8 one-bedroom suites with whirlpools. 7-8 stories, interior corridors. **Parking:** on-site. **Terms:** 30 day cancellation notice, in season. **Amenities:** voice mail, safes, irons, hair dryers. *Some:* CD players, honor bars. **Pool(s):** 3 outdoor, 2 heated outdoor, wading. **Leisure Activities:** whirlpools, steamroom, waterslide, canoeing, paddleboats, windsurfing, miniature golf, 2 lighted tennis courts, recreation programs, playground, exercise room, sports court, basketball, shuffleboard, volleyball. *Fee:* scuba diving, snorkeling, charter fishing, massage. **Guest Services:** gift shop, complimentary evening beverages, valet laundry. **Business Services:** meeting rooms. *Fee:* PC, fax. **Cards:** AX, MC, VI.

SOME UNITS

24 D / /

FIESTA AMERICANA CONDESA CANCUN — Book at aaa.com — Phone: (998)881-4200 — 28

AAA

Large-scale Hotel

All Year — 1P: $148-$280 — 2P: $148-$280 — XP: $20 — F17

Location: On the beach; windward side of Cancun Island. Blvd Kukulcan KM 16.5 77500. Fax: 998/885-1800. **Facility:** Accented by a Mediterranean-style exterior, lush landscaping and refined public areas, this property features ocean views from all rooms. 528 units. 502 one-bedroom standard units, some with whirlpools. 26 one-bedroom suites ($250-$440), some with whirlpools. 7-8 stories, exterior corridors. **Parking:** on-site. **Terms:** 3 day cancellation notice-fee imposed. **Amenities:** video games, voice mail, safes, honor bars, irons, hair dryers. **Dining:** 3 restaurants, 6:30 am-11 pm, cocktails, also, Rosato Ristorante, see separate listing, entertainment. **Pool(s):** heated outdoor, wading. **Leisure Activities:** sauna, steamroom, recreation programs. *Fee:* scuba diving, snorkeling, fishing, charter fishing, 2 lighted tennis courts, exercise room, massage. **Guest Services:** gift shop, valet laundry. **Business Services:** conference facilities, business center. **Cards:** AX, DC, JC, MC, VI.

(See color ad card insert)

SOME UNITS

24 DATA PORT / /

(See map and index starting on p. 353)

FIESTA AMERICANA GRAND CORAL BEACH
Book at aaa.com Phone: (998)881-3200 **13**

All Year 2P: $290-$590 XP: $30 F17

Location: On the beach; leeward side of Cancun Island. Blvd Kukulcan KM 9.5 77500. Fax: 998/881-3218. **Facility:** Large rooms with balconies overlook the Caribbean at this hotel offering sophisticated common areas and an extensive beachfront pool. 602 units. 599 one-bedroom standard units, some with whirlpools. 1 one- and 2 two-bedroom suites with whirlpools. 11 stories, interior corridors. **Parking:** valet. **Terms:** [MAP] meal plan available. **Amenities:** video games (fee), CD players, high-speed Internet, dual phone lines, voice mail, safes, honor bars, irons, hair dryers. *Some:* DVD players, fax. **Dining:** 5 restaurants, 6:30 am-midnight, cocktails, also, La Joya Restaurant, Le Basilic, see separate listings, entertainment. **Pool(s):** 2 outdoor, 2 heated outdoor, 2 wading. **Leisure Activities:** lifeguard on duty, rental boats, scuba diving, snorkeling, pool & ocean sun decks, golf privileges, recreation programs, fiesta kids club, playground, spa. *Fee:* sailboats, windsurfing, waterskiing, fishing, charter fishing, jet ski, 3 lighted indoor tennis courts, game room. **Guest Services:** gift shop, valet laundry, area transportation (fee). **Business Services:** conference facilities, business center. **Cards:** AX, CB, DC, JC, MC, VI.

(See color ad p 359, back cover, card inserts)

Resort
Large-scale Hotel

SOME UNITS

HILTON CANCUN BEACH & GOLF RESORT
Book at aaa.com Phone: (998)881-8000 **30**

12/22-4/6 2P: $310-$465 XP: $30 F18
4/7-11/30 2P: $230-$305 XP: $30 F18
12/1-12/21 2P: $225-$305 XP: $30 F18

Location: On the beach; windward side of Cancun Island. KM 17 Zona Hotelera, Seccion A 77500. Fax: 998/881-8080. **Facility:** Dramatic pyramid building with extensive pool areas. Also secluded villas on spectacular beach. Many rooms with balcony. All rooms with dramatic view of Caribbean. Occasionally vigorous surf. 426 units. 384 one-bedroom standard units. 36 one- and 6 two-bedroom suites ($405-$755), some with whirlpools. 2-9 stories, interior/exterior corridors. **Parking:** on-site and valet. **Terms:** 3 day cancellation notice. **Amenities:** video games, voice mail, safes, honor bars, irons, hair dryers. **Dining:** 2 restaurants, 6 am-11:30 pm, cocktails, also, Mitachi, see separate listing, nightclub, entertainment. **Pool(s):** 7 heated outdoor, wading. **Leisure Activities:** sauna, whirlpools, scuba diving, snorkeling, water polo, recreation programs, jogging, volleyball. *Fee:* sailboats, windsurfing, charter fishing, golf-18 holes, golf & tennis instruction, 2 lighted tennis courts, massage. **Guest Services:** gift shop, valet laundry, area transportation (fee). **Business Services:** conference facilities, business center. **Cards:** AX, CB, DC, MC, VI.

(See color ad p 360)

Resort
Large-scale Hotel

SOME UNITS

HOLIDAY INN EXPRESS CANCUN HOTEL ZONE
Book at aaa.com Phone: (998)883-2200 **17**

12/1-4/6 [ECP] 1P: $120 2P: $120 XP: $15 F12
7/15-8/31 [ECP] 1P: $110 2P: $110 XP: $15 F12
4/7-7/14 & 9/1-11/30 [ECP] 1P: $100 2P: $100 XP: $15 F12

Location: On north side of Cancun Island, off Blvd Kukulcan; 7 km from downtown; next to Pok-Ta-Pok Golf Club House. Located in a quiet area. (Paseo Pok-Ta-Pok Lote 21 y 22 Zona Hotel). Fax: 998/883-2532. **Facility:** 119 one-bedroom standard units. 2 stories (no elevator), interior corridors. *Bath:* combo or shower only. **Parking:** on-site. **Terms:** cancellation fee imposed, 12% service charge. **Amenities:** irons, hair dryers. **Pool(s):** outdoor, wading. **Guest Services:** gift shop, valet laundry, area transportation. **Business Services:** meeting rooms, fax (fee). **Cards:** AX, DC, MC, VI.

Small-scale Hotel

SOME UNITS

HOTEL OASIS BEACH
Phone: 998/849-4510 **5**

12/1-4/12 1P: $162-$215 2P: $162-$215 XP: $45 F12
7/13-8/31 1P: $136-$182 2P: $136-$182 XP: $35 F12
4/13-7/12 & 9/1-11/30 1P: $119-$159 2P: $119-$159 XP: $35 F12

Location: On north side of Cancun Island; at leeward side of Cancun Island. Located on the beach. Blvd Kukulcan, Seccion C, Lote 1 77500. Fax: 998/849-4509. **Facility:** Modern pyramid-shaped high-rise, colorful rooms; few with balcony. Recently remodeled. Wide, tranquil beach with palapas. Meets AAA guest room security requirements. 470 one-bedroom standard units. 8 stories, interior corridors. *Bath:* shower only. **Parking:** on-site. **Terms:** 10 day cancellation notice-fee imposed, [AP], [BP] & [CP] meal plans available, package plans. **Amenities:** voice mail, safes, honor bars, hair dryers. **Pool(s):** 2 outdoor, wading. **Leisure Activities:** sauna, steamroom, rental boats, rental sailboats, rental sailboards. *Fee:* marina, waterskiing, scuba diving, snorkeling, fishing, 2 lighted tennis courts, massage. **Guest Services:** gift shop, valet laundry. **Business Services:** meeting rooms. **Cards:** AX, MC, VI.

Resort
Large-scale Hotel

SOME UNITS

HOTEL PRESIDENTE INTERCONTINENTAL CANCUN
Book at aaa.com Phone: (998)848-8700 **9**

12/25-4/17 1P: $190-$250 2P: $190-$250 XP: $35 F18
4/18-11/30 1P: $175-$235 2P: $175-$235 XP: $35 F18
12/1-12/24 1P: $160-$220 2P: $160-$220 XP: $35 F18

Location: On the beach; north side of Cancun Island. Blvd Kukulcan KM 7.5 77500. Fax: 998/883-2602. **Facility:** Lagoon or Caribbean views. Striking pyramid-shaped pool area with whirlpools. Superb, wide beach area with palapas; usually a tranquil surf. Meets AAA guest room security requirements. 299 units. 296 one-bedroom standard units. 3 one-bedroom suites with whirlpools. 6-10 stories, interior corridors. **Parking:** on-site and valet. **Terms:** 7 day cancellation notice-fee imposed, $5 service charge. **Amenities:** voice mail, safes, honor bars, irons, hair dryers. *Some:* CD players. **Dining:** 3 restaurants, 6:30 am-11 pm, cocktails, also, The Palm, see separate listing, entertainment. **Pool(s):** outdoor, heated outdoor. **Leisure Activities:** whirlpools, rental boats, rental sailboats, rental sailboards, lighted tennis court, recreation programs, jogging, playground, exercise room, basketball. *Fee:* waterskiing, scuba diving, snorkeling, charter fishing, skin diving, motor ski, kayaks, massage. **Guest Services:** gift shop, valet laundry. **Business Services:** conference facilities, business center. **Cards:** AX, DC, JC, MC, VI.

Resort
Large-scale Hotel

SOME UNITS

A FORTUNATE FEW WILL VISIT THE CARIBBEAN MOST HONORED.

OTHERS WILL ONLY WISH THEY COULD.

FIESTAMERICANA
CORAL BEACH CANCUN *Grand*

(See map and index starting on p. 353)

HOTEL SIERRA CANCUN
Phone: (998)883-2444 **19**
▼▼▼ ▼▼ All Year [AP] 2P: $268-$368
Large-scale Hotel
Location: On the beach; windward side of Cancun Island. Blvd Kukulcan KM 10 77500 (Apdo Postal 138). Fax: 998/883-3486. **Facility:** 260 one-bedroom standard units. 9 stories, interior corridors. **Parking:** on-site. **Terms:** 7 day cancellation notice. **Amenities:** voice mail, honor bars, irons, hair dryers. **Pool(s):** 2 outdoor.
Leisure Activities: sauna, whirlpool, steamroom, boating, boat dock, miniature golf, 2 tennis courts, playground, exercise room, basketball, horseshoes, shuffleboard. *Fee:* snorkeling, massage. **Guest Services:** gift shop, valet laundry, beauty salon. **Business Services:** meeting rooms, fax (fee). **Cards:** AX, DC, MC, VI.

SOME UNITS

HYATT CANCUN CARIBE VILLAS & RESORT
Book at aaa.com Phone: (998)848-7800 **20**
(AAA)

12/1-1/1	1P: $219-$450	2P: $219-$450	XP: $30 F12
1/2-3/31	1P: $279	2P: $279	XP: $30 F12
4/1-11/30	1P: $219-$240	2P: $219-$240	XP: $30 F12

▼▼▼ ▼▼▼
Resort
Large-scale Hotel
Location: On the beach; windward side of Cancun Island. Blvd Kukulcan KM 10.5, Zona Hotelera 77500 (Apdo Postal 353). Fax: 998/884-1514. **Facility:** This beachfront property's rooms all face the Caribbean and most offer private balconies and spectacular views. 226 units. 190 one-bedroom standard units. 36 one-bedroom suites ($289-$549). 3-7 stories, interior/exterior corridors. *Bath:* combo or shower only. **Parking:** on-site.
Terms: 3 day cancellation notice-fee imposed. **Amenities:** voice mail, honor bars, irons, hair dryers. *Some:* safes. **Dining:** 6:30 am-11 pm, cocktails, also, Blue Bayou, Cafe Cocay, see separate listings, entertainment. **Pool(s):** 3 outdoor. **Leisure Activities:** whirlpools, 3 tennis courts (1 lighted), jogging, playground, exercise room, volleyball. *Fee:* scuba diving, snorkeling, charter fishing, massage. **Guest Services:** gift shop, valet laundry. **Business Services:** conference facilities, business center. **Cards:** AX, DC, JC, MC, VI.

SOME UNITS

JW MARRIOTT CANCUN RESORT & SPA
Book at aaa.com Phone: 998/848-9600 **26**
▼▼▼ ▼▼▼ All Year 1P: $219-$569 2P: $219-$569
Resort
Large-scale Hotel
Location: Adjacent to Marriott CasaMagna Cancun; 11 mi from Cancun International Airport; 2 mi s of Cancun Convention Center. Blvd Kukulcan KM 14.5 77500. Fax: 998/848-9601. **Facility:** Lavish public areas, extensive resort facilities, multiple dining outlets and excellent service comprise one of Cancun's newest hotel/spa resorts. 448 units. 374 one-bedroom standard units. 74 one-bedroom suites. 14 stories, interior corridors.
Parking: on-site. **Terms:** 3 day cancellation notice-fee imposed, package plans. **Amenities:** dual phone lines, voice mail, safes, honor bars, irons, hair dryers. **Pool(s):** 2 outdoor, indoor, wading. **Leisure Activities:** whirlpools, 2 lighted tennis courts. *Fee:* scuba diving, snorkeling, charter fishing, massage. **Guest Services:** gift shop, valet laundry, area transportation (fee). **Business Services:** conference facilities, business center. **Cards:** AX, MC, VI.

SOME UNITS

FEE

LE MERIDIEN
Book at aaa.com Phone: (998)881-2200 **24**
(AAA) All Year 1P: $150-$300 2P: $150-$300 XP: $50 F12
▼▼▼ ▼▼
Resort
Large-scale Hotel
Location: Off Blvd Kukulcan; windward side of Cancun Island. KM 14 Retorno del Rey 77500. Fax: 998/881-2201. **Facility:** Sophisticated French resort. All rooms with view of Caribbean. Expansive pool/beach area with occasionally strong, dramatic surf. 213 units. 188 one-bedroom standard units. 19 one- and 6 two-bedroom suites ($250-$450), some with whirlpools. 7 stories, interior corridors. **Parking:** on-site and valet. **Terms:** 7 day cancellation notice-fee imposed. **Amenities:** dual phone lines, voice mail, safes, honor bars, irons, hair dryers. *Some:* CD players. **Dining:** 2 restaurants, 6:30 am-11 pm, cocktails, also, Aioli, see separate listing, entertainment. **Pool(s):** 3 heated outdoor, wading. **Leisure Activities:** sauna, whirlpool, steamroom, scuba diving, snorkeling, fishing, 2 lighted tennis courts, tennis instruction, recreation programs, spa. *Fee:* charter fishing. **Guest Services:** gift shop, valet laundry. **Business Services:** conference facilities, business center. **Cards:** AX, DC, JC, MC, VI.

SOME UNITS

MARRIOTT CASAMAGNA CANCUN
Book at aaa.com Phone: (998)881-2000 **27**
▼▼▼ ▼▼▼ All Year 2P: $129-$349
Resort
Large-scale Hotel
Location: Blvd Kukulcan KM 16; on the beach; windward side of Cancun Island. Manzana 23, Lote 41, Seccion A, ZA Etapa 77500. Fax: 998/881-2085. **Facility:** A spacious, luxurious lobby and a large oceanfront pool complement the stylish rooms at this hotel. 450 units. 426 one-bedroom standard units. 24 one-bedroom suites, some with whirlpools. 6 stories, interior corridors. **Parking:** on-site. **Terms:** 3 day cancellation notice, 60 day 12/17-1/3-fee imposed. **Amenities:** voice mail, safes, honor bars, irons, hair dryers. **Dining:** Mikado, La Capilla Argentina, see separate listings. **Pool(s):** outdoor. **Leisure Activities:** saunas, whirlpools, recreation programs, exercise room, volleyball. *Fee:* waterskiing, scuba diving, snorkeling, charter fishing, 2 lighted tennis courts, massage. **Guest Services:** gift shop, valet laundry. **Business Services:** conference facilities. **Cards:** AX, MC, VI.

SOME UNITS

FEE FEE

OASIS AMERICA CANCUN
Phone: (998)848-8600 **3**
▼▼▼ ▼▼

12/1-1/3	1P: $63	2P: $63	XP: $17 F
4/2-11/30	1P: $56	2P: $56	XP: $17 F
1/4-4/1	1P: $53	2P: $53	XP: $17 F

Small-scale Hotel
Location: Off Cancun Island; in town on Ave Tulum, jct highway to beaches. Located in Old Town Cancun. Aves Tulum y Calle Brisa SM 4 CP 77500 (Apdo Postal 600). Fax: 998/884-1953. **Facility:** 178 one-bedroom standard units, some with efficiencies (no utensils). 5 stories, interior corridors. *Bath:* shower only. **Parking:** on-site. **Terms:** 14 day cancellation notice-fee imposed, [BP] & [MAP] meal plans available, 12% service charge. **Amenities:** safes, honor bars, hair dryers. **Pool(s):** outdoor, wading. **Leisure Activities:** playground. **Guest Services:** gift shop, valet laundry, area transportation. **Business Services:** conference facilities, business center. **Cards:** AX, DC, MC, VI.

SOME UNITS

(See map and index starting on p. 353)

OCCIDENTAL CARIBBEAN VILLAGES CANCUN   *Book at aaa.com*   **Phone:** (998)848-8000   ⑧
All Year [AP]   1P: $150-$180   2P: $246   XP: $80
Location: Blvd Kukulcan KM 12; on the beach; windward side of Cancun Island. Blvd Kukulcan, Lote 18 77500.
Fax: 998/848-8003. **Facility:** All inclusive resort (meals & non-motorized sports included). Room numbers
Resort   ending in 27 are larger corner units. 300 units. 294 one-bedroom standard units. 6 one-bedroom suites. 8
Large-scale Hotel   stories, interior corridors. *Bath:* combo or shower only. **Parking:** on-site. **Amenities:** voice mail, safes (fee),
hair dryers. **Pool(s):** 2 outdoor. **Leisure Activities:** whirlpool, lifeguard on duty, rental boats, paddleboats, sailboats,
windsurfing, scuba diving, snorkeling, 2 lighted tennis courts, recreation programs. *Fee:* waterskiing, fishing, massage, game
room. **Guest Services:** gift shop, valet laundry. **Business Services:** conference facilities. **Cards:** AX, MC, VI.
SOME UNITS

OMNI CANCUN HOTEL & VILLAS   *Book at aaa.com*   **Phone:** (998)881-0600   ㉙
All Year   2P: $260-$895   XP: $50   F17
Location: Blvd Kukulcan KM 16.5; windward side of Cancun Island. Located on the beach. Blvd Kukulcan L-48, M-53
77500. Fax: 998/885-0059. **Facility:** A beachfront location and a range of recreational facilities add appeal to
Resort   this property, which offers both traditional rooms and full villas. 353 units. 301 one-bedroom standard units.
Large-scale Hotel   32 one-bedroom suites, some with whirlpools. 20 vacation homes ($495-$895) with whirlpools. 3-12 stories,
interior corridors. **Parking:** on-site. **Terms:** 3 day cancellation notice, 14 day for villas. **Amenities:** voice mail, safes, irons, hair
dryers. **Pool(s):** 3 outdoor, wading. **Leisure Activities:** whirlpools, steamroom, recreation programs, spa. *Fee:* 2 lighted tennis
courts. **Guest Services:** gift shop, valet laundry. **Business Services:** conference facilities, business center. **Cards:** AX, CB,
DC, MC, VI.
SOME UNITS

PORTO REAL   **Phone:** (998)881-5500   ㉓
12/21-4/4 [AP]   1P: $237-$329   2P: $286-$396   XP: $135   F5
4/5-11/30 [AP]   1P: $183-$219   2P: $220-$264   XP: $90   F5
12/1-12/20 [AP]   1P: $212   2P: $256   XP: $87   F5
Large-scale Hotel   **Location:** On the beach; windward side of Cancun Island. Blvd Kukulcan KM 11.5 77500. Fax: 998/881-5694.
Facility: 638 units. 623 one-bedroom standard units. 15 one-bedroom suites ($340-$800). 2-6 stories, interior corridors.
Parking: on-site. **Terms:** 5 day cancellation notice-fee imposed. **Amenities:** voice mail, safes (fee), hair dryers. **Pool(s):** 3
outdoor. **Leisure Activities:** rental boats, miniature golf, 2 lighted tennis courts, recreation programs, exercise room, basketball,
volleyball. *Fee:* scuba diving, snorkeling, fishing, racquetball courts, massage. **Guest Services:** gift shop, valet laundry.
Business Services: conference facilities, fax (fee). **Cards:** AX, DC, JC, MC, VI.
FEE

THE RITZ-CARLTON CANCUN   *Book at aaa.com*   **Phone:** (998)881-0808   ㉛
(AAA)   All Year   1P: $185-$390   2P: $185-$390
Location: Blvd Kukulcan KM 17.5; on the beach; windward side of Cancun Island. #36 Retorno del Rey, Zona Hotelera
77500. Fax: 998/881-1015. **Facility:** Impressive common areas and a refined ambience enhance this hotel's
Resort   location on a prime section of beach in the middle of the hotel zone. Meets AAA guest room security
Large-scale Hotel   requirements. 365 units. 340 one-bedroom standard units. 25 one-bedroom suites ($290-$900), some with
whirlpools. 9 stories, interior corridors. **Parking:** valet. **Terms:** 7 day cancellation notice. **Amenities:** CD
players, dual phone lines, voice mail, safes, honor bars, irons, hair dryers. *Fee:* video games, high-speed
Internet. *Some:* DVD players. **Dining:** 4 restaurants, 7 am-midnight, cocktails, also, The Club Grill, Fantino, see separate
listings, entertainment. **Pool(s):** 2 heated outdoor, wading. **Leisure Activities:** saunas, whirlpool, steamrooms, recreation
programs, spa. *Fee:* scuba diving, snorkeling, fishing, charter fishing, jet ski, 3 lighted tennis courts, private palapas. **Guest
Services:** gift shop, valet laundry, area transportation (fee). **Business Services:** conference facilities, business center.
Cards: AX, CB, DC, JC, MC, VI.
SOME UNITS
FEE

SHERATON CANCUN RESORT & TOWERS   *Book at aaa.com*   **Phone:** (998)891-4400   ㉑
All Year   1P: $217-$260   2P: $217-$260   XP: $15   F17
Location: On the beach; windward side of Cancun Island. Blvd Kukulcan KM 12.5 77500 (Apdo Postal 834).
Fax: 998/885-0204. **Facility:** Rooms with ocean or lagoon view. Well-landscaped grounds. Tower section
Resort   with larger rooms than pyramid building. Many rooms with balcony. 471 units. 435 one-bedroom standard
Large-scale Hotel   units. 36 one-bedroom suites ($340-$520) with whirlpools. 6-7 stories, interior corridors. **Parking:** on-site.
Terms: 3 day cancellation notice, in season-fee imposed, [AP] & [CP] meal plans available. **Amenities:** voice mail, safes, honor
bars, hair dryers. *Some:* irons. **Pool(s):** outdoor, wading. **Leisure Activities:** sauna, steamroom, miniature golf, 4 lighted tennis
courts, recreation programs, playground. *Fee:* scuba diving, snorkeling, massage. **Guest Services:** gift shop, valet laundry.
Business Services: conference facilities, business center. **Cards:** AX, CB, DC, MC, VI. *(See color ad p 8)*
SOME UNITS
FEE

SUNSET LAGOON HOTEL & MARINA   **Phone:** 998/881-4500   ④
All Year [AP]   1P: $150-$200   2P: $240-$340
Location: On the north side of Cancun Island; facing the lagoon. Blvd Kukulcan KM 5.8 77500. Fax: 998/883-4959.
Small-scale Hotel   **Facility:** 60 one-bedroom standard units. 2 stories, exterior corridors. *Bath:* shower only. **Parking:** on-site.
Terms: 3 day cancellation notice. **Amenities:** voice mail, safes. **Pool(s):** outdoor, wading. **Leisure
Activities:** whirlpool, boating, paddleboats, sailboats, windsurfing, scuba diving, snorkeling, recreation programs, playground.
Fee: marina, waterskiing, charter fishing. **Guest Services:** gift shop, valet laundry. **Business Services:** fax (fee). **Cards:** AX,
MC, VI.

(See map and index starting on p. 353)

THE WESTIN REGINA RESORT CANCUN — *Book at aaa.com* — Phone: (998)848-7400 — **34**

	12/1-1/1	1P: $143-$308	2P: $268-$308	XP: $40	F17
	1/2-4/6	1P: $215-$272	2P: $225-$272	XP: $40	F17
	4/7-11/30	1P: $150-$182	2P: $150-$182	XP: $40	F17

Resort
Large-scale Hotel — **Location:** On the beach; windward side of Cancun Island. Blvd Kukulcan KM 20 Lote 70 y Zona Hotel 77500 (Apdo Postal 1808). Fax: 998/885-0779. **Facility:** Ocean and lagoon views, excellent public, pool and beach areas. Bright colors, open areas; some units with private balcony. 379 units. 376 one-bedroom standard units. 3 one-bedroom suites ($252-$333), some with whirlpools. 6 stories, interior corridors. **Parking:** on-site. **Terms:** 3 day cancellation notice-fee imposed, [AP], [BP], [CP] & [MAP] meal plans available. **Amenities:** dual phone lines, voice mail, safes, honor bars, irons, hair dryers. **Pool(s):** 5 outdoor, wading. **Leisure Activities:** sauna, whirlpool, steamroom, boat dock, recreation programs. *Fee:* waterskiing, scuba diving, snorkeling, charter fishing, 2 lighted tennis courts, massage. **Guest Services:** gift shop, valet laundry, area transportation (fee), beauty salon. **Business Services:** conference facilities, business center. **Cards:** AX, DC, MC, VI.
(See color ad p 8)

SOME UNITS

The following lodgings were either not evaluated or did not meet AAA rating requirements but are listed for your information only.

HOTEL RIU CANCUN — Phone: 998/848-7151
(fyi)   Not evaluated. **Location:** Blvd Kukulcan Lote. Facilities, services, and decor characterize a mid-range property.

HOTEL RIU CARIBE — Phone: 998/848-7850
(fyi)   Not evaluated. **Location:** Blvd Kukulcan KM 5.5. Facilities, services, and decor characterize a mid-range property.

HOTEL RIU PALACE LAS AMERICAS — Phone: 998/891-4300
(fyi)   Not evaluated. **Location:** Blvd Kukulcan Manz 50, Lote 4. Facilities, services, and decor characterize a mid-range property.

OASIS VIVA CANCUN — Phone: 998/883-0800
(fyi)   Not evaluated. **Location:** Blvd Kukulcan; Zona Hotelera. Blvd Kukulcan KM 8.5 77500 (Apdo Postal 673). Facilities, services, and decor characterize a mid-range property.

--- **WHERE TO DINE** ---

AIOLI — Lunch: $12-$16 — Dinner: $30-$65 — Phone: 998/881-2260 — **29**
Regional Mediterranean — **Location:** Off Blvd Kukulcan; windward side of Cancun Island; in Le Meridien. KM 14 Retorno del Rey 77500. **Hours:** 6:30 am-11 & 6-11 pm. **Reservations:** suggested. **Features:** Ocean views are exceptional from either the large terrace or the dramatic floor-to-ceiling windows inside this distinctively designed dining room. Specialty Mediterranean entrees include duck breast with potato galette, served with a honey lavender sauce, or pan-seared grouper with a paste of black olives, crushed potato and tomato. Lighter fare also is available, particularly on the lunch bistro menu. The "fifth element" dessert is renowned. Dressy casual; cocktails; entertainment. **Parking:** on-site and valet. **Cards:** AX, DC, MC, VI.

BLUE BAYOU — Dinner: $18-$30 — Phone: 998/883-0044 — **24**
Regional International — **Location:** On the beach; windward side of Cancun Island; in Hyatt Cancun Caribe Villas & Resort. Blvd Kukulcan KM 10.5, Zona Hotelera 77500. **Hours:** 6 pm-11 pm. **Reservations:** suggested. **Features:** Distinctive bayou decor is fitting at this semi-formal restaurant, which specializes in Cajun preparations. Dressy casual; cocktails; entertainment. **Parking:** on-site and valet. **Cards:** AX, DC, DS, MC, VI.

CAFE COCAY — Lunch: $5-$15 — Dinner: $12-$22 — Phone: 998/848-7800 — **18**
Regional International — **Location:** On the beach; windward side of Cancun Island; in Hyatt Cancun Caribe Villas & Resort. Blvd Kukulcan KM 10.5, Zona Hotelera 77500. **Hours:** 6:30 am-1 & 6-10 pm. **Reservations:** accepted. **Features:** On the ground level of a boutique resort, the dining room displays colorful yet elegant Caribbean decor. Breakfast includes a vast buffet, including omelets made on-the-spot, as well as a la carte selections. Casual dress. **Parking:** on-site and valet. **Cards:** AX, CB, DC, JC, MC, VI.

CASA ROLANDI'S — Lunch: $10-$15 — Dinner: $11-$25 — Phone: 998/883-2557 — **9**
Northern Italian — **Location:** On lagoon side of Blvd Kukulcan; in Plaza Caracol Shopping Mall. Site 32-34 Plaza Caracol Shopping Mall 77500. **Hours:** 1 pm-12:30 am. **Reservations:** accepted. **Features:** In the heart of a popular mall, this local favorite is well known for its grotto walls, attentive servers and tasty dishes prepared with fresh ingredients and pasta. Casual dress; cocktails. **Parking:** on-site and street. **Cards:** AX, MC, VI.

CENACOLA IL RISTORANTE ITALIANO — Dinner: $14-$22 — Phone: 998/885-3603 — **23**
Italian — **Location:** In Plaza Kukulcan. Blvd Kukulcan KM 13 77500. **Hours:** 5 pm-11:30 pm; hours may vary in season. **Reservations:** suggested. **Features:** A Cancun flair punctuates preparations of fine Italian cuisine. In addition to traditional gourmet pizzas and homemade pasta, the menu incorporates exotic choices, such as sea salt gulf shrimp. There is a choice of elegant indoor seating, where guests are surrounded by large European wall murals, as well as space on the patio, where candlelit tables and robust Italian music set a decidedly romantic tone. Service is detailed and attentive. Casual dress; cocktails. **Parking:** on-site. **Cards:** AX, MC, VI.

(See map and index starting on p. 353)

THE CLUB GRILL
Dinner: $32-$45   **Phone:** 998/881-0808   **33**

AAA
Continental

Location: Blvd Kukulcan KM 17.5; on the beach; windward side of Cancun Island; in The Ritz-Carlton Cancun. #36 Retorno del Rey, Zona Hotelera 77500. **Hours:** 7 pm-11 pm. Closed: Mon. **Reservations:** suggested. **Features:** The lavish, clublike setting sets the stage for a refined, romantic dining experience. Seafood, steak and game dishes are vividly presented and augmented by local Yucatan and Caribbean flavors. Service is formal and precise. The adjoining lounge is ideal for dancing or enjoying a Cuban cigar. Dressy casual; cocktails; entertainment. **Parking:** valet. **Cards:** AX, CB, DC, JC, MC, VI.

FANTINO
Dinner: $35-$40   **Phone:** 998/881-0808   **34**

AAA
Northern Italian

Location: Blvd Kukulcan KM 17.5; on the beach; windward side of Cancun Island; in The Ritz-Carlton Cancun. #36 Retorno del Rey, Zona Hotelera 77500. **Hours:** 7 pm-11 pm. Closed: Sun. **Reservations:** suggested. **Features:** The specialty restaurant features surprising presentations and refined service. Caribbean flavors lend a distinctive taste to Italian dishes. Dressy casual; cocktails; entertainment. **Parking:** valet. **Cards:** AX, CB, DC, JC, MC, VI.

HACIENDA EL MORTERO RESTAURANTE
Dinner: $14-$32   **Phone:** 998/883-1133   **17**

Mexican

Location: Blvd Kukulcan KM 9 77500. **Hours:** 6 pm-midnight. **Reservations:** suggested. **Features:** For true Mexican flavor in both food and atmosphere, this cozy restaurant is a great choice. Wandering mariachis entertain diners as they feast on homemade, tasty meals in the bright, festive atmosphere of a center courtyard. Menu highlights include fresh fish, seafood, Mexican crepes and more traditional favorites along the lines of ranch steaks and sizzling fajitas. Casual dress; cocktails; entertainment. **Parking:** street. **Cards:** AX, MC, VI.

LA BRISA
Lunch: $12-$25   **Dinner:** $10-$30   **Phone:** 998/848-7083   **15**

Regional Seafood

Location: On the beach at Punta Cancun; in Camino Real Cancun. Punta Cancun 77500. **Hours:** noon-midnight. **Reservations:** suggested. **Features:** Overlooking the Caribbean Sea, the restaurant is a classic spot for romantic dining. Regional influences enhance artistically presented seafood from around the world, including fresh, mesquite-grilled specialties. The outstanding Contoy Island shrimp steak is marinated with lemon and aromatic herbs, grilled, then served on a bed of parpadelle with curry. Another good choice is the hogfish filet served with clam butter on a bed of wild mushrooms and fresh clams. Casual dress; cocktails; entertainment. **Parking:** valet and street. **Cards:** AX, CB, DC, MC, VI.

LA CAPILLA ARGENTINA
Dinner: $15-$30   **Phone:** 998/881-2000   **26**

Argentine

Location: Blvd Kukulcan KM 16; on the beach; windward side of Cancun Island; in Marriott CasaMagna Cancun. **Hours:** 6:30 am-11 & 5:30-11 pm. **Reservations:** suggested. **Features:** Among the comfortable restaurant's decor touches are a Spanish tile floor and Mexican fountain. However, the food is the clear highlight. Servers display fresh cuts of beef and tempting starters such as gaucho sausage to enhance the experience. Expect huge portions of freshly prepared and perfectly spiced cuisine with an Argentine flair. Casual dress; cocktails. **Parking:** on-site and valet. **Cards:** AX, CB, DC, DS, JC, MC, VI.

LA DESTILERIA
Lunch: $8   **Dinner:** $14   **Phone:** 998/885-1086   **25**

Mexican

Location: Blvd Kukulcan; in Zona Hotelera. KM 13 Blvd Kukulcan 77500. **Hours:** 1 pm-midnight. **Reservations:** suggested. **Features:** Resembling a turn-of-the-20th-century tequila-making ranch, the restaurant is reminiscent of another time. The menu centers on Mexican fare. Guests are told their satisfaction is guaranteed. Casual dress; cocktails. **Parking:** on-site. **Cards:** AX, MC, VI.

LA DOLCE VITA
Lunch: $12-$28   **Dinner:** $12-$28   **Phone:** 998/885-0161   **27**

Italian

Location: Across from Marriott CasaMagna Cancun and JW Marriott Cancun Resort & Spa; facing lagoon. KM 14.6 Blvd Kulkulcan 77500. **Hours:** noon-11:30 pm. Closed: 1/1. **Reservations:** suggested, for dinner. **Features:** Overlooking the beautiful Nichupte Lagoon, the 18-year-old establishment features Italian specialties in a contemporary setting. The ample wine list includes a good selection of by-the-glass choices. Recommended is the tripasta dolce vita, consisting of cannelloni, ravioli and gnocchi. For a touch of the Caribbean, try tagliolini with lobster medallions. Seating is available indoors or on the terrace. Casual dress; cocktails; entertainment. **Parking:** on-site. **Cards:** AX, MC, VI.

LA DOLCE VITA CENTRO
Lunch: $8-$12   **Dinner:** $8-$21   **Phone:** 998/884-3393   **5**

Regional Italian

Location: 1 blk w from bridge to Cancun Island. Ave Coba 87, SM 3 77500. **Hours:** 1 pm-11 pm. **Reservations:** suggested. **Features:** Located in Old Town Cancun just off of the island proper, this is one of Cancun's earliest Italian restaurants brought back to life after 30 years. Casual dress; cocktails. **Parking:** street. **Cards:** AX, MC, VI.

LA FISHERIA
Lunch: $8-$17   **Dinner:** $12-$28   **Phone:** 998/883-1395   **11**

Regional Seafood

Location: In Plaza Caracol. Blvd Kukulcan KM 8.5 Plaza Caracol 77500. **Hours:** 11 am-11:30 pm. **Reservations:** accepted. **Features:** This restaurant, located in a popular shopping area, serves a variety of fresh seafood in a pleasant atmosphere. Casual dress; cocktails. **Parking:** on-site and street. **Cards:** AX, MC, VI.

LA HABICHUELA
Lunch: $15-$25   **Dinner:** $15-$25   **Phone:** 998/884-3158   **2**

Regional Mexican

Location: 2 blks n of Ave Tulum at Calle Azucenas; behind the theater; downtown. Margaritas 25. **Hours:** noon-midnight. **Reservations:** suggested, for dinner. **Features:** Mayan stone relief carvings complement the tropical garden setting where patrons dine on Caribbean dishes under the stars. Food is prepared using fresh fruit sauces, such as mango, guava and guanabana. Good choices include the specialty "cocobichuela" entree, a light curry with chunks of lobster and shrimp served in a coconut with tropical fruits, and jumbo shrimp in a ginger/mushroom sauce. For a wonderful ending, try strawberries flambe with a "cafe maya" prepared tableside. Casual dress; cocktails. **Parking:** on-site and street. **Cards:** AX, MC, VI.

(See map and index starting on p. 353)

LA JOYA RESTAURANT   **Dinner: $30-$50**   Phone: 998/881-3200 ⑬
Location: On the beach; leeward side of Cancun Island; in Fiesta Americana Grand Coral Beach. KM 9.5 Blvd Kukulcan 77500. **Hours:** 6:30 pm-11 pm. **Reservations:** suggested. **Features:** Those who dine in the main
Nouvelle Mexican plaza of this quaint place can discover authentic Mexican haute cuisine. Distinctive and artistic dishes combine national and classic flavors. Live mariachi music enhances the splendid dining atmosphere. Semi-
formal attire; cocktails; entertainment. **Parking:** valet. **Cards:** AX, DC, JC, MC, VI.

LA MADONNA   **Lunch: $15-$35**   **Dinner: $25-$35**   Phone: 998/883-4837 ⑧
Location: Blvd Kukulcan; at La Isla Shopping Village. Blvd Kukulcan KM 12.5 77500. **Hours:** noon-11:30 pm.
Reservations: suggested. **Features:** Homemade rich pasta, gourmet pizzas, live lobster and fresh local
Italian seafood are just some of the menu highlights. Huge statues, floor-to-ceiling murals and ornate decor
enhance the distinctive European setting. Overlooking activities at La Isla Shopping Village, the small patio
area on the ground or second level is a nice spot for drinks. Casual dress; cocktails. **Parking:** street. **Cards:** AX, MC, VI.

LA PARRILLA   **Lunch: $5-$15**   **Dinner: $6-$20**   Phone: 998/887-6141 ④
Location: Near jct aves Uxmal and Yaxchilan; downtown. Ave Yaxchilan 51 77500. **Hours:** 12:30 pm-2 am, Sun-1
am. **Reservations:** accepted. **Features:** Since 1975, this downtown institution has served delicious
Mexican "parrilla"—grilled specialties of pork, steak, chicken and sausage—in a festive, open-air courtyard
atmosphere. For an appetizer, try squash flower crepes. The staff can prepare grilled dishes, or diners can
cook them at the table on a mini-charcoal grill. Favorite tableside options include flaming dagger brochette or shrimp au tequila,
as well as seven varieties of fajitas. Casual dress; cocktails; entertainment. **Parking:** valet. **Cards:** AX, MC, VI.

LE BASILIC   **Dinner: $23-$47**   Phone: 998/881-3200 ⑩
Location: On the beach; leeward side of Cancun Island; in Fiesta Americana Grand Coral Beach. Blvd Kukulcan KM
9.5 77500. **Hours:** 6:30 pm-11 pm. **Closed:** Sun. **Features:** The newest arrival in Cancun is where
Regional Mediterranean creations meet with subtle undertones of French haute cuisine. The elegant dining room,
Mediterranean with its pianist and attentive service, encourages romance and celebration. After dinner, diners can step out
to the lounge for a nightcap and live nightly entertainment. Semi-formal attire; cocktails. **Parking:** valet.
Cards: AX, CB, DC, JC, MC, VI.

LORENZILLO'S   **Lunch: $12-$20**   **Dinner: $40-$50**   Phone: 998/883-1254 ⑲
Location: Opposite Hotel Continental Villas Plaza Cancun. Blvd Kukulcan 77500. **Hours:** noon-11:30 pm.
Reservations: suggested, for dinner. **Features:** Named after legendary French pirate Lorenzillo, who came
Seafood to Mexico in 1683, the long-established restaurant is built over the water on Nichupte Lagoon. The specialty,
live lobster, can be selected from the water-filled boat moored in the dining room. Seafood dishes can be
cooked in several ways. Seating is available outside or inside in the open-air dining room under the large palapa (thatched)
roof. Casual dress; cocktails. **Parking:** valet. **Cards:** AX, MC, VI.

MARIA BONITA   **Dinner: $12-$22**   Phone: 998/883-0100 ⑭
Location: On the beach at Punta Cancun; in Camino Real Cancun, near main entrance. Punta Cancun Lote 17 77500.
Hours: 6:45 pm-midnight. **Reservations:** required, in season. **Features:** This high-energy, family-oriented
Regional Mexican restaurant takes diners on a fun-filled gastronomical tour through Mexican regions, customs, foods and
people. Strolling musicians enliven the atmosphere. Authentic, colorfully presented Mexican dishes—
including the smoked marlin appetizer, the chef's specialty of chicken almond mole and the delicious poblano chilies stuffed with
lobster and seafood—are made with fresh, quality ingredients. Casual dress; cocktails; entertainment. **Parking:** on-site and
valet. **Cards:** AX, CB, DC, MC, VI.

MIKADO   **Dinner: $18-$30**   Phone: 998/881-2000 ㉚
Location: Blvd Kukulcan KM 16; on the beach; windward side of Cancun Island; in Marriott CasaMagna Cancun.
Hours: 5:30 pm-11 pm. **Reservations:** suggested. **Features:** Near the entrance of the hotel, the restaurant
Asian enables diners to choose from both Japanese and Thai selections amid sleek, contemporary Asian decor.
Choices include tempura, yellow and green curries, Pad Thai and extensive sushi varieties. Also available
are teppan-style grill seating and sunset dinners. Dressy casual; cocktails. **Parking:** on-site and valet. **Cards:** AX, CB, MC, VI.

MITACHI   **Lunch: $10-$25**   **Dinner: $18-$35**   Phone: 998/881-8000 ㉜
Location: On the beach; windward side of Cancun Island; in Hilton Cancun Beach & Golf Resort. KM 17 Blvd Kukulcan
77500. **Hours:** 12:30 pm-3 & 5-midnight, Sun-11:30 pm. **Reservations:** suggested. **Features:** Authentic
Regional Japanese creations are served in a relaxed, inviting dining room located steps from the turquoise
Japanese Caribbean. Casual dress; cocktails. **Parking:** on-site and valet. **Cards:** AX, CB, DC, JC, MC, VI.

THE PALM   **Lunch: $10-$18**   **Dinner: $25-$40**   Phone: 998/848-8700 ⑦
ⒶⒶⒶ
Location: On the beach; north side of Cancun Island; in Hotel Presidente InterContinental Cancun. KM 7.5 Blvd
Kukulcan 77500. **Hours:** noon-11 pm. **Reservations:** suggested. **Features:** The classic American steak
house features oversized portions, white linens, knowledgeable staff and a view of the Caribbean sea.
Steak & Seafood Casual dress; cocktails. **Parking:** on-site and valet. **Cards:** AX, CB, DC, DS, JC, MC, VI.

PERICOS RESTAURANTE-CANTINA   **Lunch: $8-$12**   **Dinner: $10-$26**   Phone: 998/884-3152 ③
Location: In town; near jct aves Uxmal and Yaxchilan. Ave Yaxchilan 61 77500. **Hours:** noon-1 am.
Reservations: accepted. **Features:** This not-to-be-missed cantina features live marimba and mariachi
Traditional music in an eclectic, high-energy atmosphere. On the menu are several styles of brochettes flambeed with
Mexican orange liqueur, as well as sizzling fajitas, fresh seafood ceviche and other Mexican favorites. The wait
staff—also known as the bandoleros—serves up food and plenty of entertainment. Casual dress; cocktails;
entertainment. **Parking:** street. **Cards:** AX, MC, VI.

(See map and index starting on p. 353)

THE PLANTATION HOUSE   Lunch: $15-$30   Dinner: $25-$40   Phone: 998/883-1455   16

Caribbean

Location: Across from Hyatt Cancun Caribe Villas & Resort. Blvd Kukulcan KM 14.8. **Hours:** noon-midnight. **Reservations:** suggested. **Features:** The covered, open-air dining room has a distinct Caribbean theme and is a good spot in which to sample island flavors. The dining room combines Old World charm with a casual, tropical ambience. Polished wood floors and elegantly set tables with crystal stemware and signature china lend to the sophistication. The menu lists regional specialties from each of the Caribbean islands, with a strong focus on seafood. Dressy casual; cocktails. **Parking:** valet. **Cards:** AX, MC, VI.

RESTAURANT EL CALAMAR   Lunch: $5-$20   Dinner: $10-$20   Phone: 998/884-0190   1

Regional Seafood

Location: From North/South Monument, 0.5 km e to Revolution Monument, left on Ave Uxmal, then just e of jct; near bus terminal. Margaritas Retorno 2. **Hours:** noon-8 pm. **Features:** For the past 25 years, fresh seafood and Mexican dishes have been served at this simple cantina, not far from the main bus station downtown. The tradition continues today, with fish being brought to the table for approval prior to being cooked and several dishes prepared in the tasty tikin-xick style. For starters, diners can munch on assorted bocadillos. Fresh ceviches, including caracol (conch), and desserts such as coconut flan round out the menu nicely. Casual dress; cocktails. **Parking:** on-site and street. **Cards:** MC, VI.

ROSATO RISTORANTE   Dinner: $15-$35   Phone: 998/881-4200   31

Italian

Location: On the beach; windward side of Cancun Island; in Fiesta Americana Condesa Cancun. Blvd Kukulcan KM 16.5 77500. **Hours:** 6 pm-11 pm. **Reservations:** suggested. **Features:** Patrons can relax in a comfortable dining room while enjoying an excellent variety of Italian-based dishes presented with artistic flair. Nice touches include a wide variety of imported cheeses and a focused wine list with some by-the-glass selections. Dressy casual; cocktails. **Parking:** on-site and valet. **Cards:** AX, DC, MC, VI.

RUTH'S CHRIS STEAK HOUSE   Lunch: $30-$40   Dinner: $50-$60   Phone: 998/885-0500   21

Steak House

Location: Blvd Kukulcan; in Kukulcan Plaza Mall. Blvd Kukulcan KM 13 77500. **Hours:** 1 pm-11:30 pm. **Reservations:** suggested. **Features:** Hearty portions of sizzling steaks are served with accompaniments large enough to share. Diners with a craving for meat never leave hungry. Save room for the pecan pie, made from a Southern recipe. The Kukulkan Plaza location is central and in the heart of the Zona Hotelera. Casual dress; cocktails. **Parking:** on-site. **Cards:** AX, MC, VI.

SAVIO'S   Lunch: $10-$14   Dinner: $16-$25   Phone: 998/883-2085   12

Italian

Location: Street level of Plaza Caracol facing Blvd Kukulcan. Blvd Kukulcan KM 8.5 77500. **Hours:** 11 am-11:30 pm. **Reservations:** suggested, for dinner. **Features:** In the Plaza Caracol Shopping Mall near the convention center, this airy, greenhouse-style restaurant features homemade pasta with sauces made from scratch. Tasty seafood dishes include shrimp manicotti and shrimp and lobster sauteed in a garlic white wine sauce. The sounds of soft jazz echo through the dining room each night. Casual dress; cocktails; entertainment. **Parking:** on-site and street. **Cards:** AX, MC, VI.

The following restaurants have not been evaluated by AAA but are listed for your information only.

CRAB HOUSE RESTAURANT & BAR   Phone: 998/885-0722

fyi   Not evaluated. **Location:** Blvd Kukulcan KM 14.8. **Features:** In addition to the fabulous seafood selections featuring crab and lobster, the menu also offers pastas, steaks and a fun children's menu.

EL PESCADOR   Phone: 998/884-2673

fyi   Not evaluated. **Location:** Downtown. **Features:** This restaurant (the name translates to "The Fisherman") offers fresh seafood in an open, casual atmosphere in downtown Cancun.

MAMA ROMA   Phone: 998/883-4467

fyi   Not evaluated. **Location:** Forum by the Sea, street level. Blvd Kukulcan KM 9.5 77500. **Features:** A casual Italian menu featuring lots of fun pastas and a relaxed setting with indoor or outdoor patio dining are the highlights here.

This ends listings for Cancun.
The following page resumes the alphabetical listings
of cities in Yucatan Peninsula.

CHICHEN ITZA, YUCATAN pop. 1,000

—— WHERE TO STAY ——

CLUB MED VILLAS ARQUEOLOGICAS
Phone: (985)851-0180

▼▼▼ All Year 1P: $90-$170 2P: $90-$170

Location: On Merida-Valladolid Hwy. Located adjacent to the main archeological area. KM 120 Carr Merida-Valladolid.
Small-scale Hotel **Fax:** 985/851-0018. **Facility:** 40 one-bedroom standard units. 2 stories (no elevator), exterior corridors. *Bath:* shower only. **Parking:** on-site. **Terms:** [MAP] meal plan available. **Pool(s):** outdoor. **Guest Services:** valet laundry. **Business Services:** fax (fee). **Cards:** AX, MC, VI.

HACIENDA CHICHEN RESORT *Book at aaa.com*
Phone: (985)851-0045

▼▼▼ All Year 1P: $100-$117 2P: $100-$117 XP: $10 F11

Location: On Merida-Puerto Juarez Hwy (Mex 180-D). Located at entrance to archeological zone. KM 120 on Merida-
Classic Historic Puerto Juarez Hwy 97751 (Apdo Postal 708, MERIDA, YU). Fax: 985/851-0119. **Facility:** The main hacienda
Country Inn building was built in the 16th century. Cabins with excellent spacing nestled around large pool courtyard area in a jungle setting. 28 one-bedroom standard units. 1 story, exterior corridors. *Bath:* combo or shower only. **Parking:** on-site. **Terms:** [AP], [BP], [CP] & [MAP] meal plans available. **Amenities:** honor bars, hair dryers. **Dining:** Restaurante Hacienda Chichen, see separate listing. **Pool(s):** outdoor. **Leisure Activities:** hiking trails, jogging. **Business Services:** meeting rooms, fax. **Cards:** AX, MC, VI.

SOME UNITS

HOTEL MAYALAND AND BUNGALOWS
Phone: (985)851-0100

▼▼▼ 11/1-11/30 2P: $158-$223 XP: $20 F12
12/1-4/30 2P: $138-$194 XP: $20 F12
Small-scale Hotel 5/1-10/31 2P: $88-$134 XP: $20 F12

Location: 120.5 km e of Merida on Merida-Puerto Juarez Hwy. Located adjacent to the main archeological zone. (Robalo #30 SM 3, CANCUN, QR, 77500). Fax: 985/851-0129. **Facility:** 103 one-bedroom standard units, some with whirlpools. 3 stories, interior/exterior corridors. *Bath:* combo or shower only. **Parking:** on-site. **Terms:** 15 day cancellation notice-fee imposed, [AP], [BP], [CP], [ECP] & [MAP] meal plans available. **Pool(s):** 3 outdoor. **Leisure Activities:** jogging. *Fee:* horseback riding. **Guest Services:** gift shop. **Business Services:** conference facilities. **Cards:** AX, MC, VI.

SOME UNITS

—— WHERE TO DINE ——

RESTAURANTE HACIENDA CHICHEN **Lunch:** $4-$10 **Dinner:** $8-$13 **Phone:** 985/851-0045

▼▼▼ **Location:** On Merida-Puerto Juarez Hwy (Mex 180-D); in Hacienda Chichen Resort. KM 120 on Merida-Puerto Juarez
Hwy 97751. **Hours:** 7 am-9 pm. **Features:** In addition to traditional American selections, the menu lists
Regional Mexican classic Mayan offerings. Seating is offered in the air-conditioned dining room or on the spectacular garden terrace. Casual dress; cocktails. **Parking:** on-site. **Cards:** AX, MC, VI.

COZUMEL, QUINTANA ROO pop. 64,100

—— WHERE TO STAY ——

DAYS INN-VILLA IGUANAS *Book at aaa.com*
Phone: (987)872-1600

▼▼▼ 12/21-4/15 1P: $58-$68 2P: $58-$68 XP: $10 F12
4/16-11/30 1P: $48-$58 2P: $48-$58 XP: $10 F12
Motel 12/1-12/20 1P: $45-$55 2P: $45-$55 XP: $10 F12

Location: 1.3 km s of San Miguel town center. Located in a quiet residential area. Calle 11, Sur 460 77600.
Fax: 987/872-1692. **Facility:** Meets AAA guest room security requirements. 43 one-bedroom standard units, some with efficiencies. 2-4 stories, exterior corridors. *Bath:* shower only. **Parking:** on-site. **Terms:** 7 day cancellation notice. **Pool(s):** outdoor. **Business Services:** fax (fee). **Cards:** AX, MC, VI. *(See color ad opposite inside front cover)*

SOME UNITS

PLAYA AZUL HOTEL
Phone: 987/872-0199

▼▼▼ All Year 1P: $160-$295 2P: $160-$295

Location: Zona Hotelera norte. Located on a quiet beach. Carr San Juan KM 4 77600 (Apdo Postal 31).
Small-scale Hotel Fax: 987/872-0110. **Facility:** 50 units. 45 one-bedroom standard units. 4 one- and 1 three-bedroom suites, some with kitchens and/or whirlpools. 3 stories, interior corridors. **Parking:** on-site. **Amenities:** safes (fee). **Pool(s):** outdoor, wading. **Leisure Activities:** scuba equipment rental, snorkeling. *Fee:* charter fishing. **Business Services:** meeting rooms, fax (fee). **Cards:** AX, MC, VI.

PRESIDENTE INTERCONTINENTAL COZUMEL
Phone: (987)872-0322

ⒶⒶⒶ 12/21-4/17 1P: $270-$670 2P: $270-$670 XP: $50 F18
4/18-11/30 1P: $220-$670 2P: $220-$670 XP: $50 F18
▼▼▼▼ 12/1-12/20 1P: $200-$650 2P: $200-$650 XP: $50 F18

Large-scale Hotel **Location:** 6.5 km s of San Miguel on beach road; at La Caleta Yacht Basin. Carr Chankanaab KM 6.5 77600.
Fax: 987/872-1360. **Facility:** Spacious, tropically landscaped grounds. Private balcony or terrace. Most rooms with ocean view. Beautiful, quiet beach areas and snorkeling at doorstep. 253 units. 251 one-bedroom standard units. 2 one-bedroom suites, some with kitchens. 2-5 stories, interior/exterior corridors. *Bath:* combo or shower only. **Parking:** on-site and valet. **Terms:** 7 day cancellation notice-fee imposed, $10 service charge. **Amenities:** honor bars, hair dryers. *Some:* CD players, safes, irons. **Dining:** 7 am-midnight, cocktails, entertainment. **Pool(s):** outdoor. **Leisure Activities:** rental boats, boat dock, fishing, jet ski, 2 lighted tennis courts, tennis equipment & instruction, art instruction, playground, exercise room. *Fee:* windsurfing, scuba diving, snorkeling, charter fishing, scuba & snorkel instruction, massage. **Guest Services:** gift shop, valet laundry. **Business Services:** conference facilities, business center. **Cards:** AX, DC, JC, MC, VI.

SOME UNITS

SCUBA CLUB COZUMEL   Phone: (987)872-1800

All Year Wkly   1P: $1015   2P: $1470

◇ *Small-scale Hotel*

Location: 1.5 km s of San Miguel on beach road. (Apdo Postal 11, 77600). Fax: 987/872-1883. **Facility:** 55 one-bedroom standard units. 2 stories (no elevator), exterior corridors. *Bath:* shower only. **Parking:** on-site. **Terms:** 30 day cancellation notice-fee imposed, [AP] meal plan available. **Pool(s):** outdoor. **Leisure Activities:** boat dock. *Fee:* scuba diving, snorkeling, charter fishing. **Cards:** MC, VI.

———— *The following lodging was either not evaluated or did not* ————
meet AAA rating requirements but is listed for your information only.

EL CID LA CEIBA   Phone: 987/872-0844

[fyi]   Not evaluated. **Location:** Carr Chankanaab KM 4.5. Facilities, services, and decor characterize a mid-range property.

———— **WHERE TO DINE** ————

CARLOS 'N CHARLIE'S   Lunch: $7-$12   Dinner: $8-$12   Phone: 987/872-0191

American

Location: In mall centro commercial, next to new city pier. Punta Langosta 77600. **Hours:** 10 am-midnight. Closed: 1/1; also 12/24. **Reservations:** accepted. **Features:** Overlooking the main pier and busy seafront promenade, the second-floor restaurant boasts a high-spirited crowd. On the menu are "gringo" favorites—hamburgers, barbecued ribs and shrimp—as well as Mexican favorites, including enchiladas, fajitas and the house specialty, molcajete served in a lava-style pot. Beer and drinks are served by the yard. Casual dress; cocktails. **Parking:** on-site. **Cards:** AX, MC, VI.

FRENCH QUARTER   Lunch: $10-$15   Dinner: $15-$25   Phone: 998/872-6321

Regional Cajun

Location: 4 blks e of Ave Rafael Melgar; 2nd floor. Sa Ave Sur 77600. **Hours:** 1 pm-11 pm. **Features:** A surprising find on the island—typical New Orleans dining on the second level of an open-air restaurant, with a refreshing evening breeze. A wide selection of classic New Orleans-style cuisine is offered. Casual dress; cocktails. **Parking:** street. **Cards:** AX, MC, VI.

LA CHOZA   Lunch: $6-$10   Dinner: $9-$15   Phone: 987/872-0958

Regional Mexican

Location: 3 blks e of Ave Rafael Melgar. Ave 10 Sur esq con Ave Rosando Salas 77600. **Hours:** 7:30 am-11:30 pm. **Features:** Featuring authentic Mexico island dishes, the local favorite offers a fun and casual experience under the open breeze palapa. Casual dress; cocktails. **Parking:** street. **Cards:** AX, MC, VI.

PEPE'S GRILL   Dinner: $15-$35   Phone: 987/872-0213

Continental

Location: On the malecon; opposite ferry pier. Ave Rafael Melgar esq con Rosardo Salas 77600. **Hours:** 5 pm-11:30 pm. **Reservations:** suggested. **Features:** A long time island favorite, the eatery features quality steaks, chops, seafood, pasta and more. Many dishes are prepared at your table, which offers a great view of Cozumel's promenade. Casual dress; cocktails. **Parking:** street. **Cards:** AX, MC, VI.

RESTAURANT ACUARIO   Lunch: $10-$20   Dinner: $10-$20   Phone: 987/872-0300

Regional Seafood

Location: 0.5 km s of San Miguel on beach road. Ave Rafael Melgar Sur 77600. **Hours:** 2 pm-11:30 pm **Reservations:** accepted. **Features:** Formerly an aquarium, this oceanside restaurant features a good selection of regional dishes, including grilled shrimp, Yucatan red snapper filet stuffed with shrimp and herbs, real Mexican fajitas and grilled steaks. Seating is available beneath the outside awning or inside amid aquariums with colorful fish. A shark tank is out back. Casual dress; cocktails. **Parking:** on-site. **Cards:** AX, MC, VI.

ISLA MUJERES, QUINTANA ROO pop. 10,800

———— **WHERE TO STAY** ————

AVALON REEF CLUB   Phone: (998)999-2050

1/4-4/26 [AP]	1P: $192-$213	2P: $256-$284	XP: $80	F12
4/27-8/23 [AP]	1P: $174-$195	2P: $222-$260	XP: $80	F12
12/1-1/3 & 8/24-11/30 [AP]	1P: $161-$180	2P: $214-$240	XP: $80	F12

Resort
Small-scale Hotel

Location: On Yunque Iset, across wood bridge from Isla Mujeres northern tip. Located on its own island. Calle Zaziltla S/N 7 Islote Yunque 77500. Fax: 998/999-2010. **Facility:** Situated on a private island and connected by a wooden bridge, this lodging features wide beaches, tranquil surf and ample resort activities. 136 units. 130 one-bedroom standard units. 6 one-bedroom suites ($206-$412). 1-6 stories, interior/exterior corridors. *Bath:* shower only. **Parking:** no self-parking. **Terms:** 14 day cancellation notice, in season, [MAP] meal plan available. **Amenities:** honor bars. **Pool(s):** outdoor, wading, saltwater. **Leisure Activities:** saunas, canoeing, paddleboats, sailboats, windsurfing boat dock, snorkeling, 2 lighted tennis courts, exercise room. *Fee:* charter fishing, massage. **Guest Services:** gift shop, valet laundry. **Business Services:** meeting rooms, fax. **Cards:** AX, MC, VI.

SOME UNITS

HOTEL NA BALAM   Phone: 998/877-0279

All Year   1P: $136-$182   2P: $136-$182   XP: $20   F8

Small-scale Hotel

Location: Northern end of island; on the beach. Calle Zazil Ha 118 77400. Fax: 998/877-0446. **Facility:** 31 units. 30 one-bedroom standard units. 1 one-bedroom suite. 2 stories (no elevator), exterior corridors. *Bath:* shower only. **Parking:** on-site. **Terms:** office hours 7 am-11 pm, 14 day cancellation notice. **Amenities:** safes. **Pool(s):** outdoor. **Leisure Activities:** Fee: scuba diving, snorkeling, fishing, charter fishing, massage. **Guest Services:** valet laundry. **Cards:** AX, MC, VI.

SECRETO.COM   *Book at aaa.com*   Phone: (998)877-1039
▼▼▼   All Year [CP]   1P: $125-$200   2P: $125-$200   XP: $25   F5
Small-scale Hotel   **Location:** On north beach. Located in a quiet, secluded area. Seccion Rocas, Lote 11, Punta Norte 77400. Fax: 998/877-1048. **Facility:** 9 one-bedroom standard units. 3 stories (no elevator), interior corridors. *Bath:* shower only. **Parking:** on-site. **Terms:** age restrictions may apply, 30 day cancellation notice, in season. **Amenities:** CD players, honor bars, irons, hair dryers. **Pool(s):** outdoor. **Leisure Activities:** Fee: massage. **Business Services:** fax (fee). **Cards:** MC, VI.

(D) ⊠ ☎

VILLA VERA PUERTO ISLA MUJERES   Phone: 998/877-0330
▼▼▼   All Year [CP]   1P: $180-$270   2P: $180-$270
Small-scale Hotel   **Location:** Towards southern end of island; south of airstrip. Laguna Makax S/N 77400. Fax: 998/877-0330. **Facility:** 24 units. 20 one-bedroom standard units with whirlpools. 4 one-bedroom suites ($210-$330) with efficiencies and whirlpools. 2 stories, exterior corridors. *Bath:* shower or tub only. **Parking:** on-site. **Terms:** 21 day cancellation notice, in season. **Amenities:** video library, CD players, safes, honor bars, hair dryers. **Pool(s):** heated outdoor, wading. **Leisure Activities:** scuba diving, snorkeling. *Fee:* marina, charter fishing. **Guest Services:** gift shop, valet laundry. **Business Services:** meeting rooms, fax (fee). **Cards:** AX, MC, VI.

SOME UNITS
⊞ ⊤ (D) ⊠ ⊠ (VCR) ☎ (DATA PORT) / ⊠ ▣

──── *The following lodgings were either not evaluated or did not* ────
meet AAA rating requirements but are listed for your information only.

CASA DE LOS SUENOS   Phone: 998/877-0651
[fyi]   Not evaluated. **Location:** Carr Garrafon KM 6 77400. Facilities, services, and decor characterize an upscale property.

ROLANDI GOURMET BEACH CLUB   Phone: 998/877-0700
[fyi]   Not evaluated. **Location:** Laguna Mar section of Sac-bajo. Lotes 15 y 16 Carr Sac-ba 77400. Facilities, services, and decor characterize an upscale property.

──── **WHERE TO DINE** ────

The following restaurant has not been evaluated by AAA
but is listed for your information only.

THE PORTERHOUSE STEAK & SEAFOOD GRILL   Phone: 998/999-2050
[fyi]   Not evaluated. **Location:** On Yunque Iset, across wood bridge from Isla Mujeres northern tip; in Avalon Reef Club. Calle Zazil Ha S/N 7 Islote 77500. **Features:** The upscale restaurant, located in the Avalon Reef Club, offers imported cuts of American beef and fresh seafood.

MERIDA, YUCATAN pop. 680,300

──── **WHERE TO STAY** ────

BEST WESTERN MARIA DEL CARMEN   *Book at aaa.com*   Phone: 999/930-0390
▼▼ ◊◊   All Year   1P: $65-$130   2P: $65-$130   XP: $7   F12
Small-scale Hotel   **Location:** 3 blks w of main plaza; between Calle 68 and 70. Calle 63 #550 97000 (Apdo Postal 411). Fax: 999/930-0393. **Facility:** 90 units. 6 stories, interior/exterior corridors. *Bath:* combo or shower only. **Parking:** on-site. **Terms:** 3 day cancellation notice-fee imposed, small pets only. **Amenities:** hair dryers. **Pool(s):** outdoor. **Guest Services:** valet laundry. **Business Services:** meeting rooms, fax (fee). **Cards:** AX, DC, MC, VI.

SOME UNITS
(S D) ⊠ ⊞ ⊤ ⊠ ☎ (DATA PORT) ▣ / ⊠ /

DEL GOBERNADOR HOTEL   *Book at aaa.com*   Phone: (999)930-4141
▼▼ ◊◊   All Year   1P: $80-$110   2P: $80-$110   XP: $11   F12
Small-scale Hotel   **Location:** Jct calles 59 and 66. Located in a quiet area. 535 Calle 59 97000. Fax: 999/930-4149. **Facility:** 86 one-bedroom standard units, some with whirlpools. 3 stories (no elevator), exterior corridors. *Bath:* shower only. **Parking:** on-site. **Terms:** 5 day cancellation notice-fee imposed, [MAP] meal plan available. **Amenities:** voice mail. *Some:* hair dryers. **Pool(s):** 2 small outdoor. **Guest Services:** valet laundry. **Business Services:** meeting rooms, fax. **Cards:** AX, DC, DS, MC, VI.

(S D) ⊞ ⊤ (fi) ⊠ ☎

FIESTA AMERICANA MERIDA   *Book at aaa.com*   Phone: (999)942-1111
◊◊◊   All Year   1P: $120-$250   2P: $120-$250   XP: $25   F17
▼▼ ◊◊   **Location:** Paseo de Montejo at Ave Colon; 1 km n of main plaza. Facing historic Paseo de Montejo. Paseo de Montejo #451 97127. Fax: 999/942-1112. **Facility:** Set just off Paseo de Montejo, this large-scale hotel offers a refined atmosphere, full service and a striking atrium lobby. 350 units. 327 one-bedroom standard units. 22 one-
Large-scale Hotel   and 1 two-bedroom suites, some with whirlpools. 5 stories, interior corridors. **Parking:** on-site. **Terms:** 3 day cancellation notice, [AP], [BP] & [MAP] meal plans available. **Amenities:** video games (fee), voice mail, safes, honor bars, hair dryers. *Some:* high-speed Internet .(fee). **Dining:** 2 restaurants, 6:45 am-midnight, cocktails, entertainment. **Pool(s):** heated outdoor. **Leisure Activities:** sauna, whirlpool, steamroom, tennis court, exercise room, spa. **Guest Services:** gift shop, valet laundry. **Business Services:** conference facilities, business center. **Cards:** AX, DC, MC, VI. *(See color ad card insert)*

SOME UNITS
⊞ (24) ⊤ (fi) (S) (D) ⊠ ⊠ ☎ (DATA PORT) ▣ / ⊠ /

HACIENDA TEYA

Phone: 999/988-0800

Classic Country Inn

All Year [CP]   1P: $100   2P: $100   XP: $10
Location: On Merida to Cancun Hwy. KM 12.5 Carr Merida-Cancun 97300. Fax: 999/924-5853. **Facility:** Upon arriving, the bright pink and rich brown buildings of this hacienda welcome both group functions and the individual traveler. 6 units. 3 one-bedroom standard units with whirlpools. 3 one-bedroom suites ($100) with whirlpools. 2 stories (no elevator), exterior corridors. **Parking:** on-site. **Terms:** office hours 8 am-6 pm. **Dining:** Hacienda Teya Restaurante, see separate listing. **Pool(s):** outdoor. **Guest Services:** gift shop. **Business Services:** meeting rooms, fax (fee). **Cards:** AX, MC, VI.

HOLIDAY INN

Phone: (999)942-8800

Large-scale Hotel

All Year   1P: $84-$120   2P: $84-$120   XP: $12   F12
Location: 1 km n of main plaza; jct Calle 60 and Ave Colon, just off Paseo de Montejo. Located behind the US Consulate. Ave Colon 498 97000. Fax: 999/942-8811. **Facility:** Meets AAA guest room security requirements. 212 one-bedroom standard units. 4 stories, interior corridors. **Parking:** on-site. **Amenities:** voice mail, irons, hair dryers. *Some:* safes. **Pool(s):** outdoor, wading. **Leisure Activities:** exercise room. *Fee:* lighted tennis court, massage. **Guest Services:** valet laundry. **Business Services:** conference facilities, business center. **Cards:** AX, DC, MC, VI.

SOME UNITS

HOTEL CARIBE

Phone: (999)924-9022

Small-scale Hotel

All Year   1P: $50-$70   2P: $50-$70   XP: $4
Location: In front of Plaza Parque Hidalgo. Located adjacent to old town square. Calle 59 #500 97000. Fax: 999/924-8733. **Facility:** 53 one-bedroom standard units. 3 stories (no elevator), exterior corridors. *Bath:* shower only. **Parking:** on-site. **Amenities:** safes. *Some:* hair dryers. **Pool(s):** small outdoor. **Guest Services:** gift shop, valet laundry. **Business Services:** meeting rooms. *Fee:* PC, fax. **Cards:** AX, MC, VI.

SOME UNITS

HOTEL CASA DEL BALAM   *Book at aaa.com*

Phone: (999)924-8844

Small-scale Hotel

All Year   1P: $100-$150   2P: $100-$150   XP: $10   F12
Location: 2 blks n of main plaza; jct calles 60 and 57. Calle 60 #488 97000. Fax: 999/924-5011. **Facility:** 52 units. 49 one-bedroom standard units. 3 one-bedroom suites ($120-$170). 6 stories, exterior corridors. **Parking:** on-site. **Terms:** [BP] & [CP] meal plans available. **Amenities:** honor bars, hair dryers. **Dining:** 7 am-11 pm, cocktails, entertainment. **Pool(s):** small outdoor. **Guest Services:** valet laundry. **Business Services:** meeting rooms, fax (fee). **Cards:** AX, CB, DC, MC, VI.

SOME UNITS

HOTEL EL CONQUISTADOR

Phone: (999)926-2155

Large-scale Hotel

All Year   1P: $115-$180   2P: $115-$180   XP: $15   F12
Location: 13 blks n of main plaza. Paseo de Montejo #458 97000. Fax: 999/926-8829. **Facility:** 159 one-bedroom standard units. 8 stories, interior corridors. **Parking:** on-site. **Terms:** [AP], [BP], [CP], [ECP] & [MAP] meal plans available. **Amenities:** safes (fee), honor bars, hair dryers. **Dining:** 2 restaurants, 7 am-midnight, cocktails, entertainment. **Pool(s):** outdoor. **Leisure Activities:** recreation programs. **Guest Services:** gift shop, valet laundry. **Business Services:** conference facilities. business center. **Cards:** AX, CB, DC, MC, VI.

SOME UNITS

FEE

HOTEL LOS ALUXES   *Book at aaa.com*

Phone: 999/924-2199

Large-scale Hotel

All Year   1P: $100-$130   2P: $100-$130   XP: $20   F12
Location: 5 blks n of main plaza; jct calles 60 and 49. Calle 60 #444 97000. Fax: 999/923-3858. **Facility:** 155 units. 137 one-bedroom standard units, some with whirlpools. 18 one-bedroom suites ($170-$210). 3-5 stories, interior corridors. **Parking:** on-site. **Terms:** 7 day cancellation notice, [BP] & [MAP] meal plans available. **Amenities:** voice mail, hair dryers. *Some:* honor bars. **Pool(s):** outdoor. **Guest Services:** gift shop, valet laundry. **Business Services:** conference facilities, business center. **Cards:** AX, MC, VI.

HOTEL MISION MERIDA   *Book at aaa.com*

Phone: (999)923-9500

Large-scale Hotel

All Year   1P: $90-$120   2P: $90-$120   XP: $12   F12
Location: 2 blks n of main plaza; jct calles 60 and 57. Calle 60 #491 97000. Fax: 999/923-7665. **Facility:** 145 one-bedroom standard units. 11 stories, interior corridors. *Bath:* combo or shower only. **Parking:** on-site. **Terms:** [AP], [BP], [CP] & [MAP] meal plans available. **Amenities:** *Some:* safes, honor bars, hair dryers. **Pool(s):** outdoor. **Leisure Activities:** *Fee:* game room. **Guest Services:** gift shop, valet laundry. **Business Services:** fax (fee). **Cards:** AX, DC, MC, VI.

SOME UNITS

HOTEL RESIDENCIAL   *Book at aaa.com*

Phone: (999)924-3099

Small-scale Hotel

All Year   1P: $85-$150   2P: $85-$150   XP: $15   F12
Location: Jct calles 59 and 76. Calle 59 #589 97000. Fax: 999/924-0266. **Facility:** Meets AAA guest room security requirements. 66 units. 64 one-bedroom standard units. 2 one-bedroom suites with whirlpools. 5 stories, interior/exterior corridors. *Bath:* shower only. **Parking:** on-site. **Terms:** 3 day cancellation notice, [AP], [BP], [CP], [ECP] & [MAP] meal plans available. **Amenities:** hair dryers. **Dining:** 7 am-11 pm, cocktails, entertainment. **Pool(s):** small outdoor. **Guest Services:** valet laundry. **Business Services:** meeting rooms, fax (fee). **Cards:** AX, MC, VI.

HOTEL VILLA MERCEDES *Book at aaa.com*

Phone: 999/942-9000

▽▽▽▽

Small-scale Hotel

All Year 1P: $150-$170 2P: $190-$220 XP: $25 F12
Location: 1 km n of main plaza; jct Calle 60 and Ave Colon, just off Paseo de Montejo. Ave Colon 500 97000. Fax: 999/942-9001. **Facility:** Meets AAA guest room security requirements. 84 units. 81 one-bedroom standard units. 3 one-bedroom suites with whirlpools. 5 stories, interior corridors. **Parking:** on-site and valet. **Amenities:** dual phone lines, voice mail, safes, honor bars, hair dryers. **Pool(s):** outdoor. **Leisure Activities:** exercise room. *Fee:* massage. **Guest Services:** gift shop, valet laundry. **Business Services:** meeting rooms, business center. **Cards:** AX, MC, VI.

SOME UNITS

⊞ 24↑ ⊤ ♿ S D ⊅ ※ DATA PORT / ✕ /

HYATT REGENCY MERIDA *Book at aaa.com*

Phone: (999)942-1234

▽▽▽▽

Large-scale Hotel

All Year 1P: $120-$185 2P: $120-$185 XP: $25 F12
Location: 1 km n of main plaza; jct Calle 60 and Ave Colon, just off Paseo de Montejo. Calle 60 #344 97000. Fax: 999/925-7002. **Facility:** Meets AAA guest room security requirements. 299 units. 295 one-bedroom standard units. 4 one-bedroom suites ($190) with whirlpools. 17 stories, interior corridors. **Parking:** on-site and valet. **Terms:** 3 day cancellation notice, [AP], [BP], [CP] & [MAP] meal plans available. **Amenities:** voice mail, honor bars, hair dryers. *Some:* safes. **Pool(s):** outdoor. **Leisure Activities:** whirlpool, steamroom, 2 lighted tennis courts, exercise room. *Fee:* massage. **Guest Services:** gift shop, valet laundry. **Business Services:** conference facilities, business center. **Cards:** AX, MC, VI.

SOME UNITS

S D ⊞ 24↑ ⊤ ♿ S D ⊅ ✕ ※ DATA PORT / ■ /

LA HACIENDA XCANATUN CASA DE PIEDRA

Phone: (999)941-0213

ⓐ

▽▽▽

Classic Historic
Country Inn

All Year [CP] 1P: $240-$305 2P: $240-$305
Location: Just e of Mex 261 at KM 12 Merida-Progresso Hwy. Adjacent to Xcanatun hamlet. KM 12 Carr Merida-Progresso 97300 (Apdo Postal 1161, Admon de Correos Siglo). Fax: 999/941-0319. **Facility:** The beautifully restored former hacienda features Mayan relics, lush gardens and luxurious accommodations in the midst of the Yucatan jungle. Meets AAA guest room security requirements. 18 one-bedroom suites, some with whirlpools. 1-2 stories (no elevator), exterior corridors. **Parking:** on-site. **Terms:** 5% service charge. **Amenities:** CD players, safes, honor bars, hair dryers. **Dining:** Casa de Piedra, see separate listing. **Pool(s):** 2 outdoor. **Leisure Activities:** hiking trails, spa. **Guest Services:** valet laundry, area transportation (fee). **Business Services:** meeting rooms, fax (fee). **Cards:** AX, MC, VI.

SOME UNITS

✈ ⊞ D ⊅ ⋈ / ✕ /
FEE

LA MISION DE FRAY DIEGO *Book at aaa.com*

Phone: (999)924-1111

▽▽▽ ▽▽

Country Inn

All Year 1P: $85-$100 2P: $85-$100 XP: $10 F11
Location: 2 blks w of main city plaza; between calles 64 and 66. Calle 61 #524 97000. Fax: 999/923-7397. **Facility:** 26 units. 24 one-bedroom standard units. 2 one-bedroom suites ($125-$135) with whirlpools. 2-3 stories (no elevator), exterior corridors. **Parking:** on-site. **Amenities:** safes, honor bars. *Some:* hair dryers. **Pool(s):** outdoor. **Guest Services:** valet laundry. **Business Services:** fax (fee). **Cards:** AX, MC, VI.

⊞ D ⊅ ※

––––––– **WHERE TO DINE** –––––––

ALBERTO'S CONTINENTAL PATIO

Lunch: $6-$20 Dinner: $6-$20 **Phone: 999/928-5367**

▽▽ ▽▽

Regional
International

MC, VI. **Historic**

Location: Corner of calles 57 and 64. Calle 64 #482 97000. **Hours:** 1 pm-11 pm; from 5 pm 12/25 & 1/1. Closed: Mardi Gras Tues & Holy Friday. **Reservations:** accepted. **Features:** Lebanese specialties are among the international dishes prepared in this converted 17th-century home. Decorated with artifacts from the city's rich colonial past, the museum-like restaurant offers seating in the open-air patio or the air-conditioned dining room. Tour groups occasionally flood this place. Casual dress; cocktails. **Parking:** street. **Cards:** AX,

⊤

CASA DEL PASEO

Lunch: $8-$12 Dinner: $10-$22 **Phone: 999/920-0528**

▽▽▽

Regional Mexican

Location: On Paseo del Montejo; next to US Consulate. Paseo de Montejo #405 97000. **Hours:** 1 pm-2 am. Closed: Sun. **Reservations:** suggested. **Features:** The stylish interior decor and the terrace seating area cater to diners' wishes. Representative of the wide selection of Continental and Yucatan offerings are varied pates and rich cream soups. Dressy casual; cocktails. **Parking:** valet. **Cards:** AX, CB, DC, MC, VI.

✕

CASA DE PIEDRA

Lunch: $10-$18 Dinner: $15-$25 **Phone: 999/941-0213**

ⓐ

▽▽▽▽

Regional
Mexican

Location: Just e of Mex 261 at KM 12 Merida-Progresso Hwy; in La Hacienda Xcanatun Casa de Piedra. KM 12 Carr Merida-Progresso 97300. **Hours:** 7:30 am-11 pm. **Reservations:** suggested. **Features:** The restaurant offers haute cuisine, featuring regional and European dishes artistically presented by highly trained staff in an upscale dining room. Dressy casual; cocktails. **Parking:** on-site and valet. **Cards:** AX, MC, VI.

⊤ ✕

HACIENDA TEYA RESTAURANTE

Lunch: $6-$12 Dinner: $10-$18 **Phone: 999/928-1885**

▽▽ ▽▽

Regional Mexican

Location: On Merida to Cancun Hwy; in Hacienda Teya. KM 12.5 Carr Merida-Cancun 97300. **Hours:** noon-6 pm. **Reservations:** suggested. **Features:** On the main highway to Chichen Itza, the restored henequen hacienda has original furnishings and specializes in Mayan cuisine. Casual dress; cocktails. **Parking:** on-site. **Cards:** AX, CB, DC, DS, JC, MC, VI.

LA BELLA EPOCA

Dinner: $12-$25 **Phone: 999/928-1928**

▽▽▽▽

Regional Mexican

Location: 2 blks n of main plaza. Calle 60 #497 97000. **Hours:** 4 pm-midnight. **Reservations:** suggested. **Features:** The Yucatan is the focus of traditional Mexican dishes. Most distinctive grilled dishes are a worthy first choice. The setting is casual on several floors, but second-floor balcony tables offer the best views and cool breezes. Casual dress; cocktails. **Parking:** street. **Cards:** AX, MC, VI.

⊤

LA PIGUA

▽▽▽
Regional Seafood

Lunch: $7-$10   **Dinner:** $12-$20   **Phone:** 999/920-3605
Location: 2 blks w of Fiesta Americana Merida; off Cupules Ave. Calle 33 #505 97127. **Hours:** noon-6 pm. **Reservations:** suggested. **Features:** Widely varied fresh seafood is prepared using both classic and innovative approaches. The service staff is knowledgeable. Dressy casual; cocktails. **Parking:** on-site. **Cards:** AX, MC, VI.

LOS ALMENDROS

▽▽▽
Regional Mexican

Lunch: $7-$10   **Dinner:** $10-$18   **Phone:** 999/928-5459
Location: 7 blks n of main plaza. Calle 50 #493 97127. **Hours:** 11 am-11 pm. **Reservations:** accepted. **Features:** Classic Yucatan cuisine includes pibil-style dishes, fried plantains, pork and chicken marinated in citrus fruits. A favorite choice is a plate of tender, oversized tamales wrapped in banana leaves. Leon beer is popular. Casual dress; cocktails. **Parking:** street. **Cards:** AX, MC, VI.

The following restaurants have not been evaluated by AAA but are listed for your information only.

LA CASONA

fyi

Phone: 999/923-8348
Not evaluated. **Location:** 7 blks n of main plaza; between calles 49 and 47. Calle 60 #434 97127. **Features:** Classic Italian selections made with homemade pasta and served in a turn-of-the-20th-century garden courtyard. Limited seating in air-conditioned area. Attentive staff ensures a more than pleasant dining experience.

PANCHO'S

fyi

Phone: 999/923-0942
Not evaluated. **Location:** 1 blk n of main plaza. Calle 59 #509 97000. **Features:** Mexico comes alive in the drinks, food and dancing at the high-energy dining choice.

PLAYA DEL CARMEN, QUINTANA ROO pop. 47,200

——— WHERE TO STAY ———

THE GRAND MAYAN RIVIERA MAYA

fyi

Resort
Large-scale Hotel

Phone: 984/206-4000
All Year   1P: $191-$286   2P: $224-$336   XP: $70   F12
Too new to rate, opening scheduled for July 2004. **Location:** Mex 307, 35 km s of Cancun International Airport. KM 48 Carr Federal Cancun 77710. Fax: 984/206-4050. **Amenities:** 376 units, restaurant, coffeemakers, microwaves, refrigerators, pool, golf, tennis. **Terms:** check-in 5 pm, 3 night minimum stay - seasonal and/or weekends, 30 day cancellation notice. **Cards:** AX, MC, VI.

MAYAN PALACE RIVIERA MAYA

▽▽▽▽
Resort
Large-scale Hotel

Phone: (984)206-4000
All Year   1P: $139-$209   2P: $173-$259   XP: $59   F12
Location: Mex 307, 35 km s of Cancun International Airport. KM 48 Carr Federal Cancun 77710. Fax: 984/206-4050. **Facility:** Newly completed, the complex has the Caribbean on one side and 18 holes of rolling turf on the other; rooms are well appointed and generous in size. 336 units. 168 one-bedroom standard units. 168 one-bedroom suites with efficiencies. 3 stories, interior corridors. **Parking:** on-site and valet. **Terms:** check-in 5 pm, 3 night minimum stay - seasonal and/or weekends, 30 day cancellation notice. **Amenities:** voice mail, hair dryers. *Fee:* video games, safes. *Some:* irons. **Pool(s):** outdoor. **Leisure Activities:** whirlpools, lifeguard on duty, rental sailboats, recreation programs, bicycles, volleyball. *Fee:* scuba diving, snorkeling, golf-18 holes, 2 lighted tennis courts, massage. **Guest Services:** gift shop, valet and coin laundry. **Business Services:** *Fee:* PC, fax. **Cards:** AX, MC, VI.

SOME UNITS

[🅂🄳] [✈] [🍴] [24🕐] [🍸] [D] [🏊] [✕] [📷] [DATA PORT] / [✕] [📶] [📠] [▭] /
FEE

OCCIDENTAL ROYAL HIDEAWAY RESORT & SPA   *Book at aaa.com*   **Phone:** (984)873-4500

ΛΛΛ

▽▽▽ ▽▽▽
Resort
Large-scale Hotel

All Year [AP]   1P: $263-$735   2P: $536-$1236   XP: $655
Location: In Playacar development; e off Mex 307; on the beach. Located in a modern, upscale area. Lote Hotelera #7 Fracc Playacar 77710. Fax: 984/873-4506. **Facility:** This all-inclusive resort offers luxurious rooms, full concierge service, elegant dining and an abundance of resort activities. 200 units. 198 one-bedroom standard units with whirlpools. 2 one-bedroom suites with whirlpools. 2-3 stories (no elevator), exterior corridors. **Parking:** on-site. **Terms:** age restrictions may apply. **Amenities:** video library, video games, CD players, voice mail, safes, irons, hair dryers. *Some:* fax. **Dining:** 7 restaurants, 7 am-1 am, cocktails, entertainment. **Pool(s):** 6 outdoor. **Leisure Activities:** whirlpools, rental boats, canoeing, paddleboats, sailboats, windsurfing, marina, scuba diving, snorkeling, poolside aerobics, introductory scuba instruction, 2 lighted tennis courts, recreation programs, library, non-motorized sports, ping pong, theater, bicycles, spa. *Fee:* waterskiing, charter fishing. **Guest Services:** gift shop, complimentary evening beverages, valet laundry, area transportation (fee). **Business Services:** conference facilities, business center. **Cards:** AX, CB, DC, JC, MC, VI. *(See color ad p 356)*

SOME UNITS

[✈] [🍴] [24🕐] [🍸] [D] [🏊] [👨] [✕] [VCR] [📷] [DATA PORT] [📶] [▭] / [✕] /

The following lodgings were either not evaluated or did not meet AAA rating requirements but are listed for your information only.

DESEO HOTEL & LOUNGE

fyi

Phone: 984/879-3620
Not evaluated. **Location:** 5A Ave y Calle 12 77710. Facilities, services, and decor characterize a mid-range property.

GRAN PORTO REAL RESORT AND SPA

fyi

Phone: 984/873-4000
Not evaluated. **Location:** On the beach, in town; just off Mex 307. Constituyentes #1 77710. Facilities, services, and decor characterize a mid-range property.

HOTEL RIU PALACE

fyi

Phone: 984/877-4200
Not evaluated. **Location:** In Playacar development. Ave Xaman-Ha Lote 3 77710. Facilities, services, and decor characterize an upscale property.

HOTEL RIU PLAYACAR   Phone: 984/877-2300
[fyi]   Not evaluated. **Location:** In Playacar development. Ave Xarnan-Ha Mz 3 Lote 0 77710. Facilities, services, and decor characterize an upscale property.

HOTEL RIU TEQUILA   Phone: 984/873-4300
[fyi]   Not evaluated. **Location:** In Playacar development. Ave Xarnan-Ha Mz 25 Lote 19 77710. Facilities, services, and decor characterize an upscale property.

HOTEL RIU YUCATAN   Phone: 984/873-1300
[fyi]   Not evaluated. **Location:** In Playacar complex. Ave Xarnan-Ha Mz 3 77710. Facilities, services, and decor characterize an upscale property.

ROYAL PORTO REAL RESORT & SPA   Phone: 984/873-4000
[fyi]   Not evaluated. **Location:** On the beach; just off Mex 307. Constituyentes #2 77780. Facilities, services, and decor characterize a mid-range property.

———— **WHERE TO DINE** ————

LA CASA DEL AGUA   Lunch: $7-$15   Dinner: $10-$22   Phone: 984/803-0232
◆◆◆ ◆◆◆   **Location:** On 5th Ave walkway. 5th Ave Esquina 2 Norte, Col Centro 77710. **Hours:** noon-midnight. **Reservations:** suggested, for dinner. **Features:** A charming restaurant offering ocean views and a varied
Regional Mexican   menu of European, Mexican and seafood selections. Casual dress; cocktails. **Parking:** no self-parking. **Cards:** MC, VI.

PALAPA HEMINGWAY   Lunch: $8-$18   Dinner: $15-$35   Phone: 984/803-0003
◆◆◆ ◆◆◆   **Location:** On 5th Ave walkway; between 12th and 14th sts. 5th Ave #230 77700. **Hours:** 8 am-midnight. **Reservations:** accepted. **Features:** A lively ambience and a distinctly Cuban menu make this a popular
Regional Mexican   choice with tourists and locals alike. Casual dress; cocktails. **Parking:** no self-parking. **Cards:** MC, VI.

YAXCHE-MAYA CUISINE   Lunch: $9-$14   Dinner: $12-$15   Phone: 984/873-2502
◆◆◆ ◆◆◆   **Location:** Just n off 5th Ave pedestrian area. Calle 8 entre Ave 5 & 10 77700. **Hours:** noon-11 pm. **Reservations:** accepted. **Features:** For a true ancient Mexican experience, dine at Yaxche, where both the
Regional Mexican   menu and decor take diners back in time. Casual dress; cocktails. **Parking:** no self-parking. **Cards:** AX, MC, VI.

PUERTO MORELOS, QUINTANA ROO pop. 800

──────── WHERE TO STAY ────────

CEIBA DEL MAR HOTEL & SPA *Book at aaa.com* Phone: (998)872-8060
▼▼◇◇▼ All Year [CP]   1P: $250-$315   2P: $250-$315   XP: $35   F8
Location: Off Mex 307, 6 km e. Costera Norte Lote 1 M26 S/N 77580. Fax: 998/872-8061. **Facility:** 125 units. 120
Small-scale Hotel one-bedroom standard units. 5 one-bedroom suites ($395-$700). 2 stories, exterior corridors. *Bath:* shower
only. **Parking:** on-site and valet. **Terms:** 14 day cancellation notice, in season, [MAP] meal plan available.
Amenities: video library, CD players, safes, honor bars, hair dryers. **Pool(s):** 2 outdoor. **Leisure Activities:** scuba diving &
rental equipment, snorkeling & rental equipment, spa. *Fee:* charter fishing. **Guest Services:** gift shop, valet laundry. **Business
Services:** fax (fee). **Cards:** AX, MC, VI.

⊘ 🍽 24🏧 ⊻ D ⊛ ✕ VCR ⊮

PARADISUS RIVIERA CANCUN   Phone: (998)872-8383
▼▼◇◇ ◇◇▼ 7/1-8/21 [AP]   1P: $400-$560   2P: $800-$1120   XP: $96   F6
          12/1-6/30 & 8/22-11/30 [AP] 1P: $384-$464   2P: $726-$978   XP: $96   F6
Resort **Location:** Off Mex 307, 3 km n, follow signs. SM 11 Manzana 9, Lote 10 77509 (PO Box MEXICO Ave Xpuhil #3 Ste
Large-scale Hotel 167 SM27, CANCUN, QR, 77500). Fax: 998/872-8388. **Facility:** The upscale all-inclusive resort's open air
lobby, Mayan theme and beautiful beach activities area make it a special destination for families. 496 units.
458 one-bedroom standard units, some with whirlpools. 38 one-bedroom suites with whirlpools. 2-3 stories, exterior corridors.
Parking: on-site and valet. **Terms:** 4 day cancellation notice. **Amenities:** voice mail, safes, irons, hair dryers. **Pool(s):** 4
outdoor, wading. **Leisure Activities:** paddleboats, sailboats, snorkeling, spa. *Fee:* scuba diving, charter fishing. **Guest
Services:** gift shop, valet laundry, area transportation (fee). **Business Services:** meeting rooms, fax (fee). **Cards:** AX, DS, JC,
MC, VI.
                                                                        SOME UNITS
✈ 🍽 24🏧 ⊻ S D ⊛ ✕ ⊮ DATA⎇PORT ⊟ /✕/

PARAISO DE LA BONITA RESORT AND THALASSO   Phone: (998)872-8300
▼▼◇◇◇ ◇◇▼ 12/1-1/4   1P: $500-$850   2P: $500-$850   XP: $90   F17
           1/5-5/31   1P: $425-$750   2P: $425-$750   XP: $90   F17
           6/1-11/30   1P: $395-$750   2P: $395-$750   XP: $90   F17
Resort **Location:** Mex 307, 22 km s of Cancun International Airport. Carr Chetumal-Cancun KM 328 77580 (PO Box 461).
Small-scale Hotel Fax: 998/872-8301. **Facility:** The small, secluded resort is comprised of palatial guest rooms and public
areas, a world-class spa and highly personalized service. 90 units. 82 one- and 8 two-bedroom suites. 3 stories, exterior
corridors. **Parking:** on-site and valet. **Terms:** age restrictions may apply, cancellation fee imposed, 8% service charge.
Amenities: video library, DVD players, CD players, voice mail, safes, honor bars, hair dryers. **Dining:** La Canoa, see separate
listing. **Pool(s):** heated outdoor, saltwater. **Leisure Activities:** saunas, whirlpools, steamrooms, boat dock, lighted tennis court,
spa. *Fee:* boats, sailboats, scuba diving, snorkeling, charter fishing, Thalasso Therapy Center. **Guest Services:** gift shop, valet
laundry. **Business Services:** meeting rooms, business center. **Cards:** AX, DC, MC, VI.
                                                                        SOME UNITS
S🄳 ✈ 🍽 24🏧 ⊻ D ⊛ ⓦ ✕ ⊮ DATA⎇PORT /✕/

──────── *The following lodging was either not evaluated or did not* ────────
meet AAA rating requirements but is listed for your information only.

MOON PALACE   Phone: 998/881-6000
fyi **Not evaluated. Location:** Mex 307, 16 km s of Cancun International Airport. Carr Chetumal-Cancun (Apdo Postal
1730, CANCUN, QR, 77500). Facilities, services, and decor characterize an upscale property.

──────── WHERE TO DINE ────────

LA CANOA   **Dinner:** $22-$35   Phone: 998/872-8300
▼▼◇◇ ◇◇▼ **Location:** Mex 307, 22 km s of Cancun International Airport; in Paraiso de la Bonita Resort and Thalasso. Carr
Chetumal-Cancun KM 328 77580. **Hours:** 6 pm-11 pm. **Reservations:** suggested. **Features:** The flavors of
International North Africa, France and Mexico gracefully collide at the top-notch eatery, making for a dining adventure.
Those who are unsure of what to have should ask the chef as he passes the table, and maybe a surprise
will be whipped up in their honor. Dressy casual; cocktails. **Parking:** valet. **Cards:** AX, DC, JC, MC, VI.
                                                                        ⊻

TEMOZON, YUCATAN

──────── WHERE TO STAY ────────

──────── *The following lodging was either not evaluated or did not* ────────
meet AAA rating requirements but is listed for your information only.

HACIENDA TEMOZON   Phone: 999/923-8089
fyi **Not evaluated. Location:** Off Mex 281, Merida to Uxmal Hwy. KM 182 Carr Merida-Uxmal 97825. Facilities, services,
and decor characterize an upscale property.

──────── WHERE TO DINE ────────

RESTAURANTE HACIENDA TEMOZON   **Lunch:** $8-$12   **Dinner:** $10-$18   Phone: 999/923-8089
▼▼◇▼ **Location:** Off Mex 281; Merida to Uxmal Hwy; in Hacienda Temozon. KM 183 Carr Merida-Uxmal 97825. **Hours:** 7
am-11 pm. **Reservations:** suggested. **Features:** The secluded restaurant overlooks the lush gardens of
Regional Mexican world famous Hacienda Temozon and features authentic Yucatan dishes. Casual dress; cocktails. **Parking:**
on-site. **Cards:** AX, DC, MC, VI.
                                                                        ⊻ 🅐🅒

TIXKOKOB, YUCATAN

──── WHERE TO STAY ────

──── *The following lodging was either not evaluated or did not* ────
meet AAA rating requirements but is listed for your information only.

HACIENDA SAN JOSE   Phone: 999/910-4617
[fyi]   Not evaluated. **Location:** KM 30 Carr Tixkokob-Tekanto 97470. Facilities, services, and decor characterize an upscale
               property.

TULUM, QUINTANA ROO

──── WHERE TO STAY ────

──── *The following lodgings were either not evaluated or did not* ────
meet AAA rating requirements but are listed for your information only.

BAHIA PRINCIPE TULUM   Phone: 984/875-5000
[fyi]   Not evaluated. **Location:** KM 250 Carr Cancun-Chetumal, Benito Juarez Local B. KM 250 Carr Chetumal, Benito
               Juarez. Facilities, services, and decor characterize a mid-range property.

COPA CABANA BEACH RESORT   Phone: 984/875-1800
[fyi]   Not evaluated. **Location:** Mex 307 at KM 264.5 (beachfront). Carr Cancun-Chetumal 77790. Facilities, services, and
               decor characterize an upscale property.

UMAN, YUCATAN

──── WHERE TO STAY ────

──── *The following lodging was either not evaluated or did not* ────
meet AAA rating requirements but is listed for your information only.

HACIENDA SANTA ROSA   Phone: 999/910-4875
[fyi]   Not evaluated. **Location:** 42 km s on Mex 180. KM 129 Carr Merida Campeche 97800. Facilities, services, and decor
               characterize an upscale property.

UXMAL, YUCATAN pop. 2,200

──── WHERE TO STAY ────

HOTEL HACIENDA UXMAL   *Book at aaa.com*   Phone: (997)976-2013
▼▼▼▼ ▼▼▼▼   11/1-11/30   2P: $131-$223   XP: $20   F12
                  12/1-4/30   2P: $114-$194   XP: $20   F12
Small-scale Hotel 5/1-10/31   2P: $89-$134   XP: $20   F12
Location: 85 km s of Merida on Mex 261. Located at main entrance to archeological zone. (Robalo #30 SM 3,
CANCUN, QR, 77500). Fax: 997/976-2011. **Facility:** 72 one-bedroom standard units, some with whirlpools. 3 stories (no elevator),
interior/exterior corridors. **Parking:** on-site. **Terms:** 15 day cancellation notice-fee imposed, [AP], [BP], [CP], [ECP] & [MAP]
meal plans available. **Amenities:** honor bars. **Pool(s):** 2 outdoor. **Guest Services:** gift shop, valet laundry. **Business Services:**
meeting rooms, fax (fee). **Cards:** AX, MC, VI.

SOME UNITS

[icons]

THE LODGE AT UXMAL   Phone: (997)976-2010
▼▼▼   12/1-4/30   2P: $228-$285   XP: $20   F12
             11/1-11/30   2P: $223-$257   XP: $20   F12
Classic   5/1-10/31   2P: $134-$188   XP: $20   F12
Country Inn **Location:** 85.5 km s of Merida on Mex 261. Located at main entrance to archeological zone. (Robalo #30 SM 3,
CANCUN, QR, 77500). Fax: 997/976-2102. **Facility:** Handmade furniture and stained-glass windows reveal a
Mayan theme at this property located at the Uxmal ruins. 40 one-bedroom standard units, some with whirlpools. 2 stories (no
elevator), exterior corridors. **Parking:** on-site. **Terms:** 15 day cancellation notice-fee imposed, [AP], [BP], [CP], [ECP] & [MAP]
meal plans available. **Amenities:** honor bars. **Pool(s):** 2 outdoor. **Guest Services:** valet laundry, area transportation fee.
Business Services: fax (fee). **Cards:** AX, MC, VI.

SOME UNITS

[icons]

BAJA CALIFORNIA

BUENAVISTA, BAJA CALIFORNIA SUR pop. 5,000

——— WHERE TO STAY ———

HOTEL BUENA VISTA BEACH RESORT
Phone: (624)141-0033
Resort Motel
All Year [AP]   1P: $90-$120   2P: $140-$170   XP: $50   D12
Location: On the shore of Bahia de Palmas off Mex 1. KM 105 Carr al Sur 23580 (130 27th St, CHULA VISTA, CA, 91911). Fax: 624/141-0133. **Facility:** One-story buildings down the hillside to the beach with lush gardens, flowers and fountains. Meets AAA guest room security requirements. 60 one-bedroom standard units. 1 story, exterior corridors. *Bath:* shower only. **Parking:** on-site. **Terms:** office hours 6 am-10 pm, 30 day cancellation notice, 15 day off season-fee imposed, [AP] meal plan available, 10% service charge. **Pool(s):** outdoor. **Leisure Activities:** whirlpools, boat ramp, scuba diving, snorkeling, fishing, 2 tennis courts. *Fee:* boats, canoes, charter fishing, horseback riding, massage. **Guest Services:** gift shop. **Business Services:** conference facilities. **Cards:** AX, MC, VI.

① ⛑ ⤴ ✗ Ⓦ ☎ ▣

——— *The following lodging was either not evaluated or did not* ———
meet AAA rating requirements but is listed for your information only.

RANCHO LEONERO RESORT
Phone: 624/141-0216
[fyi]
Resort Motel
Did not meet all AAA rating requirements for locking devices in some guest rooms at time of last evaluation on 10/20/2003. **Location:** 8 km e of Mex 1 at KM 103.5, via unpaved road. Located in a remote area. (1560 N Hwy 101, LEUCADIA, CA, 92024). Facilities, services, and decor characterize a basic property.

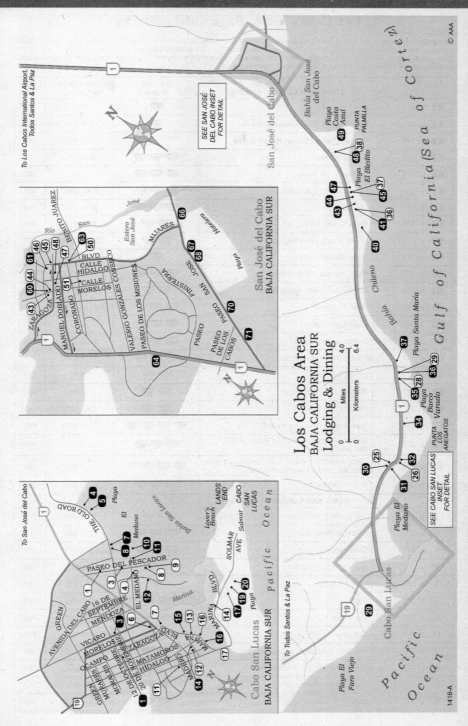

Los Cabos Area
BAJA CALIFORNIA SUR
Lodging & Dining

San José del Cabo
BAJA CALIFORNIA SUR

Cabo San Lucas
BAJA CALIFORNIA SUR

Los Cabos Area, Baja California Sur

This index helps you "spot" where approved accommodations and restaurants are located on the corresponding detailed maps. Lodging rate ranges are for comparison only and show the property's high season; rates are per night, unless only weekly (W) rates are available. Restaurant rate range is for dinner, unless only lunch (L) is served. Turn to the listing page for more detailed rate information and consult display ads for special promotions.

Spotter/Map Page Number	OA	CABO SAN LUCAS - Lodgings	Diamond Rating	Rate Range High Season	Listing Page
1 / p. 377		Hotel Santa Fe	◈	$87	382
3 / p. 377		Best Western Hotel Cabo Las Flores	◈	$75-$79	380
4 / p. 377	AAA	**Villa del Palmar Beach Resort & Spa**	◈◈◈	$246-$697	384
5 / p. 377		Villa La Estancia	◈◈◈	$316-$531	384
7 / p. 377		Pueblo Bonito Rose	◈◈◈	$300	383
8 / p. 377		Pueblo Bonito Los Cabos	◈◈◈	$315-$360	383
10 / p. 377		Melia San Lucas	◈◈◈	$280-$435	383
11 / p. 377		Bahia Condo Hotel	◈◈	$129-$149	380
12 / p. 377		Marina Fiesta Resort Hotel	◈◈	$200-$480	382
14 / p. 377		Siesta Suites Hotel	◈	$44-$55	384
15 / p. 377		Plaza Nautica Condominiums	◈◈◈	$150-$300	383
16 / p. 377		Costa Real Cabo Resorts & Suites	◈◈	$150-$188	380
17 / p. 377		Hotel Finisterra	◈◈	$140-$195	380
19 / p. 377		Playa Grande Resort	◈◈◈	$260	383
20 / p. 377		Solmar Suites Resort	◈◈◈	$135-$265	384
29 / p. 377		Pueblo Bonito Sunset Beach	◈◈◈	$195-$350	384
30 / p. 377		Los Patios Hotel	◈◈	$99	382
31 / p. 377		Calinda Cabo San Lucas	◈◈	$178	380
32 / p. 377		Misiones del Cabo	◈◈	$165-$275	383
34 / p. 377		Esperanza An Auberge Resort	◈◈◈◈	$550-$925	380
35 / p. 377		Sheraton Hacienda Del Mar Resort & Spa - see color ad p 8	◈◈◈	$399-$430	384
36 / p. 377		Fiesta Americana Grand Los Cabos - see color ad p 381, back cover, card inserts	◈◈◈◈	$344-$381	380
37 / p. 377		Hotel Twin Dolphin	◈◈◈	$350-$395	382
		CABO SAN LUCAS - Restaurants			
1 / p. 377		The Trailer Park Restaurant (La Golondrina)	◈◈	$14-$48	386
3 / p. 377		Peacocks Restaurant	◈◈◈	$18-$40	385
4 / p. 377		Casa Rafael's	◈◈◈	$19-$43	385
6 / p. 377		Stop Light Bar & Grill	◈	$6-$40	386
7 / p. 377		Margaritavilla	◈	$12-$40	385
8 / p. 377		Edith's	◈◈	$13-$55	385
9 / p. 377		The Office	◈◈	$12-$35	385
11 / p. 377		Mi Casa	◈◈	$11-$18	385
12 / p. 377		Pancho's Restaurant & Tequila Bar	◈◈	$12-$40	385
13 / p. 377		Senor Greenberg's Mexicatessen	◈	$7-$12	386
14 / p. 377		Galeon Italian Restaurant	◈◈	$8-$20	385
16 / p. 377		Sancho Panza	◈◈	$16-$30	386

Spotter/Map Page Number	OA	CABO SAN LUCAS - Restaurants (continued)	Diamond Rating	Rate Range High Season	Listing Page
⑰ / p. 377		Romeo y Julieta Ristorante	◈◈	$6-$20	386
㉕ / p. 377		Latitude 22+	◈	$9-$20	385
㉖ / p. 377		Ristorante Da Giorgio	◈◈◈	$10-$20	386
㉘ / p. 377		Pitahayas	◈◈	$25-$40	386
㉙ / p. 377		Rosato	◈◈◈	$16-$22	386
		SAN JOSE DEL CABO - Lodgings			
㊵ / p. 377		Melia Los Cabos All Suites Oceanfront, Spa & Golf Resort	◈◈◈	$281-$381	398
㊶ / p. 377		Casa Del Mar Golf Resort & Spa	◈◈◈	$430-$480	397
㊸ / p. 377	—	Las Ventanas Al Paraiso	◈◈◈◈◈	$575-$4000	398
㊹ / p. 377		Melia Cabo Real Beach & Golf Resort, All Inclusive	◈◈◈	$254-$446	398
㊺ / p. 377	◬◬◬	**Hilton Los Cabos Beach & Golf Resort** - see color ad p 382	◈◈◈◈	$330-$380	398
㊼ / p. 377		Marquis Los Cabos Beach, Golf, Spa & Casitas Resort	◈◈◈◈	$405	398
㊽ / p. 377	◬◬◬	**The Westin Regina Golf & Beach Resort, Los Cabos** - see color ad p 8	◈◈◈◈	$419	399
㊾ / p. 377		One & Only Palmilla	[fyi]	$430-$745	399
60 / p. 377		El Encanto Inn & Suites	◈◈	$65-$99	397
61 / p. 377		Casa Natalia	◈◈◈	$250-$385	397
63 / p. 377		Tropicana Inn	◈	$80	399
64 / p. 377		Suites Las Palmas	◈◈	$78-$99	399
66 / p. 377		Presidente InterContinental Los Cabos Resort	◈◈◈	$250-$310	399
67 / p. 377		Royal Solaris Los Cabos-Deluxe All Inclusive Resort	◈◈◈	$252-$270	399
68 / p. 377		Crowne Plaza Los Cabos Beach Resort-All Inclusive Resort	◈◈◈	$230-$320	397
70 / p. 377		Best Western Posada Real Los Cabos	◈◈	$145	397
71 / p. 377		Fiesta Inn An All Inclusive Resort - see color ad card insert	◈	$212-$235	398
		SAN JOSE DEL CABO - Restaurants			
36 / p. 377		The Restaurant	◈◈◈◈	$25-$45	400
37 / p. 377		Restaurant Fenicia	◈◈◈	$18-$30	400
38 / p. 377		Arrecifes	◈◈◈	$25-$45	400
43 / p. 377		Baan Thai	◈◈◈	$8-$18	400
44 / p. 377		Morgan's Encore	◈◈	$16-$24	400
45 / p. 377		Damiana	◈◈	$12-$28	400
46 / p. 377		Mi Cocina	◈◈◈	$16-$28	400
47 / p. 377		Morgan's Restaurant & Cellar	◈◈◈	$19-$25	400
48 / p. 377		Tequila Restaurante	◈◈	$14-$28	400
50 / p. 377		Tropicana Bar & Grill	◈◈	$10-$28	401
51 / p. 377		El Chilar	◈◈	$10-$20	400

CABO SAN LUCAS, BAJA CALIFORNIA SUR pop. 40,300

(See map and index starting on p. 377)

------- WHERE TO STAY -------

BAHIA CONDO HOTEL
Phone: (624)143-1888 **11**

12/15-4/20	1P: $129-$149	2P: $129-$149	XP: $20 F12
12/1-12/14 & 4/21-11/30	1P: $95-$115	2P: $95-$115	XP: $20 F12

Condominium **Location:** 1 km s of Mex 1 via Paseo del Pescador. Playa El Medano S/N 23400 (16175 Monterey Rd, Suite B, MORGAN HILL, CA, 95037). Fax: 624/143-1891. **Facility:** Meets AAA guest room security requirements. 76 one-bedroom standard units with efficiencies. 5 stories, exterior corridors. *Bath:* shower only. **Parking:** on-site. **Terms:** 30 day cancellation notice-fee imposed. **Pool(s):** heated outdoor. **Leisure Activities:** whirlpool. *Fee:* massage. **Guest Services:** gift shop, coin laundry. **Business Services:** meeting rooms. **Cards:** MC, VI.

SOME UNITS

BEST WESTERN HOTEL CABO LAS FLORES
Phone: (624)143-6199 **3**

All Year	1P: $75-$79	2P: $75-$79	XP: $10 F12

Motel **Location:** Just n of Lazaro Cardenas. Leona Vicario at 20 Noviembre 23410. Fax: 624/143-7500. **Facility:** 105 one-bedroom standard units. 3 stories (no elevator), exterior corridors. *Bath:* shower only. **Parking:** on-site. **Terms:** 7 day cancellation notice-fee imposed. **Amenities:** hair dryers. **Pool(s):** outdoor, wading. **Business Services:** fax (fee). **Cards:** AX, MC, VI.

CALINDA CABO SAN LUCAS
Phone: (624)145-7300 **31**

All Year	1P: $178	2P: $178	XP: $40 F12

Small-scale Hotel **Location:** Mex 1, 4.5 km e of town. KM 4.5 Carr Transpeninsular 23410. Fax: 624/145-8057. **Facility:** 125 units. 124 one-bedroom standard units. 1 two-bedroom suite. 2-3 stories (no elevator), exterior corridors. *Bath:* combo or shower only. **Parking:** on-site. **Terms:** 3 day cancellation notice-fee imposed. **Amenities:** voice mail, safes, honor bars, hair dryers. **Pool(s):** 3 outdoor. **Leisure Activities:** whirlpools. **Guest Services:** gift shop, valet laundry. **Business Services:** meeting rooms. **Cards:** AX, CB, MC, VI.

SOME UNITS

COSTA REAL CABO RESORTS & SUITES
Phone: (624)143-1220 **16**

12/1-12/23 & 4/5-11/30		2P: $150-$188	XP: $40 F12
12/24-4/4		2P: $144-$173	XP: $40 F12

Large-scale Hotel **Location:** In town; at marina. Blvd Marina Lote 9 y 10 23410. Fax: 624/143-1238. **Facility:** 287 units. 277 one-bedroom standard units, some with efficiencies. 10 two-bedroom suites with kitchens. 5 stories, interior corridors. **Parking:** on-site. **Terms:** check-in 4 pm, 5 day cancellation notice-fee imposed, 10% service charge. **Amenities:** voice mail, safes, honor bars, hair dryers. **Pool(s):** outdoor. **Leisure Activities:** whirlpool. *Fee:* massage. **Guest Services:** gift shop, valet laundry, area transportation. **Business Services:** conference facilities, fax (fee). **Cards:** AX, MC, VI.

SOME UNITS

ESPERANZA AN AUBERGE RESORT *Book at aaa.com*
Phone: (624)145-6400 **34**

12/1-6/30 & 10/15-11/30	1P: $550-$925	2P: $550-$925	
7/1-10/14	1P: $350-$725	2P: $350-$725	

Resort Small-scale Hotel **Location:** On Mex 1, 6 km n of town. Located at Punta Ballena. Carr Transpeninsular KM 7, Punta Ballena 23410 (2225 Broadway, Suite A, SANTA MONICA, CA, 90404). Fax: 624/145-6499. **Facility:** This intimate, luxury, seaside resort offers rooms of 925 square feet and larger, all with indoor and outdoor living spaces. 53 units. 50 one-bedroom standard units, some with whirlpools. 3 two-bedroom suites ($3000-$5000) with kitchens and whirlpools. 3-4 stories, exterior corridors. **Parking:** on-site and valet. **Terms:** 28 day cancellation notice, 15% service charge. **Amenities:** video library, DVD players, CD players, high-speed Internet, dual phone lines, voice mail, safes, honor bars, irons, hair dryers. **Pool(s):** 2 heated outdoor. **Leisure Activities:** whirlpools, steamrooms, exercise room, spa. **Guest Services:** gift shop, valet laundry. **Business Services:** meeting rooms, PC, fax. **Cards:** AX, DC, MC, VI.

FIESTA AMERICANA GRAND LOS CABOS *Book at aaa.com*
Phone: 624/145-6200 **36**

12/21-5/31		2P: $344-$381	XP: $20
12/1-12/20 & 6/1-11/30		2P: $265-$352	XP: $20

Resort Large-scale Hotel **Location:** On Mex 1, 10 km e of town. Located at Cabo del Sol. Carr Transpeninsular KM 10.3, Lote A-1 23410. Fax: 624/145-6201. **Facility:** On a hillside facing the sea, this resort well-suited for groups offers large guest rooms, ocean-view balconies and marble bathrooms. 284 units. 264 one-bedroom standard units. 18 one- and 2 two-bedroom suites with kitchens and whirlpools. 1-6 stories, exterior corridors. **Parking:** valet. **Terms:** 5 day cancellation notice, 10% service charge. **Amenities:** dual phone lines, voice mail, safes, honor bars, irons, hair dryers. **Dining:** Rosato, see separate listing. **Pool(s):** 5 heated outdoor. **Leisure Activities:** whirlpools, steamrooms, spa. *Fee:* saunas, scuba diving, snorkeling, charter fishing, golf-18 holes, 2 lighted tennis courts, exercise room. **Guest Services:** gift shop, valet and coin laundry. **Business Services:** conference facilities, business center. **Cards:** AX, CB, DC, DS, MC, VI.
(See color ad p 381, back cover, card inserts)

SOME UNITS
FEE

HOTEL FINISTERRA
Phone: (624)143-3333 **17**

12/1-4/30 & 10/1-11/30		2P: $140-$195	XP: $30 F12
5/1-9/30		2P: $125-$150	XP: $30 F12

Resort Large-scale Hotel **Location:** 1 km s of town via Blvd Marina. Located at Land's End. (Apdo Postal #1). Fax: 624/143-0590. **Facility:** Palapa-style thatched umbrellas and large free-form pools bring the tropical touch to this hotel set amid sand and cliffs at the water's edge. 286 units. 281 one-bedroom standard units. 3 one- and 2 two-bedroom suites ($245-$850). 1-8 stories, interior/exterior corridors. *Bath:* combo or shower only. **Parking:** on-site. **Terms:** check-in 4 pm, cancellation fee imposed, $10 service charge. **Amenities:** safes, irons, hair dryers. *Some:* honor bars. **Pool(s):** 3 outdoor. **Leisure Activities:** whirlpools, 2 lighted tennis courts, limited exercise equipment. *Fee:* massage. **Guest Services:** gift shop, valet laundry. **Business Services:** conference facilities. **Cards:** AX, MC, VI.

SOME UNITS

Some of México's most *beautiful* sands you don't want to *feel* between your toes.

In addition to our beautiful yet challenging Jack Nicklaus-designed golf course, Fiesta Americana Grand Los Cabos offers magnificent ocean-view accommodations, impeccable guest service, sensational dining, plus a variety of beachside activities that let you focus on things like sandcastles rather than sand traps.

FIESTA AMERICANA GRAND LOS CABOS

FIESTA AMERICANA
LOS CABOS *Grand*

one of
The Leading Hotels of the World

For reservations, contact your travel professional or call 1 800 FIESTA1.
For a free brochure, call 1 800 FIESTA2. www.fiestamericana.com

(See map and index starting on p. 377)

HOTEL SANTA FE   *Book at aaa.com*   Phone: 624/143-4401   **1**
    12/1-4/30 & 11/1-11/30   2P: $87   XP: $10   F12
    5/1-10/31   2P: $72   XP: $10   F12
Motel   **Location:** 1 km n of Lazaro Cardenas; in town. Calle Ignacio Zaragoza at Alvaro Obregon 23410. Fax: 624/143-4403. **Facility:** 46 one-bedroom standard units with efficiencies. 4 stories (no elevator), exterior corridors. *Bath:* shower only. **Parking:** on-site. **Terms:** 7 day cancellation notice, $5 service charge. **Pool(s):** outdoor. **Guest Services:** valet and coin laundry. **Business Services:** business center. **Cards:** AX, DS, MC, VI.

HOTEL TWIN DOLPHIN   Phone: (624)145-8190   **37**
    12/1-5/31 & 10/1-11/30   2P: $350-$395   XP: $55   F4
    6/1-9/30   2P: $235-$295   XP: $40   F4
Resort   **Location:** 12 km e of town on Mex 1. KM 12 Carr Transpeninsular 23410. Fax: 624/145-8196. **Facility:** A secluded
Large-scale Hotel   setting and serene pool give the resort a retreatlike ambience; guest rooms without telephones or televisions further the sense of escape. 50 units. 44 one-bedroom standard units. 6 one-bedroom suites ($395-$545). 1 story, exterior corridors. *Bath:* shower only. **Parking:** on-site and valet. **Terms:** 14 day cancellation notice-fee imposed, [AP] & [MAP] meal plans available, 18% service charge. **Amenities:** safes, hair dryers. **Pool(s):** heated outdoor. **Leisure Activities:** whirlpool, putting green, 2 lighted tennis courts, hiking trails, jogging, exercise room. *Fee:* horseback riding, massage. **Guest Services:** gift shop, valet laundry, area transportation. **Business Services:** business center. **Cards:** AX, DC, DS, MC, VI.

LOS PATIOS HOTEL   Phone: 624/145-6070   **30**
    All Year   1P: $99   2P: $99   XP: $10   F12
    Location: Mex 1, 4.5 km e of town. Carr Transpeninsular KM 4.5 23450. Fax: 624/145-6071. **Facility:** 76 one-
Small-scale Hotel   bedroom standard units. 2 stories (no elevator), exterior corridors. *Bath:* shower only. **Parking:** on-site. **Amenities:** voice mail, safes, honor bars, irons, hair dryers. **Pool(s):** heated outdoor. **Leisure Activities:** whirlpool. **Business Services:** meeting rooms, business center. **Cards:** AX, MC, VI.

                                                        SOME UNITS

MARINA FIESTA RESORT HOTEL   *Book at aaa.com*   Phone: (624)145-6020   **12**
    12/1-4/30   1P: $200-$480   2P: $200-$480   XP: $30   F12
    5/1-11/30   1P: $190-$260   2P: $190-$260   XP: $35   F12
Condominium   **Location:** On the east side of the marina. Lote 37 Col La Marina 23410. Fax: 624/145-6021. **Facility:** 155 units. 60 one-bedroom standard units with efficiencies. 93 one- and 2 two-bedroom suites ($480) with kitchens. 4-7 stories, exterior corridors. *Bath:* combo or shower only. **Parking:** on-site. **Terms:** check-in 4 pm, 3 day cancellation notice-fee imposed, $5 service charge. **Amenities:** irons, hair dryers. *Some:* safes. **Pool(s):** outdoor, heated outdoor. *Fee:* saunas. **Leisure Activities:** whirlpools, steamrooms, marina, playground, exercise room, spa. **Guest Services:** gift shop, valet laundry. **Business Services:** meeting rooms. **Cards:** AX, MC, VI.

(See map and index starting on p. 377)

MELIA SAN LUCAS *Book at aaa.com*
Phone: (624)145-7800 **10**

12/24-4/19	1P: $280-$435	2P: $280-$435	XP: $45	F12
4/20-11/30	1P: $250-$355	2P: $250-$355	XP: $45	F12
12/1-12/23	1P: $250-$322	2P: $250-$322	XP: $45	F12

Resort
Large-scale Hotel
Location: 1 km e of Mex 1 via Paseo del Pescador. Located at El Medano Beach. Playa El Medano 23410. **Fax:** 624/143-0420. **Facility:** Pueblo-style buildings distinguish this family-oriented resort located close to town; rooms are comfortable with modern baths and amenities. Meets AAA guest room security requirements. 150 units. 144 one-bedroom standard units. 6 one-bedroom suites. 6 stories, exterior corridors. **Parking:** on-site. **Terms:** 7 day cancellation notice, 10% service charge. **Amenities:** safes, honor bars, hair dryers. **Pool(s):** 2 heated outdoor, wading. **Leisure Activities:** 2 lighted tennis courts. *Fee:* massage. **Guest Services:** gift shop, valet laundry, area transportation. **Business Services:** conference facilities, PC. **Cards:** AX, MC, VI.

MISIONES DEL CABO
Phone: 624/145-8090 **32**

12/1-4/30	2P: $165-$275
5/1-11/30	2P: $120-$225

Condominium
Location: 5 km e on Mex 1. KM 5.5 Carr Transpeninsular 23410 (Apdo Postal 283). Fax: 624/145-8097. **Facility:** 42 units. 2 one-bedroom standard units with efficiencies. 23 one- and 17 two-bedroom suites with kitchens. 6-8 stories, exterior corridors. **Parking:** on-site. **Terms:** 10% service charge. **Pool(s):** outdoor. **Leisure Activities:** 2 lighted tennis courts. **Guest Services:** coin laundry. **Cards:** AX, MC, VI.

PLAYA GRANDE RESORT
Phone: 624/143-7575 **19**

12/1-4/30 & 10/1-11/30	2P: $260	XP: $40
5/1-9/30	2P: $235	XP: $40

Resort
Condominium
Location: 1.5 km s of town via Blvd Marina. Located at Land's End. Ave Playa Grande #1 23410 (PO Box 383, PACIFIC PALISADES, CA, 90272). Fax: 624/143-6655. **Facility:** Resembling a colorful seaside village, this condominium resort sits on the sands at the tip of the peninsula; expansion is ongoing. Meets AAA guest room security requirements. 260 units. 42 one-bedroom standard units with efficiencies. 188 one- and 30 two-bedroom suites ($310-$445) with kitchens, some with whirlpools. 4-8 stories, exterior corridors. **Parking:** on-site. **Terms:** check-in 4 pm, 7 day cancellation notice, 10% service charge. **Amenities:** voice mail, safes, irons, hair dryers. **Pool(s):** 4 outdoor. **Leisure Activities:** whirlpools, exercise room, spa. **Guest Services:** gift shop, valet and coin laundry. **Business Services:** conference facilities, business center. **Cards:** MC, VI.

PLAZA NAUTICA CONDOMINIUMS
Phone: (624)143-1688 **15**

12/1-4/30 & 10/16-11/30	2P: $150-$300
5/1-10/15	2P: $100-$150

Condominium
Location: In town; at marina. Located in a shopping complex. Blvd Marina Plaza Nautica 23451. Fax: 624/143-1688. **Facility:** This high-rise condominium is conveniently located in the downtown shopping district with a 24-hour deli, restaurants and a marina. 42 units. 4 one-, 32 two- and 6 three-bedroom suites ($300-$800) with kitchens. 8 stories, exterior corridors. **Parking:** on-site. **Terms:** 60 day cancellation notice-fee imposed, 10% service charge. **Amenities:** irons. *Some:* safes. **Pool(s):** heated outdoor. **Leisure Activities:** whirlpool. *Fee:* massage. **Cards:** MC, VI.

PUEBLO BONITO LOS CABOS *Book at aaa.com*
Phone: 624/142-9797 **8**

12/1-1/1	1P: $315-$360	2P: $315-$360	XP: $40	F18
1/2-4/25	1P: $275-$325	2P: $275-$325	XP: $40	F18
11/1-11/30	1P: $245-$285	2P: $245-$285	XP: $40	F18
4/26-10/31	1P: $225-$275	2P: $225-$275	XP: $40	F18

Resort
Condominium
Location: Mex 1, 1 km n of town to Mex 19, 0.5 mi e to the "Old Road", then just s. Playa El Medano 23410 (Apdo Postal 460). Fax: 624/143-1995. **Facility:** Mediterranean in style and painted all white, this condominium property is on sandy grounds near town; units have a balcony, living room and kitchen. 147 units. 30 one-bedroom standard units with efficiencies. 113 one-, 3 two- and 1 three-bedroom suites ($730-$1800) with kitchens. 5 stories, exterior corridors. **Parking:** on-site and valet. **Terms:** check-in 4 pm, 14 day cancellation notice, 10% service charge. **Amenities:** voice mail, safes, irons, hair dryers. **Pool(s):** heated outdoor. **Leisure Activities:** lighted tennis court, exercise room. *Fee:* massage. **Guest Services:** gift shop, valet and coin laundry. **Business Services:** business center. **Cards:** AX, MC, VI.

PUEBLO BONITO PACIFICA
Phone: 624/142-9696

[fyi]
All Year 2P: $220-$425

Resort
Large-scale Hotel
Too new to rate, opening scheduled for November 2004. **Location:** Marina Blvd, 1.8 km w via Lazaro Cardenas and Miguel Herrera. Predio Paraiso Escondido S/N 23410 (Apdo Postal 60, Sucurn Arcoiris, 23452). **Amenities:** 200 units, restaurant, coffeemakers, pool, tennis. **Terms:** check-in 4 pm, 14 day cancellation notice. **Cards:** AX, MC, VI.

PUEBLO BONITO ROSE *Book at aaa.com*
Phone: 624/142-9898 **7**

12/1-1/1	1P: $300	2P: $300	XP: $40	F18
1/2-4/30	1P: $255	2P: $255	XP: $40	F18
11/1-11/30	1P: $220	2P: $220	XP: $40	F18
5/1-10/31	1P: $200	2P: $200	XP: $40	F18

Resort
Condominium
Location: Mex 1, 1 km n of town to Mex 19, 0.5 mi e to the "Old Road", then just s. Playa El Medano 23410 (Apdo Postal 460). Fax: 624/143-5972. **Facility:** The elegant lobby and grounds feature classic Italian sculptures, a large reflection pool, a giant free-form pool, koi ponds and tropical birds. Meets AAA guest room security requirements. 260 units. 40 one-bedroom standard units with efficiencies. 147 one- and 73 two-bedroom suites with efficiencies. 6 stories, interior corridors. *Bath:* combo or shower only. **Parking:** on-site and valet. **Terms:** check-in 4 pm, 14 day cancellation notice, $10 service charge. **Amenities:** voice mail, safes, irons, hair dryers. **Pool(s):** heated outdoor, wading. **Leisure Activities:** steamrooms, lighted tennis court, exercise room, spa. *Fee:* saunas, whirlpools. **Guest Services:** gift shop, valet laundry. **Business Services:** meeting rooms, fax (fee). **Cards:** AX, MC, VI.

(See map and index starting on p. 377)

PUEBLO BONITO SUNSET BEACH   *Book at aaa.com*

Phone: 624/142-9999   **29**

All Year	2P: $195-$350	XP: $40	F18

Resort
Large-scale Hotel

Location: Marina Blvd, 1.8 km w via Lazaro Cardenas and Miguel Herrera. Predio Paraiso Escondido S/N 23410 (Apdo Postal 60, Sucum Arcoiris, 23452). Fax: 624/142-9957. **Facility:** The resort's hacienda-style buildings are terraced on the hillside, providing all rooms with a sunset view over the Pacific and a beachside pool. Meets AAA guest room security requirements. 360 units. 181 one-bedroom standard units. 112 one-, 44 two- and 23 three-bedroom suites ($350-$450), some with kitchens and/or whirlpools. 2-6 stories, exterior corridors. **Bath:** combo or shower only. **Parking:** valet. **Terms:** check-in 4 pm, 15 day cancellation notice, 10% service charge. **Amenities:** video games (fee), voice mail, safes, honor bars, irons, hair dryers. **Pool(s):** 3 heated outdoor. **Leisure Activities:** whirlpools, steamrooms, exercise room, spa. **Fee:** saunas, 2 lighted tennis courts. **Guest Services:** gift shop, valet laundry, area transportation. **Business Services:** conference facilities, business center. **Cards:** AX, MC, VI.

SOME UNITS

SHERATON HACIENDA DEL MAR RESORT & SPA   *Book at aaa.com*

Phone: (624)145-8000   **35**

12/1-1/1	1P: $399-$430	2P: $399-$430	XP: $50	F12
1/2-4/29	1P: $329-$360	2P: $329-$360	XP: $50	F12
4/30-11/30	1P: $239-$280	2P: $239-$280	XP: $50	F12

Resort
Large-scale Hotel

Location: 10 km e on Mex 1. Located at Cabo del Sol. Corredor Turistico KM 10, Lote D 23410. Fax: 624/145-8002. **Facility:** Designed like a Mexican hacienda with fountains and stonework, the resort offers large rooms with a whirlpool tub and private patio or balcony. 171 units. 140 one-bedroom standard units with efficiencies and whirlpools. 15 one- and 16 three-bedroom suites with kitchens and whirlpools. 4-7 stories, interior/exterior corridors. **Parking:** on-site. **Terms:** 3 day cancellation notice, $3 service charge. **Amenities:** dual phone lines, voice mail, safes, honor bars, irons, hair dryers. **Dining:** Pitahayas, see separate listing. **Pool(s):** 2 outdoor, heated outdoor, wading. **Leisure Activities:** whirlpools, spa. **Fee:** golf-18 holes, exercise room. **Guest Services:** gift shop, valet laundry. **Business Services:** conference facilities, business center. **Cards:** AX, DC, MC, VI. *(See color ad p 8)*

SOME UNITS

SIESTA SUITES HOTEL

Phone: (624)143-2773   **14**

All Year	1P: $44-$50	2P: $49-$55	XP: $10	F10

Motel

Location: Just n of Marina Blvd and Miguel Hidalgo; downtown. Calle E Zapata I Guerrero 23410 (PO Box 9416, PHOENIX, AZ, 85068). Fax: 624/143-2773. **Facility:** 20 units. 5 one-bedroom standard units. 15 one-bedroom suites with kitchens. 4 stories (no elevator), exterior corridors. **Bath:** shower only. **Parking:** street. **Terms:** 15 day cancellation notice. **Pool(s):** small outdoor. **Leisure Activities:** whirlpool. **Business Services:** PC, fax. **Cards:** MC, VI.

SOME UNITS

SOLMAR SUITES RESORT

Phone: (624)143-3535   **20**

All Year	1P: $135-$265	2P: $135-$265	XP: $28	F12

Resort
Large-scale Hotel

Location: 1.5 km s of town via Blvd Marina. Located at Land's End. Ave Solmar #1 23410 (PO Box 383, PACIFIC PALISADES, CA, 90272). Fax: 624/143-0410. **Facility:** This beachfront resort features expansive grounds and ample lounging areas; rooms and suites each have a private patio or balcony. 193 units. 124 one-bedroom standard units, some with kitchens. 48 one- and 21 two-bedroom suites ($300-$330), some with kitchens. 2-5 stories, exterior corridors. **Parking:** on-site. **Terms:** check-in 4 pm, 7 day cancellation notice, 10% service charge. **Amenities:** safes, honor bars. **Pool(s):** 3 outdoor. **Leisure Activities:** whirlpool, exercise room. **Fee:** scuba diving, snorkeling, fishing, charter fishing, lighted tennis court, massage. **Guest Services:** gift shop, valet and coin laundry. **Business Services:** meeting rooms. **Fee:** PC, fax. **Cards:** AX, MC, VI.

SOME UNITS

VILLA DEL PALMAR BEACH RESORT & SPA   *Book at aaa.com*

Phone: (624)145-7000   **4**

12/1-1/2	1P: $246-$697	2P: $246-$697	XP: $20	F12
1/3-4/30 & 11/1-11/30	1P: $226-$624	2P: $226-$624	XP: $20	F12
5/1-10/31	1P: $168-$555	2P: $168-$555	XP: $20	F12

Resort
Condominium

Location: Mex 1, 1 km n of town to Mex 19, 0.5 mi e to the "Old Road", then just n. KM 0.5 Camino Viejo a San Jose 23410. Fax: 624/143-2664. **Facility:** Notable features include a seashell chandelier, a nine-story atrium lobby, waterfalls, two tiered pools and a waterslide. Meets AAA guest room security requirements. 458 units. 170 one-bedroom standard units. 228 one-, 50 two- and 10 three-bedroom suites ($1086-$1178) with kitchens, some with whirlpools. 7-8 stories, exterior corridors. **Bath:** combo or shower only. **Parking:** on-site. **Terms:** 3 day cancellation notice-fee imposed, 10% service charge. **Amenities:** voice mail, safes, hair dryers. **Dining:** 2 restaurants, 7 am-10:30 pm, cocktails, entertainment. **Pool(s):** 3 heated outdoor, wading. **Leisure Activities:** whirlpools, steamrooms, waterslide, 2 lighted tennis courts, recreation programs, spa, shuffleboard. **Fee:** saunas. **Guest Services:** gift shop, valet and coin laundry. **Business Services:** meeting rooms, business center. **Cards:** AX, MC, VI.

FEE

VILLA LA ESTANCIA

Phone: 624/145-6900   **5**

12/1-1/2	1P: $316-$531	2P: $316-$531	
1/3-4/30 & 11/1-11/30	1P: $256-$504	2P: $256-$504	
5/1-10/31	1P: $188-$467	2P: $188-$467	

Resort
Condominium

Location: Mex 1, 1 km n of town to Mex 19, 0.5 km e to the "Old Road", then just n. KM 0.5 Camino Viejo a San Jose 23450. Fax: 624/143-2664. **Facility:** A luxury condominium complex on Medano Beach with private balconies and views of the ocean and Land's End. 327 units. 162 one-bedroom standard units. 162 one- and 3 three-bedroom suites ($882-$1382) with kitchens and whirlpools. 7 stories, interior corridors. **Parking:** on-site and valet. **Terms:** 3 day cancellation notice, 10% service charge. **Amenities:** high-speed Internet, voice mail, hair dryers. **Some:** CD players, safes. **Pool(s):** 3 heated outdoor. **Leisure Activities:** saunas, whirlpools, steamrooms, 2 lighted tennis courts, exercise room, spa. **Business Services:** meeting rooms, business center. **Cards:** AX, MC, VI.

SOME UNITS

(See map and index starting on p. 377)

——————— *The following lodgings were either not evaluated or did not* ———————
meet AAA rating requirements but are listed for your information only.

HOTEL CABO SAN LUCAS   Phone: 624/144-0017
[fyi]   Not evaluated. **Location:** On Mex 1, 16 km e. KM 14.5 Carr Transpeninsular 23400. Facilities, services, and decor
characterize a mid-range property.

HOTEL HACIENDA BEACH RESORT   Phone: 624/143-0663
[fyi]   Not evaluated. **Location:** 2 km s of Mex 1, Camino al Hacienda. Box 34 23410. Facilities, services, and decor
characterize a mid-range property.

——————— **WHERE TO DINE** ———————

CASA RAFAEL'S   Dinner: $19-$43   Phone: 624/143-0739   [4]
▽▽▽▽▽   **Location:** 1 km s of Mex 1, Camino al Hacienda. Playa El Medano 23410. **Hours:** Open 12/1-9/14 & 10/1-11/30; 6
pm-10 pm. **Reservations:** suggested. **Features:** Skilled staff members at this quaint Mexican-colonial inn
Continental   provide refined service to guests in the garden room, ocean room or poolside. Chicken Allison is a house
specialty on a menu that also includes chiote red snapper, scampi, ribs and steak. Dressy casual; cocktails.
Parking: street. **Cards:** AX, MC, VI.

EDITH'S   Dinner: $13-$55   Phone: 624/143-0801   [8]
▽▽▽   **Location:** 1.1 km s of Mex 1. Paseo de Pescador & Playa El Medano 23410. **Hours:** Open 12/1-8/31 & 10/1-11/30;
5 pm-10 pm. **Reservations:** suggested. **Features:** Affording an impressive view of Land's End, the popular
Seafood   palapa dining room is a favorite for seafood. Steaks, lamb and chicken are also on the menu. As patrons
enter, they pick up the aroma of the mesquite grill and see tortillas being made. Casual dress; cocktails.
Parking: street. **Cards:** MC, VI.

GALEON ITALIAN RESTAURANT   Dinner: $8-$20   Phone: 624/143-0443   [14]
▽▽▽   **Location:** 1 km s of town. Blvd Marina S/N 23410. **Hours:** 4 pm-11 pm. **Reservations:** accepted.
Features: Overlooking the town and bay, the restaurant offers seating in the relaxed dining room and on the
Italian   balcony. Offered is a nice selection of seafood, pasta, veal and pizza. Dressy casual; cocktails. **Parking:** on-
site. **Cards:** AX, MC, VI.

LATITUDE 22+   Lunch: $6-$12   Dinner: $9-$20   Phone: 624/143-1516   [25]
▽▽   **Location:** Mex 1, 4.5 km e of town. KM 4.5 Carr Transpeninsular 23410. **Hours:** 9 am-10 pm. Closed: Tues.
Features: The small cafe and bar can boast great food and attitude. Funky memorabilia is pinned to the
American   walls and ceiling. On the menu are not only great hamburgers and barbecue sandwiches, but also ribs,
prime rib, chicken-fried steak and pasta dishes. Fishermen can bring in their catch for preparation. Casual
dress; cocktails. **Parking:** street. **Cards:** MC, VI.

MARGARITAVILLA   Lunch: $4-$15   Dinner: $12-$40   Phone: 624/143-0010   [7]
▽▽   **Location:** At the marina; in Plaza Bonita Shopping Center. Blvd Marina #17, Lote 38 23410. **Hours:** 7 am-11 pm.
Features: Casual and sometimes noisy, the restaurant offers seating overlooking the marina and main
Mexican   street. The food is good and the servers friendly. Casual dress; cocktails. **Parking:** on-site. **Cards:** AX,
MC, VI.

MI CASA   Lunch: $8-$10   Dinner: $11-$18   Phone: 624/143-1933   [11]
▽▽   **Location:** 1 km w of Blvd Marina via Lazaro Cardenas; in town. Ave Cabo San Lucas 23410. **Hours:** noon-3 & 5:30-
10:30 pm, Sun from 5:30 pm. Closed: 1/1; also for lunch 7/1-10/31. **Reservations:** suggested.
Mexican   **Features:** Colorful murals surround the enchanting courtyard, a place best experienced after dark. Authentic
regional dishes from throughout Mexico include such popular choices as mole poblano fish, roasted pork,
filet of beef and grilled chicken. Casual dress; cocktails. **Parking:** street. **Cards:** MC, VI.

THE OFFICE   Lunch: $8-$20   Dinner: $12-$35   Phone: 624/143-3464   [9]
▽▽   **Location:** 1.2 km se of Mex 1 via Paseo de Pescador. Playa El Medano 23410. **Hours:** 7 am-10 pm.
Reservations: suggested. **Features:** This is a prototype casual restaurant, with tables and chairs on the
Mexican   sand. Stop in for breakfast after a morning walk or sunset as the shadows fall on the "Arch." Office
assistants serve fun with an assortment of special beverages, hamburgers, chicken enchiladas and
Tampiquena top sirloin. Party favors and entertainment enliven theme nights on Monday, Thursday and Sunday at 6:30 pm.
Casual dress; cocktails. **Parking:** street. **Cards:** MC, VI.

PANCHO'S RESTAURANT & TEQUILA BAR Lunch: $5-$35   Dinner: $12-$40   Phone: 624/143-0973   [12]
▽▽▽   **Location:** Just w of Blvd Marina; in town. Miguel Hildago at Calle Zapata 23410. **Hours:** 6 am-11 pm. Closed: 1/1.
Reservations: suggested. **Features:** The colorfully decorated restaurant treats diners to friendly service
Mexican   and more than 250 selections of tequila. Tender pork posole, pico de gallo salad, shredded-beef omelet and
large hamburgers are a sampling of the comfort foods offered. Casual dress; cocktails. **Parking:** street.
Cards: MC, VI.

PEACOCKS RESTAURANT   Dinner: $18-$40   Phone: 624/143-1858   [3]
▽▽▽   **Location:** 0.5 km e of Mex 1. Paseo del Pescador 23410. **Hours:** 6 pm-10:30 pm. Closed: 1/1.
Reservations: suggested. **Features:** European cuisine is served in the palapa dining room and on the
Continental   patio. Boned Chilean salmon in cream sauce, baked whole red snapper and cabo dorado in pecan crust are
among seafood dishes. Other dishes include grilled New York steak in peppercorn sauce and New Zealand
rack of lamb in a mustard crust. Dressy casual; cocktails. **Parking:** street. **Cards:** AX, MC, VI.

(See map and index starting on p. 377)

PITAHAYAS
Pacific Rim

Dinner: $25-$40 Phone: 624/145-6126 (28)
Location: 10 km e on Mex 1; in Sheraton Hacienda Del Mar Resort & Spa. Corredor Turistico KM 10, Lote D 23410. **Hours:** 5 pm-11 pm. **Reservations:** suggested. **Features:** Pacific Rim and Asian influences are employed in the preparation of seafood, meat and pasta dishes. The oceanfront setting is suitable for comfortable relaxation. Dressy casual. **Parking:** on-site. **Cards:** AX, MC, VI.

RISTORANTE DA GIORGIO
Italian

Lunch: $7-$20 Dinner: $10-$20 Phone: 624/145-8160 (26)
Location: 5 km e on Mex 1, 1 km s, past Misiones del Cabo. Carr Transpeninsular KM 5.5 23410. **Hours:** 8 am-10 pm. **Reservations:** suggested. **Features:** The impressive, open-air, palapa-covered restaurant affords views of the ocean and Land's End. The menu centers on pasta, seafood and pizza. Dressy casual; cocktails. **Parking:** on-site. **Cards:** MC, VI.

ROMEO Y JULIETA RISTORANTE
Italian

Dinner: $6-$20 Phone: 624/143-0225 (17)
Location: 0.5 km s of town via Blvd Marina. Camino del Cerro 23410. **Hours:** 4 pm-11 pm. **Reservations:** accepted. **Features:** Pasta, seafood and specialty pizzas are served in this quaint, family-friendly hacienda. Dressy casual; cocktails. **Parking:** street. **Cards:** AX, MC, VI.

ROSATO
Northern
Italian

Dinner: $16-$22 Phone: 624/145-6200 (29)
Location: On Mex 1, 10 km e of town; in Fiesta Americana Grand Los Cabos. Carr Transpeninsular KM 10.3, Lote A-1 23410. **Hours:** 6 pm-10 pm. **Reservations:** suggested. **Features:** Overlooking the resort and Sea of Cortez, the sophisticated dining room incorporates subdued lighting, candles and soft music into its intimate setting. Delicious examples of Northern Italian cooking include kelp bass, gnocchi in shrimp sauce and veal ravioli. Dressy casual; cocktails. **Parking:** valet. **Cards:** AX, CB, DC, DS, MC, VI.

SANCHO PANZA
Mediterranean

Dinner: $16-$30 Phone: 624/143-3212 (16)
Location: Located in town beside the Plaza Las Glorias Hotel. Blvd Marina 23410. **Hours:** 3 pm-11 pm. **Closed:** 1/1. **Reservations:** suggested. **Features:** The Art Deco and Cuban art hangings are what stand out when you enter the restaurant, along with the aroma of Mediterranean cuisine with a Latin twist, and eclectic blend of everything. Offering the best and fairest wine list in all of Cabo San Luis. Entrees vary from osso bucco and liver mousse to a tasteful ribeye Florentine. You will be tempted to try their homemade desserts. Live jazz and blues nightly. Casual dress; cocktails. **Parking:** street. **Cards:** MC, VI.

SENOR GREENBERG'S MEXICATESSEN
Deli/Subs
Sandwiches

Lunch: $6-$9 Dinner: $7-$12 Phone: 624/143-5630 (13)
Location: In town. Blvd Marina, Plaza Nautica 23410. **Hours:** 24 hours. **Features:** Located right off the main street, the bright green and white deli is as popular for coffee and pastries as for the food items on the extensive menu. Hot dogs, burritos, baked meatloaf and barbecue ribs are ordered as often as the corned beef and pastrami. Breakfast is served around the clock, and all menu items are prepared to go. Casual dress; cocktails. **Parking:** on-site. **Cards:** MC, VI.

STOP LIGHT BAR & GRILL
Mexican

Lunch: $6-$40 Dinner: $6-$40 Phone: 624/143-4740 (6)
Location: Just e of Calle Zaragoza; in town. Blvd Lazaro Cardenas (Blvd Marina) 23410. **Hours:** 8 am-1 am. **Features:** Simple dishes, such as hamburgers, tamales and tacos, share menu space with fresh seafood plates, steaks, pork chops and chicken. On the main drag, the open, streetside restaurant always offers daily specials. Casual dress; cocktails. **Parking:** street. **Cards:** MC, VI.

THE TRAILER PARK RESTAURANT (LA GOLONDRINA)
Mexican

Dinner: $14-$48 Phone: 624/143-0542 (1)
Location: Just e of Mex 1. Paseo del Pescador S/N 23410. **Hours:** 5 pm-10:30 pm. **Closed:** 1/1. **Reservations:** suggested. **Features:** At a historic trading post, this popular restaurant lets diners relax on the patio while savoring Mexican-style combination plates of seafood, chicken and beef. Casual dress; cocktails. **Parking:** street. **Cards:** MC, VI. **Historic**

CATAVINA, BAJA CALIFORNIA pop. 1,500

———— WHERE TO STAY ————

The following lodging was either not evaluated or did not meet AAA rating requirements but is listed for your information only.

HOTEL LA PINTA Phone: 555/151-4604

Not evaluated. **Location:** On Mex 1. (Apdo Postal 179, SAN QUINTIN, BA). Facilities, services, and decor characterize a basic property.

EL ROSARIO, BAJA CALIFORNIA

———— WHERE TO DINE ————

The following restaurant has not been evaluated by AAA but is listed for your information only.

MAMA ESPINOSA'S Phone: 616/165-8770
Not evaluated. **Location:** On Mex 1; in town center. KM 55 Carr Transpeninsular. **Features:** Baja-influenced lobster, fish and beef dishes are served in this historic restaurant, the home of Dona Anita.

ENSENADA, BAJA CALIFORNIA pop. 237,700

——— WHERE TO STAY ———

BEST WESTERN EL CID
Phone: 646/178-2401

Small-scale Hotel

All Year — 2P: $46-$72

Location: Just w of Ave Blancarte; center. Located in the tourist area. Ave Lopez Mateos #993 22800 (PO Box 786, CHULA VISTA, CA, 91910). Fax: 646/178-3671. **Facility:** Meets AAA guest room security requirements. 52 units. 46 one-bedroom standard units. 6 one-bedroom suites ($110-$130), some with whirlpools. 3 stories (no elevator), interior corridors. *Bath:* combo or shower only. **Parking:** on-site. **Amenities:** voice mail, hair dryers. **Pool(s):** outdoor. **Business Services:** meeting rooms. **Cards:** AX, DC, DS, MC, VI.

SOME UNITS

CASA DEL SOL MOTEL
Phone: 646/178-1570

Motel

All Year — 1P: $48-$60 — 2P: $53-$80 — XP: $10 — F12

Location: At Ave Blancarte; center. Located in the tourist area. Ave Lopez Mateos #1001 22800 (PO Box 7561, CHULA VISTA, CA, 91912). Fax: 646/178-2025. **Facility:** Meets AAA guest room security requirements. 40 one-bedroom standard units. 2 stories (no elevator), exterior corridors. *Bath:* shower only. **Parking:** on-site. **Pool(s):** outdoor. **Cards:** AX, MC, VI.

SOME UNITS

CORONA HOTEL
Phone: 646/176-0901

Small-scale Hotel

6/1-8/31 — 2P: $65-$95 — XP: $10 — F12
9/1-11/30 — 2P: $52-$65 — XP: $10 — F12
12/1-5/31 — 2P: $46-$52 — XP: $10 — F12

Location: 1 km s. Blvd Lazaro Cardenas #1442 22800 (482 W San Ysidro Blvd #303, SAN YSIDRO, CA, 92173). Fax: 646/176-4324. **Facility:** Meets AAA guest room security requirements. 91 units. 89 one-bedroom standard units. 2 one-bedroom suites ($150-$1300), some with whirlpools. 4 stories, interior corridors. **Parking:** on-site. **Terms:** cancellation fee imposed, pets (in limited units). **Pool(s):** heated outdoor. **Leisure Activities:** whirlpool, exercise room, spa. **Business Services:** meeting rooms, business center. **Cards:** AX, DC, DS, MC, VI.

DAYS INN-VILLA FONTANA HOTEL   *Book at aaa.com*
Phone: 646/178-3434

Motel

All Year — 1P: $54-$86 — 2P: $54-$86 — XP: $10 — F12

Location: Just w of Ave Blancarte; center. Located in the tourist area. Ave Lopez Mateos 1050 22800. Fax: 646/178-3434. **Facility:** Meets AAA guest room security requirements. 65 units. 64 one-bedroom standard units, some with whirlpools. 1 one-bedroom suite ($88-$120). 2 stories, exterior corridors. *Bath:* combo or shower only. **Parking:** on-site. **Terms:** cancellation fee imposed. **Pool(s):** outdoor. **Leisure Activities:** whirlpool. **Cards:** AX, DC, JC, MC, VI. *(See color ad opposite inside front cover)*

SOME UNITS

ESTERO BEACH RESORT HOTEL
Phone: 646/176-6230

Resort
Small-scale Hotel

4/1-9/30 — 2P: $80-$140 — XP: $10 — F5
12/1-3/31 & 10/1-11/30 — 2P: $60-$120 — XP: $5 — F5

Location: 10.5 km s of town on Mex 1, 1.5 km w on Ave Jose Ma Moreles and Lupita Novelo O. (482 W San Ysidro Blvd; PMB 1186, SAN YSIDRO, CA, 92173). Fax: 646/176-6925. **Facility:** A family-oriented resort on several acres of beachfront grounds. Units are located in several buildings, from modest to upscale. 98 units. 91 one-bedroom standard units. 2 two-bedroom suites ($120-$400) with efficiencies. 5 cottages. 2 stories (no elevator), exterior corridors. *Bath:* combo or shower only. **Parking:** on-site. **Pool(s):** heated outdoor. **Leisure Activities:** whirlpools, boat ramp, 3 lighted tennis courts, rental bicycles, playground, basketball, volleyball. *Fee:* fishing, horseback riding. **Guest Services:** gift shop, valet and coin laundry. **Cards:** MC, VI.

SOME UNITS

HACIENDA BAJAMAR
Phone: 646/155-0151

Resort
Small-scale Hotel

All Year — 2P: $109-$176 — XP: $30 — F12

Location: On Mex 1-D (toll road), exit Baja Mar, 33 km n of town. Carr Escenica Tijuana KM 77.5 22760 (416 W San Ysidro Blvd #L-732, SAN YSIDRO, CA, 92173). Fax: 646/155-0150. **Facility:** A golf resort located along a picturesque and peaceful coastline, this Mexican colonial-style hotel surrounds a secluded courtyard. 81 units. 71 one-bedroom standard units. 10 one-bedroom suites ($184-$208) with kitchens. 2 stories (no elevator), interior/exterior corridors. **Terms:** check-in 4 pm, 3 day cancellation notice-fee imposed. **Amenities:** safes, hair dryers. **Pool(s):** outdoor. **Leisure Activities:** whirlpool, 2 tennis courts, playground. *Fee:* golf-27 holes, massage. **Guest Services:** gift shop, valet laundry. **Business Services:** meeting rooms. **Cards:** AX, MC, VI.

SOME UNITS

HOTEL CORAL & MARINA RESORT   *Book at aaa.com*
Phone: 646/175-0000

Large-scale Hotel

All Year — 2P: $135-$600 — XP: $20 — F12

Location: On Mex 1-D (toll road), 3 km n of town at KM 103. Carr Tijuana-Ensenada #3421 22860. Fax: 646/175-0005. **Facility:** Meets AAA guest room security requirements. 147 units. 20 one-bedroom standard units. 122 one-, 4 two- and 1 three-bedroom suites ($135-$600), some with kitchens (no utensils). 6 stories, interior corridors. **Parking:** on-site. **Terms:** 3 day cancellation notice-fee imposed. **Amenities:** hair dryers. **Pool(s):** outdoor, heated indoor, wading. **Leisure Activities:** saunas, whirlpools, steamrooms, 2 lighted tennis courts. *Fee:* boats, sailboats, marina, charter fishing, massage. **Guest Services:** gift shop, valet laundry. **Business Services:** meeting rooms. **Cards:** AX, MC, VI.

SOME UNITS

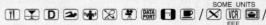
FEE

HOTEL CORTEZ   *Book at aaa.com*

Phone: 646/178-2307

All Year   1P: $70-$80   2P: $70-$80   XP: $8   F12

Small-scale Hotel

Location: At Ave Castillo; center. Located in the tourist area. Ave Lopez Mateos #1089 22800 (PO Box 5356, CHULA VISTA, CA, 91912). **Fax:** 646/178-3904. **Facility:** Meets AAA guest room security requirements. 82 units. 75 one-bedroom standard units. 7 one-bedroom suites ($105-$130). 2 stories (no elevator), interior/exterior corridors. *Bath:* combo or shower only. **Parking:** on-site. **Terms:** 3 day cancellation notice-fee imposed. **Pool(s):** heated outdoor. **Leisure Activities:** limited exercise equipment, basketball. **Guest Services:** gift shop, valet laundry. **Business Services:** meeting rooms, business center. **Cards:** AX, MC, VI.

SOME UNITS

HOTEL LA PINTA

Phone: 646/176-2601

All Year   2P: $36-$62   XP: $15   F17

Small-scale Hotel

Location: 1 km s of town on Blvd Lazaro Cardenas, 0.4 km e on Ave Club Rotario. Ave Floresta y Bucaneros 22800 (Apdo Postal 929). **Fax:** 646/172-4950. **Facility:** Meets AAA guest room security requirements. 50 units. 46 one-bedroom standard units. 4 one-bedroom suites ($100-$120). 3 stories (no elevator), exterior corridors. *Bath:* shower only. **Parking:** on-site. **Amenities:** *Some:* safes, hair dryers. **Pool(s):** outdoor. **Cards:** AX, MC, VI.

SOME UNITS

HOTEL PARAISO LAS PALMAS

Phone: 646/177-1701

All Year   2P: $55-$65   XP: $5   F14

Small-scale Hotel

Location: 2 km s of town on blvds Costero and Lazaro Cardenas, just e. Calle Augustin Sangines 206 22800. **Fax:** 646/176-0985. **Facility:** Meets AAA guest room security requirements. 67 units. 56 one-bedroom standard units. 11 one-bedroom suites ($70-$90). 3 stories (no elevator), exterior corridors. *Bath:* shower only. **Parking:** on-site. **Terms:** cancellation fee imposed. **Pool(s):** outdoor. **Leisure Activities:** whirlpool, playground. **Business Services:** meeting rooms. **Cards:** AX, MC, VI.

SOME UNITS

HOTEL SANTO TOMAS   *Book at aaa.com*

Phone: 646/178-1503

All Year   2P: $70-$80   XP: $8   F12

Small-scale Hotel

Location: On Blvd Larazo Cardenas at Ave Miramar. Located across from the port. Blvd Costero #609 22800 (PO Box 5356, CHULA VISTA, CA, 91912). **Fax:** 646/178-1504. **Facility:** Meets AAA guest room security requirements. 80 units. 78 one-bedroom standard units. 2 one-bedroom suites ($115-$140). 3 stories, interior corridors. *Bath:* shower only. **Parking:** on-site. **Amenities:** hair dryers. **Guest Services:** gift shop, valet laundry. **Business Services:** meeting rooms, business center. **Cards:** AX, MC, VI.

SOME UNITS

LAS ROSAS HOTEL

Phone: 646/174-4310

All Year   2P: $132-$192   XP: $23   F12

Small-scale Hotel

Location: On Mex 1, 7 km n of town. Carr Tijuana-Ensenada KM 105.5 22800 (374 E H St, Suite APMB-455, CHULA VISTA, CA, 91910-7484). **Fax:** 646/174-4595. **Facility:** Meets AAA guest room security requirements. 48 units. 47 one-bedroom standard units, some with whirlpools. 1 cottage. 4 stories, exterior corridors. *Bath:* combo or shower only. **Parking:** on-site. **Terms:** 3 day cancellation notice-fee imposed. **Amenities:** hair dryers. **Pool(s):** heated outdoor. **Leisure Activities:** sauna, whirlpool, exercise room. *Fee:* lighted tennis court, massage. **Guest Services:** gift shop, valet laundry. **Business Services:** meeting rooms, business center. **Cards:** MC, VI.

POSADA EL REY SOL   *Book at aaa.com*

Phone: 646/178-1601

All Year   1P: $65-$90   2P: $65-$90   XP: $15   F12

Motel

Location: Just n of Ave Lopez Mateos; center. Located in the tourist area. Ave Blancarte #130 22800 (4492 Camino de la Plaza, PMB 8118, SAN YSIDRO, CA, 92173-3097). **Fax:** 646/174-0005. **Facility:** Meets AAA guest room security requirements. 52 units. 51 one-bedroom standard units, some with whirlpools. 1 one-bedroom suite ($175-$275) with whirlpool. 3 stories, exterior corridors. *Bath:* shower only. **Parking:** on-site. **Amenities:** high-speed Internet, voice mail, safes, honor bars, hair dryers. **Dining:** El Rey Sol Restaurant, see separate listing. **Pool(s):** outdoor. **Leisure Activities:** whirlpool, limited exercise equipment. **Guest Services:** valet laundry. **Business Services:** meeting rooms, business center. **Cards:** AX, MC, VI.

SOME UNITS

PUNTA MORRO RESORT

Phone: 646/178-3507

All Year [CP]   2P: $108   XP: $25   F12

Small-scale Hotel

Location: 5 km n of town on Mex 1, 0.5 km w. KM 106 Carr Tijuana-Ensenada 22800 (PO Box 434263, SAN DIEGO, CA, 92143). **Fax:** 646/174-4490. **Facility:** Meets AAA guest room security requirements. 24 units. 3 one-bedroom standard units. 9 one-, 9 two- and 3 three-bedroom suites ($135-$290). 3 stories, exterior corridors. *Bath:* shower only. **Parking:** on-site. **Terms:** 3 day cancellation notice-fee imposed. **Amenities:** hair dryers. **Dining:** The Restaurant at Punta Morro, see separate listing. **Pool(s):** outdoor. **Leisure Activities:** whirlpool. *Fee:* massage. **Business Services:** meeting rooms. **Cards:** MC, VI.

─────── **WHERE TO DINE** ───────

EL CID

Lunch: $8-$16   **Dinner:** $11-$28   **Phone: 646/178-1809**

Mexican

Location: Just w of Ave Blancarte; center; next to Best Western El Cid. Ave Lopez Mateos #995-A Zona Centro 22800. **Hours:** 7 am-11 pm. **Features:** Nestled on the main strip in downtown with indoor and outdoor seating. The variety of menu selections depicts the flavor of Mexican delicacies starting off with chips and homemade salsa. Try their combination platter if you can't make up your mind. Flan is a typical Mexican dessert which will satisfy any sweet tooth. Casual dress; cocktails. **Parking:** street. **Cards:** MC, VI.

EL REY SOL RESTAURANT

French
Cards: AX, MC, VI.

Lunch: $9-$22   **Dinner:** $15-$35   **Phone:** 646/178-1733
Location: Just n of Ave Lopez Mateos; center; in Posada El Rey Sol. Ave Lopez Mateos 1000 22800. **Hours:** 7:30 am-11 pm. **Features:** Family operated since 1947, the award-winning French restaurant offers formal dining, fresh baked pastries and a tea room. The extensive menu includes swordfish with cilantro sauce, fish and shrimp broiled with butter and garlic and chicken chipotle. Casual dress; cocktails. **Parking:** street.

HALIOTIS
Seafood
Cards: AX, MC, VI.

Lunch: $9-$35   **Dinner:** $9-$35   **Phone:** 646/176-3720
Location: Mex 1, 1 km e; at south end of town. Calle Delante 179 22800. **Hours:** noon-10 pm. Closed: 1/1, 12/25; also 5/1. **Features:** Popular with locals, the family-operated restaurant is just outside the tourist area. Spacious dining rooms are appointed with nautical decor and family pictures. The menu centers on fresh seafood, including the specialty: pacifico abalone grilled in a wine and butter sauce. Other choices include scallops in garlic sauce, fish stuffed with cheese, broiled clams and lobster tacos. Casual dress; cocktails. **Parking:** on-site.

LA EMBOTELLADORA VIEJA RESTAURANTE
Mediterranean

Lunch: $8-$17   **Dinner:** $8-$17   **Phone:** 646/174-0807
Location: 0.5 km n of downtown. Ave Miramar #666 22800. **Hours:** noon-10 pm. Closed: 1/1, 12/25; also Sun. **Features:** At the Bodegas de Santo Tomas Winery, the restaurant has a large dining room—formerly the bottling room—with brick pillars and massive wine barrels. Well matched with wine list recommendations, menu selections include fish filet with scallions, salmon in cream sauce, veal and mushrooms and pasta with shrimp. Service is attentive. Diners can take the winery tour for no additional fee. Casual dress; beer & wine only. **Parking:** street. **Cards:** AX, DC, DS, MC, VI.

LAS CAZUELAS RESTAURANT

Mexican

Lunch: $6-$20   **Dinner:** $6-$20   **Phone:** 646/176-1044
Location: 2 km s of town on blvds Lazaro Cardenas and Costero, just e. Ave Sangines #6 22800. **Hours:** 7 am-11 pm. **Features:** Fast, friendly service and generous portions of comfort food attract business and family diners all day long to the busy dining room. Breakfast is a special draw. Lobster, abalone, jumbo shrimp stuffed with lobster, chicken adobo, chillaques with chicken and grilled or baked fish with garlic are a few of the dishes. Casual dress; cocktails. **Parking:** on-site. **Cards:** MC, VI.

THE RESTAURANT AT PUNTA MORRO
International

Lunch: $15-$25   **Dinner:** $20-$35   **Phone:** 646/178-3507
Location: 5 km n of town on Mex 1, 0.5 km w; in Punta Morro Resort. KM 106 Carr Tijuana-Ensenada 22600. **Hours:** noon-11 pm, Sat & Sun from 9 am. **Reservations:** accepted. **Features:** Set atop a rock overlooking the ocean, this restaurant offers sunset views across the ocean and views of the city lights. The waves lap beneath the dining room, which offers calamari steak with "Pinguica" sauce scented with lime-leafed sage, New Zealand rack of lamb with sangrita sauce, prime rib with a poblanas corn basket and chicken breast marinated in balsamic vinegar and virgin olive oil. The large wine list and the flan with Irish cream will complete any meal. Dressy casual; cocktails. **Parking:** on-site. **Cards:** MC, VI.

RESTAURANT CASAMAR
Steak & Seafood

Lunch: $9-$20   **Dinner:** $9-$20   **Phone:** 646/174-0417
Location: Across from marina. Blvd Lazaro Cardenas #987 22800. **Hours:** noon-11 pm. **Reservations:** accepted. **Features:** This long-established restaurant, patronized by loyal diners, prepares such steak and seafood dishes as grilled sea bass, salmon with cilantro sauce and steak rinconada. Dressy casual; cocktails. **Parking:** street. **Cards:** MC, VI.

SE DE VINO
Mediterranean

Lunch: $7-$24   **Dinner:** $7-$24   **Phone:** 646/178-3433
Location: Northeast end of town; between 1st and 2nd sts. Ave Ruiz 138, Zona Centro 22899. **Hours:** noon-midnight, Sun 1 pm-6 pm. Closed: Mon. **Features:** Modern and ideally located in the heart of downtown, the restaurant attracts on-lookers with its floor-to-ceiling glass entrance. The menu selection offers a variety of poultry, meat and fish entrees. Desserts are to die for; try their crepe tower. Situated in the center of the restaurant is a full-service bar with high chairs if you're in the mood for cocktails only. You can also look over their display of T-shirts, wine glasses, books and bottled wine. Casual dress; cocktails. **Parking:** street. **Cards:** AX, MC, VI.

GUERRERO NEGRO, BAJA CALIFORNIA SUR pop. 10,900

——— WHERE TO STAY ———

——— *The following lodging was either not evaluated or did not* ———
meet AAA rating requirements but is listed for your information only.

HOTEL LA PINTA
[fyi]

Phone: 615/157-1304
Not evaluated. **Location:** 7.5 km ne of town on Mex 1; at 28th parallel. (Apdo Postal 929, ENSENADA, BA, 22800). Facilities, services, and decor characterize a basic property.

——— WHERE TO DINE ———

——— *The following restaurant has not been evaluated by AAA* ———
but is listed for your information only.

MALARRIMO RESTAURANT
[fyi]

Phone: 615/157-0250
Not evaluated. **Location:** 1 km w of Mex 1; at east edge of town. Blvd Emiliano Zapata 23940. **Features:** The long-established restaurant counts its specialties as preparations of local seafood and beef.

LA PAZ, BAJA CALIFORNIA SUR pop. 168,600

——— WHERE TO STAY ———

ARAIZA INN PALMIRA
Phone: (612)121-6200

▼▼▼ ▼▼▼

Small-scale Hotel

All Year   1P: $102-$136   2P: $102-$136   XP: $7   F12
Location: 2.5 km n of town on Carr a Pichilingue. Blvd Alberto Alvarado Aramburo S/N 23000 (Col Lomas de Palmira, 23010). Fax: 612/121-6227. **Facility:** Meets AAA guest room security requirements. 120 one-bedroom standard units. 3 stories, interior corridors. *Bath:* shower only. **Parking:** on-site. **Terms:** 15 day cancellation notice. **Amenities:** hair dryers. **Pool(s):** outdoor, wading. **Leisure Activities:** lighted tennis court, playground. **Guest Services:** valet laundry, area transportation. **Business Services:** conference facilities, business center. **Cards:** AX, MC, VI.

SOME UNITS

CABANAS DE LOS ARCOS
Phone: 612/122-2744

▼▼▼ ▼▼▼

Motel

All Year   1P: $85-$90   2P: $85-$90   XP: $10   F12
Location: Just off Paseo Alvaro Obregon opposite the malecon; center; adjacent to Hotel Los Arcos. Alvaro Obregon 490 23000 (Apdo Postal 112). Fax: 612/125-4313. **Facility:** Meets AAA guest room security requirements. 52 units. 48 one- and 2 two-bedroom standard units. 2 one-bedroom suites ($105). 1-4 stories, interior/exterior corridors. *Bath:* shower only. **Parking:** street. **Terms:** 30 day cancellation notice-fee imposed. **Amenities:** high-speed Internet, voice mail, honor bars, irons. **Pool(s):** heated outdoor. **Leisure Activities:** Fee: sauna, massage. **Guest Services:** gift shop, valet laundry. **Business Services:** meeting rooms, business center. **Cards:** AX, MC, VI.

CLUB EL MORO
Phone: (612)122-4084

▼▼▼ ▼▼▼

Motel

All Year   2P: $60-$70
Location: 2 km n of town. KM 2 Carr a Pichilingue 23010 (Apdo Postal 357). Fax: 612/125-2828. **Facility:** 25 units. 10 one-bedroom standard units, some with efficiencies or kitchens. 12 one- and 3 two-bedroom suites ($80-$110) with kitchens. 2 stories (no elevator), exterior corridors. *Bath:* shower only. **Parking:** on-site. **Terms:** office hours 7 am-11 pm, 15 day cancellation notice-fee imposed, [BP] meal plan available, pets (in designated units). **Pool(s):** outdoor. **Leisure Activities:** whirlpools. **Guest Services:** coin laundry. **Cards:** MC, VI.

SOME UNITS

CROWNE PLAZA HOTEL AND RESORT   *Book at aaa.com*
Phone: (612)124-0830

▼▼▼▼ ▼▼▼▼

Large-scale Hotel

All Year   1P: $150-$200   2P: $150-$200   XP: $20   F19
Location: 5.5 km sw on Mex 1 (Abasolo). Lote A Marina Fidepaz 23090 (Apdo Postal 482, 23000). Fax: 612/124-0837. **Facility:** Meets AAA guest room security requirements. 54 units. 24 one-bedroom standard units. 19 one-, 10 two- and 1 three-bedroom suites ($270), some with whirlpools. 2-3 stories (no elevator), exterior corridors. **Parking:** on-site. **Amenities:** safes, irons, hair dryers. *Some:* CD players. **Pool(s):** 3 outdoor. **Leisure Activities:** sauna, whirlpool, playground, exercise room, sports court. **Guest Services:** gift shop, valet laundry, area transportation. **Business Services:** conference facilities, PC. **Cards:** AX, MC, VI.

SOME UNITS

HOTEL LA CONCHA BEACH RESORT
Phone: (612)121-6161

▼▼▼

Large-scale Hotel

All Year   1P: $95   2P: $95   XP: $15   F12
Location: 5 km ne of town. KM 5 Carr a Pichilingue 23010 (Apdo Postal 607). Fax: 612/121-6218. **Facility:** 112 units. 96 one- and 6 two-bedroom standard units, some with efficiencies. 6 one-, 2 two- and 2 three-bedroom suites ($125-$300) with kitchens, some with whirlpools. 3 stories (no elevator), exterior corridors. *Bath:* shower only. **Parking:** on-site. **Terms:** age restrictions may apply, 7 day cancellation notice. **Pool(s):** outdoor, wading. **Leisure Activities:** whirlpool, exercise room. *Fee:* boats, windsurfing, scuba diving, snorkeling, fishing, charter fishing, massage. **Guest Services:** gift shop, valet laundry, area transportation. **Business Services:** conference facilities. **Cards:** AX, MC, VI.

HOTEL LA POSADA DE ENGELBERT
Phone: (612)122-4011

▼▼

Motel

All Year   1P: $75-$95   2P: $75-$95
Location: 3 km s of town on Mex 1 (Abasolo), turn w; just s of Volkswagen Agency, 0.5 km w. Nueva Reforma y Playa Sur 23000 (Apdo Postal 152). Fax: 612/122-0663. **Facility:** 26 units. 20 one-bedroom standard units. 6 one-bedroom suites ($110). 1 story, exterior corridors. *Bath:* combo or shower only. **Parking:** on-site. **Terms:** 8 day cancellation notice. **Pool(s):** outdoor. **Guest Services:** valet and coin laundry. **Business Services:** meeting rooms. **Cards:** AX, MC, VI.

SOME UNITS

HOTEL LOS ARCOS   *Book at aaa.com*
Phone: (612)122-2744

▼▼▼ ▼▼▼

Large-scale Hotel

All Year   1P: $85-$90   2P: $85-$90   XP: $10   F12
Location: Center of town. Paseo Alvaro Obregon 498 23000 (Apdo Postal 112). Fax: 612/125-4313. **Facility:** Meets AAA guest room security requirements. 130 units. 126 one-bedroom standard units. 4 one-bedroom suites ($105). 3 stories, interior corridors. *Bath:* shower only. **Parking:** on-site. **Terms:** 30 day cancellation notice-fee imposed. **Amenities:** voice mail, safes, honor bars, irons. **Dining:** Restaurant Bermejo, see separate listing. **Pool(s):** outdoor. **Leisure Activities:** Fee: sauna, massage. **Guest Services:** gift shop, valet laundry. **Business Services:** meeting rooms, business center. **Cards:** AX, MC, VI.

SOME UNITS

HOTEL MARINA
Phone: (612)121-6254

▼▼▼ ▼▼▼

Large-scale Hotel

All Year   1P: $85-$135   2P: $85-$135   XP: $16   F12
Location: 2.5 km n of town. KM 2.5 Carr a Pichilingue 23010 (Apdo Postal 194). Fax: 612/121-6177. **Facility:** Meets AAA guest room security requirements. 91 units. 86 one-bedroom standard units, some with efficiencies. 5 one-bedroom suites ($135-$185) with kitchens. 5 stories, exterior corridors. *Bath:* combo or shower only. **Parking:** on-site. **Terms:** office hours 7 am-11 pm, cancellation fee imposed. **Amenities:** hair dryers. *Some:* safes. **Pool(s):** outdoor, wading. **Leisure Activities:** whirlpool, rental boats, lighted tennis court. *Fee:* marina, charter fishing. **Guest Services:** gift shop, valet laundry. **Business Services:** conference facilities, PC. **Cards:** AX, JC, MC, VI.

SOME UNITS

HOTEL MEDITERRANE

▽▽▽▽
Motel

12/1-4/30 & 10/1-11/30   1P: $60-$80   2P: $65-$80   XP: $10
5/1-9/30   1P: $50-$75   2P: $55-$75   XP: $10

Phone: (612)125-1195

Location: Just e of Paseo Alvaro Obregon; in town. Allende 36 23000. Fax: 612/125-1195. **Facility:** 9 one-bedroom standard units. 2 stories (no elevator), exterior corridors. *Bath:* shower only. **Parking:** street. **Terms:** office hours 7 am-10 pm, 7 day cancellation notice-fee imposed. **Amenities:** video library. *Some:* CD players. **Dining:** La Pazta Restaurante, see separate listing. **Leisure Activities:** bicycles. **Cards:** AX, MC, VI.

HOTEL PERLA

▽▽▽
Large-scale Hotel

All Year   1P: $78   2P: $78   XP: $16

Phone: (612)122-0777
F12

Location: In town. Paseo Alvaro Obregon #1570 23000 (Apdo Postal 207). Fax: 612/125-5363. **Facility:** 110 one-bedroom standard units. 5 stories, interior corridors. *Bath:* shower only. **Parking:** on-site and valet. **Amenities:** irons. **Dining:** Restaurant La Terraza, see separate listing. **Pool(s):** outdoor. **Leisure Activities:** whirlpool, playground. **Guest Services:** valet laundry. **Business Services:** meeting rooms. **Cards:** AX, MC, VI.

LA CASA JALISCO   *Book at aaa.com*

▽▽▽▽▽
Motel

All Year [CP]   1P: $60-$100   2P: $60-$100   XP: $10

Phone: 612/128-4311
F6

Location: 3.3 km s of town on Mex 1 (Abasolo), just e. Jalisco 480 Esq I Ramirez Col Pueblo Nuevo 23060. Fax: 612/128-5311. **Facility:** 10 units. 9 one- and 1 two-bedroom standard units. 3 stories (no elevator), interior corridors. **Parking:** on-site. **Terms:** office hours 8 am-10 pm, check-in 4 pm. **Pool(s):** outdoor. **Business Services:** meeting rooms. **Cards:** AX, MC, VI.

SOME UNITS

LA CASA MEXICANA INN

▽▽▽▽
Bed & Breakfast

12/1-6/15 & 10/15-11/30 [ECP]   2P: $65-$95   XP: $10

Phone: (612)125-2748

Location: Paseo Alvaro Obregon, turn e, just past Hotel Los Arcos on Rosales, 1 blk n on Madero, then just w. Calle Bravo #106 23000. **Facility:** A Spanish-deco home, steps from the bay and tourist area, the inn has individually themed rooms featuring art, antiques and hand-woven textiles. Smoke free premises. 5 one-bedroom standard units, some with efficiencies or kitchens. 2 stories (no elevator), interior corridors. *Bath:* combo or shower only. **Parking:** street. **Terms:** open 12/1-6/15 & 10/15-11/30, age restrictions may apply, 7 day cancellation notice-fee imposed.

SOME UNITS

POSADA DE LAS FLORES LA PAZ

▽▽▽▽
Bed & Breakfast

All Year [BP]   2P: $140-$199

Phone: 612/125-5871

Location: On northern end of town along the malecon. Paseo Alvaro Obregon 440 23000. Fax: 612/122-8748. **Facility:** Not too far from the romantic walkway, this reddish brick-colored hotel sits fronting stunning views of the sunrise and sunset. This antique Mexican house exemplifies authenticity in its furnishings and decor, tapered by crafted workmanship and tile floors. The lovely inner courtyards offer a serene ambience with an opportunity to relax, read and comtemplate the sun or enjoy short walks to nearby shops and restaurants. Smoke free premises. 7 units. 6 one-bedroom standard units. 1 one-bedroom suite ($450). 3 stories (no elevator), exterior corridors. *Bath:* combo or shower only. **Parking:** street. **Terms:** office hours 7 am-11 pm, check-in 4 pm, age restrictions may apply. **Amenities:** safes, hair dryers. **Pool(s):** small outdoor. **Cards:** MC, VI.

SOME UNITS

SEVEN CROWN HOTEL

▽▽▽ ▽▽▽
Small-scale Hotel

All Year   1P: $85-$100   2P: $85-$100   XP: $20

Phone: 612/128-7788

Location: In town. Paseo Alvaro Obregon y Lerdo de Tejeda 23000. Fax: 612/128-9090. **Facility:** 52 one-bedroom standard units, some with efficiencies. 6 stories, interior corridors. *Bath:* shower only. **Parking:** valet. **Terms:** 7 day cancellation notice, 4% service charge. **Amenities:** hair dryers. **Dining:** El Aura, see separate listing. **Leisure Activities:** whirlpool. *Fee:* massage. **Guest Services:** valet laundry. **Business Services:** meeting rooms, PC. **Cards:** AX, MC, VI.

SOME UNITS

--------- **WHERE TO DINE** ---------

BOUGAINVILLEA RESTAURANTE

▽▽▽ ▽▽▽
Steak & Seafood

Lunch: $5-$9   **Dinner:** $10-$18   **Phone:** 612/122-7744

Location: Paseo Alvaro Obregon, just w via Marquez de Leon. Malecon de Vista Coral, Local #5. **Hours:** 1 pm-11 pm. Closed: Tues. **Features:** At the end of Coral Marina Wharf with strings of lights that match the city view back across the bay, the restaurant provides attentive service in a circular dining room, on the patio and waterside on the wharf. Among menu choices are quality steaks, fresh seafood and pizza. Casual dress; cocktails. **Parking:** on-site. **Cards:** MC, VI.

EL AURA

▽▽▽ ▽▽▽
International

Lunch: $8-$16   **Dinner:** $8-$16   **Phone:** 612/128-7787

Location: In town; in Seven Crown Hotel. Paseo Alvaro Obregon y Lerdo de Tejeda 23000. **Hours:** 7 am-11 pm. **Features:** On the fourth floor of the hotel, the restaurant is made of glass walls and offers a spectacular view of the bay. The young chef creates new and artfully prepared dishes with touches of Mexican, Italian and Continental influence. The setting is also popular for breakfast. Casual dress; cocktails. **Parking:** street. **Cards:** AX, MC, VI.

EL TASTE

▽▽▽
Mexican

Lunch: $7-$25   **Dinner:** $7-$25   **Phone:** 612/122-8121

Location: In town. Paseo Alvaro Obregon #780 23000. **Hours:** 8 am-midnight. Closed: 1/1, 12/25. **Features:** On the popular malecon, the open-air restaurant overlooks the bay. Guests watch such sights as boats navigating the harbor, sunsets and street activity. Lining the menu are good, basic dishes: breaded or grilled fish or shrimp in garlic butter, T-bone or pepper steak, carne asada and grilled lobster. Casual dress; cocktails. **Parking:** street. **Cards:** MC, VI.

LA PAZ-LAPA DE CARLOS 'N CHARLIE'S **Lunch:** $5-$13 **Dinner:** $5-$13 **Phone:** 612/122-9290

Mexican

Location: On the malecon at Calle 16 de Septiembre. Paseo Alvaro Obregon 23010. **Hours:** 8 am-1 am. **Features:** Many factors contribute to the restaurant's boisterous atmosphere: the upbeat streetside patio and sidewalk, the festive dining room, lively music and comedic waiters. Guests can survey the town while enjoying such menu offerings as hamburgers, tacos, rellenos or full dinners of grilled beef filet, ribs, chicken or fish. Casual dress; cocktails. **Parking:** street. **Cards:** AX, MC, VI.

LA PAZTA RESTAURANTE **Dinner:** $7-$12 **Phone:** 612/125-1195

Italian

Location: Just e of Paseo Alvaro Obregon; in town; in Hotel Mediterrane. Allende 36 23000. **Hours:** 3 pm-10:30 pm. Closed: Tues. **Features:** In front of the hotel, the converted house has black and white tile floors, open walls and contemporary decor. Guests can sit in one of several rooms or on the front patio. Made fresh daily on the premises, pasta is used in such preparations as pasta with squid in wine and cream sauce. Other favorites include chicken with lemon cream sauce, mushroom-stuffed ravioli and pizza. Casual dress; cocktails. **Parking:** street. **Cards:** AX, MC, VI.

LE BISTROT FRANCAIS **Lunch:** $5-$15 **Dinner:** $5-$15 **Phone:** 612/125-6080

French

Location: Paseo Alvaro Obregon, just e on Lerdo Degollado, just n. Calle Esquerro #10. **Hours:** 9 am-11 pm. **Features:** Paintings, sculptures and wall murals in the historic building give patrons the feeling of dining in a gallery. Seating in the garden also can be requested. The relocated French family has created a menu of traditional dishes, such as crepes polo, lamb chops with capers and fresh seafood, shrimp and lobster served steamed or flambeed. Casual dress; cocktails. **Parking:** street. **Cards:** MC, VI.

RESTAURANT BERMEJO **Lunch:** $7-$12 **Dinner:** $8-$18 **Phone:** 612/122-2744

Mexican

Location: Center of town; in Hotel Los Arcos. Paseo Alvaro Obregon 498 23000. **Hours:** 7 am-11 pm, Sun from 9 am. **Features:** Brick columns, arches and windows overlooking bobbing sailboats on the bay lend to the pleasant atmosphere in the hotel dining room. Formal servers present a selection of steaks and seafood. Chicken breast stuffed with lobster over a demi-glace sauce and brandy is a signature item. Dressy casual; cocktails. **Parking:** street. **Cards:** AX, MC, VI.

RESTAURANT LA TERRAZA **Lunch:** $3-$12 **Dinner:** $5-$12 **Phone:** 612/122-0777

Mexican

Location: In town; in Hotel Perla. Paseo Alvaro Obregon #1570 23000. **Hours:** 7 am-10:30 pm. **Features:** Popular for its window to the bay and streetside views, the coffee shop-style restaurant offers good food and prompt service. The varied menu lists Mexican favorites, chicken cordon bleu, T-bone steak and filet mignon. Casual dress; cocktails. **Parking:** street. **Cards:** AX, MC, VI.

LORETO, BAJA CALIFORNIA SUR pop. 10,600

— WHERE TO STAY —

CAMINO REAL LORETO BAJA *Book at aaa.com* **Phone:** 613/133-0010

All Year [AP] 2P: $143-$241 XP: $83 F12

Resort
Large-scale Hotel

Location: 8 km s on Mex 1, 1 km w on Mision San Ignacio, then 1 km s; in Nopolo. Blvd Mision de Loreto S/N Fracc Napolo 23880. Fax: 613/133-0020. **Facility:** This hotel is on the beach, with a large swimming pool, palapas in the sand and an adjacent golf course; all rooms face the ocean. Meets AAA guest room security requirements. 155 one-bedroom standard units, some with whirlpools. 3 stories, exterior corridors. *Bath:* shower only. **Parking:** on-site and valet. **Amenities:** voice mail, safes, honor bars, hair dryers. **Pool(s):** outdoor, wading. **Leisure Activities:** whirlpools, golf-18 holes, 3 lighted tennis courts. **Guest Services:** gift shop, valet laundry. **Business Services:** meeting rooms, PC. **Cards:** AX, MC, VI.

SOME UNITS

HACIENDA SUITES **Phone:** 613/135-0202

All Year 2P: $69-$79 XP: $10 F12

Motel

Location: 1 km e of Mex 1; at town entrance. Salvatierra #152 23880. Fax: 613/135-0202. **Facility:** Meets AAA guest room security requirements. 25 units. 24 one-bedroom standard units. 1 one-bedroom suite ($95). 2 stories, exterior corridors. *Bath:* shower only. **Parking:** on-site. **Terms:** 7 day cancellation notice. **Amenities:** safes. **Pool(s):** outdoor, wading. **Leisure Activities:** Fee: charter fishing. **Cards:** MC, VI.

SOME UNITS

HOTEL LA PINTA **Phone:** 613/135-0025

All Year 1P: $79-$89 2P: $79-$89 XP: $15

Small-scale Hotel

Location: Mex 1, 1.5 km e to Calle Indepencia, 0.5 km n to Calle Pinta, then just e. Calle Davis S/N 23880 (Apdo Postal 28). Fax: 613/135-0026. **Facility:** Meets AAA guest room security requirements. 48 one-bedroom standard units. 2 stories, exterior corridors. *Bath:* shower only. **Parking:** on-site. **Amenities:** hair dryers. **Pool(s):** outdoor. **Guest Services:** gift shop, valet laundry. **Cards:** AX, MC, VI.

POSADA DE LAS FLORES LORETO **Phone:** 613/135-1165

All Year [BP] 2P: $140-$199

Country Inn

Location: Mex 1, 1.5 km e to Calle Indepencia, just n to Blvd Benito Juarez, then 0.5 km s. Salvatierra Esq Madero Col Centro 23880. Fax: 613/135-1099. **Facility:** Colorful walls, heavy wood furniture and stone floors accent this hacienda; a glass-bottomed rooftop swimming pool forms the lobby ceiling. Designated smoking area. 15 one-bedroom standard units. 3 stories (no elevator), exterior corridors. *Bath:* shower only. **Parking:** street. **Terms:** age restrictions may apply. **Amenities:** safes, hair dryers. **Dining:** The Roof Garden, see separate listing. **Pool(s):** outdoor. **Guest Services:** valet laundry, area transportation. **Cards:** MC, VI.

VILLAS DE LORETO
Phone: (613)135-0586
Motel
All Year   2P: $78-$123   XP: $20   F12
Location: 1 km s of town center via Francisco Madero. Colonia Zaragoza 23880 (Apdo Postal 132). Fax: 613/135-0355. **Facility:** Meets AAA guest room requirements. Smoke free premises. 13 units. 11 one-bedroom standard units. 2 cottages. 1 story, exterior corridors. *Bath:* shower only. **Parking:** on-site. **Terms:** 30 day cancellation notice-fee imposed. **Amenities:** *Some:* safes. **Pool(s):** outdoor. **Leisure Activities:** scuba diving & rental equipment, bicycles. **Guest Services:** coin laundry. **Cards:** MC, VI.

SOME UNITS

THE WHALES INN BEACH AND GOLF RESORT
Phone: 613/133-0700
Resort
Large-scale Hotel
All Year   1P: $170   2P: $230   D12
Location: 8 km s on Mex 1, 1 km e on Mision San Ignacio; in Nopolo. Blvd Mision de Loreto, Lotes 8 y 9 23880. Fax: 613/133-0837. **Facility:** The hotel lies on a beautiful coastal view of the Sea of Cortez offering exclusive beaches. Almost every room has a view of the center courtyard. 246 units. 238 one-bedroom standard units. 8 one-bedroom suites. 3 stories, exterior corridors. *Bath:* combo or shower only. **Parking:** on-site. **Terms:** age restrictions may apply. **Amenities:** safes. **Pool(s):** 2 outdoor. **Leisure Activities:** whirlpool, windsurfing, bicycles, exercise room, game room. *Fee:* massage. **Guest Services:** gift shop, valet laundry. **Business Services:** meeting rooms. **Cards:** AX, DC, MC, VI.

SOME UNITS

──────── **WHERE TO DINE** ────────

EL NIDO STEAK HOUSE
Lunch: $4-$17   **Dinner:** $9-$17   **Phone:** 613/104-4016
Steak House
Location: 1 km e of Mex 1; at town entrance. Salvatierra #154 23880. **Hours:** 1:30 pm-10:30 pm. **Features:** Rough brick walls, heavy wood doors and tables with wagon wheel lights contribute to the hacienda-style, ranch atmosphere. The aromas of mesquite-grilled steaks fill the air. Also offered are pork chops, fish and shrimp with garlic butter, tacos, chiles rellenos and hamburgers. Casual dress; cocktails. **Parking:** on-site.

THE ROOF GARDEN
Dinner: $8-$20   **Phone:** 613/135-1162
Mexican
Location: Mex 1, 1.5 km e to Calle Indepencia, just n to Blvd Benito Juarez, then 0.5 km s; in Posada de las Flores Loreto. Salvatierra Esq Madero Col Centro 23880. **Hours:** 6 pm-9 pm. Closed: Sun. **Features:** Atop an enchanting inn, the third-floor rooftop restaurant is enclosed by walls of glass that afford views of the ocean and the blue sky across the rooftops. Pleasant locals meet the demands of guests with flavorful Mexican dishes such as the house special mariscada, steamed clams, adobo chicken, grilled prawns and grilled chicken poblano. Casual dress; cocktails. **Parking:** on-site. **Cards:** MC, VI.

LOS BARRILES, BAJA CALIFORNIA SUR

──────── **WHERE TO STAY** ────────

HOTEL PUNTA PESCADERO
Phone: 624/141-0101
Resort Motel
All Year   1P: $125   2P: $125   XP: $25   F11
Location: 12 km n off Mex 1, via unpaved road. Located in a remote area. Camino de los Barriles a El Cardonal (Apdo Postal 362, LA PAZ, BS, 23000). Fax: 612/126-1771. **Facility:** Secluded resort on uncrowded beaches with underwater sea life for diving and expansive waters to explore by canoe or dinghy. Spacious units with fireplace, sitting area and private tiled terrace overlooking the sea. 23 units. 21 one-bedroom standard units. 1 one- and 1 two-bedroom suites. 1 story, exterior corridors. *Bath:* shower only. **Parking:** on-site. **Terms:** office hours 7 am-10 pm, 15 day cancellation notice, 15% service charge. **Pool(s):** outdoor. **Leisure Activities:** rental boats, rental canoes, scuba diving & rental equipment, snorkeling & rental equipment, fishing, lighted tennis court, game room. *Fee:* charter fishing. **Guest Services:** gift shop. **Business Services:** business center. **Cards:** MC, VI.

LOS BARRILES HOTEL
Phone: (624)141-0024
Motel
All Year   1P: $43   2P: $53   XP: $10
Location: 1 km e of Mex 1, 1 km n. Bahia de Palmas 23501 (Apdo Postal 50). Fax: 624/141-0024. **Facility:** 20 one-bedroom standard units. 2 stories (no elevator), exterior corridors. *Bath:* shower only. **Parking:** on-site. **Terms:** 7 day cancellation notice, 5% service charge. **Pool(s):** outdoor, wading. **Leisure Activities:** whirlpool. *Fee:* massage. **Cards:** MC, VI.

──────── **WHERE TO DINE** ────────

OTRA VEZ RESTAURANT
Lunch: $6-$14   **Dinner:** $7-$15   **Phone:** 624/141-0249
American
Cards: MC, VI.
Location: 1 km e of Mex 1, 1.5 km n. Bahia de Palmas 23501. **Hours:** Open 12/1-8/1 & 10/1-11/30; 7 am-10 pm, Mon from 11 am. **Features:** The local cafe, with indoor and patio seating, serves American-style dishes with a Mexican accent. The menu lists such items as fish and chips, hamburgers, blackened fish and spicy Thai chicken. At breakfast, look for prime rib hash or an omelet. Casual dress; cocktails. **Parking:** on-site.

TIO PABLO'S BAR & GRILL
Lunch: $5-$17   **Dinner:** $6-$17   **Phone:** 624/141-0330
American
Cards: MC, VI.
Location: 1 km e of Mex 1, just n; in town. Camino al Cardonal S/N 23501. **Hours:** 11 am-10 pm. **Features:** Diners who visit the local-favorite gathering place unwind in the large palapa or on the garden patio. The casual setting and service match the menu, which lists such choices as hamburgers, sandwiches, fajitas, pasta, pizza, ribeye steak, Santa Fe chicken and vegetarian enchiladas. Casual dress; cocktails. **Parking:** on-site.

MEXICALI, BAJA CALIFORNIA pop. 575,300

——— WHERE TO STAY ———

ARAIZA HOTEL **Book at aaa.com**
Phone: (686)564-1100

▼▼▼▼ All Year 2P: $65-$97 XP: $30 F12
Location: From the border, 4.5 km e on Ave Cristobal Colon, 3 km s on Calzada Justo Sierra and Blvd Benito Juarez.
Large-scale Hotel Blvd Benito Juarez 2220 21270 (233 Pauline Ave, Suite 947, CALEXICO, CA, 92231). Fax: 686/564-1113.
Facility: Meets AAA guest room security requirements. 269 units. 220 one-bedroom standard units. 49 one-bedroom suites ($110-$122). 3-6 stories, interior corridors. *Bath:* combo or shower only. **Parking:** on-site. **Amenities:** hair dryers. *Some:* safes. **Pool(s):** 2 outdoor, heated outdoor, wading. **Leisure Activities:** exercise room. *Fee:* lighted tennis court.
Guest Services: gift shop, valet laundry. **Business Services:** meeting rooms. **Cards:** AX, MC, VI.
SOME UNITS

CALAFIA INN
Phone: 686-568-3311

▼▼ All Year 2P: $72-$85 XP: $8
Location: From the border, 4.5 km e on Ave Cristobal Colon, 2.4 km s. Calzada Justo Sierra #1495 21230 (233 Pauline
Small-scale Hotel Ave, Suite 947, CALEXICO, CA, 92231). Fax: 686/568-2010. **Facility:** Meets AAA guest room security requirements. 171 units. 164 one-bedroom standard units. 7 one-bedroom suites ($149). 2-4 stories (no elevator), exterior corridors. *Bath:* shower only. **Parking:** on-site. **Amenities:** *Some:* hair dryers. **Pool(s):** outdoor. **Guest Services:** valet laundry. **Business Services:** meeting rooms. **Cards:** AX, MC, VI.
SOME UNITS

CROWNE PLAZA HOTEL AND RESORT **Book at aaa.com**
Phone: (686)557-3600

▼▼▼ All Year 2P: $120-$186 XP: $40 F16
Location: 4.5 km s of border on Blvd Lopez Mateos, just w. Ave de los Heroes #201 21000. Fax: 686/557-0555.
Large-scale Hotel **Facility:** Meets AAA guest room security requirements. 158 units. 151 one-bedroom standard units. 7 one-bedroom suites ($236). 8 stories, interior corridors. **Parking:** on-site. **Terms:** 3 day cancellation notice.
Amenities: irons, hair dryers. **Dining:** The Premiere, see separate listing. **Pool(s):** outdoor. **Leisure Activities:** exercise room.
Guest Services: gift shop, valet laundry. **Business Services:** meeting rooms, business center. **Cards:** AX, MC, VI.
SOME UNITS

HOTEL LUCERNA **Book at aaa.com**
Phone: (686)564-7000

▼▼▼ All Year [CP] 1P: $125-$140 2P: $125-$140 XP: $15 F12
Location: From the border, 4.5 km e on Ave Cristobal Colon, 3.8 km s on Calzada Justo Sierra and Blvd Benito Juarez.
Large-scale Hotel Blvd Benito Juarez #2151 21270 (PO Box 2300, CALEXICO, CA, 92231). Fax: 686/566-4706. **Facility:** Meets AAA guest room security requirements. 175 units. 167 one-bedroom standard units. 8 one-bedroom suites ($175-$240). 1-6 stories, interior/exterior corridors. *Bath:* combo or shower only. **Parking:** on-site. **Amenities:** high-speed Internet, voice mail, irons, hair dryers. **Dining:** Mezzosole Restaurante Italiano, see separate listing. **Pool(s):** 2 outdoor. **Leisure Activities:** sauna, exercise room. **Guest Services:** gift shop, valet laundry. **Business Services:** meeting rooms, business center. **Cards:** AX, MC, VI.
SOME UNITS

HOTEL POSADA DEL SOL
Phone: 686-558-7475

▼▼ All Year 2P: $65-$95 XP: $20
Location: 4.5 km s of the border on Blvd Lopez Mateos, just w. Calle Calafia 400 21200 (120-A Rockwood Ave, PMB
Motel 43-527, CALEXICO, CA, 92231). Fax: 686/558-7162. **Facility:** 56 one-bedroom standard units. 2 stories (no elevator), exterior corridors. **Parking:** on-site. **Cards:** MC, VI.
SOME UNITS

MOTEL COLONIAL LAS FUENTES
Phone: 686-556-1312

▼▼▼ All Year [CP] 1P: $88 2P: $88 XP: $10
Location: 4.5 km s of the border; at Calle Calafia. Blvd Lopez Mateos #1048 21200 (PO Box 722, Suite 9, CALEXICO,
Motel CA, 92232). Fax: 686/556-1141. **Facility:** Meets AAA guest room security requirements. 149 units. 147 one-bedroom standard units. 2 one-bedroom suites ($124). 2 stories (no elevator), exterior corridors. **Parking:** on-site. **Pool(s):** outdoor, wading. **Guest Services:** valet laundry. **Business Services:** meeting rooms. **Cards:** AX, MC, VI.
SOME UNITS

——— WHERE TO DINE ———

CASINO DE MEXICALI
Lunch: $6-$12 Dinner: $8-$17 Phone: 686-552-5893

▼▼▼ **Location:** 4 km e of the border on Ave Francisco Madero, 0.5 km s on Calle K, then just e to Calle L. Pino Suarez
International #2001 21230. **Hours:** 8 am-11 pm, Sun-7 pm. **Reservations:** accepted. **Features:** A local favorite for special occasions, the stylish restaurant has a stone entrance, white linen tablecloths, a sprig of greens on each table, designer lighting and a display kitchen. On the menu are prime steaks, chicken parmigiana, fresh fish with herbs, gourmet hamburgers, tacos and burritos. Dressy casual; cocktails. **Parking:** street. **Cards:** AX, MC, VI.

LOS ARCOS RESTAURANT
Lunch: $7-$15 Dinner: $7-$15 Phone: 686-556-0903

▼▼▼ **Location:** 4.5 km s of the border via Blvd Lopez Mateos, just w. Calle Calafia #454 21200. **Hours:** 11 am-10 pm.
Seafood **Features:** Festively decorated with fish netting, sculptures and bright colors, the restaurant has lively servers to match. Fresh fish from local waters is the specialty. Open-faced fish tacos with lime are a treat, as is the seafood fiesta for two, which includes a variety of stews of squid and octopus, shredded fish, smoked fish and shrimp, stuffed peppers and perch. Steaks also are available. Top dessert choices are bananas flambe and crepes Suzette. Casual dress; cocktails. **Parking:** on-site. **Cards:** MC, VI.

MEZZOSOLE RESTAURANTE ITALIANO   **Lunch:** $8-$18   **Dinner:** $8-$18   **Phone:** 686/564-7000
Location: From the border, 4.5 km e on Ave Cristobal Colon, 3.8 km s on Calzada Justo Sierra and Blvd Benito Juarez; in Hotel Lucerna. Blvd Benito Juarez #2151 21270. **Hours:** noon-midnight. **Closed:** Sun.
Italian   **Reservations:** suggested. **Features:** A cool and relaxing atmosphere exudes through the intimate dining room, which has wall and ceiling murals and overlooks a swimming pool. Popular dishes on a menu of pasta, pizza and seafood entrees include seafood linguine, Gorgonzola and beef and chicken prosciutto. Dressy casual. **Parking:** on-site. **Cards:** AX, CB, DC, MC, VI.

THE PREMIERE   **Lunch:** $8-$22   **Dinner:** $8-$22   **Phone:** 686/557-3600
Location: 4.5 km s of border on Blvd Lopez Mateos, just w; in Crowne Plaza Hotel and Resort. Ave de los Heroes #201 21200. **Hours:** 7 am-11 pm. **Reservations:** suggested. **Features:** The refined staff contributes to an elegant dining experience. Examples of artfully presented dishes include filet mignon in braised mushroom sauce, International   seared ahi, grilled shrimp with scallions, rosemary chicken and made-to-order pasta. Flaming desserts and gourmet coffees top off the meal. Dressy casual; cocktails. **Parking:** on-site. **Cards:** AX, MC, VI.

RESTAURANT LA MISION DRAGON   **Lunch:** $7-$14   **Dinner:** $7-$18   **Phone:** 686/566-4320
Location: From the border, 4.5 km e on Ave Cristobal Colon, 5.5 km s on Calzada Justo Sierra and Blvd Bonito Juarez, then just e. Blvd Lazaro Cardenas #555 21270. **Hours:** 11 am-11 pm. **Reservations:** accepted.
Chinese   **Features:** Guests feel as though they are entering the Emperor's Palace as they cross bridges and pass waterfalls on the grounds. Inside, the room comprises wood-paneled walls, a large red dragon mural and numerous areas for private dining. Dragon plaza duck is a signature dish among offerings of Cantonese fare. Casual dress; cocktails. **Parking:** on-site. **Cards:** MC, VI.

SAKURA RESTAURANT   **Lunch:** $7-$12   **Dinner:** $7-$14   **Phone:** 686/566-4848
Location: 4.5 km s of the border on Blvd Lopez Mateos, just w. Blvd Lazaro Cardenas y Calz Fco L Monte 21270. **Hours:** 7 am-11 pm. **Closed:** Mon. **Reservations:** accepted. **Features:** The large complex houses a video bar and karaoke club. Wood paneling, bridges and a rock and water garden with live turtles decorate the
Japanese   dining room. The sushi bar and teppanyaki tables occupy separate areas. Locals frequent the buffet lunch from noon-4 pm daily. Dressy casual; cocktails. **Parking:** on-site. **Cards:** AX, MC, VI.

MULEGE, BAJA CALIFORNIA SUR pop. 3,100

——— **WHERE TO DINE** ———

LAS CASITAS RESTAURANT   **Lunch:** $5-$8   **Dinner:** $8-$15   **Phone:** 615/153-0019
Location: Callejon de los Estudiantes and Ave Independencia; in town center. Madero #50. **Hours:** 7 am-10 pm. **Features:** Popular for breakfast and lunch, the casual patio setting gets lively Friday nights, when a mariachi band and folkloric dancers accompany the fiesta buffet. Grilled lobster, fried or ranchero-style garlic
Mexican   chicken, baby back pork ribs and breaded, charcoal-broiled or grilled fish or shrimp are among tried-and-true entrees. Casual dress; cocktails. **Parking:** street. **Cards:** MC, VI.

PUNTA CHIVATO, BAJA CALIFORNIA SUR

——— **WHERE TO STAY** ———

POSADA DE LAS FLORES PUNTA CHIVATO   **Phone:** 615/153-0188
All Year   1P: $130-$230   2P: $160-$260
Location: Mex 1 at Palo Verde, 17 km e on gravel and dirt road. Located in a remote area. Domicilio Conocido Punta Chivato (Salvatierra esq Madero Col Centro, LORETO, BS, 23880). Fax: 615/155-5600. **Facility:** A resort of 7.5
Resort   acres at the sea has been created with colorful yellow/gold buildings and brick red walkways that lead to
Small-scale Hotel   inner grounds with coral walls and stone arches. The place to relax, read and contemplate the sun. Willows and palms sway with the breezes out over the white caps. Units have patios with umbrellas, heavy wood furniture on tile floors with colorful walls. 20 one-bedroom standard units. 1 story, exterior corridors. *Bath:* shower only. **Parking:** on-site. **Terms:** age restrictions may apply, 15% service charge. **Pool(s):** outdoor. **Leisure Activities:** tennis court, bicycles. **Cards:** MC, VI.

ROSARITO, BAJA CALIFORNIA pop. 53,700

——— **WHERE TO STAY** ———

BRISAS DEL MAR HOTEL BY VENTANA ROSA   **Phone:** 661/612-2547
3/1-9/30 [BP]   2P: $60-$90   XP: $20   F12
12/1-2/28 & 10/1-11/30 [BP]   2P: $45-$70   XP: $10   F12
Location: Mex 1-D (toll road), exit south end of town, just prior to toll station, then n into town. Blvd Benito Juarez #22 22710 (808 4th Ave, Suite 511, SAN DIEGO, CA, 92101-6153). Fax: 661/612-2547. **Facility:** Meets AAA guest
Small-scale Hotel   room security requirements. 71 one-bedroom standard units, some with whirlpools. 2 stories, exterior corridors. **Parking:** on-site. **Dining:** 7 am-10 pm, cocktails. **Pool(s):** heated outdoor. **Leisure Activities:** whirlpool, volleyball. **Business Services:** meeting rooms. **Cards:** MC, VI.

SOME UNITS

LAS ROCAS RESORT & SPA   **Phone:** 661/614-0354
5/1-9/30   2P: $89-$279   XP: $15   F12
12/1-4/30 & 10/1-11/30   2P: $74-$199   XP: $15   F12
Location: On Mex 1, 10 km s of town. KM 38.5 Carr Libre Tijuana-Ensenada 22710 (PO Box 189003 HLR,
Small-scale Hotel   CORONADO, CA, 92178-9003). Fax: 661/614-0360. **Facility:** Meets AAA guest room security requirements. 74 one-bedroom standard units. 4 stories (no elevator), exterior corridors. **Parking:** on-site. **Terms:** 3 day cancellation notice. **Pool(s):** outdoor, heated outdoor. **Leisure Activities:** whirlpools, tennis court, spa, volleyball. *Fee:* exercise room. **Cards:** MC, VI.

SOME UNITS

ROSARITO BEACH HOTEL & SPA
AAA
▼▼ ▼▼
Resort
Large-scale Hotel

Phone: 661/612-0144

| 6/18-9/5 | 2P: $129-$299 | XP: $30 | F12 |
| 12/1-6/17 & 9/6-11/30 | 2P: $99-$279 | XP: $20 | F12 |

Location: On Mex 1-D (toll road), exit south end of town, just prior to the toll station, circle right, then just n. Blvd Bonito Juarez #31 22710 (PO Box 430145, SAN DIEGO, CA, 92143-0145). Fax: 661/612-1125. **Facility:** In town, this historic resort continues to re-build to provide modern accommodations. Units are modest to upscale in high rise and one-story buildings. 276 units. 202 one-bedroom standard units. 42 one- and 32 two-bedroom suites ($229-$549), some with efficiencies. 1-8 stories, interior/exterior corridors. *Bath:* combo or shower only. **Parking:** on-site (fee). **Terms:** check-in 4 pm. **Amenities:** voice mail. **Dining:** Chabert's Restaurant, Azteca Restaurant, see separate listings. **Pool(s):** 2 heated outdoor. **Leisure Activities:** whirlpools, fishing, spa, sports court. **Guest Services:** gift shop, valet laundry. **Business Services:** meeting rooms. **Cards:** MC, VI.

SOME UNITS

――――――― **WHERE TO DINE** ―――――――

AZTECA RESTAURANT   *Menu on aaa.com*
AAA
▼▼ ▼▼
Mexican

Lunch: $5-$8   Dinner: $9-$12   Phone: 661/612-0144

Location: On Mex 1-D (toll road), exit south end of town, just prior to the toll station, circle right, then just n; in Rosarito Beach Hotel & Spa. Blvd Bonito Juarez #31 22710. **Hours:** 7:30 am-10 pm. **Features:** Enjoy the picturesque view from the dining room where your taste buds will water with Mexican delicacies flavored with fresh herbs. Typical local dishes are prepared to reflect the local culture and ambience with their new tile decor and fireplace setting. Try their seafood Baja omelette stuffed with shrimp and lobster. Machaca (shredded beef) is always a favorite. Ceviche, diced filet of fish marinated in lemon, tomato and chiles and a tortilla, is a meal in itself. Casual dress; cocktails. **Parking:** on-site. **Cards:** MC, VI.

CHABERT'S RESTAURANT
AAA
▼▼ ▼▼
International

Dinner: $11-$21   Phone: 661/612-0144

Location: On Mex 1-D (toll road), exit south end of town, just prior to the toll station, circle right, then just n; in Rosarito Beach Hotel & Spa. **Hours:** 5 pm-midnight. Closed: Mon in winter & Tues. **Features:** In the stately mansion of the founder of the Rosarito Beach Hotel & Spa, the elegant dining room is well-attended by formal servers. Food preparations reflect European and Mexican influences. Shining examples are New York and pepper steaks, salmon medallions, Puerto Nuevo lobster, chicken Mediterranean and guindas duck. Caesar and spinach salads are prepared tableside. Dressy casual; cocktails. **Parking:** on-site. **Cards:** MC, VI.

EL NIDO STEAKHOUSE
▼▼▼ ▼▼▼
Steak House

Lunch: $5-$23   Dinner: $7-$23   Phone: 661/612-1431

Location: Center. Blvd Benito Juarez 67 21850. **Hours:** 8 am-11:30 pm. Closed: 9/16; also Mexico Independence Day. **Features:** Rough brick walls, heavy wood doors and tables with wagon wheel lights contribute to the hacienda-style, ranch atmosphere. The aromas of mesquite-grilled steaks fill the air. Also offered are pork chops, fish and shrimp with garlic butter, tacos, chiles rellenos and hamburgers. Casual dress; cocktails. **Parking:** street.

LOS PELICANOS
▼▼▼ ▼▼
Steak House

Lunch: $7-$23   Dinner: $7-$23   Phone: 661/612-1757

Location: Just w of Blvd Benito Juarez; on the beach. Calle Ebano 113 21850. **Hours:** 8 am-midnight. Closed: 9/16. **Features:** Mesquite-broiled steaks and seafood are served in the dining room or on the patio, both of which overlook the ocean. Casual dress; cocktails. **Parking:** on-site. **Cards:** AX, MC, VI.

SAN FELIPE, BAJA CALIFORNIA pop. 14,000

――――――― **WHERE TO STAY** ―――――――

―――――――― *The following lodging was either not evaluated or did not* ――――――――
meet AAA rating requirements but is listed for your information only.

SAN FELIPE MARINA RESORT
[fyi]

Phone: 686/577-1455

Not evaluated. **Location:** 4.5 km s on road to airport. KM 4.5 Carr San Felipe Aero Puerto 21850 (PO Box 9019, CALEXICO, CA, 92232). Facilities, services, and decor characterize a basic property.

――――――― **WHERE TO DINE** ―――――――

EL NIDO STEAKHOUSE
▼▼▼ ▼▼▼
Steak House
Parking: on-site.

Dinner: $7-$20   Phone: 686/577-1660

Location: 1 km s of town center. Ave Mar de Cortez Sur #348 21850. **Hours:** 2 pm-10 pm. Closed: Wed. **Features:** Rough brick walls, heavy wood doors and tables with wagon wheel lights contribute to the hacienda-style, ranch atmosphere. The aromas of mesquite-grilled steaks fill the air. Also offered are pork chops, fish and shrimp with garlic butter, tacos, chiles rellenos and hamburgers. Casual dress; cocktails.

GEORGE'S RESTAURANT & BAR
▼▼
Mexican

Lunch: $5-$14   Dinner: $5-$14   Phone: 686/577-1057

Location: 1 km s of town center. Ave Mar de Cortez Sur #336 21850. **Hours:** 6:30 am-9:30 pm. **Features:** Families favor the modern, coffee shop-style restaurant, which offers seating in leather booths. Steaks, seafood, burritos, tacos and sandwiches are available all day. The American-style breakfast is popular with locals who meet to exchange stories. Casual dress; cocktails. **Parking:** on-site.

RICE & BEANS
▼▼
Mexican
Cards: MC, VI.

Lunch: $4-$15   Dinner: $4-$15   Phone: 686/577-1775

Location: On the malecon. Ave Malecon #262 21850. **Hours:** 7 am-10 pm. **Features:** The popular patio above the street is filled in the afternoon with patrons sipping cool beverages and watching the beach scene. Enchiladas, burritos, tacos and fajitas are offered a la carte or with dinner plates of rice, beans and salsa. Fresh seafood, chicken and steak complete the casual menu. Casual dress. **Parking:** street.

ROSITA RESTAURANT **Lunch:** $4-$15 **Dinner:** $4-$15 **Phone:** 686/577-1770

Mexican

Cards: MC, VI.

Location: At north end of the malecon. Ave Malecon #381 21850. **Hours:** 7 am-10 pm. **Features:** The modest, bayfront restaurant's patio lets guests refuel while watching fishermen return with their catches. The casual staff serves a dozen types of fresh fish either prepared grilled, breaded, Veracruz-style or with garlic and butter. Grilled butterfly shrimp, octopus cocktail and clams are popular. Casual dress. **Parking:** street.

SAN IGNACIO, BAJA CALIFORNIA SUR pop. 800

———— WHERE TO STAY ————

———— *The following lodging was either not evaluated or did not* ————
meet AAA rating requirements but is listed for your information only.

HOTEL LA PINTA **Phone:** 615/154-0300

[fyi]

Not evaluated. **Location:** 2.5 km w of jct Mex 1, towards town plaza. (Apdo Postal 37). Facilities, services, and decor characterize a basic property.

SAN JOSE DEL CABO, BAJA CALIFORNIA SUR pop. 33,000

(See map and index starting on p. 377)

———— WHERE TO STAY ————

BEST WESTERN POSADA REAL LOS CABOS *Book at aaa.com* **Phone:** (624)142-0155 **70**

12/1-3/22	1P: $145	2P: $145	XP: $15	F12
3/23-11/30	1P: $140	2P: $140	XP: $15	F12

Large-scale Hotel

Location: 0.8 km e, off Mex 1. Blvd San Jose 23400 (Apdo Postal 51). Fax: 624/142-0460. **Facility:** Meets AAA guest room security requirements. 148 units. 140 one-bedroom standard units. 8 one-bedroom suites ($225). 3 stories, interior corridors. **Parking:** on-site. **Terms:** 3 day cancellation notice-fee imposed. **Amenities:** safes, hair dryers. **Fee:** high-speed Internet. **Pool(s):** heated outdoor, wading. **Leisure Activities:** whirlpool, putting green, tennis court. **Guest Services:** gift shop, valet laundry. **Business Services:** meeting rooms, PC, fax. **Cards:** AX, DC, MC, VI.

SOME UNITS

CASA DEL MAR GOLF RESORT & SPA **Phone:** (624)145-7700 **41**

1/17-3/21	1P: $430-$480	2P: $430-$480	XP: $54	F12
12/1-1/16	1P: $395-$445	2P: $395-$445	XP: $54	F12
3/22-11/30	1P: $290-$445	2P: $290-$445	XP: $54	F12

Resort
Large-scale Hotel

Location: 11.5 km w on Mex 1. Located in Cabo Real. Carr Transpeninsular KM 19.5 23400. Fax: 624/144-0034. **Facility:** With its stone archways, massive wooden doors, courtyard, and verdant garden, the resort calls to mind a classic Mexican hacienda. 56 units. 31 one-bedroom standard units with whirlpools. 25 one-bedroom suites with whirlpools. 1-3 stories, interior corridors. **Parking:** on-site. **Terms:** 5 day cancellation notice-fee imposed, $10 service charge. **Amenities:** safes, honor bars, hair dryers. **Pool(s):** 4 outdoor, wading. **Leisure Activities:** whirlpools, steamrooms, exercise room, spa. **Fee:** saunas, golf-18 holes, 4 lighted tennis courts. **Guest Services:** gift shop, valet laundry. **Business Services:** meeting rooms, fax (fee). **Cards:** AX, MC, VI.

CASA NATALIA *Book at aaa.com* **Phone:** 624/142-5100 **61**

12/1-4/30 & 11/1-11/30 [CP]	2P: $250-$385	
5/1-10/31 [CP]	2P: $180-$305	

Small-scale Hotel

Location: Downtown; at town plaza. Blvd Mijares 4 23400. Fax: 624/142-5110. **Facility:** 16 one-bedroom standard units, some with whirlpools. 2-3 stories (no elevator), interior corridors. *Bath:* shower only. **Parking:** street. **Terms:** 2 night minimum stay - seasonal, age restrictions may apply, 15 day cancellation notice. **Amenities:** safes, hair dryers. **Dining:** Mi Cocina, see separate listing. **Pool(s):** small heated outdoor. **Leisure Activities:** Fee: massage. **Guest Services:** valet laundry, area transportation. **Business Services:** PC, fax. **Cards:** AX, MC, VI.

SOME UNITS

CROWNE PLAZA LOS CABOS BEACH RESORT-ALL
INCLUSIVE RESORT *Book at aaa.com* **Phone:** 624/142-9292 **68**

All Year	2P: $230-$320	

Resort
Large-scale Hotel

Location: 1 km e off Mex 1. Blvd San Jose 23400. Fax: 624/142-9290. **Facility:** Whether for business or families, this all-inclusive resort offers an abundance of activities with numerous restaurants, bars and swimming pools. 333 one-bedroom standard units, some with whirlpools. 5 stories, interior corridors. *Bath:* combo or shower only. **Parking:** on-site and valet. **Terms:** 3 day cancellation notice, $5 service charge. **Amenities:** high-speed Internet, voice mail, safes, honor bars, irons, hair dryers. *Some:* CD players. **Pool(s):** 4 heated outdoor, wading. **Leisure Activities:** whirlpool, 2 tennis courts, racquetball court, recreation programs, jogging, exercise room. *Fee:* bicycles, massage. **Guest Services:** gift shop, valet laundry. **Business Services:** conference facilities, business center. **Cards:** AX, MC, VI.

SOME UNITS

EL ENCANTO INN & SUITES *Book at aaa.com* **Phone:** 624/142-0388 **60**

12/1-12/31	2P: $65-$99	XP: $10	F10
1/1-6/30 & 10/1-11/30	2P: $65-$89	XP: $10	F10
7/1-9/30	2P: $55-$79	XP: $10	F10

Small-scale Hotel

Location: Just n of Zaragosa and the town square. Calle Morelos #133 23400. Fax: 624/142-4620. **Facility:** 25 units. 24 one-bedroom standard units, some with efficiencies. 1 two-bedroom suite ($95-$119). 2 stories (no elevator), exterior corridors. *Bath:* shower only. **Parking:** street. **Terms:** 14 day cancellation notice-fee imposed. **Pool(s):** outdoor. **Cards:** AX, MC, VI.

SOME UNITS

(See map and index starting on p. 377)

FIESTA INN AN ALL INCLUSIVE RESORT
Phone: (624)142-9300   **71**

◈

	1P: $212	2P: $235	XP: $32
12/19-4/11 [AP]	1P: $212	2P: $235	XP: $32
4/12-11/30 [AP]	1P: $176	2P: $199	XP: $23
12/1-12/18 [AP]	1P: $123	2P: $148	XP: $35

Large-scale Hotel   **Location:** 0.5 km e off Mex 1. Blvd San Jose 23400 (Apdo Postal 124). Fax: 624/142-0480. **Facility:** Meets AAA guest room security requirements. 153 one-bedroom standard units. 3 stories, exterior corridors. **Parking:** on-site. **Terms:** 3 day cancellation notice-fee imposed. **Pool(s):** outdoor. **Leisure Activities:** fishing, recreation programs, limited exercise equipment. *Fee:* scuba diving, snorkeling, charter fishing. **Guest Services:** gift shop, valet laundry. **Business Services:** meeting rooms, PC, fax. **Cards:** AX, DC, DS, JC, MC, VI. *(See color ad card insert)*

SOME UNITS

⊞ ▦ ⊞ ⊠ ▦ ⊞ /⊠/

HILTON LOS CABOS BEACH & GOLF RESORT
Book at aaa.com   Phone: (624)145-6500   **45**

AAA

	1P: $330-$380	2P: $330-$380	XP: $20	F18
12/25-4/26	1P: $330-$380	2P: $330-$380	XP: $20	F18
12/1-12/24 & 4/27-11/30	1P: $229-$334	2P: $229-$334	XP: $20	F18

◈◈ ◈◈   **Location:** 11 km w on Mex 1. Located at Cabo Real. Carr Transpeninsular KM 19.5 23447. Fax: 624/145-6501. **Facility:** This large resort on a hillside overlooks an infinity swimming pool and the sea and is adjacent to Resort two world-class golf courses. 375 units. 345 one-bedroom standard units. 28 one- and 2 two-bedroom Large-scale Hotel suites ($459-$2500) with whirlpools, some with kitchens. 5-6 stories, interior corridors. **Parking:** valet. **Terms:** 7 day cancellation notice, 10% service charge. **Amenities:** high-speed Internet (fee), dual phone lines, voice mail, safes, honor bars, irons, hair dryers. **Dining:** 7 am-10 pm, cocktails, also, Restaurant Fenicia, see separate listing. **Pool(s):** 2 heated outdoor, wading. **Leisure Activities:** whirlpools, steamrooms, 2 lighted tennis courts, spa. *Fee:* saunas, golf-18 holes, exercise room. **Guest Services:** gift shop, valet laundry. **Business Services:** conference facilities, business center. **Cards:** AX, MC, VI. *(See color ad p 382)*

SOME UNITS

⊞ 24 ⊞ Ⓢ Ⓓ ⊠ ▦ ⊞ ▦ ⊞ /⊠/

LAS VENTANAS AL PARAISO
Book at aaa.com   Phone: (624)144-0300   **43**

◈◈ ◈◈◈ ◈◈

		2P: $575-$4000
12/1-5/31 & 10/1-11/30		2P: $575-$4000
6/1-9/30		2P: $375-$1400

Resort   **Location:** 11.5 km w on Mex 1. Located at Cabo Real. KM 19.5 Carr Transpeninsular 23400. Fax: 624/144-0301. Small-scale Hotel   **Facility:** Accenting this elegant and serene oceanfront resort are native-specimen plants and waterways; all rooms have a fireplace, patio and whirlpool. 61 units. 56 one-bedroom standard units with whirlpools. 4 one- and 1 three-bedroom suites ($2300-$4000) with whirlpools. 2 stories (no elevator), exterior corridors. **Parking:** on-site and valet. **Terms:** 28 day cancellation notice-fee imposed, [AP] & [MAP] meal plans available, 15% service charge. **Amenities:** video library, DVD players, CD players, high-speed Internet, dual phone lines, voice mail, safes, honor bars, hair dryers. **Dining:** The Restaurant, see separate listing. **Pool(s):** 3 outdoor, heated outdoor. **Leisure Activities:** saunas, whirlpools, steamrooms, 2 lighted tennis courts, spa. *Fee:* golf-18 holes. **Guest Services:** gift shop, valet laundry. **Business Services:** meeting rooms, PC, fax. **Cards:** AX, CB, DC, DS, MC, VI.

⊞ 24 ⊞ ⊠ ▦ ⊠ ▦ VCR ▦ ▦

MARQUIS LOS CABOS BEACH, GOLF, SPA & CASITAS RESORT
Phone: 624/144-2000   **47**

◈◈ ◈◈ ◈◈

	1P: $405	2P: $405	XP: $25
All Year	1P: $405	2P: $405	XP: $25

Resort   **Location:** 11 km w on Mex 1. Located at Cabo Real. Carr Transpeninsular KM 21.5 23447. Fax: 624/144-2001. Large-scale Hotel   **Facility:** The resort is designed with an open-air arch and a 36-foot waterfall splashing through the lobby into the pool bar; rooms have contemporary decor. 240 units. 206 one-bedroom standard units with whirlpools. 34 one-bedroom suites ($560-$3500) with whirlpools. 2-5 stories, interior corridors. **Parking:** valet. **Terms:** check-in 4 pm, $25 service charge. **Amenities:** CD players, high-speed Internet, dual phone lines, voice mail, safes, honor bars, hair dryers. **Pool(s):** 3 heated outdoor, wading. **Leisure Activities:** whirlpools, steamrooms, exercise room, spa. *Fee:* saunas, golf-18 holes. **Guest Services:** gift shop, valet laundry. **Business Services:** meeting rooms, business center. **Cards:** AX, MC, VI.

SOME UNITS

⊞ 24 ⊞ Ⓢ Ⓓ ⊠ ▦ ▦ ▦ /⊠/

MELIA CABO REAL BEACH & GOLF RESORT, ALL INCLUSIVE
Phone: 624/144-2222   **44**

◈◈ ◈◈

	1P: $254-$335	2P: $338-$446	XP: $147	D12
12/1-4/19 [AP]	1P: $254-$335	2P: $338-$446	XP: $147	D12
4/20-11/30 [AP]	1P: $233-$365	2P: $311-$392	XP: $127	D12

Resort   **Location:** 11 km w on Mex 1. Located at Cabo Real. KM 19.5 Carr Transpeninsular 23400. Fax: 624/144-0101. Large-scale Hotel   **Facility:** Wrapping around palm-shaded grounds and a large free-form pool, these recently remodeled units have marble floors and light, airy decor. 302 one-bedroom standard units. 4 stories, exterior corridors. **Parking:** on-site. **Terms:** 15 day cancellation notice. **Amenities:** voice mail, safes, honor bars, irons, hair dryers. **Pool(s):** outdoor, wading. **Leisure Activities:** whirlpool, steamrooms, 2 tennis courts, exercise room. *Fee:* saunas, golf-18 holes, massage. **Guest Services:** gift shop, valet laundry, area transportation. **Business Services:** conference facilities, business center. **Cards:** AX, MC, VI.

▦ ⊞ 24 ⊞ Ⓓ ⊠ ⊠ ▦ ▦ ▦

MELIA LOS CABOS ALL SUITES OCEANFRONT, SPA & GOLF RESORT
Phone: (624)145-7600   **40**

◈◈ ◈◈

	1P: $281-$381	2P: $281-$381	XP: $55	F12
12/24-4/19	1P: $281-$381	2P: $281-$381	XP: $55	F12
4/20-11/30	1P: $240-$366	2P: $240-$366	XP: $55	F12
12/1-12/23	1P: $240-$336	2P: $240-$336	XP: $55	F12

Resort   **Location:** 12 km w on Mex 1. Located at Cabo Real. KM 18.5 Carr Transpeninsular 23400. Fax: 624/144-0216. Large-scale Hotel   **Facility:** Wide arches open this Spanish hacienda-style resort's airy lobby to a free-form pool, a sandy beach and the sea. 160 units. 111 one-bedroom standard units. 49 one-bedroom suites ($438-$606). 4-6 stories, exterior corridors. **Parking:** on-site. **Terms:** 15 day cancellation notice, [AP] & [MAP] meal plans available, $10 service charge. **Amenities:** safes, honor bars, irons, hair dryers. **Pool(s):** 2 heated outdoor, wading. **Leisure Activities:** whirlpool, steamrooms, waterslide, recreation programs, exercise room, spa. *Fee:* saunas, golf-18 holes, 2 lighted tennis courts. **Guest Services:** gift shop, valet laundry, area transportation. **Business Services:** meeting rooms, business center. **Cards:** AX, MC, VI.

SOME UNITS

Ⓢ ⊞ 24 ⊞ ⊠ ⊠ ▦ ▦ ▦ /▦/

(See map and index starting on p. 377)

ONE & ONLY PALMILLA
Phone: (624)146-7000   49

[fyi]	12/21-4/15 [CP]	1P: $430-$745	2P: $450-$745
	4/16-11/30 [CP]	1P: $345-$650	2P: $345-$650
Resort	12/1-12/20 [CP]	1P: $325-$625	2P: $325-$625

Large-scale Hotel Under major renovation, scheduled to be completed February 2004. **Last rated:** ♦♦♦ **Location:** 4 km w on Mex 1. KM 7.5 Carr Transpeninsular 23400 (Apdo Postal 52). Fax: 624/146-7001. **Facility:** Nine hundred acres of lush, palm-covered grounds surround this long-established Colonial Mexican-style property. 172 units. 152 one-bedroom standard units. 20 one-bedroom suites ($650-$3150). 1-3 stories, exterior corridors. **Parking:** valet. **Terms:** 3 night minimum stay - weekends, 28 day cancellation notice-fee imposed, 15% service charge. **Amenities:** video library, voice mail, safes, honor bars, irons, hair dryers. **Pool(s):** 2 heated outdoor. **Leisure Activities:** 2 lighted tennis courts, exercise room, spa. *Fee:* scuba diving, snorkeling, charter fishing, golf-27 holes. **Guest Services:** gift shop, valet laundry. **Business Services:** meeting rooms, business center. **Cards:** AX, MC, VI.

SOME UNITS

PRESIDENTE INTERCONTINENTAL LOS CABOS
RESORT   *Book at aaa.com*
Phone: (624)142-0211   66

♦♦♦

	1/1-4/10	1P: $250-$310	2P: $250-$310	XP: $40	F18
	4/11-11/30	1P: $245-$305	2P: $245-$305	XP: $40	F18
Resort	12/1-12/31	1P: $235-$295	2P: $235-$295	XP: $40	F18

Large-scale Hotel **Location:** 2.5 km e of Mex 1. Blvd Mijares S/N 23400 (Apdo Postal 2). Fax: 624/142-1733. **Facility:** Next to a fresh-water estuary and natural park, this property accents its scenic setting with pools, organized sports and numerous buffets. Meets AAA guest room security requirements. 395 units. 388 one-bedroom standard units. 7 one-bedroom suites. 3 stories, exterior corridors. *Bath:* shower only. **Parking:** on-site. **Terms:** cancellation fee imposed, $8 service charge. **Amenities:** voice mail, irons, hair dryers. *Some:* honor bars. **Pool(s):** 3 heated outdoor, wading. **Leisure Activities:** 3 lighted tennis courts, recreation programs, bicycles, exercise room, volleyball. *Fee:* massage. **Guest Services:** gift shop, valet laundry. **Business Services:** conference facilities, PC, fax. **Cards:** AX, MC, VI.

SOME UNITS

ROYAL SOLARIS LOS CABOS-DELUXE ALL
INCLUSIVE RESORT   *Book at aaa.com*
Phone: 624/145-6800   67

♦♦♦

	All Year [AP]		2P: $252-$270	XP: $99

Location: Mex 1, 0.6 km e. Blvd San Jose Lote 10 23400. Fax: 624/145-6811. **Facility:** Themed parties are among the many activities organized at this family-friendly resort located on the beach. 389 one-bedroom standard units. 6 stories, interior corridors. *Bath:* shower only. **Parking:** on-site. **Terms:** 3 day cancellation notice-fee imposed. **Amenities:** safes, hair dryers. **Pool(s):** 2 outdoor, wading. **Leisure Activities:** whirlpools, steamrooms, lighted tennis court, recreation programs, bicycles, basketball, game room. *Fee:* massage. **Guest Services:** gift shop, valet laundry. **Business Services:** meeting rooms, PC, fax. **Cards:** AX, MC, VI.

SUITES LAS PALMAS
Phone: (624)142-2341   64

♦♦♦

	All Year	1P: $78-$99	2P: $78-$99	XP: $15	F12

Small-scale Hotel **Location:** On Mex 1; at edge of town. Carr Transpeninsular KM 31 23500. Fax: 624/142-4442. **Facility:** 62 units. 19 one-bedroom standard units. 38 one- and 5 two-bedroom suites ($110-$160) with kitchens. 3 stories, exterior corridors. *Bath:* shower only. **Parking:** on-site. **Terms:** 15 day cancellation notice. **Amenities:** *Some:* hair dryers. **Pool(s):** outdoor. **Guest Services:** gift shop, coin laundry. **Cards:** AX, MC, VI.

SOME UNITS

TROPICANA INN
Phone: 624/142-2311   63

♦♦

	12/1-4/30 [CP]		2P: $80	XP: $10	F12
	5/1-11/30 [CP]		2P: $65	XP: $10	F12

Small-scale Hotel **Location:** In town. Blvd Mijares #30 23400. Fax: 624/142-1590. **Facility:** Meets AAA guest room security requirements. 41 one-bedroom standard units. 2-3 stories (no elevator), exterior corridors. *Bath:* shower only. **Parking:** on-site. **Terms:** 3 day cancellation notice, [BP] meal plan available. **Amenities:** hair dryers. **Dining:** Tropicana Bar & Grill, see separate listing. **Pool(s):** outdoor. **Cards:** AX, MC, VI.

THE WESTIN REGINA GOLF & BEACH RESORT,
LOS CABOS   *Book at aaa.com*
Phone: (624)142-9000   48

AAA

	12/19-12/31	1P: $419	2P: $419	XP: $50	F17
	1/1-10/3	1P: $339	2P: $339	XP: $50	F17
♦♦♦♦	12/1-12/18	1P: $299	2P: $299	XP: $50	F17
Resort	10/4-11/30	1P: $269	2P: $269	XP: $50	F17

Large-scale Hotel **Location:** 10 km w on Mex 1. Carr Transpeninsula KM 22.5 23400 (Apdo Postal 145). Fax: 624/142-9011. **Facility:** Extraordinary architecture creating a window to the sea is the signature of this resort, providing private ocean views from every room. Meets AAA guest room security requirements. 243 units. 229 one-bedroom standard units. 14 one-bedroom suites ($575-$775), some with whirlpools. 3-9 stories, exterior corridors. **Parking:** on-site. **Terms:** 7 day cancellation notice-fee imposed, $4 service charge. **Amenities:** dual phone lines, voice mail, safes, honor bars, irons, hair dryers. *Some:* DVD players, CD players, fax. **Dining:** 2 restaurants, 7 am-11 pm, cocktails, also, Arrecifes, see separate listing. **Pool(s):** 3 outdoor, wading. **Leisure Activities:** whirlpool, steamrooms, 2 lighted tennis courts, recreation programs, spa. *Fee:* saunas, golf-18 holes, exercise room. **Guest Services:** gift shop, valet laundry. **Business Services:** conference facilities, business center. **Cards:** AX, DC, MC, VI. *(See color ad p 8)*

SOME UNITS

The following lodging was either not evaluated or did not meet AAA rating requirements but is listed for your information only.

HUERTA VERDE
Phone: 624/148-0511

[fyi]   Not evaluated. **Location:** 1.7 km e of Mex 1 at Santa Rosa. Located in a secluded area. Las Animas Altos 23400 (7674 Reed St, ARVADA, CO, 80003). Facilities, services, and decor characterize a mid-range property.

(See map and index starting on p. 377)

──────── WHERE TO DINE ────────

ARRECIFES   **Dinner:** $25-$45   **Phone:** 624/142-9000   38

▽▽▽▽
Continental
Location: 10 km w on Mex 1; in The Westin Regina Golf & Beach Resort, Los Cabos. Carr Transpeninsular KM 22.5 23400. **Hours:** 6 pm-11 pm. Closed: Wed. **Reservations:** suggested. **Features:** Diners should visit just prior to sunset to enjoy the dramatic views from this cliffside location. Upscale table settings and attentive servers complement a sophisticated menu of Continental- and Mexican-influenced dishes. Grilled scallops, salmon with cream cheese and red snapper on a bed of bell peppers are among seafood specialties. Semi-formal attire. **Parking:** onsite and valet. **Cards:** AX, MC, VI.

BAAN THAI   **Dinner:** $8-$18   **Phone:** 624/142-3344   43

▽▽▽▽
Asian
Location: Just n of Zaragosa and town square. Morelos at Alvaro Obregon 23400. **Hours:** 3 pm-10 pm. Closed: Sun. **Reservations:** accepted. **Features:** Asian teak and bamboo furnishings add to the relaxing effect of the dining room and patio. Seafood curry, Pad Thai, lamb shank with herbs, green mango salad and lettuce-wrapped chicken soon are among the Thai- and Asian-influenced dishes with crisp flavors. Casual dress; cocktails. **Parking:** street. **Cards:** MC, VI.

DAMIANA   **Lunch:** $6-$14   **Dinner:** $12-$28   **Phone:** 624/142-0499   45

▽▽▽▽
Mexican
Location: Downtown; at town plaza. Blvd Mijares 8 23400. **Hours:** 11:30 am-10:30 pm. Closed: 12/25; also Tues 8/1-9/30. **Reservations:** accepted. **Features:** Traditional Mexican seafood and regional dishes are served on the garden patio and in the quaint, colorful dining room. Chayote salad is a menu specialty. Omelets are served with shrimp, fish, lobster or chicken. Brunch is offered daily until 5 pm. Casual dress; cocktails. **Parking:** street. **Cards:** AX, MC, VI.

EL CHILAR   **Dinner:** $10-$20   **Phone:** 624/142-2544   51

▽▽▽
Mexican
Location: Just w of Blvd Mijares; downtown. Blvd Benito Juarez 1490, Col Centro 23400. **Hours:** 3 pm-10 pm. Closed: Sun. **Reservations:** suggested. **Features:** Chef Montano changes the menu monthly, using chili for flavor not heat. In the simple, comfortable, candlelit dining room, guests can sample imaginative dishes such as zucchini blossom quesadilla, green mole enchilada, marinated flank steak with cumin and chili and chicken breast over polenta. Casual dress. **Parking:** street.

MI COCINA   **Dinner:** $16-$28   **Phone:** 624/142-5100   46

▽▽▽▽
International
Location: Downtown; at town plaza; in Casa Natalia. Blvd Mijares 4, Centro 23400. **Hours:** 6:30 pm-10:30 pm. **Reservations:** suggested. **Features:** A casual, yet sophisticated ambience sets the stage for nouvelle Mexican-Euro cuisine. International wines accompany such dishes as grilled shrimp with risotto, pan-seared sea bass on buckwheat soba, grilled lamb with pasta and spinach saffron, and filet mignon on potato leek galette. Dressy casual; cocktails. **Parking:** street. **Cards:** AX, MC, VI.

MORGAN'S ENCORE   **Dinner:** $16-$24   **Phone:** 624/142-4737   44

▽▽▽ ▽
Italian
Location: Just n of Zaragosa and town square. Morelos at Obregon 23400. **Hours:** Open 12/1-7/31 & 10/16-11/30; 6 pm-10:30 pm. **Reservations:** suggested. **Features:** Indoor seating offers a glimpse into the open kitchen, but folks may prefer seats on the enchantingly lit patio or on the rooftop, which has a fireplace and soft lights. This offshoot from the well-established Morgan's restaurant presents an ever-changing Italian menu. Casual dress; cocktails. **Parking:** street. **Cards:** AX, MC, VI.

MORGAN'S RESTAURANT & CELLAR   **Dinner:** $19-$25   **Phone:** 624/142-3825   47

▽▽▽▽
International
Location: In town; 1 blk from town center; corner of M Hidalgo. Manuel Doblado #107 23400. **Hours:** Open 12/1-7/31 & 10/1-11/30; 6 pm-10:30 pm. **Reservations:** suggested. **Features:** Twinkling lights, a fountain, soft music and an open kitchen set the stage for an enchanting experience in the open-air courtyard. The highly trained staff serves dishes with a Mexican touch, including tuna mignon with risotto, grilled prawns, beef tenderloin and rack of lamb with herbs. Among specialties are fish in Veracruz sauce and rice with raisins and curry. Dressy casual. **Parking:** street. **Cards:** MC, VI.

THE RESTAURANT   **Lunch:** $15-$30   **Dinner:** $25-$45   **Phone:** 624/144-0300   36

▽▽▽ ▽▽▽▽
Mexican
Location: 11.5 km w on Mex 1; in Las Ventanas Al Paraiso. KM 19.5 Carr Transpeninsular 23400. **Hours:** 7 am-10 pm. **Reservations:** required. **Features:** Patrons can enjoy elegant dining under the palapa roof or on the open-air patio, which affords views of the sea. A private wine room and beach dining in the sand are also available. Attentive service complements the menu, which lists high-quality dishes prepared with fresh ingredients and a Mexican flair. Steamed parrot fish, roasted cabrilla, Parmesan gnocchi and tender braised short ribs are a few of the items on the ever-changing menu. Semi-formal attire; cocktails. **Parking:** valet. **Cards:** AX, CB, DC, DS, MC, VI.

RESTAURANT FENICIA   **Dinner:** $18-$30   **Phone:** 624/145-6500   37

▽▽▽▽
Mediterranean
Location: 11 km w on Mex 1; in Hilton Los Cabos Beach & Golf Resort. Carr Transpeninsular KM 19.5 23447. **Hours:** 6 pm-11 pm. Closed: Mon. **Reservations:** suggested. **Features:** The pleasant hotel setting overlooks the pool and sea. Although the Mediterranean menu specializes in seafood, it also lists well-presented preparations of steaks and lamb. Dressy casual; cocktails. **Parking:** valet. **Cards:** AX, MC, VI.

TEQUILA RESTAURANTE   **Dinner:** $14-$28   **Phone:** 624/142-1155   48

▽▽▽ ▽▽
Mediterranean
Location: In town; just w of Blvd Mijares. Manuel Doblado #1011 23400. **Hours:** 6 pm-10:30 pm. **Reservations:** accepted. **Features:** Mexican and Asian flavors punctuate Mediterranean-influenced cuisine on a limited menu. The pleasant garden setting occasionally bustles with groups. Dressy casual; cocktails. **Parking:** street. **Cards:** AX.

(See map and index starting on p. 377)

TROPICANA BAR & GRILL
♦♦♦♦ ♦♦♦♦
Seafood

Lunch: $5-$28   **Dinner:** $10-$28   **Phone:** 624/142-1580   (50)
Location: In town; in Tropicana Inn. Blvd Mijares #30. **Hours:** 8 am-11 pm. **Reservations:** accepted. **Features:** Fresh seafood and friendly service abound in the large palapa dining room, the comfortable palapa bar and the sidewalk seating area. Specialties are lobster, mahi mahi, ahi tuna and whole red snapper. Breakfasts are popular. Casual dress; cocktails. **Parking:** street. **Cards:** AX, MC, VI.

SAN QUINTIN, BAJA CALIFORNIA pop. 2,000

───── WHERE TO STAY ─────

───── *The following lodging was either not evaluated or did not meet AAA rating requirements but is listed for your information only.* ─────

HOTEL LA PINTA
[fyi]

Phone: 616/165-9008
Not evaluated. **Location:** 16 km s on Mex 1, 4.5 km w to outer San Quintin Bay. (Apdo Postal 168). Facilities, services, and decor characterize a basic property.

TECATE, BAJA CALIFORNIA pop. 55,200

───── WHERE TO DINE ─────

LA MISION
♦♦♦♦ ♦♦♦♦
Mexican

Lunch: $5-$18   **Dinner:** $8-$18   **Phone:** 665/654-2105
Location: 1 km w of town center. Ave Juarez #1110. **Hours:** 7 am-10 pm, Sat-11 pm. **Reservations:** required. **Features:** Known locally for friendly service and good food. A variety of sandwiches, soups and salads are offered with seafood, steaks and chicken entrees prepard with a choice of traditional Mexican sauces. A Sunday bruch buffet is available each week. Casual dress; cocktails. **Parking:** on-site. **Cards:** MC, VI.

TIJUANA, BAJA CALIFORNIA pop. 1,228,700

───── WHERE TO STAY ─────

CAMINO REAL TIJUANA   *Book at aaa.com*
(AAA)
♦♦♦♦♦
Large-scale Hotel

All Year   2P: $175   XP: $40   F12
Phone: (664)633-4000
Location: 2.5 km se of the border. Paseo de los Heroes #10305, Zona Rio 22320 (4630 Border Village, Suite 38, SAN YSIDRO, CA, 92173). Fax: 664/633-4001. **Facility:** Meets AAA guest room security requirements. 263 units. 256 one-bedroom standard units. 7 one-bedroom suites ($390-$520), some with whirlpools. 7 stories, interior corridors. **Parking:** on-site and valet. **Amenities:** voice mail, safes, honor bars, irons, hair dryers. **Dining:** 7 am-11 pm, cocktails. **Leisure Activities:** exercise room. **Guest Services:** gift shop, valet laundry. **Business Services:** conference facilities, business center. **Cards:** AX, MC, VI.

SOME UNITS

EMPORIO HOTEL   *Book at aaa.com*
♦♦♦♦♦
Large-scale Hotel

All Year   2P: $180-$240   XP: $15   F12
Phone: (664)622-6600
Location: 3 km se of the border on Paseo de los Heroes, 0.5 km s on Ave Rodriguez, then 1 km e. Blvd Agua Caliente #11553 22420 (PO Box 43-1588, SAN YSIDRO, CA, 92173). Fax: 664/622-6602. **Facility:** 210 units. 207 one-bedroom standard units. 1 one- and 2 two-bedroom suites ($255-$455) with kitchens. 10 stories, interior corridors. **Parking:** on-site and valet. **Terms:** cancellation fee imposed. **Amenities:** voice mail, safes, honor bars, irons, hair dryers. **Pool(s):** heated outdoor. **Leisure Activities:** whirlpools, exercise room. *Fee:* massage. **Guest Services:** gift shop, valet laundry. **Business Services:** conference facilities, business center. **Cards:** AX, MC, VI.

SOME UNITS

FIESTA INN   *Book at aaa.com*
♦♦♦♦
Small-scale Hotel

All Year   2P: $100-$130   XP: $15   F12
Phone: 664/636-0000
Location: 3 km se of the border on Paseo de los Heroes to Ave Rodriguez, just n to Poniente, then 0.5 km e. Paseo de los Heroes #18818, Zona Rio 22320. Fax: 664/636-0003. **Facility:** 127 units. 123 one-bedroom standard units. 4 one-bedroom suites ($150-$175). 4 stories, interior corridors. *Bath:* combo or shower only. **Parking:** on-site. **Terms:** cancellation fee imposed. **Amenities:** voice mail, hair dryers. *Some:* high-speed Internet, irons. **Pool(s):** outdoor. **Leisure Activities:** whirlpool, limited exercise equipment, spa. **Guest Services:** valet laundry. **Business Services:** meeting rooms, business center. **Cards:** AX, MC, VI. *(See color ad card insert)*

SOME UNITS

GRAND HOTEL TIJUANA   *Book at aaa.com*
♦♦♦♦♦
Large-scale Hotel

All Year   2P: $100-$135   XP: $10   F13
Phone: (664)681-7000
Location: 3 km se of the border via Paseo de los Heroes, 0.5 km s on Ave Rodriguez, then just e. Located in a commercial area. Blvd Agua Caliente #4500 22420 (PO Box BC, CHULA VISTA, CA, 91912). Fax: 664/681-7016. **Facility:** Meets AAA guest room security requirements. 422 units. 402 one-bedroom standard units. 20 one-bedroom suites. 22 stories, interior corridors. **Parking:** on-site and valet. **Amenities:** irons, hair dryers. *Some:* high-speed Internet, safes, honor bars. **Pool(s):** heated outdoor. **Leisure Activities:** saunas, whirlpool, 2 lighted tennis courts. **Guest Services:** gift shop, valet laundry. **Business Services:** conference facilities, business center. **Cards:** AX, MC, VI.

SOME UNITS

HOTEL BUGAMBILIAS

Phone: 664/623-8411

All Year   2P: $88-$89   XP: $10

Small-scale Hotel

Location: From Otay Mesa border crossing, 3 km sw via Carr al Aeropuerto and Calle 16. Ave Tijuana 1600; CD Industrial 22500. Fax: 664/623-8416. **Facility:** 141 units. 136 one-bedroom standard units. 5 one-bedroom suites ($95-$105). 4 stories, interior corridors. **Parking:** on-site. **Amenities:** hair dryers. **Pool(s):** heated outdoor. **Leisure Activities:** sauna, whirlpool, limited exercise equipment. **Guest Services:** valet laundry. **Business Services:** meeting rooms, business center. **Cards:** MC, VI.

SOME UNITS

HOTEL COUNTRY CLUB

Phone: (664)681-7733

All Year   2P: $65   XP: $10   F12

Motel

Location: 3 km se of border on Paseo de los Heroes to Ave Rodriguez, 0.5 km s to Blvd Agua Caliente, 1.5 km e, then just s. Located between the Tijuana Country Club and Caliente Race Track. Calle Tapachula #1 22420 (1181 Broadway, Suite 2, CHULA VISTA, CA, 91911). Fax: 664/681-7692. **Facility:** 135 units. 124 one-bedroom standard units. 11 one-bedroom suites ($60-$90). 2-4 stories (no elevator), interior corridors. *Bath:* shower only. **Parking:** on-site. **Pool(s):** heated outdoor. **Leisure Activities:** whirlpool. **Guest Services:** gift shop, valet laundry. **Business Services:** meeting rooms, business center. **Cards:** AX, MC, VI.

SOME UNITS

HOTEL HACIENDA DEL RIO

Phone: (664)684-8644

All Year   2P: $87   F12

Motel

Location: 3 km se of the border on Paseo de los Heroes to Ave Rodriguez, just s, then just w. Blvd Rodolfo Sanchez Taboada #10606 22320 (1181 Broadway, Suite 2, CHULA VISTA, CA, 91911). Fax: 664/684-8620. **Facility:** 131 units. 126 one-bedroom standard units. 5 one-bedroom suites. 3 stories (no elevator), exterior corridors. *Bath:* combo or shower only. **Parking:** on-site. **Terms:** 3 day cancellation notice-fee imposed. **Amenities:** hair dryers. **Pool(s):** outdoor. **Leisure Activities:** exercise room. **Guest Services:** gift shop, valet laundry, beauty salon. **Business Services:** meeting rooms, business center. **Cards:** AX, MC, VI.

SOME UNITS

HOTEL LA MESA INN

Phone: (664)681-6522

All Year   2P: $65-$75   XP: $10   F12

Motel

Location: 3 km se of the border on Paseo de los Heroes, 0.5 km s on Ave Rodriguez, then 2.5 km e on Blvd Agua Caliente (Blvd Diaz Ordaz). Located in the La Mesa area. Blvd Diaz Ordaz Esq con Cardenias #50 22440 (1181 Broadway, Suite 2, CHULA VISTA, CA, 91911). Fax: 664/681-2871. **Facility:** 122 units. 120 one-bedroom standard units. 2 one-bedroom suites ($95). 1-3 stories, interior/exterior corridors. *Bath:* combo or shower only. **Parking:** on-site. **Amenities:** *Some:* hair dryers. **Pool(s):** heated outdoor. **Business Services:** meeting rooms, business center. **Cards:** AX, MC, VI.

SOME UNITS

HOTEL LUCERNA   *Book at aaa.com*

Phone: 664/633-3900

All Year   2P: $84-$156   XP: $17   F12

Large-scale Hotel

Location: 3 km se of the border. Paseo de los Heroes #10902, Zona Rio 22320 (PMB-110 PO Box 439056, SAN DIEGO, CA, 92143-9056). Fax: 664/634-2400. **Facility:** Meets AAA guest room security requirements. 167 units. 162 one-bedroom standard units. 5 one-bedroom suites ($275-$324), some with whirlpools. 2-6 stories, interior/exterior corridors. **Parking:** on-site and valet. **Terms:** cancellation fee imposed. **Amenities:** voice mail, irons, hair dryers. **Dining:** Rivoli's, see separate listing. **Pool(s):** heated outdoor. **Leisure Activities:** limited exercise equipment. **Guest Services:** valet laundry. **Business Services:** meeting rooms, business center. **Cards:** AX, DC, MC, VI.

SOME UNITS

HOTEL REAL DEL RIO   *Book at aaa.com*

Phone: 664/634-3100

All Year   2P: $86-$110   XP: $17   F12

Small-scale Hotel

Location: 2.5 km se of the border on Paseo de los Heroes to Diego Rivera, just n to Poniente, just e, then just s. Jose Ma Velasco 1409-A, Zona Rio 22320 (PMB 270-555 Saturn Blvd, Suite B, SAN DIEGO, CA, 92143). Fax: 664/634-3053. **Facility:** Meets AAA guest room security requirements. 105 units. 103 one-bedroom standard units. 2 one-bedroom suites ($208-$269) with whirlpools. 5 stories, interior/exterior corridors. **Parking:** on-site. **Terms:** 3 day cancellation notice-fee imposed. **Amenities:** high-speed Internet, voice mail, safes, hair dryers. **Dining:** 7 am-11 pm, cocktails. **Business Services:** meeting rooms. **Cards:** AX, MC, VI.

SOME UNITS

PALACIO AZTECA HOTEL

Phone: 664/681-8100

All Year   1P: $75-$82   2P: $89-$99   XP: $10   F12

Large-scale Hotel

Location: 2.2 km s of the border on Paseo de los Heroes, 0.6 km s on Ave Cuauhtemoc (Ave 16 de Septiembre) to Ibarro, just e, then just n. Blvd Cuauhtemoc Sur #213 Col Davila 22400. Fax: 664/681-8100. **Facility:** Meets AAA guest room security requirements. 200 one-bedroom standard units, some with whirlpools. 7 stories, interior corridors. **Parking:** on-site and valet. **Terms:** 3 day cancellation notice-fee imposed. **Amenities:** safes, irons, hair dryers. **Pool(s):** outdoor. **Leisure Activities:** limited exercise equipment. **Guest Services:** gift shop, valet laundry. **Business Services:** meeting rooms, business center. **Cards:** AX, DS, JC, MC, VI.

SOME UNITS

PUEBLO AMIGO HOTEL   *Book at aaa.com*

Phone: 664/624-2700

All Year   2P: $140-$150   XP: $25   F12

Large-scale Hotel

Location: 0.8 km s of border, 1st right after border, veer left under bridge to Paseo de Gruta Rivera, just e to Alfonso Reyes, then just s. Via Oriente 9211 22320. Fax: 664/683-5032. **Facility:** Meets AAA guest room security requirements. 106 units. 104 one-bedroom standard units. 2 one-bedroom suites with whirlpools. 7 stories, interior corridors. **Parking:** on-site. **Amenities:** hair dryers. *Some:* safes. **Leisure Activities:** limited exercise equipment. **Guest Services:** gift shop, valet laundry. **Business Services:** meeting rooms, business center. **Cards:** AX, MC, VI.

SOME UNITS

RESIDENCE INN BY MARRIOTT-REAL DEL MAR
All Year
Small-scale Hotel
2P: $119-$159
XP: $15
F12
Phone: (664)631-3670
Location: Mex 1-D (toll road), exit Real Del Mar, just e; 19.5 km s of the border. KM 19.5 Carr Cuota 22605 (4492 Camino de la Plaza, #1246, SAN YSIDRO, CA, 92173-3097). Fax: 664/631-3677. **Facility:** Meets AAA guest room security requirements. 76 units. 18 one-bedroom standard units with efficiencies, some with whirlpools. 58 one-bedroom suites with efficiencies. 2 stories (no elevator), exterior corridors. **Parking:** on-site and valet. **Terms:** 3 day cancellation notice. **Amenities:** high-speed Internet, voice mail, safes, irons, hair dryers. **Pool(s):** heated outdoor. **Leisure Activities:** saunas, whirlpool, steamrooms, 2 lighted tennis courts, exercise room, spa, basketball, volleyball. *Fee:* golf-18 holes. **Guest Services:** gift shop, complimentary evening beverages, valet and coin laundry. **Business Services:** meeting rooms, business center. **Cards:** AX, MC, VI.

SOME UNITS

——— WHERE TO DINE ———

CAFE LA ESPECIAL
Mexican
Lunch: $4-$12
Dinner: $4-$12
Phone: 664/685-6654
Location: 1 km across the border via Carrillo Puerto Calle #3A (downtown), just s; lower level below Hotel Lafayette. Ave Revolucion #718 22220. **Hours:** 9 am-10:30 pm. **Features:** Operating since 1952, the festive, friendly restaurant offers a convenient stop during shopping. The menu is full of familiar dishes, including tamales, enchiladas and chiles rellenos, but char-broiled steaks are the specialty. Casual dress; cocktails. **Parking:** no self-parking. **Cards:** AX, CB, DC, DS, JC, MC, VI.

CASA PLASENCIA
Spanish
Lunch: $8-$15
Dinner: $8-$15
Phone: 664/686-3604
Location: 3 km se of the border via Paseo de los Heroes to Blvd Agua Caliente, 0.5 km e, then just s. Calle Robirosa #250. **Hours:** noon-11 pm. Closed: Mon. **Reservations:** accepted. **Features:** Attentive servers attend to guests in the comfortable dining room. Traditional Spanish recipes are used to prepare numerous tapas and paellas, as well as such dishes as shredded beef with chiles and seasoned chicken breast. Casual dress; cocktails. **Parking:** on-site and valet. **Cards:** MC, VI.

CHAN'S CUISINE
Sichuan
Lunch: $11-$18
Dinner: $11-$18
Phone: 664/634-2766
Location: 3 km se of border on Paseo de los Heroes to Ave Rodriguez, just s, then just e. Blvd Sanchez Taboada 10880. **Hours:** noon-11:30 pm. **Features:** Offering a selection of tasty platters of Szechuan and Mandarin cuisine, the restaurant features ambiance that befits the artwork, and Asian porcelain vases displayed throughout the restaurant. The variety of authentic Oriental selections ranges from mild to spicy dishes. Each dish has its own individual flavor which will water your palate and can be served as combinations dinners or on their own. You will be sure to leave with leftovers in hand. Casual dress. **Parking:** on-site. **Cards:** AX, MC, VI.

EL POTRERO
Mexican
Lunch: $6-$15
Dinner: $6-$15
Phone: 664/686-3626
Location: 3 km se of the border on Paseo de los Heroes to Ave Rodriguez to Blvd Agua Caliente, 1 km e, then circle left. Blvd Salinas #4700, Col Aviacion 22320. **Hours:** 7 am-11 pm. **Features:** Shaped like a large hat, the popular restaurant has walls covered with cultural artifacts and pictures. Service is thoughtful and informal. Ribeye steak, New York cut and carne Asada are popular steak choices. Chicken can be marinated in polano, conejo or parrilla sauce. Samplings of seafood dishes include poached salmon and fish filet in Veracruz sauce. Casual dress; cocktails. **Parking:** on-site. **Cards:** MC, VI.

EL RODEO
Mexican
Lunch: $13-$22
Dinner: $13-$22
Phone: 664/686-5640
Location: 3 km se of the border on Paseo de los Heroes, 0.5 km s on Ave Rodriguez, just e on Blvd Agua Caliente, just n on Calle Escuadron, then just w. Blvd Salinas #1647 22190. **Hours:** 11 am-midnight. **Features:** The steak house, which has been serving guests since 1972, specializes in Sonora-style cooking and charcoal-broiled meats. Meals include marinated vegetables, beans, beef broth, a salad and dessert. Casual dress; cocktails. **Parking:** on-site. **Cards:** MC, VI.

LA ESPANADA
Mexican
Lunch: $6-$14
Dinner: $6-$14
Phone: 664/634-1488
Location: 3 km se of the border on Paseo de los Heroes to Ave Rodriguez, just s, then just e. Blvd Sanchez Taboada #10813, Zona Rio 22320. **Hours:** 7:30 am-11 pm, Sun-10 pm. **Features:** A friendly village-feeling envelops the hacienda-style mission building. Popular for families and business companions, the energetic restaurant provides fast service, but there sometimes can be a wait for seating. Among reliable menu offerings are chiles rellenos, chicken with mole sauce, pork ribs, grilled beef, enchiladas and fresh pastries. Breakfast is a favorite time. Casual dress; cocktails. **Parking:** on-site. **Cards:** MC, VI.

LOS ARCOS RESTAURANT
Seafood
Lunch: $8-$17
Dinner: $8-$17
Phone: 664/686-3171
Location: 3 km se of the border on Paseo de los Heroes, 0.5 km s on Ave Rodriguez, just e on Blvd Agua Caliente, then just n on Calle Escuadron. Blvd Salinas #1000 22320. **Hours:** 11 am-10 pm, Sat & Sun-midnight. **Features:** Festively decorated with fish netting, sculptures and bright colors, the restaurant has lively servers to match. Fresh fish from local waters is the specialty. Open-faced fish tacos with lime are a treat, as is the seafood fiesta for two, which includes stews of squid and octopus, shredded fish, smoked fish and shrimp, stuffed peppers and perch. Steaks also are available. Top dessert choices are bananas flambe and crepes Suzette. Dressy casual; cocktails. **Parking:** on-site and valet. **Cards:** MC, VI.

RESTAURANTE LA COSTA
Seafood
Lunch: $8-$10
Dinner: $10-$29
Phone: 664/685-8494
Location: 1 km across the border on Carrillo Puerto Calle #3A (downtown) to Ave Revolucion, just s, then just w. Calle 7A #150 22220. **Hours:** 10 am-10 pm, Fri & Sat-11 pm. **Features:** Near jai alai and shopping areas, the long-established restaurant is popular for business meetings and family gatherings. The nautical theme is matched by "old time" service from the staff. The menu lists many types of seafood: shrimp, fish kebabs, stone crabs, abalone, squid, salt cod and Alaskan king crab. Meals include soup, salad and rice. Casual dress; cocktails. **Parking:** on-site. **Cards:** MC, VI.

RINCON SAN ROMAN
AAA
International
Lunch: $5-$20   Dinner: $7-$20   Phone: 664/631-2241
Location: 19.5 km s of the border on Mex 1-D (toll road), exit Real Del Mar, just e. KM 19.5 Carr Cuota 22605. **Hours:** 1 pm-10 pm, Fri & Sat-11 pm. **Features:** In the hillside center at Real Del Mar, the intimate dining room overlooks red-tile roofs, the golf course and the ocean. White tablecloths and candelabra lights set a sophisticated mood, which attentive servers continue to foster. The ever-changing menu might include such choices as filet of beef with rosemary, salmon in a bed of scallions and chiles rellenos with cheese. Dressy casual; cocktails. **Parking:** on-site. **Cards:** MC, VI.

RIVOLI'S
International
Lunch: $8-$17   Dinner: $8-$17   Phone: 664/633-3900
Location: 3 km se of the border; in Hotel Lucerna. Paseo de los Heroes #10902 22320. **Hours:** 7 am-11 pm, Sun-8 pm. **Features:** Mural-painted walls decorate the pleasant, peaceful dining room, which has a wall of glass overlooking the courtyard. The well-trained staff serves from a menu offering duck in fig sauce with aromatic lavender, shrimp or lobster with coconut and mango chutney, beef filet Singapore with pureed sweet potato sauce and wasabi. Penne with Gorgonzola, ricotta and mozzarella cheeses and ginger linguine with chicken and shrimp are among pastas. Dressy casual; cocktails. **Parking:** on-site and valet. **Cards:** AX, MC, VI.

VILLA SAVERIOS
Italian
Lunch: $17-$24   Dinner: $17-$24   Phone: 664/686-6502
Location: 3 km se of border on Paseo de los Heroes, 0.5 km s on Ave Rodriguez, just e on Blvd Agua Caliente, then just n. Escuadron #201, Rio Zona 22320. **Hours:** noon-11 pm, Sun-10 pm. **Reservations:** accepted. **Features:** An attractive, modern, Italian-style building houses the large, aroma-filled dining room. Italian and Greek influences are evident in delicious pasta, chicken, beef and seafood dishes. The extensive wine collection surrounds a private dining room in the cellar. Dressy casual; cocktails. **Parking:** on-site. **Cards:** AX, MC, VI.

TODOS SANTOS, BAJA CALIFORNIA SUR pop. 2,400

——— WHERE TO STAY ———

POSADA LA POZA
Small-scale Hotel
Phone: 612/145-0400
12/1-4/30 & 11/16-11/30 [BP]   2P: $150-$225
5/1-11/15 [BP]   2P: $135-$185
Location: Mex 19, 1.9 km s via Olachea; southside of town; at La Poza. (Apdo Postal 10, 23305). Fax: 612/145-0453. **Facility:** Designated smoking area. 7 units. 5 one-bedroom standard units. 2 one-bedroom suites ($380-$500) with whirlpools. 2 stories, exterior corridors. *Bath:* combo or shower only. **Parking:** on-site. **Terms:** office hours 7 am-10 pm, 30 day cancellation notice. **Amenities:** CD players, safes, honor bars. **Dining:** El Gusto! Restaurant, see separate listing. **Pool(s):** saltwater. **Leisure Activities:** fishing. *Fee:* massage. **Cards:** MC, VI.
SOME UNITS

TODOS SANTOS INN
Historic
Small-scale Hotel
Phone: 612/145-0040
All Year   2P: $95-$135
Location: Mex 19, just w on Obregon, just s; in town. Calle Legaspi #33 23305. Fax: 612/145-0040. **Facility:** Within the town's historic district, this restored inn has tastefully furnished rooms with tranquil gardens; a gallery is on the premises. Designated smoking area. 6 units. 4 one-bedroom standard units. 2 one-bedroom suites. 1 story, exterior corridors. *Bath:* combo or shower only. **Parking:** street. **Terms:** 30 day cancellation notice. **Pool(s):** heated outdoor. **Cards:** MC, VI.
SOME UNITS

——— WHERE TO DINE ———

CAFE SANTA FE
Italian
Lunch: $12-$25   Dinner: $12-$25   Phone: 612/145-0340
Location: In town center. Calle Centenario #4 23305. **Hours:** Open 12/1-8/1 & 11/1-11/30; noon-9 pm. Closed: 1/1, 12/25; also Tues. **Reservations:** suggested. **Features:** Refined Italian dishes are served in an attractively decorated dining room and on the lush, tropical patio. Casual dress; cocktails. **Parking:** street. **Cards:** MC, VI.

EL GUSTO! RESTAURANT
International
Lunch: $12-$18   Dinner: $12-$18   Phone: 612/145-0400
Location: Mex 19, 1.9 km s via Olachea; southside of town; at La Poza; in Posada La Poza. **Hours:** 11:30 am-8 pm. Closed: Thurs. **Reservations:** accepted. **Features:** Mexican gourmet cuisine is prepared with an international flair. The full-size bar is spacious. The restaurant sits high enough to offer a breathtaking view of the sunset and is ideal for memorable weddings and private events. The wine list comprises a nice selection of local bottled and by-the-glass choices. Poultry, fish and meat entrees are pleasantly decorated with fresh vegetables and herbs. A European influence is seen in the presentations of homemade desserts. Dressy casual; cocktails. **Parking:** on-site. **Cards:** MC, VI.

LOS ADOBES DE TODOS SANTOS

Mexican
Lunch: $8-$22   Dinner: $10-$22   Phone: 612/145-0203
Location: Between Juarez and Militar; in town. Calle Hidalgo 23305. **Hours:** Open 12/1-8/1 & 10/1-11/30; 11:30 am-9 pm, Sun-5 pm. **Reservations:** accepted. **Features:** Regional dishes from throughout Mexico have been given a light new touch. Fresh local ingredients enhance such dishes as white fish with cilantro, amaretto and garlic or herbs, chicken mole poblano and pork loin stuffed with mushroom in plum sauce. The kitchen is in a restored historic house, and seating is on the patio. Also on the premises are an internet cafe with coffee and lighter fare, and a wine and tequila bar set in the garden. Casual dress; cocktails. **Parking:** on-site. **Cards:** MC, VI.

NORTHWESTERN MEXICO

ALAMOS, SONORA pop. 6,100

——— WHERE TO STAY ———

CASE DE LOS TESOROS

Phone: (647)428-0010

▼△▼△▼△▼

All Year   1P: $65-$95   2P: $65-$95   XP: $15   F12

Historic Country Inn

Location: Just se of Plaza de Armas. Calle A Obregon 10 85763 (PO Box 4395, SANTA FE, NM, 87502). Fax: 647/428-0400. **Facility:** Unique 18th-century converted convent. Period furniture; fireplaces. Indian dances every Saturday night in season. Strolling musicians in the evening. 15 one-bedroom standard units. 1 story, exterior corridors. *Bath:* combo or shower only. **Parking:** on-site. **Terms:** 14 day cancellation notice, pets ($5 extra charge). **Pool(s):** outdoor. **Cards:** AX, MC, VI.

SOME UNITS
🛏 🍴 🍸 🐾 📶 🅿 / ✕ /
FEE

CASA ENCANTADA DE LOS TESOROS

Phone: 647/428-0482

▼△▼△▼△

12/1-6/1 [BP]   2P: $60-$80   XP: $15

Historic Bed & Breakfast

Location: Next to Palacio Municipal. Ave Juarez 20 85763 (PO Box 4395, SANTA FE, NM, 87502). Fax: 647/428-0400. **Facility:** This is a converted 280-year-old hacienda, large rooms, high ceilings and attractive inner courtyard. Smoke free premises. 10 one-bedroom standard units. 1 story, exterior corridors. *Bath:* shower only. **Parking:** on-site. **Terms:** open 12/1-6/1, 14 day cancellation notice, pets ($5 extra charge). **Pool(s):** wading. **Cards:** AX, MC, VI.

🛏 ✕ 🅺 📶 🅿
FEE

HACIENDA DE LOS SANTOS

Phone: 647/428-0222

▼△▼△ ▼△▼△

All Year [BP]   1P: $200-$1200   2P: $200-$1200

Small-scale Hotel

Location: 2 blks s of main plaza. Calle Molina #8 85760 (3795 E Calle Cayo, TUCSON, AZ, 85718). Fax: 647/428-0367. **Facility:** Built in the late 17th century, this beautifully restored stately hacienda offers manicured, Mexican gardens; all units have fireplaces. Smoke free premises. 25 units. 21 one-bedroom standard units. 4 one-bedroom suites. 1-2 stories (no elevator), exterior corridors. **Parking:** on-site. **Amenities:** CD players, safes, honor bars, irons, hair dryers. **Dining:** restaurant, see separate listing. **Pool(s):** 2 outdoor, 2 small outdoor. **Leisure Activities:** whirlpool, exercise room, spa. **Guest Services:** gift shop, valet laundry. **Business Services:** meeting rooms, business center. **Cards:** AX, MC, VI.

SOME UNITS
✈ 🍴 🍸 Ⓓ 🐾 ✕ ✕ 📺 📠 / 📶 VCR /

LA MANSION

Phone: 647/428-0221

▼△ ▼△

All Year [BP]   1P: $60-$80   2P: $60-$80

Bed & Breakfast

Location: Just se of Plaza de Armas; center. Calle Obregon 2 85763. Fax: 647/428-0400. **Facility:** 12 one-bedroom standard units. 1 story, exterior corridors. *Bath:* shower only. **Parking:** on-site. **Terms:** pets ($5 extra charge).

🛏 🍴 🍸 ✕ 📶 🅿
FEE

——— *The following lodging was either not evaluated or did not* ———
meet AAA rating requirements but is listed for your information only.

LA PUERTA ROJA INN

Phone: 647/428-0142

[fyi]

Not evaluated. Location: 4 blks w of Plaza de Armas. Galeana #46 85760. Facilities, services, and decor characterize a basic property.

——— WHERE TO DINE ———

HACIENDA DE LOS SANTOS RESTAURANT   Lunch: $8-$15   Dinner: $18-$30   Phone: 647/428-0222

▼△▼△▼△

Continental

Location: 2 blks s of main plaza; in Hacienda de los Santos. Calle Molina #8 85760. **Hours:** 7 am-11 pm. **Reservations:** suggested. **Features:** Featuring fine dining in an elegant cantina-style dining room, the restaurant offers well-prepared Mexican and Continental fare and attentive service. Casual dress; cocktails. **Parking:** on-site and street. **Cards:** AX, MC, VI.

🍸 🅺 ✕

LA PUERTA ROJA RESTAURANT   Lunch: $5-$10   Dinner: $25   Phone: 647/428-0142

▼△ ▼△

Continental

Location: 4 blks w of Plaza de Armas; in La Puerta Roja Inn. Calle Galeana #46 85760. **Hours:** Open 12/1-4/30 & 9/2-11/30; 6:30 pm seating for prix fixe dinner, Thurs-Sat also 12:30 pm-2:30 pm. **Reservations:** required. **Features:** Enjoy tasty, creative food items while relaxing in the portal overlooking the fountain and gardens. Many food items are fresh from the garden. Recommended for lunch is the chicken salad served with artichoke souffle; or stay for a prix fixe dinner. A colorful collection of Mexican folk art is on display in this casual, 1870 home with eclectic decor. Casual dress. **Parking:** street.

🅺

BAHIA KINO, SONORA pop. 3,100

——— WHERE TO DINE ———

JORGE'S RESTAURANT   Lunch: $6-$14   Dinner: $6-$14   Phone: 662/242-0049

▽▽

Mexican

Location: 8 km nw on beach highway; near pavement ending New Kino. Mar de Cortez y Alicantes 83340. **Hours:** 9 am-10 pm. **Features:** The restaurant serves fresh seafood, as well as beef and chicken, with a nice view of the beach and sea, especially from the available outside seating; lobster is available in season. Casual dress; cocktails. **Parking:** street.

CEROCAHUI, CHIHUAHUA pop. 2,100

------ WHERE TO STAY ------

HOTEL MISION   Phone: 668/818-7046

◆◆ ◆◆   All Year [AP]   1P: $165   2P: $247

Small-scale Hotel   **Location:** 18 km from Bahuichivo Station. Located in a remote area; accessible only by train. Bahuichivo Station. Fax: 668/818-0046. **Facility:** 39 one-bedroom standard units. 1 story, interior/exterior corridors. *Bath:* shower only. **Parking:** on-site. **Terms:** 20 day cancellation notice-fee imposed. **Pool(s):** heated indoor. **Leisure Activities:** game room. *Fee:* horseback riding. **Guest Services:** gift shop, area transportation. **Business Services:** meeting rooms. **Cards:** AX, DC, MC, VI.

------ *The following lodging was either not evaluated or did not* ------
meet AAA rating requirements but is listed for your information only.

CEROCAHUI WILDERNESS LODGE   Phone: 635/456-0245

[fyi]   Not evaluated. **Location:** 22 km from Cerocahui. Bahuichivo Station 33200. Facilities, services, and decor characterize a basic property.

CHIHUAHUA, CHIHUAHUA pop. 678,000

------ WHERE TO STAY ------

BEST WESTERN MIRADOR MOTOR INN   Phone: (614)413-2200

◆◆◆◆   All Year   1P: $90   2P: $90   XP: $8   F12

Small-scale Hotel   **Location:** On Mex 45; 6 blks s of Pancho Villa Monument. Ave Universidad 1309 31240. Fax: 614/413-8906. **Facility:** 90 one-bedroom standard units. 2 stories, exterior corridors. *Bath:* shower only. **Parking:** on-site. **Terms:** 3 day cancellation notice. **Amenities:** voice mail, safes, irons, hair dryers. **Pool(s):** outdoor, wading. **Guest Services:** valet laundry. **Business Services:** meeting rooms, business center. **Cards:** AX, DC, DS, MC, VI.

SOME UNITS

FIESTA INN   *Book at aaa.com*   Phone: (614)429-0100

◆◆◆◆   7/1-11/30   1P: $129-$140   2P: $139-$150   XP: $10
         1/1-6/30   1P: $126-$137   2P: $135-$146   XP: $9
         12/1-12/31   1P: $112-$121   2P: $120-$129   XP: $8

Small-scale Hotel   **Location:** 2 km w on Blvd Ortiz Mena at Minnesota St. Located in a commercial area. 2801 Blvd Ortiz Mena 31250. Fax: 614/429-0110. **Facility:** Meets AAA guest room security requirements. 152 units. 145 one-bedroom standard units. 7 one-bedroom suites ($125-$154). 7 stories, interior corridors. **Parking:** on-site. **Terms:** 7 day cancellation notice. **Amenities:** voice mail, irons, hair dryers. **Pool(s):** heated outdoor. **Leisure Activities:** exercise room. **Business Services:** meeting rooms, business center. **Cards:** AX, DC, MC, VI. *(See color ad card inserts)*

SOME UNITS

HOLIDAY INN EXPRESS   *Book at aaa.com*   Phone: (614)442-2200

◆◆◆◆   All Year [ECP]   1P: $79-$108   2P: $79-$108   XP: $15   F18

Small-scale Hotel   **Location:** 8 km n on Mex 45. Located next to Denny's Restaurant. Ave Cristobal Colon 11390 31109. Fax: 614/442-2211. **Facility:** Meets AAA guest room security requirements. 96 one-bedroom standard units. 2 stories (no elevator), interior corridors. **Parking:** on-site. **Amenities:** high-speed Internet, dual phone lines, voice mail, safes, irons, hair dryers. **Pool(s):** heated outdoor. **Leisure Activities:** whirlpool, exercise room, game room. **Guest Services:** gift shop, valet and coin laundry. **Business Services:** conference facilities, business center. **Cards:** AX, DC, MC, VI.

SOME UNITS

HOLIDAY INN HOTEL & SUITES CHIHUAHUA   *Book at aaa.com*   Phone: (614)439-0000

◆◆◆◆   All Year [BP]   1P: $114-$142   2P: $114-$142   XP: $15   F18

Small-scale Hotel   **Location:** On Mex 45, 6 blks s of Pancho Villa Monument. Escudero 702 31000. Fax: 614/414-3313. **Facility:** Meets AAA guest room security requirements. 74 units. 60 one- and 14 two-bedroom standard units with kitchens. 2 stories (no elevator), exterior corridors. **Parking:** on-site. **Amenities:** high-speed Internet, dual phone lines, voice mail, safes, irons, hair dryers. **Pool(s):** heated outdoor, heated indoor. **Leisure Activities:** sauna, whirlpool, exercise room, sports court. **Guest Services:** valet and coin laundry. **Business Services:** meeting rooms, business center. **Cards:** AX, DC, DS, MC, VI.

SOME UNITS

HOTEL HAMPTON INN CHIHUAHUA   *Book at aaa.com*   Phone: 614/439-8000

◆◆◆◆   All Year [ECP]   1P: $76   2P: $89

Small-scale Hotel   **Location:** Jct Mex 16 to Ave Cuauhtemoc. Periferico de la Juventud #6100 31236. Fax: 614/439-8010. **Facility:** 95 one-bedroom standard units. 4 stories, interior corridors. **Parking:** on-site. **Amenities:** dual phone lines, voice mail, irons, hair dryers. **Pool(s):** heated outdoor. **Leisure Activities:** exercise room. **Guest Services:** complimentary and valet laundry, area transportation. **Business Services:** meeting rooms, business center. **Cards:** AX, MC, VI.

SOME UNITS

HOTEL PALACIO DEL SOL   *Book at aaa.com*   Phone: 614/416-6000

◆◆◆◆   All Year   1P: $115-$135   2P: $115-$135   XP: $10   F12

Small-scale Hotel   **Location:** Just n of Plaza de Armas; downtown. Ave Independencia 116 31000. Fax: 614/415-9947. **Facility:** 182 one-bedroom standard units, some with efficiencies. 17 stories, interior corridors. **Parking:** on-site. **Amenities:** irons. *Some:* hair dryers. **Dining:** Las Truffas Restaurante, see separate listing. **Leisure Activities:** exercise room. **Guest Services:** gift shop, valet and coin laundry. **Business Services:** meeting rooms, business center. **Cards:** AX, DC, MC, VI.

SOME UNITS

HOTEL SAN FRANCISCO PARK PLACE
◆◆◆◆ All Year   1P: $80   2P: $85   XP: $10   F12
Phone: (614)439-9000
Small-scale Hotel   **Location:** Just off main plaza; center of downtown. Calle Victoria 409 31000. Fax: 614/415-3538. **Facility:** Meets AAA guest room security requirements. 131 one-bedroom standard units. 4 stories, interior corridors. **Parking:** on-site. **Amenities:** dual phone lines, voice mail, irons, hair dryers. **Dining:** Restaurante Dega, see separate listing. **Leisure Activities:** exercise room. **Guest Services:** valet laundry. **Business Services:** meeting rooms, business center. **Cards:** AX, MC, VI.
SOME UNITS

HOTEL SICOMORO   *Book at aaa.com*
◆◆◆◆ All Year   1P: $79   2P: $79   XP: $10   F12
Phone: (614)413-5445
Small-scale Hotel   **Location:** 3.2 km nw on Ave Universidad to VW dealer, 0.3 km sw on Americas to Pemex Station, then 1.6 km s. Blvd Ortiz Mena 411 31230 (Apdo Postal 1121). Fax: 614/413-1411. **Facility:** 128 one-bedroom standard units. 2 stories (no elevator), interior corridors. *Bath:* shower only. **Parking:** on-site. **Amenities:** high-speed Internet, dual phone lines, voice mail. *Some:* irons, hair dryers. **Dining:** Restaurant El Trigal, see separate listing. **Pool(s):** outdoor. **Guest Services:** valet laundry. **Business Services:** meeting rooms, business center. **Cards:** AX, DC, MC, VI.
SOME UNITS

POSADA TIERRA BLANCA
◆◆◆◆ All Year   1P: $61   2P: $68
Phone: (614)415-0000
Small-scale Hotel   **Location:** Just n of Plaza de Armas. (Ave Independencia y Ninos Heroes). Fax: 614/416-0063. **Facility:** 102 one-bedroom standard units. 3 stories (no elevator), interior/exterior corridors. *Bath:* shower only. **Parking:** on-site. **Terms:** 3 day cancellation notice. **Pool(s):** outdoor. **Leisure Activities:** exercise room. **Cards:** AX, DS, MC, VI.
SOME UNITS

RADISSON HOTEL CASA GRANDE   *Book at aaa.com*
◆◆◆◆ All Year   1P: $85-$95   2P: $95-$105   XP: $10   F12
Phone: 614/439-4444
Small-scale Hotel   **Location:** 7 km n on Mex 45. Ave Tecnologico 4702 31160. Fax: 614/439-4461. **Facility:** Meets AAA guest room security requirements. 115 one-bedroom standard units. 2 stories (no elevator), interior corridors. **Parking:** on-site. **Terms:** cancellation fee imposed. **Amenities:** irons, hair dryers. **Pool(s):** outdoor. **Leisure Activities:** tennis court, exercise room, sports court, basketball, game room. **Guest Services:** gift shop, valet laundry. **Business Services:** meeting rooms, business center. **Cards:** AX, MC, VI.
SOME UNITS

THE WESTIN SOBERANO CHIHUAHUA   *Book at aaa.com*
◆◆◆◆ All Year   1P: $122-$164   2P: $122-$164   XP: $20   F12
Phone: (614)429-2929
Large-scale Hotel   **Location:** 8 km nw on Cuauhtemoc Bypass. Barranca del Cobre #3211 31125 (Fracc Barrancas 31125). Fax: 614/429-2900. **Facility:** Meets AAA guest room security requirements. 204 units. 194 one-bedroom standard units. 10 one-bedroom suites ($500-$1500), some with whirlpools. 5 stories, interior corridors. **Parking:** on-site. **Terms:** cancellation fee imposed. **Amenities:** high-speed Internet, dual phone lines, voice mail, safes, honor bars, irons, hair dryers. **Dining:** Los Candiles, see separate listing. **Pool(s):** heated outdoor. **Leisure Activities:** whirlpool, steamroom, 2 tennis courts, racquetball court. *Fee:* massage. **Guest Services:** gift shop, valet laundry. **Business Services:** meeting rooms, business center. **Cards:** AX, DC, MC, VI. *(See color ad p 8)*
SOME UNITS

―――――― *The following lodging was either not evaluated or did not* ――――――
meet AAA rating requirements but is listed for your information only.

HOTEL DIVISADERO BARRANCAS
[fyi]   Not evaluated. **Location:** Near Divisadero Train Station. Divisadero Station. Facilities, services, and decor characterize a mid-range property.
Phone: 614/415-1199

―――――― **WHERE TO DINE** ――――――

EL RETABLO   **Lunch:** $6-$24   **Dinner:** $6-$24   **Phone: 614/415-5545**
◆◆◆◆
Mexican
Cards: MC, VI.
Location: 3.2 km nw. Blvd Ortiz Mena 1810 59214. **Hours:** 8 am-11 pm, Fri & Sat-1 am. **Reservations:** suggested. **Features:** This is a favorite lunch stop for the local folks who enjoy traditional northern Mexican cuisine, such as green chile salsa with a real kick to it. Slow-cooked pork melts in the mouth. The restaurant is an archetypical example of the genre. Casual dress; cocktails. **Parking:** on-site.

GARUFA RESTAURANTE ARGENTINO   **Lunch:** $7-$24   **Dinner:** $7-$24   **Phone: 614/430-0417**
◆◆
Argentine
Location: On Periferico de la Juventud, jct Mex 16 to Ave Cuauhtemoc. Periferico de la Juventud #3108 31320. **Hours:** 1 pm-midnight, Sun-9 pm. **Reservations:** suggested. **Features:** You'll enjoy the excellent quality, well-prepared beef at this eating establishment serving Argentinian-style food. Casual dress; cocktails. **Parking:** on-site. **Cards:** AX, MC, VI.

LAS TRUFFAS RESTAURANTE   **Lunch:** $8-$12   **Dinner:** $8-$12   **Phone: 614/416-6000**
◆◆
Continental
Location: Just n of Plaza de Armas; downtown; in Hotel Palacio del Sol. Ave Independencia 116 31000. **Hours:** 7 am-midnight. **Reservations:** accepted. **Features:** Operating as the dining room of a downtown hotel, the restaurant prepares a number of Continental selections as well as traditional Mexican dishes. This place can be quite busy at lunchtime. Casual dress; cocktails. **Parking:** on-site. **Cards:** AX, MC, VI.

LOS CANDILES
Continental
Lunch: $9-$27   **Dinner:** $9-$27   **Phone:** 614/429-2929
Location: 8 km nw on Cuauhtemoc Bypass; in The Westin Soberano Chihuahua. Barranca del Cobre #3211 31125. **Hours:** 1 pm-midnight. Closed: Sun & Holy Week. **Reservations:** suggested. **Features:** In the Hotel Westin Soberano, the elegant, fine dining restaurant is appointed in upscale decor and affords commanding city views. Features on the eclectic menu include beef, seafood and fowl prepared in a blend of International and Mexican styles. Dressy casual; cocktails. **Parking:** on-site. **Cards:** AX, DC, MC, VI.

LOS VITRALES
Continental
Lunch: $7-$19   **Dinner:** $7-$19   **Phone:** 614/437-1200
Location: Jct aves Juarez and Cristobal Colon; 1.8 km e on Mex 45. Ave Juarez #3300 31000. **Hours:** noon-11 pm, Fri & Sat-midnight. **Reservations:** suggested. **Features:** Elegant, refined dining in a gracefully restored, colonial-style home with stained glass windows, or vitrales. Specializing in seafood, steaks, poultry and Mexican dishes, the restaurant also offers upstairs dining and outside dining on the second floor terrace in season. Casual dress; cocktails. **Parking:** on-site and valet. **Cards:** AX, MC, VI.

RESTAURANTE BAR LA CALESA
Continental
Lunch: $9-$24   **Dinner:** $9-$24   **Phone:** 614/416-0222
Location: 1.8 km e on Mex 45. Ave Juarez 3300 Col Centro 31000. **Hours:** noon-midnight. **Reservations:** accepted. **Features:** Uniformed staff circulate through the semi-formal dining room, which is appointed with crisp linens. On the menu is a fine selection of steaks, Mexican food and delectable desserts. Dressy casual; cocktails; entertainment. **Parking:** on-site (fee). **Cards:** AX, MC, VI.

RESTAURANTE DEGA
Continental
Lunch: $7-$18   **Dinner:** $7-$18   **Phone:** 614/439-9000
Location: Just off main plaza; center of downtown; in Hotel San Francisco Park Place. Calle Victoria 409 31000. **Hours:** 7 am-11 pm. **Reservations:** accepted. **Features:** Inside a popular downtown hotel, the dining room is usually busy with local business people and patrons from the hotel. The cuisine is a mix of Continental and Mexican dishes. Casual dress; cocktails. **Parking:** on-site. **Cards:** AX, MC, VI.

RESTAURANT EL TRIGAL
Continental
Lunch: $6-$9   **Dinner:** $7-$15   **Phone:** 614/413-5445
Location: 3.2 km nw on Ave Universidad to VW dealer, 0.3 km sw on Americas to Pemex Station, then 1.6 km s; in Hotel Sicomoro. Blvd Ortiz Mena 411 31230. **Hours:** 6 am-midnight. **Reservations:** accepted. **Features:** Popular with both locals and visitors, the colorful eatery builds a menu on Continental dishes and Mexican fare. Quick, competent servers add to the friendly feel of the busy, lively dining room. Casual dress; cocktails. **Parking:** on-site. **Cards:** AX, DC, MC, VI.

RINCON MEXICANO RESTAURANT-BAR
Mexican
Lunch: $12-$22   **Dinner:** $12-$22   **Phone:** 614/411-1510
Location: 2 km sw on Calle Victoria. Ave Cuauhtemoc 2224 31020. **Hours:** 7 am-midnight. **Reservations:** suggested. **Features:** Well-prepared steak and seafood specialties are at the heart of the menu at the traditional restaurant, which is set in a residential neighborhood. Casual dress; cocktails. **Parking:** on-site. **Cards:** AX, MC, VI.

YI HE YUAN
Chinese
Lunch: $7-$8   **Dinner:** $7-$11   **Phone:** 614/425-6965
Location: Just e of jct Periferico de la Juiventud. Ave Francisco Villa #5514 31250. **Hours:** 1 pm-10 pm. Closed: 12/25. **Features:** The all-you-can-eat Chinese buffet lines up all the favorite dishes, including sweet and sour pork, Chinese fried chicken, beef with vegetables and chicken with bamboo shoots, as well as such American-style desserts as apple pie. Casual dress; cocktails. **Parking:** on-site. **Cards:** MC, VI.

CIUDAD JUAREZ, CHIHUAHUA pop. 1,257,200

──── WHERE TO STAY ────

FIESTA INN CD JUAREZ   *Book at aaa.com*
Small-scale Hotel
Phone: (656)686-0700

7/1-11/30 [BP]	1P: $80-$95	2P: $90-$100	XP: $10	F11
1/15-6/30 [BP]	1P: $75-$85	2P: $85-$95	XP: $10	F11
12/1-1/14 [BP]	1P: $65-$75	2P: $75-$85	XP: $10	F11

Location: 3.7 km e on Mex 45. Paseo Triunfo de la Republica 3451 32315. Fax: 656/686-0701. **Facility:** Meets AAA guest room security requirements. 166 one-bedroom standard units. 9 stories, interior corridors. **Parking:** on-site. **Terms:** 5 day cancellation notice. **Amenities:** voice mail, irons, hair dryers. **Pool(s):** heated indoor. **Leisure Activities:** whirlpool, exercise room. **Guest Services:** gift shop, valet laundry. **Business Services:** conference facilities, business center. **Cards:** AX, DC, MC, VI. *(See color ad card insert)*

SOME UNITS

HILTON GARDEN INN   *Book at aaa.com*
Small-scale Hotel
Phone: (656)629-0994

7/1-11/30	1P: $100	2P: $100	XP: $15	F12
1/1-6/30	1P: $90	2P: $90	XP: $10	F12
12/1-12/31	1P: $80	2P: $80	XP: $10	F12

Location: 10 km e on Mex 45. Ave Tecnologico 3750 32612. Fax: 656/618-5827. **Facility:** Meets AAA guest room security requirements. 120 one-bedroom standard units. 5 stories, interior corridors. **Parking:** on-site. **Terms:** cancellation fee imposed. **Amenities:** voice mail, irons, hair dryers. **Pool(s):** heated indoor. **Leisure Activities:** whirlpool, exercise room. **Guest Services:** valet laundry, area transportation. **Business Services:** meeting rooms, business center. **Cards:** AX, DC, MC, VI.

SOME UNITS

HOLIDAY INN EXPRESS   *Book at aaa.com*
Small-scale Hotel
Phone: (656)629-6000

All Year [CP]	1P: $92-$97	2P: $92-$97	XP: $9	F12

Location: 4 km e on Mex 45. 3745 Paseo Triunfo de la Republica 32310. Fax: 656/629-6020. **Facility:** Meets AAA guest room security requirements. 147 one-bedroom standard units. 4 stories, interior corridors. **Parking:** on-site. **Terms:** 3 day cancellation notice. **Amenities:** voice mail, irons, hair dryers. **Pool(s):** heated indoor. **Leisure Activities:** exercise room. **Guest Services:** sundries, valet and coin laundry. **Business Services:** meeting rooms, business center. **Cards:** AX, MC, VI.

SOME UNITS

HOLIDAY INN LINCOLN CIUDAD JUAREZ
Phone: (656)613-1310
All Year 1P: $63-$66 2P: $63-$66 XP: $10 F18
Small-scale Hotel **Location:** 3.5 km s of Bridge of the Americas. Ave Lincoln & Coyoacan 32315. Fax: 656/611-2451. **Facility:** 170 units. 165 one- and 5 two-bedroom standard units. 2 stories (no elevator), exterior corridors. **Parking:** on-site. **Terms:** [BP] meal plan available, 15% service charge. **Amenities:** voice mail, irons, hair dryers. **Pool(s):** heated outdoor. **Leisure Activities:** exercise room. **Guest Services:** valet and coin laundry. **Business Services:** meeting rooms, business center. **Cards:** AX, DC, MC, VI.

SOME UNITS

HOTEL COLONIAL
Phone: (656)613-5161
All Year 1P: $60-$85 2P: $60-$85 XP: $6 F12
Small-scale Hotel **Location:** 3 km s of Bridge of the Americas. aves Lincoln & de las Americas 32310. Fax: 656/613-4081. **Facility:** Meets AAA guest room security requirements. 229 one-bedroom standard units. 2 stories (no elevator), exterior corridors. **Parking:** on-site. **Terms:** [ECP] meal plan available. **Pool(s):** 2 heated outdoor, wading. **Business Services:** conference facilities, business center. **Cards:** MC, VI.

SOME UNITS

HOTEL LUCERNA
Phone: (656)629-9900
All Year 1P: $130-$150 2P: $130-$150 XP: $12 F12
Small-scale Hotel **Location:** 3.9 km e on Mex 45. P T de la Rep 3976 32310. Fax: 656/613-3778. **Facility:** Meets AAA guest room security requirements. 138 one-bedroom standard units. 8 stories, interior corridors. **Parking:** on-site. **Terms:** cancellation fee imposed. **Amenities:** voice mail, hair dryers. **Pool(s):** outdoor. **Leisure Activities:** exercise room. **Guest Services:** gift shop, valet laundry. **Business Services:** meeting rooms, business center. **Cards:** AX, DC, MC, VI.

SOME UNITS

RADISSON HOTEL CASA GRANDE CD JUAREZ *Book at aaa.com*
Phone: 656/629-4000
All Year 1P: $118 2P: $170 XP: $15 F12
Small-scale Hotel **Location:** 10 km e on Chihuahua Hwy (Mex 45). Ave Tecnologico 3620 32617. Fax: 656/629-4033. **Facility:** Meets AAA guest room security requirements. 145 one-bedroom standard units. 4 stories, interior corridors. **Parking:** on-site. **Amenities:** dual phone lines, voice mail, irons, hair dryers. **Pool(s):** heated outdoor. **Leisure Activities:** exercise room. **Guest Services:** gift shop, valet laundry. **Business Services:** meeting rooms, business center. **Cards:** AX, DC, MC, VI.

SOME UNITS

——— WHERE TO DINE ———

SHANGRI-LA RESTAURANT
Lunch: $8-$20 Dinner: $8-$20 Phone: 656/613-0033
Chinese **Location:** 4.5 km sw of Bridge of the Americas. Ave de las Americas 133 32310. **Hours:** 11 am-11 pm. **Reservations:** suggested. **Features:** A popular dining spot for tourists, local business people and El Paso residents who live just across the border, the restaurant serves authentic Chinese dishes in a semi-formal setting. Dressy casual; cocktails. **Parking:** on-site. **Cards:** AX, MC, VI.

CIUDAD OBREGON, SONORA pop. 220,000

——— WHERE TO STAY ———

HOLIDAY INN CIUDAD OBREGON
Phone: 644/410-5090
All Year 2P: $92-$105 XP: $5 F12
Small-scale Hotel **Location:** Center. Located in a commercial area. Ave Miguel Aleman 200 Nte y Allende 85000. Fax: 644/413-5343. **Facility:** 89 one-bedroom standard units. 3 stories, exterior corridors. *Bath:* shower only. **Parking:** on-site. **Terms:** pets (must remain caged). **Amenities:** hair dryers. *Some:* irons. **Pool(s):** outdoor, wading. **Leisure Activities:** exercise room. **Business Services:** meeting rooms, business center. **Cards:** AX, DS, MC, VI.

SOME UNITS

HOTEL VALLE GRANDE OBREGON
Phone: 644/410-6500
All Year 2P: $73 XP: $10 F12
Small-scale Hotel **Location:** 1.2 km n on Mex 15. Ave Miguel Aleman y Tetabiate 85000. Fax: 644/413-4194. **Facility:** 135 units. 131 one-bedroom standard units. 4 one-bedroom suites. 2 stories (no elevator), exterior corridors. *Bath:* combo or shower only. **Parking:** on-site. **Amenities:** voice mail, safes, irons, hair dryers. *Some:* honor bars. **Pool(s):** outdoor, wading. **Leisure Activities:** exercise room. **Business Services:** meeting rooms, business center. **Cards:** AX, MC, VI.

SOME UNITS

CREEL, CHIHUAHUA pop. 3,100

——— WHERE TO STAY ———

BEST WESTERN THE LODGE AT CREEL *Book at aaa.com*
Phone: (635)456-0071
All Year [CP] 2P: $95-$110 XP: $12 F6
Country Inn **Location:** Center. Calle Lopez Mateos 61 33200. Fax: 635/456-0082. **Facility:** 30 units. 29 one-bedroom standard units, some with whirlpools. 1 one-bedroom suite ($120-$150) with kitchen. 1 story, exterior corridors. *Bath:* combo or shower only. **Parking:** on-site. **Terms:** 30 day cancellation notice-fee imposed, [AP], [BP] & [MAP] meal plans available. **Amenities:** video library (fee), voice mail, hair dryers. **Dining:** Sierra Madre Restaurant, see separate listing. **Leisure Activities:** sauna, whirlpool, playground, exercise room. *Fee:* bicycles, massage. **Guest Services:** gift shop, valet and coin laundry. **Business Services:** meeting rooms. **Cards:** AX, MC, VI.

SOME UNITS

MARGARITA'S PLAZA MEXICANA
Small-scale Hotel
All Year   1P: $50   2P: $62   XP: $3
Phone: (635)456-0245
Location: Center. Elefido Batista S/N 33200. Fax: 635/456-0245. **Facility:** 29 units. 27 one-bedroom standard units. 2 cabins. 2 stories, exterior corridors. *Bath:* combo or shower only. **Parking:** on-site. **Leisure Activities:** Fee: bicycles.
SOME UNITS

MOTEL PARADOR DE LA MONTANA
Small-scale Hotel
All Year   2P: $65-$85   XP: $3   F12
Phone: 635/456-0023
Location: Center. Calle Lopez Mateos 44 32300 (Apdo Postal 15, 32428). Fax: 635/456-0085. **Facility:** 50 one-bedroom standard units. 2 stories, exterior corridors. *Bath:* shower only. **Parking:** on-site. **Business Services:** meeting rooms. **Cards:** AX, MC, VI.

VILLA MEXICANA
Cabin
All Year   2P: $90-$120   XP: $15   F12
Phone: (635)456-0666
Location: 1 km se. Located adjacent to RV park. Calle Lopez Mateos S/N 33200. Fax: 635/426-0665. **Facility:** 22 cabins. 1 story, exterior corridors. *Bath:* shower only. **Parking:** on-site. **Terms:** 3 day cancellation notice. **Leisure Activities:** playground, basketball, volleyball. **Guest Services:** gift shop, coin laundry, area transportation. **Business Services:** meeting rooms, PC (fee). **Cards:** AX, MC, VI.
SOME UNITS

——— **WHERE TO DINE** ———

EL CABALLO BAYO STEAK HOUSE
Steak House
Lunch: $9-$10   **Dinner:** $9-$10   **Phone:** 635/456-0136
Location: Center. Calle Lopez Mateos #58 33200. **Hours:** 1 pm-11 pm. Closed: 1/1, 12/25. **Reservations:** accepted. **Features:** The American-style steak house caters to the tourists who visit Creel. In addition to steaks, the menu lists tasty salads, well-prepared chicken and favorite desserts. Casual dress; cocktails. **Parking:** street.

SIERRA MADRE RESTAURANT
Mexican
Lunch: $4-$8   **Dinner:** $6-$18   **Phone:** 635/456-0071
Location: Center; in Best Western The Lodge at Creel. Calle Lopez Mateos 61 33200. **Hours:** 7 am-10 pm. **Reservations:** accepted. **Features:** Tasty food, such as roasted pork served with grilled apples, is served in a lodge-style atmosphere that includes a fireplace. Casual dress; cocktails. **Parking:** on-site. **Cards:** AX, MC, VI.

CULIACAN, SINALOA pop. 367,000

——— **WHERE TO STAY** ———

FIESTA INN
Small-scale Hotel
All Year   2P: $110-$150
Phone: 667/759-5900
Location: 2 km n of historic centro; in Plaza Forum Center Mall. Blvd Jose Diego Valadez #1676 Ote 80000. Fax: 667/759-5999. **Facility:** Meets AAA guest room security requirements. 142 one-bedroom standard units. 4 stories, interior corridors. **Parking:** on-site. **Amenities:** high-speed Internet (fee), dual phone lines, voice mail, hair dryers. **Pool(s):** outdoor. **Leisure Activities:** exercise room. **Business Services:** meeting rooms, business center. **Cards:** AX, DC, MC, VI. *(See color ad card insert)*
SOME UNITS

HOTEL EXECUTIVO   *Book at aaa.com*
Large-scale Hotel
All Year   2P: $76-$114   XP: $12   F12
Phone: (667)713-9300
Location: Just n of jct Blvd Francisco I Madero and Ave Alvaro Obregon; center of town. Blvd Francisco Madero & Ave Obregon 80000. Fax: 667/713-9300. **Facility:** 230 one-bedroom standard units. 6 stories, interior corridors. **Parking:** on-site. **Amenities:** voice mail. **Pool(s):** small outdoor. **Leisure Activities:** exercise room. **Guest Services:** valet laundry. **Business Services:** meeting rooms, business center. **Cards:** AX, MC, VI.
SOME UNITS

HOTEL SAN LUIS LINDA VISTA   *Book at aaa.com*
Small-scale Hotel
All Year   1P: $100-$135   2P: $100-$135   XP: $15   F12
Phone: 667/716-7010
Location: 1.8 km s on Ave Alvaro Obregon. Ave Las Palmas 1 80220 (Apdo Postal 312). Fax: 667/715-0815. **Facility:** 90 units. 85 one- and 5 two-bedroom standard units. 2-5 stories, interior corridors. *Bath:* combo or shower only. **Parking:** on-site. **Dining:** El Mirador, see separate listing. **Pool(s):** small outdoor. **Guest Services:** valet laundry. **Business Services:** meeting rooms. **Cards:** AX, MC, VI.
SOME UNITS

——— *The following lodging was either not evaluated or did not* ———
meet AAA rating requirements but is listed for your information only.

HOTEL LUCERNA CULIACAN
[fyi]
Phone: 667/759-0000
Not evaluated. **Location:** 2 km n of historic town center; adjacent to Forum Mall Shopping Ctr. Blvd Carlos Salinas #99 80000. Facilities, services, and decor characterize a mid-range property.

------- **WHERE TO DINE** -------

EL MIRADOR
◆◆◆ ◆◆◆
Mexican
Lunch: $10-$18   **Dinner:** $10-$18   **Phone:** 667/716-7010
Location: 1.8 km s on Ave Alvaro Obregon; in Hotel San Luis Linda Vista. Ave Las Palmas #1 80220. **Hours:** 7 am-11 pm. **Reservations:** suggested. **Features:** Perched atop the hotel, the well-known restaurant provides not only traditional Mexican food but also a splendid view of the city below. The setting is casual. Casual dress; cocktails. **Parking:** on-site. **Cards:** AX, MC, VI.
⊠

DELICIAS, CHIHUAHUA pop. 87,400

------- **WHERE TO STAY** -------

HOTEL CASA GRANDE   *Book at aaa.com*
◆◆◆ ◆◆◆
Small-scale Hotel
Phone: (639)474-0404
All Year   1P: $70-$80   2P: $70-$80   XP: $10   F12
Location: 6 blks e of center, just w of Mex 45. Ave 6 Oriente 601 33000. Fax: 639/474-0404. **Facility:** 89 one-bedroom standard units. 3 stories, interior corridors. **Parking:** on-site. **Amenities:** voice mail. **Dining:** Los Nogales Restaurante, see separate listing. **Pool(s):** heated outdoor, wading. **Guest Services:** gift shop, valet laundry. **Business Services:** meeting rooms, business center. **Cards:** AX, MC, VI.
SOME UNITS
⦅⏐⦆ ⊇ 🎥 [DATA PORT] 🖥 / ⊠ 🛏 /

------- **WHERE TO DINE** -------

LOS NOGALES RESTAURANTE
◆◆ ◆◆
Mexican
Lunch: $8-$15   **Dinner:** $8-$15   **Phone:** 639/474-0404
Location: 6 blks e of center; just w of Mex 45; in Hotel Casa Grande. Ave 6 Oriente 601 33000. **Hours:** 7 am-11 pm. **Features:** Featured here are well-prepared Mexican specialties, as well as a good selection of meat, poultry and seafood selections. The well-appointed dining room is in the covered atrium of the Hotel Casa Grande. Casual dress; cocktails. **Parking:** on-site. **Cards:** AX, MC, VI.
⊻ ⊠

EL FUERTE, SINALOA pop. 10,300

------- **WHERE TO STAY** -------

HOTEL POSADA DEL HIDALGO
◆◆ ◆◆
Historic
Small-scale Hotel
Phone: 698/893-0242
All Year   1P: $117   2P: $130
Location: Mex 15, just s of KM 55, 55 km e on rural paved road; just ne of main plaza. Hidalgo 101 81200 (Apdo Postal 24). Fax: 698/892-0046. **Facility:** Some guest rooms and public areas constructed in 1890. Attractive gardens. Historic building located in center of town. 54 units. 51 one-bedroom standard units. 3 one-bedroom suites. 2 stories, exterior corridors. *Bath:* shower only. **Parking:** on-site. **Terms:** 10 day cancellation notice-fee imposed. **Pool(s):** small outdoor. **Leisure Activities:** whirlpool. **Business Services:** meeting rooms. **Cards:** AX, MC, VI.
⦅⏐⏐⦆ ⊻ ⊇ ⊠ 🎥 🅩

GOMEZ PALACIO, DURANGO pop. 164,100

------- **WHERE TO STAY** -------

HOTEL POSADA DEL RIO BEST WESTERN
◆◆ ◆◆
Small-scale Hotel
Phone: 871/714-3399
All Year   1P: $88   2P: $88   XP: $7   F12
Location: 4 km s on Mex 49 (becomes Fco Madero) to Ave Juarez; downtown. Fco Madero y Ave Juarez 35000. Fax: 871/714-7483. **Facility:** 100 one-bedroom standard units. 2 stories (no elevator), interior/exterior corridors. *Bath:* shower only. **Parking:** on-site. **Amenities:** *Some:* honor bars. **Dining:** El Parador, see separate listing. **Pool(s):** heated outdoor. **Leisure Activities:** exercise room. **Guest Services:** gift shop. **Business Services:** meeting rooms, business center. **Cards:** AX, MC, VI.
SOME UNITS
✈ ⦅⏐⏐⦆ ⊻ ⊇ 🎥 🖥 / ⊠ /

------- **WHERE TO DINE** -------

EL PARADOR
◆◆ ◆◆
Continental
Lunch: $6-$10   **Dinner:** $6-$10   **Phone:** 871/714-3399
Location: 4 km s on Mex 49 (becomes Fco Madero) to Ave Juarez; downtown; in Hotel Posada del Rio Best Western. Fco Madero y Ave Juarez 35000. **Hours:** 7 am-11 pm. **Features:** Well-prepared meat, poultry and seafood specialties are at the heart of a menu that also includes soup, sandwiches and some Mexican specialties. Casual dress; cocktails. **Parking:** on-site. **Cards:** AX, MC, VI.

GUAMUCHIL, SINALOA pop. 34,000

------- **WHERE TO STAY** -------

MOTEL YORK SA DE CV
ⒶⒶⒶ
◆◆
Small-scale Hotel
Phone: 673/732-5611
All Year   1P: $45   2P: $58
Location: 1.5 km n on Mex 15. (Apdo Postal 152). Fax: 673/732-0500. **Facility:** 80 units. 77 one-bedroom standard units. 1 one- and 2 two-bedroom suites ($98), some with whirlpools. 2 stories, exterior corridors. *Bath:* shower only. **Parking:** on-site. **Dining:** 7 am-11 pm, cocktails, entertainment. **Pool(s):** outdoor. **Leisure Activities:** playground. **Guest Services:** gift shop, valet laundry. **Business Services:** meeting rooms. **Cards:** AX, MC, VI.
SOME UNITS
🐾 ⦅⏐⏐⦆ ⊻ ⊇ 🎥 🛏 / ⊟ 🖥 /

HERMOSILLO, SONORA pop. 559,600

—— WHERE TO STAY ——

ARAIZA HOTEL Y CENTRO DE CONVENCIONES *Book at aaa.com*   Phone: (662)210-2717
▽▽/▽▽   All Year [BP]   1P: $78-$110   2P: $78-$110   XP: $7   F12
Small-scale Hotel   **Location:** 4 km ne on Mex 15. Located in a commercial area. Blvd Eusebio Kino 353 83010. Fax: 662/210-4541. **Facility:** 156 units. 150 one-bedroom standard units. 6 one-bedroom suites ($90). 4 stories, interior/exterior corridors. **Parking:** on-site. **Amenities:** irons, hair dryers. **Pool(s):** outdoor. **Leisure Activities:** tennis court, exercise room. **Guest Services:** valet and coin laundry. **Business Services:** meeting rooms, business center. **Cards:** AX, MC, VI.

SOME UNITS

BEST WESTERN PLAZA DEL SOL   Phone: (662)215-5958
▽▽/▽▽   All Year [CP]   1P: $43-$63   2P: $55-$95   XP: $5   F12
Small-scale Hotel   **Location:** 3.6 km ne on Mex 15. Located in a commercial area. Guillermo Carpena 203 83010. Fax: 662/215-5093. **Facility:** 59 one-bedroom standard units, some with whirlpools. 5 stories, interior corridors. **Parking:** on-site. **Terms:** 3 day cancellation notice. **Pool(s):** outdoor. **Guest Services:** valet laundry. **Business Services:** meeting rooms. **Cards:** AX, MC, VI.

SOME UNITS

FIESTA INN   *Book at aaa.com*   Phone: 662/289-2200
▽▽/▽▽   All Year   2P: $110   XP: $12
Small-scale Hotel   **Location:** 4.5 km n on Mex 15. Blvd Eusebio Kino 375 83010. Fax: 662/289-2200. **Facility:** 155 units. 72 one-bedroom standard units. 83 one-bedroom suites ($185). 4 stories, interior corridors. **Parking:** on-site. **Amenities:** voice mail, hair dryers. **Pool(s):** small heated indoor, wading. **Leisure Activities:** exercise room. **Guest Services:** sundries, valet laundry. **Business Services:** conference facilities, business center. **Cards:** AX, DC, MC, VI. *(See color ad card insert)*

SOME UNITS

HOLIDAY INN HERMOSILLO   *Book at aaa.com*   Phone: (662)289-1700
▽▽/▽▽   All Year   2P: $85-$98   XP: $12   F12
Small-scale Hotel   **Location:** 3.8 km ne on Mex 15. Blvd Eusebio Kino y Ramon Corral 83010. Fax: 662/214-6473. **Facility:** 132 units. 124 one-bedroom standard units. 8 one-bedroom suites. 3 stories, exterior corridors. *Bath:* combo or shower only. **Parking:** on-site. **Terms:** cancellation fee imposed. **Amenities:** voice mail, safes, irons, hair dryers. **Pool(s):** outdoor, wading. **Leisure Activities:** exercise room. **Guest Services:** gift shop. **Business Services:** meeting rooms, business center. **Cards:** AX, MC, VI.

SOME UNITS

HOTEL BUGAMBILIA   *Book at aaa.com*   Phone: 662/289-1600
▽   All Year [BP]   1P: $63   2P: $63
Small-scale Hotel   **Location:** 3.8 km ne on Mex 15. Located in a commercial area. Blvd Eusebio Kino 712 83010. Fax: 662/289-1600. **Facility:** 104 one-bedroom standard units. 1-3 stories (no elevator), exterior corridors. *Bath:* shower only. **Parking:** on-site. **Terms:** 3 day cancellation notice. **Pool(s):** heated outdoor. **Leisure Activities:** exercise room privileges. **Business Services:** meeting rooms. **Cards:** AX, MC, VI.

HOTEL FIESTA AMERICANA HERMOSILLO   *Book at aaa.com*   Phone: (662)259-6000
▽▽/▽▽   All Year   2P: $158   XP: $16
Large-scale Hotel   **Location:** 4.5 km n on Mex 15. Blvd Eusebio Kino 369 83010. Fax: 662/259-6060. **Facility:** 221 one-bedroom standard units. 9 stories, interior corridors. **Parking:** on-site. **Terms:** cancellation fee imposed. **Amenities:** voice mail, honor bars, hair dryers. *Some:* safes. **Dining:** El Rincon, see separate listing. **Pool(s):** outdoor, wading. **Leisure Activities:** lighted tennis court, exercise room. **Guest Services:** gift shop, valet laundry. **Business Services:** conference facilities, business center. **Cards:** AX, DC, MC, VI.

SOME UNITS

The following lodging was either not evaluated or did not meet AAA rating requirements but is listed for your information only.

HOTEL SAN MARTIN   Phone: 662/210-4105
[fyi]   Not evaluated. **Location:** Jct Blvd Eusebio Kino and Calle San Javier; in Zona Hotelera. Blvd Eusebio Kino #498 83010. Facilities, services, and decor characterize a mid-range property.

—— WHERE TO DINE ——

EL RINCON   Lunch: $12-$25   Dinner: $12-$25   Phone: 662/259-6000
▽▽/▽▽   **Location:** 4.5 km n on Mex 15; in Hotel Fiesta Americana Hermosillo. Blvd Eusebio Kino 369 83010. **Hours:** 8 am-11 pm. Closed: Sun & Mon. **Reservations:** suggested. **Features:** Patrons who visit this high-end dining room can expect an extensive selection of prime Sonoran steaks cooked to order over a wood fire. Casual dress; cocktails. **Parking:** on-site. **Cards:** AX, DC, MC, VI.
Steak House

MEDITERRANEOS   Lunch: $7-$15   Dinner: $7-$15   Phone: 662/214-9129
▽▽/▽▽   **Location:** Behind Best Western Senorial; in Zona Hotelera. Nayarit #208 83010. **Hours:** 7:30 am-midnight, Sun from noon. Closed major holidays. **Reservations:** accepted. **Features:** A variety of antipasti, pizzas and pastas, along with fish, chicken and beef dishes prepared Italiano. Also enjoy the relaxing outdoor patio with garden area. Casual dress; cocktails. **Parking:** on-site and street. **Cards:** MC, VI.
Italian

SANBORNS RESTAURANT
♦♦♦ ♦♦♦
Mexican

Lunch: $5-$12   **Dinner:** $5-$12   **Phone:** 662/214-7350
Location: 2 km sw on Blvd Eusebio Kino. Blvds Navarrete y Luis Encinas 83010. **Hours:** 7 am-1 am.
Features: Restaurants in the casual chain, which includes more than 100 locations throughout Mexico, offer a good selection of American-style sandwiches, salads, soups and both Mexican and US entrees. The selection of desserts is impressive. Casual dress; cocktails. **Parking:** on-site. **Cards:** AX, MC, VI.

SONORA STEAK
♦♦♦ ♦♦♦
Steak House
Cards: DC, MC, VI.

Lunch: $5-$22   **Dinner:** $5-$22   **Phone:** 662/210-0313
Location: On Mex 15; in Zona Hotelera. Blvd Eusebio Kino 914 83150. **Hours:** noon-midnight. Closed major holidays. **Features:** At Sonora Steak you'll find jumbo steaks cut from premium local beef, charcoaled to perfection "al carbon." The New York cut is particularly flavorful, and makes for a grand meal when accompanied by one of their tasty, decoratively prepared salads. Casual dress; cocktails. **Parking:** on-site.

LOS MOCHIS, SINALOA pop. 204,900

------ **WHERE TO STAY** ------

EL DORADO HOTEL Y MOTEL   **Book at aaa.com**
♦
Small-scale Hotel
Activities: playground. **Guest Services:** valet laundry. **Business Services:** meeting rooms. **Cards:** AX, MC, VI.

Phone: (668)815-1111
All Year   2P: $56-$87   XP: $10   F11
Location: 3.5 km w of Mex 15. Ave Gabriel Leyva y H Valdez 81200 (Apdo Postal 812). Fax: 668/812-0179. **Facility:** 93 one-bedroom standard units. 2-3 stories (no elevator), interior/exterior corridors. *Bath:* shower only. **Parking:** on-site. **Terms:** 8 day cancellation notice-fee imposed. **Pool(s):** outdoor. **Leisure**

HOTEL SANTA ANITA
♦♦♦ ♦♦♦
Small-scale Hotel
Dining: Restaurante Santa Anita, see separate listing. **Guest Services:** gift shop, valet laundry. **Business Services:** conference facilities, business center. **Cards:** AX, DC, MC, VI.

Phone: 668/818-7046
All Year   1P: $117   2P: $130
Location: Downtown. Ave Gabriel Leyva y Hidalgo 81200 (Apdo Postal 159). Fax: 668/812-0046. **Facility:** 116 units. 115 one-bedroom standard units. 1 one-bedroom suite. 5 stories, interior corridors. *Bath:* shower only. **Parking:** on-site. **Terms:** 10 day cancellation notice-fee imposed. **Amenities:** *Some:* hair dryers.

SOME UNITS

PLAZA INN HOTEL & CONVENTION CENTER   **Book at aaa.com**
♦♦♦ ♦♦♦
Small-scale Hotel
only. **Parking:** on-site. **Amenities:** dual phone lines, voice mail, hair dryers. *Some:* high-speed Internet, safes. **Dining:** Mr Owen's Restaurant & Bar, see separate listing. **Pool(s):** outdoor. **Leisure Activities:** exercise room. **Guest Services:** valet laundry. **Business Services:** conference facilities, business center. **Cards:** AX, MC, VI.

Phone: (668)816-0800
All Year   1P: $110   2P: $120   XP: $15   F12
Location: 0.5 km e. Aves Gabriel Leyva y L Cardenas S/N 81200 (Apdo Postal 159). Fax: 668/818-1590. **Facility:** Meets AAA guest room security requirements. 122 units. 112 one-bedroom standard units. 10 one-bedroom suites ($160), some with whirlpools. 5 stories, interior/exterior corridors. *Bath:* combo or shower

SOME UNITS

------ **WHERE TO DINE** ------

MR OWEN'S RESTAURANT & BAR
♦♦♦ ♦♦♦
Continental
cocktails. **Parking:** on-site. **Cards:** AX, MC, VI.

Lunch: $8-$18   **Dinner:** $8-$18   **Phone:** 668/816-0800
Location: 0.5 km e; in Plaza Inn Hotel & Convention Center. Aves Gabriel Leyva y L Cardenas S/N. **Hours:** 6 am-1 am. **Reservations:** suggested, 11/1-3/31. **Features:** Although this place is decorated much like an American coffee shop, the service and cuisine it offers are more refined. In addition to a fine breakfast selection, food choices include a wide variety of steaks. At dinner, service is semi-formal. Casual dress;

RESTAURANTE SANTA ANITA
♦♦♦ ♦♦♦
Continental

Lunch: $8-$18   **Dinner:** $10-$25   **Phone:** 668/818-7046
Location: Downtown; in .Hotel Santa Anita. Ave Gabriel Leyva & Hidalgo 81200. **Hours:** 7 am-11 pm. **Reservations:** accepted. **Features:** Mexican charm prevails at this hotel restaurant. The food represents a good selection of international cuisine, as well as some pleasing Mexican selections. Casual dress; cocktails; entertainment. **Parking:** on-site. **Cards:** AX, DC, MC, VI.

NAVOJOA, SONORA pop. 82,600

------ **WHERE TO STAY** ------

BEST WESTERN HOTEL DEL RIO
⬧⬧⬧
♦♦♦ ♦♦♦
Small-scale Hotel
Dining: 7 am-10:30 pm, cocktails, entertainment. **Pool(s):** outdoor, wading. **Leisure Activities:** sauna, tennis privileges. **Guest Services:** gift shop, valet laundry, airport transportation (fee)-Obregon Airport. **Business Services:** meeting rooms, business center. **Cards:** AX, CB, DC, MC, VI.

Phone: 642/425-5300
All Year   1P: $65   2P: $65   XP: $10   F12
Location: On Mex 15, at south end of bridge over Rio Mayo. Pesquiera Norte S/N 85800 (Apdo Postal 228). Fax: 642/425-5309. **Facility:** Meets AAA guest room security requirements. 77 units. 74 one- and 1 two-bedroom standard units. 2 one-bedroom suites ($97-$129). 2 stories (no elevator), exterior corridors. *Bath:* shower only. **Parking:** on-site. **Terms:** 7 day cancellation notice, small pets only. **Amenities:** hair dryers.

SOME UNITS

FEE

MOTEL EL MAYO

Phone: 642/422-6828

Small-scale Hotel

All Year [CP]   2P: $45-$80
Location: Just s of jct Mex 15 and SR 162/10 to Otero y Jimenez, just e. Otero y Jimenez 85870 (Apdo Postal 234). Fax: 642/422-6515. **Facility:** Meets AAA guest room security requirements. 48 units. 45 one-bedroom standard units, some with efficiencies and/or whirlpools. 3 one-bedroom suites ($65-$75) with efficiencies. 2 stories, exterior corridors. *Bath:* combo or shower only. **Parking:** on-site. **Terms:** 7 day cancellation notice, small pets only. **Amenities:** video library. **Pool(s):** heated outdoor. **Leisure Activities:** whirlpool, exercise room. **Guest Services:** valet laundry, area transportation. **Business Services:** meeting rooms. **Cards:** AX, MC, VI.

SOME UNITS

——— WHERE TO DINE ———

TIP'S RESTAURANTE

Lunch: $3-$6   **Dinner:** $7-$10   **Phone: 642/422-9028**

Mexican

Location: On Mex 15 through town; 2 blks s of Alamos turn off; center. Pesquiera y J O de Dominguez 85870. **Hours:** 7 am-10 pm. **Features:** Although it resembles a US coffee shop, the restaurant offers mostly Mexican cuisine. Patrons find all the traditional dishes, such as enchiladas, tacos and burritos. Try the carne adobada plate; it's exceptional. Casual dress; beer & wine only. **Parking:** on-site. **Cards:** DC, DS, MC, VI.

POSADA BARRANCA, CHIHUAHUA pop. 1,000

——— WHERE TO STAY ———

HOTEL POSADA BARRANCA CONVENTION CENTER

Phone: 668/818-7046

Small-scale Hotel

All Year [AP]   1P: $162   2P: $230   XP: $100
Location: Just n of Posada Barranca Train Station. Estacion Posada Barranca. Fax: 668/818-0046. **Facility:** 26 one-bedroom standard units. 1 story, exterior corridors. *Bath:* shower only. **Parking:** on-site. **Terms:** 15 day cancellation notice-fee imposed. **Leisure Activities:** hiking trails. *Fee:* bicycles, horseback riding. **Business Services:** conference facilities, business center. **Cards:** AX, MC, VI.

HOTEL POSADA BARRANCA MIRADOR

Phone: (668)818-7046

Small-scale Hotel

All Year [AP]   1P: $162   2P: $230   XP: $100
Location: Just s of Posada Barranca Train Station. Estacion Posada Barranca. Fax: 668/818-0046. **Facility:** 51 one-bedroom standard units. 3 stories, exterior corridors. *Bath:* shower only. **Parking:** on-site. **Terms:** 5 day cancellation notice. **Leisure Activities:** hiking trails. *Fee:* horseback riding. **Guest Services:** gift shop, area transportation. **Business Services:** meeting rooms. **Cards:** AX, MC, VI.

PUERTO PENASCO, SONORA pop. 31,600

——— WHERE TO STAY ———

HOTEL PLAYA BONITA

Phone: 638/383-2586

Small-scale Hotel

All Year   1P: $92-$130   2P: $92-$130   XP: $15
Location: Center. Located on Playa Bonita beach. Paseo Balboa #100 83550 (PO Box 276, LUKEVILLE, AZ, 85341). Fax: 638/383-5566. **Facility:** 128 units. 122 one-bedroom standard units. 6 two-bedroom suites. 4 stories, interior corridors. **Parking:** on-site. **Pool(s):** outdoor. **Cards:** MC, VI.

HOTEL PLAYA INN   *Book at aaa.com*

Phone: 638/383-5015

Small-scale Hotel

All Year [ECP]   1P: $65-$110   2P: $65-$110
Location: Jct Juarez Blvd, just e on Fremont Blvd, just s; center. Calle Sinaloa #18 83550. Fax: 638/383-5016. **Facility:** 80 one-bedroom standard units. 2 stories (no elevator), exterior corridors. *Bath:* shower only. **Parking:** on-site. **Terms:** small pets only ($10 fee). **Pool(s):** outdoor. **Cards:** AX, DC, MC, VI.

SOME UNITS

HOTEL PLAZA LAS GLORIAS   *Book at aaa.com*

Phone: 638/383-6010

Resort
Small-scale Hotel

All Year   1P: $116-$192   2P: $116-$192
Location: At the end of 13th St; center. Paseo Las Glorias #1 83550. Fax: 638/383-6015. **Facility:** Right on the oceanfront, the hotel offers modern, comfortable rooms, a spacious lobby and proximity to restaurants and shops. 210 units. 160 one-bedroom standard units. 50 one-bedroom suites with efficiencies (no utensils). 5 stories, interior corridors. **Parking:** on-site. **Terms:** check-in 4 pm. **Amenities:** safes. **Pool(s):** heated outdoor, wading. **Leisure Activities:** whirlpool. **Guest Services:** sundries, valet laundry. **Business Services:** conference facilities. **Cards:** MC, VI.

HOTEL SENORIAL

Phone: 638/383-2120

Small-scale Hotel

All Year   1P: $45-$95   2P: $45-$95
Location: Center. Calle Trece #81 83550. Fax: 638/383-3055. **Facility:** 79 one-bedroom standard units. 2 stories (no elevator), exterior corridors. *Bath:* shower only. **Parking:** on-site. **Pool(s):** outdoor, wading. **Cards:** AX, DC, DS, MC, VI.

MAYAN PALACE PUERTO PENASCO

Resort
Large-scale Hotel

All Year   1P: $139-$209   2P: $173-$259   XP: $59   F12

Phone: (638)383-0400

Location: Jct Sonora Hwy 8, 24 km e, then 5.7 km. KM 24 Carr Puerto Penasco Caborca 83550. Fax: 638/383-0450. **Facility:** In addition to well-appointed rooms and striking public areas, this new luxury resort features a really fine beach. Meets AAA guest room security requirements. 114 units. 48 one-bedroom standard units. 56 one- and 10 two-bedroom suites, some with efficiencies. 3 stories, interior corridors. **Parking:** on-site and valet. **Terms:** check-in 5 pm, 3 night minimum stay - seasonal and/or weekends, 30 day cancellation notice. **Amenities:** voice mail, safes. *Some:* irons, hair dryers. **Pool(s):** heated outdoor, heated indoor. **Leisure Activities:** saunas, steamrooms, waterskiing, 2 lighted tennis courts, exercise room, spa, volleyball, game room. *Fee:* boats, scuba diving, snorkeling, fishing, charter fishing. **Guest Services:** gift shop, valet and coin laundry. **Business Services:** meeting rooms. **Cards:** AX, MC, VI.

SOME UNITS

SONORAN SEA RESORT

Condominium

All Year   1P: $100-$405   2P: $100-$405

Phone: 638/382-8250

Location: Jct Mex 8 and Cholla Bay Rd, 3.7 km w, follow signs. Located on a sandy beach. Camino de la Cholla KM 3.7 83550. Fax: 638/382-8257. **Facility:** Amenities abound at these luxury condominium vacation accommodations set on a great stretch of beach; units have individualized decor. 39 units. 18 one-, 14 two- and 7 three-bedroom suites with kitchens, some with whirlpools. 10 stories, interior corridors. **Parking:** on-site. **Terms:** check-in 4 pm. **Amenities:** CD players. **Pool(s):** outdoor, heated outdoor, wading. **Leisure Activities:** whirlpool, exercise room. **Guest Services:** complimentary laundry. **Business Services:** PC. **Cards:** MC, VI.

SONORAN SPA RESORT

Condominium

All Year   1P: $90-$350   2P: $90-$350

Phone: 638/382-8060

Location: Jct Mex 8 and Cholla Bay Rd, 3.7 km w, follow signs. Located on a sandy beach. Camino de la Cholla KM 3.7 S/N 83550 (PO Box 87540, PHOENIX, AZ, 85080). Fax: 638/383-8063. **Facility:** A sister property to the adjacent Sonoran Sea Resort, these well-appointed beachside condominiums offer ample amenities including pools and a gym. 116 units. 45 one-, 67 two- and 4 three-bedroom suites with kitchens. 8 stories, interior corridors. *Bath:* shower only. **Parking:** on-site. **Terms:** office hours 9 am-5 pm, check-in 4 pm. **Pool(s):** outdoor, heated outdoor. **Leisure Activities:** whirlpool, exercise room, spa. **Guest Services:** sundries, complimentary laundry. **Business Services:** PC. **Cards:** MC, VI.

SOME UNITS

————— WHERE TO DINE —————

CASA DEL CAPITAN

International

Lunch: $6-$8   Dinner: $9-$15   Phone: 638/383-5558
Location: Center; on hill. Lote 1 y 2 Fracc del Cerro 83550. **Hours:** 10 am-10 pm. **Reservations:** accepted. **Features:** Marvelous ocean and bay views abound from the setting atop a hill overlooking the harbor. The abundant local seafood is the specialty here, and it's prepared in the Mexican style. Bacon-wrapped shrimp is memorable. Dressy casual; cocktails. **Parking:** on-site. **Cards:** MC, VI.

JR'S BBQ
American

Lunch: $5-$7   Dinner: $9-$15   Phone: 638/383-5824
Location: Jct calles Trece and Suarez; center. Calles Suarez y Trece 83550. **Hours:** 7 am-11 pm. **Reservations:** accepted. **Features:** The boisterous Texas-style barbecue house and saloon welcomes a friendly crowd of American snowbirds and RVers. There is an all-you-can-eat fish fry on Friday night, and the barbecue is great. Casual dress; cocktails. **Parking:** on-site.

THE LIGHTHOUSE RESTAURANT BAR
International

Dinner: $9-$16   Phone: 638/383-2389
Location: Center; on top of hill. Fracc del Cerro Lotes 2 y 2Bis 83550. **Hours:** 4 pm-10 pm; to 9 pm in summer. Closed: 12/25; also Mon 7/4-9/5. **Reservations:** accepted. **Features:** Patrons can dine by rock 'n' roll or jazz music at the lively eatery and lounge, which overlooks the town and the harbor. Local seafood and beef are prepared in a variety of international styles. Casual dress; cocktails. **Parking:** on-site. **Cards:** MC, VI.

MAX'S CAFE
American

Lunch: $3-$5   Phone: 638/383-1011
Location: Center; across from Plaza Las Glorias. Calle Sinaloa #15 83550. **Hours:** 7:30 am-3 pm. Closed: 12/25. **Features:** A pleasant, informal atmosphere prevails at the cafe, which serves a great breakfast burrito and a fine selection of espressos, coffee and lattes. Lunch guests can choose from a good selection of sandwiches and a daily soup special. Wireless internet access allows patrons to log on while enjoying a meal. Casual dress. **Parking:** on-site.

OCEAN KING RESTAURANT & BAR
Seafood

Lunch: $6-$11   Dinner: $6-$11   Phone: 638/383-8420
Location: Center; on the malecon. Malecon Fco Kino #17 Planta Alta 83550. **Hours:** 7 am-10 pm. **Reservations:** accepted. **Features:** Seafood plucked from the nearby bay is king here. Guests can order succulent jumbo shrimp or fish dishes cooked with a European flair. Try Italian-style whitefish, covered with a dreamy sauce. Casual dress; cocktails. **Parking:** street.

————— *The following restaurants have not been evaluated by AAA* —————
but are listed for your information only.

PORTOFINO ITALIAN RESTAURANT & BAR   Phone: 638/383-6838
[fyi]   Not evaluated. **Location:** Center; on the malecon. Malecon Kino y Primero de Junio 83550. **Features:** This restaurant on the Malecon comes alive in the evening, serving succulent local seafood prepared Italian style.

SONORAN GRILL RESTAURANT & BAR   Phone: 638/382-8089
[fyi]   Not evaluated. **Location:** Jct Mex 8 and Cholla Bay Rd, 3.7 km w, follow signs; in Sonoran Spa Resort. Camino de la Cholla KM 3.7 S/N 83550. **Features:** The eatery's owners are expatriate Americans and the cuisine is a mixture of the best of Mexican and American food.

SAN CARLOS, SONORA pop. 4,000

————— WHERE TO STAY —————

————— *The following lodging was either not evaluated or did not* —————
meet AAA rating requirements but is listed for your information only.

BEST WESTERN HACIENDA TETA KAWI   Phone: 622/226-0220
[fyi]   Not evaluated. **Location:** 10.7 km nw on Mex 15, 9.3 km w on San Carlos turn-off. (Apdo Postal 71). Facilities, services, and decor characterize a basic property.

————— WHERE TO DINE —————

————— *The following restaurant has not been evaluated by AAA* —————
but is listed for your information only.

CHARLY'S ROCK   Phone: 622/226-1805
[fyi]   Not evaluated. **Location:** 10.7 km nw on Mex 15, 9.3 km w on San Carlos turn-off. Blvd M F Beltrones KM 9. **Features:** This quaint establishment provides a spectacular view of the sea. Enjoy grilled lobster in season, seafood salads, soups and fresh fish prepared in several ways.

NORTHEASTERN MEXICO

Monterrey

This index helps you "spot" where approved accommodations and restaurants are located on the corresponding detailed maps. Lodging rate ranges are for comparison only and show the property's high season; rates are per night, unless only weekly (W) rates are available. Restaurant rate range is for dinner, unless only lunch (L) is served. Turn to the listing page for more detailed rate information and consult display ads for special promotions.

Spotter/Map Page Number	OA	MONTERREY - Lodgings	Diamond Rating	Rate Range High Season	Listing Page
1 / p. 418		Hampton Inn Monterrey Galerias Obispado	♦♦♦	$95-$160	420
3 / p. 418		Safi Monterrey	♦♦♦	$85-$130	421
4 / p. 418		Days Inn Alameda-Monterrey - see color ad opposite inside front cover	♦♦	$70-$160	419
5 / p. 418	AAA	**DoubleTree Hotel Rio**	♦♦♦	$90-$150	419
6 / p. 418		Hotel Howard Johnson Macroplaza Monterrey	♦♦	$180-$250	420
7 / p. 418		Fiesta Americana Centro Monterrey - see color ad card inserts	♦♦♦	$110-$200	419
8 / p. 418		Fiesta Inn Centro - see color ad card inserts	♦♦♦	$57-$95	420
9 / p. 418	AAA	**Sheraton Ambassador Hotel & Towers Monterrey** - see color ad p 8	♦♦♦♦	$160-$250	421
10 / p. 418		Radisson Gran Ancira Plaza Hotel - see color ad p 477	♦♦♦	$120-$180	421
11 / p. 418		Crowne Plaza Monterrey	♦♦♦	$150-$230	419
13 / p. 418		Best Western Royal Courts	♦♦	$75-$90	419
15 / p. 418		Hampton Inn & Suites Monterrey Norte - see color ad p 420	♦♦♦	$105-$185	420
17 / p. 418	AAA	**Courtyard by Marriott Monterrey Aeropuerto**	♦♦♦	$100-$200	419
18 / p. 418		Hampton Inn Monterrey Aeropuerto - see color ad p 420	♦♦♦	$90-$140	420
19 / p. 418		Fairfield Inn by Marriott	♦♦	$49-$72	419
21 / p. 418		Holiday Inn Express Galerias-San Jeronimo	♦♦♦	$140-$170	420
22 / p. 418		Hotel Quinta Real Monterrey	♦♦♦♦	$130-$200	421
23 / p. 418		Presidente InterContinental Monterrey	♦♦♦♦	$269-$309	421
		MONTERREY - Restaurants			
2 / p. 418		Luisiana Restaurant	♦♦♦	$18-$30	422
6 / p. 418		El Gran Pastor	♦♦♦	$10-$15	421
7 / p. 418		Wall St. Steakhouse	♦♦♦	$22-$45	422
8 / p. 418		Los Arcos	♦♦	$12-$25	422

1409-M

To Mariano Escobedo International Airport, **17** **18** & **19**

To Reynosa & Brownsville

To Pastora Park

To Niños Héroes Park, Nuevo León State Univ., Plaza de Toros

Bullring; Laredo, **13** & **15**

To Horsetail Falls, El Cercado, Ciudad Victoria, Ciudad Valles & Mexico City, D.F.

GOMEZ

A. PRIETO

ALT

AV CHAPULTEPEC

GUERRERO

AV COLON

FCO I MADERO

CALZADA

FELIX

ARAMBERRI

WASHINGTON

PADRE MIER

MORELOS

LEON GUZMAN

AYUTLA

ZUAZUA

ZARAGOZA

ESCOBEDO

GALEANA

Gran Plaza

River

MARTINEZ

JUAREZ

BENITO

5 DE MAYO

ALLENDE

SEE INSET MAP FOR DETAIL

BARRAGAN

VICTORIA

CALZ

CUAUHTEMOC

SUAREZ

PINO

HIDALGO

VILLAGRAN

SERAFIN

Alameda General Escobedo

6 **1**

PEÑA

ARAMBERRI

WASHINGTON

5 DE MAYO

MIER

Santa Catarina

PRIETO

VIADUCTO

FCO I MADERO

V CARRANZA

AV COLON

CALZADA

URDIALES

LOS

ALT

AV

BOLIVAR

CALZ

F G SADA

J BENITEZ

E ZOLA

HIDALGO

CONSTITUCION

DOMINGUEZ

PADRE

MORONES

8

AV

GONZALEZ

P

J ELEUTERIO

7

21 **22** & **7**

To Nuevo Laredo

PROLONGACION

MADERO

SUR AMERICA

GRAL PABLO GONZALEZ GARZA

GONZALEZ

To Garcia Caves, Huasteca Canyon, Saltillo, Mexico City, D.F. & **23**

N

© AAA

Monterrey
NUEVO LEON
Lodging & Dining

Miles 0 — 0.6
Kilometers 0 — 1.0

Inset map:

DR COSS

MIER

JARDIN

ZUAZUA

ZARAGOZA

Plaza Zaragoza

ESCOBEDO

2

GALEANA

6

7

10 **11**

MORELOS

GUERRERO

HIDALGO

9

JUAREZ

OCAMPO

CONSTITUCION VIADUCTO

Santa Catarina River

PADRE

GARIBALDI

5

To Alta Cultural Center, **21** **22** & **7**

CUAUHTEMOC

3 **4**

SUAREZ

PINO

HIDALGO

RAYON

8

MORONES PRIETO

AV

MONTERREY, NUEVO LEON pop. 1,127,000 (See map and index starting on p. 418)

———— WHERE TO STAY ————

BEST WESTERN ROYAL COURTS
Phone: (81)8305-1900 **13**
All Year [BP] 1P: $75-$90 2P: $75-$90 XP: $5 F17
Location: On Mex 85, 8.5 km s of toll road to Nuevo Laredo; on northern city outskirts. Located in a busy commercial
Small-scale Hotel area. Ave Universidad 314 66450. Fax: 81/8305-1919. **Facility:** 82 one-bedroom standard units. 2-3 stories (no elevator), exterior corridors. *Bath:* shower only. **Parking:** on-site. **Terms:** 3 day cancellation notice.
Amenities: safes, hair dryers. **Pool(s):** heated outdoor. **Guest Services:** valet laundry, area transportation. **Business Services:** meeting rooms, business center. **Cards:** AX, DC, MC, VI.

SOME UNITS

COURTYARD BY MARRIOTT MONTERREY
AEROPUERTO *Book at aaa.com*
Phone: (81)8625-5050 **17**
All Year 1P: $100-$200 2P: $100-$200
Location: At entrance to international airport. Carr Miguel Aleman KM 24.5 66600. Fax: 81/8625-5071. **Facility:** 205 units. 197 one-bedroom standard units. 8 one-bedroom suites ($170). 5 stories, interior corridors. *Bath:* combo or shower only. **Parking:** on-site. **Amenities:** dual phone lines, voice mail, irons, hair dryers.
Small-scale Hotel **Pool(s):** outdoor. **Leisure Activities:** exercise room. **Guest Services:** valet and coin laundry, area transportation-within 15 km. **Business Services:** meeting rooms, business center. **Cards:** AX, DC, MC, VI.

SOME UNITS

CROWNE PLAZA MONTERREY *Book at aaa.com*
Phone: (81)8319-6060 **11**
All Year 1P: $150-$230 2P: $150-$230 XP: $30 F19
Location: Just w of Plaza Hidalgo. Located adjacent to downtown historic center. Ave Constitution Ote 300 64000
Large-scale Hotel (Apdo Postal 1619). Fax: 81/8344-3007. **Facility:** Meets AAA guest room security requirements. 403 units. 398 one-bedroom standard units. 5 one-bedroom suites ($369-$609). 15 stories, interior corridors. **Parking:** on-site (fee) and valet. **Amenities:** video games (fee), high-speed Internet, dual phone lines, voice mail, honor bars, irons, hair dryers. **Pool(s):** heated indoor. **Leisure Activities:** sauna, whirlpool, exercise room. *Fee:* lighted tennis court, massage. **Guest Services:** gift shop, valet laundry, area transportation (fee). **Business Services:** conference facilities, business center. **Cards:** AX, DC, MC, VI.

SOME UNITS
FEE

DAYS INN ALAMEDA-MONTERREY
Phone: (81)8150-7100 **4**
All Year 1P: $70-$150 2P: $80-$160 XP: $10 F16
Location: Ave Pino Suarez, jct 5 de Mayo. Pino Suarez 343 Sur Col Centro 64000 (1209 San Diego Ave PMB 7-419,
Small-scale Hotel LAREDO, TX, 78040-4505). Fax: 81/8150-7102. **Facility:** 70 units. 68 one-bedroom standard units. 2 one-bedroom suites. 5 stories, interior corridors. **Parking:** on-site. **Leisure Activities:** sauna, exercise room.
Guest Services: valet laundry. **Business Services:** meeting rooms, business center. **Cards:** AX, CB, DC, MC, VI.
(See color ad opposite inside front cover)

SOME UNITS

DOUBLETREE HOTEL RIO
Phone: (81)8625-4000 **5**
All Year 1P: $90-$150 2P: $90-$150 XP: $10 F18
Location: 0.7 km w of Grand Plaza, jct Padre Mier and Ave Garibaldi. Located in a busy commercial area. Padre Mier 194 Pte 64000 (Apdo Postal 35). Fax: 81/8625-4015. **Facility:** Meets AAA guest room security requirements. 394 units. 393 one-bedroom standard units. 1 one-bedroom suite ($250). 9-14 stories, interior corridors.
Large-scale Hotel *Bath:* combo or shower only. **Parking:** on-site (fee) and valet. **Amenities:** voice mail, safes, irons, hair dryers. *Some:* CD players. **Dining:** 6 am-1 am, cocktails, entertainment. **Pool(s):** heated outdoor. **Leisure Activities:** tennis court, exercise room, sports court. **Guest Services:** gift shop, valet laundry, area transportation (fee).
Business Services: conference facilities, business center. **Cards:** AX, DC, MC, VI.

SOME UNITS
FEE

FAIRFIELD INN BY MARRIOTT
Phone: (81)8625-2000 **19**
All Year 1P: $49-$72 2P: $49-$72
Location: At entrance to international airport on Carr Miguel Aleman. Ave Rogelio Gonzalez Caballero #150 66600.
Small-scale Hotel Fax: 81/8625-2010. **Facility:** 103 one-bedroom standard units. 3 stories, interior corridors. *Bath:* combo or shower only. **Parking:** on-site. **Amenities:** irons. **Leisure Activities:** exercise room. **Guest Services:** area transportation. **Business Services:** business center. **Cards:** AX, CB, DC, JC, MC, VI.

SOME UNITS

FIESTA AMERICANA CENTRO MONTERREY *Book at aaa.com*
Phone: (81)8319-0900 **7**
All Year 1P: $110-$200 2P: $110-$200 XP: $15 F12
Location: In downtown Historic Zona Rosa District. Corregidora 519 Zona Rosa 64000. Fax: 81/8319-0980.
Large-scale Hotel **Facility:** Meets AAA guest room security requirements. 207 units. 189 one-bedroom standard units. 18 one-bedroom suites ($145-$165). 13 stories, interior corridors. **Parking:** on-site (fee). **Terms:** cancellation fee imposed, [BP] meal plan available. **Amenities:** video games, voice mail, safes, honor bars, irons, hair dryers. **Pool(s):** heated indoor. **Leisure Activities:** exercise room. *Fee:* massage. **Guest Services:** gift shop, valet laundry. **Business Services:** conference facilities, business center. **Cards:** AX, DC, MC, VI. *(See color ad card inserts)*

SOME UNITS

(See map and index starting on p. 418)

FIESTA INN CENTRO
Phone: (81)8150-2232   **8**

All Year   1P: $57-$95   2P: $57-$95   XP: $7   F15

Small-scale Hotel

Location: Jct aves Pino Suarez and Ocampo. Ave Pino Suarez #1001, Col Centro 64000. Fax: 81/8150-2222. **Facility:** 231 one-bedroom standard units. 13 stories, interior corridors. **Terms:** [BP] meal plan available. **Amenities:** video games (fee), high-speed Internet, voice mail, hair dryers. **Pool(s):** indoor. **Leisure Activities:** whirlpool, exercise room. **Guest Services:** valet laundry. **Business Services:** meeting rooms, business center. **Cards:** AX, CB, MC, VI. *(See color ad card inserts)*

SOME UNITS

HAMPTON INN & SUITES MONTERREY NORTE
Phone: 81/8625-2600   **15**

All Year [ECP]   1P: $105-$185   2P: $105-$185   XP: $10   F18

Small-scale Hotel

Location: 8 km s of Mex 85 and Monterrey-Nuevo Laredo toll road; on northern outskirts. Ave Universidad 501 Nte 66450. Fax: 81/8625-2601. **Facility:** Meets AAA guest room security requirements. 225 units. 213 one-bedroom standard units. 12 one-bedroom suites ($130-$190). 6 stories, interior corridors. **Bath:** combo or shower only. **Parking:** on-site. **Amenities:** voice mail, irons. **Pool(s):** outdoor. **Leisure Activities:** exercise room. **Guest Services:** complimentary evening beverages: Mon-Thurs, valet laundry, area transportation. **Business Services:** meeting rooms, business center. **Cards:** AX, DC, MC, VI. *(See color ad below)*

SOME UNITS

HAMPTON INN MONTERREY AEROPUERTO   *Book at aaa.com*
Phone: (81)8625-2900   **18**

All Year [CP]   1P: $90-$140   2P: $90-$140

Small-scale Hotel

Location: At entrance to international airport. Carr Miguel Aleman KM 23.7 66600. Fax: 81/8625-2908. **Facility:** 181 one-bedroom standard units. 5 stories, interior corridors. **Bath:** combo or shower only. **Parking:** on-site. **Terms:** 15 day cancellation notice-fee imposed. **Amenities:** dual phone lines, voice mail, irons, hair dryers. **Pool(s):** outdoor. **Leisure Activities:** exercise room, sports court. **Guest Services:** valet and coin laundry, area transportation. **Business Services:** meeting rooms, business center. **Cards:** AX, DC, MC, VI. *(See color ad below)*

SOME UNITS

HAMPTON INN MONTERREY GALERIAS OBISPADO
Phone: (81)8625-2450   **1**

All Year   1P: $95-$160   2P: $95-$160

Small-scale Hotel

Location: Across from Galerias Mall. Located in the upscale Galerias District. Ave Gonzalitos 415 S 64060. Fax: 81/8625-2451. **Facility:** Meets AAA guest room security requirements. 223 one-bedroom standard units. 7 stories, interior corridors. **Bath:** combo or shower only. **Parking:** on-site. **Terms:** 3 day cancellation notice. **Amenities:** high-speed Internet, dual phone lines, voice mail, irons, hair dryers. **Pool(s):** outdoor. **Leisure Activities:** exercise room. **Guest Services:** valet laundry, area transportation. **Business Services:** meeting rooms, business center. **Cards:** AX, DC, MC, VI.

SOME UNITS

FEE

HOLIDAY INN EXPRESS GALERIAS-SAN JERONIMO
Phone: (81)8389-6000   **21**

All Year   1P: $140-$170   2P: $140-$170   XP: $10   F17

Small-scale Hotel

Location: Just w of Galerias Mall. 1082 Ave San Jeronimo 64640. Fax: 81/8389-6020. **Facility:** 170 units. 166 one-bedroom standard units. 4 one-bedroom suites with whirlpools. 5 stories, interior corridors. **Bath:** combo or shower only. **Parking:** on-site. **Amenities:** voice mail, honor bars, irons, hair dryers. **Some:** high-speed Internet. **Pool(s):** heated outdoor. **Leisure Activities:** exercise room. **Guest Services:** gift shop, complimentary evening beverages: Wed, valet and coin laundry. **Business Services:** meeting rooms, business center. **Cards:** AX, DC, MC, VI.

SOME UNITS

HOTEL HOWARD JOHNSON MACROPLAZA MONTERREY
Phone: (81)8380-6000   **6**

All Year [BP]   1P: $180-$250   2P: $180-$250   XP: $20   F12

Large-scale Hotel

Location: In front of Plaza Zaragoza; downtown historic center. Located in a busy commercial area. Morelos 574 Nte 64000 (Apdo Postal 349). Fax: 81/8344-7378. **Facility:** Meets AAA guest room security requirements. 198 units. 186 one-bedroom standard units. 12 one-bedroom suites ($85). 9 stories, interior corridors. **Bath:** combo or shower only. **Parking:** on-site. **Amenities:** voice mail, safes, irons, hair dryers. **Pool(s):** heated indoor. **Leisure Activities:** sauna, steamroom, exercise room. **Guest Services:** gift shop, valet laundry, area transportation (fee). **Business Services:** conference facilities, business center. **Cards:** AX, DC, MC, VI.

SOME UNITS

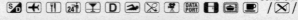

(See map and index starting on p. 418)

HOTEL QUINTA REAL MONTERREY

Small-scale Hotel

All Year — 2P: $130-$200 — XP: $20 — **Phone:** (81)8368-1000 — **22** — F16

Location: Across from Plaza Fiesta San Agustin. Located in an upscale, financial district. Diego Rivera #500 66260. **Fax:** 81/8368-1070. **Facility:** Colonial architecture and upscale decor enhance the property, which features a rotunda registration area, life-size artwork and palatial furnishings. 125 units. 120 one-bedroom standard units, some with whirlpools. 5 one-bedroom suites ($170-$320) with whirlpools. 5 stories, interior corridors. **Amenities:** voice mail, honor bars, irons, hair dryers. *Some:* dual phone lines, safes. **Leisure Activities:** whirlpool, jogging, exercise room. *Fee:* massage. **Guest Services:** valet laundry. **Business Services:** conference facilities, business center. **Cards:** AX, DC, MC, VI.

SOME UNITS

PRESIDENTE INTERCONTINENTAL MONTERREY

Book at aaa.com

Large-scale Hotel

1/13-11/30	1P: $269-$309	2P: $269-$309	XP: $20 — F18
12/1-1/12	1P: $259-$299	2P: $259-$299	XP: $20 — F18

Phone: (81)8368-6000 — **23**

Location: In financial district. Located in an upscale neighborhood. Ave Vasconcelos 300 Ote 66260. **Fax:** 81/8368-6040. **Facility:** Expansive public areas. Outdoor courtyard area with waterfalls. Tastefully decorated guest rooms. Meets AAA guest room security requirements. 305 units. 248 one-bedroom standard units. 57 one-bedroom suites, some with kitchens (no utensils). 10 stories, interior corridors. **Parking:** on-site. **Terms:** cancellation fee imposed. **Amenities:** high-speed Internet, voice mail, safes, honor bars, irons, hair dryers. **Dining:** Wall St. Steakhouse, see separate listing. **Pool(s):** heated indoor, wading. **Leisure Activities:** whirlpool, lighted tennis court. *Fee:* massage. **Guest Services:** gift shop, valet laundry. **Business Services:** conference facilities, business center. **Cards:** AX, DC, JC, MC, VI.

SOME UNITS

RADISSON GRAN ANCIRA PLAZA HOTEL

Book at aaa.com

Historic
Large-scale Hotel

All Year — 1P: $120-$180 — 2P: $120-$180 — XP: $15 — **Phone:** (81)8150-7000 — **10** — F12

Location: Southwest corner of Plaza Hidalgo; entrance only by one-way eastbound Ave Hidalgo. Located in the historic main plaza. Ocampa #443 Ote 64000 (Apdo Postal 697). **Fax:** 81/8344-5226. **Facility:** Neoclassic landmark boasting a grand marbled lobby combined with contemporary amenities and service. 263 units. 237 one-bedroom standard units. 26 one-bedroom suites ($300), some with whirlpools. 5 stories, interior corridors. **Parking:** on-site (fee) and valet. **Terms:** 5 day cancellation notice. **Amenities:** voice mail, honor bars, irons, hair dryers. **Pool(s):** small heated outdoor. **Leisure Activities:** sauna, whirlpool, exercise room. **Guest Services:** gift shop, valet laundry. **Business Services:** conference facilities, business center. **Cards:** AX, DC, MC, VI. *(See color ad p 477)*

SOME UNITS

RADISSON HOTEL CASA GRANDE GARZA GRACIA MONTERREY

[fyi]

Small-scale Hotel

Under construction, scheduled to open December 2004. **Location:** Ave Lazaro Cardenas, 2305 Col Valle Or.

SAFI MONTERREY

Small-scale Hotel

All Year — 1P: $85-$130 — 2P: $85-$130 — XP: $12 — **Phone:** 81/8399-7000 — **3** — F12

Location: From Monterrey-Nuevo Laredo toll road, s on Ave Universidad to Ave Pino Suarez, s to northern edge of downtown. Located adjacent to Alameda Park. Ave Pino Suarez 444 Sur 64000. **Fax:** 81/8399-7020. **Facility:** Meets AAA guest room security requirements. 158 one-bedroom standard units. 7 stories, interior/exterior corridors. **Parking:** on-site. **Amenities:** hair dryers. **Pool(s):** heated outdoor. **Leisure Activities:** whirlpool, exercise room. **Guest Services:** gift shop, valet laundry. **Business Services:** meeting rooms, fax. **Cards:** AX, MC, VI.

SOME UNITS

SHERATON AMBASSADOR HOTEL & TOWERS MONTERREY

Book at aaa.com

[AAA]

Large-scale Hotel

All Year — 1P: $160-$250 — 2P: $160-$250 — XP: $20 — **Phone:** (81)8380-7000 — **9** — F17

Location: Just w of Plaza Hidalgo at Ave Hidalgo and E Carranza. Located in heart of historic area. Ave Hidalgo 310 Ote 64000 (Apdo Postal 1733). **Fax:** 81/8345-1984. **Facility:** Turn-of-the-20th-century ambience. Elegant public areas. Spacious units. Meets AAA guest room security requirements. 239 units. 222 one-bedroom standard units. 16 one- and 1 two-bedroom suites ($180-$360), some with whirlpools. 12 stories, interior corridors. **Parking:** on-site (fee) and valet. **Amenities:** high-speed Internet, dual phone lines, voice mail, safes, honor bars, irons, hair dryers. *Some:* CD players. **Dining:** 24 hours, cocktails, entertainment. **Pool(s):** outdoor, wading. **Leisure Activities:** whirlpool, tennis court, racquetball court, racquetball equipment. *Fee:* massage. **Guest Services:** gift shop, valet laundry. **Business Services:** conference facilities, business center. **Cards:** AX, DC, MC, VI. *(See color ad p 8)*

SOME UNITS

The following lodging was either not evaluated or did not meet AAA rating requirements but is listed for your information only.

FIESTA INN MONTERREY PONIENTE

[fyi]

Phone: 81/8389-8989

Not evaluated. **Location:** Ave Fidel Velasquez #3000 64270. Facilities, services, and decor characterize a mid-range property. *(See color ad card insert)*

--- **WHERE TO DINE** ---

EL GRAN PASTOR

Regional Mexican

Lunch: $10-$12 — **Dinner:** $10-$15 — **Phone:** 81/8333-3391 — **6**

Location: Just n of jct Ave Constitucion. Ave Gonzalitos 702 64640. **Hours:** noon-midnight. **Reservations:** accepted, except Sat. **Features:** Located in the business district, this well-known city landmark specializes in roasted baby goat, split on a rack and charbroiled over a wood fire. Casual dress; cocktails. **Parking:** on-site. **Cards:** AX, DC, MC, VI.

(See map and index starting on p. 418)

LOS ARCOS

Regional Seafood

Lunch: $10-$18 **Dinner:** $12-$25 **Phone:** 81/8347-2301 [8]
Location: In financial center. Ave Ignacio Morones Prieta #2414 64710. **Hours:** 1 pm-11 pm, Fri & Sat-midnight. **Features:** A well-known local favorite, the casual Monterrey-style seafood house prepares a wide selection of excellent seafood and distinctive preparations. Try the light and refreshing shrimp ball soup. Casual dress; cocktails. **Parking:** on-site. **Cards:** AX, MC, VI.

LUISIANA RESTAURANT

Continental

Lunch: $10-$17 **Dinner:** $18-$30 **Phone:** 81/8343-1561 [2]
Location: In downtown historic center. Plaza Hidalgo 530 64000. **Hours:** noon-midnight. Closed major holidays. **Reservations:** suggested. **Features:** Diners who patronize this classic establishment get a feel for the true meaning of the word restaurant: to restore. Soft piano music, a quiet dining room and formally attired staff members with crisp, white napkins draped perfectly over their forearms invite those who dine here to relax and rejuvenate. The mood is distinctly European. Dressy casual; cocktails; entertainment. **Parking:** on-site. **Cards:** AX, CB, DC, MC, VI.

WALL ST. STEAKHOUSE

Regional Steak & Seafood

Lunch: $15-$30 **Dinner:** $22-$45 **Phone:** 81/8368-6000 [7]
Location: In financial district; in Presidente InterContinental Monterrey. Ave Vasconcelos 300 Ote 66260. **Hours:** 1 pm-10 pm, Fri & Sat-midnight. **Reservations:** suggested. **Features:** The classic New York-style steak house features rich woods, starched white linens and sparkling glassware. Attentive, well-trained staffers serve large portions of high-quality imported steaks, chops and seafood. Dressy casual; cocktails. **Parking:** on-site (fee) and valet. **Cards:** AX, CB, DC, JC, MC, VI.

NUEVO LAREDO, TAMAULIPAS pop. 322,100

—— WHERE TO STAY ——

HILTON GARDEN INN

Small-scale Hotel

Phone: (867)711-4600
All Year 1P: $80-$120 2P: $80-$120 XP: $6 F17
Location: 4 mi s of International Bridge. Located in a commercial area. Ave Reforma 5102 88290. Fax: 867/711-4601. **Facility:** 120 units. 117 one-bedroom standard units. 3 one-bedroom suites ($180-$220). 4 stories, interior corridors. **Parking:** on-site. **Amenities:** dual phone lines, voice mail, irons, hair dryers. **Pool(s):** heated indoor. **Leisure Activities:** whirlpool, exercise room. **Business Services:** meeting rooms, business center. **Cards:** AX, MC, VI.

SOME UNITS

SALTILLO, COAHUILA pop. 581,400

—— WHERE TO STAY ——

CAMINO REAL SALTILLO *Book at aaa.com*

Small-scale Hotel

Phone: (844)438-0000
All Year [CP] 1P: $100-$180 2P: $100-$180 XP: $30 F12
Location: 6 km se on Mex 57 from Mex 40; on eastern city outskirts. Located in a quiet area. #2000 Blvd Los Fundadores 25015. Fax: 844/438-0007. **Facility:** On mountain slope above Saltillo Valley. Extensive landscaped gardens. 164 units. 161 one-bedroom standard units. 2 one- and 1 two-bedroom suites ($220-$300) with whirlpools. 1-2 stories (no elevator), exterior corridors. **Parking:** on-site. **Amenities:** voice mail, safes, honor bars, irons, hair dryers. **Dining:** 2 restaurants, 5:30 am-midnight, also, Buena Vista, see separate listing. **Pool(s):** heated outdoor. **Leisure Activities:** putting green, miniature golf, 2 lighted tennis courts, playground, exercise room. **Guest Services:** valet laundry. **Business Services:** conference facilities, business center. **Cards:** AX, DC, MC, VI.

SOME UNITS

HAMPTON INN ZONA AEROPUERTO

Small-scale Hotel

Phone: (844)438-8787
All Year 1P: $99-$109 2P: $99-$109 XP: $12 F18
Location: 19 km n. 6580 Carr Saltillo-Monterrey 25270. Fax: 844/432-3939. **Facility:** 149 units. 143 one-bedroom standard units. 6 one-bedroom suites. 4 stories, interior corridors. **Parking:** on-site. **Terms:** 10% service charge. **Amenities:** high-speed Internet, dual phone lines, voice mail, irons, hair dryers. **Pool(s):** outdoor. **Leisure Activities:** exercise room. **Guest Services:** valet and coin laundry. **Business Services:** meeting rooms, business center. **Cards:** AX, CB, DC, JC, MC, VI.

SOME UNITS

HOLIDAY INN EUROTEL *Book at aaa.com*

Small-scale Hotel

Phone: (844)438-8888
All Year 1P: $120-$160 2P: $120-$160 XP: $12 F12
Location: 1 km s from Glorieta; at N Ortiz G and Blvd V Carranza. Located in a modern, commercial area. Blvd V Carranza #4100 25230. Fax: 844/488-8886. **Facility:** 182 units. 179 one-bedroom standard units. 3 one-bedroom suites ($165-$180). 3 stories, interior corridors. **Parking:** on-site. **Terms:** [AP], [BP], [CP], [ECP] & [MAP] meal plans available. **Amenities:** voice mail, safes, honor bars, irons, hair dryers. *Some:* dual phone lines. **Pool(s):** heated indoor. **Leisure Activities:** sauna, whirlpool, playground, exercise room. **Guest Services:** gift shop, valet laundry. **Business Services:** conference facilities, business center. **Cards:** AX, DC, MC, VI.

SOME UNITS

HOLIDAY INN RAMOS ARIZPE *Book at aaa.com*

Small-scale Hotel

Phone: (844)438-8800
All Year 1P: $85-$150 2P: $85-$150 XP: $12 F18
Location: 18 km n. Carr Saltillo-Monterrey #9000 25015. Fax: 844/438-8818. **Facility:** 124 units. 123 one-bedroom standard units, some with efficiencies (no utensils). 1 one-bedroom suite. 2 stories (no elevator), interior corridors. **Parking:** on-site. **Amenities:** dual phone lines, voice mail, honor bars, irons, hair dryers. *Some:* high-speed Internet. **Pool(s):** heated indoor, wading. **Leisure Activities:** whirlpool, exercise room. **Guest Services:** valet and coin laundry, area transportation (fee). **Business Services:** meeting rooms, business center. **Cards:** AX, DC, MC, VI.

SOME UNITS

——— WHERE TO DINE ———

BUENA VISTA
Continental
Lunch: $12-$20   **Dinner:** $15-$30   **Phone:** 844/438-0000
Location: 6 km se on Mex 57 from Mex 40; on eastern city outskirts; in Camino Real Saltillo. #2000 Blvd Los Fundadores 25015. **Hours:** noon-11 pm. **Reservations:** accepted. **Features:** Diners who unwind amid the restaurant's upscale Western decor are treated to a beautiful view of the surrounding mountains. Dressy casual; cocktails. **Parking:** on-site. **Cards:** AX, DC, MC, VI.

RESTAURANT LA CANASTA
Continental
Lunch: $7-$10   **Dinner:** $10-$20   **Phone:** 844/415-8050
Location: 0.8 mi from Glorieta; at N Ortiz G and Blvd V Carranza. Blvd V Carranza 2485 25280. **Hours:** noon-midnight. **Reservations:** suggested. **Features:** Fireplaces lend to the restaurant's elegant, yet informal, country-style decor. Ample parking is offered behind this place, which is north of downtown. Among examples of popular regional Mexican dishes is the house specialty: mole poblano. Casual dress; cocktails. **Parking:** on-site and valet. **Cards:** AX, MC, VI.

TORREON, COAHUILA pop. 439,400

——— WHERE TO STAY ———

HOLIDAY INN EXPRESS TORREON
Small-scale Hotel
Book at aaa.com
Phone: (871)729-6000
All Year [CP]   1P: $125   2P: $125
Location: Just ne on Mex 30. Located in a financial district. Blvd Independencia 1133 Ote 27000. Fax: 871/729-6020. **Facility:** Meets AAA guest room security requirements. 165 one-bedroom standard units. 5 stories, interior corridors. **Parking:** on-site. **Terms:** cancellation fee imposed. **Amenities:** dual phone lines, voice mail, irons, hair dryers. **Pool(s):** small heated outdoor. **Leisure Activities:** exercise room. **Guest Services:** valet and coin laundry. **Business Services:** meeting rooms, business center. **Cards:** AX, MC, VI.
SOME UNITS

PARAISO DEL DESIERTO GRAND HOTEL
Small-scale Hotel
Phone: (871)716-1122
All Year [BP]   1P: $85   2P: $85
Location: 2 km ne on Mex 30. Blvd Independencia 100 Pte 27000. Fax: 871/716-1122. **Facility:** 153 units. 152 one- and 1 two-bedroom standard units. 4-6 stories, interior/exterior corridors. *Bath:* combo or shower only. **Parking:** on-site. **Amenities:** hair dryers. **Pool(s):** outdoor, wading. **Leisure Activities:** exercise room. **Guest Services:** valet and coin laundry. **Business Services:** meeting rooms, business center. **Cards:** AX, MC, VI.
SOME UNITS

——— *The following lodgings were either not evaluated or did not meet AAA rating requirements but are listed for your information only.* ———

BEST WESTERN HOTEL DEL RIO EXPRESS
[fyi]
Phone: 871/750-7500
Not evaluated. **Location:** On Mex 30, near Industrial City turn off. Blvd Independencia #3837 27100. Facilities, services, and decor characterize a mid-range property.

CROWNE PLAZA TORREON
[fyi]
Phone: 871/729-9600
Not evaluated. **Location:** Center. Blvd Torreon Matamoros #4050 27260. Facilities, services, and decor characterize a mid-range property.

FIESTA INN TORREON
[fyi]
Phone: 871/729-4300
Not evaluated. **Location:** Jct Paseo de las Rositas and Diagonal de los Fuentes, just w. Paseo de las Rositas #910 27250. Facilities, services, and decor characterize a mid-range property. *(See color ad card insert)*

——— WHERE TO DINE ———

MARTIN'S RESTAURANT
Mexican
Lunch: $4-$16   **Dinner:** $4-$16   **Phone:** 871/729-6000
Location: Just ne on Mex 30. Blvd Independencia 1133 Ote 27000. **Hours:** 7 am-midnight, Fri & Sat 24 hours. **Features:** Locally popular, the coffee shop-style restaurant serves a good selection of reasonably priced American sandwiches, soups and Mexican food, in addition to some luscious desserts. Casual dress; beer only. **Parking:** on-site. **Cards:** AX, MC, VI.

THE PACIFIC COAST
Acapulco

This index helps you "spot" where approved accommodations and restaurants are located on the corresponding detailed maps. Lodging rate ranges are for comparison only and show the property's high season; rates are per night, unless only weekly (W) rates are available. Restaurant rate range is for dinner, unless only lunch (L) is served. Turn to the listing page for more detailed rate information and consult display ads for special promotions.

Spotter/Map Page Number	OA	ACAPULCO - Lodgings	Diamond Rating	Rate Range High Season	Listing Page
3 / p. 425		Qualton Club Acapulco-An All Inclusive Resort	◆◆	$228-$297	428
4 / p. 425		Grand Acapulco	fyi	$175-$275	427
5 / p. 425		Radisson Resort Acapulco - see color ad p 477	◆◆◆	$95-$100	429
6 / p. 425		Hotel Acapulco Tortuga	◆	$75-$100	427
7 / p. 425		Fiesta Americana Condesa Acapulco - see color ad card insert	◆◆◆	$135-$195	426
8 / p. 425		Fiesta Inn Acapulco - see color ad card insert	◆◆◆	$130-$180	427
9 / p. 425		Calinda Beach Acapulco	◆◆◆	$150-$200	426
10 / p. 425		Villa Vera Hotel Spa & Racquet Club	◆◆◆	$250-$1500	429
11 / p. 425		Quinta Real Acapulco	◆◆◆◆	$350-$420	428
12 / p. 425		Hotel Elcano	◆◆◆	$350	427
13 / p. 425	◬	**Hotel Copacabana**	◆◆	$150-$200	427
14 / p. 425		Hotel Las Hamacas	◆	$90-$120	428
16 / p. 425		El Mirador Acapulco	◆◆	$80-$110	426
18 / p. 425	◬	**Hyatt Regency Acapulco**	◆◆◆	$195-$295	428
19 / p. 425		Hotel Villas La Marina	◆◆	$75-$125	428
20 / p. 425		Hotel La Jolla	◆	$40	427
21 / p. 425		Hotel Las Brisas Acapulco - see color ad opposite title page	◆◆◆	$315-$515	427
23 / p. 425		Camino Real Acapulco Diamante	◆◆◆	$220-$420	426
24 / p. 425		The Fairmont Acapulco Princess	◆◆◆◆	$245-$290	426
25 / p. 425		The Fairmont Pierre Marques	◆◆◆◆	$154-$190	426
27 / p. 425		Mayan Palace Acapulco	◆◆◆	$139-$259	428
28 / p. 425		Mayan Sea Garden Acapulco	◆◆	$93-$190	428
		ACAPULCO - Restaurants			
1 / p. 425		La Mansion	◆◆◆	$14-$27	430
2 / p. 425		El Faro	◆◆◆	$15-$30	429
3 / p. 425		El Olvido	◆◆◆	$10-$19	429
4 / p. 425		El Fogon Mexican Restaurant	◆	$4-$10	429
5 / p. 425		Suntory Acapulco	◆◆◆	$11-$24	430
6 / p. 425		Su Casa	◆◆	$14-$29	430
7 / p. 425		Coyuca 22	◆◆◆	$20-$38	429
8 / p. 425		Kookaburra	◆◆◆	$10-$29	429
9 / p. 425		Baikal	◆◆◆◆	$18-$40	429
10 / p. 425		CasaNova	◆◆◆◆	$20-$45	429
11 / p. 425		La Hacienda	◆◆◆	$20-$30	430
12 / p. 425		Tabachin	◆◆◆◆	$16-$36	430

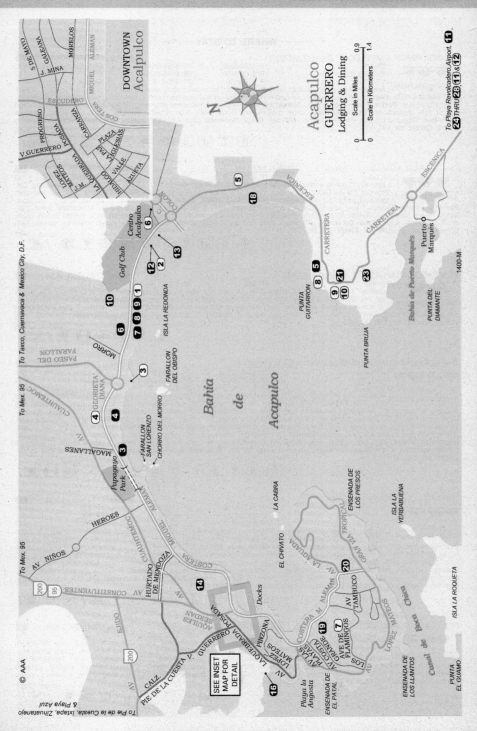

DOWNTOWN Acapulco

Acapulco GUERRERO
Lodging & Dining

Scale in Miles
Scale in Kilometers

© AAA

ACAPULCO, GUERRERO pop. 516,300 (See map and index starting on p. 425)

──────── WHERE TO STAY ────────

CALINDA BEACH ACAPULCO *Book at aaa.com* Phone: (744)484-0410 **9**
▼▼▼ ▼▼▼ 12/1-1/5 1P: $150-$200 2P: $150-$200 XP: $15 F12
1/6-4/15 & 7/11-11/30 1P: $100-$130 2P: $100-$130 XP: $10 F12
4/16-7/10 1P: $70-$100 2P: $70-$100 XP: $10 F12
Large-scale Hotel **Location:** 5.6 km e. Located on the bay in a heavy-commercial area. Costera Miguel Aleman 1260 39690. Fax: 744/484-4676. **Facility:** 357 units. 350 one-bedroom standard units. 7 one-bedroom suites, some with kitchens. 26 stories, interior corridors. **Parking:** on-site and valet. **Terms:** 14 day cancellation notice-fee imposed, [BP] meal plan available, package plans, 15% service charge. **Amenities:** voice mail, safes, honor bars, hair dryers. **Pool(s):** outdoor, wading. **Leisure Activities:** lifeguard on duty, exercise room, volleyball. **Guest Services:** gift shop, valet laundry. **Business Services:** meeting rooms. **Cards:** AX, MC, VI.
SOME UNITS
[🍴 🍸 📶 S D 🏊 ✕ 🎥 DATA/PORT 🖥] / ✕ /

CAMINO REAL ACAPULCO DIAMANTE *Book at aaa.com* Phone: (744)435-1010 **23**
▼▼▼ ▼▼▼ All Year 1P: $220-$420 2P: $220-$420 XP: $50 F12
Large-scale Hotel **Location:** 13 km se on Mex 200; overlooking Bahia de Puerto Marques. Located in a secluded, residential area. Carr Escenica KM 14 39867 (Calle Baja Catita S/N). Fax: 744/435-1020. **Facility:** 157 units. 145 one-bedroom standard units. 12 one-bedroom suites ($470-$680), some with whirlpools. 5 stories, interior corridors. **Parking:** on-site. **Terms:** 7 day cancellation notice-fee imposed, [BP] & [MAP] meal plans available. **Amenities:** voice mail, safes, honor bars, hair dryers. *Some:* irons. **Pool(s):** 3 outdoor. **Leisure Activities:** lifeguard on duty, lighted tennis court, exercise room, spa. **Guest Services:** gift shop, valet laundry, beauty salon. **Business Services:** meeting rooms. *Fee:* administrative services, PC. **Cards:** AX, DC, MC, VI.
SOME UNITS
[✈ 🍴 24 🍸 📶 D 🏊 ✕ 🎥 DATA/PORT] / 🖥 /
FEE

EL MIRADOR ACAPULCO *Book at aaa.com* Phone: (744)483-1155 **16**
▼▼▼ ▼▼▼ All Year 1P: $80 2P: $110 XP: $15
Small-scale Hotel **Location:** 1 km w; on La Quebrada Cliffs. Located in a commercial area. Plazoleta de la Quebrada #74 39300. Fax: 744/482-4564. **Facility:** 133 units. 130 one- and 3 two-bedroom standard units, some with whirlpools. 1-3 stories, exterior corridors. *Bath:* combo or shower only. **Parking:** on-site. **Terms:** 7 day cancellation notice, 3 day off season, [AP], [BP] & [CP] meal plans available. **Pool(s):** 3 outdoor, saltwater. **Guest Services:** gift shop, valet laundry. **Cards:** AX, CB, DC, MC, VI.
SOME UNITS
[S/D 🍴 🍸 🏊 🖥 🖥] / ✕ /

THE FAIRMONT ACAPULCO PRINCESS *Book at aaa.com* Phone: (744)469-1000 **24**
▼▼▼ ▼▼▼ 12/21-4/10 1P: $245-$290 2P: $245-$290 XP: $35 F18
4/11-11/30 1P: $170-$220 2P: $170-$220 XP: $35 F18
Resort 12/1-12/20 1P: $165-$220 2P: $165-$220 XP: $35 F18
Large-scale Hotel **Location:** 19.3 km se, off Mex 200 (Airport Hwy). Located in a quiet area. Playa Revolcadero S/N 39300 (Apdo Postal 1351). Fax: 744/469-1015. **Facility:** An enormous hotel with beautiful, sprawling, tropical grounds, this property is oceanfront, away from the hustle and bustle of downtown. 1017 units. 967 one-bedroom standard units. 50 one-bedroom suites ($260-$1450), some with kitchens and/or whirlpools. 14 stories, interior corridors. **Parking:** on-site and valet. **Terms:** cancellation fee imposed, [BP] & [MAP] meal plans available, package plans. **Amenities:** voice mail, safes, hair dryers. *Some:* high-speed Internet (fee), irons. **Dining:** La Hacienda, see separate listing. **Pool(s):** 4 outdoor, 2 wading, saltwater. **Leisure Activities:** lifeguard on duty, spa, basketball, volleyball, game room. *Fee:* golf-36 holes, 8 tennis courts (2 indoor, 8 lighted), exercise room. **Guest Services:** gift shop, valet laundry. **Business Services:** conference facilities, business center. **Cards:** AX, MC, VI.
SOME UNITS
[🍴 24 🍸 📶 S D 🏊 ✕ 🎥] / ✕ DATA/PORT 🖥 🖥 /

THE FAIRMONT PIERRE MARQUES Phone: (744)466-1000 **25**
▼▼▼ ▼▼▼ 12/19-3/31 1P: $154-$190 2P: $154-$190 XP: $30 F17
4/1-11/30 1P: $108-$154 2P: $108-$154 XP: $30 F17
Resort 12/1-12/18 1P: $108-$117 2P: $108-$117 XP: $30 F17
Large-scale Hotel **Location:** 17.5 km se, off Mex 200 (Airport Hwy). Located in a quiet beachside setting. Playa Revolcadero S/N 39300 (Apdo Postal 474). Fax: 744/466-1046. **Facility:** On sprawling grounds, the property offers a variety of elegant room types including bungalows and villas, some with ocean views. 335 units. 326 one-bedroom standard units. 9 one-bedroom suites ($200-$475). 1-5 stories, exterior corridors. *Bath:* combo or shower only. **Parking:** on-site and valet. **Terms:** [AP] & [BP] meal plans available. **Amenities:** voice mail, safes. *Some:* CD players, high-speed Internet, honor bars, irons, hair dryers. **Dining:** Tabachin, see separate listing. **Pool(s):** 3 outdoor, 2 wading. **Leisure Activities:** lifeguard on duty, playground, exercise room, basketball, volleyball. *Fee:* golf-36 holes, 5 lighted tennis courts. **Guest Services:** gift shop, valet laundry. **Business Services:** conference facilities, business center. **Cards:** AX, MC, VI.
SOME UNITS
[🍴 🍸 📶 & 🏊 ✕ 🎥 DATA/PORT] / ✕ VCR 🖥 /

FIESTA AMERICANA CONDESA ACAPULCO *Book at aaa.com* Phone: (744)484-2828 **7**
▼▼▼ All Year 2P: $135-$195 XP: $25 F12
Large-scale Hotel **Location:** 5.3 km e. Located on the bay in a busy commercial area. Costera Miguel Aleman 97 39690. Fax: 744/484-1828. **Facility:** 500 units. 496 one-bedroom standard units. 4 one-bedroom suites, some with whirlpools. 18 stories, interior corridors. *Bath:* combo or shower only. **Parking:** on-site. **Terms:** 3 day cancellation notice-fee imposed. **Amenities:** voice mail, safes, honor bars, hair dryers. **Pool(s):** outdoor, wading. **Leisure Activities:** lifeguard on duty. **Guest Services:** gift shop, valet laundry. **Business Services:** meeting rooms, business center. **Cards:** AX, DC, MC, VI. *(See color ad card insert)*
SOME UNITS
[S/D 🍴 🍸 📶 & D 🏊 🖥] / ✕ /

(See map and index starting on p. 425)

FIESTA INN ACAPULCO *Book at aaa.com*   **Phone:** (744)435-0500   **8**
▽▼▽ ◇▽◇   All Year   1P: $130   2P: $180   XP: $25   F12
     Location: 5.4 km e. Located on the bay in a heavy-commercial area. Costera Miguel Aleman #2311 39690.
Large-scale Hotel   Fax: 744/435-0509. **Facility:** 220 units. 216 one-bedroom standard units. 4 one-bedroom suites. 14 stories,
interior corridors. **Parking:** valet. **Terms:** 3 day cancellation notice. **Amenities:** video games (fee), voice
mail. *Some:* honor bars, hair dryers. **Pool(s):** outdoor. **Leisure Activities:** exercise room. **Guest Services:** valet laundry.
Business Services: meeting rooms, business center. **Cards:** AX, DC, MC, VI. *(See color ad card insert)*

SOME UNITS

[icons] SÞ ¶¶ ▲ S D ➾ ⌖ DATA/PORT ▭ / ✕ /

GRAND ACAPULCO   **Phone:** (744)440-5555   **4**
[fyi]   12/24-3/31   1P: $175-$275   2P: $175-$275   XP: $30   F12
     4/1-11/30   1P: $160-$235   2P: $160-$235   XP: $30   F12
Large-scale Hotel   12/1-12/23   1P: $145-$220   2P: $145-$220   XP: $30   F12
     Under major renovation, scheduled to be completed December 2004. **Last rated:** ▽▽▽ **Location:** 4.5 km
w. Located on the bay in a busy commercial area. Costera Miguel Aleman 123, Fracc Magallanes 39670. Fax: 744/485-9811. **Facility:** 506
units. 427 one-bedroom standard units. 79 one-bedroom suites, some with whirlpools. 28 stories, interior corridors. **Parking:**
valet. **Terms:** 3 day cancellation notice-fee imposed. [AP], [BP], [CP] & [MAP] meal plans available. **Amenities:** voice mail,
safes. *Some:* honor bars. **Pool(s):** 4 outdoor, 3 small outdoor. **Leisure Activities:** recreation programs. *Fee:* massage, game
room. **Guest Services:** gift shop, valet laundry. **Business Services:** conference facilities, business center. **Cards:** AX, DC,
MC, VI.

SOME UNITS

[icons] SÞ ¶¶ ▼ D ➾ ✕ DATA/PORT / ✕ /

THE GRAND MAYAN ACAPULCO   **Phone:** 744/469-6000
[fyi]   All Year   1P: $191-$286   2P: $224-$336   XP: $70   F12
     Too new to rate, opening scheduled for July 2004. **Location:** 22 km se, off Mex 200 (Airport Hwy). Ave de las
Resort   Palmas #1121 39900. Fax: 744/469-6050. **Amenities:** 360 units, restaurant, pool. **Terms:** check-in 5 pm, 3
Large-scale Hotel   night minimum stay - seasonal and/or weekends, 30 day cancellation notice. **Cards:** AX, MC, VI.

HOTEL ACAPULCO TORTUGA   **Phone:** (744)484-8889   **6**
▽▼▽   All Year   2P: $75-$100   XP: $20
     Location: 5 km e. Located in a busy commercial area. Costera Miguel Aleman 132 39690. Fax: 744/484-7385.
Small-scale Hotel   **Facility:** 252 one-bedroom standard units. 7 stories, interior corridors. *Bath:* combo or shower only.
Parking: on-site. **Terms:** 7 day cancellation notice, 3 day off season, [AP] & [BP] meal plans available.
Pool(s): outdoor, wading. **Leisure Activities:** exercise room. **Guest Services:** gift shop, valet laundry. **Business Services:**
meeting rooms. **Cards:** AX, DC, DS, MC, VI.

SOME UNITS

[icons] ¶¶ ▼ ▲ ⅃ ➾ ⌖ / ✕ /

HOTEL COPACABANA *Book at aaa.com*   **Phone:** (744)484-3260   **13**
ⒶⒶⒶ   12/1-12/31   2P: $150-$200   XP: $15   F12
   1/1-4/14   2P: $100-$140   XP: $10   F12
▽▼▽ ◇▽◇   4/15-11/30   2P: $80-$120   XP: $10   F12
     Location: 6 km e of downtown; off Costera Miguel Aleman. Located on the bay. Tabachines 2 39690.
Large-scale Hotel   Fax: 744/484-6268. **Facility:** 428 one-bedroom standard units. 18 stories, interior corridors. *Bath:* shower
only. **Parking:** on-site. **Terms:** 7 day cancellation notice, 3 day off season-fee imposed. **Amenities:** voice
mail, hair dryers. **Dining:** 2 restaurants, 8 am-11 pm, cocktails, entertainment. **Pool(s):** outdoor, wading. **Leisure
Activities:** whirlpools. *Fee:* jet ski, massage. **Guest Services:** gift shop, valet laundry. *Fee:* beauty salon. **Business Services:**
conference facilities, business center. **Cards:** AX, DC, MC, VI.

SOME UNITS

[icons] SÞ ¶¶ ▼ ▲ ➾ ✕ ⌖ DATA/PORT / ✕ /

HOTEL ELCANO *Book at aaa.com*   **Phone:** (744)435-1500   **12**
▽▼▽ ◇▽◇   12/1-12/31   1P: $350   2P: $350   XP: $45   F12
   1/1-4/5   1P: $105-$192   2P: $105-$192   XP: $30   F12
Small-scale Hotel   4/6-11/30   1P: $100-$168   2P: $105-$192   XP: $25   F12
     Location: 6 km e. Located on the bay in a commercial area. Costera Miguel Aleman 75 39690. Fax: 744/484-2230.
Facility: 180 units. 163 one-bedroom standard units. 16 one- and two-bedroom suites, some with whirlpools. 9 stories, interior
corridors. **Parking:** on-site. **Terms:** 3 day cancellation notice. **Amenities:** safes, honor bars, hair dryers. **Pool(s):** outdoor.
Leisure Activities: whirlpool, steamroom, lifeguard on duty, exercise room. *Fee:* massage. **Guest Services:** gift shop, valet
laundry. **Business Services:** meeting rooms. **Cards:** AX, DC, MC, VI.

[icons] SÞ ¶¶ ▼ ▲ ➾ ✕ DATA/PORT

HOTEL LA JOLLA   **Phone:** 744/482-5862   **20**
▽▼▽   All Year   1P: $40   2P: $40   XP: $5   F10
     Location: 1 km s at Caletilla Beach; downtown. Located in a residential area. Costera Miguel Aleman 506 39390.
Motel   Fax: 744/482-5862. **Facility:** 73 one-bedroom standard units. 3 stories, exterior corridors. *Bath:* shower
only. **Parking:** on-site. **Pool(s):** outdoor, wading. **Cards:** MC, VI.

SOME UNITS

[icons] ➾ ▮ / ⊞ /

HOTEL LAS BRISAS ACAPULCO *Book at aaa.com*   **Phone:** (744)469-6900   **21**
▽▼◆▽▼   12/23-4/15 [CP]   1P: $315-$515   2P: $315-$515   XP: $50   F11
   12/1-12/22 & 4/16-11/30 [CP]   1P: $240-$400   2P: $240-$400   XP: $50   F11
Resort   **Location:** 11.3 km se on Mex 200. Located on a mountainside in a residential area. Carr Escenica 5255 39868.
Large-scale Hotel   Fax: 744/446-5328. **Facility:** Picturesque mountainside location with commanding view. Duplex cottages
with private or semi-private swimming pool. 263 units. 233 one-bedroom standard units. 30 one-bedroom
suites ($720-$1450), some with whirlpools. 1 story, exterior corridors. *Bath:* combo or shower only. **Parking:** on-site.
Terms: age restrictions may apply, 7 day cancellation notice, 3 day off season-fee imposed, $20 service charge.
Amenities: voice mail, safes, honor bars, irons, hair dryers. **Pool(s):** outdoor, saltwater. **Leisure Activities:** exercise room,
spa. *Fee:* 5 lighted tennis courts. **Guest Services:** gift shop, valet laundry. **Business Services:** meeting rooms, business
center. **Cards:** AX, DC, JC, MC, VI. *(See color ad opposite title page)*

SOME UNITS

[icons] ¶¶ 24¶ ▼ ▲ ⅃ ➾ ✕ ⌖ DATA/PORT ▭ / ✕ /

(See map and index starting on p. 425)

HOTEL LAS HAMACAS
Phone: 744/483-7006   **14**

12/16-4/26	2P: $90-$120	XP: $10
12/1-12/15	2P: $70-$120	XP: $10
4/27-11/30	2P: $70-$100	XP: $10

Small-scale Hotel **Location:** 1 km e, just n of the beach. Located in a busy commercial area. Costera Miguel Aleman 239 39360. Fax: 744/483-0575. **Facility:** 127 units. 122 one-bedroom standard units. 5 one-bedroom suites ($150-$200). 5 stories, exterior corridors. *Bath:* shower only. **Parking:** on-site. **Terms:** 15 day cancellation notice, 7 day off season, [AP], [CP] & [MAP] meal plans available. **Pool(s):** outdoor, wading. **Leisure Activities:** playground. **Guest Services:** valet laundry. **Business Services:** meeting rooms. **Cards:** AX, MC, VI.

HOTEL VILLAS LA MARINA
Phone: 744/482-8556   **19**

All Year   1P: $75-$125   2P: $75-$125   XP: $25

Location: 1.7 km sw of Zocalo; downtown. Located in a residential area. Costera Miguel Aleman 222 39390. Small-scale Hotel Fax: 744/482-8595. **Facility:** Meets AAA guest room security requirements. 44 one-bedroom standard units. 1-2 stories (no elevator), exterior corridors. **Parking:** on-site. **Terms:** [BP] meal plan available. **Amenities:** safes, irons, hair dryers. **Pool(s):** outdoor, 2 wading. **Guest Services:** valet laundry, area transportation. **Business Services:** meeting rooms. **Cards:** AX, MC, VI.

SOME UNITS

HYATT REGENCY ACAPULCO   *Book at aaa.com*
Phone: (744)469-1234   **18**

12/23-4/19	1P: $195-$295	2P: $195-$295	XP: $25	F12
12/1-12/22 & 4/20-11/30	1P: $170-$270	2P: $170-$270	XP: $25	F12

Large-scale Hotel **Location:** 8 km e. Located on the bay next to the Icacos Naval Base. Costera Miguel Aleman 1 39869. Fax: 744/484-3087. **Facility:** 640 units. 601 one-bedroom standard units. 39 one-bedroom suites. 22 stories, interior corridors. **Parking:** on-site (fee) and valet. **Terms:** 3 day cancellation notice-fee imposed. **Amenities:** voice mail, hair dryers. *Some:* honor bars. **Dining:** 3 restaurants, 7 am-2 am, cocktails. **Pool(s):** 2 outdoor, wading. **Leisure Activities:** lifeguard on duty. *Fee:* massage. **Guest Services:** gift shop, valet laundry. **Business Services:** meeting rooms, business center. **Cards:** AX, DC, MC, VI.

SOME UNITS

FEE

MAYAN PALACE ACAPULCO
Phone: (774)469-6000   **27**

All Year   1P: $139-$209   2P: $173-$259   XP: $59   F12

Resort
Large-scale Hotel **Location:** 22 km se, off Mex 200 (Airport Hwy). Located in a quiet beachside setting. Ave de las Palmas #1121 39900. Fax: 744/469-6050. **Facility:** An enormous resort on the beach with unique Aztec construction, the property features lush gardens and has a huge reflecting pool in the lobby. 360 one-bedroom suites, some with kitchens. 1-7 stories, exterior corridors. *Bath:* combo or shower only. **Parking:** on-site and valet. **Terms:** check-in 5 pm, 3 night minimum stay - seasonal and/or weekends, 30 day cancellation notice. **Amenities:** voice mail, hair dryers. **Pool(s):** 2 outdoor, wading. **Leisure Activities:** whirlpool, steamrooms, lifeguard on duty, recreation programs, exercise room, spa, volleyball. *Fee:* canoes, paddleboats, golf-18 holes, 10 lighted tennis courts. **Guest Services:** gift shop, valet laundry. *Fee:* beauty salon. **Business Services:** PC (fee). **Cards:** AX, MC, VI.

SOME UNITS

FEE

MAYAN SEA GARDEN ACAPULCO
Phone: (744)466-1850   **28**

All Year   1P: $93-$139   2P: $127-$190   XP: $49   F12

Location: 22 km se, off Mex 200 (Airport Hwy). Located adjacent to the beach. Ave de las Palmas #1121 39900. Small-scale Hotel Fax: 744/466-6515. **Facility:** 114 units. 24 one-bedroom standard units. 90 one-bedroom suites with kitchens. 2-3 stories (no elevator), interior corridors. **Parking:** on-site. **Terms:** check-in 5 pm, 3 night minimum stay - seasonal and/or weekends, 30 day cancellation notice. **Amenities:** safes (fee), hair dryers. **Pool(s):** outdoor, 2 wading. **Leisure Activities:** lifeguard on duty, playground. *Fee:* golf-18 holes. **Guest Services:** gift shop, valet laundry, area transportation. **Cards:** AX, MC, VI.

SOME UNITS

QUALTON CLUB ACAPULCO-AN ALL INCLUSIVE RESORT
Phone: 744/469-1360   **3**

All Year   2P: $228-$297   XP: $30

Location: 4.2 km e. Located on the bay in a busy commercial area. Costera Miguel Aleman 159 39670. Resort Fax: 744/486-8324. **Facility:** High-rise towers on beachfront. Average-size rooms with contemporary decor. Small-scale Hotel Most with balcony and ocean view. 240 one-bedroom standard units. 11-14 stories, interior corridors. *Bath:* combo or shower only. **Parking:** on-site. **Amenities:** safes (fee). **Pool(s):** outdoor, wading. **Leisure Activities:** recreation programs, exercise room. *Fee:* snorkeling. **Guest Services:** gift shop, valet laundry. **Business Services:** meeting rooms. **Cards:** AX, DC, MC, VI.

SOME UNITS

QUINTA REAL ACAPULCO   *Book at aaa.com*
Phone: (744)469-1500   **11**

All Year   1P: $350-$420   2P: $350-$420   XP: $45   F12

Location: 2 km off Mex 200; in Punta Diamante. Located in a quiet, cliffside area. Paseo de la Quinta #6 Fracc Real Small-scale Hotel Diamante 39907. Fax: 744/469-1516. **Facility:** Located in upscale Punta Diamante Beach, this is a boutique resort built into the side of a cliff, with spectacular views of Acapulco Bay. 72 units. 63 one-bedroom standard units, some with whirlpools. 8 one- and 1 two-bedroom suites ($480-$950), some with whirlpools. 5 stories, exterior corridors. **Parking:** on-site and valet. **Terms:** 2 night minimum stay - weekends, 3 day cancellation notice-fee imposed, package plans. **Amenities:** voice mail, honor bars, irons, hair dryers. *Some:* safes. **Pool(s):** outdoor, wading. **Leisure Activities:** lifeguard on duty, exercise room, spa. **Guest Services:** gift shop, valet laundry. **Business Services:** meeting rooms. **Cards:** AX, DC, MC, VI.

SOME UNITS

(See map and index starting on p. 425)

RADISSON RESORT ACAPULCO   *Book at aaa.com*   Phone: 744/440-6565   **5**
▼▼◆▼▼   12/24-11/30   2P: $95-$100   XP: $15   F11
12/1-12/23   2P: $85-$95   XP: $15   F11
Resort   **Location:** 9.5 km se off Carr Escencia, follow signs. Located on the bay in a residential area. Costera Guitarron 110
Large-scale Hotel   Fracc Playa Guitarron 39359. Fax: 744/440-6098. **Facility:** Perched on the side of a mountain, the hotel
overlooks Acapulco Bay and has an elegant lobby and a unique trolley system to take guests to their rooms.
224 units. 211 one-bedroom standard units. 5 one- and 8 two-bedroom suites. 4-7 stories, interior/exterior corridors. **Parking:**
valet. **Terms:** [BP] meal plan available. **Amenities:** voice mail, safes, honor bars, irons, hair dryers. **Pool(s):** 2 outdoor. **Leisure
Activities:** spa, volleyball. *Fee:* exercise room. **Guest Services:** gift shop, valet laundry. **Business Services:** meeting rooms.
Cards: AX, DC, MC, VI. *(See color ad p 477)*

SOME UNITS

▯▮ ▼ ▥ D ≈ ✕ 🎥 ▭ / ✕ /

VILLA VERA HOTEL SPA & RACQUET CLUB   *Book at aaa.com*   Phone: (744)484-0334   **10**
▼▼◆▼▼   All Year   1P: $250-$1500   2P: $250-$1500   XP: $35
Small-scale Hotel   **Location:** 6 km e, 5 blks opposite from Beach Blvd. Located in a residential area. Lomas del Mar 35 39690.
Fax: 744/484-7479. **Facility:** 70 one-bedroom standard units, some with whirlpools. 1-2 stories (no
elevator), exterior corridors. **Parking:** on-site. **Terms:** check-in 4 pm, 7 day cancellation notice-fee imposed.
Amenities: voice mail, safes, honor bars, irons, hair dryers. *Some:* CD players. **Pool(s):** 4 outdoor. **Leisure Activities:** sauna,
whirlpool, racquetball courts, exercise room, spa. *Fee:* 2 lighted tennis courts. **Guest Services:** gift shop, valet laundry.
Business Services: meeting rooms. **Cards:** AX, DC, MC, VI.

S/D ▯▮ ▼ ▥ ≈ ✕ 🎥 DATA PORT ▭

─────── **WHERE TO DINE** ───────

BAIKAL   **Dinner:** $18-$40   Phone: 744/446-6845   **9**
▼▼◆▼▼   **Location:** 9.5 km se. Carr Escenica #16 & #22 Playa Guitarron 39359. **Hours:** 7 pm-midnight. Closed: Mon.
French   **Reservations:** suggested. **Features:** The visually stunning fine dining restaurant is set on a cliff overlooking
Acapulco Bay. From the glass enclosed lobby surrounded by a reflecting pool to the spiral staircase, marble
floors, large white columns, lovely art pieces and fabulous views, Baikal introduces a unique dining
experience for its guests. Fresh fish, seafood, poultry, pasta and prime beef cuts make up some of the changing menu's
choices. A video light show is featured during dinner along with live music. Dressy casual; cocktails. **Parking:** valet. **Cards:** AX,
DC, MC, VI.

Ġ M ▼

CASANOVA   **Dinner:** $20-$45   Phone: 744/446-6237   **10**
▼▼◆▼▼   **Location:** 12 km se on Mex 200. Escenica Las Brisas 5256 39868. **Hours:** 7 pm-11 pm, Fri & Sat-midnight.
Northern   **Reservations:** suggested. **Features:** Both indoors and on the outdoor patio, the atmosphere is elegant and
Italian   the hilltop vantage point ideal for looking out on Acapulco Bay. The attentive wait staff is dressed in semi-
formal attire. The menu features varieties of veal, shrimp, fresh fish, beef, lamb and pasta, as well as
traditional antipasto and desserts. Dressy casual; cocktails; entertainment. **Parking:** on-site and valet.
Cards: AX, DC, MC, VI.

▼ ✕

COYUCA 22   **Dinner:** $20-$38   Phone: 744/482-3468   **7**
▼▼◆▼▼   **Location:** From Caleta Beach, follow signs. Coyuca 22 39390. **Hours:** Open 12/1-4/30 & 11/1-11/30; 7 pm-11 pm.
Continental   **Reservations:** suggested. **Features:** In an open-air setting on the mountainside, the attractive restaurant
affords a panoramic view of Acapulco Bay. Menu feature includes succulent lobster and prime rib. Dressy
casual; cocktails. **Parking:** valet and street. **Cards:** AX, DC, DS, MC, VI.

▼ 𝒜𝒞

EL FARO   **Lunch:** $15-$30   **Dinner:** $15-$30   Phone: 744/484-3100   **2**
▼▼◆▼▼   **Location:** 6 km e; in front of Hotel Elcano. Costera Miguel Aleman 75 39690. **Hours:** 1:30 pm-11 pm. Closed: Mon.
Mediterranean   **Reservations:** suggested. **Features:** A refined nautical theme is featured at this fine dining restaurant. The
lighthouse tower-style construction outside and the large anchor with fountain inside set the stage for a
unique dining experience. The two-tier dining room is elegant with its cloth-covered tables, polished white
granite flooring and lovely cherry wood millwork. The menu has excellent variety, with options such as lamb, fish, seafood,
pasta, steaks or chicken. Dressy casual; cocktails. **Parking:** on-site and valet. **Cards:** AX, MC, VI.

▼

EL FOGON MEXICAN RESTAURANT   **Lunch:** $4-$10   **Dinner:** $4-$10   Phone: 744/484-3607   **4**
▼   **Location:** 4.6 km e; near Diana Glorieta traffic circle. Costera Miguel Aleman S/N 39670. **Hours:** 24 hours.
Mexican   **Features:** A casual eatery set along Acapulco's busiest thoroughfares, this open-air restaurant features an
enormous menu of classic Mexican comfort food. The service is laid back and friendly. Casual dress; beer &
wine only. **Parking:** street. **Cards:** AX, DC, MC, VI.

𝒜𝒞

EL OLVIDO   **Dinner:** $10-$19   Phone: 744/481-0214   **3**
▼▼◆▼▼   **Location:** 5 km e of Zocalo; adjacent to Diana Glorieta traffic circle. Costera Miguel Aleman S/N 39690. **Hours:** 6 pm-
Continental   midnight. **Reservations:** accepted. **Features:** Dishes reflect a fusion of French and Mexican styles at this
open-breezeway restaurant on Acapulco Bay. Mood lighting lends a romantic feel to multi-tiered terraces
among palm trees. Tabletop candles flicker to the soothing sound of crashing waves. Dressy casual;
cocktails. **Parking:** on-site and street. **Cards:** AX, DC, MC, VI.

𝒜𝒞

KOOKABURRA   **Lunch:** $8-$26   **Dinner:** $10-$29   Phone: 744/446-6039   **8**
▼▼◆▼▼   **Location:** 10 km e, 3 km s of Costera Miguel Aleman. Carr Escenica S/N 39359. **Hours:** noon-midnight.
Seafood   **Reservations:** suggested. **Features:** Perched on a hill beside Acapulco Bay, the open-air restaurant
presents creative preparations of quail, duck, local red snapper and beef filet, many tinged with citrus
flavorings. Desserts are fun and tempting. The staff is gracious and friendly. Casual dress; cocktails.
Parking: valet. **Cards:** MC, VI.

▼ 𝒜𝒞

(See map and index starting on p. 425)

LA HACIENDA

Mexican

Dinner: $20-$30

Phone: 744/469-1000   ⑪

Location: 19.3 km se, off Mex 200 (Airport Hwy); in The Fairmont Acapulco Princess. Playa Revolcadero 39300. **Hours:** 7 pm-11 pm, Sun noon-6 pm. Closed: Mon. **Reservations:** required. **Features:** At La Hacienda, guests dine amid the sounds of the lovely ballads sung by the mariachi singers and the peaceful echoes of the ocean waves rolling ashore. The menu has an excellent variety ranging from the more traditional Mexican cuisine to plenty of fish, seafood and steak options. The service staff are welcoming and are dressed in traditional Mexican clothing. Dressy casual; cocktails. **Parking:** on-site and valet. **Cards:** AX, MC, VI.

LA MANSION

Mexican

Dinner: $14-$27

Phone: 744/481-0796   ①

Location: 6 km e. Costera Miguel Aleman 81 Fracc Deportivo CP 39690. **Hours:** 2 pm-midnight. **Reservations:** accepted. **Features:** Prime beef cuts are the main attraction at the restaurant, which counts sharply dressed servers and tables draped in white cloths among the features lending to its upscale ambience. Those wanting traditional Mexican food will find suitable selections on the large menu. Steaks are served on heavy wood plates with handles. Dressy casual; cocktails. **Parking:** valet. **Cards:** AX, MC, VI.

SU CASA

Continental

Dinner: $14-$29

Phone: 744/484-4350   ⑥

Location: Jct Costera Miguel Aleman and Calle Cristobal Colon, 1 km nw. Anahuac #110, Lomas de Costa Azul 39850. **Hours:** 5 pm-11:30 pm. **Reservations:** suggested. **Features:** Perched on a mountainside, this intimate restaurant offers fabulous views of Acapulco Bay. The dining area is on a large open-air terrace with archways that are lined with twinkling lights and flower baskets. The ambience is romantic and the food is well-prepared. While Su Casa offers a wide variety of Continental cuisine, the adjoining dining room and sister restaurant, La Margarita, offers the more traditional Mexican food. Casual dress; cocktails. **Parking:** street. **Cards:** MC, VI.

SUNTORY ACAPULCO

Japanese

Dinner: $11-$24

Phone: 744/484-8088   ⑤

Location: 7.5 km e. Costera Miguel Aleman 36 39850. **Hours:** 2 pm-midnight. **Reservations:** accepted. **Features:** Dishes are prepared tableside at the Japanese restaurant, which features combinations of fresh seafood, poultry and beef, as well as sushi and rice. Dining room windows look over a manicured garden. The dining room is a nice spot for groups and conversation. Casual dress; cocktails. **Parking:** street. **Cards:** AX, DC, MC, VI.

TABACHIN

French

Dinner: $16-$36

Phone: 744/466-1000   ⑫

Location: 17.5 km se, off Mex 200 (Airport Hwy); in The Fairmont Pierre Marques. Playa Revolcadero S/N 39300. **Hours:** 7 pm-11 pm. **Reservations:** required. **Features:** It is daring. It is exciting. It is French fusion and Asian-inspired cuisine. It is Tabachin! It is out of the ordinary! And, it is one of Acapulco's best and most 'civilized' restaurants. Dressy casual; cocktails; entertainment. **Parking:** on-site and valet. **Cards:** AX, MC, VI.

This ends listings for Acapulco.
The following page resumes the alphabetical listings
of cities in The Pacific Coast.

BAHIAS DE HUATULCO, OAXACA pop. 1,900

———— WHERE TO STAY ————

BARCELO HUATULCO BEACH RESORT   *Book at aaa.com*   Phone: 958/581-0055
All Year   1P: $78-$175   2P: $78-$175   XP: $65
Location: In Tangolunda Hotel Zone. Blvd Benito Juarez 70989. Fax: 958/581-0113. **Facility:** Wide sandy beach. All rooms with balcony view of Pacific Ocean. In-season entertainment and social activities. 344 one-bedroom standard units. 6 stories, interior corridors. **Parking:** on-site. **Terms:** 3 day cancellation notice, [AP], [BP] & [MAP] meal plans available. **Amenities:** safes, honor bars, hair dryers. **Pool(s):** 2 outdoor, wading. **Leisure Activities:** 4 lighted tennis courts, recreation programs, playground, exercise room, volleyball. *Fee:* sailboats, windsurfing, waterskiing, charter fishing, golf-18 holes, massage. **Guest Services:** gift shop, valet laundry. **Business Services:** conference facilities, fax (fee). **Cards:** AX, DC, MC, VI.
Resort
Large-scale Hotel
SOME UNITS

CROWN PACIFIC HUATULCO   *Book at aaa.com*   Phone: 958/581-0044
All Year   2P: $170
Location: In Tangolunda Hotel Zone. Blvd Benito Juarez #8 70989. Fax: 958/581-0221. **Facility:** Lavish, built on terraced hillside overlooking ocean. Flamboyant design. Some rooms reached by funicular. Large, attractive suites. Meets AAA guest room security requirements. 135 one-bedroom standard units, some with whirlpools. 2-3 stories, exterior corridors. **Parking:** on-site. **Terms:** 20 day cancellation notice-fee imposed. **Amenities:** safes, hair dryers. *Some:* honor bars. **Pool(s):** 2 outdoor, wading. **Leisure Activities:** steamroom, lighted tennis court, recreation programs, playground, exercise room. **Guest Services:** gift shop, valet laundry, area transportation. **Business Services:** conference facilities, fax. **Cards:** AX, DC, MC, VI.
Resort
Large-scale Hotel
SOME UNITS

HOTEL MEIGAS BINNIGUENDA   Phone: 958/587-0077
All Year   1P: $70-$110   2P: $70-$110   XP: $10
Location: In Santa Cruz Bay area. (Blvd Santa Cruz 201). Fax: 958/587-0284. **Facility:** 165 one-bedroom standard units. 2 stories, interior corridors. *Bath:* shower only. **Parking:** on-site. **Amenities:** safes. **Pool(s):** outdoor, wading. **Guest Services:** area transportation. **Cards:** AX, MC, VI.
Small-scale Hotel

———— WHERE TO DINE ————

——— *The following restaurant has not been evaluated by AAA* ———
but is listed for your information only.

LOS PORTALES   Phone: 958/587-0070
[fyi]   Not evaluated. **Location:** Center of La Crucecita. Bugambilia #603 70989. **Features:** The small and modest restaurant located in plaza of La Crucecita features a variety of tacos, and is a welcome break from the plethora of hotel restaurants.

BUCERIAS, NAYARIT pop. 2,000

———— WHERE TO STAY ————

——— *The following lodging was either not evaluated or did not* ———
meet AAA rating requirements but is listed for your information only.

HOTEL VILLA SERENA   Phone: 329/298-1288
[fyi]   Not evaluated. **Location:** 0.5 km s of central plaza. Calle Lazaro Cardenas #35 63732. Facilities, services, and decor characterize a basic property.

———— WHERE TO DINE ————

CAFE' MAGANA   Lunch: $3-$6   Dinner: $7-$15   Phone: 329/298-1761
Location: Mex 200, 2 blks w at center, just n; 0.5 km s of the plaza. Calle Lazaro Cardenas #40 63732. **Hours:** 11 am-9:30 pm. **Reservations:** accepted. **Features:** Guests can stop by for a drink and watch world-class soccer on TV at the friendly English-style pub. The menu includes barbecued ribs "a la USA," and there is a tasty dinner special every evening. Casual dress; cocktails. **Parking:** on-site.
International

CLAUDIO'S MESON BAY RESTAURANT   Lunch: $4-$7   Dinner: $7-$15   Phone: 329/298-1634
Location: Center. Calle Lazaro Cardenas #17 63732. **Hours:** 11 am-10 pm. **Reservations:** accepted. **Features:** At the beachside eatery, patrons can watch the breakers while dining on fresh seafood. Shrimp, lobster and fresh red snapper are perfectly baked. There's a bar here, too, with giant margaritas that demand quick attention. Casual dress; cocktails. **Parking:** street.
Seafood

ESPRESSIONS CAFE'   Lunch: $5-$6   Dinner: $7-$10   Phone: 329/298-0749
Location: 2 blks w from Mex 200, just e of beach; center. Calle Lazaro Cardenas #50 63732. **Hours:** 11 am-10 pm. Closed: Sun & Mon. **Reservations:** accepted. **Features:** A delightful patio dining area is a feature of this cafe, which is popular with the expatriate community. On the menu is a selection of American-style salads, sandwiches and desserts. Live music is featured Tuesday through Saturday evening. Casual dress.
American
Parking: street.

SANDRINA'S RESTAURANT **Lunch:** $5-$7 **Dinner:** $7-$9 **Phone:** 329/298-0273

International street.

Location: Mex 200, 2 blks e, just n; center. Calle Lazaro Cardenas #33 63732. **Hours:** 10:30 am-10:30 pm. Closed: Tues. **Reservations:** accepted. **Features:** The restaurant prepares US-style sandwiches, salads and burgers, as well as some Greek dishes. Pastries, cakes and pies—including the exceptional Key lime pie—are made on site. This internet cafe allows patrons to check e-mail. Casual dress; cocktails. **Parking:**

COLIMA, COLIMA pop. 123,500

---------- **WHERE TO STAY** ----------

MOTEL LOS CANDILES **Phone:** (312)312-3212

Small-scale Hotel

All Year 2P: $50-$90 XP: $10 F12
Location: 1.5 km ne on Mex 54. Blvd Camino Real #399. Fax: 312/313-1707. **Facility:** 75 one-bedroom standard units. 3 stories, interior/exterior corridors. *Bath:* shower only. **Parking:** on-site. **Pool(s):** outdoor. **Guest Services:** gift shop. **Business Services:** meeting rooms. **Cards:** AX, MC, VI.

IXTAPA, GUERRERO pop. 1,000

---------- **WHERE TO STAY** ----------

ALL INCLUSIVE BARCELO PREMIUM-IXTAPA *Book at aaa.com* **Phone:** (755)555-2000

Large-scale Hotel

All Year [AP] 1P: $138-$176 2P: $230-$280 XP: $30 F17
Location: South end of hotel zone. Blvd Ixtapa S/N 40880 (Apdo Postal 201). Fax: 755/553-2438. **Facility:** 336 one-bedroom standard units. 12 stories, interior corridors. **Parking:** on-site. **Terms:** 3 day cancellation notice-fee imposed. **Amenities:** voice mail, safes, honor bars, hair dryers. **Dining:** Sunset Terrace, see separate listing. **Pool(s):** outdoor, wading. **Leisure Activities:** 3 tennis courts (1 lighted), recreation programs, playground, exercise room, volleyball. *Fee:* massage. **Guest Services:** gift shop, valet laundry. **Business Services:** meeting rooms, PC (fee). **Cards:** AX, DC, MC, VI.

SOME UNITS

COSTA REAL IXTAPA RESORT & SUITES **Phone:** (755)553-1175

Small-scale Hotel

12/21-4/4	1P: $144-$272	2P: $144-$272	XP: $30	F12
4/5-11/30	1P: $131	2P: $131	XP: $30	F12
12/1-12/20	1P: $127	2P: $127	XP: $30	F12

Location: North end of hotel zone. Blvd Ixtapa S/N Lote #5 40880. Fax: 755/553-0790. **Facility:** 154 one-bedroom standard units. 7 stories, interior corridors. **Parking:** on-site. **Terms:** check-in 4 pm, 5 day cancellation notice-fee imposed. **Amenities:** safes, honor bars. **Pool(s):** outdoor, wading. **Leisure Activities:** recreation programs, volleyball. *Fee:* massage. **Guest Services:** gift shop, valet laundry. **Business Services:** meeting rooms. **Cards:** AX, MC, VI.

SOME UNITS

HOTEL FONTAN IXTAPA BEACH RESORT **Phone:** (755)553-1666

Large-scale Hotel

All Year 1P: $116-$160 2P: $130-$170 XP: $20
Location: Center of hotel zone. Blvd Ixtapa S/N 40880. Fax: 755/553-2126. **Facility:** 472 one-bedroom standard units. 8 stories, interior corridors. *Bath:* shower only. **Parking:** on-site. **Terms:** check-in 4 pm, 14 day cancellation notice-fee imposed. **Pool(s):** 2 outdoor, wading. **Leisure Activities:** recreation programs, bicycles, exercise room, volleyball. *Fee:* massage. **Guest Services:** gift shop, valet laundry. **Business Services:** meeting rooms. **Cards:** AX, MC, VI.

SOME UNITS

HOTEL NH KRYSTAL IXTAPA *Book at aaa.com* **Phone:** (755)553-0333

Large-scale Hotel

All Year 1P: $92-$190 2P: $92-$190 XP: $15
Location: North end of hotel zone. Blvd Ixtapa S/N 40880 (Apdo Postal 68). Fax: 755/553-0226. **Facility:** 255 units. 252 one-bedroom standard units. 2 one- and two-bedroom suites, some with kitchens. 11 stories, interior corridors. **Parking:** on-site. **Terms:** 3 day cancellation notice. **Amenities:** honor bars. *Some:* safes, hair dryers. **Dining:** Bogarts, see separate listing. **Pool(s):** outdoor, wading. **Leisure Activities:** recreation programs, playground, exercise room, volleyball. *Fee:* fishing, racquetball court. **Guest Services:** gift shop, valet laundry. **Business Services:** meeting rooms. **Cards:** AX, MC, VI.

SOME UNITS

LAS BRISAS-IXTAPA *Book at aaa.com* **Phone:** (755)553-2121

Large-scale Hotel

| 12/1-1/2 | 1P: $307 | 2P: $307 | XP: $40 |
| 1/3-11/30 | 1P: $218 | 2P: $218 | XP: $40 |

Location: On beach at Playa Vistahermosa. Playa Vistahermosa S/N 40880 (Apdo Postal 97). Fax: 755/553-1091. **Facility:** All rooms at this architecturally rich property feature ocean views and private balconies with hammocks; some rooms have private pools. 416 one-bedroom standard units, some with whirlpools. 12 stories, interior corridors. **Parking:** no self-parking. **Terms:** check-in 4 pm, 3 day cancellation notice-fee imposed. **Amenities:** voice mail, safes, honor bars, hair dryers. **Dining:** 6 restaurants, 7 am-midnight, also, Portofino Ristorante, Restaurant El Mexicano, La Brisa II, see separate listings, entertainment. **Pool(s):** 3 outdoor, wading. **Leisure Activities:** recreation programs, exercise room. *Fee:* 4 lighted tennis courts, massage. **Guest Services:** gift shop, valet laundry. *Fee:* beauty salon. **Business Services:** meeting rooms, business center. **Cards:** AX, DC, MC, VI.
(See color ad opposite title page)

SOME UNITS

PRESIDENTE INTERCONTINENTAL-IXTAPA, AN ALL INCLUSIVE RESORT *Book at aaa.com*   Phone: (755)553-0018

12/20-4/17 [AP]	1P: $355-$425	2P: $355-$425	XP: $60	F6
4/18-11/30 [AP]	1P: $235-$300	2P: $235-$300	XP: $60	F6
12/1-12/19 [AP]	1P: $225-$290	2P: $225-$290	XP: $50	F6

Large-scale Hotel **Location:** Center of hotel zone. Blvd Ixtapa S/N 40880 (Apdo Postal 95). Fax: 755/553-2312. **Facility:** 420 one-bedroom standard units. 3-11 stories, interior/exterior corridors. **Parking:** on-site. **Terms:** 3 day cancellation notice-fee imposed, package plans, $5 service charge. **Amenities:** voice mail. **Pool(s):** 2 outdoor, wading. **Leisure Activities:** sauna, steamroom, 2 lighted tennis courts, recreation programs, exercise room. *Fee:* massage. **Guest Services:** gift shop, valet laundry. *Fee:* beauty salon. **Business Services:** meeting rooms, business center. **Cards:** AX, DC, JC, MC, VI.

SOME UNITS

QUALTON CLUB IXTAPA ALL INCLUSIVE   Phone: (755)552-0080

12/15-4/30 [AP]	1P: $150	2P: $300
12/1-12/14 & 5/1-11/30 [AP]	1P: $120	2P: $240

Resort Motel **Location:** At Playa Linda. Located across from Ixtapa Island. Carr Escenica S/N 40880. Fax: 755/552-0070. **Facility:** All rooms have balcony or terrace, spacious grounds. 150 one-bedroom standard units. 1-2 stories, exterior corridors. *Bath:* shower only. **Parking:** on-site. **Terms:** 3 day cancellation notice. **Amenities:** safes. **Pool(s):** 2 outdoor, wading. **Leisure Activities:** windsurfing, snorkeling, recreation programs, bicycles, exercise room, basketball, volleyball, game room. *Fee:* 2 lighted tennis courts, massage. **Guest Services:** gift shop. **Business Services:** meeting rooms. **Cards:** AX, MC, VI.

SOME UNITS

RADISSON RESORT-IXTAPA *Book at aaa.com*   Phone: (755)553-0003

All Year	1P: $132-$165	2P: $132-$165	XP: $30

Large-scale Hotel **Location:** North end of hotel zone. Blvd Ixtapa S/N Lote #5-A 40880. Fax: 755/553-1555. **Facility:** 275 units. 263 one-bedroom standard units. 12 one-bedroom suites with whirlpools. 13 stories, interior corridors. *Bath:* combo or shower only. **Parking:** on-site. **Terms:** 7 day cancellation notice. **Amenities:** hair dryers. **Pool(s):** outdoor. **Leisure Activities:** sauna, recreation programs, playground, exercise room, basketball, volleyball, game room. **Guest Services:** gift shop, valet laundry. **Business Services:** meeting rooms. **Cards:** AX, DC, MC, VI. *(See color ad p 477)*

SOME UNITS

RIVIERA BEACH RESORT IXTAPA *Book at aaa.com*   Phone: 755/553-1066

12/1-1/2	1P: $150	2P: $150	XP: $30	F12
1/3-3/26	1P: $90	2P: $90	XP: $30	F12
3/27-11/30	1P: $80	2P: $80	XP: $30	F12

Small-scale Hotel **Location:** Center of hotel zone. Blvd Ixtapa S/N 40880 (Apdo Postal 50). Fax: 755/553-0400. **Facility:** Meets AAA guest room security requirements. 173 units. 150 one-bedroom standard units. 17 one- and 6 two-bedroom suites. 11 stories, interior corridors. *Bath:* shower only. **Parking:** on-site. **Terms:** 3 day cancellation notice. **Amenities:** safes, honor bars, hair dryers. **Pool(s):** outdoor, wading. **Leisure Activities:** sauna, whirlpool, recreation programs, exercise room, spa. *Fee:* 2 lighted tennis courts. **Guest Services:** gift shop, valet laundry, beauty salon. **Business Services:** meeting rooms, business center. **Cards:** AX, MC, VI.

SOME UNITS

FEE

───── WHERE TO DINE ─────

BECCOFINO RESTAURANT AND BAR   Lunch: $10-$25   Dinner: $10-$25   Phone: 755/553-1770

Northern Italian **Location:** 1.5 km n of hotel zone, via Blvd Ixtapa; at marina. **Hours:** 8 am-1 & midnight. **Reservations:** suggested. **Features:** A Mediterranean atmosphere pervades the seaside dining room and the beautiful teak wood deck, which perches right on the water. Plentiful seafood is well-prepared in Continental-style dishes. Casual dress; cocktails. **Parking:** on-site. **Cards:** AX, MC, VI.

BOGARTS   Dinner: $20-$30   Phone: 755/553-0333

Continental **Location:** North end of hotel zone; in Hotel NH Krystal Ixtapa. Blvd Ixtapa S/N 40880. **Hours:** 6 pm-11 pm. **Reservations:** suggested. **Features:** Appointments reflect a theme based on the movie "Casablanca," complete with a staff costumed in North African garb. Among creative menu choices are seafood, steaks and several flambeed selections prepared tableside, as well as attractive desserts. Dressy casual; cocktails; entertainment. **Parking:** on-site. **Cards:** AX, MC, VI.

BUCANERO'S RESTAURANT   Lunch: $8-$15   Dinner: $15-$40   Phone: 755/553-0916

International **Location:** 1.5 km n of hotel zone, via Blvd Ixtapa; at marina. **Hours:** 8 am-midnight. **Reservations:** suggested. **Features:** With outdoor dining overlooking the marina, the popular dining spot presents a creative, Italian-based menu. Featured are many preparations of abundant local seafood, such as fresh shrimp and sea bass, as well as pasta dishes. A light luncheon menu also is available. Cocktails. **Parking:** on-site. **Cards:** AX, MC, VI.

CAFE SALSA   Lunch: $8-$20   Dinner: $8-$20   Phone: 755/553-0939

International **Location:** South end of hotel zone; across from Barcelo Hotel. Blvd Ixtapa S/N 40880. **Hours:** 8 am-11 pm. **Features:** This large dining room features covered patio dining and a casual relaxed ambience. The menu is varied and caters to all cravings, offering pizzas, pasta, kebobs and grilled meats and seafoods. Mexican specialties are also featured with quite an extensive fajita list. Come hungry, as portions are hearty and the desserts are tempting. It's also a popular spot for breakfast, within easy walking distance of most hotels in the zone. Casual dress; cocktails. **Parking:** no self-parking. **Cards:** AX, MC, VI.

CARLOS 'N CHARLIE'S

International

Lunch: $8-$14 **Dinner:** $8-$14 **Phone:** 755/553-0085

Location: North end of hotel zone; Posada Real. Blvd Ixtapa S/N 40880. **Hours:** 10 am-midnight. **Features:** In the hotel area along the beach, the lively and busy beach club, which incorporates a bar and restaurant, serves a variety of American and Mexican dishes and scores of popular drinks, including this place's classic margarita. Casual dress; cocktails. **Parking:** on-site. **Cards:** AX, MC, VI.

CASA MORELOS

Mexican

Lunch: $7-$20 **Dinner:** $10-$30 **Phone:** 755/553-0578

Location: Center of hotel zone. Zona Commercial, La Puerta Local 18 40880. **Hours:** 7:30 am-11:30 pm. **Reservations:** accepted. **Features:** Authentic Mexican fare in an open-air, cantina-like setting keeps the tourists and locals coming back. Situated in the shopping area/restaurant row of the hotel zone, this popular eatery attracts diners for breakfast, lunch and dinner with a menu mixing the flavors of Mexico with some of the favorites from back home. Whether it's hot and spicy fajitas, enchiladas or simply broiled steak and seafood, you are sure to be pleased, as they cater to all taste buds here. Casual dress; cocktails. **Parking:** no self-parking. **Cards:** MC, VI.

EL GALEON

International

Lunch: $7-$14 **Dinner:** $7-$14 **Phone:** 755/553-2150

Location: 1.5 km n of hotel zone, via Blvd Ixtapa; at marina. **Hours:** 9 am-midnight. **Reservations:** suggested. **Features:** The distinctive, open-air restaurant resembles a Spanish galleon, parked pierside, and affords a good view of the many yachts and boats housed at the marina. The menu includes pasta, seafood, chicken and beef selections, prepared in the Continental style, as well as some Mexican dishes. Casual dress; cocktails. **Parking:** on-site. **Cards:** AX, MC, VI.

J J'S LOBSTER AND SHRIMP

Steak & Seafood

Lunch: $8-$25 **Dinner:** $8-$25 **Phone:** 755/553-2494

Location: In hotel zone; across from Riviera Beach Resort Ixtapa. Ixtapa Plaza Local 5 40880. **Hours:** 7:30 am-11 pm. **Reservations:** accepted. **Features:** This delightful two-story restaurant features covered open-air dining. The menu features a tempting selection of grilled lobster, fresh jumbo shrimp, steaks and pastas. Many entrees include skilled tableside flambé preparation, creating a romantic tone. At breakfast and lunch expect more casual fare, with tasty pancakes, burgers and sandwiches. Casual dress; cocktails. **Parking:** street. **Cards:** MC, VI.

LA BRISA II

Continental

Dinner: $14-$30 **Phone:** 755/553-2121

Location: On beach at Playa Vistahermosa; in Las Brisas-Ixtapa. Playa Vistahermosa S/N 40880. **Hours:** Open 12/1-4/30 & 11/1-11/30; 6 pm-11:30 pm. **Reservations:** accepted. **Features:** The romantic terrace overlooks the sea below. On the menu are delicious fresh seafood, steaks and pasta. Some items—such as shrimp with garlic and white wine and the mango fruit dessert—are flambéed tableside. Casual dress; cocktails. **Parking:** valet. **Cards:** AX, DC, MC, VI.

LAGUNA RESTAURANT AND AMERICAN BAR

Steak & Seafood

Lunch: $10-$20 **Dinner:** $10-$20 **Phone:** 755/553-1103

Location: In center of hotel zone; adjacent to Senor Frogs. Paseo de Ixtapa S/N 40880. **Hours:** noon-1 am. **Reservations:** accepted. **Features:** This open-air dining room features a display case of meats and fish at the entrance to entice diners. The thatched roof creates a real holiday feel, and the ambience is loud and bustling. Casual dress; cocktails. **Parking:** no self-parking. **Cards:** AX, MC, VI.

LOBSTER HOUSE

Seafood

Lunch: $10-$20 **Dinner:** $10-$30 **Phone:** 755/553-0621

Location: In center of hotel zone. Centro Comercial Galerias Altus (Terraza) 40880. **Hours:** 1 pm-10:30 pm. **Reservations:** accepted. **Features:** This well-established eatery has been keeping diners happy since 1985. Located on the second level, it features a covered open-air setting in a dining room filled with greenery. In addition to the lobster, the menu also specializes in fresh shrimp prepared in a variety of ways, as well as many other seafood, steak and pasta options. It offers a casual, relaxed dining experience. Casual dress; cocktails. **Parking:** no self-parking. **Cards:** MC, VI.

MAMA NORMA AND DEBORAH

American

Lunch: $7-$23 **Dinner:** $7-$23 **Phone:** 755/553-0274

Location: In center of hotel zone; across from Presidente InterContinental-Ixtapa, An All Inclusive Resort. Ixtapa Plaza Local 5 40880. **Hours:** 8 am-11 pm. **Reservations:** accepted. **Features:** A casual covered patio and a menu featuring wholesome home cooked cuisine make this a popular favorite with locals and tourists alike for breakfast, lunch and dinner. Menu highlights include homemade soups, salads and sandwiches, as well as some Mexican specialties and grilled items such as chicken, steak and seafood. Desserts are homemade and tasty; the chocolate cake is just like mom's. Casual dress; cocktails. **Parking:** street.

PORTOFINO RISTORANTE

Italian

Dinner: $15-$33 **Phone:** 755/553-2121

Location: On beach at Playa Vistahermosa; in Las Brisas-Ixtapa. Playa Vistahermosa S/N 40880. **Hours:** 6 pm-midnight; open every other night. **Reservations:** suggested. **Features:** Part of the Las Brisas Beach Resort, the formal, fine dining restaurant is characterized by an elegant dining room, tuxedoed maitre d' and imaginatively prepared Italian cuisine. Dressy casual; cocktails. **Parking:** on-site and valet. **Cards:** AX, DC, MC, VI.

RAFFAELLO RISTORANTE

Italian

Dinner: $6-$18 **Phone:** 755/553-0092

Location: In the hotel zone. Paseo de Ixtapa #6 40880. **Hours:** 5 pm-midnight. **Features:** This popular spot features casual sidewalk cafe dining and an extensive menu offering casual Italian fare. In addition to the tasty pizzas and pastas, grilled items such as steak, chicken and seafood are also offered. The location is great: within easy walking distance of the major hotels and in the heart of the shopping area. Casual dress; cocktails. **Parking:** no self-parking. **Cards:** AX, MC, VI.

RESTAURANT EL MEXICANO

▼▼▼ ▼▼▼

Mexican

Dinner: $13-$28   **Phone:** 755/553-2121

Location: On beach at Playa Vistahermosa; in Las Brisas-Ixtapa. Playa Vistahermosa S/N 40880. **Hours:** 7 pm-midnight; open every other night. **Reservations:** required. **Features:** Within Las Brisas Beach Resort, the moderately upscale spot prepares steaks, chicken and seafood in a traditional Mexican style. The atmosphere is reflective of a 16th-century colonial hacienda. Casual dress; cocktails. **Parking:** valet.
Cards: AX, DC, MC, VI.

SOLEIADO

▼▼▼ ◆◆◆

Italian

Lunch: $7-$10   **Dinner:** $7-$22   **Phone:** 755/553-2101

Location: North end of hotel zone; across from Radisson Resort-Ixtapa. Plaza Ambiente Locales 14,15 Paseo Ixtapa 40880. **Hours:** 8 am-10:30 pm. **Reservations:** accepted. **Features:** Diners enjoy the pleasant stroll to this lovely open air cafe, located in the north end of the hotel zone. The cheery ambience is peaceful at breakfast and lunch; at night it takes on a more elegant feel with the fairy-lit bushes and candlelit tables. The menu caters to all taste buds, featuring a good selection of fine Italian fare, in addition to steaks, seafood and Mediterranean-influenced cuisine. Casual dress; cocktails. **Parking:** street. **Cards:** AX, MC, VI.

SUNSET TERRACE

▼▼▼ ▼▼▼

Steak & Seafood

Dinner: $18-$35   **Phone:** 755/555-2000

Location: South end of hotel zone; in All Inclusive Barcelo Premium-Ixtapa. Blvd Ixtapa S/N 40880. **Hours:** Open 12/15-4/18; 7 pm-10:30 pm. Closed: 1/1; also Fri & Sat. **Reservations:** required. **Features:** Patrons of the seaside restaurant can dine under the stars. Grilled food, prepared artfully, is the specialty. Casual dress; cocktails. **Parking:** on-site. **Cards:** AX, DC, MC, VI.

VILLA DE LA SELVA

▼▼▼ ◆◆◆

Continental

Dinner: $25-$30   **Phone:** 755/553-0362

Location: On beach at Playa Vistahermosa; next to Las Brisas-Ixtapa. Paseo de la Roca Lote D 40880. **Hours:** Open 12/1-8/31 & 10/1-11/30; 6 pm-1 am. **Reservations:** suggested. **Features:** Soft music, formal service and a breathtaking, cliffside view of the ocean add to the inviting atmosphere of this moderately upscale spot, a favorite with knowledgeable tourists. The menu centers on well-prepared Continental and Mexican cuisine. Dressy casual; cocktails. **Parking:** on-site. **Cards:** AX, MC, VI.

MANZANILLO, COLIMA pop. 100,200

——— **WHERE TO STAY** ———

EL CAREYES BEACH RESORT

▼▼▼ ▼▼▼

Resort
Small-scale Hotel

All Year   1P: $270-$559   2P: $270-$559   XP: $50   **Phone:** 315/351-0000
Location: KM 53.5, Mex 200, 2 km w, follow signs. KM 53.5 Carr Barra de Navidad 48970. Fax: 315/351-0100. **Facility:** A scenic beach, a pool, an open-air fine-dining restaurant and luxury rooms with private hot tubs all help make this secluded resort a standout. 51 units. 29 one-bedroom standard units, some with whirlpools. 12 one- and 7 two-bedroom suites, some with efficiencies and/or whirlpools. 3 vacation homes with whirlpools. 3 stories (no elevator), interior/exterior corridors. **Bath:** combo or shower only. **Parking:** on-site. **Amenities:** video library, safes, honor bars, hair dryers. **Pool(s):** heated outdoor. **Leisure Activities:** saunas, whirlpools, steamrooms, paddleboats, miniature golf, 2 lighted tennis courts, bicycles, hiking trails, exercise room, spa. *Fee:* boats, snorkeling, fishing. **Guest Services:** gift shop, valet laundry. **Business Services:** meeting rooms. **Cards:** AX, MC, VI.

SOME UNITS

GRAND BAY HOTEL-ISLA NAVIDAD RESORT-A
WYNDHAM LUXURY RESORT   *Book at aaa.com*

ⒶⒶⒶ

▼▼▼ ◆◆◆

Resort
Large-scale Hotel

Phone: (315)355-5050

12/18-1/2	1P: $285-$370	2P: $285-$370	XP: $50	F17
1/3-4/22	1P: $250-$300	2P: $250-$300	XP: $50	F17
12/1-12/17	1P: $205-$255	2P: $205-$255	XP: $25	F17
4/23-11/30	1P: $199-$249	2P: $199-$249	XP: $50	F17

Location: Mex 200, 6 km n of Cihuatlan, 18 km w. Circuito de los Marinos S/N 28830 (Apdo Postal 20, BARRA DE NAVIDAD, JA, 48987). Fax: 315/355-6071. **Facility:** An extremely impressive, luxurious resort hotel complex that features golf, beach and spa facilities, it also offers excellent, refined service. 198 units. 158 one-bedroom standard units. 39 one- and 1 three-bedroom suites, some with whirlpools. 10 stories, interior/exterior corridors. **Parking:** valet. **Terms:** cancellation fee imposed, $15 service charge. **Amenities:** voice mail, safes, honor bars, hair dryers. **Dining:** 2 restaurants, 7 am-midnight, cocktails, also, Antonio's, see separate listing. **Pool(s):** 2 outdoor, heated outdoor, wading. **Leisure Activities:** whirlpools, waterslide, jogging, exercise room, volleyball. *Fee:* boats, sailboats, windsurfing, marina, scuba diving, snorkeling, fishing, golf-27 holes, 3 lighted tennis courts, bicycles, massage. **Guest Services:** gift shop, valet laundry, area transportation (fee)-Manzanillo area. **Business Services:** conference facilities, business center. **Cards:** AX, MC, VI. *(See color ad p 436)*

SOME UNITS

HOTEL LA POSADA

▼▼▼ ▼▼▼

Motel

Phone: (314)333-1899

12/1-5/1 [BP]	1P: $58	2P: $78	XP: $20
5/2-11/30 [BP]	1P: $38	2P: $58	XP: $20

Location: 3 km off Mex 200; in Las Brisas; on Playa Azul. Lazaro Cardenas 201 28210 (Apdo Postal 135, 28200). Fax: 314/333-6690. **Facility:** Meets AAA guest room security requirements. 23 one-bedroom standard units. 1-2 stories, exterior corridors. **Bath:** shower only. **Parking:** on-site. **Terms:** 10 day cancellation notice. **Pool(s):** outdoor. **Guest Services:** coin laundry. **Cards:** MC, VI.

SOME UNITS

KARMINA PALACE ALL SUITE, ALL INCLUSIVE   *Book at aaa.com*

ⒶⒶⒶ

▼▼▼ ◆◆◆

Resort
Large-scale Hotel

Phone: 314/334-1313

All Year [AP]   1P: $215-$250   2P: $350-$430   XP: $160
Location: On Mex 200, Peninsula de Santiago. Ave Vistahermosa #13 28200. Fax: 314/334-1108. **Facility:** An all-suites resort with seven connected pools that eventually lead down to a private sheltered lagoon and lots of ocean activities. 324 units. 226 one-bedroom standard units. 98 one-bedroom suites. 7 stories, interior corridors. **Parking:** on-site and valet. **Amenities:** voice mail, safes, irons, hair dryers. **Dining:** 3 restaurants, 7 am-11 pm, cocktails, entertainment. **Pool(s):** 7 outdoor, wading. **Leisure Activities:** steamroom, waterslide, snorkeling, kayaks, recreation programs, bicycles, playground, exercise room, spa, volleyball. *Fee:* scuba diving, golf-18 holes, game room. **Guest Services:** gift shop, valet laundry. **Business Services:** meeting rooms, business center. **Cards:** AX, MC, VI.

SOME UNITS

LAS ALAMANDAS

Phone: 322/285-5500

12/1-5/31 & 10/1-11/30 [ECP]	1P: $430-$1590	2P: $430-$1590
6/1-9/30 [ECP]	1P: $320-$1330	2P: $320-$1330

Small-scale Hotel **Location:** Mex 200, KM 83.5; entry to property, follow signs. KM 83.5 Carr Barra de Navidad 48980 (PO Box 201, SAN PATRICIO MELAQUE, JA). Fax: 322/285-5027. **Facility:** Set on 1,500 acres of a private reserve, this exclusive resort feature a private airstrip and three beaches. 14 units. 12 one-bedroom standard units. 2 one-bedroom suites. 1-2 stories, exterior corridors. **Parking:** on-site. **Terms:** office hours 8 am-10 pm. check-in 4 pm, 2 night minimum stay, 30 day cancellation notice, [AP] meal plan available. **Amenities:** honor bars, hair dryers. **Pool(s):** outdoor. **Leisure Activities:** snorkeling, exercise room, horseshoes. **Guest Services:** gift shop, coin laundry. **Cards:** AX, MC, VI.

FEE

LAS HADAS GOLF RESORT & MARINA   *Book at aaa.com*

Phone: 314/331-0101

All Year [BP]	2P: $150-$240	XP: $40 F12

Location: 11.5 km nw on Mex 200, 2.5 km s on Peninsula Santiago. Ave Vistahermosa S/N 28867. Fax: 314/331-0123. **Facility:** Arabesque buildings set in a private cove at the base of rugged hills form a striking sight at this property complete with beach and marina. 234 units. 230 one-bedroom standard units. 1 one- and 3 two-bedroom suites ($300-$900), some with whirlpools. 2-5 stories, interior/exterior corridors. *Bath:* combo or shower only. **Parking:** on-site and valet. **Terms:** 7 day cancellation notice-fee imposed. **Amenities:** voice mail, safes, honor bars. *Some:* irons, hair dryers. *Dining:* 3 restaurants, 7 am-midnight, cocktails, also, Restaurant Legazpi, Los Delfines, see separate listings, entertainment. **Pool(s):** 2 outdoor, wading. **Leisure Activities:** kayaking, recreation programs, exercise room, volleyball. *Fee:* sailboats, marina, waterskiing, scuba diving, snorkeling, fishing, golf-18 holes, 10 lighted tennis courts, massage. **Guest Services:** gift shop, valet and coin laundry, area transportation-Casa club & golf course. **Business Services:** meeting rooms. *Fee:* PC, fax. **Cards:** AX, CB, DC, DS, MC, VI.

SOME UNITS

MESON DONA PAZ

Phone: 315/355-6441

All Year	1P: $200-$500	2P: $200-$520 XP: $50

Country Inn **Location:** Mex 200, 6 km n of Cihuatlan, 18 km w on Circuito de los Marinos, then just s. Rinconada del Capitan S/N 28830. Fax: 315/355-6155. **Facility:** The former luxury residence of a wealthy family, this inn has manicured grounds, a beach and a fine-dining restaurant. 13 units. 11 one-bedroom standard units. 2 one-bedroom suites, some with whirlpools. 3 stories, exterior corridors. **Parking:** on-site. **Amenities:** dual phone lines, safes, honor bars, hair dryers. **Pool(s):** outdoor, wading. **Leisure Activities:** whirlpool, paddleboats, exercise room. *Fee:* fishing, lighted tennis court, massage. **Guest Services:** valet laundry, area transportation (fee). **Business Services:** meeting rooms. **Cards:** AX, MC, VI.

SOME UNITS

FEE

SIERRA HOTEL MANZANILLO

Phone: (314)333-2000

All Year [AP]   2P: $185-$250   XP: $80   F12

Resort
Large-scale Hotel

Location: 11.5 km nw on Mex 200, 2.5 km s on Peninsula Santiago. Ave de La Audencia #1 28860 (Apdo Postal 777, 28200). Fax: 314/333-2272. **Facility:** Frequented by tourists from the United States and Canada, this resort has lively entertainment as well as fine beaches. 332 units. 330 one-bedroom standard units. 2 one-bedroom suites. 19 stories, interior corridors. **Parking:** on-site. **Terms:** 3 day cancellation notice. **Amenities:** Some: hair dryers. **Pool(s):** outdoor, wading. **Leisure Activities:** sauna, whirlpool, steamroom, fishing, 4 lighted tennis courts, exercise room, spa. Fee: boats, windsurfing, waterskiing, golf-18 holes. **Guest Services:** gift shop, valet laundry. **Business Services:** meeting rooms. **Cards:** AX, MC, VI.

SOME UNITS

The following lodging was either not evaluated or did not meet AAA rating requirements but is listed for your information only.

HOTELITO DESCONOCIDO

Phone: 322/222-2526

[fyi]

Not evaluated. **Location:** S from Puerto Vallarta, Mex 200, KM 133.5, Cruz de Loretto, 11 km. Facilities, services, and decor characterize a mid-range property.

——— WHERE TO DINE ———

ANTONIO'S

Dinner: $15-$35   **Phone:** 314/331-0500

Continental

Location: Mex 200, 6 km n of Cihuatlan, 18 km w; in Grand Bay Hotel-Isla Navidad Resort-A Wyndham Luxu. Circuito de los Marinos S/N 28830. **Hours:** 7 pm-midnight. **Reservations:** suggested. **Features:** The fine dining restaurant of the hotel, Antonio's features several tableside preparations of salad, delectable seafood dishes and desserts such as cherries jubilee. It's appropriate that in this hacienda-style setting, the bar would feature over 200 tequilas from which to choose. Dressy casual; cocktails. **Parking:** valet. **Cards:** AX, MC, VI.

LA TOSCANA AKA "WILLY'S"

Dinner: $9-$20   **Phone:** 314/333-2515

Seafood

Location: 3 km off Mex 200, on Playa Azul. Bulevar Miguel de la Madrid KM 7 28218. **Hours:** 7 pm-11:30 pm. **Reservations:** accepted. **Features:** While the name has changed from Willy's, the food and staff are still the same. Diners walk past the open outdoor kitchen as they enter the restaurant and then wait at their table for other guests to finish ordering so they can have the dry erase board brought over that proclaims the night's dining selection of Mexican and seafood choices. Most seating is on the outdoor patio where a live band plays and the sound of crashing waves can be heard. Casual dress; cocktails. **Parking:** on-site. **Cards:** MC, VI.

LOS DELFINES

Lunch: $10-$35   **Dinner:** $10-$35   **Phone:** 314/331-0101

Seafood

Location: 11.5 km nw on Mex 200, 2.5 km s on Peninsula Santiago; in Las Hadas Golf Resort & Marina. Ave Vistahermosa S/N 28867. **Hours:** noon-midnight. **Reservations:** suggested. **Features:** A stunning oceanfront setting perfectly complements the fine menu of freshly prepared seafood. The covered, open-air dining room features a cool ocean breeze and a relaxed, romantic ambience. Casual dress; cocktails. **Parking:** on-site (fee). **Cards:** AX, CB, DC, MC, VI.

RESTAURANT LEGAZPI

Dinner: $10-$35   **Phone:** 314/331-0101

Continental

CB, DC, DS, MC, VI.

Location: 11.5 km nw on Mex 200, 2.5 km s on Peninsula Santiago; in Las Hadas Golf Resort & Marina. Ave Vistahermosa S/N 28867. **Hours:** 6 pm-midnight. Closed: Sun. **Reservations:** suggested. **Features:** A new fine dining restaurant at the hotel that shows promise. An extensive Continental menu, as well as local favorites, are offered in an opulent setting. Dressy casual; cocktails. **Parking:** on-site and valet. **Cards:** AX,

---

RESTAURANT L'RECIF

Dinner: $9-$23   **Phone:** 314/335-0900

International

Location: On Peninsula de Juluapan; in Vida del Mar Complex. Cerro del Cenicero S/N 28860. **Hours:** Open 12/1-4/30; 5 pm-11 pm. **Reservations:** suggested. **Features:** A must try classic, this treasure is a ways out of town so if arriving by taxi, ask the driver to wait while you dine. When making your reservation, the best seats are on the outer edge of a stone terrace where flood lights illuminate the crashing waves and rock outcropping far below while softly lit palm fronds dance overhead with the stars. The International menu is well-rounded with items like chicken breast in mango sauce, mahi mahi with dill sauce, beef brochette and tamarindo shrimp. Casual dress; cocktails. **Parking:** on-site. **Cards:** MC, VI.

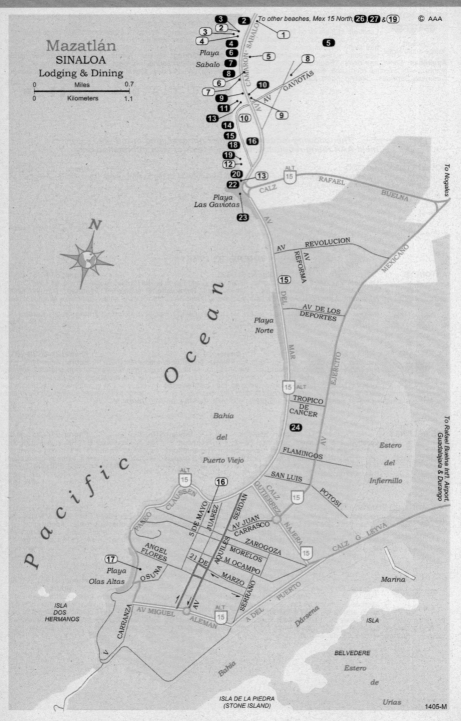

Mazatlán
SINALOA
Lodging & Dining

Miles 0   0.7
Kilometers 0   1.1

To other beaches, Mex 15 North, **26** **27** & **19**

© AAA

Playa
Sabalo

Playa
Las Gaviotas

Pacific Ocean

Bahía
del
Puerto Viejo

Playa
Norte

AV REVOLUCION

AV REFORMA

AV DE LOS
DEPORTES

TROPICO
DE
CANCER

FLAMINGOS

SAN LUIS

RAFAEL
BUELNA

MEXICANO

EJERCITO

Estero
del
Infiernillo

To Nogales

To Rafael Buelna Intl. Airport,
Guadalajara & Durango

Playa
Olas Altas

ISLA
DOS
HERMANOS

ANGEL
FLORES

21 DE
MARZO

5 DE MAYO
JUAREZ
AQUILES
SERDAN
AV JUAN
CARRASCO
ZAROGOZA
MORELOS
M OCAMPO
SERRANO

OSUNA
CARRANZA

AV MIGUEL
ALEMAN

CLAUSSEN
PASEO

CALZ
GUTIERREZ
NAJERA
A DEL PUERTO

Marina

ISLA

BELVEDERE

Dársena

Estero

de

Urías

Bahía

ISLA DE LA PIEDRA
(STONE ISLAND)

1405-M

Mazatlan

This index helps you "spot" where approved accommodations and restaurants are located on the corresponding detailed maps. Lodging rate ranges are for comparison only and show the property's high season; rates are per night, unless only weekly (W) rates are available. Restaurant rate range is for dinner, unless only lunch (L) is served. Turn to the listing page for more detailed rate information and consult display ads for special promotions.

Spotter/Map Page Number	OA	MAZATLAN - Lodgings	Diamond Rating	Rate Range High Season	Listing Page
2 / p. 438		Faro Mazatlan All Inclusive Beach Resort	▽▽▽	$170-$340	440
3 / p. 438		Hotel Pueblo Bonito	▽▽▽	$125-$195	441
4 / p. 438		All Inclusive Luna Palace	▽▽▽	$100-$160	440
5 / p. 438		Pueblo Bonito at Emerald Bay	▽▽▽	$225-$375	442
6 / p. 438		All Inclusive Oceano Palace	▽▽	$85-$100	440
7 / p. 438		Fiesta Inn - see color ad card insert	▽▽▽	$100-$135	440
8 / p. 438	AAA	**Holiday Inn SunSpree Resort Mazatlan - see color ad p 441**	▽ ▽▽	$120-$140	441
9 / p. 438		El Cid El Moro Beach Hotel	▽▽▽	$122-$262	440
10 / p. 438		El Cid Granada Country Club	▽▽	$62-$190	440
11 / p. 438		Hotel Costa de Oro	▽▽▽	$130	441
13 / p. 438		El Cid Castilla Beach Hotel	▽▽▽	$77-$283	440
14 / p. 438		Motel Marley	▽▽	$80-$95	442
15 / p. 438		Suites Lindamar	▽▽	$80-$95	442
16 / p. 438		Azteca Inn	▽▽	$50-$70	440
18 / p. 438		Motel Los Arcos	▽	$90-$110	442
19 / p. 438		Hotel Suites Las Flores	▽▽	$90-$135	442
20 / p. 438		Hotel Playa Mazatlan	▽▽▽	$93-$111	441
22 / p. 438		Los Sabalos Resort Hotel	▽▽▽	$90-$130	442
23 / p. 438		Riviera Beach Resort Mazatlan	▽▽▽	$130-$180	442
24 / p. 438		Hotel Aguamarina-Mazatlan	▽▽	$65-$90	441
26 / p. 438	AAA	**Villas El Rancho**	▽▽	$110-$230	443
27 / p. 438		Marina El Cid Hotel & Yacht Club	▽▽▽	$130-$250	442
		MAZATLAN - Restaurants			
① / p. 438		Sr Pepper	▽▽▽	$20-$35	444
② / p. 438		Angelo's Restaurant	▽▽▽	$20-$35	443
③ / p. 438		La Costa Marinera	▽▽	$12-$25	443
④ / p. 438		The Place	▽	$8-$20	443
⑤ / p. 438		Villa Italia	▽▽	$11-$16	444
⑥ / p. 438		El Parador Espanol	▽▽▽	$15-$30	443
⑦ / p. 438		Carlos & Lucia's Restaurant Bar & Grill	▽▽	$7-$16	443
⑧ / p. 438		Restaurant Casa Loma	▽▽	$15-$22	443
⑨ / p. 438		Tequila's Sports Bar & Grill	▽▽	$5-$12	444
⑩ / p. 438		Blue Cactus	▽▽	$12-$25	443
⑫ / p. 438		Terraza Playa	▽▽	$8-$17	444
⑬ / p. 438		Vittore	▽▽▽	$10-$20	444
⑮ / p. 438		Senor Frog's Mazatlan	▽▽	$8-$16	444
⑯ / p. 438		Restaurant Mamucas	▽▽	$6-$18	443
⑰ / p. 438		El Shrimp Bucket	▽▽	$8-$20	443
⑲ / p. 438		Restaurante La Marina	▽▽▽	$12-$20	443

MAZATLAN, SINALOA pop. 335,900 (See map and index starting on p. 438)

——— WHERE TO STAY ———

ALL INCLUSIVE LUNA PALACE
Phone: (669)914-6299 **4**
All Year [AP]   1P: $100-$135   2P: $150-$160   XP: $30
Resort
Large-scale Hotel
Location: 12 km nw. Ave Camaron Sabalo S/N 82100 (Apdo Postal 971). Fax: 669/913-9666. **Facility:** This property is on attractive grounds with secure parking; some rooms include a balcony with ocean views, and all rooms have an efficiency kitchen. 71 units. 47 one-bedroom standard units with efficiencies (no utensils). 24 one-bedroom suites with efficiencies (utensils extra charge). 8 stories, exterior corridors. **Parking:** on-site. **Amenities:** safes, hair dryers. **Pool(s):** heated outdoor, wading. **Guest Services:** valet laundry. **Business Services:** meeting rooms, fax (fee). **Cards:** AX, MC, VI.

ALL INCLUSIVE OCEANO PALACE
Phone: (669)913-0666 **6**
All Year [AP]   1P: $85   2P: $100   XP: $40
Resort
Large-scale Hotel
Location: 12 km nw. Ave Camaron Sabalo S/N 82100 (Apdo Postal 971). Fax: 669/913-9666. **Facility:** Many rooms with ocean view and balcony. 200 one-bedroom standard units. 6 stories, interior corridors. *Bath:* combo or shower only. **Parking:** on-site. **Amenities:** safes (fee). **Pool(s):** outdoor, wading. **Guest Services:** gift shop, valet laundry. **Business Services:** meeting rooms, fax (fee). **Cards:** AX, MC, VI.
SOME UNITS

AZTECA INN   *Book at aaa.com*
Phone: (669)913-4477 **16**
All Year   2P: $50-$70   XP: $5   F12
Small-scale Hotel
Location: 7.3 km nw. Ave Playa Gaviotas #307 82110 (Apdo Postal 841). Fax: 669/913-7476. **Facility:** 74 one-bedroom standard units. 3 stories (no elevator), exterior corridors. *Bath:* shower only. **Parking:** on-site. **Terms:** 5 day cancellation notice. **Pool(s):** small heated outdoor. **Leisure Activities:** whirlpool. **Guest Services:** valet laundry. **Business Services:** fax (fee). **Cards:** AX, MC, VI.

EL CID CASTILLA BEACH HOTEL   *Book at aaa.com*
Phone: 669-913-3333 **13**
All Year   1P: $77-$283   2P: $77-$283   XP: $26
Resort
Large-scale Hotel
Location: In Camaron Sabalo Hotel Zone. Ave Camaron Sabalo S/N 82110. Fax: 669/914-1311. **Facility:** A high-rise with a big lobby and ample public areas, this large mid-level hotel is part of the massive El Cid Resort complex. 600 one-bedroom standard units. 1-17 stories, interior corridors. **Parking:** on-site and valet. **Amenities:** hair dryers. **Pool(s):** outdoor. **Leisure Activities:** sauna, whirlpool, golf-27 holes, 9 tennis courts (5 lighted), recreation programs, exercise room, spa, basketball, volleyball. **Business Services:** conference facilities, business center. **Cards:** AX, MC, VI.

EL CID EL MORO BEACH HOTEL   *Book at aaa.com*
Phone: 669-913-3333 **9**
All Year   1P: $122-$262   2P: $122-$262   XP: $34
Resort
Large-scale Hotel
Location: 8.7 km nw; in Camaron Sabalo Hotel Zone. Ave Camaron Sabalo S/N 82110. Fax: 669/914-1311. **Facility:** Next to El Cid Castilla Beach Hotel, this impressive tower property has a mall with fine shops, as well as a beach, swimming pools and restaurants. 390 units. 40 one-bedroom standard units. 350 one-bedroom suites with kitchens. 25 stories, interior corridors. **Parking:** on-site. **Amenities:** safes, hair dryers. **Pool(s):** 2 outdoor. **Leisure Activities:** whirlpool, golf-27 holes, 9 tennis courts (5 lighted), recreation programs, exercise room, spa, basketball, volleyball. **Guest Services:** gift shop, valet laundry. **Business Services:** conference facilities, business center. **Cards:** AX, MC, VI.
SOME UNITS

EL CID GRANADA COUNTRY CLUB   *Book at aaa.com*
Phone: 669-913-3333 **10**
All Year   1P: $62-$190   2P: $62-$190   XP: $22
Resort
Small-scale Hotel
Location: 8.7 km nw; in Camaron Sabalo Hotel Zone; across from El Moro Tower. Ave Camaron Sabalo S/N 82110. Fax: 669/914-1311. **Facility:** Next to a golf course and across the street from the beach, the property offers modest guest units designed to accommodate families. 120 units. 36 one-bedroom standard units with efficiencies. 84 one-bedroom suites with efficiencies. 3 stories, interior corridors. *Bath:* tub only. **Parking:** on-site and valet. **Amenities:** safes. **Pool(s):** outdoor. **Leisure Activities:** sauna, whirlpool, golf-27 holes, 9 tennis courts (5 lighted), exercise room, spa. **Guest Services:** valet laundry. **Cards:** AX, MC, VI.

FARO MAZATLAN ALL INCLUSIVE BEACH RESORT   *Book at aaa.com*
Phone: (669)913-1111 **2**
All Year [AP]   1P: $170   2P: $340   XP: $35
Resort
Large-scale Hotel
Location: 13 km nw; on north end of Zona Hotelera. Punta del Sabalo S/N 82110 (Apdo Postal 538). Fax: 669/916-5144. **Facility:** On promontory. Some rooms with oceanview. 165 one-bedroom standard units. 4 stories, interior corridors. **Parking:** on-site. **Terms:** 7 day cancellation notice. **Amenities:** honor bars. **Pool(s):** outdoor. **Leisure Activities:** 2 tennis courts, recreation programs, exercise room, basketball, volleyball. **Fee:** fishing. **Guest Services:** gift shop, valet laundry. **Business Services:** meeting rooms. **Fee:** PC, fax. **Cards:** AX, JC, MC, VI.
SOME UNITS

FIESTA INN   *Book at aaa.com*
Phone: (669)989-0100 **7**
All Year   1P: $100-$135   2P: $100-$135   XP: $15   F12
Resort
Small-scale Hotel
Location: 10 km nw. Ave Camaron Sabalo 1927 82110. Fax: 669/989-0130. **Facility:** Featuring a beach and attractive public areas, this property offers very good-size, well-appointed rooms, many with ocean views and balconies. 117 one-bedroom standard units. 2-9 stories, interior corridors. **Parking:** on-site. **Terms:** [AP] meal plan available. **Amenities:** voice mail, irons, hair dryers. **Pool(s):** heated outdoor, wading. **Leisure Activities:** fishing, exercise room. **Fee:** sailboats, charter fishing. **Guest Services:** gift shop, valet laundry. **Business Services:** meeting rooms, business center. **Cards:** AX, MC, VI. *(See color ad card insert)*
SOME UNITS

(See map and index starting on p. 438)

HOLIDAY INN SUNSPREE RESORT MAZATLAN   *Book at aaa.com*   Phone: (669)913-2222   **8**
All Year   1P: $120-$140   2P: $120-$140   XP: $10   F12
Location: 9.2 km nw. Ave Camaron Sabalo 696 82100. Fax: 669/914-1287. **Facility:** 190 units. 161 one-bedroom standard units, some with efficiencies. 29 one-bedroom suites ($140-$180) with efficiencies. 6 stories, interior corridors. **Terms:** 4 day cancellation notice. **Pool(s):** outdoor, wading.
Large-scale Hotel **Amenities:** irons, hair dryers. **Dining:** 2 restaurants, 7 am-10:30 pm, cocktails. **Guest Services:** gift shop, valet and coin laundry. **Business Services:** meeting rooms, business center. **Cards:** AX, MC, VI.
(See color ad below)

SOME UNITS

HOTEL AGUAMARINA-MAZATLAN   *Book at aaa.com*   Phone: (669)981-7080   **24**
All Year   2P: $65-$90   XP: $12   F12
Location: 3.3 km nw. Ave del Mar 110 82000. Fax: 669/982-4624. **Facility:** 112 units. 104 one-bedroom
Small-scale Hotel standard units. 8 one-bedroom suites ($117) with efficiencies. 3 stories (no elevator), interior/exterior corridors. *Bath:* shower only. **Parking:** on-site. **Terms:** 3 day cancellation notice-fee imposed.
Amenities: *Some:* hair dryers. **Pool(s):** heated outdoor. **Guest Services:** valet laundry. **Business Services:** meeting rooms;
PC. **Cards:** AX, MC, VI.

SOME UNITS

HOTEL COSTA DE ORO   *Book at aaa.com*   Phone: 669/913-5344   **11**
All Year   1P: $130   2P: $130   XP: $10   F12
Location: 8.8 km nw. Calz Camaron Sabalo #710 82110 (Apdo Postal 130). Fax: 669/914-4209. **Facility:** On beach; some rooms with balcony. 290 units. 285 one- and 5 two-bedroom standard units, some with
Resort **Large-scale Hotel** efficiencies. 3-10 stories, exterior corridors. *Bath:* shower only. **Parking:** on-site. **Terms:** 3 day cancellation notice. **Pool(s):** outdoor, wading. **Leisure Activities:** whirlpool. *Fee:* scuba diving, snorkeling, fishing, 3 tennis courts. **Guest Services:** gift shop, valet laundry. **Business Services:** meeting rooms, PC (fee). **Cards:** AX, DS, MC, VI.

SOME UNITS

HOTEL PLAYA MAZATLAN   Phone: (669)989-0555   **20**
12/1-4/5   2P: $93-$111   XP: $10   F12
4/6-11/30   2P: $83-$94   XP: $10   F12
Location: 7.3 km nw; on Las Gaviotas Beach. Ave Playa Gaviotas #202 82110 (Apdo Postal 207).
Resort **Large-scale Hotel** Fax: 669/916-5125. **Facility:** Well-appointed rooms, many with ocean view. Balcony or patio. Very attractive grounds, beach and restaurant facilities. 413 units. 410 one-bedroom standard units. 3 one-bedroom suites. 3-5 stories, interior/exterior corridors. *Bath:* shower only. **Parking:** on-site. **Terms:** 7 day cancellation notice-fee imposed. **Amenities:** hair dryers. **Dining:** Terraza Playa, see separate listing. **Pool(s):** 3 outdoor, wading. **Leisure Activities:** whirlpools, recreation programs, exercise room, volleyball. *Fee:* charter fishing. **Guest Services:** gift shop, valet laundry. *Fee:* beauty salon. **Business Services:** meeting rooms, business center. **Cards:** AX, MC, VI.

SOME UNITS

HOTEL PUEBLO BONITO   Phone: (669)989-8900   **3**
All Year   2P: $125-$195   XP: $20   F18
Location: 12.5 km nw. Ave Camaron Sabalo 2121 82110 (Apdo Postal 6). Fax: 669/914-1723. **Facility:** Beach-view balconies and efficiency kitchens are features of some rooms at this well-maintained facility. 247 units. 149
Resort **Large-scale Hotel** one-bedroom standard units with efficiencies. 98 one-bedroom suites with efficiencies. 4-5 stories, exterior corridors. **Parking:** on-site. **Terms:** check-in 4 pm. **Amenities:** voice mail, irons, hair dryers.
Dining: Angelo's Restaurant, see separate listing. **Pool(s):** 2 heated outdoor, 2 wading. **Leisure Activities:** whirlpool, recreation programs, exercise room, volleyball. *Fee:* massage. **Guest Services:** gift shop, valet laundry. **Business Services:** meeting rooms. *Fee:* PC, fax. **Cards:** AX, MC, VI.

(See map and index starting on p. 438)

HOTEL SUITES LAS FLORES — *Book at aaa.com* — Phone: (669)913-5100 [19]

Resort
Large-scale Hotel

All Year — 1P: $90 — 2P: $135 — XP: $10 — F12
Location: 7.3 km nw; on Las Gaviotas Beach. Ave Playa Gaviotas 212 82110 (Apdo Postal 583). Fax: 669/914-3422. **Facility:** Most rooms with balcony and ocean view. 119 units. 15 one-room standard units. 104 one-bedroom suites ($125-$155) with efficiencies. 12 stories, interior/exterior corridors. **Bath:** combo or shower only. **Parking:** on-site. **Terms:** check-in 4 pm, 3 day cancellation notice. **Pool(s):** outdoor. **Guest Services:** gift shop, valet laundry. **Business Services:** PC, fax (fee). **Cards:** AX, MC, VI.

SOME UNITS

LOS SABALOS RESORT HOTEL — Phone: (669)983-5409 [22]

Resort
Large-scale Hotel

All Year — 2P: $90-$130 — XP: $10 — F12
Location: 7 km nw; on Las Gaviotas Beach. Ave Playa Gaviotas #100 82110 (Apdo Postal 944). Fax: 669/983-8156. **Facility:** This mid-level Mexican hotel features well-tended grounds, a swimming pool and a beach-view restaurant. 200 units. 150 one- and 30 two-bedroom standard units. 20 one-bedroom suites. 8 stories, exterior corridors. **Bath:** combo or shower only. **Parking:** on-site. **Terms:** 4 day cancellation notice. **Amenities:** safes, hair dryers. **Pool(s):** outdoor. **Leisure Activities:** spa, volleyball. *Fee:* sauna, whirlpool, scuba diving, snorkeling. **Guest Services:** gift shop, valet laundry. **Business Services:** meeting rooms, business center. **Cards:** AX, MC, VI.

SOME UNITS

MARINA EL CID HOTEL & YACHT CLUB — *Book at aaa.com* — Phone: 669/913-3333 [27]

Resort
Large-scale Hotel

All Year — 2P: $130-$250 — XP: $20
Location: 13.5 km nw; north end of Zona Hotelera. Punta del Sabalo S/N 82110. Fax: 669/914-1040. **Facility:** Situated around a private marina, the resort consists of many smaller buildings, so it feels more residential than hotel in scope. 204 units. 83 one-bedroom standard units with efficiencies. 114 one-, 1 two- and 6 three-bedroom suites ($800) with efficiencies, some with whirlpools. 3-7 stories, exterior corridors. *Bath:* shower only. **Parking:** on-site. **Amenities:** safes, irons, hair dryers. **Dining:** Restaurante La Marina, see separate listing. **Pool(s):** outdoor, heated outdoor, wading. **Leisure Activities:** whirlpool, recreation programs, playground, spa, shuffleboard, volleyball. *Fee:* marina, golf-27 holes, miniature golf, 9 tennis courts (4 lighted). **Guest Services:** gift shop, valet and coin laundry. **Business Services:** meeting rooms. *Fee:* PC, fax. **Cards:** AX, MC, VI.

SOME UNITS

MOTEL LOS ARCOS — Phone: 669/913-5066 [18]

Small-scale Hotel

All Year — 2P: $90-$110 — XP: $10
Location: 7.5 km nw; on Las Gaviotas Beach. Ave Playa Gaviotas #214 82110 (Apdo Postal 132). Fax: 669/913-5066. **Facility:** 22 units. 13 one- and 9 two-bedroom standard units, some with efficiencies. 2 stories (no elevator), exterior corridors. *Bath:* shower only. **Parking:** on-site. **Terms:** office hours 7 am-9 pm, small pets only ($10 extra charge, in designated units). **Pool(s):** outdoor. **Business Services:** fax (fee). **Cards:** MC, VI.

SOME UNITS
FEE

MOTEL MARLEY — Phone: 669/913-5533 [14]

Motel

All Year — 2P: $80-$95 — XP: $8
Location: 7.5 km nw; on Las Gaviotas Beach. Ave Playa Gaviotas #226 82110 (Apdo Postal 214). Fax: 669/913-5533. **Facility:** 16 units. 12 one- and 4 two-bedroom suites with efficiencies. 2 stories (no elevator), exterior corridors. *Bath:* shower only. **Parking:** on-site. **Terms:** office hours 7 am-10 pm, 7 day cancellation notice. **Pool(s):** outdoor. **Cards:** MC, VI.

PUEBLO BONITO AT EMERALD BAY — *Book at aaa.com* — Phone: 669/989-0525 [5]

Resort
Large-scale Hotel

All Year — 2P: $225-$375 — XP: $20
Location: In Zona Mueva de Mazatlan; just n of Culiacan turn off, on Mex 15. Ave Ernesto Coppel Campana S/N 82110. Fax: 669/988-0718. **Facility:** A luxury beach hotel in a recently developed area, Pueblo Bonito features an impressive marble lobby, gardens and an upscale restaurant and lounge. Meets AAA guest room security requirements. 144 one-bedroom standard units with efficiencies. 2-4 stories, interior corridors. **Parking:** on-site and valet. **Terms:** check-in 4 pm. **Amenities:** high-speed Internet, voice mail, safes, irons, hair dryers. **Pool(s):** 2 heated outdoor, 2 wading. **Leisure Activities:** whirlpools, steamroom, recreation programs, exercise room, basketball, horseshoes, volleyball. *Fee:* snorkeling, fishing. **Guest Services:** gift shop, valet laundry. **Business Services:** meeting rooms, business center. **Cards:** AX, DS, MC, VI.

FEE

RIVIERA BEACH RESORT MAZATLAN — *Book at aaa.com* — Phone: (669)983-4822 [23]

Large-scale Hotel

All Year — 2P: $130-$180 — XP: $15 — F12
Location: 6.5 km nw. Ave Camaron Sabalo 51 82110 (Apdo Postal 795). Fax: 669/984-4532. **Facility:** 176 one-bedroom standard units, some with efficiencies. 4 stories, exterior corridors. *Bath:* shower only. **Parking:** on-site. **Amenities:** safes, hair dryers. **Pool(s):** 3 heated outdoor. **Leisure Activities:** whirlpools, recreation programs, volleyball. **Guest Services:** gift shop, valet laundry. **Business Services:** meeting rooms. *Fee:* PC, fax. **Cards:** AX, MC, VI.

SUITES LINDAMAR — Phone: 669/913-5533 [15]

Small-scale Hotel

All Year — 2P: $80-$95 — XP: $8
Location: 7.5 km nw; on Las Gaviotas Beach. Ave Playa Gaviotas #222 82110 (Apdo Postal 214). Fax: 669/913-5533. **Facility:** 12 one-bedroom suites with kitchens. 3 stories (no elevator), exterior corridors. *Bath:* shower only. **Parking:** on-site. **Terms:** office hours 7 am-10 pm, 7 day cancellation notice. **Cards:** MC, VI.

(See map and index starting on p. 438)

VILLAS EL RANCHO

Phone: 669/988-0090 [26]

AAA
◇◇ ◇◇
Cottage

All Year
2P: $110-$230
Location: Just n of marina on beach road. Sabalo-Cerritos #3000 82000 (Jm Terrazas #20, Ampl Los Angeles, 27140). Fax: 669/988-0190. **Facility:** 27 cottages. 2 stories (no elevator), exterior corridors. **Parking:** on-site. **Terms:** office hours 7 am-9 pm, check-in 4 pm. **Dining:** 7 am-8 pm, cocktails. **Pool(s):** outdoor, wading. **Leisure Activities:** whirlpool, fishing. **Guest Services:** sundries, valet laundry. **Business Services:** meeting rooms, PC. **Cards:** AX, MC, VI.

🛗 🍸 🅳 🏊 🎥 📷 🛗 💻

----------- **WHERE TO DINE** -----------

ANGELO'S RESTAURANT

Dinner: $20-$35
Phone: 669/989-8900 [2]

◇◇◇◇ ◇◇◇◇
Italian

Location: 12.5 km nw; in Hotel Pueblo Bonito. Ave Camaron Sabalo 2121 Nte Norte Fracc 82110. **Hours:** 6 pm-11 pm. **Reservations:** required. **Features:** The popular restaurant features Italian specialties, as well as great, cooked-to-order steaks. The setting is casual yet refined. Casual dress; cocktails; entertainment. **Parking:** no self-parking. **Cards:** AX, MC, VI.

🍸

BLUE CACTUS

Lunch: $12-$25   Dinner: $12-$25   Phone: 669/914-1020 [10]

◇◇◇◇ ◇◇◇◇
Continental

Location: 7.5 km nw; on Las Gaviotas Beach. Ave Playa Gaviotas 505 82110. **Hours:** 8 am-1 am. **Reservations:** accepted. **Features:** Blue is the theme of this newer restaurant where diners can elect to sit indoors in the brightly lit blue dining room while drinking a Mary Blue or on the porch next to a row of blue agave cactus. A traditional Mexican menu is accented with some international choices. Casual dress; cocktails. **Parking:** street. **Cards:** MC, VI.

🍸

CARLOS & LUCIA'S RESTAURANT BAR & GRILL

Lunch: $4-$8   Dinner: $7-$16   Phone: 669/913-8238 [7]

◇◇ ◇◇
Cuban

Location: On Ave Camaron Sabalo; just s of Holiday Inn SunSpree Resort Mazatlan. Camaron Sabalo S/N 82110. **Hours:** 8 am-10 pm, Sun from 10 am. Closed: Mon. **Reservations:** accepted. **Features:** Cuban cuisine is served in a relaxed, pleasant atmosphere. Guests can sit on the patio or in the indoors dining room. The Cuban sandwich is a must-try, and imperial shrimp is fabulous. Casual dress; cocktails. **Parking:** street.

🍸 🎦

EL PARADOR ESPANOL

Lunch: $15-$30   Dinner: $15-$30   Phone: 669/913-0767 [6]

◇◇◇◇ ◇◇◇◇
Spanish

Location: 9 km nw. Ave Camaron Sabalo 714 82110. **Hours:** 7 am-11:30 pm. **Reservations:** accepted. **Features:** If you're not sure what you want for dinner, the tapas menu is sure to please with small portions and plenty of variety from which to choose. If you're looking for something really light, then perhaps try the tortilla soup with lemon broth and chicken or maybe the white fish ceviche. Casual dress; cocktails. **Parking:** street. **Cards:** MC, VI.

🍸

EL SHRIMP BUCKET

Lunch: $7-$10   Dinner: $8-$20   Phone: 669/961-6350 [17]

◇◇◇◇ ◇◇◇◇
Seafood

Location: 5 blks sw of Plaza de la Republica. Olas Atlas #11 82110. **Hours:** 6 am-11 pm, Thurs-Sat to 2 am. **Reservations:** accepted. **Features:** Shrimp served in a clay bucket with fries is the signature dish at the popular cafe, which features an outdoor sidewalk section that affords fine views of the malecon and ocean. Sunsets here are a treat. Casual dress; cocktails. **Parking:** street. **Cards:** AX, MC, VI.

LA COSTA MARINERA

Lunch: $12-$25   Dinner: $12-$25   Phone: 669/916-1599 [3]

◇◇◇◇ ◇◇◇◇
Seafood

Location: 12 km nw. Privada del Camaron y Privada de la Florida 82110. **Hours:** 10 am-11 pm. **Reservations:** accepted. **Features:** If you're looking for a fun beach shack environment set just above the sand where venders can still lean through the windows with trinkets and the setting sun can be enjoyed over a margarita and prawns Bombay, then this is for you! Casual dress; cocktails. **Parking:** street. **Cards:** MC, VI.

🍸 🎦

THE PLACE

Lunch: $8-$20   Dinner: $8-$20   Phone: 669/916-1301 [4]

◇◇
Mexican

Location: 12 km nw. Ave Camaron Sabalo 5504 82110. **Hours:** 7 am-10:30 pm. **Reservations:** accepted. **Features:** This is the place where "all you can eat & drink" is taken seriously with bottomless margaritas, platters of ribs and a dinner special that includes three lobsters. Set right on the sidewalk, diners can take in the Petalumas rumbling by and do some great people watching. Festive music and a friendly staff make for a very relaxed and fun meal. Casual dress; cocktails. **Parking:** street. **Cards:** DS, MC, VI.

🎦

RESTAURANT CASA LOMA

Lunch: $15-$22   Dinner: $15-$22   Phone: 669/913-5398 [8]

◇◇◇◇ ◇◇◇◇
Continental

Location: 7.8 km nw. Ave Playa Gaviotas, #104 Fracc Gaviotas 82110. **Hours:** 1:30 pm-10:30 pm. **Reservations:** suggested. **Features:** In a quiet residential neighborhood, the popular restaurant blends well-prepared Italian cuisine and some Mexican dishes on its diverse menu. Casual dress; cocktails. **Parking:** on-site. **Cards:** MC, VI.

🍸

RESTAURANTE LA MARINA

Lunch: $7-$9   Dinner: $12-$20   Phone: 669/913-3333 [19]

◇◇◇◇ ◇◇◇◇
International

Location: 13.5 km nw; north end of Zona Hotelera; in Marina El Cid Hotel & Yacht Club. Punta del Sabalo S/N 82110. **Hours:** 7 am-11 pm. **Reservations:** accepted. **Features:** A stylish dining experience awaits. From the open patio, patrons are treated to a marvelous view of white yachts in the marina. Seafood, as well as fowl and meats, is skillfully prepared and attractively presented. Dressy casual; cocktails. **Parking:** on-site and valet. **Cards:** AX, MC, VI.

RESTAURANT MAMUCAS

Lunch: $4-$8   Dinner: $6-$18   Phone: 669/981-3490 [16]

◇◇◇◇ ◇◇◇◇
Seafood

Location: Jct Paseo Claussen and Ave Nelson, just e, just s; in Old Mazatlan. Simon Bolivar #404 Pte 82110. **Hours:** 10:30 am-9:30 pm. **Reservations:** accepted. **Features:** First-timers shouldn't let the modest looks of the cafe fool them; this is where local folks go for seafood. Jumbo shrimp grilled with butter is absolutely fantastic, and this place serves everything available on the local seafood market. Octopus is a standout. Casual dress; cocktails. **Parking:** street. **Cards:** MC, VI.

🎦

(See map and index starting on p. 438)

SENOR FROG'S MAZATLAN
Lunch: $7-$10   **Dinner:** $8-$16   **Phone:** 669/985-1110   (15)
▼▼▼ ▼▼▼
International
Location: On the Malecon; between aves Insurgentes and de los Deportes. Ave del Mar #882, Zona Costera 82110. **Hours:** 11 am-2 am. **Reservations:** accepted. **Features:** Part of the popular restaurant chain native to Mexico, this location features tempting seafood as well as a good selection of steaks, soups and well-prepared desserts; the lounge can be a bit raucous in the evenings. Casual dress; cocktails. **Parking:** street. **Cards:** AX, MC, VI.   ⵖ

SR PEPPER
Dinner: $20-$35   **Phone:** 669/914-0101   (1)
▼▼▼ ▼▼▼
Steak & Seafood
Location: 13 km nw; on north end of Zona Hotelera. Ave Camaron Sabalo Nte S/N 82110. **Hours:** 6 pm-midnight. **Reservations:** accepted. **Features:** Gilded mirrors and polished brass are visible throughout the dining room so as to reflect the rich wood paneling, linen-draped tables and tuxedo-attired staff, which all create an atmosphere that makes this a perfect stop for a special occasion or just a super night out. The menu has a few seafood selections but focuses primarily on select cuts of fresh beef that are brought to the table for viewing prior to ordering. Live music and dancing Tuesday through Sunday. Casual dress; cocktails. **Parking:** on-site. **Cards:** AX, MC, VI.   ⵖ

TEQUILA'S SPORTS BAR & GRILL
Lunch: $5-$12   **Dinner:** $5-$12   **Phone:** 669/913-5344   (9)
▼▼▼ ▼▼▼
Mexican
Location: 8.8 km nw; across from Hotel Costa de Oro. Ave Camaron Sabalo S/N 82110. **Hours:** noon-11 pm. **Reservations:** accepted. **Features:** At the lively sports bar and eatery, diners can nibble on tasty American and Mexican dishes while viewing sporting events on a big-screen television. Casual dress; cocktails. **Parking:** on-site. **Cards:** AX, MC, VI.   ⵖ

TERRAZA PLAYA
Lunch: $8-$13   **Dinner:** $8-$17   **Phone:** 669/989-0555   (12)
▼▼▼ ▼▼▼
Continental
Location: 7.3 km nw; on Las Gaviotas Beach; in Hotel Playa Mazatlan. Ave Playa Gaviotas #202 82110. **Hours:** 6 am-11 pm. **Features:** On beachside terrace. Casual dress; cocktails; entertainment. **Parking:** on-site. **Cards:** AX, MC, VI.   ⵖ ⵜ

VILLA ITALIA
Lunch: $11-$16   **Dinner:** $11-$16   **Phone:** 669/913-0311   (5)
▼▼▼ ▼▼▼
Italian
Location: 8 km nw; in front of Hotel El Cid. Ave Camaron Sabalo S/N 82100. **Hours:** noon-midnight. **Reservations:** suggested. **Features:** Casual, well-prepared Italian specialties are served indoors and on the casual patio. The outdoor brick oven is used to prepare bread and pizza. Casual dress; cocktails. **Parking:** on-site. **Cards:** MC, VI.

VITTORE
Lunch: $10-$20   **Dinner:** $10-$20   **Phone:** 669/983-5333   (13)
▼▼▼ ▼▼▼
Italian
Location: 7 km nw; on Las Gaviotas Beach; across from Los Sabalos Resort Hotel. Ave Playa Gaviotas #100 82110. **Hours:** noon-midnight. **Reservations:** suggested. **Features:** A wood-burning pizza oven, trattoria ambience, open dining room and pleasant patio all add up to an enjoyable Italian dining experience. Casual dress; cocktails. **Parking:** on-site. **Cards:** AX, MC, VI.   ⵖ

MISMALOYA, JALISCO

———— **WHERE TO STAY** ————

CASA IGUANA HOTEL DE MISMALOYA   *Book at aaa.com*
Phone: 322/228-0186

▼▼▼ ▼▼▼
Motel

	1P: $85	2P: $85	XP: $15
12/1-4/15			
4/16-11/30	1P: $60	2P: $60	XP: $15

Location: 11.5 km s of center of Puerto Vallarta. Ave 5 de Mayo #455 48394 (Apdo Postal 2-248, 48351). Fax: 322/228-0087. **Facility:** 53 units. 50 two- and 3 three-bedroom suites with efficiencies. 4 stories (no elevator), exterior corridors. *Bath:* shower only. **Parking:** on-site. **Terms:** 3 day cancellation notice, 17% service charge. **Pool(s):** heated outdoor, wading. **Leisure Activities:** whirlpool. **Guest Services:** sundries, coin laundry. **Business Services:** meeting rooms, PC (fee). **Cards:** AX, MC, VI.

SOME UNITS
⏏ ⵖ ⚓ ▯ ▭ / ✕ /

LA JOLLA DE MISMALOYA   *Book at aaa.com*
Phone: (322)226-0660

▼▼▼ ▼▼▼
Resort
Large-scale Hotel

	1P: $330-$350	2P: $330-$350	XP: $45	F12
12/1-1/1				
1/2-4/18	1P: $230-$272	2P: $230-$272	XP: $45	F12
4/19-11/30	1P: $194-$214	2P: $194-$214	XP: $45	F12

Location: 11.5 km s of Puerto Vallarta. Zona Hotelera Sur KM 11.5 48394 (Apdo Postal 158B). Fax: 322/228-0500. **Facility:** This resort is loaded with recreational activities, guest room amenities and a great view of Los Arcos. 303 units. 108 two-bedroom standard units. 179 one- and 16 two-bedroom suites ($650-$1200), some with efficiencies and kitchens. 9 stories, exterior corridors. *Bath:* combo or shower only. **Parking:** on-site. **Terms:** 15 day cancellation notice-fee imposed, [AP] meal plan available. **Amenities:** dual phone lines, voice mail, safes, honor bars, irons, hair dryers. **Dining:** The Set of the Night of the Iguana, see separate listing. **Pool(s):** 3 heated outdoor, wading. **Leisure Activities:** whirlpools, steamrooms, snorkeling, lighted tennis court, recreation programs, playground, spa, volleyball. *Fee:* boats, paddleboats, windsurfing, scuba diving, fishing, charter fishing, horseback riding, game room. **Guest Services:** gift shop, valet and coin laundry. **Business Services:** conference facilities, business center. **Cards:** AX, MC, VI.

SOME UNITS
⒮ᴅ ✈ ⏏ 24 ⵖ ♠ S D ⚓ ⟟ ✕ ⛱ DATA PORT ▭ / ✕ ▯ ▱ /
FEE

———— **WHERE TO DINE** ————

THE SET OF THE NIGHT OF THE IGUANA
Lunch: $10-$24   **Dinner:** $10-$24   **Phone:** 322/226-0660
▼▼▼ ▼▼▼
Continental
Location: 11.5 km s of Puerto Vallarta; in La Jolla de Mismaloya. Zona Hotelera Sur KM 11.5 48394. **Hours:** 8 am-midnight. **Reservations:** suggested. **Features:** A short 10-minute cab ride south from Puerto Vallarta, diners will walk onto the set of a Tennessee Williams movie shot in 1963. The large brick patio is softly lit and casually set for a fun night with strolling musicians, lively diners and tasteful entrees. Casual dress; cocktails. **Parking:** on-site. **Cards:** AX, MC, VI.   ⵖ ⵜ

NUEVO VALLARTA, NAYARIT pop. 4,000

———— WHERE TO STAY ————

THE GRAND MAYAN RESORT

Phone: 322/226-4000

[fyi]

Small-scale Hotel

All Year   1P: $191-$286   2P: $224-$336   XP: $70   F12

Too new to rate, opening scheduled for October 2004. **Location:** Paseo de las Moras S/N 63735. Fax: 322/226-4032. **Amenities:** 460 units, coffeemakers, microwaves, refrigerators, pool. **Terms:** 3 night minimum stay - seasonal and/or weekends, 30 day cancellation notice. **Cards:** AX, MC, VI.

HOTEL SIERRA-NUEVO VALLARTA ALL INCLUSIVE

Phone: 322/297-1300

Resort
Large-scale Hotel

All Year [AP]   1P: $274   2P: $330   XP: $112   F12

Location: Mex 200, exit Nuevo Vallarta, 2 km n. Paseo de los Cocoteros #19, Villa 8 63732. Fax: 322/297-1400. **Facility:** This all-inclusive beach resort offers a full complement of attractions including pools, restaurants and a white-sand beach. Meets AAA guest room security requirements. 362 units. 355 one-bedroom standard units. 7 one-bedroom suites with whirlpools. 6 stories, interior corridors. **Parking:** on-site. **Terms:** check-in 4 pm. **Amenities:** safes, honor bars, hair dryers. **Pool(s):** outdoor, heated outdoor, wading. **Leisure Activities:** saunas, whirlpool, steamrooms, windsurfing, snorkeling, putting green, lighted tennis court, recreation programs, bicycles, horseback riding, playground, exercise room, spa, shuffleboard, volleyball. **Guest Services:** gift shop, valet laundry. **Business Services:** meeting rooms. **Cards:** AX, DC, DS, MC, VI.

SOME UNITS
[icons] / [icon] /

MAYAN PALACE NUEVO VALLARTA

Phone: (322)226-4000

Resort
Large-scale Hotel

All Year   1P: $139-$209   2P: $179-$259   XP: $59   F12

Location: Mex 200, 2 km n via Nuevo Vallarta exit. Paseo de las Moras S/N 63735. Fax: 322/226-4032. **Facility:** Guests are transported to their rooms via a water taxi on the lagoon or a small train service; the impressive resort's huge pool overlooks the ocean. 523 units. 174 one-bedroom standard units. 349 one-bedroom suites with efficiencies. 4-7 stories, interior corridors. *Bath:* combo or shower only. **Parking:** on-site (fee) and valet. **Terms:** check-in 5 pm, 3 night minimum stay - seasonal and/or weekends, 30 day cancellation notice. **Amenities:** voice mail, safes (fee), irons, hair dryers. **Pool(s):** outdoor. **Leisure Activities:** steamroom, recreation programs, spa. *Fee:* whirlpool, golf-18 holes, bicycles, game room. **Guest Services:** gift shop, valet and coin laundry. **Business Services:** meeting rooms. **Cards:** AX, MC, VI.

SOME UNITS
[icons] FEE ... FEE / [icons] /

MAYAN SEA GARDEN NUEVO VALLARTA

Phone: (322)266-4000

Small-scale Hotel

All Year   1P: $93-$139   2P: $127-$190   XP: $49   F12

Location: Mex 200, 2 km n via Nuevo Vallarta exit. Paseo de las Moras S/N 63735. Fax: 322/226-4505. **Facility:** 182 units. 78 one-bedroom standard units. 104 one-bedroom suites with efficiencies. 7 stories, exterior corridors. **Parking:** on-site and valet. **Terms:** check-in 5 pm, 3 night minimum stay - seasonal and/or weekends, 30 day cancellation notice. **Amenities:** voice mail, safes (fee), hair dryers. **Pool(s):** heated outdoor, wading. **Leisure Activities:** recreation programs. **Guest Services:** gift shop, valet and coin laundry. **Cards:** AX, MC, VI.

SOME UNITS
[icons] FEE / [icons] /

OCCIDENTAL GRAND NUEVO VALLARTA ALL INCLUSIVE

Phone: (322)297-0400

Resort
Large-scale Hotel

All Year [AP]   1P: $130   2P: $240   XP: $70

Location: Mex 200, exit Nuevo Vallarta, 2 km n. Paseo de los Cocoteros #18 63732. Fax: 322/297-0082. **Facility:** Large modern facility, very good beach, pools. Well-appointed rooms, lots of activities and opportunities to enjoy the sun, sand and water. 294 one-bedroom standard units. 7 stories, interior corridors. *Bath:* shower only. **Parking:** on-site. **Terms:** 14 day cancellation notice-fee imposed. **Amenities:** safes, irons, hair dryers. **Pool(s):** heated outdoor, wading. **Leisure Activities:** sailboats, 2 lighted tennis courts, recreation programs, bicycles, playground, exercise room, horseshoes, shuffleboard, volleyball. *Fee:* boats, scuba diving, snorkeling, fishing, massage. **Guest Services:** gift shop, valet laundry. **Business Services:** meeting rooms. **Cards:** AX, MC, VI.

SOME UNITS
[icons] / [icon] /

PARADISE VILLAGE BEACH RESORT & SPA

Book at aaa.com   **Phone: 322/226-6770**

Resort
Large-scale Hotel

All Year   1P: $130-$406   2P: $130-$406   XP: $15

Location: Mex 200, 2 km n via exit Nuevo Vallarta. Paseo de los Cocoteros #1 63732. Fax: 322/226-6759. **Facility:** Even a zoo is featured at this large-scale resort with all the amenities; there are also three pools, a fine beach, five restaurants and many shops. 495 units. 177 one-bedroom standard units with efficiencies. 163 one-, 111 two- and 44 three-bedroom suites ($490-$656) with kitchens. 8 stories, interior corridors. **Parking:** on-site. **Terms:** check-in 4 pm, [AP] meal plan available. **Amenities:** safes, irons, hair dryers. **Dining:** El Faro de Tulum, see separate listing. **Pool(s):** 3 heated outdoor. **Leisure Activities:** windsurfing, snorkeling, 2 lighted tennis courts, bicycles, playground, spa, basketball, shuffleboard, volleyball. *Fee:* scuba diving, fishing, charter fishing, golf-18 holes, exercise room. **Business Services:** conference facilities. **Cards:** AX, MC, VI.

[icons]

———— The following lodging was either not evaluated or did not ————
meet AAA rating requirements but is listed for your information only.

CLUB HOTEL RIU JALISCO

Phone: 322/226-6600

[fyi]

Not evaluated. **Location:** 15 km n of Puerto Vallarta; on Playa de Flamingos Beach. Paseo de los Cocoteros S/N Lote K 63732. Facilities, services, and decor characterize a mid-range property.

──────── **WHERE TO DINE** ────────

EL FARO DE TULUM

Mexican

Lunch: $10-$25　　　**Dinner:** $10-$25　　　**Phone:** 322/226-6770
Location: Mex 200, 2 km n via exit Nuevo Vallarta; in Paradise Village Beach Resort & Spa. Paseo de los Cocoteros #1 63732. **Hours:** 7 am-10:30 pm. **Reservations:** suggested. **Features:** Open-air dining and an oceanfront setting attract diners to the lovely restaurant, but tasty and creative dishes keep them coming back. The menu blends contemporary Mexican cuisine and seafood specialties. Service is warm and personable, and the setting is comfortable. Casual dress; cocktails. **Parking:** on-site. **Cards:** AX, MC, VI.

IL PESCATORE RISTORANTE
Italian

Dinner: $15-$30　　　**Phone:** 322/226-6670
Location: Mex 200, 2 km n via exit Nuevo Vallarta; in marina of Paradise Village Beach Resort & Spa. Paseo de los Cocoteros #1 63732. **Hours:** 6 pm-10:30 pm. **Reservations:** suggested. **Features:** Set on the peaceful side of the marina, the open-air restaurant boasts a romantic setting and a fine menu of freshly prepared Italian cuisine. The chef features fresh local seafood, including a particularly popular grilled lobster entree served with a side of tasty pasta. The eatery proves to be a wonderful spot to linger over a glass of wine and a fine meal. Casual dress; cocktails. **Parking:** on-site. **Cards:** AX, MC, VI.

THE JUNGLE
Mexican

Dinner: $10-$25　　　**Phone:** 322/226-6770
Location: Mex 200, 2 km n on Nuevo Vallarta exit, follow signs; at Paradise Plaza. Paseo de los Cocoteros #1 63732. **Hours:** 5 pm-11 pm. **Reservations:** suggested. **Features:** Fun, casual decor revolves around a jungle theme in the family-oriented restaurant, which has a live snake tank and many stuffed jungle animals. Guests can sample hearty portions of tasty Mexican and Mediterranean cuisine with a strong focus on fresh local seafood. At night after the kitchen closes, this place transforms into a lively disco. Casual dress; cocktails. **Parking:** on-site. **Cards:** AX, MC, VI.

PUERTO ESCONDIDO, OAXACA pop. 19,000

──────── **WHERE TO STAY** ────────

HOTEL BEST WESTERN POSADA REAL PUERTO ESCONDIDO　　　*Book at aaa.com*
Small-scale Hotel

Phone: (954)582-0133
All Year　　　1P: $90-$115　　　2P: $90-$115　　　XP: $15　　　F12
Location: 2.2 km n of jct Mex 200 and 131, just w of tourist information booth. Blvd Benito Juarez S/N 71980. Fax: 954/582-0192. **Facility:** Meets AAA guest room security requirements. 100 one-bedroom standard units. 3 stories, interior/exterior corridors. *Bath:* shower only. **Parking:** on-site. **Terms:** 3 day cancellation notice-fee imposed. **Amenities:** voice mail. **Pool(s):** 2 outdoor, 2 wading. **Leisure Activities:** putting green, recreation programs, sports court. *Fee:* tennis court, game room. **Guest Services:** gift shop, valet laundry, area transportation. **Business Services:** fax (fee). **Cards:** AX, DC, MC, VI.

SOME UNITS

HOTEL SANTA FE
Country Inn

Phone: (954)582-0170
All Year　　　2P: $110　　　XP: $15
Location: At Playa Zicatela, off Mex 200; at south end of town. Calle del Morro S/N 71980 (Apdo Postal 96). Fax: 954/582-0260. **Facility:** 61 one-bedroom standard units. 3 stories (no elevator), exterior corridors. *Bath:* combo or shower only. **Parking:** on-site. **Terms:** 30 day cancellation notice. **Amenities:** *Some:* safes. **Pool(s):** 3 outdoor, 2 wading. **Guest Services:** gift shop, valet laundry. **Business Services:** fax (fee). **Cards:** AX, MC, VI.

SOME UNITS

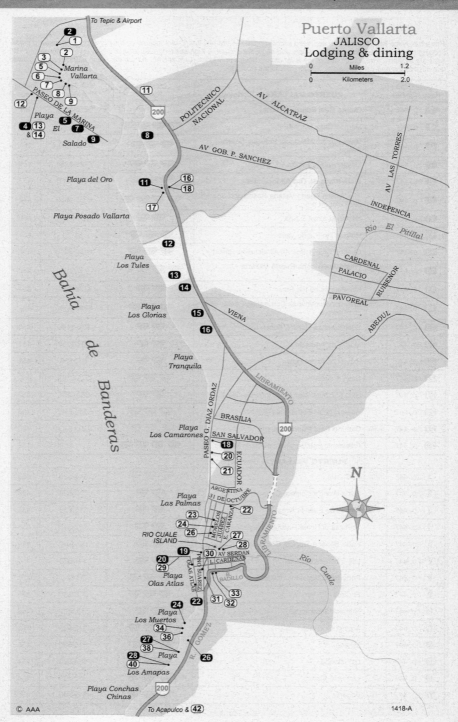

Puerto Vallarta
JALISCO
Lodging & dining

Puerto Vallarta, Jalisco

This index helps you "spot" where approved accommodations and restaurants are located on the corresponding detailed maps. Lodging rate ranges are for comparison only and show the property's high season; rates are per night, unless only weekly (W) rates are available. Restaurant rate range is for dinner, unless only lunch (L) is served. Turn to the listing page for more detailed rate information and consult display ads for special promotions.

Spotter/Map Page Number	OA	PUERTO VALLARTA - Lodgings	Diamond Rating	Rate Range High Season	Listing Page
2 / p. 447	AAA	Quinta Real Puerto Vallarta	◆◆◆◆	$275-$450	452
4 / p. 447		Marriott Casa Magna	◆◆◆◆	$129-$239	451
5 / p. 447		Melia Puerto Vallarta All Inclusive Beach Resort	◆◆◆	$110-$272	451
7 / p. 447		Mayan Palace Puerto Vallarta	◆◆◆	$139-$259	451
8 / p. 447	AAA	Vista Playa de Oro All Inclusive	◆◆◆	$149-$238	452
9 / p. 447		The Westin Puerto Vallarta Resort and Spa - see color ad p 8	◆◆◆◆	$265-$589	452
11 / p. 447		Hacienda Hotel & Spa	◆◆	$53-$132	450
12 / p. 447		Holiday Inn Puerto Vallarta	◆◆◆	$175	451
13 / p. 447		Qualton Club & Spa An All Inclusive Resort	◆◆◆	$100-$310	452
14 / p. 447	AAA	Fiesta Americana Puerto Vallarta - see color ad card insert	◆◆◆◆	$327	450
15 / p. 447		Las Palmas by the Sea	◆◆	$130-$200	451
16 / p. 447		Sheraton Buganvilias Convention Center - see color ad p 8	◆◆◆	$259-$350	452
18 / p. 447		Buenaventura Hotel & Beach Club	◆◆	$75-$150	450
19 / p. 447		Molino de Agua Hotel	◆◆	$97-$150	451
20 / p. 447		Playa Los Arcos Hotel	◆◆	$62-$89	451
22 / p. 447		Casa Andrea	◆◆◆	$75-$130	450
24 / p. 447		Club Meza del Mar An All Inclusive Hotel	◆◆	$82-$206	450
26 / p. 447		Casa Mirador Bed & Breakfast	◆◆◆	$160-$180	450
27 / p. 447	AAA	Camino Real Puerto Vallarta	◆◆◆	$290-$430	450
28 / p. 447		Presidente InterContinental Puerto Vallarta	◆◆◆◆	$314-$699	452
		PUERTO VALLARTA - Restaurants			
1 / p. 447	AAA	El Candil	◆◆◆	$14-$29	453
2 / p. 447		Suzie Wong's Chinese Cuisine	◆◆	$10-$28	456
3 / p. 447		Rincon de Buenos Aires	◆◆	$10-$30	455
5 / p. 447		Terrazza di Roma Ristorante Italiano	◆◆	$12-$18	456
6 / p. 447		Fajita Banana Tropical Grill & Bar	◆◆	$7-$14	454
7 / p. 447		Las Palomas Doradas	◆◆	$11-$20	454
8 / p. 447		Porto Bello Ristorante Italiano	◆◆◆	$8-$27	455
9 / p. 447		El Circo	◆◆◆	$16-$30	453
11 / p. 447		Outback Steakhouse	◆◆	$8-$20	455
12 / p. 447		Andrea Gourmet	◆◆◆	$15-$35	453
13 / p. 447		Mikado	◆◆◆	$15-$30	455
14 / p. 447		La Estancia	◆◆◆	$14-$20	454
16 / p. 447		La Petite France	◆◆◆	$12-$35	454
17 / p. 447		Bogart's	◆◆◆	$12-$40	453

Spotter/Map Page Number	OA	PUERTO VALLARTA - Restaurants (continued)	Diamond Rating	Rate Range High Season	Listing Page
⑱ / p. 447		La Hacienda	◈◈◈	$18-$21	454
⑳ / p. 447		La Dolce Vita Ristorante Bar	◈◈	$8-$18	454
㉑ / p. 447		Paradise Burger	◈	$7-$15	455
㉒ / p. 447		Cafe des Artistes	◈◈◈	$20-$25	453
㉓ / p. 447	▲▲▲	**Los XiTomates**	◈◈◈	$18-$35	454
㉔ / p. 447		Trio Restaurant	◈◈◈	$12-$30	456
㉖ / p. 447		The Blue Shrimp Restaurant	◈◈◈	$18-$40	453
㉗ / p. 447		The River Cafe	◈◈◈	$12-$30	455
㉘ / p. 447		Le Bistro Jazz Cafe	◈◈◈	$15-$20	454
㉙ / p. 447		Kaiser Maximilian	◈◈◈	$9-$20	454
㉚ / p. 447		Mezzaluna Ristorante Italiano	◈◈	$15-$23	455
㉛ / p. 447		Pie in the Sky-Puerto Vallarta	◈	$3-$6	455
㉜ / p. 447		Restaurante Argentino Los Pibes	◈◈	$20-$40	455
㉝ / p. 447		Pancake House	◈◈	$3-$6(L)	455
㉞ / p. 447	▲▲▲	**La Palapa Restaurante and Bar**	◈◈◈	$16-$38	454
㊱ / p. 447		El Dorado	◈◈	$6-$30	453
㊳ / p. 447		Maria Bonita	◈◈◈	$14-$22	455
㊵ / p. 447		Da Antonio	◈◈◈	$15-$25	453
㊷ / p. 447		Le Kliff Restaurante and Bar	◈◈◈	$15-$45	454

PUERTO VALLARTA, JALISCO pop. 94,700 (See map and index starting on p. 447)

———— WHERE TO STAY ————

BUENAVENTURA HOTEL & BEACH CLUB   *Book at aaa.com*   Phone: (322)226-7000   **18**
▼▼ ▼▼   All Year   1P: $75-$150   2P: $75-$150   XP: $16
Location: 1 km n on Airport Hwy (Mex 200). Ave Mexico 1301, Col 5 de Diciembre 48350. Fax: 322/226-3546.
Resort   **Facility:** Near downtown. Traditional room decor. 236 units. 232 one-bedroom standard units, some with
Large-scale Hotel   whirlpools. 4 one-bedroom suites ($215) with efficiencies. 5 stories, interior corridors. *Bath:* shower only.
Parking: street. **Terms:** 21 day cancellation notice, 7 day off season-fee imposed. **Amenities:** *Some:* safes.
Pool(s): 3 heated outdoor, wading. **Leisure Activities:** whirlpool, boating, recreation programs. *Fee:* massage. **Guest Services:** gift shop, valet laundry. **Cards:** AX, MC, VI.

CAMINO REAL PUERTO VALLARTA   *Book at aaa.com*   Phone: (322)221-5000   **27**
(AAA)   12/18-1/2   2P: $290-$430   XP: $40   F30
1/3-4/21   2P: $220-$315   XP: $40   F30
▼▼ ▼▼   4/22-11/30   2P: $201-$265   XP: $30   F30
12/1-12/17   2P: $142-$189   XP: $30   F30
Resort   **Location:** 3.5 km s on Mismaloya Hwy (Mex 200). Playa Las Estacas S/N KM 3.5 48300 (Apdo Postal 95).
Large-scale Hotel   Fax: 322/221-6000. **Facility:** Private cove and beach. Fine public facilities. All rooms with ocean views;
some with balcony. Excellent staff. 337 units. 326 one-bedroom standard units, some with whirlpools. 11
one-bedroom suites. 11 stories, interior/exterior corridors. **Parking:** on-site and valet. **Terms:** 3 day cancellation notice, [MAP]
meal plan available. **Amenities:** voice mail, safes, honor bars. *Some:* irons, hair dryers. **Dining:** 3 restaurants, 7 am-midnight,
cocktails, also, Maria Bonita, see separate listing, entertainment. **Pool(s):** outdoor, heated outdoor, wading. **Leisure
Activities:** rental boats, playground, exercise room. *Fee:* waterskiing, scuba diving, snorkeling, fishing, 2 lighted tennis courts,
massage. **Guest Services:** gift shop, valet laundry. **Business Services:** meeting rooms, business center. **Cards:** AX, DC,
MC, VI.
SOME UNITS

CASA ANDREA   Phone: 322/222-1213   **22**
▼▼▼ ▼▼▼   All Year [CP]   1P: $75-$130   2P: $75-$130   XP: $15
Location: Just e of Olas Altas St; center; in Zona Romantica. Located a block from the beach. Francisca Rodriguez
Bed & Breakfast   #174 48384. Fax: 322/222-1213. **Facility:** A pleasant, well-decorated and -maintained lodging choice,
Andrea's is close to the beach and restaurants. 10 units. 8 one- and 2 two-bedroom suites with kitchens. 2
stories (no elevator), exterior corridors. *Bath:* shower only. **Parking:** street. **Pool(s):** outdoor. **Leisure Activities:** whirlpool.
Guest Services: TV in common area.

CASA MIRADOR BED & BREAKFAST   Phone: (322)221-5597   **26**
▼▼▼ ▼▼▼   12/1-4/14 [BP]   1P: $160-$180   2P: $160-$180   XP: $20
4/15-6/14 & 11/15-11/30 [CP]   1P: $120-$135   2P: $120-$135   XP: $20
Bed & Breakfast   6/15-11/14 [CP]   1P: $105-$120   2P: $105-$120   XP: $20
Location: 2 km s. 1200 Carr a Barra de Navidad Mex #200 48399 (5837 Deerfield, PORTAGE, MI, 49024).
Fax: 322/221-5597. **Facility:** Colorful, comfortable rooms that open to beach and ocean views await you here, but be ready to
climb some stairs and get some good exercise. 5 units. 4 one- and 1 two-bedroom standard units with efficiencies. 5 stories (no
elevator), exterior corridors. *Bath:* combo or shower only. **Parking:** on-site. **Terms:** office hours 9 am-8 pm, 60 day cancellation
notice, no pets allowed (owner's pet on premises). **Amenities:** safes, hair dryers. **Pool(s):** small outdoor. **Guest Services:** valet
laundry. **Business Services:** fax.
SOME UNITS

CLUB MEZA DEL MAR AN ALL INCLUSIVE HOTEL   Phone: (322)222-4888   **24**
▼▼ ▼▼   All Year [AP]   1P: $82-$206   2P: $82-$206   XP: $35
Location: 1 km s, on Playa de los Muertos. Amapas 380, Col E Zapata 48380. Fax: 322/222-2308. **Facility:** 128
Small-scale Hotel   units. 74 one-bedroom standard units. 41 one- and 13 three-bedroom suites. 4-8 stories, interior corridors.
Bath: shower only. **Parking:** street. **Terms:** office hours 9 am-6 pm, 3 day cancellation notice.
Amenities: safes (fee). **Pool(s):** 2 outdoor, wading. **Leisure Activities:** tennis court. **Guest Services:** gift shop, valet laundry.
Cards: MC, VI.
SOME UNITS

FIESTA AMERICANA PUERTO VALLARTA   Phone: (322)226-2100   **14**
(AAA)   12/1-1/2   2P: $327   XP: $24   F12
1/3-4/13   2P: $239   XP: $20   F12
▼▼ ▼▼   ▼▼ ▼▼   4/14-11/30   2P: $153   XP: $20   F12
Location: 4 km n on Paseo de las Palmas, off Airport Hwy (Mex 200). Blvd Fco Medina Ascencio KM 2.5 48300 (Apdo
Large-scale Hotel   Postal 270). Fax: 322/224-2108. **Facility:** All rooms with ocean view from balcony. 291 units. 288 one-
bedroom standard units. 3 one-bedroom suites, some with whirlpools. 9 stories, interior corridors. *Bath:*
combo or shower only. **Parking:** on-site. **Terms:** 15 day cancellation notice, [MAP] meal plan available. **Amenities:** video
games (fee), voice mail, safes, honor bars, hair dryers. **Dining:** 3 restaurants, 7 am-midnight, cocktails, entertainment. **Pool(s):**
heated outdoor, wading. **Leisure Activities:** recreation programs. *Fee:* massage. **Guest Services:** gift shop, valet laundry.
Business Services: conference facilities. **Cards:** AX, DC, MC, VI. *(See color ad card insert)*
SOME UNITS

HACIENDA HOTEL & SPA   *Book at aaa.com*   Phone: 322/226-6667   **11**
▼▼ ▼▼   All Year   1P: $53-$66   2P: $106-$132   XP: $16   F12
Location: 4.8 km n just off Airport Hwy (Mex 200). Blvd Fco Medina Ascencio 2699 48310 (Apdo Postal 95-B).
Small-scale Hotel   Fax: 322/226-6672. **Facility:** 155 one-bedroom standard units. 2-4 stories (no elevator), interior corridors.
Bath: combo or shower only. **Parking:** street. **Terms:** [AP] meal plan available. **Amenities:** *Some:* safes.
Pool(s): heated outdoor, wading. **Leisure Activities:** whirlpool, spa, shuffleboard. **Guest Services:** gift shop, valet laundry.
Business Services: meeting rooms, fax (fee). **Cards:** AX, MC, VI.

(See map and index starting on p. 447)

HOLIDAY INN PUERTO VALLARTA   *Book at aaa.com*   Phone: (322)226-1700   12

12/20-4/20	1P: $175	2P: $175	XP: $10 F12
12/1-12/19 & 4/21-11/30	1P: $111	2P: $111	XP: $10 F12

Large-scale Hotel **Location:** 4 km n on Airport Hwy (Mex 200). Blvd Fco Medina Ascencio S/N KM 3.5 48300 (Apdo Postal 555). Fax: 322/224-5683. **Facility:** 231 one-bedroom standard units. 9 stories, interior corridors. **Parking:** on-site. **Terms:** cancellation fee imposed, 17% service charge. **Amenities:** voice mail, safes. *Some:* irons, hair dryers. **Pool(s):** 2 outdoor, wading. **Leisure Activities:** whirlpools, steamrooms, rental boats, fishing, exercise room. *Fee:* waterskiing, scuba diving, charter fishing, 2 lighted tennis courts, massage. **Guest Services:** gift shop, valet laundry. **Business Services:** meeting rooms, business center. **Cards:** AX.

SOME UNITS

LAS PALMAS BY THE SEA   *Book at aaa.com*   Phone: (322)226-1220   15

All Year [AP]   1P: $130   2P: $200   XP: $80   F6

Resort / Large-scale Hotel **Location:** 2.5 km n off Airport Hwy (Mex 200). Blvd Fco Medina Ascencio KM 2.5 48300. Fax: 322/226-1268. **Facility:** Balconies and patios. Beachfront dining. 221 one-bedroom standard units. 4 stories, interior/exterior corridors. *Bath:* shower only. **Parking:** on-site. **Terms:** check-in 4 pm. **Amenities:** voice mail. *Some:* safes (fee). **Pool(s):** 2 outdoor. **Leisure Activities:** whirlpool, recreation programs, volleyball. *Fee:* boats, windsurfing, waterskiing, scuba diving, snorkeling. **Guest Services:** gift shop, valet laundry. **Business Services:** fax (fee). **Cards:** AX, CB, JC, MC, VI.

SOME UNITS

MARRIOTT CASA MAGNA   Phone: (322)226-0000   4

All Year   2P: $129-$239

Resort / Large-scale Hotel **Location:** 5 km n on Mex 200; at Marina Vallarta. Paseo de la Marina 5 48354. Fax: 322/226-0060. **Facility:** Fine location, very attractive grounds and public facilities. Pleasant, well-appointed rooms. 433 units. 415 one-bedroom standard units. 18 one-bedroom suites ($225-$1950), some with whirlpools. 9 stories, interior corridors. **Parking:** on-site. **Terms:** check-in 4 pm, 7 day cancellation notice-fee imposed, [AP] & [BP] meal plans available. **Amenities:** voice mail, safes, honor bars, irons, hair dryers. **Dining:** Mikado, La Estancia, see separate listings. **Pool(s):** heated outdoor, wading. **Leisure Activities:** saunas, whirlpool, recreation programs, exercise room. *Fee:* 3 lighted tennis courts, massage. **Guest Services:** gift shop, valet laundry. **Business Services:** conference facilities, business center. **Cards:** AX, DC, MC, VI.

SOME UNITS

MAYAN PALACE PUERTO VALLARTA   Phone: (322)226-6000   7

All Year	1P: $139-$209	2P: $173-$259	XP: $59 F12

Resort / Large-scale Hotel **Location:** 5 km off Mex 200; in Marina District. Paseo de la Marina Sur 220 48354. Fax: 322/226-6000. **Facility:** Authentic Mexican decor is found throughout this resort, which features a peaceful lagoon in addition to a huge pool, all in an oceanfront setting. 200 units. 80 one-bedroom standard units. 120 one-bedroom suites with efficiencies. 5-7 stories, interior corridors. *Bath:* combo or shower only. **Parking:** on-site. **Terms:** check-in 4 pm, 3 night minimum stay - seasonal and/or weekends, 30 day cancellation notice. **Amenities:** hair dryers. *Some:* irons. **Pool(s):** 2 heated outdoor, wading. **Leisure Activities:** whirlpool, recreation programs, volleyball. *Fee:* boats, scuba diving, snorkeling, charter fishing, miniature golf, lighted tennis court. **Guest Services:** gift shop. **Business Services:** meeting rooms. **Cards:** AX, MC, VI.

SOME UNITS   FEE

MELIA PUERTO VALLARTA ALL INCLUSIVE BEACH RESORT   *Book at aaa.com*   Phone: (322)226-3000   5

1/1-4/3 [AP]	1P: $110-$136	2P: $220-$272	XP: $90 F7
12/1-12/31 & 4/4-11/30 [AP]	1P: $95-$118	2P: $190-$236	XP: $80 F7

Resort / Large-scale Hotel **Location:** 5 km n off Mex 200. Located in the Marina District. Paseo de la Marina Sur Lote #7 48354. Fax: 322/221-0118. **Facility:** Very good recreational facilities. Modern, well-appointed rooms, attractive grounds. 352 one-bedroom standard units. 5-9 stories, interior corridors. **Parking:** on-site. **Terms:** 7 day cancellation notice. **Amenities:** voice mail, safes, hair dryers. **Pool(s):** outdoor, wading. **Leisure Activities:** 2 lighted tennis courts, recreation programs, playground, exercise room, shuffleboard, volleyball, game room. *Fee:* sailboats, waterskiing, scuba diving. **Guest Services:** gift shop, valet laundry. **Business Services:** meeting rooms. **Cards:** AX, MC, VI.

SOME UNITS

MOLINO DE AGUA HOTEL   Phone: (322)222-1907   19

12/1-4/15		2P: $97-$150	XP: $15 F12
4/16-11/30		2P: $67-$128	XP: $15 F12

Motel **Location:** Just s of Puente Cuale, bordering Rio Cuale and Playa Ozas Altas. Ignacio L Vallarta 130 48380 (Apdo Postal 54). Fax: 322/222-6056. **Facility:** 60 units. 32 one-bedroom standard units. 4 one-bedroom suites ($135-$160). 24 cottages. 1-3 stories (no elevator), exterior corridors. *Bath:* combo or shower only. **Parking:** on-site. **Terms:** 15 day cancellation notice-fee imposed. **Pool(s):** 2 outdoor. **Leisure Activities:** whirlpool. *Fee:* massage. **Guest Services:** valet laundry. **Cards:** AX, MC, VI.

SOME UNITS

PLAYA LOS ARCOS HOTEL   *Book at aaa.com*   Phone: (322)222-1583   20

1/3-4/6	1P: $62-$82	2P: $67-$89	XP: $10 F12
4/7-11/30	1P: $52-$64	2P: $57-$70	XP: $10 F12
12/1-1/2	1P: $50-$62	2P: $55-$68	XP: $10 F12

Small-scale Hotel **Location:** Center; in Zona Romantica. Olas Altas 380 48380. Fax: 322/226-7104. **Facility:** 175 units. 163 one-bedroom standard units. 12 one-bedroom suites ($115-$125) with kitchens. 4 stories, interior/exterior corridors. *Bath:* shower only. **Parking:** on-site. **Terms:** 7 day cancellation notice-fee imposed, [AP], [BP] & [MAP] meal plans available. **Amenities:** hair dryers. **Pool(s):** 2 heated outdoor. **Leisure Activities:** recreation programs. **Guest Services:** gift shop, valet laundry. **Business Services:** fax (fee). **Cards:** AX, MC, VI.

SOME UNITS

(See map and index starting on p. 447)

PRESIDENTE INTERCONTINENTAL PUERTO
VALLARTA   *Book at aaa.com*   **Phone:** (322)228-0191   **28**

4/18-11/30	1P: $314-$699	2P: $314-$699 XP: $30 F18
12/26-4/17	1P: $289-$699	2P: $289-$699 XP: $30 F18
12/1-12/25	1P: $169-$544	2P: $169-$544 XP: $30 F18

Large-scale Hotel   **Location:** On Mex 200, 8.5 km s. KM 8.5 Mex 200, Carr Puerto Vallarta 48300 (Apdo Postal 448).
Fax: 322/228-0603. **Facility:** Fine location on pretty beach. Beautiful landscaping. All guest rooms have balcony overlooking the
ocean. 120 units. 116 one-bedroom standard units, some with whirlpools. 4 two-bedroom suites with whirlpools. 10 stories,
exterior corridors. **Parking:** on-site. **Terms:** age restrictions may apply, 3 day cancellation notice-fee imposed, $8 service
charge. **Amenities:** video library (fee), voice mail, hair dryers. *Some:* DVD players, CD players. **Dining:** Da Antonio, see
separate listing. **Pool(s):** heated outdoor. **Leisure Activities:** exercise room. *Fee:* scuba diving, snorkeling, fishing, lighted
tennis court, massage. **Guest Services:** gift shop, valet laundry. **Business Services:** meeting rooms, business center.
Cards: AX, DC, JC, MC, VI.

SOME UNITS
FEE

QUALTON CLUB & SPA AN ALL INCLUSIVE RESORT   *Book at aaa.com*   **Phone:** (322)224-4446   **13**

12/20-4/26 [AP]	1P: $100-$155	2P: $250-$310 XP: $85
12/1-12/19 & 4/27-11/30 [AP]	1P: $80-$100	2P: $160-$200 XP: $75

Resort   **Location:** 4 km n on Ave de las Palmas, off Airport Hwy (Mex 200). KM 2.5 Blvd Fco Medina Ascencio S/N 48300
Large-scale Hotel   (Apdo Postal 308). Fax: 322/224-4445. **Facility:** Extensive spa facilities. 218 one-bedroom standard units,
some with whirlpools. 4-14 stories, interior corridors. **Parking:** valet. **Terms:** 3 day cancellation notice.
Amenities: voice mail, safes (fee). *Some:* hair dryers. **Pool(s):** outdoor. **Leisure Activities:** saunas, whirlpools, steamrooms,
paddleboats, windsurfing, lighted tennis court, recreation programs, spa. *Fee:* scuba diving. **Guest Services:** gift shop, valet
laundry. **Business Services:** meeting rooms. *Fee:* PC, fax. **Cards:** AX, MC, VI.

SOME UNITS

QUINTA REAL PUERTO VALLARTA   *Book at aaa.com*   **Phone:** 322/226-6688   **2**

All Year   1P: $275-$450   2P: $275-$450   XP: $50

Location: In Marina Vallarta Golf Course. 311 Pelicanos Marina Vallarta 48354. Fax: 322/226-6699. **Facility:** This
gated resort features private villas or spacious guestrooms, many with private dip pool and views of the
adjoining golf course. 84 units. 67 one-bedroom standard units, some with whirlpools. 8 one-, 8 two- and 1
Resort   three-bedroom suites ($475-$786) with whirlpools. 3 stories, interior/exterior corridors. **Parking:** on-site and
Small-scale Hotel   valet. **Amenities:** CD players, dual phone lines, voice mail, safes, honor bars, irons, hair dryers. **Dining:** 7
am-11 pm, cocktails, also, El Candil, see separate listing. **Pool(s):** 2 heated outdoor. **Leisure
Activities:** saunas, whirlpools, steamrooms, beach club privileges, 2 lighted tennis courts, bicycles, exercise room, spa. *Fee:*
golf privileges. **Guest Services:** gift shop, valet laundry. **Business Services:** meeting rooms, PC. **Cards:** AX, MC, VI.

SHERATON BUGANVILIAS CONVENTION CENTER   *Book at aaa.com*   **Phone:** 322/226-0404   **16**

All Year   1P: $259-$350   2P: $259-$350   XP: $30

Location: Just n of town center. Blvd Fco Medina Ascencio 99 48300. Fax: 322/222-3111. **Facility:** This large
complex features two large pools with swim-up bars and a fine oceanfront location; it is walking distance
Resort   from the popular downtown area. 674 units. 670 one-bedroom standard units, some with efficiencies and/or
Large-scale Hotel   whirlpools. 4 one-bedroom suites ($365-$430) with whirlpools. 13-15 stories, interior corridors. *Bath:* combo
or shower only. **Parking:** on-site. **Terms:** [AP] meal plan available. **Amenities:** voice mail, safes, hair dryers. *Some:* honor bars.
Pool(s): 2 heated outdoor, 2 wading. **Leisure Activities:** whirlpool, recreation programs, exercise room, spa. *Fee:* 4 tennis
courts (2 lighted). **Business Services:** conference facilities, business center. **Cards:** AX, MC, VI. *(See color ad p 8)*

SOME UNITS

VISTA PLAYA DE ORO ALL INCLUSIVE   *Book at aaa.com*   **Phone:** 322/226-6868   **8**

12/24-4/27 [AP]	1P: $149	2P: $238 XP: $89 F5
12/1-12/23 & 4/28-11/30 [AP]	1P: $129	2P: $218 XP: $89 F5

Location: 4.8 km n off Airport Hwy (Mex 200). Ave Las Garzas #1 48333. Fax: 322/226-6810. **Facility:** Attractive
grounds. Pleasant rooms, some with ocean view; balcony. 250 one-bedroom standard units, some with
Resort   whirlpools. 4 stories (no elevator), exterior corridors. *Bath:* shower only. **Parking:** on-site. **Terms:** check-in 4
Large-scale Hotel   pm, 3 day cancellation notice-fee imposed. **Amenities:** voice mail, hair dryers. *Some:* safes. **Dining:** 4
restaurants, 7 am-1 am, cocktails, nightclub, entertainment. **Pool(s):** heated outdoor, wading. **Leisure
Activities:** steamroom, rental boats, windsurfing, snorkeling, boogie boards, kayaks, non-motorized watersports, recreation
programs, playground, exercise room, shuffleboard, volleyball, game room. *Fee:* waterskiing, scuba diving, fishing, 3 lighted
tennis courts, massage. **Guest Services:** gift shop, valet laundry. **Business Services:** meeting rooms, fax (fee). **Cards:** AX,
MC, VI.

THE WESTIN PUERTO VALLARTA RESORT AND
SPA   *Book at aaa.com*   **Phone:** (322)226-1100   **9**

12/19-1/3	1P: $265-$589	2P: $265-$589 XP: $40 F18
1/4-4/17	1P: $159-$425	2P: $159-$425 XP: $40 F18
12/1-12/18 & 4/18-11/30	1P: $120-$379	2P: $120-$379 XP: $40 F18

Resort   **Location:** 5 km n on Mex 200; in Marina Vallarta. Paseo de la Marina Sur 205 48354 (Apdo Postal 4-100).
Large-scale Hotel   Fax: 322/226-1107. **Facility:** Handsome beachfront hotel with excellent facilities and very attractive rooms.
280 units. 264 one-bedroom standard units, some with whirlpools. 16 one-bedroom suites ($320-$1369), some with whirlpools.
14 stories, interior corridors. **Parking:** on-site. **Terms:** 7 day cancellation notice-fee imposed. [BP] meal plan available.
Amenities: dual phone lines, voice mail, safes, honor bars, irons, hair dryers. **Pool(s):** 4 outdoor. **Leisure Activities:** sauna,
whirlpools, steamrooms, recreation programs, playground, spa. *Fee:* 3 lighted tennis courts. **Guest Services:** gift shop, valet
laundry. **Business Services:** conference facilities, business center. **Cards:** AX, DC, MC, VI. *(See color ad p 8)*

SOME UNITS
FEE

(See map and index starting on p. 447)

———— *The following lodging was either not evaluated or did not* ————
meet AAA rating requirements but is listed for your information only.

HOTEL SAN MARINO   Phone: 322/222-1555
[fyi]   Not evaluated. **Location:** Center. Rodolfo Gomez #111 Col E Zapata 48300. Facilities, services, and decor
characterize a mid-range property.

———— **WHERE TO DINE** ————

ANDREA GOURMET   **Lunch:** $10-$20   **Dinner:** $15-$35   **Phone:** 322/221-0091   ⑫
▼▼▼▼   **Location:** 5 km n of Mex 200; in Marina Vallarta; in Hotel Velas Vallarta. Paseo de la Marina 48354. **Hours:** 7:30 am-
noon, 12:30-5 & 6-10:30 pm. **Reservations:** suggested. **Features:** The elegant dining room features
Continental   candlelit tables and both indoor and outdoor terrace seating. Mexico-influenced contemporary decor
complements a fine menu of Continental and Italian cuisine. Casual dress; cocktails. **Parking:** street.
Cards: AX, MC, VI.

THE BLUE SHRIMP RESTAURANT   **Lunch:** $18-$40   **Dinner:** $18-$40   **Phone:** 322/222-4246   ㉖
▼▼▼▼   **Location:** Center of downtown; east of the malecon. Morelos #779 Col Centro 48300. **Hours:** noon-midnight.
Reservations: suggested. **Features:** This is the spot for shrimp lovers. As the name suggests, the popular
Seafood   restaurant specializes in fresh shrimp in everything from tangy cocktails to pay-by-the-pound options. The
chef cooks them in a variety of ways, including tequila, freshly breaded coconut and the often-ordered
garlic-seasoned. Also featured are fresh local lobsters of huge proportions, some meat options and a tasty salad bar. After
dinner, guests can head upstairs to the Martini Bar, which has live entertainment. Casual dress; cocktails. **Parking:** street.
Cards: AX, MC, VI.
                                                                            Ⓨ Ⓧ

BOGART'S   **Dinner:** $12-$40   **Phone:** 322/224-0202   ⑰
▼▼▼▼   **Location:** 4.5 km n, off Mex 200; at Krystal Vallarta. Ave de las Garzas S/N 48300. **Hours:** 6 pm-midnight.
Reservations: suggested. **Features:** Exotic decor contributes to a strong Moroccan theme. The interior is
Steak & Seafood   filled with flowing pools, fresh tropical plants and dim lighting that make guests feel as though they are in
another land. The equally intriguing menu merges Continental and local dishes. Dressy casual; cocktails.
Parking: street. **Cards:** AX, MC, VI.
                                                                            Ⓨ Ⓧ

CAFE DES ARTISTES   **Dinner:** $20-$25   **Phone:** 322/222-3228   ㉒
▼▼▼▼   **Location:** Center. Guadalupe Sanchez 740 48300. **Hours:** 6 pm-11:30 pm. **Reservations:** required.
Features: Innovative cuisine combines French and Mexican preparation styles. For a real treat, try the
French   custom-prepared "menu de degustacion." Piano performances are offered nightly on the deck, where the
secluded atmosphere is romantic. Dressy casual; cocktails; entertainment. **Parking:** on-site. **Cards:** AX,
MC, VI.
                                                                            Ⓨ Ⓚ

DA ANTONIO   **Dinner:** $15-$25   **Phone:** 322/228-0191   ㊵
▼▼▼ ▼▼▼   **Location:** On Mex 200, 8.5 km s; in Presidente InterContinental Puerto Vallarta. KM 8.5 Mex 200, Carr Puerto Vallarta
48300. **Hours:** 6 pm-11:30 pm. Closed: Sun. **Reservations:** suggested. **Features:** An elegant dining room
Italian   with live piano entertainment and views overlooking the ocean sets the stage. The romantic restaurant
presents diners a menu of freshly prepared fine Italian cuisine. Service is professional and polished. Dressy
casual; cocktails. **Parking:** on-site. **Cards:** AX, DC, MC, VI.
                                                                            Ⓧ

EL CANDIL   **Lunch:** $14-$29   **Dinner:** $14-$29   **Phone:** 322/226-6688   ①
ⒶⒶⒶ   **Location:** In Marina Vallarta Golf Course; in Quinta Real Puerto Vallarta. 311 Pelicanos Marina Vallarta 48354.
Hours: 7 am-11 pm. **Reservations:** accepted. **Features:** Guests enter through the secured gates and
▼▼▼▼   graceful lobby of the hotel before being awed by the cascading pools leading down to the midnight blue pool
which will be the backdrop for an enjoyable meal, which might include sweet plantain and black bean
Continental   turnover in a sweet cream sauce, a salad of tender lobster and sliced pineapple in a citric vinaigrette or
maybe beef medallions in a blue agave sauce with cracked black pepper. Casual dress; cocktails. **Parking:**
valet. **Cards:** AX, MC, VI.
                                                                            Ⓨ

EL CIRCO   **Dinner:** $16-$30   **Phone:** 322/221-2404   ⑨
▼▼▼▼   **Location:** In Marina Vallarta. Condominios Marina del Rey, Local 13 48354. **Hours:** 6 pm-11 pm. Closed major
holidays; also Sun. **Reservations:** suggested. **Features:** An innovative menu with a distinct Caribbean flair
Caribbean   and a fun upscale atmosphere make the restaurant a popular choice for those seeking a memorable
evening. This place is designed like a circus tent. Brightly colored paper animals surround diners seated on
striped chair cushions. The food, which blends exotic spices and fresh ingredients, is the star here. Dressy casual; cocktails.
Parking: street. **Cards:** AX, MC, VI.
                                                                            Ⓚ

EL DORADO   **Lunch:** $6-$30   **Dinner:** $6-$30   **Phone:** 322/222-1511   ㊱
▼▼▼ ▼▼▼   **Location:** On Playa de los Muertos. Pulpito #102 Playa de los Muertos 48380. **Hours:** 8 am-10 pm. Closed: 5/1.
Reservations: accepted. **Features:** A prime beachfront location and a mixed menu of casual fare make this
Continental   a popular choice for diners both day and night. In the day, in addition to the fully-serviced dining room, the
restaurant also features a beach club, where diners can enjoy meals while relaxing in their lounge chairs.
The menu features such light fare favorites as burgers, clubhouse sandwiches and salads, as well as a good variety of fresh
local seafood. Shrimp dishes, offered in several sauces, are superb. Casual dress; cocktails. **Parking:** street. **Cards:** AX,
MC, VI.
                                                                            Ⓚ

(See map and index starting on p. 447)

FAJITA BANANA TROPICAL GRILL & BAR **Lunch:** $7-$14 **Dinner:** $7-$14 **Phone:** 322/221-3154 ⑥
'American
Location: In Marina Vallarta. Puesta del Sol Loc 17 Marina Vallarta 48354. **Hours:** 8 am-11 pm. **Reservations:** accepted. **Features:** US-style ribs, burgers and, of course, fajitas, are served at the eatery, which lets guests sit in an open-air setting and view the boats in the marina. Indoors is a bar and lounge. Patrons might overindulge on the all-you-can-eat ribs. Casual dress; cocktails. **Parking:** street.
Cards: MC, VI.

KAISER MAXIMILIAN **Dinner:** $9-$20 **Phone:** 322/223-0760 ㉙
Continental
Location: In older part of town. Olas Altas #380 B 48380. **Hours:** 6 pm-11 pm. Closed: Sun. **Reservations:** suggested. **Features:** European decor and ambience punctuate the indoor dining room and the sidewalk area. A few Austrian specialties stand out on the menu. Coffee and pastries are served at a separate coffee bar. Casual dress; cocktails. **Parking:** on-site. **Cards:** AX, MC, VI.

LA DOLCE VITA RISTORANTE BAR **Lunch:** $7-$10 **Dinner:** $8-$18 **Phone:** 322/222-3852 ⑳
Italian
Location: On the malecon, along beachfront road; center. Ave P Diaz Ordaz #674 48300. **Hours:** noon-midnight. **Features:** The beachfront cafe serves traditional pasta dishes, as well as fresh, well-prepared Italian-style seafood. Views of the busy Malecon can be enjoyed from most tables. Casual dress; cocktails. **Parking:** street. **Cards:** MC, VI.

LA ESTANCIA **Lunch:** $8-$14 **Dinner:** $14-$20 **Phone:** 322/226-0000 ⑭
Mexican
Location: 5 km n on Mex 200; at Marina Vallarta; in Marriott Casa Magna. Paseo de la Marina 5 48354. **Hours:** 6:30 am-11:30, noon-5 & 6-11 pm. **Reservations:** suggested. **Features:** High ceilings, marble floors and lots of tropical plants add to the perfect setting for an enjoyable meal. Service is friendly and personable. Among options are items on a daily changing buffet and selections of fine Mexican fare from the a la carte menu. For a tasty local food adventure, try tortilla soup and shrimp fajitas. Casual dress; cocktails. **Cards:** AX, DC, MC, VI.

LA HACIENDA **Dinner:** $18-$21 **Phone:** 322/226-2100 ⑱
Continental
Location: 4 km n on Paseo de las Palmas, off Airport Hwy (Mex 200); in Fiesta Americana Puerto Vallarta. Blvd Fco Medina Ascencio KM 2.5 48300. **Hours:** 6 pm-midnight. **Reservations:** suggested. **Features:** Lending to the Mexican atmosphere are wonderful displays of hand-painted pottery and festive artwork. Diners can peruse the fine Continental menu at candlelit tables in the main dining room or on the romantic patio. Dressy casual; cocktails. **Parking:** on-site. **Cards:** AX, MC, VI.

LA PALAPA RESTAURANTE AND BAR **Lunch:** $9-$30 **Dinner:** $16-$38 **Phone:** 322/222-5225 ㉞
International
Location: On Playa de los Muertos. Pulpito 103 48380. **Hours:** 9 am-11:30 pm. Closed: 5/1. **Reservations:** suggested, for dinner. **Features:** Casual elegance and a prime beachfront setting are the main attractions. During the day, diners can take a break from the sun and have a wonderful light or full entree lunch on the sand or in the main dining room. At night, the setting is romantic as diners hear the roar of the waves. Live entertainment is featured in the lounge day and night. The menu features a range of local and international fare including fresh seafood, fajitas and beef selections. Casual dress; cocktails. **Parking:** no self-parking. **Cards:** AX, DC, DS, MC, VI.

LA PETITE FRANCE **Lunch:** $7-$15 **Dinner:** $12-$35 **Phone:** 322/293-0901 ⑯
French
Location: 4 km n on Paseo de las Palmas, off Airport Hwy (Mex 200). Blvd Fco Medina Ascencio KM 2.5 48300. **Hours:** 8 am-midnight. **Features:** A European feel is re-created in the large but cozy dining room. Pictures of old-day Paris adorn the walls. Fine French cuisine is prepared with wonderful sauces. Whether choosing tableside-prepared Caesar salad, traditional French onion soup or mussels in wine or cream sauce, guests are sure to have a wonderful beginning. Among entrees are duck a l'orange, coq au vin and varied meat and seafood selections. Dressy casual; cocktails. **Parking:** street. **Cards:** AX, MC, VI.

LAS PALOMAS DORADAS **Lunch:** $8-$11 **Dinner:** $11-$20 **Phone:** 322/221-0470 ⑦
Continental
Location: In Marina Vallarta. Club de Tenis, Puesta Local Marina Vallarta 48354. **Hours:** Open 12/1-8/31 & 10/1-11/30; 8 am-11 pm. Closed: 12/25. **Features:** Close to the sailboats and yachts in the marina, the boardwalk cafe serves fresh fish, US-style steaks and Mexican cuisine. Margaritas are enormous, and the food is deftly prepared. Casual dress; cocktails. **Parking:** street. **Cards:** AX, MC, VI.

LE BISTRO JAZZ CAFE **Lunch:** $15-$20 **Dinner:** $15-$20 **Phone:** 322/222-0283 ㉘
Continental
Location: On Rio Cuale Island; center of city. Rio Cuale Island 16A 48300. **Hours:** 9 am-midnight. Closed: Sun. **Features:** Casual. Outdoor and covered dining. Casual dress; cocktails. **Parking:** on-site. **Cards:** AX, DC, DS, MC, VI.

LE KLIFF RESTAURANTE AND BAR **Lunch:** $15-$45 **Dinner:** $15-$45 **Phone:** 322/228-0666 ㊷
Seafood
Location: On Carr A Barra de Navidad KM 17.5. Carr A Barra de Navidad KM 17.5 48300. **Hours:** noon-10:30 pm. **Reservations:** required. **Features:** On a cliff overlooking the ocean, the restaurant is known for its spectacular views. Many patrons reserve a table so they can dine while watching the sunset. Marriage proposals are common in this romantic setting. The menu lists a wonderful selection of fine Continental cuisine, with fresh local seafood a specialty. Casual dress; cocktails. **Parking:** on-site. **Cards:** AX, MC, VI.

LOS XITOMATES **Dinner:** $18-$35 **Phone:** 322/222-1694 ㉓
Mexican
Location: Downtown. Morelos 570 Centro 48300. **Hours:** 6 pm-11:30 pm. **Reservations:** accepted. **Features:** The casually elegant and tranquil setting of this dining room makes it worth the couple of blocks walk off the malecon, and once you've enjoyed a meal of sauteed octopus, red snapper with heart of palm sauce and Toluca ice cream cake, you will have a hard time not returning the next night. The owner describes the cuisine as "high Mexican cuisine". Casual dress; cocktails. **Parking:** street. **Cards:** AX, MC, VI.

(See map and index starting on p. 447)

MARIA BONITA — Mexican
Dinner: $14-$22 **Phone:** 322/226-5023 ⊞ 38
Location: 3.5 km s on Mismaloya Hwy (Mex 200); in Camino Real Puerto Vallarta. Playa Las Estacas S/N KM 3.5 48300. **Hours:** 6:30 pm-midnight. **Reservations:** suggested. **Features:** Fine Mexican cuisine and lively entertainment delight diners. Brightly decorated like a cantina, the restaurant displays hand-painted Mexican pottery. On the menu is a wonderful mix of freshly prepared fare, including fresh seafood, fajitas and some Tex-Mex specialties. Casual dress; cocktails. **Parking:** on-site. **Cards:** AX, DC, DS, MC, VI.

MEZZALUNA RISTORANTE ITALIANO — Italian
Dinner: $15-$23 **Phone:** 322/222-0393 ⊞ 30
Location: Southeast corner of Hidalgo St and Corona; downtown. Hidalgo St 550 48300. **Hours:** 6 pm-11:30 pm. **Reservations:** accepted. **Features:** An eclectic mix of furnishings can make for a romantic dinner for two on the patio or for a lively group of friends on the balcony. A fairly traditional Italian menu with items like grilled mozzarella, potato dumplings and homemade flan and tiramisu make for a nice change from seafood and Mexican meals. Casual dress; cocktails. **Parking:** street. **Cards:** MC, VI.

MIKADO — Sushi
Dinner: $15-$30 **Phone:** 322/221-0004 ⊞ 13
Location: 5 km n on Mex 200; at Marina Vallarta; in Marriott Casa Magna. Paseo de la Marina 5 48354. **Hours:** 6 pm-11 pm. **Reservations:** suggested. **Features:** The restaurant incorporates a Japanese sushi bar and teppanyaki tableside cooking done by entertaining chefs. Dressy casual; cocktails. **Parking:** on-site. **Cards:** AX, DC, MC, VI.

OUTBACK STEAKHOUSE — Steak House
Lunch: $8-$20 **Dinner:** $8-$20 **Phone:** 322/225-4906 ⊞ 11
Location: Just s of Marina District (north Hotel Zone). Blvd Fco Medina Ascencio 4690 48324. **Hours:** 1:30 pm-11 pm, Fri & Sat-midnight. **Features:** Ready to satisfy your craving for tastes from back home, the restaurant offers the same hearty portions of sizzling steaks, lamb, chicken and juicy burgers. In addition to these popular favorites, the menu is also packed with choices of sizzling fajitas to add that Mexican touch. Come with a hearty appetite, as the portions are generous. Casual dress; cocktails. **Parking:** on-site. **Cards:** AX, MC, VI.

PANCAKE HOUSE — American
Lunch: $3-$6 **Phone:** 322/222-6272 ⊞ 33
Location: 4 blks s of Rio Cuale. 289 Basilio Badillo 48380. **Hours:** 8 am-2 pm. Closed major holidays. **Features:** The mood is casual at this restaurant, which prepares a good selection of American-style breakfast dishes, waffles, pancakes and blintzes. Authentic Mexican dishes are at the heart of the dinner menu. Casual dress; cocktails. **Parking:** on-site.

PARADISE BURGER — American
Lunch: $7-$15 **Dinner:** $7-$15 **Phone:** 322/223-2328 ⊞ 21
Location: On the malecon, facing the ocean. Paseo Diaz Ordaz #740 48300. **Hours:** 10:30 am-midnight. **Features:** In the mood for a juicy burger or some tasty onion rings? This eatery fills the bill. Also on the menu are wings, fish and chips, hearty sandwiches, salads and ribs. The great location has some balcony seating offering a great view. Casual dress; cocktails. **Parking:** street. **Cards:** MC, VI.

PIE IN THE SKY-PUERTO VALLARTA — Bakery/Desserts
Lunch: $3-$6 **Dinner:** $3-$6 **Phone:** 322/222-8411 ⊞ 31
Location: Just s of Puente Cuale; bordering Rio Cuale and Playa Ozas Altas. Ignacio L Vallarta #150 48380. **Hours:** 8 am-11 pm. **Features:** The first choice of locals and tourists alike looking for a wakeup cup of coffee and a fresh bagel, or perhaps one last bite of dessert before retiring for the night. The specialties include tres leche pastel cake and a beso, which is a brownie with a molten fudge center. Light lunch might include a slice of pizza and a scoop of ice cream. Casual dress. **Parking:** street.

PORTO BELLO RISTORANTE ITALIANO — Italian
Lunch: $8-$27 **Dinner:** $8-$27 **Phone:** 322/221-0003 ⊞ 8
Location: In Marina Vallarta. Marina del Sol Local 7 Marina Vallarta 48354. **Hours:** 11 am-11 pm. **Features:** This elegant restaurant offers diners a choice of indoor or outdoor patio in the relaxed, yet sophisticated style that is so common in the area. The menu features a wide variety of fine Italian cuisine with antipasta platters for sharing, fresh homemade pastas, veal and seafood offerings. Although portions are hearty, try to save room for the fabulous selection of homemade desserts: the ultimate in decadence. Dressy casual; cocktails. **Parking:** street. **Cards:** AX, MC, VI.

RESTAURANTE ARGENTINO LOS PIBES — Argentine
Dinner: $20-$40 **Phone:** 322/223-1557 ⊞ 32
Location: Center; Zona Romantica. Basilio Badillo #261. **Hours:** Open 12/1-6/30 & 10/1-11/30; 6 pm-midnight. Closed: Sun. **Reservations:** suggested. **Features:** For those looking for good grilled beef, this restaurant is a nice change of pace. Gaucho-attired servers show diners the various appetizers and entrees that will be grilled. Casual dress; cocktails. **Parking:** street. **Cards:** AX, DC, MC, VI.

RINCON DE BUENOS AIRES — Steak House
Dinner: $10-$30 **Phone:** 322/221-2260 ⊞ 3
Location: In Marina Vallarta. Malecon de la Marina Royal Pacific Local 12 6127 48354. **Hours:** 5 pm-11 pm. Closed: 12/14. **Reservations:** suggested. **Features:** This casual eatery features hearty portions of prime beef. Servers will display the huge cuts of meat tableside to help diners make their selection. Kebobs, seafood, and poultry are also featured. The chefs grill all meals to order over a wood fire, making the flavor sensational. Casual dress; cocktails. **Parking:** street. **Cards:** AX, MC, VI.

THE RIVER CAFE — Continental
Lunch: $8-$20 **Dinner:** $12-$30 **Phone:** 322/223-0788 ⊞ 27
Location: Center; at Isla Rio Cuale. Isla Rio Cuale Local 4 48354. **Hours:** 9 am-11:30 pm. **Reservations:** suggested, for dinner. **Features:** A tranquil setting awaits diners who wish to escape from the bustling city streets to a peaceful oasis overlooking the river. Lucky diners may spot some large iguanas sunning themselves in the heat of the day. At night, a romantic atmosphere is created with candlelit tables and pleasant background music. The menu offers light and full lunch entrees and a sophisticated dinner menu featuring fine Continental cuisine. Dressy casual; cocktails. **Parking:** no self-parking. **Cards:** AX, MC, VI.

(See map and index starting on p. 447)

SUZIE WONG'S CHINESE CUISINE   **Lunch:** $6-$15   **Dinner:** $10-$28   **Phone:** 322/221-2057   ②

    Location: In Marina Vallarta; close to the light house. Condominio Royal Pacific #124 48354. **Hours:** noon-11 pm.

Chinese   **Features:** The casual restaurant features both indoor and outdoor patio seating. Tropical foliage, a fish pond and a water fountain lend to a tranquil setting. The menu lists a selection of tasty Chinese cuisine, and daily lunch specials offer excellent value. Casual dress; cocktails. **Parking:** street. **Cards:** MC, VI.

TERRAZZA DI ROMA RISTORANTE ITALIANO   **Lunch:** $6-$9   **Dinner:** $12-$18   **Phone:** 322/221-0871   ⑤

    Location: In Marina Vallarta. Condominio Puesta del Sol Local 2 48354. **Hours:** 8:30 am-11 pm.

Italian   **Reservations:** accepted. **Features:** A charming, awning-covered pier at the water's edge is part of the setting at this restaurant. The menu lists pizza and a full range of Italian pasta and meat dishes, as well as both American and Mexican breakfast selections. Casual dress; cocktails. **Parking:** street. **Cards:** AX, MC, VI.

TRIO RESTAURANT   **Lunch:** $10-$17   **Dinner:** $12-$30   **Phone:** 322/222-2196   ㉔

    Location: 3 blks n of the malecon; center. Guerrero #264 48300. **Hours:** 6 pm-11:30 pm; also noon-3:30 pm 11/1-4/30. **Reservations:** suggested. **Features:** Fine European cuisine is what you'll find at this very popular

Mediterranean   dining spot located in the central part of the city. It also features a pleasant mix of local and bistro decor, live music and generous drinks. It is popular with the American and European expatriate communities. Dressy casual; cocktails. **Parking:** street. **Cards:** AX, MC, VI.

The following restaurant has not been evaluated by AAA but is listed for your information only.

LA CAVE RESTAURANT   **Phone:** 322/222-4790

  fyi   Not evaluated. **Location:** Just s of Cuale Island bridge; downtown. Hidalgo St #113 48300. **Features:** In the Zona Romantica, the full-service restaurant prepares a mix of Mexican and North American cuisine. Breakfast is also served.

This ends listings for Puerto Vallarta.
The following page resumes the alphabetical listings
of cities in The Pacific Coast.

PUNTA MITA, NAYARIT

———— WHERE TO STAY ————

CASA LAS BRISAS
Phone: 322/306-2122

▼▼▼ ▼▼▼ All Year [AP]   1P: $335   2P: $385
Bed & Breakfast **Location:** Mex 200, 18 km on Punta Mita Rd, Higuena Blanco turn off, 1.8 km w to bridge Puente Cauyeros, then 1.1 km on beach access road. Calle Playa Caneyeras S/N (827 Union Pacific, PO Box 078-369, LAREDO, TX, 78045). Fax: 329/298-4112. **Facility:** Casa Las Brisas is an exclusive, luxury, seaside B&B where the included meals emphasize fine dining. Designated smoking area. 7 one-bedroom standard units. 2 stories (no elevator), interior/exterior corridors. *Bath:* shower only. **Parking:** on-site. **Terms:** office hours 8 am-11 pm, age restrictions may apply, pets (with prior approval). **Amenities:** video library, CD players, safes, honor bars. **Pool(s):** heated outdoor. **Leisure Activities:** snorkeling. *Fee:* massage. **Guest Services:** valet laundry. **Cards:** MC, VI.

FOUR SEASONS RESORT PUNTA MITA, MEXICO
Phone: (329)291-6000

(AAA)   12/1-4/20   1P: $420-$845   2P: $420-$845   XP: $80   F18
▼▼▼ ▼▼▼ ▼▼ 4/21-11/30   1P: $290-$740   2P: $290-$740   XP: $80   F18
Resort   **Location:** Puerto Vallarta Airport, 29 mi n (KM 47). (350 S Beverly Dr, Suite 220, BEVERLY HILLS, CA, 90212).
Large-scale Hotel Fax: 329/291-6060. **Facility:** This exclusive resort overlooks the ocean and a beach. It caters to couples and families who enjoy outdoor activities rather than nightlife. 140 units. 114 one-bedroom standard units. 26 one-bedroom suites ($875-$4270), some with whirlpools. 1-3 stories (no elevator), exterior corridors. **Parking:** valet. **Terms:** 30 day cancellation notice-fee imposed, [AP] & [MAP] meal plans available, small pets only. **Amenities:** video library, DVD players, CD players, high-speed Internet (fee), dual phone lines, voice mail, safes, honor bars, irons, hair dryers. **Dining:** 3 restaurants, 6:30 am-11:30 pm, cocktails, also, Aramara Restaurant and Bar, see separate listing, entertainment. **Pool(s):** heated outdoor, wading. **Leisure Activities:** whirlpool, steamrooms, paddleboats, windsurfing, snorkeling, fishing, kayaks, golf & tennis instruction, recreation programs, ATV, hiking trails, jogging, playground, spa, volleyball, game room. *Fee:* boats, sailboats, scuba diving, charter fishing, swim with dolphins, golf-19 holes, 4 lighted tennis courts, canopy tours, horseback riding. **Guest Services:** gift shop, complimentary and valet laundry. **Business Services:** conference facilities. **Cards:** AX, CB, DC, MC, VI.

VIVA WYNDHAM VALLARTA
Phone: 329/226-9900

▼▼▼ ▼▼ All Year [AP]   1P: $178-$320   2P: $178-$320   XP: $100
Resort   **Location:** Mex 200, exit Punta Mita Rd, 11 km s to entrance. Costa Banderas KM 8 & 9 63737. Fax: 329/226-9910.
Large-scale Hotel **Facility:** This all-inclusive resort offers a relaxing, fun atmosphere and a stunning oceanfront location; activities are available for all ages. 420 one-bedroom standard units. 3 stories, exterior corridors. **Parking:** on-site. **Amenities:** hair dryers. **Pool(s):** 2 outdoor, wading. **Leisure Activities:** saunas, whirlpool, windsurfing, snorkeling, 2 lighted tennis courts, recreation programs, spa, volleyball, game room. *Fee:* scuba diving. **Guest Services:** gift shop, complimentary evening beverages. **Business Services:** meeting rooms. **Cards:** AX, MC, VI.

———— WHERE TO DINE ————

ARAMARA RESTAURANT AND BAR
Dinner: $21-$35   **Phone:** 329/291-6000

▼▼▼ ▼▼▼ **Location:** Puerto Vallarta Airport, 29 mi n (KM 47); in Four Seasons Resort Punta Mita, Mexico. **Hours:** 6:30 pm-
International 11:30 pm. **Reservations:** suggested. **Features:** This elegant dining room features both indoor and outdoor terrace dining. The chef has created an innovative menu referred to as "Chino Latino" cuisine, which is a Latin American menu infused with Asian influences, and it's a big hit with diners. Take for example the cold prawn and rice noodle spring roll, the rack of lamb with sake sauce or the tangerine glazed cornish hen with stir-fry vegetables. Every visit is a night to remember. Dressy casual; cocktails. **Parking:** valet. **Cards:** AX, DC, MC, VI.

TEPIC, NAYARIT pop. 270,000

———— WHERE TO STAY ————

HOTEL BUGAMVILLAS
Phone: 311/218-0227

▼▼ ▼▼ All Year   1P: $77-$108   2P: $77-$108   XP: $10   F10
Small-scale Hotel **Location:** 3 km n on Mex 15. Ave Insurgentes y Libramiento Pte 63117. Fax: 311/218-0225. **Facility:** 50 one-bedroom standard units. 2 stories (no elevator), exterior corridors. *Bath:* combo or shower only. **Parking:** on-site. **Terms:** 8 day cancellation notice, [AP] meal plan available, small pets only. **Pool(s):** heated outdoor. **Guest Services:** valet laundry. **Business Services:** fax (fee). **Cards:** AX, MC, VI.

HOTEL LAS PALOMAS
Phone: (311)214-0239

▼▼▼ ▼▼ All Year   1P: $75   2P: $95   XP: $8   F12
Small-scale Hotel **Location:** 3 km w on Mex 15. Ave Insurgentes 2100 Ote 63170. Fax: 311/214-0948. **Facility:** 61 one-bedroom standard units. 2 stories, exterior corridors. *Bath:* combo or shower only. **Parking:** on-site. **Terms:** 7 day cancellation notice-fee imposed. **Pool(s):** outdoor. **Leisure Activities:** whirlpool. **Guest Services:** valet laundry. **Business Services:** fax (fee). **Cards:** AX, MC, VI.

HOTEL MELANIE
Phone: (311)214-2310

▼▼▼ ▼▼ All Year   1P: $75   2P: $150
Small-scale Hotel **Location:** 2 km se on Tepic-Puerto Vallarta Hwy. Blvd Tepic-Xalixco 109 63168. Fax: 311/213-9846. **Facility:** 56 units. 55 one-bedroom standard units. 1 one-bedroom suite. 4 stories, interior corridors. *Bath:* shower only. **Parking:** on-site. **Guest Services:** gift shop, valet laundry. **Business Services:** meeting rooms. **Cards:** AX, CB, MC, VI.

MOTEL LA LOMA
Phone: (311)213-2222

Small-scale Hotel

All Year   1P: $36-$110   2P: $36-$110   XP: $10

Location: Just w of Mex 15. Located opposite Loma Park. Paseo de la Loma 301 63000. Fax: 311/213-2222. **Facility:** 47 units. 41 one-bedroom standard units. 1 one- and 5 two-bedroom suites. 2 stories (no elevator), exterior corridors. *Bath:* shower or tub only. **Parking:** on-site. **Terms:** 4 day cancellation notice, small pets only. **Pool(s):** outdoor, wading. **Business Services:** meeting rooms. **Cards:** AX, MC, VI.

SOME UNITS
FEE

──────── *The following lodging was either not evaluated or did not* ────────
meet AAA rating requirements but is listed for your information only.

HOTEL NEKIE TEPIC
Phone: 311/211-5000

[fyi]

Not evaluated. **Location:** On Mex 15, east end of town. Ave Insurgentes/Lago Victoria 63000. Facilities, services, and decor characterize a mid-range property.

──────── **WHERE TO DINE** ────────

ROBERTO'S RESTAURANT
Lunch: $7-$12   **Dinner:** $9-$15   **Phone:** 311/213-2085

International

Location: Jct Ave Insurgentes and Paseo de la Loma. Paseo de la Loma y Ave Insurgentes 63000. **Hours:** 1 pm-2 am. Closed major holidays; also Sun. **Reservations:** accepted. **Features:** Operating for 29 years in the same location, the restaurant is a longtime favorite. Steaks, seafood and poultry are served in a cozy, intimate setting. The delicately flavored sea bass dinner is a must-try. Dressy casual; cocktails. **Parking:** street. **Cards:** AX, DC, DS, MC, VI.

ZIHUATANEJO, GUERRERO pop. 37,300

──────── **WHERE TO STAY** ────────

CATALINA BEACH HOTEL   *Book at aaa.com*
Phone: 755/554-2137

Small-scale Hotel

All Year   2P: $85-$176   XP: $25

Location: Playa La Ropa, 9 km n of airport. Playa La Ropa S/N 40880 (Apdo Postal 23). Fax: 755/554-9327. **Facility:** 40 one-bedroom standard units, some with efficiencies. 1-4 stories (no elevator), exterior corridors. *Bath:* shower only. **Parking:** on-site. **Pool(s):** outdoor. **Guest Services:** valet laundry. **Cards:** AX, DC, MC, VI.

SOME UNITS

HOTEL VILLA DEL SOL   *Book at aaa.com*
Phone: (755)555-5500

Small-scale Hotel

All Year   2P: $285-$330   XP: $80

Location: 10 km n of airport. Playa La Ropa S/N 40880 (Apdo Postal 84). Fax: 755/554-2758. **Facility:** Palms and tropical gardens surround this service-oriented hotel, which features a fine restaurant; 40 rooms have private plunge pools. 70 units. 62 one-bedroom standard units. 1 one- and 7 two-bedroom suites ($485-$1050). 1-3 stories (no elevator), exterior corridors. *Bath:* shower only. **Parking:** on-site and valet. **Terms:** age restrictions may apply, 30 day cancellation notice, 15 day in summer-fee imposed, [MAP] meal plan available, small pets only. **Amenities:** safes, honor bars, hair dryers. *Some:* CD players. **Dining:** Villa del Sol Restaurant, see separate listing. **Pool(s):** 4 outdoor, lap. **Leisure Activities:** exercise room, spa. *Fee:* 2 lighted tennis courts. **Guest Services:** gift shop, valet laundry. **Business Services:** meeting rooms, business center. **Cards:** AX, MC, VI.

SOME UNITS

LA CASA CUITLATECA
Phone: 755/554-2448

Bed & Breakfast

All Year [BP]   1P: $165-$340   2P: $165-$340   XP: $50

Location: Playa La Ropa, 9 km n of airport. Playa La Ropa S/N 40880. Fax: 755/554-7394. **Facility:** A distinctive B&B with sweeping ocean views from the patio, the property offers an infinity pool that seems to end in the horizon. 4 one-bedroom standard units. 3 stories (no elevator), interior/exterior corridors. *Bath:* combo or shower only. **Parking:** on-site. **Terms:** age restrictions may apply, 30 day cancellation notice. **Pool(s):** outdoor. **Leisure Activities:** whirlpool. *Fee:* massage. **Guest Services:** valet laundry. **Business Services:** meeting rooms. **Cards:** AX, DS, MC, VI.

LA CASA QUE CANTA   *Book at aaa.com*
Phone: (755)555-7030

Country Inn

All Year   2P: $415-$835

Location: Playa La Ropa; Mirador sector; 9 km n of airport. Camino Escenico S/N Playa La Ropa 40880. Fax: 755/554-7900. **Facility:** On a cliff with bay views. Elegance with Mexican folk art. Requires stair climbing to reach most areas of hotel. Only a few rooms with elevator access. 28 one-bedroom suites. 3-6 stories, exterior corridors. *Bath:* shower only. **Parking:** on-site. **Terms:** age restrictions may apply, 30 day cancellation notice-fee imposed. **Amenities:** voice mail, safes, honor bars, hair dryers. **Pool(s):** 2 outdoor, saltwater. **Leisure Activities:** whirlpool, exercise room, Well Being Center. *Fee:* massage. **Guest Services:** gift shop, valet laundry. **Business Services:** meeting rooms, PC. **Cards:** AX, MC, VI.

SOME UNITS

SOTAVENTO BEACH RESORT   *Book at aaa.com*
Phone: (755)554-2032

Small-scale Hotel

12/16-4/15   1P: $85-$110   2P: $95-$120   XP: $25   F11
12/1-12/15 & 4/16-11/30   1P: $60-$72   2P: $65-$75   XP: $15   F11

Location: Playa La Ropa, 9 km n of airport. Camino Escenico S/N Playa La Ropa 40880 (Apdo Postal 2). Fax: 755/554-2975. **Facility:** 91 units. 86 one- and 5 two-bedroom standard units. 5-8 stories (no elevator), exterior corridors. *Bath:* shower only. **Parking:** on-site. **Terms:** 20 day cancellation notice, [AP], [CP] & [MAP] meal plans available. **Pool(s):** outdoor, wading. **Guest Services:** valet laundry. **Cards:** AX, DC, MC, VI.

SOME UNITS

VILLA VERA PUERTO MIO ZIHUATANEJO *Book at aaa.com* Phone: (755)553-8165

All Year 2P: $235-$860 XP: $30

▼▼▼▼ Location: 3 km w of Mex 200 interchange; follow Morelos. Paseo del Morro #5 Col el Almacen 40880 (Apdo Postal 84).

Small-scale Hotel Fax: 755/553-8168. Facility: 15 units. 14 one- and 1 two-bedroom standard units, some with whirlpools. 4 stories (no elevator), interior/exterior corridors. *Bath:* combo or shower only. Parking: on-site.

Terms: check-in 4 pm, 46 day cancellation notice, [AP] & [MAP] meal plans available. Amenities: safes, honor bars, hair dryers. Dining: Altura, see separate listing. Pool(s): outdoor. Leisure Activities: Fee: massage. Guest Services: valet laundry, area transportation. Cards: AX, MC, VI.

SOME UNITS

✈ ⊺↥ ⊻ ⇝ 🎥 ▣ /⊠/
FEE

──── WHERE TO DINE ────

ALTURA Lunch: $8-$15 Dinner: $10-$20 Phone: 755/553-8165

▼▼▼ Location: 3 km w of Mex 200 interchange; follow Morelos; in Villa Vera Puerto Mio Zihuatanejo. Paseo del Morro #5 Col El Almacen 40880. Hours: 7 am-11 pm. Reservations: accepted. Features: With a spectacular view

International overlooking a private cove, the restaurant prepares Mexican-inspired cuisine. Casual dress; cocktails. Parking: on-site. Cards: AX, MC, VI.

⊻ 🄐

CASA ELVIRA RESTAURANT Lunch: $4-$7 Dinner: $6-$13 Phone: 755/554-2061

▼▼▼ ▼▼▼ Location: Center; on the waterfront; just e of town pier. Paseo del Pescador #32 40880. Hours: 9 am-2:30 pm. Reservations: accepted. Features: The eatery has been in operation for almost 50 years. Fish tacos are

Seafood terrific, and quesadillas are well worth trying. Casual dress; cocktails. Parking: street. Cards: MC, VI.

⊻ 🄐

KAU KAN Dinner: $12-$18 Phone: 755/554-8446

▼▼▼ Location: On La Ropa Beach Rd; at taxi stand. Carr Escencia Lote #7 Cd La Madera 40880. Hours: Open 12/1-8/31 & 10/1-11/30; 5 pm-11 pm. Reservations: accepted. Features: A romantic view of the bay is available from

Continental the rooftop patio, where patrons can watch the sun set as they dine. A fine selection of wine and spirits complements a menu of great seafood. Dressy casual; cocktails. Parking: no self-parking. Cards: AX,

MC, VI.

⊻ 🄐

LA PERLA Lunch: $8-$10 Dinner: $10-$17 Phone: 755/554-2700

▼▼▼ Location: On La Ropa Beach. Playa La Ropa S/N 40880. Hours: 9 am-11 pm. Reservations: accepted. Features: Right on the beach, the eatery prepares fresh seafood a la minute. Jumbo shrimp is plentiful, and

Seafood patrons can order it cooked the way they like it. Casual dress; cocktails. Parking: on-site. Cards: AX, MC, VI.

⊻ 🄐

VILLA DEL SOL RESTAURANT Lunch: $10-$18 Dinner: $10-$50 Phone: 755/554-2239

▼▼▼▼ Location: 10 km n of airport; in Hotel Villa del Sol. Playa La Ropa S/N 40880. Hours: 8 am-10:30 pm. Reservations: suggested. Features: Under a giant palapa, a thatched roof supported by wooden timbers,

Continental the classy outdoor restaurant features fine Continental and Mexican cuisine in a beachside setting. Dressy casual; cocktails. Parking: on-site. Cards: AX, MC, VI.

🄐

──── *The following restaurant has not been evaluated by AAA* ──── *but is listed for your information only.*

CASA CUITLATECA RESTAURANT Phone: 755/554-2448

fyi Not evaluated. Location: Playa La Ropa, 9 km n of airport. Playa La Ropa S/N 40880. Features: Cross the swing bridge, then enjoy the sunset, infinity pool and lily pond while dining at this restaurant.

⊻

MEXICO CITY AND VICINITY

Cuernavaca & Vicinity

This index helps you "spot" where approved accommodations and restaurants are located on the corresponding detailed maps. Lodging rate ranges are for comparison only and show the property's high season; rates are per night, unless only weekly (W) rates are available. Restaurant rate range is for dinner, unless only lunch (L) is served. Turn to the listing page for more detailed rate information and consult display ads for special promotions.

Spotter/Map Page Number	OA	CUERNAVACA - Lodgings	Diamond Rating	Rate Range High Season	Listing Page
❶ / p. 461		Racquet Club Cuernavaca	▽▽▽	$175-$235	462
❷ / p. 461		Hotel Argento	▽▽▽	$135-$145	462
❸ / p. 461		Hotel Vista Hermosa	▽▽▽	$120-$130	462
❹ / p. 461		Hotel Hacienda de Cortez	▽▽	$130-$150	462
❺ / p. 461		Camino Real Sumiya, Cuernavaca	▽▽▽	$130-$180	462
❻ / p. 461		Las Mananitas	▽▽▽▽	$140-$424	462
❼ / p. 461		Hosteria Las Quintas	▽▽▽	$170-$225	462
		CUERNAVACA - Restaurants			
① / p. 461		Restaurante Hacienda de Corte	▽▽	$10-$30	463
② / p. 461		Restaurant Sumiya	▽▽▽	$8-$15	463
③ / p. 461		Las Mananitas Restaurant	▽▽▽▽	$20-$30	463
⑤ / p. 461		La Adelita	▽	$5-$9	463
⑥ / p. 461		Restaurante Jade	▽▽▽	$10-$19	463
		TEQUESQUITENGO - Lodgings			
⑩ / p. 461		Hotel Hacienda Vista Hermosa	▽▽	$107-$215	484

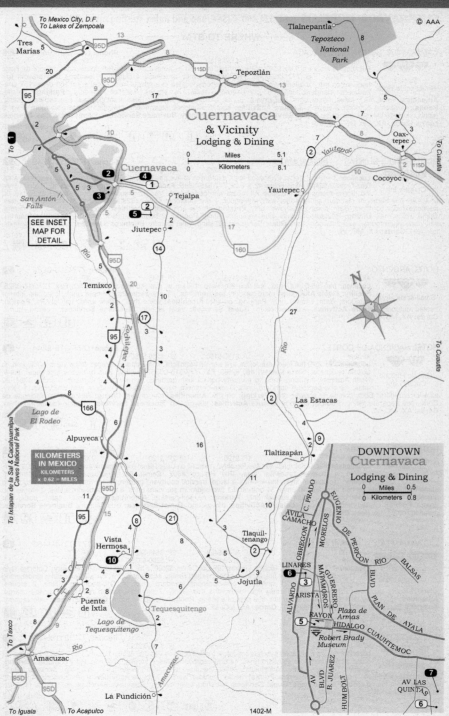

To Mexico City, D.F.
To Lakes of Zempoala

Tlalnepantla

Tepozteco National Park

Tres Marías

13

95D

8

20

95

9

95D

17

115D

Tepoztlán

13

Cuernavaca
& Vicinity
Lodging & Dining

10

2

To 1

San Antón Falls

5

9

5 3

Cuernavaca

4
1

3

5

5

2

SEE INSET
MAP FOR
DETAIL

Tejalpa

2

5

Jiutepec

14

Río

5

95D

Temixco

20

10

2

17

3

95

3

4

4

Zochitepec

4

4

8

166

Lago de
El Rodeo

6

Alpuyeca

To Ixtapan de la Sal & Cacahuamilpa
Caves National Park

KILOMETERS
IN MEXICO
KILOMETERS
x 0.62 = MILES

16

11

95D

95

15

4

11

8

21

Vista
Hermosa

8

10

1

3

4

2

8

Puente
de Ixtla

6

Tequesquitengo

2

Lago de
Tequesquitengo

7

Río

Amacuzac

95D

95D

To Taxco

8

La Fundición

Oax-
tepec

3

7

7

8

2

Yautepec

10

Cocoyoc

2

115D

To Cuautla

Yautepec

2

17

160

27

To Cuautla

N

Las Estacas

2

4

2

9

Tlaltizapán

11

10

Tlaquil-
tenango

3

5

2

5

Jojutla

5

6

DOWNTOWN
Cuernavaca
Lodging & Dining

AVILA
CAMACHO

C. PRADO

EUGENIO DE PERICON

RIO

BALSAS

OBREGON

MORELOS

LINARES

6

3

ALVARADO

ARISTA

GUERRERO

MAYAMOROS

BLVD
PLAN
DE
AYALA

RAYON

5

Plaza de
Armas

HIDALGO

CUAUHTEMOC

Robert Brady
Museum

AV
BLVD
B. JUAREZ

HUMBOLT

AV LAS
QUINTAS

7

6

To Iguala

To Acapulco

1402-M

CUERNAVACA, MORELOS pop. 334,400 (See map and index starting on p. 461)

———— WHERE TO STAY ————

CAMINO REAL SUMIYA, CUERNAVACA
Phone: (777)329-9888 **5**
All Year 1P: $130-$180 2P: $130-$180 XP: $25 F16
Location: 3 km se of Mex 95-D (toll road), exit Mex 160 (Cuernavaca-Cuautla Rd); follow signs. Interior de Fracc Sumiya 62550. Fax: 777/329-9888. **Facility:** Authentic Japanese architecture, gardens and artwork are featured on the expansive grounds of this property located in a private, residential area. 163 units. 157 one-bedroom standard units. 6 one-bedroom suites. 4 stories, exterior corridors. **Parking:** on-site.
Resort Small-scale Hotel
Amenities: voice mail, safes, honor bars, hair dryers. *Some:* CD players. **Dining:** Restaurant Sumiya, see separate listing. **Pool(s):** 2 heated outdoor, 2 wading. **Leisure Activities:** sauna, whirlpool, steamroom, playground, exercise room. *Fee:* 8 tennis courts (6 lighted), massage. **Guest Services:** gift shop, valet laundry. **Business Services:** conference facilities, business center. **Cards:** AX, CB, DC, MC, VI.

SOME UNITS

HOSTERIA LAS QUINTAS *Book at aaa.com*
Phone: (777)318-3949 **7**
All Year 1P: $170-$225 2P: $170-$225 XP: $30 F12
Location: 3 km e of Cortez Palace, off Ave Cuauhtemoc at Ave Las Quintas 107. Located in a quiet residential area. Diaz Ordaz 9 62440 (Apdo Postal 427). Fax: 777/318-3895. **Facility:** Spacious, tropical grounds. Colonial-style inn. Some rooms with fireplace. All rooms with ceiling fans. Variety of suites and junior suites available. 90 units. 86 one-bedroom standard units, some with whirlpools. 4 one-bedroom suites ($230-$260) with whirlpools. 2 stories, interior/exterior corridors. *Bath:* combo or shower only. **Parking:** on-site and valet. **Amenities:** safes, honor bars, hair dryers. *Some:* voice mail. **Dining:** Restaurante Jade, see separate listing. **Pool(s):** 2 heated outdoor. **Leisure Activities:** saunas, whirlpool, steamrooms, exercise room, spa. **Guest Services:** gift shop, valet laundry. **Business Services:** conference facilities, fax (fee). **Cards:** AX, MC, VI.
Country Inn

SOME UNITS

HOTEL ARGENTO
Phone: 777/316-3282 **2**
All Year 1P: $135 2P: $145 XP: $10
Location: Mex 95-D (toll road), exit Ave Rio Mayo, 1.9 km w. Ave Rio Mayo 1001 62290. Fax: 777/316-0825. **Facility:** Meets AAA guest room security requirements. 51 one-bedroom standard units. 2 stories, interior corridors. *Bath:* shower only. **Parking:** on-site. **Amenities:** voice mail, safes, irons, hair dryers. **Pool(s):** heated outdoor. **Leisure Activities:** exercise room. **Guest Services:** valet laundry. **Business Services:** meeting rooms. **Cards:** AX, MC, VI.
Small-scale Hotel

HOTEL HACIENDA DE CORTEZ
Phone: (777)315-8844 **4**
All Year 1P: $130-$150 2P: $130-$150
Location: Mex 95-D (toll road), exit Jojutla, just e to 1st traffic light, then 2 km s to Jiutepec, follow signs; in Atlacomulco Colonia of Jiutepec. Plaza Kennedy #90 62560. Fax: 777/315-0035. **Facility:** Said to be the first sugar mill in North America, this long-standing property boasts lush gardens, rich history and massive stone walls. 22 units. 19 one-bedroom standard units. 3 one-bedroom suites ($200-$270), some with whirlpools. 1 story, exterior corridors. *Bath:* combo or shower only. **Parking:** on-site. **Amenities:** hair dryers. **Dining:** Restaurante Hacienda de Corte, see separate listing. **Pool(s):** outdoor. **Leisure Activities:** playground. **Business Services:** meeting rooms, fax (fee). **Cards:** AX, MC, VI.
Classic Historic Country Inn

SOME UNITS

HOTEL VISTA HERMOSA
Phone: 777/315-2374 **3**
All Year 1P: $120 2P: $130 XP: $10 F12
Location: Mex 95-D (toll road), exit Ave Rio Mayo, 1 km sw on Calle Diana, 0.4 km sw on Ave Rio Mayo, then 1.2 km s. Located in a quiet residential area. (Rio Panuco #600, Corner Rio Papaloapan). Fax: 777/315-2374. **Facility:** Colonial in style, the inn has a large, tranquil courtyard garden; guest rooms have tile floors and some feature private garden terraces. 40 units. 34 one- and 1 two-bedroom standard units. 5 one-bedroom suites. 2 stories (no elevator), interior/exterior corridors. *Bath:* shower only. **Parking:** no self-parking. **Amenities:** voice mail, safes, irons, hair dryers. **Pool(s):** heated outdoor, wading. **Leisure Activities:** playground. **Guest Services:** valet laundry. **Business Services:** meeting rooms, fax (fee). **Cards:** AX, MC, VI.
Country Inn

LAS MANANITAS *Book at aaa.com*
Phone: (777)314-1466 **6**
4/20-11/30 1P: $140-$424 2P: $140-$424 XP: $35
12/1-4/19 1P: $200-$325 2P: $200-$325 XP: $35
Location: Just e of Mex 95. Ricardo Linares 107 Col Centro 62000. Fax: 777/318-3672. **Facility:** Colonial-style inn. Tropical gardens. Few fireplaces. Large meeting facility adjacent to the inn with extensive landscaping including a waterfall. 21 units. 17 one-bedroom standard units. 4 one-bedroom suites. 2 stories, interior/exterior corridors. **Parking:** valet. **Terms:** age restrictions may apply, 7 day cancellation notice, $5 service charge. **Amenities:** safes, hair dryers. **Dining:** restaurant, see separate listing. **Pool(s):** heated outdoor. **Guest Services:** valet laundry. **Business Services:** meeting rooms, fax (fee). **Cards:** AX, MC, VI.
Classic Country Inn

RACQUET CLUB CUERNAVACA
Phone: (777)311-2400 **1**
All Year 1P: $175-$235 2P: $175-$235 XP: $18 F12
Location: 0.8 km n of Zapata's monument, follow signs. Francisco Villa 100 62120. Fax: 777/317-5483. **Facility:** 52 units. 38 one-bedroom standard units. 14 one-bedroom suites. 4 stories, interior/exterior corridors. **Parking:** on-site. **Terms:** 3 day cancellation notice-fee imposed, [MAP] meal plan available, package plans. **Amenities:** safes (fee), honor bars, hair dryers. **Pool(s):** heated outdoor, wading. **Leisure Activities:** 9 tennis courts (4 lighted), exercise room, game room. *Fee:* massage. **Guest Services:** gift shop, valet laundry. **Business Services:** conference facilities, fax. **Cards:** AX, MC, VI.
Large-scale Hotel

SOME UNITS

(See map and index starting on p. 461)

──────── WHERE TO DINE ────────

LA ADELITA
Mexican

Lunch: $5-$9   Dinner: $5-$9   Phone: 777/318-5697   [5]
Location: Downtown; facing Cortez Palace. Ave Hidalgo #1 (Colonia Centro) 62000. **Hours:** 7:30 am-midnight. **Reservations:** accepted. **Features:** This centrally located restaurant is a perfect way to enjoy a respite from sightseeing; ample sidewalk sitting and a menu of classic Mexican dishes with reasonable prices are offered. Casual dress; cocktails. **Parking:** street. **Cards:** MC, VI.

LAS MANANITAS RESTAURANT
Regional
Continental

Lunch: $15-$25   Dinner: $20-$30   Phone: 777/314-1466   [3]
Location: Just e of Mex 95; in Las Mananitas. Ricardo Linares 107 Col Centro 62000. **Hours:** 1 pm-5 & 7-10:30 pm, Fri & Sat-11 pm. **Reservations:** suggested. **Features:** In a colonial country inn, the restaurant offers upscale dining on the terrace or amid meticulously manicured lawns and gardens. Extensive selections line the daily-changing menu. Semi-formal attire; cocktails. **Parking:** valet. **Cards:** AX.

RESTAURANTE HACIENDA DE CORTE
Regional Mexican

Lunch: $8-$12   Dinner: $10-$30   Phone: 777/315-8844   [1]
Location: Mex 95-D (toll road), exit Jojutla, just e to 1st traffic light, then 2 km s to Jiutepec, follow signs; in Atlacomulco Colonia of Jiutepec; in Hotel Hacienda de Cortez. Plaza Kennedy #90 62560. **Hours:** 8 am-9 pm, Fri & Sat-midnight. **Reservations:** accepted. **Features:** Established in the 1500s, the famous hacienda offers a quiet dining respite in its cool garden courtyard or inside the historic restaurant. Casual dress; cocktails. **Parking:** on-site. **Cards:** AX, MC, VI.

RESTAURANTE JADE
Regional
Continental

Lunch: $10-$16   Dinner: $10-$19   Phone: 777/362-3949   [6]
Location: 3 km e of Cortez Palace, off Ave Cuauhtemoc at Ave Las Quintas 107; in Hosteria Las Quintas. Diaz Ordaz 9 62440. **Hours:** 7 am-11 pm. **Reservations:** suggested, for dinner. **Features:** In the city of "eternal spring," the restaurant is renowned for its lush, tropical gardens and refined colonial setting. Lining the menu is a combination of authentic regional preparations and Continental dishes. Dressy casual; cocktails; entertainment. **Parking:** on-site and valet. **Cards:** AX, MC, VI.

RESTAURANT SUMIYA
Japanese

Lunch: $8-$15   Dinner: $8-$15   Phone: 777/320-9199   [2]
Location: 3 km se from Mex 95-D (toll road), exit Mex 160 (Cuernavaca-Cuautla Rd), follow signs; in Camino Real Sumiya, Cuernavaca. **Hours:** 12:30 pm-11 pm, Fri-midnight, Sat-12:30 am. Closed: Mon & Tues. **Reservations:** accepted. **Features:** Overlooking expansive gardens, the restaurant replicates the Japanese Imperial Palace. A detour here is well worth the effort. Although the menu centers on Japanese fare, it also features some regional Mexican cuisine. Casual dress; cocktails. **Parking:** on-site. **Cards:** AX, DC, MC, VI.

──────── *The following restaurant has not been evaluated by AAA* ────────
but is listed for your information only.

CASA HIDALGO
[fyi]

Phone: 777/312-2749
Not evaluated. **Location:** Downtown; facing Cortez Palace. Jardin de los Ninos Heroes #6 62440. **Features:** This stylish restaurant is easy to spot with its yellow exterior and lovely iron work around the windows and balcony areas. Its central location makes it a suitable stop for those in the downtown area.

IXTAPAN DE LA SAL, MEXICO pop. 16,600

──────── WHERE TO STAY ────────

DEL REY IXTAPAN DE LA SAL RESORT & SPA (AN ALL INCLUSIVE RESORT) *Book at aaa.com*
Resort
Large-scale Hotel

Phone: 721/143-2010
All Year [AP]   2P: $250-$350
Location: Just w of Mex 55. Jose Ma Morelos S/N Fracc Bugambilias 51900. Fax: 721/143-1977. **Facility:** Scenic mountain views accent this all-inclusive resort offering spacious guest rooms, many with a terrace or patio; a small chapel is on the premises. Meets AAA guest room security requirements. 189 units. 187 one-bedroom standard units. 2 one-bedroom suites. 5 stories, interior corridors. **Parking:** valet. **Amenities:** voice mail, safes, hair dryers. **Pool(s):** 2 heated outdoor, heated indoor. **Leisure Activities:** whirlpool, waterslide, 2 lighted tennis courts, recreation programs, bicycles, playground, exercise room, spa, basketball, game room. **Guest Services:** gift shop, valet laundry. **Business Services:** conference facilities, business center. **Cards:** AX, MC, VI.

SOME UNITS

HOTEL BUNGALOWS LOLITA
Small-scale Hotel

Phone: 721/143-0016
All Year [AP]   2P: $60   XP: $45
Location: 1.5 km n on Mex 55. Blvd Arturo San Roman 33 51900. Fax: 721/143-0230. **Facility:** 39 units. 31 one- and 2 two-bedroom standard units. 6 three-bedroom suites. 1-2 stories, interior/exterior corridors. *Bath:* shower only. **Parking:** on-site. **Pool(s):** heated outdoor, wading. **Leisure Activities:** playground. *Fee:* massage. **Guest Services:** gift shop, valet laundry. **Cards:** AX, DS, MC, VI.

HOTEL VILLA VERGEL
Small-scale Hotel

Phone: (721)143-0349
All Year [AP]   1P: $110-$170   2P: $170-$320   XP: $45   F10
Location: 1.5 km n on Mex 55. Blvd Arturo San Roman y Ave Juarez S/N 51900. Fax: 721/143-0842. **Facility:** 67 units. 65 one-bedroom standard units. 2 two-bedroom suites. 2-3 stories, interior corridors. *Bath:* combo, shower or tub only. **Parking:** on-site. **Terms:** 15 day cancellation notice-fee imposed. **Amenities:** *Some:* honor bars. **Pool(s):** heated outdoor, wading. **Leisure Activities:** spa, game room. **Guest Services:** valet laundry. **Business Services:** meeting rooms. **Cards:** AX, MC, VI.

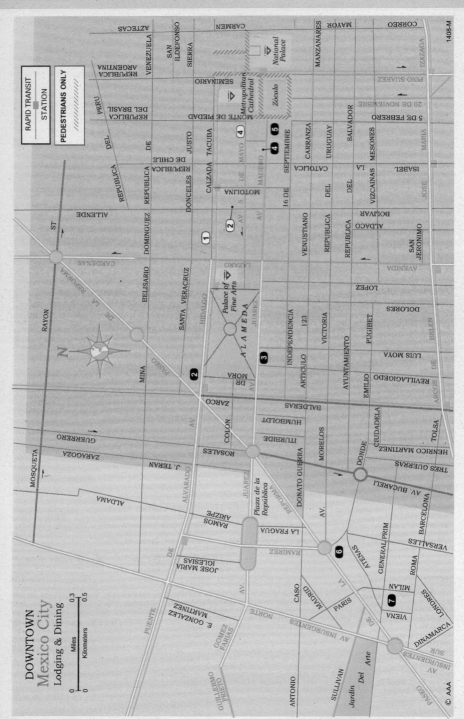

DOWNTOWN
Mexico City
Lodging & Dining

Miles   0   0.3
Kilometers   0   0.5

RAPID TRANSIT
STATION
PEDESTRIANS ONLY

1408-M

© AAA

Downtown Mexico City

This index helps you "spot" where approved accommodations and restaurants are located on the corresponding detailed maps. Lodging rate ranges are for comparison only and show the property's high season; rates are per night, unless only weekly (W) rates are available. Restaurant rate range is for dinner, unless only lunch (L) is served. Turn to the listing page for more detailed rate information and consult display ads for special promotions.

Spotter/Map Page Number	OA	**MEXICO CITY** - Lodgings	Diamond Rating	Rate Range High Season	Listing Page
2 / p. 464		Best Western Hotel De Cortes	▽▽	$95-$130	473
3 / p. 464		Sheraton Centro Historico Hotel & Convention Center Mexico City - see color ad p 8	▽▽▽▽	$185-$250	478
4 / p. 464		Holiday Inn Zocalo	▽▽	$60-$110	474
5 / p. 464		Best Western-Hotel Majestic	▽▽	$80-$180	473
6 / p. 464		Fiesta Americana Reforma - see color ad card inserts	▽▽▽	$120-$160	473
7 / p. 464		Suites Mi Casa	▽	$70-$80	478
		MEXICO CITY - Restaurants			
1 / p. 464		Los Girasoles	▽▽▽	$7-$15	480
2 / p. 464		Primer Cuadro	▽▽▽	$6-$12	481
4 / p. 464		Restaurante Mercaderes Cafe	▽▽▽	$7-$20	481

Mexico City
DISTRITO FEDERAL
Lodging & Dining

Miles 0 — 0.5
Kilometers 0 — 0.8

To Villa Gustavo A. Madero

N

AV GRANJAS

CALZ

RIO CONSULADO

CEDRO

DIAZ

CALZ MARINA

MOLINO DEL REY

MEXICO-TACUBA

AV

RIVERA DE

EJERCITO

CALZ

OCAMPO

M.M. CONTRERAS

MIGUEL SCHULTZ

ALF HERRER

A. CAS

AV HORACIO

NACIONAL

ASCENCION

BAHIA

VILLALONGIN

SULLIVAN

AV

NACIONAL

GUTEMBERG

RIO TIBER

RIO AMAZONAS

RIO RHIN

(30) (31)

To 33 & 36

(26)

(1)

(32)

THIERS

RIO LERMA

RIO

(12)

PRESIDENTE

MASARYK

GRAL. MARIANO ESCOBEDO

(34) (27)

ELISEOS

MELCHOR

(9)

(13)

(14)

(2)

CAMPOS ELISEOS

CAMPOS

DARIO

LIEBNITZ

(8)

(7)

(14)

(3)

RUBEN

(10)

(12)

(11)

NIZA

(8)

PASEO

CALZ

(9)

VICTOR HUGO

CALZ

MISSISSIPPI

(17)

FLORENCIA

(11)

(17)

(1)

DE

(6)

(17)

(19)

(18)

(19)

(3)

LA

(13)

REFORMA

SEVILLA

(21)

To 28 & 39

(4) (2)

(15)

PINK ZONE

(18)

LONDRES

(20)

(4) & (7)

MOLINO DEL REY

Lake Chapultepec

Museum of Modern Art

(16)

AV HAMBURGO

(20)

ANILLO

Chapultepec Park

CHAPULTEPEC

(26)

OAXACA

(24)

LOS SANTOS

DURANGO

SUR

Plaza Rio de Janeir

PERIFERICO

National Museum of Anthropology

AV

SONORA

AV

AV

CONSTITUYENTES

GOMEZ PEDRAZA

VERACRUZ

(25)

AV J ESCUTIA

AV

MEDELLIN

YUCATAN

GRAL CANO

VASCONCELOS

TAMAULIPAS

Parque México

INSURGENTES

COAHUILA

LOS

PARQUE

AV DE

NUEVO

ALFONSO REYES

AV BAJA CALIFORNIA

MONTERREY

LIRA

AV JOSE

AV

AV

LEON

PERIFERICO

JALISCO

PUENTE

REVOLUCION

MORENA

ALEMAN

VIADUCTO

1407-M   To Villa Álvaro Obregón

To Plaza México, Villa Álvaro Obregón & Olympic Stadium

MIGUEL

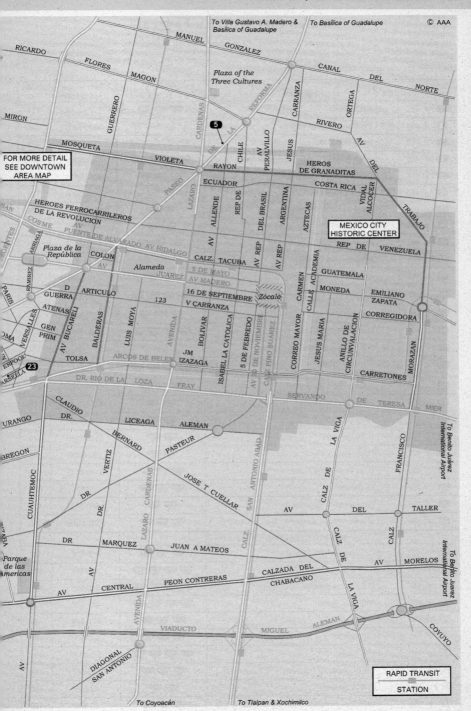

© AAA

To Villa Gustavo A. Madero &
Basílica of Guadalupe

To Basílica of Guadalupe

RICARDO

MANUEL

GONZALEZ

FLORES

MAGON

Plaza of the
Three Cultures

CANAL

DEL

NORTE

GUERRERO

MIRON

MOSQUETA

VIOLETA

CARDENAS

REFORMA

CARRANZA

CHILE

PERALVILLO

JESUS

RIVERO

ORTEGA

AV

DEL

TRABAJO

5

FOR MORE DETAIL
SEE DOWNTOWN
AREA MAP

PASEO

LAZARO

RAYON

ECUADOR

ALLENDE

REP DE

DEL BRASIL

ARGENTINA

AZTECAS

HEROS
DE GRANADITAS

COSTA RICA

VIDAL
ALCOCER

HEROES FERROCARRILEROS
DE LA REVOLUCION

COSME

AV

PUENTE DE ALVARADO, AV HIDALGO

AV

AV REP

AV REP

CARMEN

CALLE ACADEMIA

MEXICO CITY
HISTORIC CENTER

REP DE

VENEZUELA

Plaza de la
República

COLON

AV

Alameda

JUAREZ

CALZ. TACUBA

5 DE MAYO

AV MADERO

GUATEMALA

MONEDA

EMILIANO
ZAPATA

RAMIREZ

D
GUERRA

ARTICULO

123

16 DE SEPTIEMBRE

V CARRANZA

Zócalo

CORREGIDORA

PARIS

ATENAS

GEN
PRIM

BUCARELI

BALDERAS

LUIS MOYA

AVENIDA

BOLIVAR

ISABEL LA CATOLICA

5 DE FEBRERO

CORREO MAYOR

JESUS MARIA

ANILLO DE
CIRCUNVALACION

MORAZAN

VERSALLES

TOLSA

ARCOS DE BELEN

JM
IZAZAGA

CARRETONES

23

DR. RIO DE LA LOZA

FRAY

SERVANDO

DE

TERESA

MIER

CLAUDIO

DR.

LICEAGA

ALEMAN

LA VIGA

To Benito Juarez
International Airport

URANGO

BERNARD

PASTEUR

SAN ANTONIO ABAD

FRANCISCO

BREGON

VERTIZ

JOSE T CUELLAR

CALZ DE

DEL

TALLER

CUAUHTEMOC

DR.

DR

LAZARO CARDENAS

CALZ.

AV

CALZ

To Bejíío Juarez
International Airport

DR

MARQUEZ

JUAN A MATEOS

CALZ DE

AV

MORELOS

Parque
de las
americas

AV

CENTRAL

PEON CONTRERAS

CALZADA DEL

CHABACANO

LA VIGA

AV

DIAGONAL
SAN ANTONIO

VIADUCTO

MIGUEL

ALEMAN

COYUYO

RAPID TRANSIT

STATION

To Coyoacán

To Tlalpan & Xochimilco

Mexico City Distrito Federal

This index helps you "spot" where approved accommodations and restaurants are located on the corresponding detailed maps. Lodging rate ranges are for comparison only and show the property's high season; rates are per night, unless only weekly (W) rates are available. Restaurant rate range is for dinner, unless only lunch (L) is served. Turn to the listing page for more detailed rate information and consult display ads for special promotions.

Spotter/Map Page Number	OA	MEXICO CITY - Lodgings	Diamond Rating	Rate Range High Season	Listing Page
❶ / p. 466		Habita Hotel	◆◆◆	$195-$265	474
❷ / p. 466	AAA	JW Marriott Hotel Mexico City	◆◆◆◆	$180-$300	477
❸ / p. 466	AAA	Hotel Nikko Mexico	◆◆◆◆	$300	475
❹ / p. 466		Hotel Presidente InterContinental Mexico City	◆◆◆◆	$260-$320	476
❺ / p. 466		Gran Melia Mexico Reforma	◆◆◆	$150-$175	474
❻ / p. 466	AAA	Camino Real Mexico City	◆◆◆◆	$150-$300	473
❼ / p. 466		Hotel Casa Inn Mexico	◆◆	$90-$120	474
❽ / p. 466		Hotel Suites San Marino	◆◆	$145	476
❾ / p. 466		NH Mexico City	◆◆◆	$115-$165	477
⓫ / p. 466	AAA	Hotel Sevilla Palace	◆◆◆	$108	476
⓬ / p. 466		Hotel Jardin Amazonas	◆◆	$80-$150	475
⓭ / p. 466		Fiesta Americana Grand Chapultepec - see color ad back cover, card inserts	◆◆◆◆	$140-$200	473
⓮ / p. 466		Hotel Marco Polo	◆◆◆	$170-$190	475
⓯ / p. 466		Marquis Reforma Hotel	◆◆◆◆	$125-$230	477
⓰ / p. 466	AAA	Four Seasons Hotel Mexico D.F.	◆◆◆◆◆	$315-$430	474
⓱ / p. 466		Sheraton Maria Isabel Hotel & Towers - see color ad p 8	◆◆◆◆	$285	478
⓲ / p. 466		Galeria Plaza Hotel	◆◆◆	$105-$200	474
⓳ / p. 466		Hotel Plaza Florencia	◆◆	$130-$150	475
⓴ / p. 466		Hotel Century	◆◆	$121-$151	475
㉑ / p. 466		Hotel Geneve	◆◆	$100-$155	475
㉓ / p. 466		Hotel Posada Viena	◆◆	$65-$100	476
㉔ / p. 466		Hotel Royal Zona Rosa	◆◆◆	$120-$180	476
㉕ / p. 466		La Casona	◆◆◆	$160	477
㉖ / p. 466		Hotel Segovia Regency	◆◆	$50-$65	476
㉘ / p. 466		Sheraton Suites Santa Fe - see color ad p 8	◆◆◆	$320-$1350	478
		MEXICO CITY - Restaurants			
① / p. 466		La Galvia Restaurante	◆◆◆	$16-$30	479
② / p. 466		Au Pie de Cochon	◆◆◆◆	$25-$65	479
③ / p. 466		El Lago Chapultepec	◆◆◆◆	$40-$65	479
④ / p. 466		Alfredo di Roma	◆◆◆◆	$22-$38	479
⑦ / p. 466		The Palm	◆◆◆	$20-$40	480
⑧ / p. 466		Los Almendros	◆◆◆	$20-$30	480
⑨ / p. 466		Le Cirque	◆◆◆◆	$50-$130	480
⑩ / p. 466		Los Azulejos	◆◆◆	$20-$40	480
⑪ / p. 466		Manhattan Deli	◆◆	$7-$15	480
⑫ / p. 466		1926 Bice Ristorante	◆◆◆	$9-$20	479

Spotter/Map Page Number	OA	**MEXICO CITY** - Restaurants (continued)	Diamond Rating	Rate Range High Season	Listing Page
⑬ / p. 466		Passy	◈◈	$15-$35	481
⑭ / p. 466		Les Moustaches	◈◈◈	$20-$40	480
⑰ / p. 466		Los Tres Soles Focolare Restaurant	◈◈◈	$8-$12	480
⑱ / p. 466		Restaurante Fonda El Refugio	◈◈◈	$20-$40	481
⑲ / p. 466		Chalet Suizo	◈◈	$16-$22	479
⑳ / p. 466		Restaurante Tezka	◈◈◈◈	$15-$38	481
㉖ / p. 466		Torre d Castilla	◈◈◈	$9-$20	481
㉗ / p. 466		Bondy Restaurant y Pasteleria	◈◈	$6-$17	479
㉚ / p. 466		Ruth's Chris Steak House	◈◈◈	$19-$36	481
㉛ / p. 466		Il Dani Ristorante Italiano	◈◈	$7-$14	479
㉜ / p. 466	AAA	**Pujol Restaurante**	◈◈◈◈	$9-$20	481
㉝ / p. 466		La Hacienda de los Morales	◈◈◈	$7-$18	480
㉞ / p. 466		Izote	◈◈◈	$8-$23	479
㊱ / p. 466		Chez Wok	◈◈◈	$22-$45	479
㊲ / p. 466		Palmas 500 Restaurante	◈◈◈	$9-$30	480

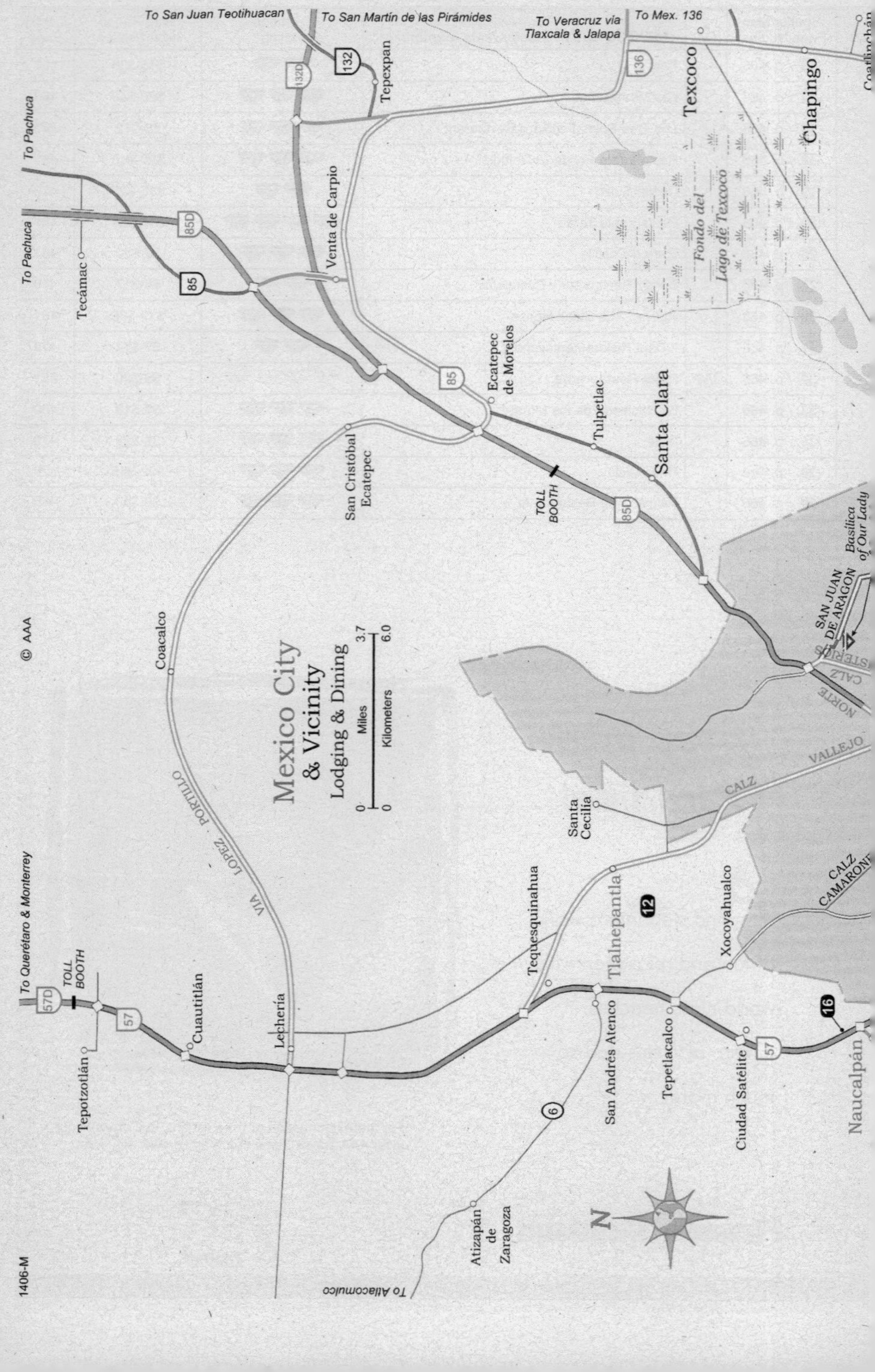

Mexico City & Vicinity

Lodging & Dining

Miles
0 — 3.7

Kilometers
0 — 6.0

To San Juan Teotihuacan

To San Martín de las Pirámides

To Veracruz via Tlaxcala & Jalapa

To Mex. 136

132

190D

Tepexpan

136

Texcoco

Chapingo

Venta de Carpio

To Pachuca

To Pachuca

85D

85

Tecámac

Fondo del Lago de Texcoco

Ecatepec de Morelos

85

San Cristóbal Ecatepec

Tulpetlac

Santa Clara

TOLL BOOTH

85D

Coacalco

SAN JUAN DE ARAGÓN

Basílica of Our Lady

CALZ NORTE

CALZ VALLEJO

CALZ

Santa Cecilia

Tequesquinahua

Tlalnepantla

12

Xocoyahualco

CALZ CAMARONE

VIA LOPEZ PORTILLO

To Querétaro & Monterrey

57D

TOLL BOOTH

57

Cuautitlán

Lechería

Tepotzotlán

San Andrés Atenco

Tepetlacalco

Ciudad Satélite

57

16

Naucalpan

6

Atizapán de Zaragoza

To Atlacomulco

N

© AAA

1406-M

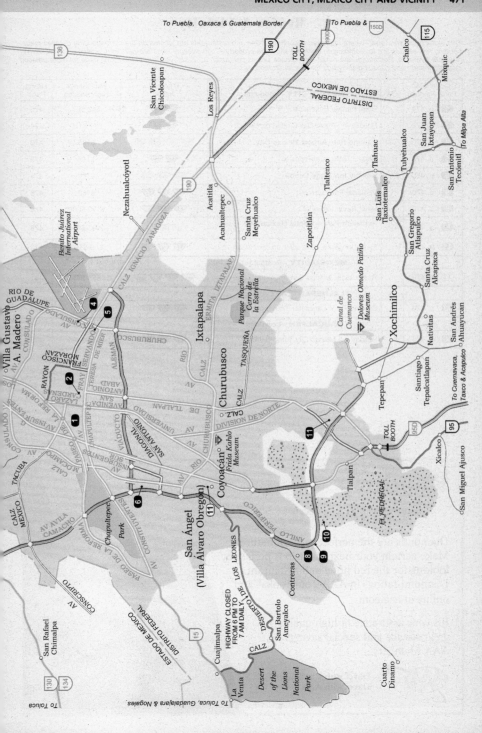

Mexico & Vicinity

This index helps you "spot" where approved accommodations and restaurants are located on the corresponding detailed maps. Lodging rate ranges are for comparison only and show the property's high season; rates are per night, unless only weekly (W) rates are available. Restaurant rate range is for dinner, unless only lunch (L) is served. Turn to the listing page for more detailed rate information and consult display ads for special promotions.

Spotter/Map Page Number	OA	MEXICO CITY - Lodgings	Diamond Rating	Rate Range High Season	Listing Page
1 / p. 470		Hotel Parque Ensenada	◆◆	$42-$57	475
2 / p. 470		Holiday Inn Plaza Dali Ciudad de Mexico	◆◆	$80-$150	474
4 / p. 470	AAA	**Camino Real Airport Mexico City**	◆◆◆◆	$185	473
5 / p. 470		Hotel J R Plaza Aeropuerto	◆◆	$115	475
6 / p. 470	AAA	**Holiday Inn Trade Center**	◆◆◆	$150	474
8 / p. 470		Pedregal Palace Hotel	◆◆◆	$150	478
9 / p. 470		Hotel Royal Pedregal	◆◆◆	$180-$290	476
10 / p. 470	AAA	**Radisson Paraiso Hotel Mexico City** - see color ad p 477	◆◆◆	$165-$210	478
11 / p. 470		Fiesta Inn Gran - see color ad card insert	◆◆◆	$85-$150	473
		MEXICO CITY - Restaurant			
11 / p. 470		Restaurante Antiguo San Angel Inn	◆◆◆◆	$25-$45	481
		TLALNEPANTLA - Lodgings			
12 / p. 470		Crowne Plaza Lancaster Tlalnepantla	◆◆◆	$80-$100	484
		NAUCALPAN - Lodgings			
16 / p. 470		Holiday Inn Mexico City Toreo-Satelite	◆◆◆	$69-$99	483

MEXICO CITY, DISTRITO FEDERAL pop. 10,000,000

(See maps and indexes p. 464-465, 466-468, 470-472)

——— WHERE TO STAY ———

BEST WESTERN HOTEL DE CORTES *Book at aaa.com* **Phone:** (55)5518-2182 **②**
▽▽▽ All Year 1P: $95-$130 2P: $95-$130 XP: $12 F16
Location: Across from Alameda Park; in historic downtown. (Ave Hidalgo 85/Paseo de la Reforma).
Historic Fax: 55/5512-1863. **Facility:** Authentic 18th-century guest house with beautiful patio featuring rooms with
Small-scale Hotel fans, windows that open and disposable slippers. 29 units. 20 one-bedroom standard units. 2 one- and 7
two-bedroom suites ($140-$170). 2 stories (no elevator), exterior corridors. *Bath:* combo or shower only.
Parking: on-site. **Terms:** 3 day cancellation notice. **Amenities:** safes, honor bars, hair dryers. **Guest Services:** valet laundry.
Business Services: meeting rooms, fax (fee). **Cards:** AX, DC, MC, VI.
SOME UNITS
Ⓢ🅓 🍴 📶 / 🎭 /

BEST WESTERN-HOTEL MAJESTIC **Phone:** (55)5521-8600 **⑤**
▽▽▽ All Year 1P: $80-$180 2P: $80-$180 XP: $15 F12
Location: In heart of Old Mexico City. Located adjacent to the Zocalo. Madero 73 Col Centro 06000.
Historic Fax: 55/5512-6262. **Facility:** Colonial-style hotel. Old World atmosphere. Public areas decorated with hand
Small-scale Hotel painted ceramic tiles from the 1700s. Teeming with Mexican diversity. Meets AAA guest room security
requirements. 85 one-bedroom standard units. 7 stories, interior corridors. **Parking:** on-site (fee).
Terms: cancellation fee imposed. **Amenities:** safes. *Some:* hair dryers. **Guest Services:** valet laundry. **Business Services:**
meeting rooms, fax (fee). **Cards:** AX, DC, MC, VI.
🍴 🎭 📶 💻

CAMINO REAL AIRPORT MEXICO CITY *Book at aaa.com* **Phone:** (55)3003-0033 **④**
🅰🅰🅰 All Year 1P: $185 2P: $185
Location: Adjacent to airport; connected via skywalk in front of Terminal B. Puerto Mexico 80 15520.
▽▽▽ ▽▽▽ Fax: 55/3003-0034. **Facility:** Rooms in series 51 or 57 are larger than other rooms. Rooms in series 56 or
Large-scale Hotel 06 with tight floor space. Boarding pass service for guests with carry-on luggage provided with specific
airlines. Meets AAA guest room security requirements. 600 units. 599 one-bedroom standard units. 1 one-
bedroom suite. 8 stories, interior corridors. **Parking:** on-site (fee) and valet. **Amenities:** voice mail, safes,
honor bars, irons, hair dryers. **Dining:** 2 restaurants, 5 am-1 am, cocktails, entertainment. **Pool(s):** heated indoor. **Leisure
Activities:** steamroom. *Fee:* massage. **Guest Services:** gift shop, valet laundry. **Business Services:** conference facilities,
business center. **Cards:** AX, DC, MC, VI.
SOME UNITS
Ⓢ🅓 🍴 24📶 🍸 🄶M Ⓢ Ⓓ ⇆ 🛗 📶 💻 / 🗙 /
FEE

CAMINO REAL MEXICO CITY *Book at aaa.com* **Phone:** (55)5263-8888 **⑥**
🅰🅰🅰 All Year 1P: $150-$300 2P: $150-$300
Location: Between Victor Hugo and Kent, just n of Diana Cir; Periferico, exit Ave Presidente Masaryk, then w. Mariano
▽▽▽ ▽▽▽ Escobedo 700 11590. Fax: 55/5531-0839. **Facility:** Distinguished atmosphere. Expansive public areas. Very
large rooms and bathrooms. Multi-lingual staff. 714 units. 669 one-bedroom standard units. 36 one- and 9
Large-scale Hotel two-bedroom suites ($300-$2750), some with kitchens (utensils extra charge). 5 stories, interior corridors.
Bath: combo or shower only. **Parking:** on-site (fee) and valet. **Terms:** cancellation fee imposed.
Amenities: video games, voice mail, safes, honor bars, irons, hair dryers. *Some:* CD players, dual phone lines. **Dining:** 2
restaurants, 24 hours, cocktails, also, Los Azulejos, Le Cirque, see separate listings, entertainment. **Pool(s):** outdoor, heated
outdoor. **Leisure Activities:** *Fee:* 4 lighted tennis courts, massage. **Guest Services:** gift shop, valet laundry, area transportation
(fee). **Business Services:** conference facilities, business center. **Cards:** AX, CB, DC, MC, VI.
SOME UNITS
🖃 🍴 24📶 🍸 🏕 Ⓓ ⇆ 🛗 📶 / 🗙 🔒 🄴 💻 /
FEE

FIESTA AMERICANA GRAND CHAPULTEPEC *Book at aaa.com* **Phone:** (55)2581-1500 **⑬**
▽▽▽ ▽▽▽ All Year 1P: $140-$200 2P: $140-$200 XP: $20 F12
Location: On Mariano Escobedo, jct Paseo de la Reforma. Mariano Escobedo 756 Col Anzures 11590.
Large-scale Hotel Fax: 55/2581-1501. **Facility:** Overlooking famed Chapultepec Park, these contemporary guest rooms
feature jewel-tone color schemes; 14 corner rooms offer sweeping views of the park. 203 units. 189 one-
bedroom standard units. 14 one-bedroom suites, some with efficiencies. 20 stories, interior corridors. **Parking:** on-site (fee).
Terms: [AP], [BP], [CP], [ECP] & [MAP] meal plans available. **Amenities:** dual phone lines, voice mail, safes, honor bars, irons,
hair dryers. *Fee:* video games, high-speed Internet. *Some:* CD players. **Leisure Activities:** whirlpool, spa. **Guest Services:**
valet laundry, area transportation (fee). **Business Services:** meeting rooms, business center. **Cards:** AX, MC, VI.
(See color ad back cover, card inserts)
SOME UNITS
Ⓢ🅓 🖃 🍴 24📶 🍸 🄳 📶 💻 / 🗙 🄴 /
FEE

FIESTA AMERICANA REFORMA *Book at aaa.com* **Phone:** (55)5140-4100 **⑥**
▽▽▽ All Year 1P: $120-$160 2P: $120-$160 XP: $12
Location: Southwest quarter of Glorieta Cristobal Colon. Paseo de la Reforma 80 06600. Fax: 55/5140-4150.
Large-scale Hotel **Facility:** 622 units. 600 one-bedroom standard units. 22 one-bedroom suites. 25 stories, interior corridors.
Parking: on-site. **Amenities:** dual phone lines, voice mail, honor bars, hair dryers. *Fee:* video games, high-
speed Internet. *Some:* safes. **Leisure Activities:** sauna, steamroom, exercise room. *Fee:* massage. **Guest Services:** gift shop,
valet laundry. **Business Services:** conference facilities, business center. **Cards:** AX, DC, DS, MC, VI.
(See color ad card inserts)
SOME UNITS
🍴 24📶 🍸 Ⓓ 🗙 🄳 📶 💻 / 🗙 /

FIESTA INN GRAN *Book at aaa.com* **Phone:** 55/5096-9300 **⑪**
▽▽▽ All Year 1P: $85-$150 2P: $85-$150
Location: On Periferico Sur, just s of Tlalpan Ave. Periferico Sur 5530 Col Pedregal de 14020. Fax: 55/5096-9300.
Small-scale Hotel **Facility:** 212 one-bedroom standard units. 12 stories, interior corridors. **Parking:** on-site and valet.
Amenities: video games, high-speed Internet, voice mail, hair dryers. **Pool(s):** heated indoor. **Leisure
Activities:** whirlpool, exercise room. **Guest Services:** gift shop, valet laundry, area transportation (fee). **Business Services:**
meeting rooms, business center. **Cards:** AX, CB, DC, JC, MC, VI. *(See color ad card insert)*
SOME UNITS
🖃 🍴 🍸 Ⓢ Ⓓ 🄳 📶 💻 / 🗙 /
FEE

(See maps and indexes p. 464-465, 466-469, 470-472)

FOUR SEASONS HOTEL MEXICO D.F. — *Book at aaa.com*
Phone: (55)5230-1818 [16]
All Year 1P: $315-$400 2P: $345-$430 XP: $30
Location: On Paseo de la Reforma. Located adjacent to Chapultepec Park. Paseo de la Reforma 500 06600. Fax: 55/5230-1817. **Facility:** Elegant and refined public areas. Spacious, tastefully appointed units. Most units overlook beautifully landscaped courtyard. Meets AAA guest room security requirements. 240 units. *Large-scale Hotel* 200 one-bedroom standard units. 40 one-bedroom suites ($450-$2500). 8 stories, interior corridors. **Parking:** valet. **Terms:** cancellation fee imposed. **Amenities:** video library, CD players, dual phone lines, voice mail, safes, honor bars, irons, hair dryers. *Fee:* video games, high-speed Internet. *Some:* DVD players, fax. **Dining:** 6:30 am-11:30 pm, cocktails, also, Reforma 500, see separate listing, entertainment. **Pool(s):** heated outdoor. **Leisure Activities:** saunas, whirlpool. *Fee:* massage. **Guest Services:** gift shop, valet laundry, area transportation (fee). **Business Services:** conference facilities, business center. **Cards:** AX, CB, DC, DS, JC, MC, VI.
SOME UNITS

GALERIA PLAZA HOTEL — *Book at aaa.com*
Phone: (55)5230-1717 [18]
All Year 1P: $105-$200 2P: $105-$200
Location: In the Pink Zone. Hamburgo #195 Col Juarez 06600. Fax: 55/5207-5867. **Facility:** 439 units. 400 one-*Large-scale Hotel* bedroom standard units. 39 one-bedroom suites ($200-$400). 12 stories, interior corridors. **Parking:** on-site (fee) and valet. **Amenities:** dual phone lines, voice mail, safes, honor bars, irons, hair dryers. **Pool(s):** small heated outdoor. **Leisure Activities:** exercise room. *Fee:* massage. **Guest Services:** gift shop, valet laundry, area transportation (fee). **Business Services:** meeting rooms, business center. **Cards:** AX, CB, DC, DS, JC, MC, VI.
SOME UNITS

GRAN MELIA MEXICO REFORMA
Phone: 55/5128-5000 [5]
All Year 1P: $150-$175 2P: $150-$175
Location: Jct Ave de la Republica. Paseo de la Reforma #1 06030. **Facility:** 490 one-bedroom standard units. *Large-scale Hotel* Interior corridors. **Parking:** valet. **Amenities:** video games, high-speed Internet, voice mail, safes, honor bars, irons, hair dryers. **Pool(s):** heated indoor. **Leisure Activities:** exercise room, spa. **Guest Services:** gift shop. **Business Services:** conference facilities, business center. **Cards:** AX, MC, VI.

HABITA HOTEL
Phone: 55/5282-3100 [1]
All Year 1P: $195-$265 2P: $195-$265
Location: In the Polanco Zone. Ave Presidente Masaryk 201 11560. Fax: 55/5282-3101. **Facility:** 32 one-bedroom *Small-scale Hotel* standard units. 6 stories, interior corridors. *Bath:* shower or tub only. **Parking:** valet. **Amenities:** high-speed Internet, voice mail, safes, honor bars, irons, hair dryers. *Some:* DVD players. **Pool(s):** lap. **Leisure Activities:** sauna, whirlpool, exercise room. *Fee:* massage. **Business Services:** meeting rooms, business center. **Cards:** AX, MC, VI.
SOME UNITS

HOLIDAY INN PLAZA DALI CIUDAD DE MEXICO — *Book at aaa.com*
Phone: (55)5768-2020 [2]
All Year 1P: $80-$150 2P: $80-$150
Location: On Viaducto Rio de la Piedad, 0.8 km n of Congreso de la Union Ave. Viaducto Rio de la Piedad; Col *Large-scale Hotel* Magdalena Mix 15860. Fax: 55/5552-0895. **Facility:** 150 units. 140 one-bedroom standard units. 10 one-bedroom suites ($150-$220) with whirlpools. 6 stories, interior corridors. *Bath:* combo or shower only. **Parking:** on-site. **Terms:** 3 day cancellation notice-fee imposed, [AP], [BP], [CP] & [MAP] meal plans available, package plans - weekends. **Amenities:** safes, irons, hair dryers. **Leisure Activities:** exercise room. **Guest Services:** gift shop, valet laundry, area transportation (fee). **Business Services:** meeting rooms, business center. **Cards:** AX, JC, MC, VI.
SOME UNITS

HOLIDAY INN TRADE CENTER — *Book at aaa.com*
Phone: 55/5278-9950 [6]
All Year 1P: $150 2P: $150 XP: $15
Location: Colonia San Pedro de los Pinos; Ave Revolucion S at Calle 23. Ave Revolucion 583 03800. Fax: 55/5278-9980. **Facility:** 188 units. 180 one-bedroom standard units. 8 one-bedroom suites with whirlpools. 7 stories, interior corridors. **Parking:** on-site (fee). **Terms:** 7 day cancellation notice. *Small-scale Hotel* **Amenities:** dual phone lines, voice mail, safes, honor bars, irons, hair dryers. **Dining:** 6:30 am-midnight, cocktails, entertainment. **Leisure Activities:** exercise room. **Guest Services:** gift shop, valet and coin laundry. **Business Services:** conference facilities, business center. **Cards:** AX, MC, VI.
SOME UNITS

HOLIDAY INN ZOCALO — *Book at aaa.com*
Phone: (55)5521-2121 [4]
All Year 1P: $60-$110 2P: $60-$110 XP: $10 F
Location: Just w of the Zocalo. Cinco de Mayo y Zocalo Centro Historica 06000. Fax: 55/5521-2122. **Facility:** 118 units. 110 one-bedroom standard units. 8 one-bedroom suites, some with whirlpools. 7 stories, interior *Small-scale Hotel* corridors. *Bath:* shower only. **Parking:** on-site (fee) and valet. **Amenities:** safes, irons, hair dryers. **Guest Services:** gift shop, valet laundry, area transportation (fee). **Business Services:** meeting rooms, business center. **Cards:** AX, MC.
SOME UNITS

HOTEL CASA INN MEXICO — *Book at aaa.com*
Phone: 55/5242-7750 [7]
All Year 1P: $90-$120 2P: $90-$120 XP: $10
Location: Just n of Paseo de la Reforma; corner of Rio Lerma and Rio Mississippi. Rio Lerma 237 06500. Fax: 55/5242-7760. **Facility:** Meets AAA guest room security requirements. 165 units. 154 one-bedroom *Small-scale Hotel* standard units. 11 one-bedroom suites. 13 stories, interior corridors. *Bath:* shower only. **Parking:** on-site and valet. **Amenities:** voice mail, safes, hair dryers. **Leisure Activities:** exercise room. **Guest Services:** gift shop, valet laundry. **Business Services:** meeting rooms. *Fee:* PC, fax. **Cards:** AX, DC, MC, VI.
SOME UNITS

(See maps and indexes p. 464-465, 466-469, 470-472)

HOTEL CENTURY — *Book at aaa.com*

Phone: (55)5726-9911   20

All Year   1P: $121-$151   2P: $121-$151   XP: $18   F12

Small-scale Hotel

Location: In the Pink Zone. Liverpool 152 06600. **Fax:** 55/5525-7475. **Facility:** 142 one-bedroom standard units. 21 stories, interior corridors. *Bath:* combo or shower only. **Parking:** valet. **Terms:** 8 day cancellation notice-fee imposed. **Amenities:** video games (fee), safes, honor bars. *Some:* hair dryers. **Pool(s):** heated outdoor. **Leisure Activities:** exercise room. **Guest Services:** valet laundry. **Business Services:** meeting rooms. **Cards:** AX, DC, MC, VI.

SOME UNITS

HOTEL GENEVE — *Book at aaa.com*

Phone: (55)5080-0800   21

All Year   1P: $100-$155   2P: $100-$155   XP: $15   F12

Small-scale Hotel

Location: In the Pink Zone; 0.5 km s of Paseo de la Reforma. Londres 130 06600. **Fax:** 55/5208-0831. **Facility:** Meets AAA guest room security requirements. 270 one-bedroom standard units. 5 stories, interior corridors. **Parking:** on-site (fee). **Terms:** cancellation fee imposed, package plans, 15% service charge. **Amenities:** voice mail, safes, honor bars, hair dryers. **Leisure Activities:** saunas, steamrooms, exercise room. *Fee:* massage. **Guest Services:** gift shop, valet laundry. **Business Services:** meeting rooms, business center. **Cards:** AX, DC, MC, VI.

SOME UNITS

HOTEL JARDIN AMAZONAS

Phone: 55/9151-5555   12

All Year   1P: $80-$150   2P: $80-$150

Small-scale Hotel

Location: Just n of Paseo de la Reforma. Rio Amazonas 73 06600. **Fax:** 55/9151-5555. **Facility:** 50 units. 45 one-bedroom standard units. 5 one-bedroom suites with kitchens (utensils extra charge). 4 stories (no elevator), exterior corridors. *Bath:* shower only. **Parking:** on-site. **Terms:** 3 day cancellation notice. **Amenities:** safes, honor bars. **Pool(s):** heated outdoor. **Guest Services:** valet laundry. **Business Services:** fax. **Cards:** AX, DC, MC, VI.

SOME UNITS

HOTEL J R PLAZA AEROPUERTO

Phone: 55/5785-5200   5

All Year   1P: $115   2P: $115   XP: $20

Small-scale Hotel

Location: Opposite international airport. Blvd Puerto Aereo 390 15500. **Fax:** 55/5784-3221. **Facility:** 106 units. 97 one-bedroom standard units. 9 one-bedroom suites ($150) with whirlpools. 4 stories, interior corridors. **Parking:** valet. **Amenities:** hair dryers. **Guest Services:** valet laundry. **Business Services:** meeting rooms, fax (fee). **Cards:** AX, CB, DC, DS, MC, VI.

SOME UNITS

HOTEL MARCO POLO

Phone: (55)5080-0063   14

All Year   1P: $170   2P: $190   XP: $25   F12

Small-scale Hotel

Location: In the Pink Zone; 4 blks s of Paseo de la Reforma. Amberes 27 06600. **Fax:** 55/5080-0063. **Facility:** Meets AAA guest room security requirements. 73 units. 64 one-bedroom standard units with efficiencies. 9 one-bedroom suites ($209-$260) with kitchens, some with whirlpools. 6 stories, interior corridors. **Parking:** on-site (fee) and valet. **Terms:** 5 day cancellation notice-fee imposed. **Amenities:** safes, honor bars, hair dryers. *Some:* fax. **Leisure Activities:** exercise room. **Guest Services:** valet laundry. **Business Services:** meeting rooms, business center. **Cards:** AX, DC, MC, VI.

SOME UNITS

HOTEL NIKKO MEXICO — *Book at aaa.com*

Phone: (55)5283-8700   3

All Year   1P: $300   2P: $300   XP: $15   F12

Large-scale Hotel

Location: In the Polanco Zone; jct Campos Eliseos and Andres Bello sts; 1 blk from National Museum of Anthropology. Campos Eliseos 204 Col Polanco 11560. **Fax:** 55/5280-9191. **Facility:** A rotating art exhibit occupies the lobby of this Mexico City high-rise, which provides a full array of business and tourism facilities. 744 units. 23 one-bedroom standard units. 23 one-bedroom suites ($550-$800), some with kitchens. 38 stories, interior corridors. **Parking:** on-site and valet. **Amenities:** video games (fee), high-speed Internet, voice mail, safes, honor bars, irons, hair dryers. **Dining:** 4 restaurants, 6:30 am-1 am, cocktails, entertainment. **Pool(s):** heated indoor. **Leisure Activities:** saunas, steamrooms, putting green, 3 lighted tennis courts, spa. *Fee:* rooftop golf driving range. **Guest Services:** gift shop, valet laundry, area transportation (fee). **Business Services:** conference facilities, business center. **Cards:** AX, DC, JC, MC, VI.

SOME UNITS

FEE

HOTEL PARQUE ENSENADA — *Book at aaa.com*

Phone: (55)5208-0052   1

All Year   1P: $42-$50   2P: $57   XP: $5   F11

Small-scale Hotel

Location: Colonia Roma; jct aves Cuauhtemoc y Alvaro Obregon; downtown. Ave Alvaro Obregon 13 06700. **Fax:** 55/5208-0052. **Facility:** 132 one-bedroom standard units. 7 stories, interior corridors. *Bath:* shower only. **Parking:** on-site and valet. **Terms:** [AP] meal plan available. **Amenities:** safes. *Some:* honor bars. **Guest Services:** valet laundry. **Business Services:** meeting rooms, business center. **Cards:** AX, MC, VI.

SOME UNITS

HOTEL PLAZA FLORENCIA

Phone: 55/5242-4700   19

All Year   1P: $130   2P: $150   XP: $11

Small-scale Hotel

Location: In the Pink Zone; 2 blks s of Paseo de la Reforma. Florencia 61 St 06600. **Fax:** 55/5242-4785. **Facility:** Meets AAA guest room security requirements. 142 units. 134 one-bedroom standard units. 8 one-bedroom suites ($160). 12 stories, interior corridors. *Bath:* combo or shower only. **Parking:** on-site (fee) and valet. **Terms:** 7 day cancellation notice. **Amenities:** voice mail, honor bars. *Some:* high-speed Internet. **Leisure Activities:** exercise room. **Guest Services:** valet laundry. **Business Services:** meeting rooms, business center. **Cards:** AX, MC, VI.

SOME UNITS

(See maps and indexes p. 464-465, 466-469, 470-472)

HOTEL POSADA VIENA   *Book at aaa.com*   **Phone:** (55)5566-0700   **23**

◆◆◆ ◆◆◆   All Year   2P: $65-$100

Small-scale Hotel   **Location:** Just off Dinamarca. Located in a quiet area. Marsella 28 06600. Fax: 55/5592-7302. **Facility:** 88 units. 71 one-bedroom standard units. 11 one- and 6 two-bedroom suites. 4-5 stories, interior corridors. *Bath:* combo or shower only. **Parking:** on-site. **Terms:** 3 day cancellation notice. **Guest Services:** valet laundry.
Business Services: meeting rooms, business center. **Cards:** AX, MC, VI.

[⊓] [24⊓] [⊤] [ℳ] [▣]

HOTEL PRESIDENTE INTERCONTINENTAL MEXICO
  CITY   *Book at aaa.com*   **Phone:** (55)5327-7700   **4**

◆◆◆◆ ◆◆◆◆   1/13-11/30   1P: $260-$320   2P: $260-$320   XP: $50   F18
       12/1-1/12   1P: $255-$305   2P: $255-$305   XP: $50   F18

Large-scale Hotel   **Location:** In the Polanco Zone; on Paseo de la Reforma, 1.3 km w of Periferico; opposite Chapultepec Park and the National Auditorium. Campo Eliseos 218 Col Pol 11560. Fax: 55/5327-7783. **Facility:** Very modern hotel across from Chapultepec Park. Impressive view from most rooms. Complimentary passes to local museums and attractions. Some connecting rooms. Outstanding business center services. Home to visiting heads of state and rock stars, such as President Clinton, Janet Reno, the King of Spain, Michael Jackson, Don King and Gloria Estefan. Meets AAA guest room security requirements. 657 units. 600 one-bedroom standard units. 55 one- and 2 two-bedroom suites, some with kitchens (utensils extra charge). 42 stories, interior corridors. **Parking:** on-site (fee) and valet. **Terms:** cancellation fee imposed. **Amenities:** video games, high-speed Internet, voice mail, honor bars, irons, hair dryers. *Some:* fax. **Dining:** Alfredo di Roma, The Palm, Au Pie de Cochon, see separate listings. **Leisure Activities:** exercise room. *Fee:* massage. **Guest Services:** gift shop, valet laundry, area transportation (fee). **Business Services:** conference facilities, business center. **Cards:** AX, DC, JC, MC, VI.

SOME UNITS
[S�] [✈] [⊓] [24⊓] [⊤] [⊞] [S] [D] [▣] [DATA PORT] [▣] [/] [✕] [▣] [/]
FEE

HOTEL ROYAL PEDREGAL   *Book at aaa.com*   **Phone:** (55)5449-4000   **9**

◆◆◆ ◆◆◆   All Year   2P: $180-$290   XP: $20   F14

Large-scale Hotel   **Location:** Adjacent to main Periferico, in southern part of city, 0.5 km n from Periferico Sur Mall. Periferico Sur 4363 14210. Fax: 55/5645-7964. **Facility:** 314 units. 297 one-bedroom standard units. 16 one- and 1 two-bedroom suites ($420-$650) with whirlpools. 5 stories, interior corridors. *Bath:* combo or shower only. **Parking:** valet. **Terms:** cancellation fee imposed, [AP], [BP] & [MAP] meal plans available. *Fee:* video games, safes. **Amenities:** voice mail, honor bars, irons, hair dryers. *Fee:* video games, safes. **Pool(s):** heated outdoor, heated indoor. **Leisure Activities:** sauna, whirlpool, spa. **Guest Services:** gift shop, valet laundry. **Business Services:** conference facilities, business center. **Cards:** AX, DC, MC, VI.

SOME UNITS
[S⊟] [⊓] [24⊓] [⊤] [⊠] [D] [⇆] [⊕] [✕] [▣] [DATA PORT] [▣] [/][✕]/
FEE

HOTEL ROYAL ZONA ROSA   *Book at aaa.com*   **Phone:** (55)5228-9918   **24**

◆◆◆ ◆◆◆   All Year   1P: $120-$180   2P: $120-$180   XP: $15   F

Small-scale Hotel   **Location:** In the Pink Zone; jct Ave Chapultepec and Liverpool St. 78 Amberes St 06600. Fax: 55/5514-3330. **Facility:** 162 units. 161 one-bedroom standard units. 1 one-bedroom suite ($250-$400) with whirlpool. 20 stories, interior corridors. *Bath:* combo or shower only. **Parking:** valet. **Amenities:** video games (fee), safes, honor bars, hair dryers. **Dining:** Restaurante Tezka, see separate listing. **Pool(s):** small heated outdoor. **Leisure Activities:** steamroom, exercise room. *Fee:* massage. **Guest Services:** gift shop, valet laundry. **Business Services:** meeting rooms, business center. **Cards:** AX, DC, MC, VI.

SOME UNITS
[S⊟] [⊓] [⊤] [D] [⇆] [✕] [▣] [DATA PORT] [/][✕]/

HOTEL SEGOVIA REGENCY   *Book at aaa.com*   **Phone:** 55/5208-8454   **26**

◆◆◆ ◆◆◆   All Year   1P: $50   2P: $65   XP: $6   F15

Small-scale Hotel   **Location:** Jct aves Monterrey and Oaxaca; adjacent to the Pink Zone. Ave Chapultepec 328 06700. Fax: 55/5525-0391. **Facility:** 120 one-bedroom standard units. 7 stories, interior corridors. *Bath:* shower only. **Parking:** on-site. **Amenities:** safes, hair dryers. **Guest Services:** valet laundry, area transportation (fee). **Business Services:** meeting rooms, fax (fee). **Cards:** AX, DC, MC, VI.

[S⊟] [✈] [⊓] [⊤] [DATA PORT]
FEE

HOTEL SEVILLA PALACE   **Phone:** (55)5566-8877   **11**

Ⓐ   All Year   1P: $108   2P: $108   XP: $10   F12

◆◆◆ ◆◆◆   **Location:** Southwest quarter of Glorieta Cristobal Colon Monumento; center. Paseo de la Reforma 105 06030. Fax: 55/5703-1521. **Facility:** 414 one-bedroom standard units, some with whirlpools. 23 stories, interior corridors. *Bath:* combo or shower only. **Parking:** valet. **Terms:** cancellation fee imposed. **Amenities:** voice mail, safes, honor bars, irons, hair dryers. *Some:* high-speed Internet. **Dining:** 2 restaurants, 7 am-midnight, cocktails, nightclub, entertainment. **Pool(s):** heated indoor. **Leisure Activities:** whirlpool, exercise room. *Fee:* massage. **Guest Services:** gift shop, valet laundry. **Business Services:** conference facilities, business center. **Cards:** AX, MC, VI.

Large-scale Hotel

SOME UNITS
[S⊟] [⊓] [⊤] [D] [⇆] [✕] [▣] [DATA PORT] [▣] [/][✕]/

HOTEL SUITES SAN MARINO   **Phone:** 55/5525-4886   **8**

◆◆◆ ◆◆◆   All Year [BP]   1P: $145   2P: $145   XP: $10

Small-scale Hotel   **Location:** Just n of Paseo de la Reforma and the Pink Zone. Tiber 107 06500. Fax: 55/5511-7800. **Facility:** 77 units. 74 one-bedroom standard units with efficiencies. 2 one- and 1 two-bedroom suites with kitchens; some with whirlpools. 12 stories, interior corridors. *Bath:* combo or shower only. **Parking:** valet. **Amenities:** irons. *Some:* safes. **Leisure Activities:** exercise room. **Guest Services:** valet laundry. **Business Services:** meeting rooms, business center. **Cards:** AX, DC, MC, VI.

SOME UNITS
[⊓] [⊤] [D] [▣] [DATA PORT] [⊟] [▣] [/][✕] [VCR] [▣] [/]

(See maps and indexes p. 464-465, 466-469, 470-472)

JW MARRIOTT HOTEL MEXICO CITY   *Book at aaa.com*   Phone: (55)5999-0000   **2**
All Year   1P: $180-$300   2P: $180-$300
Location: On Paseo de la Reforma; opposite Chapultepec Park and National Auditorium. Andres Bello #29 11560.
Fax: 55/5999-0009. **Facility:** This hotel has a large entrance with 3 huge columns, handsomely appointed public areas and a state-of-the-art spa. 317 units. 299 one-bedroom standard units. 15 one- and 3 two-bedroom suites ($250-$600), some with kitchens and/or whirlpools. 26 stories, interior corridors. *Bath:* combo or shower only. **Parking:** valet. **Amenities:** video games (fee), high-speed Internet, dual phone lines, voice mail, safes, honor bars, hair dryers. *Some:* CD players, fax, irons. **Dining:** 2 restaurants, 6:30 am-midnight, cocktails. **Pool(s):** heated outdoor. **Leisure Activities:** saunas, whirlpool, steamrooms, spa. **Guest Services:** gift shop, valet laundry. **Business Services:** conference facilities, business center. **Cards:** AX, CB, DC, DS, JC, MC, VI.

Large-scale Hotel

SOME UNITS
⊘ 🍴 24🕐 🍷 🖾 Ⓢ Ⓓ 🏊 📶 ✕ 📹 / ✕ 📠 📺 💻 /

LA CASONA   Phone: 55/5286-3001   **25**
All Year [CP]   1P: $160   2P: $160   XP: $15   F13
Location: Corner of Durango and Cozumel. Durango 280 Colonia Roma 06700. Fax: 52/5211-0871. **Facility:** 29 one-bedroom standard units, some with whirlpools. 3 stories (no elevator), interior corridors. **Parking:** on-site (fee) and valet. **Terms:** age restrictions may apply, [BP] meal plan available. **Amenities:** safes, hair dryers. **Leisure Activities:** exercise room. **Guest Services:** valet laundry. **Business Services:** meeting rooms, PC. **Cards:** AX, DC, DS, MC, VI.

Small-scale Hotel

SOME UNITS
🍴 Ⓓ 📶 📠 / ✕ 📹
FEE

MARQUIS REFORMA HOTEL   *Book at aaa.com*   Phone: (55)5229-1200   **15**
All Year   1P: $125-$230   2P: $125-$230   XP: $30   F12
Location: 0.8 km sw of jct Insurgentes; opposite Chapultepec Park. Paseo de la Reforma 465 06500. Fax: 55/5229-1212. **Facility:** Dramatic exterior of pink granite and blue glass. Expensive furnishings in public areas. Well-appointed rooms. Meets AAA guest room security requirements. 208 units. 123 one-bedroom standard units. 85 one-bedroom suites ($165-$650), some with whirlpools. 11 stories, interior corridors. **Parking:** valet. **Terms:** [BP] meal plan available. **Amenities:** dual phone lines, voice mail, fax, safes, honor bars, hair dryers. *Fee:* video games, high-speed Internet. *Some:* CD players. **Leisure Activities:** saunas, whirlpools, exercise room, spa. **Guest Services:** gift shop, valet laundry, area transportation. **Business Services:** conference facilities, business center. **Cards:** AX, CB, DC, DS, JC, MC, VI.

Small-scale Hotel

SOME UNITS
Ⓢ 🍴 24🕐 🍷 📶 Ⓢ Ⓓ ✕ 📹 📠 / ✕ 📹 📺 💻 /

NH MEXICO CITY   *Book at aaa.com*   Phone: (55)5228-9928   **9**
All Year   1P: $115-$165   2P: $115-$165   XP: $15
Location: In the Pink Zone. Liverpool 155 Zona Rosa 06600. Fax: 55/5511-3490. **Facility:** 302 units. 292 one-bedroom standard units. 9 one- and 1 two-bedroom suites, some with kitchens (utensils extra charge) and/or whirlpools. 17 stories, interior corridors. **Parking:** on-site (fee). **Terms:** cancellation fee imposed. **Amenities:** video games (fee), voice mail, safes, honor bars, hair dryers. *Some:* dual phone lines. **Pool(s):** heated outdoor, wading. **Leisure Activities:** exercise room. **Guest Services:** gift shop, valet laundry. **Business Services:** conference facilities, business center. **Cards:** AX, DS, MC, VI.

Large-scale Hotel

SOME UNITS
🍴 24🕐 🍷 Ⓓ 🏊 📶 💻 / ✕ /

(See maps and indexes p. 464-465, 466-469, 470-472)

PEDREGAL PALACE HOTEL   *Book at aaa.com*   Phone: 55/5681-6855   8
All Year   1P: $150   2P: $150   XP: $20
Small-scale Hotel   **Location:** Just off Periferico Sur, exit Luis Cabrera. 3487 Periferico Sur 10400. Fax: 55/5595-4394. **Facility:** Meets AAA guest room security requirements. 64 units. 57 one-bedroom standard units. 7 one-bedroom units, some with whirlpools. 7 stories, interior corridors. *Bath:* shower only. **Parking:** on-site and valet. **Amenities:** voice mail, safes, honor bars, hair dryers. **Leisure Activities:** whirlpool, steamroom, exercise room. **Guest Services:** valet laundry. **Business Services:** meeting rooms, PC (fee). **Cards:** AX, DC, MC, VI.
SOME UNITS

RADISSON PARAISO HOTEL MEXICO CITY   *Book at aaa.com*   Phone: (55)5927-5959   10
All Year   1P: $165-$210   2P: $165-$210   XP: $30   F12
Large-scale Hotel   **Location:** Adjacent to main Periferico in southern part of city. Located in front of Periferico Sur Mall. Cuspide 53 Parques del Pedregal 14020. Fax: 55/5606-4006. **Facility:** Meets AAA guest room security requirements. 236 units. 234 one-bedroom standard units. 2 one-bedroom suites ($380-$800), some with whirlpools. 12 stories, interior corridors. *Bath:* shower only. **Parking:** on-site (fee) and valet. **Terms:** 3 day cancellation notice. **Amenities:** dual phone lines, voice mail, safes, honor bars, irons, hair dryers. *Fee:* video games, high-speed Internet. **Dining:** 2 restaurants, 7 am-11 pm, cocktails, entertainment. **Leisure Activities:** sauna, exercise room. *Fee:* massage. **Guest Services:** gift shop, valet laundry, area transportation-local malls, beauty salon. **Business Services:** conference facilities, business center. **Cards:** AX, DC, MC, VI. *(See color ad p 477)*
FEE   SOME UNITS

SHERATON CENTRO HISTORICO HOTEL &
CONVENTION CENTER MEXICO CITY   Phone: 55/5130-5300   3
All Year   1P: $185-$250   2P: $185-$250
Large-scale Hotel   **Location:** Facing Alameda Park in the historic center. Ave Juarez #70 Col Centro. Fax: 55/5130-5255. **Facility:** The downtown high-rise features upscale, contemporary decor; the upper rooms offer a spectacular view of the city. 457 units. 422 one-bedroom standard units. 34 one- and 1 two-bedroom suites ($200-$600), some with kitchens and/or whirlpools. 20 stories, interior corridors. **Parking:** valet. **Amenities:** video games, high-speed Internet, dual phone lines, voice mail, safes, honor bars, irons, hair dryers. *Some:* CD players. **Pool(s):** heated indoor, wading. **Leisure Activities:** exercise room. *Fee:* massage. **Guest Services:** gift shop, valet laundry, area transportation (fee). **Business Services:** conference facilities, business center. **Cards:** AX, CB, DC, DS, JC, MC, VI. *(See color ad p 8)*
FEE   SOME UNITS

SHERATON MARIA ISABEL HOTEL & TOWERS   *Book at aaa.com*   Phone: (55)5242-5555   17
All Year   1P: $285   2P: $285   XP: $15   F12
Large-scale Hotel   **Location:** Next to US Embassy, opposite Angel de la Independencia Monument. Paseo de la Reforma 325 06500. Fax: 55/5207-0684. **Facility:** This long-time four-diamond is on the famed Paseo de la Reforma; executive rooms feature comfortable, overstuffed chairs with ottomans. Meets AAA guest room security requirements. 755 units. 730 one-bedroom standard units. 24 one- and 1 two-bedroom suites ($320-$1800), some with efficiencies, kitchens (utensils extra charge) and/or whirlpools. 19-22 stories, interior corridors. **Parking:** on-site (fee). **Terms:** [BP] & [ECP] meal plans available. **Amenities:** voice mail, safes, honor bars, irons, hair dryers. *Some:* CD players, fax. **Dining:** 1926 Bice Ristorante, Manhattan Deli, see separate listings. **Pool(s):** heated outdoor. **Leisure Activities:** saunas, steamrooms, 2 lighted tennis courts, exercise room. *Fee:* massage. **Guest Services:** gift shop, valet laundry. **Business Services:** conference facilities, business center. **Cards:** AX, CB, DC, DS, JC, MC, VI. *(See color ad p 8)*
SOME UNITS

SHERATON SUITES SANTA FE   *Book at aaa.com*   Phone: (55)5258-8500   28
All Year   1P: $320-$1350   2P: $320-$1350   XP: $30   F16
Small-scale Hotel   **Location:** In the Santa Fe District; 12 km w of Paseo de la Reforma. 200 Guillermo Gonzalez Camarena 01210. Fax: 55/5258-8501. **Facility:** 194 one-bedroom suites ($360-$1350) with efficiencies, some with whirlpools. 10 stories, interior corridors. **Parking:** valet. **Terms:** 3 day cancellation notice-fee imposed. **Amenities:** high-speed Internet (fee), dual phone lines, voice mail, safes, honor bars, irons, hair dryers. *Some:* fax. **Leisure Activities:** steamrooms. *Fee:* exercise room, massage. **Guest Services:** gift shop, valet laundry. **Business Services:** conference facilities, business center. **Cards:** AX, CB, DC, DS, MC, VI. *(See color ad p 8)*
SOME UNITS
FEE

SUITES MI CASA   Phone: 55/5566-6711   7
All Year   1P: $70-$80   2P: $70-$80   XP: $10
Small-scale Hotel   **Location:** Just s of Paseo de la Reforma, at General Prim and Milan St. General Prim 106 06600. Fax: 55/5566-6010. **Facility:** 27 units. 26 one-bedroom standard units with kitchens. 1 two-bedroom suite ($90-$100) with kitchen. 7 stories, interior corridors. *Bath:* combo or shower only. **Parking:** on-site. **Terms:** 4 day cancellation notice-fee imposed. **Amenities:** safes. **Guest Services:** valet laundry. **Cards:** AX, MC, VI.

---

*The following lodgings were either not evaluated or did not
meet AAA rating requirements but are listed for your information only.*

RADISSON FLAMENCO   Phone: 52/5627-0220
fyi   Not evaluated. **Location:** Ave Revolucion #333 11870. Facilities, services, and decor characterize a mid-range property.

W MEXICO CITY   Phone: 55/9138-1800
fyi   Not evaluated. **Location:** Campos Eliseos 252 11560. Facilities, services, and decor characterize a mid-range property.

(See maps and indexes p. 464-465, 466-469, 470-472)

──────── **WHERE TO DINE** ────────

1926 BICE RISTORANTE   **Lunch:** $9-$20   **Dinner:** $9-$20   **Phone:** 55/5242-5555 ⑫
▽▽▽▽ ▽▽▽▽   **Location:** Next to US Embassy, opposite Angel de la Independencia Monument; in Sheraton Maria Isabel Hotel & Towers. Paseo de la Reforma 325 06500. **Hours:** 7 am-11 & 1-11 pm, Sat from 1 pm. Closed major holidays; also Sun. **Reservations:** suggested. **Features:** A contemporary look throughout the dining room complements the innovative menu at this popular spot, which specializes in fine Italian cuisine. Menu highlights include fresh tomato and mozzarella cheese salads, Caesar salads or homemade soups, followed by an extensive array of rich pastas, veal, poultry or fish selections. The desserts are a menu highlight worth saving room for. Dressy casual; cocktails. **Parking:** on-site (fee) and valet. **Cards:** AX, MC, VI.
  Italian ☒

ALFREDO DI ROMA   **Lunch:** $12-$18   **Dinner:** $22-$38   **Phone:** 55/5327-7700 ④
▽▽▽▽ ▽▽▽▽   **Location:** In the Polanco Zone; on Paseo de la Reforma, 1.3 km w of Periferico; opposite Chapultepec Park and the National Auditorium; in Hotel Presidente InterContinental Mexico City. Campos Eliseos 218 11560. **Hours:** 1 pm-midnight. **Reservations:** suggested. **Features:** Servers navigate knowingly through the elegant dining room, bringing authentic Italian dishes to appreciative diners. House specialties include imported prosciutto and fettuccine Alfredo prepared tableside. The wine list is extensive. Hedonistic desserts are a sweet way to amplify the experience. Casual dress; cocktails. **Parking:** on-site (fee) and valet. **Cards:** AX, CB, DC, DS, JC, MC, VI.
  Italian ☒

AU PIE DE COCHON   **Lunch:** $18-$38   **Dinner:** $25-$65   **Phone:** 55/5377-7700 ②
▽▽▽▽ ▽▽▽▽   **Location:** In the Polanco Zone; on Paseo de la Reforma, 1.3 km w of Periferico; opposite Chapultepec Park and the National Auditorium; in Hotel Presidente InterContinental Mexico City. Campo Eliseos 218 Col Pol 11560. **Hours:** 24 hours. **Reservations:** suggested. **Features:** Elegant French dining can be enjoyed 24 hours a day. The menu comprises the highest-quality seafood, shellfish, pasta, rich livers and sumptuous breakfasts dishes. The hot spot is usually jam-packed with the avant garde of the capital. Dressy casual; cocktails. **Parking:** on-site (fee) and valet. **Cards:** AX, CB, DC, JC, MC, VI.
  Regional Seafood ☒

BONDY RESTAURANT Y PASTELERIA   **Lunch:** $6-$17   **Dinner:** $6-$17   **Phone:** 55/5281-1818 ㉗
▽▽ ▽▽   **Location:** In the Polanco Zone; just off Paseo de la Reforma. Galileo 38 11560. **Hours:** 9 am-10 pm. Closed: Mon & 4/5-4/11. **Reservations:** suggested. **Features:** In the swank Polanco area, the restaurant and bakery serves many Europe-inspired dishes in small, cozy dining rooms. Save room for a choice from the many tempting pastries on display. Casual dress; beer & wine only. **Parking:** valet. **Cards:** MC, VI.
  Bakery/Desserts ☒

CHALET SUIZO   **Lunch:** $12-$16   **Dinner:** $16-$22   **Phone:** 55/5511-7529 ⑲
▽▽ ▽▽   **Location:** In the Pink Zone; just s of Paseo de la Reforma. Niza 37 06600. **Hours:** 1 pm-11 pm. **Reservations:** accepted. **Features:** A variety of well-prepared German and Swiss food is offered in an authentic Swiss setting with low ceilings and Tudor-style wood accents. The owners usually visit each table to look after diners' needs. Dressy casual; cocktails. **Parking:** no self-parking. **Cards:** AX, CB, DC, MC, VI.
  Ethnic

CHEZ WOK   **Lunch:** $18-$30   **Dinner:** $22-$45   **Phone:** 55/5281-3410 ㊱
▽▽▽ ▽▽▽   **Location:** In the Polanco Zone. Calle Tennyson #117 11560. **Hours:** 1 pm-11 pm, Fri & Sat-1 am. **Reservations:** suggested. **Features:** With an elegant setting on 2nd floor level, this spot offers fresh, creative dishes served by a refined staff in an upscale setting. Dressy casual; cocktails. **Parking:** valet. **Cards:** AX, MC, VI.
  Nouvelle Chinese ⬛☒

EL LAGO CHAPULTEPEC   **Lunch:** $20-$30   **Dinner:** $40-$65   **Phone:** 55/5515-9586 ③
▽▽▽▽ ▽▽▽▽   **Location:** In new section of Chapultepec Park; near National Museum of Natural History. Chapultepec Park 11870. **Hours:** 7:30 am-11:30 & 1-10:30 pm. Closed major holidays. **Reservations:** suggested. **Features:** Elegant dining spot overlooking the lake. Sunday buffet. Semi-formal attire; cocktails; entertainment. **Parking:** on-site (fee) and valet. **Cards:** AX, CB, DC, MC, VI.
  Regional New World ⬛☒

IL DANI RISTORANTE ITALIANO   **Lunch:** $7-$14   **Dinner:** $7-$14   **Phone:** 55/5280-5086 ㉛
▽▽ ▽▽   **Location:** At Paso a desnivel Peatonal. Monte Elbruz #132 Polanco Lomas 11000. **Hours:** 1 pm-11 pm, Fri & Sat-1 am. Closed major holidays; also Sun. **Reservations:** suggested. **Features:** A cozy cantina atmosphere complete with piano and guitar entertainment makes this a wonderful choice for a casual meal of hearty Italian fare. The menu features traditional favorites such as pizzas, pastas, veal and fish and tasty sweet pastries for dessert. Dressy casual; cocktails. **Parking:** valet. **Cards:** AX, MC, VI.
  Italian ☒

IZOTE   **Lunch:** $8-$23   **Dinner:** $8-$23   **Phone:** 55/5280-1671 ㉞
▽▽▽ ▽▽▽   **Location:** In the Polanco Zone. Ave Presidente Masaryk #513 Local 3 11560. **Hours:** 1 pm-midnight, Sun-6 pm. **Reservations:** suggested. **Features:** The menu offers superbly prepared Mexican cuisine done with a very contemporary spin. The dining room is understated with reminders of the country's indigenous roots subtly presented on its walls. Even with minimal knowledge of the Spanish language you can feel confident, as this restaurant is heavily patronized by foreign tourists. Dressy casual; cocktails. **Parking:** on-site. **Cards:** AX, MC, VI.
  Mexican

LA GALVIA RESTAURANTE   **Lunch:** $16-$30   **Dinner:** $16-$30   **Phone:** 55/5281-2310 ①
▽▽▽▽ ▽▽▽▽   **Location:** Opposite JW Marriott Hotel Mexico City. Campos Elisesus 247 Col Polanco 11560. **Hours:** 1:30 pm-11 pm, Sun 2 pm-5 pm. **Reservations:** suggested. **Features:** A warm welcome awaits at this restaurant, where you will find a charming dining room filled with plants and trees, offering a garden-like setting. In addition to the regular menu, which features a good selection of beef and seafood items, a complete light menu is offered with all the calories counted. The service is detailed and professional. Dressy casual; cocktails. **Parking:** on-site (fee). **Cards:** AX, MC, VI.
  Continental ☒

(See maps and indexes p. 464-465, 466-469, 470-472)

LA HACIENDA DE LOS MORALES　　**Lunch:** $7-$18　　**Dinner:** $7-$18　　**Phone:** 55/5096-3055　　�33
▼▼▼▼　**Location:** Just s of Ejercito Nacional. Vazquez de Mella 525 06300. **Hours:** 1 pm-1 am. Closed: 1/1, 12/25.
Reservations: suggested. **Features:** Surrounded by beautiful gardens with fountains, the restored
hacienda boasts large courtyards and dining rooms suited to relaxing, refined dining. Excellent quality
Regional Mexican　ingredients go into dishes that are served in ample portions, The staff is formal. Dressy casual; cocktails;
entertainment. **Parking:** valet. **Cards:** AX, CB, DC, MC, VI.　　　　　　　　　　　　　　　Ⓨ

LE CIRQUE　　　**Lunch:** $30-$60　　　**Dinner:** $50-$130　　　**Phone:** 55/5263-8884　　⑨
▼▼▼ ▼▼▼　**Location:** Between Victor Hugo and Kent, just n of Diana Cir; Periferico, exit Ave Presidente Masaryk, then w; in
Camino Real Mexico City. Mariano Escobedo 700 11590. **Hours:** 1 pm-11:30 pm, Sat from 6 pm, Sun noon-5 pm.
Regional New　Closed: 12/25. **Reservations:** required. **Features:** The whimsical yet upscale circus decor includes chrome
World　monkeys gazing down on guests from their rosewood perches. Dishes are complex and created with the
very best ingredients from around the world, all presented in unique, dazzling compositions for an
indubitably world-class experience. Semi-formal attire; cocktails. **Parking:** on-site (fee) and valet. **Cards:** AX, CB, DC, DS, JC,
MC, VI.　　　　　　　　　　　　　　　　　　　　　　　　　　　　　　　　　　Ⓨ Ⓧ

LES MOUSTACHES　　　**Lunch:** $15-$25　　　**Dinner:** $20-$40　　　**Phone:** 55/5533-3390　　⑭
▼▼▼▼　**Location:** In the Pink Zone. 88 Rio Sena 06500. **Hours:** 1:45 pm-10:30 pm. Closed: 1/1, 12/25; also 5/1 & Sun.
Reservations: suggested. **Features:** Elegant surroundings and a refined atmosphere are hallmarks of the
sophisticated restaurant. Distinctive presentations add to the appeal of menu offerings. Diners can request
French　seating in the main dining room, garden courtyard or upstairs private area. Coats and ties are required on
weekdays, but attire is casual on Saturday. Dressy casual; cocktails. **Parking:** valet and street. **Cards:** AX, DC, MC, VI.
　　　　　　　　　　　　　　　　　　　　　　　　　　　　　　　　　　　Ⓨ Ⓧ

LOS ALMENDROS　　　**Lunch:** $15-$25　　　**Dinner:** $20-$30　　　**Phone:** 55/5531-7307　　⑧
▼▼▼▼　**Location:** In the Polanco Zone; just e, corner of Campos Eliseos and Arquimedes. #164 Campos Eliseos 11560.
Hours: 7 am-11 pm, Sun 8 am-10:30 pm. **Reservations:** suggested. **Features:** Known for Mayan-
influenced cuisine, the restaurant transports diners to the Yucatan. A must on any tourist's itinerary, this spot
Regional Mexican　offers an unforgettable experience. A well-rounded meal might start with savory, but not spicy, panuchos de
cochinita pibil; center on arroz con pollo con platanos fritos; and end with cerveza Leon. Dressy casual; cocktails;
entertainment. **Parking:** valet and street. **Cards:** AX, DC, MC, VI.　　　　　　　　　　　　Ⓧ

LOS AZULEJOS　　　**Lunch:** $10-$25　　　**Dinner:** $20-$40　　　**Phone:** 55/5263-8888　　⑩
▼▼▼▼　**Location:** Between Victor Hugo and Kent, just n of Diana Cir; Periferico, exit Ave Presidente Masaryk, just w; in Camino
Real Mexico City. Mariano Escobedo 700 11590. **Hours:** 7 am-noon & 1:30-11 pm. **Reservations:** suggested.
Features: On the garden level of a world-famous hotel, the restaurant offers seating indoors or on the
Regional Mexican　terrace. Varied dishes are prepared with the highest quality ingredients and served in an upscale yet
informal dining room. Dressy casual; cocktails. **Parking:** on-site (fee). **Cards:** AX, CB, DC, JC, MC, VI.
　　　　　　　　　　　　　　　　　　　　　　　　　　　　　　　　　　　　Ⓧ

LOS GIRASOLES　　　**Lunch:** $7-$15　　　**Dinner:** $7-$15　　　**Phone:** 55/5510-0630　　①
▼▼▼▼　**Location:** Between calles 8 and 10; in front of Plaza Manuel Tolsa; in the historic district; downtown. Calle Tacuba entre
el 8 y el 10 06000. **Hours:** 1 pm-1 am, Mon & Sun-8 pm. Closed: 1/1, 12/25. **Reservations:** accepted.
Features: Created as a place to serve pre-Columbian recipes that have been handed down for generations,
Regional Mexican　the restaurant is conveniently near museums and the Zocalo. Menu items range from traditional tortilla soup
and duckling in blackberry sauce to such adventurous items as fried worms, ant eggs and grasshoppers. Casual dress;
cocktails. **Parking:** valet. **Cards:** AX, MC, VI.　　　　　　　　　　　　　Ⓨ Ⓚ Ⓧ

LOS TRES SOLES FOCOLARE RESTAURANT　　**Lunch:** $8-$12　　**Dinner:** $8-$12　　**Phone:** 55/5207-8055　　⑰
▼▼▼▼　**Location:** In the Pink Zone. Hamburgo 87, just off Niz 06600. **Hours:** 7:30 am-2 am, Sat & Sun from 9 am.
Reservations: suggested, for dinner. **Features:** From the large, festive dining room, diners can hear the
cocks crow as they select excellent regional specialties from Puebla, Yucatan and Veracruz. A nightly
Regional Mexican　folkloric show begins at 9 pm. Casual dress; cocktails; entertainment. **Parking:** valet. **Cards:** AX, CB, DC,
MC, VI.　　　　　　　　　　　　　　　　　　　　　　　　　　　　　　　　　Ⓨ

MANHATTAN DELI　　　**Lunch:** $7-$15　　　**Dinner:** $7-$15　　　**Phone:** 55/5242-5555　　⑪
▼▼ ▼▼　**Location:** Next to US Embassy, opposite Angel de la Independencia Monument; in Sheraton Maria Isabel Hotel &
Towers. Paseo de la Reforma 325 06500. **Hours:** noon-midnight. Closed major holidays; also Sat & Sun.
Features: Finding a New York-style deli in the heart of Mexico City is quite a surprise, but this one is
American　located directly beside the US Embassy so it fits right in. In addition to the traditional deli fare, diners will
also find some Mexican influences such as tacos, quesadillas and jalapeno poppers. An extensive salad bar is also offered.
Casual dress; cocktails. **Parking:** on-site (fee) and valet. **Cards:** AX, CB, DC, JC, MC, VI.　　　　Ⓧ

THE PALM　　　**Lunch:** $20-$40　　　**Dinner:** $20-$40　　　**Phone:** 55/5327-7700　　⑦
▼▼▼▼　**Location:** In the Polanco Zone; on Paseo de la Reforma, 1.3 km w of Periferico; in Polanco, opposite Chapultepec Park
and the National Auditorium; in Hotel Presidente InterContinental Mexico City. Campo Eliseos 218 11560. **Hours:** 1
pm-midnight. Closed: Sun. **Reservations:** suggested. **Features:** Offering seating on two tiers, the dining
Steak & Seafood　room has a sophisticated aura, with rich wood appointments and starched, white table linens. Huge bibs are
tied around the necks of diners before they feast on house specialties of steak and lobster, all fresh and served in ample
portions. Dressy casual; cocktails. **Parking:** on-site (fee) and valet. **Cards:** AX, CB, DC, DS, JC, MC, VI.　Ⓨ Ⓧ

PALMAS 500 RESTAURANTE　　　　　　　**Dinner:** $9-$30　　　　　　**Phone:** 55/5540-6004　　㊴
▼▼▼▼　**Location:** Jct Sierra Gamon. Palmas 500 Col Lomas de Chapultepec 11000. **Hours:** 2 pm-1 am, Sun & Mon-6 pm.
Closed major holidays. **Reservations:** suggested. **Features:** The innovative contemporary decor sets the
International　tone at this upscale restaurant, where diners are met with an African/Asian motif in decorative accents. The
slick look is complemented by the unique menu that offers diners a choice of International cuisine, including
Mexican favorites such as tacos and quesadillas for starters to exotic beef and seafood fare. At night, it takes on a club-like
atmosphere. Be sure to bring your translation book if you don't speak Spanish, as there are no English menus. Dressy casual;
cocktails. **Parking:** on-site (fee). **Cards:** AX, MC, VI.

(See maps and indexes p. 464-465, 466-469, 470-472)

PASSY
Lunch: $10-$15   Dinner: $15-$35   Phone: 55/5208-2087   [13]
Traditional Continental
Location: Just s of Paseo de la Reforma. Amberes 10 06600. **Hours:** 1 pm-6 pm. Closed major holidays; also Sun. **Reservations:** suggested. **Features:** Classic Continental selections. Dressy casual; cocktails. **Parking:** valet. **Cards:** AX, CB, DC, MC, VI.

PRIMER CUADRO
Lunch: $6-$12   Dinner: $6-$12   Phone: 55/5521-2016   [2]
Regional Mexican
Location: Downtown; in the historic district; close to the Zocalo. Bolivar 12 06600. **Hours:** 8 am-10 pm, Thurs-Sat to midnight, Sun 9 am-6 pm. **Reservations:** suggested. **Features:** On a quiet side street, the newcomer has a simple entrance and minimalist decor, but the focus on food has been achieved. Works by local artists are displayed, and book readings occur regularly. Traditional Mexican dishes are served in a relaxed atmosphere. Casual dress; cocktails. **Parking:** valet. **Cards:** AX, MC, VI.

PUJOL RESTAURANTE
Lunch: $9-$20   Dinner: $9-$20   Phone: 55/5545-4111   [32]
Continental
Location: Between Horacio and Homero. F Petrarca 254 Polanco 11570. **Hours:** 1 pm-11 pm, Mon-6 pm. Closed major holidays; also Sun. **Reservations:** suggested. **Features:** This dining room features an upscale contemporary interior, a fine Continental menu, and an extensive wine list. If you don't speak Spanish, you may want to bring a language book to translate the fabulous menu, as you won't want to miss the tempting choices. Starters include mussels, goat cheese salad or calamari, followed by mains such as Cornish hen in orange sauce, rack of lamb and several innovative seafood selections. The wine list features "flights of wine" for the adventuresome diner. Dressy casual; cocktails. **Parking:** valet. **Cards:** AX, MC, VI.

REFORMA 500
Lunch: $15-$25   Dinner: $20-$35   Phone: 55/5230-1818
Mediterranean
Location: On Paseo de la Reforma; in Four Seasons Hotel Mexico D.F. Paseo de la Reforma 500 06600. **Hours:** 6:30 am-11:30 pm. **Reservations:** suggested. **Features:** Mediterranean concepts employ premium quality ingredients. Preparations are complex and presentations distinctive. Patrons can dine in the elegant dining room or on the outdoor terrace overlooking the refined courtyard. Dressy casual; cocktails. **Parking:** valet. **Cards:** AX, CB, DC, DS, JC, MC, VI.

RESTAURANTE ANTIGUO SAN ANGEL INN
Lunch: $19-$29   Dinner: $25-$45   Phone: 55/5616-2222   [11]
Traditional Continental
Location: 7 blks w of Insurgentes Sur; 5 blks e of Anrillo Periferico; in Col San Angel Inn. Palmas & Altavista 01060. **Hours:** 1 pm-1 am, Sun-10 pm. Closed major holidays. **Reservations:** required. **Features:** In a renovated 18th-century hacienda, the renowned dining room is surrounded by gardens and patios. Sip a beverage in any of the courtyard gardens or elegant rooms, then unwind in the large ornate main dining room and appreciate the excellent service. The menu focus is on haute Mexican cuisine. Dressy casual; cocktails; entertainment. **Parking:** valet. **Cards:** AX, CB, DC, MC, VI. **Historic**

RESTAURANTE FONDA EL REFUGIO
Lunch: $15-$39   Dinner: $20-$40   Phone: 55/5525-8128   [18]
Regional Mexican
Location: In the Pink Zone. Liverpool 166 06600. **Hours:** 1 pm-midnight, Sun-10 pm. Closed: 1/1, 12/25. **Features:** Quaint countryside decor lends to the informal atmosphere at this long-time local favorite restaurant. Excellent preparation marks dishes that journey through the culinary regions of Mexico. Casual dress; cocktails. **Parking:** street. **Cards:** AX, DC, MC, VI.

RESTAURANTE MERCADERES CAFE
Lunch: $7-$20   Dinner: $7-$20   Phone: 55/5510-2213   [4]
Steak House
Location: In historical center; across from cathedral. Ave Cinco de Mayo #57 Centro Historico 06000. **Hours:** 8 am-7 pm, Wed-Fri to 9 pm. Closed major holidays; also Sun. **Reservations:** suggested. **Features:** A great location in the historical center of the city across from the cathedral and a few blocks from the Palace of Fine Arts makes this the perfect spot to break or end your sightseeing day. Although the menu is in Spanish only, the waiters will display the various cuts of steaks that are the featured specialty. They are grilled to order and arrive in hearty portions. Also offered are seafood, pasta and Mexican selections. Dressy casual. **Parking:** valet. **Cards:** AX, MC, VI.

RESTAURANTE TEZKA
Lunch: $12-$18   Dinner: $15-$38   Phone: 55/5228-9918   [20]
Regional New World
Location: In the Pink Zone; jct Ave Chapultepec and Liverpool St; in Hotel Royal Zona Rosa. 78 Amberes St 06600. **Hours:** 1 pm-5 pm, Thurs & Fri also 8 pm-11 pm. Closed: Sun & 12/25-1/1. **Reservations:** required. **Features:** Continental cuisine at this well-known local favorite is infused with fresh regional ingredients and presented in an elegant and refined dining room. Servers are attentive, knowledgeable and well trained. Dressy casual; cocktails. **Parking:** on-site (fee). **Cards:** AX, DC, MC, VI.

RUTH'S CHRIS STEAK HOUSE
Lunch: $19-$36   Dinner: $19-$36   Phone: 55/5395-5135   [30]
Steak House
Location: Entrance at Homero. Jaime Balmes 8 11510. **Hours:** 1:30 pm-11 pm, Sun-Tues to 7 pm. Closed major holidays. **Reservations:** suggested. **Features:** Famed for the hearty portions of sizzling steaks, this location is no exception. Located in a busy commercial area, diners can enjoy indoor or outdoor patio dining. The menu offers huge cuts of beef and equally large sides that are perfect for sharing. Dressy casual; cocktails. **Parking:** on-site (fee) and valet. **Cards:** AX, MC, VI.

TORRE D CASTILLA
Lunch: $9-$20   Dinner: $9-$20   Phone: 55/5281-0906   [26]
Spanish
Location: Opposite Cuban Embassy. Esopo 31 Polanco 11530. **Hours:** 1 pm-11 pm, Sun-7 pm. **Reservations:** suggested. **Features:** Set in a castle, this restaurant gives diners a true sense of medieval Europe with its distressed wood floors, wall murals and stone walls. The menu features a wonderful mixture of fine Spanish cuisine, complete with an extensive selection of hot and cold appetizers, or "tapas," and a good selection of meat, poultry and seafood. The jumbo shrimp in garlic sauce is a popular selection. The menu is in Spanish so be sure to bring your language book and a sense of adventure. Dressy casual; cocktails. **Parking:** valet. **Cards:** AX, MC, VI.

(See maps and indexes p. 464-465, 466-469, 470-472)

———— *The following restaurants have not been evaluated by AAA* ————
but are listed for your information only.

AGUILA Y SOL   **Phone:** 55/5281-8354
fyi Not evaluated. **Location:** Moliere 42 Polanco 06000. **Features:** This restaurant features innovative Mexican fare incorporating the old and the new.

CAFE DE TACUBA   **Phone:** 55/5518-4950
fyi Not evaluated. **Location:** Downtown; near the Zocalo. Tacuba #28 06010. **Features:** The eatery is tremendously popular with tourists but is still not to be missed. The menu offers a variety of traditional Mexican dishes; the Oaxacan tamale is a treat.

COMO   **Phone:** 55/5250-1596
fyi Not evaluated. **Location:** Horacio 253 Polanco 11560. **Features:** Diners here enjoy the casual ambience and the good menu selection featuring an extensive pasta selection, as well as meat and poultry offerings.

LA PIGUA   **Phone:** 55/5281-1302
fyi Not evaluated. **Location:** Alejandro Dumas 16. **Features:** This pleasant restaurant features an interesting seafood menu which highlights specialties from the Gulf Coast and the Yucatan Peninsula.

LE BOUCHON   **Phone:** 55/5281-7902
fyi Not evaluated. **Location:** Julio Verne 102, at Virgilio. **Features:** This popular restaurant features a cozy setting with indoor and outdoor patio dining and a menu of Country French cuisine.

MASACCIO   **Phone:** 55/5281-6265
fyi Not evaluated. **Location:** Newton 53-A. **Features:** A casual atmosphere and hearty portions of tasty pastas and other Italian fare make this a popular choice with locals.

MESON EL CID   **Phone:** 55/5521-6999
fyi Not evaluated. **Location:** Humbolt #61. **Features:** Classic elements from Spain are the hallmarks of this distinguished Mexico City favorite.

PORTA PORTESE RISTORANTE   **Phone:** 55/5281-4020
fyi Not evaluated. **Location:** Ave Presidente Masaryk 513-101. **Features:** Diners here enjoy the innovative Italian cuisine and the modern upscale setting.

RINCON ARGENTINO   **Phone:** 55/5254-8744
fyi Not evaluated. **Location:** Ave Presidente Masaryk #177. **Features:** The name translates into 'corner of Argentina,' which manifests as a bohemian atmosphere, tender cuts of beef and attentive personalized service.

SIR WINSTON CHURCHILL'S   **Phone:** 55/5280-6070
fyi Not evaluated. **Location:** Avila Camacho 67. **Features:** A touch of Britain in the heart of Mexico City, the eatery features traditional favorites such as roast beef and Yorkshire pudding.

This ends listings for Mexico City.
The following page resumes the alphabetical listings
of cities in Mexico City and Vicinity.

NAUCALPAN, DISTRITO FEDERAL   (See map and index starting on p. 470)

──── WHERE TO STAY ────

HOLIDAY INN MEXICO CITY TOREO-SATELITE   Phone: 55/5300-4828   **16**
▼▼▼▼ All Year   1P: $69-$99   2P: $69-$99
Small-scale Hotel **Location:** San Luis Tlatilco #2 53370. **Facility:** 114 units. 110 one-bedroom standard units. 4 one-bedroom suites with whirlpools. 6 stories, interior corridors. *Bath:* combo or shower only. **Parking:** valet. **Amenities:** high-speed Internet, voice mail. **Leisure Activities:** sauna, whirlpool, playground, exercise room. **Guest Services:** gift shop, coin laundry. **Business Services:** meeting rooms, business center.

SOME UNITS

〽️ 24📶 ⅄ D ⌧ 🚶 DATA PORT 💳 / ⌧ /

TEOTIHUACAN, MEXICO

──── WHERE TO STAY ────

CLUB MED VILLAS ARQUEOLOGICAS   Phone: (594)956-0909
▼▼▼ ▼▼▼ All Year   1P: $70-$80   2P: $70-$80
Small-scale Hotel **Location:** Adjacent to main archeological zone, off Mex 132. Periferico Sur S/N 55800. **Facility:** 41 units. 39 one-bedroom standard units. 2 one-bedroom suites ($130-$240) with whirlpools. 2 stories (no elevator), exterior corridors. *Bath:* shower or tub only. **Parking:** on-site. **Terms:** 3 day cancellation notice. **Amenities:** hair dryers. **Pool(s):** outdoor. **Leisure Activities:** lighted tennis court, playground. **Guest Services:** gift shop, valet laundry. **Business Services:** meeting rooms, fax (fee). **Cards:** AX, CB, DC, JC, MC, VI.

SOME UNITS

〽️ D 🏊 🍴 / ⌧ /

──── WHERE TO DINE ────

──── *The following restaurant has not been evaluated by AAA* ────
but is listed for your information only.

LA GIRUTA   Phone: 594/956-0104
[fyi] Not evaluated. **Location:** Adjacent to main archeological zone. **Features:** At the entrance to the pyramids, the restaurant occupies an immense cave at the foot of mountains.

TEQUESQUITENGO, MORELOS pop. 2,800   (See map and index starting on p. 461)

WHERE TO STAY

HOTEL HACIENDA VISTA HERMOSA   *Book at aaa.com*   Phone: 734/345-5361   🔟
▼▼ ▼▼
All Year   1P: $107-$150   2P: $150-$215
Location: 8.5 km se of Alpuyeca interchange off Mex 95 and 95-D (toll road); 1.5 km n of Lake Tequesquitengo. KM 7
Carr Alpuyeca 62680. Fax: 734/345-5360. **Facility:** This time-tested structure in the countryside south of
Classic Historic   Cuernavaca was the 16th-century hacienda of Hernan Cortes; gardens adorn the grounds. 105 units. 83
Country Inn   one-bedroom standard units. 12 one-bedroom suites ($220-$298). 10 cottages. 2 stories, exterior corridors.
Bath: combo or shower only. **Parking:** on-site. **Terms:** 20 day cancellation notice-fee imposed, [AP] meal plan available.
Pool(s): 2 outdoor. **Leisure Activities:** tennis court, playground, basketball, volleyball. *Fee:* horseback riding, massage. **Guest
Services:** gift shop, valet laundry. **Business Services:** conference facilities, fax (fee). **Cards:** AX, DC, MC, VI.

SOME UNITS
🍽 🔜 ⊠ / 🅺 🆅

TLALNEPANTLA, MEXICO pop. 130,000   (See map and index starting on p. 470)

WHERE TO STAY

CROWNE PLAZA LANCASTER TLALNEPANTLA   Phone: (55)5228-9500   1️⃣2️⃣
▼▼ ▼▼
All Year   1P: $80-$100   2P: $80-$100   XP: $30   F12
Location: 0.5 mi e of jct Mex 57 at Tlalnepantla de Baz, n of Mexico City limits. Ave Roberto Fulton 2-A 54000.
Large-scale Hotel   Fax: 55/5228-9528. **Facility:** Meets AAA guest room security requirements. 129 units. 122 one-bedroom
standard units. 7 one-bedroom suites ($180-$285) with whirlpools. 7 stories, interior corridors. **Parking:** on-
site. **Terms:** cancellation fee imposed. **Amenities:** voice mail, honor bars, irons, hair dryers. **Leisure Activities:** sauna,
whirlpool, steamroom, lighted tennis court, jogging, exercise room. **Guest Services:** gift shop, valet laundry. **Business
Services:** conference facilities, business center. **Cards:** AX, MC, VI.

SOME UNITS
🆂 🍽 24 🍸 D ⊠ 📽 DATA PORT ▭ / ⊠ /

TOLUCA, MEXICO pop. 461,400

WHERE TO STAY

DEL REY INN HOTEL   Phone: (722)277-1010
AAA
All Year   1P: $105-$120   2P: $105-$120
Location: 4 km e on Mex 15. Carr Mex Toluca KM 63.5 50160 (Apdo Postal 325, 50000). Fax: 722/277-1030.
▼▼ ▼▼   **Facility:** 252 one-bedroom standard units, some with whirlpools. 2-5 stories, interior corridors. **Parking:** on-
site. **Terms:** 7 day cancellation notice. **Amenities:** voice mail, safes, irons, hair dryers. *Some:* honor bars.
Large-scale Hotel   **Dining:** 7 am-midnight, cocktails, entertainment. **Pool(s):** heated indoor, wading. **Leisure Activities:** sauna,
whirlpool, playground, exercise room, game room. *Fee:* massage. **Guest Services:** gift shop,
complimentary evening beverages: Mon-Sat, valet laundry. **Business Services:** meeting rooms, business center. **Cards:** AX,
DC, MC, VI.

SOME UNITS
🆂 🍽 🍸 🔜 ⊠ 🅺 📽 DATA PORT / ▭ /

QUINTA DEL REY   *Book at aaa.com*   Phone: 722/275-8000
AAA
All Year   2P: $131   XP: $25   F10
Location: 9.5 km e on Mex 15. Paseo del Tollacan Ote KM 5 52140. Fax: 722/216-7233. **Facility:** 66 units. 63
one- and 3 two-bedroom standard units. 3 stories (no elevator), interior corridors. **Parking:** on-site.
▼▼ ▼▼   **Amenities:** voice mail, safes, irons, hair dryers. **Dining:** 6:30 am-11 pm, cocktails, entertainment. **Pool(s):**
Small-scale Hotel   heated indoor. **Leisure Activities:** sauna, whirlpool, tennis court, playground, exercise room, game room.
Fee: massage. **Guest Services:** gift shop, valet laundry, airport transportation-Toluca Airport, area
transportation. **Business Services:** meeting rooms, business center. **Cards:** AX, DC, MC, VI.

SOME UNITS
✈ 🍽 🍸 🔜 ⊠ 🅺 📽 DATA PORT / ⊠ VCR ▭ /

──────── *The following lodgings were either not evaluated or did not* ────────
meet AAA rating requirements but are listed for your information only.

CROWNE PLAZA HOTEL TOLUCA LANCASTER   Phone: 722/275-4475
[fyi]   Not evaluated. **Location:** Paseo Tollocan #750 52170. Facilities, services, and decor characterize a mid-range
property.

GRAN HOTEL   Phone: 722/213-9888
[fyi]   Not evaluated. **Location:** Center. Ave Allende #124 Col Centro 50000. Facilities, services, and decor characterize a
mid-range property.

──────── **WHERE TO DINE** ────────

──────── *The following restaurant has not been evaluated by AAA* ────────
but is listed for your information only.

EL ROBLE   Phone: 722/199-3399
[fyi]   Not evaluated. **Location:** On Paseo del Tollocan; just e of Del Rey Inn. Paseo del Tollocan Ote 1208 50160.
Features: Mexican and International cuisines are featured in a formal upscale setting. Steaks, poultry,
exciting salads and decorative desserts are prepared and served with great care.

CENTRAL MEXICO

ABASOLO, GUANAJUATO pop. 20,300

──────── **WHERE TO STAY** ────────

HOTEL BALNEARIO SPA LA CALDERA

Phone: (429)693-0020

All Year — 1P: $90-$120 — 2P: $135-$150 — XP: $20 — F10

Resort
Small-scale Hotel

Location: On Mex 90. (Apdo Postal 16). Fax: 429/693-0020. **Facility:** A family-oriented resort hotel built around a natural hot spring, La Caldera offers a retreatlike ambience. 117 units. 113 one- and 4 two-bedroom standard units. 2-3 stories, exterior corridors. *Bath:* combo or shower only. **Parking:** on-site. **Terms:** check-in 5 pm, 8 day cancellation notice. **Pool(s):** 2 wading. **Leisure Activities:** whirlpool, 2 tennis courts, playground. **Guest Services:** gift shop. **Business Services:** meeting rooms. **Cards:** MC, VI.

SOME UNITS

AGUASCALIENTES, AGUASCALIENTES pop. 618,400

──────── **WHERE TO STAY** ────────

FIESTA INN AGUASCALIENTES   *Book at aaa.com*

Phone: (449)978-0808

6/1-11/30 — 1P: $120-$135 — 2P: $120-$135

Small-scale Hotel

Location: 1 km s on Leon Hwy (Mex 45). Located adjacent to large shopping center. Mahatma Gandhi 302 Sur 20280. Fax: 449/978-0100. **Facility:** 125 one-bedroom standard units. 3 stories (no elevator), interior corridors. **Parking:** on-site. **Terms:** open 6/1-11/30, [AP] meal plan available. **Amenities:** video games (fee), high-speed Internet, irons. **Pool(s):** heated outdoor. **Leisure Activities:** exercise room. **Guest Services:** valet laundry. **Business Services:** meeting rooms, business center. **Cards:** AX, DC, MC, VI. *(See color ad card insert)*

SOME UNITS

HOTEL DE ANDREA ALAMEDA

Phone: (449)970-3800

All Year — 1P: $100-$135 — 2P: $100-$135 — XP: $20 — F12

Small-scale Hotel

Location: On east side, 3 blks e of Ave de la Convencion. Located in a quiet residential area. Alameda Esq Tecnologico 20170. Fax: 449/970-3757. **Facility:** 48 units. 44 one-bedroom standard units. 4 one-bedroom suites. 2 stories (no elevator), interior corridors. *Bath:* combo or shower only. **Parking:** on-site. **Terms:** 10 day cancellation notice. **Amenities:** honor bars, hair dryers. **Pool(s):** heated indoor. **Leisure Activities:** exercise room. **Guest Services:** gift shop. **Business Services:** meeting rooms. **Cards:** AX, MC, VI.

HOTEL FRANCIA   *Book at aaa.com*

Phone: 449/918-7300

All Year — 1P: $60 — 2P: $65

Small-scale Hotel

Location: Center. Ave Fco I Madero #113-A 20000. Fax: 449/915-7317. **Facility:** 74 units. 72 one-bedroom standard units. 2 two-bedroom suites. 5 stories, interior corridors. *Bath:* combo or shower only. **Parking:** valet. **Amenities:** voice mail, safes, honor bars, hair dryers. **Guest Services:** gift shop, valet laundry. **Business Services:** meeting rooms, business center. **Cards:** AX, DC, DS, MC, VI.

SOME UNITS

QUINTA REAL AGUASCALIENTES   *Book at aaa.com*

Phone: 449/978-5818

All Year — 1P: $119-$305 — 2P: $119-$305 — XP: $30

Small-scale Hotel

Location: On south side, just e of jct Blvd Jos Chavez and Ave Aguascalientes on highway to Leon. Located along a busy boulevard. Ave Aguascalientes Sur 601 20270. Fax: 449/978-5616. **Facility:** This stylish hotel features elegantly decorated rooms with unique art and a fountained courtyard that provides a fine level of colonial charm. 85 one-bedroom standard units, some with whirlpools. 3 stories, interior/exterior corridors. **Parking:** valet. **Terms:** cancellation fee imposed. **Amenities:** honor bars, irons, hair dryers. **Pool(s):** heated outdoor. **Guest Services:** gift shop, valet laundry. **Business Services:** meeting rooms, business center. **Cards:** AX, MC, VI.

SOME UNITS

AJIJIC, JALISCO pop. 13,300

──────── **WHERE TO STAY** ────────

AJIJIC PLAZA SUITES

Phone: (376)766-0383

All Year — 1P: $55-$65 — 2P: $55-$65 — XP: $6

Motel

Location: Center. Located across the street from the main plaza. Calle Colon 33 45920. Fax: 376/766-2331. **Facility:** 10 one-bedroom standard units. 1 story, exterior corridors. *Bath:* shower only. **Parking:** street. **Terms:** 3 day cancellation notice, small pets only. **Amenities:** video library. **Pool(s):** outdoor. **Guest Services:** valet laundry. **Business Services:** meeting rooms.

HOTEL REAL DE CHAPALA

Phone: 376/766-0014

All Year — 1P: $90 — 2P: $110

Small-scale Hotel

Location: In La Floresta area; between Blvd Ajijic and Chapala. Paseo del Prado #20 45920. Fax: 376/766-0025. **Facility:** 85 units. 80 one-bedroom standard units. 5 one-bedroom suites with whirlpools. 2 stories (no elevator), interior/exterior corridors. **Parking:** on-site. **Amenities:** safes. **Pool(s):** heated outdoor. **Leisure Activities:** 2 lighted tennis courts, volleyball. **Guest Services:** sundries, valet laundry. **Business Services:** meeting rooms. **Cards:** AX, MC, VI.

LA NUEVA POSADA

Phone: 376/766-1344

▼▼▼▼ All Year [BP]   1P: $56-$73   2P: $65-$90   XP: $12   F12

Country Inn   **Location:** 0.4 km se of main plaza. Donato Guerra #9 45920 (Apdo Postal 30). Fax: 376/766-1444. **Facility:** La Nueva Posada overlooks Lake Chapala. Some rooms have balconies, all display Mexican-Colonial decor, colorful artwork, and comfortable furnishings. 23 units. 21 one- and 2 two-bedroom standard units. 3 stories (no elevator), interior corridors. *Bath:* shower or tub only. **Parking:** on-site. **Terms:** 21 day cancellation notice, small pets only. **Amenities:** *Some:* irons. **Dining:** Restaurante La Nueva Posada, see separate listing. **Pool(s):** outdoor. **Guest Services:** gift shop. **Business Services:** meeting rooms. **Cards:** MC, VI.

SOME UNITS

LOS ARTISTAS BED & BREAKFAST

Phone: 376/766-1027

▼▼▼ All Year [BP]   1P: $55-$77   2P: $55-$77

Bed & Breakfast   **Location:** Center. #105 Constitucion 45920 (827 Union Pacific, PMB 71-387, LAREDO, TX, 78045). Fax: 376/766-1762. **Facility:** An eclectically decorated guest lounge is adorned with the owner's art collection, and a manicured garden offers outside interest. Smoke free premises. 7 one-bedroom standard units. 1 story, interior/exterior corridors. *Bath:* shower only. **Parking:** on-site. **Pool(s):** small outdoor.

--------- **WHERE TO DINE** ---------

JOHANNA'S

Lunch: $8-$10   **Dinner:** $8-$10   **Phone: 376/766-0437**

▼▼ ▼▼   **Location:** Center; along Main St through town. Blvd Ajijic 118-A 45920. **Hours:** 12:30 pm-8 pm. Closed: 12/25; also Mon. **Reservations:** accepted. **Features:** Austrian and German food is the specialty. Noteworthy are the fine schnitzels and the wonderful Leipziger filet with Dijon sauce. Apfelstrudel is magnificent. Guests can choose from a fine selection of wines and imported German beers. Casual dress; beer & wine only.

German
Parking: street.

PEDRO'S GOURMET

Lunch: $4-$15   **Dinner:** $4-$15   **Phone: 376/766-4747**

▼▼ ▼▼   **Location:** Jct Ocampo and Aquiles Serdan; just e; center. Ocampo #71 45920. **Hours:** noon-9 pm. Closed: Sun & Mon. **Reservations:** accepted. **Features:** The open-air cafe serves US-style fare melded with Mexican accents. Attractively priced daily specials reflect the best of both cuisines. Casual dress; cocktails. **Parking:** street.

Continental

RESTAURANTE LA NUEVA POSADA

Lunch: $10-$14   **Dinner:** $10-$14   **Phone: 376/766-1344**

▼▼▼▼   **Location:** 0.4 km se of main plaza; in La Nueva Posada. Donato Guerra #9 45920. **Hours:** 8 am-9 pm, Fri & Sat-10 pm. **Reservations:** accepted. **Features:** Popular with the town's American residents, the restaurant features Continental, American and Mexican cuisine. Some tables in the elegantly furnished dining room offer views of the garden and patio. Cocktails; entertainment. **Parking:** on-site. **Cards:** MC, VI.

Continental

--------- *The following restaurant has not been evaluated by AAA but is listed for your information only.* ---------

BRUNO'S RESTAURANTE

Phone: 376/766-1674

[fyi]   Not evaluated. **Location:** Center; on main road through town. Carr Ote 20 45920. **Features:** Steaks are the specialty. Excellent cuts of beef are expertly grilled and served Mexican style with such side dishes as guacamole and refried beans. The combinations are exquisite.

CELAYA, GUANAJUATO pop. 214,900

--------- **WHERE TO STAY** ---------

HOTEL CELAYA PLAZA

Phone: (461)598-7000

▼▼▼▼ All Year   2P: $100-$250   XP: $15

Small-scale Hotel   **Location:** Mex 45, west side of town. Located across from the Pepsi Cola plant. Ave Constituyentes #100 38060 (Apdo Postal 566). Fax: 461/614-6889. **Facility:** 97 units. 89 one-bedroom standard units, some with whirlpools. 8 one-bedroom suites. 3 stories (no elevator), interior/exterior corridors. **Parking:** on-site. **Amenities:** safes, hair dryers. *Some:* DVD players. **Pool(s):** heated outdoor. **Leisure Activities:** sauna, lighted tennis court, playground, exercise room. **Fee:** massage. **Guest Services:** gift shop, valet laundry. **Business Services:** meeting rooms, fax (fee). **Cards:** AX, MC, VI.

SOME UNITS

--------- **WHERE TO DINE** ---------

--------- *The following restaurant has not been evaluated by AAA but is listed for your information only.* ---------

MARISCOS CHAVA

Phone: 461/617-6777

[fyi]   Not evaluated. **Location:** 3 km n of Mex 45. Eje Norponiente SN 38060. **Features:** Shellfish and other seafood are expertly prepared, as are pasta and beef dishes. Friendly staffers wearing island shirts and straw hats welcome diners.

CIHUATLAN, JALISCO

——— WHERE TO STAY ———

EL TAMARINDO GOLF RESORT   *Book at aaa.com*   **Phone: 315/351-5032**
◆◆◆◆
Resort
Small-scale Hotel
All Year 1P: $356-$765 2P: $356-$765 XP: $50
Location: Mex 200, KM 7.5, 8 km w, follow signs. KM 7.5 Carr Barra de Navidad 48970. **Fax:** 315/351-5070. **Facility:** A secluded coastal jungle setting, a world-class golf course and the privacy of individual casitas give this property appeal. All with private plunge pools. 29 one-bedroom suites, some with whirlpools. 1 story, exterior corridors. *Bath:* shower only. **Parking:** on-site. **Amenities:** CD players, safes, honor bars, irons, hair dryers. **Dining:** La Higuera Restaurant, see separate listing. **Pool(s):** outdoor. **Leisure Activities:** sailboats, windsurfing, boat dock, snorkeling, 2 tennis courts, bicycles, hiking trails, spa. *Fee:* scuba diving, fishing, golf-18 holes. **Guest Services:** TV in common area, gift shop, valet laundry, area transportation (fee). **Business Services:** meeting rooms, PC. **Cards:** AX, MC, VI.

——— WHERE TO DINE ———

LA HIGUERA RESTAURANT   **Lunch:** $10-$38   **Dinner:** $10-$38   **Phone: 315/351-5032**
◆◆◆◆
Mexican
Location: Mex 200, KM 7.5, 8 km w, follow signs; in El Tamarindo Golf Resort. KM 7.5 Carr Barra de Navidad 48970. **Hours:** 7:30 am-10:30 pm. **Reservations:** required, for non-hotel guests. **Features:** The open-air restaurant is the perfect spot to stop for a wonderful lunch on the drive between Puerto Vallarta and Manzanillo. In the jungle setting of the resort, the restaurant occupies a stunning oceanfront location. The daily changing menu of fine, freshly prepared Mexican cuisine offers a touch of local flavor. Casual dress; cocktails. **Parking:** on-site. **Cards:** AX, MC, VI.

DOLORES HIDALGO, GUANAJUATO pop. 52,100

——— WHERE TO STAY ———

POSADA HIDALGO   **Phone: 418/182-2683**
◆◆
Small-scale Hotel
All Year 1P: $28 2P: $33
Location: 2 blks e of main plaza. Located across from a hospital and half a block from bus terminal. Hidalgo #15 Centro 37800. **Fax:** 418/182-0477. **Facility:** 30 one-bedroom standard units. 3 stories (no elevator), interior corridors. *Bath:* shower only. **Parking:** on-site and street. **Terms:** office hours 6 am-midnight. **Leisure Activities:** steamroom. **Guest Services:** sundries, valet laundry. **Business Services:** fax. **Cards:** MC, VI.

——— WHERE TO DINE ———

EL CARUAJE DE CAUDILLO   **Lunch:** $4-$8   **Dinner:** $5-$10   **Phone: 418/182-0474**
◆◆◆
Regional Mexican
Location: Across from east side of main plaza. Plaza Principal #8 37800. **Hours:** 9 am-10 pm, Fri & Sat-10:30 pm. **Closed:** Sun. **Features:** Facing historic Dolores Hidalgo Plaza, the family restaurant specializes in provincial dishes served with flair. Casual dress; cocktails. **Parking:** street. **Cards:** AX, MC, VI.

RESTAURANTE PLAZA   **Lunch:** $5-$10   **Dinner:** $8-$15   **Phone: 418/182-2004**
◆◆◆
Regional Mexican
Location: Opposite south side of main plaza. Plaza Principal #17 37800. **Hours:** 8:30 am-11 pm. **Features:** Facing the plaza and church made famous by "El Grito" of Padre Hidalgo, the restaurant offers a focused menu, homemade dishes and friendly service; also great for breakfast. Casual dress; cocktails. **Parking:** street. **Cards:** AX, MC, VI.

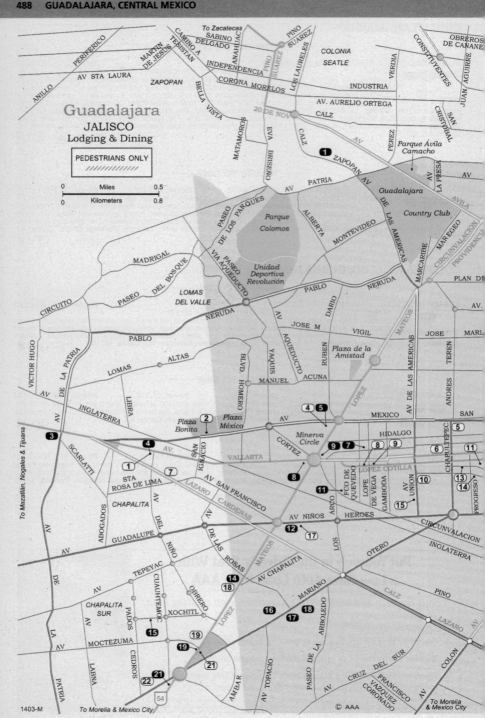

Guadalajara
JALISCO
Lodging & Dining

PEDESTRIANS ONLY
//////////////

Miles		
0		0.5
0		0.8
Kilometers		

1403-M

To Morelia & Mexico City

© AAA

DOWNTOWN
Guadalajara

0   Miles   0.2
0   Kilometers   0.3

Guadalajara

This index helps you "spot" where approved accommodations and restaurants are located on the corresponding detailed maps. Lodging rate ranges are for comparison only and show the property's high season; rates are per night, unless only weekly (W) rates are available. Restaurant rate range is for dinner, unless only lunch (L) is served. Turn to the listing page for more detailed rate information and consult display ads for special promotions.

Spotter/Map Page Number	OA	GUADALAJARA - Lodgings	Diamond Rating	Rate Range High Season	Listing Page
1 / p. 488	AAA	Hotel Country Plaza	◊◊◊	$130-$220	492
4 / p. 488	AAA	Camino Real Guadalajara	◊◊◊◊	$238-$305	491
5 / p. 488		Quinta Real Guadalajara	◊◊◊◊	$250	493
7 / p. 488		Las Pergolas Gran Hotel	◊	$60-$80	493
8 / p. 488		Hotel Fiesta Americana Guadalajara - see color ad card insert	◊◊◊	$186-$194	492
9 / p. 488		Moralva Suites	◊◊	$175-$220	493
11 / p. 488		Hotel Plaza Diana	◊◊◊	$120-$160	493
12 / p. 488		Holiday Inn Select	◊◊◊	$165-$200	492
14 / p. 488		Guadalajara Plaza Lopez Mateos	◊◊◊	$140-$190	491
15 / p. 488		Suites Marysol	◊◊	$85-$105	493
16 / p. 488		Fiesta Inn Guadalajara - see color ad card insert	◊◊◊	$120-$170	491
17 / p. 488		Hotel Guadalajara Plaza Expo	◊◊◊	$165-$180	492
18 / p. 488		Hilton Guadalajara	◊◊◊◊	$130-$240	491
19 / p. 488		Hotel Presidente InterContinental Guadalajara	◊◊◊◊	$225-$335	493
21 / p. 488	AAA	Crowne Plaza Hotel and Resort Guadalajara	◊◊◊◊	$122-$165	491
23 / p. 488		Hotel de Mendoza	◊◊◊	$103-$119	492
25 / p. 488		Hotel El Frances	◊◊	$65-$75	492
27 / p. 488		Holiday Inn Hotel & Suites	◊◊◊	$130	492
29 / p. 488		Best Western Hotel Plaza Genova	◊◊◊	$85-$125	491
31 / p. 488		Hotel Casa Grande Aeropuerto Guadalajara	◊◊	$100-$170	492
		GUADALAJARA - Restaurants			
1 / p. 488	AAA	Aquellos Tiempos	◊◊◊	$20-$40	493
2 / p. 488		Sanborns Plaza Bonita	◊◊	$8-$18	494
4 / p. 488		Quinta Real Restaurant	◊◊◊	$22-$40	494
5 / p. 488		Los Itacates	◊◊	$5-$9	494
6 / p. 488		Sandy's Cafe Plaza del Sol	◊◊	$5-$12	495
7 / p. 488		Tony Roma's Guadalajara	◊◊	$7-$20	495
8 / p. 488		Hard Rock Cafe'	◊◊	$8-$18	494
9 / p. 488		Chili's	◊◊	$8-$16	493
10 / p. 488		Santo Coyote	◊◊◊	$20-$25	495
11 / p. 488	AAA	Villa Chianti Ristorante	◊◊◊	$25-$30	495
12 / p. 488		El Sacromonte	◊◊	$9-$16	494
13 / p. 488		Recco Restaurant	◊◊	$9-$17	494
14 / p. 488		Suehiro	◊◊	$15-$24	495
15 / p. 488		Formosa Gardens Restaurante	◊◊	$8-$17	494
17 / p. 488		La Trattoria Pomodoro de Guadalajara	◊◊	$6-$11	494

Spotter/Map Page Number	OA	GUADALAJARA - Restaurants (continued)	Diamond Rating	Rate Range High Season	Listing Page
18 / p. 488		Club Biwon	▽▽	$8-$12	494
19 / p. 488		Sanborns Restaurant Plaza del Sol	▽▽	$12-$30	495
21 / p. 488		Sandy's Cafe	▽	$5-$12	495
22 / p. 488		Restaurant Jacarandas	▽▽▽	$10-$24	494
24 / p. 488		La Chatta de Guadalajara	▽	$4-$7	494

GUADALAJARA, JALISCO pop. 3,456,100 (See map and index starting on p. 488, 491)

------ WHERE TO STAY ------

BEST WESTERN HOTEL PLAZA GENOVA *Book at aaa.com*   Phone: (33)3613-7500   **29**
▽▽▽▽▽ All Year   2P: $85-$125   XP: $6
Small-scale Hotel **Location:** Center. Ave Juarez 123 44100. Fax: 33/3614-8253. **Facility:** 197 units. 196 one- and 1 two-bedroom standard units. 7 stories, interior corridors. *Bath:* shower only. **Parking:** on-site (fee). **Terms:** 5 day cancellation notice. **Amenities:** honor bars, irons, hair dryers. **Leisure Activities:** steamroom, exercise room. **Guest Services:** valet laundry. **Business Services:** meeting rooms, business center. **Cards:** AX, DC, MC, VI.
SOME UNITS

CAMINO REAL GUADALAJARA   Phone: (33)3134-2434   **4**
(AAA) All Year   1P: $238   2P: $305   XP: $30   F12
▽▽▽▽ ▽▽▽▽ **Location:** 6 km nw on Mex 15. Ave Vallarta 5005 45040. Fax: 33/3134-2404. **Facility:** Manicured gardens and distinctive Mexican architecture are features of this family-oriented luxury hotel. 205 one-bedroom standard units. 2 stories (no elevator), interior/exterior corridors. **Parking:** on-site and valet. **Terms:** cancellation fee imposed. **Amenities:** high-speed Internet, voice mail, safes, honor bars, irons, hair dryers. **Dining:** 7 am-midnight, also, Aquellos Tiempos, see separate listing, nightclub. **Pool(s):** outdoor, 3 heated outdoor, wading. **Leisure Activities:** putting green, lighted tennis court, playground, exercise room. **Guest Services:** gift shop, valet laundry. **Business Services:** meeting rooms, business center. **Cards:** AX, DC, MC, VI.
Small-scale Hotel
SOME UNITS

CROWNE PLAZA HOTEL AND RESORT GUADALAJARA   Phone: (33)3634-1034   **21**
(AAA) All Year   1P: $122-$165   2P: $122-$165   XP: $30   F12
▽▽▽▽ ▽▽▽ **Location:** 7.2 km s on Mex 15 and 80; off Glorieta Mariana Otero. Ave Lopez Mateos Sur #2500 45050. Fax: 33/3631-9393. **Facility:** An upscale hotel built around a lush garden, the Crowne Plaza caters to business travelers who frequent the finer hotels of Guadalajara. 294 units. 290 one- and 4 two-bedroom standard units. 2-9 stories, interior/exterior corridors. **Parking:** on-site (fee) and valet. **Terms:** cancellation fee imposed. **Amenities:** dual phone lines, voice mail, safes, honor bars, irons, hair dryers. **Dining:** 2 restaurants, 6 am-midnight, cocktails, also, Restaurant Jacarandas, see separate listing, entertainment. **Pool(s):** heated outdoor, wading. **Leisure Activities:** sauna, whirlpool, putting green, 2 lighted tennis courts, playground, exercise room. *Fee:* massage. **Guest Services:** gift shop, valet laundry, beauty salon. **Business Services:** conference facilities, business center. **Cards:** AX, DC, MC, VI.
Large-scale Hotel
SOME UNITS

FIESTA INN GUADALAJARA   Phone: 33/3669-3200   **16**
▽▽▽▽ All Year   1P: $120-$170   2P: $120-$170   XP: $10
Small-scale Hotel **Location:** 3.5 km w; near Expo Center. Ave Otero 1550 45055. Fax: 33/3669-3247. **Facility:** 158 one-bedroom standard units. 9 stories, interior corridors. **Parking:** on-site. **Terms:** cancellation fee imposed. **Amenities:** video games (fee), hair dryers. **Pool(s):** heated outdoor. **Leisure Activities:** exercise room. **Guest Services:** gift shop, valet laundry. **Business Services:** meeting rooms, business center. **Cards:** AX, DC, MC, VI.
(See color ad card insert)
SOME UNITS

GUADALAJARA PLAZA LOPEZ MATEOS *Book at aaa.com*   Phone: (33)3208-4400   **14**
▽▽▽▽ All Year   1P: $140-$190   2P: $140-$190   XP: $9   F12
Small-scale Hotel **Location:** 7 km s on Mex 15 and 80. Ave Lopez Mateos Sur 2128 45050. Fax: 33/3122-1703. **Facility:** 142 units. 112 one-bedroom standard units. 30 one-bedroom suites. 2-7 stories, interior/exterior corridors. *Bath:* shower only. **Parking:** valet. **Amenities:** *Some:* irons, hair dryers. **Pool(s):** heated outdoor. **Business Services:** meeting rooms, business center. **Cards:** AX, DC, DS, MC, VI.
SOME UNITS

HILTON GUADALAJARA   Phone: (33)3678-0505   **18**
▽▽▽▽ ▽▽▽▽ All Year   1P: $130-$240   2P: $130-$240   XP: $20   F18
Large-scale Hotel **Location:** At Expo and World Trade Center. Ave de las Rosas 2933 44540. Fax: 33/3678-0511. **Facility:** A spacious lobby, meeting and dining facilities, a shopping area and attentive service contribute to the upscale ambience of this big-city hotel. 450 units. 449 one-bedroom standard units. 1 one-bedroom suite. 20 stories, interior corridors. **Parking:** on-site (fee) and valet. **Terms:** cancellation fee imposed. **Amenities:** video games (fee), high-speed Internet, dual phone lines, voice mail, safes, honor bars, irons, hair dryers. **Pool(s):** heated outdoor. **Leisure Activities:** steamroom, exercise room. *Fee:* massage. **Guest Services:** gift shop, valet laundry. **Business Services:** conference facilities, business center. **Cards:** AX, DC, MC, VI.
SOME UNITS

(See map and index starting on p. 488)

HOLIDAY INN HOTEL & SUITES   *Book at aaa.com*   Phone: 33/3613-1763   27
All Year   1P: $130   2P: $130   XP: $15   F12
Location: Center. Located in a historic area of the city. Ave Juarez 211-103 44100. Fax: 33/3613-1763.
Small-scale Hotel   **Facility:** Meets AAA guest room security requirements. 90 one-bedroom standard units, some with efficiencies and/or whirlpools. 5 stories, interior corridors. *Bath:* shower only. **Parking:** on-site.
Terms: cancellation fee imposed, [AP], [BP], [CP] & [MAP] meal plans available. **Amenities:** voice mail, safes, honor bars, irons, hair dryers. **Leisure Activities:** exercise room. **Guest Services:** valet laundry. **Business Services:** meeting rooms, business center. **Cards:** AX, MC, VI.
SOME UNITS

HOLIDAY INN SELECT   *Book at aaa.com*   Phone: (33)3122-2020   12
All Year   1P: $165-$200   2P: $165-$200   XP: $30   F12
Location: 0.5 km s of Minerva Fountain. Ave Ninos Heroes 3089 44500. Fax: 33/3647-7778. **Facility:** Meets AAA
Small-scale Hotel   guest room security requirements. 220 one-bedroom standard units. 14 stories, interior corridors. **Parking:** on-site (fee). **Terms:** 15% service charge. **Amenities:** voice mail, honor bars, irons, hair dryers. **Pool(s):** heated outdoor. **Leisure Activities:** steamrooms, exercise room. **Guest Services:** gift shop, valet laundry. **Business Services:** meeting rooms, business center. **Cards:** AX, MC, VI.
SOME UNITS

HOTEL CASA GRANDE AEROPUERTO
GUADALAJARA   Phone: (33)3678-9000   31
All Year   1P: $100-$150   2P: $125-$170   XP: $7   F12
Location: At Guadalajara International Airport. Calle Interior Aeropuerto 45640. Fax: 33/3678-9002. **Facility:** 177
Small-scale Hotel   units. 175 one-bedroom standard units. 1 one- and 1 two-bedroom suites with whirlpools. 4 stories, interior corridors. *Bath:* combo or shower only. **Parking:** on-site (fee) and valet. **Amenities:** high-speed Internet.
Pool(s): heated outdoor. **Leisure Activities:** exercise room. **Guest Services:** valet laundry, area transportation. **Business Services:** meeting rooms, business center. **Cards:** AX, DC, MC, VI.
SOME UNITS

HOTEL COUNTRY PLAZA   Phone: (33)3208-4633   1
All Year   2P: $130-$220   XP: $15   F12
Location: 8 km w. Prolonguacion Ave Americas 1170 45160. Fax: 33/3656-2522. **Facility:** 119 units. 95 one- and
9 two-bedroom standard units. 15 one-bedroom suites ($188-$220), some with whirlpools. 4 stories, interior
Small-scale Hotel   corridors. *Bath:* combo or shower only. **Parking:** on-site. **Terms:** cancellation fee imposed, [CP] meal plan available. **Amenities:** voice mail, hair dryers. **Dining:** 7 am-midnight, cocktails, entertainment. **Pool(s):** heated indoor. **Leisure Activities:** whirlpool, exercise room. **Guest Services:** gift shop, valet laundry.
Business Services: meeting rooms, business center. **Cards:** AX, MC, VI.

HOTEL DE MENDOZA   Phone: (33)3613-4646   23
All Year   1P: $103-$119   2P: $103-$119   XP: $15   F12
Location: Opposite Degollado Theatre. Located in the historic district. Venustiano Carranza 16 44100 (Apdo Postal 1-
2453). Fax: 33/3613-7310. **Facility:** 104 one-bedroom standard units. 5 stories, interior corridors. *Bath:*
Small-scale Hotel   combo or shower only. **Parking:** on-site (fee). **Terms:** [AP], [BP], [CP], [ECP] & [MAP] meal plans available.
Amenities: voice mail, hair dryers. *Some:* irons. **Pool(s):** small outdoor. **Leisure Activities:** whirlpool, exercise room. **Guest Services:** gift shop, valet laundry. **Business Services:** meeting rooms, business center. **Cards:** AX, DC, MC, VI.
SOME UNITS

HOTEL EL FRANCES   Phone: 33/3613-1190   25
All Year   1P: $65-$75   2P: $65-$75   XP: $4
Location: Center. Located in the historic district. Maestranza 35 44100. Fax: 33/3658-2831. **Facility:** Constructed
Classic Historic   in 1610. Old World charm. All rooms with ceiling fan. 60 units. 40 one- and 10 two-bedroom standard units,
Small-scale Hotel   some with whirlpools. 10 three-bedroom suites ($74-$100). 4 stories, interior corridors. *Bath:* combo or shower only. **Parking:** on-site. **Terms:** 3 day cancellation notice. **Business Services:** meeting rooms.
Cards: AX, MC, VI.
SOME UNITS

HOTEL FIESTA AMERICANA GUADALAJARA   *Book at aaa.com*   Phone: (33)3825-3434   8
1/1-11/30   1P: $186-$194   2P: $186-$194   XP: $15   F12
12/1-12/31   1P: $169-$176   2P: $169-$176   XP: $14   F12
Location: On Minerva Cir, jct aves Vallarta and Lopez Mateos. Located in a busy commercial area. Aurelio Aceves 225
Large-scale Hotel   44110. Fax: 33/3630-3725. **Facility:** 391 one-bedroom standard units, some with kitchens and/or whirlpools.
22 stories, interior corridors. **Parking:** on-site and valet. **Terms:** cancellation fee imposed. **Amenities:** voice mail, honor bars, hair dryers. *Fee:* video games, high-speed Internet. *Some:* irons. **Pool(s):** heated outdoor. **Leisure Activities:** exercise room.
Fee: 2 lighted tennis courts. **Guest Services:** gift shop, valet laundry. **Business Services:** conference facilities, business center. **Cards:** AX, DC, MC, VI. *(See color ad card insert)*
SOME UNITS

FEE

HOTEL GUADALAJARA PLAZA EXPO   Phone: (33)3669-0215   17
All Year   1P: $165-$180   2P: $165-$180   XP: $10   F12
Location: At the Expo and World Trade Center. Ave Otero 3261 44550. Fax: 33/3122-2850. **Facility:** 204 one-
Small-scale Hotel   bedroom standard units. 5 stories, interior corridors. **Parking:** on-site and valet. **Amenities:** high-speed Internet, voice mail, hair dryers. **Pool(s):** heated outdoor. **Leisure Activities:** jogging, exercise room. **Guest Services:** gift shop, valet laundry. **Business Services:** meeting rooms. **Cards:** AX, DC, DS, MC, VI.
SOME UNITS

(See map and index starting on p. 488)

HOTEL PLAZA DIANA
Phone: (33)3540-9700   **11**
All Year   1P: $120-$160   2P: $120-$160   XP: $20   F12
Small-scale Hotel
Location: 5 km n. Agustin Yanez 2760, Dept 30 44130. Fax: 33/3540-9715. **Facility:** 151 units. 141 one-bedroom standard units. 10 one-bedroom suites ($344-$382). 5 stories, interior corridors. *Bath:* combo or shower only. **Parking:** on-site and valet. **Terms:** 7 day cancellation notice. **Amenities:** video games (fee), safes, hair dryers. **Pool(s):** heated indoor. **Leisure Activities:** whirlpool, exercise room. **Guest Services:** gift shop, valet laundry, area transportation. **Business Services:** meeting rooms. **Cards:** AX, DC, MC, VI.

SOME UNITS

HOTEL PRESIDENTE INTERCONTINENTAL
GUADALAJARA   *Book at aaa.com*   Phone: (33)3678-1234   **19**
All Year   1P: $225-$335   2P: $225-$335   XP: $45   F18
Large-scale Hotel
Location: 7 km s on Mex 15 and 80; across from Plaza del Sol. (Ave Lopez Mateos Sur y Moctezuma). Fax: 33/3678-1222. **Facility:** This large, upscale, city hotel features impressive marble-trimmed public areas, secured parking and proximity to a high-end shopping mall. 409 units. 385 one-bedroom standard units. 24 one-bedroom suites with whirlpools. 13 stories, interior corridors. **Parking:** on-site (fee) and valet. **Terms:** cancellation fee imposed. **Amenities:** dual phone lines, voice mail, safes, honor bars, irons, hair dryers. *Fee:* video games, high-speed Internet. *Some:* fax. **Pool(s):** heated outdoor. **Leisure Activities:** whirlpools, steamroom, exercise room, spa. *Fee:* saunas. **Guest Services:** gift shop, valet laundry. **Business Services:** conference facilities, business center. **Cards:** AX, DC, JC, MC, VI.

SOME UNITS
FEE

LAS PERGOLAS GRAN HOTEL
Phone: 33/3630-1727   **7**
All Year   1P: $60-$80   2P: $60-$80   XP: $10
Small-scale Hotel
Location: 3 blks e of Minerva Cir, just n of Ave Vallarta. Ave Morelos 2244 44290. Fax: 33/3630-0576. **Facility:** 158 one-bedroom standard units. 4 stories, interior corridors. *Bath:* shower only. **Parking:** on-site. **Terms:** 30 day cancellation notice. **Amenities:** *Some:* safes. **Pool(s):** heated outdoor, wading. **Leisure Activities:** exercise room. *Fee:* sauna. **Guest Services:** gift shop, valet laundry. **Business Services:** meeting rooms. **Cards:** MC, VI.

SOME UNITS

MORALVA SUITES
Phone: 33/3615-4805   **9**
All Year   1P: $175-$220   2P: $175-$220
Condominium
Location: Just e of Minerva Cir. Ave Vallarta 2477 44100. Fax: 33/3616-3817. **Facility:** 20 units. 2 one- and 18 two-bedroom suites, some with efficiencies or kitchens. 10 stories, interior corridors. *Bath:* combo or shower only. **Parking:** on-site. **Amenities:** safes. *Some:* hair dryers. **Leisure Activities:** exercise room privileges. **Cards:** AX, MC, VI.

SOME UNITS

QUINTA REAL GUADALAJARA
Phone: (33)3669-0627   **5**
12/23-11/30   1P: $250   2P: $250   XP: $30   F
12/1-12/22   1P: $235   2P: $235   XP: $30   F
Small-scale Hotel
Location: 2 blks n of Minerva Fountain near Ave Lopez Mateos. Ave Mexico 2727 44680. Fax: 33/3669-0601. **Facility:** Fine art, well-appointed rooms and manicured grounds add an elegant sophistication to this property. 76 one-bedroom standard units, some with whirlpools. 3-5 stories, interior corridors. **Parking:** on-site and valet. **Terms:** 7 day cancellation notice-fee imposed. [AP], [CP] & [MAP] meal plans available, 15% service charge. **Amenities:** voice mail, safes, honor bars, irons, hair dryers. *Some:* CD players. **Dining:** restaurant, see separate listing. **Pool(s):** small outdoor. **Leisure Activities:** whirlpool. **Guest Services:** valet laundry. **Business Services:** meeting rooms, business center. **Cards:** AX, MC, VI.

SOME UNITS

SUITES MARYSOL
Phone: 33/3631-1932   **15**
All Year   1P: $85   2P: $105
Condominium
Location: Corner of Tezozomoc and Kabah sts, just w. Tezozomoc St 409 45050. Fax: 33/3632-9575. **Facility:** 20 units. 3 one- and 17 two-bedroom suites with efficiencies. 2-3 stories (no elevator), interior corridors. *Bath:* shower only. **Parking:** on-site. **Terms:** 30 night minimum stay. **Cards:** AX, MC, VI.

——— WHERE TO DINE ———

AQUELLOS TIEMPOS
Lunch: $20-$40   Dinner: $20-$40   Phone: 33/3134-2434   **1**
Continental
Location: 6 km nw on Mex 15; in Camino Real Guadalajara. Ave Vallarta 5005 45040. **Hours:** 7 am-1 am. Closed major holidays; also Sun. **Reservations:** suggested. **Features:** Meaning the "Golden Age," the name of the elegant, fine-dining restaurant is fitting of such an accolade. Imaginative international and local cuisine tempts the palate, and the service and setting are superlative. Salad and dessert offerings are exceptional. Dressy casual; cocktails; entertainment. **Parking:** on-site and valet. **Cards:** AX, DC, MC, VI.

CHILI'S
Lunch: $8-$16   Dinner: $8-$16   Phone: 33/3616-5216   **9**
American
Location: In Centro Magno; near Minerva Cir. Ave Vallarta 2425 Local A2 44160. **Hours:** 11 am-11 pm. **Features:** Homesick travelers can visit this import from the States. On the menu are comfort foods to which Americans are accustomed, and the setting is familiar. Casual dress; cocktails. **Parking:** on-site (fee). **Cards:** MC, VI.

(See map and index starting on p. 488)

CLUB BIWON   Lunch: $6-$9   Dinner: $8-$12   Phone: 33/3123-0730   [18]
♥♥ ♥♥
International
Location: 0.4 km n of Plaza del Sol. Ave Lopez Mateos Sur #2198 45050. **Hours:** 8:30 am-12:30 am. Closed major holidays. **Reservations:** accepted. **Features:** Known by many as the secret garden, the restaurant has an unassuming exterior that leads down a brick path to several large coconut-thatched open-air huts. Diners can choose from buffet or a la carte Mexican and international items while unwinding in an outstanding garden setting with several waterfalls and secret paths. Dressy casual; cocktails. **Parking:** on-site (fee) and valet. **Cards:** AX, MC, VI.

EL SACROMONTE   Lunch: $9-$16   Dinner: $9-$16   Phone: 33/3825-5447   [12]
♥♥ ♥♥
Mexican
Location: Just e of Ave Chapultepac. Pedro Moreno #1398 Col Americana 44100. **Hours:** 1 pm-midnight. Closed major holidays; also Sun. **Reservations:** accepted. **Features:** Billowy fabric drapes the ceiling, while the soft glow of candlelight emanating from punctured-tin light fixtures reflects off small mirrors along yellow and ochre stucco courtyard walls. Locals and a few knowledgeable international visitors love both the casual pace and the honest Nuevo Mexican cuisine in the neighborhood restaurant. Dressy casual; cocktails. **Parking:** valet. **Cards:** AX, MC, VI.

FORMOSA GARDENS RESTAURANTE   Lunch: $8-$15   Dinner: $8-$17   Phone: 33/3615-7415   [15]
♥♥ ♥♥
Chinese
Location: N of Ave Ninos Heroes. Ave Union 322 44150. **Hours:** 8 am-noon & 1:30-midnight, Sun-6 pm. Closed: 12/25. **Reservations:** accepted. **Features:** Popular with the local business community, the restaurant features most of the better-known Chinese dishes, such as sweet and sour pork, Peking duck and kung pao chicken. Casual dress; cocktails. **Parking:** on-site and valet. **Cards:** DC, MC, VI.

HARD ROCK CAFE'   Lunch: $8-$18   Dinner: $8-$18   Phone: 33/3616-4560   [8]
♥♥ ♥♥
American
Location: In Centro Magno center; near Minerva Cir. Ave Vallarta 2425 Col Americana 44160. **Hours:** 1 pm-2 am. Closed: 12/25. **Reservations:** accepted. **Features:** As popular in Guadalajara as it is in other famous cities, the restaurant presents a similar menu that includes Mexican twists here and there. Casual dress; cocktails. **Parking:** on-site (fee). **Cards:** AX, MC, VI.

LA CHATTA DE GUADALAJARA   Lunch: $4-$7   Dinner: $4-$7   Phone: 33/3613-0588   [24]
♥♥
Mexican
Location: Jct Aves Juarez and Ramon Corona; centro. Ave Ramon Corona #126 44100. **Hours:** 8 am-midnight. **Features:** While it may be difficult to find bilingual staff members, the menu of traditional favorites—from fresh guacamole and zesty chiles rellenos to spicy meat dishes—enables guests and servers alike to speak a common language. Hand-painted tile accents decorate the cheerful, bright yellow dining room, a block from Place d'Arms and a nice respite from the crowds in the historic town center. Casual dress; cocktails. **Parking:** street. **Cards:** AX, MC, VI.

LA TRATTORIA POMODORO DE GUADALAJARA   Lunch: $6-$11   Dinner: $6-$11   Phone: 33/3122-1817   [17]
♥♥ ♥♥
Italian
Location: Just e of jct Ave Lopez Mateos. Ave Ninos Heroes 3051 44520. **Hours:** 1 pm-midnight. Closed: 12/25. **Features:** Popular with locals and tourists alike, the restaurant features authentic Italian entrees and an accomplished selection of appetizers and wines. Casual dress; cocktails. **Parking:** on-site. **Cards:** AX, MC, VI.

LOS ITACATES   Lunch: $4-$8   Dinner: $5-$9   Phone: 33/3825-1106   [5]
♥♥ ♥♥
Mexican
Location: Jct aves Chapultapec and Mexico, just s. Ave Chapultapec Nte #110 44100. **Hours:** 8 am-11 pm, Fri & Sat-midnight, Sun-7 pm. Closed: 1/1, 12/25. **Reservations:** accepted. **Features:** Mexican traditional "campestre" (country cooking) is the specialty at the friendly, colorfully decorated Guadalajara cafe. Expect a terrific meal. Casual dress; cocktails. **Parking:** street. **Cards:** MC, VI.

QUINTA REAL RESTAURANT   Lunch: $22-$40   Dinner: $22-$40   Phone: 33/3669-0627   [4]
♥♥♥ ♥♥♥
Continental
Location: 2 blks n of Minerva Fountain near Ave Lopez Mateos; in Quinta Real Guadalajara. Ave Mexico 2727 44680. **Hours:** 7 am-midnight. **Reservations:** suggested. **Features:** The high-quality, fine-dining establishment enjoys a good reputation for its imaginatively prepared and presented food and smooth, professional service. Dressy casual; cocktails; entertainment. **Parking:** on-site and valet. **Cards:** AX, MC, VI.

RECCO RESTAURANT   Lunch: $9-$17   Dinner: $9-$17   Phone: 33/3825-0724   [13]
♥♥ ♥♥
Italian
Location: Just e of Ave Chapultepec. Libertad 1981 44100. **Hours:** 1 pm-11 pm. Closed major holidays. **Reservations:** suggested. **Features:** The Italian restaurant provides a nice change of pace, with such choices as hearty servings of lasagna and tasty osso buco. The Caesar salad is "magnifico," as are the desserts. Dressy casual; cocktails. **Parking:** on-site. **Cards:** AX, MC, VI.

RESTAURANT JACARANDAS   Lunch: $10-$22   Dinner: $10-$24   Phone: 33/3634-1034   [22]
♥♥♥ ♥♥♥
Continental
Location: 7.2 km s on Mex 15 and 80; off Glorieta Mariana Otero; in Crowne Plaza Hotel and Resort Guadalajara. Ave Lopez Mateos Sur 2500 45050. **Hours:** 8 am-noon & 1-1 am. Closed major holidays; also Sun. **Reservations:** suggested. **Features:** The panoramic city view is a highlight of this restaurant, atop the hotel. Elegance is evident in the dining room, where imaginative salads, appetizers, high-quality beef entrees and desserts are served. Cuisine preparation styles range from local to international. Dressy casual; cocktails; entertainment. **Parking:** on-site (fee) and valet. **Cards:** AX, DC, MC, VI.

SANBORNS PLAZA BONITA   Lunch: $8-$18   Dinner: $8-$18   Phone: 33/3813-2062   [2]
♥♥ ♥♥
Mexican
Location: 2 km w of Minerva Fountain. Ave Mexico 3370 34000. **Hours:** 7 am-1 am, Sun-midnight. **Features:** Restaurants in the casual chain, which includes more than 100 locations throughout Mexico, offer a good selection of American-style sandwiches, salads, soups and both Mexican and US entrees. The selection of desserts is impressive. Casual dress; cocktails; entertainment. **Parking:** on-site. **Cards:** AX, MC, VI.

(See map and index starting on p. 488)

SANBORNS RESTAURANT PLAZA DEL SOL   **Lunch:** $12-$30   **Dinner:** $12-$30   **Phone:** 33/3121-3675   (19)

Mexican

Location: 7 km s on Mex 15 and 80; across from Plaza del Sol Mall. Ave Lopez Mateos 2718 45050. **Hours:** 7 am-1 am. **Features:** Restaurants in the casual chain, which includes more than 100 locations throughout Mexico, offer a good selection of American-style sandwiches, salads, soups and both Mexican and US entrees. The selection of desserts is impressive. Casual dress; cocktails; entertainment. **Parking:** on-site. **Cards:** AX, MC, VI.

SANDY'S CAFE   **Lunch:** $5-$12   **Dinner:** $5-$12   **Phone:** 33/6616-1841   (21)

American

Location: Ave Chapultepec and Pedro Moreno; just n of Ave Vallarta. Lopez Cotilla/Ave Chapultepec. **Hours:** 8 am-10:30 pm, Tues, Fri & Sat-midnight. Closed major holidays. **Features:** Part of a small chain in the Guadalajara area, the restaurant offers a good selection of American-style sandwiches, burgers and entrees, as well as preparations of local cuisine, at attractive prices. Casual dress; cocktails. **Parking:** street. **Cards:** AX, MC, VI.

SANDY'S CAFE PLAZA DEL SOL   **Lunch:** $5-$12   **Dinner:** $5-$12   **Phone:** 33/3121-9714   (6)

American

Location: Plaza del Sol Shopping Mall, west entrance. 13 Zone D. **Hours:** 8 am-10:30 pm, Fri & Sat-midnight. Closed major holidays. **Features:** Part of a small chain in the Guadalajara area, the restaurant offers a good selection of American-style sandwiches, burgers and entrees, as well as preparations of local cuisine, at attractive prices. Casual dress; cocktails. **Parking:** on-site (fee). **Cards:** AX, MC, VI.

SANTO COYOTE   **Lunch:** $15-$20   **Dinner:** $20-$25   **Phone:** 33/3616-6978   (10)

Mexican

Location: 0.4 km e of Ave Chapultepec. Lerdo de Tejada #2379 44100. **Hours:** 1 pm-1 am. Closed major holidays. **Reservations:** accepted. **Features:** In the former US Consul General's residence, the Nuevo Mexican eatery features several open-air rooms with hand-painted murals, romantic pixie and candle lighting and views of a courtyard garden. Cabrito (goat) and excellent baby back ribs, topped with tamarind and pepper sauce, are roasted over a wood fire in the open kitchen and grill. Dressy casual; cocktails. **Parking:** valet. **Cards:** AX, MC, VI.

SUEHIRO   **Lunch:** $15-$24   **Dinner:** $15-$24   **Phone:** 33/3826-0094   (14)

Japanese

Location: 4 blks e of Ave Chapultepec. Ave La Paz 1701 44100. **Hours:** 1 pm-6 & 7:30-11 pm. Closed: 1/1, 12/25; also 5/1. **Reservations:** suggested. **Features:** Japanese-style tableside preparation is the specialty of this ethnic restaurant. Table grills are skillfully employed to give diners wonderfully flavorful, freshly cooked beef, shrimp and chicken dishes. Cocktails. **Parking:** valet. **Cards:** AX, MC, VI.

TONY ROMA'S GUADALAJARA   **Lunch:** $7-$20   **Dinner:** $7-$20   **Phone:** 33/3121-7203   (7)

American

Location: In Zapopan. Ave Lazaro Cardenas #4002 45040. **Hours:** 1 pm-11 pm, Fri-midnight, Sat noon-midnight, Sun noon-10 pm. **Reservations:** accepted. **Features:** This spot is the place for those who develop a craving for ribs while in Guadalajara. Also on the menu are American-style burgers and other dishes for which this chain is known north of the border. Casual dress; cocktails. **Parking:** valet. **Cards:** AX, MC, VI.

VILLA CHIANTI RISTORANTE   **Lunch:** $20-$25   **Dinner:** $25-$30   **Phone:** 33/630-2250   (11)

Italian

Location: Just w of Ave Chapultepac. Jose Guadalupe Zuno 2152 Col Americana 44100. **Hours:** 1 pm-midnight, Fri & Sat-1 am. Closed major holidays; also Sun. **Reservations:** accepted. **Features:** Several Mexican accents sneak into the Italian menu at the restaurant, which occupies a converted Victorian mansion. Intricate marble Marquette-bordered floors contribute to the upscale yet romantic tone in the dining rooms. Bilingual servers are fluent in describing both impeccably prepared regular dishes and daily features. Dressy casual; cocktails. **Parking:** valet and street. **Cards:** AX, MC, VI.

This ends listings for Guadalajara.
The following page resumes the alphabetical listings
of cities in Central Mexico.

To The Mummy Museum

© AAA

Avenida Subterránea Miguel Hidalgo is for inbound traffic only with street level exits just beyond the Hidalgo Market, at Plazuela de los Ángeles, at Jardín Unión and terminus at Plaza de Allende. It is 3 km. long.

To Mexico City, D.F. or León, Pipila Statue 13 14 & 6

110

C. PARDO

Cantador Park

11

110

To Valenciana Church & Mine, Dolores Hidalgo, Cubilete Mountain, 1 & 10

ESCALERA SALGADO

AV. SUBTERRÁNEA MIGUEL HIDALGO

JUÁREZ 5 DEMAYO

MENDIZABAL

1

JUAN VALLE

Plazuela de los Ángeles

POCITOS

ALONZO

Diego Rivera Museum

3

Plaza de la Paz

State Historical Museum of Guanajuato

4

4

5

TENAZA

6

Jardín Unión

2

EL SOL

5

MANUEL DOBLADO

HIDALGO

7

BELAUNZARAN

CALLE

Plaza de Allende

CALLE SANGRE DE CRISTO

Las Embajadoras Park

C. SEBASTIAN

San Jerónimo Park

N

PASEO DE LA PRESA

CALLE PASTITA

8

Antillón Park

Presa de la Olla

Acacia Park

Guanajuato
GUANAJUATO
Lodging & Dining

Miles 0   0.2
Kilometers 0   0.3

1404-L

City Layout

Unlike many Mexican cities, where the streets are laid out in an orderly grid pattern radiating from a central plaza, downtown Guanajuato's twisting thoroughfares simply follow the dictates of the terrain. Streets are winding, congested and often unmarked, which can make exploring on your own a challenge. The two main streets, Avenida Juárez and Calle Pocitos, run roughly east-west; once past Plaza de la Paz, Avenida Juárez's name changes to Avenida Sopeña.

Avenida Subterránea Miguel Hidalgo, an antiquated tunnel which in the mid-1960s was transformed into a vehicular subway for inbound traffic, follows the original course of the Río Guanajuato under the city-roughly parallel with Avenida Juárez/Sopeña-for about 1.5 miles. Mexican engineers rerouted the river's course following a flood in 1905. The traffic tunnel passes by the foundations of old buildings; street-level exits are just beyond the Hidalgo Market, at Plazuela de Los Ángeles, at Jarín de la Unión and at the subway terminus at Plaza Allende. Little more than illumination and paving stones were required to turn the tunnel into a traffic artery.

A confusing network of subsidiary tunnels have since been added in a not-too-successful effort to alleviate the heavy traffic; Guanajuato's layout was never intended to accommodate automobiles. Even horse-drawn carriages cannot fully negotiate the steep streets. It's best to travel on foot whenever possible, unless you want to experience an appropriately eerie night drive through the tunnel. Fortunately, most of the city's downtown tourist attractions are within walking distance of the Jardín de la Unión, a tree-shaded park that makes a delightful meeting place.

Guanajuato

This index helps you "spot" where approved accommodations and restaurants are located on the corresponding detailed maps. Lodging rate ranges are for comparison only and show the property's high season; rates are per night, unless only weekly (W) rates are available. Restaurant rate range is for dinner, unless only lunch (L) is served. Turn to the listing page for more detailed rate information and consult display ads for special promotions.

Spotter/Map Page Number	OA	GUANAJUATO - Lodgings	Diamond Rating	Rate Range High Season	Listing Page
1 / p. 496		Suites Casa de las Manrique	◆	$75-$82	499
3 / p. 496	AAA	Hotel San Diego	◆◆	$95-$120	498
4 / p. 496		El Meson de los Poetas	◆◆	$80-$125	498
5 / p. 496		Hotel Posada Santa Fe	◆◆	$80-$95	498
6 / p. 496		Hosteria del Frayle	◆	$70-$140	498
7 / p. 496		Hotel Hostel Cantarranas	◆	$45-$65	498
8 / p. 496	AAA	Quinta Las Acacias	◆◆◆◆	$200-$300	499
10 / p. 496		Casa Estrella de la Valenciana	◆◆◆	$190-$225	498
11 / p. 496		Howard Johnson Parador San Javier Hotel	◆◆	$110-$120	499
13 / p. 496		Hotel Mision Guanajuato	◆◆	$100-$160	498
14 / p. 496		Holiday Inn Express Guanajuato	◆◆◆	$93-$103	498
		GUANAJUATO - Restaurants			
1 / p. 496		Restaurant Real de la Esperanza	◆◆◆	$10-$18	499
2 / p. 496		Restaurante Hotel Posada Santa Fe	◆◆	$10-$20	499
4 / p. 496		El Gallo Pitagorico	◆◆	$6-$11	499
5 / p. 496		Casa Valadez	◆◆	$8-$18	499
6 / p. 496		Chez Nicole at Hacienda de Marfil	◆◆◆	$9-$20	499

GUANAJUATO, GUANAJUATO pop. 76,900 (See map and index starting on p. 496)

──────── WHERE TO STAY ────────

CASA ESTRELLA DE LA VALENCIANA Phone: 473/732-1784 🔟
◆◆◆ 12/1-1/3 [BP] 2P: $190-$225
1/4-11/30 [BP] 2P: $170-$200
Bed & Breakfast **Location:** 3.5 km nw on Mex 110 to Dolores Hidalgo Hwy, just w, follow signs. Callejon Jalisco #10 36000 (PO Box 22654, LONG BEACH, CA, 90801-5654). Fax: 562/430-0648. **Facility:** Across from the noted Valenciana church, the property overlooks a valley and offers elegant accommodations. Designated smoking area. 6 units. 5 one-bedroom standard units, some with whirlpools. 1 one-bedroom suite. 2 stories (no elevator), interior/exterior corridors. *Bath:* combo or shower only. **Parking:** on-site. **Terms:** check-in 4 pm, age restrictions may apply, 15 day cancellation notice-fee imposed. **Amenities:** video library, DVD players, CD players, irons, hair dryers. **Pool(s):** heated outdoor. **Leisure Activities:** whirlpool. *Fee:* massage. **Guest Services:** complimentary evening beverages, valet laundry. **Business Services:** meeting rooms, fax (fee). **Cards:** AX, DS, MC, VI.

SOME UNITS
🚲 Ⓓ ➿ ✕ 🅺 📺 🆅🅲🆁 🈯 / 🖥 /

EL MESON DE LOS POETAS Phone: 473/732-5406 4️⃣
◆◆◆ All Year 1P: $80 2P: $125
Small-scale Hotel **Location:** Just w of Jardin; center. Positos #35 36000. Fax: 473/732-6657. **Facility:** 31 units. 27 one-bedroom standard units, some with kitchens (no utensils). 4 one-bedroom suites with kitchens (no utensils). 9 stories (no elevator), interior corridors. *Bath:* combo or shower only. **Parking:** street. **Guest Services:** valet laundry. **Business Services:** fax (fee). **Cards:** MC, VI.

🅺

HOLIDAY INN EXPRESS GUANAJUATO *Book at aaa.com* Phone: (473)735-2000 1️⃣4️⃣
◆◆◆◆ All Year [ECP] 1P: $93-$103 2P: $93-$103
Small-scale Hotel **Location:** On Mex 110 (toll road); at entrance to town; sw on Mex 10 (non toll), 0.6 mi e on GT067. Euquerio Guerrero #120 36250. Fax: 473/735-2020. **Facility:** Meets AAA guest room security requirements. 165 one-bedroom standard units. 5 stories, interior corridors. **Parking:** on-site. **Amenities:** dual phone lines, voice mail, irons, hair dryers. **Pool(s):** heated indoor. **Leisure Activities:** exercise room. **Guest Services:** valet and coin laundry, area transportation. **Business Services:** conference facilities, business center. **Cards:** AX, MC, VI.

SOME UNITS
🆂🅳 🍴 🆂 Ⓓ ➿ 📷 DATA PORT 🖥 / ✕ 🖥 /

HOSTERIA DEL FRAYLE Phone: 473/732-1179 6️⃣
◆ All Year 1P: $70-$85 2P: $120-$140 XP: $10
Historic **Location:** Center. Sopena #3 36000. Fax: 473/732-1179. **Facility:** Hotel converted from 17th-century gold and
Small-scale Hotel silver coin mint; some very steep steps. 37 units. 34 one-bedroom standard units. 3 one-bedroom suites. 4 stories (no elevator), interior corridors. *Bath:* shower only. **Parking:** street. **Terms:** 15 day cancellation notice. **Amenities:** safes. **Guest Services:** beauty salon. **Business Services:** fax (fee). **Cards:** MC, VI.

🅺

HOTEL HOSTEL CANTARRANAS Phone: (473)732-5241 7️⃣
◆ All Year 1P: $45 2P: $65 XP: $10 F12
Small-scale Hotel **Location:** Center. Calle Cantarranas 50 36000. Fax: 473/732-5241. **Facility:** 8 units. 4 one-bedroom standard units. 4 one-bedroom suites with efficiencies. 3 stories (no elevator), exterior corridors. *Bath:* shower only. **Parking:** street. **Terms:** 15 day cancellation notice. **Business Services:** fax (fee).

SOME UNITS
🅺 📷 / 🖥 /

HOTEL MISION GUANAJUATO *Book at aaa.com* Phone: (473)732-3980 1️⃣3️⃣
◆◆◆ ◆◆◆ All Year 2P: $100-$160 XP: $10 F12
Small-scale Hotel **Location:** 2.5 km w; at entrance to town on Mex 110 (Dolores Hidalgo Hwy). Camino Antiguo A Marfil KM 2.5 36050. Fax: 473/732-3980. **Facility:** 138 units. 137 one-bedroom standard units. 1 one-bedroom suite with whirlpool. 2-3 stories (no elevator), interior corridors. *Bath:* combo or shower only. **Parking:** on-site. **Terms:** 3 day cancellation notice. **Amenities:** *Some:* safes, honor bars, hair dryers. **Pool(s):** heated outdoor. **Leisure Activities:** lighted tennis court. **Guest Services:** gift shop, valet laundry, area transportation. **Business Services:** meeting rooms, fax (fee). **Cards:** AX, MC, VI.

SOME UNITS
🍴 🍷 ➿ 🅺 📷 DATA PORT / 🖥 /

HOTEL POSADA SANTA FE Phone: 473/732-0084 5️⃣
◆◆◆ ◆◆◆ All Year 1P: $80 2P: $95 XP: $22 F12
Historic **Location:** Take vehicular subway to exit Jardin de la Union, left 1 short blk on Ave Juarez, then right on Calle del Turco.
Small-scale Hotel Jardin de la Union 12 36000. Fax: 473/732-4653. **Facility:** Restored 1862 building. 47 one-bedroom standard units. 3 stories (no elevator), interior corridors. *Bath:* combo or shower only. **Parking:** on-site. **Terms:** 15 day cancellation notice. **Dining:** restaurant, see separate listing. **Leisure Activities:** whirlpools. **Guest Services:** valet laundry. **Business Services:** meeting rooms, fax (fee). **Cards:** AX, DS, MC, VI.

SOME UNITS
🍴 🍷 🅺 📷 / 🖥 🖥 /

HOTEL SAN DIEGO Phone: 473/732-1300 3️⃣
AAA All Year 1P: $95-$120 2P: $95-$120 XP: $12 F10
Location: Center. Located in a historic commercial district. Jardin de la Union #1 36000. Fax: 473/732-5626. **Facility:** 43 units. 41 one-bedroom standard units. 1 one- and 1 two-bedroom suites ($105-$137). 4 stories,
◆◆◆ ◆◆◆ interior corridors. *Bath:* shower only. **Parking:** street. **Terms:** 10 day cancellation notice. **Dining:** 7 am-11
Small-scale Hotel pm. **Guest Services:** valet laundry. **Business Services:** meeting rooms, fax. **Cards:** MC, VI.

🆂🅳 🍴 🍷 🅺

(See map and index starting on p. 496)

HOWARD JOHNSON PARADOR SAN JAVIER HOTEL   Phone: (473)732-2222   **11**
All Year   1P: $110   2P: $120   XP: $10
Small-scale Hotel   **Location:** 2 km ne on Mex 110 (Dolores Hidalgo Hwy). Plaza Aldama #92 36020. Fax: 473/732-3114. **Facility:** 113 units. 98 one-bedroom standard units. 13 one- and 2 two-bedroom suites ($150-$300). 6 stories, interior/exterior corridors. **Bath:** combo or shower only. **Parking:** on-site. **Terms:** 8 day cancellation notice-fee imposed. **Amenities:** safes. **Pool(s):** heated outdoor. **Leisure Activities:** waterslide. **Guest Services:** valet laundry. **Business Services:** meeting rooms, fax (fee). **Cards:** AX, MC, VI.
SOME UNITS

QUINTA LAS ACACIAS   *Book at aaa.com*   Phone: (473)731-1517   **8**
12/24-11/30 [BP]   2P: $200-$300   XP: $30
12/1-12/23 [BP]   2P: $185-$200   XP: $30
Country Inn   **Location:** Across from Acacia Park; center. Paseo de la Presa #168 36000. Fax: 473/731-1862. **Facility:** This property offers two styles of rooms, the traditional New England room with hardwood floors and antiques, or rooms done in a colonial Mexican motif. 10 units. 9 one-bedroom standard units, some with whirlpools. 1 one-bedroom suite. 5 stories (no elevator), interior/exterior corridors. **Parking:** street. **Terms:** age restrictions may apply. 7 day cancellation notice. **Amenities:** safes, hair dryers. **Dining:** 7:30 am-11 pm. **Leisure Activities:** whirlpool. *Fee:* massage. **Guest Services:** valet laundry. **Business Services:** meeting rooms, fax (fee). **Cards:** AX, MC, VI.
FEE

SUITES CASA DE LAS MANRIQUE   Phone: 473/732-7678   **1**
All Year   1P: $75-$82   2P: $75-$82   XP: $8   F12
Historic Small-scale Hotel   **Location:** Center. Located across from the Mercado Hidalgo. Ave Juarez 116 36000. Fax: 473/732-8306. **Facility:** Converted 1882 home. 8 one-bedroom suites, some with whirlpools. 3 stories (no elevator), interior corridors. *Bath:* shower only. **Parking:** on-site. **Terms:** 15 day cancellation notice. **Amenities:** safes. **Guest Services:** valet laundry. **Business Services:** meeting rooms, fax (fee). **Cards:** AX, MC, VI.

——— **WHERE TO DINE** ———

CASA VALADEZ   Lunch: $6-$12   Dinner: $8-$18   Phone: 473/732-1157   **5**
Mexican   **Location:** Center. Jardin de la Union #3 36000. **Hours:** 8:30 am-11 pm. **Features:** Attentive staff welcome guests to a tearoom setting across from Jardin de la Union and the Teatro Juarez. Casual dress; cocktails. **Parking:** street. **Cards:** MC, VI.

CHEZ NICOLE AT HACIENDA DE MARFIL   Lunch: $9-$20   Dinner: $9-$20   Phone: 473/733-1148   **6**
Continental   **Location:** Jct Mex 110, 0.6 mi w on Marfil; across from Parraquia de San Jose in Marfil. Arcos de Guadalupe #3 36250. **Hours:** 1:30 pm-6:30 pm. Closed: Mon & 12/15-12/26. **Reservations:** accepted. **Features:** Tucked into the courtyard of a 200-year-old hacienda with many established plants, the restaurant employs an attentive staff. Among delicately seasoned and beautifully presented foods are rabbit, mixed grill, chicken and fondue bourguignonne. Save room for profiteroles or crepes with chocolate. Casual dress; cocktails. **Parking:** street. **Cards:** AX, CB, DC, DS, JC, MC, VI.

EL GALLO PITAGORICO   Dinner: $6-$11   Phone: 473/732-9489   **4**
Mediterranean   **Location:** Just w of Jardin de la Union; center. Constancia 10 36000. **Hours:** 2 pm-11 pm. Closed: 1/1, 12/25. **Reservations:** accepted. **Features:** Climbing the steps to the dining room, which is perched above the city center, allows for wonderful views. Offerings include fresh salads and rich sauces on meats, seafood and pasta. Casual dress; cocktails. **Parking:** street. **Cards:** MC, VI.

RESTAURANTE HOTEL POSADA SANTA FE   Lunch: $8-$15   Dinner: $10-$20   Phone: 473/732-0084   **2**
Mexican   **Location:** Take vehicular subway to exit Jardin de la Union, left 1 short blk on Ave Juarez, then right on Calle del Turco; in Hotel Posada Santa Fe. Jardin de la Union 12 36000. **Hours:** 7:30 am-11 pm. **Features:** In the heart of the main "jardin," the restaurant has a relaxed ambience that invites diners to spend countless hours just people-watching. Casual dress; cocktails. **Parking:** street. **Cards:** AX, DS, MC, VI.

RESTAURANT REAL DE LA ESPERANZA   Lunch: $7-$12   Dinner: $10-$18   Phone: 473/732-1041   **1**
Continental   **Location:** 5.5 km on Dolores Hidalgo Hwy. Carr A Dolores Hidalgo KM 5 36000. **Hours:** 1 pm-9 pm. **Features:** On the outskirts of the city, the eatery is well worth the short drive. Examples of the traditional Mexican fare include milanesa (breaded steak), arrachera (marinated skirt steak) and fideo (Mexican pasta soup). Room should be left to enjoy the delicious crepes with "cajeta," a sweet creamy sauce popular with the locals. Casual dress; cocktails. **Parking:** on-site. **Cards:** AX, MC, VI.

LAZARO CARDENAS, MICHOACAN

——— **WHERE TO STAY** ———

HOTEL NH KRYSTAL EXPRESS LAZARO CARDENAS   *Book at aaa.com*   Phone: 753/533-2900
All Year   1P: $65-$70   2P: $65-$70   XP: $15
Small-scale Hotel   **Location:** 6 km w on Mex 200. Circuito de las Universidades #60, 2 undo se 60950. Fax: 753/533-2922. **Facility:** 118 one-bedroom standard units. 4 stories, interior corridors. **Parking:** on-site. **Amenities:** high-speed Internet, dual phone lines, voice mail. **Leisure Activities:** whirlpool, exercise room. **Guest Services:** valet laundry. **Business Services:** meeting rooms, business center. **Cards:** AX, MC, VI.
SOME UNITS

LEON, GUANAJUATO pop. 760,400

─── **WHERE TO STAY** ───

FIESTA INN LEON   *Book at aaa.com*   Phone: (477)710-0500
▼▼✦✦▼   All Year   2P: $130-$160   XP: $12
Small-scale Hotel   **Location:** 8 km se on Mex 45. Ave Lopez Mateos 2702 Ote 37530. Fax: 477/710-0506. **Facility:** 160 one-bedroom standard units. 3 stories, interior corridors. **Parking:** on-site. **Amenities:** video games (fee), voice mail, irons, hair dryers. **Pool(s):** outdoor. **Leisure Activities:** exercise room. **Guest Services:** gift shop, valet laundry. **Business Services:** meeting rooms, business center. **Cards:** AX, DC, MC, VI. *(See color ad card insert)*

SOME UNITS
🍽️ 🍷 S D 🏊 📹 [DATA PORT] 🖥️ / ✕ VCR /

HOLIDAY INN CENTRO DE CONVENCIONES   Phone: 477/710-0041
▼▼✦✦▼   All Year   1P: $110-$160   2P: $110-$160   XP: $15   F
Small-scale Hotel   **Location:** 7 km se on Mex 45. Ave Lopez Mateos #1501 37270. Fax: 477/710-0041. **Facility:** Meets AAA guest room security requirements. 177 units. 171 one-bedroom standard units. 6 one-bedroom suites. 5 stories, interior corridors. *Bath:* combo or shower only. **Parking:** on-site. **Amenities:** voice mail, safes, irons, hair dryers. **Pool(s):** heated indoor. **Leisure Activities:** exercise room. **Guest Services:** valet laundry. **Business Services:** meeting rooms, business center. **Cards:** AX, DC, DS, MC, VI.

SOME UNITS
🍽️ S D 🏊 📹 [DATA PORT] 🖥️ / ✕ /

HOLIDAY INN LEON MEXICO   *Book at aaa.com*   Phone: (477)710-0003
▼▼✦✦▼   12/1-12/31 & 7/1-11/30   1P: $98-$107   2P: $98-$107   XP: $15   F
            1/1-6/30   1P: $95-$105   2P: $95-$105   XP: $15   F
Small-scale Hotel   **Location:** 3.5 km se on Mex 45. Ave Lopez Mateos 1308 37270. Fax: 477/710-0003. **Facility:** Meets AAA guest room security requirements. 170 units. 166 one-bedroom standard units. 4 one-bedroom suites ($180-$200). 5 stories, interior corridors. **Parking:** on-site. **Terms:** 15% service charge. **Amenities:** voice mail, irons, hair dryers. *Some:* safes. **Pool(s):** heated indoor. **Leisure Activities:** exercise room. **Guest Services:** valet laundry. **Business Services:** meeting rooms, business center. **Cards:** AX, MC, VI.

SOME UNITS
[S🔓] 🍽️ S D 🏊 📹 [DATA PORT] 🖥️ / ✕ /

HOTEL FIESTA AMERICANA-LEON   *Book at aaa.com*   Phone: (477)719-8000

(AAA)

🔻🔻🔻 🔻🔻🔻

Large-scale Hotel

All Year   1P: $190   2P: $190   XP: $16   F12
Location: On Mex 45; downtown. Located across from Centro Estrella. Ave Lopez Mateos 1102 37270. Fax: 477/719-8028. **Facility:** This hotel houses not only well-appointed rooms, but shares its space with boutiques and retail stores. 211 units. 177 one-bedroom standard units, some with whirlpools. 34 one-bedroom suites ($208). 6 stories, interior corridors. **Parking:** on-site. **Terms:** cancellation fee imposed, [BP] meal plan available. **Amenities:** video games (fee), voice mail, safes, honor bars, hair dryers. **Dining:** 6 am-midnight, cocktails, also, Romanza, see separate listing, entertainment. **Pool(s):** heated outdoor. **Leisure Activities:** saunas, whirlpool, 2 lighted tennis courts, children's playhouse, exercise room. **Fee:** tennis instruction, massage. **Guest Services:** gift shop, valet laundry. **Business Services:** conference facilities, business center. **Cards:** AX, DC, MC, VI.

(See color ad card insert)

SOME UNITS

(🛎️) (🍴) (24T) (🍸) (♿) (D) (🏊) (✕) (🎥) (DATA PORT) (🖥️) / (✕) (VCR) / FEE

HOTEL LA ESTANCIA   Phone: (477)716-3939

🔻🔻🔻

Small-scale Hotel

All Year   1P: $135   2P: $170   XP: $12
Location: East entrance via Mex 45. Located adjacent to Centro Estrella. Ave Lopez Mateos 1311 Ote 37000 (Apdo Postal 1-759). Fax: 477/716-3940. **Facility:** 76 units. 68 one-bedroom standard units. 8 one-bedroom suites, some with whirlpools. 2 stories (no elevator), interior corridors. **Parking:** valet. **Amenities:** voice mail, safes, hair dryers. **Pool(s):** outdoor, wading. **Guest Services:** gift shop, valet laundry. **Business Services:** meeting rooms, business center. **Cards:** AX, DS, MC, VI.

SOME UNITS

(🍴) (🍸) (D) (🏊) (🎥) (🖥️) / (✕) /

──────── **WHERE TO DINE** ────────

ARGENTILIA RESTAURANT   Dinner: $10-$20   Phone: 477/718-3394

🔻🔻

Argentine

Location: 2 km n on Ave Lopez Mateos to Ave Campestre, 2.1 km w. Ave Cerro Gordo #12 37160. **Hours:** 2 pm-11 pm, Fri & Sat-midnight, Sun-6 pm. Closed: 1/1, 12/25. **Reservations:** suggested. **Features:** Meat lovers will enjoy this steak house. Cuts of beef are prepared Argentine-style and grilled over mesquite wood. Casual dress; cocktails. **Parking:** no self-parking. **Cards:** AX, MC, VI.

FRASCATI RISTORANTE-PIZZERIA   Dinner: $8-$18   Phone: 477/773-7123

🔻🔻

Italian

Location: 2 km on Ave Lopez Mateos to Blvd Campestre, 1 km w. Blvd Campestre 1403 37160. **Hours:** 2 pm-11:30 pm, Fri-midnight, Sun-6 pm. **Reservations:** suggested. **Features:** Pasta, pizza and other Italian staples can be sampled in a casual atmosphere. Casual dress; cocktails. **Parking:** no self-parking. **Cards:** AX, MC, VI.

ROMANZA   Lunch: $9-$18   Dinner: $10-$35   Phone: 477/719-8000

🔻🔻🔻

Continental

Location: On Mex 45; downtown; in Hotel Fiesta Americana-Leon. Ave Lopez Mateos 1102 37270. **Hours:** 1:30 pm-midnight. **Reservations:** suggested. **Features:** The name of this elegantic fine dining restaurant reflects the special occasions its patrons celebrate therein. The service is formal, the steaks prepared to perfection, and the wine selection is glorious. Dressy casual; cocktails. **Parking:** valet. **Cards:** AX, DC, MC, VI.   (✕)

────── The following restaurant has not been evaluated by AAA ──────
but is listed for your information only.

LOS AGAVES   Phone: 477/772-5588

(fyl)

Not evaluated. **Location:** 9.3 km e via Blvd Lopez Mateos (Mex 45); between airport and town. Blvd Aeropuerta KM 8 37230. **Features:** Midway between the airport and town, the pleasant restaurant has attractive rooms and an attentive staff. Among well-prepared regional dishes are salmon with mango and guajillo chili sauce and quesadillas with squash blossoms and cheese.

MATEHUALA, SAN LUIS POTOSI pop. 54,700

────── **WHERE TO STAY** ──────

────── The following lodgings were either not evaluated or did not ──────
meet AAA rating requirements but are listed for your information only.

LAS PALMAS MIDWAY INN   Phone: 488/882-0002

(fyl)

Not evaluated. **Location:** On Mex 57, by north jct entrance road to town. Hwy 57 KM 617 78700 (Apdo Postal 73). Facilities, services, and decor characterize a basic property.

MOTEL EL DORADO   Phone: 488/882-0174

(fyl)

Not evaluated. **Location:** On Mex 57; jct Dr Arroyo Hwy. (Apdo Postal 73). Facilities, services, and decor characterize a basic property.

────── **WHERE TO DINE** ──────

LAS PALMAS RESTAURANT   Lunch: $5-$9   Dinner: $6-$10   Phone: 488/882-0001

🔻🔻🔻

Continental

Location: On Mex 57, by north jct entrance road to town; in Las Palmas Midway Inn. **Hours:** 7 am-10:30 pm. **Features:** Diners take to the relaxing atmosphere to unwind and replenish, with the help of the well-trained staff. The menu centers on Continental fare. Casual dress; cocktails. **Parking:** on-site. **Cards:** AX, MC, VI.

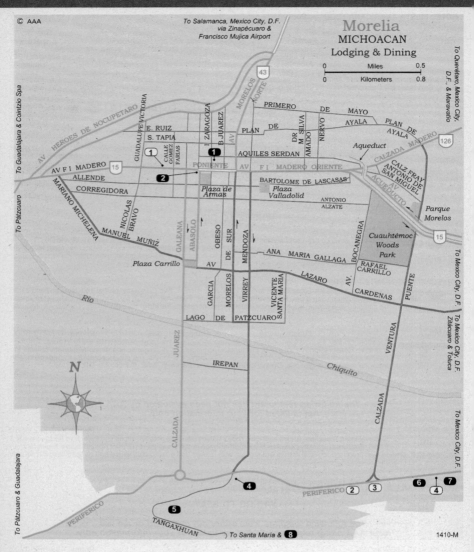

Morelia
MICHOACAN
Lodging & Dining

© AAA

1410-M

Morelia

This index helps you "spot" where approved accommodations and restaurants are located on the corresponding detailed maps. Lodging rate ranges are for comparison only and show the property's high season; rates are per night, unless only weekly (W) rates are available. Restaurant rate range is for dinner, unless only lunch (L) is served. Turn to the listing page for more detailed rate information and consult display ads for special promotions.

Spotter/Map Page Number	MORELIA - Lodgings	Diamond Rating	Rate Range High Season	Listing Page
❶ / p. 502	Hotel de la Soledad	◈◈	$85-$110	504
❷ / p. 502	Hotel Virrey de Mendoza	◈◈◈	$150-$350	504
❹ / p. 502	CasaCamelinas	◈◈	$65-$85	504
❺ / p. 502	Villa Montana	◈◈◈◈	$180-$300	504
❻ / p. 502	Holiday Inn-Morelia	◈◈◈	$115	504
❼ / p. 502	Holiday Inn Express Morelia	◈◈◈	$95-$105	504
❽ / p. 502	Villa San Jose Hotel & Suites	◈◈◈	$160-$333	504
	MORELIA - Restaurants	Diamond Rating	Rate Range High Season	Listing Page
① / p. 502	Fonda Las Mercedes	◈◈◈	$7-$15	505
② / p. 502	Las Trojes Restaurant-Bar	◈◈◈	$8-$15	505
③ / p. 502	San Miguelito Restaurante	◈◈	$7-$14	505
④ / p. 502	Carlos 'N Charlie's	◈◈	$6-$15	504

MORELIA, MICHOACAN pop. 562,400   (See map and index starting on p. 502)

------- WHERE TO STAY -------

CASACAMELINAS
Phone: 443/324-5194   **4**

Bed & Breakfast

All Year [BP]   2P: $65-$85
Location: 3.3 km s off Mex 15 via Periferico, just s. Located on terraced slope in residential area. (Jacarandas #172, Col Nueva Jacarandas). Fax: 443/324-5194. **Facility:** 5 one-bedroom standard units, some with kitchens. 3 stories (no elevator), exterior corridors. *Bath:* shower only. **Parking:** on-site. **Terms:** 17% service charge, no pets allowed (owner's pet on premises). **Amenities:** *Some:* irons, hair dryers. **Leisure Activities:** spanish language studies available. **Guest Services:** valet laundry.

SOME UNITS

HOLIDAY INN EXPRESS MORELIA   *Book at aaa.com*
Phone: (443)315-7100   **7**

Motel

All Year [ECP]   1P: $95-$105   2P: $95-$105   XP: $18   F18
Location: 6.7 km se on Periferico. Ave Camelinas 5000 58270. Fax: 443/315-7257. **Facility:** Meets AAA guest room security requirements. 80 one-bedroom standard units. 2 stories (no elevator), exterior corridors. **Parking:** on-site. **Terms:** 7 day cancellation notice-fee imposed. **Amenities:** voice mail, honor bars, irons, hair dryers. **Pool(s):** heated outdoor, wading. **Guest Services:** valet laundry. **Cards:** AX, MC, VI.

SOME UNITS

HOLIDAY INN-MORELIA
Phone: 443/314-3111   **6**

Small-scale Hotel

All Year [BP]   2P: $115
Location: 6.3 km se on Periferico. Located opposite Plaza Las Americas. 3466 Camelinas Ave 58279. Fax: 443/314-3643. **Facility:** Meets AAA guest room security requirements. 123 units. 120 one-bedroom standard units. 3 one-bedroom suites. 3 stories, interior corridors. **Parking:** on-site. **Terms:** 15 day cancellation notice. **Amenities:** voice mail, honor bars, irons, hair dryers. **Pool(s):** heated outdoor, wading. **Leisure Activities:** whirlpool, tennis court, jogging, exercise room. **Guest Services:** gift shop, valet laundry. **Business Services:** meeting rooms, business center. **Cards:** AX, DC, JC, MC, VI.

SOME UNITS

HOTEL DE LA SOLEDAD
Phone: (443)312-1888   **1**

Small-scale Hotel

All Year   2P: $85-$110   XP: $6   F12
Location: Just n of cathedral. Zaragoza 90 y Melchor Oca, Colonia 58000. Fax: 443/312-2111. **Facility:** 58 units. 49 one-bedroom standard units. 9 one-bedroom suites. 2 stories, exterior corridors. *Bath:* combo or shower only. **Parking:** valet. **Terms:** [CP] & [MAP] meal plans available. **Amenities:** safes. **Guest Services:** valet laundry. **Business Services:** meeting rooms. **Cards:** AX, CB, DC, MC, VI.

HOTEL VIRREY DE MENDOZA
Phone: (443)312-0633   **2**

Historic
Small-scale Hotel

All Year   2P: $150-$350   XP: $15   F12
Location: Just w of cathedral; center. Ave Madero Poniente 310, Colonia Cen 58000 (Portal Matamdros 16). Fax: 443/312-6719. **Facility:** From a stained-glass ceiling to original art, Old World elegance imbues this hotel built in the 17th century; some units furnished in superb antiques. 55 one-bedroom standard units. 3 stories, interior corridors. **Parking:** on-site. **Terms:** 7 day cancellation notice. **Amenities:** voice mail, hair dryers. **Guest Services:** valet laundry. **Business Services:** meeting rooms, business center. **Cards:** AX, MC, VI.

VILLA MONTANA   *Book at aaa.com*
Phone: (443)314-0231   **5**

Small-scale Hotel

All Year   1P: $180-$300   2P: $180-$300   XP: $15   F12
Location: 3.3 km s off Mex 15 via Periferico and s on Tangaxhuan. Patzimba 201 58090 (Apdo Postal 233). Fax: 443/315-1423. **Facility:** The villa's accommodations, terraced on a mountain slope above the city, feature tasteful interiors with colonial design. 36 units. 14 one- and 12 two-bedroom standard units. 6 one- and 4 two-bedroom suites. 2 stories, exterior corridors. **Parking:** on-site. **Terms:** age restrictions may apply, 7 day cancellation notice-fee imposed, $10 service charge, small pets only. **Amenities:** voice mail, safes, hair dryers. **Pool(s):** heated outdoor. **Leisure Activities:** tennis court, exercise room. **Fee:** massage. **Guest Services:** gift shop, valet laundry. **Business Services:** meeting rooms, business center. **Cards:** AX, MC, VI.

VILLA SAN JOSE HOTEL & SUITES
Phone: (443)324-4545   **8**

Motel

All Year   2P: $160-$333   XP: $13   F12
Location: 3.3 km s off Mex 15 via Periferico and s on Tangaxhuan. 77 Patzimba Col Vista Bella 58090. Fax: 443/324-4545. **Facility:** 42 units. 39 one- and 1 two-bedroom standard units. 2 two-bedroom suites. 2 stories, exterior corridors. *Bath:* combo or shower only. **Parking:** on-site. **Terms:** 3 day cancellation notice, small pets only (with prior approval). **Amenities:** hair dryers. **Pool(s):** heated outdoor. **Leisure Activities:** tennis court. **Guest Services:** gift shop, valet laundry. **Business Services:** meeting rooms, business center. **Cards:** AX, MC, VI.

SOME UNITS

------- WHERE TO DINE -------

CARLOS 'N CHARLIE'S
Lunch: $6-$15   **Dinner:** $6-$15   **Phone:** 443/341-3741   **4**

American

Location: 6.3 km se on Periferico. Ave Camelinas #3340 58270. **Hours:** 1 pm-2 am. **Features:** The popular, lively restaurant specializes in barbecue chicken, ribs and American-style steaks. Also served is a traditional Aztec dish called molcajete, which is baked in a lava pot. The full bar prepares a great selection of drinks, some of which are served in jumbo containers. Casual dress; cocktails. **Parking:** on-site and valet. **Cards:** MC, VI.

(See map and index starting on p. 502)

FONDA LAS MERCEDES
Lunch: $7-$15   **Dinner:** $7-$15   **Phone:** 443/312-6113   ①

Continental

Location: Just w of cathedral, corner of Ave Madero Pte; in historic district. Leon Guzman #47 58000. **Hours:** 1:30 pm-midnight. Closed: 12/25; also 5/1. **Reservations:** suggested. **Features:** The downtown restaurant serves a combination of local specialties and some Continental dishes. Distinctively decorated dining rooms mix colonial and contemporary styles. Check out the lounge ceiling, which is adorned with numerous pots. Dressy casual; cocktails. **Parking:** street. **Cards:** MC, VI. **Historic**

LAS TROJES RESTAURANT-BAR
Lunch: $8-$15   **Dinner:** $8-$15   **Phone:** 443/324-3283   ②

Regional Mexican

Location: 3.3 km s off Mex 15 via Periferico, just s on Mozart, then just e. Juan Sebastian Bach #51. **Hours:** 1 pm-midnight, Sun-6 pm. **Reservations:** accepted. **Features:** The popular family dining spot serves steaks, soups and salads prepared Mexican style. Service is attentive and somewhat formal. Casual dress; cocktails. **Parking:** valet and street. **Cards:** AX, MC, VI.

SAN MIGUELITO RESTAURANTE
Dinner: $7-$14   **Phone:** 443/324-4411   ③

Mexican

MC, VI.

Location: 3.5 km off Mex 15 via Periferico; across from convention center. F Chopin #45 Fracc La Loma 58290. **Hours:** 2 pm-11 pm, Thurs-Sat to 2 am, Sun 2 pm-5 pm. Closed: 12/25. **Features:** A lively crowd gathers at the colonial-styled cafe for lunch in the afternoon. On the menu is a good selection of steaks, chicken dishes and salads, reinforced by tasty margaritas. Casual dress; cocktails. **Parking:** valet. **Cards:** AX,

----

***The following restaurant has not been evaluated by AAA
but is listed for your information only.***

SANBORN'S RESTAURANTE
Phone: 443/315-1049

[fyi]

Not evaluated. **Location:** 6.3 km se on Periferico; in Plaza Las Americas. Camelinas 5030-26 58270. **Features:** The chain restaurant prepares American-style sandwiches and serves popular Mexican foods from a buffet.

PATZCUARO, MICHOACAN pop. 48,400

--------- **WHERE TO STAY** ---------

LA CASA DE LOS SUENOS HOTEL
Phone: 434/342-5708

Country Inn

All Year   1P: $200   2P: $400

Location: Center. Ibarra #15, Centro 61600. Fax: 434/342-5718. **Facility:** Luxurious rooms full of local art and beautifully crafted furniture will impress, and the restaurant is a gem in itself. Designated smoking area. 11 one-bedroom standard units. 1-2 stories, interior corridors. **Parking:** valet and street. **Amenities:** honor bars, hair dryers. **Dining:** Priscilla's, see separate listing. **Leisure Activities:** whirlpool. *Fee:* massage. **Guest Services:** gift shop, complimentary evening beverages, valet laundry. **Cards:** AX, MC, VI.

POSADA DE DON VASCO-BEST WESTERN
Phone: 434/342-2490

Small-scale Hotel

All Year   2P: $99-$200

Location: 2.5 km n on Calz de las Americas. Ave de Lazaro Cardenas #450 61600 (Apdo Postal 15). Fax: 434/342-0262. **Facility:** 103 units. 101 one-bedroom standard units. 2 one-bedroom suites with whirlpools. 2 stories (no elevator), exterior corridors. *Bath:* combo or shower only. **Parking:** on-site. **Terms:** 3 day cancellation notice, [CP] & [MAP] meal plans available. **Amenities:** hair dryers. **Dining:** 7 am-11 pm, entertainment. **Pool(s):** heated outdoor. **Leisure Activities:** tennis court, playground, game room. **Guest Services:** valet laundry. **Business Services:** meeting rooms. **Cards:** AX, MC, VI.

--------- **WHERE TO DINE** ---------

PRISCILLA'S
Lunch: $10-$30   **Dinner:** $10-$30   **Phone:** 434/342-5708

Regional Continental

Location: Center; in La Casa De Los Suenos Hotel. Ibarra #15, Centro 61600. **Hours:** 8 am-10:30 pm. **Reservations:** suggested. **Features:** Menu offerings are presented in an elegant, refined dining room or in the more casual setting of a courtyard under the stars. Dressy casual; cocktails. **Parking:** street. **Cards:** AX, MC, VI.

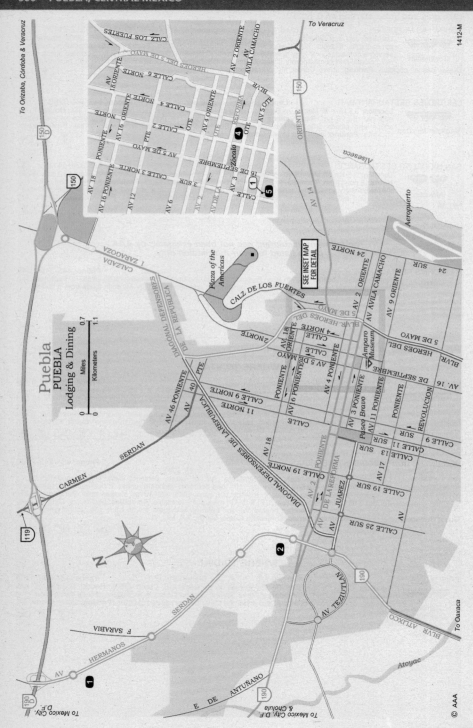

Puebla
PUEBLA
Lodging & Dining

To Orizaba, Córdoba & Veracruz

To Veracruz

To Mexico City, D.F.

To Mexico City, D.F. & Cholula

To Oaxaca

Plaza of the Americas

SEE INSET MAP FOR DETAIL

Amparo Museum

Paseo Bravo

1412-M

© AAA

Puebla

This index helps you "spot" where approved accommodations and restaurants are located on the corresponding detailed maps. Lodging rate ranges are for comparison only and show the property's high season; rates are per night, unless only weekly (W) rates are available. Restaurant rate range is for dinner, unless only lunch (L) is served. Turn to the listing page for more detailed rate information and consult display ads for special promotions.

Spotter/Map Page Number	PUEBLA - Lodgings	Diamond Rating	Rate Range High Season	Listing Page
1 / p. 506	Puebla Marriott	◆◆◆	$145-$195	507
2 / p. 506	Crowne Plaza Hotel and Resort	◆◆◆	$152-$190	507
4 / p. 506	Hotel del Portal	◆	$45-$60	507
5 / p. 506	Camino Real Puebla	◆◆◆◆	$185	507

Spotter/Map Page Number	PUEBLA - Restaurant	Diamond Rating	Rate Range High Season	Listing Page
1 / p. 506	El Convento	◆◆◆	$10-$20	507

PUEBLA, PUEBLA pop. 1,320,600   (See map and index starting on p. 506)

───── WHERE TO STAY ─────

CAMINO REAL PUEBLA   *Book at aaa.com*   **Phone:** (222)229-0909   **5**
◆◆◆◆   All Year   1P: $185   2P: $185   XP: $25   F12
Classic Historic Small-scale Hotel   **Location:** Just sw of the plaza. 7 Poniente 105 Centro Historico 72000. Fax: 222/232-9251. **Facility:** A courtyard accents this handsome 16th-century convent; large rooms feature high ceilings, carved wooden headboards and talavera tile baths. 84 units. 82 one-bedroom standard units. 2 one-bedroom suites ($280-$450). 4 stories, interior/exterior corridors. *Bath:* combo or shower only. **Parking:** on-site (fee) and valet. **Terms:** [BP] & [CP] meal plans available. **Amenities:** honor bars, hair dryers. *Some:* irons. **Dining:** El Convento, see separate listing. **Guest Services:** gift shop, valet laundry. **Business Services:** conference facilities, business center. **Cards:** AX, DC, MC, VI.
SOME UNITS

CROWNE PLAZA HOTEL AND RESORT   *Book at aaa.com*   **Phone:** (222)213-7070   **2**
◆◆◆   All Year   1P: $152-$190   2P: $152-$190   XP: $20   F14
Large-scale Hotel   **Location:** S of Mex 190-D (toll road); jct Ave Hermanos Serdan. Ave Hermanos Serdan 141 72140. Fax: 222/213-7000. **Facility:** Meets AAA guest room security requirements. 214 units. 210 one-bedroom standard units. 3 one- and 1 two-bedroom suites, some with whirlpools. 5 stories, interior/exterior corridors. *Bath:* combo or shower only. **Parking:** on-site. **Terms:** cancellation fee imposed, [BP] meal plan available. **Amenities:** CD players, voice mail, honor bars, irons, hair dryers. *Some:* fax. **Pool(s):** heated outdoor, wading. **Leisure Activities:** playground, exercise room. **Guest Services:** gift shop, valet laundry, beauty salon. **Business Services:** conference facilities, business center. **Cards:** AX, MC, VI.
SOME UNITS

HOTEL DEL PORTAL   **Phone:** 222/246-0211   **4**
◆   All Year   1P: $45-$48   2P: $55-$60   XP: $10
Small-scale Hotel   **Location:** Opposite Zocalo. Juan de Palafox y Mendoza 205 72000. Fax: 222/232-3194. **Facility:** 92 one-bedroom standard units. 4 stories, interior corridors. *Bath:* shower only. **Parking:** on-site (fee). **Terms:** 3 day cancellation notice. **Guest Services:** valet laundry. **Business Services:** meeting rooms. **Cards:** AX, MC, VI.

PUEBLA MARRIOTT   **Phone:** (222)223-8300   **1**
◆◆◆   All Year [ECP]   1P: $145-$195   2P: $160-$195   XP: $25   F14
Small-scale Hotel   **Location:** S of Mex 190-D (toll road); jct Ave Hermanos Serdan. Ave Hermanos Serdan 807 72100. Fax: 222/223-8301. **Facility:** Meets AAA guest room security requirements. 192 units. 181 one-bedroom standard units, some with whirlpools. 11 one-bedroom suites ($190-$220). 2-3 stories (no elevator), interior/exterior corridors. **Parking:** on-site. **Amenities:** voice mail, safes, honor bars, hair dryers. *Some:* irons. **Pool(s):** outdoor, heated outdoor. **Leisure Activities:** lighted tennis court, playground, exercise room. **Guest Services:** gift shop, valet laundry. **Business Services:** conference facilities, business center. **Cards:** AX, CB, DC, MC, VI.
SOME UNITS

───── WHERE TO DINE ─────

EL CONVENTO   **Lunch:** $8-$15   **Dinner:** $10-$20   **Phone:** 222/229-0909   **1**
◆◆◆   **Location:** Just sw of the plaza; in Camino Real Puebla. **Hours:** 1 pm-midnight. Closed: Mon.
Continental   **Reservations:** required. **Features:** The elegant specialty restaurant, a 16th-century convent, serves international fare. Surrounding walls and arches are adorned with beautiful, hand-painted frescoes. Some seating faces the courtyard. The lunch buffet may help those on a budget. Cocktails. **Parking:** valet.
Cards: AX, DC, MC, VI.

QUERETARO, QUERETARO pop. 565,400

———— WHERE TO STAY ————

AZTECA PARADOR HOTEL
Phone: 442/234-0592

▼▼▼
Motel

All Year   1P: $40   2P: $45

Location: Mex 57, exit Juriquilla northbound; exit Juriquilla southbound to access northbound lanes, 14.5 km n of jct Mex 45. Located adjacent to Pemex Station. KM 15.5 Queretaro-Juriquilla Hwy 76000 (Apdo Postal 98-C). Fax: 442/234-0592. **Facility:** 44 one-bedroom standard units. 2 stories, interior/exterior corridors. *Bath:* shower only. **Parking:** on-site. **Dining:** restaurant, see separate listing. **Pool(s):** heated outdoor. **Guest Services:** valet laundry. **Cards:** AX, MC, VI.

[icons]

HOLIDAY INN-QUERETARO CENTRO HISTORICO   *Book at aaa.com*
Phone: (442)192-0202

▼▼▼▼
Small-scale Hotel

All Year   1P: $88   2P: $88   XP: $10   F12

Location: On Mex 57, 1 km n of jct Mex 45 and 45-D (toll road), exit Cinco de Febrero. Ave 5 de Febrero 110 Col Ninos Heroes 76010 (Apdo Postal 95). Fax: 442/216-8902. **Facility:** Meets AAA guest room security requirements. 218 units. 209 one-bedroom standard units. 9 one-bedroom suites. 3 stories, interior corridors. *Bath:* combo or shower only. **Parking:** on-site. **Terms:** cancellation fee imposed, 8% service charge. **Amenities:** voice mail, irons, hair dryers. *Some:* safes, honor bars. **Pool(s):** heated outdoor, wading. **Leisure Activities:** whirlpool, 2 lighted tennis courts, playground, exercise room, sports court. **Guest Services:** gift shop, valet laundry. **Business Services:** conference facilities, business center. **Cards:** AX, DC, MC, VI.

SOME UNITS
[icons]

HOTEL HACIENDA JURICA QUERETARO   *Book at aaa.com*
Phone: (442)218-0022

▼▼▼▼
Large-scale Hotel

All Year   1P: $120-$300   2P: $120-$300

Location: Mex 57, exit Jurica, 4 km w; at end of Jurica development. (Apdo Postal 338). Fax: 442/218-0136. **Facility:** 182 units. 178 one-bedroom standard units. 4 one-bedroom suites, some with whirlpools. 2 stories (no elevator), interior corridors. *Bath:* shower or tub only. **Parking:** on-site. **Terms:** 5 day cancellation notice. **Amenities:** honor bars, hair dryers. **Dining:** Los Hules, see separate listing. **Pool(s):** heated outdoor, wading. **Leisure Activities:** playground. *Fee:* golf-18 holes, miniature golf, 2 lighted tennis courts, bicycles, horseback riding. **Guest Services:** gift shop, valet laundry, area transportation (fee). **Business Services:** conference facilities, business center. **Cards:** AX, DC, MC, VI.

SOME UNITS
[icons]
FEE

HOTEL MESON DE SANTA ROSA
Phone: 442/224-2623

▼▼▼▼
Classic Historic
Country Inn

All Year   1P: $110-$170   2P: $110-$170   XP: $16   F12

Location: Center. Located on Plaza de Independencia. Pasteur Sur #17 76000. Fax: 442/212-5522. **Facility:** This restored 18th-century guest house sits on the main plaza; spacious rooms, a few with private balconies, overlook an inner courtyard. Meets AAA guest room security requirements. 21 one-bedroom standard units. 2 stories (no elevator), interior corridors. **Parking:** on-site (fee) and valet. **Terms:** [BP] & [CP] meal plans available. **Amenities:** safes, honor bars, hair dryers. **Pool(s):** heated outdoor. **Guest Services:** valet laundry. **Business Services:** meeting rooms. *Fee:* PC, fax. **Cards:** AX, MC, VI.

SOME UNITS
[icons]

HOTEL REAL DE MINAS TRADICIONAL
Phone: (442)216-0444

▼▼▼
Small-scale Hotel

All Year   1P: $80-$120   2P: $80-$120   XP: $20   F16

Location: On Mex 45 (Celaya Libre), 0.3 km w of jct Mex 57. Located next to the bull ring. Ave Constituyentes 124 Pte 76180. Fax: 442/216-0662. **Facility:** 200 one-bedroom standard units. 2 stories (no elevator), interior corridors. **Parking:** on-site. **Amenities:** safes, hair dryers. **Pool(s):** heated outdoor, wading. **Leisure Activities:** 2 tennis courts, playground, exercise room, basketball. **Guest Services:** gift shop, valet laundry. **Business Services:** meeting rooms, business center. **Cards:** AX, CB, DC, MC, VI.

SOME UNITS
[icons]

LA CASA DE LA MARQUESA   *Book at aaa.com*
Phone: 442/212-0092

▼▼▼ ▼▼▼
Classic Historic
Country Inn

All Year   1P: $125-$235   2P: $125-$235   XP: $14

Location: Downtown. Located in a historic district. Madero 41 Esquina Allende 76000. Fax: 442/212-0098. **Facility:** Beautiful courtyards and luxurious rooms characterize this stunning 1700s country inn, formerly home to emperors and presidents. 25 one-bedroom standard units, some with whirlpools. 3 stories (no elevator), exterior corridors. *Bath:* combo or shower only. **Parking:** valet and street. **Terms:** age restrictions may apply, 3 day cancellation notice-fee imposed. **Amenities:** hair dryers. **Dining:** El Comedor de la Marquesa, see separate listing. **Guest Services:** complimentary evening beverages, valet laundry. **Business Services:** meeting rooms, PC, fax (fee). **Cards:** AX, MC, VI.

[icons]

RADISSON HOTEL PLAZA CAMELINAS   *Book at aaa.com*
Phone: 442/441-1600

[AAA]
▼▼▼▼
Small-scale Hotel

All Year   1P: $150   2P: $150   XP: $25

Location: Between aves Zaragoza and Constituyentes. Ave 5 de Febrero #28 76170. Fax: 442/441-1617. **Facility:** 156 units. 155 one-bedroom standard units. 1 one-bedroom suite ($210-$330) with whirlpool. 3 stories (no elevator), interior corridors. *Bath:* combo or shower only. **Parking:** on-site (fee). **Amenities:** *Some:* safes, hair dryers. **Dining:** 7 am-11 pm, cocktails. **Pool(s):** heated outdoor, wading. **Leisure Activities:** playground, exercise room. **Guest Services:** gift shop, valet laundry. **Business Services:** meeting rooms, business center. **Cards:** AX, MC, VI. *(See color ad p 477)*

SOME UNITS
[icons]

———— The following lodging was either not evaluated or did not ————
meet AAA rating requirements but is listed for your information only.

HOTEL DONA URRACA
Phone: 442/238-5400

[fyi]

Not evaluated. **Location:** In historic downtown. Ave 5 de Mayo #117 76000. Facilities, services, and decor characterize a basic property.

——— WHERE TO DINE ———

EL COMEDOR DE LA MARQUESA **Lunch:** $10-$15   **Dinner:** $15-$20   **Phone:** 442/212-0092
Mexican
Location: Downtown; in La Casa de la Marquesa. Madero 41 Esquina Allende 76000. **Hours:** 7 am-11 pm. **Reservations:** suggested. **Features:** Although the menu is Mexican, it exhibits notable European influences in such dishes such as lamb chops with mint sauce and fusilli Alfredo. Dressy casual; cocktails; entertainment. **Parking:** valet and street. **Cards:** AX, MC, VI. **Historic**

JOSECHO **Lunch:** $10-$16   **Dinner:** $12-$35   **Phone:** 442/216-0201
Regional Continental
Location: Mex 57, exit Ave Constituyentes, 1.5 km w. Dalia #1, Fracc Orquideas 76000. **Hours:** 1 pm-8 pm. Closed: Sun. **Reservations:** accepted. **Features:** Offering refined dining in a lodge-like setting, the restaurant features Continental and Mexican dishes served by well-trained staff. Dressy casual; cocktails. **Parking:** no self-parking. **Cards:** AX, CB, DC, JC, MC, VI.

LA CASTA DIVINA **Lunch:** $6-$19   **Dinner:** $10-$19   **Phone:** 442/214-4912
Mexican
Location: Just w of Plaza de Armas. Ave 5 de Mayo #46 76000. **Hours:** 1:30 pm-11 pm, Sun 1 pm-7 pm. Closed: Mon. **Features:** For a memorable experience, try the Yucatan-inspired cuisine at La Casta Divina, meaning the "divine caste." Servers dressed in white guayaberas will offer you a menu of traditional dishes such as the savory cochinita pibil, which is made with chunks of tender pork served in a red sauce. Panuchos and salbutes are also recommended for a taste of the Yucatan. Casual dress; cocktails. **Parking:** street. **Cards:** MC, VI.

LOS HULES **Lunch:** $5-$8   **Dinner:** $10-$20   **Phone:** 442/218-0022
Regional Mexican
Location: Mex 57, exit Jurica, 4 km w; at end of Jurica development; in Hotel Hacienda Jurica Queretaro. **Hours:** 7:30 am-10 pm. **Reservations:** accepted. **Features:** Overlooking the majestic grounds of a 1600s former hacienda, the restaurant lets guests savor Mexican cuisine indoors or on a garden terrace. Casual dress; cocktails. **Parking:** on-site and valet. **Cards:** AX, CB, DC, DS, JC, MC, VI.

RESTAURANTE AZTECA PARADOR **Lunch:** $5   **Dinner:** $9   **Phone:** 442/234-0592
Mexican
Location: On Mex 57 northbound, 14.5 km n of jct Mex 45; exit Juriquilla southbound to access northbound lanes; in Azteca Parador Hotel. KM 15.5 Queratero-Juriquilla. **Hours:** 7 am-9 pm. **Features:** Travelers can stop in the small, simple roadside restaurant for a quick refresher before continuing on the long road to San Luis Potosi. Casual dress. **Parking:** on-site. **Cards:** AX, MC, VI.

RESTAURANTE BAR 1810 **Lunch:** $6-$8   **Dinner:** $6-$8   **Phone:** 442/214-3324
Continental
Location: Plaza de Independencia; in historic district. Andador La Libertad 60 76000. **Hours:** 8 am-11 pm. Closed: 12/24. **Reservations:** suggested. **Features:** International and Mexican specialties are served in a lively atmosphere. The outdoor patio is on the main city plaza and provides prime opportunities for interesting people-watching. Casual dress; cocktails. **Parking:** street. **Cards:** AX, MC, VI.

SUSHI ITTO **Lunch:** $8-$12   **Dinner:** $10-$20   **Phone:** 442/215-6048
Japanese
Location: Mex 57, exit Ave Constituyentes, 1.5 km w. Ave Constituyentes Poniente #180 76000. **Hours:** 11 am-10 pm, Sun 1 pm-8 pm. **Features:** Featuring Japanese food served fast in a casual setting, the restaurant boasts an extensive menu, a full bar and both indoor and outdoor seating. Casual dress; cocktails. **Parking:** on-site and street. **Cards:** AX, CB, DC, JC, MC, VI.

SAN JUAN DEL RIO, QUERETARO pop. 105,600

——— WHERE TO STAY ———

FIESTA AMERICANA HACIENDA GALINDO *Book at aaa.com*   **Phone:** 427/271-8200
Large-scale Hotel
All Year   1P: $150-$350   2P: $150-$350
Location: On Mex 45 and 57, exit KM 172, 6 km s on Mex 120 toward Galindo. Located in the country side. (Apdo Postal 16). Fax: 427/275-0300. **Facility:** Large, converted 16th-century hacienda, extensively decorated with period art. Beautiful grounds. 166 units. 142 one-bedroom standard units. 24 one-bedroom suites ($120-$140), some with whirlpools. 3 stories, interior corridors. **Parking:** on-site. **Amenities:** voice mail, honor bars, hair dryers. **Dining:** 7 am-11 pm, Fri & Sat-1 am, entertainment. **Pool(s):** heated outdoor, wading. **Leisure Activities:** miniature golf, racquetball court, tennis instruction, mini farm, soccer, hiking trails, jogging, playground. *Fee:* 6 tennis courts (3 lighted), horseback riding. **Guest Services:** gift shop, valet laundry. **Business Services:** conference facilities, business center. **Cards:** AX, DC, MC, VI. *(See color ad card insert)*
SOME UNITS

HOTEL MISION SAN GIL *Book at aaa.com*   **Phone:** (427)271-0030
Large-scale Hotel
All Year   1P: $120-$150   2P: $120-$150
Location: On Mex 45 and 57, 37 km e at KM 172. Located in a rural area. KM 172 Carr Mex-Qro 76800 (Apdo Postal 128). Fax: 427/271-0096. **Facility:** 134 units. 112 one-bedroom standard units. 21 one- and 1 two-bedroom suites ($120-$320), some with kitchens and/or whirlpools. 2 stories (no elevator), interior corridors. *Bath:* combo or shower only. **Parking:** on-site. **Terms:** cancellation fee imposed. **Amenities:** honor bars. *Some:* safes, hair dryers. **Pool(s):** heated outdoor, wading. **Leisure Activities:** 2 tennis courts, jogging, playground, basketball. *Fee:* golf-18 holes. **Guest Services:** gift shop, valet laundry. **Business Services:** conference facilities, business center. **Cards:** AX, DC, DS, MC, VI.

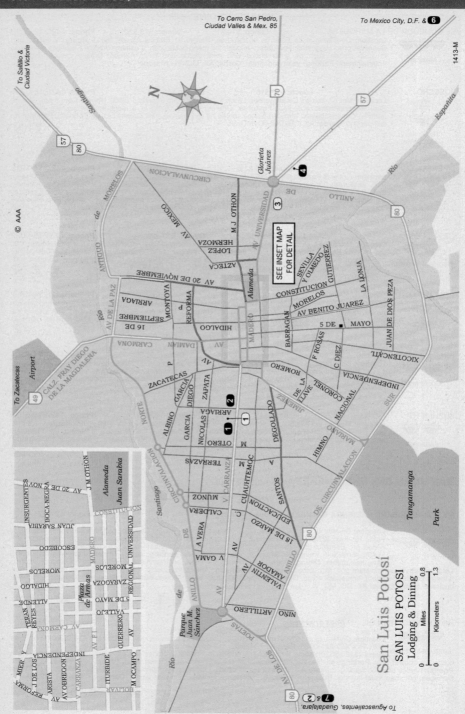

© AAA

N

To Cerro San Pedro,
Ciudad Valles & Mex. 85

To Mexico City, D.F. & 6

1413-M

To Saltillo &
Ciudad Victoria

To Zacatecas

Airport

Glorieta
Juárez

San Luis Potosí

SAN LUIS POTOSI
Lodging & Dining

Miles
0   0.8

Kilometers
0   1.3

To Aguascalientes, Guadalajara, 7 & 2

Tanganmanga
Park

SEE INSET MAP
FOR DETAIL

Parque
Juan M.
Sánchez

Alameda
Juan Sarabia

Plaza
de Armas

San Luis Potosi

This index helps you "spot" where approved accommodations and restaurants are located on the corresponding detailed maps. Lodging rate ranges are for comparison only and show the property's high season; rates are per night, unless only weekly (W) rates are available. Restaurant rate range is for dinner, unless only lunch (L) is served. Turn to the listing page for more detailed rate information and consult display ads for special promotions.

Spotter/Map Page Number	OA	SAN LUIS POTOSI - Lodgings	Diamond Rating	Rate Range High Season	Listing Page
1 / p. 510		Hotel Real Plaza	◊◊	$76-$100	512
2 / p. 510		Country Inn & Suites by Carlson - see color ad below	◊◊◊	$60-$160	511
4 / p. 510		Hotel Real de Minas	◊◊	$65-$105	512
6 / p. 510		Holiday Inn	◊◊◊	$160-$190	511
7 / p. 510		The Westin San Luis Potosi - see color ad p 8	◊◊◊◊	$120-$225	512
		SAN LUIS POTOSI - Restaurants			
① / p. 510		Restaurante La Virreina	◊◊	$12-$22	512
② / p. 510		Restaurante Cantera	◊◊◊	$10-$30	512
③ / p. 510		La Casa de las Flores	◊◊◊	$12-$25	512

SAN LUIS POTOSI, SAN LUIS POTOSI pop. 644,300 (See map and index starting on p. 510)

——— WHERE TO STAY ———

COUNTRY INN & SUITES BY CARLSON *Book at aaa.com* **Phone: (444)826-9900** **2**
◊◊◊ All Year [BP] 1P: $60-$160 2P: $60-$160
Small-scale Hotel **Location:** On Mex 57, 1 km se. Carr 57 #1530, Zona Industrial 78399. Fax: 444/826-9909. **Facility:** 120 units. 100 one-bedroom standard units. 20 one-bedroom suites ($150-$230). 4 stories, interior corridors. **Parking:** on-site. **Amenities:** high-speed Internet, dual phone lines, voice mail, irons, hair dryers. **Pool(s):** heated indoor, wading. **Leisure Activities:** whirlpool, exercise room. **Guest Services:** valet laundry, area transportation (fee). **Business Services:** meeting rooms, business center. **Cards:** AX. *(See color ad below)* SOME UNITS
[✈] [Ⅱ] [S] [D] [⊸] [🎥] [DATA PORT] [▭] / [✕] [🛏] [📷] /

HOLIDAY INN *Book at aaa.com* **Phone: (444)834-4100** **6**
◊◊◊ All Year 1P: $160-$190 2P: $160-$190 XP: $15 F16
Large-scale Hotel **Location:** 5 km se on Mex 57. (Apdo Postal F-1893). Fax: 444/818-6105. **Facility:** Meets AAA guest room security requirements. 210 units. 200 one-bedroom standard units. 5 one- and 5 two-bedroom suites with whirlpools. 2-3 stories, interior/exterior corridors. **Parking:** on-site. **Amenities:** high-speed Internet, voice mail, safes, honor bars, irons, hair dryers. *Some:* CD players. **Pool(s):** heated outdoor, wading. **Leisure Activities:** lighted tennis court, playground, exercise room. **Guest Services:** gift shop, valet laundry. **Business Services:** conference facilities, business center. **Cards:** AX, CB, DC, JC, MC, VI. SOME UNITS
[✈] [🐾] [Ⅱ] [24] [Y] [⊸] [✕] [🎥] [DATA PORT] [▭] / [✕] [📷] /

(See map and index starting on p. 510)

HOTEL REAL DE MINAS
Phone: 444/818-2616   **4**
▼▼▼▼   All Year   1P: $65-$105   2P: $65-$105
Small-scale Hotel   **Location:** On Mex 57; 1 km se of Glorieta Juarez; 0.5 km s of Distribuidora Juarez. Carr Central KM 426.6 78090 (Apdo Postal F-1371). Fax: 444/818-6915. **Facility:** 170 units. 168 one-bedroom standard units. 2 one-bedroom suites ($140-$200), some with whirlpools. 2 stories, interior/exterior corridors. *Bath:* combo or shower only. **Parking:** on-site. **Amenities:** hair dryers. *Some:* irons. **Pool(s):** outdoor. **Leisure Activities:** recreation programs. **Guest Services:** gift shop, valet laundry, area transportation (fee). **Business Services:** meeting rooms, business center. **Cards:** AX, CB, DC, DS, JC, MC, VI.

SOME UNITS

HOTEL REAL PLAZA
Phone: (444)814-6055   **1**
▼▼▼▼   All Year   1P: $76-$100   2P: $76-$100   XP: $6   F14
Large-scale Hotel   **Location:** In heart of downtown. Located in a busy commercial area. Ave Vicente Carranza 890 78250. Fax: 444/814-6639. **Facility:** 268 one-bedroom standard units. 9 stories, interior corridors. *Bath:* shower only. **Parking:** on-site. **Terms:** 3 day cancellation notice. **Amenities:** hair dryers. **Guest Services:** gift shop, valet laundry, area transportation (fee). **Business Services:** meeting rooms, business center. **Cards:** AX, MC, VI.

THE WESTIN SAN LUIS POTOSI   *Book at aaa.com*
Phone: (444)825-0125   **7**
▼▼▼▼ ▼▼▼▼   All Year   1P: $120-$225   2P: $120-$225   XP: $10   F12
Large-scale Hotel   **Location:** 3.5 km sw on Carr SLP-Guadalajara. Located in an upscale, commercial area. Real de Lomas 1000 78210. Fax: 444/825-0200. **Facility:** Upscale colonial themes. Quiet courtyard areas. 123 units. 105 one-bedroom standard units. 18 one-bedroom suites ($180-$290). 3 stories, exterior corridors. **Parking:** on-site and valet. **Terms:** cancellation fee imposed. **Amenities:** safes, honor bars, irons, hair dryers. **Dining:** Restaurante Cantera, see separate listing. **Pool(s):** heated outdoor. **Guest Services:** gift shop, valet laundry. **Business Services:** conference facilities, fax. **Cards:** AX, CB, DC, MC, VI. *(See color ad p 8)*

SOME UNITS

────── **WHERE TO DINE** ──────

LA CASA DE LAS FLORES
Lunch: $8-$15   Dinner: $12-$25   Phone: 444/813-4333   **3**
▼▼▼▼   **Location:** Arista at Ave Emilio Carranza; 1 blk s of Jardin de Tequisquiapan; in Zona Rosa. Arista 1205 78220. **Hours:** 8 am-midnight, Sun-6 pm. **Reservations:** accepted. **Features:** European influences continue to dominate this upscale restaurant. Featured cuisine includes Potosino dishes along with traditional Regional Mexican   Continental selections. Dressy casual; cocktails. **Parking:** no self-parking. **Cards:** AX, CB, DC, JC, MC, VI.

RESTAURANTE CANTERA
Lunch: $6-$12   Dinner: $10-$30   Phone: 444/825-0125   **2**
▼▼▼▼ ▼▼▼▼   **Location:** 3.5 km sw on Carr SLP-Guadalajara; in The Westin San Luis Potosi. Real de Lomas 1000 78210. **Hours:** 6:30 am-10 pm, Fri & Sat-11 pm. **Reservations:** suggested. **Features:** This elegant dining room is Continental   located in an upscale boutique hotel. A formal staff serves unique dishes incorporating fresh, quality ingredients. Dressy casual; cocktails. **Parking:** on-site and valet. **Cards:** AX, CB, DC, MC, VI.

RESTAURANTE LA VIRREINA
Lunch: $8-$14   Dinner: $12-$22   Phone: 444/812-3750   **1**
▼▼▼▼   **Location:** 1 km w on Mex 80; center of downtown. Ave Vicente Carranza 830 78230. **Hours:** 1 pm-11 pm, Sun-7 pm: Closed: 1/1, 12/25. **Reservations:** suggested, for dinner. **Features:** The Maximilian-period mansion is Continental   a refined spot for classic, Old World dining. Traditional Continental dishes make up the menu. Service is **Historic**   sophisticated. Casual dress; cocktails; entertainment. **Parking:** on-site and street. **Cards:** AX, MC, VI.

SAN MIGUEL DE ALLENDE, GUANAJUATO pop. 62,200

────── **WHERE TO STAY** ──────

ABADIA CASA SCHUCK BOUTIQUE B&B
Phone: (415)152-0657
▼▼▼▼   All Year [BP]   2P: $135-$195   XP: $35
Bed & Breakfast   **Location:** 4 blks e of main plaza. Bajada de la Garita #3 37700. Fax: 415/152-0657. **Facility:** A lovely fountained courtyard and rooftop patio with a view to the Parroquia provides guests a tranquil environment and scenic surroundings. Designated smoking area. 6 one-bedroom standard units. 2 stories (no elevator), exterior corridors. **Parking:** street. **Terms:** 30 day cancellation notice-fee imposed. **Amenities:** safes, hair dryers. **Pool(s):** heated outdoor. **Leisure Activities:** spa. **Guest Services:** TV in common area, valet laundry. **Business Services:** meeting rooms, fax (fee). **Cards:** DC, DS, MC, VI.

ANTIGUA VILLA SANTA MONICA
Phone: 415/152-0427
▼▼▼▼   All Year [CP]   2P: $179-$229   XP: $25
Country Inn   **Location:** Facing Benito Juarez Park. Baeza #22 37700 (Apdo Postal 686). Fax: 415/152-0518. **Facility:** Very attractive, intimate inn. All rooms unique; all facing interior courtyard. Well-landscaped. Building is over 230 years old. 14 one-bedroom standard units, some with whirlpools. 1 story, exterior corridors. *Bath:* combo, shower or tub only. **Parking:** on-site. **Terms:** check-in 3:30 pm, 10 day cancellation notice-fee imposed. **Amenities:** *Some:* honor bars, hair dryers. **Pool(s):** heated outdoor. **Guest Services:** valet laundry. **Business Services:** fax (fee). **Cards:** AX, MC, VI.

SOME UNITS

CASA DE LIZA VILLAS EN EL PARQUE

Book at aaa.com

Phone: (415)152-0352

	2P: $170-$360	XP: $30	F12
12/1-4/30 & 7/1-11/30 [BP]			
5/1-6/30 [BP]	2P: $140-$300	XP: $30	F12

Bed & Breakfast

Location: 3 blks se of main plaza. Located at the edge of the historic district. Bajada del Chorro #7-Centro 37700 (PMB 24-203, McPherson, LAREDO, TX, 78041). Fax: 415/152-6144. **Facility:** Lush gardens invite outdoor lounging at this B&B notable for its personalized service and exceptional guest-room decor. Designated smoking area. 7 units. 5 one-bedroom standard units, some with kitchens and/or whirlpools. 2 one-bedroom suites. 2 stories (no elevator), exterior corridors. **Bath:** combo or shower only. **Parking:** on-site. **Terms:** 7 day cancellation notice-fee imposed, small pets only (with prior approval, owner's pets on premises). **Amenities:** Some: dual phone lines, safes, hair dryers. **Leisure Activities:** whirlpool. **Fee:** massage. **Guest Services:** valet laundry. **Business Services:** meeting rooms, fax (fee). **Cards:** AX, MC, VI.

SOME UNITS

CASA DE SIERRA NEVADA QUINTA REAL

Book at aaa.com

Phone: (415)152-7040

| All Year | 1P: $220 | 2P: $366 | XP: $30 | F12 |

Historic Country Inn

Location: Just se of main plaza. Hospicio 46 37700 (Hospicio 35). Fax: 415/152-1436. **Facility:** Rated among the top lodgings in Latin America, this property provides luxurious rooms, impeccable service and world-class dining. Some rooms are near El Parque. 33 units. 31 one-bedroom standard units. 2 one-bedroom suites. 2 stories (no elevator), exterior corridors. **Bath:** combo or shower only. **Parking:** valet. **Terms:** 2 night minimum stay - weekends, age restrictions may apply, 3 day cancellation notice, weekly rates available, [AP] meal plan available, 15% service charge. **Amenities:** safes, honor bars, hair dryers. **Dining:** Sierra Nevada Restaurant, Casa de Sierra Nevada en el Parque, see separate listings. **Pool(s):** heated outdoor. **Leisure Activities:** exercise room, spa. **Guest Services:** valet laundry. **Business Services:** meeting rooms, fax (fee). **Cards:** AX, MC, VI.

SOME UNITS

CASA PUESTA DEL SOL

Phone: 415/152-0220

| All Year [BP] | 1P: $98-$165 | 2P: $98-$165 | XP: $35 |

Bed & Breakfast

Location: Jct Pedro Vargas (Queretero Hwy), 0.4 km e on Santo Domingo, just ne. Fuentes #12 37700 (413 Interamerica Blvd, Suite 1, LAREDO, TX, 78045). Fax: 415/152-7232. **Facility:** High in the residential area above the village and tucked into a tiered garden, you'll find a waterfall and fountains to cool the day at this inn. Designated smoking area. 7 units. 6 one-bedroom standard units. 1 two-bedroom suite with kitchen. 2 stories (no elevator), interior/exterior corridors. **Parking:** street. **Terms:** age restrictions may apply, 14 day cancellation notice, small pets only (with prior approval). **Leisure Activities:** Fee: massage. **Guest Services:** valet laundry. **Business Services:** PC, fax (fee). **Cards:** MC, VI.

SOME UNITS

GUADIANA BED AND BREAKFAST ON THE PARK

Phone: (415)152-4948

| All Year [BP] | 2P: $65 | XP: $11 | D18 |

Bed & Breakfast

Location: 0.5 mi s of main plaza. Located in a quiet residential area. Mesquite #11 37700. **Facility:** 9 one-bedroom standard units. 3 stories (no elevator), interior corridors. **Bath:** shower only. **Parking:** street. **Terms:** age restrictions may apply, 15 day cancellation notice. **Guest Services:** TV in common area, complimentary evening beverages, valet laundry. **Cards:** MC, VI.

SOME UNITS

HACIENDA DE LAS FLORES

Phone: (415)152-1808

| All Year [CP] | 2P: $85-$160 | XP: $30 |

Bed & Breakfast

Location: 2.5 blks s of main plaza. Hospicio 16 37700. Fax: 415/152-8383. **Facility:** Colonial-style converted hacienda. Very pretty setting. Attractive, well-maintained guest rooms. Roof garden overlooks bull ring. 16 units. 11 one-bedroom standard units. 5 one-bedroom suites with kitchens. 2 stories, exterior corridors. **Parking:** street. **Terms:** 10 day cancellation notice. **Pool(s):** outdoor. **Guest Services:** valet laundry. **Business Services:** meeting rooms. **Cards:** MC, VI.

SOME UNITS

HACIENDA EL SANTUARIO HOTEL, SPA & GOLF

Phone: (415)185-2036

| All Year | 1P: $180-$260 | 2P: $180-$260 |

Country Inn

Location: 13 km n on San Miguel de Allende Dolores Hidalgo Hwy (Mex 51), follow signs. Dolores Hidalgo Hwy KM 13 37700. Fax: 415/185-2076. **Facility:** Outside of town you will find this property with very attractive guest rooms and grounds that will make for a relaxing stay. 9 units. 8 one-bedroom standard units. 1 one-bedroom suite ($180-$260) with whirlpool. 1 story, exterior corridors. **Bath:** combo or shower only. **Parking:** on-site. **Terms:** 3 day cancellation notice-fee imposed, [AP] & [ECP] meal plans available. **Amenities:** CD players, safes, hair dryers. **Pool(s):** outdoor. **Leisure Activities:** whirlpool, golf-9 holes, tennis court, bicycles, exercise room, spa. **Guest Services:** valet laundry. **Business Services:** fax (fee). **Cards:** AX, DC, JC, MC, VI.

FEE

HOTEL ARISTOS SAN MIGUEL

Book at aaa.com

Phone: (415)152-0149

| All Year | 2P: $88-$110 | XP: $12 |

Small-scale Hotel

Location: 1.3 km s on Mex 49 (Celaya Hwy). Calzada del Cardo #2 37700 (Apdo Postal 588). Fax: 415/152-1631. **Facility:** 60 units. 58 one-bedroom standard units. 2 one-bedroom suites. 2 stories (no elevator), interior corridors. **Bath:** combo or shower only. **Parking:** on-site. **Terms:** 5 day cancellation notice. **Pool(s):** outdoor. **Leisure Activities:** Fee: 2 tennis courts. **Guest Services:** valet laundry. **Business Services:** meeting rooms, fax (fee). **Cards:** AX, MC, VI.

SOME UNITS

HOTEL HACIENDA TABOADA, SA DE CV

Phone: (415)152-9250

| All Year | 1P: $190 | 2P: $244 |

Small-scale Hotel

Location: 8 km on San Miguel de Allende Dolores Hidalgo Hwy (Mex 51), 3 km w, follow signs. Located in a quiet area. KM 8 Carr a Dolores Hidalgo Hwy 37700 (Apdo Postal 100). Fax: 415/152-1798. **Facility:** 70 one-bedroom standard units. 3 stories (no elevator), exterior corridors. **Parking:** on-site. **Terms:** cancellation fee imposed, [AP] & [BP] meal plans available. **Pool(s):** heated outdoor, 2 wading. **Leisure Activities:** 2 tennis courts, hiking trails, horseback riding, playground, exercise room, volleyball. **Guest Services:** gift shop, valet laundry. **Business Services:** meeting rooms. **Cards:** AX, DC, MC, VI.

HOTEL LA SIESTA
Motel
Phone: (415)152-0207
All Year [CP]　　　　2P: $55-$75
Location: 2 km s on Mex 49 (Celaya Hwy). Salida A Celaya Hwy 82 37765. Fax: 415/152-4357. **Facility:** 29 one-bedroom standard units. 1 story, exterior corridors. *Bath:* shower only. **Parking:** on-site. **Terms:** 5 day cancellation notice. **Pool(s):** heated outdoor. **Guest Services:** valet laundry. **Business Services:** fax (fee).
Cards: AX, MC, VI.

HOTEL POSADA DE LA ALDEA
Small-scale Hotel
Phone: 415/152-1022
All Year [BP]　　1P: $80　　2P: $100　　XP: $20
Location: 1 km s on Mex 49 (Celaya Hwy). Calle Ancha de San Antonio #15 37700 (Apdo Postal 410). Fax: 415/152-1296. **Facility:** 65 one-bedroom standard units. 3 stories, interior corridors. *Bath:* shower only. **Parking:** on-site. **Terms:** 5 day cancellation notice. **Pool(s):** heated outdoor, wading. **Leisure Activities:** 2 tennis courts. *Fee:* exercise room. **Guest Services:** valet laundry. **Business Services:** meeting rooms, fax (fee). **Cards:** AX, MC, VI.
SOME UNITS

HOTEL POSADA DE SAN FRANCISCO
Small-scale Hotel
Phone: (415)152-7213
All Year　　1P: $70-$90　　2P: $70-$90　　XP: $15　　F12
Location: N of main plaza; center. Plaza Principal #2 Centro 37700. Fax: 415/152-0072. **Facility:** 46 one-bedroom standard units. 3 stories, interior corridors. *Bath:* combo or shower only. **Parking:** valet. **Terms:** 3 day cancellation notice-fee imposed. **Guest Services:** gift shop, valet laundry. **Business Services:** meeting rooms, fax (fee). **Cards:** AX, MC, VI.

HOTEL VILLA JACARANDA　*Book at aaa.com*
Small-scale Hotel
Phone: (415)152-1015
All Year　　1P: $165　　2P: $210　　XP: $47　　F11
Location: 3 blks s of main plaza. Aldama 53 37700. Fax: 415/152-0883. **Facility:** 16 units. 8 one-bedroom standard units. 8 one-bedroom suites. 2 stories, interior/exterior corridors. **Parking:** on-site. **Terms:** 3 day cancellation notice, 30 day 12/15-4/15. **Amenities:** safes, hair dryers. **Dining:** restaurant, see separate listing. **Leisure Activities:** whirlpool. **Guest Services:** valet laundry. **Business Services:** meeting rooms, fax (fee). **Cards:** AX, MC, VI.
SOME UNITS
FEE

LA PUERTECITA BOUTIQUE OTEL'S SA DE CV　*Book at aaa.com*
Country Inn
Phone: (415)152-5011
All Year　　1P: $168-$480　　2P: $168-$480
Location: Jct Pedro Vargas (Queretero Hwy), 0.6 km e. Located in the affluent Atascadero neighborhood. Santo Domingo 75 37740. Fax: 415/152-5505. **Facility:** The property's picturesque gardens and waterfalls create a retreat-like ambience; many rooms feature fireplaces. Designated smoking area. 33 units. 25 one-bedroom standard units, some with whirlpools. 8 one-bedroom suites with whirlpools, some with whirlpools. 3 stories (no elevator), interior/exterior corridors. **Parking:** on-site. **Terms:** cancellation fee imposed. **Amenities:** safes, hair dryers. **Dining:** 8 am-10 pm, cocktails. **Pool(s):** outdoor, heated outdoor. **Leisure Activities:** whirlpool, library, exercise room. *Fee:* mountain bike tours, country club privileges offering golf, tennis, gym, walking tours, painting and Spanish instruction. **Guest Services:** valet laundry, area transportation-town center. **Business Services:** meeting rooms, fax (fee). **Cards:** AX, MC, VI.
SOME UNITS
FEE

RANCHO HOTEL SAKKARAH
Country Inn
Phone: (415)185-2061
All Year　　2P: $80-$100　　XP: $13
Location: 15 km n on San Miguel de Allende Dolores Hidalgo Hwy (Mex 51), 2 km e via signs. Located in a quiet area. (Apdo Postal 729). Fax: 415/185-2062. **Facility:** For those who want a real getaway, this hotel is located away from town and truly serves as an oasis as there is little else in the area. 8 one-bedroom standard units. 1 story, exterior corridors. *Bath:* shower only. **Parking:** on-site. **Terms:** 15 day cancellation notice. **Pool(s):** outdoor. **Leisure Activities:** whirlpool, fishing, basketball, volleyball. **Guest Services:** valet laundry. **Business Services:** conference facilities. **Cards:** AX, MC, VI.

VILLA MIRASOL HOTEL
Small-scale Hotel
Phone: (415)152-6685
All Year　　2P: $78-$110　　XP: $10
Location: Just sw of main plaza. Pila Seca #35 37700. Fax: 415/152-1564. **Facility:** Designated smoking area. 10 one-bedroom standard units. 2 stories (no elevator), exterior corridors. *Bath:* combo or shower only. **Parking:** street. **Terms:** 15 day cancellation notice-fee imposed. [MAP] meal plan available. **Guest Services:** sundries, valet laundry. **Business Services:** fax (fee). **Cards:** AX, MC, VI.
FEE

VILLA RIVERA HOTEL　*Book at aaa.com*
Small-scale Hotel
Phone: 415/152-2289
All Year　　1P: $176　　2P: $242　　XP: $30
Location: 1 blk s of main plaza; center. Cuadrante #3 37700. Fax: 415/152-2289. **Facility:** 12 one-bedroom standard units, some with whirlpools. 3 stories, interior/exterior corridors. **Parking:** valet. **Amenities:** honor bars, hair dryers. **Pool(s):** outdoor. **Leisure Activities:** *Fee:* massage. **Guest Services:** valet laundry. **Business Services:** fax (fee). **Cards:** MC, VI.

—— **WHERE TO DINE** ——

ANTIGUA TRATTORIA ITALIAN
Italian
Phone: 415/152-3790
Lunch: $8-$17　　**Dinner:** $8-$17
Location: 3 blks s of main plaza. CODO #9 37700. **Hours:** noon-11 pm. Closed: Wed & 5/15-5/31. **Reservations:** accepted. **Features:** Popular with the locals, the restaurant prepares a modest selection of pasta entrees in a friendly, laid-back, village-style atmosphere. Casual dress; cocktails. **Parking:** street. **Cards:** AX, DC, MC, VI.

BUGAMBILIA

Mexican

Lunch: $6-$15   **Dinner:** $8-$20   **Phone:** 415/154-5180

Location: Just n of main plaza; center. Hidalgo 42 37700. **Hours:** noon-11 pm. **Reservations:** accepted. **Features:** Attentive service, a casual atmosphere and evening entertainment only enhance the good food. Try such freshly prepared dishes as caldo Xochitl soup or the locally famous chili en nogada, with colors representing the Mexican flag. Casual dress; cocktails; entertainment. **Parking:** street. **Cards:** MC, VI.

CASA DE SIERRA NEVADA EN EL PARQUE   **Lunch:** $9-$22   **Dinner:** $9-$22   **Phone:** 415/152-7154

Mexican

Location: Just se of main plaza; in Casa de Sierra Nevada Quinta Real. Santa Elena 2. **Hours:** 8 am-11 pm. **Reservations:** suggested. **Features:** Mexican specialties are prepared in a colonial Mexican atmosphere. The dining room has an elegant feel, while the patio is tranquil. Weekend entertainment lends to the mood. Casual dress; cocktails. **Parking:** street. **Cards:** AX, MC, VI.

CASA PAYO-ARGENTINIAN GRILL   **Lunch:** $9-$16   **Dinner:** $9-$16   **Phone:** 415/152-7277

Argentine

Location: Southeast corner of Pila Seca; center. Zacateros 26 37700. **Hours:** 1 pm-11 pm. **Features:** Steaks are custom-cooked, and the portions are plentiful. With stars overhead and strolling musicians, the attractive courtyard dining area is charming. Casual dress; cocktails. **Parking:** street. **Cards:** AX, MC, VI.

EL PEGASO

International

Lunch: $4-$9   **Dinner:** $4-$9   **Phone:** 415/152-1351

Location: 1 blk w of main plaza; center. Corregidora #6 37700. **Hours:** 8:30 am-10 pm. Closed major holidays; also Sun. **Reservations:** accepted. **Features:** Few of the city's many restaurants offer the charming service for which this place is known—friendly and laid-back but with an eye and instinct for anticipating a diner's every need. The International menu offers something for everyone, including chicken enchiladas, Reubens, shark tacos, sushi and daily specials. Casual dress; cocktails. **Parking:** street. **Cards:** MC, VI.

EL TOMATO

Vegetarian

Lunch: $6-$8   **Dinner:** $6-$8   **Phone:** 415/151-6057

Location: Just n of main plaza. Mesones #62 A & B, Centro 37700. **Hours:** 9 am-9 pm. Closed: 1/1, 12/25; also Sun. **Reservations:** accepted. **Features:** The menu comprises simply prepared healthy and vegetarian foods. Daily specials, natural juices, smoothies, salads and unusual vegetarian burgers made from eggplant and spinach are just some of the offerings. Casual dress; beer & wine only. **Parking:** street.

HARRY'S NEW ORLEANS CAFE   **Lunch:** $7-$10   **Dinner:** $9-$25   **Phone:** 415/152-2645

Cajun

Location: Just n of main plaza; center. Hidalgo #12 37700. **Hours:** noon-midnight. **Reservations:** suggested. **Features:** Cajun fare served in stylish, contemporary surroundings offering a definite American experience. Casual dress; cocktails. **Parking:** street. **Cards:** AX, CB, DC, DS, MC, VI.

HECHO EN MEXICO   **Lunch:** $9-$11   **Dinner:** $9-$13   **Phone:** 415/154-6383

Mexican

Cards: MC, VI.

Location: 1 km s on Mex 49 (Celaya Hwy). Calle Ancha de San Antonio 8 37700. **Hours:** noon-10 pm. Closed: 1/1, 11/24, 12/25. **Features:** The bilingual staff greets guests with friendly smiles. Southern touches enhance such dishes as sweet potato casserole, which others, such as napoles and cactus salad, center on Mexican elements. Dessert portions are ample enough to share. Casual dress; cocktails. **Parking:** street.

LA CAPILLA

Continental

Lunch: $8-$30   **Dinner:** $17-$30   **Phone:** 415/152-0698

Parking: street. **Cards:** AX, MC, VI.

Location: 1 blk s of main plaza; center. Cuna de Allende 10 Centro Historico 37700. **Hours:** 1 pm-11 pm. Closed: Tues. **Reservations:** suggested. **Features:** In a restored 16th-century building, the restaurant is set against a Gothic-style church. The changing menu incorporates cuisine from Mexico as well as other countries. Al fresco dining on the upstairs terrace includes views of the mountains and church. Casual dress; cocktails.

L'INVITO

Italian

Lunch: $7-$14   **Dinner:** $7-$14   **Phone:** 415/152-7333

Location: 2 km s of plaza; in Instituto Allende. Calle Ancha de San Antonio #20 37700. **Hours:** 1 pm-midnight. **Reservations:** suggested. **Features:** The owner, who started cooking at age 4 with her Italian grandmother, prepares imported Italian pasta al dente, along with beef and chicken dishes, using extra virgin olive oil from Tuscany. A fireplace warms each of the intimate dining rooms on chilly nights. The restaurant is tucked quietly in a courtyard passage. Casual dress; cocktails. **Parking:** street. **Cards:** AX, CB, DC, DS, MC, VI.

NIRVANA

International

Lunch: $6-$12   **Dinner:** $10-$13   **Phone:** 415/150-0067

Location: Just w of main plaza; center. Canal #17 37700. **Hours:** 8 am-11 pm. Closed: 1/1, 12/25. **Reservations:** accepted. **Features:** Upscale decor and friendly, attentive service are found in the casual bistro. Chef Juan Carlos, who trained at the Culinary Institute of America, brings a fresh view to traditional regional foods. Casual dress; cocktails. **Parking:** street. **Cards:** MC, VI.

SIERRA NEVADA RESTAURANT   **Lunch:** $12-$20   **Dinner:** $12-$20   **Phone:** 415/152-7040

Continental

Cards: AX, MC, VI. **Historic**

Location: Just se of main plaza; in Casa de Sierra Nevada Quinta Real. Hospicio 35 37700. **Hours:** 8 am-11 pm. **Reservations:** required. **Features:** Most would never guess the eatery sits just east of the bustling main plaza; its lovely garden courtyard provides tranquility. For a more formal outing, request the dining room, where jackets are required. The Continental menu is diverse in its offerings, with such selections as chicken and squash crepes and desserts that highlight the chef's dedication to his art. Dressy casual; cocktails. **Parking:** street.

VILLA JACARANDA RESTAURANT **Lunch:** $8-$12   **Dinner:** $8-$12   **Phone:** 415/152-1015
▼▼▼▼
Continental
Location: 3 blks s of main plaza; in Hotel Villa Jacaranda. Aldama 53 37700. **Hours:** 8 am-10 pm. **Reservations:** suggested. **Features:** The menu lists a varied sampling of food, ranging from chicken Kiev and steak Tampiquena to shrimp bisque soup. The chef's meticulous preparation is award-winning. Casual dress; cocktails. **Parking:** on-site. **Cards:** AX, MC, VI.

SILAO, GUANAJUATO

——— WHERE TO STAY ———

HOLIDAY INN EXPRESS SILAO-AEROPUERTO
BAJIO   *Book at aaa.com*   **Phone:** (472)722-8000

▼▼▼▼	10/1-11/30 [ECP]	1P: $123	2P: $123	XP: $15	F12
	12/1-9/30 [ECP]	1P: $115	2P: $115	XP: $15	F12

Small-scale Hotel   **Location:** On Mex 45 at Silao exit. Libramiento Norte #3360 36169. **Fax:** 472/722-8020. **Facility:** Meets AAA guest room security requirements. 165 one-bedroom standard units. 5 stories, interior corridors. *Bath:* combo or shower only. **Parking:** on-site. **Terms:** cancellation fee imposed. **Amenities:** high-speed Internet, dual phone lines, voice mail, irons, hair dryers. **Pool(s):** heated indoor. **Leisure Activities:** exercise room. **Guest Services:** valet and coin laundry, area transportation. **Business Services:** meeting rooms, business center. **Cards:** AX, MC, VI.

SOME UNITS

TLAQUEPAQUE, JALISCO pop. 467,900

——— WHERE TO STAY ———

CASA DE LAS FLORES   **Phone:** (33)3659-3186
▼▼▼▼   All Year [BP]   2P: $88-$100
Bed & Breakfast
Location: 4 blks s of Plaza Hidalgo; center. Santos Degollado #175 45500. **Fax:** 33/3659-3186. **Facility:** Near the center of town, in a restored historic home, this B&B features colorful local decor and artwork; a well-cared-for garden is relaxing. 7 one-bedroom standard units. 2 stories (no elevator), exterior corridors. *Bath:* shower only. **Parking:** on-site. **Terms:** 14 day cancellation notice-fee imposed, [ECP] meal plan available. **Guest Services:** valet laundry. **Cards:** MC, VI.

SOME UNITS

LA VILLA DEL ENSUENO   **Phone:** (33)3635-8792
▼▼▼▼   All Year [ECP]   2P: $75-$120   XP: $15   F12
Bed & Breakfast
Location: 1 km w of El Parian. Florida 305 45500. **Fax:** 33/3659-6152. **Facility:** Although a wall makes the exterior of the property seem nondescript, the interior features fine examples of uniquely Mexican decor. 18 units. 14 one- and 4 two-bedroom standard units, some with efficiencies. 2 stories (no elevator), interior corridors. *Bath:* combo or shower only. **Parking:** on-site. **Terms:** 14 day cancellation notice, no pets allowed (owner's cats on premises). **Amenities:** *Some:* hair dryers. **Pool(s):** 2 heated outdoor. **Guest Services:** gift shop, valet laundry. **Cards:** AX, MC, VI.

SOME UNITS

QUINTA DON JOSE B&B HOTEL   **Phone:** 33/3635-7522
▼▼▼▼   All Year [BP]   1P: $65   2P: $90
Bed & Breakfast
Location: Center. Reforma #139 Centro 45500. **Fax:** 33/3659-9315. **Facility:** This in-town B&B has a variety of rooms from singles to family units; classical Mexican decor includes colorful tile, furniture and artwork. 14 units. 9 one-bedroom standard units. 4 one- and 1 two-bedroom suites ($105), some with efficiencies or kitchens. 2 stories (no elevator), interior/exterior corridors. *Bath:* combo or shower only. **Parking:** on-site. **Terms:** small pets only. **Pool(s):** outdoor. **Guest Services:** valet laundry. **Business Services:** PC. **Cards:** AX, MC, VI.

——— WHERE TO DINE ———

ADOBE RESTAURANTE & BAR   **Lunch:** $7-$12   **Phone:** 33/3657-2792
▼▼▼
Mexican
Location: Center. Francisco de Miranda #27 45500. **Hours:** noon-6:30 pm. Closed major holidays. **Reservations:** accepted. **Features:** Combined with a pottery and crafts shop, the colorful, lively restaurant and cantina serves large portions of well-prepared beef and chicken as well as a good selection of spirits. Casual dress; cocktails; entertainment. **Parking:** on-site (fee). **Cards:** MC, VI.

TUXPAN, MICHOACAN pop. 6,800

——— WHERE TO STAY ———

MOTEL QUINTA MITZI   **Phone:** 786/155-0112
▼▼   All Year   2P: $35   XP: $5
Motel
Location: 1.5 km se. Ave Morelos Sur S/N 61420. **Facility:** 9 one-bedroom standard units. 1 story, exterior corridors. *Bath:* shower only. **Parking:** on-site. **Terms:** 8 day cancellation notice. **Cards:** MC, VI.

URUAPAN, MICHOACAN pop. 229,400

———— WHERE TO STAY ————

HOTEL MANSION DEL CUPATITZIO
Phone: (452)523-2100

▼▼▼▼   All Year   1P: $115-$150   2P: $115-$150   XP: $15   F12
Location: 0.5 km se of Mex 37 on Calz Fray Juan de San Miguel. Calz de La Rodilla del Diablo #20 60000 (Apdo
Small-scale Hotel   Postal 63). Fax: 452/524-6772. **Facility:** 57 one-bedroom standard units. 2 stories, exterior corridors. *Bath:*
combo or shower only. **Parking:** on-site. **Terms:** 3 day cancellation notice-fee imposed. **Amenities:** hair
dryers. *Some:* safes, irons. **Pool(s):** heated outdoor. **Leisure Activities:** exercise room. **Guest Services:** gift shop, valet
laundry. **Business Services:** meeting rooms. **Cards:** AX, MC, VI.

SOME UNITS
⊞ 🍴 ⛨ ➥ Ⓚ / ⊟ ⊞

ZACATECAS, ZACATECAS pop. 115,700

———— WHERE TO STAY ————

HOTEL EMPORIO ZACATECAS   *Book at aaa.com*
Phone: 492/915-6500

▼▼▼▼   All Year   1P: $112   2P: $163   XP: $10   F12
Location: On Plaza de Armas; center. Located in historic district; opposite Cathedral and Governor's. Ave Hidalgo 703
Historic   98000. Fax: 492/922-6245. **Facility:** Many of the property's rooms overlook a courtyard with a fountain, while
Small-scale Hotel   some have patios. 113 one-bedroom standard units. 6 stories, interior corridors. *Bath:* combo or shower
only. **Parking:** on-site. **Amenities:** voice mail. **Guest Services:** gift shop, valet laundry. **Business**
Services: meeting rooms, business center. **Cards:** AX, MC, VI.

SOME UNITS
🍴 ⛨ 🏃 D Ⓚ ⚒ / ⊠ /

HOTEL HACIENDA DEL BOSQUE   *Book at aaa.com*
Phone: (492)924-6666

▼▼▼   All Year   1P: $95-$185   2P: $95-$185   XP: $13   F12
Location: 4 km ne of center on Guadalajara Rd; at crossroads on Hwy 54. Heroes de Chapultepec 801 98054.
Small-scale Hotel   Fax: 492/924-6666. **Facility:** 80 units. 79 one-bedroom standard units. 1 one-bedroom suite ($185) with
kitchen and whirlpool. 2 stories (no elevator), interior corridors. **Parking:** on-site. **Terms:** 30 day cancellation
notice-fee imposed. **Amenities:** irons, hair dryers. *Some:* honor bars. **Pool(s):** heated indoor. **Leisure Activities:** steamroom,
playground, exercise room. *Fee:* bicycles. **Guest Services:** gift shop, valet laundry, area transportation. **Business Services:**
meeting rooms, business center. **Cards:** AX, MC, VI.

SOME UNITS
✈ 🍴 ⊞ D ➥ ⊠ ⚒ [DATA PORT] ⊟ / ⊠ /

HOWARD JOHNSON PLAZA HOTEL   *Book at aaa.com*
Phone: 492/922-3311

▼▼ ▼▼   All Year   2P: $100-$120
Location: 3 blks s of cathedral, on Mex 45; center. (Blvd Lopez Mateos y Callejon del Barro). Fax: 492/922-3415.
Small-scale Hotel   **Facility:** Meets AAA guest room security requirements. 126 units. 114 one-bedroom standard units. 12 one-
bedroom suites, some with whirlpools. 5 stories, interior corridors. **Parking:** on-site. **Terms:** 21 day
cancellation notice-fee imposed. **Amenities:** hair dryers. **Pool(s):** small indoor. **Leisure Activities:** sauna, exercise room.
Guest Services: gift shop, valet laundry. **Business Services:** meeting rooms, business center. **Cards:** AX, MC, VI.

SOME UNITS
🍴 ⊞ S D ➥ ⚒ [DATA PORT] / ⊠ /

QUINTA REAL ZACATECAS   *Book at aaa.com*
Phone: (492)922-9104

▼▼▼ ▼▼▼   All Year   1P: $125-$160   2P: $125-$160   XP: $35   F12
Location: 5 blks w of cathedral; beside Elcubo Aqueduct on Ave Gonzalez Ortega. Ave Rayon 434 98000.
Small-scale Hotel   Fax: 492/922-8440. **Facility:** With its facade built around the ruins of an old bull ring, this hotel is considered
to be the most beautiful hotel in all of Mexico. 49 units. 38 one-bedroom standard units. 11 one-bedroom
suites ($750), some with whirlpools. 5 stories, interior corridors. **Parking:** on-site. **Terms:** 3 day cancellation notice, 15% service
charge. **Amenities:** voice mail, honor bars, irons, hair dryers. **Dining:** dining room, see separate listing. **Guest Services:** gift
shop, valet laundry. **Business Services:** meeting rooms, business center. **Cards:** AX, MC, VI.

[S D] 🍴 ⚒ [DATA PORT]

———— WHERE TO DINE ————

LOS DORADOS DE VILLA   **Dinner:** $4-$6
Phone: 492/922-5722

▼▼ ▼▼   **Location:** N of cathedral, next to Museo Rafael Coronel; center. Plazuela de Garcia #1314 98000. **Hours:** 3 pm-1
am. Closed: 1/1. **Reservations:** suggested. **Features:** For traditional northern Mexican cuisine, there is no
Mexican   better place. Try the enchiladas Zacatecanas to get a true taste of regional cuisine—as they say "When in
Rome...". The staff takes great pride in making menu items a la minute so sit back, relax, and rest assured it
will be worth the wait. Casual dress; beer only. **Parking:** street.

Ⓚ ⊠

QUINTA REAL DINING ROOM   **Lunch:** $10-$15   **Dinner:** $10-$20   **Phone:** 492/922-9104

▼▼▼   **Location:** 5 blks w of cathedral; beside Elcubo Aqueduct on Ave Gonzalez Ortega; in Quinta Real Zacatecas. Ave
Rayon 434 98000. **Hours:** 7 am-11 pm. **Reservations:** suggested. **Features:** The elegant, formal dining room
Continental   overlooks picturesque bull ring ruins. Featured on the menu are some seafood and Mexican items. Dressy
casual; cocktails. **Parking:** on-site. **Cards:** AX, MC, VI.

⊞ ⊠

SOUTHERN MEXICO

Oaxaca

This index helps you "spot" where approved accommodations and restaurants are located on the corresponding detailed maps. Lodging rate ranges are for comparison only and show the property's high season; rates are per night, unless only weekly (W) rates are available. Restaurant rate range is for dinner, unless only lunch (L) is served. Turn to the listing page for more detailed rate information and consult display ads for special promotions.

Spotter/Map Page Number	OA	OAXACA - Lodgings	Diamond Rating	Rate Range High Season	Listing Page
❶ / p. 519		Best Western Fortin Plaza	▽▽	$110-$120	518
❷ / p. 519	AAA	**Camino Real Oaxaca**	▽▽▽◆	$220-$360	518
❸ / p. 519		Casa Oaxaca	▽▽▽	$110-$196	518
❹ / p. 519		Casa Antiqua	▽▽▽	$100-$190	518
		OAXACA - Restaurants			
① / p. 519		El Asador Vasco	▽▽	$8-$24	519
③ / p. 519		La Flor de Oaxaca	▽	$4-$6	519

OAXACA, OAXACA pop. 257,000   (See map and index starting on p. 519)

──────── WHERE TO STAY ────────

BEST WESTERN FORTIN PLAZA   Phone: (951)515-7777   ❶
▽▽ ▽▽   All Year   1P: $110   2P: $120   XP: $10
Small-scale Hotel   **Location:** On north side; in Colonia Estrella on Mex 190. Ave Venus 118 68040. Fax: 951/515-1328. **Facility:** 92 one-bedroom standard units. 6 stories, interior/exterior corridors. *Bath:* combo or shower only. **Parking:** on-site. **Terms:** 3 day cancellation notice. **Amenities:** hair dryers. **Pool(s):** outdoor. **Guest Services:** valet laundry. **Business Services:** meeting rooms, business center. **Cards:** AX, DC, MC, VI.

SOME UNITS

CAMINO REAL OAXACA   *Book at aaa.com*   Phone: (951)501-6100   ❷
AAA   All Year   1P: $220-$360   2P: $220-$360   XP: $50   F18
▽▽▽ ▽▽▽   **Location:** 4 blks n of Zocalo; between Murguia and Abasolo sts; center. 5 de Mayo 300 68000. Fax: 951/516-0732.
Classic Historic   **Facility:** The picturesque 16th-century convent has colonnaded cloisters and a fountain courtyard; rooms
Country Inn   have high ceilings, colorful decor and modern amenities. 91 one-bedroom standard units. 2 stories (no elevator), interior/exterior corridors. **Parking:** on-site (fee) and valet. **Amenities:** voice mail, safes, honor bars, hair dryers. *Some:* irons. **Dining:** 7 am-11 pm, cocktails, entertainment. **Pool(s):** heated outdoor. **Guest Services:** gift shop, valet laundry. **Business Services:** conference facilities, fax (fee). **Cards:** AX, DC, MC, VI.

SOME UNITS

FEE

CASA ANTIQUA   Phone: 951/501-1240   ❹
▽▽▽▽   All Year   1P: $100-$190   2P: $100-$190   XP: $40
Small-scale Hotel   **Location:** In historic downtown. 5 de Mayo 206 68000. Fax: 951/501-1240. **Facility:** 15 units. 14 one-bedroom standard units. 1 one-bedroom suite with whirlpool. 2 stories, interior corridors. *Bath:* combo or shower only. **Parking:** street. **Amenities:** safes, hair dryers. **Cards:** AX, CB, DC, DS, MC, VI.

CASA OAXACA   *Book at aaa.com*   Phone: 951/514-4173   ❸
▽▽▽   All Year [BP]   1P: $110-$196   2P: $163-$196
Bed & Breakfast   **Location:** 4 blks n of Zocalo; in historic downtown. Garcia Vigil 407 68000. Fax: 951/516-4412. **Facility:** Rooms surround a lovely courtyard where local artists' work is displayed. The property's environment is very quiet and serene. Designated smoking area. 7 units. 6 one-bedroom standard units. 1 one-bedroom suite. 2 stories, interior corridors. *Bath:* combo or shower only. **Parking:** on-site. **Amenities:** safes, hair dryers. **Pool(s):** outdoor. **Leisure Activities:** sauna. *Fee:* massage. **Guest Services:** complimentary laundry. **Business Services:** business center. **Cards:** AX, MC, VI.

SOME UNITS

──────── *The following lodgings were either not evaluated or did not* ────────
meet AAA rating requirements but are listed for your information only.

LA CASA DE LOS MILAGROS   Phone: 951/501-2262
fyi   Not evaluated. **Location:** In historic downtown. Matamoros #500-C 68000. Facilities, services, and decor characterize a basic property.

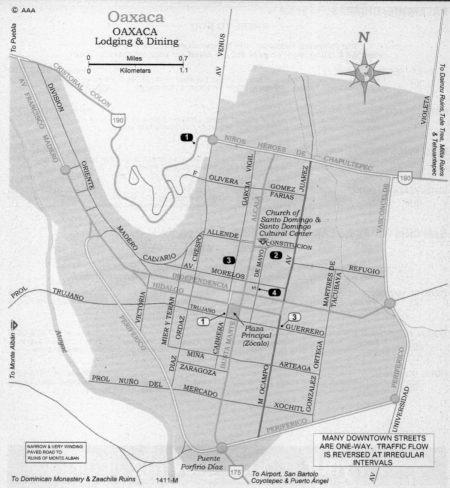

© AAA

Oaxaca

OAXACA
Lodging & Dining

Miles   0.7
Kilometers   1.1

N

To Puebla

MANY DOWNTOWN STREETS
ARE ONE-WAY. TRAFFIC FLOW
IS REVERSED AT IRREGULAR
INTERVALS

NARROW & VERY WINDING
PAVED ROAD TO
RUINS OF MONTE ALBAN

To Dominican Monastery & Zaachila Ruins   1411-M

*Puente
Porfirio Díaz*   175   To Airport, San Bartolo
Coyotepec & Puerto Ángel

LAS BUGAMBILIAS   **Phone:** 951/516-1165

[fyi]   Not evaluated. **Location:** In historic downtown. Reforma #402 68000. Facilities, services, and decor characterize a basic property.

PARADOR SAN MIGUEL   **Phone:** 951/514-9331

[fyi]   Not evaluated. **Location:** In historic downtown. Ave Independencia #503 68000. Facilities, services, and decor characterize a basic property.

─────── **WHERE TO DINE** ───────

EL ASADOR VASCO   **Lunch:** $5-$8   **Dinner:** $8-$24   **Phone:** 951/514-4755   ①

▼▼ ▼▼   **Location:** On west side of Zocalo. Portal de Flores #10A 68000. **Hours:** 1 pm-11:30 pm. **Reservations:** accepted.
Features: The restaurant enables guests to dine amid the entertaining surroundings of the Zocalo. On the
Regional Mexican   second floor of a historic building facing the main square, terrace seating is highly sought after on any given night. The menu's International influences provide variety. Service is consistent. Casual dress; cocktails.
Parking: no self-parking. **Cards:** AX, MC, VI.   ⏁ ⎇

LA FLOR DE OAXACA   **Lunch:** $4-$6   **Dinner:** $4-$6   **Phone:** 951/516-5522   ③

▼▼▼   **Location:** Just e of Zocalo; adjacent to chapel. Armenta y Lopez 311 68000. **Hours:** 8 am-10 pm, Sun 9 am-3 pm.
Features: Tucked away next to and a bit overshadowed by the adjacent church, the restaurant centers on
Regional Mexican   classic local dishes. Among simply prepared favorites are the varied moles for which this state is known. The environment is modest and casual. Casual dress; cocktails. **Parking:** no self-parking. **Cards:** DC, DS,
MC, VI.   ⎇

PALENQUE, CHIAPAS pop. 31,800

——— WHERE TO STAY ———

——— *The following lodgings were either not evaluated or did not* ———
meet AAA rating requirements but are listed for your information only.

CHAN-KAH RESORT VILLAGE   **Phone:** 916/345-1100
[fyi]   Not evaluated; located in area of political unrest. **Location:** 3.5 km on hwy to archaeological ruins. KM 3 Carr A
Las Ruinas 29960. Facilities, services, and decor characterize a basic property.

HOTEL CALINDA NUTUTUN PALENQUE   **Phone:** 916/345-0100
[fyi]   Not evaluated; located in area of political unrest. **Location:** 5 km s on Mex 199 to Agua Azul. KM 3.5 Carr
Palenque-Ocosingo 29960. Facilities, services, and decor characterize a basic property.

HOTEL MISION PALENQUE PARK PLAZA   **Phone:** 916/345-0241
[fyi]   Not evaluated; located in area of political unrest. **Location:** 4 blks e of center, follow signs. Rancho San Martin de
Porres 29960. Facilities, services, and decor characterize a mid-range property.

HOTEL PLAZA PALENQUE   **Phone:** 916/345-0555
[fyi]   Not evaluated; located in area of political unrest. **Location:** 1 km n on Mex 199. KM 27 Carr Caletaja-Palenque
29960 (Apdo Postal 58). Facilities, services, and decor characterize a mid-range property.

SAN CRISTOBAL DE LAS CASAS, CHIAPAS pop. 118,200

——— WHERE TO STAY ———

——— *The following lodgings were either not evaluated or did not* ———
meet AAA rating requirements but are listed for your information only.

DIEGO DE MAZARIEGOS HOTEL   **Phone:** 967/678-0833
[fyi]   Not evaluated; located in area of political unrest. **Location:** Just n of Parque Espinosa. Ma Adelina Flores 2
29240. Facilities, services, and decor characterize a mid-range property.

HOSTAL FLAMBOYANT ESPANOL   **Phone:** 967/678-0045
[fyi]   Not evaluated; located in area of political unrest. **Location:** In town; just n of Parque Espinosa. Ave 16 de
Septiembre y Primero 29200 (Apdo Postal 12). Facilities, services, and decor characterize an upscale property.

HOTEL BONAMPAK   **Phone:** 967/678-1621
[fyi]   Not evaluated; located in area of political unrest. **Location:** On Mex 190, north entrance to town at statue. Calzada
Mexico 5 29310 (Apdo Postal 75). Facilities, services, and decor characterize a basic property.

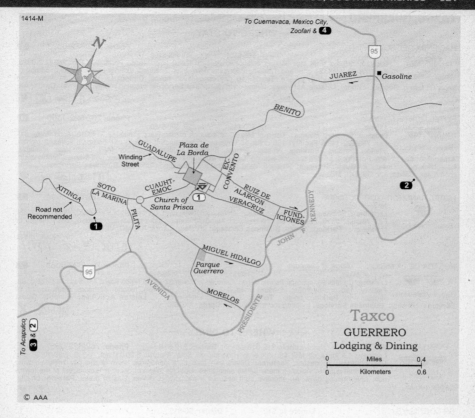

1414-M

To Cuernavaca, Mexico City,
Zoofari & **4**

95

JUAREZ ■ *Gasoline*

BENITO

GUADALUPE

Plaza de
La Borda

Winding
Street

EX-CONVENTO

2

SOTO
LA MARINA

CUAUHT-
EMOC

RUIZ DE
ALARCON
VERACRUZ

KENNEDY

XITINGA

Church of
Santa Prisca

1

FUND-
ICIONES

Road not
Recommended

1

PILITA

JOHN F.

MIGUEL HIDALGO

95

Parque
Guerrero

AVENIDA

MORELOS

PRESIDENTE

To Acapulco
3 & **2**

Taxco
GUERRERO
Lodging & Dining

| 0 | Miles | 0.4 |
| 0 | Kilometers | 0.6 |

© AAA

Taxco

This index helps you "spot" where approved accommodations and restaurants are located on the corresponding detailed maps. Lodging rate ranges are for comparison only and show the property's high season; rates are per night, unless only weekly (W) rates are available. Restaurant rate range is for dinner, unless only lunch (L) is served. Turn to the listing page for more detailed rate information and consult display ads for special promotions.

Spotter/Map Page Number	**TAXCO - Lodgings**	Diamond Rating	Rate Range High Season	Listing Page
1 / above	Hotel Rancho Taxco-Victoria	◈	$55-$80	522
2 / above	Posada de la Mision	◈ ◈	$140-$170	522
3 / above	Hacienda del Solar	◈ ◈	$65-$100	522
4 / above	Hotel Monte Taxco	◈ ◈	$90-$150	522

Spotter/Map Page Number	**TAXCO - Restaurants**	Diamond Rating	Rate Range High Season	Listing Page
① / above	Sr Costilla's	◈	$8-$15	522
② / above	La Ventana de Taxco	◈ ◈ ◈	$12-$18	522

TAXCO, GUERRERO pop. 51,500 (See map and index starting on p. 521)

------ WHERE TO STAY ------

HACIENDA DEL SOLAR　　　　　　　　　　　　　　　　Phone: 762/622-0323　**3**
All Year　　　　　　1P: $65-$100　　　　2P: $65-$100
Location: 3.5 km s off Mex 95, just e. Located opposite tourist office. (Apdo Postal 96). Fax: 762/622-0323.
Small-scale Hotel　**Facility:** 22 units. 21 one- and 1 two-bedroom standard units. 2 stories, exterior corridors. *Bath:* combo or shower only. **Parking:** on-site. **Terms:** 10 day cancellation notice. **Dining:** La Ventana de Taxco, see separate listing. **Pool(s):** outdoor. **Leisure Activities:** tennis court. **Business Services:** meeting rooms, fax (fee). **Cards:** AX, MC, VI.

HOTEL MONTE TAXCO　　　　　　　　　　　　　　　　Phone: 762/622-1300　**4**
All Year　　　　　　1P: $90-$150　　　　2P: $90-$150
Location: On steep mountain, just n of Mex 95 at entrance of city. Fracc Lomas de T 40210 (Apdo Postal 84).
Small-scale Hotel　Fax: 762/622-1428. **Facility:** 156 units. 153 one-bedroom standard units. 3 one-bedroom suites. 2 stories, interior corridors. **Parking:** on-site. **Terms:** 3 day cancellation notice, [AP] meal plan available. **Amenities:** hair dryers. **Pool(s):** 2 heated outdoor, wading. **Leisure Activities:** exercise room. *Fee:* golf-9 holes, tennis court, horseback riding, massage. **Guest Services:** gift shop, valet laundry, area transportation (fee). **Business Services:** meeting rooms, fax. **Cards:** AX, CB, DC, MC, VI.

HOTEL RANCHO TAXCO-VICTORIA　　　　　　　　　　Phone: 762/622-0004　**1**
All Year　　　　　　1P: $55-$80　　　　2P: $55-$80
Location: 2 1/2 blks s of Santa Prisca Church; on hill overlooking town. Carlos J Nibbi 5 y 7 40200 (Apdo Postal 83).
Small-scale Hotel　Fax: 762/622-0010. **Facility:** 64 one-bedroom standard units. 2 stories, exterior corridors. *Bath:* combo or shower only. **Parking:** on-site. **Business Services:** fax (fee). **Cards:** AX, MC, VI.

SOME UNITS

POSADA DE LA MISION　*Book at aaa.com*　　　　　　Phone: 762/622-0063　**2**
All Year [MAP]　　　　1P: $140-$170　　　2P: $140-$170　　XP: $20　　F12
Location: On Mex 95, opposite Pemex station. Cerro de la Mision 32 40230 (Apdo Postal 88). Fax: 762/622-2198.
Small-scale Hotel　**Facility:** 150 one-bedroom standard units. 1-3 stories (no elevator), exterior corridors. *Bath:* combo or shower only. **Parking:** on-site. **Terms:** 3 day cancellation notice. **Leisure Activities:** whirlpool. **Guest Services:** gift shop. **Business Services:** meeting rooms, fax (fee). **Cards:** AX, MC, VI.

------ WHERE TO DINE ------

LA VENTANA DE TAXCO　　**Lunch:** $12-$18　　**Dinner:** $12-$18　　Phone: 762/622-0587　**2**
Location: 3.5 km s off Mex 95, just e; in Hacienda del Solar. **Hours:** 8:30-11 am, 1-5 & 7:30-10:30 pm.
Continental　**Reservations:** suggested. **Features:** Diners can take in a panoramic view of the city while enjoying International cuisine, including many Italian specialties. Upscale Western decor is reminiscent of the town's rich, silver-mining days. An attentive staff ensures a memorable dinner. Casual dress. **Parking:** on-site.
Cards: AX, MC, VI.

SR COSTILLA'S　　　　**Lunch:** $7-$12　　　**Dinner:** $8-$15　　Phone: 762/622-3215　**1**
Location: Downtown; overlooking main plaza. **Hours:** noon-midnight. **Features:** Rustic decor and an informal atmosphere characterize this laid-back spot, which has many balcony tables overlooking the town square.
Traditional American　Menu specialties are barbecue chicken, steak and ribs. The young wait staff is energetic and friendly. Casual dress; cocktails. **Parking:** no self-parking. **Cards:** MC, VI.

TUXTLA GUTIERREZ, CHIAPAS pop. 445,100

------ WHERE TO STAY ------

------ *The following lodgings were either not evaluated or did not meet AAA rating requirements but are listed for your information only.* ------

CAMINO REAL TUXTLA GUTIERREZ　　　　　　　　　　Phone: 961/617-7777
[fyi]　Not evaluated. **Location:** 1.5 mi e. #1195 Blvd Belisario Dominguez 29060. Facilities, services, and decor characterize an upscale property.

HOLIDAY INN　　　　　　　　　　　　　　　　　　　Phone: 961/615-0888
[fyi]　Not evaluated. **Location:** 4.5 km w on Mex 190. Blvd Belisario Dominguez 29000. Facilities, services, and decor characterize an upscale property.

------ WHERE TO DINE ------

------ *The following restaurant has not been evaluated by AAA but is listed for your information only.* ------

MONTEBELLO　　　　　　　　　　　　　　　　　　　Phone: 961/617-7777
[fyi]　Not evaluated. **Location:** 1.5 mi e; in Camino Real Tuxtla Guitierfor. #1195 Blvd Belisario Dominguez 29060.
Features: Contemporary decor and a high degree of tableside service characterize this comfortably upscale restaurant. Ingredients are blended in complex compositions—ranging from regional Yucatan or Chapeneco dishes to more Continental selections—that are presented artistically.

VERACRUZ, VERACRUZ pop. 544,800

——— WHERE TO STAY ———

CROWNE PLAZA VERACRUZ TORREMAR

Phone: (229)989-2100

All Year 1P: $144 2P: $144 XP: $20 F12

Location: 8 km sw from Plaza de Armas on Blvd Veracruz Mocambo. Located on the beach. Blvd Aldolfo Ruiz Cortines 4300 94260. Fax: 229/989-2121. **Facility:** Meets AAA guest room security requirements. 230 units. 210 one-bedroom standard units. 20 one-bedroom suites, some with whirlpools. 9 stories, interior/exterior corridors. Large-scale Hotel **Parking:** on-site. **Terms:** cancellation fee imposed. **Amenities:** CD players, high-speed Internet, voice mail, safes, honor bars, irons, hair dryers. **Dining:** 2 restaurants, 7 am-11 pm, nightclub, entertainment. **Pool(s):** 2 outdoor, wading. **Leisure Activities:** playground, exercise room. *Fee:* sailboats, windsurfing, massage. **Guest Services:** gift shop, valet laundry, area transportation-Veracruz World Trade Center. **Business Services:** conference facilities, business center. **Cards:** AX, MC, VI.

SOME UNITS

FIESTA AMERICANA VERACRUZ *Book at aaa.com*

Phone: (229)989-8989

All Year 1P: $120-$200 2P: $120-$200 XP: $10 F17

Location: 6 km sw from Plaza de Armas on Ave Avila Camacho. Located on the beach, in modern, commercial area. Prol Blvd Avila Camacho 94299. Fax: 229/922-4343. **Facility:** Located on the beach in an upscale area of town, this is a full service business and resort hotel. The friendly staff is bilingual. 233 units. 209 one-Large-scale Hotel bedroom standard units. 23 one- and 1 two-bedroom suites ($180-$400), some with whirlpools. 7 stories, interior corridors. **Parking:** on-site and valet. **Amenities:** video games (fee), voice mail, safes, honor bars, irons, hair dryers. *Some:* CD players. **Dining:** 3 restaurants, 7 am-midnight, entertainment. **Pool(s):** heated indoor/outdoor, wading. **Leisure Activities:** sauna, bicycles, exercise room. *Fee:* charter fishing, massage. **Guest Services:** gift shop, valet laundry. **Business Services:** meeting rooms, business center. **Cards:** AX, DC, MC, VI. *(See color ad card insert)*

SOME UNITS

FEE

HOTEL VERACRUZ *Book at aaa.com*

Phone: (229)931-2233

All Year 1P: $60-$85 2P: $60-$85 XP: $8 F12

Location: Jct Ave Independencia at M Lerdo St. Located in a busy commercial area. Ave Independencia S/N Esquina Small-scale Hotel Mig 91700. Fax: 229/931-5134. **Facility:** 116 one-bedroom standard units. 6 stories, interior corridors. *Bath:* shower only. **Parking:** on-site and valet. **Terms:** [CP] meal plan available. **Amenities:** hair dryers. **Guest Services:** valet laundry. **Business Services:** *Fee:* PC, fax. **Cards:** AX, MC, VI.

SOME UNITS

VILLAHERMOSA, TABASCO pop. 342,200

——— WHERE TO STAY ———

——— *The following lodgings were either not evaluated or did not* ———
meet AAA rating requirements but are listed for your information only.

CALINDA VIVA SPA VILLAHERMOSA

Phone: 993/315-0000

Not evaluated. **Location:** 1.5 km n on Mex 180; near Tabasco 2000 Commercial Complex. Adolfo Ruiz Cortinez con Paseo 86050. Facilities, services, and decor characterize a mid-range property.

CAMINO REAL VILLAHERMOSA

Phone: 993/316-4400

Not evaluated. **Location:** 1.5 km n on Mex 180; in Tabasco 2000 Commercial Complex. Ave Paseo Tabasco 1407 86030. Facilities, services, and decor characterize an upscale property.

HOTEL HYATT REGENCY VILLAHERMOSA

Phone: 993/315-1234

Not evaluated. **Location:** 1.5 km n on Mex 180; near Tabasco 2000 Commercial Complex. (Ave Juarez 106, LINDAVISTA, CL, 86050). Facilities, services, and decor characterize an upscale property.

——— WHERE TO DINE ———

——— *The following restaurant has not been evaluated by AAA* ———
but is listed for your information only.

BOUGANVILLAS RESTAURANT

Phone: 993/315-1234

Not evaluated. **Location:** 1.5 km n on Mex 180; near Tabasco 2000 Commercial Complex; in Hotel Hyatt Regency Villahermosa. Ave Juarez 106 86050. **Features:** Elegant continental dining.

Club Contacts in Mexico

The Asociación Mexicana Automovilística (Mexican Automobile Association, or AMA) has nine club offices throughout Mexico that are able to assist visiting AAA/CAA members; for information phone (55) 5242-0262 in Mexico City, or (800) 010-7100 (toll-free long distance within Mexico). AMA headquarters is located at Av. Orizaba #7 at Avenida Chapultepec, just outside the Zona Rosa in the Roma neighborhood (M: Insurgentes, line 1).

As part of AAA's "Show Your Card & Save" program and a SYC&S alliance between AAA/CAA and AMA, U.S. and Canadian members can enjoy savings from Mexicana Airlines, Tony Roma restaurants and Six Flags of Mexico. AMA is continuously expanding the number of "Ahorra con AMA" (SYC&S) program partners; for up-to-date information members can visit the SYC&S section of www.aaa.com on their local club's Web site.

Speaking of Spanish

ON THE FOLLOWING PAGES are listed some of the Spanish phrases and sentences that are most useful to an English-speaking visitor in Mexico. Although not essential, a basic knowledge of the language will be helpful. Most Mexicans who deal with tourists speak at least some English, and those who don't will be only too glad to help you along with your attempts at Spanish. Fortunately, the language is not that difficult to speak. A little study of the following rules of pronunciation will be sufficient to make yourself understood.

Even if your knowledge of Spanish is rudimentary, using such everyday expressions as por favor (please), gracias (thank you), buenos días (good morning), buenas tardes (good afternoon) and buenas noches (good evening) shows respect. Mexicans are very polite and use these terms all the time; you should also. Good manners mean more than being able to speak the language fluently.

Pronunciation

The pronunciation of the Spanish language presents very few difficulties. The spelling is almost phonetic; nearly every letter has one sound that it retains at all times.

Vowels

A—pronounced as "a" in father.
E—pronounced as "e" in them.
I—pronounced as "e" in me.
O—pronounced as "o" in hold.
U—pronounced as "oo" in food.

Consonants

Consonants do not differ materially from those in English. The few differences are as follows:

b and v—in Mexico are pronounced as in "boy."

c—is pronounced with an "s" sound before e and i. Otherwise it has a "k" sound. Ex. cinco—seen-koh.

g—is soft, like a strong English "h," when it precedes e and i. Ex. gente—hente. In all other cases, it is a hard "g" as in go. Ex. gato—gahtoh. If gu precedes an e or i, the "g" has a hard sound and the "u" is not pronounced. Ex. guerra—geh-rah, guiso—geeh-so. If the "u" has an umlaut it is pronounced güera—gweh-rah, güiro—gwee-roh.

h—always silent, except after c, which makes a "ch" sound as in English.

j—pronounced like the English "h."

ll—pronounced like the English "y." Ex. caballo—kah-BAH-yo.

ñ—combination of "n" and "y," like cognac. Ex. niño—neenyoh.

qu—pronounced like "k." Ex. que—keh.

r—in Mexico the "r" is trilled; the "r" at the beginning of a word and the double "rr" are trilled quite strongly.

x—pronounced as in English, and also pronounced like the English "s" as in Xochimilco (soh-chih-MEEL-coh), and the English "h," as in México (ME-hee-coh). In Mexico "x" also is used to represent the "sh" sound in native languages, as in Xel-Há (Shehl-AH).

z—in Mexico is always pronounced like the English "s."

ch, ll, ñ—these are all letters in the Spanish alphabet and are found after the single letter: "ch" after "c," "ll" after "l," "ñ" after "n."

Diphthongs

Spanish diphthongs are pronounced as very swift omissions of the component vowels.

Ex. "ue" as in weh—fuente.
Ex. "au" as in English ouch—gaucho.

Accent or Stress

1. The stress falls on the next to the last syllable when a word ends in a vowel, "n" or "s."
Ex. hombre—OHM-breh.
Ex. hablan—AH-blahn.
Ex. estos—EHS-tos.

2. The stress falls on the last syllable when the word ends in a consonant other than "n" or "s."
Ex. hablar—ah-BLAR.

3. In some cases an accent mark will be found over a vowel. This does not change the pronunciation of that vowel but indicates that the stress falls on that syllable.
Ex. gramática—grah-MAH-teeh-cah.

Words and Phrases

Note: All nouns in Spanish are either masculine or feminine, and there are two words meaning "the": *el* is used before masculine nouns, *la* before feminine nouns. Masculine words end with an *o*, feminine words end with an *a* (although there are a few exceptions). An adjective agrees in gender with the noun it modifies. The plural of *el* is *los*, of *la* is *las*. After words given on these pages the gender is indicated by (m.) for masculine, (f.) for feminine. For instance, say *el hotel* and *los hoteles; la posada* and *las posadas*. The word *"usted,"* meaning "you," is always abbreviated *Ud.* (*Vd.* in old writings).

Language

Do you understand English?	¿Entiende Ud. el inglés?
I do not speak Spanish	No hablo español.
Yes, sir; no, madam	Sí, señor; no, señora.
Very little	Muy poco.
I do not understand	No entiendo.
Do you understand me?	¿Me entiende Ud.?
Please speak slowly	Por favor hable despacio.
I wish to speak with an interpreter	Quisiera hablar con un intérprete.
What did you say?	¿Cómo dice?

Polite Phrases

Good morning	Buenos días.
Good afternoon	Buenas tardes.
Good night	Buenas noches.
Goodbye; see you later	Adios; hasta la vista.
Thank you	Gracias.
Yes; very good	Sí; muy bien.
Please	Por favor.
Excuse me	Perdóneme.
I am very sorry	Lo siento mucho.

To Explain Your Needs

I need; we need	Necesito; necesitamos.
I would like to telephone	Quisiera telefonear.
I am hungry; we are hungry	Tengo hambre; tenemos hambre.
I am thirsty; we are thirsty	Tengo sed; tenemos sed.
I am cold; we are cold	Tengo frío; tenemos frío.
I am warm; we are warm	Tengo calor; tenemos calor.
I am tired; we are tired	Estoy cansado; estamos cansados.
I am sick; we are sick	Estoy enfermo; estamos enfermos.
The child is sick; tired	El niño (la niña) está enfermo (a); cansado (a).
Men's room, ladies' room	El baño de hombres, de damas.
Fire	Fuego (m.).
Help	Auxilio; socorro (m.).

Time

today	hoy
the morning	a mañana
tomorrow	mañana
noon	el mediodía
yesterday	ayer
the afternoon	la tarde

tonight	esta noche
night	la noche
last night	anoche
midnight	la media noche
What time is it?	¿Qué hora es?
It is one o'clock	Es la una.
It is ten minutes past two	Son las dos y diez.
It is quarter past three	Son las tres y cuarto.
It is a quarter of five	Es un cuarto para las cinco.
It is 25 minutes of six	Son veinticinco para las seis.
It is half past four	Son las cuatro y media.

Days of the Week

Sunday	domingo (m.)
Monday	lunes (m.)
Tuesday	martes (m.)
Wednesday	miércoles (m.)
Thursday	jueves (m.)
Friday	viernes (m.)
Saturday	sábado (m.)

Months of the Year

January	enero (m.)
February	febrero (m.)
March	marzo (m.)
April	abril (m.)
May	mayo (m.)
June	junio (m.)
July	julio (m.)
August	agosto (m.)
September	septiembre (m.)
October	octubre (m.)
November	noviembre (m.)
December	diciembre (m.)

Colors

white	blanco
black	negro
gray	gris
brown	café
red	rojo
pink	rosa
blue; dark blue	azul; azul oscuro
green; light green	verde; verde claro
purple	morado
yellow	amarillo

Useful Adjectives

Note: These adjectives are in their masculine forms. End them with an "a" if you want the feminine form (except for grande, tarde and fácil, which are used for both genders).

bad	malo
high	alto
beautiful	bello
kind	bondadoso
cheap	barato.
large	grande
clean	limpio
late	tarde
difficult	difícil
low	bajo
dirty	sucio
polite	cortés
early	temprano
sharp	agudo
easy	fácil
slow	lento
expensive	caro

small	pequeño
fast	rápido
ugly	feo
good	bueno
unkind	despiadado, duro
long	largo
short	corto
narrow	angosto
dangerous	peligroso

Numerals

1. uno	8. ocho	15. quince	30. treinta
2. dos	9. nueve	16. diez y seis	31. treinta y uno
3. tres	10. diez	17. diez y siete	40. cuarenta
4. cuatro	11. once	18. diez y ocho	50. cincuenta
5. cinco	12. doce	19. diez y nueve	60. sesenta
6. seis	13. trece	20. veinte	70. setenta
7. siete	14. catorce	21. veintiuno	80. ochenta

90. noventa
100. cien
200. doscientos
500. quinientos
1,000. mil
1,000,000. un millón

Points of the Compass

north ....norte (m.)   south ....sur (m.)   east ....este (m.)   west ....oeste (m.)
Note: In addresses, east is oriente, abbreviated Ote.; west is poniente, abbreviated Pte.

At the Border

passport	pasaporte
tourist card	tarjeta de turista
age	edad
marital status	estado civil
single	soltero
married	casado
widowed	viudo
divorced	divorciado
profession or occupation	profesión; ocupación
vaccination card	certificado de vacuna
car owner's title (registration)	título de propiedad (registro)
driver's license	licencia de manejar
year of car	modelo (o año)
make (Ford, Plymouth, etc.)	marca
license plate number and state	número y estado de placa
chassis and motor number	número de chasis y motor
number of doors	número de puertas
number of cylinders	número de cilindros
number of passengers	número de pasajeros

On the Road

highway	carretera (f.)
road	camino (m.)
street	calle (f.)
avenue	avenida (f.)
boulevard	bulevar (m.)
corner	esquina (f.)
kilometer	kilómetro (m.)
block	cuadra (f.)
left side	lado izquierdo (m.)
right side	lado derecho (m.)

Please show me the road to	Enséñeme el camino a...
How far is?	¿Qué tan lejos está...
Can we get to.. .before dark?	¿Podemos llegar a.. . .antes del anochecer?
Is this road dangerous?	¿Es peligroso este camino?
Is that road in good condition?	¿Está en buen estado ese camino?
Is it paved or is it a dirt road?	¿Está pavimentado o es de tierra?
Go straight ahead.	Siga adelante.
Turn to the right; left.	Vuelta a la derecha; izquierda.
What city, town, is this?	¿Qué ciudad, pueblo, es éste?
Where does this road lead?	¿A dónde va este camino?

In Case of Car Trouble

I want to ask you a favor.	Quiero pedirle un favor.
My car broke down.	Se me descompuso el carro.
I need a tow truck.	Necesito una grúa.
My lights don't work.	Mis faros no funcionan.
My engine's overheating.	Mi motor se está sobrecalentando.
I have run out of gasoline.	Se me acabó la gasolina.
Is there a gasoline station near here?	¿Hay alguna gasolinería cerca de aquí?
Is there a garage near here?	¿Hay algún taller cerca?
Please send a mechanic.	Por favor mándeme un mecánico.
May I go with you to get a mechanic?	¿Puedo ir con usted a conseguir un mecánico?
Do you have a rope to tow my car?	¿Tiene un cable para remolcar mi carro?
The starter does not work.	El arranque no funciona.
Can you help me push the car to one side of the road?	¿Puede ayudarme a empujar el coche a un lado del camino?
Do you want to be my witness?	¿Quiere ser mi testigo?
Do you want to help me change a tire?	¿Quiere ayudarme a cambiar una llanta?

Arriving in Town

Is English spoken here?	¿Se habla inglés aquí?
Where is the center of town?	¿Dónde está el centro de la ciudad?
May I park here?	¿Puedo estacionarme aquí?
Could you recommend a good restaurant; a good small hotel; a first class hotel?	¿Puede Ud. recomendar un buen restaurante; unbuen hotel pequeño; un hotel de primera clase?
Please direct me to the nearest post office	Por favor diríjame a la oficina de correos mas cercana.
I wish to telephone, to telegraph, to cable	Quiero telefonear, telegrafiar, cablegrafiar.
Please direct me to the railroad station, the bus station	Por favor diríjame a la estación del ferrocarril, a la estación del autobús.
Where is X Street, X Square, the X Hotel?	¿Dónde está la Calle X, la Plaza X, el Hotel X?
How often does the bus go by?	¿Que tan seguido pasa el autobús?
Does the streetcar stop here?	¿Para aquí el tranvía?
I wish to change some money.	Quiero cambiar dinero.
What is the rate of exchange?	¿Cuál es el tipo de cambio?
I want to cash a check.	Quiero cambiar un cheque.
I have lost my traveler's checks.	He perdido mis cheques de viajero.
Where can I find a policeman, a hairdresser, a doctor, a drug store?	¿Dónde puedo hallar un policía, un peinador, un médico, una farmacia?
Where is the police station; the chamber of commerce; the automobile club?	¿Dónde está la comisaría, la cámara de comerciola asociación automovilística?,
Where can I find guidebooks, road maps, postcards, American newspapers?	¿Dónde se pueden hallar guías turísticas, mapas de carreteras, tarjetas postales, periódicos norteamericanos?

At the Hotel

hotel	hotel (m.)
inn	posada (f.)
guesthouse	casa de huéspedes (f.)
apartment house	apartamentos (m.)
furnished room	cuarto amueblado (m.)
stairway	escalera (f.)
bedroom	recámara (f.)
bathroom	cuarto de baño (m.)
kitchen	cocina (f.)
towel	toalla (f.)
washcloth	toallita facial (f.)
soap	jabón (m.)
air conditioning	aire acondicionado
room	cuarto (m.)
hot water	agua caliente
office	oficina (f.)
elevator	elevador (m.)

dining room	comedor (m.)
guest	huésped (m.)
manager	gerente
office employee	empleado de oficina
maid	camarera (f.)
key	llave (f.)
porter	mozo (m.) de servicios
bellboy	botones (m.)
ice water	agua con hielo

I want a single room, with bath	Deseo un cuarto para una persona, con baño.
I want a room for two, with twin beds	Deseo un cuarto para dos, con camas gemelas.
I want two connecting rooms	Deseo dos cuartos comunicados.
On the lower floor; upper floor	En el piso bajo; piso alto.
A front room; a back room	Un cuarto al frente; al fondo.
Do you have hot running water?	¿Hay agua corriente y caliente?
What is the price?	¿Cuál es el precio?
What is the minimum rate?	¿Cuál es el precio mínimo?
Do you accept checks in payment?	¿Acepta Ud. cheques en pago?
Is there a arage?	¿Hay garage?
Please call me at six o'clock	Hágame el favor de llamarme a las seis.
Where is the ladies' room, men's room?	¿Dónde está el lavabo de señoras, de señores?
Will you have the baggage brought up? down?	¿Quiere Ud. hacer subir.. . .bajar el equipaje?
We are leaving tomorrow	Partimos mañana.
We are staying several days.. .Just tonight	Nos quedaremos aquí unos pocos días.. . .solamente esta noche.
Please send these clothes to the laundry	Hágame el favor de mandar esta ropa a la lavandería.
Please clean and press this suit	Hágame el favor de limpiar y planchar este traje.
I want it today; tomorrow.	Lo quiero hoy; mañana.
Where is a barber shop?	¿Dónde hay una peluquería?
I wish my bill, please.	Quiero mi cuenta, por favor.
Please forward my correspondence to this address.	Por favor reexpida mi correspondencia a esta dirección.
Do you want to prepare a lunch for us to carry with us?	¿Quiere Ud. prepararnos un almuerzo para llevárnoslo?

At the Garage

Fill up the gasoline tank; the radiator	Llene el tanque de gasolina; el radiador.
Give me five, ten, fifteen, twenty liters	Deme cinco, diez, quince, veinte litros.
Do you have unleaded gasoline?	¿Tiene gasolina sin plomo?
How much is gasoline per liter?	¿Cuánto vale el litro de gasolina?
Check the oil; change the oil, antifreeze	Vea el aceite; cambie el aceite, anticongelante.
Please lubricate the car; wash the car	Favor de lubricar el automóvil; lavar el automóvil.
Please tighten the brakes; adjust the brakes	Favor de apretar los frenos; ajustar los frenos.
Please tune the engine; change the spark plugs	Favor de afinarme el motor; cambiar las bujías.
My tire has a puncture. Can you repair it?	Mi llanta está picada. ¿Puede repararla?
The tire is flat.	La llanta está desinflada.
Put water in the battery.	Por favor, pónga agua en la batería.
The horn is not working.	La bocina no funciona.
The battery needs charging	La batería necesita carga.
Please replace this headlamp	Por favor, cámbieme este farol.
the fan belt	la banda del ventilador.
the radiator hose	la manguera del radiador.
The gas line is clogged	La tubería de gasolina está tapada.
My engine's overheating	Mi motor se está sobrecalentando.
The exhaust is choked	Está obstruido el tubo de escape.
The steering gear is out of order	La dirección está descompuesta.
The radiator leaks	El radiador gotea.
The clutch slips	El clutch se derrapa.
The gasoline tank is leaking	El tanque de gasolina está goteando.
There is a short circuit	Hay un cortocircuito.
The windshield wiper does not work	El limpiavidrios del parabrisa no funciona.
The taillight does not work	La calavera no funciona.
The water pump does not work	La bomba de agua no funciona.
Please clean the windshield	Favor de limpiar el parabrisa.
When will the repairs be finished?	¿Cuándo terminará la reparación?

How much do I owe you? .... ¿Cuánto le debo?

In Restaurants

breakfast ....desayuno (m.)
lunch ....almuerzo (m.)
midday meal ....comida (f.)
dinner; supper ....cena (f.); merienda (f.)
spoon ....cuchara (f.)
cup ....taza (f.)
glass ....vaso (m.)
napkin ....servilleta (f.)
bill ....cuenta (f.)
tip ....propina (f.)
knife ....cuchillo (m.)
fork ....tenedor (m.)

Meat, Eggs, Fish

bacon ....tocino (m.)
beef ....carne (f.) de res (m.)
beefsteak ....bistec (m.)
chicken ....pollo (m.)
duck ....pato (m.)
egg ....huevo (m.)
fried ....frito
soft-boiled ....tibio
hard-boiled ....duro
fish ....pescado (m.)
ham ....jamón (m.)
lamb ....carne (f.) de carnero (m.)
lamb chops ....chuletas (f.) de carnero (m.)
meat ....carne (f.)
omelet ....omelete de huevo (m.)
pork ....carne (f.) de puerco (m.)
roast ....asado (m.)
sausage ....salchicha (f.)
turkey ....guajolote (m.); pavo (m.)
veal ....ternera (f.)

Vegetables

salad ....ensalada (f.)
beans ....frijoles (m.)
beets ....betabeles (f.)
cabbage ....repollo (m.); col (f.)
corn; young corn ....maíz (m.); elote (m.)
lettuce ....lechuga (f.)
onion ....cebolla (f.)
peas ....chícharos (m.)
potatoes ....papas (f.)
rice ....arroz (m.)
string beans ....ejotes (m.)
sweet potatoes ....camotes (m.)
tomatoes ....jitomates (m.)
vegetables ....legumbres (f.); verduras (f.)

Bread

bread ....pan (m.)
crackers ....galletas (f.)
toast ....pan tostado (m.)

Beverages, Liquors

beer ....cerveza (f.)
brandy ....brandy (m.)
coffee ....café (m.)
with cream ....con crema (f.)
without cream ....sin crema
gin ....ginebra (f.)
juice ....jugo (m.)

milk ....leche (f.)
rum ....ron (m.)
tea ....té (m.)
whiskey ....whisky (m.)
table wine ....vino de mesa (m.)

Sweets

dessert ....postre (m.)
sweet rolls ....pan dulce (m.)
cake ....pastel (m.)
candies ....dulces (m.)
cookies ....galletas (f.)
custard ....flan (m.)
ice cream ....helado (m.)
sherbets ....nieves (f.)
pastries ....pasteles (m.)
pie ....pastel (m.)

Fruits, Nuts

apple ....manzana (f.)
avocado ....aguacate (m.)
banana ....plátano (m.)
cantaloupe ....melón (m.)
figs ....higos (m.)
fruit ....fruta (f.)
grapes ....uvas (f.)
guava ....guayaba (f.)
grapefruit ....toronja (f.)
lemon ....limón amarillo (m.)
lime (sweet) ....limón (m.)
nuts ....nueces (f.)
olives ....aceitunas (f.)
orange ....naranja (f.)
peach ....durazno (m.)
peanuts ....cacahuates (m.)
pecans ....nueces (f.)
pineapple ....piña (f.)
strawberries ....fresas (f.)
walnut ....nuez (f.) de castilla
watermelon ....sandía (f.)

Miscellaneous

sugar ....azúcar (m.)
salt ....sal (f.)
pepper ....pimienta (f.)
butter ....mantequilla (f.)
soup; broth ....sopa (f.); caldo (m.)
cheese ....queso (m.)
honey ....miel de abejas (f.)
cigarette; cigar ....cigarrillo (m.); puro (m.)
Please bring me the menu ....Por favor tráigame el menú.
I like my meat rare, medium, well done ....Quiero la carne roja, término medio, bien cocida

Fiestas and Holidays

NOTE: The dates listed here for local celebrations are often variable and may be moved forward or back when the fiesta must be celebrated on a specific day of the week or time of the month or year. Confirm dates in advance with your hotel, at a local tourist information office or at city hall. For background information about widely observed events, *see* *"Celebrations," p. 42.*

National Holidays

All banks and most businesses close on these days.

Jan. 1	New Year's Day (Año Nuevo)
Feb. 5	Constitution Day (Día de la Constitución) commemorates the Constitutions of 1857 and 1917, by which Mexico is now governed.
Mar. 21	Birthday of Benito Juárez, Mexican president and national hero.
May 1	Labor Day (Día del Trabajo), with workers' parades throughout the country.
May 5	Battle of Puebla (Batalla de Puebla), commonly known as Cinco de Mayo, commemorates the Mexican victory over the French at Puebla in 1862.
Sept. 1	The president of Mexico delivers the annual State of the Nation Address (Informe Presidencial).
Sept. 16	Independence Day (Día de la Independencia). The president presides at the ceremony of the *Grito de Dolores* in Mexico City's *Zócalo;* or sometimes at the parish church in Dolores Hidalgo, Gto., where Father Miguel Hidalgo y Costilla issued the *Grito* in 1810. Special celebrations take place in each state capital and start the night of Sept. 15.
Oct. 12	Discovery of the New World by Christopher Columbus, known as Día de la Raza (Day of the Race).
Dec. 25	Christmas Day (Navidad). Plays, religious ceremonies.

Fiestas and Fairs in Mexico

The following fiestas and holiday periods are celebrated in many parts of the country.

Jan. 6	Day of the Three Kings (Día de Los Reyes Magos) features an exchange of gifts as on Christmas in other parts of the world. This also is the day when *Rosca de Los Reyes* (King's Loaf) is served. The round, doughnut-like cake has a plastic doll inside; if you are served the slice containing the doll, tradition says you must host a party on Candlemas Day.
Feb. 2	Candlemas (Día de la Candelaria) is celebrated with processions, dancing, music and food to observe the passing of winter.
Mar. 19	St. Joseph's Day (Día de San José). Especially colorful in Tamuín, S.L.P.
3 days preceding Ash Wednesday	Carnaval is marked with parades, processions, fireworks, music, dancing and a general celebration of fun. Especially spirited in Acapulco, Gro.; Cozumel, Q.R.; Cuernavaca, Mor.; Mazatlán, Sin.; San Cristóbal de Las Casas, Chis.; and Veracruz, Ver.
Palm Sunday to Easter Sunday	Holy Week (Semana Santa). Particularly impressive are the candlelight processions in Taxco, the Passion Play in Ixtapalapa (Mexico City), and the Processions of Silence in San Luis Potosí, S.L.P. and San Miguel de Allende, Gto. Other notable observances occur in Pátzcuaro, Mich.; Querétaro, Qro.; Tzintzuntzan, Mich.; and Zinacantán, Chis.
Holy Saturday	Judas Day. Grotesque papier-mâché figures representing Judas are burned the day before Easter Sunday. Especially dramatic in Mexico City and vicinity.
June 24	Saint John the Baptist Day (Día de San Juan Bautista) is celebrated with popular fairs, religious festivities and practical jokes associated with dunking.
Aug. 15-16 and 20-22	Celebration for the Day of the Virgin of Charity and Assumption Day (Día de la Asunción). Flowers and sawdust adorn the streets for processions and special masses. Especially significant in Huamantla, Pue. Fair, Indian dances, *tianguis.*
Oct. 4	St. Francis' Day. Especially interesting in Real de Catorce, S.L.P., and San Francisquito, Son.
Nov. 1-2	Day of the Dead (Día de Los Muertos). A 2-day religious festival celebrated throughout Mexico and marked by visits to cemeteries, flower and culinary offerings, candlelight vigils, elaborately decorated home altars and general merrymaking. It is especially impressive on Isla Janitzio, Mich. Other noteworthy observances take place in Tzintzuntzan, Mich.; Oaxaca, Oax.; and Chiapa de Corzo, Chis.

Nov. 20		Revolution Day (Día de la Revolución). Not a national holiday, but a day marking the anniversary of the Mexican Revolution of 1910 with speeches and official ceremonies.
Dec. 8		Immaculate Conception. San Juan de los Lagos, Jal., and Pátzcuaro, Mich. are among the many towns with noteworthy celebrations.
Dec. 12		Feast Day of the Virgin of Guadalupe. Religious festival that pays tribute to the Guadalupe Virgin. This is Mexico's largest religious pilgrimage. Especially dramatic in Mexico City and Monterrey, N.L., but celebrations take place throughout the country.
Dec. 24-25		Christmas. Celebrations usually begin on Dec. 16 with the *posadas*, re-enactments of Mary and Joseph's search for an inn. At Salamanca, Gto., the fiesta lasts until Feb. 2 and includes numerous Nativity scenes enhanced by moving parts and sound-and-light effects. The entire country celebrates, with particularly notable events taking place in Aguascalientes, Ags.; Oaxaca, Oax.; San Juan del Río, Qro.; San Luis Potosí, S.L.P.; San Miguel de Allende, Gto.; Santiago Tuxtla, Ver.; and Tepotzotlán, Mex.
Dec. 31		New Year's Eve and Thanksgiving (Fin de Año y Día de Gracias). Especially vibrant in Mexico City, where empty eggshells filled with confetti and food coloring are tossed into the air.

Other Selected Local Festivals and Events

Jan. 17	Taxco, Gro.	St. Anthony's Day. Blessing of pets and other animals in the parish church.
Jan. 18	Taxco, Gro.	Day of Santa Prisca, town patroness, begins with parishioners singing early morning wake-up songs *(mañanitas)* to the Virgin. Celebration and dancing last all day.
Feb. 1-3	San Blas, Nay.	Blessing of the Sea. Dancing and horse races.
Mar. 6	Taxco, Gro.	Day of Our Lord of Xalpa. Indian dances include Los Tlacololeros, Santiagos, Diablos and Pescadores.
Mar. 18-Apr. 4	Tonalá, Jal.	Ceramics Fair. Handicraft exhibits and sales.
Mar. or Apr.	Uruapan, Mich.	Palm Sunday celebration with a huge, weeklong ceramics contest and exhibition, handicraft sales.
Apr. 1-7	Cuernavaca, Mor.	Flower Fair. Exhibits and competitions in floriculture and gardening. Sound-and-light show; popular entertainers.
Apr. 16-May 6	Aguascalientes, Ags.	San Marcos Fair. A major commercial, industrial and agricultural exposition. Handicrafts, local food and beverages, bullfights, exhibits.
Apr. 20-26	Tuxtla Gutiérrez, Chis.	Fiesta of St. Mark the Evangelist. A regional commercial and crafts fair, with *charreadas*, theatrical presentations, marimba contests and sports events.
Apr. (last week)	Villahermosa, Tab.	Tabasco State Fair. People from throughout the state present their music, dances and traditions. Folkloric ballet.
May (last three weekends)	Taxco, Gro.	Alarcón Days. Cultural and artistic festival with band serenades, musical performances and presentations of plays by Taxco-born playwright Juan Ruiz de Alarcón.
May (three weeks)	Morelia, Mich.	Michoacán State Fair (Feria de Morelia). Handicrafts, livestock and agricultural exhibitions, regional dances, bullfights. Fireworks on May 18 mark the anniversary of the city's founding in 1541.
May 3-15	Tepic, Nay.	Fiesta of St. Isador the Farmer. A commercial and cultural fair that includes the blessing of seeds, animals and water.
May 19-22	Chihuahua, Chih.	Fiesta of Santa Rita. A major fair with commercial exhibits, cultural events, food and Indian dances.
May 20-June 10	Monterrey, N.L.	Commercial and agricultural fair.
May 20-30	Tequisquiapan, Qro.	National Wine and Cheese Fair. Tastings and sales, *tianguis*, cultural events.
June 1	Guaymas, Son.	Mexican Navy Day features a naval battle with fireworks.
June (1st Thurs.)	Temascalcingo, Mex.	Corpus Christi Thursday. Blessing of farm animals and equipment; children in Indian costumes.
June 15-July 2	Tlaquepaque, Jal.	National Ceramics Fair and June Fiestas. Craft competitions, exhibits and demonstrations; cultural events.
June 18	Papantla, Ver.	Corpus Christi Day and Vanilla Festival. The famous Flying Pole dancers perform in their place of origin. Regional food and beverages, booths with vanilla products.
July 25	Santiago Tuxtla, Ver.	Day of St. James the Apostle. Líseres (in which participants wear jaguar costumes), Negritos and other local Indian dances.
Mid- to late July (two successive Mondays)	Oaxaca, Oax.	Guelaguetza (Festival of Cooperation). Elaborate, dynamic folkloric festival with dances, regional costumes, music and food.
July 12-Aug. 9	Santa Ana Chiautempan, Tlax.	National Sarape Fair (Feria Nacional del Sarape). This fair takes place simultaneously with the celebration of the town's patron saint on July 26.

Aug. (variable)	Santa Clara del Cobre, Mich.	Copper Fair. Copper handicrafts. Indian dancers, floats.
Aug. 2	Mexico City, D.F.	Cuauhtémoc Day. Dances and ceremonies at Cuauhtémoc Circle honor the last Aztec emperor.
Aug. 18-31	San Luis Potosí, S.L.P.	National Fair of Potosí (Feria Nacional Potosina). Concerts, bullfights, rodeos, sports events, agricultural and livestock exhibitions. The Day of St. Louis the King Aug. 25 honors the city's patron saint with floats and *gigantes* (papier-mâché figures).
Aug. 27-Sept. 1	Zacatecas, Zac.	Festival of La Morisma. Spectacular re-enactment of a 3-day battle between Moors and Spaniards. *Pastorelas;* Indian dances, church services.
Sept. 5-21	Zacatecas, Zac.	National Fair (Feria de Zacatecas). Agricultural and livestock exhibitions, handicrafts, bullfights, rodeos, cultural events.
Sept. 10-17	Dolores Hidalgo, Gto.	Independence Fair and Regional Exposition. *El Grito de Dolores* is reissued by the president on Sept. 15 of most years; there is television coverage of the Mexico City ceremony.
Sept. 15-end of Oct.	Puebla, Pue.	International Fair, a major cultural event focusing on music. The Regional Fair of Hard Cider is an industrial, agricultural and handicrafts exposition.
Sept. 25-Oct. 10	Real de Catorce, S.L.P.	Fiesta of St. Francis and Regional Fair. More than 150,000 pilgrims flock to Real de Catorce for religious and traditional ceremonies honoring St. Francis of Assisi.
Oct. (all)	Guadalajara, Jal.	October Festivals (Fiestas de Octubre). Major fair with many shows, races and other events in the arts and sports.
Oct. (most)	Guanajuato, Gto.	Cervantes International Festival (Festival Internacional Cervantino). One of Mexico's leading cultural events, it draws participants from many countries. *Entremeses,* skits based on the author's work, are featured.
Dec. (1st week)	Taxco, Gro.	National Silver Fair. Show and sale of silver items by craftsmen from around the world.
Dec. 10-12	San Cristóbal de Las Casas, Chis.	Fiesta of the Virgin of Guadalupe. Tzotzil and Tzeltal Indians in procession; marimba music, equestrian parades.
Dec. 23	Oaxaca, Oax.	Night of the Radishes features huge radishes carved into fanciful shapes and thin, fried radish cakes covered with molasses. The cakes are served in a clay dish that must be broken after the cakes are eaten. A parade of floats through the city center takes place the following night.

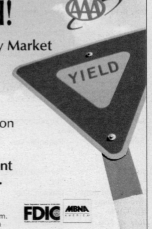

GOLDEN PASSPORTS

Golden Passports, available in three types, offer benefits and significant savings to individuals who plan to visit federal recreation sites.

The Golden Eagle Passport, available for a **$65** annual fee, is valid for entrance only to all federal recreation areas that have an entrance fee. Sites include those operated by the National Forest Service, National Park Service, Bureau of Land Management and the U.S. Fish and Wildlife Service. The passport admits all occupants of a private vehicle at locations where entrance is on a per vehicle basis. At locations where a per person fee is charged, the pass covers the pass holder, spouse, parents and children.

Citizens or permanent residents of the United States who are 62 and older can obtain *Golden Age Passports* for a one-time **$10** fee. Proof of age is required.

Golden Access Passports are free to citizens or permanent residents of the United States (regardless of age) who are medically blind or permanently disabled. Medical documention is required.

Both *Golden Age* and *Golden Access Passports* cover entrance fees for the holder and accompanying private party to all national parks and sites managed by the U.S. Fish and Wildlife Service, the U.S. Forest Service and the Bureau of Land Management, plus a 50% discount on federal recreation use fees. When a per person fee is imposed, the pass covers the pass holder, spouse and children. Apply in person at a federally operated area where an entrance fee is charged.

NATIONAL PARKS PASS

The *National Parks Pass*, valid for 1 year from its first use in a park, allows unlimited admissions to all U.S. national parks. The **$50** pass covers all occupants of a private vehicle at parks where the entrance fee is per vehicle. At parks with individual entry fees, the pass covers the pass holder, spouse, parents and children.

As a result of a partnership with the National Park Foundation, AAA members may purchase the pass for **$48**, either through AAA's internet site (www.aaa.com) or by visiting a participating AAA office. Members may also phone the National Park Foundation at **(888) 467-2757** or purchase the pass online at www.nationalparks.org. Non-members may purchase the pass through participating AAA offices for the full **$50** price or online at www.nationalparks.org.

For an upgrade fee of **$15**, a Golden Eagle Hologram sticker can be added to a *National Parks Pass*. The hologram covers entrance fees not just at national parks, but at any federal recreation area that has an admission fee. Valid for the duration of the *National Parks Pass* to which it is affixed, the Golden Eagle hologram is available at National Park Service, Fish and Wildlife Service and Bureau of Land Management fee stations.

How to Read a Campground Listing

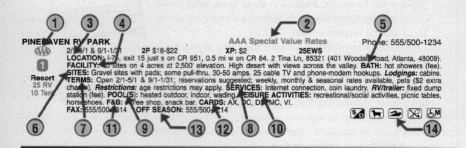

① **AAA** or **CAA** indicates an Official Appointment campground. The OA program permits privately operated campgrounds to display and advertise the **AAA** or **CAA** emblem. Red helps you easily locate those OA campgrounds that want AAA/CAA member business.

RATING - AAA Tourism Editors evaluate and rate, on a scale of 1 to 3, all privately operated campgrounds based on the overall visual appeal, environmental quality, and completeness, cleanliness and condition of the facilities. The number awarded, not the color, informs you of the overall level of quality you can expect.

❶ Surroundings are adequate with modest natural appeal and limited facilities. Sites are visibly rustic and include basic essentials. Showers, toilets and other comforts are not consistently available within direct proximity of each site.

❷ Surroundings provide an enhanced natural setting. Sites are visibly appealing, easily identifiable and well defined. There is at least one general service facility onsite such as a visitor's center, store, meeting room or mail center.

❸ Surroundings reflect the ultimate camping location featuring prominent natural elements. Extensive recreational facilities and social programs are available. All sites are groomed and enhance the natural beauty of the environment. A variety of services are offered such as a visitor's center, store, meeting room and mail center.

RESORT - A campground classified as a Resort will be denoted as such immediately below the rating. Travel packages, meal plans, entertainment, social and recreational programs, and extensive recreational facilities are typically available.

Campgrounds operated by a public/government agency are included but have not been evaluated or rated by AAA.

SITE COUNT defines the total number and type of short-term sites available.

② **RATE LINES** shown from left to right: dates or days that the fees are in effect; how many persons the rate applies to; the daily fee charged per site; fee for an extra person (XP) staying at the site; and total sites with electric, water or sewer hookups and any fees charged for the service. Rates do not include taxes.

RATE OPTIONS:

Special Value Rates - The campground not only guarantees that rates will not exceed the maximum rates printed in the CampBook, but it also offers a minimum discount of 10 percent off printed rates. This is the only rate option that contains a discount.

Guaranteed Rates - The campground guarantees that AAA/CAA members will not be charged more than the maximum rate printed in the CampBook.

Rates Subject To Change - Rates may vary for the life of the CampBook; however, they are guaranteed not to exceed a 15 percent increase on the rates printed.

Exceptions - A campground may temporarily increase rates or modify policies during a special event or for those traveling as part of a group or convention. At these times the *Special Value* and *Guaranteed* rate options and senior discounts do not apply. Members may take advantage of either the *Special Value Rate* or the senior discount, but not both.

3   **LOCATION** includes driving directions, street address and zip or postal code; and mailing address in parenthesis; U.S. directions include the following abbreviations: I (interstate highway), US (federal highway), SR (state road), CR (county road), FR (forest road) and FM (farm to market). For province directions, the following abbreviations are used: Hwy (provincial highway), Rt (route) and CR (county road). Distances are from the nearest town or community unless otherwise noted.

4   **FACILITY** details the physical attributes of the campground, including acreage, elevation and total number of campsites.

5   **BATH** describes types of bathing facilities and any associated fees. Flush toilets and hot showers are available and at no charge unless otherwise noted.

6   **SITES** describes the physical attributes of the average individual campsite, hookup availability and associated fees. *Lodgings* shows additional permanent lodgings available to rent. (These may or may not be AAA/CAA approved.)

7   **TERMS** describes reservation policies, conditions and fees imposed. At check-in, some campgrounds require full payment in cash or by credit card for the period reserved. Any subsequent cancellation or refund might then be subject to the advance notice requirement or to the re-rental of the site. *Restrictions* details any limits imposed by the campground.

8   **SERVICES** lists services and amenities available at the campground. *RV/trailer* describes special services and amenities offered for use by RV and trailers.

9   **POOL(S)** describes types and number of pools.

10   **LEISURE ACTIVITIES** lists the recreational opportunities and activities and any associated fees. Equipment available at a cost is preceded by "rental."

11   **F&B** lists the food or beverage outlets located within the campground.

12   **CARDS:**   AX = American Express   CB = Carte Blanche   DC = Diners Club
                   DS = Discover   JC = Japan Credit Bureau   MC = MasterCard   VI = Visa

13   The property's main **TELEPHONE NUMBER** appears in the upper right-hand corner. The **RESERVATION** phone number is included for public campgrounds using a central reservations service. The **OFF SEASON** phone number is included for private campgrounds not open year round.

14   **ICONS** help members quickly identify services and amenities available at the campground.

🔟 10% senior discount for members over 59	⊇ Pool	🐾 Pets Allowed
♿ Barrier-Free Facilities	⊠ Recreational Activities	⛔ No Tents

ACAPULCO, GUERRERO

Where to Camp

PLAYA SUAVE TRAILER PARK   Rates Subject to Change   Phone: 744/485-1885

❶   All Year   2P $20-$23   38EWS
38 RV/Tent   **LOCATION:** 0.5 km e; corner of Diego H de Mendoza; entrance on Calz Vasco Nunez de Balboa. Costera Miguel Aleman #276, 39300 (Apdo Postal 165). **FACILITY:** 38 sites on 3 acres. In shaded coconut grove in western bayfront hotel zone. **BATH:** cold showers. **SITES:** Sites with concrete pad, bathroom and shower. **TERMS:** reservation deposit. **SERVICES:** groceries nearby. **RV/trailer:** fixed dump station.

BAHIA KINO, SONORA

Where to Camp

KINO BAY RV PARK   Rates Subject to Change   Phone: 662/242-0216

❷   All Year   2P $15-$20   XP: $4   200EWS
200 RV/Tent   **LOCATION:** 8 km nw on beach highway; near pavement end. Mar de Cortez S/N, 83340 (Apdo Postal 57). **FACILITY:** 200 sites on 4 acres. **SITES:** Level, hardpan and gravel sites with concrete patio; some with corrugated metal sun cover for shade. 30 amps. **TERMS:** monthly rates available. **SERVICES:** propane, Internet connection, coin laundry. **RV/trailer:** fixed dump station, supplies, storage. **LEISURE ACTIVITIES:** beach, boat storage, recreational/social activities, bocci, recreation room.
FAX: 662/242-0083

BUCERIAS, NAYARIT

Where to Camp

BUCERIAS TRAILER COURT   Rates Subject to Change   Phone: 329/298-0265

❶   12/1-5/1 & 11/1-11/30   2P $24   47EWS
47 RV   **LOCATION:** 11 km n of Puerto Vallarta on Mex 200, KM 143, w at 1st light, then just n. Calle Lazaro Cardenas y Javier SN Mina, 63732 (Apdo Postal 148). **FACILITY:** 47 sites on 2 acres. On beach with tropical landscaping. **SITES:** Hardpan sites with concrete pads shaded by coconut palm trees. **TERMS:** Open 12/1-5/1 & 11/1-11/30; monthly rates available. **POOL(S):** outdoor, wading.
FAX: 329/298-0300

LAS PAROTAS RV PARK   Rates Subject to Change   Phone: 329/298-1788

❷   All Year $20   XP: $4   18EWS
18 RV   **LOCATION:** Mex 200 (Bucerias Centro), 1 mi e on Ave Estaciones, just s. #119 Ave Estaciones, 63732 (Apdo Postal 39).
12 Tent   **FACILITY:** 30 sites on 8 acres. Surrounded by a fence line of colorful bougainvillea. **SITES:** Level, well-spaced hardpan and grass sites. 30 amps. **Lodgings:** casitas (camping cabins). **TERMS:** weekly & monthly rates available. **SERVICES:** Internet connection, coin laundry, groceries nearby. **RV/trailer:** storage. **POOL(S):** heated outdoor. **LEISURE ACTIVITIES:** horseshoes, bocci, rental scooter, ATV tours. **F&B:** restaurant, lounge.
FAX: 329/298-1787

CABO SAN LUCAS, BAJA CALIFORNIA SUR

Where to Camp

VAGABUNDOS DEL MAR RV PARK   Rates Subject to Change   Phone: 624/143-0290

❷   All Year   2P $16-$18   85EWS
85 RV   **LOCATION:** On Mex 1, 3 km e of town. (Apdo Postal 197). **FACILITY:** 85 sites on 3 acres. Walled park on the edge of town, popular for caravans. **SITES:** Open, gravel sites with cement pads. 85 cable TV hookups. **TERMS:** reservation deposit, 30 day cancellation notice-fee imposed; weekly & monthly rates available. **SERVICES:** coin laundry, groceries nearby. **POOL(S):** outdoor. **F&B:** restaurant, lounge. **CARDS:** MC, VI.
FAX: 624/143-0511

VILLA SERENA RV PARK   Rates Subject to Change   Phone: 624/145-8165

❷   All Year   2P $21   XP: $2   56EWS
56 RV/Tent   **LOCATION:** Mex 1, 7.5 km e of town. Carr Transpeninsular KM 7.5, 23410. **FACILITY:** 56 sites. RV park overlooks home sites and the sea. **SITES:** Open, dirt sites. **TERMS:** weekly & monthly rates available. **SERVICES:** guest laundry, groceries nearby. **POOL(S):** outdoor. **LEISURE ACTIVITIES:** whirlpool. **F&B:** restaurant, lounge.
FAX: 624/143-1891

CANCUN, QUINTANA ROO

Where to Camp

CANCUN MECOLOCO TRAILER PARK Rates Subject to Change Phone: 998/843-0324
1 All Year 4P $16 70EWS
100 RV/Tent **LOCATION:** On beach road; between Puerto Juarez and Punta Sam. KM 3 Carr Puerto Juarez-Punta Sam, 77500. **FACILITY:** 100 sites on 5 acres. Rural location across the road from beach. Adjacent to the Mayan ruin excavation. **SERVICES:** groceries, guest laundry. **RV/trailer:** fixed dump station. **LEISURE ACTIVITIES:** scuba diving, snorkeling, fishing.
FAX: 998/880-2376

CIUDAD CONSTITUCION, BAJA CALIFORNIA SUR

Where to Camp

MANFRED'S RV PARK Rates Subject to Change Phone: 613/132-1103
1 All Year 2P $14-$16 XP: $5 40EWS
40 RV/Tent **LOCATION:** On Mex 1, 1 km n of town. Carr Transpeninsular KM 213, 23600 (Apdo Postal 120). **FACILITY:** 40 sites on 3 acres. Fully walled park on the edge of town. **SITES:** Gravel sites among flowering plants and trees. **Lodgings:** motel units. **SERVICES:** groceries nearby.
FAX: 613/132-1103

CREEL, CHIHUAHUA

Where to Camp

VILLA MEXICANA RV PARK Rates Subject to Change Phone: 635/456-0665
3 All Year 2P $10-$22 XP: $5 74EW 25S
74 RV **LOCATION:** 1 km se; adjacent to Villa Mexicana Hotel. Calle Lopez Mateos S/N, 33200. **FACILITY:** 104 sites. Very nicely
30 Tent done campground. **SITES:** Open, hardpan sites with picnic table and charcoal grill. 30-50 amps. **Lodgings:** camping cabins. **TERMS:** reservations accepted; weekly & monthly rates available. **SERVICES:** groceries, Internet connection, gift shop, coin laundry, area transportation-train & bus station. **RV/trailer:** fixed dump station, storage. **LEISURE ACTIVITIES:** playground, basketball, volleyball. **F&B:** restaurant, lounge. **CARDS:** AX, MC, VI.
FAX: 635/426-0065

CUERNAVACA, MORELOS

Where to Camp

CUERNAVACA TRAILER PARK DIAMANTE Rates Subject to Change Phone: 777/316-0761
1 All Year 2P $10-$15 XP: $3 153EWS
153 RV **LOCATION:** On Mex 95-D (toll road), exit Calle Diana, 0.4 km w, then s. Mesalina 3, Colonia Delicias, 62250. **FACILITY:** 153 sites on 2 acres. Country setting. 30 amps. **LEISURE ACTIVITIES:** 1 lighted tennis court, playground.
FAX: 777/316-0761

ENSENADA, BAJA CALIFORNIA

Where to Camp

BAJA SEASONS RV BEACH RESORT Rates Subject to Change Phone: 646/155-4015
2 3/16-11/30 2P $50-$67 XP: $10 140EWS
  12/1-3/15 2P $40-$50 XP: $10 140EWS
140 RV **LOCATION:** On Mex 1-D (toll road), exit Alisitos northbound, U-turn, then 10 km s; 42 km n of town. Carr Escencia Tijuana Ensenada 72.5 (1177 Broadway #4 PMB 329, CHULA VISTA, 91911). **FACILITY:** 140 sites on 50 acres. Beachfront RV park between Rosarito and Ensenada. **SITES:** Open sites with cement pads. 30 amps. 140 cable TV hookups. **Lodgings:** motel units, villas. **TERMS:** reservation deposit, 14 day cancellation notice; weekly & monthly rates available; check-in 3 pm; pets ($1 extra charge). **SERVICES:** groceries, coin laundry. **POOL(S):** outdoor, wading. **LEISURE ACTIVITIES:** saunas, whirlpool, steam room, 2 tennis courts, volleyball, recreation room. Fee: miniature golf, putting green. **F&B:** restaurant, lounge. **CARDS:** MC, VI.
FAX: 646/155-4019

ESTERO BEACH RV PARK Rates Subject to Change Phone: 646/176-6225
2 All Year 2P $25 XP: $10 57EWS
57 RV **LOCATION:** 10.5 km s of town on Mex 1, 1.5 km w on Ave Jose Ma Moreles and Lupita Novelo O; at Estero Beach Resort Hotel. (482 W San Ysidro Blvd, PMB 1186, SAN YSIDRO, 92173). **FACILITY:** 57 sites on 4 acres. Located at the bay. **SITES:** Open sites on extensive grounds. **TERMS:** reservation deposit, 3 day cancellation notice-fee imposed; monthly rates available; check-in 3 pm. **SERVICES:** coin laundry. **RV/trailer:** 35m limit, fixed dump station. **LEISURE ACTIVITIES:** beach, swimming, rental paddleboats, boat ramp, fishing, 3 lighted tennis courts, playground. Fee: jet skis, kayaks, waverunners, bicycles. **F&B:** restaurant, lounge. **CARDS:** MC, VI.

GUADALAJARA, JALISCO

Where to Camp

SAN JOSE DEL TAJO Rates Subject to Change Phone: 33/3686-1738

2
150 RV

All Year 2P $16 XP: $2 150EWS
LOCATION: 15.5 km s on Mex 15 and 80. Ave Presidente Lopez Mateos, 45640 (Apdo Postal 31-242, 45050). **FACILITY:** 150 sites on 16 acres. Secluded area. **SITES:** Some shaded sites. 30-50 amps. **TERMS:** reservation deposit, 30 day cancellation notice-fee imposed; monthly rates available. **SERVICES:** groceries, coin laundry. **POOL(S):** outdoor. **LEISURE ACTIVITIES:** 1 tennis court, recreational/social activities, horseshoes, shuffleboard, recreation room. **FAX:** 33/3686-1738

LA PAZ, BAJA CALIFORNIA SUR

Where to Camp

AQUAMARINA RV PARK Rates Subject to Change Phone: 612/122-3761

1
19 RV

All Year 2P $17 XP: $2 19E: $1 19WS
LOCATION: 2 km sw of town on Mex 1 (Abasolo), 1 km w. Calle Nayarit, 23094 (Apdo Postal 133). **FACILITY:** 19 sites on 5 acres. On La Paz Bay, enclosed park with modest facilities. **SITES:** Well-spaced sites with many trees. **TERMS:** weekly & monthly rates available. **SERVICES:** coin laundry. **POOL(S):** outdoor. **LEISURE ACTIVITIES:** marina, fishing. Fee: mooring, storage.
FAX: 612/125-6228

CASA BLANCA RV PARK Rates Subject to Change Phone: 612/124-0009

2
43 RV/Tent

All Year 2P $17 XP: $3 43EWS
LOCATION: On Mex 1, KM 4.5; west entrance to town. Ave Delfines, 23094 (Apdo Postal 681). **FACILITY:** 43 sites. Walled park with modest restrooms and facilities. On the edge of town. **SITES:** Open sites with cement pads. **TERMS:** monthly rates available. **SERVICES:** coin laundry. **POOL(S):** outdoor. **LEISURE ACTIVITIES:** 1 tennis court.
FAX: 612/124-0009

LA PAZ TRAILER PARK Rates Subject to Change Phone: 612/122-8787

2
35 RV

All Year 2P $17 XP: $6 35EWS
LOCATION: 3 km s of town on Mex 1 (Abasolo), turn w, just s of Volkswagen Agency, 1 km w, then just s. Brecha California #1010, 23094 (Apdo Postal 482). **FACILITY:** 35 sites on 6 acres. Walled park on edge of town. **SITES:** Open, modest sites; some pull-thru. **TERMS:** 3 day cancellation notice; weekly & monthly rates available. **SERVICES:** coin laundry. **POOL(S):** outdoor, wading.
FAX: 612/122-9938

LORETO, BAJA CALIFORNIA SUR

Where to Camp

LORETO SHORES VILLAS & RV PARK Rates Subject to Change Phone: 613/135-0629

2
30 RV

All Year 2P $17 XP: $4 30EWS
LOCATION: 1 km s of town center via Francisco Madero. Colonia Zaragoza, 23880 (Apdo Postal 219). **FACILITY:** 30 sites on 5 acres. A park at the beach. **SITES:** Open sites; mostly pull-thru. **TERMS:** reservation deposit; weekly rates available. **SERVICES:** coin laundry. **RV/trailer:** fixed dump station. **LEISURE ACTIVITIES:** beach, fishing.
FAX: 613/135-0711

TRIPUI RESORT RV PARK Rates Subject to Change Phone: 613/133-0814

1
31 RV

All Year 2P $15 XP: $4 31EWS
LOCATION: 20 km s of town via Mex 1, 1 km e at KM 94. (Apdo Postal 172, 23880). **FACILITY:** 31 sites on 5 acres. **SITES:** Open sites at the edge of a mobile home park. 31 cable TV hookups. **TERMS:** reservation deposit, 3 day cancellation notice; weekly & monthly rates available. **SERVICES:** groceries, coin laundry. **POOL(S):** outdoor, wading. **LEISURE ACTIVITIES:** playground. Fee: boat ramp. **F&B:** restaurant, lounge.
FAX: 613/133-0828

VILLAS DE LORETO Rates Subject to Change Phone: 613/135-0586

2
9 RV

All Year 2P $20 XP: $5 9EWS
LOCATION: 1 km s of town center via Francisco Madero. Colonia Zaragoza, 23880 (Apdo Postal 132). **FACILITY:** 9 sites on 4 acres. At the beach in walled park. Smoke-free premises. **SITES:** Open sites. *Lodgings:* motel units. **TERMS:** reservation deposit, 30 day cancellation notice-fee imposed; weekly rates available. **SERVICES:** coin laundry. **POOL(S):** outdoor. **LEISURE ACTIVITIES:** beach, scuba diving & rental equipment, bicycles, mountain bike tours. Fee: kayak. **F&B:** restaurant. **CARDS:** MC, VI.
FAX: 613/135-0355

LOS BARRILES, BAJA CALIFORNIA SUR

Where to Camp

MARTIN VERDUGO'S BEACH RESORT   Rates Subject to Change   Phone: 624/141-0054
[2] All Year   2P $12-$14   XP: $4   69EWS
69 RV   **LOCATION:** 1 km e of Mex 1. Bahia de Palmas, 23501 (Apdo Postal 17). **FACILITY:** 94 sites on 5 acres. RV park at the
25 Tent   bay behind motel. **SITES:** Some partially shaded sites in crowded park. *Lodgings:* motel units. **TERMS:** weekly & monthly
rates available. **SERVICES:** coin laundry, groceries nearby. **POOL(S):** outdoor. **LEISURE ACTIVITIES:** beach, boating,
boat ramp, fishing. Fee: charter fishing. **F&B:** lounge. **CARDS:** MC, VI.
FAX: 624/141-0054

MATEHUALA, SAN LUIS POTOSI

Where to Camp

LAS PALMAS TRAILER PARK   Rates Subject to Change   Phone: 488/882-0001
[1] All Year $4-$7   35EWS
35 RV   **LOCATION:** On Mex 57, by north entrance road to Matehuala; on grounds of Las Palmas Midway Inn and Restaurant.
(Apdo Postal 73, 78700). **FACILITY:** 35 sites on 4 acres at 1,524m elevation. Quiet well-maintained grounds. Valet laundry
service. **SITES:** Open, spacious sites. **TERMS:** weekly & monthly rates available. **SERVICES:** *RV/trailer:* fixed dump station. **POOL(S):** outdoor, wading. **LEISURE ACTIVITIES:** Fee: miniature golf, bowling. **F&B:** lounge. **CARDS:** AX, MC, VI.

MULEGE, BAJA CALIFORNIA SUR

Where to Camp

ORCHARD VACATION VILLAGE   Rates Subject to Change   Phone: 615/153-0300
[1] All Year   2P $18   XP: $3   16EWS
16 RV   **LOCATION:** 1.7 km s of town on Mex 1. (Apdo Postal 24, 23900). **FACILITY:** 46 sites on 15 acres. A village with mobile
30 Tent   homes, cottages and RV Park at the river. **SITES:** Many shade trees. *Lodgings:* cabanas. **TERMS:** weekly rates available.
SERVICES: *RV/trailer:* fixed dump station. **LEISURE ACTIVITIES:** rental canoes, boat ramp, fishing.
FAX: 615/153-0300

VILLA MARIA ISABEL RECREATIONAL PARK   Rates Subject to Change   Phone: 615/153-0246
[2] All Year   2P $16   XP: $2   33EW   25S
25 Tent   **LOCATION:** 2.5 km s of town on Mex 1. (Apdo Postal 5, 23900). **FACILITY:** 58 sites on 5 acres. At the river. **SITES:** Open,
33 RV/Tent   pull-thru sites; tent sites with palapas. **TERMS:** weekly rates available. **SERVICES:** coin laundry. *RV/trailer:* fixed dump
station. **POOL(S):** outdoor. **LEISURE ACTIVITIES:** boat ramp.
FAX: 615/153-0246

PATZCUARO, MICHOACAN

Where to Camp

EL POZO TRAILER PARK   Rates Subject to Change   Phone: 434/342-0937
[1] All Year   2P $15   XP: $4   20EWS
20 RV   **LOCATION:** 1.5 km ne on Mex 120 (Morelia Hwy). (Apdo Postal 142, 61600). **FACILITY:** 20 sites on 3 acres at 2,154m
elevation. Basic facilities with gravel roads. **SITES:** Large, open sites with lots of grass, good separation between sites. 15
amps. **TERMS:** reservation deposit, 7 day cancellation notice. **LEISURE ACTIVITIES:** playground.
FAX: 434/342-0937

PUERTO VALLARTA, JALISCO

Where to Camp

LAURIES "TACHOS" TRAILER PARK   Rates Subject to Change   Phone: 322/224-2163
[1] All Year   2P $19   XP: $6   135EWS
35 RV   **LOCATION:** 6.3 km n on Mex 200 (Airport Rd), 1 km e on paved road. Camino Nuevo al Pitillal S/N, 48300 (Apdo Postal
100 RV/Tent   315). **FACILITY:** 135 sites on 10 acres. **SITES:** Cobblestone and hardpan sites with brick pad; some pull-thru; some with
shade trees. 40 amps. **TERMS:** reservation deposit; weekly rates available. **POOL(S):** outdoor. **LEISURE ACTIVITIES:** pavilion, horseshoes, volleyball.

QUERETARO, QUERETARO

Where to Camp

AZTECA TRAILER PARK

1
30 RV

All Year · · · 2P $7-$8 · · · Rates Subject to Change · · · 30EWS · · · Phone: 442/234-0592
LOCATION: Mex 57, exit Juriquilla northbound; exit Juriquilla southbound to access northbound lane, 14.5 km n of jct Mex 45; on grounds of Azteca Parador Hotel. KM 15.5 Queratero-Juriquilla, 76230 (Apdo Postal 4, Juriquilla). **FACILITY:** 30 sites on 15 acres at 1,878m elevation. **SITES:** Open sites on grounds of motel. 20 amps. **TERMS:** reservation deposit. **POOL(S):** heated outdoor. **F&B:** restaurant. **CARDS:** AX, MC, VI.
FAX: 442/234-0592

SAN BARTOLO, BAJA CALIFORNIA SUR

Where to Camp

RANCHO VERDE RV PARK

1
30 RV/Tent

All Year · · · 2P $7-$11 · · · Rates Subject to Change · · · XP: $2 · · · Phone: 624/126-9103
LOCATION: On Mex 1, KM 142.5. KM 142.5 (PO Box 1050, EUREKA, 59917). **FACILITY:** 30 sites. RV park in a home-site development in remote mountain area. **SITES:** Well-spaced gravel and dirt sites. **SERVICES:** coin laundry.
FAX: 624/126-9103

SAN CARLOS, SONORA

Where to Camp

HACIENDA TETA KAWI TRAILER PARK

1
45 RV/Tent

All Year · · · 2P $20 · · · AAA Special Value Rates · · · XP: $3 · · · 45EWS · · · Phone: 622/226-0220
LOCATION: 10.7 km nw on Mex 15, 9.3 km w on San Carlos turn-off. Across from Bahia de San Carlos (Apdo Postal 71, GUAYMAS, 85506). **FACILITY:** 45 sites on 3 acres. Across from beach, behind motel. **SITES:** Open sites with concrete patio; some with sheet metal awning. 30 amps. 45 cable TV hookups. **TERMS:** reservation deposit, 14 day cancellation notice; weekly & monthly rates available. **SERVICES:** *RV/trailer:* storage. **POOL(S):** outdoor. **F&B:** lounge. **CARDS:** MC, VI.
FAX: 622/226-0248

SAN CRISTOBAL DE LAS CASAS, CHIAPAS

Where to Camp

BONAMPAK TRAILER PARK

1
8 Tent
22 RV/Tent

All Year · · · 1P $6 · · · Rates Subject to Change · · · XP: $6 · · · 22EWS · · · Phone: 967/678-1621
LOCATION: On Mex 190, north entrance to town, at statue; on grounds of Hotel Bonampak. Calz Mexico 5, 29310 (Apdo Postal 75). **FACILITY:** 30 sites at 2,113m elevation. At entrance to ruins. **TERMS:** reservation deposit, 15 day cancellation notice. **LEISURE ACTIVITIES:** playground. **F&B:** lounge. **CARDS:** AX, CB, DC, MC, VI.

SAN FELIPE, BAJA CALIFORNIA

Where to Camp

EL CACHANILLA CAMPING PRESERVE

2
100 RV/Tent

All Year · · · 4P $10 · · · Rates Subject to Change · · · XP: $5 · · · 20E: $4 · · · 14W: $4 · · · 8S: $4 · · · Phone: 686/577-0003
LOCATION: On Hwy 5, 0.6 km w; 14.5 km ne of town. Hwy 5, 21850. **FACILITY:** 100 sites on 50 acres. Desert location. **SITES:** Open, dirt sites. 50 amps. **TERMS:** check-in 3 pm. **SERVICES:** coin laundry. **LEISURE ACTIVITIES:** recreation privileges.

EL DORADO RANCH RV PARK

3
95 RV

All Year · · · 4P $20 · · · Rates Subject to Change · · · XP: $5 · · · 95EWS · · · Phone: 686/577-0003
LOCATION: On Hwy 5, 1.6 km e; 14.5 km n of town. Hwy 5, 21850. **FACILITY:** 100 sites on 50 acres. A full-service RV park and home sites on a hillside above the beach with water sports and equipment rentals. **SITES:** Open, dirt sites with bay view. 30 amps. *Lodgings:* 5 park models. **TERMS:** reservations required; check-in 3 pm. **SERVICES:** supplies, coin laundry. *RV/trailer:* fixed dump station. **POOL(S):** heated outdoor. **LEISURE ACTIVITIES:** whirlpool, beach, rental boats, 2 tennis courts, recreation room. **F&B:** restaurant, lounge.

SAN FELIPE MARINA RESORT RV PARK　　　Rates Subject to Change　　　Phone: 686/577-1455
2　All Year　　　　4P $22　　　XP: $5　　　143EWS
143 RV　**LOCATION:** 4.5 km s on road to airport. KM 4.5 Carr San Felipe Aeropuerto, 21850 (PO Box 9019, CALEXICO, 92232). **FACILITY:** 143 sites on 4 acres. Large park overlooking the marina. Adjacent hotel facilities available to guests. **SITES:** Large sites with bay view, cement pad and gravel side. 50 amps. **TERMS:** reservation deposit, 3 day cancellation notice; weekly & monthly rates available. **SERVICES:** groceries, guest laundry. **RV/trailer:** fixed dump station. **POOL(S):** outdoor. **CARDS:** MC, VI.
FAX: 686/577-1578

SAN JOSE DEL CABO, BAJA CALIFORNIA SUR

Where to Camp

BRISA DEL MAR RV RESORT　　　　Rates Subject to Change　　　Phone: 624/142-3999
2　12/1-2/28　　　2P $19-$30　　　XP: $2　　　150EWS
　3/1-11/30　　　2P $19-$25　　　XP: $2　　　150EWS
150 RV/Tent　**LOCATION:** 3 km w of town on Mex 1. Carr Transpeninsular KM 28, 23400 (Apdo Postal 287). **FACILITY:** 150 sites. On the beach. **SITES:** Open, level dirt sites. **POOL(S):** outdoor. **LEISURE ACTIVITIES:** beach, fishing. Fee: charter fishing. **F&B:** restaurant, lounge.
FAX: 624/142-3999

SAN MIGUEL DE ALLENDE, GUANAJUATO

Where to Camp

LAGO DORADO　　　　　　Rates Subject to Change　　　Phone: 415/152-2301
1　All Year　　　$10-$12　　　XP: $3-$3　　　60EW　　　20S
60 RV　**LOCATION:** 3.8 km s on Mex 49 to Villa de los Frailes, 2 km w, follow signs. Calle Bienaventura, 37700 (Apdo Postal 523). **FACILITY:** 60 sites on 10 acres at 1,800m elevation. Located in a secluded area, near lake. **SITES:** Level, grassy sites; some shaded. **SERVICES:** **RV/trailer:** fixed dump station. **POOL(S):** outdoor. **LEISURE ACTIVITIES:** playground.

TRAILER PARK LA SIESTA　　　　Rates Subject to Change　　　Phone: 415/152-0207
1　All Year　　　2P $12　　　XP: $2　　　70EWS
70 RV　**LOCATION:** 2 km s on Mex 49 (Celaya Hwy). (Apdo Postal 72, 37700). **FACILITY:** 70 sites on 5 acres at 1,800m elevation. Campground located on motel property. Guests have use of motel facilities. **SITES:** Open, grassy, level sites. **TERMS:** reservation deposit, 7 day cancellation notice. **SERVICES:** coin laundry. **POOL(S):** heated outdoor. **LEISURE ACTIVITIES:** playground. **CARDS:** AX, MC, VI.
FAX: 415/152-3722

TECATE, BAJA CALIFORNIA

Where to Camp

TECATE KOA ON RANCHO OJAI　　　Rates Subject to Change　　　Phone: 665/655-3014
3　All Year　　　2P $10-$28　　　XP: $10　　　30EWS
30 RV　**LOCATION:** On Mex 2, 20 km e of town near KM 112. Carr Mexicali-Tijuana KM 112 (PO Box 280, TECATE, 91980).
60 Tent　**FACILITY:** 90 sites on 40 acres. A working ranch in oak-covered mountains. **SITES:** Pull-thru sites with picnic table and barbecue grill. 50 amps. **Lodgings:** Kamping Kabins. **TERMS:** reservation deposit, 4 day cancellation notice; weekly & monthly rates available. **SERVICES:** groceries, gift shop, coin laundry. **RV/trailer:** fixed dump station. **POOL(S):** heated outdoor. **LEISURE ACTIVITIES:** hiking trails, playground, pavilion, horseshoes, volleyball, game room, recreation room. Fee: bicycles, horseback riding.
FAX: 665/655-3015

ZACATECAS, ZACATECAS

Where to Camp

HOTEL HACIENDA DEL BOSQUE RV PARK　　Rates Subject to Change　　　Phone: 492/924-6666
2　All Year　　　2P $19　　　34EWS
34 RV　**LOCATION:** 4 km ne of center on Guadalajara Rd; at crossroads on Mex 54. Heroes de Chapultepec 801, 98054. **FACILITY:** 34 sites on 2 acres at 5,000m elevation. This is a popular overnight stopping place. **SITES:** Flagstone paved sites. 50 amps. **TERMS:** reservation deposit, 15 day cancellation notice. **POOL(S):** heated indoor. **LEISURE ACTIVITIES:** playground, exercise room. **F&B:** lounge. **CARDS:** AX, MC, VI.
FAX: 492/924-6565

Metric Equivalents

TEMPERATURE

To convert Fahrenheit to Celsius, subtract 32 from the Fahrenheit temperature, multiply by 5 and divide by 9.
To convert Celsius to Fahrenheit, multipy by 9, divide by 5 and add 32.

ACRES

1 acre = 0.4 hectare (ha)	1 hectare = 2.47 acres

MILES AND KILOMETERS

Note: A kilometer is approximately 5/8 or 0.6 of a mile.
To convert kilometers to miles multiply by 0.6.

Miles/Kilometers		Kilometers/Miles	
15	24.1	30	18.6
20	32.2	35	21.7
25	40.2	40	24.8
30	48.3	45	27.9
35	56.3	50	31.0
40	64.4	55	34.1
45	72.4	60	37.2
50	80.5	65	40.3
55	88.5	70	43.4
60	96.6	75	46.6
65	104.6	80	49.7
70	112.7	85	52.8
75	120.7	90	55.9
80	128.7	95	59.0
85	136.8	100	62.1
90	144.8	105	65.2
95	152.9	110	68.3
100	160.9	115	71.4

Celsius ° / Fahrenheit °

Celsius °		Fahrenheit °
100	BOILING	212
37		100
35		95
32		90
29		85
27		80
24		75
21		70
18		65
16		60
13		55
10		50
7		45
4		40
2		35
0	FREEZING	32
-4		25
-7		20
-9		15
-12		10
-15		5
-18		0
-21		-5
-24		-10
-27		-15

LINEAR MEASURE

Customary	Metric
1 inch = 2.54 centimeters	1 centimeter = 0.4 inches
1 foot = 30 centimeters	1 meter = 3.3 feet
1 yard = 0.91 meters	1 meter = 1.09 yards
1 mile = 1.6 kilometers	1 kilometer = .62 miles

LIQUID MEASURE

Customary	Metric
1 fluid ounce = 30 milliliters	1 milliliter = .03 fluid ounces
1 cup = .24 liters	1 liter = 2.1 pints
1 pint = .47 liters	1 liter = 1.06 quarts
1 quart = .95 liters	1 liter = .26 gallons
1 gallon = 3.8 liters	

WEIGHT

If You Know:	Multiply By:	To Find:
Ounces	28	Grams
Pounds	0.45	Kilograms
Grams	0.035	Ounces
Kilograms	2.2	Pounds

PRESSURE

Air pressure in automobile tires is expressed in kilopascals. Multiply pound-force per square inch (psi) by 6.89 to find kilopascals (kPa).

24 psi = 165 kPa	28 psi = 193 kPa
26 psi = 179 kPa	30 psi = 207 kPa

GALLONS AND LITERS

Gallons/Liters				Liters/Gallons			
5	19.0	12	45.6	10	2.6	40	10.4
6	22.8	14	53.2	15	3.9	50	13.0
7	26.6	16	60.8	20	5.2	60	15.6
8	30.4	18	68.4	25	6.5	70	18.2
9	34.2	20	76.0	30	7.8	80	20.8
10	38.0	25	95.0	35	9.1	90	23.4

Highway Signs

Stop

No Passing

Horizontal Clearance

Maximum Weight (Metric Tons)

No Pedestrians

Parking Limit

One-Hour Parking

No Left Turn

No U Turn

No Parking

Keep to the Right

Inspection

No Trucks

Pedestrians Keep Left

Speed Limit (In K.P.H.)

Right Turn on Red Permitted

No Bicycles

Keep Right

Do Not Enter

Road Signs In Spanish	Descriptions In English
Topes, Vibradores	Speed Bumps
Un Solo Carril	One Lane
Pavimento Derrapante	Pavement Slippery
Prohibido Seguir de Frente	Do Not Enter
Vado	Dip

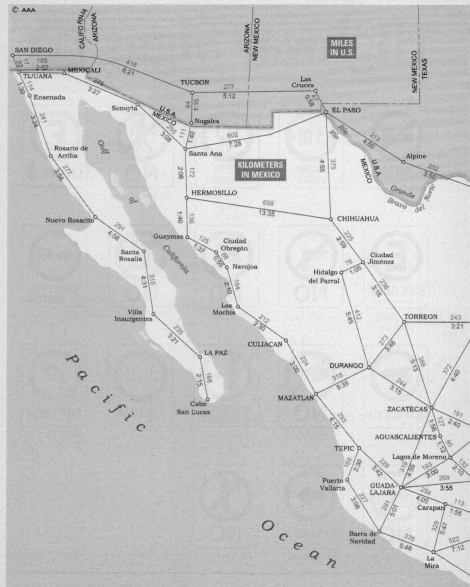

© AAA

MILES
IN U.S.

KILOMETERS
IN MEXICO

MEXICO

DRIVING DISTANCES

100 KILOMETERS IN MEXICO/MILES IN US
2:00 AVERAGE TIME (EXCLUDING STOPS)

3632-M

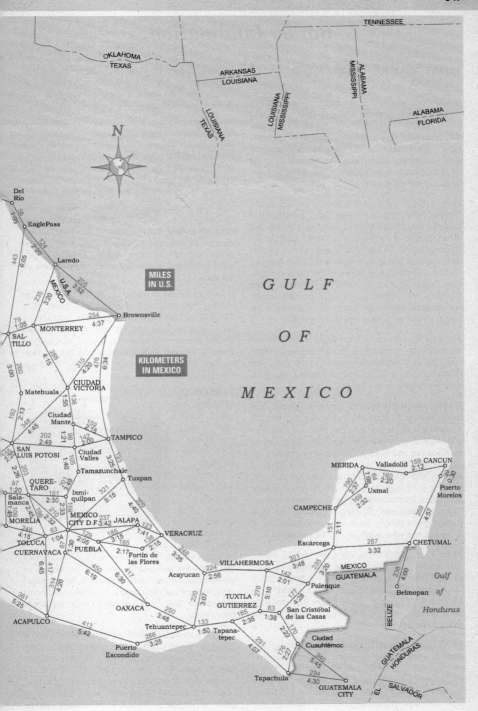

OKLAHOMA
TEXAS

ARKANSAS
LOUISIANA

ALABAMA
MISSISSIPPI

LOUISIANA
TEXAS

LOUISIANA
MISSISSIPPI

ALABAMA
FLORIDA

N

Del
Río

Eagle Pass

58
105

124
2:05

Laredo

443
6:05

235
3:20

U.S.A.
MEXICO

205
3:52

MILES
IN U.S.

254
4:37

Brownsville

G U L F

79
1:05

MONTERREY

SAL-
TILLO

288
4:15

315
4:20

476
6:34

260
3:00

O F

KILOMETERS
IN MEXICO

Matehuala

CIUDAD
VICTORIA

M E X I C O

192
3:48

2:13

4:45

136
1:55

Ciudad
Mante

159
2:15

202
2:49

98
1:21

142
2:00

TAMPICO

MERIDA

Valladolid

159
2:12

CANCUN

SAN
LUIS POTOSI

105
1:40

Ciudad
Valles

193
3:25

64
1:08

160
2:20

0:30

2:26

203

Tamazunchale

190
2:37

Uxmal

Puerto
Morelos

97
1:20

QUERE-
TARO

151

Ixmi-
quilpan

321
5:15

Tuxpan

169
2:32

CAMPECHE

359
4:57

Sala-
manca

2:30

MORELIA

2:32

MEXICO
CITY D.F.

237
3:42

JALAPA

123

270

151
2:11

Escárcega

257
3:32

CHETUMAL

246
4:15

TOLUCA

1:04

2:05

185
3:15

138
2:15

VERACRUZ

248

301
3:48

235
3:20

MEXICO
GUATEMALA

238
4:00

Gulf

CUERNAVACA

PUEBLA

2:17

Fortín de
las Flores

165

3:35

VILLAHERMOSA

224
2:56

142
2:01

Palenque

BELIZE

Belmopan

of

6:45

417
6:19

450
6:30

417

Acayucan

278
5:10

177
4:28

Honduras

361
5:25

220

3:07

TUXTLA
GUTIERREZ

83
1:38

San Cristóbal
de las Casas

170
2:22

ACAPULCO

OAXACA

250
3:48

133

165
2:35

413
5:42

Tehuantepec

1:50

Tapana-
tepec

Ciudad
Cuauhtémoc

GUATEMALA
HONDURAS

Puerto
Escondido

266
3:25

291
4:07

176
2:27

340
5:45

294
4:30

Tapachula

GUATEMALA
CITY

EL SALVADOR

Border Information

WHAT MAY BE TAKEN INTO MEXICO

If you're driving across the border, your baggage will be examined at the Mexican customs checkpoint. Although there's always the possibility that this procedure can turn into an ordeal of exasperating interactions with customs officials—or time-consuming additional inspections at customs or immigration substations—it has been streamlined for the most part.

Each vehicle must pass through an automated "traffic light" signal system. After submitting a customs declaration form or oral declarations, the driver presses a button that activates a randomly flashing signal. If the light flashes green no further action is taken; if it flashes red your luggage will be inspected, regardless of previous declarations made to customs officials. By law, if the signal is not operating properly no inspections are allowed unless the previous declaration involves goods on which fees are required.

The best time to cross the border is early in the morning on weekdays. Weekends—and especially holiday weekends—are the worst time, and there may be a long wait depending on what time you arrive at the border.

Airline passengers receive a customs declaration form (printed in English) on the flight listing all items that can be brought into Mexico duty-free and without prior authorization. The form should be filled out and is then submitted to customs officials upon arrival at the entry point. At most airports (for example, Mexico City's), after retrieving your luggage you'll proceed to a similar automated mechanism and press a button that activates a randomly flashing signal. If the light flashes green simply hand in your declaration; if it flashes red your luggage will be inspected.

Note: Complaints regarding treatment by Mexican customs officials may be registered by contacting the Comptroller and Administrative Development Secretariat (SECODAM) in Mexico City; phone (800) 001-4800 (toll-free long distance within Mexico). English is not likely to be spoken.

MONEY: Up to $10,000 in U.S. currency and traveler's checks (or the equivalent in other currencies) may be taken into Mexico; any greater amount must be declared. It is advisable to have the bulk of funds in traveler's checks. U.S. traveler's checks, particularly those issued by the most recognized institutions, are normally easy

to cash. It may be more difficult to cash Canadian currency and traveler's checks, so many Canadian travelers convert their money into U.S. currency beforehand.

Small-denomination traveler's checks and also a fair amount of cash come in handy when traveling in Baja California and the more remote areas of mainland Mexico. When presented with sufficient identification, major credit cards are accepted in the larger cities provided that the credit card company normally operates in Mexico.

You can make your dollars go further by exchanging them only as you need them. Exchange rates are posted at hotel front desks, currency exchange offices and banks. Banamex and Bancomer are two of the largest Mexican banks; most cities and towns have branches of one or the other.

If you transport or cause to be transported (including by mail or other means) more than $10,000 in currency or negotiable instruments such as traveler's checks into or out of the United States, you must file a copy of Customs Form 4790 with U.S. Customs and Border Protection, 1300 Pennsylvania Ave. NW, Washington, D.C. 20229.

PERSONAL ITEMS: You may take with you into Mexico duty free clothing, footwear and other personal items. The allowance includes jewelry, perfume,

toiletries, books and magazines (in a quantity that does not indicate them to be the object of commercialization), and medicines for personal consumption (accompanied by prescriptions as appropriate and in accordance with quantities prescribed).

Unless acceptable proof of prior ownership is presented upon return to the United States, duty may be required on personal articles that are foreign-made. This proof can be a bill of sale, insurance policy, jeweler's appraisal or original receipt of purchase. Items with serial numbers or other permanently affixed identification can be registered with the nearest Bureau of Customs and Border Protection office before departure. The certificate of registration will facilitate re-entry into the United States should any question of prior possession arise.

PHOTOGRAPHIC EQUIPMENT: One camera with up to 12 rolls of unused film, as well as one video camera and 12 blank cassettes, are admissible; this includes the camera's power source. Foreign-made cameras can be registered at the point of departure to prove that they were not purchased in Mexico. Airline passengers should have all photographic film hand-inspected at boarding points to ensure against damage from baggage inspection equipment at check-in locations.

Note: Photography must not be for commercial purposes. Tripods and flash equipment require special permits for use at archeological sites, museums and monuments.

PETS: Dogs and cats should be left at home because of special inspections and the possible refusal of hotel operators to allow pets in their establishments. However, if you must take your dog or cat into Mexico, you are required to have a veterinarian's *signed* and dated certificate (Pet Health Certificate for dogs and cats) stating the pet is in good health and stating inoculation against rabies and distemper. This certificate, available from a veterinarian's or county health department office, can be obtained up to 2 weeks prior to the date the animal enters Mexico. It is extremely difficult to temporarily import animals other than dogs or cats.

Inoculation certificates are necessary to re-enter the United States if the pet has been out of the country more than 30 days. Dogs can be left at kennels in Laredo, El Paso, Brownsville or Tucson while their owners are traveling in Mexico.

The brochure "Pets and Wildlife" can be obtained by writing U.S. Customs and Border Protection, 1300 Pennsylvania Ave. NW, Room 34A, Washington, D.C. 20229.

WEAPONS: Strict regulations govern the temporary importation of firearms and ammunition into Mexico. Tourists are not permitted to import pistols, revolvers, automatic firearms or weapons of any type. Technically this includes all knives (pocket and Swiss Army knives, as well as switchblades and other knives that could be classified as weapons). Although tourists are not likely to be fined or incarcerated for bringing in knives normally used for camping purposes, it may be safer to purchase such a knife while in Mexico.

U.S. citizens are most often arrested for firearms possession in border areas, but arrests have been made in every part of the country—including on private boats in Mexican territorial waters. Ignorance of the law in no way guarantees leniency or prevents prosecution. The only way to legally import firearms and ammunition into Mexico is to secure a permit in advance from the nearest Mexican consulate office.

DRUGS: The possession, use or sale of illegal drugs in Mexico is extremely risky. Mexican law, to which tourists in Mexico are subject, deems that trafficking in and/or possession of illegal drugs is a federal offense. All such cases are prosecuted rigorously by the Mexican government regardless of the nature of the drug. During the extensive trial process, which could possibly last more than a year, offenders are not eligible for bail; if found guilty, they are ineligible for parole.

If you require medicines containing habit-forming drugs or narcotics, take precautions to avoid any misunderstanding. Properly identify all drugs, carry only the necessary quantity and have with you a prescription or written statement from a physician. These safeguards will also help to avoid potential customs problems upon return to the United States.

OTHER DUTY-FREE ITEMS: Also allowed are one tent and camping equipment, one surfboard, two tennis rackets, a pair of skis, one pair of binoculars, one new or used laptop or other portable computer, one cellular phone, one pager, one portable radio/cassette player, one CD player, one portable television set, one VCR, up to 20 CDs or audiocassettes, up to five laser disks or DVDs, a musical instrument that can normally be carried by one person, one portable typewriter, up to five used toys (if the tourist is a minor), and personal items that compensate for or aid individuals with a disability.

The duty-free limit for the above items is usually per person or per each family member. Also admissible are gifts or items up to a total value of $300 (provided none are restricted) if arriving by air or sea, $50 if arriving by land. These duty-free limits apply per each crossing or arrival. There are no restrictions on the containers in which items are imported.

Each tourist, provided that he or she is not a minor, may bring in 3 liters of wine or another alcoholic beverage and two cartons of cigarettes, 25 cigars or 200 grams of loose tobacco. Recreational vehicle owners can bring in kitchen, dwelling and/or bedroom furniture or utensils, a videocassette player and a bicycle (with or without motor).

Tourists are *not* permitted to bring any type of live animal, fresh food products of animal or vegetable origin, or plants, flowers or fruits into Mexico. The following foodstuffs are allowed: dehydrated foods or canned fruit or vegetables, packaged roasted coffee, dried spices, dry herbal medicines, canned or bottled jellies or fruit preserves, canned or bottled nuts and sauces, and U.S.- or Canadian-processed cheeses.

CROSSING THE BORDER

All U.S. and Canadian tourists entering Mexico by land must stop at the international border to show proof of citizenship, pay a fee to have their tourist permit validated, and complete the necessary forms if temporarily bringing a vehicle into the country. Hours of operation for Mexican customs and immigration offices at major border crossing points are as follows:

CALIFORNIA/MEXICO

Calexico/Mexicali—Daily 24 hours

San Diego/Tijuana—Daily 24 hours

ARIZONA/MEXICO

Douglas/Agua Prieta—Daily 24 hours

Lukeville/Sonoita—Daily 6 a.m.-midnight

Nogales/Nogales—Daily 24 hours

TEXAS/MEXICO

Brownsville/Matamoros—Daily 24 hours

Del Rio/Ciudad Acuña—Daily 24 hours

Eagle Pass/Piedras Negras—Mon.-Fri. 8-8, Sat. 10-2

El Paso/Ciudad Juárez—Daily 24 hours

Laredo/Nuevo Laredo—Daily 24 hours

McAllen/Reynosa—Daily 24 hours

PROOF OF CITIZENSHIP: U.S. and Canadian tourists traveling to Mexico must carry proof of citizenship. A valid (unexpired) passport is the most convenient, since it ensures problem-free re-entry into the United States, serves as a photo ID and facilitates many transactions, such as cashing traveler's checks. The U.S., Canadian and Mexican governments also recognize a birth certificate, which must be a certified copy with a raised seal from the government agency that issued it and be accompanied by a photo ID. A driver's license, baptismal certificate or voter registration card is *not* considered proof of citizenship.

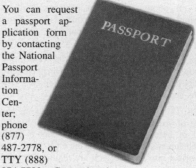

You can request a passport application form by contacting the National Passport Information Center; phone (877) 487-2778, or TTY (888) 874-7793. Comprehensive passport information and application forms also are available on the U.S. Department of State Department Web site; the address is travel.state.gov (link to "passports").

It's a good idea to carry an extra copy of your birth certificate, as well as keeping a record of your passport number. Make two photocopies of your passport identification page and other personal documents before leaving home. Leave one set at home, and carry the other set with you in a separate place from your actual documents.

Those persons holding dual U.S./Mexican citizenship should be prepared to travel into and out of both countries with the proper documentation required by both countries. This includes a Mexican passport to travel into and out of Mexico as a Mexican citizen. U.S. citizens who also are Mexican nationals are considered Mexican by local authorities, which may hamper U.S. government efforts to provide consular protection should it be necessary.

TOURIST PERMITS: The Mexican government imposes a tourist entry fee for each visitor entering Mexico. At press time, the fee was 195 pesos (approximately $20 U.S.). If traveling on business or as a student, contact the nearest Mexican consulate for information on obtaining a business or student visa. The fee must be paid in order to have your tourist permit validated if you plan to remain anywhere in Mexico for more than 72 hours, or stay less than 72 hours and travel beyond the 20-kilometer (12-mile) border zone (often referred to as the Free Trade Zone).

If you're entering Mexico by land it is advisable to obtain your tourist permit prior to leaving the United States. The government-issued permit (commonly referred to as a tourist card, but actually a form) is available upon presentation of proof of citizenship from Mexican consulates in the United States and Canada (see page 60) or immigration offices at official points of entry. Check with a Mexican consulate for current visitor entry and temporary vehicle importation permit fees. If you're arriving by air, the permit is distributed on the flight; if you're arriving by cruise ship, it is distributed upon disembarking.

If arriving by land, the tourist entry fee is paid at a branch of any bank operating in Mexico (a list of banks at which the fee can be paid is shown on the back of the tourist permit form). Upon payment the permit is stamped with an official "Fee Paid" designation. (Although the fee may be paid at any time prior to leaving the country if arriving by land, it is recommended that it be paid at the border as soon as possible.)

If arriving by air, the fee is included in the price of the ticket charged by the airline. If arriving by cruise ship, the fee is collected upon disembarking or is included in the purchase price of a cruise, but only if the stay is longer than 72 hours. **Note:** All visitors are required to produce verification of payment by showing the "Fee Paid" stamp on their tourist permit upon departing Mexico.

Exemptions are as follows:

Visitors traveling by land or sea anywhere in Mexico and staying less than 72 hours.

Visitors traveling by land to destinations within the 20-kilometer (12-mile) border zone, regardless of length of stay.

Those visiting as students (as defined by Mexican immigration laws).

Visitors traveling by land beyond the border zone and staying more than 72 hours but limiting their visit to the following routes/destinations: Tijuana to Ensenada in the state of Baja California; Mexicali to San Felipe in the state of Baja California; Sonoita to Puerto Peñasco in the state of Sonora; Ciudad Juárez to Paquime in the state of Chihuahua; Piedras Negras to Santa Rosa in the state of Coahuila; and Reynosa to China in the state of Nuevo León or Reynosa to Presa Cuchillo in the state of Tamaulipas.

Certain concessions are granted to those visiting Mexico on a recurring basis. Tourists entering by land should keep their validated tourist permit showing proof of payment, which allows unlimited visits within the permit's 6-month validity period. Business travelers entering by land should keep their validated business entry card (not a tourist permit) as proof of payment, which grants unlimited visits within a 30-day period.

Note: Any person traveling in Mexico on business with only a tourist permit is subject to a fine. For further information contact the Embassy of Mexico, 1911 Pennsylvania Ave. N.W., Washington, D.C. 20006; phone (202) 728-1600.

When applying for a tourist permit, minors (under age 18) traveling without their parents—i.e., alone or with friends or relatives—must present proof of citizenship (a valid passport or birth certificate) and a notarized, signed letter of consent from both parents granting permission for the minor to travel in Mexico. If the minor's parents are divorced or separated, the letter must be accompanied by divorce or separation papers, or proof of sole custody. Even if one parent goes along, a minor must submit from the absent parent a notarized, signed letter of consent, or when applicable, divorce, death certificate or guardianship papers.

Canadian citizens, including parents, traveling abroad with a minor should be prepared to document their legal custody of that child. If a minor is traveling with a friend or relative, the individual with the minor must have a notarized letter of consent from both parents (including a telephone number) or a custody document. In all cases it is important for the minor to have a valid Canadian passport. Mexican citizens living in the United States must go to the Mexican consulate nearest their place of residence and sign the legal documents granting permission for the minor to travel in Mexico.

The single-entry tourist permit is valid for up to 180 days and must be returned to Mexican border officials upon leaving Mexico. A multiple-entry permit allows multiple visits into and out of Mexico within the 180-day period. If a tourist permit is not used within 90 days of issuance it becomes void. Carry your tourist permit with you at all times while in Mexico. If you lose it, a duplicate can be obtained from local immigration officials.

You *must* be out of the country by the end of the validity period, or you will be subject to a fine. Extensions of up to 90 additional days can be obtained from Mexican immigration officials only when a physician verifies that you are too ill to travel.

ARRIVING BY AIR: There are international airports in all major Mexican cities and resort areas that receive regular flights from the United States and Canada, either directly or through Mexico City. Some airports receive charter flights as well. Major Mexican cities that receive direct U.S. flights are so identified in their descriptive listing. **Note:** Unlike nonstop service, a direct flight stops at least once and may involve changing planes.

The following airlines provide service from selected cities in the United States and Canada to Mexican destinations:

Aero California, (800) 237-6225 from the United States

Aeroméxico, (800) 237-6639 from the United States
www.aeromexico.com

Alaska Airlines, (800) 252-7522 from the United States
www.alaskaair.com

American Airlines, (800) 433-7300 from the United States
www.americanair.com/

America West Airlines, (800) 363-2597 from the United States
www.americawest.com/

Continental Airlines, (800) 523-3273 from the United States
www.continental.com/

Delta Air Lines, (800) 241-4141 from the United States
www.delta.com/

Mexicana Airlines, (800) 531-7921 from the United States
www.mexicana.com

Northwest Airlines, (800) 447-4747 from the United States
www.nwa.com

United, (800) 538-2929 from the United States
www.ual.com/

US Airways, (800) 622-1015 from the United States
www.usair.com

The two major domestic airlines are Mexicana and Aeroméxico, with flights linking the resorts and larger cities to Mexico City. Smaller regional airlines operate in different parts of the country. Aeromar serves central Mexico; Aviacsa the Yucatán Peninsula and southern Mexico. Other regional airlines are Aerocaribe and Aerolitoral. Traveling between destinations within the country often involves changing planes in Mexico City. Schedules, fares and routes all are subject to change. Smoking is generally prohibited on all international flights; check with the appropriate Mexican carrier regarding its smoking policy.

Airports almost always offer fixed-rate transportation via bus, minivan or taxi to downtown or hotel zone areas. Usually there is a booth at the airport where you can purchase a ticket or voucher. You also may have the option of riding in a private taxi (which costs more) or sharing the ride (and paying less). For safety reasons, never hail an unmarked cab outside the terminal.

There are frequent flights to Mexico from such "gateway" cities as Dallas/Fort Worth, Houston, Los Angeles and Miami. A bewildering array of fares, vacation packages and promotions also are available, and it often pays to search for a bargain. AAA/CAA members can obtain fare and schedule information and make reservations through AAA Travel Agencies. When making reservations, be sure you confirm all flights at least 72 hours prior to departure—particularly the return leg of a round trip.

Charter flights, while offering low fares, also are subject to the greatest number of restrictions. The charter operation can cancel a flight up to 10 days before it is scheduled to depart; if *you* cancel, you may not be able to recoup your money. When considering a charter flight, review the refund policy and contract stipulations carefully. **Note:** Mexico charges an airport tax on all departing flights. At press time the charge was about $25 (U.S.) for international flights and $16 for domestic flights; this fee normally is included in the cost of your airline ticket, but double check to make sure.

CAR RENTALS: U.S. rental cars generally cannot be driven across the border into Mexico. One exception is Hertz, which permits designated vehicles rented at airport facilities in San Diego, Tucson and Yuma to be taken across the border; special paperwork is required. Enterprise Rent-a-Car also allows rental vehicles to be driven into Mexico, contingent upon the purchase of Mexican automobile insurance; however, the policy varies according to the Enterprise location.

If you're flying into Mexico but plan on taking a side trip from your main destination, renting a car is an easy way to sidestep dealing with unfamiliar local transportation. AAA/CAA members can reserve a rental car through their local club; it is recommended that you make all necessary arrangements prior to your departure.

The major U.S. franchises are located in the larger cities. There are numerous Mexican companies as well, but although their rates are cheaper the vehicles may be less reliable. Overall, the cost of renting a car in Mexico is at least, if not more, expensive than in the United States.

It's also advisable to prepay for the vehicle in advance. Most companies require a credit card;

some will accept a cash deposit, although the amount is likely to be hefty. A U.S. or Canadian driver's license is acceptable. The usual minimum age limit is 25; special restrictions may be placed on drivers above a certain age. If you want such extras as air conditioning or automatic transmission, make sure you know what the additional cost will be.

Also take your itinerary into account when deciding how long to rent. While most companies will allow you to rent in one location and drop off at another, the drop-off charge can be quite steep. Request that a copy of the reservation confirmation be mailed to you; this should reduce the chance of overcharging, since the rate will be printed on the confirmation slip.

Booking a vehicle in advance simplifies matters, but it may not guarantee the make and model of your choice when you arrive. Many Mexican rental vehicles are Volkswagen Beetles, and if one is unavailable a company may try to send you elsewhere or charge for an upgrade. Inspect the car carefully before you drive off the lot. Check the windshield for cracks; the windshield wipers; the body and fenders for dents, rust, etc.; the head and taillights; the tires for wear and pressure; and note any missing items, such as the gas cap or floor mats. Seat belts and a fire extinguisher are required by law. A thorough inspection is well worth the time, as you will be charged for anything that is perceived damaged or missing.

Mexican automobile insurance is required; it is provided by the rental company and figured into the total cost of the contract. Standard contracts normally include both liability coverage and collision coverage after payment of a deductible. Obtaining an optional collision damage waiver (CDW) will cost more but means that you won't have to pay the deductible (which can be in excess of $2,000) in the event of an accident.

While the extras add up, they're worth it for peace of mind. In any event, the more coverage you have the better; speed bumps on many Mexican free roads, for example, can cause damage even if negotiated at slow speeds. Look into what your own automobile insurance covers—it might, for example, take care of damages to a rental car.

Keep the rental company's toll-free emergency number handy in case you run into trouble on the road. And when you return the vehicle, remember to fill the gas tank; the refueling charge will be much more expensive than any pump.

ARRIVING BY PERSONAL VEHICLE: If you're driving into Mexico, a little advance preparation can prevent crossing the border from

becoming a lengthy process. For one thing, AAA club offices at the following locations can provide Mexican automobile insurance to members. (**Note:** The Chula Vista office is 8 miles north of the Baja California border; the Tucson office is about an hour north of the Sonora border.)

TUCSON, ARIZONA
AAA Arizona
6950 N. Oracle Rd. 85704
Mon.-Fri. 8-5, Sat. 9-1 (520) 885-0694

CHULA VISTA, CALIFORNIA
Automobile Club of Southern California
569 Telegraph Canyon Rd. 91910
Mon.-Fri. 9-5, Sat. 10-2 (619) 421-0410

EL PASO, TEXAS
AAA Texas
655 Sunland Park Dr. 79912
Mon.-Fri. 9-6, Sat. 9-1 (915) 778-9521

TEMPORARY IMPORTATION OF VEHICLES: Both a temporary vehicle importation permit and a promise to return vehicle form are required for vehicle travel beyond about 20 kilometers (12 miles) of the mainland border. These documents are **not** required on the Baja California Peninsula (the states of Baja California and Baja California Sur), unless the vehicle is put on a ferry bound for the mainland.

To obtain these documents from a Mexican consulate or an immigration office at an official point of entry, the vehicle owner must be 18 years of age or older, have a valid U.S. or Canadian driver's license, present proof of citizenship (passport, birth certificate or affidavit of citizenship), and provide proof of ownership for each vehicle being taken into Mexico.

The vehicle's original title or registration constitutes proof of ownership; it is recommended that the registration be used for this purpose. Information on the application for temporary vehicle importation must match the information on the promise to return form; the same requirements apply to both.

The documents can be obtained at a Mexican consulate up to 2 months prior to your entry into Mexico. Only consulates in the cities of Chicago, Dallas, Houston, Los Angeles, Sacramento, Salt Lake City and San Bernardino are able to issue the documents. The documentation also can be accessed online by going to the Banjercito Web site; the address is www.banjercito.com.mx/site/tramiteitv_ing.jsp.

The temporary importation permit is generally issued for 90 days; extensions of up to 90 days can be obtained from Mexican immigration officials. Only one permit is issued per person, for one motorized vehicle at a time. It should be carried with you (not left in your car) at all times while in the country. If the permit or the promise to return vehicle form is lost or stolen, replacement documentation can be issued by Mexican customs offices to the vehicle importer as long as a certified document is obtained from the U.S. Embassy (U.S. residents) or the Canadian Embassy (Canadian residents) or one of their consulates attesting to the loss.

At the point of entry (mainland border crossings or transporting a vehicle by ferry from Baja California to the mainland), a $27 (U.S., plus IVA tax) administrative fee must be paid. If the vehicle importation permit is obtained at a Mexican consulate, the fee is $35.20 (U.S.).

The fee must be paid using a major credit card (American Express, MasterCard or Visa). The card must be in the registered owner's name and issued by a U.S. or Canadian bank or lending institution. Cash, checks, money orders or a credit card issued by a Mexican bank will not be accepted. The fee is paid at a Banjercito (Army Forces Bank) branch office. A sticker is applied to the vehicle's windshield at the point of entry.

In addition to the completed temporary vehicle importation permit and promise to return vehicle form, the following documents must be presented at the point of entry: acceptable proof of citizenship, a valid driver's license, a tourist permit and a current vehicle license/registration receipt, which should be carried in the car at all times while in Mexico. (Carry a copy of the registration receipt, not the original.)

Note: The temporary importation permit *must* be obtained *at* the border. "Second border" stops marking the end of the border zone (immigration checkpoints for proper documents and dutiable goods) will *not* accept the administrative fee for the permit or issue a windshield sticker. An exception is the 21-kilometer immigration checkpoint booth on Mex. 15 south of Nogales *(see "Only Sonora" Program information below).*

For leased or company-owned vehicles, a notarized letter of authorization (printed on stationery showing the company's or leasing agency's letterhead) that permits the driver to take the vehicle out of the United States or Canada and into Mexico is required, and an employee ID card must be presented. If the vehicle is not fully paid for, a notarized letter from the lienholder authorizing use of the vehicle in Mexico for a specified period must be presented.

Rented vehicles require a rental agreement and a notarized affidavit from the rental car company stating the company's permission to bring the car into Mexico. The same name must appear on the rental agreement and on the temporary vehicle importation permit.

If the owner does not have or does not wish to use a major credit card, a bond—based on the value of the vehicle—must be posted with a Mexican bonding firm (Afianzadora) at the point of entry. However, this is a costly, involved procedure that involves much paperwork; fees range from several hundred to as much as $30,000 U.S., depending on the vehicle's make and model.

To reduce the amount of time spent at the border (and to avoid potential frustration), obtain the proper forms and fill them out in advance. Have copies of all necessary documents in order. At crossings, the lanes designated *Declaración* are staffed by officials who speak English.

For the temporary importation of two vehicles, at least two persons must travel as tourists, and separate permits must be obtained for each vehicle. For example, one individual will not be allowed with both a car and a motorcycle, even if he or she owns both vehicles. One of the vehicles must be registered to another qualified driver in the same party, or a second person can obtain a permit for the additional vehicle by presenting a notarized affidavit of permission from the owner.

It is not mandatory for a group of people arriving in Mexico in the same vehicle to leave in the same vehicle; however, the individual who obtained and filled out the temporary vehicle importation permit must leave the country in the same vehicle in which he or she arrived. Drivers crossing and recrossing the border need not obtain a new temporary vehicle importation permit with each crossing, provided that the initial permit is still valid.

The temporary importation permit, promise to return form and windshield sticker **must be returned to Mexican customs officials at the border for cancellation,** either before or on the expiration date shown on the promise to return vehicle form and *prior to* re-entering the United States. Those failing to comply will be fined. There is no set fine; the amount can be up to the total value of the vehicle, and there is the possibility that the vehicle could be confiscated. You also will be denied subsequent entry into Mexico until the fine is paid.

"Only Sonora" Program: The "Only Sonora" program allows travelers staying within the state of Sonora less than 72 hours to waive the $20 tourist entry fee and the administrative fee for the 90-day temporary vehicle importation permit. If you stay in Sonora more than 72 hours a tourist permit is required, and if you plan to drive beyond the Sonora state border a temporary vehicle importation permit and windshield sticker must be obtained *(see above)*.

The free "Only Sonora" vehicle permit good for up to 180 days of travel within the state can be obtained at the 21-kilometer (13-mile) immigration checkpoint booth on Mex. 15 south of Nogales. Valid proof of citizenship, a tourist permit (which also can be obtained at this booth if you've entered Mexico by way of Nogales) and the vehicle's original current registration must be presented.

You are required to fill out a form, and a sticker is placed on the vehicle; both *must* be returned to the same booth when departing Sonora. For additional information about the "Only Sonora" Program contact the Sonora Department of Tourism; phone (800) 476-6672 in the United States.

The temporary importation regulations for automobiles also apply to recreational vehicles. Equipment and luggage should be packed to permit easy customs inspection. Vehicles exceeding 3.5 metric tons in weight require a special permit, as do buses. If in doubt as to how your vehicle will be classified, consult the nearest Mexican consulate office before starting your trip.

Trailers and motor homes can only stay in Mexico 6 months unless they are left in bond at an authorized trailer park. Such trailer parks have placed a bond with the nearest Mexican customs office, making them responsible for the storage of the recreational vehicle.

When you pay the administrative fee and enter Mexico with your own vehicle, a guarantee must be signed on your credit card, giving the Mexican government authority to track down the owner or driver if the vehicle is left behind. If a fine is incurred, it may be charged against the credit card. Should your vehicle become incapacitated, arrangements to leave without it can be made through the U.S. Embassy or one of its consulates, or through a Mexican customs (Aduana) office.

The Mexican government does not provide facilities for storing an automobile if you have to suddenly leave the country. It can be left with friends, but no one will be able to drive it; Mexican law dictates that a personal vehicle cannot be driven unless its owner is present.

Hacienda (the Mexican Treasury Department) has the authority to confiscate any vehicle that has been illegally imported into the country. Hacienda also has the authority to confiscate a vehicle whose owner (or driver) cannot produce the

proper temporary vehicle importation documentation. **Note:** It is illegal for a foreigner to sell a motor vehicle in Mexico.

INSURANCE: U.S. automobile insurance is *not* valid in Mexico. It must be replaced by insurance from a Mexican company. While some American companies may extend their coverage a certain number of miles from the border or number of days in Mexico, *only* a Mexican automobile liability policy is acceptable as evidence of financial responsibility if you have an accident in that country.

Arrange for a policy with full coverage issued through a reliable Mexican insurance company with complete adjusting facilities in cities throughout the country. AAA offices at border locations in California and Texas can provide Mexican automobile insurance to members; in Arizona offices Mexican insurance can be purchased at any AAA store location. A number of companies at border locations also provide insurance; one of the best-known is Sanborn's.

Other Automobile Club of Southern California and California State Automobile Association offices also will issue Mexican automobile insurance. However, documents for rented vehicles must include a letter of authorization, and a rental contract *must* be presented from the rental agency stating the renter has obtained permission to take the vehicle into Mexico; without them a policy cannot be written. AAA offices in Arizona are not able to issue insurance documents for rented vehicles.

Unlike the prevailing tenet of U.S. and Canadian law, Mexican law is based on the Napoleonic Code, *which presumes guilt until innocence is proven.* As a result, *all* parties (operators of vehicles, but in some cases even passengers) involved in an accident in Mexico are detained for assessing responsibility. If the accident involves no personal injury, the drivers may be asked to go with the attending officer to the police station to complete the necessary accident report, and the vehicles will usually be impounded for investigation. Once blame is established, the negligent driver's vehicle will remain impounded until he or she pays the damages.

If the accident causes injury or death, the operators will be jailed until the authorities determine who was at fault. Then only the responsible driver will remain incarcerated until he or she guarantees restitution to the victims and payment of the fine imposed for causing the accident (under Mexican law an automobile accident is a criminal offense).

A Mexican insurance policy is recognized by the authorities as a guarantee of proper payment for damages according to the terms of the policy. When presented, it can significantly reduce red tape and help to bring about an early release. However, a Mexican insurance policy may not prevent a motorist from actually being detained *if* he or she is involved in an accident that results in injury or death.

Note: Automobile Club of Southern California border offices in California and Texas offer optional coverage with their policy that provides professional legal services necessary to deal with Mexican authorities. Under this coverage, a bond will be submitted in order to obtain the release of the automobile and bail for the insured party who is involved in legal proceedings.

If an accident in which a driver is at fault results in damage to government property, such as road signs, safety fences, light or telephone poles, toll stations, street pavement or sidewalks, he or she must pay for the repairs needed even if no other vehicle was involved or no injury or death occurred.

All accidents or claims *must* be reported before leaving Mexico. If you need assistance with a claim, you should obtain it *only* from an authorized agent or adjuster of the insurance company that issued the policy. Official release papers should be kept as evidence that the case is closed, especially if the car shows obvious damage from the accident.

To obtain Mexican insurance, you will need to provide the following: current vehicle title or registration, a valid U.S. or Canadian driver's license, and proof that you currently have U.S. or Canadian automobile insurance (the policy's declaration sheet lists all coverages). Call ahead to determine what additional specific information (vehicle identification number, included accessories, etc.) is needed so that the policy can be accurately written.

If the vehicle is leased or not owned by you, a notarized letter from the leasing company or the registered owner giving you permission to take the vehicle into Mexico must be provided, and must include the vehicle identification number and the dates of your entry into and departure from Mexico.

The Mexican government has no minimum requirement for insurance; the agent will help you obtain the coverage best suiting your needs. If you obtain Mexican insurance through a AAA club office, the policy will be written by the day, with a discount for more than 30 days' coverage, and will be issued immediately upon application. Towed vehicles *must* be identified in the policy; if not, the policy can be declared void.

Rates are based on the current value of the vehicle; towed vehicles are covered separately. Policies are written in both English and Spanish. In the event of a disagreement, the Spanish text will prevail. Read your policy carefully before entering Mexico to discern what is and isn't covered. Most companies, for example, do not include lawyer's fees or bail to defend the policyholder against criminal charges, although adjusters in the larger cities may keep lawyers on a retainer who will act on behalf of the insured free of charge.

A separate policy may be required to pay for translating and notarizing a driver's license or other documents. Personal accident insurance, baggage insurance and medical coverage are all wise investments when considering the amount of coverage you think you'll need.

TRAVEL TO CENTRAL AMERICA

Anyone driving through Mexico en route to Central American countries, and intending to drive back through Mexico into the United States, must have a U.S. passport and the appropriate visa for each country visited. If tourism is the sole purpose of the trip and the 180-day travel limit has not been exceeded, it shouldn't be necessary to return the temporary vehicle importation permit, the promise to return vehicle form and the windshield sticker at the Mexico/Guatemala or Mexico/Belize border; all three documents should be retained and then returned to customs officials when departing Mexico.

Following are the current entry requirements for U.S. and Canadian citizens traveling to Central America; for additional information, contact the nearest Mexican consulate office or the U.S. consulate in Matamoros prior to departing the United States.

Belize—A visa is not required for visits of less than 3 months; visits of more than a month require a permit from Belizean immigration officials. A passport is required, as is proof of sufficient funds and proof of onward passage.

Costa Rica—A visa is not required. A passport or acceptable proof of citizenship is required, as is a tourist permit, proof of sufficient funds and proof of onward passage.

El Salvador—A visa and proof of onward passage are required. Visitors must have at least 6 months' continued validity on their passport and may be required to submit a notarized employer letter.

Guatemala—A passport and tourist permit both are required, as is proof of sufficient funds and proof of onward passage. **Note:** For safety reasons, visitors entering the country by motor vehicle along the coastal route are advised to use the Talismán/El Carmen border crossing (Mex. 200) rather than the crossing between Ciudad Hidalgo and Tecún Umán (the crossing used by most commercial traffic).

Honduras—Visitors are strongly advised to have a visa. Proof of sufficient funds and proof of onward passage also is required.

Nicaragua—A visa is not required for U.S. visitors; it is required for Canadian visitors. A passport is required for all visitors and must have at least 6 months of continued validity after the dates of stay in Nicaragua. Proof of sufficient funds and proof of onward passage also is required.

Panama—A passport, tourist permit and proof of onward passage are required. Tourist cards with a 30-day validity period are available from airlines that serve Panama.

DEPARTING MEXICO

If you entered Mexico with a car or any other motor vehicle, you must leave the country with that vehicle. *See "Temporary Importation of Vehicles," page 553.* Applicable documents (temporary vehicle importation permit, promise to return vehicle form and windshield sticker) may be collected at an interior inspection point, but usually they are returned to Mexican immigration and customs officials at the border.

Be sure to return all documents if you do not plan to re-enter Mexico on a multiple-entry tourist permit. U.S. Customs and Border Protection offices at the major border crossing points are open daily 24 hours; an exception is the Otay Mesa crossing, just east of Tijuana International Airport, which is open daily 6 a.m.-10 p.m.

Note: Motorists traveling north to the U.S. border are subject to official Mexican agricultural inspections at stations along the highways. All fruits, vegetables, houseplants and other plant matter will be inspected.

If departing by air, call the airline at least 24 hours prior to departure to confirm reservations and departure time. **Note:** Mexico charges an airport tax of around $25 or the equivalent in pesos on international departing flights, which is usually included in the price of your ticket; check with the airline to make certain.

Cruise ship passengers returning from Mexico to the United States are required to pay a $6.50 customs user fee; this is generally included in the ticket price.

Returning U.S. citizens must present to U.S. Customs and Border Protection officials valid proof of citizenship, either a valid passport or a birth certificate; the latter must be a certified copy from the government agency that issued it. A passport is required for returning naturalized citizens; it also is recommended that naturalized citizens note their naturalization certificate numbers to facilitate re-entry into the United States.

A Customs Declaration form should be prepared before you pass through U.S. customs. An oral declaration may be given to the customs inspector if all articles acquired abroad are accompanying you and do not exceed your allowable duty-free exemption. A written declaration is required for items exceeding your personal exemption in total retail value, and for more than one liter (33.8 fl. oz.) of alcoholic beverages, 200 cigarettes (one carton) or 100 cigars.

To expedite the process, keep sales slips handy and try to pack things that need to be declared separately. You must declare to customs officials items both in your possession and acquired during your trip, including:

- items purchased
- items given to you while abroad, such as wedding and birthday gifts or inherited items
- items purchased in duty-free shops or on board a carrier
- items you have been asked to bring back for another person
- items for which repairs or alterations were made, even if free of charge
- items you intend to sell or use in a business

The price actually paid for each item must be stated on your customs declaration form in U.S. currency or its equivalent in the country of acquisition and must include any value added tax (IVA) if it was not refunded prior to arrival.

The helpful booklet "Know Before You Go" lists and explains all U.S. customs regulations. Write to the U.S. Department of Homeland Security, Customs & Border Protection, 1300 Pennsylvania Ave. NW, Washington, D.C. 20229, or go to the U.S. Customs Web site and link to the online brochure; the address is www.cbp.gov.

WHAT U.S. CITIZENS MAY BRING BACK

EXEMPTIONS: Each visitor to Mexico may bring back, duty free, articles not exceeding $800 in retail value from a stay abroad of at least 48 hours. Duty must be paid on all items in excess of this amount. The personal exemption is allowed once every 30 days. A $200 exemption is granted if you cannot claim the $800 exemption because of the 30-day or 48-hour limitations. It may include 50 cigarettes, 10 cigars, 150 milliliters (5 fl. oz.) of alcoholic beverages or 4 fl. oz. of perfume containing alcohol. This individual exemption may not be grouped with other members of a family on one customs declaration.

Special regulations apply to gifts; *see "Gifts" below*. Articles purchased and left for alterations or other reasons do not qualify for the $800 exemption when shipped at a later date. Duty must be paid when the shipment is received; it cannot be prepaid. Personal-use shipments valued at less than $200 are duty free.

RESTRICTED OR PROHIBITED ITEMS: Certain items considered injurious or detrimental to the general welfare of the United States are prohibited entry by law, including lottery tickets, narcotics and dangerous drugs, obscene articles and publications, seditious and treasonable materials, hazardous articles (fireworks, dangerous toys, toxic or poisonous substances) and switchblade knives.

To prevent the introduction of plant and animal pests and diseases, the agricultural quarantine bans the importation of certain fruits, vegetables, plants, livestock, poultry and meats. All food products brought into the United States must be declared. If you attempt to conceal agricultural items, you can be fined $50-$100. For more information refer to the Department of Agriculture's Animal Products and Fruit and Vegetable manuals on their Web site at www.aphis. usda.gov/ppq/manuals/online_manuals.html.

Endangered or threatened wildlife species or products made of any part of these species are generally prohibited, unless you have a permit issued by the U.S. Fish and Wildlife Service. This includes products made from sea turtles, as well

as all ivory and ivory products made from elephant or marine mammal ivory.

If you are thinking of returning to the United States with any purchased articles made of fur, any animal skin other than cowhide leather, tortoiseshell, whalebone or any product manufactured wholly or in part from any type of wildlife, contact the U.S. Fish and Wildlife Service, Office of Management Authority, Division of Law Enforcement, P.O. Box 3247, Arlington, VA 22203-3247, phone (800) 358-2104, or visit www.fws.gov.

Such live birds as parrots, parakeets or birds of prey, widely available on the market in Mexico, can be brought into the United States subject to inspection by the U.S. Department of Agriculture. Birds must be quarantined upon arrival for at least 30 days in a USDA-operated facility at the owner's expense. Quarantine space must be reserved in advance; for more information phone (301) 734-8364.

To be taken out of Mexico, cultural artifacts or property items such as pre-Columbian monumental and architectural sculpture or murals, clay figurines, original paintings and other works of art (not handicrafts) will need an export certificate. Valuable religious and archeological relics are the property of the Mexican government and may not be taken out of the country.

Goods purchased in Mexico but originating in Cuba, Iran, Iraq, Liberia, Myanmar (Burma), North Korea or Sudan are not admissible. Gold coins, medals and bullion may be brought into the United States, but such items originating in or brought from Cuba, Iran, Iraq, Libya, Serbia and Sudan are prohibited.

One foreign-made article of a type carrying a protected U.S. trademark—for example, cameras, binoculars, musical instruments, jewelry or watches—may be brought into the United States under your personal exemption, provided the article accompanies you for private use and is not sold within 1 year of importation. Some perfumes are limited to one bottle; a few are prohibited altogether. If you intend to purchase perfume, be sure to inquire about trademark restrictions beforehand. *See "Personal Items," page 548*, for safeguards to consider when entering Mexico with foreign-made articles.

The U.S. Department of Agriculture's APHIS Web site, www.aphis.usda.gov, has a "Traveler's Tips" section with extensive information about what can and cannot be brought back, as well as information about permits allowing the importation of some restricted articles.

ALCOHOLIC BEVERAGES: The federal government permits each resident who is 21 years of age or older to bring into the United States one liter of alcohol duty free once every 30 days. However, most states restrict the quantity of alcoholic beverages that may be imported, and state law prevails if you arrive in a state that permits a lesser amount than what you have legally brought into the United States. For this reason it is important to know the import limits of your state of residence as well as the state of entry.

Taxes imposed on alcoholic beverages (which include beer and wine as well as distilled spirits) vary by state; miniature bottles are prohibited. Since these regulations can be quite complex, verify them before your trip if you intend to bring alcoholic beverages back with you.

GIFTS: Gifts accompanying you across the U.S./Mexico border are considered to be for personal use and are included in the $800 exemption.

Gifts sent in packages with a total retail value not exceeding $100 may be sent to friends or relatives in the United States free of U.S. customs duty or tax, provided that no recipient receives more than one gift shipment per day. Gifts may be sent to more than one person in the same package if they are individually wrapped and labeled with the name of the recipient.

Perfumes containing alcohol and valued at more than $5 retail, tobacco products or alcoholic beverages may not be included in gift packages. The designation "Unsolicited Gift," the name of the donor and the total value of the contents must be clearly marked on the outside.

Consolidated gift parcels should have listed on the outside the names of the recipients and the value of each gift, and labeled with the designation "Consolidated Gift Package." However, the safe arrival of gifts sent through the mail cannot be guaranteed. It also is possible to ship gifts through a broker. If you choose to do so, always obtain the name of the customs broker at the border who will handle the shipment. Make sure you understand the shipping arrangements and fees involved before signing the contract.

Note: Customs brokers are not U.S. Customs and Border Protection employees, and brokers' fees are based on the cost of delivery services, not the value of the items shipped. If the fee seems excessive in relation to the value of the shipment, opt to take purchases across the border with you if at all possible.

DUTIES: A flat rate of duty of 10 percent is applied to the first $1,000 worth (fair retail value) of merchandise in excess of your customs exemption of $800. The sales receipt functions as proof of value. Family members residing in one household and traveling together may group articles for application of the flat-duty rate. Articles must accompany you to the U.S. border. The flat-duty rate may be taken only once every 30 days.

Articles over the initial $1,000 flat-duty limit are dutiable at the rate applicable to the articles. Under the terms of the North American Free Trade Agreement, the United States offers a preferential rate of duty to many imports originating in Mexico; these items must be listed on the Customs Declaration form if returning by air or sea or declared orally if returning by land. The final authority on duty-free items and duty rates for other items is the U.S. Customs and Border Protection official at the border.

Payment of duty is required upon arrival for articles accompanying you and may be paid in U.S. currency; by personal check in the exact amount of the duty; or by government check, money order or traveler's check if not exceeding the duty amount by more than $50. MasterCard and Visa are accepted at some locations.

WHAT CANADIAN CITIZENS MAY BRING BACK

Canadian residents who have been outside Canada **at least 48 hours** may bring back, duty and tax free, articles not exceeding $200 (Canadian) in retail value. This exemption can be claimed any number of times a year. After an absence of **7 days or more** Canadian residents may bring back duty and tax free goods up to $750 in value. The $750 exemption may be claimed regardless of any $200 exemption taken on a previous trip and requires a written declaration; the two exemptions may **not** be combined at one time.

Canadian residents can claim duty- and tax-free entry for articles (excluding tobacco products or alcoholic beverages) that do not exceed a total value of $50 upon return from each trip abroad of at least 24 hours. In general, items brought into Canada under a personal exemption must be for personal or household use, souvenirs, or gifts for friends or relatives.

The following limitations apply to either the $200 or $750 exemption: 50 cigars, 200 cigarettes, 14 ounces (400 grams) of tobacco and 400 tobacco sticks, as well as 40 ounces (1.1 liters) of wine or liquor *or* 300 ounces (8.5 liters) of beer or ale (equivalent to 24, 12-ounce bottles/cans).

All exemptions are individual and may not be combined with another person's to cover an article valued at more than the maximum exemption. You may be requested to prove the length of your visit outside Canada. Dated sales receipts for goods or services received constitute valid proof and should be kept.

All declared goods associated with the $200 personal exemption must accompany the purchaser to the Canadian border; declared goods associated with the $750 personal exemption may follow the purchaser by mail. Gifts sent to friends or relatives from Mexico do not count against a resident's personal exemption as long as a gift is valued at no more than $60 Canadian and does not consist of alcoholic beverages, tobacco products or advertising matter. Make sure a gift card is enclosed to avoid misunderstanding. Since parcels to be shipped must first be examined by Mexican government customs officials, consider having a customs broker or a forwarding agent handle these important details before you leave Mexico.

Canada grants to residents who have been abroad at least 48 hours a special 8 percent combined duty and GST (Goods and Services Tax) rate on the next $500 value in goods (except tobacco and/or alcohol) in excess of the maximum amount exempted, provided the goods are of Mexican origin. Regular duties apply on any amount over that. For detailed information concerning specific duty rates and prohibited articles, consult Canadian customs before leaving on your trip.

Bed & Breakfast Lodgings Index

Some bed and breakfasts listed below might have historical significance. Those properties are also referenced in the Historical index. The indication that continental [CP] or full breakfast [BP] is included in the room rate reflects whether a property is a Bed-and-Breakfast facility.

Country Inns Index

Some of the following country inns can also be considered as bed-and-breakfast operations. The indication that continental [CP] or full breakfast [BP] is included in the room rate reflects whether a property is a Bed-and-Breakfast facility.

Historical Lodgings & Restaurants Index

Some of the following historical lodgings can also be considered as bed-and-breakfast operations. The indication that continental [CP] or full breakfast [BP] is included in the room rate reflects whether a property is a Bed-and-Breakfast facility.

562

HISTORICAL LODGINGS & RESTAURANTS (CONT'D)

Resorts Index

Many establishments are located in resort areas; however, the following places have extensive on-premises recreational facilities:

Points of Interest Index

Index Legend

◆ GEM: Points of Interest Offering a *Great Experience for Members*®

THEATERS-BUILDINGS

TOWERS

VIEWS

VISITOR CENTERS

WALKING TOURS

WATERFALLS

WATER PARKS

WAX MUSEUMS

WILDERNESS AREAS

WILDLIFE SANCTUARIES

WINERIES

ZOOLOGICAL PARKS & EXHIBITS

Crossword Puzzle

ACROSS

2

4

5

8

9

11

12

13

14

DOWN

1

3

6

7

10